THE HANDBOOK OF ADULT AND CONTINUING EDUCATION

THE HANDBOOK OF ADULT AND CONTINUING EDUCATION
2020 Edition

Edited by Tonette S. Rocco, M Cecil Smith, Robert C. Mizzi, Lisa R. Merriweather, and Joshua D. Hawley

A publication of the

First published in paperback 2024

First published 2021 by Stylus Publishing, LLC

Published 2023 by Routledge
605 Third Avenue, New York, NY 10158

and by Routledge
4 Park Square, Milton Park, Abingdon, Oxon OX14 4RN

Routledge is an imprint of the Taylor & Francis Group, an informa business

Copyright © 2021, 2023, 2024 Taylor & Francis

First Edition, 2021

All rights reserved. No part of this book may be reprinted or reproduced or utilised in any form or by any electronic, mechanical, or other means, now known or hereafter invented, including photocopying and recording, or in any information storage or retrieval system, without permission in writing from the publishers.

Trademark notice:
Product or corporate names may be trademarks or registered trademarks, and are used only for identification and explanation without intent to infringe.

Publisher's Note
The publisher has gone to great lengths to ensure the quality of this reprint but points out that some imperfections in the original copies may be apparent.

Library of Congress Cataloging-in-Publication Data
Names: Rocco, Tonette S., 1954- editor. | Smith, M. Cecil, editor. | Mizzi,
　Robert C., 1973- editor. | Merriweather, Lisa R., editor. | Hawley,
　Joshua D., editor.
Title: The handbook of adult and continuing education / edited by Tonette
　S. Rocco, M Cecil Smith, Robert C. Mizzi, Lisa R. Merriweather, and
　Joshua D. Hawley.
Description: First Edition. 2020 Edition. | Sterling, Virginia : Stylus
　Publishing, LLC, 2020. | Includes bibliographical references and index.
　| Identifiers: LCCN 2020045035 | ISBN 9781620366844 (Hardback : acid-free
　paper)
Subjects: LCSH: Adult education--Handbooks, manuals, etc. | Continuing
　education--Handbooks, manuals, etc. | Adult learning.
Classification: LCC LC5215 .H247 2020 | DDC 374--dc23
LC record available at https://lccn.loc.gov/2020045035

ISBN: 978-1-62036-684-4 (hbk)
ISBN: 978-1-03-291908-9 (pbk)
ISBN: 978-1-00-344784-9 (ebk)

DOI: 10.4324/9781003447849

This book is dedicated to adult educators working to alleviate the suffering caused by the COVID-19 outbreak.

The beautiful thing about learning is nobody can take it away from you.
B.B. King

Contents

Introduction: Advancing Adult and Continuing Education Through Critical Conversations and Diverse Perspectives   1
Robert C. Mizzi, Tonette S. Rocco, M Cecil Smith, Lisa R. Merriweather, and Joshua D. Hawley

PART ONE: FOUNDATIONS

1. Philosophical Foundations of Adult and Continuing Education   11
   Leodis Scott, Robert C. Mizzi, and Lisa R. Merriweather

2. History of Adult and Continuing Education   22
   Amy D. Rose

3. Interdisciplinarity in Adult and Continuing Education   31
   Royce Ann Collins

4. Public Policy and Adult and Continuing Education   38
   Elizabeth A. Roumell and Larry G. Martin

5. Lifelong Learning   47
   Marcie Boucouvalas

6. Internationalization of Adult and Continuing Education   61
   Mary V. Alfred and Shibao Guo

PART TWO: UNDERSTANDING ADULT LEARNING

7. Adult Learning   73
   Colleen Kawalilak and Janet Groen

8. Adult Development   81
   Thomas G. Reio Jr.

9. Motivation   91
   Margery B. Ginsberg and Raymond J. Wlodkowski

10. Access, Participation, and Support of Adult Learners   100
    David Deggs and Ellen Boeren

11. Mentoring in Adult and Continuing Education   107
    Geleana D. Alston and Catherine A. Hansman

PART THREE: TEACHING PRACTICES AND ADMINISTRATIVE LEADERSHIP

12. Organization and Administration of Adult and Continuing Education Programs   119
    Susan M. Yelich Biniecki and Steven W. Schmidt

13. Program Planning in an Era of "Wicked Problems"   128
    Thomas J. Sork

14. Assessment and Evaluation in Adult and Continuing Education 140
    Lilian H. Hill

15. Teaching Perspectives 150
    Stephen D. Brookfield

16. Pedagogy and Andragogy: Intersection for Learning 158
    Jerry Bowling and John A. Henschke

17. Adult Learning Through Everyday Engagement With Popular Culture 168
    Kaela Jubas, Jennifer A. Sandlin, Robin Redmon Wright, and Jake Burdick

18. Digital Technologies for Teaching and Learning 177
    Elisabeth E. Bennett and Rochell R. McWhorter

PART FOUR: FORMAL AND INFORMAL LEARNING CONTEXTS

19. The Cost of a Dollars and Cents Rationale for Adult Basic Education Policy 189
    Alisa Belzer and Jeounghee Kim

20. English as a Second Language 197
    Christy Rhodes and Clea A. Schmidt

21. Family Literacy 205
    Esther Prins, Carol Clymer, Anna Kaiper-Marquez, and Blaire Willson Toso

22. Prison Education 214
    Dominique T. Chlup

23. Workforce Development: Past, Present, and Future 223
    Ellen Scully-Russ and Ximena Vidal De Col

24. Military Education: Evolution and Future Directions 232
    Sarah Cote Hampson and Nancy Taber

25. International Development Education 240
    Jill Zarestky, Maren Elfert, and Daniel Schugurensky

26. Health Professions Education and Adult and Continuing Education: Working Collaboratively to Foster Educator Development 249
    Barbara J. Daley and Ronald M. Cervero

27. Continuing Professional Education 257
    Maureen Coady

28. Adult Learners in Higher Education 266
    Matt Bergman

29. Human Resource Development and Workplace Learning 275
    Henriette Lundgren and Rob F. Poell

30. Labor Education Programs: Radical Beginnings, McCarthyist Backlash, and the Rise of Neoliberal Education 287
    Corey Dolgon and Reuben Roth

31. Adult Education for Human Flourishing: A Religious and Spiritual Framework 297
    Davin Carr-Chellman, Michael Kroth, and Carol Rogers-Shaw

32. Cultural Institutions 305
    Robin S. Grenier

CONTENTS

33. Adult Environmental Education — 314
    Pierre Walter

34. Education to Change the World: Learning Within/Through Social Movements — 322
    Jude Walker and Shauna Butterwick

35. Peace-Building and Conflict Resolution Education — 330
    Robin Neustaeter and Jessica Senehi

PART FIVE: CONTEMPORARY ISSUES

36. Decolonizing Adult Education — 341
    Cindy Hanson and JoAnn Jaffe

37. Adult Education, Welfare, and New Evidence on Helping Low-Income Adults Improve Their Skills — 350
    Julie Strawn

38. Activism in/and Struggle: Teaching for a Different World — 362
    Dianne Ramdeholl and Rusa Jeremic

39. Sexual Diversity and Allyship in Adult and Continuing Education — 371
    Mitsunori Misawa and Craig M. McGill

40. Gender and Its Multiple Forms — 380
    Laura L. Bierema and André P. Grace

41. Adult Education and Disability — 392
    Jovita M. Ross-Gordon and Greg Procknow

42. Older Adults: Learning and Identity — 401
    Kathy D. Lohr, Brian Findsen, and Vivian W. Mott

43. Adult Education and Race: A Critical Race Theory Analysis — 409
    Lorenzo Bowman and Jeremy Bohonos

44. Working Class, Social Class, and Literacy Classism — 420
    Jeff Zacharakis, Margaret Becker Patterson, and Allan Quigley

45. Whiteness and Privilege — 428
    Elaine Manglitz and Stephen D. Brookfield

46. Migration and Migrant Education — 436
    Hongxia Shan and Shibao Guo

Conclusion: Reflecting on Struggles, Achievements, and Cautions in Complex Times — 445
M Cecil Smith, Robert C. Mizzi, Joshua D. Hawley, Tonette S. Rocco, and Lisa R. Merriweather

Epilogue: Considerations of the COVID-19 Pandemic and Black Lives Matter — 453
Joshua D. Hawley, Lisa R. Merriweather, M Cecil Smith, Robert C. Mizzi, and Tonette S. Rocco

Editors — 457

Contributors — 459

Name Index — 467

Subject Index — 489

Introduction

Advancing Adult and Continuing Education Through Critical Conversations and Diverse Perspectives

Robert C. Mizzi, Tonette S. Rocco, M Cecil Smith, Lisa R. Merriweather, and Joshua D. Hawley

Those who think about adult education or lifelong learning are, by nature, planners of the future, not surveyors of the past. In their view, education tends to be concerned with needs and aspirations; with imperfections or inadequacies in people, institutions and communities; and with how life can be made better by learning. (Houle, 1992, p. 35)

As Houle illustrates, the field of adult and continuing education can be fairly described as a forward-looking domain of practice and scholarship. Adult education is a discipline that foresees a better tomorrow, and this foundational value is what drives current and future plans, activisms, pedagogies, and discussions. The accomplishments and challenges of today need to be thoughtfully contested and explored in order for emancipatory possibilities to flourish and take root (Mizzi et al., 2016; Sheared & Sissel, 2001). The handbooks create an important legacy in our field; they help us envision the future in light of ongoing provocations among the various disciplines that shape. Previous editions of the *Handbook of Adult and Continuing Education* had similar ambitions but with different approaches reflective of their contexts and historical eras.

A handbook on adult education as a field has been published since the 1930s. The early handbooks were focused on programs (Kasworm et al., 2010) and sharing of practical information. During the 1960s the focus of the handbooks began to change, with concerns being raised about what was missing from the previous handbooks in the series. Namely, issues of race, gender, sexuality, and power and privilege were missing. A reflective and critical lens was needed to provide insights on the content updated every 10 years. The 2000 *Handbook of Adult and Continuing Education* (Wilson & Hayes, 2000) was the first handbook that intentionally "embraced critical reflection as a significant hope for improving what we take to be an increasingly marginalized professional practice of adult and continuing education" (p. 1). This handbook carved out a necessary critical lens to include lives and perspectives on the social periphery with a discussion of implications for adult education.

The 2000 *Handbook of Adult and Continuing Education* (Wilson & Hayes, 2000) introduced the field to 21st-century notions, while the 2010 *Handbook of Adult and Continuing Education* (Kasworm et al., 2010) situated the field in this century, focusing on adult and continuing education as a discipline that requires specific skills and understandings. Across the broad spectrum of institutions, programs, opportunities, and scenarios in which adults have opportunities to learn, increase their skills and knowledge, earn certifications and degrees, and improve their chances and quality of life, adult and continuing education represents growth, progress, and achievement for individuals and advancement for society (Kasworm et al., 2010). With these ideas in mind, the 2020 *Handbook of Adult and Continuing Education*, while respecting past accomplishments in the field, is a forward-looking volume. The 2020 edition draws on insights gained from the past, describes the present, and looks forward to the future of the field in light of current trends and challenges facing adult and continuing education. Shifting across time in such a way aims to reflect on existent complex insights and topics in the field, explore how they shift in the present, and conceptualize new possibilities in light of ongoing social and political changes.

We recognize that this is a tumultuous time for the field. Researchers situated within adult and continuing education programs must argue to maintain their funding (Fenwick, 2010) and struggle with a new managerialism that expects accountability and evidence of program effectiveness (see Hill, chapter 14). The field, as a result, is less visible than it was in decades past, largely due to diminishing resources and nonrenewal of adult education positions and programs in the postsecondary education sector and reduction of funding support in the community education sector. Administrators of adult education programs now need to be more creative in locating funds to support their initiatives (see Yelich Biniecki and Schmidt, chapter 12). This handbook provides opportunity for adult educators to reflect on and consider how the theory and practice of adult and continuing education can respond to our swiftly changing society. Diversity is a core premise that orients this particular edition, which is perhaps more pronounced than previous editions, and reflects our current sociality. For instance, diversity is seen in the editors' educational backgrounds which include international education and social policy; educational psychology; language, culture, and teaching; human resource development; and adult education. For some of us, equity and social justice are dominant concerns; for others, pragmatism and evidence-based practice are guiding principles.

Diversity as/in/of Adult and Continuing Education

We have observed remarkable and, sometimes, troubling changes in society since the publication of the 2010 *Handbook of Adult and Continuing Education*. American society appears more divisive and fractured than at any time since the Vietnam War and civil rights movement. To many Americans, it seems something of a pleasant surprise whenever Congressional leaders representing the two major political parties can find their way toward compromise and agree to pass legislation that benefits our citizens. Social movements such as Black Lives Matter harken back to the civil rights movement of a half-century past with a renewed focus on justice, racial equality, and the limits of policing (Miller & Schwartz, 2016). Around the country, important conversations about race and other matters of equity and inclusion are taking place in schools and classrooms, churches, community centers, and workplaces. There are other issues that are deepening the discourse, such as the #MeToo movement that raises awareness of sexual harassment and gender-based violence (Bierema & Grace, chapter 40; Lange & Young, 2019), the rise of gun violence in public and private spaces (Brown & Barthelemy, 2019), and the struggle for respect for migrants and their families alongside the rise of neofascism and xenophobia (Ramdeholl & Jeremic, chapter 38). It is becoming paramount for adult educators to be at the forefront of contributing to and facilitating conversations that lead to more civil discourse and equitable treatment for all.

That said, fair and respectful treatment of people with diverse backgrounds are not the only concerns that weave throughout these chapters. Other aspects of diversity include varied work and learning situations, perspectives, and religious and political views. Diversity can be a strength of any society, but to be a strength, pedagogy must be skillfully used to encourage civil dialogue about our differences. Incivility can paralyze development, stifle cohesion, and generate blowback and regressive policies (Hill, 2009). We recognize diversity as a necessary value in this handbook, in identity, in perspectives, in work practices, in social realities, in interpretations, and in beliefs. Because we believe diversity is a necessary value, we have included chapters on migration and migrant education (Shan & Guo, chapter 46), decolonization (Hanson & Jaffe, chapter 36), Whiteness and privilege (Manglitz &

Brookfield, chapter 45), gender and its multiple forms (Bierema & Grace, chapter 40), and sexual diversity perspectives (Misawa & McGill, chapter 39) for the first time in an adult education handbook.

An aspect of diverse work situations is that workers experience less job security as corporate offices and manufacturers relocate overseas, new technologies replace workers, and labor unions shrink in size and influence, all hallmarks of neoliberalism (Harvey, 2016). Modern work has become more service oriented, more information driven, and less labor intensive. The "gig" economy has emerged, exemplified by the establishment of online-based ride-sharing companies such as Uber and Lyft, where drivers are considered to be contractors who can work whenever they want but have no real job security (save for their own initiative), employee-provided benefits, or fair wage. Still, there remains demand for employees to be knowledgeable, skilled, and responsive to social and professional changes and, thereby, able to help their employers compete in the volatile and neoliberal global marketplace. Such demands indicate the need for individuals to pursue lifelong learning and occasional upgrading of skills through retraining. Employers stress the need for prospective employees to be critical thinkers who can solve problems, create and innovate, and work successfully in teamwork environments. These and other so-called soft skills are in greater demand today than are physical abilities (Davidson, 2016). These changes implicate adult educators, who need to stay abreast of such developments in order to make their teaching relevant to the changing lives of learners. We hope that this handbook will assist adult educators in this awareness and so have included chapters on human resource devlopment (HRD) and workplace learning (Lundgren & Poell, chapter 29), labor education (Dolgon & Roth, chapter 30), workforce development (Scully-Russ & Vidal De Col, chapter 23), and working class adults (Zacharakis et al., chapter 44).

There are various types of formal education in society, and there is diversity in how the state views certain educational systems. Adult and continuing education is considered the "fourth leg of the chair" of the American system of education, alongside early childhood programs, K–12, and postsecondary institutions. Yet, in some ways, adult and continuing education is the weakest leg—rarely the topic of conversation on political talk shows, in public policy arenas, on Capitol Hill, or among the American public. Ironically, many—perhaps most—adults participate in adult and continuing education at some time throughout their lives, whether through a high school equivalency degree program (e.g., GED; see Belzer & Kim, chapter 19), workplace training, professional development (e.g., Coady, chapter 27), museum education (e.g., Grenier, chapter 32), courses taken at a local community college, or any of the myriad education (formal, nonformal, and informal) and training programs available to adult learners. Yet, few adults know what adult education is when the phrase is used, holding misguided perceptions of *adult educators* as mainly teachers of any age or holding a narrow view of adult education as literacy and GED programs. Adult and continuing education, as a field of study, has little name recognition because, as a field, we exert little influence on policy or engagement with policy discussions on a national or international level. Our engagement with lifelong learning policies on the international level was limited with the withdrawal of the United States from UNESCO—further weakening the field and possibly the United States' standing in the world (see Boucouvalas, chapter 5).

Given the various venues in which adults learn, adult educators are increasingly required to quickly and efficiently respond to rapid technological, political, and social changes (see Kop & Bouchard, 2011). For example, higher education institutions are moving toward a neoliberal, corporate model that is supplementing diminishing state support by reshaping educational products, such as raising tuition, increasing the role of industry in pursuit of profits, or increasing hiring of contract workers (Fish, 2009). The ever-growing prison-industrial complex is increasingly privatized in the hopes that states save money and corporations make profits while the inmates' access to basic education and development activities are limited. Prisoner rehabilitation as a philosophy seems like something out of our distant past (see Chlup, chapter 22). Adult education programs for highly vulnerable populations, such as homeless people, veterans, or women who have been abused or need basic reproductive health care and education, are being neglected at best, assaulted at worst by public institutions. Because of these events we created a handbook "based on the principles of *inclusivity* and *utility*" (Merriam & Cunningham, 1989, p. xvi, italics in original). Our editorial team members have different views on what these terms mean, and thus we felt it necessary to produce a handbook that includes "differing ideological viewpoints in conjunction with a broad definition of adult education" (Merriam & Cunningham, 1989, p. xvi).

We also recognize a diversity of approaches to adult and continuing education around the globe. Recent international comparisons of adults' competencies—specifically regarding literacy and numeracy skills, and the abilities to problem-solve in technology-rich environments—show that Americans perform, at best, in the middle of the pack compared to more than two dozen European and East Asian countries (National Center for Education Statistics, 2019). These results are a clear sign that U.S. economic and technological strength will be lost if we are unable to improve our education systems—from early childhood through adulthood—and create better and more compelling opportunities for adults to improve their skills and knowledge. The importance of collaboration with international partners remains a key element to this success. We can learn much throughout our lives about educational systems outside our borders. There are countries that have novel approaches to fostering and supporting adult and continuing education that can be adopted or adapted in the United States, and there are countries that struggle with social, political, and educational issues that are not too distant from our own. Readers will notice that many chapters have an international perspective embedded in the content to reflect this broader view of subject matter. The shift beyond the U.S. context in this handbook was indeed purposeful in light of our current era of advanced globalization. Readers can strengthen their comparative analytical skills through looking elsewhere while reflecting inwards. Through adopting a comparative view, we begin to realize how the status quo has remained constant, much to the detriment of human agency, development, and subjectivity, while other countries have begun to embed social change in adult and continuing education programs. Within this era of advanced globalization, the time is right for greater awareness of different contexts and increased collaboration and partnership across national and cultural borders. It is through this lens that we expect diversity of ideas, beliefs, and perspectives to flourish.

Exploring diversity means that researchers and practitioners must draw knowledge and skills from a variety of sociocultural sources to improve what they know and can do. In clinical disciplines, one such approach is *evidence-based practice*—defined as "the integration of the best available research with clinical expertise in the context of patient characteristics, culture, and preferences" (American Psychological Association, 2005, para. 1). Similarly, in education, evidence-based practice combines research evidence with teacher expertise. What is a significant realization through these practices is that all types of adult learning and adult education are valuable and, as such, should receive greater attention in adult and continuing education as a field and by policymakers. This realization includes confronting the forces that jeopardize adult and continuing education in the United States and seeking out opportunities to cement the education of adults as a vital policy issue. Each chapter in this handbook helps actualize and prioritize adult and continuing education amid the challenges and complexities that shape current social realities.

Organization of This Handbook

The purpose of this handbook is to inform policymakers, practitioners, learners, and scholars on the complexities of adult learning and education in its current form, on the variations in philosophy and orientation that drive teaching, practice, policy, theory, and research, and on the forward direction of the field. The *Handbook of Adult and Continuing Education* is the foundational volume in adult and continuing education, and as such provides a comprehensive overview of the knowledge and research that orient the field. There is rich information on the contemporary issues and trends that are of concern to adult and continuing education, of the programs and resources available to adult learners, and of opportunities to challenge and critique the structures embedded in the field that perpetuate inequity and social injustice. The handbook is designed to engage and inspire readers to assist the field to seek new paths in uncertain and complex times, ask questions, and to help the field flourish.

The handbook is divided into five sections, and there are chapters within each section that are connected by a central theme. First, there is the *Foundations* section. This section situates the field by describing the developments, core debates, perspectives, and key principles that form the basis of the field. The intent is to offer an overview that provides practitioners, emerging and established scholars, and those with less familiarity of adult and continuing education with a comprehensive understanding of the history, important milestones, and current trends and issues. Chapters on philosophy, history, interdisciplinarity, public policy, lifelong learning, and internationalization form this section. The central ideas to this section are that adult and continuing education has deep-seated roots in philosophy (Scott et al., chapter 1); has a history that is complex and multidimensional (Rose, chapter 2); is characterized by interdisciplinarity that fosters new ideas, concepts, and theories in adult education (Collins, chapter 3); and has policies that shape how the public values adult learning (Roumell & Martin, chapter 4). Lifelong learning is implied by adult and continuing education and includes individual and social actions (Boucouvalas, chapter 5). Globalization, internationalization, and neoliberal forces have exerted ever-greater influence over adult education in recent times (Alfred & Guo, chapter 6). This section demonstrates that interconnectedness across time, disciplines, and contexts is a core value to adult and continuing education.

Understanding Adult Learning forms the second section of the handbook. This section presents information necessary to understanding adults as students, clients, stakeholders, and consumers of knowledge. This multiple perspective-taking deconstructs the adult learner role category to show the complex ways adults learn and can be learners. This section engages contemporary and historical theory, policy making, research, and trends in adult learning. Chapters on adult learning, adult development, motivation, access, participation, and support of adult learners, and mentoring form this section. Among the ideas emerging out of this section are that adult learning theorizing has been shaped by a variety of disciplines (Kawalilak & Groen, chapter 7); an understanding of adult physical, cognitive, social, and emotional needs is paramount to supporting adult learning and development (Reio, chapter 8); motivation underpins and fuels adult learning (Ginsberg & Wlodkowski, chapter 9); adult learning programs and projects need to be invitational, accessible, and supportive (Deggs & Boeren, chapter 10); and mentoring relationships foster adult learning (Alston & Hansman, chapter 11). A core theme of this section is that adult learning is relational, and informed by emotional, psychological, and physical factors that shape adult learner experiences.

Teaching Practices and Administrative Leadership forms the third section of the handbook. This section provides information necessary for program development, maintenance, and teaching practices. It offers chapters on organization and administration, program planning, assessment and evaluation, teaching perspectives, andragogy and pedagogy, public pedagogy, and digital technologies for teaching and learning. Some ideas that shape this section are that organization and administration of programs can shape teaching and learning experiences (Yelich Biniecki & Schmidt, chapter 12), program planners need to be proactive and anticipatory in their practice (Sork, chapter 13), the construction of effective assessment and evaluation practices can sustain adult education programs (Hill, chapter 14), teaching practices should help adults learn and move forward in their development (Brookfield, chapter 15), pedagogy and andragogy can be mutually supportive (Bowling & Henschke, chapter 16), teaching can occur through popular culture (Jubas et al., chapter 17), and new teaching spaces and practices often emerge through technological advancements (Bennett & McWhorter, chapter 18). A core theme of this section is that teaching does not occur in isolation and has important connections to adult education administration, evaluation, social awareness, and technologies.

Formal and Informal Learning Contexts is the fourth section in this handbook. This section provides an overview of adult and continuing education in different areas of practice. It includes traditional organizations that practice adult and continuing education as well as newer focus areas. This overview is meant to broaden the depth of the field and show how learning context greatly varies across regions and realities and that these contexts are significant to the development and relevance of adult and continuing education. Chapter topics in this section consist of adult basic, GED, and literacy education, English as a second language programs, family literacy, prison education, workforce development, military education, international development education, health professions education, continuing professional education, higher education, human resource development and workplace learning, union and labor education, religious and spiritual education, cultural institutions, environmental education, social and political movements, and peace and conflict education. Some ideas that these chapters expand upon are that adult literacy skills can shape personal and professional well-being (Belzer & Kim, chapter 19); classrooms present diverse and complex circumstances for learners (Rhodes & Schmidt, chapter 20); learning together across the life span promotes growth and development (Prins et al., chapter 21); adult education should be meaningful and equitable and not wielded as a site for control (Chlup, chapter 22); workers can be vulnerable learners and therefore should be supported by appropriate and tailored programs (Scully-Ross & Vidal De Col, chapter 23); there are different goals associated with "training" and "education" (Hampson & Taber, chapter 24); learning sites can be contested, complex, and tied to larger political agendas (Zarestky et al., chapter 25); adult education programs can be tied to certifications and ongoing professional development and competencies (Daley & Cervero, chapter 26; Coady, chapter 27); institutions need to consider larger life struggles if they wish to promote learner retention (Bergman, chapter 28); adult educators have the capacity to foster skills development at employment sites (Lundgren & Poell, chapter 29); labor education exists within a tension between radical and neoliberal ideology (Dolgon & Roth, chapter 30); spirituality has a place and presence in adult education (Carr-Chellman et al., chapter 31); cultural institutions can foster participatory and relevant learning opportunities (Grenier, chapter 32); environmental justice and social movements require adult education interventions based on an intersectional analysis (Walker & Butterwick, chapter 34; Walter, chapter 33); and adult education can foster peaceful lives and nonviolent interventions (Neustaeter & Senehi, chapter 35). The core theme of this section is that there are multiple sites of inquiry for adult learners, and each is nuanced by a set of values and perspectives.

Contemporary Issues focus the fifth section of this handbook. This section is concerned with the development of learners who wish to build better communities through learning. It interrogates the profound learning that occurs through nonformal and informal sites. Each site is rooted in a current social, cultural, or political context that facilitates opportunities for ongoing engagement within a community of practice. Chapters in this section focus on decolonizing adult and continuing education; adult education and welfare; teaching social activism; lesbian, gay, bisexual, trans, queer, and straight allies; gender and its multiple forms; disability; older adults and intergenerational identities; race and ethnicity; working class; Whiteness and privilege; and migrants and migrant education. Some ideas put forth by chapter contributors are that: adult education can be a colonizing discourse (Hanson & Jaffe, chapter 36); adult education can alleviate poverty, and this requires a political will for inclusion (Strawn; chapter 37); adult education can make visible normalization processes and generate collective action (Ramdeholl & Jeremic; chapter 38); adult learning classrooms have a legacy as being heteronormative and gendered (Bierema & Grace, chapter 40; Misawa & McGill, chapter 39) and riddled with ableism (Ross-Gordon & Procknow, chapter 41) and ageism (Lohr et al., chapter 42); adult education is racialized and a product of racialization (Bowman & Bohonos, chapter 43); adult educators need to recognize class differences in the classroom (Zacharakis et al., chapter 44); White power and privilege shape relationships in classrooms (Manglitz & Brookfield, chapter 45); and, relatedly, institutions can screen out—or embody—social differences based on political leanings (Shan & Guo, chapter 46). The core theme of this section is that "everything is connected," and it is beneficial for adult educators to trouble the dominant assumptions and identify unconscious biases currently occupying the field.

The editors then provide a concluding chapter that suggests some of the social tensions that became clear in the creation of this handbook. They respond to ongoing provocations raised by chapter authors and offer some next steps for adult and continuing education and priorities for the future. The editors also offer an epilogue in light of the recent COVID-19 pandemic and continued devaluation of Black lives.

Conclusion

We encourage readers to read these chapters as starting points. The chapters should prompt further questions: How does an understanding of the chapter inform adult and continuing education? How may these topics compete with and work against one another? What are the key understandings, theories, and perspectives that contribute to meaning making in adult and continuing education? What are the controversies and dilemmas around policy, practice, and concerns in adult and continuing education? What is the role of power and privilege in these chapters? These questions, among others, aim to provoke further dialogue, reflection, and analysis into each chapter topic. We come to understand how political and social influences are always changing, which means continually reshaping and reviewing adult and continuing education.

Above all, a main premise of this handbook is that adult and continuing education should not simply respond to rapidly changing social, economic, technological, and political environments across the globe, but should lead the way in preparing adults to become informed, globally connected, critical citizens who are knowledgeable, skilled, and open and adaptive to change and uncertainty. While due attention is given to foundational theories and models of practice in the field, the 2020 *Handbook of Adult and Continuing Education* also emphasizes emerging theoretical perspectives, philosophies of practice, broad interdisciplinary, epistemological and methodological approaches to adult and continuing education, and identification and description of adult learner populations that have been previously invisible, unexamined, or marginalized by policymakers and educators. There is a lot of work to be done, and our aim is that this handbook, like the others before it, inspires readers to learn and work together for a greater world where adults learn, thrive, and find their place.

Acknowledgments

We, the editors, are extremely grateful for the honor extended by American Association for Adult and Continuing Education (AAACE) and the Board of Directors to develop the 2020 decennial *Handbook of Adult and Continuing Education*. The privilege of curating a body of work of this magnitude is both an incredible responsibility and humbling opportunity. We appreciate the scholars who contributed chapters and their willingness to work with us through a process that at times was tense and frustrating as we forged toward meeting necessary chronological milestones and sought to achieve continuity across the nearly 50 chapters. We learned so much from each and every one of you and gained new perspectives across a wide range of topics. You are to be applauded as this handbook would not have been possible without you. Likewise we thank our colleagues both at the university and our professional communities who offered their support, encouragement, and patience.

We would like to extend a special thanks to David Brightman and the Stylus team for their tireless efforts to assist and provide guidance as the handbook underwent a metamorphosis from its embryonic state of a cluster of ideas and topics to a rich, robust collection of chapters that promise to inform as well as inspire adult educators and adult learners to use their influence to make and be the difference for individuals and our society. David, in particular, was quick to respond and offered useful and insightful reviews from the beginning to end of the work that pushed us to create an even stronger handbook. David gently nudged us while also providing extensions of time when needed allowing us to produce this high-quality volume.

Our editorial team additionally wishes to thank Josh Hawley, a member of the team, for envisioning the unimaginable: editing this decennial handbook. It was that spark that led to conversations with Tonette S. Rocco that ultimately led to assembling a diverse team of scholars, many of whom met for the first time as strangers on a conference call but now are friends who share meals, cornball jokes, and interesting tidbits about their lives with each other. We acknowledge Tonette, our team lead, for managing our ragtag bunch and keeping the project on task but our deep appreciation stems from Tonette's skill, ability, and confidence as a leader. It was this leadership, the uncanny ability to tap into our unique individual strengths allowing us to bring the best of ourselves to the work, and the levity continually interjected that created the conditions for us to emerge from the editorial process with our sanity and with smiles on our faces and in our hearts. This process was at times grueling, but it was a gift that we, the editors, are grateful for having the opportunity for which to have been a part.

References

American Psychological Association. (2005). *Policy statement on evidence-based practice in psychology.* https://www.apa.org/practice/guidelines/evidence-based-statement

Brown, M. E., & Barthelemy, J. J. (2019). The aftermath of gun violence: Implications for social work in communities. *Health & Social Work, 44*(4), 271–275. https://doi.org/10.1093/hsw/hlz027

Davidson, K. (2016, Aug. 30). Employers find "soft skills" like critical thinking in short supply. *Wall Street Journal.* https://www.wsj.com/articles/employers-find-soft-skills-like-critical-thinking-in-short-supply-1472549400

Fenwick, T. (2010). Accountability practices in adult education: Insights from actor-network theory. *Studies in the Education of Adults, 42*(2), 170–185. https://doi.org/10.1080/02660830.2010.11661596

Fish, S. (2009, March 8). Neoliberalism and higher education. *New York Times.* https://opinionator.blogs.nytimes.com/2009/03/08/neoliberalism-and-higher-education/

Harvey, D. (2016, July 23). Neoliberalism is a political project. *Jacobin Magazine.* https://www.jacobinmag.com/2016/07/david-harvey-neoliberalism-capitalism-labor-crisis-resistance/

Hill, R. J. (2009). Incorporating queers: Blowback, backlash, and other forms of resistance to workplace diversity initiatives that support sexual minorities. *Advances in Developing Human Resources, 11*(1), 37–53. https://doi.org/10.1177/1523422308328128

Houle, C. O. (1992). *The literature of adult education. A bibliographic essay.* Jossey-Bass.

Kasworm, C. E., Rose, A. D., & Ross-Gordon, J. M. (2010). Introduction: Adult and continuing education as an intellectual commons. In C. E. Kasworm, A. D. Rose, & J. M. Ross-Gordon (Eds.), *Handbook of adult and continuing education* (pp. 1–12). SAGE.

Kop, R., & Bouchard, P. (2011). The role of adult educators in the age of social media. In M. Thomas (Ed.), *Digital education: Opportunities for social collaboration* (pp. 61–80). Palgrave Macmillan.

Lange, E., & Young, S. (2019). Gender-based violence as difficult knowledge: Pedagogies for rebalancing the masculine and feminine. *International Journal of Lifelong Education, 38*(3), 301–326. https://doi.org/10.1080/02601370.2019.1597932

Merriam, S., & Cunningham, P. (1989). Adult education as a field of professional practice. In S. Merriam & P. Cunningham (Eds.), *Handbook of adult and continuing education* (pp. 1–2). Jossey-Bass.

Miller, B., & Schwartz, J. (2016). The intersection of Black Lives Matter and adult education: One community college initiative. In B. Drayton, D. Rosser-Mims, J. Schwartz, & T. Guy (Eds.), *Swimming up stream 2: Agency and urgency in the education of Black men* (pp. 13–22). Jossey-Bass. https://doi.org/10.1002/ace.20182

Mizzi, R. C., Rocco, T., & Shore, S. (Eds.). (2016). *Disrupting adult and community education: Teaching, learning, and working in the periphery.* SUNY Press.

National Center for Education Statistics. (2019). *Explore how U.S. adults compare to their international peers and see the latest 2017 U.S. results.* https://nces.ed.gov/surveys/piaac/current_results.asp#international

Sheared, V., & Sissel, P. (Eds.). (2001). *Making space: Merging theory and practice in adult education.* Bergin & Garvey.

Wilson, A. L., & Hayes, E. R. (2000). Introduction. In A. L. Wilson & E. R. Hayes (Eds.) *Handbook of adult and continuing education* (p. 1). Jossey-Bass.

PART ONE

FOUNDATIONS

CHAPTER 1

Philosophical Foundations of Adult and Continuing Education

Leodis Scott, Robert C. Mizzi, and Lisa R. Merriweather

Adult educators, practitioners, and scholars use philosophies for informing practice, teaching, and research when pursuing the purpose of educating the society and self. This chapter outlines the philosophical foundations in adult and continuing education (ACE) that have guided adult educators in their practices and throughout the theoretical development of the field. Over time, there have been several widely accepted Western philosophies of adult education, namely liberal, behaviorist, progressive, analytical, radical/critical, postmodern, and humanistic (Darkenwald & Merriam, 1982; Elias & Merriam, 2005; Ross-Gordon et al., 2017; Zinn, 1998). Philosophers associated with the origins of these philosophies or philosophical orientations were predominantly White men representing Eurocentric values. These philosophies or philosophical orientations came to represent the purposes of educating the collective society and the individual self (i.e., society and self) and guided the practices within ACE. Merriam and Kim in 2008 interjected into the discourse the idea of non-Western philosophies as being present and paramount to understanding the purposes and practices of adult education, especially for non-White adult educators and adult learners. By highlighting the lack of universality of the Western philosophies that were permitted to function as canons, Merriam and Kim (2008) revealed how cultural hegemony influenced how those purposes and practices were framed and demonstrated that they were not inclusive.

This chapter will focus mainly on those Western, Eurocentric philosophies in ACE, as they still dominate the field and are most often seen in the literature, but will also briefly describe other culturally informed philosophies such as Eastern, African, and Indigenous models that appear on the landscape of adult education philosophy. Historically, other approaches that acquaint readers with philosophy and its application to ACE are worth revisiting. Most notable are Powell and Benne (1960), who called for adult education to pay more attention to understanding the unspoken assumptions and implicit values of adult educational concepts and principles (Ross-Gordon et al., 2017). Toward this end, an alternative conceptualization rooted in larger essential philosophical ideals—metaphysics, epistemology, logic, ethics, and aesthetics—is proffered as a means to create a more inclusive philosophical framework for sculpting the field's purposes and practices. Thus, the final intention of this chapter is to place together the widely accepted philosophical foundations and the essential philosophical questions and terms into a connected framework for understanding the historical and contemporary theories/practices of the field. This framework can also help clarify other thought systems and scholarship practices that may advance ACE in subsequent years.

Western Philosophical Foundations and Concepts in ACE

From the beginning, philosophy in the context of education has addressed the challenges of its day, focusing on the society and self. Ancient Greek philosophers, including the Sophists, Sappho, Socrates, Plato, and Aristotle and, later, Roman contributors such as Cicero and Quintilian considered a philosophy of education in terms of human virtues, the liberal arts, and moral education. They considered knowledge of philosophy as essential for teaching public service, law, or civil administration (Gutek, 2010; Murphy, 2006). Still later, medieval and Christian educational philosophers—including Augustine, Thomas Aquinas, Charlemagne—advanced the Holy Bible and classical liberal education as essential for developing intellect, preserving culture, and nurturing a moral life. These philosophers advanced the idea of the seven liberal arts that included the *trivium* (i.e., grammar, logic, rhetoric) and the *quadrivium* (i.e., arithmetic, geometry, astronomy, and music). Education and philosophy in the time of the Renaissance (ca. 1300–1600 AD) and the 16th-century Reformation started a rebirth of innovations in learning as a result of inventing the printing press, discovering the New World, and growing secular interests beyond classical Greco-Roman culture. The Enlightenment (ca. 1685–1815 AD) also brought about new ideas about education, scientific methods, and educational opportunities for wider classes of people (Gutek, 2010; Murphy, 2006).

Moving into the Modern Era, philosophy and education continued to share interest in both the society and self. According to Dewey (1910/1993), education connects to philosophy in addressing the experiences that "originate in the conflicts and difficulties of social life" (p. 324). Therefore, education and philosophy complement each other, leading Dewey to define *philosophy* as the general theory of education where education serves as the workshop of philosophy by which many philosophies and their philosophical distinctions "become concrete and . . . tested" (Dewey, 1916/1994; pp. 328–329). These historical goals of education and philosophy pertaining to both the society and self offer clarification about the contemporary philosophical positions of ACE.

Besides Dewey, there are other thought leaders even more central to understanding the philosophical foundations of ACE. Chief among these are thinkers such as Eduard Lindeman (1926) and Paulo Freire (1972). In the founding of the ACE field, Lindeman proposed the field's dual purpose of improving both the society and self in a democracy; likewise, Freire proposes social transformation and personal empowerment as inseparable processes in emancipatory practices (Merriam et al., 2007). Houle (1992) also lists authors who have put forward systematic philosophical approaches to ACE. Among these philosophical contributions are thoughts and ideas that also range from the society to the self and center on the importance of philosophy and ACE in addressing social and personal issues. In combination, these thought leaders helped to develop what is viewed as a common philosophical language of ACE.

Across the dual goals of society and self, thought leaders can be categorized within the philosophical foundations often highlighted in ACE. There are seven widely accepted philosophies of adult education: liberal, behaviorist, progressive, analytical, radical/critical, postmodern, and humanistic, which Zinn (1998) presents as a resource for adult educators to develop their own philosophical orientation. Table 1.1 attempts to make straightforward many of the diverse and complex ideas featured in the philosophical language of ACE. Each philosophy will be described later in the chapter.

According to Elias and Merriam (2005), liberal adult education highlights liberal learning and intellectual development while behaviorist adult education features learning objectives and performance measurement. The *liberal* philosophical foundation is general education with the concept of liberal learning promoted by thinkers such as Cyril Houle (1992), Horace Kallen (1962), and Mortimer Adler (1988). For example, Kallen (1962) considers philosophical issues and introduces an idea of *cultural pluralism* that allows for smaller groups in a larger society to maintain their cultural identities, beliefs, and values. The *behaviorist* philosophical foundation features the learning objectives with concepts such as competence, mastery, and performance based on contributions from Edward L. Thorndike (1927), B. F. Skinner (1971), and R. W. Tyler (2013). For example, Skinner (1971) noted that the goal of education is to bring about behavior that will ensure the survival of individuals, society, and the entire human species (Merriam et al., 2007).

TABLE 1.1. Philosophical Foundations, Purposes, Concepts, and Key Thinkers in ACE

	Society <--> *Self*						
	Liberal	*Behaviorist*	*Radical-Critical*	*Analytical*	*Postmodern*	*Progressive*	*Humanistic*
Purposes	General Education	Learning Objectives	Social Action	Logical Reasoning	Social Practices	Practical Knowledge	Personal Growth
Concepts	Liberal Learning	Competence; Performance	Critical Thinking; Social Justice	Arguments; Decision-Making	Deconstruction; Cultural Practices	Experience; Problem-Solving	Autonomy; Self-Direction
Key Thinkers	Houle, Kallen, Adler	Thorndike, Skinner, Tyler	Freire, Brookfield	Lawson, Paterson	Usher, Bryant, Johnston	Lindeman, Dewey, Bergevin	Knowles, Tough, McKenzie

Progressive adult education, in contrast, advances experience, society, and democracy, and analytical adult education introduces concept clarification. The *progressive* philosophical foundation features the purpose of practical knowledge using concepts of experience and problem-solving from Eduard Lindeman (1926), John Dewey (1910/1993), and Paul Bergevin (1967). Bergevin articulates an entire philosophy of adult education for the purpose of explaining that adult education should be everyone's concern and should be used for developing free, creative, and responsible people in every society. The *analytical* philosophical foundation includes logical reasoning for concepts of argumentation, decision-making, critical thinking, and rational thought from systematic philosophers such as K. H. Lawson (1975, 1998) and R.W.K. Paterson (1979). Paterson utilizes three concepts to conceptualize the philosophical essence of ACE: values, education, and the adult. This marks an important connection of considering one's values within philosophy and education that can be both social and personal to the adult.

Postmodern adult education proposes further questioning and deconstruction of ideas. The *postmodern* philosophical foundation argues for social practices using deconstruction and attention to cultural practices. For example, Usher et al. (1997) explain the unparalleled importance of ACE in both personal and social life. These authors further explain that in postmodern times, the field has become a part of a "culture market" that excludes as well as includes adults, also becoming a "cultural producer" with fewer distinctions among education, leisure, and entertainment, resulting in less intellectual and practical relevance (Usher et al., 1997, p. xv).

The *radical* or *critical* philosophical foundation advances the purpose of social action through concepts of social justice and critical thinking, most notably by thinkers like Paulo Freire (1972) and Stephen D. Brookfield (2010, 2019). Brookfield (2010) explains how crucial radical/critical thinking is in penetrating hegemony and realizing corporate agendas that displace individual and social well-being. Radical/critical adult education also promotes social action. Elias and Merriam (2005) describe the radical/critical philosophy of adult education as focusing on social justice and transformation-oriented education.

The radical/critical philosophical foundation is growing in prominence within ACE. For example, Bierema (2010) describes the goals of society and self concerning social justice and professional identity in adult education by embracing its diversity across multiple contexts. Tisdell and Taylor (2001) reframe the radical/critical philosophical foundation into critical-emancipatory and critical-humanistic foundations for acquiring and questioning new forms of abilities and identities. Brookfield (2010) adds to this philosophical foundation by including critical race theory, feminism, Afrocentrism, and queer theory that address race, gender, and sexual orientation by confronting social justice, identity, inequality, discrimination, and marginalization. Further, Isaac et al. (2010) consider contemporary race-based theories regarding multiculturalism and Black feminist thought, which offer philosophical positions and techniques for how cultural and racial diversity are reflected in a pluralistic society. Alhadeff-Jones (2017) also expresses the goals of the society and self through complexities of emancipation and education.

Humanistic adult education introduces freedom, autonomy, and self-direction, highlighting the role of individuality and self-actualization. The *humanistic* philosophical foundation focuses on purposes of personal growth through concepts of autonomy and self-direction from thought leaders such as Malcolm Knowles (1980), Allen Tough (1971), and Leon McKenzie (1978, 1991). For example, McKenzie (1978) considers how adult education should foster a courageous spirit in individual learners while developing understandings of self, others, and the world.

These foundational philosophies serve as a starting point for orientating adult educators to the philosophical/educational goals pertaining to society and the self. Darkenwald and Merriam (1982) explain these goals as specific aims and objectives related to social transformation, organizational effectiveness, personal/social improvement, intellectual cultivation, and individual self-actualization. Similarly, Ross-Gordon et al. (2017) suggest the need for a useful tool in working through many of the confusing philosophical orientations, dimensions, and worlds of "isms" (i.e., idealism, realism, pragmatism, instrumentalism, existentialism, feminism, multiculturalism, and cosmopolitanism) while Zinn (1998) focuses on how these philosophies can help adult educators identify a philosophical orientation that guides their effective practice and instruction.

Houle (1992) acknowledges other thinkers who have contributed broadly "philosophical" approaches to adult learning, which Ross-Gordon et al. (2017) later describe as the "philosophical enterprise" of ACE. It is important to note that the individual work, collaboration, and philosophical contributions of such thinkers are numerous and remarkable, yet rarely researched for their philosophical impact on ACE. Reasonably, this can be explained through the absence of a philosophical language, accessible framework, or useful tool by which their contributions can be assessed, compared, and evaluated—which could be provided by these widely accepted foundations. While a turn toward these foundations is necessary, it is also necessary to acknowledge that those thinkers primarily were White and represented Western, Eurocentric ideals and values. Any framework built from those alone would further perpetuate presumed cultural neutrality in the philosophizing of the field.

This is important because, as Ross-Gordon et al. (2017) suggest, "Philosophy can clarify both our own actions and those of others . . . [it]can help us understand the foundations . . . while also allowing us a chance to develop a common language" (p. 164). Ross-Gordon et al. also recognize the importance of philosophy in helping adult educators and practitioners understand the important impact of philosophy to educational practices. These philosophical foundations can provide a common language for any learner, cluster of learners, community, or society. This philosophical common language should be for everyone, especially adult educators, philosophers, professors—even common folks interested in both social and personal practices through education and learning—but failure to appreciate the detrimental impact of relying solely on values and ideas from primarily one cultural vantage point will limit the roles that philosophy can play in ACE frameworks and language.

From these historical and contemporary goals, both philosophy and education have complemented each other relating to concerns for the society and self. ACE has distinctively contributed further questions and viewpoints in developing its own unique philosophical language. Thus, the seven widely accepted philosophies of adult education align to the historical and contemporary goals of educating the society and self, but stop short of being inclusive of the diverse societies and selves participating in adult education. Merriam and Kim (2008) write, "Anchored in classical Greek thought, the dominance of Western knowledge has resulted in nonattention to, if not outright dismissal of, other systems, cosmologies, and understandings about learning and knowing" (p. 72). These widely accepted philosophies can serve as one point of reference for adult educators to understand philosophical practices within ACE but must not be framed as the only point of reference.

"Othered" Philosophical Foundations

Merriam and Kim (2008) reiterate the connection between what we believe (our philosophy) and what we do (our practice). Being aware of other philosophies broadens how we practice adult education. Merriam and Kim use the term *non-Western*—which they recognize as problematic—to reference "systems of thought different from what we in the West have come to assume about the knowledge base of adult learning theory" (p. 72). Highlighting the communal, informal, lifelong, and holistic nature of most philosophies originating from outside of Western, Eurocentric hegemony, Merriam and Kim provide a bird's-eye view of what other philosophical frameworks include and offer an understanding of practice and theory informed by these differing ideological locations.

Eastern Philosophy

Like the Western approach, there is no one single Eastern philosophy to draw from, but rather a plethora of perspectives that are insightful for informing practice. A cursory review of some Eastern philosophies suggests little distinction between adults and youth, unlike Western philosophies, which have produced sharper lines between the two types of learners. In Thailand, *khit-pen* (know how to think) is grounded in Buddhism and encourages individuals to think carefully, take initiative, and be self-reliant in their communities. People need to relate to information about the self, society, or literature before solving the problem or making a decision. If the problem is unsolved, then khit-pen is started again (Sungsri, 2018). Another philosophy is both-ways education, which is rooted in Australian Indigenous tradition. Both-ways education expects all contributors to the educational setting to recognize different knowledge traditions are in the same space, causing a convergence of different epistemologies (Campbell & Christie, 2016).

Further, in China, Neo-Confucianism is about developing self-conscious reflection. As Wang and King (2008) explain, "Westerners believe exploration should precede the development of skill, whereas Chinese educators believe skills should be developed first (which requires repetitive learning), which provides a basis to be creative with" (p. 139). Inner experience develops self-knowledge, which leads to creativity in Neo-Confucianism. Last, Rabindranath Tagore, the Indian Nobel laureate, supported the notion of free mind, free knowledge, and a free nation, leading to self-realization. His educational ideas are gleaned through his various writings rather than a single, primary text. Through self-realization, people are better able to self-educate based on three principles: independence (harmony with one's relationships and society), perfection (develop all aspects of the self), and universality (rebirth of an individual above their limitations). The goal of education, therefore, is for self-realization. The curriculum is situated in the local surroundings, and through this interaction, students write, create, and dream their ideas (O'Connell, 2003; Pushpanathan, 2013). Each of these perspectives help distinguish an Eastern philosophy of ACE.

African Philosophy

Within African philosophies, hints of Merriam and Kim's (2008) characterizations are evident. Mutamba (2012) reminds us that Africa is not monolithic, but while variations across regions and people exist, some salient philosophical concepts are present. In particular, within a traditional African philosophical framework are the two concepts of Ubuntu and communalism. Both reflect the significance of community uplift and sustenance. "Community and belonging to a community of people constitute the very fabric of traditional African life. Unlike the Western liberal notion of the individual as some sort of entity that is capable of existing and flourishing on its own" (Mutamba, 2012, pp. 5–6). Fordjor et al. (2003) highlight that within Ghanaian philosophy, virtue and character underlie the importance of community and one's social responsibility within it. Such a philosophy is more concerned with developing the individual for the benefit of the community, as opposed to developing the individual for the benefit of that individual.

Likewise, functionalism and lifelong learning as philosophical ideas are driven by the imperative of developing and sustaining community. The question becomes, "What does the community need and how are community members developed to meet those needs?" Within this viewpoint, it is people that are developed, not workers, as they need not only skill-based knowledge but also understanding of the interrelatedness between and within people and with the environment. Essential knowledge develops throughout one's lifetime and is not compartmentalized or limited by age (Fordjor et al., 2003).

In the traditional Ghanaian philosophy, knowledge is viewed as any competence that the individual possesses that can be used to solve societal problems . . . . Knowledge, therefore, is comprehensive and seen as an embodiment of all virtues in society. These include technical or vocational knowledge, intellectual, spiritual, aesthetic powers, the ability to speak in proverbs and interpret them accordingly and the ability to use words of wisdom. (Fordjor et al., 2003, p. 191)

Semali (2009) recognizes the import of African philosophy being informed by Indigenous ways of knowing and the cultural context of Black Africans and frames an African philosophy as viewing knowledge holistically, meaning "knowledge is continuous and contextual" (p. 40). Because of the history and the contemporary legacy and manifestation of colonialism, African philosophy necessarily speaks to the political, economic, and sociocultural manifestations of Black African personhood. Contemporary African philosophy "has to do with valuing and (re)valuing African heritage" (Semali, 2009, p. 46), spirituality, holistic knowledge, and community well-being (Fordjor et al., 2003; Semali, 2009). Philosophical imperatives are invoked in proverbs and in stories like that of Ananse, the spider, to communicate what matters and is valued the most.

Indigenous Philosophy

Morcom (2017) has explored Indigenous philosophy within the context of Indigenous people in Eastern Canada. Morcom noted that although, as in Africa, there is no one Indigenous philosophy, there are some similarities among them. Key concepts include holism, personalism, subjectivism, spiritualism, and transformativism. *Holism*, according to Morcom,

at one level . . . refers to the various elements that make up the self. At another level, it refers to a connection to the community, other living things, the earth, and the spiritual, and reflects Indigenous concepts of the nature of the divine. (p. 123)

The holistic self encompasses all aspects of the learner's personhood: feelings and thoughts, as well as spirit and physicality. The "medicine wheel" is often used to visually depict these dimensions of self and functions as the foundation for an Indigenous-rooted philosophy, placing learners and their contexts at the center of all learning. In Indigenous philosophy, teaching is always aimed at the "whole learner" (Morcom, 2017, p. 125). Further, learners are intimately connected and responsible to each other and the instructor as well as the community, human, and nonhuman (e.g., land, animals) and are situated nonhierarchically and collectively. Indigenous philosophy promotes egalitarianism. A final aspect highlights the importance of the spiritual. The spiritual, as Morcom explains,

ties in closely with relationships to the land; as people with millennia of history and knowledge based in specific territories, connection to place and land, as well as connection to one's ancestors and the teachings that have been passed down from them . . . . This focus on interrelationships between all things is fundamental to Indigenous ways of making sense and finding meaning. (p. 127)

Essential Philosophical Questions and Terms

The philosophical foundations of ACE are embedded within larger essential philosophical questions. These questions are:

From metaphysics: *What is universal?*
From epistemology: *What is knowledge?*
From logic: *What is reasonable?*
From ethics: *What is good or just?*
From aesthetics: *What is art, spirit, or beauty?*

These essential questions correspond to the problems of philosophy that Dewey outlined (1910/1993, 1916/1994) relating the individual to the universal/social; to physical nature/humanity; of mind/matter; to the object of knowledge (extent/limitation); and, last, of knowing (theory)/doing (practice). These questions stem from terms—*metaphysics*, *epistemology*, *logic*, *ethics*, and *aesthetics*—that Elias and Merriam (2005) refer to as subdisciplines of philosophy representing divergent viewpoints, systems, and schools of thought. Elias and Merriam assumed that such questions and terms would become apparent to adult educators, but they acknowledged that scholars and practitioners interested in the philosophy of adult (continuing) education have been attacked for being "too theoretical," "irrelevant to practice," and "far removed from educational issues" (p. 6). Their claims further support

TABLE 1.2. Essential Philosophical Questions and Terms With Related Adult-Educational Purposes

Terms	Metaphysics	Epistemology	Logic	Ethics	Aesthetics
Questions	What is universal?	What is knowledge?	What is reasonable?	What is good or just?	What is art, spirit, or beauty?
Purposes Related to Adult Education	General Education	Learning Objectives; Practical Knowledge	Logical Reasoning	Social Action	Personal Growth; Cultural Practices

the need to clarify these essential questions and terms and explain their practical relevance to the ACE field.

Table 1.2 explains connections to ACE's common purposes, which originate from its philosophical foundations. Understanding the essential philosophical terms will help adult educators and practitioners value the philosophical impact of contributions from various authors and researchers in the ACE field.

Metaphysics

ACE engages questions of metaphysics related to universal worldviews. Metaphysics, composed of the terms *meta* (meaning *after*) and *physics* (meaning *natural science*), defines exploration beyond the sciences, paying attention to the fundamental nature of reality and existence. McKenzie (1978, 1991) describes metaphysics as a more contemplative construction called *worldview*, defining social norms and values. Elias and Merriam (2005) describe metaphysics as searching out "the most general principles of reality" (p. 3). The point here is that metaphysics addresses the general claims of reality or unifying worldviews. Metaphysics also deals with questions about the philosophy of nature and humanity regarding the values people share toward humanity, the environment, and the world. An example of metaphysics within ACE comes from Lindeman's view of adult education as equivalent to life itself, meaning that ACE is universal to all of life and not merely a course subject. Another example can be situated within Tagore's view of education as being organically informed by the local environment (O'Connell, 2003).

Epistemology

Epistemology (from *episteme*, meaning *knowledge*) concerns the origins of knowledge or an understanding of how knowledge develops. This philosophical term is concerned with what we know and how we come to know. Others are familiar with the term in determining research paradigms in education such as postpositivism or constructivism (Paul, 2005). Bagnall and Hodge (2018) conduct an epistemological analysis of contemporary adult education that identifies an outline of "competing educational epistemologies" (p. 13). Bagnall and Hodge explain these four epistemologies as theories of knowledge: disciplinary, constructivist, emancipatory, and instrumental (situational) (Illeris, 2018). *Disciplinary epistemology* defines knowledge as truth. *Constructivist epistemology* expresses knowledge as authentic commitment, which can also be argued to be close to khit-pen in Thai adult education philosophy (see Sungsri, 2018). *Emancipatory epistemology* views knowledge as power. Finally, *instrumental (situational) epistemology* views knowledge as effective practice. Bagnall and Hodge's outline serves as an example of epistemology in ACE by explaining ways that adult learners come to learn and the ways adult educators' knowledge contributes to such learning.

Logic

Logic (from *logos*, meaning *reason*, *idea*, or *word*) explores the science of drawing conclusions and reasoning from information. It investigates language (propositions) as basic units of thought. In other definitions, the aim of logic is to make explicit the rules whereby interpretations can be drawn. There are four general types of logic: deductive, inductive, traditional, and modern (Blackburn, 2005). Doing the work of logic involves both analytic and critical examination of arguments. From exploring premises and conclusions, the practice of logic raises questions for the sake of clarity and understanding, pointing out contradictions from conclusions, and providing definitions, analogies, and counterarguments (Bedau, 2002; Noddings, 2015). Examples of logic in ACE can be traced to Lawson (1998), who applies logic by reaching conclusions about the concept of adult education and its reasonable use in ordinary language. Elias and Merriam (2005) encourage adult educators to achieve the work of logic for assisting the field with "language clarity, precision, and vigor" (p. 215).

Ethics

Ethics (from *ethos*, meaning *nature*, *disposition*, or *customs*) represents a broad area of concerns including values, morality, and action for doing what is right, fair, or just to oneself and others. If *logic* is a philosophical term with limited examination, *ethics* is undoubtedly more widely discussed and dominant in ACE. Jarvis (1997) believes ethics to be the "underlying principle of all morally good actions" (p. 15). Brockett (1988) explains that ethics has a place in ACE for ethical decision-making and clarifying questions of practice. Sheared et al. (2010) and Brookfield (2019) address concerns of race, racism, and adult education, and they challenge adult educators to "practice what they preach" (Brookfield, 2019, p. 147) and adult learners to "unmask" (Brookfield et al., 2019, p. 38) by engaging in critically reflective practices, examining their racial identities, and contemplating worldviews shaped through race, racism, and racial identity (Sheared et al., 2010). Another example of ethics in ACE comes from Paterson (1979), who explains ethics through moral education and developing "moral awareness" (pp. 143–144).

Aesthetics

Aesthetics (from *aisthetikos*, meaning *of sense perception*) is a philosophical term rooted in the study of beauty and art. Runes (1963) explains that the term was first used about 1750 to imply the "science of sensuous knowledge, whose aim is beauty, as contrasted with logic, whose aim is truth" (p. 6). Over time, many philosophers have viewed aesthetics as including the study of feelings, emotions, concepts, and judgments from an appreciation of the arts and the wider class of the "beautiful" or "sublime" (Barton, 1964; Blackburn, 2005; More, 1964; O'Connell, 2003). From the viewpoint of ACE, aesthetics represents learners' cultures in artful ways that advance ideals and culture. Another connection to aesthetics in ACE can be derived from Tisdell (2003), who connects culture to transformative learning experiences and advances the aesthetic, beautiful, and artful role of "spirituality" in ACE through art, music, symbols, and images.

Connected Framework for Philosophical Foundations and Essential Terms

Ross-Gordon et al. (2017) express the absence of a philosophical language, accessible framework, or useful tool in ACE where philosophical contributions can be assessed, compared, and evaluated. A connected framework, as presented in Figure 1.1, serves to link the seven widely accepted philosophies to the essential philosophical questions and terms. This connected framework serves as a response to this absence.

The explanation of this framework starts with ACE's purpose of educating the collective society and the individual self, as represented by the two continuum goals (in bold). Next, the positions of the seven widely accepted philosophies represent their relationship to the goals of the society and self. At the center of the framework is the analytical philosophy of adult education for its potential and promise in ACE. Elias and Merriam (2005) advocate for an analytical philosophy of adult education that goes beyond mere conceptual analysis to a "rational reconstruction of educational enterprise in its full dimension" (p. 215), concluding that analytical philosophy of adult education "may well provide the strongest philosophical basis for contemporary philosophy of adult education" (p. 215).

The essential philosophical term directly related to the analytical philosophy of adult education is *logic*. Lawson (1998) advocates for the importance of logic in analyzing philosophical issues, such as different concepts of adult education and the daily practices of educating adults. Ross-Gordon et al. (2017) noted that the analytical philosophy of adult education "is by far the most common philosophical approach today" (p. 162). Analytical philosophy and logic should be the start for all philosophical theory and practice, serving as the educational enterprise of ACE in its full dimension (Scott, 2015).

The other widely accepted Western philosophies—liberal, behaviorist, progressive, radical/critical, postmodern, and humanistic—also align to the goals of society and self in varying degrees. For example, liberal and behaviorist philosophies are most aligned to the society goal and the essential terms of metaphysics and epistemology, addressing general education, learning objectives, universality, reality, and knowledge; whereas the progressive and humanistic philosophies are most aligned to the self goal and the essential terms of ethics and aesthetics, addressing experience, self-direction, art, beauty, and spirituality.

The radical/critical and postmodern philosophies are most aligned to both the society goal and the self goal and are placed in the center of this figure for their convergence with educating both society and self. The radical/critical philosophy aligns closer to the essential

Figure 1.1 Connected framework of ACE philosophical foundations and essential terms.

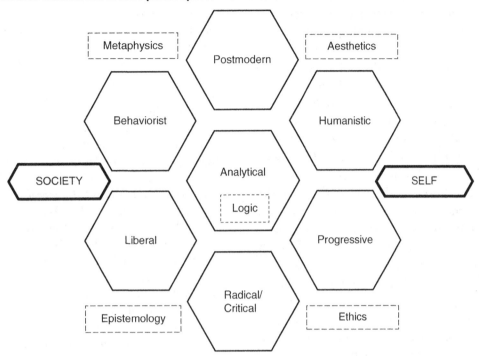

terms of epistemology and ethics; the postmodern philosophy aligns closer to the essential terms of metaphysics and aesthetics. Elias and Merriam (2005) believe that radical/critical philosophy has had a limited impact on the practice of adult education. However, Brookfield and Holst (2011) provide examples of radical/critical adult education including participatory action research and its principles of epistemology and ethics. Usher et al. (1997) explain postmodernism as a decline in universal ideals and grand narratives (metaphysics) alongside the cultures (aesthetics) that pervade everyday life, although some proponents of postmodernism would likely argue against representing this philosophical foundation between metaphysics and aesthetics terms (or even being structurally represented at all). The higher placement of the postmodern foundation supports Elias and Merriam's (2005) explanation that it "raises crucial questions about the world we live in, and the enterprise that engages us" (p. 246).

In short, the alignment of widely accepted philosophies and essential philosophical terms is helpful for simplifying how to apply specific philosophies and terms to educational goals, such as the goal of educating the collective society or of educating the individual self. For ACE scholars and practitioners interested in educating society, the philosophies of liberalism and behaviorism should be primarily considered, along with metaphysics and epistemology. For those interested in educating the self, the philosophies of progressivism and humanism should be primarily considered, along with ethics and aesthetics. Lastly, those equally interested in educating the society and self should primarily start with the radical/critical and postmodern philosophies and the essential terms of epistemology and ethics, and metaphysics and aesthetics, respectively. This connected framework represents a start but fails to incorporate "othered" philosophies such as Eastern, African, and Indigenous, to name only a few. Further development of the connected framework is needed and welcomed.

Conclusion

In searching the extant literature during this past decade, literature focused on or using "other"-informed philosophies in education, especially adult education, was scarce. The widely accepted philosophies of ACE involve understanding the essential philosophical questions and terms that undergird, strengthen, and bind the field together. As framed, the seven commonly accepted philosophies of adult education collectively fail to allow space for philosophical orientations not rooted in a Western value and belief system. These philosophies are essentially othered within the context of adult education philosophy. The essential philosophical terms (and purposes) described in this chapter—metaphysics (universality), epistemology (knowledge), logic (reasoning), ethics (goodness/justice), and aesthetics (art/spirit/beauty)—should be looked at more broadly and from multiple cultural–historical locations to create space for "othered" philosophies. When this is done, these essential terms can be aligned specifically to the widely accepted philosophies of ACE as well as "othered" philosophies forming a framework for understanding adult learning and practice in ways that authentically honor and engage the diversity among adult learners. This chapter considered how philosophy, and the adult-educational contributions to philosophy, can be more relevant and more efficiently researched through using a connected framework. Although the focus of this chapter was mainly Western in scope, including Eastern, African, and Indigenous philosophies of education provides a broader range of insights and questions that can inform ACE practice.

In all, these philosophical foundations and essential terms may serve as the common language for the goals of educating society and self within the enterprise of ACE. Such an enterprise will invite, for decades to come, all learners, clusters, or communities of learners. Hopefully, this enterprise will also summon teachers, researchers, and professors, and equip them for better practice, teaching, and research in the societal and solitary interplay—of our continued adult educational philosophy.

References

Adler, M. J. (1988). *Reforming education: The opening of the American mind*. Macmillan.

Alhadeff-Jones, M. (2017). *Time and the rhythms of emancipatory education: Rethinking the temporal complexity of self and society*. Routledge.

Bagnall, R. G., & Hodge, S. (2018). Contemporary adult and lifelong education and learning: An epistemological analysis. In M. Milana, S. Webb, J. Holford, R. Waller, & P. Jarvis (Eds.), *The Palgrave international handbook on adult and lifelong education and learning* (pp. 13–34). Palgrave Macmillan.

Barton, G. E. (1964). *Ordered pluralism: A philosophic plan of action for teaching*. Center for the Study of Liberal Education for Adults.

Bedau, H. (2002). *Thinking and writing about philosophy* (2nd ed.). Bedford/St. Martin's.

Bergevin, P. (1967). *A philosophy for adult education*. Seabury Press.

Bierema, L. L. (2010). Professional identity. In C. E. Kasworm, A. D. Rose, & J. M. Ross-Gordon (Eds.), *Handbook of adult and continuing education* (pp. 135–145). SAGE.

Blackburn, S. (2005). *The Oxford dictionary of philosophy*. Oxford University Press.

Brockett, R. G. (Ed.). (1988). *Ethical issues in adult education*. Teachers College Press.

Brookfield, S. (2010). Theoretical frameworks for understanding the field. In C. E. Kasworm, A. D. Rose, & J. M. Ross-Gordon (Eds.), *Handbook of adult and continuing education* (pp. 71–81). SAGE.

Brookfield, S. D. (2019). *Teaching race: How to help unmask and challenge racism*. Jossey-Bass.

Brookfield, S. D., & Holst, J. D. (2011). *Radicalizing learning: Adult education for a just world*. Jossey-Bass.

Campbell, M., & Christie, M. (2016). Shopping at Pine Creek: Rethinking both-ways education through the context of remote Aboriginal Australian Ranger Training. In R. C. Mizzi, T. S. Rocco, & S. Shore (Eds.), *Disrupting adult and community education: Teaching, learning, and working in the periphery* (pp. 147–160). SUNY Press.

Darkenwald, G. G. & Merriam, S. B. (1982). *Adult education: Foundations of practice*. Harper & Row.

Dewey, J. (1993). *Philosophy & education in their historic relations* (E. R. Clapp, Transcriber; J. J. Chambliss, Ed.). Westview Press. (Original work published 1910)

Dewey, J. (1994). *Democracy and education: An introduction to the philosophy of education*. The Free Press. (Original work published 1916)

Elias, J. L., & Merriam, S. B. (2005). *Philosophical foundations of adult education* (3rd ed.). Krieger.

Fordjor, P., Kotoh, A., Kpeli, K., Kwamefio, A., Mensa, Q., Owusu, E., & Mullins, B. (2003). A review of traditional Ghanaian and Western philosophies of adult education. *International Journal of Lifelong Education, 22*(2), 182–199. https://doi.org/10.1080/0260137032000055321

Freire, P. (1972). *Pedagogy of the oppressed* (M. Bergman Ramos, Trans.). Herder.

Gutek, G. L. (2010). *Historical and philosophical foundations of education* (5th ed.). Pearson.

Houle, C. O. (1992). *The literature of adult education: A bibliographic essay*. Jossey-Bass.

Illeris, K. (2018). *Contemporary theories of learning* (2nd ed.). Routledge.

Isaac, E. P., Merriweather, L. R., & Rogers, E. E. (2010). Chasing the American dream: Race and adult and continuing education. In C. E. Kasworm, A. D. Rose, & J. M. Ross-Gordon (Eds.), *Handbook of adult and continuing education* (pp. 359–368). SAGE.

Jarvis, P. (1997). *Ethics and education for adults*. National Institute of Adult and Continuing Education.

Kallen, H. M. (1962). *Philosophical issues in adult education*. Charles C. Thomas.

Kasworm, C. E., Rose, A. D., & Ross-Gordon, J. M. (2010). Adult and continuing education as an intellectual common. In C. E. Kasworm, A. D. Rose, & J. M. Ross-Gordon (Eds.), *Handbook of adult and continuing education*, (pp. 1–10). SAGE.

Knowles, M. S. (1980). *The modern practice of adult education: From pedagogy to andragogy*. Prentice Hall.

Lawson, K. H. (1975). *Philosophical concepts and values in adult education*. Open University Press.

Lawson, K. H. (1998). Philosophical foundations. In J. M. Peters, P. Jarvis, & Associates (Eds.), *Adult education: Evolution and achievements in a developing field of study* (pp. 282–300). Jossey-Bass.

Lindeman, E. C. (1926). *The meaning of adult education in the United States*. Harvest House.

McKenzie, L. (1978). *Adult education and the burden of the future*. University Press of America.

McKenzie, L. (1991). *Adult education and worldview construction*. Krieger.

Merriam, S. B., Caffarella, R. S., & Baumgartner, L. M. (2007). *Learning in adulthood: A comprehensive guide* (3rd ed.). Jossey-Bass.

Merriam, S., & Kim, Y. (2008). Non-Western perspectives on learning and knowing. *New Directions for Adult and Continuing Education, 2018*(119), 71–81. https://doi.org/10.1002/ace

Morcom, L. A. (2017). Indigenous holistic education in philosophy and practice, with wampum as a case study. *Foro de Educación, 15*(23), 121–138. http://dx.doi.org/10.14516/fde.572

More, W. S. (1964). *Emotions and adult learning*. Heath.

Murphy, M. M. (2006). *The history and philosophy of education: Voices of educational pioneers*. Pearson.

Mutamba, C. (2012). *21st century African philosophy of adult and human resource education in southern Africa* (ED546475). ERIC. https://files.eric.ed.gov/fulltext/ED546475.pdf

Noddings, N. (2015). *Philosophy of education* (4th ed.). Westview Press.

O'Connell, K. M. (2003). Rabindranath Tagore on education. *Infed*. https://infed.org/mobi/rabindranath-tagore-on-education/

Paterson, R. W. K. (1979). *Values, education, and the adult*. Routledge & Kegan Paul.

Paul, J. L. (2005*). Introduction to the philosophies of research and criticism in education and the social sciences*. Pearson.

Powell, J. W., & Benne, K. (1960). Philosophies of adult education. In M. S. Knowles (Ed.), *Handbook of adult education in the United States* (pp. 50–52). Education Association of the U.S.A.

Pushpanathan, T. (2013). Rabindranath Tagore's philosophy of education and its influence on Indian Education. *International Journal of Current Research and Academic Review, 1*(4), 42–45.

Ross-Gordon, J. M., Rose, A. D., & Kasworm, C. E. (2017). *Foundations of adult and continuing education*. Jossey-Bass.

Runes, D. D. (1963). *Dictionary of philosophy: Ancient-medieval-modern*. Littlefield, Adams.

Scott, L. (2015). Learning cities for all: Directions to a new adult education and learning movement [Themed issue]. *New Directions for Adult and Continuing Education, 2015*(145).

Semali, L. (2009). Cultural perspectives in African adult education: Indigenous ways of knowing in lifelong learning. In A. Abdi & D. Kapoor (Eds.), *Global perspectives on adult education,* (pp. 35–52). Palgrave Macmillan.

Sheared, V., Johnson-Bailey, J., Colin III, S. A. J., Peterson, E., Brookfield, S. D., & Associates. (Eds.). (2010). *The handbook of race and adult education*. Jossey-Bass.

Skinner, B. F. (1971). *Beyond freedom and dignity*. Knopf.

Stewart, D. W. (1987). *Adult learning in America: Eduard Lindeman and his agenda for lifelong education*. Krieger.

Sungsri, S. (2018). Nonformal and informal education in Thailand. In G. W. Fry (Ed.), *Education in Thailand: An old elephant in search of a new mahout* (pp. 189–222). Springer.

Thorndike, E. L. (1927). The law of effect. *The American Journal of Psychology, 39*(1/4), 212–222.

Tight, M. (2001). *Key concepts in adult education and training*. Routledge Falmer.

Tisdell, E. J. (2003). *Exploring spirituality and culture in adult and higher education*. Jossey-Bass.

Tisdell, E. J., & Taylor, E. W. (2001). Adult education philosophy informs practice. *Adult Learning, 11*(2), 6–10. https://doi.org/10.1177/104515959901100203

Tough, A. (1971). *The adult's learning projects: A fresh approach to theory and practice in adult learning*. OISE.

Tyler, R. W. (2013). Basic principles of curriculum and instruction. In D. J. Flinders & S. J. Thornton (Eds.), *Curriculum studies reader* (rev. ed., pp. 60–68). Routledge.

Usher, R., Bryant, I., & Johnston, R. (1997). *Adult education and the postmodern challenge: Learning beyond the limits*. Routledge.

Wang, V., & King, K. P. (2008). Transformative learning and ancient Asian educational perspectives. *Journal of Transformative Education, 6*(2), 136–150. https://doi.org/10.1177/0002764208322760

Zinn, L. M. (1998). Identifying your philosophical orientation. In M. W. Galbraith (Ed.), *Adult learning methods* (2nd ed., pp. 37–72). Krieger.

CHAPTER 2

History of Adult and Continuing Education

Amy D. Rose

The history of adult and continuing education is hardly a pressing area of concern. Indeed, there is often a deep separation between the history of the field and its actual practice. It is not the intent here to dissect the ways that history can be used; however, it is important to understand that although nothing is preordained, the past does affect how we view the present (Rose, 2017, 2018).

Each year, a few historically oriented pieces appear in the United States, but there is usually very little development of new ideas or trends in the historical scholarship. In fact, the entire approach to adult and continuing education history lies in the interests of individual authors. This is fine in some respects, but it also leaves big gaps and misunderstandings about the field and its development. In this chapter, I will describe the varying ways that the history of adult and continuing education has been portrayed and will discuss some of the more interesting aspects of recent historical research in the field.

All history writing is complex and multidimensional. However, adult and continuing education history has an extra level of complexity because there are so many different definitions and approaches. If one is serious about trying to understand the history of the field, one needs to examine articles within the histories of higher education, communities, the professions, business and industry, and schooling itself. Additionally, the histories of immigration, nation-building, journalism, social change movements, group learning, and communication need to be considered. This is probably a task that no one person can ever accomplish (and this list is hardly even exhaustive). The first questions that anyone needs to ask are, what am I trying to achieve here? How do I approach such a broad field? What are the imperative questions? There are no simple answers.

Historiography of the Field

Historiography is the history of history or the study of how historians have portrayed a particular event or phenomenon. Historians are constantly reevaluating or revising history, either through reinterpretation or by analyzing newly acquired data sets or documents (Rose, 2018). Here I am examining how historians have presented the history of adult continuing education. Starting in the 1940s, there have been five major histories of the adult and continuing education field in the United States (although the exact definition of the field was not fully explored in most of these works). In the first history, Adams (1944) framed the history of adult education in terms of the diffusion of culture. Lacking an institutional framework, Adams saw adult education in terms of culture and looked at the varying institutions involved with that. In the words of Stubblefield and Keane (1994), Adams "found an 'adult education jumble,' which gave him a feeling of helplessness when he tried to rationalize his task" (p. 4). Taking another tack, Grattan (1955) portrayed the long development of adult education from ancient Greece to the present. Adams and Grattan were both commissioned to write their works to prove the breadth and depth of adult education history. They were making the case that adult education has always existed and that it existed to serve a particular function within society either to strengthen democracy (Grattan) or the diffusion of culture and knowledge (Adams).

Malcolm Knowles (1977) looked at the history from a different perspective. Not a trained historian, Knowles saw the history of American adult continuing education as one long journey of advancement culminating in the development of a field and a professional organization. Finally, two newer works approach the broad history from different perspectives. Kett (1994) examined not adult continuing education but the myriad ways that adults learn on their own. He was not interested in the field, but rather in what we can call *voluntary learning*. He lost interest when adult education became an organized, institutionalized entity, ending his preface with this somber statement, "Today, no one can plausibly describe adult education as a marginal activity, but professional adult educators have become increasingly marginal to the education of adults" (p. xviii). Stubblefield and Keane (1994) wrote the last overview history of American adult education. They tried to remedy many of the critiques made by other writers, looking at the complexity of the adult education experience and including previously excluded groups such as Native Americans, African Americans, and women. Since 1994, no one has written a book-length history of U.S. adult continuing education, although Welton (2013) looked at the history of Canadian adult education. Welton eschewed the big thematic issues that Grattan, Adams, and Knowles attempted, opting instead for a brief but in-depth treatment.

Aside from book-length overviews, there have been other specialized treatments of particular time periods or issues, as well as chapters that have attempted to summarize the history of adult continuing education. The most recent chapter treatment was the historical overview included in the introductory textbook by Ross-Gordon et al. (2017). They consider several historical themes, including: adults and adulthood; diffusion of knowledge; higher education; basic education and literacy; work-related learning; and learning for social justice or advocacy.

The most prevalent approach to historical research in adult continuing education lies in the study of particular issues or individuals, rather than an overview or synthesis. These studies are continuous and focus on myriad concerns. They also come from a variety of disciplines. Historians may study some of these because they are interested in labor history or women's history, although a few of these histories were written by adult educators. One of the more recent efforts in this vein is an edited book by Imel and Bersch (2015) that examined the role of women in the field of adult education.

Finally, writers have occasionally looked at the biographies of learners and teachers as ways of understanding a particular aspect or approach within adult and continuing education. There have been relatively few of these studies published over the past 10 years. In general, the field has moved toward integrating biography into the fabric of its history. Yet large questions remain. These include the expansion of our understanding of the role of Latina/o adult continuing education history. Additionally, there has been little integration of the various historical case studies into a broader narrative of the history of adult education. In the remainder of this chapter I will discuss some of the ways that the historical narratives have been conceptualized and presented. I will draw from some of the more recent research but, of necessity, much will be left out.

Overview of Recent Research

There is no easy way to summarize the most recent historical research. First of all, the research is disseminated through so many different journals and disciplines that it is virtually impossible to consult all of the possibilities. Using a search engine such as Google Scholar or ERIC and entering the phrase "adult education history" yields an extremely limited output. A cursory study of the past 10 years of *Adult Education Quarterly* (*AEQ*) shows only two historical articles (Boshier & Huang, 2010; Platt & Hill, 2014). Since one of these papers concerns prostitution in New Orleans from 1897 to 1917 and the other deals with China in the 1930s, it is difficult to make any statements about current historiography based on these articles alone. In addition, several articles—while not, strictly speaking, historical studies—did draw on the study of history. These were philosophical works that pulled from published works to analyze a particular issue. For example, Glassman et al. (2012) discussed the development of action research and the ways that it has changed over time. This study may be viewed as a piece of intellectual history although its focus is much more present-centered. Examining previous issues of *History of Education Quarterly* (*HEQ*) was somewhat more fruitful. While historical research in *AEQ* is sporadic and discrete, some major themes emerge from *HEQ*. Since 2010, there has been an explosion of research on African American, Latinx, and Native American topics. Some of these touch on issues relating to adult education in terms of either community development, teacher training, or the diffusion of culture.

Additionally, many books published since 2010 afford an elucidation of some aspect of adult education. Some of these, particularly as they relate to the history of African Americans, social change, and higher education will be discussed later.

Central Tensions and Questions

In thinking about the history of adult education, the first problem lies in the following questions: What is to be included and what are the implications of any accepted definition of *adult continuing education*? The next issue is, how do we think about the historical narrative? What story is actually being told? What is to be included and what, if anything, is to be omitted? This leads to another question, already briefly discussed: What is history for? This is a broad question, but it is also important to think about the ways our understanding of history have framed our concept of adult continuing education today. Finally, it is important to analyze some of the basic trends in adult education, in particular the tension in a field that has defined itself in terms of both individual development and community improvement or social change. While foci on the individual and on the group are not necessarily mutually exclusive, they do need to be parsed or interrogated more closely.

Problems of Definition: Setting Parameters?

Stubblefield and Rachal (1992) traced the history of the term *adult education* from its earliest use until the 1920s, by which time it had become a contentious term. In fact, the term was the center of battle within the nascent American Association for Adult Education (AAAE). Stubblefield and Rachal noted that, by 1912, the term *adult education* had been used to "convey several very different concepts derived from such contexts as scientific societies, public school free lectures, library activities, university extension, and farm demonstration" (p. 107). This umbrella term was adopted during a "gestational phase" (p. 114) of 1891 to 1916, but moved into general usage in the 1920s. This development shows that early attempts to create a single term coalesced around adult education, but the exact definition was not fully developed. In fact, the early years of the AAAE focused on securing a footing for adult education by looking for commonalities among the disparate aspects of the field (Rose, 1989).

If we look at the development of the field over time, we can see that the tension over definition has affected how we currently view adult education as a professional area. This is partly related to the particular lens that we bring to the endeavor. For example, individuals in adult basic education often talk about *adult education* generally when they really mean *basic education* or *secondary education*. This began with the passage of the Adult Education Act of 1966 and continues through to the present with the 2016 passage of the Adult Education and Family Literacy Act, which is Title II of the Workforce Innovation and Opportunity Act (OCTAE, n.d.; Rose, 1991).

This confusing nomenclature has resulted in a search for commonalities that transcend particular organizational ties. Part of this effort stems from an attempt to build an academic field with recognition within the university and research communities (Rose & Hansman, 2015). In effect, the U.S. field has defined itself around the unique attributes of adult learning and the concomitant instructional, administrative, and organizational implications of this emphasis. We can see this confusion play out in a number of ways.

Critically, the emphasis on adult learning, as opposed to adult education as a unifying theme, has both strengthened the field and created a centrifugal force that identifies almost all aspects of life as adult education. Emanating from this viewpoint, all changes or transformations are conceptually converted into educational experiences. Historical research, as with all research, focuses on questions that arise from previous research. It seems incumbent on educators to ask historical questions that bind history to broader questions of social, labor, intellectual, or educational history.

What Is to Be Included in the Historical Record?

As noted, historians approach history with specific questions that then affect every aspect of their research. It is important to understand the historical questions being asked in order to understand where a specific piece of research might fit into a general narrative of adult education history. For example, the history of adults in higher education would look very different depending on the kinds of questions being asked. Justice (2011) analyzed the Civil Affairs Training School at Stanford during World War II as an example of how progressive education infiltrated education at all levels and in many diverse ways. However, his approach could have also looked at the Civil Affairs Training School from an adult education perspective, which would have explained the ways that adult educators adopted and then adapted principles of progressive education to adult education generally.

Additionally, as this discussion indicates, there are many different stories of adult education to be told and it is difficult—almost impossible—to combine them into a totality. Much of the recent work within adult education is predicated on the idea that specific groups have been systematically (and systemically) ignored. For example, Imel and Bersch's (2015) book examines the lives of women who were involved in and helped shape adult education from the 1920s until the 1950s. Some of the chapters focus on the development of the field (see, particularly, Rose, 2015) and the women involved in the early years of the AAAE, such as Mary Ely (Bersch, 2015), Dorothy Canfield Fisher (Sexton, 2015) and Jessie Allen Charters (Wanstreet, 2015), among others. However, other individuals covered in this book were active as adult educators without being engaged with the field. Are they less important? This book says no, but their contributions are different.

Additionally, the history of African Americans in adult education has been increasingly explored over the past 25 years. Of particular interest is the recent work on Alain Locke (Stewart, 2018), and the civil rights movement. Some of the work focuses on the role of Locke himself and the continuing debate about his place in either adult education history or African American history (e.g., Guy & Brookfield, 2009). There is no single way to think about what should be included within the history of adult education.

Thus, the study of history and historical inquiry stem from many different impulses. Within adult education, the interest is usually provoked by one of several circumstances. Initially history was used to justify the field—that is, adult education has always existed, and it is a genuine area or discipline. Additionally, history can give a sense about how a particular problem first developed or how a particular phenomenon has changed or evolved. Finally—and this is actually a strong point even if it feels like belittlement—history is inherently interesting. While colonial history may feel removed from the present, the dilemmas presented—from the development of slavery to the status of women—have had a profound effect on our understanding of the United States in general, and adult education specifically.

What Is History For?

Historians of education have grappled with the issue of meaning for decades. They have questioned whether the history of education is a history of schooling or something more. Bailyn (1960) called for an examination of the education that occurs outside of schools. Similarly, Cremin (1970), in the first of his foundational three-volume history of American education, expanded on this idea, calling for all aspects of the transmission of culture, both formal and informal, to be included under the broad umbrella of education. He posited that the complex process of cultural transmission and change were both part of the educational narrative and the result of it. Thus, for Cremin, the study of education (which included the education of adults) was necessary in order to understand American culture in all of its diversity. In fact, Cremin's view of the history of American education encompassed what he called *educational configurations*, that is, institutions and organizations for the transmission of culture. These include the family, religion, schools, workplaces, cultural and helping institutions, and popular culture. Of course, these comprise the purview of adult education as well.

However, what Cremin did not emphasize is that individuals oppress others and that, too, is learned. Additionally, others learn to resist. All of this needs to be included in any history of adult education. Therefore, we are looking at the development of multiple cultures, the resistance to the transmission of these cultures (in some cases), and the efforts to annihilate or suppress other cultural traditions. This, then, is the history of adult education.

Individual, Community, or Organizational Approaches

The study of history starts with questions. The approach to adult education history is often narrow because the questions asked are narrow. Yet, although the questions seem to be rather narrow, they have broader implications. In addition, since much of the writing and research of this history is accomplished by historians in other fields, their questions may have limited relevance for adult educators. However, their questions may also open our eyes to the narrative that we have constructed about adult education. As historians reimagine the histories of, for example, lyceums, Americanization, or a host of other issues, we begin to see the ways that adult education has connected to many broader social movements (both conservative and liberal).

For adult educators, this may mean thinking about groups that use but are not dedicated to adult education, such as a health agency that uses adult education to promote community health. There is ample evidence that, historically, adult education has had a strong agenda of working for social change. For example, Stubblefield and Keane (1994) point to many social movements that utilized adult education in quests for change, while Holst (2002) analyzes the intersection between movements for social change and adult education. Yet, the historical record is more complex and ambiguous than these views would lead us to believe. In fact, several, often contradictory impulses make up the narrative history of adult education. Thus, while it is certainly true that social justice and social change have been an undercurrent in much adult education programming, it is also true that adult education has served an essentially conservative function. For example, historians have studied adult education as a progressive movement that brought adult education methods to diverse settings working for social change. These settings include organizations such as trade unions, the Folk School movement (especially Highlander Folk School), and civil rights organizations, to name a few (see Stubblefield & Keane, 1994). However, while the Americanization movement of the early 20th century has been portrayed as a reform effort, with assimilation as a positive end, it has also been seen a means of social control (e.g., Glazer, 1993). This is not due necessarily to the movement into the university, as Grace (2000) maintained, although the search for the legitimacy that an association with higher education conveys is certainly important (Rose & Hansman, 2015).

The Complexities of Social Change

Looking at the phenomenon of learning within community organizations and autonomous groups leads to the uncomfortable conclusion that all political persuasions have utilized adult education. Blee (1993) emphasizes the ways that historians limit themselves by not looking at social change as both a conservative and liberal phenomenon. She focuses specifically on oral history, but the point can probably be made about adult education more generally. She writes, "Historians have paid less attention to the life stories of ordinary people whose political agendas they find unsavory, dangerous, or deliberately deceptive" (p. 596). This is also true within adult education, where writers have focused on the liberal (or progressive) aspects of change, but not on the other kinds of organizations that have used adult education methods to further their ends.

The story of women's clubs and groups within adult education has been sporadically told (e.g., Imel & Bersch, 2015). In writing about the women of the Ku Klux Klan (Blee, 2008) and women in hate groups more generally (Blee, 2002), Blee expands our understanding of social change and women's groups. She attempts to shift the narrative from women's participation in social change and social action as inherently liberal and pacifist to women's roles in shaping the Far Right. She also maintains that they participated as purveyors, consumers, and maintainers of culture. To cite another example, June Melby Benowitz (2015) discusses the ways that women on the right mobilized to control the school curriculum and prevent desegregation. These women used a self-help model that focused on community-based organizations and the development of school curricula to send out their message. They often concentrated on education as a traditionally feminine area, but they also adopted forceful political tactics that relied on diverse elements of persuasion to make their points.

These works emphasize the fact that *self-help* and even *social change movements* are inherently neutral terms. It is the actual work done that lends them their political cast. One more example will have to suffice to substantiate this view.

Disrupting the Narrative

The narrative is also disrupted by the multifaceted approaches to historical research that we think we understand. Reinterpreting the meaning of historical events is an important part of the historical enterprise.

Alain Locke is often painted as a luminary within adult education circles. As a Howard University philosophy professor who was active in the AAAE and later became president of its successor, the Adult Education Association (AEA), he blended his interest in the philosophy of aesthetics with projects that would enhance understanding and appreciation of African art (Ross-Gordon et al., 2017; Stewart, 2018). Locke's approach has been much debated. He is usually seen as an antagonist of the much-better-known (at least today) W. E. B. Du Bois, whose reputation has remained intact while Locke's has oscillated. Nocera (2018) argues that Locke's Harlem Experiments, which are often portrayed as important adult education efforts, were instead an extension of what he calls elite democratic liberalism. He adds:

> Despite having roots in radical forms of Black expression that had been popularized in 1920s Harlem, the Carnegie-funded program represented something else: a far-reaching negotiation over whether Black culture, politics, and protest could be incorporated in a broader paradigm of elite liberalism that had developed in the interwar era. (p. 4)

Nocera (2018) continues that Locke was a member of the "Black reform elite" (p. 5), that is, individuals who served as communicators of Black culture to White liberals. In this sense, Nocera conveyed the idea that Locke was a supreme popularizer, an idea with which Locke might have agreed. Of course, this is not an entirely new idea, as the animus between Locke and Du Bois makes evident (Guy & Brookfield, 2009). There is the added problem, however, that it is unclear whether Du Bois objected to Locke's ideas, his personality, or his homosexuality—or some combination of all three. Locke's focus on aesthetics often led to his being labeled an elitist snob, although his primary interest was in equalizing the value placed on differing artistic approaches (Stewart, 2018).

Additionally, there are many dimensions to the analysis of self-help movements and organizations. Thus, the use of adult education for social change and social justice is just one aspect of a broader and conflicting narrative. Virtually every reform movement in U.S. history has been viewed as both ameliorative and oppressive. Starting with literacy programs and programs for immigrants, the assessments and reassessments have been unrelenting. Initially presented as early examples of adult education, both of these types of programs have been questioned in recent years. The Moonlight Schools founded in Kentucky in the early 20th century were originally viewed as important innovations that allowed working people of all races, but especially African Americans, to gain literacy. Its founder, Cora Wilson Stewart, was a very prominent educator in Kentucky and acted as a proselytizer for the evening literacy programs she helped found (Greer, 2015). The Moonlight Schools are often presented as a reform effort to ameliorate the plight of Southern illiterates. Later works, however, point to the needs of a modernizing South as the key to understanding the focus on literacy by Stewart and other likeminded reformers (NeCamp, 2014). Thus, we see that an event originally framed as a humanitarian effort can also be presented as a more complex phenomenon.

In a like manner, the Americanization programs directed toward new immigrants in the early 20th century have been hotly debated and excoriated for decades. From the beginning, these programs have been portrayed as debasing of other cultures. Jane Addams, for example, felt that instead of looking at immigrant deficiencies, Americans needed to observe immigrants' gifts (Fischer, 2014).

I could add many more of these reassessments. They are extremely important to all areas of historical inquiry. In fact, one could argue that the lack of agreement lies at the heart of the disconnect between adult education and its history. In fact, nothing is fixed. As new information is found and integrated into the prevailing narrative, the very history itself changes. In my view, the central narrative tension within adult education history is between an emphasis on the individual and/or the community. Interestingly, there are some counterintuitive aspects to these dichotomous perspectives. In the previous examples, we can see that what were initially portrayed as philanthropic efforts to improve the lives of individuals and of democracy were also connected to the needs of business and industry—and, in the case of Cora Stewart, to improve the reputation of the Southern states in order to ready them for modernization. Individual development and enrichment through adulthood is the primary subject of Kett's (1994) book. Informal or nonformal groupings such as the lyceum movement, Benjamin Franklin's Junto, scientific societies, or Chautauqua have collectively served the purpose of helping individuals grow and change. At times, there has been an underlying presumption that social change will emanate from individual change. This was certainly true of the lyceum movement, which began as an effort to persuade the public of the importance of public education (Kett, 1994; Ross-Gordon et al., 2017).

Much of this history has led to a focus on adult learning (as opposed to adult education) as the thread that binds a disparate field. Although social learning and learning in groups have never been exactly ignored by historians, the primary interest has been in individual learning, especially among adults. From the early days of the founding of the formal U.S. adult and continuing education field in the 1920s, much of the writing on adult education has focused on the individual aspect of adult education. Lindeman (1926) wrote that adult education was a search for meaning. For Lindeman, as for many of the early writers on adult education, the term adult education was meant to espouse a nonvocational, postcollegiate educational experience. Basic education and job-related learning experiences were not to be included. This adult education was meant to embody a new entity, a fourth continuous tier in the educational system (albeit operating outside of all systems). Because of this, there was deep distrust of this new movement among labor leaders, magnified by their distrust of the principal funder, the Carnegie Corporation of New York (Rose, 1989).

The library was envisioned as the model for the adult education of the 1920s. Educators were to be even more talented than librarians in figuring out individual interests and helping to guide the learning process. Thus, the development or enrichment of the individual was presumed to lie in the nonformal learning opportunities provided by the Chautauqua Institution (and the related tent Chautauquas scattered across the country), the lyceum movement, Mechanics Institutes, Benjamin Franklin's Junto, and Anna Ticknor's Society to Encourage Study at Home (Rose, 1989; Scheil, 2012; Scott, 1999).

At the other end of the spectrum, political and social movements utilizing educational efforts to bring about change operated outside the purview of formal adult education. These works illustrate the fact that social change has varying meanings. The educational process can be utilized with multiple agendas. The research here is limitless, so of necessity, I have chosen a few interesting examples.

Nembhard (2014) examines the cooperative movement through the lens of African American history. She uses the cooperative movement to highlight African Americans' commitment to both self-sufficiency and social change. Placing her work within the larger sociological framework of autonomous groups, Nembhard describes the long history of African American self-help and collective action. Her essential questions are not about adult education, but they have implications for thinking about African American adult education, especially its informal, community-based aspect.

In fact, it is probably safe to say that much of the historical research on community-based groups has an important adult education component. Mathes (2012) writes of the political work of the Women's National Indian Association. Although not the purpose of her work, Mathes presents an interesting picture of the ways that women's benevolent organizations worked and the ways that they used education (both formal and informal) to pressure legislators for change and to pressure Native Americans to change.

Finally, we need to think about the difference between education and propaganda. From the earliest days of a formal field, adult educators have been concerned with this distinction. While adult educators today continue to be concerned, they are remarkably uninformed about the long history of this preoccupation (Kloubert, 2018).

Conclusion

In many ways, the narrative of adult education history mirrors the concerns of history (and especially educational history) in general. Just as American historiography has gone through waves of democratic fervor, focusing on great men, and excluding native peoples and African Americans, so has adult education history. Much of the recent historical research (especially that done by non-adult educators) has focused on who has been left out—but there is still much more to be done. The general narrative that starts with the cultural transmissions of the Native Americans; moves to the informal learning and nonformal learning of the colonial and revolutionary periods; expands to the beginnings of learning societies, mechanics institutes, and lecture circuits in the antebellum period; and results in more formalized adult education organizations such as night schools for immigrants, and for college students, extension and other similar organizations. All are part of the adult and continuing education story. The ways that clubs, newspapers, and other organizations engage in educational activities is also important, as is the work of political organizations, unions, other social movements. All of these examples combine into a multifaceted and complex educational endeavor that needs more historical study.

References

Adams, J. T. (1944). *Frontiers of American culture: A study of adult education in a democracy.* Scribner's.

Bailyn, B. (1960). *Education in the forming of American society: Needs and opportunities for study.* University of North Carolina Press; Institute of Early American History and Culture.

Benowitz, J. M. (2015). *Challenge & change: Right-wing women, grassroots activism & the baby boom generation.* University Press of Florida.

Bersch, G. T. (2015). Mary L. Ely: Dedicated adult educator. In S. Imel & G. Bersch (Eds.), *North American handbook of early women adult educators, 1925–1950* (pp. 107–114). Information Age.

Blee, K. M. (1993). Evidence, empathy, and ethics: Lessons from oral histories of the Klan. *The Journal of American History, 80*(2), 596–606.

Blee, K. M. (2002). *Inside organized racism: Women in the hate movement.* University of California Press.

Blee, K. M. (2008). *Women of the Klan: Racism and gender in the 1920s.* University of California Press.

Boshier, R., & Huang, Y. (2010). More important than guns: Chinese adult education after the Long March. *Adult Education Quarterly, 60*(3), 284–302.

Cremin, L. A. (1970). *American education: The colonial experience, 1607–1785.* Harper & Row.

Fischer, M. (2014). Addams on cultural pluralism, European immigrants, and African Americans. *The Pluralist, 9*(1), 38–58.

Glassman, M., Erdem, G., & Barthomew, M. (2012). Action research and its history as an adult education movement for social change. *Adult Education Quarterly, 63*(3), 272–288. https://doi.org/10.1177/0741713612471418.

Glazer, N. (1993). Is assimilation dead? *The Annals of the American Academy of Political and Social Science, 530*(1), 122–136.

Grace, A. P. (2000). Canadian and U.S. adult learning (1945–1970) and the cultural politics and place of lifelong learning. *International Journal of Lifelong Education, 19*(2), 141–158.

Grattan, C. H. (1955). *In quest of knowledge: A historical perspective on adult education.* Association Press.

Greer, J. (2015). Expanding working-class rhetorical traditions: The Moonlight Schools and alternative solidarities among Appalachian women, 1911–1920. *College English, 77*(3), 216–235.

Guy, T. C., & Brookfield, S. (2009). W. E. B. Du Bois's basic American Negro creed and the associates in Negro folk education: A case of repressive tolerance in the censorship of radical Black discourse on adult education. *Adult Education Quarterly, 60*(1), 65–76.

Holst, J. D. (2002). *Social movements, civil society, and radical adult education. Critical studies in education and culture series.* Bergin & Garvey.

Imel, S., & Bersch, G. (Eds.). (2015). *North American handbook of early women adult educators, 1925–1950.* Information Age.

Justice, B. (2011). When the Army got progressive: The Civil Affairs Training School at Stanford University, 1943–1945. *History of Education Quarterly, 51* (3), 330–361.

Kett, J. F. (1994). *The pursuit of knowledge under difficulties: From self-improvement to adult education in America, 1750–1990.* Stanford University Press.

Kloubert, T. (2018). Propaganda as a (new) challenge of civic education. *European Journal for Research on the Education and Learning of Adults 9*(2), 139–159.

Knowles, M. S. (1977). *A history of the adult education movement in the United States: Includes adult education institutions through 1976.* Krieger.

Lindeman, E. C. (1926). *The meaning of adult education.* New Republic Books.

Mathes, V. S. (2012). *Divinely guided: The California work of the Women's National Indian Association.* Texas Tech University Press.

NeCamp, S. (2014). *Adult literacy and American identity: The moonlight schools and Americanization programs.* Southern Illinois University Press.

Nembhard, J. G. (2014). *Collective courage: A history of African American cooperative economic thought and practice.* Pennsylvania State University Press.

Nocera, A. (2018). Negotiating the aims of African American adult education: Race and liberalism in the Harlem Experiment, 1931–1935, *History of Education Quarterly, 58* (1), 1–32. https://doi.org/10.1017/heq.2017.47

OCTAE. (n.d.). *Reports and resources*. https://www2.ed.gov/about/offices/list/ovae/resource/index.html

Platt, R. E., & Hill, L. H. (2014). A Storyville education: Spatial practices and the learned sex trade in the city that care forgot. *Adult Education Quarterly, 64*(4), 285–305.

Rose, A. D. (1989). Beyond classroom walls: The Carnegie Corporation and the founding of the American Association for Adult Education. *Adult Education Quarterly, 39*(3), 140–151.

Rose, A. D. (1991). *Ends or means: An overview of the history of the Adult Education Act*. ERIC Clearinghouse on Adult, Career, and Vocational Education.

Rose, A. D. (2015). Searching for the women in a defeminized past: America adult education between the wars. In S. Imel & G. Bersch (Eds.), *North American handbook of early women adult educators, 1925–1950* (pp. 3–16). Information Age.

Rose, A. D. (2017). Historical research in adult continuing education. In A. B. Knox, S. C. O. Conceição, & L. G. Martin (Eds.), *Mapping the field of adult and continuing education: An international compendium* (pp. 597–600). Stylus; American Association for Adult and Continuing Education.

Rose, A. D. (2018). Thinking historically: Writing and understanding historical research. In V. C. X. Wang & T. G. Reio, Jr. (Eds.), *Handbook of research on innovative techniques, trends, and analysis for optimized research methods* (pp. 220–232). IGI Global. https://doi.org/10.4018/978-1-5225-5164-5

Rose, A. D., & Hansman, C. A. (2015, May 19). Consolidating the profession? The professoriate in the 1950s and 1960s. In J. Zacharakis & R. A. Collins (Eds.), *Proceedings of the 56th Annual Adult Education Research Conference* (pp. 415–416). Kansas State University Press.

Ross-Gordon, J. M., Rose, A. D., & Kasworm, C. E. (2017). *Foundations of adult and continuing education*. Wiley.

Scheil, K. W. (2012). *She hath been reading: Women and Shakespeare clubs in America*. Cornell University Press.

Scott, J. C. (1999). The Chautauqua Movement: Revolution in popular higher education. *The Journal of Higher Education 70*(4), 389–412.

Sexton, C. A. (2015). Dorothy Canfield Fisher: Strengthening democracy through adult education. In S. Imel & G. Bersch (Eds.), *North American handbook of early women adult educators, 1925–1950* (pp. 115–124). Information Age.

Stewart, J. C. (2018). *The new negro: The life of Alain Locke*. Oxford University Press.

Stubblefield, H. W., & Keane, P. (1994). *Adult education in the American experience: From the colonial period to the present*. Jossey-Bass.

Stubblefield, H. W., & Rachal, J. R. (1992). On the origins of the term and meanings of "adult education" in the United States. *Adult Education Quarterly, 42*(2), 106–116.

Wanstreet, C. E. (2015). Jessie Allen Charters: "Giving the best we know to mothers and fathers." In S. Imel & G. Bersch (Eds.), *North American handbook of early women adult educators, 1925–1950* (pp. 81–90). Information Age.

Welton, M. R. (2013). *Unearthing Canada's hidden past: A short history of adult education*. Thompson.

CHAPTER 3

Interdisciplinarity in Adult and Continuing Education

Royce Ann Collins

The field of adult and continuing education (ACE) has always been interdisciplinary, intertwined with other formal academic disciplines. ACE evolved out of a need to understand problems focused on how adults learn and interact with society. The study of these problems borrowed ideas and approaches from other academic disciplines, thus driving the interdisciplinary nature of ACE. While the field has many areas of study—continuing education (Houle, 1961), literacy (Hayes & Valentine, 1989), human resource development (Nadler & Wiggs, 1986), adult learning (Knowles, 1980), and workplace learning (Marsick, 1987)—some ACE scholars have based their work in a particular discipline such as psychology (Tennant & Pogson, 1995), sociology (Cunningham, 2000; Jarvis, 1985), and history (Stubblefield & Keane, 1994). ACE, utilizing a variety of theories (i.e., feminist theory, critical race theory, critical theory), intertwines the study of social justice and social justice education, bridging to other disciplines. This chapter defines interdisciplinarity and its influence on ACE practice and research.

Defining Interdisciplinarity

In the academy, *discipline* refers to a body of knowledge (concepts, theories, methods, and factual base) (Newell, 1992). A discipline distinguishes itself by several factors: questions asked, worldview, the set of assumptions used, and methods used to build the body of knowledge (Newell & Green, 1982). "One way of looking at disciplines is through a structural framework, noting how they are manifested in the basic organizational components of the higher education system" (Becher & Trowler, 2001, p. 410). Academic disciplines began organizing the structure of American higher education and thus knowledge in the 19th century (Klein, 1990, 2010; Kockelmans, 1979). It was a cost-effective and organized way to educate as the arts, humanities, and scientific and technology areas developed across the academy. Disciplines grouped themselves by problems, topics, and issues that shaped their subject matter and created scholarly communities that study and advance relevant concepts, theories, and methods of investigation. "What demarcates one disciplinary perspective from another is a theme or topic which they share may vary between a distinction in style or emphasis, a division of labor or difference in conceptual framework" (Becher & Trowler, 2001, p. 60). The assumption is that academic knowledge can be grouped into distinct disciplines. While in some cases there are distinct boundaries for what counts as disciplinary knowledge and fields of inquiry, in others, the lines are blurred.

Interdisciplinarity, as defined by Klein (1990), is "a methodology, a concept, a process, a way of thinking, a philosophy, and a reflexive ideology" (p. 196). Rhoten et al. (2009) emphasize it as a "process and a practice by which a set of purposive arrangements and a sense of community are established and ultimately integrates ideas with others to form an end product" (p. 87). *Inter* refers to integration of fields of studies, which often leads to new insights in the "in between space" (Repko, 2012, p. 7) or between disciplines. Repko also stresses the importance of integration and "developing a distinctively interdisciplinary theory-based research" (p. 2). This allows individuals to be responsive and expansive in their thinking. Interdisciplinary is the combination of two or more fields of study, and interdisciplinary theory-based research draws on several disciplines, integrating and reorganizing knowledge to broaden understanding and solve problems (Vickers, 1992). Interdisciplinary differs from multidisciplinary. *Multidisciplinary* refers to bringing side-by-side the perspectives of different disciplines on a central topic and there is no attempt to integrate the perspectives. Multidisciplinary is collective information, merely bringing insights to the forefront (Repko, 2012). In multidisciplinary teams, researchers join together to work on a common problem, but each makes a separate and discrete contribution. They also leave this exchange without assimilating the information or a synthesis of ideas or methods. Given this distinct understanding of interdisciplinary and multidisciplinary, interdisciplinarity therefore "seeks to combine disciplines to enhance the learning in one or more of the disciplines, or to apply discipline-based methods to real life situations" (Mathison & Freeman, 1998, p. 11). Interdisciplinarity requires complexity and synthesis of information from various disciplines to address new problems or issues. The research teams must include a variety of researchers and practitioners from a variety of fields. As a result of interdisciplinarity, there has been a great deal of poaching across all discipline borders. Since the 1960s, this poaching has led to difficulty in clearly characterizing any particular discipline as pure (Becher & Trowler, 2001).

Adult Education and Interdisciplinarity

Adult education has never been seen as a single field of practice or scholarly focus. The field of ACE has been influenced by and has influenced other fields. A cursory examination of the history of adult education has provided several examples of scholars (e.g., Lindeman, McClusky) synthesizing information from various fields in order to address the issues facing adult learners (Stubblefield & Keane, 1994). As Jarvis (1991) states, "The body of adult education knowledge is a complex and ever-changing phenomenon, overlapping and subdividing" (p. 5).

The Commission of Professors in Adult Education (CPAE) received funding in 1957 from the Kellogg Foundation to better understand the field through "formulat[ing] a theoretical framework for adult education" (Kreitlow, 1964, p. 3). Members of CPAE met with scholars and professionals from psychology, sociology, and philosophy and other disciplines to build a literature base for the field (Merriam et al., 2007; Tennant, 2006). Even though "it was clear from earlier explorations that there would be research findings of value to the adult educator in fields such as psychology, sociology, anthropology, vocational education, and communications" (Kreitlow, 1964, p. 3), the discussions were hampered by a lack of research in these fields on educating adults. Adult education research, which is focused on understanding the way adults learn and the utilization of that learning in their lives and the society around them, began to fill this gap (Kreitlow, 1964).

The report, *Facilitating Interdisciplinary Research* (Institute of Medicine, 2005), outlined four "drivers" of interdisciplinary research and learning: (a) the inherent complexity of nature and society, (b) the desire to explore problems and questions at the interfaces of disciplines, (c) the need to solve social problems, and (d) the need to produce revolutionary insights and generative technologies. The first driver, the inherent complexity of nature and society, demonstrates the necessity for interdisciplinarity in the field of adult education. The study of adult learners, the hallmark of the ACE field (Kasworm et al., 2010), represents a complex system that depends on insights from multiple disciplines—for instance, understanding how the brain functions requires input from neurobiology, neuroscience, psychology, and biomedical engineering. Learning is in itself a complex system influenced by the environment, culture, history, and spiritual traditions of the adult learner (Bryant et al., 2016; Jarvis, 2010; Kolb, 1984). Because adult learners live and learn within complex systems, they must be understood from a variety of perspectives. For example, the adult learner has been examined through the lens of psychology and cognitive psychology in order to understand the many facets of learning (King & Kitchener, 1994; Perry, 1999; Tennant, 2006). In another instance, Swartz (2011) examined wisdom and adult learning with insights from neuroscience, using knowledge from another discipline to show how adult learning is part of a larger complex system. Researchers further investigating the role of the body in learning and knowledge focus on two facets: embodied learning and somatic learning (Jordi, 2011; Tobin & Tisdell, 2015). Paramount to this work is how interdisciplinary efforts are critical to a deeper understanding of adult learning.

The second driver of interdisciplinarity is the "desire to explore problems and questions that extend beyond the confines of a single discipline" (Institute of Medicine, 2005, p. 16). Closson (2010) noted that the field of adult education draws information from sociology, psychology, economics, and anthropology, and Swartz and Triscari (2011) noted that business and social science were also disciplines from which adult education draws. Sodhi and Cohen (2012) combined adult education research and social work while Roessger (2012) did so with motor learning literature. One specific example of the second driver is the field's focus on adult learning whose research and theories have benefited from numerous other fields, especially primary and secondary school education. While there is separation between elementary and secondary curricular education and adult education, these disciplines exchange ideas around pedagogy and learning contexts, and professional development and teacher education explores adult learning. Collaboration has long been a practice of educators, and "the basic research in education is as meaningful for the adult educator as for the kindergarten teacher" (Kreitlow, 1964, p. 18).

Dewey (1938), whose work focused on the classroom teacher and the American educational system, inspired the research and theories of experiential learning for adult learners. A fundamental ideal of adult education is that adults learn through connecting new ideas, theories, or concepts to experiences. Experience and its effect on learning holds a central role in andragogy, a key adult learning theory (Knowles et al., 2012). Of Knowles's (1980) four assumptions of the adult learner, two focused on experience. First, adults have an increasing reservoir of experience and learn better when they can connect new information to an experience. Second, adults are positioned to learn new information when they experience a necessity for it to resolve a real-life problem or task (Knowles, 1980). Tennant and Pogson (1995) also noted the significance of experience and classified experience in four areas (prior experience, current experience, new experience, and learning from experience).

The third driver is that interdisciplinarity solves social problems. The field of adult education emerged through practitioners' work with social injustices. The 1936 handbook addressed numerous social problems (training, vocational education, vocational guidance, and schools for women workers) and how the discipline works to support adults, such as adult prisoners, immigrants, and people with physical disabilities (Wilson & Hayes, 2000). Addressing social problems continued through subsequent handbooks addressing topics such as public forums, federal emergency adult education programs, settlement houses, and educating African Americans (Wilson & Hayes, 2000). Solving social problems has included discussions of social justice and social change at many adult education conferences and in previous handbooks (Butterwick & Egan, 2010; Rachal, 1990; Wilson & Hayes, 2000).

A variety of theoretical frameworks has been employed to further the discussion of social problems. One particular theoretical framework is critical race theory (CRT) (Brookfield, 2010). CRT has been used by diverse fields including ACE to address different forms of oppression (e.g., Clover et al., 2017; Murray-Johnson, 2013) and the social inequity problems facing many marginalized groups. For example, Schwartz (2015) used CRT as the conceptual framework to investigate unequal educational opportunities for formerly incarcerated Black and Latino males.

The fourth primary driver of interdisciplinary research is the need to produce "novel and revolutionary insights" (Institute of Medicine, 2005, p. 35). The best way to illustrate this driver in ACE is through integrative approaches to learning or the "knit[ting] together information from disparate sources" (Repko, 2012, p. 41) and filling gaps in knowledge. An example of integrative approaches in adult education is the exploration and incorporation of public pedagogy, which is "educational activity and learning in extrainstitutional spaces and discourses" (Sandlin et al., 2011, p. 338). While *public pedagogy* was not a new term, scholars' interest in it grew in the 1990s, and public pedagogy was incorporated into adult education as a new research subject (Kreber, 2015; McLean, 2013; Sandlin et al., 2011; Sandlin et al., 2013; Zorrilla & Tisdell, 2016).

Another example of a new integration of sources is the exploration of cosmopolitanism (Coryell et al., 2014; Coryell et al., 2018). "Cosmopolitanism is rooted in the belief in a shared global community, openness to different cultures and perspectives, and recognition of universal values across cultures and peoples" (Coryell et al., 2018, p. 180). While cosmopolitanism has ancient origins (Kleingeld & Brown, 2014), Coryell et al.'s (2018) review of literature introduced and demonstrated two predominant categories that integrated with adult education: "methods for developing adult learners' cosmopolitan values and skills and the ways in which adult educators', researchers' and workers', and students' cosmopolitan orientations are manifested in work and learning" (p. 188).

ACE research advanced out of the use of the interdisciplinary process of defining a problem; incorporating relevant concepts, theories, and methods from other disciplines; and generating new insights from the context of the adult learner. When authors take adult learning principles and theories and merge them with other disciplines, such as human resource development, religious education, and technology, they begin the process of engaging interdisciplinarity.

The Influence of Interdisciplinarity in ACE Research

The interdisciplinarity of ACE research has made it difficult to describe the field. The field has been described as a big tent, referring to the scope and breadth of practice and research. An illustration of this scope and breadth is seen in the American Association for Adult and Continuing Education's (AAACE) list of 26 units that represent adult educators (Henschke, 2007). This ACE big tent of 26 units ranging from adults in high school to popular education illustrates the four drivers of interdisciplinarity. These units represent the complexity of society and ACE and the need to solve problems in multiple areas. Further units illustrate the exploration of problems and questions dealing with adult learning from high school to college to older adults and in settings from correctional institutions, military, to international development. New insights and revolutionary ideas are being added to the field through research and practice with adults in different contexts including distance education, higher education, and human resource development

and training. ACE research has long focused on adult education practice across these units, drawing from numerous fields and disciplines to examine specific research questions that emanated from these contextual units (Rose, 2000).

To illustrate the connection between the units specified by AAACE and ACE research, two different literature searches were conducted. The first investigated journal publications outside the primary adult education journals associated with AAACE to show how other disciplines are incorporating ACE research. The second was within the primary adult education journals associated with AAACE to explore the interdisciplinarity within ACE research.

The first literature search was conducted excluding the primary adult education journals (*Adult Education Quarterly, New Directions for Adult and Continuing Education, Adult Basic Education and Literacy, Journal of Transformative Education,* and *Adult Learning*). These were excluded to isolate the primary ACE publications and investigate other scholarly journals outside of the field for the incorporation of ACE research. Using a PROQUEST database, a search of publications that included "adult education" or "adult learning" terms compiled a list of 423 articles published between 2010 and 2018 from U.S. publications. The majority of these were in a health-related field (e.g., nursing, public health, health care for poor and underserved, health affairs). The second highest number of articles that rose from the review was management and leadership, which included occupational health and safety, educational leadership, and ethics. The third highest that surfaced was educational technology and the application of adult learning principles to online pedagogy. The remaining were a variety of higher education, secondary education, law, and international student journals. Clearly ACE research has been cited in other discipline journals when the topic was related to adults. However, this literature search also illustrates the diverse and interwoven nature of ACE research and the focus on specific research questions (Rose, 2000).

The second database search focused on ACE research in the United States. A review of articles published in *Adult Education Quarterly* from 2010 through the first third of 2018 was limited to U.S. authors and yielded 147 articles. As stated earlier, ACE earns this distinction of interdisciplinarity because it consciously and deliberately integrates sociology, psychology, history, literature, biology, and economics, among other disciplines. Interdisciplinarity was most evident in articles that incorporated some aspect of social justice: critical race theory, critical pedagogy, social capital, power relations, empowerment, oppression, and conscientization. This was not surprising, as the field of adult education has a long history and deep roots in social justice education (Johnson-Bailey et al., 2010). It also demonstrated that new ideas continue to be contributed as adult education integrates neuroscience, educational technology, cosmopolitanism, and public pedagogy, to name a few, into the field's research.

Interdisciplinarity involves a "range of phenomena, with a diversity of rationales, forms, outcomes, and problems" (Squires, 1992, p. 204). The interdisciplinarity in ACE research is further illustrated by authors who specialize within the field on a range of questions and diversity of problems within a specified context, population, or theory. For example, Kasworm (2010) is known for her research on adult learners in higher education, while spirituality has been the focus of Tisdell's (2010) research for decades. The unity of ACE's interdisciplinarity is its focus on the subject of adults.

Interdisciplinarity research does have challenges (Erichsen & Goldenstein, 2011). One challenge is that "knowledge itself has been rigidly categorized and compartmentalized in libraries and repositories" (p. 2), but knowledge produced through interdisciplinarity does not fit neatly within those categories. Further, disciplines do not use common terminology, but develop their own unique language, making it difficult to locate research crossing disciplines. Even within the field of adult education, terminology has different meanings to distinctive populations. "Because of the fluidity of its self-definition, adult education has a difficult time building a body of knowledge" (Rose, 2000, p. 28). *Andragogy* is an example of this differing terminology. For Alexander Kapp in 1833, it was an element of practice (Reischmann, 2005); for Knowles (1980) it was a set of assumptions; in Europe, it was described as an academic discipline (Reischmann, 2005). These challenges erect barriers to interdisciplinary in ACE research.

While the interdisciplinarity of ACE research allows for diverse voices, professions, and specializations, it can also hinder finding it. ACE is intertwined with other disciplines, but is it its own distinct field? Is the terminology that demonstrates integration of ideas from ACE simply worded too inconsistently? Is the problem one of integration or invisibility? Interdisciplinarity within the field promotes diversification with a central focus on the adult. Interdisciplinarity may also lead to invisibility by weakening the academic disciplinary distinction.

Conclusion

The concern for a field is its disciplinary status and visibility. Disciplinary perceptions and affiliations are core to the academic culture and disciplinary identities are many times associated with the department of alignment. The core of a discipline is its boundaries, terminology, theories, methodology, professional organizations, culture and shared norms (Squires, 1992). Adult education professors and their discipline are integrated into a variety of departments where adult education units are housed across various programs and departments, such as lifelong learning, higher education, continuing education, organization and leadership, educational leadership and administration, policy studies, student affairs and academic advising, and human resource development. Scholars are expected to specialize and focus their research areas and demonstrate connections to traditional understandings of these various programs and departments. Even though there are some distinct specializations within the field, such as the theoretical frameworks of transformative learning and self-directed learning, specializing and focusing its research areas presents a unique challenge to adult education which has had to create its own space while integrating with other knowledge bases and disciplines. Adult education professors and scholars pull from a variety of fields and publish in other discipline journals freely. Furthermore, there are multiple ways to classify, organize, and operationalize ACE knowledge areas and activities which are evident in internet search engines, journal databases, and bibliographic databases that have discipline specific collections, making it difficult to identify adult education within interdisciplinary research.

In contrast, the interdisciplinarity of ACE demonstrates the diversity within the field and the integration in numerous disciplines, but this leads to an erosion of identity when divided into specializations and enmeshed with other disciplines. A keyword search may miss articles because they may use different terminology to describe the same concept (e.g., self-regulated learning versus self-directed learning, or adult students versus nontraditional students versus mature students in higher education). While interdisciplinarity is endorsed by grant funders, policymakers, and academic fields, every discipline also must argue for its importance, uniqueness, and valuable contribution to the academy.

Rachal (1990) once described the adult education discipline using a tree metaphor, allowing it to always grow and change. The roots of the tree are buried deep in the foundations of ACE. These strong roots allow scholars to branch out and touch different disciplines along the various branches increasing interdisciplinarity. These branches are all part of the ACE tree, but they move in different directions, touching and learning from other parts of the whole complex system. ACE must maintain a strong connection to the foundation of the field as well and argue for its place and presence in the academy.

References

Becher, T., & Trowler, P. (2001). *Academic tribes and territories* (2nd ed.). Society for Research into Higher Education; Open University Press.

Brookfield, S. (2010). Theoretical frameworks for understanding the field. In C. Kasworm, A. Rose, & J. Ross-Gordon (Eds.), *Handbook of adult and continuing education* (pp. 71–81). Jossey-Bass.

Bryant, L., Bowman, L., & Isaac-Savage, E. P. (2016). Adult education and spirituality: A "liberatory spaces" for Black gay men. *New Directions for Adult and Continuing Education, 2016*(10), 59–69. https://doi.org/10.1002/ace.20186

Butterwick, S., & Egan, J. (2010). Sociology of adult and continuing education: Some key understandings for the field of practice. In C. Kasworm, A. Rose, & J. Ross-Gordon (Eds.), *Handbook of adult and continuing education* (pp. 113–122). Jossey-Bass.

Closson, R. (2010). Critical race theory and adult education. *Adult Education Quarterly, 60*(3), 261–283.

Clover, D., Etmanski, C., & Reimer, R. (2017). Gendering collaboration: Adult education in feminist leadership. *New Directions for Adult and Continuing Education, 2017*(156), 21–31. https://doi.org/10.1002/ace.20205

Coryell, J., Sehin, O., & Peña, C. (2018). Adult education through a cosmopolitanism lens: A review of the research literature. *Adult Education Quarterly, 68*(3), 179–196.

Coryell, J., Spencer, B., & Sehin, O. (2014). Cosmopolitan adult education and global citizenship: Perceptions from a European itinerant graduate professional study abroad program. *Adult Education Quarterly, 64*(2), 145–164.

Cunningham, P. (2000). A sociology of adult education. In A. Wilson & E. Hayes (Eds.), *Handbook of adult and continuing education* (pp. 573–591). Jossey-Bass.

Dewey, J. (1938). *Experience and education*. Touchstone.

Erichsen, E. A., & Goldenstein, C. (2011). Fostering collaborative and interdisciplinary research in adult education: Interactive resource guides and tools. *SAGE Open, 1*(1), 1–11. https://doi.org/10.1177/2158244011403804

Hayes, E., & Valentine, T. (1989). The functional literacy needs of low-literate adult basic education students. *Adult Education Quarterly, 40*(1), 1–14.

Henschke, J. A. (2007). *Adult education professional societies*. https://cdn.ymaws.com/aaace.site-ym.com/resource/resmgr/About/Who_We_Are/ch_20_adult_education_profes.pdf

Houle, C. O. (1961). *The inquiring mind: A study of the adult who continues to learn*. University of Wisconsin Press.

Institute of Medicine. (2005). *Facilitating interdisciplinary research*. National Academies Press.

Jarvis, P. (1985). *The sociology of adult education*. Croom Helm.

Jarvis, P. (1991). Growth and challenge in study of adult education. In J. M. Peters, P. Jarvis, & Associates (Eds.), *Adult education: Evolution and achievements in a developing field of study* (pp. 1–17). Jossey-Bass.

Jarvis, P. (2010). *Towards a comprehensive theory of human learning*. Routledge.

Johnson-Bailey, J., Baumgartner, L., & Bowles, T. (2010). Social justice in adult and continuing education. In C. Kasworm, A. Rose, & J. Ross-Gordon (Eds.), *Handbook of adult and continuing education* (pp. 339–349). Jossey-Bass.

Jordi, R. (2011). Reframing the concept of reflection: Consciousness, experiential, and reflective learning practices. *Adult Education Quarterly, 61*(2), 181–197.

Kasworm, C. (2010). Adult learners in a research university: Negotiating undergraduate student identity. *Adult Education Quarterly, 60*(2), 143–160.

Kasworm, C., Rose, A., & Ross-Gordon, J. (Eds.). (2010). *Handbook of adult and continuing education*. Jossey-Bass.

King, P. M., & Kitchener, K. S. (1994). *Developing reflective judgment*. Jossey-Bass.

Klein, J. T. (1990). *Interdisciplinarity: History, theory, and practice*. Wayne State University Press.

Klein, J. T. (2010). A taxonomy of interdisciplinarity. In R. Frodeman (Ed.), *The Oxford handbook of interdisciplinarity* (pp. 15–30). Oxford University Press.

Kleingeld, P., & Brown, E. (2014). Cosmopolitanism. In E. N. Zalta (Ed.), *The Stanford encyclopedia of philosophy*. https://plato.stanford.edu/archives/fall2014/entries/cosmopolitanism/

Knowles, M. (1980). *The modern practice of adult education: From pedagogy to andragogy*. Prentice Hall.

Knowles, M., Holton, E., & Swanson, R. (2012). *The adult learner: The definitive classic in adult education and human resource development* (7th ed.). Routledge.

Kockelmans, J. J. (1979). Why interdisciplinarity? In J. J. Kockelmans (Ed.), *Interdisciplinarity and higher education* (pp. 123–160). Pennsylvania State University Press.

Kolb, D. (1984). *Experiential learning: Experience as the source of learning and development*. Prentice Hall.

Kreber, C. (2015). Transforming employment-oriented adult education to foster Arendtian action: Rebuilding bridges between community and vocational education. *Adult Education Quarterly, 65*(2), 100–115.

Kreitlow, B. (1964). *Relating adult education to other disciplines*. University of Wisconsin Press.

Marsick, V. (1987). *Learning in the workplace*. Croom Helm.

Mathison, S., & Freeman, M. (1998). *The logic of interdisciplinary studies* (Report series 2.33.1998). National Research Center on English Learning & Achievement.

McLean, S. (2013). Public pedagogy, private lives: Self-help books and adult learning. *Adult Education Quarterly, 63*(4), 373–388.

Merriam, S. B., Caffarella, R., & Baumgartner, L. (2007). *Learning in adulthood* (3rd ed.). Jossey-Bass.

Murray-Johnson, K. (2013). Cultural (de)coding and racial identity among women of the African diaspora in U.S. adult higher education. *Adult Learning, 24*(2), 55–62.

Nadler, L., & Wiggs, G. (1986). *Managing human resource development*. Jossey-Bass.

Newell, W. (1992). Academic disciplines and undergraduate interdisciplinary education: Lessons from the school interdisciplinary studies at Miami University, Ohio. *European Journal of Education, 27*(3), 211–221.

Newell, W., & Green, W. (1982). Defining and teaching interdisciplinary studies. *Improving College and University Teaching, 30*(1), 23–30.

Perry, W. G. (1999). *Forms of intellectual and ethical development in the college years: A scheme*. Jossey-Bass.

Rachal, J. (1990). *The adult education "tree": Revision* (ED367908). ERIC. https://files.eric.ed.gov/fulltext/ED367908.pdf

Reischmann, J. (2005). Andragogy. In L. M. English (Ed.), *International encyclopedia of adult education* (pp. 58–63). Palgrave Macmillan.

Repko, A. (2012). *Interdisciplinary research: Process and theory* (2nd ed.). SAGE.

Rhoten, D., O'Connor, E., & Hackett, E. (2009). The act of collaborative creation and the art of integrative creativity: Originality, disciplinarity, and interdisciplinarity. *Thesis Eleven, 96*(1), 83–108.

Roessger, K. (2012). Toward an interdisciplinary perspective: A review of adult learning frameworks and theoretical models of motor learning. *Adult Education Quarterly, 62*(4), 371–392.

Rose, A. (2000). What is the state of adult education research today? *Adult Learning, 11*(4), 28–29.

Sandlin, J., O'Malley, M., & Burdick, J. (2011). Mapping the complexity of public pedagogy scholarship: 1894–2010. *Review of Educational Research, 81*(3), 338–375.

Sandlin, J., Redmon Wright, R., & Clark, C. (2013). Reexamining theories of adult learning and adult development through the lenses of public pedagogy. *Adult Education Quarterly, 63*(1), 3–23. https://doi.org/10.1177/0741713611415836

Schwartz, J. (2015). After incarceration and adult learning. *Adult Learning, 26*(2), 51–58.

Sodhi, M., & Cohen, H. (2012). The manifestation and integration of embodied knowing into social work practice. *Adult Education Quarterly, 62*(2), 120–137.

Squires, G. (1992). Interdisciplinarity in higher education in the United Kingdom. *European Journal of Education, 25*(3), 201–209.

Stubblefield, H., & Keane, P. (1994). *Adult education in the American experience: From the colonial period to the present*. Jossey-Bass.

Swartz, A. (2011). Wisdom, the body, and adult learning: insights from neuroscience. *New Directions for Adult and Continuing Education, 2011*(131), 15–24. https://doi.org/10.1002/ace.417

Swartz, A., & Triscari, J. (2011). A model of transformative collaboration. *Adult Education Quarterly, 61*(4), 324–340.

Tennant, M. (2006). *Psychology and adult learning* (3rd ed.). Routledge.

Tennant, M., & Pogson, J. (1995). *Learning and change in the adult years*. Jossey-Bass.

Tisdell, E. (2010). The role of spirituality in Irish adult education in culturally responsive teaching. *Adult Learner: The Irish Journal of Adult and Community Education* (EJ907234, pp. 91–104). ERIC. https://eric.ed.gov/?id=EJ907234

Tobin, J., & Tisdell, E. (2015). "I know down to my ribs": A narrative research study of the embodied adult learning or creative writers. *Adult Education Quarterly, 65*(3), 215–231.

Vickers, J. (1992). *Comparing disciplinary and interdisciplinary claims: How much discipline* [Working document on interdisciplinarity] (pp. 5–41). Association for Canadian Studies.

Wilson, A., & Hayes, E. (Eds.). (2000). *Handbook of adult and continuing education*. Jossey-Bass.

Zorrilla, A., & Tisdell, E. (2016). Art as critical public pedagogy: A quantitative study of Luis Camnitzer and his conceptual art. *Adult Education Quarterly, 66*(3), 273–291.

CHAPTER 4

Public Policy and Adult and Continuing Education

Elizabeth A. Roumell and Larry G. Martin

Major historical events and social trends, ongoing shifts in international and national economic labor demands, and changes in requirements for training and education throughout the life span situate learning in the adult years squarely within the public policy domain. Adult and continuing education (ACE) public educational policy serves as a mechanism for determining how public values regarding learning, development, and growth across the life span and in adulthood are formulated and codified to create educational programming to support the design and implementation of services for the public. In the case of ACE, policy and programming have historically been initiated in response to public issues that are both economic and social in nature. Given the evolving nature of policy discourse and the emerging challenges for ACE policy—particularly as governing bodies try to address the rapid changes in the social, economic, environmental, technological, and political spheres—it is critical for professionals in the field to understand the origins and nature of U.S. federal ACE policy and its implications for current practice (Roumell et al., 2020).

ACE policy continues to be an important locus of public responsibility and programming for learning opportunities in adulthood. Yet, the policy arena has proven to be challenging to locate and define as a basis for national- and state-level policy formulation because many of the relevant policies are embedded within other areas of focus and legislation (e.g., Department of Education [ED], Department of Labor [DOL], Department of Defense [DOD], etc.). This chapter addresses working definitions pertaining to ACE public policy, the purpose and framing of ACE policies, a synopsis of ACE policy development, and an analysis of ACE policy development and related problems and issues.

Working Definitions

For ACE, national public policy provides for a broad spectrum of educational programming and practices that are carried out by governments, not-for-profit organizations, and private institutions. Policy is also created as a function of regulating the economic and social dynamics that shape the circumstances of adult learning. In this chapter, for the purpose of identifying relevant policy, *adult education* refers to "all practices and processes that consider adults to be pedagogical subjects, independently of age, responsibilities, educational attainment or socioeconomic conditions, and the venues in which such practices take place" (Milana & Nesbit, 2015, p. 1). Here, *education* stresses "the intentionality, by adults as social actors, to create the conditions for them to extend and develop their knowledge, skills, judgments, and sense-making actions and capacities" (Milana & Nesbit, 2015, p. 1). Under these definitions, education and training for adults in the *ACE policy arena* include: adult basic education programming; vocational, career, and technical training; continuing education; community education and programming; workforce education and development; learning in the workplace; and others. In a broad sense, *public policy* refers to a course of action that has been codified by a governing body as guiding principles and procedures that influence and determine present and future decisions regarding programs and services for the public. *ACE public policy* denotes the extent of legislation, regulatory developments, and the instrumentalization of educational programs within the ACE policy domain (Martens et al., 2007). *Policy development* connotes ongoing changes that are indicative of the broader policy area as a whole, and not just specific pieces of legislation (Martens et al., 2007).

A *policy domain* is constituted of different societal and political wills and drives (literacy, adult basic education, career and technical education, continuing education, developmental education, English language learning, etc.) expressed by multiple actors to determine and carry out education policy through multiple sites and scales (local providers, workforce development boards, state programs, federal programs and agencies, etc.). Historically, ACE policy has been constructed through joint political action, as a product of multiple agencies at multiple levels of governance, capturing the coordination of mutual interdependencies among a variety of ACE political actors (typically involving the leadership and membership of national adult education associations) and their arenas of influence. Therefore, it is necessary to identify the structure of the polity that determines ACE policy, the key actors and their motives, and the environment in which policy is established and implemented.

Purpose and Framing of ACE Public Policy

Public policy in the ACE area has, by and large, been developed in response to economic developments and downturns and has been intended to serve as a stimulus for the economy, primarily being rationalized through a lens of human capital theory (Rose, 1999). In 1944, President Roosevelt presented an Economic Bill of Rights to the American people, with the aim to ensure that every individual has the right to a useful and remunerative job in an atmosphere of economic security, which neatly sums up the framing of most federal ACE policy over the past 7 decades. To endorse this right, Roosevelt's advisers set as the nation's post–World War II economic goal full and stable national productivity, income, and employment (Roosevelt, 1944). Within the postwar economy, the framing of policy emphasized that literacy and other forms of education and training would be necessary to assist adults in successfully (re)integrating themselves into the new economy. As the U.S. economy has continued to navigate economic transitions over the decades, social and educational policies have been further developed to respond to perceived needs and to expand the available education systems and programs to meet those needs.

In this vein, the point of departure for the majority of federal ACE legislation has been remediation for basic education and the equalization of economic opportunity and productivity. More recently, according to the Workforce Innovation and Opportunity Act of 2014 (WIOA), the purposes of ACE policy, embedded in the broader workforce development system, include:

(1) To increase, for individuals in the United States, particularly those individuals with barriers to employment, access to and opportunities for the employment, education, training, and support services they need to succeed in the labor market.

(2) To support the alignment of workforce investment, education, and economic development systems in support of a comprehensive, accessible, and high-quality workforce development system in the United States. (WIOA, 2014, Sec. 2)

These WIOA goals aim to expand on the original goals of improving adult literacy and skills of the public on average, provide additional learning opportunities for those without traditional compulsory, public education completion; improve the abilities and skills of individuals to provide for themselves toward the end of economic and social stability; and improve the abilities of individuals to effectively participate as citizens in the democratic process (Adult Education Act, 1966). As the focus on economic viability and efficiency of the system has been increasingly foregrounded over the past 20 years in response to global neoliberal economic trends, ACE educational policies have progressively been combined with workforce development and social services policies in an effort to further build social and educational systems in support of the national economy (Roumell et al., 2020).

Synopsis of ACE Policy Development

Historically, the focus of federal ACE policy was engendered with the recognition at the federal level that national economic interests and growing social inequalities needed to be addressed (Houle, 1968). In contrast to the compulsory education system, which has been predominantly governed at the local level, the origins and evolution of ACE policy in the United States has been principally driven as a national agenda from the federal level, although program delivery and much of the fiscal responsibilities remain within the purview of state and local governance. The development of ACE policy can be organized into four eras that will help guide the overview of its historical trajectory to follow.

During the initial era of ACE policy (ca. 1862–1917), seven laws were passed in response to the industrial revolution to develop and distribute agricultural and technological information to the general population across the states through agricultural extension services and provide education and training related to new agricultural and technological advances. In the second era (ca. 1918–1961), five laws were passed as legislative efforts primarily concentrated on the rehabilitation and reintegration of World War I and World War II veterans into the changing U.S. economy. This legislation included the creation of many community college systems and the GI bill, and programs which were housed and driven by the federal DOL and DOD.

Beginning in the early 1960s, the ACE policy area bloomed with the passage of 16 laws during the advent of its third era (ca. 1962–1997). The first legislation formally establishing federally funded adult basic education programs originated from the Economic Opportunity Act of 1964, which provided a suite of federal programs to address issues related to poverty in the United States (ED, 1991; Sticht, 2002). Within a span of 2 years, every state in the nation implemented a system of adult education and delivered instruction via local programs per the mandates of this act. The civil rights movement also spurred the expansion of these adult literacy services, and adult educators argued that the field should also embrace learner emancipation; the fight against racial, gender, cultural, and other forms of discrimination; developing critical thinking skills; and pursuing equity and social justice (Quigley, 2000). During the 1990s ACE funding priorities and programming options were impacted by New Federalism policies of devolution (Hayes, 1999). Devolution sought to transfer policy responsibilities from the federal government to state and local governments, permanently changing the social contract for obtaining welfare assistance (especially for women and mothers of dependent children), and compelling individuals to seek and obtain unsubsidized employment. Several legislative acts were passed which provided the basis for welfare reform and shaped the role of adult literacy education (Hayes, 1999). The Personal Responsibility and Work Opportunity Reconciliation Act (PRWORA) of 1996 reformed the nation's welfare laws and instituted the Temporary Assistance for Needy Families (TANF) system for providing block grants to states. The DOL's 1997 Welfare-to-Work Program was implemented to assist individuals to obtain and keep unsubsidized employment. The Workforce Investment Act (WIA) of 1998 included the Adult Education and Family Literacy Act aiming to provide federal funding and oversight of state-based adult literacy programs (Hayes, 1999).

The fourth era (ca. 1998–present) of ACE policy witnessed the implementation of 18 policy initiatives, beginning with the far-reaching reforms under WIA. The 1998 act aimed to foster greater interagency cooperation in order to serve clientele held in common (offering literacy programs and job placement programs in the same location, i.e., "one-stop shops") leading to a paradigm shift through the provision of joint adult education and job training (ED Office of Vocational and Adult Education, 2013). Equally important was the mandate that ACE programs partner with state and local workforce development systems, and the continued expansion of non-traditional policy actors (including public libraries, community centers, faith organizations, and a variety of not-for profit, private, and public service providers). Title II of WIA also legislated the creation of a performance accountability system which, unlike previous accountability measures that made local programs accountable to their state agencies, made states accountable in a systematic way to the federal-level Department of

Education (ED Office of Vocational and Adult Education, 2013). The 2006 Carl D. Perkins Career and Technical Education Act (Perkins Act) was enacted with the goal of transforming Career and Technical Education (CTE), and the initiation of Career Pathways–focused initiatives, further facilitated efforts to improve the integration of a variety of programming within the ACE domain.

The WIOA of 2014 signaled a renewed federal effort at systematically reforming ACE policy, where many of the policies appeared to increasingly align with a dominant market–oriented economic agenda. During the 1990s, in response to globalization and automation, neoliberal policies were developed to support adult education programs and services to strengthen the ability of adult learners to become more employable, mobile (especially with the completion of degrees and certificate programs), and flexible in their pursuit of economic benefits. These policies are premised on the notion that competitiveness and flexibility must be maintained and that extending the reach of economic markets in all areas of social life will create wealth and maximize individual choice (Finnegan, 2016). Consequently, the WIOA legislation introduced several changes to improve systems integration and interoperability between the multiple state- and federal-level government agencies, with the aim of developing and extending a more clearly defined system of adult education and workforce development programming (ED Office of Vocational and Adult Education, 2013).

The aim of the new legislation was to coordinate programs housed within multiple agencies, bringing them together under the scope of the Career Pathways initiative (DOL, 2012). Under WIOA, ACE programming was further integrated under and embedded within the expanding workforce development system at the local, state, and federal levels. While most ACE program implementation remains local and is still primarily the responsibility of states, the dictates of federal legislation and requirements for federal funding have implemented another element of neoliberalism (i.e., systematically measuring competences and outcomes) via mandating a greater centralization of standards, data requirements, accountability, and focus on evidence-based programming and practices. Consequently, these policies have increased overall federal oversight of state and local programming.

Title I of WIOA (Workforce Development Activities) outlines the structure of a more comprehensive, efficient, and effective workforce development system and the placement and assignment of ACE programming responsibilities within that broader workforce development system (DOL, 2016). The current architecture of WIOA policy is intended to formalize the relationships between the levels of governance and create feedback loops between various levels and kinds of education providers and their local workforce stakeholders to better respond to the current labor climate. Local workforce development boards report to regional boards, which report to state boards, and so on, with the intent of creating programs that are responsive to local workforce, learning, and training needs. At each of these levels, the boards are required to complete local and regional needs analyses and education and workforce development plans that are then forwarded to the next level for review and approval. It is within this framework that additional programming requirements have been added, and the mission and purpose of various kinds of education and workforce programming were brought together under the Career Pathways initiative (DOL, 2012).

For example, data and reporting requirements have been instated in order to gather information regarding the impact of programming within local contexts and at varied levels, meaning that local providers have had to adjust in order to meet the new reporting requirements beyond their normal responsibilities. As states create workforce development plans, they are increasingly required to work toward aligning ACE curriculum and education standards with those across education levels (K–12, postsecondary, and higher education), and across local, state, and federal levels. Collaboration between a variety of organizations and stakeholders has also become an ingrained expectation, along with the coordination of funding streams.

Workforce development plans are also required to streamline their programming under the Career Pathways initiative. Programs are encouraged to make the necessary steps in training and educational attainment for learners more explicit by developing *stackable credentials* and more clearly articulating *career pathways* for learners to follow to accumulate the education and qualifications necessary for gainful employment. WIOA's overall aims include: to more formally integrate a variety of educational and training programming that have been offered across several agencies over the decades, to diversify but also streamline funding streams, to decrease duplication of programming, and to reduce time and confusion for adult learners on their path toward more sustainable and living wages (Roumell et al., 2020).

ACE policies and programming have been incorporated across and carried out through numerous contexts and providers. The development of ACE policy has been in response to diverse interest groups over the decades, including: training needs for government employees; military education and training; workforce development; vocational, occupational, career, and technical education; adult and family literacy initiatives; community education and enrichment; distance and continuing education; correctional education; social services, unemployment, and welfare; veterans services and occupational transitions; Native American, ethnic minorities, and marginalized populations; and language and civics classes for newly arrived residents and citizens. The diverse public interests and actors within the ACE policy arena also function on several levels, including multiple federal agencies, state agencies, local boards, and service providers. In addition to formal policy actors in public ACE programming, several other policy actors and stakeholders have been integrated: from business and industry (which now hold seats on workforce development boards, for example); nongovernmental and not-for-profit organizations; independent research institutes and think tanks; civil society organizations; and actors from other levels of education (K–12, higher education, community college systems, etc.) (Belzer, 2007). The aim of WIOA legislation was to orchestrate improved collaboration and coordination between these levels and kinds of actors, requiring more clearly defined partnerships, clarifying fiduciary remit, and sharing responsibilities in the implementation of ACE programs and initiatives.

Despite this growing number and diversity of actors, U.S. policy researchers (Mitchell et al., 2017) have observed a gradual consolidation of policy control at the state and federal levels, with compounding pressure on institutions and service providers to become more uniform in practice and more compliant with nationally defined policy goals and reporting requirements. While most ACE programming is still primarily the responsibility of states (especially fiscally) and program delivery remains local, the dictates of federal legislation have increased federal oversight targeting state and local ACE programming. Even so, there has also been a notable proliferation of innovative state and regional initiatives to create and improve adult and workforce education enterprises, particularly under the Career Pathways initiative (e.g., the Career and Technical Education Research Network's current studies being conducted in several states [CTE, 2019]).

ACE Policy Development: Related Problems and Issues

The ACE policy efforts of WIOA notwithstanding, it does not provide a complete story of ACE policy development. Any telling of that story should be cognizant of the tangled sense of self-identity and social policy positionality in the field. This identity has been inherited from the loosely structured nature of the broader ACE policy arena—which formed in great part through piecemeal policy responses to economic and social issues over the decades—and the process of professionalization in the field, involving an increasing number of specialized subfields, for example, human resource development, distance education, adult literacy and basic education, workforce education and training, education in the health professions, and others (Quigley, 2000). Signaling the policy weakness derived from a fractured field, Quigley cited Collins's (1991) observation that it seems "there is less and less for adult education to claim as the sum of its parts" (p. 209), rendering it difficult to exercise coordinated policy influence in service to adult learners and our democratic institutions. Beyond the policy actors identified by WIOA, there is a need to understand the policy interests of all stakeholders in the ACE field. However, recent publications suggest that what Quigley (2000) identified as differences based on the loosely structured nature of the ACE policy arena may actually signal more deeply embedded problems and issues: the turn toward neoliberalism in ACE policy; divergent policy interests of national adult education associations; and the need for diversity in methodological research approaches.

Neoliberalism and ACE Policy

The overhaul of our current WIOA-based ACE policies has incorporated ACE programming under an instrumental economic agenda by embedding adult education programs within the broader workforce development structure, to serve as a means of individual wealth production in a knowledge economy and knowledge society (Patrick, 2013). As a highly utilitarian and ideologically biased approach to education, the neoliberal focus on the commodification of education and the commodification of the learner as a potential knowledge worker has weakened the ability of adult educators to attend to the complex multidimensional nature of adult learning (Finnegan, 2016; Patrick, 2013). In an age of digital learning and educational entrepreneurs, ACE programs/organizations are pushed to respond to the waves of technological innovations such as omnipresent internet services, cell phones, and apps (e.g., Facebook, Google, YouTube, Twitter, and others) by increasingly utilizing these broader innovations to provide specific programs and learning opportunities to targeted demographics. Continuing education learning opportunities are also now available on demand through courses and programs (via massive open online courses [MOOCs], e.g., Coursera, edX, FUN, FutureLearn, and others) that are flexible, immediately accessible, fully online, self-paced, and allow students to enroll and start learning immediately. Continuing and higher education programs are customizing the delivery of course content by experimenting with innovative delivery systems (e.g., minidegrees, micromasters, and nanodegrees) and multiple delivery models (e.g., in-person, self-paced online, synchronized online, and hybrid) (Horn et al., 2006). It remains to be seen, however, whether these targeted populations benefit from these interventions, whether learners may have been inadvertently further marginalized, and which technologies and tools have effectively advanced adult learning. Trends notwithstanding, the extent to which these innovative efforts provide an equitable distribution of education programs, credentials, and services to all adult learners remains unclear. Also unclear is whether these approaches further exacerbate knowledge and skills gaps by stereotypically serving the learners who are most likely to demonstrate success.

The efforts to develop and distribute adult education programs as purchasable commodities for people not only raises questions related to educational policy but also ultimately engender debates about the meaning of education and learning in adulthood. Is adult education simply an instrumental tool for employment, or can adult learning programs still serve as cultural spaces which encourage students and teachers to engage in critical discourse? If education simply becomes an end of obtaining objectified, measurable, and transferable certificates and degrees (Patrick, 2013)—obtained in the interest of documenting individual achievement as potential economic value—what is the meaning of lifelong learning for the individual beyond its market value? In a utilitarian policy environment, will adult education programs still be able to thrive by assisting learners in leading personally fulfilling lives by providing learning opportunities that enhance learners' discovery of the meaning of experience (Lindeman, 1961)? ACE stakeholders currently face a categorical imperative to more deeply engage in a deliberate conversation about the affordances and delimitations of the current policies; unfortunately, many key stakeholders (e.g., national associations) have remained routinely disinterested observers or cynical armchair commentators.

Divergent Policy Interests of National Associations

National and international adult education associations are composed of members (professional adult educators and key ACE stakeholders) who assist with the provision of educational opportunities for people engaged in targeted occupations (e.g., administration, clergy, medicine, nursing, teaching, and others) (Cordie, 2017). Some of these associations (e.g., American Association for Adult and Continuing Education [AAACE], Association for Continuing Higher Education [ACHE], the Council for Adult and Experiential Learning [CAEL], and others) indicate policy advocacy in their mission and/or vision statements; however, their policy actions have not been highly visible in the policy arena. While the voices and actions of a wide variety of adult education organizations and associations are notably silent on matters of national adult education policy, the Coalition on Adult Basic Education (COABE) has been steadfastly engaged with the process. Representing over 55,000 adult education practitioners and providers, the association has developed the infrastructure to enable its membership to directly engage with state and national legislators. For example, according to its website, the organization launched a national public awareness campaign and an advocacy campaign that enabled more than 50,000 connections with legislators since April 2017.

The membership of COABE notwithstanding, ACE professional associations provide an infrastructure for professional adult educators to become more actively involved in ACE policy discourse. Some states and regions have professional associations for adult and lifelong learning, while others do not. The former National Council of State Directors of Adult Education has also recently turned into the National Adult Education Professional Development

Consortium and aims to be a leading voice for adult education in the country. However, there exists no formal architecture designed to incorporate all stakeholders into a comprehensive ACE policy domain. The field has not yet addressed several fundamental questions: Who should be the primary actors in ACE policy design and development? Who are the primary stakeholders? Which networks should be involved, and how should they interrelate? What key policy issues should be addressed? There is a need to conduct a network analysis and for adult education associations to coalesce around a common policy agenda that can be effectively communicated to legislators. The agenda should be based on empirical data and evidence.

The Need for Diversity in Methodological Research Approaches

Although the WIOA legislation demonstrates a heavy economic focus, it also provides a means for adult education researchers to develop data-based findings of the successes or failures of adult education programs and services (i.e., a requirement that providers systematically maintain quantitative data files on all participants and programs). Although databases and information infrastructures have been growing rapidly, the field exhibits deficiencies in quantitative data analysis expertise in two areas: first, adult education programs and providers need further training and development in the areas of assessment, evaluation, and accountability measures; and second, ACE researchers do not appear to be well positioned to conduct quantitative research with large data sets or utilizing big data analytics.

In her analysis of 1,089 articles published between 2000 and 2014 in *Adult Education Quarterly, Studies in Continuing Education*, and *International Journal of Lifelong Learning*, Boeren (2018) found qualitative research methods have become the norm in the field, and quantitative methods were noted as "the methodological underdog" among adult education researchers. That is, her analysis found that our leading journals feature more qualitative than quantitative studies. She argued for the use of different methods and methodologies to enhance the quality of research via the exploration of similar topics from different angles and employing different empirical approaches. Daley et al. (2018) agreed with this assessment and called for methodological diversity and plurality in current research and evaluation approaches. These weaknesses may have contributed to a lack of advanced research in the adult learning sciences, resulting in a shortage of adult education scholars who can effectively link learning theory to adult education practices (Roessger, 2017).

To better inform policy-making decisions and to galvanize support for a concrete policy agenda, it would be helpful for adult education stakeholders and scholars to increase the dissemination of findings from large scale regional and country-wide projects (e.g., program evaluation results, Program for the International Assessment of Adult Education Competencies [PIAAC], etc.). For example, Patterson (2018) analyzed 2012/2014 PIAAC-USA data. She found that 90% of U.S. adults aged 20 years and older (considered the least educated) did not participate recently in formal or nonformal education. These findings suggest that WIOA's market-based, entrepreneurial interventions may not be having the desired effects for the least-educated adults in our society. In another study using PIAAC data, Yamashita et al. (2018) investigated the relationship between general skill proficiencies and employment outcomes among older (45 years–65 years) adults in the United States. The results showed literacy skills were positively associated with being employed as opposed to being either unemployed or out of the labor force. They argued there is a need for policies that facilitate opportunities for employment-related training and education programs. Consequently, the array of ACE programs should include not only adult education and workforce training but also efforts to assist these learners in improving outcomes in other life domains, such as health and social networks—both at the individual and aggregate levels (Yamashita et al., 2018).

Conclusion

The current ACE policy arena has been incorporated into WIOA legislation and its focus on consolidating federal influence on the design, development, and delivery of market-based adult education programs. While the effectiveness of the current legislation is still early in implementation, there is a pressing need for the entire range of adult education stakeholders to join the national policy conversation. There is a need for a coordinated ACE public policy research agenda to provide data-based analyses and findings regarding the strengths and weaknesses of WIOA initiatives and the impacts on learners. National ACE professional associations need to coalesce around the common policy interests of their members; develop coordinated ACE policy platforms; and communicate these to appropriate legislative representatives. They are uniquely positioned to provide member updates on legislative items, platforms via annual conferences to present policy-related research and discussion papers, and work with other associations to forge alliances in support of legislative priorities. Professors of adult education (and graduates of degree programs) should more actively engage in state- and national-level programming initiatives and processes. They can provide critical skills in the design, development, implementation, and evaluation of programs offered under the Career Pathways initiatives (DOL, 2012). Similarly, graduate degree programs should incorporate ACE policy literature into the core curriculum and work toward ensuring our graduates are competent in a broader range of research methodologies.

References

Adult Education Act. (1966). Title III of the Elementary and Secondary Education Act Amendments, Pub. L. 89-750, 80 Stat. 1191–1222. http://www.govtrack.us/congress/bills/89/hr13161

Belzer, A. (2007). Implementing the Workforce Investment Act from in between: State agency responses to federal accountability policy in adult basic education. *Educational Policy*, 21(4), 555–588.

Boeren, E. (2018). The methodological underdog: A review of quantitative research in the key adult education journals. *Adult Education Quarterly*, 68(1), 63–79.

Career and Technical Education Research Network. (2019). *Career and technical education research network*. https://cteresearchnetwork.org/

Collins, M. (1991). *Adult education as a vocation: A critical role for the adult educator*. Routledge.

Cordie, L. A. (2017). Professional associations. In A. B. Knox, S. C. O. Conceição, & L. G. Martin (Eds.), *Mapping the field of adult and continuing education: An international compendium*, (p. 54). Stylus; American Association for Adult and Continuing Education.

Daley, B. J., Martin, L. G., & Roessger, K. M. (2018). A call for methodological plurality: Reconsidering research approaches in adult education. *Adult Education Quarterly*, 68(2), 157–169.

Department of Education. (1991). *History of the Adult Education Act: An overview*. Office of Vocational and Adult Education, Division of Adult Education and Literacy.

Department of Education Office of Vocational and Adult Education. (2013). *An American heritage—federal adult education: A legislative history 1964–2013*. Author.

Department of Labor. (2012). *Career pathways joint letter*. https://careerpathways.workforcegps.org/resources/2016/04/27/12/12/Career_Pathways_Joint_Letter_2016

Department of Labor. (2016). *WIOA fact sheet*. https://www.doleta.gov/WIOA/Docs/Top-Line-Fact-Sheet.pdf

Economic Opportunity Act. (1964). Pub. L. 88-452, 78 Stat. 508. http://www.govtrack.us/congress/bills/88/s2642

Finnegan, F. (2016). The future is unwritten: Democratic adult education against and beyond neoliberalism. *Adult Learner: The Irish Journal of Adult and Community Education*, 46, 58.

Hayes, E. (1999). Policy issues that drive the transformation of adult literacy. *New Directions for Adult and Continuing Education*, 1999(83), 3–14.

Horn, M. B., Laxton, A., and Lifshits, Y. (2006). *10 trends ahead for continuing education*. http://entangled.solutions/docs/10-trends-ahead-for-continuing-education.pdf

Houle, C. O. (1968, June). Federal policies concerning adult education. *The School Review*, 76(2), 166–189.

Lindeman, E. C. (1961). *The meaning of adult education* (Vol. 1). Ravenio Books.

Martens, K., Rusconi, A. & Leuze, K. (Eds.). (2007). *New arenas of education governance: The impact of international organizations and markets on education policy making*. Palgrave Macmillan.

Milana, M. & Nesbit, T. (Eds.). (2015). *Global perspectives on adult education and learning policy*. Palgrave Macmillan.

Mitchell, D. E., Shipps, D., & Crowson, R. L. (2017). *Shaping education policy: Power and process*. Routledge.

Patrick, F. (2013). *Neoliberalism, the knowledge economy, and the learner: Challenging the inevitability of the commodified self as an outcome of education*. ISRN Education.

Patterson, M. B. (2018). The forgotten 90%: Adult nonparticipation in education. *Adult Education Quarterly*, 68(1), 41–62.

Quigley, B. A. (2000). Adult education and democracy: Reclaiming our voice through social policy. In A. L Wilson & E. R. Hayes (Eds.), *Handbook of adult and continuing education* (pp. 208–223). SAGE.

Roessger, K. M. (2017). From theory to practice: A quantitative content analysis of adult education's language on meaning making. *Adult Education Quarterly*, 67(3), 209–227.

Roosevelt, F. D. (1844, January 11). *The Economic Bill of Rights*. Independence Hall Association. https://www.ushistory.org/documents/economic_bill_of_rights.htm

Rose, A. (1999). Adult education as a means, not an end: United States policy in the 20th century. *Adult Learning, 10*(3), 4–6.

Roumell, E. A., Salajan, F. D., & Todora, N. C. (2020). A review of U.S. education policy regarding the education of adults. *Educational Policy.* https://doi.org/10.1177/0895904818802416

Sticht, T. G. (2002). The rise of the adult education and literacy system in the United States: 1600–2000. *Review of Adult Learning and Literacy* (ED508720). ERIC. https://files.eric.ed.gov/fulltext/ED508720.pdf

Workforce Innovation and Opportunity Act (WIOA). (2014). Pub. L. 113–128. https://www.congress.gov/113/bills/hr803/BILLS-113hr803enr.pdf

Workforce Investment Act (WIA). (1998). Pub. L. 105-220, 29 U.S.C. §2801. http://www.govtrack.us/congress/bills/105/hr1385

Yamashita, T., Cummins, P. A., Arbogast, A., & Millar, R. J. (2018). Adult competencies and employment outcomes among older workers in the United States: An analysis of the Program for the International Assessment of Adult Competencies. *Adult Education Quarterly, 68*(3), 235–250. https://doi.org/10.1177/0741713618773496

CHAPTER 5

Lifelong Learning

Marcie Boucouvalas

In 1875, having been urged to write a poem for his 50th class reunion at Bowdoin College (Class of 1825), the American poet Henry Wadsworth Longfellow had this to say to his classmates:

> Ah, nothing is too late,
>
> Til the tired heart should cease to palpitate.
>
> Cato learned Greek at eighty;
>
> Sophocles wrote his grand Oedipus, and
>
> Simonides bore off the prize from his compeers,
>
> When each had numbered more than fourscore years.
>
> And Theophrastus at fourscore and ten,
>
> Had but begun his "Characters of Men."
>
> Chaucer, at Woodstock with the nightingales,
>
> At sixty wrote the Canterbury Tales;
>
> Goethe at Weimar, toiling to the last,
>
> Completed Faust when eighty years were past.
>
> These are indeed exceptions, but they show
>
> How far the gulf-stream of our youth may flow.
> (Longfellow, 1893, p. 313, lines 238–251)

Longfellow's position and encouragement are clear: Regardless of age, much is possible. While he recognized that these examples might be exceptions, the implied point of his message is the importance of maintaining a healthy attitude toward learning as a lifelong process and, I would add, even as we acknowledge that disease, disuse, or disability might give rise to challenges and limitations.

The concept of lifelong learning also holds much richer dimensions that move beyond the individual to include society. Individuals do not live or unfold in a vacuum; we live and grow in the contexts in which we navigate: relationships, groups, organizations, communities, nations, and our planet. Collectives and the macro environment become an important part of the lifelong learning trajectory. Learning is multifaceted and often leads to development. The potential for an individual's development within such contexts as well as development of the contexts themselves are important and mutually beneficial. This vital relationship between the development of the individual and society is increasingly recognized globally in both policy and practice, as is discussed later. While this handbook focuses on the American setting and milieu, we live in a global world. Accordingly, attention is addressed to such a contextualization, where appropriate.

The purpose of this chapter is to illuminate the depth and breadth of this foundational concept of lifelong learning, its long-standing history, philosophical foundations, misunderstandings and partial understandings, criticisms and dialogues it has generated over decades, and advances in the present context. The chapter is designed to address these facets of lifelong learning as a movement, a process, along with its programmatic dimensions. Programs and learning activities are the most concrete manifestation of recognition that the process of learning continues throughout life, but both are part of a continually evolving lifelong learning movement, a force permeating society and influencing the social order.

The discussion begins with an examination of three key concepts that provide a fundamental foundation: Lifelong learning, lifelong education, and learning society, followed by a brief historic journey harkening to ancient times and illuminating as well the social and other forces catalyzing and characterizing the contemporary movement. Consideration is also given to how professionalization of adult education as a field of study and practice, and the impact of key global bodies in the field, further contributed to lifelong learning as a movement in the United States. The discussion also raises awareness as to key tensions and controversies, some new, but others long-standing, that have appeared as concerns even in earlier literature. In a complementary manner, and with an eye to the future, attention is focused on the importance of understanding and exploring the multiple meanings given to the term *lifelong learning* and the significance of current ongoing advances and activities such as the United Nations' Sustainable Development Goals (SDGs). The chapter concludes with a discussion of challenges and opportunities for our future and invites the reader to consider where we will want to be in 2030 when the next handbook emerges—and beyond.

Key Concepts

Lifelong learning and the accompanying concepts of *lifelong education* and *learning society* (which will be discussed in more detail) have added richness and depth and provided a fundamental foundation to adult education as a field of both study and practice. Unfortunately, lifelong learning and lifelong education have sometimes, erroneously, been used interchangeably. To briefly clarify: *Lifelong learning* can refer to a movement permeating society at large, a process, a way of navigating life, an attitude, or a guiding philosophy, setting forth the position that preparation of a learner for continuous inquiry is an essential condition of living. Some focus more concretely, however, on its programmatic aspects. *Lifelong education*, often contrasted with *terminal education*, has been proposed as an organizing principle (as well as master concept) to rethink the meaning of education that continues throughout life, which can be provider driven by many agents, in addition to those outside the formal educational system, or in which one can be one's own planning agent. The ultimate goal is a *learning society*, in which education is interwoven with the social, political, and economic fabric such that it becomes a responsibility of the entire society in the twofold venture of promoting the accessibility of learning opportunities to all individuals throughout their lives and the cultivation of self-directing learners. The learning society has a long trajectory. The term, originally coined by McGhee (1959), was followed with publications by Thomas (1961); Hutchins (1968); and, from the United Nations Educational, Scientific and Cultural Organization (UNESCO), Faure et al. (1972). Although outside the scope of the present chapter, the concept then gained attention in other countries as well: Sweden (Husén, 1974, 1986), although more focused on school reform, and New Zealand (Boshier, 1980), as examples.

Ohliger (1975) expressed serious concern with McGhee's proposal, suggesting that it was too narrow in scope and could result in an instructional, training, or credentialing society—quite a contemporary potential concern as well, as discussed later. Thomas's proposal, however, 2 years after McGhee's, leaves no such doubt in a reader's mind. He clearly promoted learning, not education, as a central and common concern of a multitude of agencies, leading to the creation of a learning environment in society at large, a democratic society in which every individual can and is encouraged to learn. His very rich description emphasizes, among many other things, the importance of an educated citizenry and the opportunity for international learning exchanges. Given that his prescient ideas were presented at the National Conference of Adult Education in Ottawa, Canada, in 1961, they may have become a bit buried in history. A 1968 publication, also titled *The Learning Society*, written by Robert M. Hutchins, former president of the University of Chicago, however, also focused on the development of responsible citizens but received greater attention, possibly due to his status. Some have even mistakenly suggested that Hutchins originated the concept (see, e.g., Davies, 2009). By 1972, when UNESCO published *Learning to Be* (known as the Faure report), the concept of a learning society attracted global attention, expressing a difference in the relationship between society and education, as foreshadowed in earlier publications:

> The very nature of the relationship between society and education is changing. . . . It deserves a name of its own—the learning society. Its advent can only be conceived as a process of close interweaving between education and the social, political, and economic fabric. (Faure et al., 1972, p. 163)

The impact of UNESCO on the lifelong learning movement in the United States is discussed later in this chapter. Elements of a learning society, however, can also be evidenced in ancient concepts.

Lifelong Learning in Ancient and Earlier Times

The idea as well as practical manifestations of learning as a lifelong process are evident in ancient Greece, China, and India, to name a few. References to the notion of learning as a lifelong process have been documented in the scriptures of India (e.g., Vedas and Upanishads), and the philosophies of ancient China under both Confucianism and Taoism. Although some efforts may have been viewed as catering to the elite, advances such as those enacted under the administration of Pericles in ancient Athens earmarked funds for the poorest citizens to attend theater. In those years, theater was not merely for entertainment value, but was considered educative in nature, where one had the opportunity to learn about the human condition and enact one's own cathartic experience that had the potential to lead to developmental growth. Such funds (called the Theorikon) were not to be touched even in times of war. Later, during the Byzantine era, depending upon the ruler or emperor of the time, an educative environment was created permitting citizens to avail themselves of the palace libraries. Among some emperors, of course, the converse was true and learned individuals were sometimes held in disdain. Even more comprehensive was the ancient Greek concept of *paideia*. Although allegedly focusing more on the elite, the concept referred to the total development of the individual and the city-state, which were considered intertwined. The responsibility of many agents in society to form a matrix that would contribute to an educated citizenry was also clearly articulated (Boucouvalas, 1988; Jaeger, 1943, 1944, 1945).

During a later period and moving beyond an elitist proclivity, Johann Amos Comenius (1592–1670), emerged as a champion of education for all throughout one's life. In his *Pampaedia* (1600s/1987), he advocated that learning should be a lifelong process. While heralded by school educators for his curriculum theory and teaching methods and considered the father of modern education, a careful reading illuminates his advocacy for all regardless of age, status, disabilities, and so on, and thus earns him a place of recognition in a chapter on lifelong learning. He recognized the complexity of humans, and his vision of education addressed the development of humanity in general. In 1992, on the 400th anniversary of his birth, UNESCO established the Comenius Medal, which recognizes individuals, groups, or organizations for important and substantial contributions to educational innovation and research. Significant to any discussion regarding the role of adult education in lifelong learning was receipt of the award in 1994 by renowned adult educator Paulo Freire.

History and Philosophy of the Lifelong Learning Movement in Our Modern Era

A confluence of forces preceded the emergence and recognition of lifelong learning as a foundational concept to the field, including professionalization of adult education as a field of study and practice and the advent of social forces that, among other things, signified the transformation of industrial society to an information society, with the accompanying vision of developing a learning society.

As early as 1919, the Adult Education Committee of the British Ministry of Reconstruction (from World War I, 1914–1918) recognized the importance of adult education, but as part of a much larger, more inclusive process that they termed, in fact, *lifelong education*. Adult education was considered an integral new thrust of lifelong education and a national necessity, providing learning opportunities for all and rejecting the idea of adult education as a luxury (Great Britain Ministry of Reconstruction, 1919). In that same year the London-based World Association for Adult Education was formed, holding its first gathering for global dialogue in 1929, in which the United States participated.

In North America (especially the United States), while apprentice opportunities and informal activities of equal importance to society such as Benjamin Franklin's Juntos abounded during the 1700s, and the lyceum movement and Chautauqua flourished during the 1800s, it was during the 1920s that professionalization of adult education took root, including the development of a professional association—the American Association for Adult Education, supported by the Carnegie Foundation, which lent much impetus to viewing both learning and education from an expanded perspective (i.e., lifelong). This emergence of adult education, as a field of both study and practice, planted seeds for what eventually emerged as the current lifelong learning movement, initially conceived as lifelong education.

Eduard Lindeman's 1926 classic *On the Meaning of Adult Education* offered a philosophical foundation for the newly emerging field, and the scientific work by Thorndike et al. (1928) provided further evidence and, consequently, impetus that adults had the ability to learn and all was not decremental after age 25. These key complementary forces from philosophical and scientific streams lent further momentum to the contemporary emergence and recognition of learning as a lifelong process.

The first book specifically titled *Lifelong Education* is credited to British educator Basil Yeaxlee, published in 1929, 3 years after American philosopher/educator Eduard Lindeman's classic *On the Meaning of Adult Education,* which Yeaxlee cites—especially in his chapter titled "Learning From Life."

In addition, Cross-Durrant (1984, 1987) offers further insights into Yeaxlee, considering him a man who was ahead of his time and who did not receive the recognition he deserved. For Yeaxlee, learning and living were an inseparable developmental process and integral to life itself in all its spheres and throughout one's life. Despite his Christian religious background, he was able to advocate for inclusion of a spiritual attitude toward life and moral education without necessarily promoting the embrace of a religious orientation or any specific religion.

The clear need for continuous learning was further catalyzed in an array of writings by Malcolm S. Knowles, who repeatedly cited philosopher Alfred North Whitehead (1861–1947), with whom he studied at Harvard, for his recognition and illumination that at the cusp of the 20th century the life span of an individual was increasing while, simultaneously, the time span of knowledge was decreasing. These analyses and observations added more impetus to the need for lifelong learning.

Adult education, evolving as a field of study and practice, also contributed much to the lifelong learning movement. Its increasing professionalization led to the establishment of university programs, including the establishment of graduate degrees, university extension activities, and other modalities. The first doctorate degree in adult education, awarded by Columbia University to Wilbur Hallenbeck in 1932, further professionalized the field, its visibility, and societal recognition regarding the importance of learning as a lifelong process, along with birthing a cadre of recognized professionals equipped to guide the process.

By the 1940s, particularly in the aftermath of World War II, public policies and legislation such as the Servicemen's Readjustment Act (1944), known as the G.I. Bill, was created to help veterans of World War II. Among other benefits (e.g., unemployment insurance and help with housing), it ensured that veterans had access to education, and granted stipends covering tuition and expenses. Given the sheer magnitude of the veteran population that took advantage of this program, estimated at 7,800,000 million, adults continuing to learn obviously became more visible in society, thus normalizing to some extent the position that adults can and do continue to learn ("G.I. School Law," 1956). Moreover, research such as that of Mettler (2005) shed further light on the social and economic impact, such as further development of the middle class and an active citizenry. Her numerous first-person interviews likewise illuminate and corroborate the impact on the soldier and future generations who started viewing themselves as continuing learners and acting accordingly.

During this post–World War II period, global advances started affecting the further development of the lifelong learning movement in the United States and abroad. By October 1945, the United Nations was officially chartered and by November UNESCO was born with the express mission to contribute to the building of a culture of peace by providing an opportunity for professionals to mutually explore potential solutions to common concerns. Functioning for decades, UNESCO works to create the conditions for dialogue among civilizations, cultures, and people, based upon respect for commonly shared values. It is through this dialogue that the world can achieve global visions of sustainable development encompassing observance of human rights, mutual respect, and the alleviation of poverty, all of which are at the heart of UNESCO's mission and activities (UNESCO, n.d).

UNESCO rapidly recognized the need to learn throughout life (for the benefit of the individual as well as society); the importance of making provisions toward that end; and, consistent with its mission, the need to encourage dialogue among such professionals around the world. It offered a space for that to evolve. Quickly, UNESCO became involved in catalyzing such efforts and was to become a key force in the further development of lifelong education and ultimately lifelong learning as guiding beacons. Beginning in 1949 (in Elsinore, Denmark), and approximately every 10 to 12 years thereafter, World Assemblies on Adult Education were held to which the United States sent key delegations: Montreal, Canada, in 1960; Tokyo, Japan, in 1972; Paris, France, in 1985; Hamburg, Germany, in 1997 (a key turning point in which the UNESCO Assemblies began using adult learning rather than education as a descriptor); and Belém, Brazil, in 2009. The next Assembly is scheduled for 2022, with Morocco as host. Each Assembly reflects on progress made since the previous one and results in declarations and agendas for the forthcoming decade. In addition, reports and reflections ensue wherein each country (i.e., delegations, as well as individual delegates and participants), bring back the information, knowledge, and any wisdom they may have digested for consideration, relevance, and implementation to their specific contexts.

One example is Adult Learners' Week, a concept initially operationalized in the United States during the 1980s, and now heralded around the world. The 1997 UNESCO Assembly on Adult Learning resulted in a formal recommendation to establish Adult Learners' Weeks, and the recommendation was unanimously approved by November 1999 at UNESCO's 30th General Assembly in Paris. Currently an increasing number of countries around the world host Adult Learners' Weeks. While implementation varies in different countries, a general aim is to celebrate and promote adult learning by raising awareness, celebrating achievements, and so on. Such efforts involve media events and free learning opportunities during the week by public and private agents of learning in communities. Some countries even offer recognition awards to adult learners.

Historically, the first international assembly in 1949 helped provide a global arena and establish a more solid identity for the field. The second assembly, held in Montreal during 1960, was organized around the theme of Adult Education in a Changing World, and was the "first international assembly [to] set lifelong education as a goal for future policies of governments" (Lowe, 1975, p. 10). Very significantly, the third assembly held in Tokyo during 1972, adopted the theme of Adult Education in the Context of Lifelong Learning. The school was viewed as one of a spectrum of agents and adult education was perceived as an integral part of a much larger concept: lifelong education/learning.

The United States withdrew from UNESCO in 1984. Consequently, at the 1985 and 1997 assemblies the U.S. delegation participated as observers, which meant they could not vote, and if they wanted to submit resolutions it had to be done by another country that resonated with the suggestion. While rejoining UNESCO in 2002, again as of December 31, 2018, the United States has withdrawn from UNESCO and if nothing changes will remain an observer for the 2022 assembly. The implication is that, as a non-member observer, while the right to vote is lost, the United States will still be able to engage in activities and debates and it currently maintains an interest in resuming full membership once noted concerns and reformations are addressed.

The full preparatory process for each assembly on local and regional levels is beyond the scope of the present chapter, but a few historical points are noteworthy. At the 1972 assembly a group of internationally oriented colleagues—spearheaded by the efforts of J. R. (Roby) Kidd of the Ontario Institute for Studies in Education (OISE) in Canada—including Alex Charters (USA) and some from other countries, catalyzed a discussion and resulting commitment that led to the development of the International Council for Adult Education (ICAE). ICAE is still fully functional today, primarily as an organization of civil society organizations, with opportunities for individual memberships as well. They not only host their own assemblies but also partake in the UNESCO assemblies. From its inception, ICAE had formed a strong collaborative relationship with UNESCO that continues to this day. For the fourth UNESCO assembly in 1985, under a contractual arrangement with UNESCO, ICAE published a volume of papers as a discussion and follow-up, reflecting upon the assembly and considering the role of NGOs (International Council for Adult Education, 1986).

As I have repeatedly emphasized, in various forms over the past 40 years, few fields can claim two mega international bodies (a governmental and a nongovernmental) addressing common issues and coalescing professionals in a common identity. Together they play a complementary part in illuminating the role of adult education as an integral part of the lifelong learning movement. ICAE is the only global organization doing advocacy for adult education in the United Nations and related organizations, has consultative status to the United Nations Economic and Social Council, is cochair of the Education and Academia Stakeholder Group (the formal representative of the global education community in the policy making sphere), and is member of the Steering Group of United Nations Coordination Mechanism of all stakeholders, which enables coordination and cooperation with all other groups and communities. Three key organizations in the United States are members of ICAE: the American Association for Adult and Continuing Education (AAACE), ProLiteracy, and the Coalition of Lifelong Learning Organization (COLLO) (which changed its name during the 1990s from the Coalition of Adult Education Organizations [CAEO], a further signifier of the movement from lifelong education to lifelong learning). The Coalition, as the name implies, is an organization of organizations that includes ProLiteracy and AAACE, as well as a host of other professional organizations and groups that have a focus on adult learners and learning.

UNESCO also continues to fuel discussions regarding the entire spectrum of lifelong learning and its importance, including the recognition of the integral and essential role of professionals working with the adult years. Three key publications continue to enrich the lifelong learning movement: The first, *Learning to Be: The World of Education Today and Tomorrow* (Faure et al., 1972) positioned lifelong education as a master concept. Building on the 1972 publication, the second, *Learning: The Treasure Within* (DeLors et al., 1996), set forth the following "pillars": learning to be, as well as learning to do, think, live together, as well as the later added learning to transform self and society. The vision of the most recent publication, *Rethinking Education: Toward a Global Common Good?* (Mohammed et al., 2015) focuses on "a central concern for sustainable human development . . . understood as the responsible action of individuals and societies toward a better future for all, locally and globally—one in which social justice and environmental stewardship guide socio-economic development" (p. 20). The publication resonates with the United Nations SDGs Project, Agenda UN 2030, to transform the world (United Nations, 2015), discussed later. Regional consultations and discussions on the book *Rethinking Education* were held. For North America, sessions were convened by AAACE at their International Pre Conference in 2016 followed by an on-site (Washington DC) and virtual session hosted by COLLO. The consultancies from all regions of the globe were coordinated by ICAE in collaborative sponsorship by UNESCO. Both UNESCO and ICAE are currently directing much energy to what is called Agenda 2030, and the United Nations SDGs, discussed more fully in a later section of this chapter.

As noted earlier, more fundamental shifts were occurring in society. Social forces were shifting that presaged a potentially new arrangement between society and education. The 1950s became a watershed point as it became increasingly apparent that society was in the midst of a transformation comparable to the move from an agricultural to an industrial society; this time from industry to information as a central project and a focal point of employability. Most compelling, however, was the work of cultural historian Lewis Mumford, who presaged the advent of lifelong learning.

Mumford (1956) was among the first to predict and recognize that during the then-forthcoming transformation that education and learning would come to the forefront such that "education would constitute the principal business of life" (p. 241). Further, "this change was so profound that one must emphasize it by bestowing upon it a new name to indicate that the process of infusing values and meaning into every phase of life will not stop with the formal school" (pp. 241–242). The "new name" seems to have eventually morphed into lifelong learning.

Meaning and Usefulness of the Concept of Lifelong Learning

Illuminating the multilayered meaning currently accorded to lifelong learning as well as its historical antecedents is warranted both for clarity of communication among professionals as well as for its usability—that is, how it has been and could be applied in practice.

From Lifelong Education to Lifelong Learning: Lifelong, Life-Wide, Life-Deep

A currently popular expression refers to learning as lifelong, life-wide, and life-deep. Although there are those who consider such terms and framework newly coined, the rootedness of the concepts harkens to earlier discussions articulating vertical and horizontal dimensions to lifelong learning, discussed as far back as the 1960s and 1970s. *Vertical*, the temporal aspect of lifelong, recognizes learning as a lifelong process. The *horizontal* dimension is spatial in nature and cuts across a spectrum of learning agents, spheres, and formats: Many agents of learning coexist within a community: formal, nonformal, and informal. Learning may be planned as well as incidental. The formal educational system of schools and postsecondary institutions is only one component, complemented by nonformal forces of workplaces, libraries, museums, religious institutions, and mass media, as well as informal sources such as family, friends, peers, and of course the internet. A *depth dimension* was proposed by Kidd (1973, 1975) to serve an integrative function, recognizing a continuum of needs from simple to sublime. Inspired by my continuing correspondence with Kidd until his passing in 1982, my own work in this sphere has focused on the significance in any lifelong learning framework of understanding the complementarity of transpersonal and personal development. The importance is stressed of considering all the levels, states, and structures of consciousness that inform our ways of knowing, including the role of wisdom in our developmental trajectories. These efforts began with completion of my dissertation in 1980, which Kidd so graciously reviewed, and continued thereafter. As the term implies, depth also refers to development that leads and moves one beyond centrisms, such as egocentrism, ethnocentrism, and others, such that one's identity expands and is able to accommodate a greater sense of self in which inclusivity, transcendence, and honoring differences are more easily embraced and enabled—a movement sorely needed in today's world.

As noted, the term *lifelong education* appears to have rooted early on, until a shift began to appear from the 1950s and accelerated during the 1970s to lifelong learning as a broader concept, a wider, deeper container and framework. In fact, the 1970s was an extremely pivotal period: The Nongovernmental International Council for Adult Education (ICAE) was born during the 1972 UNESCO assembly, the then CAEO, later named COLLO, was established in the United States during 1973. CAEO provided an opportunity to the executive directors of the member associations of the Coalition to meet four times a year in Washington DC, to keep apprised of and connected to the government, to learn from each other, and to provide visibility to the important role of adult education in the context of lifelong learning. One of the major collaborative efforts of the group was to influence the passage of lifelong learning legislation, having invested time and energy in educating Congress and others.

The Movement Toward Legislation

In September–October 1975, then-Senator Walter Mondale introduced to the Congress of the United States the Lifetime Learning Act. With a few minor revisions, it succeeded in being enacted as Public Law 94-482 of October 12, 1976 (Lifelong Learning Act, 1976). Ultimately titled the Lifelong Learning Act, provisions cited the definition, scope, rationale, and projected lifelong learning activities, all discussed in the following section. Although the act was not ultimately funded, and is now purportedly in sunset legislation, it is quite instructive and illuminating to witness the details of what the founders had in mind in understanding the importance of and need for lifelong learning. Moreover, it was an unprecedented opportunity for an array of professional associations and groups to collaborate under a common concern. As noted, CAEO (now COLLO), spearheaded such efforts. Research and input offered by the array of professional associations who were members of the CAEO "educated" Congress, resulting in recognition of the necessity for lifelong learning. The details are worth citing here as it is quite stunning how much could be equally applied to our contemporary era, but in a more accelerated manner and in a more technologically and tumultuous context (e.g., proliferation of the internet and social media, with their pluses and minuses; immigration and refugee issues; increasingly uncertain times when massacres of innocent people occur, horrifyingly, in public places and in our universities and schools; the rapid spread of COVID-19;

other global pandemics; etc.). A different kind of learning and education may be needed with more emphasis on the process to complement the programmatic emphasis here but it seems clear that many of the points elucidated by the then legislation may still apply.

The Congress finds that

1. Accelerating social and technological change have had impact on the duration and quality of life;
2. The American people need lifelong learning to enable them to adjust to social, technological, political, and economic change;
3. Lifelong learning has a role in developing the potential of all persons, including their personal well-being, upgrading their workplace skills, and preparing them to participate in the civic, political, and cultural life of the Nation;
4. Lifelong learning is important in meeting the needs of the growing number of older and retired persons;
5. Learning takes place through formal and informal instruction, through educational programs provided through public and private educational and other institutions and organizations, through independent study, and through the efforts of business, industry, and labor;
6. Planning is necessary at the national, State, and local levels to assure effective use of existing resources in the light of changing characteristics and learning needs of the population;
7. More effective use should be made of the resources of the Nation's educational institutions in order to assist the people of the United States in solution of community problems in areas such as housing, poverty, government, recreation, employment, youth opportunities, transportation, health, and land use; and
8. American Society should have as a goal the availability of appropriate opportunities for all of its citizens without regard to restrictions of previous education or training, sex, age, handicapping conditions, social or ethnic background, or economic circumstances. (Lifelong Learning Act, 1976, p. 2086)

With regard to the then-recognized scope of lifelong learning (Section 132):

Lifelong learning includes, but is not limited to, adult basic education, continuing education, independent study, agricultural education, business education and labor education, occupational education and job training programs, parent education, postsecondary education, preretirement and education for older and retired remedial education, special educational programs for groups or for individuals with special needs, and also educational activities designed to upgrade occupational and professional skills, to assist businesses, public agencies, and other organizations in the use or innovation and research results, and to serve family needs and personal development. (Lifelong Learning Act, 1976, p. 2087)

While seemingly comprehensive, the narrative seems to focus more on the programmatic rather than process aspects and is more relevant to lifelong education. It also focuses more on the adult years.

Section 133 proceeds to list an array of "Lifelong Learning Activities." This section is very extensive and only highlights can be offered here, but it does evidence a depth and breadth of intent had matters been funded. Some examples are provisions to make grants to "state agencies, institutions of higher education, and public and private nonprofit organizations," "act as a clearinghouse for information regarding lifelong learning," "review existing major foreign lifelong learning . . . in order to determine the applicability . . . to this country," and many other elements that suggest collaborative efforts (Lifelong Learning Act, 1976, p. 2087).

Even though it never materialized with regard to appropriations, the effort was there and is an important part of the United States' strides. Some ambitious and inspired reader(s) may want to help urge Congress to resurrect, amend or augment, and reintroduce such or similar legislation, with further compelling arguments, in whatever form, for reconsideration. Clarification might also be in order that adult learning and education are part of a larger focus on learning as a lifelong process.

Controversies and Tensions

One could drown in the voluminous literature that has emerged under the moniker of lifelong learning. With a grasp of the trajectory of publications, presentations, dialogues, and discussions, however, it seems clear that some seminal controversies and tensions continue to loom. For example, during the 1970s, John Ohliger (e.g., Ohliger, 1975; see also Grace & Rocco, 2009; Zacharakis, 2003) provided a strong voice in his concern that we might be headed for a "training" or "credentialing" society and mandatory continuing education might usurp matters. Indeed, the credentialing thrust seems to have increased, especially with the proliferation of online certificates that purportedly increase employability for individuals (or at least might be sold that way) and provide economic growth as well for organizations. Moreover, there might be organizations and for-profit enterprises that have merely coopted the lifelong learning banner, or maybe just employ a term that has now come into common usage.

In 1976, Dave expressed concern as well with matters that are still of concern today:

> There is a serious danger that some aspects of lifelong learning would serve primarily to make lifelong learning "profitable" to capital, or to stifle educational dissent. For example, it could serve as a device for rapidly adapting the labor force to the changing needs of industry, or for keeping surplus labor docile and under control. If "collectively" financed, it could shift the burden of cost of upgrading and retraining off the shoulders of industry, while providing a ready-made market for the products of education. (p. 363)

Discourse is still alive, however, about the importance of a social justice perspective on lifelong learning, especially in regard to the marginalized. Discussions have taken on newer focal points as well, with publications such as such as UNESCO's 2019 Global Education Monitoring Report (GEM) (Global Education Monitoring Report Team, 2018) that focuses on migrant and refugee education, complemented by a virtual issue of the AAACE periodical *Adult Learning* titled *Immigration, Adult Education, and Learning Today*, posted in November 2018 (Brooks & Alston, 2018). The 2020 GEM, titled *Inclusion and Education: All Means All*, focuses on barriers faced especially by the most vulnerable due to disadvantage, disability, and so on. It also addresses progress on SDG #4 Education, discussed later. The 2021 GEM, as its title suggests, is scheduled to tackle *Non-State Actors in Education*.

Then there are wider tensions, as well, in society at large. The DeLors (1996) report, cited earlier, listed seven such tensions generated by technological, economic, and social change that the 2015 report on *Rethinking Education* recorroborated:

> Tensions between the global and the local; the universal and the particular; tradition and modernity; the spiritual and the material; long term and short term considerations; the need for competition and the ideal of equality of opportunity; and the expansion of knowledge and our capacity to assimilate it. (DeLors et al., 1996, cited in Mohammed et al., 2015, p. 20)

The 2015 report also added that "patterns of economic growth characterized by rising vulnerability, growing inequality, increased ecological stress, and rising intolerance and violence" (pp. 20–21). For 2020, we certainly should add the COVID-19 pandemic.

Violence in the United States is particularly troublesome along with the uncertainty it brings when massacres of innocent people continue to occur in public places such as entertainment events (concerts, movie theaters, etc.), shopping malls, churches, hospitals, and even schools and universities. Learning to live with such uncertainty can certainly become an integral part of a lifelong learning trajectory.

The continually escalating sprawling crawling nature and availability of the internet (including social media as well) as a source for independent lifelong learning endeavors can be a blessing but also a curse to individuals as well as society. The blessing is welcome, but there are households and individuals still without access in the United States. Moreover, a belief has become entrenched among some individuals that a search of the internet is sufficient to retrieve most material and, even more troublesome, that one only need go back 5 years or so to find relevant data. The reality is that not all material and discussions from the seminal years of the lifelong learning movement have been digitized, resulting sometimes in articles and publications discussing similar positions or making claims that others offered decades prior. At minimum, staying mindful of that possibility may help modify claims made.

For regular users there is yet the discernment factor regarding the validity and credibility of information in general, and understanding of ways in which cults and hate groups might proliferate. While control of access might be more prevalent in authoritarian regimes (with often unfortunate consequences), the mass populace is still subject to manipulative tactics even in the United States. An educated, critically reflective citizenry is essential. Vis à vis society, it is one thing regarding the freedom of speech that permits an array of persuasions to set up sites and create dialogues; it is another when such opportunities spill over into society in deleterious ways as a result of easy information on, for example, how to create homemade bombs or inspiration to kill some offensive "other" due to group reinforcement, and so on.

Another tension is the scarcity or diminishing funding for the adult sector of the lifelong learning movement by governments on a global scale. While of serious concern, in the United States many professional associations; NGOs; and, of course, private and corporate arenas are not as dependent upon governmental funding as is the case in other countries. In addition, a strong cadre of committed volunteers still graces the country.

Toward the Future

As we move through the next decade, and beyond, the future presents us with challenges as well as opportunities. Reflecting on the past, maintaining some grounding in the present, while visioning the future provides dynamic guidance to move forward.

Embracing Multiple Levels of Meaning

In this chapter, lifelong learning has been described as a movement, a process, along with its programmatic aspects. Programs, of course, are the most concrete, often with practical goals and a product orientation. It seems important to embrace an understanding of all levels of conceptualization for a holistic understanding of lifelong learning.

In 1979, Cropley wrote of *maximimalist* and *minimalist* approaches. What Cropley termed the *minimalist approach* tends to focus more on programmatic aspects of lifelong learning and is often used interchangeably with the term *adult education*. By contrast, the maximalist perspective focuses on a fundamental transformation of society.

From a 2020 lens, might it be timely for each perspective to understand the other in a both/and rather than either/or manner, with minimalist perspective understanding that lifelong learning pertains to all of life, not just the adult years, and the maximalist perspective welcoming the practical orientation as one way of operationalizing the lifelong learning concept? It seems useful not to mistake the part for the whole. In general, staying mindful of the many meanings given to the concept, as well as partial understandings and even misunderstandings, will facilitate communication along professionals. Such a feat requires action.

Toward that end, since spring 2018, COLLO in the United States has been conducting a needs analysis among member organizations and others to determine today's major issues in providing lifelong learning opportunities for adults and actions to resolve them. Expected outcomes include clarification of key professionals' understanding of the concept of lifelong learning, challenges, promising practices and approaches, needed resources, and policies.

Adult Education, Part of Lifelong Learning Within the Context of Societal Transformation

Concepts as broad and deep as lifelong learning and lifelong education, however, cannot be left to or are not solely the domain of the discipline of education alone. Recalling the prediction of cultural historian Lewis Mumford (1956) regarding our then-coming transformation, encouraging advances are on the horizon. Two seem particularly promising: (a) the learning cities movement (moving, in part, toward operationalization of the learning society, a key concept of the contemporary lifelong learning movement since inception), and (b) United Nations Agenda 2030, the SDGs, with which the world is awash.

Learning Cities

Since publication of the Faure report in 1972, discussions have ensued about ways to bring the ideal of a *learning society* to fruition. Longworth, beginning in 1999 and in many publications thereafter, as well as Longworth and Osborne (2010) seem to be key informants with regard to the historical backdrop of pilots and projects undertaken over decades alternatively called *learning regions, educating cities*, as well as *learning cities*.

Current advances are breathing interesting life into the early concept of *learning societies* and, driven mostly by UNESCO and the UNESCO Institute for Lifelong Learning (2017a, 2017b), are expending mega efforts at developing Learning Cities, local and regional concrete efforts that include the development of partnerships and economic viability, but connected to a larger network of learning cities throughout the globe: UNESCO Global Network of Learning Cities (GNLC).

Supplanting an earlier concept of the 1970s of educative communities and transcending the phenomenon of one discipline as a change agent, four biennial global conferences on Learning Cities have transpired, each with a resulting report for current and future use: Beijing, China, October 21–23, 2013; Mexico City, Mexico, September 28–30, 2015; Cork, Ireland, September 18–20, 2017; Medellín, Colombia, South America, October 1–3, 2019. The next conference is scheduled for 2021. Reports are available and searchable in the UNESCO digital library (http://unesdoc.unesco.org).

The United States has not joined this particular movement spearheaded by UNESCO and is now unable because it is not a member of UNESCO, and the official application must be endorsed by the country's National UNESCO Commission. Discussion is emerging, however, regarding the way in which some of the elements might already be in place in specific cities and thoughts are under consideration about how to further catalyze dialogue and action in the United States (e.g., Scott, 2015; Tisdell et al., 2012). Moreover, Edwin Lee, the late mayor of San Francisco, speaking at the 3rd International Conference on Learning Cities (UIL, 2017a), indicated that San Francisco was working to become a Learning City. Action is now intensifying in the United States with efforts to form the European-American Network of Learning Cities and with activities such as those in South Bend, Indiana, and Lowell, Massachusetts, which are deeply engaged in declaring, developing, and promoting themselves as Cities of Lifelong Learning. Moreover, the first North American Learning Cities Networking Conference with Workshops on How to Develop Learning Cities took place during November 2019 in Lowell, Massachussetts.

UN Agenda 2030: SDGs

"Transforming Our World: 2030 Agenda for Sustainable Development" was adopted by 193 United Nations member states on September 15, 2015, at the United Nations World Summit and launched on January 1, 2016, as a road map and universal call to action to creating a better more sustainable future for all. Seventeen key goals are specified, each with indicators to monitor progress. The United States continually monitors and provides updated progress and statistics on this feat (U.S. Government, n.d.). An array of websites, continually expanding and developing, also offer resources and activities for the public that are quite comprehensive in scope (SDGs, n.d.; UNESCO, 2019; United Nations, n.d.a., n.d.b.). Included are resource materials for adults as well as children, teachers, and parents to better understand the goals, some of which are simplified to engage young children in a storytelling format. Much work remains, however, to raise awareness of the importance of adult education and the development of materials as well that target adults and educators of adults. Specific actions and activities that individuals and groups, as well as cities and countries, can do to support the goals are also included, though. An action database is offered to keep one apprised of what is being done, and a dedicated space is devoted as well to submit for upload consideration what one's locale is doing (good practices, success stories, lessons learned). Each of the 17 goals is replete with targets, explanatory videos, key facts and figures, and suggestions on how one can help achieve them, take action, and more. Goal 4 specifically targets "quality education" to "ensure inclusive and equitable quality education and promote lifelong learning opportunities for all" (United Nations, 2015, p. 21), but we must acknowledge that adult and lifelong learning can help catalyze many of the other goals as well. Interestingly, Goal 11 is addressed to creating sustainable cities and communities (i.e., "Make cities and human settlements inclusive, safe, resilient and sustainable" [United Nations, 2015, p. 26]), thus interfacing with the Learning Cities movement.

Collaborative efforts among government, civil society, and the private sector are also urged. In the United States, the Hilton Foundation is raising awareness and engagement as to how philanthropy can contribute to the achievement of the SDGs (Conrad N. Hilton Foundation, n.d., 2016, 2017). The nonprofit Sustainable Development Solutions Network of researchers, knowledge, workers, and thought leaders is equally concerned with promoting domestic implementation of the United Nations SDGs adapted to the U.S. context and has published its third yearly report of strides in the United States, ranking U.S. cities on progress toward the SDGs (Lynch et al., 2019).

Specifically relevant to the field of adult education, COLLO has sponsored a symposium (on site in Washington DC, and virtually globally) raising awareness and discussing action steps regarding what the field can do and needs to be doing to promote the SDGs. COLLO (2019) provides insights into the symposium as well as resources for continuing inquiry. The target date for realization of the United Nations' "plan of action for people, planet, and prosperity" is the year 2030 (United Nations, 2015, p. 5).

Blazing Trails Ahead

In another 10 years, the 2030 handbook will be published. How will the field have been impacted, but more important, what impact will the field of adult and continuing education have made and what role will it have played in such endeavors, both with regard to the SDGs as well as the lifelong learning movement in general?

Will we have or develop the capacity to understand that when the term *lifelong learning* is used individuals and institutions may define it differently? Will we be able to embrace the multiple meanings and respect the role that various individuals and collective contribute? How equipped might we be or become to understand the more market driven approaches to lifelong learning as balanced with the human services orientation and educate each that they are part of a larger movement.

This chapter presented lifelong learning as a foundational concept to the field of adult and continuing education—as a movement, a process, along with it more concrete programmatic aspects—but with a much broader reach that applies across one's life span. One is reminded, however, that throughout history, harkening to ancient times, voices have arisen heralding the importance of lifelong learning, expressing the need to examine and improve the relationship between society and learning for all humanity, and calling upon lifelong learning, although not necessarily named as such. Advocates and forerunners such as Pericles, Comenius, Yeaxlee, and others understood the importance of lifelong learning not just to the individual but also to society. Sometimes they appeared as lone voices or ahead of their time, and in some instances their contributions may have lain fallow awaiting current recognition.

In our contemporary era, many more forces have converged to solidify the concept of lifelong learning. Among those discussed are the advent of the profession of adult education itself as a catalyst, coupled with an array of social forces that created an appropriate zeitgeist. We live in uncertain times, however, which has bred an array of tensions and controversies discussed that will require attention by many disciplines and sectors of society. As a critical component of the lifelong learning movement, the field of adult education has a key role to play in shedding light on these challenges and contributing to their resolution.

Consider this chapter an invitation to further dialogue. The future is in our hands.

References

Boshier, R. (1980). *Towards a learning society: New Zealand adult education in transition.* Learning Press.

Boucouvalas, M. (1988). *Adult education in Greece.* University of British Columbia; International Council for Adult Education.

Brooks, A. K., & Alston, G. D. (Eds.). (2018, November). Virtual issue: Immigration, adult education, and learning today. *Adult Learning.* https://journals.sagepub.com/page/alx/collections/virtual-issue/immigration-adult-education-learning-today?pbEditor=true

Coalition of Lifelong Learning Organizations. (2019). *COLLO. The Coalition of Lifelong Learning Organizations.* www.thecollo.org

Comenius, J. A. (1987). *Pampaedia* (A. M. O. Dobbie, Trans.). Regency Press. (Original work published in Latin during the 1600s)

Conrad N. Hilton Foundation. (n.d.). *Our work and the sustainable development goals.* www.hiltonfoundation.org/sdgs

Conrad N. Hilton Foundation. (2016, July). *From global goals to local impact: How philanthropy can help achieve the U.N. Sustainable Development Goals in the U.S.* https://hiltonfoundation.org/news/our-news/from-global-goals-to-local-impact-how-philanthropy-can-help-achieve-the-u-n-sustainable-development-goals-in-the-u-s

Conrad N. Hilton Foundation. (2017, November). *Sustainable development goals in the United States.* https://www.hiltonfoundation.org/learning/sustainable-development-goals-in-the-united-states

Cropley, A. J. (1979). Lifelong education: Some theoretical and practical considerations. In A. J. Cropley (Ed.), *Lifelong education: A stocktaking* (pp. 99–115). UNESCO Institute for Education.

Cross-Durrant, A. (1984). Basil Yeaxlee and lifelong education: Caught in time. *International Journal of Lifelong Education, 3*(4), 279–291.

Cross-Durrant, A. (1987). Basil Yeaxlee and the origins of lifelong education. In P. Jarvis (Ed.), *Twentieth-century thinkers in adult education* (pp. 38–61). Croom Helm.

Dave, R. H. (1976). *Foundations of lifelong education.* UNESCO Institute for Education; Pergamon Press.

Davies, K. (2009). A learning society. In A. Stibbe (Ed.), *The handbook of sustainability literacy* (pp. 215–220). Green Books.

DeLors, J., Al Mufti, I., Amagi, I., Caeneiro, R., Chung, F., Geremek, B., Gorham, W., Singh, K., Komhauser, A., Manley, M., Quero, M.P., Savané, M-A. P., Singh, K., Stavenhagen, R., Suhr, M.W., & Zhou, N. (1996). *Learning: The treasure within* [report to UNESCO of the International Commission on Education for the Twenty-first Century]. UNESCO.

Faure, E., Herrera, F., Kaddoura, A-R., Lopes, H., Petrovsky, A. V., Rahnema, M., & Ward, F. C. (1972). *Learning to be: The world of education today and tomorrow.* UNESCO.

"G.I. school law ends Wednesday." (1956, July 22). *The New York Times.* ProQuest Historical Newspapers: The New York Times.

Global Education Monitoring Report Team. (2018). Global education monitoring report, 2019: *Migration, displacement, and education: Building bridges, not walls.* UNESCO. https://en.unesco.org/gem-report/2019

Global Education Monitoring Report Team. (2020). *Global education monitoring report, 2020: Inclusion and education: All means all.* UNESCO. https://en.unesco.org/gem-report/2020

Grace, A. P., & Rocco, T. S. (Eds.). (2009). *Challenging the professionalization of adult education: John Ohliger and contradiction in modern practice.* Jossey-Bass.

Great Britain Ministry of Reconstruction. Adult Education Committee (1919). *Final report* [Great Britain House of Commons Command Paper 321]. H.M.S.O.

Husén, T. (1974). *The learning society.* Methuen.

Husén, T. (1986). *The learning society revisited.* Pergamon.

Hutchins, R. M. (1968). *The learning society.* Praeger.

International Council for Adult Education. (1986). *Making the connection: The adult education movement and the fourth UNESCO conference.* ICAE.

Jaeger, W. (1943). *Paideia: The ideals of Greek culture: In search of the divine center* (Vol. 2) (G. Highet, Trans.). Oxford University Press. (Original work published 1939)

Jaeger, W. (1944). *The ideals of Greek culture: The conflict of cultural ideals in the age of Plato* (Vol. 3) (G. Highet, Trans.). Oxford University Press. (Original work published 1939)

Jaeger, W. (1945). *The ideals of Greek culture: Archaic Greece and the mind of Athens.* (Vol. 1) (G. Highet, Trans.). Oxford University Press. (Original work published 1939)

Kidd, J. R. (1973). *Relentless verity: Education for being, becoming, belonging* (ED 094 158). ERIC. https://files.eric.ed.gov/fulltext/ED094158.pdf

Kidd, J. R. (1975). The inner continuum: Some notes on the application of a third dimension to reflection and research about lifelong education. In R. J. Dave (Ed.), *Reflections on lifelong continuing education and the school* (pp. 27–30). UNESCO Institute for Education.

Lifelong Learning Act, PL 94-482. (1976, 12 October). Part B Lifelong Learning of the Educational Amendments of 1976. Stat. 90, 20 USC 1015, Sections 131–134. *Congressional Record* (pp. 2086–2089). U.S. Government Printing Office.

Lindeman, E. (1926). *The meaning of adult education.* New Republic.

Longfellow, H. W. (1893). Morituri Salutamus. In H. E. Scudder (Ed.), *Complete poetical works of Henry Wadsworth Longfellow.* Houghton, Mifflin. (Original work published 1875)

Longworth, N. (1999). *Lifelong learning at work: Learning cities for a learning century.* Kogan Page.

Longworth, N., & Osborne, M. (2010). Six ages toward a learning region: A retrospective. *European Journal of Education, 45*(3), 368–401.

Lowe, J. (1975). *The education of adults: A world perspective.* UNESCO Press.

Lynch, A., LoPresti, A., & Fox, C. (2019). *The 2019 US cities sustainable development report.* Sustainable Development Solutions Network. www.sustainabledevelopment.report/2019USCities

McGhee, P. (1959). *The learning society.* Center for the Study of Liberal Education for Adults.

Mettler, S. (2005). *Soldier to citizen: The GI bill and the making of the greatest generation.* Oxford University Press.

Mohammed, A. J., Morgan, W. J., DeSouza, P. R., Haddad, G., Kiwan, F., van Leeuwen, F., Sato, T., & Schmelk, S. (2015). *Rethinking education: Toward a global common good?* UNESCO.

Mumford, L. (1956). *The transformations of man.* Harper & Row.

Ohliger, J. (1975). Prospects for a learning society. *Adult Leadership, 24*(1), 37–39.

Scott, L. (Ed.). (2015). Learning cities for adult learners. [Themed issue]. *New Directions for Adult and Continuing Education, 2015*(145).

Servicemen's Readjustment Act. (1944). P.L. 346, Chapter 268, S. 1767.

Sustainable Development Goals. (n.d.). *Student resources.* https://www.un.org/sustainabledevelopment/student-resources/

Thomas, A. (1961). The learning society. *Food for Thought, 21*(B), 70–75 (ED 012 433). ERIC. https://files.eric.ed.gov/fulltext/ED012433.pdf

Thorndike, E. L., Bregman, E. O., Tilton, J. W., & Woodyard, E. (1928). *Adult learning.* Macmillan.

Tisdell, E. J., Chang, W. J., Bush, P. L., & Boyd, G. C. (2012, July 3–6). *A U.S. perspective on the learning city: Efforts on lifelong learning in Harrisburg, PA* [Paper presentation]. SCUTREA 42nd Annual Conference, Leicester, England. http://www.leeds.ac.uk/educol/documents/209882.pdf

UNESCO. (n.d.). *UNESCO in brief: Mission and mandate.* https://en.unesco.org/about-us/introducing-unesco

UNESCO. (2019). *SDG resources for educators: Quality Education.* https://en.unesco.org/themes/education/sdgs/material/04

UNESCO Institute for Lifelong Learning. (2017a, September 18–20). *Global goals, local actions—Toward lifelong learning for all in 2030* [Conference report]. 3rd International Conference on Learning Cities (ICLC), Cork, Ireland, Hamburg, Germany.

UNESCO Institute for Lifelong Learning. (2017b). *Learning cities and the SDGs: A guide to action* (ED 590 193). ERIC. https://files.eric.ed.gov/fulltext/ED590193.pdf

United Nations. (n.d.a). *17 goals to transform our world.* Sustainable development goals. https://www.un.org/sustainabledevelopment/

United Nations. (n.d.b). *Student resources.* Sustainable development goals. https://www.un.org/sustainabledevelopment/student-resources/

United Nations. (2015). *Transforming our world: The 2030 agenda for sustainable development.* https://sustainabledevelopment.un.org/post2015/transformingourworld

U.S. Government. (n.d.). *U.S. national statistics for the U.N. sustainable development goals.* https://sdg.data.gov/

Yeaxlee, B. (1929). *Lifelong education: A sketch of the range and significance of the adult education movement.* Cassell.

Zacharakis, J. (2003). Placing John Ohliger in his proper historical context. *Adult Learning, 14*(3), 24–27.

CHAPTER 6

Internationalization of Adult and Continuing Education

Mary V. Alfred and Shibao Guo

For this chapter, we set out to investigate, through a review of the extant literature, the phenomenon of internationalization within adult and continuing education. Upon our initial review and from our prior research on the topic, we found much of the scholarship and case examples of internationalization to be framed within higher education, with implications for adult education practice (see Alfred & Guo, 2012; Coryell et al., 2012; Egetenmeyer, 2017; Guo et al., 2010; Tolliver et al., 2018; Xiao, 2018). Moreover, much of the scholarship points to the impact of globalization as a determinant in the internationalization practices of higher and adult education, to be discussed later in this chapter.

While the terms *internationalization* and *globalization* are used interchangeably, Altbach and Knight (2007) define *globalization* as the economic, political, and societal forces pushing systems of higher education toward greater international engagements. Hence, we use internationalization to encompass activities of engagement within higher education that cross international borders.

We approach this chapter by first presenting a history of internationalization of the field. Second, we explore the phenomenon of globalization and its complementary features of neoliberalism and marketization, highlighting impact on administration and practices within higher education. Finally, we explore internationalization within adult education and highlight case examples of practice and research activities among faculty globally.

History of Internationalization of Adult Education

International discourse on adult education can be traced to the establishment of the World Association of Adult Education (WAAE) in London in 1919. The organization, which continued until the start of World War II, was founded with an expressed purpose of using adult education as a platform to make visible and address the challenges that confronted individuals, communities, and societies across the globe (Boucouvalas, 2002). According to Knoll (2002), the vision for the organization was the promotion of cultural awareness; promotion of international cooperation and understanding; and advancement of an agenda for policy, research, and practice to solve problems confronting adults. In 1929, the WAAE organized the first world conference on adult education in Cambridge, England, with 85 delegates from Europe and across the globe to set an international agenda for the academic discipline of adult education. Knoll (2002) affirms that the WAAE was the first concrete step in collaboration among the academic discipline of adult education in Europe and other countries. John Field (2016), in his blog post titled "The World Conference on Adult Education,

1929," confirmed the historic significance of the association in its attempt to internationalize adult education across the globe. However, according to Field, the WAAE did not survive beyond World War II.

Following the WAAE, two international bodies made significant contributions to the internationalization of adult education, namely the United Nations Educational, Scientific and Cultural Organization (UNESCO) and the International Council of Adult Education (ICAE) (Boucouvalas, 2011). Similar to the concept of the WAAE, internationalization in that regard refers to an international approach among government and nongovernment organizations (NGOs), educators, and other leaders to advance adult education as a platform to address global issues of social justice, education disparities, gender inequalities, poverty, health, vulnerable population, peace, and the environment (Ireland & Spezia, 2014; Knoll, 2014). While UNESCO is a government-based organization, ICAE draws its membership from NGOs; however, both organizations have a similar mission (Boucouvalas, 2011; Charters, 2011; Ireland & Spezia, 2014).

While the WAAE was the start of an international discourse on adult education, consistent efforts at implementing an international agenda can be traced to the adult education world conferences sponsored by UNESCO, the first of which was held at Elsinore, Denmark, in 1949. Following the first conference, five other International Conferences on Adult Education (CONFINTEA) were held in various world regions to include, in succeeding order, Montreal, Canada (1960); Tokyo, Japan (1972); Paris, France (1985); Hamburg, Germany (1997); and Belém, Brazil (2009). These conferences are held approximately every 12 years, and with each assembly, world leaders and other representatives gather to discuss the status of education for adults and to develop strategies and make recommendations for future development across world nations. The UNESCO's world regions include the African Continent, the Arab States, Asia and the Pacific Region, Europe and North America, and Latin America and the Caribbean.

With a parallel agenda, the ICAE was founded in 1972 during the third UNESCO world conference. It draws its membership from NGOs and works in concert with UNESCO "to strengthen the structures of adult education and the role of adult education in the face of critical global issues" (ICAE, n.d., p. 2). With the emergence of social movements in the 1980s, for example, the women's movement, the peace movement, trade union movements, and movement of indigenous peoples (ICAE, n.d.), the organization promoted international adult education as a platform whereby organizations for social change could launch and advance their transformative agenda—one that is aligned with the philosophy of the field.

Although in recent times, UNESCO has had a more global presence, the underlying themes of social justice, equity, democracy, and environmental sustainability drive the mission of both organizations. Unlike the WAAE, UNESCO was not concerned with adult education as an academic discipline, but focused primarily on humanitarian, political, and social crises in developing countries that could be mitigated by practical, applied adult education (Knoll, 2014).

Over the past 70 years, reports following each of UNESCO's international conferences documented varying levels of progress throughout the world regions (Ireland & Spezia, 2014), but some global challenges persist: gender inequality, poverty, health and education disparities, among others. While these challenges are endemic to all of the world regions, contemporary globalization is noted to be the overarching influence that disrupts the promotion of an international agenda for education and human development globally (Burbules & Torres, 2000; Giroux, 2008; Giroux & Myrsiades, 2001; Jarvis, 2007, 2011).

Moreover, some adult education scholars argue the demands of the knowledge economy in an era of contemporary globalization are also responsible for the limited progress in the agenda for adult education and lifelong learning in civil society (Folkman, 2006; Guo et al., 2010; Jarvis, 2007, 2011; Schied, 2006; Schied et al., 2005). While some lament the problem and its devastating impact on adult education, others simultaneously highlight the problem and offer recommendations for advancing the field of adult education in the current era of neoliberal globalization.

Adult education as a discipline in higher education is impacted by the globalizing effects on that enterprise and, therefore, much of the discourses and practices of internationalization is situated within that context (see Coryell et al., 2012; Egetenmeyer, 2017; Guo et al., 2010; Jarvis, 2011; Tolliver et al., 2018; Xiao, 2018). In this literature, authors highlighted internationalization activities within higher education, driven by policies and strategic imperatives at promoting global competitiveness. We will discuss some of these cases later in the chapter.

Globalization and Education

Higher education and its related discipline of adult and continuing education is historically grounded in values that have shaped their legitimacy, governance structures, organizational arrangements, traditions, cultures, and academic orientations (Vaira, 2004). According to Hill et al. (2005), higher education provides considerable value to individuals, the economies where they work, and society at large. Historically, with support from state and federal government, education leaders focused primarily on research, teaching, learning, and service activities as avenues for the transmission of values to the individuals, communities, and society. Today the traditional education enterprise is being challenged by the globalization process that emphasizes capitalism within a free market system, one that is often in conflict with traditional institutionalized values of education for the common good, for citizenship building, and transmission of knowledge for civil society (Kandiko, 2010; Olssen & Peters, 2007; Vaira, 2004). With the decrease in state funding and the increase in federal and state expectations of higher education, leaders are now focused on education as a business enterprise with a capitalist agenda.

As the global knowledge economy becomes increasingly competitive, the role of education comes under intense scrutiny. Moreover, as globalization intensifies the processes of corporatization, marketization, and capitalism, the value of education as a public good is being redefined and assessed based on its value for contributing to the global competitiveness of nation states.

Globalization, Neoliberalism, and Academic Capitalism

From an oversimplistic perspective, globalization is conceptualized as a process of interaction among people, corporations, and governments of different nations. It represents a process of international trade and investment, facilitated by information technology (Burbules & Torres, 2000; Olssen & Peters, 2005; Vaira, 2004). However, the day-to-day occurrence of globalization and its impact is not that simple. It is essentially a contested concept that incites controversy (Robertson & White, 2007). It is not surprising then, that there is no agreed-on definition. Attempts at definition focus on the dimensions of speed and time, processes and flows, space, and increasing integration and interconnection (Ritzer, 2007).

In the current literature on globalization, there is a neglect of questions of social inequality, power and the global–local relationship (Robertson & White, 2007). There is evidence suggesting that we are experiencing widening gaps between the "haves" and the "have nots" in global society, devastating environmental problems, declining civic participation and community, and increasing mistrust and alienation among citizenries (Welch, 2001). Global capitalism, it seems, has created a global society that is unequal and unjust (Giroux, 2008; Jarvis, 2007). Many have argued this new societal culture is not the result of globalization, a phenomenon which has been around for a while, but the result of a form of globalization referred to as neoliberal globalization (Giroux, 2008; Saad-Filho & Johnston, 2005).

From Globalization to Neoliberal Globalization

The concepts of globalization and neoliberalism, while closely connected, have some subtle variations. While globalization is not a new phenomenon, the current wave is driven by public policies that have opened market economies both nationally and internationally. Hence, public policy and technology are the two main drivers of today's globalization (Burbules & Torres, 2000; Kandiko, 2010; Mitchell & Nielsen, 2012).

Many critics agree that liberal public policies, facilitated by technology, have transformed globalization into a neoliberal phenomenon. According to Burbules and Torres (2000), neoliberalism dominates modern globalization. Neoliberal globalization assumes markets are self-regulating social systems and, if allowed to function without governmental interference, have the potential to serve all economic needs, make efficient use of economic resources, and create full employment for everyone who is willing to work (Saad-Filho & Johnston, 2005; Vaira, 2004). While this simplistic definition is commonly offered, it is the opinion of many scholars that articulating a theoretical definition of neoliberalism is an impossible task, as it involves a range of social, political, and economic arrangements with varying levels of complexity, some of which are abstract and some are more concrete (Burbules & Torres, 2000; Giroux, 2008; Saad-Filho & Johnston, 2005; Vaira, 2004). The growing power of multinational corporations and the erosion of democracy and social justice, for example, represent the abstract characteristic of the phenomenon while privatization of social welfare and other public service exemplifies its concrete and more visible influence (Saad-Filho & Johnston, 2005).

Taking into consideration the undergirding concepts of neoliberalism and its impact on the fabric of the world, many critical scholars are concerned that the educational enterprise is increasingly affected by the process of neoliberal globalization that threatens the autonomy of national educational systems (Giroux, 2003, 2004; Kandiko, 2010; Mitchell & Nielsen, 2012). There is the concern that the educational enterprise, which was once viewed as an enterprise of the state, is now left to the open market and influenced by neoliberal ideals of global competition, corporatization, and marketization.

Neoliberal Globalization and Academic Capitalism

The influence of globalization on education can be understood within the concepts of neoliberalism, namely ideologies of the free market, a system of economics based on cost recovery and entrepreneurship, accountability and assessment, and new forms of institutional leadership which Ball (1998) refers to as *neoliberal managerialism*. Neoliberal managerialism, according to Ball, is the commercialization of universities to gain efficiency and remain competitive. The neoliberal concept of the new managerialism in higher education is not new. As Levidow (2005) explains, since 1995, universities worldwide have been urged to adopt a commercial model of knowledge, skills, curriculum, finance, accounting, and organization management. Moreover, continued Levidow, the World Bank has been promoting a global reform agenda for higher education, one that emphasizes the neoliberal features of privatization, deregulation, and marketization. The model envisioned by the World Bank is that

> the market orientation of higher education include (a) tuition, fees, and the sale of research and instruction via grants, contracts, and entrepreneurial training; (b) the private sector, including both nonprofit and proprietary providers of tertiary education; (c) regional decentralization, or the devolution of authority from the central government to the regions; and (d) institutional autonomy, or the devolution of authority from government at whatever level, to institutions. (Levidow, 2005, p. 4)

Although the World Bank agenda has little support among educators, Johnstone et al. (1998) noted some key elements being implemented. In the United States and Canada, for example, many universities have adopted entrepreneurial ventures, acting as not only business partners but businesses themselves, using university resources with faculty and students as labor (Levidow, 2005; Slaughter & Rhodes, 2004).

Similarly, in research universities, there is a strong focus on grant funding activities as a marker of faculty excellence and a requirement for tenure and/or promotion. In the absence of external funding for adult education research, some faculty engage in entrepreneurial activities to include delivery of workshops and certificate programs to education, business, and industry, here and abroad, to generate funding in lieu of funded research activities. In other instances, faculty of adult education, for example, abandon their research agenda to support funded projects in other disciplines, especially in the sciences, to demonstrate evidence of engagement in extramural activities. This expectation of income generation is inherent in the neoliberal ideology of marketization and entrepreneurship to enhance competition. After all, external funding is a marker of excellence in higher education and a criterion by which research universities are ranked.

Similarly, within the environment of academic capitalism, the relationship between faculty and administration is rapidly shifting from permanent employees with full-time jobs to a work arrangement that involves contingent, intermittent, and contracting work (Kandiko, 2010; Mitchell & Nielsen, 2012). The acceleration of online education, with institutions competing for students on a global sphere, for example, has contributed to this arrangement where loyalty between higher education institutions and employees is being derailed (Slaughter & Leslie, 1997; Slaughter & Rhodes, 2004). The use of part-time contingent workers to deliver instruction is aligned with the neoliberal practice of using low-wage, temporary workers to maximize profit. This practice is quite prevalent in adult and continuing education programs, where it is not uncommon in U.S. graduate adult education programs to have one or two permanent faculty, supplemented by part-time contingent workers in the form of adjunct faculty.

With the eradication of labor unions within the neoliberal capitalist landscape, Berry and Worthen (2012) contend higher education administrators are left to adapt to this capitalist labor utilization to maximize their resources and maintain a competitive position among their peer institutions. This positionality is characterized by the number of top tier student admissions, number of students enrolled, time to degree, number of students retained and graduated, employability of students upon graduation, external funding and patents per faculty, faculty publications and citations, and national faculty award recognition, among other performance indicators.

A major indicator of competitive performance and university ranking is engagement in international activities. As a result, global education in the form of international recruitment of faculty and students, study abroad programs, offshore campuses and disciplinary programs, and research collaborations are examples of internationalization activities within higher and adult education (Coryell et al., 2012; Guo et al., 2010; Mitchell & Nielsen, 2012). According to Mitchell and Nielsen (2012),

> Colleges and universities are internationalizing their behavior when they reshape their purposes to attract international students, to deploy their programs across national borders, concentrate on internationally advantageous education program niches, restructure work roles or compensation systems to recruit, retain, or manage employees. (p. 10)

The globalizing practices in higher education have implications for adult and continuing education programs and, thus, guide the directions, curricula, and practices of such programs.

Internationalization of Adult and Higher Education

Internationalization is a contested term which means different things to different people. For some people, it means a series of international activities (e.g., academic mobility of students and faculty), international linkages and partnerships, and new international academic programs and research initiatives, while for others it means the delivery of education to other countries through satellite programs (Knight, 2004). For critical scholars such as Luke (2010), internationalization is viewed as a reflection of "a complex, chaotic and unpredictable *edubusiness*, whose prioritization of the financial 'bottom line' has supplanted clear normative educational and, indeed, overtly ideological intents" (p. 44, italics in original). Knight (2004) defines *internationalization of higher education* as "the process of integrating an international, intercultural or global dimension into the purpose, functions or delivery of post-secondary education" (p. 11). This definition acknowledges the relationship between and among nations, cultures, or countries and conveys that internationalization is an ongoing effort to make universities "more responsive to the challenges of the globalization of the economy and society" (Elliott, 1998, p. 32). A recent study published by the European Parliament revised Knight's widely cited definition to read:

> [Internationalization is] the intentional process of integrating an international, intercultural, or global dimension into the purpose, functions, and delivery of postsecondary education, in order to enhance the quality of education and research for all students and staff, and to make a meaningful contribution to society. (de Wit et al., 2015, p. 29)

This revision places a focus on intentionality and broadens internationalization from mobility to include curriculum and learning outcomes. Internationalization of the curriculum aims to incorporate "international, intercultural, and/or global dimensions into the content of the curriculum as well as the learning outcomes, assessment tasks, teaching methods, and support services of a program of study" (Leask, 2009, p. 209).

The literature on the internationalization of higher education presents two major discourses: market driven (i.e., related to fostering economic performance and competitiveness) and ethically driven (i.e., related to charitable concerns for enhancing the quality of life of disadvantaged students) discourses (Khoo, 2011). Financial crises are driving profit-seeking policies of internationalization in higher education as seen in the recruitment of international students and faculty, establishing academic programs and research initiatives in international countries, and marketing online programs to students of other countries.

Many critics highlight the exploitation of international students, claiming they are being treated like "cash cows" (Canadian Association of University

Teachers, 2016, p. A9). Guo and Guo (2017) urge us to pay attention to discrepancies between internationalization policies and international student experiences (such as racism) and advocate for more ethically oriented policies and practices as opposed to profit-seeking. Recent literature (Abdi & Shultz, 2008; Andreotti, 2013) also indicates that concepts expressed in internationalization policies and initiatives such as governments' and institutions' social responsibility, transnational mobility of students, and students' interculturality that are associated with global citizenship have come to combine both market and ethical influences for positive outcomes on students' global learning. Evidence of global learning, albeit minimal, can be found in the research, teaching, and service activities of adult education faculty worldwide.

Discourses and Practices of Internationalization in Adult Education

The concept and practice of internationalization has been an ongoing phenomenon in adult education. Approaches at internationalization were first made with attempts from world organizations like WAAE, UNESCO, and ICAE to assemble world leaders of government and nongovernment organizations to develop a common agenda for the field—one that would address the problems confronting human and societal development endemic to nations across the globe. Adult education was and continues to be a platform for promoting human rights, economic justice, gender equality, and environmental sustainability—issues that remain constant in the international agenda for adult education (Ireland & Spezia, 2014).

While the global discourse on adult education continues with the work of UNESCO and ICAE, today's universities, influenced by the forces of neoliberal globalization, have escalated their efforts at internationalizing their curricular, research, teaching, and engagement activities. We refer to this practice as internationalization at the institutional level to differentiate it from the global assemblies of UNESCO and ICAE. Egetenmeyer (2017) refers to today's internationalization activities as cross-border education, a phenomenon with many dimensions. As a panelist on the discussion on internationalization of adult education in Canada and beyond, Schugurensky identified some of these dimensions to include short-term study-abroad programs; faculty exchanges, such as short-term leaves for teaching and research at international universities; establishing satellite campuses in other countries; and curricular exchanges among international university faculty of adult education programs (Guo et al., 2010).

In our review of the literature, we found more scholars in higher education than in adult education were writing about the concept and practices of internationalization. Among the works of adult education scholars we reviewed were those of Alfred and Guo (2012), Coryell et al. (2012), Egetenmeyer (2017), Guo et al. (2010), Jarvis (2007, 2011), Tolliver et al. (2018), and Xiao (2018). In each case, the scholars situated their research and/or collaborative practice within higher education and referenced adult education as an academic program or discipline within that institution. This is to suggest that as a discipline in higher education, adult education is bound by the philosophy and priorities of the institution which, in turn, guide internationalization practices. Therefore, internationalization of adult education must be understood within the broader internationalization activities in higher education.

One area of internationalization that is most evident is the increasing enrollment of international students in both Canadian and U.S. higher education institutions. As of December 31, 2019, Canada hosted 642,480 international students as the fourth-largest host country of postsecondary international students after the United States, United Kingdom, and China (Canadian Bureau for International Education, 2020). The United States remains the top receiving country with 1.1 million international students in 2017 (Zong & Batalova, 2018). While universities are engaged in various forms of globalization activities, we profile a few case examples specific to adult education practice and research.

In the first case example, the partnerships involved the University of Free State (UFS) in South Africa and DePaul University's School of New Learning (SNL) in the United States. The second partnership was with Tangaza University College in Kenya and the same U.S. institution (Tolliver et al., 2018). Drawing from the competency-based model at SNL, the goal of the partnership was the development and implementation of a competency-based adult education program to support workforce education, leading to a bachelor of management leadership undergraduate degree, exclusively for working adults. According to the authors, South Africa and Kenya are among several African nations working to internationalize their curriculum, drawing on models from the West. These institutions were in search of programs that would guide their efforts at effective educational reform and meet the growing needs of their workforce (Tolliver et al., 2018). Specific to South Africa, the collaboration was the government's attempt to address exclusion and inequality in the postapartheid era. While the partners from the U.S. university delivered on content, structure, and process, the authors concluded the most important aspect of the paradigm shift for the institution would be to examine "faculty, staff, and administration's historical and contemporary perspectives about culture, gender, and power relations" (Tolliver et al., 2018, p. 30), vestiges of apartheid that must be addressed with education reform.

In the second case example, Egetenmeyer (2017) addressed the internationalization in adult and continuing education across several universities in Europe. Recognizing the growing need for international awareness among graduates in adult and continuing education and the growing commitment of universities to internationalize teaching and learning activities (Egetenmeyer, 2017), seven European universities collaborated to develop a joint module designed to provide an international education program for their masters and doctoral students. Adult education professors from the different nations collaborated in developing the consortium with support of their universities. The countries represented in this consortium included Denmark, Italy, Germany (with two universities represented), Portugal, Italy, and Hungary. This example consisted of the integration of a joint module on internationalization into the curricular of masters and doctoral studies of adult education at each of the universities represented.

The third example is one presented by Coryell et al. (2012), who reported findings from their study that explored internationalization activities within four universities from the United States and the United Kingdom. As part of that investigation, Coryell et al., who are from a Hispanic- and minority-serving institution in the United States, were charged by the administration "to examine how the institution is currently situated with respect to offering internationally focused educational experiences and to find ways to provide these experiences more widely to students, faculty, administration, and staff" (p. 77).

To collect data for the study, the researchers visited four universities in the United States and the United Kingdom that were engaged in internationalization activities. Since internationalization often involves border crossing, the researchers were particularly interested in the experiences and perspectives of faculty and administrators from intuitions at home and abroad. The findings supported those of prior studies that found internationalization activities in higher education to include research collaborations among scholars, student and faculty mobility across borders, institutional mobility in terms of satellite campuses and program offerings in other countries, and curricular exchanges among disciplinary programs. What is missing from these global activities, according to Coryell et al. (2012), is robust evaluation of impact beyond the number of participants who engage in internationalization activities.

As a final example, we present the work of Alfred and Guo (2012), who conducted a study "to examine the extent to which adult education faculty and programs in Canada and the United States were moving toward the internationalization of research, curricular, and practice to adequately prepare graduate students for responsible citizenship in a civil society" (p. 56). The authors reviewed and analyzed conference proceedings from 1995 to 2010 from the U.S.-based Adult Education Research Conference (AERC) and the Canadian Association for the Study of Adult Education (CASAE) conference for evidence of faculty engagement in international/intercultural research. They also reviewed curricular and program offerings from selected universities for evidence of international perspectives.

The findings revealed 7.52% of the CASAE papers and 7.64% of the AERC papers focused on issues beyond local concerns. The study found much of the research with an international dimension to be those authored by visible minorities who were not born in Canada or the United States. However, there was evidence of collaboration among international and native-born faculty and students. From the review of program offerings and course descriptions of programs at selected universities, the study found six programs from the United States and five from Canada to have at least one course that showed evidence of an international perspective. Granted this study was conducted several years ago, but results from our extensive review of the literature for this chapter reveal limited progress in the scholarship of internationalization of the field.

Conclusion

Adult education has a long history of internationalization activities that started at the global level with the WAAE in 1929, followed by UNESCO and ICAE. While UNESCO and ICAE are still actively engaged with documented scholarship of their engagement, adult educators within colleges and universities demonstrate some engagement, guided by priorities of the institution and individual interests. Yet, there is a paucity of publications on the internationalization of adult and continuing education, particularly among U.S. scholars. Ruther (2002) suggested the task of advancing internationalization is the responsibility of actors within the institution. Adult educators are actors in that enterprise and, therefore, share the responsibility of advancing internationalization as an integral part of the curricula, scholarship, and practice of the field. Similarly, Ruther (2002) argued for higher education associations to play a serious role in advancing and supporting internationalization efforts. To that end, adult and continuing education associations like AAACE with its Commission of Professors of Adult Education in the United States and CASAE in Canada, for example, can serve as platforms to raise awareness, incite interests, and advance the internationalization of the field. Most importantly, these associations can create opportunities to promote the scholarship of this phenomenon through its conferences, proceedings, book sponsorships, and other avenues. While many adult educators are engaged in various internationalization activities, there is a dire need to publish reports of these activities to address the void that currently exist in the adult education literature, particularly that of the United States.

References

Abdi, A. A., & Shultz, L. (2008). *Educating for human rights and global citizenship*. State University of New York Press.

Alfred, M. V., & Guo, S. (2012). Toward global citizenship: Internationalization of adult education in Canada and the U.S. *Canadian Journal for the Study of Adult Education, 24*(2), 51–70.

Altbach, P. G., & Knight, J. (2007). The internationalization of higher education: Motivations and realities. *Journal of Studies in International Education, 11*(3/4), 290–305.

Andreotti, V. D. O. (Ed.). (2013). *The political economy of global citizenship education*. Routledge.

Ball, S. J. (1998). Big policies/small world: An introduction to international perspectives in education policy. *Comparative Education, 34*(2), 119–130.

Berry, J., & Worthen, H. (2012, November/December). Higher education as a workplace. *Dollars & Sense.* http://depts.washington.edu/uwaaup/berry-worthen.pdf.

Boucouvalas, M. (2002). International adult education: Past, present, and into the future. *Adult Learning, 13*(4), 23–26.

Boucouvalas, M. (2011). UNESCO and ICAE as catalysts. *Adult Learning, 22*(4), 4–8.

Burbules, N. C., & Torres, C. A. (2000). *Globalization and education: Critical perspectives*. Routledge.

Canadian Association of University Teachers. (2016, May). Academics warn of dangerous dependency on international fees. *CAUT Bulletin.* http://www.caut.ca

Canadian Bureau for International Education. (2020). *International students in Canada continue to grow in 2019.* https://cbie.ca/international-students-in-canada-continue-to-grow-in-2019/

Charters, A. N. (2011). Reflections on involvement with six UNESCO international conferences on adult education and suggestions for the future. *Adult Learning, 22*(4), 14–17.

Coryell, J. E., Durodoye, B. A., Wright, W. R., Pate, P. E., & Nguyen, S. (2012). Case studies of internationalization in adult and higher education: Inside the processes of four universities in the United States and the United Kingdom. *Journal of Studies in International Education, 16*(1), 75–98.

de Wit, H., Hunter, F., Egron-Polak, E., & Howard, L. (2015). *Internationalisation of higher education*. European Parliament.

Egetenmeyer, R. (2017). The internationalization of studies in adult education: The example of Compall: Comparative studies in adult education and lifelong learning. *Androgoska spoznanja, 23*(4), 121–134.

Elliott, D. (1998). Internationalization in British higher education: Policy perspectives. In P. Scott (Ed.), *The globalization of higher education* (pp. 32–43). Open University Press.

Field, J. (2016, April 8). *The world conference on adult education, 1929*. The Learning Professor. https://thelearningprofessor.wordpress.com/tag/world-association-for-adult-education/

Folkman, D. V. (2006). Framing a critical discourse on globalization. In S. Merriam, S. Courtenay, & R. Cervero (Eds.), *Global issues and adult education: Perspectives from Latin America, Southern Africa, and the United States* (pp. 78–89). Jossey-Bass.

Giroux, H. A. (2003). Selling out higher education. *Policy Futures in Higher Education, 1*(1), 179–200.

Giroux, H. A. (2004). Neoliberalism, corporate culture and the promise of higher education: The University as a democratic public sphere. *Harvard Educational Review, 72*(4), 425–463.

Giroux, H. A. (2008). *Against the terror of neoliberalism: Politics beyond the age of greed.* Paradigm.

Giroux, H. A., & Myrsiades, K. (2001). *Beyond the corporate university: Culture and pedagogy in the new millennium.* Rowman & Littlefield.

Guo, Y., & Guo, S. (2017). Internationalization of Canadian higher education: Discrepancies between policies and international student experiences. *Studies in Higher Education, 42*(5), 851–868. https://doi.org/10.1080/03075079.2017.1293874

Guo, S., Schugurensky, D., Hall, B., Rocco, T., & Fenwick, T. (2010). Connected understanding: internationalization of adult education in Canada and beyond. *Canadian Journal for the Study of Adult Education, 23*(1), 73–89.

Hill, K., Hoffman. D., & Rex, T. (2005). *The value of higher education: Individual and societal benefits (with special consideration for the state of Arizona).* Arizona State University, W. P. Carey School of Business.

International Council for Adult Education. (n.d.). *History of ICAE.* http://icae.global/en/about/history-of-icae/

Ireland, T. D., & Spezia, C. J. (2014). *Adult education in retrospective—60 years of CONFINTEA.* UNESCO.

Jarvis, P. (2002). Globalization, citizenship, and the education of adults in contemporary European society. *Compare: A Journal of Comparative Education, 32*(1), 5–19.

Jarvis, P. (2007). *Globalization, lifelong learning and the learning society.* Routledge.

Jarvis, P. (2011). Adult education and the changing international scene: Theoretical perspectives. *PAACE Journal of Lifelong Learning, 20,* 37–50.

Johnstone, D. B., Arora, A., & Experton, W. (1998). *The financing and management of higher education: A status report on worldwide reforms.* The World Bank Human Development Network. https://www.researchgate.net/publication/44823223

Kandiko, C. B. (2010). Neoliberalism in higher education: A comparative approach. *International Journal of Arts and sciences, 31*(4), 153–175.

Khoo, S. M. (2011). Ethical globalization or privileged internationalization? Exploring global citizenship and internationalisation in Irish and Canadian universities. *Globalisation, Societies and Education, 9*(3–4), 337–53. https://doi.org/10.1080/14767724.2011.605320

Knight, J. (2004). Internationalization remodeled: Definition, approaches, and rationales. *Journal of Studies in International Education, 8*(1), 5–31.

Knoll, J. H. (2002). Adult and continuing education in international and supranational organizations. *Journal of Adult Education and Development, 59.* https://www.dvv-international.de/adult-education-and-development/ausgaben/number-59/

Knoll, J. H. (2014). The history of the UNESCO international conferences on adult education—from Helsingor (1949) to Hamburg (1997): International education policy through people and programmes. In T. D. Ireland & C. J. Spezia (Eds.), *Adult education in retrospective—60 years of CONFINTEA* (pp. 13–28). UNESCO.

Leask, B. (2009). Using formal and informal curricular to improve interactions between home and international students. *Journal of Studies in International Education, 13*(2), 205–221. https://doi.org/10.1177/1028315308329786.

Levidow, L. (2005). Neoliberal agendas for higher education. In A. Saad-Filho & D. Johnston (Eds.), *Neoliberalism: A critical reader* (pp. 156–162). Pluto Press.

Luke, A. (2010). Educating the "other" standpoint and internationalization of higher education. In V. Carpentier & E. Unterhaler (Eds.), *Global inequalities in higher education: Whose interests are you serving?* (pp. 1–25). Palgrave Macmillan.

Mitchell D. E., & Nielsen, S. Y., (2012). *Internationalization and globalization in higher education.* https://www.intechopen.com/books/globalization-education-and-management-agendas/internationalization-and-globalization-in-higher-education

Olssen, M., & Peters, M. A. (2005). Neoliberalism, higher education, and the knowledge economy: From the free market to knowledge capitalism. *Journal of Education Policy, 20*(3), 313–345. https://doi.org/10.1080/02680930500108718

Ritzer, G. (2007). Introduction. In G. Ritzer (Ed.), *The Blackwell companion to globalization* (pp. 1–13). Blackwell.

Robertson, R., & White, K. E. (2007). What is globalization? In G. Ritzer (Ed.), *The Blackwell companion to globalization* (pp. 54–66). Blackwell.

Ruther, N, L. (2002). *Barely there, powerfully present: Years of U.S. policy on international higher education.* Routledge.

Saad-Filho, A., & Johnston, D. (2005). *Neoliberalism: A critical reader.* Pluto Press.

Schied, F. (2006). In the belly of the beast: Globalization and adult education in the United States. In S. Merriam, S. Courtenay, & R. Cervero (Eds.), *Global issues and adult education: Perspectives from Latin America, Southern Africa, and the United States* (pp. 53–63). Jossey-Bass.

Schied, F. M., Mulenga, D., & Baptiste, I. (2005). *Lifelong learning in global contexts: Towards a reconceptualization of adult education* [Paper presentation]. Adult Education Research Conference, Athens, GA, United States. http://newprairiepress.org/aerc/2005/papers/31

Slaughter, S., & Leslie, L. L. (1997). *Academic capitalism: Politics, policies, and the entrepreneurial university.* The Johns Hopkins University Press.

Slaughter, S., & Rhoades, G. (2004). *Academic capitalism and the new economy: Markets, states, and higher education.* The Johns Hopkins University Press.

Tolliver, D. E., Martin, A., & Salome, N. (2018). Competency based education, lifelong learning and adult students: Insights from international partnerships between East Africa, Southern Africa and the USA-based institutions of higher education. *Africology: The Journal of Pan African Studies, 12*(1), 123–135.

Vaira, M. (2004). Globalization and higher education organizational change: A framework for analysis. *Higher Education, 48*, 483–510.

Welch, A. R. (2001). Globalization, post-modernity and the state: comparative education facing the third millennium. *Comparative Education, 37*(4), 475–492.

Xiao, J. (2018). Internationalization of higher education: Considerations for adult education. *Alberta Journal of Educational Research, 64*(2), 202–207.

Zong, J., & Batalova, J. (2018). *International students in the United States.* Migration Policy Institute. https://www.migrationpolicy.org/article/international-students-united-states

PART TWO

UNDERSTANDING ADULT LEARNING

CHAPTER 7

Adult Learning

Colleen Kawalilak and Janet Groen

Adult learning is a circuitous pathway, influenced by diverse factors in every social context. Boucouvalas and Lipson Lawrence (2010) observed that the *Handbook(s) of Adult and Continuing Education* published prior to 2010 applied a more standard lens to discern how adults learn. They referred to a lens that "repeatedly stressed that any inability of adults to change and adapt was predicated primarily on habituation, or fixed habits . . . reflect[ing] the context of the time" (p. 35). In the "Adult Learning" chapter of the 2010 handbook, Boucouvalas and Lipson Lawrence drew from scholarly advancements, deepening the discourse by recognizing conditions extending beyond habituation and contexts of time to include social contexts, complexities, and influences regarding where adults live, work, and learn. Scholars have increasingly acknowledged that learning is experienced in multiple ways—formally, nonformally, informally, incidentally, and through tacit learning. This recognition has influenced the development of learning theories and continues to guide the praxis of adult educators.

Formal and *nonformal learning* share common ground; both are intentional and based on organized educational activities that provide structures for learning. Formal learning, once completed, organized in structured learning contexts by educational institutions (Merriam & Bierema, 2014), leads to a credential. Nonformal learning "is sponsored by organizations, agencies and institutions . . . [where] education might be a secondary mission employed to carry out the main reason for existence" (Merriam & Bierema, 2014, p. 16). Alternatively, Coombs (1985) described *informal learning* as "spontaneous, unstructured [daily] learning" (p. 92) taken up "in all the private and nonorganized contexts of everyday life" (p. 151). Although learners are consciously aware of learning acquired through informal learning activities, capturing and understanding informal learning is, indeed, a challenge due to the plethora of informal learning opportunities in day-to-day living (Merriam & Bierema, 2014). *Incidental learning* and *tacit learning* are also identified as types of informal learning (Merriam & Bierema, 2014). Incidental learning is learning that is not organized and often experienced unexpectedly and unpredictably. Tacit learning is "perhaps the most subtle form of informal learning [that] we regularly draw upon in negotiating our lives" (Merriam & Bierema, 2014, p. 19).

In this chapter, we begin by situating the emergence and progression of *foundational* and *contemporary* theories of adult learning in the broader landscape of *traditional learning theories*. Systematic studies on how adults learn were spawned in the early 20th century. Lindeman's (1961) *The Meaning of Adult Education*, originally published in 1926, and the launch of the *Handbook of Adult Education (Adult Learning)* series by Thorndike et al. (1928), are early examples that recognized learning in adulthood as deserving attention. As Merriam (2017) noted, early studies were taken up "by behavioral and cognitive scientists . . . [most] interested in memory, intelligence, and information processing, and in particular, how age impacted these processes" (p. 22).

Drawing on Merriam and Bierema's (2014) framework on traditional learning theories, we discuss five orientations to learning that "offer helpful insights into adult learning" (Merriam et al., 2007, p. 277): behaviorist, humanist, cognitivist, social cognitivist, and constructivist/social constructionism. Over time, a variety of disciplines—including psychology, sociology, anthropology, political sciences, and, more recently, the neurosciences—have contributed to theorizing about learning.

We then narrow our focus on adult learning—to andragogy and foundational theories including self-directed, transformational, and experiential learning. These theories have been pivotal in further developing the field of adult learning. Despite being recognized as theories "created in a White, male, middle-class context" (Baumgartner et al., 2003, p. 10), foundational adult learning theories have, since the 1950s, strongly influenced perceptions of scholars and practitioners as to how adults learn. A heightened awareness of valuing other ways of learning and knowing in adult learning has recently emerged. Thus, we provide an overview of more recent research, acknowledging more holistic and tacit ways of knowing.

Traditional Theories That Inform Adult Learning: Historical and Current Perspectives

Early 20th-century influences from psychology contributed to learning being viewed as mechanical and individualistic. Behaviorism (Skinner, 1953) focused on measurable and observable change in behavior. Merriam et al. (2007) maintained that this way of learning is still emphasized in human resource development and vocational education.

In the past 40 years, however, our understanding of learning has expanded. Humanism is one of the earliest theories recognizing that learning involves the whole person in a broader context. Humanism recognizes the human potential for growth and development (Maslow, 1970). Rogers (1961) also had a pivotal influence on earlier understandings, further emphasizing self-directed growth and self-actualization. Critics of humanism (Muller, 1992; Pratt, 1993) suggested it primarily focused on individual growth, sidestepping the sociocultural context of learners.

Constructivism and social constructionism emerged in the later half of the 20th century, signaling a shift toward locating learners within this broader milieu. Constructivism posits that learning involves the process of updating one's sense of the world based on new experiences (Piaget, 1973). Through such experiences, individuals rework and revise their histories, narratives, emotions, physical sensations, thoughts, and beliefs to construct an understanding of the world. Social constructionism shifts its focus toward "interpersonal dynamics and collective activity across learners; therefore, social status, gender and cultural background play a central role in how we make meaning" (Groen & Kawalilak, 2014, p. 129). This theoretical approach, associated with Vygotsky (1978), linked cognition to both the learner and the social context.

During the 1960s and 1970s, a more concerted movement emerged, challenging dominant discourses and focusing on the social context of individual learners. Critical theory, drawing from anthropology and political science, addressed the social implications of education systems regarding power and privilege (Nesbit et al., 2013). Adult educators customarily refer to Freire's (1970) work as the harbinger of the shift toward critical theory. Freire's concept of *conscientização* (*conscientization*), the raising of consciousness through reflection and action, denotes "the effort to render explicit the cultural conditions that delimit possible worlds and acceptable identities" (p. 54).

Over the past 2 decades, disciplines such as biochemistry and environmental studies have explored how we learn generating the emergence of ecological, systems, and complexity in learning theories (Swartz & Sprow, 2010). Remaining attentive to the centrality of the relational, we are now challenged to consider global and even interspecies relationships. In adult learning, Swartz and Tisdell (2012) drew on complexity theory, suggesting we make multiple system connections to ourselves, to one another, and to the world as cocreators. The result profoundly impacts our work as adult educators.

Foundational Theories of Adult Learning

The role of experience becomes apparent in this summary of four foundational theories of adult learning: andragogy; self-directed learning; experiential learning; and transformative learning.

Andragogy

Malcolm Knowles (1980) defined *andragogy* as "the art and science of helping adults learn" (p. 43), in contrast to pedagogy, which focuses on helping children learn. Over several decades, Knowles expanded andragogy to include the centrality of experience in adult learning processes (Knowles, 1950, 1984, 1990). The core of andragogy was Knowles's understanding of the development of adults' self-concept—being self-directed and responsible for learning. Knowles (1980) first developed four assumptions about how adults learn:

1. As a person matures, his or her self-concept moves from that of a dependent personality toward one of a self-directing human being.
2. An adult accumulates a growing reservoir of experience, which is a rich resource for learning.
3. The readiness of an adult to learn is closely related to the developmental tasks of his or her social role.
4. There is a change in time perspective as people mature—from future application to knowledge to immediacy of application. Thus, an adult is more problem centered than subject centered in learning.

Later, Knowles (1984) added these assumptions:

1. The most potent motivations are internal rather than external.
2. Adults need to know why they need to learn something.

Some scholars (Grace, 1996; Hartree, 1984; Sandlin, 2005) argued that Knowles's assumptions failed to constitute a theory of learning; rather, they emphasized best practices. Addressing concerns regarding artificial distinctions between pedagogy and andragogy, Knowles (1990) nuanced his interpretation to suggest a *continuum of learning* no longer associated with age. Notwithstanding the criticism, andragogy has had a profound impact on current understandings of adult learning, taking its place in university courses on adult learning and in the practices of adult educators.

Self-Directed Learning

Tough (1967, 1979, 1982) developed a particular dimension of andragogy by studying the intentional and nonformal practices taken up by adults when learning. In self-directed learning (SDL), two aspects of learning are highlighted: *processes* of learning where learners have the primary responsibility for their learning pathway, and *products* of learning (Tough, 1967). Ultimately, the goal is to develop self-directed, internally motivated learners (Brookfield, 1985). Critiques of SDL focused on individuals not being autonomous learners involved in a systematic process of learning (Tough, 1979). Adult educators were then invited to challenge Western perspectives where conceptions of the self as individualistic, unitary, rational, and decontextualized are privileged (Boucouvalas & Lipson Lawrence, 2010; Usher et al., 1997).

Experiential Learning

As with andragogy and SDL, experiential learning theory highlights that much of learning draws from experience (Kolb, 1984). Learning "occurs when the learner directly experiences the realities of the theory, concept, or fact that they are learning" (Kolb, 1984, p. 21). Kolb deconstructed this process into a four-part model: concrete experience, reflective observation, abstract conceptualization, and active experimentation. Like previous critiques of andragogy and SDL, Kolb's model was assessed as overly individualistic and rational. Fenwick (2003) summarized more recent advancements in this theory by introducing five conceptualizations. The first upheld knowledge as constructed by reflecting on concrete experience. Further conceptualizations appeased some earlier critics, suggesting that experiential learning can occur in groups, fears and unconscious desires can be attended to intentionally as part of the process, experiential learning can inform the resistance of dominant ideas, and adult learners can draw on systems and ecological ways of learning as part of the process (Fenwick, 2003). Additional advancements in experiential learning (Weil & McGill, 1989) discussed the potential of experience in contributing to individual and societal growth. The evaluation and accreditation of experiential learning through prior learning assessment processes has received much scholarly attention, as has drawing on experiential learning for informing consciousness raising, community action, and social change. A key contribution of experiential learning resides in the realm of practice, encouraging adult educators and learners to recognize, design, engage in, and value learning beyond formal, classroom-based, cognitive activities.

Transformative Learning

Recognizing experience as central to adult learning, transformative learning shifts from the acquisition and expansion of knowledge to learning that fundamentally changes how adults view and experience the world (Boucouvalas & Lipson Lawrence, 2010). Mezirow (1978) introduced this theory, drawing from research that explored learning journeys of women returning to college. Through this transition, fundamental assumptions and perspectives about themselves and their world were challenged and changed. As Mezirow developed this learning approach, he situated his research in a psychological, rational, and cognitive framework. Critics of transformative learning discussed the narrowness of the process (Mezirow, 1991), prompting the development of additional perspectives. Drawing from Taylor and Cranton (2012), "[t]ransformative learning [can be] described as cognitive and rational, as imaginative and intuitive . . . spiritual . . . related to individuation . . . relational, and . . . relating to social change" (p. 7). However, Taylor and Cranton (2012) also noted that the growth of approaches to transformative learning can contribute to the perception that this area of research is fragmented and lacking in coherence.

Taylor and Cranton (2012) and Hoggan (2015) pointed to transformative learning theory as accomplishing what earlier scholars of andragogy and adult education practitioners had hoped to achieve. That is, transformative learning offers "a framework for both understanding adult learning . . . mov[ing] from the margins to the center of study of adult learning in both adult education and a variety of other disciplines" (Taylor & Cranton, 2012, p. 16). Understanding how we learn has, indeed, grown in complexity and continues to draw from multiple disciplines and perspectives to support more holistic and interdependent factors.

Contemporary Theories and Practices

Present-day adult educators continue to be guided by traditional and foundational adult learning theories to inform the development and design of adult education programs and to form pedagogical practices for adults who work, live, and learn in diverse contexts.

Discourses and practices have expanded considerably and now include more contemporary perspectives, methodologies, and recognition of the multiple roadways adults navigate on their learning journeys. These learning journeys invite engagement with others and with all aspects of one's self as a learner. Contemporary adult learning theories broadly captured under the umbrella terms of integrated ways of learning and narrative spaces of knowing, explicate the multiple ways with which adult learners engage.

Integrated Ways of Learning

While earlier research on traditional and foundational learning theories emphasized an intellectual orientation, we consider learning to be more than rational processing—our bodies, emotions, and spirit are deeply involved. Drawing from neuroscience research on brain hemispheres and learning, we recognize the brain as a concatenation of networks that requires integrated ways of learning. For example, while the left hemisphere values words, reasoning, and logic, the right hemisphere embodies sense-making, invoking images, feelings and intuition in the learning process (Taylor & Marienau, 2016).

Scholars (Boucouvalas & Lipson Lawrence, 2010; Taylor & Marienau, 2016) have indicated the neurosciences—in particular, how the brain processes information—is the next critical discipline in furthering understanding of integrative ways in which adults learn. "Brains have been shaped by evolution to adapt and readapt to an ever-changing world . . . [and] the ability to learn is dependent on modification of the brain's chemistry and architecture in a process called 'neural plasticity'" (Cozolino & Sprokay, 2006, p. 12). However, while all brains undergo this synaptic process when learning, Taylor and Marienau (2016) asserted the sense-making process for each person remains unique. "Because experience is the basis of all learning, adults' greater variety of life experiences set them apart from younger learners, as well as from one another" (p. 33). Further, once an experience has garnered our attention, our brain sorts it as being familiar or unfamiliar, seeking similarities between this and previous experiences in order to relate it to existing patterns (Taylor & Marienau, 2016). This results in rewiring or modifying existing neural pathways in the brain.

Because integrative ways of learning involve the body, emotions, and spirit, we offer a brief overview of these dimensions. Kinesthetic or somatic learning is typically associated with the *body* being required to achieve a task. Freiler (2008) encouraged awareness of the body and sensations experienced when engaged in activities. Further, embodiment and embodied learning (Freiler, 2008) refer to the body as a site of learning. We sometimes refer to this as "gut feelings," where our body conveys important situational information or prompts us to take the next step (Lawrence, 2012a). Indeed, tacit knowing may also begin with the body: "Every time we make sense of the world, we rely on our tacit knowledge of impacts made by the world on our body and complex responses of our body to these impacts" (Polyani, 1969, pp. 147–148).

Emotions are integral to learning and emerge unconsciously and unexpectedly throughout the learning process (Dirkx, 2008; Grams & Jurowetski, 2015). Emotions are often associated with dynamics in the context of learning and/or with personal narratives constructed outside the current setting. As emotions often reside close to the surface (Dirkx, 2008; Griffin, 2001), adult educators play a role in encouraging adult learners to connect, engage, and make meaning of emotions. Regarding experiential and transformative learning and the interconnectivity of cognition and emotions, scholars acknowledge the central role of emotions, both during and after experiences, in influencing learning processes associated with change (Hathaway, 2017; Wilson & Beard, 2003).

Research on *spirituality* and adult learning examines learning processes in order to incorporate multifaceted ways of being and knowing in the world. Dirkx (1997), one of the first to recognize the importance of spirituality in a "whole-person approach to the transformative learning process" (Piercy, 2013, p. 30), identified the vital role of emotions in undergoing change. Dirkx (1997) asserted that changes necessitate delving deeper into spiritual and soulful dimensions of learning. Likewise, English and Tisdell (2010) suggested that spirituality and adult learning involved meaning making and connecting to something greater than one's self.

Additionally, arts-based learning provides opportunities for reflection and knowledge acquisition beyond the rational (Lawrence, 2012b), "bring[ing] out the affective self, hence contributing to whole person knowing" (Gaby et al., 2014, p. 205). Aesthetic endeavors such as painting, drama, and music have the potential to ignite the body, emotions, and spirit by providing pathways to acquiring knowledge not otherwise accessible (Clover & Butterwick, 2013; Klein, 2018) and by prompting reflection.

Narrative Spaces of Knowing

Adults' biographies of learning are shaped by cultural/contextual influences, relationships, events, opportunities, and challenges. Their learning stories provide rich fodder when reflecting on their personal *narratives*. Through these narratives, adult learners create a sense of self, make meaning of their experiences, and experience a sense of agency. Groen and Kawalilak (2014) observe that the "telling and retelling of our stories reflect a *narrating notion of identity*, in which the self is understood as an ever-unfolding and changing story" (p. 48, emphasis in original). Consequently, adult learners often reconstruct their narratives, as both an impetus for, and a consequence of, change and action. Narrative learning is one way to deepen understanding of self, others, and the world. Narratives are *not* constructed in isolation; stories are meant to be shared. For receivers of stories, narratives become intertwined and subsequently reshaped. By continuing to make new meaning of experiences through narrative learning, this network of conversations—of dialogue with self, others, and the world around us—serves to construct a larger personal narrative.

Narratives and stories are also embedded in ways of knowing extending beyond the Western, Eurocentric paradigm of knowledge acquisition traditions. For example, *Indigenous ways of knowing* value situatedness, relatedness, and the centrality of learners and knowledge to all aspects of the environment and the power of story in oral knowledge sharing traditions (Tuhiwai Smith, 1999). Risku and Harding (2013) asserted: "People of Western cultures have a tendency to see indigenous peoples as 'others' . . . to assess their practices and beliefs with a conscious or unconscious bias that stems from their own culture and education" (p. 10). Relationality is central to Indigenous ways of knowing, connecting individuals' growth, development, and learning to a greater, communal good. Indigenous ways of knowing involve responding to physical, natural, spiritual, and social aspects of the world (Tuhiwai Smith, 1999). Indigenous knowledge is relational, existing beyond formal education structures and systems, and is traditionally imparted by elders in the community. Embedded in stories is a framework of values—the interconnectedness of how values are taken up and lived, in contributing to collective humanity and well-being.

Also vital is the interrelationality of Indigenous values with Indigenous languages in the formation and preservation of cultural identity. Revitalizing Indigenous languages encourages knowledge sharing and the development of a culturally relevant curriculum in learning contexts that span education for children, youth, and adults. Hermes et al. (2012) cited "longstanding efforts of change characterized by community building and collaboration with academics across disciplines, cultures, and ideologies" (p. 131) as evidence of a changing narrative.

Blurring the Boundaries: Impacts and Influences

How adult learners come *to know* and *be* in the world is multifaceted, interconnected, nonlinear, complex, and often experienced fortuitously (Groen & Kawalilak, 2014). The complexity of diversity within and across cultures and contexts challenges adult educators to deepen and broaden their understanding and pedagogy. Moreover, adopting new ways of learning can be uncomfortable, as gathering the will to learn requires openness—a willingness to reflect on long-held assumptions and biases, and to respond to learning opportunities presented.

Boucouvalas and Lipson Lawrence (2010) referred to the importance of employing a holistic framework to better understand how adults learn, stressing that "adults [are] embedded in many systems [and] any effort at understanding the adult as learner calls for contextualization" (p. 36). We herald this call with an even greater emphasis on the interplay and array of complexities of internal processes and external influences impacting adult learning. Indeed, in this time of escalating economic and demographic change, attention to relationality (relational learning) cannot be overstated. Relational learning, described by Belenky et al. (1986), referred to connected knowing and to "engag[ing] in multiple and simultaneous relationships: with our ongoing narratives within ourselves . . . with the ideas and concepts being explored, and with the larger community" (Groen & Kawalilak, 2014, pp. 170–171). We recognize elements of relational learning throughout traditional, foundational, and contemporary learning theories discussed in this chapter. We feature relational learning as a focal point, with relationality encompassing *all* aspects of learning, significantly impacting *how* we teach and *how* we engage with a diverse demographic of adult learners. The interconnectivity of the relational with *how* adults learn is embedded in much of the literature on adult teaching and learning.

It is also paramount to highlight the deep interconnectivity (relationship) of the learning context to individual growth and to a deepening of critical consciousness for individuals and communities. Rapidly changing demographics, political and economic trends, and shifting workplace realities challenge adult educators to revisit and renew the historical foundations and purposes of adult education. In particular, we need to step back to reclaim the humanity rooted in the teaching–learning relationship. Indeed, current political dynamics and competing ideologies favor nationalism over globalism and individualism over community. Nevertheless, we maintain that the world remains an interconnected place, however complex and conflicted.

Relationality encompasses logical, natural, dynamic, and functional interactions (Thayer-Bacon, 2003) and may help to blur the boundaries that sometimes situate theories as being disassociated from one another and from practice. Mapping foundational and contemporary adult learning theories to the broader landscape of human learning is imperative, as what we have come to know about how adults learn has been shaped by the scholarship of traditional learning theorists, such as Dewey (1938) and Maslow (1970). Relational ways of knowing reveal the interconnectivity of humankind, "not only personally, but also to our social environment, our cultures, past, present, and future, as well as the natural environment [and to] how much our individual ideas are caught up within webs of related ideas" (Thayer-Bacon, 2003, p. 73).

Another challenge for adult educators is to navigate these tensions with thoughtfulness, purpose, intentionality, care, and compassion and to convey with authenticity that we value multiple and diverse ways of knowing and being in the world. If as adult educators we are committed to conveying to learners that we recognize and value the teacher and learner within all of us, we are more able to see and appreciate adult learners and ourselves as being situated within a much broader social narrative. Conveying these beliefs, authentically and with transparency, has the potential to significantly contribute to healthy relational dynamics, enhancing and enriching the learning experiences of adult learners.

References

Baumgartner, L., Lee, M., Firden, S., & Flowers, D. (2003). *Adult learning theory: A primer.* Information Series, 392 (ED482337). ERIC. https://files.eric.ed.gov/fulltext/ED482337.pdf

Belenky, M. F., Clinchy, B. M., Goldberger, N. R., & Tarule, J. M. (1986). *Women's ways of knowing.* Basic Books.

Boucouvalas, M., & Lipson Lawrence, R. (2010). Adult learning. In C. E. Kasworm, A. D. Rose, & J. M. Ross-Gordon (Eds.), *Handbook of adult and continuing education* (pp. 35–48). SAGE.

Brookfield, S. D. (1985). Self-directed learning: A critical review of the literature. *New Directions for Adult and Continuing Education, 1985*(25), 5–16.

Clover, D. E., & Butterwick, S. (2013). Fear of glue, fear of thread: Reflections on teaching arts-based practice. In D. E. Clover & K. Sanford (Eds.), *Lifelong learning, the arts, and community cultural engagement in the contemporary university: International perspectives* (pp. 66–78). Manchester University Press.

Coombs, P. H. (1985). *The world crisis in education: A view from the eighties.* Oxford University Press.

Cozolino, L., & Sprokay, S. (2006). Neuroscience and adult learning. *New Directions for Adult and Continuing Education, 2006*(110), 11–19.

Dewey, J. (1938). *Experience and education.* Collier Books.

Dirkx, J. M. (1997). Nurturing soul in adult learning. *New Directions for Adult and Continuing Education, 1997*(74), 79–88.

Dirkx, J. M. (2008). The meaning and role of emotions in adult learning. *New Directions for Adult and Continuing Education, 2008*(120), 7–18.

English, L. M., & Tisdell, E. J. (2010). Spirituality and adult education. In C. E. Kasworm, A. D. Rose, & J. M. Ross-Gordon (Eds.), *Handbook of adult and continuing education* (pp. 35–48). Jossey-Bass.

Fenwick, T. (2003). Reclaiming and re-embodying experiential learning through complexity science. *Studies in the Education of Adults, 35*(2), 123–141.

Freiler, T. J. (2008). Learning through the body. *New Directions for Adult and Continuing Education, 2008*(119), 37–47.

Freire, P. (1970). *Pedagogy of the oppressed.* Continuum International.

Gaby, R., Kwong, W., Rosini, E., & Segree, R. (2014, June 4–7). *Arts as a catalyst for adult learning* [Paper presentation]. Adult Education Research Conference, Harrisburg, PA, United States. http://newprairiepress.org/aerc/2014/papers/33

Grace, A. P. (1996). Striking a critical pose: Andragogy—missing links, missing values. *International Journal of Lifelong Education, 15*(5), 382–392.

Grams, S. L., & Jurowetski, R. (2015). Emotions in the classroom. In B. Lund & T. Chemi (Eds.), *Dealing with emotions: A pedagogical challenge to innovative learning* (pp. 81–98). Sense.

Griffin, V. R. (2001). Holistic learning. In T. Barer-Stein & M. Kompf (Eds.), *The craft of teaching adults* (3rd ed., pp. 107–139). Culture Concepts.

Groen, J., & Kawalilak, C. (2014). *Pathways of adult learning: Professional and education narratives.* Canadian Scholars' Press.

Hartree, A. (1984). Malcolm Knowles' theory of andragogy: A critique. *International Journal of Lifelong Education, 3*(3), 203–210.

Hathaway, M. (2017). Activating hope in the midst of crisis: Emotions, transformative learning, and "the work that reconnects." *Journal of Transformative Education, 15*(4), 296–314.

Hermes, M., Bang. M., & Marin, A. (2012). Indigenous language revitalization and documentation in the United States: Collaboration despite colonialism. *Wiley Researcher Academy, 6*(3), 131–142. https://doi.org/10.1002/Inc3.327

Hoggan, C. (2015, May 19–22). *Bringing clarity to transformative learning research* [Paper presentation]. Adult Education Research Conference, Manhattan, KS, United States. http://newprairiepress.org/aerc/2015/papers/26

Klein, S. R. (2018). Coming to our senses: Everyday landscapes, aesthetics, and transformative learning. *Journal of Transformative Education, 16*(1), 3–16. https://doi.org/10.1177/1541344617696969

Knowles, M. S. (1950). *Informal adult education.* Association Press.

Knowles, M. S. (1980). *The modern practice of adult education: From pedagogy to andragogy* (2nd ed.). Cambridge Books.

Knowles, M. S. (1984). *Andragogy in action: Applying principles of adult learning.* Jossey-Bass.

Knowles, M. S. (1990). *The adult learner: A neglected species.* Gulf.

Kolb, D. (1984). *Experiential learning: Experience as the source of learning and development.* Prentice Hall.

Lawrence, R. L. (2012a). Intuitive knowing and embodied consciousness. *New Directions for Adult and Continuing Education, 2012*(134), 5–13.

Lawrence, R. L. (2012b). Transformative learning through artistic expression: Getting out of our heads. In E. W. Taylor & P. Cranton (Eds.), *Handbook of transformative learning: Theory, research, and practice* (pp. 471–485). Jossey-Bass.

Lindeman, E. C. (1961). *The meaning of adult education.* Harvest House. (Original work published in 1926)

Maslow, A. H. (1970). *Motivation and personality* (2nd ed.). McGraw-Hill.

Merriam, S. B. (2017). Adult learning theory: Evolution and future directions. *PAACE Journal of Lifelong Learning, 26,* 21–37.

Merriam, S. B., & Bierema, L. L. (2014). *Adult learning: Linking theory and practice.* Jossey-Bass.

Merriam, S. B., & Caffarella, R. S., & Baumgartner, L. M. (2007). *Learning in adulthood: A comprehensive guide* (3rd ed.). Jossey-Bass.

Mezirow, J. (1978). Perspective transformation. *Adult Education Quarterly, 28*(2), 100–110.

Mezirow, J. (1991). *Transformative dimensions of adult learning.* Jossey-Bass.

Muller, L. (1992). *Progressivism and United Stated adult education: A critique of mainstream theory as embodied in the work of Malcolm Knowles.* UMI Dissertation Services.

Nesbit, T., Brigham, S., M., & Taber, N. (Eds.). (2013). *Building on critical traditions: Adult education and learning in Canada.* Thompson Educational Publishing.

Piaget, J. (1973). *The child's conception of the world.* Paladin.

Piercy, G. (2013). Transformative learning theory and spirituality: A whole-person approach. *Journal of Instructional Research, 2,* 30–42.

Polyani, M. (1969). *Knowing and being: Essays by Michael Polyani.* University of Chicago Press.

Pratt, D. D. (1993). Andragogy after twenty-five years. *New Directions for Adult and Continuing Education, 1993*(57), 15–23.

Risku, M., & Harding, L. (2013). *Education for tomorrow: A biocentric, student-focused model for reconstructing education.* SensePublishers.

Rogers, C. R. (1961). *On becoming a person.* Houghton Mifflin.

Sandlin, J. A. (2005). Andragogy and its discontents: An analysis of andragogy from three critical perspectives. *PAACE Journal of Lifelong Learning, 1*(14), 25–42.

Skinner, B. F. (1953). *Science and human behavior.* Simon and Schuster.

Swartz, A. L., & Sprow, K. (2010, June 4–6). *Is complexity science embedded in transformative learning?* [Paper presentation]. Adult Education Research Conference, Sacramento, CA, United States. http://newprairiepress.org/aerc/2010/papers/73

Swartz, A. L., & Tisdell, E. J. (2012, June 1–3). *Wisdom, complexity, and adult education: Emerging theory and meanings for practice* [Paper presentation]. Adult Education Research Conference, Saratoga Springs, NY, United States. http://newprairiepress.org/aerc/2012/papers/45

Taylor, E. W., & Cranton, P. (2012). *The handbook of transformative learning: Theory, research, and practice.* John Wiley.

Taylor, K., & Marienau, C. (2016). *Facilitating learning with the adult brain in mind: A conceptual and practical guide.* Jossey-Bass.

Thayer-Bacon, B. J. (2003). *Relational "(e)pistemologies."* Peter Lang.

Thorndike, E. L., Bregman, E. O., Tilton, J. W., & Woodyard, E. (1928). *Adult learning.* Macmillan.

Tough, A. M. (1967). *Learning without a teacher.* Ontario Institute for Studies in Education.

Tough, A. M. (1979). *The adult's learning projects: A fresh approach to theory and practice in adult learning* (2nd ed.). Learning Concepts.

Tough, A. M. (1982). *Intentional changes: A fresh approach to helping people change.* Cambridge University Press.

Tuhiwai Smith, L. (1999). *Decolonizing methodologies: Research and indigenous peoples.* Zed Books.

Usher, R., Bryant, I., & Johnson, R. (1997). *Adult education and the postmodern challenge: Learning beyond the limits.* Routledge.

Vygotsky, L. S. (1978). *Mind in society: The development of higher mental process.* Harvard University Press.

Weil, S. W., & McGill, I. (1989). *Making sense of experiential learning: Diversity in theory and practice.* Open University Press.

Wilson, J. P., & Beard, C. (2003). The learning combination lock—An experiential approach to learning design. *Journal of European Industrial Training, 27*(2/3/4), 88–97.

CHAPTER 8

Adult Development

Thomas G. Reio Jr.

We must understand the needs and facilities of adults of all ages if we are going to support them as learners and advance as a society (Arnett et al., 2020). Knowledge of adult developmental principles can help adult educators design and implement learning endeavors that facilitate adults' adaptation to their environments (Ackerman & Kanfer, 2020). Boucouvalas (1989) noted that development is closely linked to adult learning in that it "leads to changes in the nature, modes, interest, and content of learning, and learning often leads to further development" (p. 184). This chapter presents understandings of physical, cognitive, social, and emotional development and their respective links to learning during adulthood. The notion is to understand constancy and change across adulthood beyond mere biological losses. *Development* is defined as systematic changes in behavior over time resulting from constant interactions between the individual and environment (Baltes et al., 2006). Knowles (1968), through his theory of andragogy, was among the first to make the direct link between adult development and adult education and learning (Boucouvalas, 1989). For example, Knowles's andragogical assumption that adults learn best when they are ready to learn was based upon Havighurst's (1953) developmental task theory and the "teachable moment."

Baltes's (1987) metatheory will be the overarching theoretical lens where development is theorized to be lifelong and consisting of the joint occurrence of gain and loss, multidirectionality and plasticity in development, and in which development is viewed as multidisciplinary, historically embedded, and contextual. Baltes's metatheory draws heavily upon sociology, anthropology, and the humanities (e.g., art history, social images of the life course). It was developed as a response to demographic pressures where there were proportionally more older adults than any time in history, as well as the need to integrate extant theory and research into a meaningful framework for understanding adult development. Thus, his contribution was to pull together diverse perspectives from varied disciplines into a framework for guiding developmental research. Baltes stressed that the goal of adult development is to increase one's adaptation to the environment, realized through learning. Further, he stated that adult development is characterized by gains and losses, depending on one's age and contextual influences. Context is important in that development is a function of the outcomes of the interactions of three systems of influences: age-graded (e.g., menopause, retirement), history-graded (e.g., obesity epidemic, economic depression), and nonnormative (e.g., traumatic brain injury, death of parent at an early age), each of which is subject to change over time.

Physical development is presented first because it is the foundation of optimal human functioning that includes learning. Normative declines in sensory, hormonal, and reproductive systems—particularly after middle adulthood—can impact how adults think, feel, and learn (Cashman, 2007; Kunzman, 2008). Physical activity and being fit are thus explored as means to combat the normative effects of aging. Through providing health education activities, for instance, adult educators can promote fitness and physical development (Jiannine & Reio, 2018). *Curiosity*, defined as the desire for new information and sensory experience that results in exploratory behavior (Reio et al., 2006), and its link to adult development and learning will be examined as well. Finally, emerging adult developmental theory will be presented to provide new directions for thinking about adult educational practice.

Physical Development

Physical development refers to the physical gains and losses that occur across the life span (Baltes, 1987). Declines in visual and auditory acuity can greatly influence learning, as anyone who strains to see and hear can attest. Engaging in moderate exercise to remain physically fit cannot be emphasized enough. Being physically active and fit has been shown to be protective against the onset of cardiovascular disease, Type 2 diabetes, osteoporosis, obesity, depression, loss of cognitive functioning, and dementia (Ogden et al., 2012).

Early adulthood tends to be a time of vigor and health. Muscle mass and body fat continue to develop, with the average male and female gaining 15 pounds between ages 18 and 25 (Keller & Engelhardt, 2013). Typically, early adults have their maximum strength, coordination, and motor skills at this time (DiPietro, 2001). At age 30, the first signs of progressive deterioration in health and strength begin. Because of the combination of lower testosterone levels and increasingly inefficient muscle fibers, there is a 10% to 15% reduction of strength and mass through adulthood (Keller & Engelhardt, 2013). Calcium loss at this time, linked to not having a proper diet, can lead to osteoporosis in later life (Cashman, 2007).

In middle adulthood, the period between 40 years and 65 years old, over half of middle-age American adults are moderately or completely inactive, and only 28.6% are at a healthy weight. In Europe, obesity ranges from 6% to 20%, as compared to 34% in the United States (Ogden et al., 2012). Muscle and bone mass continue to deteriorate and recovery time after strenuous activity increases, accompanied by deterioration in vision and hearing.

In late adulthood, 65 years of age and older, adults become more sedentary and gain weight, and experience changes in posture and balance, hormonal levels, and disease (Notthoff & Cartenson, 2014). Cardiovascular diseases that include hypertension, arrhythmia, and congestive heart failure are the world's leading cause of death, hitting women and African American women hard because they have a higher risk of having a heart attack and dying than males (Akintunde et al., 2015). Approximately 30% of postmenopausal women in the United States and Europe have osteoporosis, often undiagnosed until after suffering a fall (Giangregorio et al., 2014). Although men can contract the disease, it is 80% more prevalent among women.

Finally, 35.6 million people are estimated to be living with dementia worldwide, with numbers expected to double every 20 years. The most common form of dementia, Alzheimer's disease, affects 5.7 million in the United States and is the fifth leading cause of death. Roughly two thirds of those with Alzheimer's disease are women; Hispanics are one and one-half times and African Americans twice as likely as older Whites to have the disease (National Center for Disease Prevention and Health Promotion, 2018). Prevention efforts aimed at maintaining an ideal weight, increasing habitual moderate physical activity (i.e., three, $\geq$ 30-minute, moderately intense physical activities per week, like brisk walking [> 4 miles per hour]) and fitness, increasing educational activities, and having a diet high in omega-3 fatty acids are among the strategies shown to be helpful in mediating cognitive declines (DiPietro, 2001). There is some evidence that social support networks help mediate optimal cognitive functioning, serving as a protective factor (Crooks et al., 2008).

Thus, healthy lifestyle choices that embrace engaging in moderate physical activity and remaining physically fit are vital to protecting against the onset of disease and cognitive declines. Telling adults they need to exercise and be fit is insufficient; they need to have safe access to walking and bicycle paths and other recreational areas that have low to no vehicular traffic and are well-lighted and patrolled (DiPietro, 2001). Moreover, the lack of funds to join supervised exercise groups or recreational facilities and lack of transportation can be all-too-real barriers to active physical activity (DiPietro, 2001). Clearly, there are inequities in the distribution of educational resources that must be overcome if we are to promote safe access to physical activities that promote optimal health.

Cognitive Development

Cognitive development is characterized by changes in thought processes as impacted by age-graded (e.g., brain maturation), history-graded (e.g., internet revolution) and nonnormative (e.g., traumatic brain injury) influences over the life span (Baltes, 1987). The role of learning in cognitive development is somewhat controversial in that with some theorists, developmental stage leads learning (e.g., Piaget, 1952); to others, learning leads development (e.g., Vygotsky, 1978). For the purposes of this chapter, curiosity will be highlighted to demonstrate the role of motivation in cognitive development.

The brain continues to develop into early adulthood, particularly in the prefrontal cortex where attention, risk taking, planning, and self-regulation are controlled. As an age-graded influence on cognitive development, brain volume decreases roughly 15% across the life span, which has been linked to loss of cognitive function—for example, memory, executive functioning (Paus, 2010). There is some evidence also that neurogenesis, the growth and development of neurons, continues throughout adulthood in the hippocampus—that is, dentate gyrus region (Eriksson et al., 1998), which plays an important role in learning and memory. In addition to regular exercise and a healthy diet, increased cognitive effort in the form of engaging in educational activities has been shown to support neurogenesis and protect the aging brain (Bekinschtein et al., 2011).

Piaget's Cognitive Development Theory

Piaget (1952) was interested in the development of qualitatively different ways of reasoning logically across four stages of cognitive development that he described—sensorimotor, preoperational, concrete operational, and formal operational. Piaget's theory focuses on gains in cognitive development and ignores possible losses (i.e., it is not possible to regress once a stage of development has been attained). He theorized that cognitive development was a function of age-graded brain maturation, quality physical and social experiences, and equilibration. Recent brain research using functional magnetic resonance imaging (fMRI), positron emission technology (PET), and multichannel electroencephalography (EEG) has demonstrated that his stages are closely aligned with anatomical and physiological development of the brain, especially in the prefrontal cortex (Bolton & Hattie, 2017).

This is a curiosity-driven model of development and learning in that it is a state of cognitive conflict that impels the individual to be curious when confronted with a problem or a lack of information. Through acquiring the information necessary to solve the problem or answer the question, one can assimilate new information into existing knowledge structures (i.e., schemata) or accommodate (transform) the information into new schemata.

As with any theory, it has its limits, as scholars have decried the lack of sufficient focus on social stimuli as a source of development or gender and cultural differences. Additionally, atypical development (e.g., someone with special needs) was not addressed by his theory and the degree of difficulty of some of his research protocols led him to underestimate reasoning abilities. Perhaps, most of all, his theory has been criticized because it may not satisfactorily reflect the nature of adult cognitive development. His four stages of cognitive development are well known to educators and psychologists and can serve as a guide to presenting concepts at age-appropriate moments and fostering learner-led, discovery learning.

Piaget's work has been extended by a wide range of neo-Piagetians who have retained at least part of Piaget's notions of stages or phases of development. Most neo-Piagetians (e.g., Commons, 2008; Sinnott, 2014), however, have moved beyond Piaget's idea that there is no further development of thinking sophistication beyond the formal operational stage. Other cognitive development theorists maintain that adult cognitive development is decidedly more complex than formal operational reasoning in that it is dialectical (process, context, relationship and transformation of thought; Riegel, 1979), relativistic (highest form of reflective judgment; Perry, 1970), and pragmatic (transition from idealistic to practical and realistic possibilities; Labouvie-Vief, 1980).

Vygotsky's Sociocultural Theory

In Vygotsky's (1979, 1986) sociocultural theory, one must consider the social, cultural, and historical contexts in which development occurs. The significance of the sociocultural perspective cannot be overemphasized because it was one of the first to highlight the importance of context when researching learning and development. Like Piaget, Vygotsky focused on cognitive development gains but acknowledged that cognitive development losses and, therefore, regression was possible. The source of motivation for cognitive development is both the learner's curiosity and the motivation of a more knowledgeable peer to pass along cultural tools (e.g., language, mathematics, and theories). The peer's demonstration of how to use the cultural tools in service of solving a problem helps the learner develop higher psychological processes for advanced, refined thought. In addition, cognitive development must be understood also in a historical context; major historical events (history-graded) can have a profound impact on members of a culture's cognitive development. In one of the more interesting ethnographic studies ever done, Luria (1976) described how the Bolshevik revolution in 1920s USSR had a great impact on the cognitive development of collectivized nomadic tribe members who had never been exposed to more educated ways of thinking.

Vygotsky supported the notion of developmental stages; he proposed that learning could lead development up to 2 years beyond one's demonstrated cognitive level, constrained by the learners' stage of development. Through working with a more-knowledgeable peer, tutor, or mentor who helps scaffold learning through one's zone of proximal development (ZPD), the learner can learn more quickly and accurately than discovery-based approaches to learning. The ZPD is "the distance between the actual developmental level as determined by independent problem-solving and the level of potential development as determined through problem-solving . . . in collaboration with more capable peers" (Vygotsky, 1978, pp. 85–86).

Overall, Vygotsky's sociocultural notions are useful for understanding how and why apprenticeships, internships, and mentoring facilitate adult learning and development. Learning with the assistance of a mentor/teacher leads to the development of greater cognitive capabilities (e.g., critical thinking). Knowledgeable peers can help the learner proceed through his or her ZPD by breaking the learning endeavor into more easily digestible parts and providing meaningful feedback to the learner (i.e., scaffolding). The entire learning and development process depends on two sources of motivation; that is, the (a) learner's curiosity and (b) mentor/tutor's motivation to help the learner grasp tasks that are beyond their current demonstrated ability.

Information Processing Theory

Using the computer as a metaphor for human processing of information, information processing (IP) theory has been another means for researching normative age-graded and nonnormative influences on cognitive development. It has provided significant insights into how we perceive, store, and access information. IP theory posits that a combination of brain maturation and development is associated with an increase in complex processing ability. Unlike Piagetian and Vygotskyan theories, IP theory was developed first for use with adults and then extended to children. Similar to Baltes (1987), researchers use IP as a theoretical lens to examine age-graded gains and losses in cognitive functions across the life span, especially in middle and late adulthood. Cognitive functions include memory, selective attention, visual processing, reasoning, and processing speed and efficiency. Atkinson and Shiffrin's (1968) three-level model (sensory, working, and long-term memory) demonstrates how multiple stimuli are attended to and encoded in the sensory memory system, processed by working memory, and made sense of when the encoded stimulus is compared and contrasted to existing schema stored in long-term memory. As in Piagetian theory, schema are built as new information is acquired and transformed when confronted by novel, discrepant stimuli. The source of motivation is the individual's intrinsic desire to be curious and gain knowledge to make meaning of the world.

IP theory has been useful for undergirding research about the aging brain and how and why cognitive functions change over the life span. For example, both changes in global processing speed (Kail & Park, 1992) and processing efficiency (Anderson, 1992) have been shown to contribute to gains and losses in cognitive functions. A major contribution of the IP perspective has been its utility in fostering understandings of individual differences in cognitive development, something largely ignored in Piagetian and Vygotskyan theory. Sex and cultural differences have been explored, but the large majority of research has focused on age differences in cognitive functioning. IP theory has also been helpful for gaining insights into disabilities like ADHD, dyscalculia, agraphia, and dyslexia and how interventions might be designed and targeted to help overcome difficulties associated with the disabilities. Because it allows the instructor to break the learning process into meaningful parts, adult educative interventions can be targeted at that part of the learning process requiring refinement.

Schaie and Willis's Theory of Adult Cognitive Development

Schaie and Willis's (2000) theory of cognitive development consists of seven stages: acquisitive, achieving, responsibility, executive, reorganizational, reintegrative, and legacy leaving. All but the acquisitive stage are part of adult development. Like Baltes (1987), they acknowledged the impact of contextual influences on adult cognitive functioning. Schaie and Willis maintained that basic intellectual abilities and processes (akin to what is attained through Piaget's four stages) are genotypic forms of intelligence that are universal across cultures and are therefore relatively context- and culture-free. Alternatively, the competencies associated with daily living are phenotypic expressions of intelligence (e.g., ability to apply computer-based technology to solve problems at work) that are context-, culture-, and age-specific. Phenotypic expressions of intelligence vary by the individual's age, their social roles, and the historical and environmental context. The theorists, however, do little to acknowledge the role of curiosity in intellectual development, but do link increasingly complex decision-making during the stages to success in attaining short- and long-term goals.

The Seattle Longitudinal Study (SLS; Schaie et al., 2014) has been influential in studying individual differences in successful cognitive aging. This longitudinal study has a number of phases designed to examine whether intelligence changed uniformly throughout adulthood and whether there was reliable evidence of cognitive decrements. The primary mental abilities examined include vocabulary, verbal memory, number, spatial orientation, inductive reasoning, and perceptual speed. The fifth cycle of the study was a cognitive intervention (Willis directed this part of the study) designed to test whether such an intervention would remediate cognitive decline and increase skills beyond those attained in earlier stages. Four of the six intellectual abilities improved and peaked with middle adults: vocabulary; verbal memory; spatial orientation; and inductive reasoning. Overall, the data generated from the study have shown general support for fluid abilities (e.g., induction) declining earlier than crystallized abilities (e.g., sequential reasoning), although there are ability-by-age, ability-by-gender, and ability-by-cohort interactions. Crystallized ability dropped off precipitously after age 77. The researchers identified six factors related to reducing the risk of cognitive decline, which included the absence of chronic disease (e.g., cardiovascular), an advantageous educational environment mediated by high socioeconomic status, complex and intellectually stimulating engagement, flexible personality style in midlife, high cognitive status of spouse, and high perceptual speed maintenance. Hypothesizing that cognitive decline may be more a function of disuse and was reversible, cognitive functioning was shown experimentally to improve meaningfully with training, even among those who had declined previously over 14 years.

The upshot of Schaie et al.'s (2014) rigorous, longitudinal work is that normative change in intellectual ability over the adult life span differs not only by age, but by gender and cohort. Decrements can be protected against primarily by leading a healthy lifestyle, involvement with intellectually stimulating occupations and people, and proactively participating in educative activities. Adult educators can target interventions that can improve cognitive ability and deter and reverse cognitive decline.

Social Development

Social development is characterized as the development of relationships across the life span (Bühler & Nikitin, 2020). Optimal use of social and emotional skills are vital to forming positive relationships that influence learning with not only one's family but also teachers, friends, peers, coworkers, and fellow citizens.

Attachment Theory

Attachment relationships are fashioned when an individual forms a lasting emotional bond to another person. Bowlby (1969) theorized that attachment experiences become internalized related to individuals' perceptions of their worthiness of love and the reliability of significant others to help handle stressful situations. Ainsworth (1979) extended Bowlby's work to individual differences in infants' attachment styles (secure and insecure—anxious-avoidant and anxious-resistant). Hazan and Shaver (1987) widened Ainsworth's attachment style work to include forming love relationships during adolescence and adulthood. Moving beyond love relationships, Reio et al. (2009) argued that emotional bonds and therefore attachments are also formed with instructors and schools like adult education centers. Possessing a secure attachment style is linked to being curious and exploratory, self-reliant, and socially competent, as well as doing better in school than those with an insecure attachment style. Adult educators can embrace the idea that emotional bonding and attachment can be best supported by making it safe for learners to be curious in learning settings and cultivating social and emotional skills through being caring, nurturing, and competent educators.

Erikson's Psychosocial Theory
Erikson (1968, 1980) examined how emotional changes are linked to biology and the sociocultural and historical context and how each interacts to influence one's ego development across the life span. His views are congruent with Baltes (1987) concerning the relevance of age-graded (biology) and history-graded influences on development, as well as Vygotsky's (1978, 1986) sociocultural view that development cannot be understood apart from the social and historical context. As one of the first life span theorists, he proposed eight stages of psychosocial development (his wife and lifelong collaborator Joan Erikson [1997] later proposed a ninth stage—very old age [late 80s and beyond]: hope and faith versus despair), each with a unique developmental task/issue that confronts the individual with a crisis or turning point that must be addressed successfully for healthy psychological development. Motivation to Erikson was searching for alternatives when confronted with a crisis. Erikson stressed that although a task/issue has its ascendancy in a particular stage, the issue is never fully resolved and reappears in a different form in later stages. The formation of an identity, for example, is the primary task/issue in adolescence, yet one's initial identity and sense of an authentic self will be refined and transformed many times in a wide range of domains (e.g., gender, ethnic, racial, sexual, religious, and professional) during adulthood. Four of the stages go beyond childhood and are relevant to adult educators: adolescent identity formation, young adult intimacy development, middle adult generativity development, and late adult ego integrity development. The strength of this theory is its breadth, compatibility with other theories (e.g., career development), and stimulation of new theories (e.g., emerging adulthood). Its weaknesses include lack of specificity of the behaviors associated with each stage (e.g., how do we know someone has achieved an identity?), little attention to nonnormative influences, and unclear applicability to women, ethnic, racial, and sexual minorities, and persons having disabilities.

Emerging Adulthood Theory
Building upon G. Stanley Hall's (1904) life span, Erikson's (1968, 1980) psychosocial, and Perry's (1970) student intellectual development theories, Arnett (2000) "propose[d] a new theory of development from the late teens through the twenties" (p. 469), that is, a new stage of development called emerging adulthood that should only be applied to those in industrialized cultures. Arnett extended Erikson's notion of identity formation from adolescence through the 20s. Arnett claimed that emerging adults are distinct demographically (postponing marriage until the late 20s is becoming normative), with their subjective perceptions (regard themselves as neither adolescents nor entirely adults), and in their identity explorations (in areas of love, work, and worldviews). Identity work explorations, for example, are more serious and focused than in adolescence, while love explorations are more intimate and serious, and worldviews, as Perry noted, evolve to challenge conventional societal views. The source of motivation is being curious and exploratory, with perhaps a greater tolerance for adaptive risk taking for the sake of exploring alternatives. Adult educators need to be aware of the normative aspects of the emerging adult's risk taking and delaying being an autonomous and financially independent "adult" when considering career development planning and delivery.

Moral Development
Moral development is the examination of how an individual's ideas, beliefs, and behaviors concerning the ethical treatment of others changes across the life span. Lawrence Kohlberg (1973) and Carol Gilligan (1982) followed Piaget's (1952) theoretical notions that logic and morality develop through stages where moral thinking becomes increasingly sophisticated. Kohlberg, with an ethic of justice as the defining feature of moral reasoning, proposed three levels (each with two substages) of moral development. He based his research, however, on an all-male sample and extrapolated from his findings that male moral reasoning was superior because males typically reasoned morally at his fourth stage (one should abide by rules and laws that were established for the good of everyone), while most females were at stage three (one

should abide by family and community values to be perceived as a *good* person). Gilligan, Kohlberg's student, theorized that Kohlberg's work was flawed in that it was biased toward males. She wondered how one could extrapolate to females from an all-male sample. From her all-female sample, using Kohlberg's three levels (with no substages), she identified an ethics of care orientation where women were more likely to value and exhibit relational, connected orientations to moral decision-making, rather than justice orientations. Gilligan's work, like Kohlberg's, has been critiqued heavily, especially in the sense that she presents little evidence that women typically favor a caring position over one of justice, as compared to men.

Notwithstanding, the contributions of Gilligan's (1982) work cannot be overstated because hers is among the first to challenge the conventional wisdom of conducting research with all-male samples and extrapolating to females. This challenge was then extended by scholars to taking theories and research developed and normed with White, U.S., or European samples and applying them to ethnic, racial, sexual, linguistic, and cultural minorities. Adult educators need to be aware that theory and research based on one group or U.S. or European samples does not necessarily apply directly to other groups or diverse contexts outside the United States and Europe. This does not negate the value of such theories and research; rather, they are an appropriate starting place for generating new research testing the validity of their claims with different groups and within differing cultural settings.

Emotional Development

Emotional development refers to the ways emotions change or remain stable over the life span. Emotions have considerable implications for understanding human thinking, behaving, and learning. Panksepp (1998) proposed a "foraging/exploration/investigation/curiosity/interest/expectancy/SEEKING" (p. 145) motivational system (for the sake of clarity, he shortened the name to a "SEEKING system") that undergirds learning and developing higher cognitive functions. Panksepp (1998) noted that the emotional function of the brain was the impulse to "search, investigate, and make sense of the environment—[and it] emerges from the circuits of the LH [lateral hypothalamus]" (p. 145). In combination with the dopamine (reward) circuits of the brain, the SEEKING system "*drives* and *energizes*" (p. 145, italics in original) numerous complex mental operations that humans experience as continuing feelings of curiosity, interest, and sensation seeking and the "search for higher meaning" (p. 145). The SEEKING system is instrumental then in that it leads one to be curious and interested and as it becomes more integrated with new layers of learning as we age, helps support higher-order mental functions like creativity and emotional regulation.

Consedine and Magai (2006) identified five major elements of adult emotional development research. The five elements concerned normative age-graded differences in experience, expression, elicitation, physiology and cognition, and emotion regulation. Gains and losses in each are a function of aging (Baltes, 1987), with losses tending to outpace gains after age 75.

Emotion experience entails developmental changes in the frequency of experiencing positive and negative affect (Panksepp, 1998). Negative affect tends to decrease across the life span until the late 60s, when it levels off. Small increases in positive affect across adulthood have been found, but then declines after age 85 (Kunzman, 2008). The frequency of experiencing discrete negative emotions (e.g., anger) decreases and experiencing positive emotions (e.g., happiness) increases across the life span, reflecting perhaps changes in learning regulatory skills (Isen, 2002). Affective intensity remains stable once emotions have been aroused. Reflecting the interaction between cognition and emotion, the complexity of emotional experiences and their understanding increases until midlife (Labouvie-Vief et al., 2003).

Emotional expressivity remains stable, while there may be a slight decrease in recognizing the emotional signals of others (Livingstone et al., 2015). Physiologically speaking, normative aging is associated with lower heart rate in response to arousal (Panksepp, 1998). Older adults then are less emotionally reactive when confronted with emotionally arousing situations (Labouvie-Vief et al., 2003). Emotional regulation changes in that as age increases, control of aggression, impulsivity, and inhibition increases, while ruminating about negative events decreases. Up until age 65, regulating aversive negative emotions *before* they are aroused increases, leveling off after age 65. It may be that older adults have learned to shape their environments, such that they seek out individuals and settings where they can avoid negative affect and conflict (Isen, 2002). Consequently, adult educators might be able to assist learners in developing strategies to accentuate positive experiences and downgrade negative experiences, which could serve as important tension-relieving coping mechanisms to counteract age-graded losses in cognitive and physical performance.

Emerging Theories

Bioecological theory (Bronfenbrenner, 1979) posits five environmental systems that range from the inputs of direct interactions from social agents (e.g., parents, teachers, siblings) to the broad-based inputs (e.g., beliefs) of culture. The five environmental systems consist of the microsystem, mesosystem, exosystem, macrosystem, and chronosystem. The point of this theory is that individual development can be best understood by observing interactions and conducting research in multiple settings, such as family, peer, school, work, and cultural contexts over the life span. The nonlinearity of development is not emphasized, but it can be bidirectional.

Spirituality is emerging as an important domain of human development. As adults explore and search for meaning in their lives, many turn to religion (beliefs and practices associated with an organized religion) and spirituality (personal, transcendent) as a way to move toward an understanding of their connection with a divine being and an ultimate reality or truth. Both Eastern and Western religions advocate regulating negative destructive emotions like envy, anger, or lust and promoting positive emotions such as hope, joy, and compassion. Fowler (1981) described six stages of faith development where religion was not synonymous with faith; one can have faith but no religious commitments. Adults' faith moves from being conformist in early adulthood to appreciating the unknowable and perceiving a universal community in late adulthood. Parents, peers, and the media have been shown to be socializing agents of religious and spiritual development, with variations by culture, community, and gender (Barry et al., 2010). Spirituality and religion are positively associated with social development and subjective well-being because they not only help individuals find meaning in their lives but also provide social support that fosters hope and optimism. Tapping into one's spirituality and religious beliefs have been shown to help adults (e.g., veterans) manage stress and reduce the symptoms of depression (Sharma et al., 2017). Adult educators can apply formal and informal learning strategies (e.g., self-directed learning) to help foster religious and spiritual development and enhance their learners' subjective well-being.

Conclusion

Adults change across the life span as a result of age-graded, history-graded, and nonnormative influences. There are gains and losses, but mostly gains until late adulthood. Moderate physical activity and fitness are closely tied to optimal cognitive and emotional functioning, being protective against the negative effects of aging. There are clearly individual differences by gender, ethnicity, race, sexual orientation, disability, and culture that matter when considering the nature of adult development and how development influences the adult's involvement with learning. Existing theories of development lack completeness and need further validation across different groups and contexts to support theory-building and new rigorous research. Curiosity was highlighted as being central to a number of developmental theories. As adult educators, understanding that one's perceptions and beliefs can be limited by developmental stage and its related issues, we must find ways to spark and sustain learner curiosity for the sake of fostering the lifelong learning required for supporting optimal adult development.

References

Ackerman, P. L., & Kanfer, R. (2020). Work in the 21st century: New directions for aging and adult development. *American Psychologist, 75*(4), 486–498.

Ainsworth, M. D. S. (1979). Infant-mother attachment. *American Psychologist, 34*(10), 932–937.

Akintunde, A. L., Akintunde, T. S., & Opadijo, O. G. (2015). Knowledge of heart disease risk factors among workers in a Nigerian university: A call for concern. *Nigerian Medical Journal, 56*(2), 91–95. https://doi.org/10.4103/0300-1652.150688

Anderson, M. (1992). *Intelligence and development: A cognitive theory*. Blackwell.

Arnett, J. J. (2000). Emerging adulthood: A theory of development from the late teens through the twenties. *American Psychologist, 55*(5), 469–480.

Arnett, J. J., Robinson, O., & Lachman, M. E. (2020). Rethinking adult development: Introduction to the special issue. *American Psychologist, 75*(4), 425–430. http://dx.doi.org/10.1037/amp0000633

Atkinson, R. C., & Shiffrin, R. M. (1968). Human memory: A proposed system and its control processes. In K. Spence & J. Spence (Eds.), *The psychology of learning and motivation* (Vol. 2, pp. 13–119). Academic Press.

Baltes, P. (1987). Theoretical propositions of life-span developmental psychology: On the dynamics between growth and decline. *Developmental Psychology, 23*(5), 611–626.

Baltes, P. B., Lindenberger, U., & Staudinger, U. (2006). Life span theory in developmental psychology. In R. M. Lerner (Ed.), *Handbook of child psychology: Vol. 1. Theoretical models of human development* (6th ed., pp. 569–664). John Wiley.

Barry, C. M., Nelson, L., Davarya, S., & Urry, S. (2010). Religiosity and spirituality during the transition to emerging adulthood. *International Journal of Behavioral Development, 34*(4), 311–324.

Bekinschtein, P., Oomen, C. A., Saksida, L. M., & Bussey, Y. J. (2011). Effects of environmental enrichment and voluntary exercise on neurogenesis, learning and memory, and pattern separation: BDNF as a critical variable? *Seminars in Cell & Developmental Biology, 22*(5), 536–542.

Bolton, S., & Hattie, J. (2017). Cognitive and brain development: Executive function, Piaget, and the prefrontal cortex. *Annals of Psychology, 1*(3), 1–36.

Boucouvalas, M. (with Krupp, J.). (1989). Adult development and learning. In S. B. Merriam & P. M. Cunningham (Eds.), *Handbook of adult and continuing education* (pp. 183–200). Jossey-Bass.

Bowlby, J. (1969). *Attachment and love* (Vol. 1). Hogarth.

Bronfenbrenner, U. (1979). *The ecology of human development: Experiments by nature and design*. Harvard University Press.

Bühler, J. L., & Nikitin, J. (2020). Sociocultural context and adult social development: New directions for 21st century research. *American Psychologist, 75*(4), 457–469.

Cashman, K. D. (2007). Diet, nutrition, and bone health. *The Journal of Nutrition, 137*(11), 2507S–2512S.

Commons, M. L. (2008). Introduction to the model of hierarchical complexity and its relationship to postformal action. *World Futures, 64*, 305–320.

Consedine, N. S. & Magai, C. (2006). Emotion development in adulthood: A developmental functionalist review and critique. In C. Hoare (Ed.), *The Oxford handbook of adult development and learning* (pp. 209–244). Oxford University Press.

Crooks, V. C., Little, D., & Chiu, V. (2008). Social network, cognitive function, and dementia incidence among elderly women. *American Journal of Public Health, 98*(7), 1221–1227.

DiPietro, L. (2001). Physical activity in aging: Changes in patterns and their relationships to health and function. *Journal of Gerontology, 56A*, 13–22.

Erikson, E. H. (1968). *Identity, youth and crisis*. W. W. Norton.

Erikson, E. H. (1980). *Identity and the life cycle*. W. W. Norton.

Erikson, J. M. (1997). *The life cycle completed: Extended version*. W. W. Norton.

Eriksson, P. S., Perfilieva, E., Björk-Akesson, T., Alborn, A., Nordberg, C., Peterson, D. A., & Gage, F. H. (1998). Neurogenesis in the adult human hippocampus. *Nature Medicine, 4*, 1313–1317.

Fowler, J. W. (1981). *Stages of faith: The psychology of human development and the quest for meaning*. Harper & Row.

Giangregorio, L. M., MacIntyre, N. J., Heinonen, A., Cheung, A. M., Wark, J. D., Shipp, K., McGill, S., Ashe, M. C., Laprade, J., Jain, R., Keller, H., & Papaioannou, A. (2014). Too fit to fracture: A consensus on future research priorities in osteoporosis and exercise. *Osteoporosis International, 25*(5), 1465–1472.

Gilligan, C. (1982). *In a different voice: Psychological theory and women's development*. Harvard University Press.

Hall, G. S. (1904). *Adolescence: Its psychology and its relation to physiology, anthropology, sociology, crime, religion, and education* (Vol. 1). Prentice Hall.

Havighurst, R. J. (1953). *Human development and education*. Longmans, Green.

Hazan, C., & Shaver, P. (1987). Romantic love conceptualized as an attachment process. *Journal of Personality and Social Psychology, 52*(3), 511–524.

Isen, A. M., (2002). Missing in action in the AIM: Positive affect's facilitation of cognitive flexibility, innovation, and problem-solving. *Psychological Inquiry, 13*(1), 57–65.

Jiannine, L. M., & Reio, T. G., Jr. (2018). The physiological and psychological effects of exercise on sexual functioning: A literature review for adult health education professionals. *New Horizons in Adult Education and Human Resource Development, 30*(2), 3–22.

Kail, R., & Park, Y. (1992). Global developmental change in processing time. *Merrill-Palmer Quarterly, 38*(4), 525–541.

Keller, K., & Engelhardt, M. (2013). Strength and muscle mass loss with aging process. Age and strength loss. *Muscles, Ligaments, and Tendons Journal, 34*(4), 346–350.

Knowles, M. S. (1968). Andragogy, not pedagogy. *Adult Leadership, 16*(10), 350–352, 386.

Kohlberg, L. (1973). The claim to moral adequacy of a highest stage of moral judgment. *Journal of Philosophy, 70*(18), 630–646.

Kunzman, U. (2008). Differential age trajectories of positive and negative affect: Further evidence from the Berlin Aging Study. *The Journals of Gerontology: Series B, 63*, P261–P270.

Labouvie-Vief, G. (1980). Beyond formal operations: Use and limits of pure logic in life-span development. *Human Development, 23*(3), 141–161.

Labouvie-Vief, G., Lumley, M. A., Jain, E., & Heinze, H. (2003). Age and gender differences in cardiac reactivity and subjective emotions responses to emotional autobiographical memories. *Emotion, 3*(2), 115–126.

Livingstone, S. R., Thompson, W. F., Wanderly, M. M., & Palmer, C. (2015). Common cues to emotion in the dynamic facial expressions of speech and song. *Quarterly Journal of Experimental Psychology, 68*(5), 952–970.

Luria, A. L. (1976). *Cognitive development: Its cultural and social foundations* (M. Cole, Ed.). Harvard University Press.

National Center for Disease Prevention and Health Promotion. (2018). *Alzheimer's disease: Promoting health and independence for an independent population.* https://www.cdc.gov/chronicdisease/pdf/healthybrain-aag-2018-H.pdf

Notthoff, N., & Cartensen, L. L. (2014). Positive messaging promotes walking in older adults. *Psychology and Aging, 29*(2), 329–341.

Ogden C. L., Carroll, M. D., Kit, B. K., & Flegal, K. M. (2012). Prevalence of obesity in the United States, 2009–2010. *NCHS Data Brief, 82,* 1–8.

Panksepp, J. (1998). *Affective neuroscience: The foundations of human and animal emotions.* Oxford University Press.

Paus, T. (2010). Sex differences in the human brain: A developmental perspective. *Progress in Brain Research, 186,* 13–28.

Perry, W. G. (1970). *Forms of intellectual and ethnical development in the college years.* Holt, Rinehart, & Winston.

Piaget, J. (1952). *The language and thought of a child.* World.

Reio, T. G., Jr., Marcus, R. F., & Sanders-Reio, J. (2009). The contribution of student and instructor relationships and attachment style to school completion. *The Journal of Genetic Psychology, 170*(1), 53–72.

Reio, T. G., Jr., & Petrosko, J. M., Wiswell, A. K., & Thongsukmag, J. (2006). The measurement and conceptualization of curiosity. *The Journal of Genetic Psychology, 167*(2), 117–135.

Riegel, K. F. (1979). *The foundations of dialectical psychology.* Academic Press.

Schaie, K. W., & Willis, S. L. (2000). A stage model of adult cognitive development revisited. In R. L. Rubenstein, M. Moss, & M. H. Kleban (Eds.), *The many dimensions of aging* (pp. 175–193). Springer.

Schaie, K. W., Willis, S. L., & Caskie, G. I. L. (2014). The Seattle longitudinal study: Relation between personality and cognition. *Aging, Neuropsychology and Cognition, 11*(2–3), 304–324.

Sharma, V., Marin, D. B., Koenig, H. K., Feder, A., Iacoviello, B. M., Southwick, S. M., & Pietrzak, R. H. (2017). Religion, spirituality, and mental health of U.S. military veterans: Results from the National Health and Resilience Study. *Journal of Affective Disorders, 217,* 197–204.

Sinnott, J. D. (2014). *Adult development: Cognitive aspects of thriving close relationships.* Oxford University Press.

Vygotsky, L. S. (1978). *Mind in society: The development of higher mental processes.* Harvard University Press.

Vygotsky, L. S. (1986). *Thought and language.* Harvard University Press.

CHAPTER 9

Motivation

Margery B. Ginsberg and Raymond J. Wlodkowski

Motivation to learn, as initially described by Brophy (2004), is the tendency to find learning activities meaningful and worthwhile and to benefit from them—to try to make sense of available information, relate this information to prior knowledge, and develop additional knowledge and skills. Motivation is basic to survival. It is the natural human process that fuels the energy and direction of human behavior (Reeve, 2009). Being motivated means being purposeful; achieving goals through attention, concentration, imagination, and other processes to accomplish our intentions. Yet attempting to understand what human motivation is requires the realization that the causes of human behavior evade any simple explanation or prescription. Depending on their discipline and cultural context, the definition of motivation and the concept of *motivation to learn* varies among scholars.

This overview of adult motivation to learn addresses the range of topics upon which researchers in this field have primarily focused. We begin with a review of the multidisciplinary orientation to understanding human motivation to learn and then proceed to how the concept of adult motivation and its relationship to adult characteristics has evolved. We then discuss the elements that comprise an educational and instructional perspective of adult motivation to learn. These take into consideration intrinsic motivation, a motivational framework for teaching adults, online learning, and transformative learning. The chapter concludes with a discussion of educational programs and improvements designed to increase persistence and degree completion among underserved adult learners.

Motivation to Learn: A Multidisciplinary Perspective

Most social scientists regard motivation as a concept that explains why people think and behave as they do (Weiner, 1992). We know from psychological research that it is part of human nature to be curious, to be active, to make meaning from experience, and to be effective at what we value (Lambert & McCombs, 1998). These are primary sources of motivation that reside in all human beings and are basic to our survival and our capacity to thrive.

Neuroscience provides a biological perspective. Within this rapidly emerging field, motivation is a process that determines how much energy and attention the brain and body assign to a given stimulus—whether a thought or a situation (Ratey, 2001). This effects the initiation, mediation, and outcome of a learning experience. How we start, how we continue, and how we complete a learning endeavor are all motivational processes that are indivisible from learning itself. In reality, motivation is not an either/or condition, but when motivation to learn is low, we can generally assume that learning will be diminished (Reeve & Lee, 2012).

Motivation and learning are inherently cultural (O'Brien & Rogers, 2016). Culture is the deeply learned mix of language, beliefs, values, and behaviors that pervade every aspect of our lives (Geertz, 1973). The cultural group(s) within which we are socialized influence systems throughout our brains, the language we use to think, the way we travel through our thoughts, how we communicate, and how we make sense of and mediate moral decisions. Although how we interact and make sense of the world may change as we age, the influence of early socialization is significant. Emotions as basic as joy and fear are initially felt and understood within the cultural contexts of our communities, families, and peers (Barrett, 2005). In any situation, and certainly when we feel threatened, emotions mediate what and how we prioritize. Every moment is a competition among our senses to perceive what matters most (Ahissar et al., 1992). Emotions add relevance and human beings are compelled to pay attention to what matters.

In learning and life, relevance guides attention and is basic to survival. In this regard, engagement with any learning task is always in a state of flux, diminishing, strengthening, or changing emotionally. From the written words on a single page of a book or in the span of 5 minutes in a course, learners may experience a range of emotions: inspiration, curiosity, futility, and inspiration once again. This dynamic makes sustaining learning a nuanced endeavor that warrants careful instructional planning. As discussed later, when instructional plans are also motivational plans, educators increase the likelihood that students will direct their energy, attention, and interest to educational tasks throughout an entire learning experience.

Adult Motivation to Learn: Research and Conceptual Understandings

A review of the literature on the relationship between adult motivation and learning is international in its scope and includes wide-ranging considerations: cultural contexts, learning environments, academic levels, multiple disciplines, motivational theories, and stages of development. Most of the research on adult motivation and learning outcomes are small-scale studies or case studies of specific teaching practices in relation to adult learning. Often, the term *adult learner* is synonymous with *nontraditional learner*, which may mean one or more of the following: entry to college delayed by at least a year following high school, having dependents, being a single parent, being employed full time, being financially independent, attending part time, and not having a high school diploma (Ross-Gordon, 2011).

There are large-scale studies that consider instruction as one of several institutional factors that influence student success, for example Kuh et al. (2010). However, few, if any, specifically focus on adult motivation, cultural diversity, or are grounded in a comprehensive synthesis of research on postsecondary teaching and learning. Given increased attention to college completion, marketable skills for learners from a wide range of backgrounds, and persistent disparities in postsecondary graduation rates, the need for large scale studies that connect teaching adults to learning outcomes and persistence has never been greater (Silva & White, 2013).

Some of the strongest analyses of the relationship of motivation to learning are found in youth education. In this body of research, there is substantial evidence that motivation is consistently and positively related to engagement, learning, and educational achievement (Hulleman & Barron, 2016). Several studies include precise investigations that range from targeted interventions to comprehensive interventions that also consider curriculum and teaching methods (Lazowski & Hulleman, 2016).

Since motivation is situation specific, its meaning, purpose, and context will affect its quality and intensity. For example, an adult might be highly motivated to play an instrument with their family, but not motivated to play music with other people or, for that matter, not motivated to perform in front of an audience.

Within the last decade, research on learners' engagement has gained considerable attention. As concepts, motivation and engagement are related (Shernoff, 2013). Motivation can be seen as an individual's behavior, goals, beliefs, emotions, and thoughts. Research on engagement focuses more on the observable interaction between the person and a system or environment with emphasis on activities or relationships. When applied to learning, motivation and engagement studies converge and include active participation in academic activities, the role of energy and effort, and the influence of culture and context on learners (Christenson et al., 2012). Thus, we consider engagement to be a motivational construct.

Characteristics of Adult Learners

Responsibility is the cornerstone of adult motivation. Most cultural communities view adults as more responsible for their actions than children. The deep social value of responsibility is why competence—being effective at what one values—looms so large as a force for adult learning. Most employers and educational institutions value and reward self-directed competence and many adults are socialized with these values. These cultural conventions account for one of the most widely accepted generalizations in adult education: Adults are highly pragmatic learners.

The second major characteristic that distinguishes adults' motivation to learn is accumulated experience and learning. The sum of adults' personal knowledge contributes to a higher regard for learning that is useful, relevant, and interesting. Neuroscientifically, prior knowledge determines what adults are attuned to and will likely concentrate on (Zull, 2006). Maturity of brain development makes a difference. In the United States, the legal age for many privileges and responsibilities of adulthood is 18, for example voting and eligibility for military service. However, emerging evidence suggests that the prefrontal cortex is often not mature until at least the age of 25, with some evidence that women develop somewhat earlier than men (Arnett, 2015). Across genders, it continues to develop throughout life (Audesirk et al., 2008).

The neurons in the frontal lobe form rules from learned experiences that support cognitive processes such as self-control and planning complex tasks (Wallis et al., 2001). This is where we create holistic views of what the world is, what we want to do about it, and what direction we want to pursue (Zull, 2011). These findings may reflect adults' greater desire to learn for a sense of accomplishment, effectiveness, and the value of what is being learned.

What these differences in biology and experience mean motivationally is that adults are likely to have certain characteristics, some of which overlap with youth motivation:

- To be sensitive to and require respect from their teachers as a condition for learning
- To use relevance (what matters rather than what is playful or stimulating) as the ultimate criteria for sustaining their interest
- To be more critical and more self-assured about their judgment of the value of what they are learning
- To be reluctant to learn what they cannot endorse by virtue of its value, usefulness, or contribution to their goals
- To want to actively test what they are learning in work and other settings
- To want to use their experience and prior learning as consciously and directly as possible while learning
- To want to integrate new learning with their roles in family, work, and community

There are other distinguishing characteristics in terms of motivation to learn, but research, theory, and our own history as educators suggest that the influences of responsibility and experience are the most notable.

Intrinsic Motivation and Adult Learning

Theories of intrinsic motivation strongly associate with characteristics of adult learners. As defined by Ryan and Deci (2000), "intrinsic motivation is entailed whenever people behave for the satisfaction inherent in the behavior itself" (p. 16). For example, someone reads a novel because they find it innately interesting. Behavior that people find intrinsically satisfying likely conforms to what they are physiologically, psychologically, and culturally disposed to want or need, for example, being effective at work or in their communities. When adults see that what they are learning makes sense and is important according to their values and perspectives, their motivation emerges. Such circumstances elicit intrinsic motivation.

Intrinsic motivation is evoked. It is a form of physical energy that emerges within supportive and relevant environments, for example, environments with familiar cultural values, behavioral norms, and roles. As conceived by Barrett (2017), such motivation is an interoceptive activity, a feeling constructed from all of the sensations in our bodies and the instantaneous melding of our neuronal networks. When adults feel respected, care about what they are learning, and know they are becoming more effective at what they value, intrinsic motivation surfaces like a cork rising through water.

Intrinsically motivated learning promotes enduring learning, the genesis of which is usually an engrossing and successful learning experience. This contributes to the trait of lifelong learning (Nakamura, 2001). It is commonly understood that being a lifelong learner is a highly valued trait within communities and work contexts. Fostering the will to learn may be of greater consequence than learning a specific thing at a specific time. Generally, people who eventually find satisfaction in reading, writing, calculating, communicating, exploring technology, and expanding their knowledge and skills are productive lifelong learners.

Researchers Richard Ryan and Edward Deci (2017), who have spent most of their lives studying the phenomenon of intrinsic motivation, believe the key to finding the act of learning worthwhile throughout life is developing motivation as an autonomous process. Intrinsically motivated lifelong learners possess a broad and deep goal orientation to learning. They find new learning to be challenging, interesting, worth mastering, and something they are capable of achieving. In general, learning experiences that foster autonomy (that feel volitional, self-regulated, and congruent with one's interests), competence (that indicate accomplishment and effectiveness), and relatedness (that feel socially connected to and cared about by others) encourage and develop lifelong learning. In addition, they probably increase an adult's sense of personal agency. Although contexts of cultures vary widely, there is emerging international evidence that intervention programs personally chosen by adults, and in which they are willing participants rather than externally controlled, are enterprises in which they are more likely to persist and experience the value of personal determination (Ibrahim & Alkire, 2007).

Such learning experiences may also contribute to feelings of flow. People are intrinsically motivated during flow: absorbed in an activity with little self-consciousness, realizing full participation with adequate skill in a challenging endeavor (Nakamura & Csikszentmihalyi, 2003). In such situations, there may be a feeling of transcendence or a merging with the activity and environment. Writers, dancers, therapists, surgeons, lawyers, pilots, and instructors report feelings of flow in repertoires of engrossing tasks. In fact, when interviewed, they report that flow experiences are among the major reasons why they enjoy and pursue the work they do.

Most adults have had flow experiences while engaged in challenging learning activities. If we think of our favorite courses and most effective instructors, we often remember being captivated by challenging and creative activities. With effort and concentration, we participated at heightened levels of motivation and skill that extended our capabilities. Because flow occurs throughout the world, this optimal state may have developed to help human beings recognize and preserve certain patterns of action.

As a guide to construct learning activities, flow experiences have remarkably similar characteristics:

- Goals are clear and compatible. For example, comparing different opening repertoires in chess to understand their cultural and competitive implications.
- Feedback is immediate, continuous, and relevant as the activity unfolds. For example, receiving auditory feedback while writing a piece of music.
- The challenge is in balance with our skills or knowledge but stretches existing capacities. For example, applying an analytical protocol to an existing set of data for insight into a medical problem in a health education course.

According to Nakamura (2001), at its highest qualitative level, intrinsic motivation is vital engagement: the experience of learning "characterized by both felt meaning (subjective significance) and enjoyed absorption" (p. 8). This kind of motivation occurs in the immediate experience of learning and over time as an enduring relationship or personal trait—a love of learning surrounding a particular subject. While vitally engaged, adults take what they learn seriously, possibly for years, realizing the subject has inherent worth to sustain concentration and energy. This allows for a range of commitments and vocational callings such as computer programming, architectural design, or political organizing—sustained actions that are personally significant to adults. Many educators are lifelong learners who know that vital engagement is most likely to occur when there is a "felt conviction" that the learning task is part of something "inherently important" (Nakamura & Csikszentmihalyi, 2003, p. 100).

A Motivational Framework for Teaching Adults

Psychological, biological, and cultural studies offer an essential understanding of adult motivation to learn: All adults want to make sense of their world, find meaning, and become effective at what they value. This is what fuels adult motivation to learn. The key to adult teaching is to evoke and encourage this natural inclination among adult learners from a range of backgrounds and identities. But how?

In her study of motivation and its impact on personal development, Dweck (2018) highlights a broader understanding of this question. She asks, "Within this field, many new motivational interventions have been designed and tested, but how do they all fit together and how can we evaluate and increase their efficacy?" (p. 42). The motivational framework for culturally responsive teaching (Wlodkowski & Ginsberg, 1995) responds to this query. Since its inception over 2 decades ago, it has become internationally recognized as an integrative application of research findings on intrinsic motivation, teaching, and learning. It has a cross-curricular reach. Adult educators continue to apply and research the framework in fields such as nursing, teacher professional development, ethnic studies, engineering, computer programming, and game design (Barnes, 2012; Rhodes, 2017; Zigarelli, 2017).

As a metaframework for instructional design it respects an essential tenet: No learning situation is culturally neutral. Learners are individuals with complex identities, personal histories, and unique living contexts. For example, a person is not just older or African American or female; she is older, African American, and female. This example is still too simple because it does not include her religious or spiritual beliefs, sexual orientation, and income or professional status, among other influences. Each of us has a variety of identities through which we make sense of things. The framework's four-question protocol requires instructors to reflect on learner diversity as a central consideration while planning instruction (Ginsberg & Wlodkowski, 2009).

The motivational conditions and related questions are:

1. Establishing inclusion: *How do we create or affirm a learning environment in which we feel respected by and connected to one another?*
2. Developing a positive attitude: *How do we create or affirm a favorable disposition toward learning through personal relevance and learner volition?*
3. Enhancing meaning: *How do we create engaging and challenging learning experiences that include learners' perspectives and values?*
4. Engendering competence: *How do we create or affirm an understanding that learners have effectively learned something they value and consider authentic for application in the world?*

Colleges and universities have more students than ever before whose perceptions and ways of making sense of interactions and information vary from one another and from their instructors. In 2013, just 14% of Latinos, 15% of Native Americans, 16% of Pacific Islanders, and 19% of Black adults over the age of 25 had earned a bachelor's degree, compared with 33% of White adults (Musu-Gillette et al., 2016). For learners with low incomes, disparities in educational attainment are even more pronounced (Snyder et al., 2016). Without an instructional architecture, adult educators tend to rely on intuition and a few "best practices" to elicit motivation among a broad range of learners. The motivational framework offers a theoretically coherent set of practices to codify, research, and experiment with for enhanced inclusion, diversity, and learning (Rhodes, 2018).

Online Learning

The internet has created access to knowledge more than any technological innovation in history. It is a force behind the acceleration of online learning in higher education and training. Nearly 90% of postsecondary institutions in the United States offer online courses and approximately 65% offer complete online degree programs (Allen & Seaman, 2012). The majority of online enrollees are nontraditional adult learners (Stavredes, 2011).

Most online adult learners reflect adult pragmatism. They want their education to prepare them for their careers, job changes, and to update their skills. Flexibility and convenience are important attributes of the programs they select. However, findings regarding retention in online programs are neither clear nor consistent (Meyer, 2014). They vary widely from institution to institution, and program dropout rates are generally higher for online learners than for traditional, on-campus students (Allen & Seaman, 2012). Studies offer ample evidence that a direct increase in the interactions of online learners with instructors and in activities such as collaborative learning and group projects, encourages persistence and certificate or degree completion (Meyer, 2014).

In addition, there is broad consensus among researchers and adult educators that instructional methods and activities that encourage adult motivation and engagement in face-to-face learning environments are useful and adaptable for online learning formats (Meyer, 2014). Through their review of research on instructional methods for enhancing intrinsic motivation, Wlodkowski and Ginsberg (2017) found 24 effective strategies for teaching adults in both online *and* classroom environments. These include such classic teaching methods as effective feedback; solving relevant problems; and a clear, inviting, and inclusive course syllabus.

Transformative Learning

Intrinsically motivated learning (Ryan & Deci, 2017) and transformative learning (Cranton, 2016) have the potential to encourage nondefensive awareness and personal change among adults. Each are associated with caring and accepting social relationships, qualities basic to motivated learning.

Kroth and Cranton (2014) define *transformative learning* as a process by which individuals engage in critical reflection and self-reflection, and intuitive and imaginative explorations, which results in developmental changes leading to a deep shift in perspective and habits of mind that are more open, permeable, and discriminating. Individual change may lead to social change, and social change may promote individual change (p. 9). Although transformative learning may not always be enjoyable, it is usually absorbing and significant to adults—qualities integral to vital engagement. From a developmental perspective, such as a period from 20 years to 40 years of age, it is likely that vital engagement and transformative learning are at times reciprocal processes.

In recent years, there has been a trend among scholars of adult education to use storytelling to foster transformative learning. Less bound by real time, stories allow adult learners to reflect over longer periods of living at a more emotional and deeper level. Personal stories are relevant, engaging, and offer insight into how the lives of adults have changed. Kroth and Cranton (2014) have used storytelling to encourage people to explore the potential for transformative learning in their own lives, practices, and communities. The personal nature of stories allows people to readily know how others have reconsidered hidden assumptions and offers hope for making changes to heighten personal fulfillment and social contribution. Because they provide insight into real, complex lives, narratives such as biography and memoir may also allow a better understanding of how intrinsic motivation and transformative learning enhance each other as they work in concert to drive adult learning and change (Wlodkowski, 2019).

Underserved and Low-Income Adult Learners

Over 90 million adults participate in formal and informal education including postsecondary education, adult basic education, English language learning, workplace learning, and personal development classes (Paulson & Boeke, 2006). When this number is examined through the lens of income, race, ethnicity, disability, and credential and degree completion, troubling disparities emerge.

The most underserved group in adult education are low-income adults (Hartle & Nellum, 2015). While postsecondary institutions are becoming more culturally and economically diverse, the degree attainment gap for low-income individuals is widening. A 45-year trend report by the Pell Institute for the Study of Opportunity in Higher Education (Cahalan & Perna, 2015) shows that while bachelor's degree attainment among students from wealthy families has increased significantly, it has barely moved for low-income learners. Although slowly changing, workplace learning, especially in large organizations and corporations, tends to prioritize learning programs for top management rather than low-skilled learners (Watkins & Marsick, 2009).

Some states (e.g., Tennessee and California) are eliminating noncredit remedial courses. In these courses, most of the students are low income. Historically, the record of success with developmental classes is dismal (Rutschow et al., 2019). With limited time and resources to improve their practice, faculty too often rely heavily on ineffective instructional methods such as prolonged lectures. Low rates of completion are exacerbated by financial constraints as well as family and work responsibilities.

As an institution, community colleges offer an extraordinary benefit to society. They are the largest gateway for adults and nontraditional learners, who comprise 70% of their student body. Most community colleges in the United States are open-access institutions enrolling a much broader variety of students than 4-year colleges. In 2012, 49% of all Black undergraduates and 56% of all Latino undergraduates were enrolled at community colleges (American Association of Community Colleges, 2013). However, as of 2011, only 30% of African Americans and 20% of Latinos ages 25 years to 34 years had attained an associate degree. This compares to 49% of White Americans of European background (Lee & Ransom, 2011).

Data from the Century Foundation (2013) indicates that, although community colleges enroll a disproportionate number of historically underserved students, they are underfunded and underresourced. This amounts to a separate and unequal educational system with completion rates impeded by one or more of the following: unwelcoming institutional climates, understaffing, and insufficient instructional support for faculty (Center for Community College Student Engagement, 2014).

Thus far, no single policy or program has significantly raised the persistence and degree completion of adult learners at a national scale. There is widespread agreement that goal completion among adult learners (and all students) requires system-wide efforts to strengthen financial assistance, provide proactive advising, and expand teaching centers to improve instruction (Haras et al., 2018; Rutschow et al., 2019). Researchers have found that improvements in instruction contribute to increased learner motivation and persistence in postsecondary education (Fong et al., 2017).

Research by the Center for Community College Student Engagement (2014), with 30 student focus groups comprising Black, Latino, and White males across the country, reveals four commonly agreed-upon needs. These are classic instructor and instructional qualities to encourage adult motivation to learn (Wlodkowski & Ginsberg, 2017) and include:

- personal connections for students that create a sense of belonging and that someone believes in them;
- high expectations for excellence;
- faculty commitment, with a demonstrated interest in students, enthusiasm for subject matter, and support for academic success; and
- engagement in learning.

Conclusion

Throughout this chapter we have offered a research-based perspective on adult motivation to learn. Motivation to learn can serve as a foundation for systemic endeavors to improve adult learning in training and postsecondary settings. While practices, policies, and politics are influential arbiters of equitable and effective motivational opportunities for the learning of adults, the role of instructors cannot be underestimated. Their own love of learning, professional craft, personal mission, and social contributions change the lives of adult learners every day. This is the platform upon which to build.

References

Ahissar, E., Vaadia, E., Ahissar, M., Bergman, H., Arieli, A., & Abeles, M. (1992). Dependence of cortical plasticity on correlated activity of single neurons and on behavioral context. *Science, 257*(5075), 1412–1415.

Allen, E. I., & Seaman, J. (2012). *Changing course: Ten years of tracking online education in the United States*. Babson Survey Research Group.

American Association of Community Colleges. (2013). *Community college fact sheet*. Author.

Arnett, J. J. (2015). *Emerging adulthood: The winding road from the late teens through the twenties* (2nd ed.). Oxford University Press.

Audesirk, T., Audesirk, G., & Byers, B. E. (2008). *Biology: Life on earth with physiology*. Pearson Prentice Hall.

Barnes, P. (2012). *Motivational conditions experienced by diverse adult learners in cohort-based accelerated degree programs: Quantifying learner perceptions for assessment and enhancement of adult motivation to learn* [Unpublished doctoral dissertation]. Kansas State University.

Barrett, L. F. (2005). Feeling is perceiving: Core affect and conceptualization in the experience of emotion. In L. F. Barret, P. M. Niedenthal, & P. Winkielman (Eds.), *Emotion and consciousness* (pp. 255–284). Guilford Press.

Barrett, L. F. (2017). *How emotions are made: The new science of the mind and brain.* Houghton Mifflin Harcourt.

Brophy, J. (2004). *Motivating students to learn* (2nd ed.). Lawrence Erlbaum.

Cahalan, M., & Perna, L. (2015). *Indicators of higher education equity in the United States: 45 year trend report.* Pell Institute for the Study of Opportunity in Higher Education.

Center for Community College Student Engagement. (2014). *Aspirations to achievement: Men of color and community colleges.* www.ccsse.org/docs/MoC_Special_Report.pdf.

Century Foundation Task Force on Preventing Community Colleges From Becoming Separate and Unequal. (2013). *Bridging the higher education divide.* Century Foundation Press.

Christenson, S. L., Reschly, A. L., & Wylie, C. (Eds.). (2012). *Handbook of research on student engagement.* Springer.

Cranton, P. (2016). *Understanding and promoting transformative learning.* Stylus.

Dweck, C. (2018, July/August). What's next? *Monitor on Psychology,* 42–43.

Fong, C. J., Davis, C. W., Kim, Y., Kim, Y. W., Marriott, L, & Kim, S. Y. (2017). Psychosocial factors and community college student success: A meta-analytic investigation. *Review of Educational Research, 87,* 388–424.

Geertz, C. (1973). *The interpretation of cultures.* Basic Books.

Ginsberg, M., & Wlodkowski, R. (2009). *Diversity & motivation: Culturally responsive teaching in college.* Jossey-Bass.

Haras, C. A., Taylor, S. C., Sorcinelli, M. D., & von Hoene, L. (Eds.). (2018). *Institutional commitment to teaching excellence: Assessing the impacts and outcomes of faculty development.* American Council on Education.

Hartle, T., & Nellum, C. (2015, November). *Where have all the low-income students gone?* American Council on Education.

Hulleman, C. S., & Barron, K. F. (2016). Motivation interventions in education: Bridging theory, research, and practice. In L. Corno & E. M. Anderman (Eds.), *Handbook of educational psychology* (3rd ed., pp. 160–171). Routledge.

Ibrahim, S., & Alkire, S. (2007). Agency and empowerment: A proposal for internationally comparable indicators. *Oxford Development Studies, 35*(4), 379–403.

Kroth, M., & Cranton, P. (2014). *Stories of transformative learning.* Sense.

Kuh, G. D., Kinzie, J., Schuh, J. H., & Whitt, E. J. (2010). *Student success in college: Creating conditions that matter.* Jossey-Bass.

Lambert, N. M., & McCombs, B. L. (1998). Introduction: Learner-centered schools and classrooms as a direction for school reform. In N. M. Lambert & B. L. McCombs (Eds.), *How students learn: Reforming schools through learner-centered education* (pp. 1–22). American Psychological Association.

Lazowski, R. A., & Hulleman, C. S. (2016). Motivation interventions in education: A meta-analytic review. *Review of Educational Research, 86*(2), 602–640.

Lee, J. M., & Ransom, T. (2011). *The educational experience of young men of color: A review of research, pathways and progress.* College Board Advocacy and Policy Center.

Meyer, K. A. (2014). Student engagement online: What works and why. *ASHE Higher Education Report, 40*(6). Jossey-Bass. https://doi.org/10.1002/aehe.20018

Musu-Gillette, L., Robinson, J., McFarland, J., KewalRamani, A., Zhang, A., & Wilkinson-Flicker, S. (2016). *Status and trends in the education of racial and ethnic groups* (NCES 2016-007). U.S. Department of Education, National Center for Education Statistics.

Nakamura, J. (2001). The nature of vital engagement in adulthood. *New Directions for Child and Adolescent Development, 93,* 5–18.

Nakamura, J., & Csikszentmihalyi, M. (2003). The construction of meaning through vital engagement. In C. Keyes & J. Haidt (Eds.), *Flourishing: Positive psychology and the life well-lived* (pp. 83–104). American Psychological Association.

O'Brien, D., & Rogers, T. (2016). Sociocultural perspectives on literacy and learning. In L. Corno & E. M. Anderman (Eds.), *Handbook of educational psychology* (3rd ed., pp. 311–337). Routledge.

Paulson, K., & Boeke, M. (2006). *Adult learners in the United States: A national profile.* American Council on Education.

Ratey, J. J. (2001). *A user's guide to the brain: Perception, attention, and the four theatres of the brain.* Pantheon.

Reeve, J. (2009). *Understanding motivation and emotion* (5th ed). John Wiley.

Reeve, J., & Lee, W. (2012). Neuroscience and human motivation. In R. M. Ryan (Ed.), *The Oxford handbook of human motivation* (pp. 365–380). Oxford University Press.

Rhodes, C. M. (2017). A validation study of the culturally responsive teaching survey. *Universal Journal of Educational Research, 5,* 45–53.

Rhodes, C. M. (2018). Culturally responsive teaching with adult learners: A review of the literature. *International Journal of Adult Vocational Education and Technology, 9*(4), 33–41.

Ross-Gordon, J. (2011). Research on adult learners: Supporting the needs of a student population that is no longer nontraditional. *Peer Review, 13,* 26–29.

Rutschow, E. Z., Cormier, M. S., Dukes, D., & Zamora, D. E. C. (2019). *The changing landscape of developmental education practices: Findings from a national survey and interviews with postsecondary institutions.* Center for the Analysis of Postsecondary Readiness. https://www.mdrc.org/sites/default/files/CAPR_Landscape_Report_2019.pdf

Ryan, R. M., & Deci, E. L. (2000). When rewards compete with nature: The undermining of intrinsic motivation and self-regulation. In C. Sansone & J. M. Harackiewicz (Eds.), *Intrinsic and extrinsic motivation: The search for optimal motivation and performance* (pp. 13–54). Academic Press.

Ryan, R. M., & Deci, E. L. (2017). *Self-determination theory: Basic psychological needs in motivation, development, and wellness.* The Guilford Press.

Shernoff, D. J. (2013). *Optimal learning environments to promote student engagement.* Springer.

Silva, E., & White, T. (2013). *Pathways to improvement: Using psychological strategies to help college students master developmental math.* Carnegie Foundation for the Advancement of Teaching.

Snyder, T. D., de Brey, C., & Dillow, S. A. (2016). *Digest of education statistics, 2014 NCES 2016-006. Table 104.92* (p. 10). National Center for Education Statistics, Institute of Education Science, U.S. Department of Education.

Stavredes, T. (2011). *Effective online teaching: Foundations and strategies for student success.* Jossey-Bass.

Wallis, J. D., Anderson, K. C., & Miller, E. K. (2001). Single neurons in pre-frontal cortex encode abstract rules. *Nature, 411,* 953–956.

Watkins, K. E., & Marsick, V. J. (2009). Trends in lifelong learning in the U.S. workplace. In P. Jarvis (Ed.). *The Routledge international handbook of lifelong learning* (pp. 129–138). Routledge.

Weiner, B. (1992). *Human motivation: Metaphors, theories, and research.* SAGE.

Wlodkowski, R. J. (2019). *Living a motivated life: A memoir and activities.* Brill/Sense.

Wlodkowski, R. J., & Ginsberg, M. B. (1995). *Diversity and motivation: Culturally responsive teaching.* Jossey-Bass.

Wlodkowski, R. J., & Ginsberg, M. B. (2017). *Enhancing adult motivation to learn: A comprehensive guide for teaching all adults* (4th ed). Jossey-Bass.

Zigarelli, J. (2017). *The role of motivation in changing teacher beliefs: an investigation of a strengths based intervention* [Unpublished doctoral dissertation]. University of Washington.

Zull, J. E. (2006). Key aspects of how the brain learns. *New Directions for Adult and Continuing Education, 2006*(110), 3–9.

Zull, J. E. (2011). *Brain to mind: Using neuroscience to guide change in education.* Stylus.

CHAPTER 10

Access, Participation, and Support of Adult Learners

David Deggs and Ellen Boeren

Those who think about adult education or lifelong learning are, by nature, planners of the future, not surveyors of the past. In their view, education tends to be concerned with needs and aspirations; with imperfections or inadequacies in people, institutions and communities; and with how life can be made better by learning. (Houle, 1992, p. 35)

The issues and challenges associated with access, participation, and support of adult learners are situated centrally in the statement made by Houle. As adult educators, we are called to address the needs and aspirations of learners. We want to address the imperfections and inadequacies in the systems that have negated opportunity for adults. We want to see families, social and civic organizations, communities, and places of employment thrive. More importantly, most adult educators are driven by a desire to improve life circumstances for adult learners through learning opportunities. The challenges associated with ensuring equitable access, encouraging full participation, and providing the appropriate type of support often create an imperfect system for adult learners throughout the world.

The issues of access, participation, and support are somewhat nebulous across the field of adult and continuing education. This chapter will attempt to provide historical context for each term; yet more importantly, recent research findings and evidence-based practices that support adult learners as they attempt to fully engage in learning opportunities in various contexts will be described. Broadly speaking, international statistics on participation rates, for example, generated through the Organisation for Economic Co-operation and Development's (OECD) Programme on the International Assessment of Adult Competencies (PIAAC; OECD, 2013) divides adult education and training into formal and nonformal education and training programs and activities (Desjardins, 2017). While formal learning opportunities tend to be credential-based and nonformal opportunities not necessarily so, both types of learning take place in organized and structured contexts (Colley et al., 2003). This is in contrast to informal learning, which tends to take place in nonstructured contexts and can be either intentional or nonintentional on the learner's part. More specific typologies of education and training have been developed by a number of scholars. For example, Myers et al. (2014) distinguished among (a) foundational learning, (b) higher education, (c) workplace-related learning, (d) other labor market–related learning, and (e) personal/social learning. Desjardins (2017) distinguished among (a) adult basic and general education, (b) adult higher education, (c) adult vocational education, and (d) adult liberal education.

Boeren (2016) developed a typology of learning opportunities that are specifically available for low-qualified adults in a European context and which included the following categories: (a) basic skills and basic education, (b) second-chance education at upper secondary levels, (c) postsecondary vocational education and training (VET), (d) apprenticeships, (e) training that forms part of active labor market policies, (f) workplace or job-related learning, and (g) personal or social learning. Several similar categories can be identified in the United States. While these different categories are important to further guarantee that suitable learning opportunities are available for everyone, statistics are more difficult to generate for each of these different types of education and training. Therefore, statistical evidence presented in this chapter will relate to formal and nonformal education and training.

Participation in Adult Education

Participation in the adult education context refers to the act of taking part in a learning activity. This does not necessarily mean that the adult learner will automatically learn a wide range of new skills or knowledge; instead, it refers to being enrolled in a course or other type of learning activity. As such, the first step in a participation process is for the adult to access an adult education course. It is important that adult educators distinguish between these two actions—enrolling and learning—on the part of the adult learner. Many policy efforts and adult learning initiatives assume that enrollment equates to taking part in a learning activity, but many adult learners enroll in programs yet never attend—for a variety of reasons, including fear, unanticipated barriers, and life events.

Efforts to expand adult learning access and opportunity are documented through Congressional efforts toward policy articulation and program development in the United States. The early development of government-supported adult education dates from the early 20th century within the U.S. Office of Education with an effort to promote lifelong learning among Americans and to assist with solving many of the problems experienced by citizens at that time. The passage of the Adult Education Act in 1966 created a larger role in adult education by the federal government. Initial federal investments focused on general services and training programs such as occupational training, on-the-job training, and cooperative extension. However, the emphasis of federal investments in adult education soon shifted to adult basic education for English literacy and basic skills instruction targeted at immigrants, unemployed, and undereducated adults. Programs to stimulate economic growth were then established in the 1960s (e.g., the Area Redevelopment Act and Manpower Development and Training Act). Youth employment and demonstration projects were added in 1977 (Eyre & Pawloski, 2014).

While these programs and initiatives represent the long-standing strategic investment of the federal government to support adult education programs for the citizenry, they are silent as to the issue on the specific learning of the adults enrolled in education. Title II of the Workforce Investment Act of 1998 provided for the development of the National Reporting System for Adult Education. That was the first effort to measure and document learning outcomes of adult learners in federally supported adult education programs in the United States.

Closely aligned to these efforts is the General Educational Development (GED) test which is used to determine adults' attainment of the knowledge and skills associated with high school completion. The GED was developed in the 1940s as a means to credential servicemen who had not completed high school prior to enlisting in the armed services—a not-uncommon occurrence in those days. Arguably, the most substantial changes to the GED occurred in 2011 when it was redeveloped. The new version of the GED includes both a High School Equivalency (HSE) level and a College and Career Readiness (CCR) level. The HSE means that GED credential earners have greater opportunities for postsecondary admission, job training, and entry-level jobs. The CCR level ensures that individuals at this performance level are ready for entry-level and credit-bearing courses, or job training programs, or somewhat more advanced jobs than HSE holders (GED Testing Service, 2019).

Another recent occurrence in the United States is the development of various Promise Programs in which individual states provide college tuition to qualified high school graduates. One of the best-known programs is the Tennessee Promise. Another program, Tennessee Reconnect (Tennessee Reconnect, n.d.), provides funding for qualified adult learners wanting to return to college or to enroll in a career- or vocational-training program. These "promise" programs provide last dollar funding for tuition after other forms of financial assistance have been applied. Such financial support eliminates one of the principal barriers to access and participation. Some programs also include additional support systems for adult learners. For example, Dallas County Promise, based in Dallas, Texas, assigns a navigator to help students manage the transition to college. This program also includes Parent Promise, which assists parents of recent high school graduates and encourages them to also pursue further education and training (Dallas County Promise, 2018).

Barriers to Participation

The seminal work of Cross (1981) provides a framework for understanding the various institutional, situational, and dispositional barriers faced by adult learners when accessing adult education and the kinds of support—institutional, situational, and dispositional—that they may obtain. Cross's work was related to the rise of the learning society (Cross, 1981) and the commensurate growth that must occur in adults due to the demographic, social, and technological changes in society. Cross developed the chain-of-response model, which explored the underlying mechanisms of adults' participation in adult learning programs and activities. Central to supporting adult learners' growth and development was the understanding of three particular barriers that many adult learners experience. Those barriers are:

- *institutional barriers* that are a result of the "practices and procedures that exclude or discourage working adults from participating in educational activities such as inconvenient schedules or locations, fulltime fees for part-time study, inappropriate courses of study, and so forth" (p. 98);
- *situational barriers* "arising from one's situation in life at a given time such as job and home responsibilities" (p. 98); and
- *dispositional barriers* "related to attitudes and self-perceptions about oneself as a learner" (p. 98).

It is important that adult and continuing education organizations and educators be cognizant of and able to recognize and respond to the different barriers experienced by adults. However, organizations cannot (and should not) assume responsibility for mitigating all barriers for adult learners. Arguably, institutions should be encouraged to lower their own barriers as much as possible. However, situational and dispositional barriers are often present among adults regardless of their potential interactions with adult education institutions. While support for the adult learner is important to mitigating these barriers, institutions should be careful to not rob the adult learner of their personal agency and autonomy and important opportunities for personal growth. Personal development is often realized through mitigation of situational and dispositional barriers (Deggs, 2018).

A relationship between life mission and adult learning was found in a study by Kroth and Boverie (2000). Within this study, the term *life mission* was developed "as the set of assumptions that each person holds about his or her life purpose, reason for being, and what he or she is to do with life" (Kroth & Boverie, 2000, p. 135). A stronger and more focused life mission can be related to both focused self-direction and motivation to learn. Adult educators must demonstrate genuine devotion to adult learners' growth to promote the development of a student-centered learning environment. A recent study was conducted of adult higher education participation in 13 European nations with low, medium, and high levels of adult participation in higher education. A study by Saar et al. (2014) provided three recommendations for education policies in support of adult learners. These recommendations are shorter duration programs of study; classes offered at times other than evenings and weekends, including distance education options; and a student financial aid system that matches adult student needs that has less restrictive policies for education grants and loans (Saar et al., 2014). The Kroth et al. and Saar et al. studies suggest that adult learner participation, especially in higher education, must be designed to focus on adult learners needs, specifically fulling one's own life mission, and coupled with institutional efforts to meet adult learner needs for time, course delivery, and financing.

The complexity of modern society can itself create barriers to participation for adult learners. Merriam and Bierema (2014) cite four factors that they deem important to understanding the context of adult learning in modern society. These factors are globalization, the knowledge society, technology, and changing demographics. Globalization refers to "the movement of goods, services, people and ideas across national borders" (p. 2). Knowledge society represents the necessity that knowledge be "weighed, organized, and structured into meaningful units of knowledge" (p. 4). Technology, which Merriam and Bierema state cannot be separated from globalization and knowledge society, is changing "how we work, carry out daily lives, and interact with other people" (p. 5). Finally, changing demographics include growth in aging populations worldwide, movement of people across borders, and increased ethnic and cultural diversity. When considering issues of equity and access for adult learners—specifically that adult learners tend to be White, middle-class, employed, younger, and better educated than nonparticipants are (Boeren, 2016)—the factors identified by Merriam and Bierema become more concerning given that adult education systems need to provide learning opportunities that are agile enough to accommodate the needs of all adult learners.

Unequal Access to Adult Education

The degree to which adult education programs address adult learners' needs and, thus, the greater needs of society should be further examined, especially when considering issues of adult learners' participation and access to adult education. The literature on participation in adult learning has documented that the majority of participants are White, middle-class, employed, younger, and better educated than are nonparticipants (Boeren, 2016). Employment-related reasons tend to dominate why adults participate in continuing education (Merriam et al., 2012). As such, participation has been discussed in relation to the Matthew principle (Boeren, 2009). That is, those who have already obtained the strongest positions in society are more likely to profit from additional participation in education and training. They receive more opportunities through access to adult education and through employer support and better understand how to navigate the existing adult education infrastructure. As such, while participation is meant to provide adults with new opportunities, it runs the risk of widening rather than narrowing the inequality gaps in society.

Worldwide, there is unequal access to adult education and social background remains an indirect influencer of participation in education by adults. To resolve this problem, policymakers and advocates should seek to "undermine the link between social background and initial educational attainment" in an effort to promote equal participation (Cincinnato et al., 2016, p. 159). Utilizing data from the PIAAC, Patterson (2018) found that most determinants of participation are situational and most nonparticipants often work in personal service, building trades, metal and machinery trades, or are truck drivers and mobile plant operators. The biggest skill deficit among nonparticipants was for numeracy skills (i.e., everyday math skills).

Differences in access to adult education is understood to result, in part, from decisions made by different governments about how they should invest their education budgets. Typically, Northern European countries are social-democratic welfare states that have strong levels of social protection in place. These countries also have high participation rates in adult education (OECD, 2013). U.S. participation rates for adult education are not as high as in the European Nordic countries, but tend to be higher than in many other regions of the world. Gender differences tend to be small but favor men in relation to nonformal education, but not for formal education. Younger adults participate more in education and training than do older adults. Those under the age of 24 who are still in college are excluded from the formal adult education and training statistics. Employers are more likely to invest in training of their younger employees because of the longer time span available for return on investments. Young adults are also more likely to invest in their education for the same reason. The observation that nonformal education is strongly job related is confirmed by the U.S. PIAAC data. Those adults who did not have a job in the previous 5 years are much less likely to have participated in work-related training. Their participation rates are also lower in formal education. Those adults who already obtained high levels of education and skills training are the most likely to pursue more education and training.

Migrants and nonnative speakers of English tend to struggle in the workplace. Many may possess foreign qualifications but have difficulties carrying out work-related tasks in English. These individuals also have lower participation rates in nonformal education. However, their participation rates in formal education (i.e., taking English as a second language courses) are slightly higher compared to those whose first language is English.

Understanding Inequalities in Access to Adult Education

In an effort to understand the impact of social and human capital on lifelong learning, Knipprath and De Rick (2015) found that social capital seems to encourage low-qualified adults to find jobs with learning opportunities. However, human capital has a stronger impact on predicting access to adult education than does social capital. Billett (2002) investigated how adults engage in workplace pedagogy to develop expert vocational practice through work and throughout their working lives. Billett found that individuals' sense of personal agency impacted how they decide to participate in workplace activities that impact the nature and quality of their learning. Billett argued that workplace pedagogy must also account for cultural, social, and situational factors among participants. As the findings of these studies suggest, adult educators and policy advocates should be careful to look more holistically at the adult learner and understand the intricate connection between social and human capital and how workplace learning is influenced by these two forces. Many programs do not consider the influence of adult learners' dispositions and their willingness to actively engage in learning—much less their retention and continued success in an education or training program.

Understanding of the complexity of the individual when it comes to accessing and succeeding in learning is an important consideration for any adult educator and policy advocate. Perna (2006) offered a conceptual framework for student college choice. While the model was confined to college choice (a choice that is clearly not available to all adults), it does speak to the various contexts that adult learners must traverse to access adult and continuing education or higher education programs. Perna's model describes four layers that represent a complex system for educational programs. These layers are also common to adult education systems and are manifested and impacted through individual attributes, the context of education providers, the delivery system itself, and finally, social, economic and policy context. The four layers of the mode, according to Perna, include:

1. the individual's habitus (e.g., demographic characteristics, cultural and social capital);
2. school and community context (e.g., available resources coupled with structural supports and barriers);
3. higher education context (e.g., institutions' marketing and recruitment efforts, location and characteristics); and
4. social, economic, and policy context (e.g., demographic, economic, and public policy characteristics).

Perna (2006) explained that human capital is the central focus of the model and that both monetary and nonmonetary benefits are to be gained through college access and completion. The role of human capital and its impact on the choice to both attend and engage in learning is addressed through Perna's model. This framework is applicable to adult and continuing education programs, as the adult learner's sense of self is often in conflict with the previous educational institution or community context. It is these conflicts that may lead to enrollment in further lifelong learning because adult learners are motivated by the challenges that are often associated with a lack of education and the ability to participate fully in all life activities, especially those associated with job attainment and advancement. The influence of the social, economic, and policy contexts is also addressed by the Perna model. Adult educators can benefit from examining this model and understanding the role of the adult learner, their previous education and community, new learning opportunities, and various social, economic, and policy influences that may shape opportunities for participation. Examination of access and participation in adult and continuing education through these various layers could serve to address the issues related to active learning participation in learning programs.

Support for Adult Education Programs

The literature on adult learner support is rather consistent regardless of the types of education and training programs that adults pursue. For example, a study by King and Lawler (1998) indicated that not all adult learners in higher education experience support in the same way. Although supportive services may be provided, this does not mean that all adult learners will perceive these services as necessarily supportive of their needs. King and Lawler's research also suggested that some adult learners find greater support among fellow classmates than from faculty or staff. In the context of participation in adult basic education programs, Gregg (2012) identified two issues that impact the success of those adult learners with disabilities (i.e., cognitive, intellectual, physical, sensory). These issues are, first, access to assessment for learning disabilities as an adult student and, second, the ability to strategically utilize provided accommodations. Gregg also underscored the importance of technology-based accommodations for adults having one or more identified disabilities. Among the barriers to participation for those who wanted to participate in adult and continuing education are the lack of time due to family or work commitments and the costs of attendance. This is in line with previous evidence from the literature (Boeren, 2016).

Directions for the Future

The efforts of adult educators and policy advocates to promote adult learner access, support, and participation in adult and continuing education are complicated by many issues. Most salient are the factors identified by Merriam and Bierema (2014): globalization, the information society, technology, and changing demographics. While some efforts have increased adults' participation, data suggest that those who frequently access, receive support, and engage as full participants in adult and continuing education are those who were successful in other educational programs, particularly White, middle-class, employed, younger, and better educated than nonparticipants (Boeren, 2016). Given the evidence outlined in the literature, adult educators and policy advocates should revisit the protocols and practices that are designed to facilitate access and support that lead to engaged participation in adult learners.

Recommendations

The following recommendations are provided to assist adult educators and policy advocates in their efforts to create a more equitable and accessible system for adult and continuing education programs:

1. Recognize that a one-size-fits-all approach cannot be applied to facilitate access, develop and deliver support systems, or promote active learner engagement. There should be varied approaches based upon individuals' economic, social, and cultural needs. Adult and continuing education programs must continue to strive to develop personalized programs that are more accessible and supportive of adult learners' needs. The shifting demographics of participants (e.g., age differences and increased diversity) should inform these efforts.
2. Initiatives to make adult and continuing education more accessible through the use of technology (e.g., online courses) and flexible scheduling of courses should be encouraged. Government agencies should also provide tuition assistance to adult learners.
3. There should also be renewed consideration given to how adult and continuing education programs operate within both formal and nonformal education settings. Participation should also be carefully considered given that individuals' motivation, especially those associated with life mission, will vary across the two domains. A more diversified and sophisticated understanding of the different types of adult education provisions will make it easier to provide targeted interventions to lower barriers in a tailor-made way.
4. Globalization will continue to influence participation in adult and continuing education because adult learners will not be bound to the borders and boundaries of countries. Adult educators and policy advocates should seek new ways to engage adults in meaningful education programs that prepare them to be competitive in a knowledge society. Such engagement will require innovative and novel ways to expand program access in a world where technology continues to facilitate access and create new means of support.

Adult and continuing education as a field of practice has a long-standing commitment to addressing imperfections or inadequacies in people, institutions, and communities. Such efforts have often been blind to issues that negate access, support, and participation among adult learners in formal, informal, and nonformal education programs. Issues of access, participation, and support cannot be decoupled from external forces that impact adult and continuing education programs, such as globalization, technological enhancements, and shifting demographics. Adult educators must experiment with methods to reconcile the needs of adult learners, specifically those associated with access, support, and participation with the social, cultural, and human capital influences. Such efforts recognize that technology will facilitate learning, learning will be enriched through diversity of experiences, and learning will continue to be expanded to more formal and nonformal settings.

References

Billett, S. (2002). Toward a workplace pedagogy: Guidance, participation, and engagement. *Adult Education Quarterly, 53*(1), 27–43.

Boeren, E. (2009). Adult education participation: The Matthew principle. *Filosofija-sociologija, 20*(2), 154–161.

Boeren, E. (2016). *Lifelong learning participation in a changing policy context: An interdisciplinary theory.* Palgrave Macmillan.

Cincinnato, S., De Wever, B., Van Keer, H., & Valcke, M. (2016). The influence of social background on participation in adult education: Applying the cultural capital framework. *Adult Education Quarterly, 66*(2), 143–168.

Colley, H., Hodkinson, P., & Malcolm, J. (2003). *Formality and informality in learning.* Learning and Skills Research Centre.

Cross, K. P. (1981). *Adults as learners: Increasing participation and facilitating learning.* Jossey-Bass.

Dallas County Promise. (2018). *Parent Promise FAQs.* http://dallascountypromise.org/about

Deggs, D. (2018). What college presidents should know about adult learners in higher education. *Journal for Research on the College President, 18*(2), 10–13.

Desjardins, R. (2017). *Political economy of adult learning systems: Comparative study of strategies, policies and constraints.* Bloomsbury.

Eyre, G. A., & Pawloski, R. (2014). *Federal adult education: A legislative history 1964–2013.* NOVA Research.

GED Testing Service (2019). *Update on outcomes & adoption of college ready levels: Learn how to advocate for GED Grads.* GED Testing Service Conference. https://ged.com/wp-content/uploads/Update-On-Outcomes-and-College-Ready-Adoption.pdf

Gregg, N. (2012). Increasing access to learning for the adult basic education learner with learning disabilities: Evidence-based accommodation research. *Journal of Learning Disabilities, 45*(1), 47–63.

Houle, C. O. (1992). *The literature of adult education: A bibliographic essay.* Jossey-Bass.

King, K. P., & Lawler, P. A. (1998). Institutional and individual support of growth among adult learners. *New Horizons in Adult Education and Human Resource Development, 12*(1), 4–11.

Knipprath, H., & De Rick, K. (2015). How social and human capital predict participation in lifelong learning: A longitudinal data analysis. *Adult Education Quarterly, 65*(1), 50–66.

Kroth, M., & Boverie, P. (2000). Life mission and adult learning. *Adult Education Quarterly, 50*(2), 134–149.

Merriam, S. B., & Bierema, L. L. (2014). *Adult learning: Linking theory and practice.* John Wiley.

Merriam, S. B., Caffarella, R. S., & Baumgartner, L. M. (2012). *Learning in adulthood: A comprehensive guide.* John Wiley.

Myers, K., Conte, N., & Rubenson, K. (2014). *Adult learning typology: adult learning and returns to training project.* Ottawa: Social Research and Demonstration Cooperation.

OECD. (2013). *Program for the International Assessment of Adult Competencies (PIAAC).* OECD.

Patterson, M. B. (2018). The forgotten 90%: Adult non-participation in education. *Adult Education Quarterly, 68*(1), 41–62.

Perna, L. W. (2006). Studying college access and choice: A proposed conceptual model. In J. C. Smart (Ed.), *Higher education: Handbook of theory and research* (Vol. 21, pp. 99–157). Springer.

Saar, E., Täht, K., & Roosalu, T. (2014). Institutional barriers for adults' participation in higher education in thirteen European countries. *Higher Education, 68*(5), 691–710.

Tennessee Reconnect. (n.d.). *Get started.* https://www.tnreconnect.gov/

CHAPTER 11

Mentoring in Adult and Continuing Education

Geleana D. Alston and Catherine A. Hansman

Mentoring relationships are essential to adult learning and development (Alston, 2014; Caffarella, 1993; Daloz, 2004; Galbraith & Cohen, 1995; Hansman, 2000, 2002; Merriam, 1983). Mentoring has been described as a form of professional support that leads to knowledge generation (Simmie & Moles, 2012) and tends "to involve a supportive relationship between a less experienced individual and a more experienced individual" (Alston, 2014, p. 10). Mentoring relationships have been described as "intense caring relationships" (Caffarella, 1993, p. 38) and as focusing on skill building and knowledge acquisition (Merriam, 1983). Kram (1983) discusses mentors as persons with more experience working with a less experienced person within the same organization, providing guidance and support for career development. Mentoring relationships occur in various adult and continuing education contexts (e.g., workplace learning, community education, higher education, continuing professional education, etc.), processes (formal versus informal), and anticipated outcomes (career enhancement, psychosocial development, personal growth and development). Adult learners, adult educators, and those who plan educational experiences for adults recognize that mentoring may be "integral to learning in the workplace [and in other formal and informal learning contexts], to receiving career help, and for developmental and psychosocial support" (Hansman, 2000, p. 494).

The purpose of this chapter is to focus on the continuing significance of mentoring to the field of adult and continuing education, extending and updating Hansman's (2000) chapter on mentoring published in the Wilson and Hays (2000) *Handbook of Adult and Continuing Education*. Specifically, the intention of this chapter is to expand the understandings and frameworks of mentoring and how they are embedded within many adult and continuing education contexts. The chapter begins with a brief review of mentoring relationships, complexities, power relationships, and mentoring models that frame mentoring in formal and informal adult education contexts. In the conclusion, we explore current and potential future mentoring challenges, issues, and research opportunities.

Forms of Mentorship

Levinson et al.'s (1978) research brought mentoring to scholarly attention while promoting mentoring as a process to help young men's career growth and personal development. Their work exemplified early research on mentoring, which focused on men's, and mostly White men's, career development. However, Kram's (1983) research examined both men's and women's mentoring relationships and categorized mentors as providing two types of developmental support to their protégés, psychosocial or career-related.

Psychosocial mentors "provide role models that may enhance protégés' esteem and self-confidence but may not necessarily provide them with career-related help . . . career-related mentors might also support the protégés' self-esteem and self-confidences, but in addition may provide career-related help" (Hansman, 2000, p. 495). The terms *mentoring* and *coaching* are sometimes used interchangeably when describing helping relationships in which learners engage; however, like Hobson (2012), we argue that mentoring is a broad term that describes overall helpful learning relationships, while coaching is one of many activities in which mentors may engage. Mentors may use coaching behaviors to help support individuals developing specific job-related skills. Both psychosocial and career-related mentors may support their protégés in informal or formal mentoring constructs.

Informal Mentoring

In their research on young university male students, Levinson et al. (1978) viewed their informal mentoring relationships as "one of the most complex and developmentally good relationships . . . a man [*sic*] can have in early adulthood" (p. 97), describing mentors as sponsoring, supporting, and teaching their protégés. Their description of mentors and protégés frame understandings of informal mentoring relationships, where there is no formal matching process, but rather mentors and protégés choose each other through mutual interests, or mentors may choose to work with a specific protégés. Informal mentoring does not follow a set structure, but relationships develop organically around the interests and goals of the protégés and mentors, and they may be especially effective if the organization's cultural norms and values support employee development (Hansman, 2000, 2002). Nevertheless, there are also weaknesses inherent in informal mentoring relationships, such as differing expectations of mentors and protégés that may cause discord; further, since there is no formal agreement between those involved, there can be little accountability for constructive interactions or learning outcomes.

Formal Mentoring

Organizations frequently develop formal mentoring programs for career development for employees (Galbraith & Cohen, 1995), planned by organizations and educational institutions to provide opportunities that potential protégés may encounter in forming mentoring relationships due to their race, class, gender, sexuality, age, or abilities (Hansman, 2000, 2002, 2016). In formal mentoring relationships, mentors and protégés may be assigned to each other through a matching process around the potential mentors' and protégés' career goals and interests. The conditions for effective formal mentoring include protégés' willingness to be mentored, organizational support for mentoring programs, effective mentor selection and pairing processes, preparing and training mentors, and designing effective mentoring strategies (Hobson, 2012). In his research concerning formal mentoring programs, Cohen (1995) identified six behavioral functions or strategies for mentors, beginning with relationship building and information sharing, then adopting a facilitative and confrontive focus to encourage protégés to reflect and engage in alternative thinking. Cohen further described mentors as modeling behaviors for protégés to adopt, as well as helping them develop future initiatives for independent growth and learning. Typically, the expectations and goals for mentoring relationships are clearly outlined and measured by the sponsoring organization or institution (Hansman, 2000, 2002).

Although formal mentoring relationships can provide opportunities for mentoring to those who may not otherwise have them, they can also "lead to mechanistic goal and outcomes rather than allowing mentors and protégés to build personal and professional relationships that might further careers or accomplish personal and professional goals" (Hansman, 2016, p. 101). Indeed, Mullen (2012) cautions that mandated formal mentoring programs have the potential to turn mentoring into a mere achievement measure for organizations or schools, rather than focusing on the psychosocial and career development of the protégés. Another concern is how protégés are chosen to participate in programs; although the process may seem to be democratic, selection criteria may include selecting the "best" employees to participate, which may exclude some members of marginalized groups from participating. In addition, mentors may be chosen from those who represent the majority group within the organization and the dominant organizational culture and values, meaning that those who hold diverse views may not become mentors (Hansman, 2000, 2002, 2012). Hegemonic cultural values thus may be passed along to the next generation, with the result that some groups may never get to participate in formal mentoring programs.

Framing Mentoring Relationships

Given that mentoring is seen as integral to learning in the workplace and adult continuing and higher education, scholars have focused on mentoring from the perspective of teaching, learning, and adult development.

Adult Development and Learning

Regardless of the context of mentoring relationships, mentors often assume various roles, such as friend, confidant, coach, adviser, and role model, to assist in enhancing their protégés' professional, personal, and psychological development. Daloz (2004) claims the goal of effective mentoring for adult educators is to foster the development of adult learners through

> an increase in the ability to perceive and hold complexity, to tolerate ambiguity, to experience one's own and others' feelings more richly, to see oneself and others in a broader context, and to make wholehearted commitments in a complex, tentative, and interdependent world. (p. 452)

Mentoring is at the crux of the pivotal moment where adult learning and development might intersect, and mentoring relationships can potentially promote critical reflection and transformative learning among all persons involved in the relationship (Taylor et al., 2000). Learning theories and models add to our understandings of mentoring relationships, such as transformative learning, self-directed learning, constructivism, critical-constructivist perspective, cognitive apprenticeships, and communities of practice (Hansman, 2014, 2016). It is difficult to discuss mentoring in adult and continuing education without acknowledging that perhaps there is an interdependent relationship between mentors and protégés that may lead to learning and development for both. For instance, Larson (2009) explored the life stories of individuals to learn how people become mentors, the motivational forces associated with mentoring, and their attitudes about exceptional mentoring. In a like manner, others have explored mentoring adult learners with the mentor as teacher or facilitator in mind. Zachary (2002) placed emphasis on the role of teacher as mentor as she encouraged the following:

> As we engage in mentoring, we bring our own cycle, our own timetable, our own history, our own individuality, and our own ways of doing things to each relationship. For learning to occur, we must understand who we are, what we bring, and what our mentoring partner brings to the relationship. We must understand the ebb and flow of the learning process. (p. 37)

While Zachary's perspective is appreciated, we caution that since mentoring is grounded in theories of adult learning, then both the mentor and mentee are adult learners involved in a partnership of iterative learning and development (Alston, 2014).

Possible Selves

From a different perspective, mentoring relationships may be influential in the learning process to help individuals recognize their potential—realize their possible selves. For example, Fletcher's (2007) research explored how mentors who include the possible-selves construct (Markus & Nurius, 1986; Ruvolo & Markus, 1992) to frame mentoring relationships can offer assistance with the personal and professional growth of protégés. Fletcher's (2007) premise is that "the realization of possible selves occurs in a social dialogic context" (p. 76) because "the emergence of possible selves is a deep, rich learning experience for all involved" (p. 85). With specific regard to mentoring, the mentor's and mentee's "repertoire of possible selves is not just any assortment of roles or identities that one can imagine, but includes only those possible selves that are psychologically accessible and personally meaningful" within the mentoring relationship (Rossiter, 2007, p. 6). With this in mind, the notion of possible selves can serve as a conduit between current interactions and desired interactions between mentors and protégés within mentoring relationships.

Incorporating 21st-Century Technology: Ementoring

With the advent of technology, electronic communications support developing and sustaining mentoring relationships (Single & Muller, 2001). Guy (2002) was one of the first scholars in the field of adult and continuing education to explore the "the online or electronic version of mentoring" (p. 34). Bierema and Merriam (2002) discussed the conceptual framework for ementoring as a "computer mediated, beneficial relationship between mentor and a protégé which provides learning, advising encouraging, promoting, and modelling" (p. 214). Cyber-mentoring, ementoring, or virtual mentoring typically involves interactions between the mentor and mentee via email, instant messaging, audio and video conferencing, or online discussion boards (Guy, 2002).

In addition, Bierema and Merriam (2002) viewed ementoring as more egalitarian and less bounded by traditional expectations than face-to-face mentoring relationships. Burgess (2007), in explaining her perspective on how mentoring can be utilized as an effective instructional online tool in workplace learning and in adult, continuing, and higher education, placed emphasis on how mentoring can be most beneficial to "students new to both the academic program and the online delivery environment or are members of historically disadvantage groups" (p. 50). She suggested that online instructors acknowledge that students need attention and nurturing beyond their technical skills and focus on their professional development.

Other scholars have specifically focused on ementoring in doctoral education and other contexts. Columbaro (2009) and Columbaro and Hansman (2014) conducted literature reviews to gain better understandings about current and future possibilities of ementoring for doctoral students in online degree programs as they prepare to enter the professoriate after graduation. Based on her findings, Columbaro (2009) suggests that ementoring assists online doctoral degree students to successfully negotiate the "virtual college environment while focusing on the intricacies of working within higher education and in one's field" (p. 13). Columbaro (2014) recommended that mentors be taught to mentor in online environments. King's (2016) flexible model of online doctoral mentoring addresses this need to teach mentors best practices for ementoring while leveraging online learning management systems, as it couples practical applications with adult learning theories so mentors can facilitate students through the dissertation process while addressing the 21st-century skills needed for virtual engagement.

Workplace learning/professional development programs also recognize that ementoring has the potential to create an additional space wherein learning, growth and professional development occur. For example, in the medical professions nurse practitioners develop professional networks that provide mutually beneficial interactions for them to address their professional development through both face-to-face and electronic means (Goolsby, 2017). In Australia, beginning public health advocates participate in an ementoring program with more experienced public health advocates to engage in knowledge and skill-building activities, resulting in a stronger public health workforce (Connell et al., 2016). Similarly, a study of midwives in New Zealand found that ementoring provides an alternate to conventional face-to-face mentoring, offering a way for midwives to reflect and debrief about specific cases, gain information concerning clinical practice, and discuss professional issues (Stewart, 2006).

Power Dynamics and Cultural Characteristics

Mentoring is relational and involves power that is socially constructed and sustained (Alston, 2014; 2016; Hansman, 2002; Johnson-Bailey & Cervero, 2004); therefore, consideration of power dynamics within these relationships is necessary. Mentoring relationships are never politically neutral and power-free, but instead reflect the complicated worlds in which adults live, learn, work, and the power and interests that frame these contexts. By virtue of their positions, mentors have power that they can employ to be helpful or hurtful to their protégés, illustrating that "the biggest paradox surrounding mentoring relationships is that although mentors seek to 'empower' their protégés, the relationships themselves are entrenched with power issues" (Hansman, 2002, pp. 45–46). Mentoring relationships require negotiation of power and interests of mentors, protégés, and the hosting institutions or organizations. Further, they may reinforce the norms within organizations or cultures by replicating the binary structures that purposely exist to sustain the power structures; however, mentoring relationships can intentionally seek to disrupt these power structures to make the organization and culture more equitable (Mott, 2002).

Cross-cultural mentoring relationships may also challenge power dynamics and present obstacles to mentors and protégés (Alston, 2014). Alston explored the nature of the cross-cultural mentoring experiences between Black female faculty mentors and their White female doctoral student protégés, revealing that in addition to race, there are other characteristics (e.g., age and academic roles) that affect power within the mentoring relationship. The findings highlighted how the tension from the power dynamics may prevent learning about cultural differences and similarities.

Critiques of early research concerning mentoring addressed the lack of attention to race, gender, class, or other considerations that might impact the quality of mentoring relationships (Hansman, 2000; Stalker, 1994). Identities are based on socially constructed images and stereotypes used to describe cultures—entities of belonging—and our positionality helps us to answer the question, "Where do I reside, or not, in the culture based on my identity?" (Alston 2014, p. 72). Mentoring relationships may be enriching for some, but with specific consideration of identity and positionality they can also be problematic for "others." Unfortunately, many times "others" may include women and people of color whose ethnicity, race, class, gender, age, (dis)ability, or sexual orientation may not be reflective of the dominant culture within their organizations, leaving them with reduced opportunities to participate in mentoring relationships or with difficulties due to these factors.

Johnson-Bailey (2012) contended "discomfort in mentoring is also influenced by demographic differences, particularly race" (p. 156). Race can be applicable in informative and meaningful ways as a critical lens for reflecting and evaluating mentoring relationships and processes (Johnson-Bailey, 2012). Mentoring relationships are affected by the present sociopolitical environment grounded in the historical and continuing protection that perpetuates White privilege and power. Individuals should take this into consideration when participating in cross-racial mentoring relationships.

Feminist critiques of mentoring purposefully seek to confront the dominant discourse that conceived mentoring as hierarchical, even in all-female dyads (Cochran-Smith & Paris, 1995; DeMarco, 1993; Standing, 1999). Mejiuni (2009) contended that "we need to acknowledge the multiple identities, including gender and professional identities, and the identity politics that women bring into relationships, and the unconscious and hidden biases that individuals in mentoring relationships have about particular groups and individuals" (p. 277). Alston (2016) argued that the traditional conceptualization of mentoring consists of a "patriarchally influenced hierarchical structures grounded in superiority and inferiority with regard to the mentor and mentee, respectively" (p. 149). Within many adult and continuing education spaces, women often lack access to professional mentors to help them understand the unwritten rules of their professional or workplace culture (Castro et al., 2005). In the midst of the #MeToo era, understanding the mentoring experiences of women is critical, and an intentional scholarly effort to increase in understanding the ways in which women make meaning of their cross-gender mentoring relationships is warranted.

While scholars have explored the influence of age and lifelong learning in the workplace (Liu & Rees, 2001; Merriweather & Morgan, 2013; Reio & Sanders-Reio, 1999), the influence of age as a cultural characteristic is an understudied topic with regard to mentoring in adult and continuing education. In a qualitative study that explored the nature of cross-age mentoring relationships between female faculty mentors and their female doctoral students, the mentees' ages influenced the power dynamics within their mentoring relationships when the mentors were younger than the mentees (Alston, 2016). A mentor may initially be uncomfortable with mentoring someone older because the mentor's perception of the roles and functions of a mentor conflict with the mentor's culturally grounded perspective of respect for elders. For instance, within African American and Asian cultures, elders are to be highly respected, obeyed, and considered a source of wisdom (Alston, 2014). Additionally, the mentee may not respect or trust the expertise of a mentor that is younger in age due to the traditional conceptualization of age and mentoring. If we consider the intergenerational demographics within current-day contexts of adult and continuing education, perhaps the notion of younger mentors is not so uncommon after all but more so understudied.

Mentoring Models and Frameworks for Adult Learners

Various types of collaborative mentoring relationships aid in psychosocial and/or career growth for both mentors and protégés (Kram & Isabella, 1985) such as peer mentoring, communities of practice (CoP), phases, and networks.

Peer Mentoring

Peer mentoring dyads or groups develop through friendships among colleagues who mentor each other—peer to peer—while providing psychosocial support and development as well as career learning (Hansman, 2012, 2016), reflecting adult learning concepts and practices. Peer mentoring involves colleagues who share the same or similar roles or status in their lives or organizations supporting each other through sharing information and resources and providing feedback, assisting others in the peer or comentoring group to develop their skills, knowledge, and expertise. During these interactions, they may exchange roles as mentors and protégés, concepts known as *mentoring constellations* (van Emmerik, 2004) or *mentoring mosaics* (Mullen et al., 2010).

Peer communities have been found to provide strong mentoring support to those engaged in them (Hansman, 2012, 2016; Mullen, 2012), allowing members to form developmental networking relationships. For example, Cherrstrom et al. (2018) researched adult doctoral students who formed a peer community for support and learning, exploring how they built the community and further, how peers provided mentoring support to facilitate learning within the community. Using a conceptual framework of zone of proximal development (Vygotsky, 1978) and CoP (Wenger, 1998), they found that the members of the peer community "progressed through their zones of proximal development by building a CoP and providing reciprocal peer mentoring . . . and benefited from socialization, peer mentoring, scholarly discussion, and multiple perspectives" (p. 49).

Community of Peer Mentors

Framed by Wenger's (1998) concept of CoP, Hansman (2012, 2014) developed the community of peer mentors model to provide the space, time, and opportunities for participants (students) to engage in learning and development for their future careers. Members share power in decision-making, opportunities for individual and group critical reflection and discourse, and foster peer relationships with other participants to sustain them as they transition from students to professionals. There are five critical points within the interactive and nonhierarchical model: forming, connecting, engaging, concluding and new beginnings, and enduring networks. In each critical point, participants engage in problem-posing questioning activities that foster self and group critical reflection to further knowledge and understanding through peer support. Further, they engage in discourse and activities, such as peer teaching, peer reviews of writing, or mock interviews to develop and perhaps change their perceptions and actions related to these skills, collaboratively making decisions concerning other activities needed to gain pertinent knowledge and competences. Thus, through supportive one-to-one and peer and group mentoring relationships, community of peer mentors' critical points provides a network that supports participants as they learn skills and knowledge to prepare them for their future careers.

Mentoring Phases

Schunk and Mullen (2013) employed Kram's (1983, 1988) concepts of mentoring to advance a phased process model for mentoring. The four phases, developed from protégés' perspectives, are initiation, cultivation, separation, and redefinition. In the initiation phase, protégés engage in intense self-reflection to determine their strengths and weaknesses, the learning and skills goals they hope to accomplish, and the psychosocial and/or career support they hope their mentor(s) might provide. During cultivation, mentors and protégés engage in self-reflective wide-ranging discussions, discerning cultural differences, asking probing questions, and giving and receiving thoughtful and constructive feedback. Crow (2012) argued that cultivation requires mentors and protégés to commit to shared purposes that are beyond career or psychosocial support; the cultivation phase is where the "real" work of mentoring is accomplished, and it may be the most challenging phase for protégés and mentors as the most learning occurs during this phase.

The third phase, separation, marks the "beginning of the end" for mentoring relationships. The phase begins as protégés seek self-sufficiency and independence, resulting in less support from their mentors than they enjoyed during the cultivation phase. Mentors work with their protégés to make separation fruitful by engaging in less-intense learning activities, evaluating their work and celebrating their protégés' achievements. If mentors are supportive of their protégés growing independence, they may help their protégés feel self-confident about their abilities, lessening the intensity of the learning process while they evaluate their work together and celebrate their protégés' achievements. Although interacting less than previously, mentors can still continue to provide support through the separation phase by endorsing their protégés' careers in professional networks and organizations. The final phase, redefinition, requires mentors and protégés to consciously "redefine" their relationships, perhaps into more egalitarian friendships where they interact as peers. Mutual support and egalitarian respect frame the relationships. However, it is up to the mentors and protégés to redefine their relationship, and they may choose to disengage at this point.

Developmental Networks

Individuals are more likely to be successful in achieving their goals if they receive support from more than one person. Developmental networks are composed of multiple developers/mentors, chosen by protégés, who take active interests in protégés' goals and interests and assist with personal and professional growth. Since the protégés identify developers/mentors, the developmental network can transcend boundaries of particular organizations, bridging and perhaps even combining formal and informal mentoring networks (Chandler et al., 2016). The advantage of developmental networks is integrating, from various contexts, both formal (professional colleagues) and informal developers/mentors (friends, family members).

Several dimensions in developmental networks are essential to sustaining them. These dimensions include: strength of tie, referring to the frequency of communication that builds trust and rapport between the protégé and her or his developers; diversity, meaning any number of differences between the protégé and developers, including race, class, gender, sexuality, and age; diversity, which also encompasses the range of social spheres and identity groups evident in developmental networks; size, connotating how many developers are within the network; developmental initiation, which encompasses the developmental—seeking behaviors of the protégé; multiplexity, which is how mentors provide more than one type of support or play more than one role for the protégé (i.e., friend as well as colleague); and inner-outer core, developers who provide high psychosocial but less career development support (Chandler et al., 2016). Chandler et al. (2016) claimed that a "network of developers can, as a collective, act as holding environment for adult learning and development . . . that individuals engage in an active process of constructing reality . . . that individuals resolve through alternating periods of growth, stability, and change" (p. 9).

Conclusion

This chapter has provided a brief examination of mentoring relationships related to adult and continuing education. However, more research should be conducted to clarify and expand understandings of mentoring's role in fostering learning and development for protégés and their mentors. For instance, much of the research seems to focus on the perspectives of protégés while little attention is paid to how mentoring relationships may also support and positively impact the professional and personal development of mentors. Additionally, if we consider mentoring as embedded in theories of adult learning and development, we argue that it is problematic to label the mentor as the adult educator or facilitator and the protégé as the adult learner. Instead, mentors and protégés may take on both roles in mentoring relationships. A more equal, perhaps democratic, playing field in mentoring relationships, as some of the models we presented in this chapter demonstrated, may provide opportunities for learning and development for mentors as well as their protégés. To that end, both the mentor and protégé are adult learners involved in a partnership of iterative learning and development that has the potential to foster transformation. Technology and social media have created many more opportunities for mentoring relationships to develop, and it holds promise to open new understandings of virtually mentoring adult learners. Finally, future research should focus on not only formal mentoring but also informal mentoring relationships, as insight into the interactions among mentors, protégés, and peers within these relationships may provide important guidance for planning educational and professional development programs.

References

Alston, G. D. (2014). *Cross-cultural mentoring relationships in higher education: A feminist grounded theory study* [Doctoral dissertation]. Texas State University. https://digital.library.txstate.edu/handle/10877/4953

Alston, G. D. (2016). "She's younger than me": A new look at age and mentoring in doctoral education. In K. Peno, E. S. Mangiante, & R. Kenahan (Eds.), *Mentoring in formal and informal contexts* (pp. 137–154). Information Age.

Bierema, L., & Merriam, S. (2002). e-Mentoring: Using computer mediated communication to enhance the mentoring process. *Innovative Higher Education, 26*(3), 211–225.

Burgess, K. R. (2007). Mentoring as holistic online instruction. *New Directions for Adult and Continuing Education, 2007*(113), 49–56.

Caffarella, R. (1993). *Psychosocial development of women: Linkages to teaching and leadership in adult education*. Information Series No. 350 (ED354386). ERIC. https://eric.ed.gov/?id=ED354386

Castro, C., Caldwell, C., & Salazar, C. F. (2005). Creating mentoring relationships between female faculty and students in counselor education: Guidelines for potential protégés and mentors. *Journal of Counseling & Development, 83*, 331–336.

Chandler, D. E., Murphy, W. M., Kram, K. E., & Higgins, M. C. (2016). Bridging formal and informal mentoring: A developmental network perspective. In K. Peno, E. S. Mangiante, & R. Kenahan (Eds.), *Mentoring in formal and informal contexts* (pp. 1–22). Information Age.

Cherrstrom, C. A., Zarestky, J., & Deer, S. (2018). "This group is vital": Adult peers in community for support and learning. *Adult Learning, 29*(2), 43–52. https://doi.org/10.1177/7045159517739701

Cochran-Smith, M., & Paris, C. (1995). Mentor and mentoring: Did Homer have it right? In J. Smyth (Ed.), *Critical discourses on teacher development* (pp. 181–202). Cassell.

Cohen, N. H. (1995). *Mentoring adult learners*. Krieger.

Columbaro, N. L. (2009). e-Mentoring possibilities for online doctoral students: A literature review. *Adult Learning, 20*(3/4), 9–15.

Columbaro, N. L. (2014). *Paving the way toward faculty careers in higher education: Student mentoring relationship experiences while completing online doctoral degrees* [Doctoral dissertation]. Cleveland State University. https://etd.ohiolink.edu/pg_10?0::NO:10:P10_ETD_SUBID:110387

Columbaro, N. L., & Hansman, C. A. (2014, June 4–7). *Mentoring relationships and experiences in online doctoral education: Perceptions, reality, and action* [Paper presentation]. Adult Education Research Conference, Harrisburg, PA, United States. http://newprairiepress.org/aerc/2014/roundtables/8

Connell, E. O., Stoneham, M., & Saunders, J. (2016). Planning for the next generation of public health advocates: Evaluation of an online advocacy mentoring program. *Health Promotions Journal of Australia, 27*, 43–47.

Crow, G. M. (2012). A critical-constructivist perspective on mentoring and coaching for leadership. In S. J. Fletcher & C. A. Mullen (Eds.), *The SAGE handbook of mentoring and coaching in education* (pp. 228–242). SAGE.

Daloz, L. A. (2004). Mentorship. In M. W. Galbraith (Ed.), *Adult learning methods: A guide for effective instruction* (3rd ed., pp. 451–472). Krieger.

DeMarco, R. (1993). Mentorship: A feminist critique of current research. *Journal of Advanced Nursing, 18*(8), 1242–1250.

Fletcher, S. (2007). Mentoring adult learners: Realizing possible selves. *New Directions for Adult and Continuing Education, 2007*(114), 75–86.

Galbraith, M. W., & Cohen, N. H. (Eds.). (1995). Mentoring: New strategies and challenges [Themed issue]. *New Directions for Adult and Continuing Education, 1995*(66). https://doi.org/10.1002/ace.36719956601

Goolsby, M. J. (2017). Effective professional networking. *Journal of the American Association of Nurse Practitioners, 29*(8), 441–445.

Guy, C. A. (2002). Telementoring: Sharing mentoring relationships in the 21st century. In C. Hansman (Ed.), *Critical perspectives on mentoring: Trends and issues* (pp. 39–48) (ED99CO0013). ERIC. https://eric.ed.gov/?id=ED465045

Hansman, C. A. (2000). Formal mentoring programs. In A. L. Wilson & E. R. Hayes (Eds.), *Handbook of adult and continuing education* (pp. 493–507). Jossey-Bass.

Hansman, C. A. (2002). Diversity and power in mentoring relationships. In C. Hansman (Ed.), *Critical perspectives on mentoring: Trends and issues* (pp. 39–48) (ED99CO0013). ERIC. https://eric.ed.gov/?id=ED465045

Hansman, C. A. (2012). Empowerment in the faculty-student mentoring relationship. In C. Mullen & S. Fletcher (Eds.), *Handbook of mentoring and coaching in education* (pp. 368–382). SAGE.

Hansman, C. A. (2014). Mentoring in graduate education: Curriculum for transformative learning. In V. Wang & V. Bryan (Eds.), *Andragogical and pedagogical methods for curriculum development* (pp. 101–117). Information Age.

Hansman, C. A. (2016). Developing rewarding mentoring relationships in doctoral education: Models from research and practice. In K. Peno, E. Silva Mangiante, & R. Kenahan (Eds.), *Mentoring in formal and informal contexts* (pp. 97–118). Information Age.

Hobson, A. J. (2012). Fostering face-to-face mentoring and coaching. In C. Mullen & S. Fletcher (Eds.), *Handbook of mentoring and coaching in education* (pp. 59–73). SAGE.

Johnson-Bailey, J. (2012). Effects of race and racial dynamics on mentoring. In S. J. Fletcher & C. A. Mullen (Eds.), *The SAGE handbook of mentoring and coaching in education* (pp. 155–168). SAGE.

Johnson-Bailey, J., & Cervero, R. (2004). Mentoring in Black and White: The intricacies of cross-cultural mentoring. *Mentoring & Tutoring: Partnership in Learning, 12*(1), 7–21.

King, K. P. (2016). Facilitating the doctoral mentoring process in online learning environments. In K. Peno, E. S. Mangiante, & R. Kenahan (Eds.), *Mentoring in formal and informal contexts* (pp. 77–96). Information Age.

Kram, K. E. (1983). Phases of the mentoring relationship. *Academy of Management Journal, 26*, 609–625.

Kram, K. E. (1988). *Mentoring at work* (2nd ed.). University Press of America.

Kram, K. E., & Isabella, L. A. (1985). Mentoring alternatives: The role of peer relationships in career development. *Academy of Management Journal, 28*, 110–132.

Larson, L. L. (2009). *A study of exceptional mentoring insights for adult education and emerging mentors* [Doctoral dissertation]. National Louis University. http://digitalcommons.nl.edu/diss/8.

Levinson, D. J., Darrow, C. N., Kelin, E. B., Levinson, M. H., & McKee, B. (1978). *The seasons of a man's life*. Ballantine Books.

Liu S., & Rees, F. (2001). The roles of adult education workplace ageism. In V. Sheared & P. A. Sissel (Eds.), *Making space: Merging theory and practice in adult education* (pp. 138–152). Greenwood.

Markus, H. R., & Nurius, P. (1986). Possible selves. *American Psychologist, 41*, 954–969.

Mejiuni, O. (2009, November 18–20). Potential for transformative mentoring relationships among women in academia in Nigeria. In P. Cranton, E. Taylor, & J. Tyler (Eds.), *Proceedings of the Eighth International Transformative Learning Conference* (pp. 277–283). http://meridianuniversity.edu/images/tlc/proceedings/TLC2009%20Proceedings.pdf

Merriam, S. B. (1983). Mentors and protégés: A critical review of the literature. *Adult Education Quarterly, 33*, 161–173.

Merriweather, L. R., & Morgan, A. J. (2013). Two cultures collide: Bridging the generation gap in a nontraditional mentorship. *The Qualitative Report, 18*(6), 1–16. https://nsuworks.nova.edu/tqr/vol18/iss6/2

Mott, V. W. (2002). Emerging perspectives on mentoring: Fostering adult learning and development. In C. Hansman (Ed.), *Critical perspectives on mentoring: Trends and issues* (pp. 5–14) (ED99CO0013). ERIC. https://eric.ed.gov/?id=ED465045

Mullen, C. A. (2012). Mentoring: An overview. In C. Mullen & S. Fletcher (Eds.), *The SAGE handbook of mentoring and coaching in education* (pp. 7–23). SAGE.

Mullen, C. A., Fish, V. L., & Hutinger, J. L. (2010). Mentoring doctoral students through scholastic engagement: Adult learning principles in action. *Journal of Further and Higher Education, 24*, 179–197.

Reio, T. G., Jr., & Sanders-Reio, J. (1999). Combating workplace ageism. *Adult Learning, 11*, 10–13.

Rossiter, M. (2007). Possible selves: An adult education perspective. *New Directions for Adult and Continuing Education, 2007*(114), 5–15.

Ruvolo, A. P., & Markus, H. R. (1992). Possible selves, and performance: The power of self-relevant imagery. *Social Cognition, 10*(1), 95–124.

Schunk, D. H., & Mullen, C. A. (2013). Toward a conceptual model of mentoring research: Integration with self-regulated learning. *Educational Psychology Review, 25*(3), 361–389.

Simmie, G. M., & Moles, J. (2012). Educating the critically reflective mentor. In C. Mullen & S. Fletcher (Eds.), *The SAGE handbook of mentoring and coaching in education* (pp. 107–121). SAGE.

Single, P., & Muller, C. (2001). When email and mentoring unite: The implementation of a nationwide electronic mentoring program. In L. K. Stromei (Ed.), *Creating mentoring and coaching programs* (pp. 107–122). American Society for Training and Development.

Stalker, J. (1994). Athene in academe: Women mentoring women in the academy. *International Journal of Lifelong Education, 13*(5), 361–372.

Standing, M. (1999). Developing a supportive/challenging and reflective/competency education (SCARCE) mentoring model and discussing its relevance to nurse education. *Mentoring & Tutoring: Partnerships in Learning, 6*(3), 3–17.

Stewart, S. (2006). A pilot study of email in an e-mentoring relationship. *Journal of Telemedicine and Telecare, 12*, 83–88.

Taylor, K., Marienau, C., & Fiddler, M. (2000). *Developing adult learners: Strategies for teachers and trainers*. Jossey-Bass.

van Emmerik, I. J. H. (2004). The more you can get the better: Mentoring constellations and intrinsic career success. *Career Development International, 9*(6), 576–594.

Vygotsky, L. S. (1978). *Mind in society: The development of higher psychological processes*. Harvard University Press.

Wenger, E. (1998). *Communities of practice: Learning, meaning, and identity*. Cambridge University Press.

Wilson, A. L., & Hayes, E. (Eds.) (2000). *Handbook of adult and continuing education*. Jossey-Bass.

Zachary, L. J. (2002). The role of teacher as mentor. *New Directions for Adult and Continuing Education, 2002*(93), 27–38.

PART THREE

TEACHING PRACTICES AND ADMINISTRATIVE LEADERSHIP

CHAPTER 12

Organization and Administration of Adult and Continuing Education Programs

Susan M. Yelich Biniecki and Steven W. Schmidt

Organization and administration of adult and continuing education (ACE) programs is a distinct aspect of adult education. Also known as *program management*, it includes a variety of functions related to how ACE programs are structured, directed, and operated. The topics associated with *educational program management*, a term used to include the functions of administration and organization, are different from many other adult education topics for several reasons. Program administration is typically done on a level that can be far removed from instructors and learners, even though much of the focus of ACE programs is on instruction, individual learners, classroom methods, program planning, and related topics. The management of educational programs takes place at a level above the instructor or learner level, above the individual course, and sometimes above the program planning level. Organization and administration focus on the structure and management of a series of courses or educational programs. The overall management of a series of educational programs is quite different from the work educators do in teaching adult learners (Schmidt & Yelich Biniecki, 2016).

Another reason why educational program administration and organization is different from other adult education topics is because it combines two disciplines: business and education. In order to successfully manage adult education programs, one must understand business or management principles as well as adult education. The multidisciplinary nature of the topic does not fit neatly into either the education or business fields. Indeed, educational program managers need to know about many different topics in order to be successful in their work. To understand this concept more completely, consider some of the different functions within program organization and administration: methods of organization, leadership, administration, budgeting, funding and support, marketing, human resources, strategic planning, program evaluation, ethical issues, and legal issues (Schmidt & Yelich Biniecki, 2016).

Educational program management is multifaceted work that typically involves the simultaneous interplay of these topics. For example, marketing is affected by strategic planning, and strategic planning depends on an organization's budget and funding and support programs. Human resource–related tasks must be done with budgetary, organizational, and legal issues in mind. Ethical issues flow through every topic and leadership and administration can influence all other aspects of program management. Nothing related to program management happens in a vacuum, and many aspects of program organization and administration involve multiple variables and complex situations.

Educational program organization and administration is important to the field of ACE because successful programs are those that are organized effectively and managed well. Even the best educational programs will not be successful if they are not marketed correctly. The best curriculum will not meet the needs of learners if the wrong instructor is hired. The most well-intentioned programs will falter if the organization does not have the budget to run them or if there are too many similar programs in a given area. Even the most effective organizations can be negatively affected by missteps that result in legal problems or ethical dilemmas.

Conversely, effective educational programs can reach more people than expected if they are marketed appropriately. Program administrators may have many qualified applicants to choose from if they are known to provide a supportive environment for their instructors. Adult education organizations may be able to expand their course and program offerings if budgeting is done correctly. Effective strategic planning may result in previously unseen opportunities for adult education organizations to reach new groups of learners. Internally, organizations that are managed appropriately may see greater efficiencies within the organization as well as improvements in job satisfaction and employee retention.

This chapter starts with discussion of methods of program organization, followed by content on effective administration. Challenges for those in organization and administration are presented along with discussion of issues in practice and research. The chapter concludes with a summary.

Educational Program Organization

Organization or *organizing* is the assembling of resources necessary to attain objectives and the arranging of those resources into a purposeful order and structure (*Business Dictionary*, n.d.). It is the grouping of activities to attain goals and it provides the framework for things like accountability, authority, and responsibility (Bhattacharyya, 2009). Organization allows for both effectiveness and efficiency in program administration.

Program organization is the function of structuring or arranging programs in effective and efficient ways (Schmidt & Yelich Biniecki, 2016). Organizing programs effectively can make the administration of those programs more effective. The phrase "form follows function" is a principle used in architecture to mean that the design of something—like a building in the case of architecture—should be based on the intended purpose or use for that thing. In a similar vein, there should be commonalities or relationships between how an organization is structured and how its educational programs are organized. Programs can be organized in several different ways (123 Help Me, 2013).

When organizing by product line, all products of a similar nature are organized together. For example, a community center may offer a variety of courses for local residents. They may offer courses on fitness, nutrition, music, sports, hobbies, and a variety of other topics. All of the fitness courses, such as yoga, Pilates, and aerobics would be organized together.

Educational programs also can be organized within the categories of the learners or customers who take advantage of those programs. Organization by customer or learner segment allows the program organizer to focus specifically on the needs of a particular market. A community center in a large urban area might organize all courses targeted at immigrants in one area. The center may organize basic skills courses for young adults who are high-school dropouts together, as well, and they may organize courses for social learners, such as those that deal with knitting or book clubs, together.

However, sometimes it makes sense for all educational products offered to a group of learners in the same geographic area or territory to be organized together. This approach is somewhat similar to the organization by customer or market segment already noted, but it is different in that all programs for all customers in a particular geographic area are organized together, rather than segmented by specific market or group of learners. Organizations that cover large geographic areas, such as professional associations, may have courses offered to residents in certain states or regions. Some, or all, of those same courses may be offered to residents in other states or regions.

Often programs are organized based on demand or the needs of stakeholders. Using this method of organization, educational programs that are run often or on a regular basis would be organized together, regardless of subject matter. Programs that are run less often are also grouped together and programs that are run very infrequently organized together as well. The human resource department of a business, for example, might organize courses run every month, such as employee orientations, together. Courses run less frequently—once or twice per year, for example—could also be together.

In addition, educational programs can be organized by the method used to deliver those programs. For example, if an organization, such as higher education, used a wide variety of delivery methods in its educational program offerings, it could organize all online programs together, all face-to-face programs together, all self-study programs together, and so on.

In another approach, organizing educational programs by function involves breaking down the individual components of those programs and grouping them by functional area. For example, within a larger for-profit training organization, needs analysis is considered one function, as are program design, program marketing, and program logistics. That means that all marketing efforts for all programs are grouped together in one function. All program development activities are grouped together by one function as well as others.

Finally, hybrid methods of program organizing pull aspects of organizing together in a way that is uniquely suited for the situation. Hybrid methods can involve the use of two or more organizing approaches. For example, a programmer may organize the educational programs for an organization by region or geographic territory. At the region or territory level, programs may be suborganized based on target market or customer.

Factors to Consider in Program Organization

Given the several ways of organizing ACE programs that have been presented in this chapter, how are systematic and methodological decisions made around organization? The following are factors to consider when making those types of decisions.

Educational programs should be structured in ways that support the mission and goals, or priorities of the organization (Johnson, n.d.). Priorities should be considered when making decisions about program organization, as well. Different from an organization's mission, which is typically fairly consistent, priorities may change over time. When priorities change, an organization's structure and way of organizing should be considered.

An organization's size, structure, and resources may dictate how ACE programs are organized (and, therefore, how the organization itself is organized) (Johnson, n.d.). For example, if an organization is very small and there is one person in charge of program organization, educational programs may be organized all together. In larger organizations with more people, there may be more elaborate and varied ways of organizing programs.

An organization's culture may affect how its educational programs are organized. For example, some organizations are more centralized, others less so. In more centralized organizations, where decisions are made from the top down, educational programs may be organized differently than in flatter organizations, where employees are empowered to make decisions. Other cultural factors may influence how programs are organized. Company hierarchy, employee roles and responsibilities, and the degree to which employees are given the freedom to make decisions are factors that affect how programs are organized.

Resources can be in the form of training budgets as well as staff or human resources—and in most organizations, budgets are developed based on organizational priorities. The more resources an organization devotes to training, the more programs it can offer, and the more complex program organization may be (Schmidt & Yelich Biniecki, 2016).

The diversity of educational programs should be considered when determining how those programs should be organized. Some organizations may focus on a single type of educational program (e.g., consulting services that offer courses in a particular subject), whereas others may offer a wide variety of programs. A narrow range of program offerings could be organized using a simpler structure than would be appropriate for the organization of a wide variety of programs.

In addition, the level of competition in an environment may affect how educational programs are organized. An organization operating in an environment that is highly competitive, with many different organizations that offer similar products, may find different ways of organizing their educational programs compared to an organization that is the only player in the market.

There are many ways educational programs can be organized, and there are many factors that influence how programs are organized. Many of the factors that affect decisions about program organization are continually changing as well. There is no one correct combination of factors to consider when making decisions about how to organize programs. Those who make these types of decisions should have a good understanding of all of these factors (Schmidt & Yelich Biniecki, 2016).

Effective Administration in ACE

Having examined the ways in which educational programs may be organized, and factors to consider when making organizational decisions, educational program administration is addressed next. Administration focuses on the management of educational programs. Because administration often is implemented on higher levels in the organization, it is a function associated with organizational leadership. There are volumes written about administration approaches and leadership theories. A deep exploration is beyond the scope of this chapter; however, the important emphasis is the symbiotic, or interactive, relationship between leadership and administration (Schmidt & Yelich Biniecki, 2016). Types of effective leadership and administration relate to context and organizational culture; therefore, what might work in one situation may not work in another.

The Symbiotic Relationship Between Leadership and Administration

The roles of leader and administrator often intersect, demonstrated in the titles of many articles, books, and academic courses, such as "Educational Administration Leadership," "Administrative Leadership in Adult and Continuing Education," or "Leadership in Higher Education Administration." Administrators usually have a formal organizational role and formal influence, whereas a leader might hold an informal or a formal role and have influence in either role. Effective leadership can help organizations to grow and thrive. However, as Rocco (2016) observed, "The results of bad leadership include poor morale, faculty attrition, distrust, and less incentive for faculty to do additional work to move the unit forward" (p. 2). Although the definition of a leader and that of an administrator is different, the aim within ACE organizations is to have effective *administrative leaders* to help create the circumstances and environments for thriving organizations with positive adult learning experiences.

Types of Leadership

Leaders may have formal or informal power and are situated differently in organizations. Northouse (2016) defined *leadership* as "a process whereby an individual influences a group of individuals to achieve a common goal" (p. 6). Dess et al. (2013) also discussed leadership as a process, but one in which leaders impose their vision to change an organization from a current to a more desirable state. Leaders also may be viewed as facilitators of learning within organizations in order to help groups and individuals grow within and toward a shared vision (Senge, 1990; Wallo, 2008). Therefore, one can view the leader as one who influences others, one who controls a process, or one who is responsible for organizational learning. Approaches to leadership are diverse with overlapping emphases.

Types of leadership approaches are grounded in theories, which inform a leader's approach within an administrative role. Although trait theory (Stogdill, 1974) assumes that leaders inherently possess certain traits and skills, the adult education field tends to gravitate toward theories that embrace leadership as a skill that can be learned (Blake & Mouton, 1964) and broadens approaches beyond the transactional or motivational systems of rewards and punishments (Weber, 1947). Several of these theories will be explored next.

Participative or democratic leadership theory (Lewin et al., 1939) embraces consulting with multiple levels and colleagues with different roles and functions to inform decision-making processes and gain support for initiatives. Rather than a top-down approach, an administrator would aim to incorporate staff and colleagues into the decision-making process to foster commitment to the organization, the goals, and the leader. Feminist and critical approaches to leading ACE organizations build on this approach with consensus building and collaborative leadership (Lawrence, 2017). In addition, servant leadership values serving others and putting others' needs first. If leaders using such an approach impact educators positively, then learners will be positively impacted as well. Servant leadership specifically is noted as a potential model for correctional educationalists (Simmons & Branch, 2015).

Situational (Hersey & Blanchard, 1969; Tannenbaum & Schmidt, 1958) and contingency approaches (Fiedler, 1964) suggest that a leader needs to look at context, which is absolutely necessary for the diverse field of ACE. For example, a leadership approach within human resource development in a manufacturing company may not transfer well to a community-based literacy organization. The situation, the followers, and the leaders need to be considered in each situation (Tannenbaum & Schmidt, 1958). Even if the people and place remain the same but the time has changed, then the context has changed, and the same leadership approach may not be as effective (Fiedler, 1964).

Additional leadership approaches relevant to ACE organizations have emerged, such as authentic (Avolio & Gardner, 2005), meta-leadership (Marcus et al., 2008), multicultural (Bordas, 2007), and global (Cabrera & Unruh, 2012). Authentic leadership at the core is being true to and understanding oneself, similar to an authentic adult educator. Authenticity may be understood as grounding actions in fortitude, prudence, temperance, and justice (Avolio & Gardner, 2005) and is modeled in diverse adult education settings such as the Highlander Research and Education Center (Glowacki-Dudka & Treff, 2016). Walumbwa et al. (2008) cited "self-awareness, relational transparency, internalized moral perspective, and balanced processing" (p. 121) as some of the qualities central to authentic leadership.

Metaleadership has emerged particularly for those ACE leaders dealing with crisis situations with an emphasis on finding order, not control. This approach is particularly salient when learning, administering, and leading take place under extraordinary and chaotic environments (Marcus et al., 2008). The leader's role is to take in the big picture and work across "silos" or divisions in order to address issues in war, natural disasters, or high-level emergencies. One could imagine relief agency administrators working to meet the needs of refugee populations across multiple countries and agencies, a higher education administrator that needs to address a massive fire in a library, or a human resource development administrator trying to address how new government regulations will impact training across multiple sectors.

Multicultural and global leadership approaches focus on leadership and administration in a diverse world. Bordas (2007) stated that a multicultural leadership approach is "[a]n inclusive approach and philosophy that incorporates the influences, practices, and values of diverse cultures in a respectful and productive manner" (p. 8). Therefore, a multicultural approach takes into account ways of getting things done that may not be within the dominant cultural paradigm. Global leadership views the leader as a connector across borders, mind-sets, and activities in order to foster creativity and contribute (Cabrera & Uruh, 2012). An administrator using a global leadership view can create value, reciprocity, and sustainability by navigating and analyzing multinational and multicultural perspectives, which may be competing. The approach grounds behavior in the ethics of understanding subordinates' positions and one's ethical use of power within a nation-state, or culture, as relevant to multinational corporations or transnational organizations such as the United Nations.

Administrative leadership behavior can be grounded in theories such as these to provide a framework for understanding diverse perspectives. ACE leaders may fall on a continuum of application as they assess the organizational context and situation.

Effective Administrative Leadership

Schmidt and Yelich Biniecki (2016) stated that "effective leaders influence and motivate others toward a shared vision, have an acute ability to navigate context, and focus on the social good" (p. 36). Some industries have standards for administrative leaders, such as those in adult basic education (Zacharakis & Glass, 2010). However, most often leadership approaches evolve collaboratively within organizational contexts and individual leaders (Lawrence, 2017).

Effective leaders possess certain knowledge, skills, and abilities and each has different strengths and weaknesses. For example, effective leaders need to have knowledge of power, people, and environments (Schmidt & Yelich Biniecki, 2016). They need to have skills in such areas as decision-making, problem-solving, cultural competency, and communication. They also must have personal attributes of being empathetic, ethical, resilient, diplomatic, and creative. While not all leaders will possess strengths in all areas, knowing what they do not know is an important input into building constructive feedback systems and selecting staff to support their visions and shared mission for the organization (Shuck et al., 2015). Misplaced leaders can lead ACE organizations to dysfunctional ends (Rocco, 2016). Many sectors, such as the military, devote considerable resources for leadership development for both military affiliated and civilian educational staff (Godinez & Leslie, 2015).

As noted previously, while the definitions of leadership and administration are different, effective leadership needs to intersect with effective administration skills. An effective administrator needs to be able to "manage people skillfully and manage resources and processes diligently" (Schmidt & Yelich Biniecki, 2016, p. 44). Just like effective leaders, effective administrators also need to possess specific knowledge, skills, and abilities. For example, effective administrators need to have knowledge of the particular adult education realm in which they are working, the context of resource management, and how best to design processes. Administrators also should be skilled leaders, supervisors, decision makers, and team builders. They should have personal attributes such as being self-directed, goal oriented, flexible, and organized.

How Administrative Leaders and Educators Can Best Support Each Other

Administrative leadership involves action and it also involves relationships. Without relationships, there is no leading. Therefore, administrative leaders need people. From the grounding of the field in adult learning, administrators and adult educators can support each other through learning and viewing roles through each other's lenses. Administrative leaders often grew into their role from their grounding in adult education and as adult educators. Sometimes the role of adult educator and administrator may overlap. However, if one is wearing the administrator hat, there is a specific lens through which one views the work.

Administrative leaders still depend on input from others to effectively do their jobs. The adult educators have the needs of the learners as their center and administrators need to know about those needs. In addition, administrators can support educators by asking for input into decision-making processes concerning programming priorities. Ultimately, administrative leaders are responsible for decision-making, and continual dialogue about why decisions were made can foster the support needed for both administrators and educators to do their jobs.

Challenges Facing ACE

There are many challenges facing those who organize and administer ACE programs. They include the tension inherent in managing people, processes, and resources; issues of funding and support; the appropriate use of marketing in the promotion of educational programs; and effective strategic planning.

Consider the three main things that effective administrators do: They skillfully and successfully manage people, resources, and processes. It is rare that any given administrative decision involves benefits to all three of these entities. Most often, a benefit to one entity means taking from another or making another less of a priority. There is a tension involved in managing people, resources, and processes, and how to make decisions that take into account the needs of all stakeholders and the fair and equitable use or treatment of people, resources, and processes. One of the challenges for administrative leaders is trying to find a balance between their concern for people and their concern for production or the management of resources (Blake & Mouton, 1964). Although there is no single prescription for finding balance, there are avenues that those who organize and administer programs can seek out to improve their skills in these areas (Schmidt & Yelich Biniecki, 2016).

It is an essential role for administrative leaders of ACE programs to secure funding and support for their programs. Often, organizations are energized by good ideas, and teams and individuals put a great deal of effort into program development; however, good ideas are not always funded or supported. Even good ideas that are implemented can find themselves subject to failure if they are not sustainable financially. It is important for the administrative leaders to think creatively about the types of funding and support needed, how to create new streams of funding and support, as well as how to leverage existing resources. Whether one is an HRD administrator in a large, for-profit corporation or an administrator in a small, grassroots adult basic education initiative, securing funding and support for programs is essential if the organization is to survive (Schmidt & Yelich Biniecki, 2016).

Another essential area for program survival is marketing—a powerful tool that is often misunderstood. Used correctly, marketing can help promote the educational services to the most appropriate people for those services. It can help an organization become more well known in the community or service area. It can spur interest in educational programs and can ultimately help an organization to increase its revenues.

On the flip side, when marketing is done incorrectly, it can be costly and time consuming and can result in little benefit for the organization. Marketing can even lead to unintended negative consequences for organizations. Marketing activities can fail, and plans can go awry, and the best intentions of marketers can be foiled by a host of variables. The difference between success and failure of marketing depends on the planning that goes into marketing efforts up front, the execution of the marketing plans, and engaging in appropriate follow-up actions.

Organizations of all types, including educational institutions, are facing increased competition, and educational customers now have many more options from which to choose when they make education-related decisions. This makes marketing more important for all types of ACE organizations, which is part of *strategic planning* (Schmidt & Yelich Biniecki, 2016).

It is easy for administrative leaders to get stuck in the daily work of their organizations and lose sight of the bigger picture. Strategic planning can help those in the organization to see that bigger picture. Strategic planning is a good way to plan for evolution and growth to meet both learner and organizational needs. However, there is often resistance to strategic planning. Chief among these negative perspectives is the idea that the process takes resources; namely, time and money (Kaufman et al., 2003). It is true that decisions based on strategic plans can involve some degree of risk. However, there is risk associated with any type of movement within an organization. In fact, not making any change involves risk. Strategic planning, if done correctly, can be a vehicle to motivate and move the organization forward. In order to be effective, however, planning must be thorough and strategic plans have to be used. This is often where organizations fail. Strategic plans must result in action plans, and those action plans must be carried out (Kaufman et al., 2003).

Change is a necessary part of the continued health of an organization, but stability is important as well. People in organizations typically prefer stability to change, so *managing change* can be difficult. External forces, such as learner needs, societal issues, competition, technological changes, and legislative changes may necessitate faster organizational change (Salmon & de Linares, 1999). The key is in knowing when each (change or stability) is a priority for the organization. Organizations must be flexible and allow for both change and stability when necessary (Lovey et al., 2007). A review of the decision-making process noted earlier in this chapter is a good start in change-making.

Issues in Practice and Research

Within the field, a tension exists between those who utilize business models in ACE and those who see neoliberalism as a detriment to ACE (Hill & Kumar, 2016). Those promoting business models in ACE emphasize the necessity to run an organization so that it is most effective, because after all, if an organization does not have the capital to exist, it will cease to exist within a competitive environment (Dess et al., 2013). That environment may be a nonprofit looking for grants, a for-profit business looking to create a cutting-edge online learning management system, a government agency trying to establish its value, or a grassroots organization seeking to organize residents to establish community gardens.

Critics of business models discuss the neoliberal approach as one in which the very vulnerable with less access are continually marginalized and pushed to the bottom, regardless of abilities and skills (Bierema & Callahan, 2014). Globalization has created environments in which access has increased for some and pushed others to the side. For example, many online resources and courses are developed to reach learner populations; however, the digital divide exists. Recent data indicate access to high-speed internet was a problem for a quarter of the rural United States (Anderson, 2018). Can adult education create an effective business model where all learners have opportunities for further learning, growth, and change? The field is struggling with answers to questions such as these.

ACE is a very broad field and includes administrative leaders and colleagues working in nonprofits, for-profits, government, and grassroots sectors, both internationally and domestically. Therefore, delineating leadership and administration best practices suited to each specific area of ACE can be elusive (Grover & Miller, 2016). What applies in one organizational context may not apply in another. It is a challenge to generate umbrella best practices in ACE to help further the field as a whole as well as interrogate the nuances of each sector to tailor theory to practice application.

Finally, the field seems to develop many student leaders and adult learning and leadership programs, but it does not write much about its own leadership capacity and effective leadership within ACE contexts. General starting points could address what effective leadership looks like within the many diverse ACE organizations in for-profit, nonprofit, governmental, higher education, and other areas. Additional qualitative, quantitative, and mixed methods studies are needed in this area to add to the literature on program administration and organization.

Conclusion

This chapter has provided an overview of the concepts of educational program organization and program administration. Although often discussed together, each is a separate concept, and knowledge of both is important for those in ACE. Effective administrative leaders are necessary for the field to remain relevant and to move it forward. The study of these topics is necessary for the next generation of administrative leader, as well. This chapter presented an overview of topics important to organizers and administrative leaders. As new sectors of adult learning, training, and development are created, there is an opportunity to develop additional conceptual frameworks for further understanding organization and administration of ACE. The broad nature of the field then can be explored on more contextual levels through developing theory to practice approaches in organizations and new course content for future administrators. ACE administrators, in particular, have an opportunity to contribute to developing this real-world knowledge base.

References

123 Help Me. (2013, January 10). *The different ways organizations can be structured and operated.* www.123HelpMe.com/view.asp?id=150297

Anderson, M. (2018, September 10). *About a quarter of rural Americans say access to high-speed internet is a major problem.* Pew Research Center. http://www.pewresearch.org/fact-tank/2018/09/10/about-a-quarter-of-rural-americans-say-access-to-high-speed-internet-is-a-major-problem/

Avolio, B., & Gardner, W. (2005). Authentic leadership development: Getting to the root of positive forms of leadership. *The Leadership Quarterly, 16,* 315–338.

Bhattacharyya, D. K. (2009). *Organizational systems, design, structure and management.* Himalaya Publishing.

Bierema, L., & Callahan, J. (2014). Transforming HRD: A framework for critical HRD practice. *Advances in Developing Human Resources, 16*(4), 429–444.

Blake, R., & Mouton, J. (1964). *The managerial grid: The key to leadership excellence.* Gulf Publishing.

Bordas, J. (2007). *Salsa, soul and spirit: Leadership for a multicultural age.* Berrett-Koehler.

Business Dictionary. (n.d.). Organizing. http://www.businessdictionary.com/definition/organizing.html

Cabrera, A., & Unruh, G. (2012). *Being global: How to think, act, and lead in a transformed world.* Harvard Business Review.

Dess, G., Lumpkin, G. T., Eisner, A., & McNamara, G. (2013). *Strategic management: Text and cases* (7th ed.). McGraw-Hill.

Fiedler, F. E. (1964). A contingency model of leadership effectiveness. *Advanced Experimental Social Psychology, 1,* 149–190.

Glowacki-Dudka, M., & Treff, M. E. (2016). Introduction to the Adult Learning special issue: Embodying authentic leadership through popular education at Highlander Research and Education Center. *Adult Learning, 27*(3), 95–97.

Godinez, E., & Leslie, B. B. (2015). Army civilian leadership development: Self-efficacy, choice, and learning transfer. *Adult Learning, 26*(3), 93–100.

Grover, K. S., & Miller, M. T. (2016). Leadership in adult education agencies: Imperatives for a new century. *Journal of Adult Education, 45*(2), 8–16.

Hersey, P., & Blanchard, K. H. (1969). An introduction to situational leadership. *Training and Development Journal, 23,* 26–34.

Hill, D., & Kumar, R. (2016). Neoliberalism and its impacts. In A. Darder, P. Mayo, & J. Paraskeva (Eds.), *International critical pedagogy reader* (pp. 77–85). Routledge.

Johnson, S. (n.d.). How to determine the best organizational structure. *azcentral.* http://yourbusiness.azcentral.com/determine-organizational-structure-11025.html

Kaufman, R., Oakley-Browne, H., Watkins, R., & Leigh, D. (2003). *Strategic planning for success: Aligning people, performance and payoffs.* Wiley.

Lawrence, R. (2017). Understanding collaborative leadership in theory and practice. *New Directions for Adult and Continuing Education, 2017*(156), 89–96.

Lewin, K., Lippit, R., & White, R. (1939). Patterns of aggressive behavior in experimentally created social climates. *Journal of Social Psychology, 10,* 271–301.

Lovey, I., Manohar, S. N., & Erdelyi, E. (2007). *How healthy is your organization?* Praeger.

Marcus, L. J., Ashkenazi, I., Dorn, B., & Henderson, J. (2008). Meta-leadership: Expanding the scope and scale of public health. *Leadership in Public Health, 8*(1–2).

Northouse, P. (2016). *Leadership theory and practice.* (7th ed.). SAGE.

Rocco, T. (2016). A reflection on dysfunctional leadership and leadership misplacement. *New Horizons in Adult Education & Human Resource Development, 28*(3), 1–2.

Salmon, R., & de Linares, Y. (1999). *Competitive intelligence: Scanning the global environment*. Economica.

Schmidt, S., & Yelich Biniecki, S. (2016). *Organization and administration of adult education programs: A guide for practitioners*. Information Age.

Senge, P. (1990). *The fifth discipline: The art & practice of the learning organization*. Currency Doubleday.

Shuck, B., Rose, K., & Bergman, M. (2015). Inside the spiral of dysfunction: The personal consequences of working for a dysfunctional leader. *New Horizons in Adult Education & Human Resource Development, 27*(4), 51–58.

Simmons, A. J., & Branch, L. M. (2015). Have you paid your rent? Servant leadership in correctional education. *Journal of Prison Education and Reentry, 2*(1), 69–72.

Stogdill, R. (1974). *Handbook of leadership: A survey of theory and research*. Free Press.

Tannenbaum, A. S., & Schmidt, W. H. (1958, March–April). How to choose a leadership pattern. *Harvard Business Review, 36*, 95–101.

Wallo, A. (2008). *The leader as a facilitator of learning at work*. Linköping University.

Walumbwa, F., Avolio, B., Gardner, W., Wernsing, T., & Peterson, S. (2008). Authentic leadership: Development and validation of a theory-based measure. *Journal of Management, 34*(1), 89–126.

Weber, M. (1947). *The theory of social and economic organization*. Free Press.

Zacharakis, J., & Glass, D. S. (2010). Why Kansas is developing standards for its adult education leaders. *Adult Basic Education & Literacy Journal, 4*(2), 109–113.

CHAPTER 13

Program Planning in an Era of "Wicked Problems"

Thomas J. Sork

On April 12, 2018, a widely reported incident occurred at a Starbucks outlet in Philadelphia, Pennsylvania. Two African American men arrived 10 minutes early for a business meeting. The press reported that one asked the White female manager if he could use the washroom and was told they were for use by paying customers. He accepted that and returned to the table where his colleague waited for their business associate to arrive, but the pair was then approached by the manager and asked if they wanted any drinks or water. The pair said they had water with them and were waiting for a meeting, although some accounts report the pair was asked to leave and they refused.

The manager then called police who arrived quickly and, after a short conversation, handcuffed and arrested both men. Reports indicated the two were neither read their rights by police nor told why they were being arrested, although they were later charged with trespassing and creating a disturbance. The charges were dropped that evening. The arrest was captured on a cell phone video, posted to Twitter, went viral, and created a crisis for Starbucks and the Philadelphia police. Reports indicated that the guidelines in place at the Philadelphia Starbucks location "were that partners [Starbucks' term for employees] must ask unpaying customers to leave the store, and police were to be called if they refused" (Siegel, 2018, para. 4).

On April 17, Starbucks announced that on May 29, all 8,000 of their U.S. stores would close for 4 hours of racial-bias education for their 175,000 employees with a curriculum designed by "nationally recognized experts" and made available for other companies to use (Starbucks, 2018).

In June 2018, 23,000 employees in Starbucks' Canadian stores experienced the same videos plus workbook exercises plus discussion program as presented in the United States. Some Canadian employees "who did not want to be named for fear of losing their jobs, said the session seemed well intentioned, but missed its mark" (Woo, 2018, para. 6), because it focused on U.S. race relations and did not address Canada's relations with Indigenous people.

It may seem unusual to begin a chapter on program planning with an incident in a Philadelphia coffee shop, but it is a useful illustration of a wide range of challenges facing adult educators—particularly program planners—at the start of the third decade of the 21st century (Sork, 2019c).

Background and Purpose

Since 1960, when the first *Handbook of Adult Education in the United States* chapter dedicated to program planning appeared (London, 1960), there have been efforts roughly every 10 years to report on recent research and theory development, changing practices, and new challenges. I've had the privilege of participating in these periodic "stocktaking" exercises since the 1989 handbook (Sork & Caffarella, 1989) so, in the spirit of full disclosure, I bring to this task a long-standing interest in understanding the theory and practice of program planning and decades of experience teaching it to both novice and experienced students. This interest includes how program planners acquire the knowledge and skills to be "effective" in a wide variety of different organizational, community, and social contexts and what it means to be a "capable planner" (Käpplinger & Sork, 2014; Sork & Käpplinger, 2019).

During previous decades there have been numerous influential contributions to the theory and practice of program planning. One of the most influential was the work of Cervero and Wilson (1994, 2006) which directed our attention away from a preoccupation with the technical aspects of planning and toward the role of power, interests, and negotiation—the "people work" of planning—in the design of programs. They posed two deceptively simple questions about the broader practice of adult education that have tremendous resonance in the current era:

- Who benefits?
- Who *should* benefit? (Cervero & Wilson, 2001, pp. 12–13)

These questions could be answered in a very narrow sense by program planners who might reference various instrumental "needs" on which many programs are based and the benefits to the "owners" of those needs and to other immediate stakeholders. But they were challenging us to address these questions in a much broader sense.

Nearly 35 years ago, Boshier (1986) offered a sober assessment of the then-dominant approach to program planning:

> North American adult education is overwhelmingly reactive and based on assessments of present and past needs. It is homeostatic, supposed to relieve tension-states, and primarily designed to maintain or adapt people to the status quo. During times of slow change this was acceptable but, in the near, short-, and long-term future, it will become increasingly dysfunctional for learners to be "served" by reactive educational systems. (p. 15)

I don't see much evidence in the literature that, as a field, we have tipped the balance from being primarily reactive and needs-based to proactive and anticipatory.

The Starbucks Incident was unusual by being captured on video, going viral, and threatening the carefully manicured corporate image of a high-profile global company. The initial learning "need" that was quickly framed from the incident was a lack of knowledge about the origins and consequences of unconscious racial bias. This was a good example of a reactive response to a persistent and deeply embedded social problem that goes far beyond who gets access to the restrooms at Starbucks. The incident was a symptom of a much larger and highly complex problem that requires more than simplistic educational solutions. And lest you regard the Starbucks Incident as unique, consider that the beauty products chain Sephora experienced a similar corporate crisis and focused their training on diversity and inclusion (Bromwich, 2019).

While reviewing work on program planning published during the past decade, I found few noteworthy research findings, novel perspectives, or insightful theoretical contributions. I am left wondering whether this apparent dearth of new ideas represents maturation or stagnation. Do we now have all the conceptual, theoretical, and practical tools needed to engage substantively with the challenges being faced—now and in the future—by adult learners and more broadly by humanity?

Changing Nature of Planning Contexts

The importance of understanding the planning context and working skillfully within it is widely recognized. But a good deal of the planning literature frames the context in overly narrow terms such as the unit, organization, or local community in which the planner is embedded. Understanding "local" contexts such as these is certainly important (Franz et al., 2015), but it is dangerous to ignore broader global developments—what some refer to as *wicked problems*—as we go about our work. The concept of wicked problems was introduced by Rittel and Webber (1973) in the context of planning theory and social policy. They differentiated "wicked problems" from "tame problems" to recognize the need for a different mind-set, skill set, and expectations when addressing each type. They proposed 10 features of wicked problems that help us understand their complexity:

1. There is no definitive formulation of a wicked problem—the formulation of a wicked problem *is* the problem.
2. Wicked problems have no "stopping rule," meaning there are no criteria that indicate when *the* or *a* solution has been found.
3. Solutions to wicked problems are not true or false, but good or bad.
4. There is no immediate and no ultimate test of a solution to a wicked problem.
5. Every solution to a wicked problem is a "one-shot operation"; because there is no opportunity to learn by trial and error, every attempt counts significantly.
6. Wicked problems do not have an enumerable (or exhaustively describable) set of potential solutions, nor is there a well-described set of permissible operations that may be incorporated into the plan.
7. Every wicked problem is essentially unique.
8. Every wicked problem can be considered a symptom of another problem.
9. The existence of a discrepancy representing a wicked problem can be explained in numerous ways. The choice of explanation determines the nature of the problem's resolution.
10. The planner has no right to be wrong. The aim is not to find the truth, but to improve some characteristics of the world where people live. (pp. 161–167)

Whether or not the following concerns strictly meet the criteria enumerated by Rittel and Webber, they are critical problems facing humanity that adult educators—along with many others—should be addressing more directly and more collaboratively (Sork, 2019a):

- Erosion of human rights
- Persistent poverty
- Growing inequality
- Forced migration and displacement
- Worsening climate crisis
- Assaults on democratic institutions
- Distrust of science, media, and the press
- Social and economic dislocation due to disruptive technologies
- Alarming water scarcity and food insecurity
- Dysfunctional economic structures

If we accept the notion that these are part of the broader context in which we plan programs, then it is reasonable to ask how often and how effectively we design programs that address them in ways large and small. How well do our current approaches to planning allow or invite engagement with these broad, complex problems? For two examples related to climate change, see Desai (2017) and Walters (2018).

These complex problems are not the only contextual features we should be aware of. Capable planners are also aware of "local" manifestations of these and other problems, some of which may seem far removed from global concerns. Capable planners are also aware of the role—and limitations—of learning and education in addressing any complex problem.

The Starbucks Incident has several features that illustrate some of the complexities planners face in contemporary adult education:

1. The incident occurred in the context of growing racial tensions (Black Lives Matter and more visible White-supremacist movements, as examples). This, along with threats of boycotts, lost profits, and a reduced share price, meant that an immediate, high-profile response was essential.
2. Although the problem was framed as unconscious racial bias (the "ascribed" learning need), Starbucks also recognized the role played by their then-existing policy, which the manager who called the police seemed to be operating within. They quickly changed their policy so that all those present in a Starbucks would be considered "customers" and therefore eligible to use the restrooms. There are noneducational elements to every complex problem that must be addressed if the problem is to be "solved" in any conventional sense.
3. Starbucks also recognized that a hastily produced, 4-hour educational program would be insufficient to address socially embedded racism, so they proclaimed that the May 29 program would be the first of a series. The first program intended specifically for managers, they announced on their website, would be Mindful Decision-Making.

4. Those handed the task of "delivering" a program on a sensitive topic within 6 weeks of the incident to 175,000 employees in 8,000 U.S. outlets faced the challenge of relying on digital technology and print resources with a highly diverse and widely distributed group of adult learners with varying levels of literacy, learning style preferences, and personal experiences with racial bias. This required making quite a few assumptions about the learners that may or may not have provided a pedagogically defensible foundation for the program.
5. Offering the same program to Canadian Starbucks employees—with apparent mixed success—illustrates the importance of understanding the historical-cultural context of learners and the limitations of assuming a program designed for one context will be effective in another.
6. Evaluating the outcomes of such a short-term program was made difficult by the rather nebulous, implicit learning objectives of the 4-hour session. In addition, any formal evaluation of outcomes would have to capture what some experts on racism predicted could be "backlash" effects—negative outcomes—of the training.
7. Beyond Starbucks, the Philadelphia police recognized that their current policy and training related to trespassing complaints contributed to the highly public, embarrassing way the incident was handled by their officers. So, they committed to change their policy and revise their training.

The Starbucks Incident is instructive because it highlights not only the impacts of the broader planning context on decision-making but also some of the challenges planners face in the current era of increasingly complex problems requiring immediate, sustained attention and a mix of educational and other forms of intervention.

Planning as Theorizing

Fundamentally, all planning involves theorizing, although that is rarely made explicit. Planning typically begins with some mental image—shared or not, implicit or explicit—of a desired outcome. Some of the many possible desired outcomes include acquiring a skill, changed perspective, or competency; becoming more critical, tolerant, empathetic, or creative; conforming to policies, procedures, rules, or standards; challenging injustice, intolerance, discrimination, or bigotry; and making informed choices about health, relationships, the environment, and politics. A plan is then developed to promote that desired outcome. Embedded—usually implicitly—in every program plan is a theory of change. Some planning models—largely in the areas of social service (Kettner et al., 2017) and health promotion planning (Eldredge et al., 2016; Green et al., forthcoming)—require that the underlying program theory be made explicit and, as far as possible, evidence-based. The mechanism for representing the theory is typically a "logic model" of the intervention or a description of the "theory of change." In cases where the program theory is made explicit, each program offering is a "test" of the theory. Did the program, if implemented as planned—that is, with a high degree of "fidelity" (Arnold, 2015)—produce the outcomes expected? If not, where is the flaw in the theory? If it wasn't implemented as planned—that is, with a low degree of fidelity—how did this disrupt the underlying program theory and achievement of outcomes? Such models generally reflect the dominant epistemological orientations and research paradigms of the contexts in which they are used.

Planning models that include the usual elements of analyzing the context and learner community, assessing needs, developing objectives, designing instruction, arranging administrative supports, and evaluating outcomes are also intended to produce a program theory of sorts, although typically it is implicit in the design. There is an underlying logic to the relationships among these planning elements that, in a sense, forces planners to theorize. But there is no clear evidence that, in practice, planning is carried out in the sequence suggested by most models or that the logical connections between planning elements necessarily result in a clearly articulated program theory.

It needs to be said here that agreeing on "desired outcomes" and the program designs to achieve them is frequently a contentious process where power and interests influence the key decisions made. This has been amply demonstrated by Cervero and Wilson (2006) and many others who have employed their theoretical lens to analyze cases of planning in a wide variety of settings. Recognizing that all decisions about "desired outcomes" reflect political-ethical commitments provides important counterpoint to the mistaken notion that planning is primarily a technical process.

Two good illustrations of planning from an explicit political-ethical position are found in the approaches suggested by Brookfield and Holst (2011), for whom the goal of "democratic socialism" drives their framework for planning radical education programs, and Harnecker and Bartolomé (2019), whose overriding commitment to social justice through popular education drives theirs. Both have their roots in Marxist analysis and critical theory.

From the opposite end of the political spectrum, we find approaches to planning in corporate and corporate-like environments where "performance" and "talent development" are the focus. For example, Chan (2010) elaborates on the application of the ADDIE model (analysis, design, development, implementation, and evaluation) in training contexts but does not acknowledge power differentials or discuss ways to challenge extant structures, assumptions, or values. Moore (2017) revisits and updates decision-making processes—which she refers to as *action mapping*—for analyzing performance problems (Mager & Pipe, 1999) and designing programs that directly address them. As with Chan, there is no critical analysis of existing power structures or recognition of how these influence key planning decisions. Silence on such matters sends a strong message that neither planners nor programs should question existing power relations, the framing of needs, the role of training in addressing organizational problems, or the moral foundations of the enterprise.

More promising within the changing contexts of workplace training is a framework for designing active learning experiences described by Bell and Kozlowski (2010). They observe that

> Traditionally, training has focused on developing routine expertise, or providing employees with competencies that directly transfer to the job. Yet, the nature of work has increasingly shifted attention toward the development of adaptive expertise, or competencies that are not only specialized but also flexible enough to be modified to changing circumstances. (p. 263)

They provide detailed advice about developing learner-centered training designs that embed self-regulatory strategies intended to promote continued learning and adaptability as jobs and workplaces change. The need to adapt planning and program designs to complex, rapidly changing circumstances is increasingly recognized as essential in the current era.

Research, Models, and Frameworks

The traditional focus of chapters in the decennial *Handbook of Adult and Continuing Education* has been to assess the current state of knowledge—and recent developments—in each area addressed. They have provided a kind of primer for those new to the field and an update for those who are more experienced. In earlier handbooks (Sork, 2000, 2010), I observed several characteristics of the English-language literature on program planning that were of concern because they can limit its relevance to practice and stifle innovative thought.

- The literature was largely dominated by White, male writers.
- Most authors were from the United States and Canada, where program planning has long been regarded as a core area of study in adult education.
- There was very little cross-referencing across contexts of practice. Planning theories and models developed in one context (e.g., workplace learning or museum education) are not referenced or recognized in other contexts (e.g., literacy or continuing professional education).
- With few exceptions, the technical aspects of planning were emphasized, while social-political and ethical dimensions received little or no attention.

Some progress has been made to address these concerns, although not as much as I had hoped. What follows are brief summaries and examples of contributions mostly from 2010 to the present which reflect progress over the past decade.

Bracken (2011) reported on an ethnographic study of program planning in a feminist community-based organization in Mexico. Bracken observed that "the most central finding from this study is deceptively simple. The role of ideology and identity in a feminist program-planning context is inseparably intertwined with the mission, philosophy, and practical actions of the organization's educators and activists" (p. 127). She posed two questions for future research:

> How can some of the specific ways in which feminists address the ideals of consensus building, leveraging power, or praxis be better understood? How can feminists make these compromises without losing their feminist identities and their ability to prioritize gendered work? (p. 135)

She concluded by saying, "The findings offer an opportunity to debate and further investigate how collective, participatory organizational structures; social change ideologies; and the concept of praxis manifest themselves via feminist program-planning practices" (p. 136). This contribution brings a gendered analysis and feminist critique to the literature on planning and illustrates how elements of feminist planning may contribute to efforts to collectively address some of the wicked problems enumerated previously.

Other contributions have expanded our understanding of planning in various cultural contexts. For example, Hiok and Haslinda (2009) reported on case studies of planning continuing professional education programs in three different professional organizations in Malaysia. They found, as have others, that the planning process followed in practice does not usually resemble the systematic, step-wise processes found in the literature. Ryu and Cervero (2011) reported on a study in Korea that examined how Confucian values influence planning. They found that values such as group harmony, respect of hierarchy, propriety, face, bond of affection, and distinct gender roles all played a part in the dynamics of planning, but that age, gender, and group harmony played particularly important roles in establishing the power relations—the human dynamics—that influenced the design of the program. They concluded that

> When planning educational programs, the lack of understanding and critical examination of the sociopolitical and sociocultural dimensions inevitably lead to an inability to construct politically and socially sound, and practically effective, programs .... Understanding Confucian values and how the values play out in the process of program planning may also help to diminish conflicts among different cultural views. (p. 156)

A rare and useful contribution to understanding variations in planning theory and practice across countries is a recent compilation of research studies presented at a conference held in Hannover, Germany, in 2015, titled *Cultures of Program Planning in Adult Education* (Käpplinger et al., 2017). Some chapters are comparative while others address planning in a single country or with a particular cultural group. We learn, for example, about the design of online higher education programs in China (Bin & Mixue); planning programs for refugees from North Korea (Lee & Roh); planning challenges and contradictions in Russia (Mukhlaeva & Sokolova); and programming for arts education in museums in Germany (Fleige & Specht). We also learn about the German research tradition of "program analysis" (Gieseke); how research is conducted using archival materials in Austria (Ganglbauer & Stifter) and Germany (Käpplinger); differences and similarities in model development in Germany and North America (von Hippel & Käpplinger); and how accreditation standards and related notions of "best practice" serve as "policy levers" that enforce conventional approaches to planning and may constrain innovation in continuing medical education (Cervero). Each of these examples illustrates a much-needed broadening of perspectives on how, why, and for whom programs are planned in different cultural contexts and why planning approaches must be compatible with the unique features of the context.

In a similar fashion but within the United States, Burnette (2010) studied program planning in public historically Black colleges and universities (HBCUs). She was interested in the strategies employed by program directors "as they negotiate sociopolitical interests in developing continuing higher education programs" (p. 3). Through interviews, she identified three prominent negotiation strategies: developing sustained networks, developing parallel support structures, and finding common ground. She addresses the asymmetrical power relations experienced by those involved in continuing education and relates her findings to other studies that have employed the theoretical orientation to planning introduced by Cervero and Wilson (2006). Once again, readers are reminded of the central role that history and culture play in enabling and constraining planning and in establishing and maintaining power relations.

Since 2010, there have been several new books published that contain planning models or frameworks. For example, St. Clair (2015) poses a series of questions to help course designers work through a process that emphasizes careful consideration of the context, learners' characteristics, and the best methods and techniques for accomplishing desired outcomes. It does not address in any detail the more administrative aspects of planning like budgeting and marketing. There are also missed opportunities to delve into common ethical issues that may arise in course design. Schmidt and Yelich Biniecki (2016) take an organizational-administrative perspective on planning and provide details on such practical matters as budgeting, marketing, human resources, strategic planning, evaluation, and legal and ethical considerations. As the authors make clear, the focus of this book is the "business side" of adult education, which is increasingly important, but addressing the key relationships between program planning, strategic planning, and program management would have enhanced its value to planners.

Caffarella and Daffron (2013) revised their "interactive planning model" and offered realistic scenarios, practical advice, examples, and worksheets to help less-experienced practitioners navigate the complexities of planning a wide range of program types. I especially appreciate their attention to planning for transfer of learning—which is often neglected in other planning models—and the section on making ethical decisions. Although arguably more practical than Cervero and Wilson's (2006) planning framework, the "interactive model" has not attracted the same level of interest in researching its utility, strengths, and limitations in different planning contexts.

Eldredge et al. (2016) recently updated the "intervention mapping" (IM) process for planning health promotion programs. IM begins with developing a logic model of the problem rather than with program outcomes. There are hundreds of published studies of programs designed using the IM protocol. These studies typically describe the program, its expected and achieved outcomes, and report on the utility of the planning process (Durks et al., 2017). One example is Wheeler et al. (2013), who used IM to develop an online continuing education program for community pharmacy staff. In relation to the utility of intervention mapping, the authors observed that

> It allowed the team of health educators, practitioners, and researchers to approach the education program in a systematic stepwise manner and bring their wide range of theoretical, practical, and experiential contributions together to make decisions . . . . As health education providers, we have a map that outlines what the intervention is expected to achieve, how it will be achieved, and if the expected outcomes are not achieved, we can return to the map to review and make further improvements. (p. 265)

Kok et al. (2017) developed a database of studies about IM, finding 750 titles in 2015. They briefly reviewed studies of six programs planned using IM and concluded that, although some authors reported IM was "complex, elaborate, tiresome, expensive, and time consuming" (p. 11), the same authors concluded it was helpful in developing more successful behavior change interventions. There seems to be good evidence that investing time and energy in complex planning processes can produce good results, but a careful cost/benefit analysis may be required to determine when the investment is likely to be justified.

The PRECEDE-PROCEED health promotion model (Green & Kreuter, 2005; Green et al., forthcoming) has been applied and researched extensively and is periodically updated based on evidence of its effectiveness (Porter, 2016). The website maintained by Green (2019) lists more than 1,000 studies of programs developed using part or all of the eight-phase PRECEDE-PROCEED model. PRECEDE-PROCEED begins with concerns about enhancing quality of life rather than specific learning outcomes and then builds educational interventions based on several types of detailed assessments: social; epidemiological; educational and ecological; and administrative and policy. The process is heavily front-loaded with analysis prior to specifying learning outcomes. This seems consistent with the challenges involved when setting out to change what are often entrenched, habitual behaviors and encourages a careful, detailed analysis required to understand possible points of intervention when addressing wicked problems.

Closely related to health promotion is work on planning health professions education programs. Owen and Schmitt (2013), for example, offer a planning process for integrating interprofessional education with continuing education and provide examples where this has been done. The mix of disciplinary backgrounds, professional orientations, embedded power relations, and varied practice contexts make working across professions particularly challenging. Schmidt and Lawson (2018) review planning approaches for health professions education programs (HPE) and explore unique features of the health professions—and the settings in which they work—that require special attention when planning.

Competency-based education (CBE) is another domain where planning follows a somewhat conventional sequence—once competencies are identified. But developing competency frameworks can be time-intensive and politically fraught because of disputes about what should be included and how the competencies should be defined and assessed. As Bushway et al. (2018) point out, CBE involves a form of design wherein "the curriculum is planned backward from the desired results to evidence of learning to the learning plan" (p. 36). If the CBE program is self-paced, then planners are faced with the challenge of building in practice, formative feedback, and authentic summative assessment activities in ways that respect the pace of progress set by learners.

I have only become aware of one fundamentally new planning model developed in the past 10 years, and it is based on work by scholars in social work (O'Connor & Netting, 2007; Netting et al., 2008). Of course, interventions in social work are different in character from those in adult education, but I was intrigued by their introduction of a new way of thinking about planning—which they refer to as *emergent approaches*, described as

> attempts to remove barriers to innovation through intense interactions, networking, and information exchange among those with a stake in change, based on the assumption that they should be empowered to create and re-create as new discoveries occur during nonlinear, unpredictable strategies. Program planning using these approaches, based on assumptions of interpretive planning, consists of several predictable dimensions, the specific content of which cannot be known in advance: engagement, discovery, sense-making, and unfolding. (Netting et al., 2008, p. 256)

These authors do not reject conventional "rational" models—that begin by identifying "end states" and then work backward to develop a plan—but insist that these alone are insufficient guides to planning in a complex world. They regard emergent approaches as important alternatives that practitioners can draw upon when rational models are not well suited to the problem at hand. O'Connor and Netting (2007) explain that emergent planning is overtly political, attends to the ideology and political will of those involved, and places feasibility at the core of decision-making.

Mayoh-Bauche (2018) melded elements of complexity theory with emergent planning to produce the *spirals model of emergent planning*. Although its many elements and graphic representations are too complex to easily summarize here, she provided six basic, interrelated principles—in no particular order—on which it is based: attend to context, iterate, be creative, disrupt, seek connection, and be playful. She went on to provide guidance on how to enact these principles while designing innovative, creative programs that address agreed-upon elements of a problem or concern. Whereas rational planning begins by asking, "What outcome do we wish to achieve?" emergent planning asks, "Where do we begin?" This model, and emergent planning generally, seems more consistent with, for example, feminist and activist approaches to planning than with conventional/rational models, with their emphasis on clear outcomes.

Educators are conditioned to focus first on outcomes rather than where to begin. There are certainly many situations where a focus on outcomes makes sense, but adding to our theoretical and practical repertoire a wide range of alternatives seems wise when confronted by complex, wicked problems that challenge us to be better planners. Rational models of planning continue to dominate the field, so the challenge is how to build, first, a "good enough" and then a richly varied and sophisticated planning repertoire. This repertoire must include how to anticipate and engage with the ethical issues that will inevitably arise, including the fundamental questions of whose interests are served and who benefits (Cervero & Wilson, 2006; Govers, 2014).

Moving From Novice to Expert Planner—and Back Again

The kind of literature that might be most useful may depend on the experience and expertise of the planner (Sork, 2019b). The less experienced students in my courses on planning typically find more technically oriented readings helpful because they want "the basics" they might need to land a new job or meet growing expectations in a current job. More experienced students—and most activists—appreciate the critical/analytical readings, those that question or problematize conventional planning concepts and practices.

Based on the five-stage theory of skill acquisition developed by Dreyfus and Dreyfus (2009), novice planners make "effortful use" of conventional/rational planning models and are comforted—falsely or otherwise—by the perception that there is a correct way of doing it: "Those at the novice stage (Stage 1) are reassured by literature that presents program planning as a linear, step-wise process with a clear beginning, well-defined processes, and a clear ending" (Sork, 2019b, p. 3). Those at the expert stage (Stage 5), by contrast, can discern what needs to be done to accomplish the task and adapt their approach to the requirements of the context. In the words of Dreyfus and Dreyfus (2009),

> A more subtle and refined discrimination ability is what distinguishes the expert from the proficient performer. This ability allows the expert to discriminate among situations all seen as similar with respect to the plan or perspective, distinguishing those situations requiring one action from those demanding another. (p. 15)

This talent is similar to expert planners "seeing what matters" and as capable of "contextual improvisation," that is, able to effectively respond based on what they "see" happening (Cervero & Wilson, 2006, p. 18). It is not clear how to best assist those who wish to move through the stages to become expert planners, but formal exposure to varied literature—including a wide range of planning approaches—critical dialogue, deep experience, and reflection-in-action all contribute to the journey through the stages. One weakness of stage-based theories is that moving through the stages may mistakenly be considered a one-way trip, which it certainly is not.

The contexts in which adult educators plan programs are continually changing. We are facing many daunting problems and may be uncertain how to begin addressing them. The learners we work with and on behalf of are becoming more diverse and are characterized by intersectionalities that defy generalization. New technologies are enabling a dizzying variety of options for program delivery as well as making it possible for many learners to satisfy their needs without engaging in formal programs. Pressures to operate within shrinking budgets or to generate more revenue are increasing for many. Fissures are opening or expanding between various groups out of a desire to control preferential access to limited resources, restrain greater social inclusion, sustain economic inequality, and stifle efforts to promote sustainability.

Those who aspire to be expert program planners have available many of the tools needed to begin addressing these daunting problems. All solutions—however partial—to wicked problems have educative components, although promising points of intervention for educators may not be obvious. A major challenge for program planners in the decade of the 2020s will be to avoid complacency and planning paralysis, to pick a critical, complex problem to which you can commit, identify a place to start, and get on with it (Nanton, 2017). As suggested by emergent planning, we—and others—can learn as we go but getting started is crucial. It is only by continually challenging our problem-solving skills that we can achieve—and hope to maintain—expertise.

References

Arnold, M. E. (2015). Connecting the dots: Improving Extension program planning with program umbrella models. *Journal of Human Sciences and Extension, 3*(2), 48–67. https://www.jhseonline.com/article/view/685/589

Bell, B. S., & Kozlowski, S. W. J. (2010). Toward a theory of learner-centered training design: An integrative framework of active learning. In S. W. J. Kozlowski & E. Salas (Eds.), *Learning, training, and development in organizations* (pp. 263–300). Routledge.

Bin, B., & Mixue, L. (2017). An empirical study of the construction of programmes for adult online higher education in China. In B. Käpplinger, S. Robak, M. Fleige, A. von Hippel, & W. Gieseke (Eds.), *Cultures of program planning in adult education: Concepts, research results, and archives* (pp. 159–175). Peter Lang.

Boshier, R. (1986). Proaction for a change: Some guidelines for the future. *International Journal of Lifelong Education,* 5(1), 15–31. https://doi.org/10.1080/0260137860050103

Bracken, S. J. (2011). Understanding program planning theory and practice in a feminist community-based organization. *Adult Education Quarterly,* 61(2), 121–138. https://doi.org/10.1177/0741713610380446

Bromwich, J. E. (2019, June 4). Sephora will shut down for an hour of diversity training tomorrow. *New York Times.* https://www.nytimes.com/2019/06/04/style/sephora-will-shut-down-for-an-hour-of-diversity-training-tomorrow.html

Brookfield, S. D., & Holst, J. D. (2011). *Radicalizing learning: Adult education for a just world.* Jossey-Bass.

Burnette, D. M. (2010). Negotiating tradition: The politics of continuing higher education program planning in public historically Black colleges and universities. *Journal of Continuing Higher Education,* 58(1), 3–11. https://doi.org/10.1080/07377360903531489

Bushway, D. J., Dodge, L., & Long, C. S. (2018). *A leader's guide to competency-based education: From inception to implementation.* Stylus.

Caffarella, R. S., & Daffron, S. R. (2013). *Planning programs for adult learners: A practical guide* (3rd ed.). Jossey-Bass.

Cervero, R. M. (2017). Provider accreditation and program planning as policy levers for continuing medical education. In B. Käpplinger, S. Robak, M. Fleige, A. von Hippel, & W. Gieseke (Eds.), *Cultures of program planning in adult education: Concepts, research results, and archives* (pp. 209–227). Peter Lang.

Cervero, R. M., & Wilson, A. L. (1994). *Planning responsibly for adult education: A guide to negotiating power and interests.* Jossey-Bass.

Cervero, R. M., & Wilson, A. L. (2001). At the heart of practice: The struggle for knowledge and power. In R. M. Cervero & A. L. Wilson (Eds.), *Power in practice: Adult education and the struggle for knowledge and power in society* (pp. 1–20). Jossey-Bass.

Cervero, R. M., & Wilson, A. L. (2006). *Working the planning table: Negotiating democratically for adult, continuing, and workplace education.* Jossey-Bass.

Chan, J. F. (2010). *Designing and developing training programs.* Wiley.

Desai, A. R. (2017). Global climate change education is all local. In A. B. Knox, S. C. O. Conceição, & L. G. Martin (Eds.), *Mapping the field of adult and continuing education: An international compendium, Vol. 1* (pp. 69–72). Stylus; American Association for Adult and Continuing Education.

Dreyfus, H. L., & Dreyfus, S. E. (2009). The relationship of theory and practice in the acquisition of skill. In P. Benner, C. Tanner & C. Chesla (Eds.), *Expertise in nursing practice: Caring, clinical judgment, and ethics* (2nd ed., pp. 1–23). Springer.

Durks, D., Fernandez-Llimos, F., Hossain, L. N., Franco-Trigo, L., Benrimoj, S. I., & Sabater-Hernández, D. (2017). Use of intervention mapping to enhance health care professional practice: A systematic review. *Health Education and Behavior,* 44(4), 524–535. https://doi.org/10.1177/1090198117709885

Eldredge, L. K. B., Markham, C. M., Ruiter, R. A. C., Fernández, M. E., Kok, G., & Parcel, G. S. (2016). *Planning health promotion programs: An intervention mapping approach* (4th ed.). Jossey-Bass/John Wiley.

Fleige, M., & Specht, I. (2017). Programs and cooperation in "adjunctive" adult education: The example of arts education in museums in Germany. In B. Käpplinger, S. Robak, M. Fleige, A. von Hippel, & W. Gieseke (Eds.), *Cultures of program planning in adult education: Concepts, research results, and archives* (pp. 177–194). Peter Lang.

Franz, N., Garst, B. A., & Gagnon, R. J. (2015). The cooperative extension program development model: Adapting to a changing context. *Journal of Human Sciences and Extension,* 3(2), 3–12. jhseonline.com/article/view/682/586.

Ganglbauer, S., & Stifter, C. H. (2017). The Austrian archives of adult education. In B. Käpplinger, S. Robak, M. Fleige, A. von Hippel, & W. Gieseke (Eds.), *Cultures of program planning in adult education: Concepts, research results, and archives* (pp. 263–268). Peter Lang.

Gieseke, W. (2017). Programs, program research, program-planning activities–Rhizome-like developments. In B. Käpplinger, S. Robak, M. Fleige, A. von Hippel, & W. Gieseke (Eds.), *Cultures of program planning in adult education: Concepts, research results, and archives* (pp. 23–42). Peter Lang.

Govers, E. (2014). An analysis of ethical considerations in programme design practice. *Journal of Further and Higher Education,* 38(6), 773–793. https://doi.org/10.1080/0309877X.2013.765942

Green, L. W. (2019). *Published studies of the application of the PRECEDE-PROCEED model.* http://lgreen.net/precede.htm

Green, L. W., Gielen, A., Kreuter, M. W., Peterson, D., & Ottoson, J. M. (Eds.). (2020). *Health program planning, implementation, and evaluation: Creating behavioral, environmental and policy change* (5th ed.). John Hopkins University Press.

Green, L. W., & Kreuter, M. W. (2005). *Health program planning: An educational and ecological approach* (4th ed.). McGraw-Hill.

Harnecker, M., & Bartolomé, J. (2019). *Planning from below: A decentralized participatory planning proposal.* Monthly Review.

Hiok, O. M., & Haslinda, A. (2009). Framing programme planning practices in continuing professional education in professional associations in Malaysia. *European Journal of Social Sciences, 8*(4), 626–639.

Käpplinger, B. (2017). Addressing 21st century learners–A comparative analysis of pictures and images in programs of adult education providers in Canada and Germany. In B. Käpplinger, S. Robak, M. Fleige, A. von Hippel, & W. Gieseke (Eds.), *Cultures of program planning in adult education: Concepts, research results, and archives* (pp. 131–140). Peter Lang.

Käpplinger, B., Robak, S., Fleige, M., von Hippel, A., & Gieseke, W. (Eds.). (2017). *Cultures of program planning in adult education: Concepts, research results, and archives.* Peter Lang.

Käpplinger, B., & Sork, T. J. (2014). Making program planning more visible: What to do when they don't know what they don't know. In S. Lattke & W. Jütte (Eds.), *Professionalisation of adult educators: International and comparative perspectives* (pp. 183–200). Peter Lang.

Kettner, P. M., Moroney, R. M., & Martin, L. L. (2017). *Designing and managing programs: An effectiveness-based approach* (5th ed.). SAGE.

Kok, G., Peters, L. W. H., & Ruiter, R. A. C. (2017). Planning theory- and evidence-based behavior change interventions: A conceptual review of the intervention mapping protocol. *Psicologia: Reflexão e Crítica, 30*(19), 1–13. https://doi.org/10.1186/s41155-017-0072-x

Lee, R., & Roh, K-R. (2017). Responsible planning for North Korean refugees as adult learners. In B. Käpplinger, S. Robak, M. Fleige, A. von Hippel, & W. Gieseke (Eds.), *Cultures of program planning in adult education: Concepts, research results, and archives* (pp. 245–259). Peter Lang.

London, J. (1960). Program development in adult education. In M. S. Knowles (Ed.), *Handbook of adult education in the United States* (pp. 65–81). Adult Education Association of the USA.

Mager, R. F., & Pipe, P. (1999). *Analyzing performance problems or you really oughta wanna* (3rd ed.). Center for Effective Performance.

Mayoh-Bauche, J. (2018). *Disrupting adult education program planning: Creating a spirals model of emergent planning for creative, connected change* [Unpublished master's thesis]. St. Frances Xavier University, Antigonish, Nova Scotia, Canada.

Moore, C. (2017). *Map it: The hands-on guide to strategic training design.* Montesa Press.

Mukhlaeva, T., & Sokolova, I. (2017). Challenges and contradictions of programme planning in Russia. In B. Käpplinger, S. Robak, M. Fleige, A. von Hippel, & W. Gieseke (Eds.), *Cultures of program planning in adult education: Concepts, research results, and archives* (pp. 229–243). Peter Lang.

Nanton, C. R. (2017). Leadership for the complexity and challenges of global adult education. In L. G. Martin, S. C. O. Conceição, & A. B. Knox (Eds.), *Mapping the field of adult and continuing education: An international compendium, Vol. 3* (pp. 445–448). Stylus; American Association for Adult and Continuing Education.

Netting, F. E., O'Connor, M. K., & Fauri, D. P. (2008). *Comparative approaches to program planning.* Wiley.

O'Connor, M. K., & Netting, F. E. (2007). Emergent program planning as competent practice: The importance of considering context. *Journal of Progressive Human Services, 18*(2), 57–75. https://doi.org/10.1300/J059v18n02_05

Owen, J. A., & Schmitt, M. H. (2013). Integrating interprofessional education into continuing education: A planning process for continuing interprofessional education programs. *Journal of Continuing Education in the Health Professions, 33*(20), 109–117. https://doi.org/10.1002/chp.21173

Porter, C. M. (2016). Revisiting Precede-Proceed: A leading model for ecological and ethical health promotion. *Health Education Journal, 75*(6), 753–764. https://doi.org/10.1177/0017896915619645

Rittel, H., & Webber, M. M. (1973). Dilemmas in a general theory of planning. *Policy Sciences, 4*(2), 155–169. https://doi.org/10.1007/sl 1077-012-9151-0

Ryu, K., & Cervero, R. M. (2011). The role of Confucian cultural values and politics in planning educational programs for adults in Korea. *Adult Education Quarterly, 61*(2), 139–160.

St. Clair, R. (2015). *Creating courses for adults: Design for learning.* Jossey-Bass.

Schmidt, S. W., & Yelich Biniecki, S. M. (2016). *Organization and administration of adult education programs: A guide for practitioners.* Information Age.

Schmidt, S. W., & Lawson, L. (2018). Program planning in health professions education. *New Directions for Adult and Continuing Education, 2018*(157): 41–50. https://doi.org/10.1002/ace.20267

Siegel, R. (2018, May 21). New Starbucks policy: No purchase needed to use restrooms or sit in cafes. *The Washington Post.* https://www.latimes.com/business/la-fi-starbucks-20180521-story.html

Sork, T. J. (2000). Planning educational programs. In A. L. Wilson & E. R. Hayes (Eds.), *Handbook of adult and continuing education* (pp. 171–190). Jossey-Bass.

Sork, T. J. (2010). Planning and delivering programs. In C. E. Kasworm, A. D. Rose & J. M. Ross-Gordon (Eds.), *Handbook of adult and continuing education* (pp. 157–166). SAGE.

Sork, T. J. (2019a). Adult education in an era of "wicked problems." *Adult Learning, 30*(4). https://doi.org/10.1177/1045159519872457

Sork, T. J. (2019b). From "effortful use" to "contextual improvisation": Skill acquisition theory and program planning. *Proceedings of the 2019 Adult Education Research Conference* (pp. 385–390). Buffalo State College/SUNY. https://newprairiepress.org/cgi/viewcontent.cgi?article=4177&context=aerc

Sork, T. J. (2019c). Luscious lattes/bitter baristas: The 'Starbucks Incident' and its implications for program planning. In J. P. Egan (Ed.), *Proceedings of the 38th Annual Conference of the Canadian Association for the Study of Adult Education* (pp. 385–390). Canadian Association for the Study of Adult Education. https://www.dropbox.com/s/04lcxsvmvek8kkh/2019_CASAE_Proceedings.pdf?dl=0

Sork, T. J. & Caffarella, R. S. (1989). Planning programs for adults. In S. B. Merriam & P. M. Cunningham (Eds.), *Handbook of adult and continuing education* (pp. 233–245). Jossey-Bass.

Sork, T. J., & Käpplinger, B. (2019). "The Politics of Responsibility" revisited: An analysis of power in program planning. In F. Finnegan & B. Brummell (Eds.), *Power and possibility: Adult education in a diverse and complex world*. Brill/Sense. https://doi.org/10.1163/9789004413320

Starbucks (2018, April 17). *Starbucks to close all stores nationwide for racial-bias education on May 29*. https://stories.starbucks.com/press/2018/starbucks-to-close-stores-nationwide-for-racial-bias-education-may-29/

von Hippel, A., & Käpplinger, B. (2017). Models of program planning in Germany and in North America–A comparison. In B. Käpplinger, S. Robak, M. Fleige, A. von Hippel, & W. Gieseke (Eds.), *Cultures of program planning in adult education: Concepts, research results, and archives* (pp. 97–112). Peter Lang.

Walters, S. (2018). The drought is my teacher: Adult learning and education in times of climate crisis. *Journal of Vocational, Adult and Continuing Education and Training, 1*(1), 146–162. https://doi.org/10.14426/jovacet.vlil.308

Wheeler, A., Fowler, J., & Hattingh, L. (2013). Using an intervention mapping framework to develop an online mental health continuing education program for pharmacy staff. *Journal of Continuing Education in the Health Professions, 33*(4), 258–266. https://doi.org/10.1002/chp.21198

Woo, A. (2018, June 11). Employees say Starbucks anti-bias training in Canada well-intentioned but missed the mark by using U.S. curriculum. *The Globe and Mail*. https://www.theglobeandmail.com/canada/article-employees-say-starbucks-anti-bias-training-in-canada-well-intentioned/

CHAPTER 14

Assessment and Evaluation in Adult and Continuing Education

Lilian H. Hill

Assessment and evaluation are critical responsibilities of educational practice. Program stakeholders require adult educators to employ direct measures of adult learning to demonstrate learner progress and program value using valid measures. Diminishing funding for all sectors of education have made funding for adult education more competitive. It is essential for adult educators to design and use effective assessment and evaluation practices in order to advocate for the value of adult education programs. Due to a lack of current texts specific to adult and continuing education, many adult educators have had to learn assessment and evaluation skills in their work and use information produced for higher education and other fields.

Differentiating Assessment From Evaluation

Assessment and evaluation are often confused with each other (Galbraith & Jones, 2010). The key difference between assessment and evaluation derive from the purposes, focus, criteria, process, and goals employed (Table 14.1). *Assessment* provides information for improvement, but in evaluation the goal is judgment and measuring value. Assessment processes provide useful diagnostic information about student learning that may be employed by instructors to influence changes in their teaching approaches and is shared with learners to guide changes in their learning strategies and activities. Assessment is attentive to adult learners' needs and learning processes that may result in continued learning. Assessment criteria may be set mutually between the instructor and students in an iterative process and dialogic, reflective relationship. The evaluative relationship tends to be prescriptive in that standards for evaluation evidence are determined in advance. *Evaluation* involves making judgments about student learning outcomes, meaning the development of expected knowledge, skills, and behaviors based on predetermined standards. Evaluation determines the degree to which goals have been met and is accountable to program sponsors, administrators, and accreditation bodies. The consequence of not making a clear distinction between assessment and evaluation is that the validity of results becomes questionable.

Assessment

Functions of assessment include screening, diagnosis, program placement, quantifying a baseline for student knowledge or skills, monitoring progress, designing educational interventions, and providing feedback to students about their progress in learning. It involves the "systematic collection, review, and use of information about educational programs undertaken for the purpose of improving student learning and development" (Banta & Palomba, 2015, pp. 1–2). Examples

TABLE 14.1. Distinguishing Between Assessment and Evaluation

	Assessment *Information for Improvement*	*Evaluation* *Measuring Value*
Purposes	Gathering useful information that can be used by teachers and students to improve learning	Making judgments about student learning outcomes based on predetermined standards
Focus	Attentive to adult learning theories and knowledge of learners' needs	Accountable to administrative, professional, and accreditation bodies
Criteria	Mutually set by instructor and students	Determined by the evaluator
Process	Iterative	Prescriptive
Goals	Continued learning, progression, and completion of learning processes	Determines whether goals have been met

of student assessment methods include pre- and post-tests, instructor-devised tests, written assignments, presentations, student-created visualizations or graphics, case studies, simulations, assignments scored with a rubric, portfolios, performances, and standardized tests. Information derived from assessments is applied by instructors to make adjustments to their teaching strategies to better meet students' learning needs and by students so that they can alter their learning strategies (Hill, 2020a). Adult educators have a responsibility to provide information about student learning to students, administrators, and to the public that provides funding for many adult education activities. This can be a relatively straightforward task in areas of adult education where normed tests are commonly used, such as adult basic education or in workplace assessments. However,

> because education and learning often happen in undocumented nonformal or informal spaces, adult learning and education can be difficult to assess with accuracy. We must continue raising the visibility of learning in all forms and strive for closer monitoring and more accurate data to inform decision-making. (UIL, 2016)

Without the ability to tell our own story, based in robust assessment and evaluation practices, there is no way to advocate for adult education teaching and learning.

Principles of Assessment Pertinent to Adult and Continuing Education

Assessment is most effective when it focuses on adult learning, meaning making, and change. Assessment should provide learners with timely, constructive, and thoughtful feedback about their performance (Ambrose et al., 2010; Su, 2015). Principles of effective assessment practice for adult and continuing education (Table 14.2) build on the principles identified by Kasworm and Marienau (1997) and incorporate information derived from additional sources.

Perspectives on Assessment

While multiple perspectives on assessment exist, four perspectives were selected for discussion in this chapter due to their relevance to adult and continuing education.

Formative and Summative Assessment

Feedback and practice are essential to effective student learning (Ambrose et al., 2010). *Formative assessment* is conducted while learning is taking place, with purposes of improvement. *Summative assessment* takes place after learning is completed with purposes of communicating students' course performance through grades or certificates of completion. Effective feedback must be timely, specific, and meaningful to help adult learners understand the difference between what they are able to do and the expected performance levels they are hoping to achieve. They

TABLE 14.2. Principles of Effective Assessment for Adult and Continuing Education

Assessment is effective when the process:

Learning	1. Answers questions instructors have about the effectiveness of their instruction in helping learners meet their goals (Bain, 2004).
	2. Serves as mechanism for instructors to communicate about learning by providing timely and meaningful feedback to students about their progress (Ambrose et al., 2010; Bain, 2004).
	3. Appreciates learners' knowledge gained from "a wide variety of informal and formal knowledge sources" (Kasworm & Marienau, 1997, p. 8).
	4. Respects cultural diversity and honors multiple ways of knowing derived from cultural experience (Marbley et al., 2008).
	5. "Accommodates adult learners' increasing differentiation from one another given varied life experiences and education" (Kasworm & Marienau, 1997, p. 8).
	6. "Recognizes and reinforces the cognitive, conative, and affective domains of learning" (Kasworm & Marienau, 1997, p. 8).
Meaning Making	7. Provides information about the criteria to be used in forming judgments so as to encourage metacognition and self-reflective learning (Bain, 2004).
	8. "Entices students into serious consideration of important questions" (Bain, 2004, p. 156).
	9. "Focuses on adults' active involvement in learning and assessment processes, including active engagement in self-assessment" (Kasworm & Marienau, 1997, p. 8).
	10. Communicates that learning is sustainable and does not stop when instruction ends (Bain, 2004).
Change	11. "Embraces adult learners' involvement in and impact on the broader world of work, family, and community" (Kasworm & Marienau, 1997, p. 8).
	12. "Is part of a larger set of conditions that promote change" (Hutchings et al., 2012, para. 18).

can then make adjustments to their learning strategies to more closely model the performance criteria. "Feedback can improve student learning when it a) focuses on the key knowledge and skills students are to learn, b) is timed when students are most likely to benefit, and c) is linked to opportunities for further practice" (Hill, 2020b, p. 22). Several authors suggest that effective feedback is supportive of lifelong learning and consequently should be based in learner values, foster self-assessment, and provide information that students can use to improve learning in future (Boud & Soler, 2016; Nguyen & Walker, 2016; Su, 2015).

Authentic Assessment
Authentic assessment is "a form of assessment in which students are asked to perform real-world tasks that demonstrate meaningful application of essential knowledge and skills" (Strachan et al., 2010, para. 7). Engaging adult students in application of what they are learning to meaningful tasks they might realistically face as citizens, consumers, or practicing professionals is often motivating. Completing authentic assessment tasks can engage students in practicing component skills, combining them, building fluency, and ultimately completing the assessment task in its entirety (Moore, 2018). Authentic assessments

provide instructors with useful information regarding their students' growth in competence (Ambrose et al., 2010). Community service, internships, demonstrations, written work, presentations, and portfolios are useful in authentic assessment.

Sustainable Assessment
Adult education that equips students with the ability to face lives' complexities, the ability to plan for future learning, and apply their learning to changing circumstances is considered to be sustainable (Boud & Soler, 2016). Assessment is a sociocultural process mutually constructed by instructors and learners with a focus on building students' abilities to judge their own performance and prepare for learning after completion of the course or program. Sustainable assessment can foster students' "independence, intellectual maturity, and creativity" (p. 403). Students need to become knowledgeable about the criteria or standards in the relevant learning domain when instructors provide instruction about learning skills, self-assessment, metacognition, and reflection.

Dynamic Assessment
In its recognition of the complexities of human relationships, communities, and influences on knowledge, dynamic assessment is holistic and authentic (Prins et al., 2015). According to Fenwick (2001), it "seeks to capture what unfolds in social environments where meanings and perceptions are complex" (p. 79). Dynamic assessment is grounded in three principles: (a) Learning is a constantly evolving and dynamic process, (b) learning occurs during interaction with other people, and (c) assessment should encompass both the *what* and *how* of learning. Therefore, assessment measures need to be repeated over time as learners are changing. The effect of language, cultural context, and social interactions on learning must be critically examined. Reflective inquiry and dialogue among learners, instructors, and assessors are essential parts of the process.

Methods of Assessment
Assessment methods may involve the use of simulations in military or professional education; standardized testing in admissions, college placement, or literacy education; and applying measures of competence and learning transfer in continuing professional education. Depending on their purposes, adult educators may assign self-reflective assessments, written assignments, presentations, or engage students in artistic endeavors. Data gathered from assessments may be used to inform diagnostic purposes, provide feedback to students, or inform program evaluation. Space limitations preclude a complete discussion of assessment methods; however, the following sections describe assessment practices in areas where considerable activity is occurring: adult literacy and basic education, prior learning assessment, and competency-based assessment.

Assessment in Adult Literacy Education
Language, literacy, and numeracy are foundational skills for adults' ability to function in society. This is reflected in the documentary film *Night School*, which portrays struggles of working adults working toward alternate high school credentials (Cohn, 2016). Belzer and Greenberg (2020) comment that assessments in adult basic and literacy education can be used for purposes of accountability, credentialing, diagnosis, and population study. Accountability is a requirement mandated by the Workforce Innovation and Opportunity Act (WIOA) of 2014, an update of the Workforce Investment Act (WIA) of 1998, and is linked to provision of federal funds for adult basic education programs. Educational gains are measured using the Tests of Adult Basic Education (TABE), Comprehensive Adult Student Assessment Systems (CASAS), and the Basic English Skills Test (BEST). Local programs report results to state agencies which relay aggregated information to the U.S. Department of Education using the National Reporting System (NRS). Based on this data, state and national policy revisions may occur.

Credentialing assessment takes place through three high school equivalency tests used to determine whether adults have attained the equivalent of a high school diploma: (a) General Equivalency Diploma (GED), (b) High School Equivalency Test (HiTest), and (c) Test Assessing Secondary Completion (TASC) (Zinth & Education Commission of the States, 2015). While the "assessments vary in length, item type, formats available, and cost" (p. 3), all address English, mathematics, sciences, and social studies. Originally created to serve returning World War II soldiers who did not complete high school (McLendon, 2017), the GED is the oldest and best-known test. The GED was revised in 2012 to be aligned with Common Core, an educational initiative sponsored by the National Governors Association and the Council of Chief State School Officers that defines the standards students should be able to meet at the conclusion of each school year (Zinth & Education Commission of the States, 2015). Until January 2014, it was the only option available. Due to concerns about the rising cost of the GED, inadequate infrastructure and staff capacity to administer computer-based testing in some settings, and some test-takers' difficulties in completing a computer-based test, new alternatives were developed (Zinth & Education Commission of the States, 2015). Now, the GED is used in 40 states (exclusively in 27 states), HiTest is used in 12 states (exclusively in 7), and TASC is used in 7 states (exclusively in 3).

Significant advances in diagnostic assessment processes reveal the complexities of reading related to adults' decoding skills, fluency, vocabulary knowledge, phonological awareness (i.e., sound structure of language), morphological awareness (i.e., essential units of meaning), and orthographic knowledge (i.e., representation of spoken language in writing) (Greenberg et al., 2017; Tighe & Fernandes, 2019). Sabatini and Educational Testing Service (2015) observed that "empirical studies in the reading literature over the past several decades have yielded a rich literature for understanding component reading processes in adults" (p. 4). Unfortunately, because diagnostic tests require specialized training and are expensive, their use in literacy programs is limited (Belzer & Greenberg, 2020).

Examples of population studies of adult literacy include the National Adult Literacy Survey (NALS) in 1992; the National Assessment of Adult Literacy (NALS) in 2002; and, more recently, the Program for the International Assessment of Adult Competencies (PIAAC), conducted in 2011. In addition to reports of results and technical reports published by OECD (n.d.), multiple researchers are receiving grants for training, gaining access to response data, and producing publications based on PIAAC data. Collecting comparative data focused on adult learners on an international scale is a relatively recent activity, beginning with the International Adult Learning Survey in 1997 (Rubenson, 2019). "The interest in data on adult learning reflects a growing recognition by policy-makers of the necessity to invest in adult learning to achieve economic efficiency" (p. 297). Rubenson comments that the indicators measured in PIAAC focus on formal learning undertaken to obtain a degree or credential. Rubenson recommends that survey instruments be developed that capture the richness of adult learning and allow for recognition of diverse motivators for adult learning.

Prior Learning Assessment

As a feature of adult higher education that has increased access for adults, prior learning assessment (PLA) involves assessment of an individual's learning from life experiences based on its equivalence for college credit, certification, or advanced standing toward further education (Ross-Gordon & Collins, 2020). PLA is focused on learning acquired outside of academic settings, including military and work experience, community service, and informal learning. Testing can be used to determine whether an individual has achieved mastery to translate learning into college credits. Higher education institutions may develop their own tests, or use standardized tests such as the College Level Examination Program (CLEP). Students may be guided in developing a portfolio to demonstrate their knowledge that consists of evidence collected in tangible form or electronically in an ePortfolio (Eynon & Gambino, 2017).

Competency-Based Assessment

Programs incorporating competency-based assessments focus on what students know and can do rather than on where and when learning has occurred.

> Instead of evaluating student progress [based] primarily on the amount of time spent in a classroom (using the credit hour, . . . the default standard for measuring progress), students receive college credit based on their actual demonstration of skills learned. (Tate et al., 2015, p. 2)

In 2005, "the Higher Education Reconciliation Act created direct assessment programs as an alternative path to Title IV financial aid eligibility for students enrolled in programs approved by the Department of Education" (Online Learning Consortium et al., 2019, para. 1).

Evaluation

Evaluation involves systematically collecting and analyzing data to make informed judgments about program quality, effectiveness, viability, and improvement

(Fitzpatrick et al., 2009). Evaluation processes entail gathering information about whether program objectives were met, program resources were used effectively, and to plan for future programming. Evaluation is best used to review the effectiveness of educational practice to help adult and continuing education professionals select practices that will prove effective at improving adult outcomes. Evaluation may be used to not only judge the value of a program but also measure its compliance with standards and agreements with program funders. The Joint Committee on Standards for Educational Evaluation defined *evaluation as* the

- systematic investigation of quality of programs, projects, subprograms, and/or any of their components or elements, together or singly,
- for purposes of decision-making, judgments, conclusions, findings, new knowledge, organization development, and capacity building in response to identified needs of stakeholders,
- leading to improvement of quality and/or accountability, and
- ultimately contributing to organizational or social value. (Yarborough et al., 2011, p. xxv)

Evaluation may be used to answer to the requirements of program stakeholders that include funding sources, regional accrediting bodies, professional accreditation bodies, and program administrators.

While information garnered from student assessment may be used to inform evaluation, due to its different purposes, program evaluators will typically gather information from additional sources. Questions that may be answered by evaluators include whether the educational program (a) met important personal and societal needs, (b) was responsive to the sociopolitical context, (c) used resources wisely, (d) assisted students with application of their learning to the personal and work needs that brought them to the educational encounter, and consequently (e) required adjustment in its delivery and management (Caffarella & Daffron, 2013).

Principles of Evaluation Pertinent to Adult and Continuing Education

Program evaluation standards were published by the Joint Committee on Standards for Educational Evaluation (2011), composed of membership from other national organizations including the American Educational Research Association (AERA), National Educational Association (NEA), American Evaluation Association (AEA), and American Psychological Association (APA), among others. Thirty standards are organized in the following categories: *utility* (value of program evaluation for stakeholders), *feasibility* (evaluation effectiveness, efficiency), *propriety* (use of fair, legal, and just processes), *accuracy* (dependability, truthfulness of findings), and *accountability* (proper documentation, focus on improvement and accountability). What is missing from the standards is a critical viewpoint about the goals and purposes of program evaluation.

Moore (2018) notes that "effective program evaluation entails a dynamic, long-term evaluation process that tracks multiple contributing factors and outcomes measurements" (p. 57). Meaningful and useful program evaluations require program staff to be thoughtful about the goals they aim to meet, criteria they use to determine success, data to collect, and which personnel are engaged in decision-making (Fitzpatrick et al., 2009). Careful planning, attentiveness to change in public demands, and flexibility are needed to prevent the possibility of being unprepared to respond to unanticipated requirements or evolving standards imposed by external stakeholders.

Evidence-based policy has become "a key concern of policymakers, funding sources, program administrators, community support groups, and current and potential program clientele" (Martin & Roessger, 2020, p. 38). *Evidence-based* refers to the use of objective evidence to guide program design or modification. Gathering and using objective evidence of student learning is "essential to improving student learning and responding to accountability expectations" (Kuh et al., 2015, p. 27). What counts as evidence should be relevant to intended outcomes and may include survey data, test results, student portfolios, or rubric scores as well as information derived from registration, attendance, absenteeism, or program continuance records. The fluid nature of adult education can lead to flaws in validity and usefulness of the evidence collected, for example, if participants' attendance is interrupted or discontinued or outcomes were ill defined at the outset (Greenberg et al., 2011). Admittedly, some adult education practices have been poorly documented and are therefore difficult to evaluate. A complexity of program evaluation is producing evidence acceptable to multiple audiences. "Stakeholders must perceive the data that are collected as part of program evaluation as credible evidence" (Moore, 2018, p. 59).

Perspectives
Similar to assessment, multiple perspectives or approaches to program evaluation exist (Stufflebeam & Coryn, 2007), but only a few pertinent to adult and continuing education are discussed in this chapter. These models can guide adult educators in conducting program evaluation (Martin & Roessger, 2020).

Four-Level Model of Evaluation
Kirkpatrick's (1994) well-known four-level model examines program outcomes: reactions; learning; behavior; and organizational results. Program evaluators using this model are interested in the impact of education in relation to: (a) participants' reactions to training, (b) whether they have increased their learning (knowledge, skills, or experience), and (c) if they are changing their behavior. The fourth level of the model is an end-of-program evaluation.

Empowerment Evaluation
This approach to evaluation is designed to help organizations and community groups develop the skills to conduct their own evaluation (Fetterman, 2017). It involves the use of "evaluation concepts, techniques, and findings to foster improvement and self-determination" (p. 112). The major issues to be determined by program evaluators are to ascertain the information needs of the community that will foster improvement and self-determination.

Participatory/Collaborative Evaluation
This model focuses on engaging program participants as stakeholders in the evaluation process (Wells, 2014). Participants directly affected by the program are in the position to provide the most critical information about program goals and results. The use of participatory methods ensures that the people involved share knowledge and control of the evaluation process, empowers marginalized people to become subjects of their own knowledge, and assures that the process remains true to the goals.

Methods
In addition to incorporating the results of assessment of student learning, multiple methods used in evaluation include observations, interviews, surveys, pre- and post-tests, portfolios, review of student products, focus groups, cost-benefit analyses, and self-assessments. All methods must be chosen carefully based on their characteristics, strengths, and weaknesses so as to meet program and evaluation goals. Space limitations preclude discussion of evaluation methods, but multiple information sources are available (Caffarella & Daffron, 2013; Fitzpatrick et al., 2009; Martin & Roessger, 2020; Moore, 2018; Yarborough et al., 2011).

Role of Bias in Assessment and Evaluation in Adult and Continuing Education

All forms of assessment and evaluation are socially constructed processes with social consequences. Racial, ethnic, and gender stereotypes are persistent and result in the use of poorly conceived or culturally inappropriate language; mismatch between learning content (knowledge, skill performance) and assessment and evaluation processes; and other forms of cultural insensitivity that interfere with ratings of student performance and which unintentionally favor some candidates over others. Biased assessments can be the result of language bias, professional bias, practice bias, and instrument bias that are generally rooted in lack of acknowledgment and understanding of diverse cultures. There is a need for the "development of culturally appropriate and culturally sensitive assessment instruments as well as the development of ethical standards and training guidelines to prepare competent professionals" (Marbley et al. 2008, p. 12). Marbley et al. comment that

> instruments used to measure achievement and competence are being more urgently called for and more widely used than ever before whereas, on the other hand, tests [and other forms of assessment] are, at the same time, being more sharply criticized and strongly opposed. (p. 13)

Critiques are based in current and historical assessment and evaluation practices that are unfair to marginalized groups, including people of color, women, immigrants, language learners, and the disabled, exemplified in biased assessments that have sometimes been expressly intended to cause harm. Leaker and Boyce (2015) comment that women, people of color, those of low socioeconomic status, and/or those with LGBT identity, pay a "self-worth tax" in that they learn to deny and subjugate their own culture to be successful in settings where Caucasian, male, and heteronormative cultural norms prevail. Lack of acknowledgment of cultural differences or application of a color-blind ideology that invalidates people's identities and negates their experiences of racism result in assessment and evaluation that perpetuate a racist culture.

Issues, Disagreements, and Problems in Practice

Currently, it is problematic to discuss assessment and evaluation without discussing societal demands for accountability of educational programs. Program staff are required to attest that educational programs are meeting public and policy requirements that focus on workforce development and cost-effectiveness, particularly when taxpayer monies are being used (Tusting, 2012). Adult education programs are often held accountable to regulatory agencies, program funders/sponsors, policy frameworks and, in some instances, accreditation agencies that require documentation of student achievement of learning outcomes (Fenwick, 2010). The public expects that students are learning skills for employability and, as a result, accountability mechanisms require the use of measures that demonstrate that students are gaining work skills, often irrespective of students' learning goals.

These increasing demands for assessment and evaluation are based in standardized metrics, competition, reduced resources, and skepticism about the value of education. The ascension of an audit culture is driven by the integration of market logic and business ideologies into social enterprises (Apple, 2013; Grace, 2016). Many aspects of our daily lives have been commodified, including education, social services, and health care, meaning that human processes are reduced to their economic value. Accountability systems are implemented to ensure that work is being done and public monies are being invested wisely (Lee, 2017; Tusting, 2012). As Fenwick (2010) observes, "in the lean streets of (post) recessionary budget cuts, adult education programs must fight to maintain what little funding is still allotted to them" (para. 2). Lee (2017) writes

Indeed, a belief has emerged that everything can be quantifiable, which has been called 'data-ism' (Brooks, Feb. 4, 2013). Data-ism, 'the rising philosophy of the day', carries 'certain cultural assumptions—that everything that can be measured and should be measured; that data is a transparent and reliable lens that allows us to filter out emotionalism and ideology; that data will help us do remarkable things—like foretell the future' (Brooks, Feb. 4, 2013). Han (2015b), however, warns against this kind of belief, given that metrics by themselves are not narratives. (p. 153, quotations in original)

The notion that everything can be quantifiable is at odds with many of adult education's goals.

In an audit culture (Apple, 2013; Grace, 2016) or evaluator state (English & Mayo, 2012), increasing levels of accountability have been introduced in a range of settings, particularly in "publicly funded arenas such as education and health care" (Tusting, 2012, p. 121). Lee (2017) argues that we have become an achievement society where adult learning is yoked to "commodifying individuals' learning experiences and outcomes in the name of [meeting evolving requirements for occupational] competence" (p. 150). A focus on financial efficiency is rendering some assessment practices unsustainable due to their consumption of financial resources, time, and labor (Boud & Soler, 2016). When the "stakeholder changes from that of the learner to that of the programme funding or sponsoring body" (Wittnebel, 2012, p. 82), evidence must be provided that documents program effectiveness in economic terms. In the face of these accountability demands, adult educators must become more sophisticated in their uses of assessment and evaluation.

Summary and Conclusions

Adult educators need to develop their knowledge of and skills in assessment and evaluation so that they are able to continue providing meaningful learning experiences to students. It is important that adult educators are able to combine critical perspectives with assessment and evaluation knowledge in order to articulate learning and assessment goals that meet students' needs, provide relevant educational experiences, and facilitate evaluation of the results. When we lack knowledge about the social consequences of assessment and evaluation we are in no position to challenge metrics of assessment, evaluation, and accountability that contradict adult education purposes. Assessment and evaluation processes should be designed by adult educators and adult learners, rather than solely in response to external stakeholders. We can contribute to society by applying critical perspectives to the role of adult education in society. Therefore, it is essential that adult educators keep the focus on the purposes of adult education and use assessment and evaluation to benefit the adult learners we serve.

References

Ambrose, S. A., Bridges, M. W., DiPietro, M., Lovett, M. C., & Norman, M. K. (2010). *How learning works: Seven research-based principles for smart teaching.* Jossey-Bass.

Apple, M. W. (2013). Audit cultures, labour, and conservative movements in the global university. *Journal of Educational Administration and History, 45*(4), 385–394.

Bain, K. (2004). *What the best college teachers do.* Harvard University Press.

Banta, T. W., & Palomba, C. A. (2015). *Assessment essentials: Planning, implementing, and improving assessment in higher education.* Jossey-Bass.

Belzer, A., & Greenberg, D. (2020). The Gordian knot of adult basic education assessment: Untangling the multiple audiences and purposes. In L. H. Hill (Ed.), *Assessment, evaluation, and accountability in adult education* (pp. 57–71). Stylus.

Boud, D., & Soler, R. (2016). Sustainable assessment revisited. *Assessment & Evaluation in Higher Education, 41*(3), 400–413. https://doi.org/10.1080/02602938.2015.1018133

Caffarella, R. S., & Daffron, S. R. (2013). *Planning programs for adult learners: A practical guide* (3rd ed.). Jossey-Bass.

Cohn, A. (Director). (2016). *Night school* [Film]. Oscilloscope.

English, L. M., & Mayo, P. (2012). *Learning with adults: A critical pedagogical introduction.* Sense Publishers.

Eynon, B., & Gambino, L. M. (2017). *High-impact ePortfolio practice: A catalyst for students, faculty, and institutional learning.* Stylus.

Fenwick, T. (2001). Dynamic assessment: Putting learners at the center of the evaluation. In T. Barer-Stein (Ed.), *The craft of teaching adults* (pp. 77–93). Irwin.

Fenwick, T. (2010). Accountability practices in adult education: Insights from actor-network theory. *Studies in the Education of Adults, 42*(2), 170–185.

Fetterman, D. (2017). Transformative empowerment evaluation and Freirean pedagogy: Alignment with an emancipatory tradition. *New Directions for Adult and Continuing Education, 2017*(115), 111–126.

Fitzpatrick, J., Christie, C., & Mark, M. M. (2009). *Evaluation in action: Interviews with expert evaluators.* SAGE.

Galbraith, M. W., & Jones, M. S. (2010). Assessment and evaluation. In C. E. Kasworm, A. D. Rose, & J. M. Ross-Gordon (Eds.), *Handbook of adult and continuing education* (pp. 167–175). SAGE.

Grace, A. (2016). Lifelong learning as critical action. In R. Mizzi, T. S. Rocco, & S. Shore (Eds.), *Disrupting adult and community education: Teaching, learning, and working in the periphery* (pp. 17–34). SUNY Press.

Greenberg, D., Ginsburg, L., & Wrigley, H. S. (2017). Research updates: Reading, numeracy, and language education. *New Directions for Adult and Continuing Education, 2017*(155), 83–94. https://doi.org/10.1002/ace.20243

Greenberg, D., Wise, J. C., Morris, R., Fredrick, L. D., Rodrigo, V., Nanda, A. & Pae, H. (2011). A randomized control study of instructional approaches for struggling adult readers. *Journal of Research on Educational Effectiveness, 4*(2), 101–117.

Hill, L. H. (Ed.). (2020a). *Assessment, evaluation, and accountability in adult education.* Stylus.

Hill, L. H. (2020b). Skillsets for assessment. In L. H. Hill (Ed.), *Assessment, evaluation, and accountability in adult education* (pp. 18–37). Stylus.

Hutchings, P., Ewell, P., & Banta, T. (2012). *AAHE principles of good practice: Aging nicely.* University of Illinois and Indiana University, National Institute for Learning Outcomes Assessment (NILOA).

Joint Committee on Standards for Educational Evaluation. (2011). *Program evaluation standards.* http://www.jcsee.org/program-evaluation-standards-statements.

Kasworm, C. E., & Marienau, C. A. (1997). Principles for assessment of adult learning. *New Directions for Adult and Continuing Education, 1997*(75), 5–16.

Kirkpatrick, D. L. (1994). *Evaluating training programs: The four levels.* Berrett-Koehler.

Kuh, G. D., Ikenberry, S. O., Jankowski, N. Cain, T. R., Hutchings, P. & Kinzie, J. (2015). *Using evidence of student learning to improve higher education.* John Wiley.

Leaker, C., & Boyce, F. A. (2015). A bigger rock, a steeper hill: PLA, race, and the color of learning. *Journal of Continuing Higher Education, 63*(3), 199–204.

Lee, M. (2017). Decoding the neoliberal subjectivity in self-directed learning in self-helping adult learners. *International Journal of Lifelong Education, 36*(1–2), 145–163.

Marbley, A. F., Bonner, F., & Berg, R. (2008). Measurement and assessment: Conversations with professional people in the field of education. *Multicultural Education, 16*(1), 12–20.

Martin, L., & Roessger, K. (2020). Skillsets for program evaluation in adult education. In L. H. Hill (Ed.), *Assessment, evaluation, and accountability in adult education* (pp. 37–53). Stylus.

McLendon, L. (2017). High school equivalency assessment and recognition in the United States: An eyewitness account. *New Directions for Adult and Continuing Education, 2017*(155), 41–49.

Moore, D. E. (2018). Assessment of learning and program evaluation in health professions education programs. *New Directions for Adult and Continuing Education, 2018*(157), 51–64.

Nguyen, T. T. H., & Walker, M. (2016). Sustainable assessment for lifelong learning. *Assessment and Evaluation in Higher Education, 41*(1), 97–111.

Online Learning Consortium, University Professional and Continuing Education Association, & WCET. (2019). *Competency-based education, direct assessment, and financial aid: Background, concerns, and guiding principles.* Online Learning Consortium.

Organisation for Economic Co-operation and Development. (n.d.). https://www.oecd.org/skills/piaac/publications/

Prins, L., Pauchulo, A. L., Brooke, A., & Corrigan, J. (2015). Learning at the center: A proposal for dynamic assessment in a combined university and community adult learning center course. *Adult Learning, 26*(2), 59–65.

Ross-Gordon, J. M., & Collins, R. A. (2020). Assessment and evaluation practices for adult students in higher education. In L. H. Hill (Ed.), *Assessment, evaluation, and accountability in adult education* (pp. 182–197). Stylus.

Rubenson, K. (2019). Assessing the status of lifelong learning: Issues with composite indexes and surveys on participation. *International Review of Education / Internationale Zeitschrift Für Erziehungswissenschaft, 65*(2), 295–317.

Sabatini, J., & Educational Testing Service (2015). *Understanding the basic reading skills of U.S. adults: Reading components in the PIAAC Literacy Survey.* ETS Center for Research on Human Capital and Education. http://www.ets.org/research/policy_research_reports/publications/report/2015/jvnx

Strachan, R., Pickard, A., Laing, C. (2010). Bringing technical authoring skills to life for students through an employer audience. *Innovation in Teaching and Learning in Information and Computer Sciences, 9*(2), 1–11.

Stufflebeam, D. L., & Coryn, C. L. S. (2007). *Evaluation theory, models, and applications* (2nd ed.). Jossey-Bass.

Su, Y. (2015). Targeting assessment for developing adult lifelong learners: Assessing the ability to commit. *Australian Journal of Adult Learning, 55*(1), 75–93.

Tate, P., Klein-Collins, R., & Council for Adult and Experiential Learning. (2015). *PLA and CBE on the competency continuum: The relationship between prior learning assessment and competency-based education.* Council for Adult and Experiential Learning.

Tighe, E. L., & Fernandes, M. A. (2019). Unraveling the complexity of the relations of metalinguistic skills to word reading with struggling adult readers: Shared, independent, and interactive effects. *Applied Psycholinguistics, 40*(3), 765–793.

Tusting, K. (2012). Learning accountability literacies in educational workplaces: Situated learning and processes of commodification. *Language and Education, 26*(2), 121–138.

UIL (UNESCO Institute for Lifelong Learning). (2016). *3rd global report on adult learning and education: The impact of adult learning and education on health and well-being; employment and the labour market; and social, civic and community life.* Author.

Wells, J. M. (2014). Investigating adult literacy programs through community engagement research: A case study. *Community Literacy Journal, 8*(2), 49–67.

Wittnebel, L. (2012). Business as usual? A review of continuing professional education and adult learning. *Journal of Adult and Continuing Education, 18*(2), 80–88.

Yarborough, D. B., Shulha, L. M., Hopson, R. M., & Caruthers, F. A. (2011). *Program evaluation standards: A guide for evaluators and evaluation users* (3rd ed.). SAGE.

Zinth, J., & Education Commission of the States. (2015). *GED, HiSET and TASC: A comparison of high school equivalency assessments.* Education Commission of the States. https://www.ecs.org/ged-hiset-and-tasc-a-comparison-of-high-school-equivalency-assessments/

CHAPTER 15

Teaching Perspectives

Stephen D. Brookfield

In the past 50 years, adult education scholarship in the United States, at least as far as the handbooks of adult and continuing education are concerned, has not viewed the teaching of adults as an important lens through which to view practice. The 1948 handbook (Ely, 1948) had a section on "Media and Methods of Instruction" but this dealt with movies, radio, materials, discussion groups, and the military. In the 1960 handbook (Knowles, 1960) the chapter on methods in adult education invoked facilitation as its organizing concept and opened with the question, "What are the conditions which facilitate adult learning?" (Schmidt & Svenson, 1960, p. 82). The topic of methods was omitted from the next two handbooks until a chapter on facilitating adult learning appeared in the 1990 edition (Brookfield, 1990). In 2000 (Wilson & Hayes, 2000) the topic of "teaching" appeared for the first time in the handbook, with two chapters authored on discourses and cultures of teaching (Pratt & Nesbit, 2000) and teaching for critical consciousness (Tisdell et al., 2000). The 2010 handbook reverted to the concept of facilitation with a chapter on the facilitation and design of learning (Smith, 2010) that fit the volume's opening section titled "The Centrality of the Adult Learner and Adult Learning" (Kasworm & Rose, 2010).

The centrality of learners and learning has framed the history of the field's understanding of practice. Since the publication of Thorndike et al.'s (1928) *Adult Learning*, adult educators have placed the learner's needs, characteristics, and experiences at the heart of their practice and then explored how to support their learning in any way that seems methodologically appropriate. Lindeman's early *The Meaning of Adult Education* (1926/1961) urged discussion group process as the emblematic form of practice in the field, a theme that was repeated in the 1948 edition of the handbook (Essert, 1948). This dialogic emphasis remains the dominant methodological paradigm in U.S. adult education because it informs two streams of thought with distinctively different ideological emphases: andragogy and critical forms of pedagogy.

Andragogy

In 1970 Knowles popularized the term *andragogy* in his hugely influential text *The Modern Practice of Adult Education*, subtitled *Andragogy Versus Pedagogy* (Knowles, 1970). Although Lindeman had briefly used the term *andragogy* several decades earlier (Brookfield, 1984), it was Knowles who developed a template for how adult educators should work with adult learners. In *The Modern Practice of Adult Education* (Knowles, 1970) and *The Adult Learner: A Neglected Species* (Knowles, 1973), he argued that adults exhibited certain inclinations as learners that irrevocably framed how their learning should be supported. Adults learned primarily to explore problems of interest to them and naturally turned toward directing these learning efforts themselves. They were self-motivated to engage in learning that had intrinsic meaning for them. Furthermore, the greater breadth and depth of their experiences meant that they were qualitatively different subjects from children and adolescents. Knowles argued that because of their natural predilection for self-directed learning, adults should be in control of their learning as much as possible as they pursued objectives they had defined as important to them.

Out of this analysis of the distinct characteristics of adult learners came the model of andragogy. Adult educators were to place a primary emphasis on helping adults design their learning needs and helping them understand which of their experiences were useful resources on which they could draw. Adult educators were to consider themselves as facilitators or helpers, in contrast to situations in which children or adolescents were learning. Because children and adolescents were at relatively early stages of their development it was impossible for them to define their true learning needs in any meaningful sense. Where this latter group was concerned, a model that emphasized teaching was more appropriate. Young people's lack of life experience meant that those with greater maturity and wisdom—teachers—typically needed to direct the learning by imparting information and skills. This latter approach was described as *pedagogy* and deemed to be the dominant method for K–12 education.

Adult educators, by way of contrast, were to practice andragogy. After working to help adults clarify their own learning needs, the educator was to consider himself or herself as a facilitator. Adult educators would stand by the side of learners, available to assist in any way directed by learners themselves. This kind of servant education paralleled the work of MacGregor Burns (1978) in leadership. In both contexts practitioners were servants and aides to learners, working primarily under their behest and direction. The adult educator as practitioner of andragogy would be a resource person who was consulted as learners ran into problems. At learners' request, adult educators would step in to provide some direction, but any guidance, information, or skill demonstration offered would always be determined by, and under the control of, the learner. Knowles made an important change to the second edition of his *Modern Practice of Adult Education* (Knowles, 1978), subtitling it *From Pedagogy to Andragogy*. In response to criticism of his initial bifurcation, he acknowledged that more pedagogical models were sometimes appropriate when working with adults and that pedagogy and andragogy were at the opposite ends of a methodological continuum that contained varying degrees of learner control. But the assumption that adult educators should move to an andragogical stance as quickly as possible was clearly evident (Knowles, 1978).

In the 1970s and 1980s the andragogy paradigm was hugely influential (Knowles & Associates, 1984). At a stroke it legitimized the professional identity of the field. If it was true that, as Knowles contended, adult learners were qualitatively different from children and adolescents, then it logically followed that an intellectual discipline and an applied field of practice of adult education were needed to study adult learners and formulate appropriate models of facilitation. Andragogy also provided the intellectual underpinning to the development of institutional practices around the accreditation of prior learning. Institutions like Empire State College in New York, the Fielding Institute in Santa Barbara, California, and Thomas Edison College in Trenton, New Jersey, were created to find ways to allow adults to earn college credit by documenting the skills and knowledge they had learned in their lives outside the academy. From being a daring outlier, the notion of granting credit for life experience is now regularly advertised on network television with accredited institutions such as Western Governors, Phoenix, and Capella universities.

In 2020 the andragogical paradigm still exerts enormous influence in the field. Enter the term *adult learning theory* into any online search engine and Knowles's ideas will still be front and center. However, practitioners and scholars of American adult education in the last 5 decades have also engaged with the methodological approach of a very different figure, Paulo Freire.

Critical Pedagogy

The same year that saw the publication of the first edition of *The Modern Practice of Adult Education* (Knowles, 1970) also marked the English publication of *Pedagogy of the Oppressed* (Freire, 1970). Freire sketched out a vision of dialogic education that sprang from very different intellectual roots than Knowles's work. Blending the early Marx of the *Economic and*

Philosophical Manuscripts (Marx, 1961) together with the Latin American tradition of liberation theology, Freire outlined a form of problem-posing education developed during his work in adult literacy in Brazil and Chile. Education was conceived of as the practice of freedom, a liberatory process designed to help peasants learn to read and write while simultaneously uncovering the forces keeping them oppressed. The pedagogy of the oppressed was one that emphasized group discussion and, on the surface, seemed akin to Knowles's desire to let learners control their own process of learning.

Crucially, however, the Marxist concept of false consciousness came into play. Freire argued that when people had been ideologically manipulated to believe their world was set and their lives unchangeable, educators needed to prompt them to realize that another world was possible. By asking people to draw pictures of their everyday situations and asking questions about these situations and who constructed them, peasants would come to see how control of land and other resources were confined to a minority who exploited the labor of the majority. The practice of andragogy was apolitical compared to Freire's conceptualization of adult literacy education as part of a revolutionary movement, as was the case with the Sandanista Nicaraguan or Cuban literacy campaigns. Behind Freire's methodology was the project of collective political liberation. Behind Knowles's approach was the project of individual growth and development.

Another superficial similarity behind Knowles and Freire was their apparent bifurcation of traditional top-down instruction and dynamic, dialogic discussion. Although Freire adopted the term *pedagogy* to refer to whatever directive actions were taken by animators or facilitators, he described institutional education as banking education. The banking metaphor was intended to communicate the manner in which teachers assumed their students' heads were empty vaults containing nothing of value until those same teachers deposited information and knowledge they regarded as necessary and valuable. U.S. adult education seized on the banking education metaphor, using it as a shorthand condemnation of top-down instructional approaches, in particular that of lecturing. It was not until Freire's (Shor & Freire, 1987) clarification that banking education could be seen just as readily in discussion-based teaching and that lectures could be critically stimulating by opening up challenging new worldviews for people, that this simple bifurcation was problematized. In two so-called talking books (Shor & Freire, 1987; Horton & Freire, 1990) Freire clarified that teachers were always directive, moving students in either a liberatory or an oppressive direction. He distinguished between authoritative and authoritarian teaching, explaining that teachers sometimes needed to exercise the necessary authority derived from their greater knowledge and experience.

Like Knowles, Freire's work reverberates to this day in American adult education. It is perhaps seen most often in work based on critical pedagogy (English & Mayo, 2012; Mayo, 2004) where the project is to radicalize adult learners ensnared by the ideological manipulation of capitalism (Brookfield & Holst, 2010). Freire's work also reverberates with that of Myles Horton at the Highlander Folk School (Horton, 1990, 2003) who encouraged activists from union, civil rights, and environmental movements to explore their experiences as a means of discovering how best to fight those controlling land, the economy, and politics. Anyone attending an adult learning workshop led by educators drawing on Knowlesian and Freirean traditions respectively would probably notice a superficial similarity. There would be groups of adults sitting in groups and talking about their experiences with each other. It would be hard to decide who was the leader or facilitator because that person would try not to dominate the conversation and would be responsible only for asking questions that stimulated more conversation. But the clue would lie in the type of questions posed. In one group, the questions would be asked with the intent of helping individual learners clarify their most important learning needs and then plan how these could be satisfied. In the other, the questions would first problematize the needs expressed, ask who benefited most from those needs being met, and inquire about the extent that individual needs could ever be extrapolated out from the collective common good.

Uneasy Pluralities: Contemporary Teaching Perspectives in Adult Education

The uneasy cohabitation of the two paradigms already explored typifies a broader theoretical plurality that marks the understanding of teaching in the field of U.S. adult education. This plurality has been explored in depth in Pratt et al.'s (2016) explication of five perspectives on teaching adults. This work is based on educators in over 100 countries completing a teaching perspectives inventory (TPI) examining the beliefs, intentions and actions of over 100,000 educators (Collins & Pratt, 2011). Pratt et al. (2016) claim that TPI research shows that of the teachers surveyed, the vast majority placed themselves within one of the following five perspectives, although they occasionally drew on others as contexts changed.

1. Transmission: This perspective views good teaching as helping adults learn necessary content and skills in a systematic and carefully sequenced way. Teachers are enthusiastic about their subject and provide frequent evaluations of how learners are progressing. The transmission mode includes the Freirean notion of banking education and Knowles's view of andragogy.
2. Apprenticeship: This perspective views teaching as a form of socialization into professional behaviors and norms. It is usually held by practitioners in applied settings who are concerned to help learners become more critically reflective practitioners (Brookfield, 2017).
3. Developmental: This perspective is learner centered in that it views good teaching as grounded in an accurate estimation of where adults are in terms of their readiness for learning and the experiences they bring to their study. Based on this knowledge, adult teachers work skillfully to move learners to more complex forms of reasoning.
4. Nurturing: This perspective regards good teaching as something close to mentoring (Daloz, 2012; Zachary, 2016). Teachers create learning environments in which adults feel respected and safe and in which providing emotional support is viewed as a prime responsibility of the teacher. In the nurturing paradigm instructors teach from the heart (Apps, 1996) and try to create authentic personal connections with learners (Cranton, 2006).
5. Social reform: This perspective is squarely in the Freirean and critical pedagogy traditions of teaching adults to critique society and learn to work collectively for democratic and transformative change. It draws on critical theory's (Brookfield, 2004) project to help people understand how ideological control works to educate them to accept their servitude. In the social reform paradigm, teaching is part of a larger project to bring about socialist, anarchist, and anticapitalist formations (Allman, 2001) that challenge dominant ideologies such as patriarchy and White supremacy (Carpenter & Mojab, 2017).

The idea that teachers work primarily within one perspective has been challenged by Brookfield (2013), who cites the Ignation pedagogical ideal of *Tantum Quantum*—the notion that context constantly alters how a practice is put into effect—to describe a typical week in which teachers move across all perspectives. A single event, for example a class designed to help adults uncover the White supremacy that lives within them (Brookfield & Associates, 2018), could involve all five paradigms. The teacher would be concerned to ensure that people knew the component elements of White supremacy and that they understood how that ideology lodged itself in their consciousness (the transmission mode). An educator would probably wish to give students the chance to role-play how to react to situations in which racial microaggressions were enacted (the apprenticeship mode). In planning the lesson there would be a concern to introduce the topic in ways that learners could understand and that connected to their experiences, perhaps through stories or narrative modeling (the developmental mode). As the class moved into the discussion of the raw and contentious topic of racism, the instructor would probably want to ensure that people's basic identity was acknowledged as the classroom moved from a safe space to a brave space (Arao & Clemens, 2013). This would entail providing emotional support as people experienced shame, fear, anxiety, and anger as they were challenged to look within their own psyches (the nurturing mode). And, of course, the topic of the class itself would be located within the project of fighting racism (the social reform mode).

The de facto understanding of teaching within adult education is that it must not be considered as performance art but as the act of helping adults learn. Helping adults learn does not mean that teachers of adults should never lecture, but that lecturing only happens when it serves learners well. Similarly, holding a discussion is not considered an inherently adult methodology. A discussion would be appropriate if teachers wanted students to realize that multiple interpretations, experiences, and viewpoints around a topic existed in the same group. It would not be the best way to teach the foundational building blocks of content. Whatever decisions and actions a "teacher as helper of learning" takes are done with the aim of helping adults move forward in their development.

This emphasis on adult teaching as embodying a plurality of different methodologies depending on context crosses several contemporary texts on the topic (Brockett, 2016; Rogers & Horrocks, 2010; Spalding, 2014; Wlodkowski & Ginsberg, 2017). Brockett (2016) writes that he uses several terms interchangeably to describe the activity of helping adults to learn: *teacher*, *instructor*, *facilitator*, *trainer*, and *guide*. He breaks teaching into a number of common tasks such as planning instruction, creating a positive learning environment, overcoming resistance to learning, and building motivation. Integrating the developing research on brain chemistry into adult education leads Taylor and Marienau (2016) to describe interweaving multifaceted approaches to helping adults create meaning.

This helping-people-learn perspective emphasizes continually shifting roles and methodologies. It places learners and learning at the conceptual heart of teaching and emphasizes teachers arriving at particular strategies only after getting to know learners (Merriam & Bierema, 2013). Despite the dialogic tradition in adult education (Vella, 2002), no single pedagogic approach is inherently privileged within this perspective. Depending on context, helping learning can best be done by a teacher staying silent or by that same person delivering a lecture. Similarly, helping learning may sometimes require substantial scaffolding, involving sequencing tasks carefully and introducing building blocks of knowledge. At other times it may require educators to step back, not direct activities, and allow learners to struggle with necessary challenges. All pedagogic decisions are guided by answering a simple question: What will best help adults learn?

Critiquing the Helping Adults Learn Paradigm

Helping Adults Learn (Knox, 1986) has served the field of adult education well as an inherently malleable descriptor that encompasses multiple forms of teaching practice. Anarchists and administrators, community organizers and CEOs in all their different guises can claim to be teachers engaged in helping adults learn skills and knowledge. But two critiques can be made of this idea: its value neutrality and its lack of power analysis.

Value Neutrality

The teaching-as-helping-adults-learn paradigm is all about empowering learners to build their confidence, realize their collective power, and shape the world to their liking. This approach seems well in line with the democratic tradition of the field and its early connections to community development and social action. Yet the matter of specific content, of curriculum, of what is actually being taught, is mostly sidestepped in this analysis.

Content or subject matter is important, and its teaching sometimes has political import. Gramsci (1971) contended that elites maintain political control through an educational process by ensuring that people actively learn ways of thinking and behaving that justify inequity as normal as they move through their daily lives. The broad field of critical theory (Brookfield, 2004) explores how people learn, and are taught, dominant ideologies such as capitalism, White supremacy, patriarchy, militarism, and representative democracy. If people learn to accept that economic, racial, and gender inequity are the natural state of affairs, then revolutionary urges to change this situation are effectively neutralized. If people are taught to believe we live in a democracy where everyone has freedom of speech and an equal opportunity to advance, and if entrepreneurial freedom and political liberty are believed to be intertwined, then monopoly capitalism and globalism are viewed as the obvious, commonsense way of ordering the world's affairs.

The helping-adults-learn paradigm flattens curriculum, assigning everything a moral equivalency. A main focus is on educational tasks such assessing learner needs, planning instruction, scaffolding activities, creating an inclusive environment, sequencing tasks from simple to complex, ensuring and developing appropriate evaluative measures. There is also a relatively unproblematized emphasis on adult educator behaviors: treating people respectfully, being authentic, demonstrating empathy, providing emotional support, and so on.

Yet curriculum is not inherently benign and there is no implied moral equivalency of content. Training agents of the state to infiltrate activist groups so as to learn the identities of leaders and the tactics of resistance is an act of helping adults learn designed to stop marginalized groups from organizing and pressing for change. Teaching marketing techniques designed to convince people that their self-worth is dependent on wearing the right designer clothes or owning the right smartphone helps adults learn how to support consumerism and keeps capitalism thriving. Using language-learning texts that perpetuate racist stereotypes, or history books that present the history of White people as the history of the world, help keep White supremacy in place. A White nationalist group teaching the innate supremacy of Aryan peoples or an internet site teaching bomb-making as an act of justified terrorism is fundamentally different from a community college class of recent immigrants studying information technology to get decent jobs or a group of tenants being taught how to organize against slum landlords or deliver an effective presentation to a committee of the state legislature.

Teaching, when conceived as the technical task of helping adults learn, risks perpetuating broader asymmetries of power and privilege, and such teaching is recognized in the most influential contemporary theoretical paradigm in the field, that of transformative learning. *Transformative learning* (Mezirow, 1991) explores how adults develop meaning schemes and perspectives that are increasingly comprehensive and discriminating. In other words, as we experience events that disrupt our lives (*disorienting dilemmas*) we broaden our understanding of the world to encompass assumptions, frameworks, and viewpoints that go far beyond those with which we have grown up. We learn that people assign very different interpretations and meanings to the same experience and become much more attuned to the importance of context. This stops us from universalizing our experience and assuming that everyone sees the world in the way we do. We learn to think dialectically and become more accepting of ambiguity and complexity.

Mezirow (1991) maintained that transformative learning was inherently democratic and inclusive. Developing more comprehensive and discriminating perspectives meant that an act of transformative learning could not encompass moving from believing that all people deserved respect and dignity to a racist commitment to White supremacy. According to him, this would be a narrowing, not a broadening of perspectives and thus could not be transformative. So it is not surprising that texts exploring the practice of transformative learning (Cranton, 2016; King 2005; Mezirow & Taylor, 2009; Taylor, 2006; Taylor & Cranton, 2012) contain an implicit or explicit commitment to democratic social change, more holistic ways of being, or creating environmentally sustaining institutions and practices (Clover et al., 2010; O'Sullivan & Taylor, 2004).

Power Analysis

Advocates of the paradigm of teaching as helping adults learn typically acknowledge that adult educators will work in more- or less-directive ways depending on the context. Sometimes educators will deliberately step aside as adults work through problems and, in the process, learn to think more creatively, develop self-confidence, and so on. At other times educators will take center stage, giving advice, offering guidance, delivering presentations, and providing explicit direction.

But the question of teacher power, of the positional or other authority of the teacher, rarely takes center stage. The assumption that teacher power is implicitly authoritarian or oppressive, something exercised by schoolteachers to keep kids in line but having no place in the democratic, inclusive world of adult education, is still widely accepted. In recent years, however, probably because of the influence of Michel Foucault's (1980) work on the field, a power analysis has increasingly been applied to adult education (Cervero & Wilson, 2001). For example, the idea that power can be exercised in an empowering way in teaching adults has warranted serious contention (Wilson & Nesbit, 2005). Brookfield (2013) has defined a powerfull technique as one that considers power dynamics, helps learners claim empowerment, illuminates how power works and renders teacher power transparent and open to critique. Baptiste (2000) has argued for a pedagogy of ethical coercion and maintained that standing on the sidelines as a neutral facilitator allows power asymmetries to remain unchallenged.

As political cultures in the United States become increasingly polarized, as English language learning for immigrants becomes entwined with political organizing and advocacy for immigrants' rights, and as asymmetries of power and privilege become ever more apparent in society, we can expect that the exercise of power by teachers of adults will become an increasing focus of attention. As an example, Freire's (Shor & Freire, 1987) already mentioned distinction between authoritarian and authoritative teaching can certainly be explored more deeply. In multiple learning contexts, it appears that adults need to trust in their teachers' authoritativeness (Brookfield, 2013, 2015; Taylor, 2006; Zachary, 2016). They need to know that the person helping them learn possesses extensive content knowledge, has relevant experience in learning and disseminating that knowledge, and can be trusted to guide them in a way that is in their own best interests. Sometimes this necessary authority will mean that teachers are correct to insist that learners engage with specific content. However, learners will feel they can challenge teachers on this insistence without fear of arbitrary repercussion. By way of contrast, an authoritarian way of teaching is viewed as a hindrance to learning with no attempt by teachers to justify their apparently capricious decisions and no opportunity to clarify or challenge teachers' actions.

The paradigm of teacher as helper of adult learning will probably continue to hold sway in adult education. It has a necessary malleability that appeals to a field that, as this handbook shows, exhibits widely varying sites of practice. Equally, however, its internal contradictions and its tendency to leave wider inequities in place will continue to be explored.

References

Allman, P. (2001). *Critical education against global capitalism: Karl Marx and revolutionary critical education*. Bergin & Garvey.

Apps, J. W. (1996). *Teaching from the heart*. Krieger.

Arao, B., & Clemens, K. (2013). From safe spaces to brave spaces: A new way to frame dialogue around diversity and social justice. In L. Landreman (Ed.), *The art of effective facilitation: Reflections from social justice educators* (pp. 135–150). Stylus.

Baptiste, I. (2000). Beyond reason and personal integrity: Toward a pedagogy of coercive restraint. *Canadian Journal for the Study of Adult Education, 14*(1), 27–50.

Brockett, R. G. (2016). *Teaching adults: A practical guide*. Jossey-Bass.

Brookfield, S. D. (1984). The contribution of Eduard Lindeman to the development of theory and philosophy in adult education. *Adult Education Quarterly, 34*(4), 185–196.

Brookfield, S. D. (1990). Facilitating adult learning. In S. B. Merriam & P. S. Cunningham (Eds.), *Handbook of adult and continuing education* (pp. 201–210). Jossey-Bass.

Brookfield, S. D. (2004). *The power of critical theory: Liberating adult learning and teaching*. Jossey-Bass.

Brookfield, S. D. (2013). *Powerful techniques for teaching adults*. Jossey-Bass.

Brookfield, S. D. (2015). *The skillful teacher: On technique, trust and responsiveness in the classroom* (3rd ed.). Jossey-Bass.

Brookfield, S. D. (2017). *Becoming a critically reflective teacher* (2nd ed.). Jossey-Bass.

Brookfield, S. D., & Associates. (2018). *Teaching race: How to help students unmask and challenge racism*. Jossey-Bass.

Brookfield, S. D. & Holst, J. D. (2010). *Radicalizing learning: Adult education for a just world*. Jossey-Bass.

Carpenter, S., & Mojab, S. (2017). *Revolutionary learning: Marxism, feminism, and knowledge*. Pluto Press.

Cervero, R. M., & Wilson, A. L. (Eds.). (2001). *Power in practice: Adult education and the struggle for knowledge and power in society*. Jossey-Bass.

Clover, D. E., Jayme, B. De'O., Fullen, S., & Hall, B. (2010). *The nature of transformation: Environmental adult education* (3rd ed.). University of Victoria.

Collins, J. B., & Pratt, D. D. (2011). The teaching perspectives inventory at 10 years and 100,000 respondents: Reliability and validity of a teacher self-report inventory. *Adult Education Quarterly, 61*(4), 358–375.

Cranton, P. A. (Ed.). (2006). Authenticity in teaching [Themed issue]. *New Directions for Adult and Continuing Education, 2006*(111).

Cranton, P. (2016). *Understanding and promoting transformative learning: A guide to theory and practice* (3rd ed.). Stylus.

Daloz, L. A. (2012). *Mentoring: Guiding the journey of adult learners* (2nd ed.). Jossey-Bass.

Ely, M. (Ed.). (1948). *Handbook of adult education in the United States*. Bureau of Publications, Teachers College.

English, L. M., & Mayo, P. (2012). *Learning with adults: A critical pedagogical introduction*. Sense.

Essert, P. L. (1948). The discussion group in adult education in America. In M. Ely (Ed.), *Handbook of adult education in the United States* (pp. 269–275). Bureau of Publications, Teachers College.

Foucault, M. (1980). *Power/Knowledge: Selected interviews and other writings, 1972–1977*. Pantheon Books.

Freire, P. (1970). *Pedagogy of the oppressed*. Continuum.

Gramsci, A. (1971). *Selections from the prison notebooks of Antonio Gramsci*. International Publishers.

Horton, M. (1990). *The long haul: An autobiography*. Doubleday.

Horton, M. (2003). *The Myles Horton reader: Education for social change*. University of Tennessee Press.

Horton, M., & Freire, P. (1990). *We make the road by walking: Conversations on education and social change*. Temple University Press.

Kasworm, E. E., & Rose, A. D. (Eds.). (2010). *Handbook of adult and continuing education*. SAGE.

King, K. P. (2005). *Bringing transformative learning to life*. Krieger.

Knowles, M. S. (Ed.). (1960). *Handbook of adult education in the United States*. Adult Education Association of the USA.

Knowles, M. S. (1970). *The modern practice of adult education: Andragogy versus pedagogy*. Association Press.

Knowles, M. S. (1973). *The adult learner: A neglected species*. Gulf Publishing.

Knowles, M. S., & Associates. (1984). *Andragogy in action: Applying model principles of adult learning*. Jossey-Bass

Knowles, M. S. (1984). *Andragogy in action: Applying modern principles of adult learning*. Jossey-Bass.

Knox, A. (1986). *Helping adults learn: A guide to planning, implementing, and conducting programs*. Jossey-Bass.

Lindeman, E. C. L. (1961). *The meaning of adult education*. Harvest House. (Original work published in 1926).

MacGregor Burns, J. (1978). *Leadership*. Harper.

Marx, K. (1961). *Economic and philosophical manuscripts: Marx's concept of man*. Frederick Ungar.

Mayo, P. (2004). *Liberating praxis: Paulo Freire's legacy for radical education and politics*. Sense.

Merriam, S. B., & Bierema, L. L. (2013). *Adult learning: Linking theory and practice*. Jossey-Bass.

Mezirow, J. (1991). *Transformative dimensions of adult learning*. Jossey-Bass.

Mezirow, J., & Taylor, E. W. (Eds.). (2009). *Transformative learning in practice: Insights from community, workplace, and higher education*. Jossey-Bass.

O'Sullivan, E., & Taylor, M. M. (Eds.). (2004). *Learning toward an ecological consciousness: Selected transformative practices*. Palgrave Macmillan.

Pratt, D., Smulders, D., & Associates. (2016). *Five perspectives on teaching: Mapping a plurality of the good*. Krieger.

Pratt, D., & Nesbit, T. (2000). Discourses and cultures of teaching. In A. L. Wilson & E. R. Hayes (Eds.), *Handbook of adult and continuing education* (pp. 117–131). Jossey-Bass.

Rogers, A., & Horrocks, N. (2010). *Teaching adults* (4th ed.). Open University Press.

Schmidt, W. H., & Svenson, E. V. (1960). Methods in adult education. In M. S. Knowles (Ed.), *Handbook of adult education in the United States* (pp. 82–95). Adult Education Association of the USA.

Shor, I., & Freire, P. (1987). *A pedagogy of liberation*. Bergin & Garvey.

Smith, R. O. (2010). Facilitation and design of learning. In C. E. Kasworm & A. D. Rose (Eds.), *Handbook of adult and continuing education* (pp. 147–156). SAGE.

Spalding, D. (2014). *How to teach adults: Plan your class, teach your students, change the world*. Jossey-Bass.

Taylor, E. E. (Ed.). (2006). Teaching for change: Fostering transformative learning in the classroom. [Themed issue]. *New Directions for Adult and Continuing Education, 2006*(109).

Taylor, E. W., & Cranton, P. (Eds.). (2012). *The handbook of transformative learning: Theory, research, and practice*. Jossey-Bass.

Taylor, K., & Marienau, C. (2016). *Facilitating learning with the adult brain in mind: A conceptual and practical guide*. Jossey-Bass.

Thorndike, E. L., Bregman, E. O., Warren Tilton, J., & Woodyard, E. (1928). *Adult learning*. Macmillan.

Tisdell, E. J., Stone Hanley, M. S., & Taylor, E. W. (2000). Different perspectives on teaching for critical consciousness. In A. L. Wilson & E. R. Hayes (Eds.), *Handbook of adult and continuing education* (pp. 132–146). Jossey-Bass.

Vella, J. (2002). *Learning to listen, learning to teach: The power of dialogue in educating adults*. Jossey-Bass.

Wilson, A. L., & Hayes, E. R. (Eds.). (2000). *Handbook of adult and continuing education*. Jossey-Bass.

Wilson, A. L., & Nesbit, T. (2005). The problem of power. In R. J. Hill, & R. Kiely (Eds.), *Proceedings of the 46th annual adult education research conference* (pp. 449–454). University of Georgia.

Wlodkowski, R. J., & Ginsberg, M. B. (2017). *Enhancing adult motivation to learn: A comprehensive guide for teaching all adults*. Jossey-Bass.

Zachary, L. J. (2016). *The mentor's guide: Facilitating effective learning relationships* (2nd ed.). Jossey-Bass.

CHAPTER 16

Pedagogy and Andragogy

Intersection for Learning

Jerry Bowling and John A. Henschke

Pedagogy and andragogy are two models that have a wide-ranging history in the theoretical discourse and process of education and learning. Historically, pedagogy and andragogy are complementary to each other. Although serving different audiences, both contribute to the overall picture of learning and education during the life span (Savicevic, 2008). Both models respond to student needs in creative ways by planning goals for learning, creating hospitable learning environments, and building organizational structures that support growth.

From its inception, pedagogy was the predominant philosophy of education for children and adults, even though its emphasis was on children. Knowles (1980) noted that there were situations when andragogy could be used effectively with children and situations when pedagogy worked well with adults. Historical characteristics of a pedagogical model are teacher-directed, a subject-centered orientation to learning and view of the learner's role as a passive one. Andragogy emphasizes the learner's experience, self-directedness, problem-centered instruction, and readiness to learn (Knowles, 1980). The andragogical model shifted away from the pedagogical model because of the realization that adult learning is connected to multiple social and personal vicissitudes such as work, employment, technology—matters that have to do with gaining confidence and dealing with uncertainty and unpredictability regarding daily living (Savicevic, 2008). Both approaches promote the distinctly human capacity for discovery and meaning making in the teacher and learner.

This chapter argues that the models of andragogy and pedagogy are distinctive and have value for their exclusive contexts in the classroom and the workplace. Pedagogy and andragogy also exhibit several common attributes and values that are compatible with one another in their shared venture of teaching. Initiatives that elect to combine andragogy and pedagogy in the same educational context could produce beneficial learning outcomes. This chapter discusses the history and conceptualizations of pedagogy and andragogy.

Pedagogy

The derivation of pedagogy comes from the Greek word *paidagogia* where *paid* translates as "child" and *agogos* describes a person who functions as a guide. When combined, these terms carry a literal meaning of "to lead a child." In classical Greek literature, Plato broadens the meaning of this same root *paideia* by noting a social integration of the child into the surrounding culture (Bertram, 1967). Interestingly, in Hellenistic and Rabbinic Judaism, the historian Philo connected the basic knowledge assumed in *paideia* with practical wisdom and spirituality (Bertram, 1967). Henschke (1998) and Savicevic (1999, 2008) note that from a review of teachers in Hellenistic, Greco-Roman, and Jewish cultures, it is possible to identify evidence of differences that existed between pedagogy and andragogy as practiced by teachers in ancient times.

The earliest usage of the term *pedagogy*, according to Merriam and Bierema (2014), appears in the 17th century CE with the establishment of monastic schools in Europe for training children. In the 19th century, the work of Pestalozzi, Herbart, and others in Europe contributed to spreading the idea of a science of pedagogy beyond primary and secondary settings, with pedagogical institutes being situated alongside and within universities (Watkins & Mortimore, 1999). Knowles (1973) traces the spread of pedagogy from the secular schools of Europe and America in the 19th and 20th centuries when the applied sciences of sociology and psychology were introduced to studying learning.

In the late 19th century, Simon (1981), an educational historian, lamented that the science of teaching in England was confused rather than coherent and that the word *pedagogy* was used less frequently than in the rest of Europe. Between 1870–1900, England's dominant educational institutions had no appetite for pedagogical theory (Selleck, 1967). This was true even though Bain's (1879) pioneering work *Education as a Science*, reprinted more than 15 times before 1900, had become nearly synonymous with student-teacher manuals and had witnessed the pedagogy of the 1890s increasingly ascribe credence to a science of learning even to the point of discussing universal education (Moon & Mayes, 1995). Simon (1981) viewed a combination of conservative legislation, social, political, and ideological reasons during this period as inhibiting the development of a scientific theory of pedagogy. Hence, in England, a science of pedagogy was neither coherent nor systematic.

Historical conceptions of pedagogy persist because they hold the archetypical foundations of how we learn. In the United States, Knowles's (1980) view of pedagogy as "the art and science of helping children learn" (p. 43) found support within Western frameworks that defined *traditional pedagogy* as principles, practices, or science of teaching (Hallam & Ireson, 1999) that contributed to any conscious activity a person designed to bring about another person's learning (Ireson et al., 1999). This narrowly defined view described pedagogy as teaching that happens in schools and, by association, a domain of knowledge with scant attention to sociocultural perspectives (Alexander, 2008) or a notion of consciousness on the part of the teacher or learner (Waring & Evans, 2015).

Conceptualizations of Pedagogy

Changing views of knowledge and an absence of congruence about approaches to pedagogy generate broad classifications germane to adult learning in North America. Three fundamental pedagogic frameworks that are operative will be discussed: (a) traditional, with its transmissive/didactic focused, teacher-centric learning; (b) holistic, with its wide-ranging constructivist-focused approaches, featuring a brief exposition on critical and contemplative pedagogy which are often practiced in adult education; and (c) blended, with its pragmatic, inclusive-centered, and diverse use of multimodality.

Traditional Pedagogy

Traditional pedagogy is described as a transmissive model of teaching characterized by objectivism, reductionism, bounded knowledge, privileged cognitive knowing (Gaard et al., 2017; Moore, 2012), and banking education (Freire, 1970). The structures or syntaxes of a traditional pedagogy prioritize a teacher's instructional role as a content expert who has responsibility for transmitting knowledge, skills, and dispositions to students in a didactic style. It views the student's role as extrinsically motivated, passive, compliant, and submissive to the teacher and to the overall educational process. From a learning theory perspective, traditional pedagogy is closely aligned with behaviorism, which claims that through operant conditioning or interaction with the environment using reward and punishment, it is possible to predict, influence, and modify behavior. B.F. Skinner is the recognized champion of behaviorism. Instructional applications connected with behaviorism are: mastery learning, which seeks to increase the likelihood that more students perform well; direct learning, a teacher-controlled practice supported through student practice under continued guidance; and various computer assisted learning approaches (Merriam & Bierema, 2014).

Holistic Pedagogy

As exemplified in the most recent fifty years, there have been numerous holistic pedagogical innovations practiced in adult education. Broadly construed, holistic pedagogy is described as eclectic, inclusive, and focused on the dynamic sociocultural interrelationships between knowledge, theory, and policy. Defining dimensions of holistic pedagogy is less causal and linear as it supports theoretical foundations and praxis that include: preference for social, emotional, spiritual, and experiential ways of knowing that shift away from a Western emphasis on cognition (Merriam & Bierema, 2014). The syntax or structure of holistic pedagogy resists following a single linear mechanistic model because predicting future growth or human potential is difficult to envision. It may converge on "unknowingness, fluidity and becoming, which in turn, has the effect of producing different knowledge" (Walshaw, 2013, p. 91). Thus, holistic pedagogy tends to support systemic and participative instructional models that are relational, ethical, and socially constructivist in scope (Gaard et al., 2017).

Holistic pedagogy tends to be culturally responsive, influenced by shifting and diverse ways of knowing, increasing learner diversity, cultural responsiveness, social awareness, and spirituality. Holistic pedagogy supports self-understanding and identity formation of adult learners (Bowling, 2012) and supports a formation of knowledge that is tacit, practical, and situated in a certain context (Traianou, 2006). Further, holistic pedagogy invites pedagogy-as-art, which involves creativity, imagination, and emotion in teaching and learning practice (Nind et al., 2016). Holistic pedagogy is less concerned with setting, age, or stage given its focus on the identity and transformation among learners (Alexander, 2008). Two holistic pedagogical examples are critical pedagogy and contemplative pedagogy, which are briefly explained in the following.

Critical Pedagogy
Paulo Freire is perhaps the most recognized voice as a pioneering exemplar of critical pedagogy. Freire's (1970) book *Pedagogy of the Oppressed* is a representative typology of holistic pedagogy. Critical pedagogy resists a unified definition (Lather, 1998). It is described within its many dimensions as a pedagogy to help adult learners achieve critical consciousness by addressing the roles of power, oppression, racism, gender oppression, praxis, and liberation (Breuing, 2011). Its structure and syntax is student-centered, concerned with learners experiencing social justice, social change, forms of democracy, and supporting learners to achieve critical consciousness while attempting to address the shortcomings of transmissive based pedagogy (Breuing, 2011).

Contemplative Pedagogy
The core of contemplative pedagogy is definitional goal change, growth, and transformation that is practical and actionable. The transformation includes: encouraging deeper learning, meditation, focused attention, introspection, reflection, and heightened awareness (Zajonic, 2013). The structures and syntax of contemplative pedagogy connects learners to their lived, embodied experience of their own learning by balancing traditional third-person perspectives with critical first-person perspectives enabling the learner to access knowledge about the nature of mind, self, and other that has been largely overlooked by traditional, Western-oriented liberal education (Roth, 2014). Contemplative pedagogy underscores a sociocultural learning context through embedding introspective practices associated with mindfulness (Barbezat & Bush, 2014). A growing number of emergent adult learners in higher education are experiencing emotional challenges and high levels of stress connected with multitasking that was absent just a decade ago (Faerm, 2020). Contemplative pedagogy has proven to lower anxiety, stress levels, and promote a greater sense of well-being. Practices such as mindfulness techniques, journaling, guided meditation, and silence strengthen memory, improve cognition, and elevate one's quality of life (Barbezat & Bush, 2014).

Blended Pedagogy
There is no agreement regarding a universal operational definition of *blended pedagogy*. However, one possible definition is "the organic integration of thoughtfully selected and complementary face-to-face and online approaches" (Garrison & Vaughn, 2008, p. 148). Put differently, blended pedagogy fuses face-to-face teaching conducted in a brick-and-mortar location with virtual online instruction (Anthony, 2019; Youde, 2018). The concept of blended pedagogy is pragmatic and seems as intuitive as it appears straightforward, yet in application it is much more complex (Garrison & Vaughn, 2008). The syntax and structure of blended pedagogy is anchored in traditional pedagogy and andragogy; however, it redesigns and extends learning beyond face-to-face or online learning paradigms. Blended pedagogy can involve a diverse number of

pedagogical approaches including a mixture of didactic methods, formal learning settings contrasted with informal outside of school, structured with unstructured learning, or custom content contrasted with off-the-shelf (Dzakiria et al., 2006; Graham, 2006; Murray & Milner, 2015). Likewise, it involves instruction that shifts from a passive model to a constructivist model that focuses on creating knowledge—a type of transformative blending (Graham, 2006). The style and shape of blended pedagogy will continue to change as emerging digital technologies continue to initiate rethinking in our understanding of pedagogy.

Blended pedagogy's multimodal design (e.g., modes of image, audio, video) opens a threshold that incorporates multiple forms of representation that generate the creation and sustainability of a community of inquiry for the adult learner (Archer & Newfield, 2014). A community of inquiry (Garrison et al., 1999) includes three interrelated types of presence: (a) cognitive (constructing knowledge, processing through reflection and dialogue), (b) social (learners identify with a trusted community and cultivating interpersonal relationships), and (c) teaching (learning climate, meaning-making, and setting instructional goals). *Presence* is defined as a teacher's virtual presence in an blended classroom. A community of inquiry has a collaborative and multimodal communication dimension that helps learners in constructing meaningful and worthwhile knowledge.

The increased attention to multimodality is cultivating advances within adult education theory and praxis. *Multimodality* is defined as practices that focus on mode as defining features of communication in learning environments (Stein, 2008). Stein and Newfield (2006) argue that multimodal dimensions of blended pedagogy have potential to make learning more democratic and inclusive since teachers act as designers and students function as agentive, resourceful, and creative meaning makers.

Holistic and blended pedagogic orientations espouse sociocultural and sociocognitive dimensions of adult learning. These associations infer mutuality between the social and cultural bases of knowledge with learning conceived as bridging between cognitive processes and social practice (Billett, 1998; Lave & Wenger, 1991). Also, mutuality suggests that a type of symbiotic relationship could exist between Garrison et al.'s (1999) notion of communities of inquiry and Wenger's (1998) notion of communities of practice.

Wenger's (1998) concept of *communities of practice* (CoP) is a social learning theory. CoP describes learning as a function of activity situated in the context and culture in which it occurs. Wenger (1998) summarizes communities of practice as groups of people who share a mutual concern or a passion for something they do and learn how to do it better as they interact regularly. Three components are required: (a) the domain, which is a shared learning need; (b) the community, a place to create a collective bond over time; and (c) the practice, interactions that produce resources that affect their practice. A CoP framework is especially relevant to blended pedagogy as it suggests identity is a nexus of membership through which belonging can integrate values from different communities. As learners participate in collective meaning-making and problem-solving, they acquire a shared competence to move from the periphery to the core of a practice. This creates a community that is sustained by the resultant reciprocal relationships as members who share their social resources, interact and learn together, and discover new knowledge that shapes their identity. The community of practitioners by sharing their experiences and stories gain competence as they continue their relationships within their domain (Wenger, 1998). Thus, a primary goal within communities of practice is to move past observation and help adults experience an increasing sense of identity as a master practitioner over time while creating critical self-awareness, wholeness, and authenticity (Lave & Wenger, 1991). Examining this diverse sociocultural capital is fertile ground for advancing generative research in our understanding of blended and holistic pedagogy in adult learning. For example, Damsa et al. (2019) argue that such an ecological learning perspective conceptualizes pedagogy that has coconstructed learning spaces that focus on promoting identity negotiation while avoiding marginalizing relationships. Participation in environments that welcome sociocultural relationships are commonly associated with holistic models of learning.

In Conclusion

Research by scholars such as Vygotsky (1980), Bruner (1996), and Lave and Wenger (1991) extended conceptions of pedagogy toward a broader range of theoretical and practical complexity (Nind et al., 2016). Understanding the diverse contexts, mediating roles in learning, influences of culture, espoused values, and diverse ways of knowing infused new thinking to the forefront expanding traditional studies in pedagogy. Holistic pedagogy underwrote an inclusive view of pedagogy that orients practices that are socially, ontologically, dialogically, and contextually situated (Edwards-Groves, 2018). Research into the pedagogic complexity, dynamic, integrative multimodal, and socioculturally layered facets of blended pedagogy has animated new theoretical investigations and discourses. In sum, Ireson et al. (1999) argue that pedagogy should be clear about its goals, maintain high expectations and motivation for learning, remain appropriate to its purposes, and continue exploring its theoretical sophistication. A diverse range of pedagogical models exist that span from traditional, holistic, and blended theories that provide impetus to transform children as well as adults. We shift the focus now to andragogy and offer a similarly nuanced discussion.

Andragogy

Savicevic (2008) presents details about the historical development of andragogy, which is understood as the art and science of educating adults. Henschke (1998) and Savicevic (2000) note that andragogy's roots can be traced back to ancient Greek and Hebrew times. Due to his influences on the writers of the 1700s, Comenius, a European education expert and one of the founders of general didactics who wrote *The Great Didactic* in 1648, is identified as the founder of andragogy (Savicevic, 1999). Comenius's primary wish was to develop the full potential of humankind, not in the privileged or the young only, but in the whole human race, regardless of age, class, sex, or nationality (Schreiner, 2019). Comenius established special institutions, forms, means, methods, and teachers for work with adults, which, in fact, is at the root of the modern concept of andragogy (Savicevic, 1999).

Andragogy as a concept was not named until the 19th century. Alexander Kapp, a German citizen, is credited with having coined the term and in an 1833 publication developed Comenius's ideas further. He argued that education, self-reflection, and educating the character are the first values in human life, as andragogy considers the education of inner, subjective personality ("character") and outer, objective competencies (education/training). Kapp (1833) contended that this type of learning could be brought about through teachers, yet it was also experienced by adults and children (both as learners) through their self-reflection and life experience.

In the early 1800s, John F. Herbart, who was an undisputable authority in the philosophy and pedagogy of his time in Germany, understood pedagogy as the education of young people. Such an understanding pitted Herbart against Kapp and was symbolic of the early conflict that erupted between andragogy and pedagogy. Kapp's ideas were not accepted at the time and *andragogy* as a term laid dormant for many years. However, andragogy did gain popularity through the Workers Education Movement in Europe between the years of 1848 and 1917.

Savicevic (1999) and Knowles (1989) both made unique contributions that advanced andragogy's modern influence. In Europe, Savicevic claimed that andragogy was best defined as a discipline that is inclusive of all forms and facets of adult education. In the United States, Knowles was instrumental in helping andragogy become popular with adult educators and their practice. In Knowles's view, theory and practice were to be congruent. Adult educators needed to be living examples of the lessons being taught, demonstrating theory in both word and deed—"walking the talk" as opposed to "do what I say, not what I do." Knowles considers congruence as a "way of being" in which we live out our life as a living, breathing, maturing picture of what we say we believe.

Savicevic (2008) called Knowles "a 'masovik', i.e., a lecturer having used it [andragogy] on mass events in 10,000 visitor stadiums, as if he was inspired by 'an ancient agonistic spirituality'!" (p. 375). This kind of spirituality could be described as tough, gung-ho, sporting, contending, grappling, challenging, vying, surpassing—all reflections of the very positive way that Knowles was committed to and conducted his work in adult education. There is no doubt that in the 31 years Knowles worked with andragogy before his death in 1997, he contributed to dissemination of andragogical thoughts through his texts and lectures. His influence is significant in the history of andragogy through his development of the model.

Conceptualizations of Andragogy

Knowles (1995) provides his sketch of andragogy, which is a combination of six assumptions and eight processes. The assumptions are that the learner (a) needs to know the reason that makes sense to them, for learning something; (b) conceptualizes how being a learner becomes increasingly self-directed; (c) perceives themselves to be a rich resource for their and others learning; (d) prepares to learn through life tasks and problems; (e) prefers to learn for immediate application; and (f) is motivated through internal curiosity, rather than through external benefits. The processes are means to engage adult learners and teachers actively and mutually in (a) preparing for what is to come; (b) setting a climate conducive to learning; (c) planning the process and content; (d) diagnosing learning needs; (e) negotiating objectives; (f) designing learning plans and contracts; (g) conducting inquiry learning projects via experiential learning techniques; and (h) learner collecting evidence validated by peers, facilitators, and experts.

Andragogy has been conceptualized in different ways. One conceptualization includes five dimensions (Knowles, 1980): (a) structure: moving from rigidity to flexibility; (b) atmosphere: changing away from being task-centered to people-centered; (c) management philosophy and attitudes: converting away from controlling personnel toward releasing their energy; (d) decision-making and policy making: modifying away from participation only at the top toward relevant participation for all; and (e) communication: transitioning from restricted, one-way flow toward open, multidirectional flow.

In response to these ideas, Grace (1996) made a compelling critique of Knowles's andragogy. Grace felt that Knowles's perspective was too much concerned with individualization, institutionalization, professionalization, techno-scientization, self-directed learning, the politics of exclusion, maintenance, and conformity. Grace also believed it ignores resistance and transformation and sees mainstream U.S. and Canadian adult education as having been complicit in sidelining cultural and social concerns, thus depoliticizing and decontextualizing adult learning.

Applications of Andragogy

Andragogy continues to be a salient idea within the discourse of adult education with far-ranging application to practice. Several contemporary examples of these applications are noteworthy. First, Henschke (1989) developed the Modified Instructional Perspectives Inventory (MIPI) as an andragogical inventory with 45 items distributed among seven factors. The seven factors are:

1. teachers' empathy with learners
2. teachers' trust of learners
3. planning and delivery of instruction
4. teachers accommodating learner uniqueness
5. teachers' insensitivity toward learners
6. teacher-centered learning process
7. learner-centered [experienced-based] learning process

Its purpose is to measure trust, beliefs, feelings, and behaviors of adult educators when they process adult education in an industry setting.

Cercone (2008) developed "a framework for integrating adult learning theories with recommendations for designing an online environment" (p. 138). She examined four adult learning theories: andragogy, self-directed learning, experiential learning, and transformational learning. She asserts that the characteristics identified in the literature provides an andragogical framework that can support the active learning approaches nascent to online learning models. She extrapolates that if facilitators integrate these adult characteristics when planning and designing their instructional online content, then they can empower adult learners to connect deeper with course content. Of the 13 characteristics developed by Cercone, andragogy is the most comprehensive approach as it considered 10 of the characteristics, which suggests that andragogy has a place in online learning.

In addition, LeNoue et al. (2011) supported the value of using andragogy with online digital learning environments, as was outlined by Cercone. They wrote, "a world increasingly characterized by high digital connectivity and a need for life-long, demand-driven learning calls for the development of andragogies specialized to DML *(digitally mediated learning)* environments" (p. 6, italics in original). King (2017) asserts that the key characteristics of andragogy align well with the 21st-century experience of adults coping with a digital age. In an era of constant digital innovation, andragogy supports lifelong learning and training. When we blend technology, problem-solving, and facilitative teaching modes, adult educators can design and deliver relevant learning experiences that are consistent with andragogy (King, 2017).

Another example is a 2-year qualitative and quantitative study conducted by Vodde (2008) involving two regional police academies. This study demonstrated the needs, readiness, orientation, and motivation of adult learners were better served through training with andragogical instructional models in police basic training for recruits and was a more effective means of training. Considering these needs, andragogy focuses on facilitating a holistic, integrative, and collaborative approach to learning that placed a strong emphasis on experiential approaches to andragogical approaches. Vodde's study found that while a traditional, pedagogical, military model of training that leans toward a behavioral school of learning may have at one time served the needs and interests of police and society, its recent applicability and efficacy have been called into question. It was theorized, and subsequently found, that an andragogical (adult-based) instructional methodology would serve as a more effective means for training police recruits.

Further, Tannehill (2009) provided one of the broadest and most encompassing examples of using andragogy for educating and servicing adult learners in post-secondary institutions. Data were gathered from 85 different higher education institutions. The five major questions focused on whether and to what extent postsecondary institutions utilize the principles of andragogy to educate adult learners, provide specialized support for the adult learners in services and program delivery options, award credit for prior nontraditional learning, apply best practices as defined by andragogy for adult learners, and employ the most common andragogical principles in institutions as categorized by the Carnegie classification. The results demonstrated the importance of increased attention to andragogy and its impact on the student experience.

Another application of andragogy is seen in Henschke (2009), who used andragogical principles to theorize characteristics of adult learners working in Brazilian corporate settings. He determined that there were 11 characteristics of adult learners, each characteristic representing a core idea found in andragogy (Figure 16.1).

Using his 11 characteristics of adult learners to inform innovative and interactive techniques, Henschke developed a workshop series in Brazil with personnel from numerous entities (corporate, business, workplace, industry, health care, government, higher education, professions, religious education, adult education, elementary, secondary, remedial education, general citizens, and community development workers). In the workshop, Henschke engaged personnel in andragogical learning experiences while they were

FIGURE 16.1 Henschke's 11 characteristics.

1. Immediate concerns
2. Low self-concept
3. Different value systems
4. Use of defense mechanisms
5. Sensitivity to nonverbal communication
6. Alienation (feeling of helplessness over control of events)
7. Reticence and lack of self-confidence
8. Hostility and anxiety toward authority
9. Fear of school, failure, and change
10. Limitations from deprived home life
11. Cultural exclusion

learning about andragogical principles. For the characteristic of immediate concerns, techniques suggested were to use realistic problems, adult-oriented materials, and concrete situations. From this list of techniques another catalog of adult learner characteristics were garnered and techniques for using andragogy with learners within industry were discovered.

From 2002 to 2004, Henschke used Knowles's (1980) conceptualization of andragogy and its five dimensions—structure, atmosphere, management philosophy and attitudes, decision-making and policy-making, and communication—to guide work with a multistate major electric company that invited the University of Missouri–St. Louis to help them strengthen the educational capacity of the 15 members of their training staff. Henschke designed and implemented andragogical and self-directed learning processes within the domains of the five dimensions. The staff participated in an organizational transformation by modeling the change and growth required for moving from being static toward becoming innovative using Knowles's suggested five dimensions. By the end of the 3 years, the team of 15 educators had begun to master these innovative individual and organizational techniques and worked well as a team.

In Conclusion

Malcolm Knowles is celebrated as the most popular andragogy theorist. Andragogy is a concept that in many ways continues to define the core attributes of the field of adult education. Many have studied and applied its ideals such as readiness to learn, self-direction, and immediacy, among others to practice. In all instances, andragogy highlights the importance of experience and honoring the experiences adults bring to learning. Yet andragogy is an unfinished theory and has room to grow, especially in fields such as online learning and nonformal education. The new forms, methods, and means for teachers to work with adults will undoubtedly advance andragogy in the future.

Conclusion

Questions about how people learn continue to captivate scholarly dialogue. There is indeed value in teaching that approaches learning through the distinctive theories of andragogy and pedagogy for the classroom and the workplace. We maintain that pedagogy and andragogy exhibit several common attributes and values that are compatible with one another in their shared venture of teaching. Similarly, Knowles (1989) asserts that there are circumstances when andragogy could provide effective instruction with children and settings when it is appropriate to begin instruction using pedagogy with adults. Initiatives that elect to intersect andragogy and pedagogy in the same educational context could produce beneficial learning outcomes. Each theory has its unique practical and theoretical foundational principles, theory, and praxis that are suitable for their exclusive contexts. Theories about pedagogy and andragogy are dynamic and therefore warrant continued research.

References

Alexander, R. (2008). Pedagogy, curriculum and culture. In K. Hall, P. Murphy, & J. Soler (Eds.), *Pedagogy and practice: Culture and identities* (pp. 3–27). SAGE.

Anthony, E. (2019). (Blended) learning: How traditional best teaching practices impact blended-learning classrooms. *Journal of Online Learning Research, 5*(1), 23–48. https://www.learntechlib.org/primary/p/183933/.

Archer, A., & Newfield, D. (2014). Challenges and opportunities of multimodal approaches to education in South Africa. In A. Archer & D. Newfield (Eds.), *Multimodal approaches to research and pedagogy: Recognition resources, and access* (pp. 1–18). Routledge.

Bain, A. (1879). *Education as a science.* Appleton.

Barbezat, D. P., & Bush, M. (2014). *Contemplative practices in higher education: Powerful methods to transform teaching and learning.* Wiley.

Bertram, G. (1967). Paideia. In G. Friedrich (Ed.), *Theological dictionary of the New Testament* (pp. 596–625). William B. Eerdmans.

Billett, S. (1998). Ontogeny and participation in communities of practice: A sociocognitive view of adult development. *Studies in the Education of Adults, 30*(1), 21–34. http://hdl.handle.net/10072/11742

Bowling, J. (2012). Experiential pedagogies for transforming student spirituality. In M. C. Fowler, J. L. Hochheimer, & M. Weiss (Eds.), *Spirituality: New reflections on theory, praxis and pedagogy* (pp. 31–43). Inter-Disciplinary Press.

Breuing, M. (2011). Problematizing critical pedagogy. *International Journal of Critical Pedagogy, 3*(3), 2–23.

Bruner, J. (1996). *The culture of education.* Harvard University Press.

Cercone, K. (2008). Characteristics of adult learners with implications for online learning design. *AACE Journal, 16*(2), 137–159.

Damsa, C., Nerland, M., & Andreadakis, Z. E. (2019). An ecological perspective on learner-constructed learning spaces. *British Journal of Educational Technology, 50*(5), 2075–2089.

Dzakiria, H., Mustafa, C., & Bakar, H. (2006). Moving forward with blended learning (BL) as a pedagogical alternative to traditional classroom learning. *Malaysian Online Journal of Instructional Technology, 3*(1), 11–18.

Edwards-Groves, C. (2018). The practice architectures of pedagogy: Conceptualizing the convergences between sociality, dialogue, ontology and temporality in teaching practices. In O. Cavero & N. Llevot-Calvet (Eds.), *New pedagogical challenges in the 21st century: Contributions of research in education* (pp. 119–140). IntechOpen.

Faerm, S. (2020). Contemplative pedagogy in the college classroom: Theory, research, and practice for holistic student development. *Cuaderno 78,* 159–182. https://fido.palermo.edu/servicios_dyc/publicacionesdc/vista/detalle_publicacion.php?id_libro=716.

Freire, P. (1970). *Pedagogy of the oppressed.* Continuum.

Gaard, G. C., Blades, J., & Wright, M. (2017). Assessing sustainability curriculum: From transmissive to transformative approaches. *International Journal of Sustainability in Higher Education, 18*(7), 1263–1278.

Garrison, D. R., Anderson, T., & Archer, W. (1999). Critical inquiry in a text-based environment: Computer conferencing in higher education. *The Internet and Higher Education, 2*(2–3), 87–105. https://doi.org/10.1016/S1096-7516(00)00016-6

Garrison, D. R., & Vaughn, N. D. (2008). *Blended learning in higher education: Framework, principles, and guidelines.* Jossey-Bass.

Grace, A. P. (1996). Striking a critical pose: Andragogy—missing links, missing values. *International Journal of Lifelong Education, 15*(5), 382–392.

Graham, C. (2006). Definition, current trends, and future directions. In C. Bonk & C. Graham (Eds.), *Handbook of blended learning: Global perspectives, local designs*. Pfeiffer.

Hallam, S., & Ireson, J. (1999). Pedagogy in the secondary school. In P. Mortimore (Ed.), *Understanding pedagogy and its impact on learning* (pp. 68–97). Paul Chapman.

Henschke, J. A. (1989). Identifying appropriate adult education practices: Beliefs, feelings and behaviors. In C. Jeffries & A. Austin (Eds.), *Proceedings of the Eighth Annual Midwest Research-to-Practice Conference in Adult, Continuing and Community Education* (pp. 81–87). University of Missouri.

Henschke, J. A. (1998, September 11). *Historical antecedents shaping conceptions of andragogy: A comparison of sources and roots* [Paper presentation]. International Conference on Research in Comparative Andragogy, Bled, Radlovjica, Slovenia.

Henschke, J. A. (2009). Engagement in active learning with Brazilian adult educators. In G. Stroschen (Ed.), *Handbook of blended shore learning: Adult program development and delivery* (pp. 121–136). Springer.

Ireson, J., Mortimore, P., & Hallam, S. (1999). The common strands of pedagogy and their implications. In P. Mortimore (Ed.), *Understanding pedagogy and its impact on learning* (pp. 212–232). Paul Chapman.

Kapp, A. (1833). *Platon's Erziehungslehre, als Paedagogik für die Einzelnen und als Staatspaedagogik*. Ferdinand Essmann.

King, K. (2017). *Technology and innovation in adult learning*. Jossey-Bass.

Knowles, M. S. (1973). *The adult learner: A neglected species*. Gulf Publishing.

Knowles, M. S. (1980). *The modern practice of adult education: From pedagogy to andragogy* (2nd ed.). Cambridge Books.

Knowles, M. S. (1989). *The making of an adult educator: An autobiographical journey*. Jossey-Bass Publishers.

Knowles, M. S. (1995). *Designs for adult learning*. American Society for Training and Development.

Lather, P. (1998). Critical pedagogy and its complicities: A praxis of stuck places. *Educational Theory, 48*(4), 487–497.

Lave, J., & Wenger, E. (1991). *Situated learning: Legitimate peripheral participation*. Cambridge University Press.

LeNoue, M., Hall, T., & Eighmy, M. (2011). Adult education and the social media revolution. *Adult Learning, 22*(2), 4–12.

Merriam, S. B., & Bierema, L. L. (2014). *Adult learning: Linking theory and practice*. Jossey-Bass.

Moon, B. & Mayes, A. (1995). *Teaching and learning in the secondary school*. Routledge.

Moore, A. (2012). *Teaching and learning: Pedagogy, curriculum and culture*. Routledge.

Murray, I., & Milner, H. (2015). Toward a pedagogy of sociopolitical consciousness in outside of school programs. *Urban Review, 47*(5), 893–913.

Nind, M., Curtin, A., & Hall, K. (2016). *Research methods in pedagogy*. Bloomsbury Academic.

Roth, H. D. (2014). Pedagogy for a new field of contemplative studies. In O. Gunnlaugson, E. W. Sarath, C. Smith, & H. Bai (Eds.), *Contemplative learning and inquiry across disciplines* (pp. 97–118). SUNY Press.

Savicevic, D. (1999). *Adult education: From practice to theory building*. Peter Lang.

Savicevic, D. (2000). *Koreni I Razvoj Andragoskih Ideja* [The roots and evolution of andragogical ideas]. Institut za pedagogijy i andragogiju Filozofskog fakulteta u Beogradu Andragosko drustvo Srbije.

Savicevic, D. (2008). Convergence or divergence of ideas on andragogy in different countries. *International Journal of Lifelong Education, 27*(4), 361–378.

Schreiner, P. (2019). The Comenius-Institute: Promoting educational discourse and practice in the spirit of public theology. In M. Pirner, J. Lähnemann, W. Haussmann, & S. Schwarz (Eds.), *Public theology perspectives on religion and education* (pp. 93–106). Routledge.

Selleck, R. (1967). The scientific educationalist, 1870–1914. *British Journal of Educational Studies, 15*(2), 148–165.

Simon, B. (1981). Why no pedagogy in England? In A. Mayes & B. Moon (Eds.), *Teaching and learning in the secondary school* (pp. 10–24). Routledge.

Stein, P. (2008). *Multimodal pedagogies in diverse classrooms*. Taylor & Francis.

Stein, P., & Newfield, D. (2006). Multiliteracies and multimodality in English in education in Africa: Mapping the terrain. *English Studies in Africa, 49*(1), 1–21. https://doi-org.nexus.harding.edu/10.1080/00138390608691341

Tannehill, D. B. (2009). *Andragogy: How do postsecondary institutions educate and service adult learners?* [Unpublished doctoral dissertation]. University of Pittsburgh.

Traianou, A. (2006). Understanding teacher expertise in primary science: A sociocultural approach. *Research papers in education, 21*(1), 63–78.

Vodde, R. F. (2008). *The efficacy of an andragogical instructional methodology in basic police training and education* [Unpublished doctoral dissertation]. University of Leicester.

Vygotsky, L. S. (1980). *Mind in society: The development of higher psychological processes*. Harvard University Press.

Walshaw, M. (2013). Explorations into pedagogy within mathematics classrooms: Insights from contemporary inquiries. *Curriculum Inquiry, 43*(1), 71–94.

Waring, M., & Evans, C. (2015). *Understanding pedagogy: Developing a critical approach to teaching and learning.* Routledge.

Watkins, C., & Mortimore, P. (1999). Pedagogy: What do we know? In P. Mortimore (Ed.), *Understanding pedagogy and its impact on learning* (pp. 1–19). Paul Chapman.

Wenger, E. (1998). *Communities of practice: Learning, meaning, and identity.* Cambridge University Press.

Youde, A. (2018). Andragogy in blended learning contexts: Effective tutoring of adult learners studying part-time, vocationally relevant degrees at a distance. *International Journal of Lifelong Education, 37*(2), 255–272. https://doi.org/10.1080/02601370.2018.1450303

Zajonic, A. (2013). Contemplative pedagogy: A quiet revelation in higher education. *New Directions for Teaching and Learning, 2013*(134), 83–94. https://doi.org/10.1002/tl.20057

CHAPTER 17

Adult Learning Through Everyday Engagement With Popular Culture

Kaela Jubas, Jennifer A. Sandlin, Robin Redmon Wright, and Jake Burdick

Across the field of adult education, the idea that learning occurs in the process of everyday experiences has become a common refrain. Despite recognition of the many contexts of informal and incidental adult learning, which unfold without a designated instructor or formal assessment and, possibly, without any intention (Marsick & Watkins, 2001), engagement with popular culture remains overlooked by many adult education scholars. From television shows and films, to novels and music videos, to video games, the popular culture that surrounds us becomes meaningful for not only its entertainment value but also its pedagogical functions. It seems fitting that a discussion of how popular culture consumption—the processes of watching, listening to, reading, playing with, and talking about texts—spurs learning among popular culture consumers is included in this handbook. Popular culture is being taken up with (re)new(ed) interest by adult education scholars. Despite a lull from the 1990s to early 2000s, adult educators have made notable, sometimes pioneering, impacts on this topic (Sandlin et al., 2010). Individually and together, we have also devoted much attention to it. Here, we share some of the insights we have encountered and developed in our work.

We begin by introducing key concepts, then outline two main perspectives informing work in this area, one stemming from critical theory's Frankfurt School and the other heavily influenced by Antonio Gramsci and potentially more poststructurally inflected. Then, we summarize some of the cultural pedagogy–focused adult education scholarship, first examining the literature on learning outside the classroom, and then turning to work on popular culture in the classroom. We conclude by considering the implications of this work for adult education theory and practice, proposing that, no matter how mundane they might seem, popular culture and cultural consumption offer serious lessons to adult educators and learners.

Key Concepts

Within the field of adult education, the understanding that popular culture functions pedagogically can be traced back at least to Gramsci's (1971) argument that culture is in constant, dynamic tension with material conditions. In this perspective, cultural texts and practices teach people how to live within the constraints of social structures. At the same time, the cultural sphere is a space where people can challenge existing structures and develop alternatives. Williams (1958/2011) extended this premise, issuing his famous statement that "culture is ordinary" (p. 53) and recognizing that, as they receive or interpret popular culture texts, people are both "trained" to receive messages in certain ways and free to bring forward "new observations and meanings which are offered and tested" (p. 54).

What, though, do we mean by "popular culture *texts*"? To instructors and students, indeed, to the general public, a text frequently is seen as a product of the written word, developed to relay information and expose readers to an author's ideas. In contrast, those who study popular culture employ the word *text* to refer to "any artifact or experience that we can read [or interpret] to produce meaning" (Maudlin & Sandlin, 2015, p. 369). Although there are variations in how the term is taken up, reflecting differences in perspectives employed by scholars, *intertextuality* refers to the idea that no text is received or interpreted in isolation; rather, texts are juxtaposed with one another, so that one text only has meaning when considered in conjunction with the meanings of other texts.

By the late 20th century, the term *public pedagogy* had been popularized in the work of Giroux (2000) and Luke (1996), in their discussions of "various forms, processes, and sites of education and learning that occur beyond the realm of formal educational institutions" (Sandlin, Wright, & Clark, 2011, p. 4). Public pedagogy is apparent in the places "where people actually live their lives and where meaning is produced, assumed, and contested in the unequal relations of power that construct the mundane acts of everyday relations" (Giroux, 2000, p. 355). Popular cultural consumption is a prime example of public pedagogy. Popular culture reinforces ideas about what or who is desirable and, in so doing, promotes certain ideals and aspirations. Popular culture texts are also replete with representations of social issues, from race or gender relations to poverty to environmental degradation, and tap into people's questions and concerns about them. With these concepts and terms explained, we move to a short discussion of theoretical perspectives from which they are taken up.

Theoretical Foundations

The two overarching theoretical trajectories that have informed public pedagogy scholarship are the Frankfurt School's version of critical theory and a neo-Gramscian approach (Burdick & Sandlin, 2013; Sandlin, O'Malley, & Burdick, 2011). We must stress that while these approaches are theoretically distinct; they are not mutually exclusive; and, in fact, much adult education work in this area uses some mixture of the two. Moreover, as we explain following an outline of key Frankfurt School and neo-Gramscian ideas, emerging theoretical perspectives are extending or, sometimes, challenging the ideas of either or both of those lines of thought.

The Frankfurt School: Ideological Transmission

Largely considered the progenitor of 20th-century cultural criticism, the theoretical approach generated by the Frankfurt School centered on Marxist political-economic theory (Adorno & Horkheimer, 1992) while comingling this conceptualization with analyses of such constructs as the aesthetic and the psychoanalytic. Frankfurt-based notions of cultural reproduction and ideology proliferation center on a largely structuralist model of the identity-culture relationship. Scholars working from this perspective argue that the economic base of a cultural order *determines* the possibilities and limits of its practices and discourse, referred to as *superstructure*. Pedagogy functions as a conduit of both knowledge and ideology, as it reproduces mainstream cultural ideas within subjects' very identities. Individuals, thus, are not viewed as possessing the agentic capacities needed to negotiate these pedagogies in ways that run counter to their intended meanings. Rather, individuals are seen as cultural products (at best) or unwitting dupes of ideological control (at worst).

Neo-Gramscian Approaches: Complexity and Agency

In contradistinction to the Frankfurt School, the neo-Gramscian approach (named for Italian theorist Antonio Gramsci) takes up a far less linear understanding of the pedagogical act and the consumer-as-learner. Ideology, for neo-Gramscians, is in tension with rather than determined by economic structure and can be contested, negotiated, recoded, and even ironically taken up. For Gramsci (1971), culture and education function as arenas where ideas promoted by those occupying positions of socioeconomic power are relayed or taught and come to be seen as what Gramsci calls *common sense*. *Hegemony* is what sets democratic societies apart from other types of society, as social order develops through a combination of ideological persuasion from those in power and consent from the people, and—when necessary—state force. Unlike the Frankfurt School perspective, neo-Gramscians adhere to agentic capacities and the possibility for counter-hegemonic forms of resistance, in which cultural forms of domination are denuded of their ideological content, negotiated, or even rejected outright. Thus, pedagogy in this approach takes on a more relational, intersectional, and complex cadence, often illustrating iterative cycles of resistance and domination around a single pedagogical artifact, act, or phenomenon (Burdick & Sandlin, 2013).

Among the proponents and developers of this perspective, Williams (1958/2011) and scholars associated with the Birmingham School offer important insertions of race, gender, nationality, and other sorts of identifications into analyses of how cultural practices and affiliations develop and become sites of learning (Hall, 1980). In general, the rise of postcritical (Lather, 1995) approaches to social inquiry have broadened the ways that Gramscian ideas continue to be taken up.

Emerging Perspectives
Paradoxically, despite the importance of the two theoretical perspectives explained in adult education, there has been scant theorization of educational processes in cultural consumption beyond the tenets outlined in the preceding paragraphs (Sandlin et al., 2011). As a result, other possibilities remain underemphasized. Even so, some public pedagogy scholarship has taken a decidedly different, postromantic turn in recent years (Burdick & Sandlin, 2013). Postcolonial, posthuman, and materialist reconceptualizations of subjectivity, identity, and pedagogy are emerging as important influences in this work. They represent extensions of and, possibly, a powerful challenge to the two dominant theoretical lenses described previously (Burdick & Sandlin, 2013). We also note that the perspectives discussed in this brief overview are not necessarily discrete, especially as other theoretical influences, including feminism, critical race theory, poststructuralism, and psychoanalysis, and interest in a range of pedagogical contexts, continue to work their way into scholarship on the links among popular culture, pedagogy, and learning.

Learning Contexts

These ideas can be used to explore how adults learn through their engagement with popular culture in a range of settings and contexts, both formal and informal. Curiously, even with the emphasis on popular culture among major figures in the development of critical theory, adult educators have been slow to take up the topic of popular culture as pedagogy as a serious concern. Despite Brookfield's (1986) earlier work as well as the involvement of adult educators such as Williams (1958/2011) in early cultural studies movements, "aside from general reference to the significance of popular culture to the media in our lives . . . , discussion of the role of entertainment media in the education of adults has been [largely] absent" (Tisdell, 2004, p. 1). Tisdell's statement suggests just how recently interest in popular culture within the field of adult education has burgeoned. In this section, we discuss how learning from engagement with popular culture is explored and apparent in both formal and informal educational contexts. Although we profile work conducted in the United States, we include work conducted elsewhere, notably in the United Kingdom and Canada, especially work that is considered important and groundbreaking in this field.

Learning From Popular Culture Outside the Classroom
Returning to the theoretical perspectives explained in the previous section, we note that both the messages that popular culture producers build into their texts and the meanings that consumers of those texts construct through engagement with them matter. Beginning with the overt messages that permeate popular films, we can find evidence that such texts represent social life in ways consistent with hegemonic common sense ideas (Gramsci, 1971). In today's world, those ideas are consistent with a neoliberal capitalist agenda (Guy, 2007; Wright, 2018). That observation makes sense, given that large movie studios and media conglomerates control production, marketing, and distribution of big-budget films and most of what is broadcast in people's homes.

How education itself is represented in popular culture has occupied the attention of a number of adult education scholars. Brown (2015) analyzed nearly a century of filmic portrayals of educators and found that, while teachers have been portrayed positively for decades, they are now often portrayed as obstacles to rather than facilitators of learning. He insisted that "understanding the way these films work, their appeal and their potency, is necessary for countering that [negative] narrative" (p. 63). Johnstone et al. (2018)

analyzed more recent depictions of higher education and educators in 11 movies released in 2014. Linking their analysis of fictional stories in these films to the reality of cuts to postsecondary education and a focus on certification of skills rather than educating for social critique, the authors argued that "film legitimizes particular ideological frameworks surrounding educational institutions and thus informs viewers' understanding of the value and process of education" (p. 26). In particular, it has become common for films to convey "skepticism about the value of humanities teaching and research in the contemporary, neoliberal moment" (p. 25). Although those analyses indicate a growing disillusionment with education and educators, even earlier, more seemingly positive representations were problematic. In their analysis of the film *Educating Rita*, Fisher et al. (2008) detailed an unrealistic, idealized representation of higher education as the key to unlock social and cultural opportunities for the (British) working class.

Other scholars have studied how films frame marginalized groups, often in ways that, for critical teachers and learners, are troubling. For example, Voelkel and Henehan (2018) discussed films' problematic influence on how Miss Laura's Social Club, a restored Victorian brothel operating as a "house museum" in Fort Smith, Arkansas, portrays the lives of sex workers and their customers. Examining films such as *Pretty Woman*, *Breakfast at Tiffany's*, and *Gone with the Wind*, they found that "Cinderella/romanticised themes in the narrative of the lives of 'the girls' that worked in the bordello" (p. 40) led to the creation of a museum that "offers a satisfying Old West fantasy to visitors, rather than taking on some of the harsh realities of prostitution" (p. 52).

On television, perhaps no other genres better exemplify the deliberate maintenance of the status quo, consistent with concerns raised by Frankfurt School scholars, than reality and talk TV. Shows dealing with working-class jobs launched alongside the expansion of neoliberal policies from 2000 to 2010. As Wright (2017) discussed, programs such as *Ice Road Truckers*, *Storage Wars*, and *Appalachian Outlaws* are saturated with the neoliberal construct of meritocracy as well as negative stereotypes of workers. They rarely mention labor abuses, deindustrialization, downsizing, or the lack of medical care, all issues that drastically affect workers. Likewise, Quail et al. (2005) provided an in-depth discussion about how daytime talk shows ignore "broader issues of injustice and exclusion" and, instead, portray an "individual [who] bears the responsibility for any failures, crises and/or alienation experienced" (p. 160). Moreover, racial and gender bias is rampant. In their quantitative analysis of 89 U.S. prime-time TV shows, Sink and Mastro (2017) found that women are "significantly underrepresented" and "harmful stereotypes that have existed for decades remain troublingly evident" (pp. 18–19). Similar results were found for racialized minorities (Tukachinsky et al., 2017).

Despite much evidence that most television programming and big-budget films support the social status quo, pockets of resistance, consistent with a neo-Gramscian perspective on popular culture's potential to provide a more critical pedagogical viewpoint, are apparent among producers of popular culture who aim to insert positive sociocultural and political messages into their texts. Wright and Wright (2015) highlighted the positive portrayals of gender and other markers of diversity in the British sci-fi program *Doctor Who*, while Taber (2015) found that the fairy tale show *Once Upon a Time* provides "complex pedagogies of gender, with women saving men and evil characters garnering understanding" (p. 130).

In reaching beyond textual analysis of popular culture content for her study of female fans of the 1962 season of the UK television drama *The Avengers*, Wright (2010, 2013) found that the *avant garde* feminist character of Dr. Cathy Gale had a profound impact on participants' lives. The character's example of an independent, educated, career woman who fought for justice using judo provided inspiration and confirmed that women were capable of much more than they had been taught growing up in the 1940s and 1950s. In another inquiry, Sandoe (2017) studied how film can serve as a catalyst for social justice-oriented learning among viewer-participants. Sandoe interviewed 10 female online activists, all of whom were inspired to fight for social justice causes by watching and reading *The Hunger Games* films and novels. Her study reveals how fandom can be an organizing factor for social justice causes and highlights "the importance of pop culture and online collaboration in the process of women learning about themselves and their role in social change" (p. 335). On a similar note, Gillig et al. (2018) found that viewers' attitudes toward transgender people were positively mediated by their engagement with an episode of the show *Royal Pains* that features transgender characters and with other positive portrayals on television. These studies embody neo-Gramscian views on popular culture and reveal how popular culture can be used in active, transgressive ways by viewers.

The novel, another form of popular culture, can fall into line with hegemonic thinking just as much as film and television; however, the fact that it is more easily and inexpensively produced than film or television makes it easier for authors and publishers to bring forward novels that deliberately offer lessons to readers about social justice issues, and a number of adult education scholars have turned to novels (Ellis, 2018; Jarvis, 2006; Jubas, 2005; Lawrence & Cranton, 2015). Reading fiction can evoke empathy for others, a necessary component of learning about social and cultural issues (Gouthro, 2014; Jarvis, 2012). In her recent analysis of deindustrialization literature by working-class writers, Linkon (2018) even reveals a new literary genre she calls "deindustrialization literature" (p. xvii), which consists of stories told from the viewpoint of the dispossessed that enable readers to vicariously experience the effects of globalized capitalism on working-class life in the Rust Belt.

Sandoe's (2017) and Wright's (2010, 2013) studies suggest that the specifics of audience members' circumstances matter in their interpretation of and learning from popular culture. This point holds even when learning is not especially critically oriented. For example, Jubas explored how medical and nursing students who watched *Grey's Anatomy* or *Scrubs*, both set in hospitals, juxtaposed their formal education with messages related to professional identity, ethics, and teaching and learning processes that they saw in the shows (Jubas, 2015; Jubas & Knutson, 2012, 2013). For participants, relating to and bonding with the shows' characters who worked as physicians, residents, or nurses helped them imagine their own educational and professional futures. Findings from a follow-up study investigating how popular culture crosses national borders to inform policy debates illuminate how Canadian fans of *Grey's Anatomy* deepened their awareness of the differences between health care in the United States and Canada, as well as their appreciation for Canada's socialized medicare insurance model (Jubas et al., 2014, 2017).

As all of this literature illustrates, consumers of popular culture learn something through their cultural engagement, illustrating the pedagogical potential of popular culture and cultural engagement even in the most everyday, mundane circumstances. Some of this work suggests that popular culture is meant to and, to some extent, functions to help socialize cultural consumers into a mainstream of hegemonic view of social life, consistent with the concerns of Frankfurt School adherents. In contrast, other work illustrates the neo-Gramscian view that cultural consumers exercise agency in interpreting cultural texts and that cultural producers themselves might intend to offer critical, counter-hegemonic representations for consumers to contemplate. Regardless of perspective, how might adult educators recognize the power of popular culture and incorporate it into curriculum?

Bringing Popular Culture Into the Classroom

Informal learning through engagement with popular culture can become a bridge to formal learning (Mills et al., 2014). Adult educators can design "new instructional models for support of the formal to informal learning continuum" (p. 333), bringing the pedagogical power of popular culture into the adult education classroom. While K–12 education saw edited volumes devoted to popular culture in the classroom appearing in earnest by the late 1980s (see, e.g., Alvermann et al., 1999), adult educators began a sustained effort to explore popular culture in the classroom only several decades later, in the mid-2000s (see, in particular, Tisdell & Thompson, 2007).

An exception to that trend in adult education, Brookfield (1986) was one of the first in this field to focus on the pedagogical importance of popular culture and has long argued for the importance of fostering critical media literacy within adult education classrooms. His now-classic article provides practical, classroom-ready tools adult educators can use to help develop media literacy among adult learners, including ways to deconstruct and decode media, with the goal to help learners develop critical consciousness. In more recent work, Brookfield (2013) has focused on how educators can use film in teaching about new perspectives, specific histories, and power. He also discussed how educators can use film to provide suggestions for further study, spur critical thinking, offer case studies for critical analysis, and illustrate complex ideas and concepts. In what follows we present some recent adult education literature that illustrates some of Brookfield's (2013) uses for popular culture in the classroom. We also discuss how learners come to deeper understandings of critical issues related to social structures and inequalities via reflection and sustained discussion with educators and peers about the popular culture texts they encounter.

In their literature review on the use of arts, including popular culture texts, in professional education, Jarvis and Gouthro (2015) found that such texts can illustrate complex concepts and dilemmas, foster empathy and insight, help learners construct professional identities and discourses, and engage learners in self-awareness and interpersonal skill development. Furthermore, drawing on the arts in their education helped professionals-in-the-making develop an understanding of the socially constructed nature of knowledge. Finally, Jarvis and Gouthro found that there was no single learning outcome to the incorporation of popular culture texts in the classroom; some students used the arts to craft more critical, antioppressive viewpoints and practices, while others embraced less critical and political, and more humanistic and empathetic perspectives.

One issue that has surfaced in the adult education literature concerns the role of a facilitator in fostering critical learning with regard to engaging with popular culture. As we have shown, adult educators have determined that audiences often make sense of popular media texts, reflect on their own pleasure, negotiate meanings, and create new meanings without the intervention of a classroom teacher, through group interactions and discussion among themselves and their peers (see also Alvermann et al., 1999). However, this does not mean that learners in more formal settings cannot benefit from bringing popular culture into the classroom. Indeed, much adult education research has found that engaging learners in discussions and activities designed to encourage critical reflection about their learning from popular culture results in deeper and more profound learning, especially around issues of race, class, gender, social justice, and power structures (Tisdell, 2008) and how learners' personal, social, and professional identities are shaped by media representations and connected to broader social contexts (Jubas & Knutsen, 2012, 2013). The movie *Crash*, for example, which places critical messages in the foreground for consumers, is one cultural text that has been used in the critically oriented adult education classroom (Guy, 2007; Tisdell, 2008). Through facilitated discussion of or an assignment focused on analyzing that film, students can construct deep meanings about issues of diversity.

In incorporating popular culture into their classrooms, adult educators need to be both purposeful and careful to avoid imposing their analyses of a cultural text and, instead, encourage students to "consider the intent of the producers and to contrast this analysis with their own or other students' interpretations" (Guy, 2007, p. 21). Drawing on earlier writing by Carmen Luke, Guy outlined how examination of a popular culture text can help students develop critical media literacy, which involves "coding practice, text-meaning practice, pragmatic practice, and critical practice" (p. 21). Through those practices, cultural consumers come to understand how objects and people become connected to ideas about what and who are good or bad, desirable or repugnant and disrupt those hegemonic understandings. Tisdell and her colleagues found that such critical discussions are even more important when learners are already fans of the media they are engaging with and when they derive pleasure from that media (Tisdell, 2008).

Taber's more recent work (Taber et al., 2014, 2017) reinforces the idea that critical learning is enhanced with scaffolded discussions that can serve to challenge learners' prior beliefs and foster more critical perspectives on social, political, and cultural issues. The authors also stressed the benefits for learners of participating in a community where they built relationships with one another. They offered five suggestions for using popular culture in the classroom to generate critical analysis and discussion: (a) provide multiple texts and counter-texts, (b) expect and accept alternative responses and resistances, (c) revisit concepts and probe for deep understanding, (d) use strategies that create respectful environments, and (e) consider positionality (Taber et al., 2014).

Research suggests that one way to help learners internalize and practice their new critical media literacy knowledge is to have them create a "practical project" (Tisdell et al., 2007, p. 611) wherein they teach others how to analyze gender, race, class, and sexual orientation in films and television programs, or take part in imagining, creating, and producing their own cultural products and experiences. Hutchins and Bierema (2013) explored students' experiences of undertaking of a media analysis project and found that, while students learned on their own from their individual analyses, they developed greater understandings as they discussed and shared with others their reflections about representations of gender, class, and race with others. Finally, Jarvis (2012) reminded her readers that learning outcomes cannot be taken for granted and encouraged adult educators to consider why some learners develop more deeply critical perspectives and qualities such as empathy through facilitated discussions of popular culture, while others do not.

Conclusion

This discussion reminds us, as adult educators, about the usefulness of considering the important role of popular culture texts and engagements as pedagogies. The work reviewed here highlights the importance of popular culture in the mediated and nonmediated learning across sites and forms of education and learning. As a pedagogical process, cultural consumption illustrates two key points related to adult learning. First, cultural consumption, which typically occurs as part of leisure life, exemplifies the multisited nature of learning, the presence of all sorts of informal educational contexts, and the possibility of incidental learning, which "may be taken for granted, tacit, or unconscious" (Marsick & Watkins, 2001, p. 26). Second, more than an intellectual process, engagement with popular culture texts, both outside and inside classrooms, and the learning associated with those engagements are multidimensional processes; in drawing in fans on an emotional level, they illustrate how learners' emotions are summoned in not only cultural consumption but also adult learning (Dirkx, 2008). We encourage other adult educators to continue exploring these important, culture-based sites of education and learning, because evidence suggests that educational engagements centered on cultural pedagogies—whether inside or outside formal classrooms—can be a "facilitator of, and catalyst for" learning that is often "far more powerful, lasting, and lifelong than learning in formal educational settings and other traditionally researched areas of teaching and learning" (Wright & Sandlin, 2009, p. 135).

References

Adorno, T., & Horkheimer, M. (1992). The concept of Enlightenment. In D. Ingram & J. Ingram (Eds.), *Critical theory: The essential readings* (pp. 49–56). Paragon.

Alvermann, D. E., Moon, J. S., & Hagood, M. C. (1999). *Popular culture in the classroom: Teaching and researching critical media literacy*. Routledge.

Brookfield, S. (1986). Media power and the development of media literacy: An adult educational interpretation. *Harvard Educational Review, 56*(2), 151–170.

Brookfield, S. (2013). Teaching through film. In V. Wang (Ed.), *Handbook of research on teaching and learning in K–20 education* (pp. 341–355). IGI Global.

Brown, T. (2015). Teachers on film: Changing representations of teaching in popular cinema from Mr. Chips to Jamie Fitzpatrick. In K. Jubas, N. Taber, & T. Brown (Eds.), *Popular culture as pedagogy: Research in adult education* (pp. 49–66). Sense.

Burdick, J., & Sandlin, J. A. (2013). Learning, becoming, and the unknowable: Conceptualizations, mechanisms, and process in public pedagogy literature. *Curriculum Inquiry, 43*(1), 142–177.

Dirkx, J. (2008). The meaning and role of emotions in adult learning. *New Directions for Adult and Continuing Education, 2008*(120), 7–18.

Ellis, J. M. (2018). Swedish crime fiction and study abroad: Literature, politics and the foreigner. *Frontiers: The Interdisciplinary Journal of Study Abroad, 30*(2), 106–116.

Fisher, R., Harris, A., & Jarvis, C. (2008). *Education in popular culture: Telling tales on teachers and learners*. Routledge.

Gillig, T. K., Rosenthal, E. L., Murphy, S. T., & Folb, K. L. (2018). More than a media moment: The influence of televised storylines on viewers' attitudes toward transgender people and policies. *Sex Roles, 78*(7–8), 515–527.

Giroux, H. A. (2000). Public pedagogy as cultural politics: Stuart Hall and the "crisis" of culture. *Cultural Studies, 14*(2), 341–360.

Gouthro, P. A. (2014). Women of mystery. *Adult Education Quarterly, 64*(4), 356–373.

Gramsci, A. (1971). *Selections from The Prison Notebooks* (Q. Hoare & G. Nowell Smith, Eds. and Trans.). International Publishers.

Guy, T. C. (2007). Learning who we (and they) are: Popular culture as pedagogy. *New Directions for Adult and Continuing Education, 2007*(115), 15–23.

Hall, S. (1980). Encoding/decoding. In S. Hall, D. Hobson, A. Lowe, & P. Willis (Eds.), *Culture, media, language* (pp. 128–138). Routledge.

Hutchins, H. M., & Bierema, L. (2013). Media analysis as critical reflexology in exploring adult learning theories. *New Horizons in Adult Education & Human Resource Development, 25*(1), 56–69.

Jarvis, C. (2006). Using fiction for transformation. *New Directions for Adult and Continuing Education, 2006*(109), 69–77.

Jarvis, C. (2012). Fiction, empathy and lifelong learning. *International Journal of Lifelong Education, 31*(6), 743–758.

Jarvis, C., & Gouthro, P. (2015). The role of the arts in professional education: Surveying the field. *Studies in the Education of Adults, 47*(1), 64–80.

Johnstone, K., Marquis, E., & Puri, V. (2018). Public pedagogy and representations of higher education in popular film: New ground for the scholarship of teaching and learning. *Teaching & Learning Inquiry, 6*(1), 25–37.

Jubas, K. (2005). *A Fine Balance* in truth and fiction: Exploring globalization's impacts on community and implications for adult learning in Rohinton Mistry's novel and related literature. *International Journal of Lifelong Education, 24*(1), 53–69.

Jubas, K. (2015). Giving substance to ghostly figures: How female nursing students respond to a cultural portrayal of "women's work" in healthcare. In K. Jubas, N. Taber, & T. Brown (Eds.), *Popular culture as pedagogy: Research in the field of adult education* (pp. 83–101). Sense.

Jubas, K., Johnston, D. E. B., & Chiang, A. (2014). Living and learning across stages and places: How transitions inform audience members' understandings pop culture and health care. *Canadian Journal for the Study of Adult Education, 26*(1), 57–75.

Jubas, K., Johnston, D., & Chiang, A. (2017). Public pedagogy as border-crossing: How Canadian fans learn about health care from American TV. *Journal of Borderlands Studies*. https://doi.org/10.1080/08865655.2017.1367319

Jubas, K., & Knutson, P. (2012). Seeing and be(liev)ing: How nursing and medical students understand representations of their professions. *Studies in the Education of Adults, 44*(1), 85–100.

Jubas, K., & Knutson, P. (2013). Fictions of work-related learning: How a hit television show portrays internship, and how medical students relate to those portrayals. *Studies in Continuing Education, 35*(2), 224–240.

Lather, P. (1995). Postcritical pedagogies: A feminist reading. In P. McLaren (Ed.), *Postmodernism, postcolonialism, and pedagogy* (pp. 167–186). James Nichols.

Lawrence, R. L., & Cranton, P. (2015). *A novel idea: Researching transformative learning in fiction*. Sense.

Linkon, S. (2018). *The half-life of deindustrialization: Working-class writing about economic restructuring*. University of Michigan Press.

Luke, C. (Ed.). (1996). *Feminisms and pedagogies of everyday life*. SUNY Press.

Marsick, V. J., & Watkins, K. E. (2001). Informal and incidental learning. *New Directions for Adult and Continuing Education, 2001*(89), 25–34.

Maudlin, J. G., & Sandlin, J. A. (2015). Pop culture pedagogies: Process and praxis. *Educational Studies, 51*(5), 368–384. https://doi.org/10.1080/00131946.2015.1075992

Mills, L. A., Knezek, G., & Khaddage, F. (2014). Information seeking, information sharing, and going mobile: Three bridges to informal learning. *Computers in Human Behavior, 32,* 323–334.

Quail, C. M., Razzano, K. A., & Skalli, L. H. (2005). *Vulture culture: The politics and pedagogy of daytime television talk shows*. Peter Lang.

Sandlin, J. A., O'Malley, M. P., & Burdick, J. (2011). Mapping the complexity of public pedagogy scholarship: 1894–2010. *Review of Educational Research, 81*(3), 338–375.

Sandlin, J. A., Schultz, B. D., & Burdick, J. (2010). Understanding, mapping, and exploring the terrain of public pedagogy. In J. A. Sandlin, B. D. Schultz, & J. Burdick (Eds.), *Handbook of public pedagogy: Education and learning beyond schooling* (pp. 1–6). Routledge.

Sandlin, J. A., Wright, R. R., & Clark, C. (2011). Reexamining theories of adult learning and adult development through the lens of public pedagogy. *Adult Education Quarterly, 63*(1), 3–23.

Sandoe, K. J. (2017). *Hungry for justice: The Hunger Games and developing an activist identity in women fans* (Publication No. 1925911753). [Doctoral dissertation: Pennsylvania State University]. ProQuest Dissertations & Theses A&I.

Sink, A., & Mastro, D. (2017). Depictions of gender on primetime television: A quantitative content analysis. *Mass Communication and Society, 20*(1), 3–22.

Taber, N. (2015). Pedagogies of gender in a Disney mashup: Princesses, queens, beasts, pirates, lost boys, and witches. In K. Jubas, N. Taber, & T. Brown (Eds.), *Popular culture as pedagogy: Research in the field of adult education* (pp. 119–134). Sense.

Taber, N., Woloshyn, V., & Lane, L. (2017). Strong Snow White requires stronger marriageable huntsman: Exploring gender in a media discussion group for women. *Canadian Journal for the Study of Adult Education, 29*(2), 21–36.

Taber, N., Woloshyn, V., Munn, C., & Lane, L. (2014). Exploring representations of super women in popular culture: Shaping critical discussions with female college students with learning exceptionalities. *Adult Learning, 25*(4), 142–150.

Tisdell, E. J. (2004, 6–8 October). *Drawing on pop culture and entertainment media in adult education practice in teaching for social change* [Paper presentation]. Midwest Research-to-Practice Conference in Adult, Continuing, and Community Education, Indianapolis, IN, United States. https://scholarworks.iupui.edu/handle/1805/279

Tisdell, E. J. (2008). Critical media literacy and transformative learning: Drawing on pop culture and entertainment media in teaching for diversity in adult higher education. *Journal of Transformative Education, 6*(1), 48–67.

Tisdell, E. J., Stuckey, H. L., & Thompson, P. M. (2007). *Teaching critical media literacy in adult and higher education: An action research study* [Paper presentation]. 48th Annual Adult Education Research Conference, Halifax, NS, Canada. https://pdfs.semanticscholar.org/5004/68d263a941125aaf96e220eba70a4590319e.pdf

Tisdell, E. J., & Thompson, P. M. (2007). Editors' notes. *New Directions for Adult and Continuing Education, 2007*(115), 1–4.

Tukachinsky, R., Mastro, D., & Yarchi, M. (2017). The effect of prime time television ethnic/racial stereotypes on Latino and Black Americans: A longitudinal national level study. *Journal of Broadcasting & Electronic Media, 61*(3), 538–556. https://doi.org/10.1080/08838151.2017.1344669

Voelkel, M., & Henehan, S. (2018). Rescuing the soiled dove: Pop culture's influence on a historical narrative of prostitution. *International Journal of Lifelong Education, 37*(1), 40–54. https://doi.org:10.1080/02601370.2017.1375036

Williams, R. (1958/2011). Culture is ordinary. In I. Szeman & T. Kaposy (Eds.), *Cultural theory: An anthology* (pp. 53–59). Wiley-Blackwell. (Original work published 1958)

Wright, R. R. (2010). Unmasking hegemony with *The Avengers*: Television entertainment as public pedagogy. In J. Sandlin, B. Schultz, & S. Burdick (Eds.), *Handbook of public pedagogy: Education and learning beyond schooling* (pp. 139–150). Routledge.

Wright, R. R. (2013). *The Avengers* and feminist identity development: Learning the example of critical resistance from Cathy Gale. In K. M. Ryan & D. Massey (Eds.), *Television and the self: Knowledge, identity and media representation* (pp. 189–204). Lexington.

Wright, R. R. (2017). Neoliberal ideology in reality television: A public pedagogy that normalizes education and income inequality in the U.S. and abroad. In G. Kong & E. Boeren (Eds.), *Adult education for inclusion and diversity conference proceedings* (pp. 412–418). Centre for Research in Education Inclusion & Diversity, University of Edinburgh and Standing Conference on Teaching and Research in the Education of Adults.

Wright, R. R. (2018). Popular culture, adult learning and identity development. In M. Milana, J. Holford, S. Webb, P. Jarvis, & R. Waller (Eds.), *Palgrave International handbook of adult and lifelong education and learning* (pp. 971–989). Palgrave Macmillan.

Wright, R. R., & Sandlin, J. A. (2009). Popular culture, public pedagogy, and perspective transformation: *The Avengers* and adult learning in living rooms. *International Journal of Lifelong Learning, 28*(4), 533–551. https://doi.org/10.1080/02601370903031389

Wright, R. R., & Wright, G. L. (2015). *Doctor Who* fandom, critical engagement, and transmedia storytelling: The public pedagogy of the Doctor. In K. Jubas, N. Taber, & T. Brown (Eds.), *Popular culture as pedagogy: Research in the field of adult education* (pp. 11–30). Sense.

CHAPTER 18

Digital Technologies for Teaching and Learning

Elisabeth E. Bennett and Rochell R. McWhorter

Advancements in digital technologies have caused a sea change in adult and continuing education (ACE) as online education grows in market share and learners and educators alike have greater access to information, collaborators, communication channels, software applications, and devices that connect them through and to the internet anywhere and anytime (Bennett & Gorman, 2018). The current era is characterized by ubiquitous computing, or the idea that digital technology diffuses into most areas of life to the extent it is no longer noticed, such as wearable technology like the Apple Watch. These devices alert the user to text and voice calls, and automation applications, or *apps*, facilitate control of other "smart" devices that communicate through the internet, even setting temperature and turning on and off lights (Adhiya, 2020). Ubiquitous computing is changing the social-historical context of ACE, both in terms of the range of digital tools available for ACE and learners' expectations for using new technologies in the classroom.

Human existence has become hybridized between the material and the virtual in the 21st century, and there is a trend toward increasing mobile learning technologies for self-directed and continuing professional education (Curran et al., 2019). Ubiquitous computing has correspondingly imbued ubiquitous learning, or learning that is anytime and anywhere, with greater emphasis on learner agency (Cope & Kalantzis, 2010), resulting in adults more quickly filling learning gaps in the moment. For example, hikers take a picture of a plant along a nature trail and use a cell phone app to identify and learn about the plant's properties. The time between self-diagnosing a learning problem and receiving an answer is vastly shortened by mobile technologies leapfrogging old, stationary technological infrastructure. Even without apps, smartphones have basic internet browsers and search capability. ACE can now reach adults in remote places serviced by satellites, which opens up unprecedented access to participation where governmental regulation allows.

Significant change is on the horizon for ACE. The world is currently going through a fourth industrial revolution advanced by artificial intelligence (AI), machine learning, and robots (Schwab, 2016; Skilton & Hovsepian, 2018) that may, on the one hand, democratize learning by lowering cost and increasing availability of advanced learning tools (i.e., robots, AI, mobile devices), but, on the other hand, may also create what Eubanks (2017) fears: inequality through automation, such as preemptive removal of children by social services based on AI risk algorithms. Concern for disparate impact of automation on the most vulnerable is an important question for ACE, especially as job losses mount. The need to reskill in this revolution will drive more adults to seek ACE, and adult educators will need to adapt and leverage new technologies to help humans thrive (Inverso et al., 2017).

In addition to solving professional learning needs, ubiquitous learning offers new pathways for personal learning and self-expression when adults create and contribute digital content through an ever-increasing palette of apps and social media. This chapter examines these digital technologies for teaching and learning, and we argue the importance of access to the internet to equalize learning opportunities and serve democratic ideals of ACE. The chapter begins with an overview of the current state of technology for ACE, discusses new trends in digital technologies, particularly the internet of things and AI, and then provides implications for ACE.

Overview of Digital Technologies for ACE

From a historical perspective, digital technologies have been part of ACE for several decades. The 2010 handbook contained two chapters focused on digital topics, including informal learning in virtual environments (King, 2010) and the history of distance education (Archer & Garrison, 2010). King's (2010) contribution provided coverage of a host of digital technologies for teaching and learning that are still relevant a decade later and identified a trend toward increased informal and self-directed learning that continues today. While there will always be a need for formal education in ACE, informal learning can leverage adults' motivations and interests, and allow them many tools to coproduce learning in a dynamic world of sociopolitical change.

Modern digital technologies are now more deeply embedded in the personal and professional lives of adults, moving beyond one-off tools to larger and more integrated systems of technology in ACE. This idea is exemplified in online sites that provide easy, curated access to ACE courses from a variety of sources (e.g., Degreed.com). Educators offer courses to adults through these sites, which help adults match learning resources with self-directed learning plans. Further, programs like these can be linked to school and workplace systems, alerting educators to newly published resources using keywords. Digital technologies can be woven together to create sophisticated learning strategies that combine human expertise and digital resources.

These networks create virtual spaces with opportunities for adult learners to connect to learning communities and materials, and easily produce learning products like presentations, blogs, instruction videos, and papers. Indeed, many people turn to online instruction videos as a first choice of new learning, such as those found on YouTube. These allow educator-to-peer and peer-to-peer sharing of knowledge and skills, which remain informal or can be linked to formal classes through learning management systems (LMSs) used by many ACE providers.

Digital technologies for adult learning include social media, online discussion boards, blogs, wikis, instant messaging, massive open online courses (MOOCs), video and screen capture, video conferencing, and topic aggregators. Each of these platforms is widespread and can be used by teachers to help adults examine areas of interest, develop skills, and engage in social networking. These technologies foster ACE that is self-directed, meaningful, and relevant (Merriam & Bierema, 2014).

Some technologies are freely available while others require purchase or subscription. For example, if a learner or educator does not have access to expensive presentation software, Prezi.com offers free basic access for adults to create and access presentations as long as an internet connection is available. Access to free, albeit stripped-down, apps gives adults a taste of a tool and encourage purchase of more expensive features, a common marketing strategy that helps equalize access to technology and benefits participation in ACE.

Table 18.1 provides an overview and sampling of tools, but it is by no means fully comprehensive given the vast array of options available to ACE. It covers some of the most popular digital technologies that can be used separately or integrated within LMSs, along with benefits and limitations of their use.

The vast array of digital technologies available today allows for a great variety of tools in ACE, and new avenues for self-expression for teachers and learners alike. The ability to create, customize, and reuse instructional materials quickly increases resources available for adult learning, which is now often accessed on-the-go through mobile technologies and cell phones. Scholars have shown that there is an increase in use of mobile technologies (e.g., cell phones, laptops, and tablets) for ACE, even among older adults and those who are low income (Inverso et al., 2017; Jelfs & Richardson, 2013). This is due to the decreasing cost of mobile technologies, such as cheap smartphones, and governmental and charitable giveaways. Additionally,

TABLE 18.1. Digital Tools and Programs for ACE

Technology Themes	Sample Tools	Benefits	Limitations
LMSs	Blackboard, Moodle, Canvas, Google Classroom (free), Learn Upon Learn	Synchronous and asynchronous learning tools, assignment submission, ability to develop learning community, multimedia files, screen capture, presentations, threaded discussions, and grading features; web links to outside technologies; some integration with talent management and student record systems possible	Oriented to formal learning; complex systems can be clumsy, time-consuming to manage, and costly; students may not be able to find resources or intuitively navigate; depends heavily on text-based communication; universal software updates may change functionality; limited ability to customize
Exploring Areas of Interest	Blogs, wikis, online discussion boards, online videos (i.e., YouTube, TED Talks), mass communication (e.g., Instagram, Twitter), MOOCs, news aggregators (e.g., AllTop)	Asynchronous access to relevant information for convenient, anytime, anywhere adult learning opportunities (i.e., online training, workshops, educational courses); available in multiple languages; most resources are free	Contributions can be deleted so adult learners may lose access to information; privacy issues; contributions can also be preserved and disseminated by others, so that the originator no longer controls; motivation by the learner determines the depth of exploration
Skill Development and Knowledge Curation	Online videos (i.e., YouTube, TED Talks); blogs, wikis, MOOCs, education and resource aggregators (e.g., Degreed.com, Pinterest.com), self-publishing (e.g., Lulu.com), digital commons, photo-sharing sites (e.g., Flickr.com), ability to purchase high-resolution pictures at low cost (e.g., Canva.com)	Asynchronous access to expert content and self-publishing; users subscribe or enroll in specific development areas, allowing focus on specific learning with pace set by the learner; available in multiple languages; some platforms allow downloading videos and learning content for later viewing offline; others provide certificates of completion for online courses	Adult learning falls on the shoulders of the learner in asynchronous environments, requiring persistence and self-direction; downloading and playing videos and course materials may require considerable bandwidth, social and hands-on learning may be more difficult; virtual reality applications approximate but differ from real-world experiences
Social Networking and Community Building	Social media (e.g., Facebook), video conferencing, instant messaging, Twitter, virtual Worlds (e.g., SecondLife)	Learners meet up with others, informally explore topics of mutual interest; share information with others, and interact with others and develop social/professional contacts; available in multiple languages; adults can try on new personas and explore new identities	Privacy and confidentiality concerns; corporate interests may sell access to users; community ground rules need to be followed; requires bandwidth for video streaming and virtual world access; takes time to learn all features; may be proprietary and require specific software for participation; interactions can become negative or misconstrued

mobile technologies that use cell service are bypassing poor telecommunications infrastructure and allowing for increased participation even in developing countries. This level of access also means an increasing need for digital literacy skills, such as understanding what information to trust and how to curate resources to limit information overload.

Knowing how learners access digital technologies is important for instructors who should no longer assume that students use desktop computers in one, stable setting for online learning. The latest digital technologies can format learning materials for multiple devices. For example, small, mobile screens on cell phones and tablets require more condensed video presentations or audio-only resources. Additionally, voice recognition software and caption services make digital technologies more accessible to adults with disabilities or who learn best through multiple modalities. Course design is also changing. The outmoded approach to online learning was to reproduce didactic teaching whereas new modes fundamentally change the relationship of adults to knowledge (Cope & Kalantzis, 2010). The new relationship is not about bypassing teachers, but increasing engagement and interactivity of ACE learners. This can be done by weaving together numerous digital technologies, such as those in Table 18.1, to create rich, participative learning environments that respect autonomy, culture, and dignity of adult learners.

The real power of digital technologies is in building multiple technologies together into a unique system or ecology in which people interact with other people, information, and digital objects like software apps and videos (Bennett & Bierema, 2010). These ecologies link together learning resources within an ACE institution's private knowledge network or intranet, creating a framework of technologies that result in a whole larger than the sum of parts. Likewise, various digital resources and apps may be webbed together in an LMS to create a customized learning environment that shifts and changes with learner needs, hyperlinking new resources over time. New digital trends on the horizon raise new possibilities and concerns for ACE.

New Trends: Internet of Things and AI

The sea change underway includes growing ubiquity of smart devices that link the world together into the Internet of Things (IoT) as well as enable cutting-edge AI. Many of the technologies covered thus far can be used in conjunction with these new trends, but the data generated from smart, internet-connected devices are often being fed back into vendor systems to increase big data needed for AI analysis and machine learning. AI makes sales calls, schedules appointments, screens job applicants, analyzes survey data, and offers suggestions for purchases on websites. This chapter section addresses these two areas that are dramatically changing education and the workplace by capitalizing on networked technologies that create IoT and AI, which create a new social milieu for ACE and enable customization of education to adult needs.

Adult Learning and the IoT

The *Internet of Things* has been defined as "a phenomenon of a growing number of connected devices, and internet-enabled services [whereby] billions of devices are now connected to one another" (Bennett, 2018, p. 166), which provides a larger digital gestalt. For example, imagine ACE for health and fitness. Sports bracelets track heart rate, sleep modes, steps, and calories burned to provide real-time biofeedback. The data can also help adults learn about their health patterns over time and set goals. Further, adults may compare goals with others in a class, allowing for collective learning and encouragement, and data can be aggregated and analyzed to discern demographic patterns and public health concerns, resulting in future education content on fitness.

According to Botta et al. (2016), IoT allows users to infer, understand, and learn from things in their environment, as in the aforementioned plant identification vignette, or other objects with built-in sensors that can be read by devices. It is conducive for adult learning as people connect with one another via social media, email, internet, and intranets through networking of myriad devices. These devices have sensors and ways to communicate encrypted data, typically through Wi-Fi, which allows for quick feedback, early warning, and exchange of high volumes of data (McWhorter, 2014). Anytime one sees the term *smart*, it means the device is digitally enabled and prepared to connect to the internet (and subsequently IoT), thus combining portability and wearability of small devices with the capability to exchange data with more resource-intensive storage servers and software applications. Smart TVs, for example, provide access to online videos and movies, facilitating ACE instructors to stream movies and instructional videos without fiddling with DVD players and other cumbersome components.

Increasingly, IoT cobbles together internal or private networks with devices that are held or worn by adults, including implantable chips. The human intranet and wearable networks, such as sports bracelets previously mentioned, link people with mobile phones and provide sources of learning about oneself using more subtle, smaller devices that are less intrusive than prior generations (Bennett, 2018). These devices often allow for two-way communication, such as text messages scrolling across small wrist-size screens, which can be used for ACE. Imagine a group problem-solving exercise in which clues and instructions are texted to members in real time. Real-time messages can enhance the reality of simulations when devices provide real data that must be cognitively assimilated in the moment, such as in medical simulations. These IoT features can help test reactions and behaviors experientially, rather than just promote knowledge gain. They go beyond original design intent and are used in new and creative ways for interactive ACE.

IoT presents a number of applications for adult learning. For example, the connectivity of the internet allows learners access to electronic books (ebooks), scholarly articles, and other digital resources on mobile devices (Business Insider Intelligence, 2016). Publishers are increasingly using electronic book formats for course texts. Ebooks are portable, interactive, cost effective, and allow learners to customize their experience with text-to-speech, highlighting and searching for keywords, and adjusting font sizes and screen brightness. These features support student differentiation, address physical limitations and disabilities, and encourage engagement with content that fosters knowledge construction. Electronic delivery means knowledge resources arrive instantaneously or are held in a central repository to be opened by multiple devices. IoT also allows cloud computing or the storage of files on central, password-protected servers. Access to these materials occurs virtually anywhere in the world, such as to academic papers or shared files for group projects.

Adults learn within networks that surround them wherever they go in this era. Wi-fi–enabled cameras upload photos and video on location, which facilitates a form of citizen journalism. Adult learning will take a leap further in the future when people are *webbed in* (Bennett, 2014) to IoT through radio-frequency identification chips and other bio-networking tools, further mediating communication, information exchange, and human decisions (Bennett, 2018). Collective learning is also part of IoT technology, such as through groupware and crowdsourcing when multiple people collaborate to solve problems using shared data and creative tools.

IoT is not without concerns for safe learning environments in ACE, including security, privacy, and data ownership issues that challenge copyright of intellectual education materials or expose users to embarrassment or legal risk. This is particularly important for always-listening devices that benefit learners as speedy, voice-activated methods of answering questions using information found on the internet; however, input can also be accidentally distributed, hacked, or misused. For example, in 2018, Amazon's Echo smart speaker recorded conversations of a user and then emailed a transcript of the conversations to contacts in the linked phone's address book without the user's consent (Panda Security, 2018). This could only occur when the phone was networked with the device. Other instances of concern include hacking digital cameras on portable devices and using baby monitors for spying. Due to IoT advancements, there is an abundance of student data being collected, worrisome to student advocacy groups, and so the benefits of IoT for ACE must be weighed against the potential for harm, especially to those already on the fringes of society. In the grand scheme, IoT is providing much of the big data needed to train AI.

AI

The social context of ACE increasingly includes advanced technologies and virtual personalities, or AI. Opportunities for adult learning include informal learning, self-directed learning, and augmenting online learning. The key point of AI is that it emulates humans as the technology comes to its own conclusions and appears to engage in natural dialogue with people, thus enhancing or replacing "human cognitive performance" (Cooney, 2016, p. 1). It is also driving the discipline of learning analytics that informs content selection and marketing of ACE. It can identify where students need extra support or those at risk of attrition, recommending intervention. Learning analytics combines learning data and statistical analysis in an effort to optimize education, analyzing at rates that are beyond human capability.

Humans must train AI for it to be useful, which is domain-specific rather than general intelligence. AI is created through machine learning, sometimes called *deep learning*. It can interact with humans and even teach adults through personas with human names and simulated voices, such as assistants: Alexa, Siri, Pepper, Cortana, Watson, and Sophia (Lin, 2018). AI assistants are useful for answering questions, playing music, making travel plans, controlling smart laboratories, and transacting online tasks. Because they are products of humans, they also are built with potentially biased gender stereotypes, since most assistants default to female voices, although Watson, used for medical diagnoses, is based on a male character in Sherlock Holmes mysteries. Use of AI-driven assistants can reinforce stereotypes in the classroom, such as female administrative assistants and male physicians. Thus, power dynamics and discriminatory assumptions may be accidentally embedded into ACE.

A new category of AI assistants, *hearables,* are "wireless, smart, micro-computers with AI that incorporate both speakers and a microphone that fit in ears and connect to other devices and the internet" (McGreal, 2018, para. 1) and are currently being built to handle foreign language translation, augment hearing above normal levels, sync to smart devices, track activity, and incorporate biometric identification (Lambda, 2020). These devices may be the future of shoulder-to-shoulder coaching in which learners are given suggestions or learning nudges.

AI has already passed the coveted Turing test—that is, when computers exhibit intelligent behaviors indistinguishable from humans. It will eventually take over some instructional tasks in the classroom, such as analyzing discussion posts and suggesting supplemental resources to students. In the near future, adults participating in ACE will learn from AI instructors that can simulate emotion and humor. AI is already being applied to adult learning through intelligent tutoring systems that customize learning for the adult student, incorporating prior performance data, identifying areas that are lacking, and building needed proficiencies into an eLearning course (BeaconLive Marketing Team, 2019); we expect this trend to continue. AI and the other digital technologies discussed here have significant implications for ACE.

Implications for ACE

The sea change of digital technology represents a paradigm shift for ACE that challenges our understanding of how knowledge is constructed in new modes of learning (Bennett, 2010; McWhorter, 2010). This paradigm shift began with ubiquity of computing and corresponding ubiquity of adult learning through digital technologies, which are increasingly mobile, networked, smart, and integrated with AI. Whether through direct use or indirectly from someone else's use, digital technologies are now integral in the current social milieu. Even remote tribes protected from outsider contact, such as the Sentinelese isolated by Indian law, may wonder about the satellites streaking overhead with regularity, monitoring, imaging, mapping their closed world. A next step in the evolution will be 5G networks that can theoretically provide global coverage, and the foundations for a global brain (Bennett, 2018).

Adults increasingly access the internet through these satellites and participate in global culture that is both particular and collective in, as yet, undefined ways. But human connection through the internet is beyond mere access; people are not only subjects of content in the internet world, they are becoming internet objects physically connected to the web through chips and wires, tracked by IoT devices. It is scary and potentially dystopian, yet intriguing, when one thinks of the greater capabilities digital technology brings to human life and learning.

The most important general implication of this chapter is that the internet, with all its applications, learning resources, and cultural communities must remain open to adults, following principles of noncensorship, academic freedom, and respect for learners, characteristic of the democratic ideals in ACE. Closing off the internet through regulation and censorship prohibits access to material for creativity and liberation from local constraints. The internet is critical for participation in ACE and activism through social movements (Bennett & McWhorter, 2019).

A second general implication likewise calls educators to recognize that digital technologies are no longer just tools that enhance old education models, but are portals to online environments imbued with humanity, culture, learning, and the highs and lows of everyday life, all integral to formal and informal learning (Bennett, 2009). Adults live a hybrid life when they step into a virtual environment or engage in virtual work, and these environments are new locations for ACE. Next, we cover opportunities and challenges.

Opportunities

Because adult learners are adopting mobile devices at unprecedented numbers, educators have an opportunity to leverage them for teaching and learning. They must understand how the mode influences virtual experiences, and therefore teachers should ensure compatibility between digital devices and the content in LMSs and course websites. This calls for professional development and organic conversations about technology integration, which may be tough on shoestring budgets, though many apps are freely available. When educators give adults flexibility, students will often embrace and use mobile tools in unexpected ways. Adult educators will need to determine best practices for virtual reality and virtual learning environments to maximize learning and to keep ethics in check given misuse of data and devices (Bennett & McWhorter, 2017b).

IoT provides a greater connection between things and people. Educational institutions increasingly use sensors to monitor physical spaces, such as labs, and components collect and relay data used in makerspaces, laboratories, and projects undertaken by students and faculty (Educause, 2014). Learning materials are more quickly secured, such as ebooks. Perhaps more important, intellectual relationships between faculty and students can be facilitated more easily and asynchronously with communication technology, which moves human connection beyond class and a defined set of office hours.

Informal learning is rampant in webbed environments, and it likely exceeds formal learning by many factors. Adults increasingly turn to the internet for help with life problems, such as support groups, product reviews for making purchase decisions, repair instructions, and for social contact, thus extending lifelong learning. Digital technologies may foster sudden insight, the classic "a-ha!" moment, given the high use of images, colors, sound, and graphics that can that trigger nonverbal cognition, such as image processing and pattern finding (Bennett, 2011, 2012).

Cope and Kalantzis (2010) indicate that technologies for ubiquitous learning blur traditional, temporal boundaries of education, emphasize learner agency, link individual thinking with social cognition, foster conceptual skills for digital technology, and contribute to collaborative knowledge cultures. Many of these map onto adult learning theory; agency is recognizable as the adult learning characteristic of self-direction (Knowles et al., 2015). However, a new theory may need to be developed as people become more integrated with technology, which may change how knowledge is constructed.

Formal and informal learning will increasingly blend to create customized education, such as personal learning pathways (Bennett et al., 2017; Christensen et al., 2008). As an example, Northeastern University's Self-Authored Integrated Learning app allows learners to capture dimensions, skills, and foundational masteries in both formal and informal learning moments across courses and internship experiences; these include intellectual agility, global mind-set, and well-being (Northeastern University, 2019). Technology documents holistic intellectual development that is difficult to represent on a student transcript but nonetheless important for learning and adult development.

Digital technology allows for impressive expansion of participation (Dinevski & Radovan, 2013) and greater poignancy of adult learning pathways, such as digital art for human rights (Black, 2017) and accommodations for learning disabilities (Gregg, 2012). Adult educators and learners will need to develop a high tolerance for ambiguity, especially given the vast and sometimes unstructured nature of the internet and the vast flow of global information. This tolerance, when paired with learning agility (Bennett & McWhorter, 2017b; Hallenbeck, 2016) will lead to greater creativity and innovation. Over time, new pedagogies and theories of learning must emerge to provide explanatory power for adult learning with digital technologies.

Challenges

Technology devices are not without risk—cyberbullying; cybersecurity; cyberstalking; scamming; computer-related injuries such as digital eyestrain and vision problems, headaches, sleep problems, pain in neck, shoulder, back, arms, hands/wrists; muscle and joint injuries; obesity; aggressive behavior and mental health problems; and photosensitive seizures (Christian, 2017). Consumers, health-care providers, and educational professionals should weigh the mental and health risks versus benefits from integrating learning technology. Digital technologies can result in repetitive motion disorders and so correct ergonomic use is important. This issue will increase as adults spend more time using digital technology. There may be other pathologies and barriers exacerbated by internet access, such as addiction and isolation. Thus, minimizing these effects and keeping accounts and devices/technologies secure to protect users should be of the utmost concern to adult educators, creators of technology, and end-users; however, many older adults who did not grow up with digital technology or those with little technology experience need extra help in this area. No amount of law, though, will protect people fully, and so humans need to understand their rights, and to recognize negative behaviors and nonauthoritative sources through new literacies.

As more networked devices are being utilized, they often overlap and compete for shared resources (Bennett, 2018), which can create personal and technological conflict. Adult educators may create overly complex technology designs when learners really need simpler solutions. This includes low-fidelity and non-digital options. In other words, technology should not be used for technology's sake; the key is to provide meaningful learning experiences with quality assurance measures (Andrade et al., 2019). Technology can be used for nefarious purposes and should be governed by standards of ethical use of data that may become seals of approval (Bennett, 2018), which may prevent surreptitious monitoring for political or corporate manipulation. There is a need for highly ethical organizations and professions to engage in self-governance and regulation with robotics, AI, and IoT applications. Policy has yet to catch up with practice. Policy needs to guide manufacturers, lawmakers, and consumers, allowing for innovation while maintaining safety (Etzioni & Etzioni, 2017). Educators need to understand the restrictions their learners face and design learning strategies that are both easy to navigate and engaging. Additionally, digital literacy training through ACE will help adults navigate virtual experiences and, hopefully, prevent the most severe concerns with automation discussed in the chapter. Research will help alleviate risks and maximize benefits of digital technologies, though this area of ACE is under-studied.

Conclusion

Engaging digital technologies for teaching and learning requires conceptualizing virtual systems and applications within educational contexts, including understanding how the technology works and how it interfaces with other technologies and systems. It also requires a realistic understanding of the current social milieu; life has become hybridized. All one has to do is look at any public space to see that humans are scrolling phones, living a portion of life in virtual realms, yet there is so much to learn about this new paradigm.

Teaching with digital technology is becoming a permanent aspect of design and delivery of ACE. Over time, affordances will make the technology, the teachers, and the learners more facile, which will push the boundaries of adult learning. Indeed, we need to prepare for a world in which technology learns before we do, such as when AI makes decisions without human intervention that we may only understand in retrospect (Bennett & McWhorter, 2017a). AI will drive both loss of jobs and development of new ones in the near future, which will have significant effect on adults to adapt and reskill through ACE. New digital technologies will also provide new capacities for learning at individual and collective levels as the world becomes more interconnected, global and, yet, simultaneously particular and local.

References

Adhiya, D. (2020). *Best home automation Apple Watch apps in @020*. iGeeks Blog. https://www.igeeksblog.com/best-home-automation-apple-watch-apps/

Andrade, M. S., Miller, R. M., Kunz, M. B., & Ratliff, J. M. (2019). Online learning in schools of business: The impact of quality assurance measures. *Journal of Education for Business.* https://www.tandfonline.com/doi/full/10.1080/08832323.2019.1596871

Archer, W., & Garrison, D. R. (2010). Distance education in the age of the internet. In C. E. Kasworm, A. D. Rose, & J. M. Ross-Gordon (Eds.), *Handbook of adult and continuing education* (pp. 317–326). SAGE.

BeaconLive Marketing Team. (2019). *3 ways AI is influencing adult learning eLearning programs*. BeaconLive. https://www.beaconlive.com/blog/artificial-intelligence-and-adult-elearning

Bennett, E. E. (2009). Virtual HRD: The intersection of knowledge management, culture, and intranets. *Advances in Developing Human Resources, 11*, 362–374. https://doi.org/10.1177/1523422309339724

Bennett, E. E. (2010). The coming paradigm shift: Synthesis and future directions for virtual HRD. *Advances in Developing Human Resources, 12*(6), 728–741. https://doi.org/10.1177/1523422310394796

Bennett, E. E. (2011). Integrative informal learning in virtual HRD: The key to tacit knowledge? In J. Storberg-Walker, C. M. Graham, & K. Dirani (Eds.), *Refereed proceedings of the 2011 Academy of Human Resource Development Conference* (pp. 4408–4437). AHRD.

Bennett, E. E. (2012). A four-part model of informal learning: Extending Schugurensky's conceptual model. *Proceedings of the Adult Education Research Conference* (pp. 24–31). AERC.

Bennett, E. E. (2014). Introducing new perspectives on virtual human resource development. *Advances in Developing Human Resource, 16*(3), 263–280. https://doi.org/10.1177/1523422314532091

Bennett, E. E. (2018). Intranets of people, things, and services: Exploring the role of virtual human resource development. In C. A. Simmers & M. Anandarajan (Eds.), *The internet of people, things and services: Workplace transformations* (pp. 166–184). Routledge.

Bennett, E. E., & Bierema, L. L. (2010). The ecology of virtual human resource development. *Advances in Developing Human Resources, 12*(6), 632–647.

Bennett, E. E., & Gorman, M. (2018). Informal and experiential learning in virtually mediated organizational leadership doctoral studies. In L. Hyatt & S. Allen (Eds.), *Advancing doctoral leadership education through technology* (pp. 97–107). Edward Elgar.

Bennett, E. E., & McWhorter, R. R. (2017a). Reaction—Organizational learning, community, and virtual HRD: Advancing the discussion. *New Horizons in Adult Education & Human Resource Development, 29*(3), 19–27.

Bennett, E. E., & McWhorter, R. R. (2017b). Virtual HRD and international HRD. In T. Garavan, A. McCarthy, & R. Carberry (Eds.), *A handbook of international HRD: Contexts, processes and people* (pp. 268–294). Edward Elgar.

Bennett, E. E., & McWhorter, R. R. (2019). Social movement learning and social innovation: Empathy, agency, and the design of solutions to unmet social needs. *Advances in Developing Human Resources, 29*(2), 224–249.

Bennett, E. E., McWhorter, R. R., Roberts, P. B., Huang, W. H., & Short, D. (2017). *Personalized learning pathways: A panel discussion* [Paper presentation]. Academy of Human Resource Development, San Antonio, Texas, United States.

Black, J. (2017). Digiart and human rights. In J. B. Cummings & M. L. Blatherwick (Eds.), *Creative dimensions of teaching and learning in the 21st century* (pp. 163–173). Sense.

Botta, A., de Donato, W., Persico, V., & Pescapé, A. (2016). Integration of cloud computing and Internet of Things: A survey. *Future Generation Computer Systems, 56*, 684–700.

Business Insider Intelligence. (2016, June 15). This exclusive report reveals the ABCs of the IoT. *Business Insider*. https://www.businessinsider.com/iot-research-report-and-ecosystem-internet-of-things-2016-2

Christensen, C., Horn, M. B., & Johnson, C. W. (2008). *Disrupting class: How disruptive innovation will change the way the world learns* (1st ed.). McGraw-Hill.

Christian, N. (2017). Comparative study to find the effect of Mulligan's Snag Technique (C1-C2) in cervicogenic headache among information technology professionals. *International Journal of Physiotherapy, 4*(3), 178–183.

Cooney, M. (2016). *Gartner: Artificial intelligence, algorithms and smart software at the heart of big network changes*. Network World. https://www.networkworld.com/article/3132006/data-center/gartner-artificial-intelligence-algorithms-and-smart-software-at-the-heart-of-big-network-changes.html

Cope, B., & Kalantzis, M. (2010). Ubiquitous learning: An agenda for educational transformation. In B. Cope & M. Kalantzis (Eds.), *Ubiquitous learning* (pp. 3–14). University of Illinois Press.

Curran, V., Gustafson, D. L., Simmons, K., Lannon, H., Wang, C., Garmsiri, M., Fleet, L, & Wetsch, L. (2019). Adult learners' perceptions of self-directed learning and digital technology usage in continuing professional education: An update for the digital age. *Journal of Adult and Continuing Education, 25*(1), 74–93.

Dinevski, D., & Radovan, M. (2013). Adult learning and the promise of new technologies. *New Directions for Adult and Continuing Education, 2013*(138), 61–69.

Educause (2014). *7 things you should know about the Internet of Things*. https://library.educause.edu/~/media/files/library/2014/10/eli7113-pdf.pdf

Etzioni, A., & Etzioni, O. (2017). Should artificial intelligence be regulated? *Issues in Science and Technology, 33*(4), 1–10. https://issues.org/perspective-should-artificial-intelligence-be-regulated/

Eubanks, V. (2017). *Automating inequality: How high-tech tools, profile, police, and punish the poor*. St. Martin's Press.

Gregg, N. (2012). Increasing access to learning for the adult basic education learner with learning disabilities. Evidence-based accommodation research. *Journal of Learning Disabilities, 45*(1), 47–63.

Hallenbeck, G. (2016). *Learning agility: Unlock the lessons of experience*. Center for Creative Leadership. https://www.ccl.org/lead-it-yourself-solutions/workshop-kits/learning-agility/

Inverso, D. C., Kobrin, J., & Hashmi, S. (2017). Leveraging technology in adult education. *Journal of Research and Practice for Adult Literacy, Secondary, and Basic Education, 6*(2), 55–58.

Jelfs, A., & Richardson, J. T. E. (2013). The use of technologies across the adult life span in distance education. *British Journal of Educational Technology, 44*(2), 338–351.

King, K. P. (2010). Informal learning in a virtual era. In C. E. Kasworm, A. D. Rose, & J. M. Ross-Gordon (Eds.), *Handbook of adult and continuing education* (pp. 421–430). SAGE.

Knowles, M. S., Holton III, Elwood F., & Swanson, R. A. (2015). *The adult learner: The definitive classic in adult education and human resource development*. Routledge.

Lambden, D. (2020, April 8). *The complete guide to hearable technology in 2020*. Clearliving. https://www.clearliving.com/hearing/technology/hearables/

Lin, M. (2018). How to write personalities for the AI around us. *The Paris Review*. https://www.theparisreview.org/blog/2018/05/02/how-to-write-personalities-for-the-ai-around-us/

McGreal, R. (2018). Hearables for online learning. *International Review of Research in Open and Distributed Learning, 19*(4). http://www.irrodl.org/index.php/irrodl/article/view/4142/4716

McWhorter, R. R. (2010). Exploring the emergence of virtual human resource development. *Advances in Developing Human Resources, 12*(6), 623–631.

McWhorter, R. R. (2014). A synthesis of new perspectives on Virtual HRD. *Advances in Developing Human Resources, 16*(3), 391–401.

Merriam, S. B., & Bierema, L. L. (2014). *Adult learning: Linking theory and practice*. Wiley.

Northeastern University (2019). *Self-authored integrated learning: The next generation of experiential learning at Northeastern*. https://sail.northeastern.edu/

Panda Security (2018, June 11). *Amazon Echo—the security risk you invite into your home?* https://www.pandasecurity.com/mediacenter/news/amazon-echo-security-risk/

Schwab, K. (2016). *The fourth industrial revolution*. World Economic Forum.

Skilton, M., & Hovsepian, F. (2018). *The 4th industrial revolution: Responding to the impact of artificial intelligence on business*. Palgrave Macmillan.

PART FOUR

FORMAL AND INFORMAL LEARNING CONTEXTS

CHAPTER 19

The Cost of a Dollars and Cents Rationale for Adult Basic Education Policy

Alisa Belzer and Jeounghee Kim

The need for *adult basic education* (ABE; defined here as including adult literacy and numeracy education, adult secondary education, and English language education) has long been recognized. Current evidence suggests that there are 36 million low-skilled adults in the United States. The recent and widely cited Program for the International Assessment of Adult Competencies (PIAAC) found that skill levels of U.S. adults in literacy, numeracy, and technology-oriented problem-solving skills are below the across-country average of the 40 participating countries despite having one of the highest high school graduation rates in the world (Organisation for Economic Co-operation and Development, 2013).

The cost of low skills is high. Adult literacy skills have repeatedly been demonstrated to play an important role in employment and individual economic well-being which in turn can contribute to broad social benefits. Most recently, PIAAC demonstrated that better skills are rewarded by a higher likelihood of employment and better wages, and the "wage reward" of higher skills is better in the United States than in almost any other country. It also demonstrated a correlation between skill level and self-reported health status and civic engagement (Organisation for Economic Co-operation and Development, 2013; Schleicher, 2013). Conversely, low skills are correlated with low wages; low family income is associated with negative economic and educational outcomes for children.

Given the correlations between skills and earnings reported by PIAAC, it is unsurprising that 40% of low-skilled Americans have earnings in the bottom fifth of the U.S. wage spectrum.

Low skills not only have a personal toll; they impact the broader economy. Although it is a somewhat questionable proxy for skill, in a study of the fiscal consequences of low educational attainment, Khatiwada et al. (2007) reported that those without a high school diploma make a negative annual fiscal contribution to the U.S. economy (cash and in-kind transfers and institutionalization costs subtracted from tax payments) of $671, or a lifetime estimated burden of $33,000 (during the employable ages of 16 to 64) to the economy. In contrast, high school graduates contribute a mean annual value of $5,464 or a lifetime average of $267,736; individuals with bachelor's degrees contribute an average of $17,664 annually or a lifetime average contribution of $865,536; and those with a master's degree or higher contribute an annual average of $26,773 and make a lifetime contribution of slightly more than $1.3 million. PIAAC findings combined with studies on the economic impact of low skills/low educational attainment point to the critical importance of ABE (Reder, 2014). Although the cost of raising adult literacy levels is high, the return on investment is estimated to be significant (Murray et al., 2009).

Although there has been adult education in the United States at least since colonial times, federal funding that supports the growth of an educational system for adults who read at a low skill level began in 1964 (Sticht, 2002). Since then, federal statutes that authorize funding for ABE have demonstrated an evolving interest in increasing access for adults who could benefit from educational services. For example, after initial federal funding in 1964, English as a second language educational services were added in 1966, and in 1968 the age of eligibility for services was lowered from 18 to 16. Later, services were expanded to include adults who needed to complete their secondary education. Amendments to the statute for ABE funding made in the 1970s expanded access by including U.S. territories and provided adult education services for incarcerated adults and refugees. Bilingual education was also added. In the 1980s, programs for homeless adults and workplace literacy programs were established. Legislation was again used to expand access in the 1991 National Literacy Act (NLA) by providing funds for classes offered in public housing. Family literacy services were included in the 1998 authorization of funds for ABE (U.S. Department of Education, Office of Vocational and Adult Education, 2013). The most recent legislation that provides federal funding for ABE, the Workforce Innovation and Opportunity Act (WIOA), was signed into law in 2014. It sustains an emphasis on access by requiring states to award contracts to programs that are serving those most in need due to low literacy and English language skills or disabilities. Although there are other funding sources for ABE, the requirements attached to federal funding aimed directly at low-skilled adults are highly influential on program provision and are the focus of this discussion (Foster & McLendon, 2012).

The statutes initially helped develop a field of practice and provided increasing focus for a nascent education system. We argue in this chapter, however, that they have more recently moved toward a narrowness that addresses a return-on-investment rationale for funding that seeks measurable outcomes related to employability but fails to address less-measurable outcomes that can serve the larger social good by developing a more informed and engaged citizenry. Similarly, they take an increasingly top-down approach to establishing learner goals and measures of success for adult learners. We see current policy that has the potential to limit who actually gets served and in what ways. This process occurs through an accountability system that encourages creaming for the highest-skilled adult learners and an ever-narrowing curricular focus in which literacy, numeracy, and problem-solving skills are treated primarily as in service or supplemental to workforce development and training.

Overview of ABE Programs: Target Population, Goals, and Funding

Despite the clear importance of a skilled adult population and need for ABE services to help us attain it, federal funding for programs and participation rates are low. ABE programs typically piece together a hodgepodge of public funding sources across education, labor, and welfare (Dunton & Alamprese, 2009). Federal money provides about 44% of support for ABE; an additional 45% comes from state funds (Foster & McLendon, 2012). Based on the 2016 federal allotment to ABE of $569.4 million (Counts, 2017) and enrollment of 1,537,160 (Office of Management and Budget, n.d.), the average per-student expenditure based on federal funding is a little less than $400 annually; when combined with other funding sources it is still less than $1,000 annually. This compares poorly, for example, to the 2016 average annual allocation per K–12 student of about $11,000 (U.S. Department of Education, National Center for Education Statistics, 2017).

The ABE system is diverse in terms of learning context, quantity and quality of services, and requirements for entry into and training for practitioners, goals, and assessments. ABE providers include education agencies, community colleges, community-based organizations, and volunteer literacy organizations. Many adult education programs also work with welfare agencies to serve clients receiving TANF funds. The ABE system is increasingly required to collaborate with the workforce development system. Despite ongoing efforts to align these systems to provide better articulation with postsecondary education, training, and employment, ABE suffers from fragmentation and inconsistency and undergoes frequent change due to shifting policy and undependable funding sources.

PIAAC data indicate that a large proportion of adults could benefit from ABE. Yet participation rates in federally funded programs suggest that only about 4% of low-skilled adults participate at any one time. Of these, according to the most recent data available, 8% are 16–18 years old, 20% are 19–24, 50%

are 25–44, 13% are 45–54, and 9% are 55 and older (Office of Management and Budget, n.d.). States are required to report participation and progress based on six literacy skill levels, from Beginning Literacy to High Adult Secondary, and six ESL levels, from beginning ESL literacy to Advanced ESL literacy. These are aggregated for reporting purposes into Adult Basic Education Level, Adult Secondary Level, and ESL. In Program Year 2016, 40.5% of learners were at the Adult Basic Education Level, 11% were at the Adult Secondary Level, and 49% were ESL and Integrated English Language and Civics Education learners. PIAAC data indicate that nearly two thirds of low-skilled adults are employed. This suggests that the vast number of adults who could benefit from ABE could be reached through their workplaces if education services were brought to them rather than requiring them to seek them out (Organisation for Economic Co-operation and Development, 2013).

Evolution of ABE Policy: From Focusing to Narrowing

Although it makes up less than half of all support for ABE, the allocation of federal funds has an impact on who gets served, under what circumstances, and what gets counted as effective practice and successful outcomes. Rose (1991) observed that the first 15 years of federal funding focused on growth and development for the field, including teacher training, curriculum development, demonstration projects, and research, in addition to providing program operating funds. This early legislation was targeted at those whose low skills were an impairment to employment. A causal link between improved skills and employment was assumed, but no specific provisions were made to ensure it. The NLA was a major reworking of the federal legislation that funds ABE. For the first time, ABE was framed not so much as a strategy for reducing poverty but rather as an important element in strengthening the economy and increasing U.S. competitiveness globally (Sticht, 2002). The Act also articulated a broad definition of *literacy* and established many new programs that helped the field move from the mentality of a temporary campaign to eliminate illiteracy to a permanent system designed to address an ongoing challenge (Fingeret, 1992). At the NLA signing ceremony, President Bush also signaled a focus on the development of human potential by stating that the act represented a significant advancement toward helping adults achieve lifelong learning goals.

The focus on human potential decreased markedly and an interest in skill development for the good of the economy and U.S. competitiveness globally became explicit in the next iteration of the federal ABE funding statute. The 1998 Workforce Investment Act (WIA) subsumed adult education into the federal workforce development system in Title II of the statute, the Adult Education and Family Literacy Act (AEFLA). Although the connection between employment and skill development had always been present, making ABE a part of a workforce development system concretized this relationship in new and significant ways. One indication of its narrowing purpose was that the phrase "to achieve one's goals and develop one's knowledge and potential" (NLA, 1991, Section 3) was dropped from the literacy definition articulated in the NLA. Thus, self-identified educational goals and lifelong learning for a broad range of purposes were no longer a policy priority.

Although the WIOA of 2014 was more of a tweak than a major revision in how ABE policy is framed, it further amplifies the connections among worker education, training, and employment. *Career Pathways* is named throughout the statute as the primary mechanism for increasing employment through workforce development. It is defined as "a combination of rigorous and high-quality education, training, and other services" (Workforce Innovation and Opportunity Act, 2014). Specific to ABE, and for the first time, a service provision approach is encoded in AEFLA in the definition of *Integrated Education and Training* (IET): "adult education and literacy activities concurrently and contextually with workforce preparation activities and workforce training for a specific occupation or occupational cluster for the purpose of educational and career advancement" (Workforce Innovation and Opportunity Act, 2014).

Both Career Pathways and IET frame education as merely a necessary step toward employment. Emphasizing the value placed on this approach, the statute states that funding decisions can be made based on the extent to which local programs adopt and effectively use IET. Adult education is positioned as the provider of education services in an integrated education and training approach, and providers applying for federal funds must submit their proposals to their local

Workforce Development Boards for review. Further supporting the workforce development focus of adult education in WIOA are the requirements that states must submit a unified plan for serving clients across all core programs (workforce development oriented) and all core programs must use the same common outcome measures which focus on participation in postsecondary education, training, employment, and earnings.

The NLA and WIA can be understood as providing much-needed focus for the field after many years of funding authorizations that largely prioritized growth, development, and stability (Rose, 1991; U.S. Department of Education, Office of Vocational and Adult Education, 2013). This focus can be positive in that it creates a clearer, richer, more detailed vision for the field. However, Belzer (2017) argued that while WIA may have started this process, WIOA explicitly shifted from focusing to narrowing the field. This narrowing is implied by subsuming ABE within the workforce development system and the revised literacy definition. It is made explicit through the accountability system, initiated in WIA and revised in WIOA, which largely measures effectiveness around a limited set of workforce-related outcomes. This can have the effect of shutting down opportunities for learning that address adults' wide range of purposes for improving their skills. It may also limit a wider set of social benefits that can accrue from a more skilled adult population. Consequentially, it could also limit who participates. Although not empirically tested, many researchers and practitioners have worried that performance measures focused on employment and earnings could discourage programs from serving the least skilled students because it is harder for them to demonstrate gains quickly in those areas (Belzer, 2007; Prins et al., 2018).

Policy Narrowing Through Performance Accountability

One of the most consequential changes in ABE policy was that WIA mandated a performance accountability system known as the National Reporting System (NRS). The NLA accountability requirements had focused primarily on evaluating program inputs and program quality. However, for the first time, the NRS was a response to the growing demand across federally funded programs for accountability that demonstrated economic returns on policy investments (Merrifield, 1998). Thus, the accountability focus shifted from process to outcomes (Merrifield, 1998). The outcomes of value were primarily employment related.

Previously, there was little consensus on what the outcomes of ABE should be (Merrifield, 1998). With the implementation of the NRS, there was convergence around narrowed attention on labor market outcomes and the academic skills that contribute to them. The initial NRS "core" outcome measures were gains in basic skills and English language, obtaining a high school credential, placement in a postsecondary or training program, and entering and retaining employment. There was no longer much attention paid to non-labor-market outcomes related to family, community, work, and lifelong learning. These were now referred to as "secondary outcomes" and were made optional in state plans and the reporting system. While they capture the effects of ABE on family, communities, and society that are beyond direct labor market outcomes, they were clearly made less important in WIA than they had been in the NLA.

Importantly, the core outcome measures were used to not only evaluate program effectiveness but also make funding decisions. What made performance accountability enacted in NRS a hallmark of WIA was that its financial incentives, sanctions, and technical assistance were tied to states exceeding the expected levels of program performance. States were required to achieve at least 80% of the negotiated performance level in order to be eligible for an incentive grant of up to $3 million. States that did not meet performance goals for 2 consecutive years were penalized with up to a 5% reduction in their WIA grant (P.L.105-220). In the program year 2010–2011, 15 states were eligible to receive incentive awards of a total of $10.4 million (U.S. Department of Education, Office of Technical, Career, and Adult Education, 2015). This performance-based funding strategy trickled down to the state level; some states began distributing funds to local providers based on their performance in order to motivate them to improve their effectiveness. Belzer (2003) found that the financial incentives and sanctions were powerful enough to influence state plans, program operations, assessment procedures, and curriculum. Specifically, she found that ABE programs tended to shift the curriculum toward a much greater emphasis on preemployment and job retention skills.

Due to expire at the end of 2003, as debates about the reauthorization of WIA dragged on through the 2000s, the NRS was criticized as ineffective and incompatible with helping low-skilled adult students achieve career and postsecondary goals quickly and efficiently (Ganzglass, 2010). Under WIOA, it continues to be used to document educational gains and labor market outcomes for ABE programs, but it has been revised to reflect the requirement that all WIOA-funded programs use the same core performance measures: employment after program exit, median earnings, obtaining a postsecondary credential, achieving measurable skill gains, and effectiveness in serving employers. The revised NRS was implemented in 2016. It maintained the same optional secondary measures for states' data collection and reporting. Yet there was little attention, elaboration, or guidance for states about using them.

Consequences of Policy Narrowing

The increasingly narrowed focus of ABE policy on employment and employment-related outcomes appears connected to at least two important changes observed in adult education programs over the years: (a) the share of the lowest skilled adults enrolled in adult education programs gradually declined, and (b) as nonemployment goals have receded in importance, the curriculum has narrowed and eroded the focus on the broad purposes of ABE (i.e., secondary outcomes). Although empirical evidence of these changes is limited and a causal assertion that links WIOA to them has not been tested, anecdotal and circumstantial evidence available from NRS data collected during the WIA era enable cautious inferences about them.

Decrease in ABE Enrollment Among the Lowest Skilled

For more than a decade, research on workforce development programs has documented that performance measures tend to affect who programs serve. This phenomenon, referred to as *creaming*, describes workforce development service providers that are incentivized to selectively serve adults who are most likely to produce the best performance outcomes (or do well even without program participation) while declining to address the needs of hard-to-serve adults (Koning & Heinrich, 2013; Trutko & Barnow, 2010). Our NRS data analysis suggests that a similar phenomenon might have occurred in ABE during the WIA period. The percentage of adults enrolled in ABE programs at the lowest literacy level (Beginning Literacy, or level 1) has steadily declined after program year 2002–2003, whereas the percentage enrolled at higher literacy levels (i.e., levels 2, 3, and 4) climbed continuously. Specifically, from 2002–2003 to 2012–2013, the percentage of adults enrolled in ABE programs at literacy level 1 more than halved from 5.86% to 2.67%, but the compatible percentages increased from 7.47% to 9.68% for adults at literacy level 2, 11.23% to 16.92% at literacy level 3, and 14.91% to 18.94% at literacy level 4. Whether and to what extent this trend indicates creaming, and if this can be attributed to increasingly narrowed performance measures, are important questions that require further analysis. Whether such an analysis is warranted depends on broad social goals and willingness to invest in the lowest skilled adults among us.

Narrowed Curriculum Focus

The wide-ranging potential outcomes of participating in adult education programs articulated in the NLA and specified to some extent in the NRS "secondary outcomes" might contribute to a rich curriculum designed to improve adults' abilities to use literacy and numeracy to participate in a range of family and community contexts as well as the workplace. Evidence indicates, however, that the narrowed policy focus, and the accountability system aligned with it, effectively eroded the importance and value of these outcomes, thus presumably narrowing the curriculum. Indeed, as Merrifield (1998) opines, "What is counted usually becomes 'what counts'" (p. 47). This potential narrowing can be exacerbated by resource-restricted programs forced to make strategic decisions about where to put their efforts in order to maximize chances for funding.

The voluntary nature of the secondary measures may explain why states were provided with little guidance or technical support in defining and measuring them, and they had no financial incentives for tracking them. This seems likely to have contributed to a considerable decrease in the number of states using these measures to evaluate and improve their ABE programs. Indeed, a U.S. Department of Education study (U.S. Department of Education, Office of Vocational and Adult Education, Division of Adult Education and Literacy, 2007) reported that the states considered the secondary measures less central in documenting learner progress and achieving program goals. In Indiana, for example, since program year 2002–2003 when the state halved its reimbursement rate for achieving secondary NRS measures, the number of secondary measures reported by local programs fell considerably, while the number of core measures achieved climbed. Our analysis of NRS data indicates that the number of states that adopted the secondary measures in their state plans was never high and declined during the WIA era (as measured from 2003–2004 through 2013–2014). For example, the number of states that reported parents' engagement in children's education as an outcome dropped from 19 to 12 states; the number for engagement in children's literacy activities, from 17 to 11; the number for citizenship skill gains, from 15 to 12; and the number for voting or registering to vote, from 11 to 8. Moreover, our review of NRS data showed that the cumulative and aggregate data on secondary measures during the WIA period are incomplete and unreliable. This may be due, at least in part, to the lack of either mandate or incentive to collect this data. This hinders research and development endeavors to improve their measurement and to demonstrate their effects for broad policy constituencies.

Clymer et al. (2017) offers an excellent case in point with regard to family literacy programs. As two of the NRS secondary measures (engagement of child literacy activities and education) indicate, AEFLA used to be a major funding source for family literacy programs that support interactive education for children and parents. The survey of 47 states and Washington DC conducted by Clymer's team (2017), however, revealed that only 11 states and Washington DC used AEFLA funds to support family literacy programs in 2015–2016. It appears that the voluntary approach to family literacy activities in AEFLA lets most states set other funding priorities (presumably oriented toward workforce development). The lack of data collection guidelines and technical support for these activities might have contributed to this diminishing impact of AEFLA on them as well.

Conclusion

The language in WIOA maintains a policy interest in maximizing access to those most in need of ABE at a time when the need has once again been demonstrated to be enormous. Nevertheless, it remains to be seen in the coming years how this will affect or reconcile with its overall, singular focus on labor market outcomes, which tends to encourage creaming from the eligible populations. That it values employment and training outcomes over all others would suggest that the potential for creaming is greater than ever. Indeed, in their descriptive study of Career Pathways programs in Chicago, Houston, and Miami, Prins et al. (2018) reported that half of their sample had some kind of grade level or test score entry requirement. This would indicate a purposeful restriction on access. Pickard (2016) has suggested that this approach is especially likely to disadvantage African American learners who are disproportionately represented among those scoring lowest on standardized tests.

Because of its focus on labor market outcomes, WIOA runs the risk of encouraging creaming even more than WIA may have. Yet creaming is counter to the stated policy concern of serving high-need individuals with barriers to employment. A return on investment rationale for funding ABE may make serving higher-level students the better bet because they may advance their skill level, employment, and earnings more quickly using fewer program resources. However, this efficiency rational belies the fact that a broader set of outcome measures may return a range of social benefits not easily measured in dollars and cents. For example, the impact of simply attending a program may help participants' children feel more motivated to go to school and do well. PIAAC analysis points to the correlation between literacy and health outcomes and social engagement. While we cannot measure the value of voting in dollars and cents, an engaged citizenry is certainly invaluable.

The limited resources dedicated to ABE might rightly beg the question of where we get the biggest bang for our buck. The narrowing curriculum and the creaming phenomenon which seems to emerge from the current policy context implies that investing in the most skilled accomplishes the most. However, we really have no way to measure that assumption given the difficulty of doing causal research in this area. Behavioral scientist Chris Anderson and economist David Sally (2013) offer us another way to evaluate the issue. They used extensive sports statistics to ask the question of whether it is better to invest in improving the strongest or the weakest players on a team. They contrast improving soccer teams, which they call a "weak-link" problem, with basketball, which presents a "strong-link" problem. Because they observed that a soccer team is interdependent on the performance of all players while a basketball team can do very well with only one or two star players, they suggest that weak-link sports should not invest in increasing their star power but rather should invest in the lowest tier of the team.

We suggest that improving adult literacy and numeracy skills may be a weak-link problem because society does best when it functions like a soccer team, interdependently, rather than a star-powered basketball team. We do not find the imagery of a weak link palatable when it comes to describing adult learners' literacy and numeracy skills, nor is the education of adults akin to a team sport. Yet the way in which Anderson and Sally argue for the importance of investing in those whose skills are weakest seems compelling. While we can not measure the results in terms of goals scored and games won, we believe that the value of investing fully in adults who present along the entire continuum of skill goes well beyond attaining the skills needed for employment. Resources should be increased and policy should be redefined to alleviate a sense of either/or that seems to undergird service provision currently. Policy should continue to evolve in ways that encourage programs to effectively serve every adult who could benefit from and, in turn, be a greater benefit to our social fabric. In this way, we make the whole team stronger.

References

Anderson, C., & Sally, D. (2013). *The numbers game: Why everything you know about soccer is wrong*. Penguin.

Belzer, A. (2003). *Living with it: Federal policy implementation in adult basic education. The cases of the Workforce Investment Act and welfare reform* (NCSALL Reports 24; ED508604). National Center for the Study of Adult Learning and Literacy. ERIC. https://files.eric.ed.gov/fulltext/ED508604.pdf

Belzer, A. (2007). Implementing the workforce investment act from in-between: State agency responses to federal accountability policy in adult basic education. *Educational Policy, 21*(4), 555–588.

Belzer, A. (2017). Focusing or narrowing: Trade-offs in the development of adult basic education, 1991–2015. In A. Belzer (Ed.), *Turning points: Recent trends in adult basic literacy, numeracy, and language education.* (pp. 11–18). Jossey-Bass.

Clymer, C., Toso, B. W., Grinder, E., & Sauder, R. P. (2017). *Changing the course of family literacy* [Policy paper]. Goodling Institute for Research in Family Literacy. ERIC. https://eric.ed.gov/?id=ED574448

Counts, D. (2017, April 4). *Federal funding for state employment and training programs covered by the WIOA*. The Council of State Governments. http://knowledgecenter.csg.org/kc/content/federal-funding-state-employment-and-training-programs-covered-wioa

Dunton, L. E., & Alamprese, J. A. (2009). *Directory of federal funding sources for adult education*. Abt Associates.

Fingeret, H. A. (1992). *Adult literacy education: Current and future directions: An update.* (ERIC Information Series No. 355). Center on Education and Training for Employment, The Ohio State University. ERIC. https://eric.ed.gov/?id=ED354391

Foster, M., & McLendon, L. (2012). *Sinking or swimming: Findings from a survey of state adult educationtuition and financing policies*. CLASP and National Council of State Directors of Adult Education.

Ganzglass, E. (2010). *New directions for workforce education and training policy require a new approach to performance accountability*. CLASP. https://www.clasp.org/sites/default/files/public/resources-and-publications/files/Workforce_Investment_Act_Recommendations_for_Shared_Accountability_System.pdf

Khatiwada, I., McLaughlin, J., Sum, A., & Palma, S. (2007). *The fiscal consequences of adult educational attainment*. National Commission on Adult Literacy.

Koning, P., & Heinrich, C. J. (2013). Cream-skimming, parking and other intended and unintended effects of high-powered, performance-based contracts. *Journal of Policy Analysis and Management, 32*(3), 461–483.

Merrifield, J. (1998). *Contested ground: Performance accountability in adult basic education*. Center for the Study of Adult Learning and Literacy.

Murray, T. S., McCracken, M., Willms, D., Jones, S., Shillington, R., & Strucker, J. (2009). *Addressing Canada's literacy challenge: A cost/benefit analysis*. DataAngel.

National Literacy Act of 1991, Pub. L. 102-73.

Office of Management and Budget. (n.d.). *National summary of the statewide performance report—WIOA title II adult education program PY 2016*. (No. OMB Control Number 1205-0526).

Organisation for Economic Co-operation and Development. (2013). *Time for the U.S. to reskill? What the survey of adult skills says*. OECD. https://doi.org/10.1787/9789264204904-en

Pickard, A. (2016). WIOA: Implications for low-scoring adult learners. *Journal of Research and Practice for Adult Literacy, Secondary, and Basic Education, 5*(2), 50–55.

Prins, E., Clymer, C., Foreman, S. S., Loa, M., Needle, M., Raymond, B., Toso, B. W., & Ziskind, A. (2018). *Career pathways for adult learners in Chicago, Houston, and Miami: Final report*. Institute for the Study of Adult Literacy.

Reder, S. (2014). *Research brief: The impact of ABE program participation on long-term economic outcomes.* U.S. Department of Education, Office of Career, Technical, and Adult Education.

Rose, A. D. (1991). *Ends or means: An overview of the history of the adult education act.* (ERIC Information Series No. 346). Center on Education and Training for Employment, The Ohio State University. ERIC. https://eric.ed.gov/?id=ED341875

Schleicher, A. (2013). *Skilled for life. Key findings from the Survey of Adult Skills.* OECD.

Sticht, T. G. (2002). The rise of the adult education and literacy system in the United States: 1600–2000. In J. Coming, B. Garner, & C. Smith (Eds.), *The annual review of adult literacy and literacy* (pp. 12–43). Jossey-Bass.

Trutko, J. W., & Barnow, B. S. (2010). *Implementing efficiency measures for employment and training programs.* U.S. Department of Labor, Employment, and Training Administration. http://capitalresearchcorp.com/assets/pdf/publications/1EJT/1.1EJT/Implementing%20Efficiency%20Measures%20for%20Employment%20and%20Training%20Programs-2010-05.pdf

U.S. Department of Education, National Center for Education Statistics. (2017). *The condition of education 2017* (NCES 2017-144), Public School Expenditures. https://nces.ed.gov/fastfacts/display.asp?id=66

U.S. Department of Education, Office of Career, Technical, and Adult Education. (2015). *Adult education and family literacy act of 1998: Annual report to Congress, program year 2011–12.* Author.

U.S. Department of Education, Office of Vocational and Adult Education, Division of Adult Education and Literacy (2007). *Performance-based funding in adult education.* Author.

U.S. Department of Education, Office of Vocational and Adult Education. (2013). *An American heritage—Federal adult education: A legislative history 1964–2013.* Author.

Workforce Innovation and Opportunity Act of 2014, Pub. L. 113-128.

Workforce Investment Act of 1998, Pub. L. 105–220.

CHAPTER 20

English as a Second Language

Christy Rhodes and Clea A. Schmidt

When entering an adult English as a second language (ESL) classroom, the multifaceted diversity and complex circumstances of the learners are striking. Subtle aspects of the diverse natures of learners and the learning environment become increasingly clear over time. These aspects include the varied ethnic, racial, linguistic, religious, gender, sexual orientation, socioeconomic backgrounds of learners, and their intersections with wider social, historical, and political forces (Anthias, 2013). Diversity is the norm rather than the exception in adult English language classes. Equally striking is that from amid this diversity, supportive and tight-knit communities of learners are often created. On any given day, a Colombian lawyer might ask her classmate, a Vietnamese grandmother, for the definition of a challenging word, or a Cuban doctor and a Mexican teacher's assistant might be discussing options for affordable daycare. If observers of the adult ESL classroom learn one lesson, it is that there is no typical classroom, learner, or teacher, and that in this diversity lies strength.

The wider sociopolitical environments in which adult ESL classrooms operate are also very complex and must be taken into account in any robust analysis of educational trends and approaches to ESL programming and policies. Current neoliberal influences on adult education across the Western world frame immigrant language learners at best as economy-boosting commodities to exploit and at worst as undesirables and burdens on society (Warriner, 2015). The notion that adult newcomers make tremendous and myriad contributions to their communities is obscured by problematic and deficit-oriented views that ESL programming serves the sole purpose of maximizing economic contributions to society. According to McHugh and Doxsee (2018), this trend has only worsened since 2014 with the introduction of the Workforce Innovation and Opportunity Act (WIOA):

> While federal adult education provisions formerly allowed a more balanced approach to teaching English and meeting learners' needs in their roles as parents, workers, and citizens, WIOA instituted mandatory performance measures that focus mainly on employment outcomes and the attainment of postsecondary credentials, placing no value on other essential integration skills or topics. (p. 2)

This chapter will describe the varied adult learning environments dedicated to English language instruction in the United States and analyze the trends and challenges these programs currently face. This chapter will help adult and continuing educators understand the diversity of adult English language learners and programs, the connection between this subfield and the larger context of adult and continuing education (ACE), and the complexities faced by teachers, learners, and program administrators in complex sociopolitical climates.

The contributors' approach is grounded in the belief that understanding the power and potential of critical and innovative practices in ethnically and linguistically heterogeneous learning environments can inform adult teaching theory and practices across the spectrum, and that now more than ever a robust critique of economic determinism as a driver of adult ESL education is warranted. Historically, ESL education has been very slow to theorize and enact critical perspectives (Ahmadian & Rad, 2014; Crookes & Lehner, 1998; Hawkins, 2011) and instead has focused on the unproblematized teaching of skills (Kumaravadivelu, 2012), often with the objective of integrating newcomers into minimum-wage employment or capitalizing on profits gleaned from international students (Warriner, 2015). A critical approach, however, questions whether profit should be the main driver of education and asserts that challenging the status quo is a precursor to enacting social justice, in which newcomers and international students are regarded as meaningful to U.S. society beyond their economic contributions.

To begin to understand the complex adult ESL learning environment, it is helpful to start with the types of programming. Two predominant areas of English language instruction for adults are adult literacy education and intensive English language programs. Adult literacy education focuses on helping immigrants acquire English language skills to assist in integration into U.S. culture. Conversely, intensive English programs are housed on university and college campuses throughout the United States and are primarily designed to help international students acquire academic English language in order to complete postsecondary education before returning to their native countries. The following section will describe the overall programming structure and learner characteristics unique to each type of English language learning environment. Next, pedagogical and philosophical principles underpinning adult ESL education are discussed, followed by an analysis of adultcentric approaches to teaching English language learners. The final section discusses current challenges and trends in adult ESL education.

Adult Literacy Education

Adult literacy ESL programs offer English language instruction to facilitate immigrants' and refugees' successful integration into the surrounding U.S. culture and community. While this primarily includes foreign-born learners, native-born individuals from non-English-speaking households may also enroll. It is challenging to provide precise demographic data about learners in adult literacy ESL programs; however, an examination of the foreign-born population provides insight into this population, yielding profiles of potential students in adult education ESL classes. According to the American Community Survey (ACS), as of 2018, the foreign-born comprised 13.7% of the total U.S. population, numbering over 44 million and residing primarily in California, New York, Texas, and Florida (U.S. Census Bureau, 2018). Although immigration has been a source of population growth throughout U.S. history, the ethnic and linguistic background of recent immigrants has changed in the past 50 years. When examined by ethnicity, or country of origin, Mexicans make up the largest single group of foreign-born individuals, followed by Chinese, Filipinos, and Indians. Therefore, Spanish is the predominant language spoken by the largest group of foreign-born individuals, but there are at least 40 languages other than English spoken in U.S. homes (Capps et al., 2002), demonstrating the linguistic diversity of America's foreign-born population.

While many adult ESL learners were born outside of the United States, there is a wider group of potential ESL students from the approximately 59.5 million individuals who use a language other than English to communicate in their homes (Batalova & Lee, 2012; Center for Applied Linguistics, 2010). According to the American Community Survey (Gambino et al., 2014), approximately 25.2 million people are described as not speaking English "at all," "not well," or only "well." Despite this need, the majority of these individuals are not enrolled in adult literacy ESL classes, with only 667,515 adult learners served in state-funded ESL classes in 2014 (Snyder et al., 2016). The highest number of students served was in California (181,926), followed by Florida (86,103), New York (59,155), Illinois (42,008), and Texas (40,248).

The diversity of the foreign-born population in the United States is mirrored in the adult ESL classroom. Classes and programs vary greatly due to the breadth and scope of needs in the local community. Students attend for a variety of reasons related to their long- and short-term goals. Furthermore, they bring to class a wide range of life experiences and knowledge sets. Demographically, they range in age, ethnicity, immigration status, and language background

(Center for Applied Linguistics, 2010). They also vary in ways that have a strong relation to second language acquisition, such as educational level, native language fluency, time of residence in the United States, and exposure to English outside of the classroom environment (Mathews-Aydinli, 2008). Adult literacy English language students are generally motivated to improve their ability to communicate in English, but also note a desire to obtain or improve their employment status; obtain U.S. citizenship, a high school diploma, or a GED certificate; enter a postsecondary educational program; or help their children with schoolwork (TESOL, 2003).

There are various ways that adult ESL programs address this diversity. Classes are held in a variety of locations, including school districts, community colleges, community organizations, correctional institutions, faith-based organizations, libraries, and museums (Center for Applied Linguistics, 2010). Scheduling and curricula are equally varied, with many state-funded programs focusing on general life skills, English, and U.S. civics. Other programs focus exclusively on employability through workplace or vocational ESL classes (Center for Applied Linguistics, 2010). Thus, in comparison with other adult literacy programs targeted at native-English speaking learners such as Adult Basic Education, ESL program goals cover a wide range of areas such as settlement, workplace English, and American history. However, increasingly, adult ESL program offerings are less representative of that diversity, as the Workforce, Innovation, and Opportunity Act (WIOA) mandates result in its narrow focus on employability and postsecondary skills (McHugh & Doxsee, 2018). Finally, various barriers and obstacles interfere with attending adult education ESL classes. As noted by the National Center for Educational Statistics (1995), these barriers include: limited time, economic resources, family responsibilities, lack of reliable transportation, and information about appropriate programs in the local area.

The underlying ESL program goal is uniformly to support immigrants, refugees, and all other non-native speakers to successfully integrate into U.S. society, particularly in terms of economic and social well-being. This "two-way process through which immigrants and refugee families become part of the civic, economic, and social mainstream" of the host country (McHugh & Doxsee, 2018, p. 3) is complex and multifaceted and can be attributed to language acquisition; understanding of government and civics; education; employment; financial literacy; health; housing; social connections; and technology. To facilitate successful integration, ESL programs incorporate these topics and use communicative approaches to language acquisition (Center for Applied Linguistics, 2010).

Intensive English Programs

Intensive English Programs (IEPs) also offer English language classes to adult learners and are found on university and college campuses throughout the United States (Grosik, 2017). These noncredit academic English programs are instrumental in helping prepare international students for postsecondary study. While some students study English in order to successfully complete a degree from a U.S. university, others do so for academic and career advancement in their native countries. Regardless of their goals, the majority of students in IEPs are in the United States for a limited time and will return to their native countries. While numbers vary, the most recent Open Doors Report (2017) found there were 86,786 international students in IEPs throughout the United States. Of those, students from China, Japan, and Saudi Arabia comprised the largest groups, with an average of 14.1 weeks of study in IEPs.

On average, IEPs offer 25 hours of English language classes per week (Friedenberg, 2002). These classes are often divided by skill (listening, speaking, reading, writing, and grammar) and proficiency. Generally, students do not take academic courses; however, students with higher-level proficiency sometimes take English for Academic Purposes (EAP) or English for Specific Purposes (ESP) classes. IEP students who want to enter U.S. academic institutions will often enroll in test preparation classes focused on the Test of English as a Foreign Language (TOEFL) or Test of English for International Communication (TOEIC).

Teaching English to Speakers of Other Languages

In light of the wide diversity of learner backgrounds in adult English language classes, also described as teaching English to speakers of other languages (TESOL), it is challenging to describe "good" teaching in these environments. While there is a general consensus that an effective ESL teacher should have a firm understanding of linguistics, educational psychology, and the cultural context of the learners (Celce-Murcia, 2014), there is no universally accepted approach to teaching a second or foreign language. Rather, there are a variety of approaches with unique strategies and philosophical principles (Celce-Murcia, 2014; Ellis, 2014).

General Overview of Linguistics

Second language teaching is based on key fundamentals of language and its use. Perhaps most important is the understanding that all languages are complex and, to a great extent, are learned without the native speaker's awareness. This explains why native speakers are able to identify an ungrammatical sentence but are often unable to explain the rule behind the error. All languages also have structure which includes systems of phonology, morphology, syntax, semantics, and pragmatics (Celce-Murcia, 2014). However, languages also evolve and change over time. An effective English language teacher understands and applies knowledge of these systems to the learning process.

Second language teaching theory has a long and storied history with its earliest movements facilitating either real-world use in listening and speaking or linguistic analysis such as learning grammatical rules (Celce-Murcia, 2014). However, recent approaches (i.e., cognitive, affective-humanistic, and communicative) take a more holistic stance and differ by philosophical foundation. As has been noted by various scholars, these approaches are often blended into an "integrated approach which would include attention to rule formation, affect, comprehension, and communication" (Celce-Murcia, 2014, p. 9).

Adult Learning Theory

Adult learning theory is informed by fundamental assumptions about adult learners (Knowles, 1973). Those tenets (e.g., self-directedness, role of learner experience, practical nature of learning, applied nature of learning, and need for adults to understand why they are learning) may not align with adult ESL learners' cultural values and norms. Therefore, it is important for ESL teachers to reflect on potential areas of cultural mismatch. For example, adult English language learners may find the process of establishing personal goals uncomfortable, as it relies heavily on an individualistic approach to learning. It is the role of the adult educator to be explicit about the role these tenets play in the classroom and be open to adapting them for use in this heterogeneous learning environment.

Cultural Context of Language Learning

Nieto (2002) and Cummins (1986) have laid the foundation for much of the literature related to the role of cultural context in language learning environments. Although developed through examinations of K–12 settings, many of the themes are relevant to adult education. In early writings, Cummins (1986) proposed examining the interactions of English language learners and the educational system. His evaluative framework was based on the tenet that English language learners are either empowered or disabled through these interactions.

Cummins's influence is clear in Nieto's (2002) work on how to prepare teachers to work with English language learners. Nieto called for a "reconceptualization of language diversity" (p. 81). This involves changing the deficit view of language diversity to one in which bilingualism is seen as an addition or resource to the learner and the wider community. She strongly supported the preservation and nurturing of heritage or native language of immigrants and refugees. Furthermore, teachers should be educated about the discriminatory nature of English-only language policies. Thus, teachers of English language learners should know about second- and first-language acquisition theories and linguistics. Moreover, they should hold additive rather than deficit beliefs about language diversity and actively foster learners' native language literacy. Nieto (2002) noted that teachers can provide students with "the time and space to work with all their peers, or with tutors or mentors, who speak the same language" (p. 95).

Adultcentric Approaches to Teaching English Language Learners

There are two approaches to working with English language learners that have emanated from the field of adult education: Alfred's (2009a, 2009b) sociocultural approach to teaching adult learners from diverse backgrounds and Ginsberg and Wlodkowski's (2009) motivational framework of culturally responsive teaching.

Sociocultural Theory and Transnational Migration

Alfred's (2009a, 2009b) advocacy of a sociocultural approach to teaching adult learners is based on the changing demographics of the foreign-born population in U.S. classrooms. She has noted that immigrants are not only more likely to be from non-Western countries but also often *transnational* and maintain contact with their native communities, commonly resisting the previous model of assimilation for biculturalism to American culture. Based on the needs of this new immigrant learner, Alfred (2009b) proposed incorporating the sociocultural framework of "a) personal, b) socio-historical, and c) community or institutional/organizational dimensions that influence learning" (p. 141) into adult education. Alfred (2009b) further made five recommendations for instructional design:

1. Integrate non-Western knowledge into the curricula to lessen the cultural divide between students and the Western-dominated classroom.
2. Acknowledge cultural differences among immigrant groups.
3. Foster inclusive learning communities through the use of learning partners or teams.
4. Deemphasize assimilation in curricula and teaching practices.
5. Consider the early schooling and work socialization of immigrant groups. (pp. 143–144)

The Motivational Framework for Culturally Responsive Teaching

The motivational framework for culturally responsive teaching (Ginsberg & Wlodkowski, 2009) was designed specifically for adult learning environments and describes norms and practices that establish an environment in which "inquiry, respect, and the opportunity for full participation by diverse adults is the norm" (Wlodkowski, 2004, p. 161). It is grounded in the assumption that culturally responsive teaching enhances minority students' motivation through the use of four elements: establishing inclusion; developing attitude; enhancing meaning; and engendering competence (Ginsberg & Wlodkowski, 2009; Wlodkowski, 2004).

Establishing Inclusion

There are many ways that teachers create a sense of community among learners. These practices lay a foundation of respect and connectedness through established routines, mutually agreed-upon norms, and equitable treatment of all learners. Frequently, that involves the use of collaborative and cooperative learning activities such as jigsaw readings or peer teaching (Ginsberg & Wlodkowski, 2009). An important aspect of establishing inclusion is getting to know students' cultural backgrounds in order to overcome cultural mismatches (Collard & Stalker, 1991; Ladson-Billings, 1995) that may interfere with learning. To do this, adult English language educators will often learn words in their students' native languages and encourage classmates to learn and use those words in class (Rhodes, 2013, 2017). Another way to increase understanding of students' backgrounds is by inviting students to share information about their families and lives outside of the English language classroom with each other.

Developing Attitude

Helping learners feel positively about content and the learning process is facilitated by building on students' personal experiences and knowledge, in addition to incorporating learner autonomy into curricular planning (Ginsberg & Wlodkowski, 2009). Addressing the relevance of the course content to students' lives and creating opportunities for student volition in the learning environment are the foundational aspects of this element. In adult English language classes, educators often find informative essays about national and ethnic groups on the internet, in addition to using international newspapers' English-language resources. These provide linguistically accessible materials that are written from the cultural point of view of the students.

Enhancing Meaning

Another element of culturally responsive teaching is making learning meaningful by engaging students in reflection and critical inquiry. Effective teachers will offer numerous opportunities for learners to explore and create new meanings together and by encouraging them to ground their understanding in their own stories and narratives. This has been described as creating classroom discussions in a "third idiom" (Ginsberg & Wlodkowski, 2009, p. 196) that privileges neither the teacher's nor the learners' language. This may be done through simulations, role-playing, or games. Central to this element is helping students make connections between their community, national, and global identities (Ladson-Billings, 1995, 2001). Adult English language teachers often ground learning activities in cross-cultural examinations. For example, adult English language teachers frequently ask learners to compare aspects of their native culture and values with those of mainstream American culture. This aids in the disarming of beliefs regarding cultural superiority and allows learners to critically evaluate aspects of their native and adopted cultural values. This, in conjunction with lessons dedicated to understanding the acculturation process, may allay some unspoken concerns about losing native identity or not fitting into their adopted country (Rhodes, 2013, 2017).

Engendering Competence
This final element comprises practices that show learners evidence of their learning and proficiency and the use of assessments that are contextualized in the learners' experiences (Ginsberg & Wlodkowski, 2009; Wlodkowski, 2004). In essence, these practices require the use of authentic and effective assessments that relate to the students' backgrounds and allow them to demonstrate mastery in a variety of ways. This often includes the use of performance-based or portfolio assessments, student-invented dialogues, focused reflections, and journals. While adult English language teachers utilize many of the same strategies mainstream adult educators use, the barrier of language proficiency may influence the implementation of some of these norms (Rhodes, 2013, 2017). Teachers in adult English language classrooms do frequently provide progress reports to students but are less apt to ask for student input or offer alternative assessments.

Career Pathways and the Narrowing of the Adult Literacy ESL Curriculum

Adult basic education, which includes literacy ESL classes, has been funded by federal–state initiatives since the early 1960s and the war on poverty (Ross-Gordon et al., 2017) through the Adult Education Act and successive legislation. All funding legislation of adult basic education has linked literacy and economic well-being, yet the current version, the Workforce Innovation and Opportunity Act (WIOA), enacted in 2015 (Ross-Gordon et al., 2017), has narrowed the scope of adult basic education to improving adult learners' readiness for both postsecondary and employment opportunities. While this focused approach on career pathways and academic readiness has been praised for its potential benefits to individuals in low-wage employment or the unemployed, it has been criticized for its debilitating effects on adult literacy ESL learners who have additional, integrative educational needs (McHugh & Doxsee, 2018). As noted previously, social integration of immigrants encompasses understanding of various aspects of daily life such as politics and history, educational systems, financial literacy, housing, health care, and employment. These topics were often covered in the general life-skills adult ESL classes in order to increase overall English language proficiency, the most foundational of necessary elements to successful integration for immigrants. However, under WIOA's employment-related program outcomes, adult literacy ESL programs are less able to provide the broad civics and in-depth language instruction instrumental to their adaptation to multiple aspects of U.S. culture (McHugh & Doxsee, 2018).

The English-Plus Integration (EPI) model has been offered as an alternative to existing program funding and organization. Based on the multifaceted understanding of successful immigrant integration, this program model would reinstate general life-skills English and focus on language acquisition, while incorporating elements which would increase adult learners' independence, such as enhanced digital literacy and the design of "individual and family success plans" (McHugh & Doxsee, 2018, p. 2). The EPI model recognizes the limited time adult ELLs are able to invest in attending class, as well as the long-term nature of language acquisition. Therefore, emphasis is placed on helping learners with general English skills as well as developing skills and strategies to help them utilize technologies to function as lifelong learners (McHugh & Doxsee, 2018).

Limited Understanding of Adult English Literacy Learners

A persistent issue affecting the advancement of the field is the dearth of research involving adult English literacy learners. In a review of literature published after 2000, Mathews-Aydinli (2008) found only 41 research articles on adult ESL classes, focusing on three areas: ethnographic studies of adult English language learners, teacher-related studies, and second-language acquisition studies. With the exception of the second-language acquisition studies, culture was a recurring theme and basis of many of these studies. Although they varied in ethnic group participation, all shared findings related to the relationship of integration and the acquisition of English. Teacher-related studies included examinations of culture and cultural identity, the results of which characterized the role of the adult education ESL teacher as "caring, patient, cultural mediators" (p. 207). Unfortunately, there have been few additions to the corpus of literature since Mathew-Aydinli's (2008) review. This critique of the paucity of research on adult English language learning remains relevant today and serves as an obstacle to a comprehensive understanding of the unique aspects of this subfield of adult education.

Conclusion

The purpose of this chapter was to describe the diversity found within a myriad of aspects of the adult English language classroom. Learners come from a variety of native countries, racial identities, educational experiences, and so on, and the learning environments established to meet learners' goals are also highly diverse. Adult education in these environments is equally eclectic and somewhat different from the teaching used with native-English-speaking students. The characteristic blending of linguistic, adult learning, and cultural identity theories has much to offer the larger field of ACE about creating successful learning communities. However, only with a broadening of legislative funding policies and an increase in research will adult English language education satisfy its full potential to help individuals assume their full roles in the United States.

References

Ahmadian, M., & Rad, S. E. (2014). Postmethod era and glocalized language curriculum development: A fresh burden on language teachers. *Journal of Language Teaching and Research, 5*(3), 592–598.

Alfred, M. (2009a). Nonwestern immigrants in continuing higher education: A sociocultural approach to culturally responsive pedagogy. *The Journal of Continuing Higher Education, 57*(3), 137–148.

Alfred, M. (2009b). Transnational identities and instructional design in adult education. In V. C. X. Wang (Ed.), *Curriculum development for adult learners in the global community (Vol. 2): Teaching and learning* (pp. 39–63). Krieger.

Anthias, F. (2013). Intersectional what? Social divisions, intersectionality and levels of analysis. *Ethnicities, 13*(3), 3–19.

Batalova, J. & Lee, A. (2012). *Frequently requested statistics on immigrants and immigration in the United States*. Migration Policy Institute. https://www.migrationpolicy.org/article/frequently-requested-statistics-immigrants-and-immigration-united-states-2

Capps, R. Ku, L., Fix, M., Furgiuele, C., Passel, J., Ramchand, & R., McNiven, S. (2002). *How are immigrants faring after welfare reform? Preliminary evidence from Los Angeles and New York City*. The Urban Institute.

Celce-Murcia, M. (2014). An overview of language teaching methods and approaches. In M. Celce-Murcia, D. Brinton, & M. Snow (Eds.), *Teaching English as a second language* (pp. 2–14). Heinle & Heinle.

Center for Applied Linguistics. (2010). *Education for adult English language learners in the United States: Trends, research, and promising practices*. Author.

Collard, S., & Stalker, J. (1991). Women's trouble: Women, gender, and the learning environment. *New Directions for Adult and Continuing Education, 1991*(50), 71–81.

Crookes, G., & Lehner, A. (1998). Aspects of process in an ESL critical pedagogy teacher education course. *TESOL Quarterly, 32*(2), 319–328.

Cummins, J. (1986). Empowering minority students: A framework for intervention. *Harvard Educational Review, 56*(1), 18–36.

Ellis, R. (2014). Principles of instructed second language learning. In M. Celce-Murcia, D. Brinton, & M. Snow (Eds.), *Teaching English as a second language* (pp. 31–45). Heinle & Heinle.

Friedenberg, J. E. (2002). The linguistic inaccessibility of U.S. higher education and the inherent inequity of U.S. IEPs: An argument for multilingual higher education. *Bilingual Research Journal, 26*(2), 309–326. https://doi.org/10.1080/15235882.2002.10668713

Gambino, C., Acosta, Y., & Grieco, E. (2014). English-speaking ability of the foreign-born population in the United States: 2012. *American Community Survey Reports, ACS-26*. U.S. Census Bureau.

Ginsberg, M., & Wlodkowski, R. (2009). *Diversity and motivation: Culturally responsive teaching in college*. Jossey-Bass.

Grosik, S. A. (2017). *The path to university admission in the United States through intensive English programs* (Order No. 10604241). ProQuest Dissertations & Theses Global. (1952045825). https://search.proquest.com/docview/1952045825?accountid=10639

Hawkins, M. R. (Ed.) (2011). *Social justice language teacher education*. Multilingual Matters.

Knowles, M. S. (1973). *The adult learner: A neglected species*. Gulf.

Kumaravadivelu, B. (2012). *Language teacher education for a global society: A modular model for knowing, analyzing, recognizing, doing, and seeing*. Routledge.

Ladson-Billings, G. (1995). But that's just good teaching! The case for culturally relevant pedagogy. *Theory Into Practice, 34*, 159–165.

Ladson-Billings, G. (2001). *Crossing over to Canaan: The journey of new teachers in diverse classrooms*. Jossey-Bass.

Mathews-Aydinli, J. (2008). Overlooked and understudied? A survey of current trends in research on adult English language learners. *Adult Education Quarterly, 58*(3), 198–213.

McHugh, M., & Doxsee, C. (2018). *English plus integration: Shifting the instructional paradigm for immigrant adult learners to support integration success*. Migration Policy Institute. https://www.migrationpolicy.org/research/english-plus-integration-instructional-paradigm-immigrant-adult-learners

National Center for Education Statistics (1995). *Participation of adults in English as a second language classes: 1994–1995*. Author. http://nces.ed.gov/pubs97/web/97319t.asp

Nieto, S. (2002). *Language, culture, and teaching: Critical perspectives for a new century*. Lawrence Erlbaum.

Open Doors Report on International Educational Exchange (2017). *IIE releases Open Doors 2017 data*. Institute of International Education. https://www.iie.org/Research-and-Insights/Publications/Open-Doors-2017

Rhodes, C. M. (2013). *Culturally responsive teaching practices of adult education English for speakers of other languages and English for academic purposes teachers* (Order No. 3559445). ProQuest Dissertations & Theses Global. (1353368116). https://search.proquest.com/docview/1353368116?accountid=10639

Rhodes, C. M. (2017). A validation study of the Culturally Responsive Teaching Survey. *Universal Journal of Educational Research, 5*, 45–53. https://doi.org/10.13189/ujer.2017.050106

Ross-Gordon, J. M., Rose, A. D., & Kasworm, C. E. (2017). *Foundations of adult and continuing education*. Jossey-Bass.

Snyder, T. D., de Brey, C., & Dillow, S. A. (2016). *Digest of education statistics 2015* (NCES 2016-014). National Center for Education Statistics, Institute of Education Sciences, U.S. Department of Education.

Teachers of English to Speakers of Other Languages. (2003). *Standards for adult education ESOL programs*. Author.

U.S. Census Bureau. (2018). *American community survey: Selected characteristics of the native and foreign-born populations 2018 ACS 1-year estimates subject tables*. https://data.census.gov/cedsci/table?q=S05&d=ACS%201Year%20Estimates%20Subject%20Tables&tid=ACSST1Y2018.S0501

Warriner, D. S. (2015). 'Here, without English, you are dead': Ideologies of language and discourses of neoliberalism in adult English language learning. *Journal of Multilingual and Multicultural Development, 37*(5), 495–508.

Wlodkowski, R. (2004). Creating motivational learning environments. In M. Galbraith (Ed.), *Adult learning: A guide for effective instruction* (3rd ed., pp. 141–164). Krieger.

CHAPTER 21

Family Literacy

Esther Prins, Carol Clymer, Anna Kaiper-Marquez, and Blaire Willson Toso

Family literacy (FL) is a multifaceted concept that includes what families do with literacy and the programs or activities that seek to enhance parents' and young children's educational, language, and literacy development and to foster parental involvement in education—primarily focusing on lower-income families (Goodling Institute for Research in Family Literacy, 2012; see also Anderson et al., 2010). Accordingly, this chapter incorporates research on programs (interventions) and on families' intergenerational language and literacy practices in everyday settings.

The chapter begins by describing the theoretical perspectives that inform our analysis, followed by an overview of FL programming and a summary of recent trends in FL policy, research, and practice. Scholarship on FL crosses disciplines including adult education, early childhood and K–12 education, human development, human services, psychology, and public policy. Although much of this research focuses on children's literacy and educational outcomes (e.g., van Steensel et al., 2012), this chapter highlights adults' experiences and outcomes in FL programs and intergenerational literacy practices. This chapter is also infused with our experiences and interests in FL research, policy, and practice as administrators at the Goodling Institute for Research in Family Literacy at Penn State (Clymer, Kaiper-Marquez, Prins) and as an FL consultant (Toso).

Theoretical Framework

We view conceptions of literacy, parenting, and parental involvement in education as historically and socially constructed, meaning that they shift over time and differ by race/ethnicity, culture, nationality, and social class (Griffith & Smith, 2005; Lareau, 2003). For instance, how a White, middle-class mother in the United States reads with, talks to, or disciplines her child may diverge from the practices of mothers who are living in poverty, who are immigrants, or who are people of color. Furthermore, the notion that parents are responsible for children's cognitive development has become normative only since the 1950s, following the institutionalization of mass schooling (Schaub, 2010). In particular, FL programming and research have been shaped by the ideology of intensive mothering (Hays, 1996), a recent Canadian and U.S. phenomenon which holds that mothers should invest great time, energy, and resources in childrearing to raise literate, academically successful children. This type of mothering helps reproduce educational and socioeconomic advantage but can also contribute to mothers' guilt and stress.

Our view of FL also incorporates three strands of sociocultural theories of literacy: social practices, multiliteracies, and critical literacy (Perry, 2012). First, in contrast to the functional perspective of literacy as a technical skill, we view literacy as a social practice that involves cognitive processes and also is shaped by specific purposes and embedded in a particular place, time, and web of power relations. Second, multiliteracies research emphasizes that literacy incorporates multiple communicative modes, including verbal, visual, aural, spatial, and gestural (Janks, 2010; Kress, 2003). The ascendance of images and digital devices (Kress, 2003) means that print is no longer the only dimension of literacy. Finally, a critical perspective elucidates how FL programming, curricula, policies, and specific literacy practices shape power inequities, the circulation of ideologies, participants' identities, and participants' abilities to exercise power within and outside the classroom (Moje et al., 2006). The critical literacy perspective particularly informs our concern with cultural responsiveness, deficit perspectives, gender equity, and recognition of participants' diverse goals (Prins & Schafft, 2009; Prins & Toso, 2008; Prins et al., 2009).

Overview of FL

FL programming began in the United States in the 1980s, arising from increased concern about the educational achievement gap based on race and social class, coupled with low levels of parental education in lower-income families. For instance, Kentucky's Parent and Child Education Program was designed to increase parents' educational expectations for preschool children, raise parents' "family skills" and educational level (by obtaining a high school equivalency degree), and improve children's "learning skills" (Devlin, 1991, n.p.). For more on the historical development of FL, see Gadsden (2017) and Wasik and Hermann (2004). FL programs simultaneously educate caregivers and young children (typically birth through lower elementary grades) to support their language and literacy growth and to help caregivers support their children's education.

Like other forms of compensatory education, the primary FL audience is families in poverty and caregivers who have unmet literacy needs, lack a secondary degree, or want to learn English or the official language(s) of the country. Immigrants represent a disproportionate share of U.S. families with young children (Park et al., 2016) and a large portion of FL participants. Increasingly, programming and research also focus on families who are not members of mainstream society, who have difficulty accessing educational services and literacy materials and whose intergenerational literacy practices deserve more attention, including homeless parents (Di Santo et al., 2016), incarcerated parents (Nutbrown et al., 2017), and refugees (Singh et al., 2015).

The most well-known comprehensive FL model is the four-component model, which includes adult education, early childhood education, parent education, and interactive parent-child literacy activities (ILAs). Developed by the National Center for Family Literacy (NCFL) and prescribed by federal Even Start legislation in 1988, this four-component model was widely adopted. Since then myriad curricular models have emerged, particularly after Even Start was defunded in 2011 (see Wasik & Hermann, 2004, for an overview of earlier FL models). Particular models may focus more on parents or children, offer different configurations of educational and social services, and vary in length and intensity, from months-long classes to one-off workshops or events. Many providers still offer some variation of the four-component model by collaborating with other organizations and/or combining funding streams (Clymer et al., 2017).

Any program, service, or activity that seeks to provide education for both adults and children, to encourage reading in families, or to help parents support their children's education could be categorized as FL. Related terms include *family learning*, *family engagement*, and *family involvement*. The *two-generation* (2Gen) approach, a recently coined term, has been championed by the U.S. Department of Health and Human Services, foundations such as the Aspen Institute, and affiliated scholars as an antipoverty strategy for providing coordinated educational and social services for children and caregivers simultaneously (e.g., Sims & Bogle, 2016). However, 2Gen programs do not necessarily provide *interactive* or *intergenerational* learning activities (ILAs). In addition, the argument that the 2Gen approach is new or substantially different than previous iterations of FL (e.g., Gardner et al., 2017; Sommer, Sabol et al., 2018) ignores more than 30 years of FL programming and scholarship and the many federal and state programs that still fund some type of FL (Clymer et al., 2017). As new FL-related initiatives and terms are created, it is important to situate them in the history and breadth of FL research, policy, and practice.

Critiques and Responses

In this section, we summarize prominent critiques of FL. First, FL policy, practice, and research have been criticized for promoting a deficit discourse that blames parents, particularly mothers, for children's language and literacy struggles, tries to "fix" families, and promotes White, middle-class literacy and parenting practices as the norm (Auerbach, 1995). Since Auerbach's seminal critique, many programs and researchers have sought to counteract deficit perspectives. However, vestiges of this problem remain. For example, 15% of the literature reviews in 213 FL publications did not mention culture, social class, race, gender, ethnicity, or language differences, and only 41% treated diversity in a substantive way (Compton-Lilly et al., 2012). Individualistic explanations for poverty and persistence in FL programs are prevalent, rooted in the debunked 1960s culture of poverty perspective—a view that Ruby Payne has propagated in education (Prins & Schafft, 2009). The deficit discourse is also evident in programs that attempt to change the quantity and quality of parent-child talk, based on Hart and Risley's (1995) methodologically suspect conclusion that by age 3, children living in poverty hear 30 million fewer words than their affluent peers. (See Sperry et al.'s 2018 critique.)

To counter deficit perspectives, educators have sought to develop more culturally responsive programming, particularly for immigrants and families in poverty. A prominent example is A. Anderson et al.'s (2015) work with rural, First Nations, immigrant, and refugee families in Canada. They have developed programs that incorporated families' strengths, language, and cultural knowledge (A. Anderson et al., 2015).

A second critique is that FL perpetuates the idea that mothers are mainly responsible for children's literacy development and educational success (Prins & Toso, 2008; Smythe & Isserlis, 2004). Despite the increased use of gender-inclusive terms like *parent*, most FL participants are women and most FL research focuses on mothers. The mothering discourse (Griffith & Smith, 2005) is problematic because it doesn't account for the material realities of mothers' lives, it subjugates women's needs and goals to those of their children, and it increases women's invisible, unpaid educational work at home (Prins & Toso, 2008). The mothering discourse also elides fathers' roles in FL; however, as we will discuss, research and practice on fathers and FL are gaining visibility.

Finally, critics have questioned whether FL is effective. The answer depends on a study's research questions, methods, measures, and length; how FL is defined; the program or intervention design; whether child and/or adult outcomes are measured; and more. The "imposition of simplistic evaluation frameworks on complex family literacy interventions" (Carpentieri, 2013, p. 548) and lack of longitudinal studies and comparison group designs are especially problematic because they fail to capture programs' multifaceted outcomes and cannot establish causality, respectively. In addition, Even Start was defunded due to national evaluations that deemed it ineffective, even though the evaluations were riddled with methodological flaws (Clymer et al., 2017).

Numerous studies have examined FL programs' influence on children, many showing positive language, literacy, and/or academic outcomes (e.g., Anderson et al., 2010; Hannon et al., 2019; van Steensel et al., 2012). The prevailing focus on children's outcomes illustrates how parents are often positioned as conduits of children's learning, rather than as learners in their own right. The few studies on adult outcomes suggest that FL programs can enhance parents' educational progress, including literacy and numeracy gains (Brooks et al., 2008); language learning (Sommer, Gomez et al., 2018); pursuit of further education and training (Swain et al., 2014); postsecondary credential attainment (Sabol et al., 2015); employability skills (Toso & Krupar, 2016); and wider benefits such as leadership, self-esteem, confidence, and self-efficacy (Brassett-Grundy, 2002; Cramer & Toso, 2015).

Trends in FL Policy, Research, and Practice

This section highlights recent developments regarding FL funding strategies, employment-focused programming, international FL, digital literacies, involvement of fathers and extended family, and family service-learning.

Funding Strategies

Although the 2008 recession and 2011 defunding of Even Start decreased the number of FL programs in the United States, many programs remain, supported by organizations such as the National Center for Families Learning, Barbara Bush Foundation, American Library Association, and several states that have continued to provide FL through state and/or federal funding via the Adult Education and Family Literacy Act (AEFLA), Title II of the 2014 Workforce Innovation and Opportunity Act (WIOA; Clymer et al., 2017). In 2016–2017, some states allowed grantees to use their AEFLA funding for FL; in addition, 10 states and the District of Columbia had dedicated funding for FL (Clymer et al., 2017). As of 2017, AEFLA was one of 18 federal programs that included FL as an allowable expenditure (Clymer et al., 2017). Further, many local programs offer FL services by combining funding from federal, state, private, and local sources and partnering with other organizations to provide specific components. Although the need outpaces funding availability, FL professionals have been creative and resourceful in finding ways to serve local families.

Focus on Employment Outcomes

As adult basic education and FL programs strive to comply with funders' accountability measures, they increasingly emphasize employment outcomes (Belzer, 2017). WIOA frames "adult education as essentially in support of federal employment goals," signaling "a shift away from conceptions of adult education as helping learners more effectively fulfill a range of roles in addition to that of worker" (Belzer, 2017, p. 15). Specifically, WIOA requires providers—including FL programs that use federal funds—to report outcomes on employment and transition to postsecondary education and training, including earnings and credentials.

The addition of the latter measures complicated a key purpose of FL programs: to help parents obtain the education and skills necessary for becoming "full partners" in their children's educational development (WIOA, 2014, p. 184). The employment turn is contested because WIOA measures do not capture FL programs' and participants' multiple purposes and goals. Although WIOA goals are important, others that cultivate adult and child literacy, parenting, and advocacy skills are equally critical. Moreover, programs may be deemed ineffective if they do not meet WIOA employment and postsecondary targets (Clymer et al., 2017; Park et al., 2016).

In response to this policy emphasis, many FL programs now include employment- and/or postsecondary-related programming. A 2016–2017 Goodling Institute survey (Toso & Clymer, 2017) found that 16 of 87 programs (18%) offered employability programming (e.g., tracked employment placement and retention and postsecondary transitions). However, only six programs were using AEFLA funds, indicating that the employability emphasis spans funding sources. Programs offered a range of employment-related services such as soft skills development (e.g., teamwork), career exploration, job searching, bridge programs, and integrated education and training. Some states (e.g., Connecticut, Pennsylvania, South Carolina) also emphasized career development in their FL programming.

Our informal discussions with practitioners suggest that they recognize the need to help families achieve economic stability but want to continue serving parents who are not looking for work, including grandparents and stay-at-home parents. Applying WIOA's employment and postsecondary accountability measures to FL means that other goals, such as navigating school systems or learning English, will not be valued or counted (Park et al., 2016). In light of these policy changes, FL practitioners must discern how to meet funders' employment-related requirements (and secure adequate resources to do so) while supporting participants' broader goals as caregivers and community residents.

International FL Programming

The field of FL began in the United States and is well developed in Anglophone countries, including Australia (Hill & Diamond, 2013), Canada (Anderson et al., 2015), England (Brooks et al., 2012), Ireland (Rose, 2013), New Zealand (Furness, 2013), and Scotland (Tett, 2000). Research in England (Swain et al., 2014) found positive impacts of FL programs on children's literacy and parental learning, leading to suggestions for national policies that support FL. In Canada, FL researchers are accounting for Indigenous forms of knowledge and broadening language practices to include refugees' and immigrants' multilingual literacies (Anderson et al., 2015). However, reduced government funding has been a challenge in England (Brooks et al., 2012) and Canada (Shohet, 2012).

Research in Western countries is vital for expanding FL, yet "intergenerational learning is rooted in many cultures and exists everywhere in the world, in the North as well as the South" (Desmond & Elfert, 2008, p. v). UNESCO promotes FL as a strategy for achieving Sustainable Development Goal 4, "which emphasizes the need to promote lifelong learning opportunities for all" (Hanemann et al., 2017, p. 7). Research on FL and intergenerational literacy practices is expanding in Europe and Scandinavia (e.g., Wright et al., 2010) and lower income countries in Africa, Asia, Latin America, and the Middle East (e.g., Desmond & Elfert, 2008).

For example, Desmond (2012) found that the South African Family Literacy Project supported parents' engagement in their children's educational practices, a practice vital in a country where 12% of sixth-grade children are at a prereading level. In Chile, Mendive et al. (2017) examined the influence of mothers' literacy practices on children's literacy and contended that research must expand beyond English-speaking, North American family contexts. In the Middle East, Al-Maadadi et al. (2017) investigated Qatari parents' and teachers' perceptions of FL programs, finding a strong correlation between parents' positive perceptions of FL and home literacy practices. A review of research on FL in China (Leung & Li, 2012) covered topics such as parent-child reading and home literacy practices, highlighting how parents can help children learn to read and write a complex, nonalphabetic language. Further research is needed on cross-cultural comparisons of intergenerational literacy practices and FL programming, including culturally specific ways to support family learning.

Digital Literacies

In addition to crossing geographic borders, FL research has expanded to encompass multimodality (Kress, 2003). With the growth of digital devices, parent–child literacy interactions now incorporate visual, aural, spatial, and gestural modes and many adult literacy practices also require technology. As such, FL programs are helping adults to develop digital literacy and use these skills to enhance children's learning (Lee et al., 2018). In particular, digital storytelling has gained traction as a participatory way to teach content (technology, literacy, language, etc.) while also documenting family stories, addressing community problems, organizing parents, designing meaningful texts, and validating participants' knowledge (Beckett et al., 2013; Pahl, 2011; Prins, 2017).

A related strand of research explores intergenerational digital literacy in homes and communities, including topics such as how digital technologies shape home literacy environments and children's language and literacy development (Kucirkova, 2017; Marsh et al., 2017). As smartphones, tablets, computers, social media, video-calling, and other digital devices and applications have proliferated, literacy practices for adults and children frequently incorporate music, symbols, emojis, gestures, images, video, and other modes (e.g., reading a book to a grandchild on Skype, parent and child cowriting a Facebook photo caption). However, we must also recognize that access to digital technologies and the internet is still restricted by income, education, race, nationality, rurality, and language.

Involvement of Fathers and Extended Family

Although FL research and practice still focus primarily on mothers, scholars and educators have sought to include fathers and other family members. The growing literature on fathers' role in FL is vital because the prevalent emphasis on mothers ignores the diversity of roles and responsibilities of mothers and fathers (Gadsden, 2012) and fathers' influence on literacy development (Baker, 2013; Palm, 2013). For example, Duursma (2014) found that paternal book reading with children in Head Start was a significant predictor of children's story comprehension, cognitive development, and language skills. Qualitative studies have examined topics such as Latino fathers' involvement in children's literacy development (Santos & Alfred, 2016); how Hmong refugees' father-daughter relationships shaped daughters' literacy, ultimately changing traditional gender dynamics and daughters' agency (Simon, 2017); and Irish fathers' Photovoice documentation of their FL work at home (Hegarty, 2016).

Research on practice has investigated fathers' experiences in FL programs (Morgan et al., 2009), why programs have not attracted more men (Rose & Atkin, 2011), and the growth of fathering programs and father-focused FL programs in the United States (Gadsden, 2012) and beyond. Father-only FL initiatives are mainly designed to help fathers support early literacy and engage in shared reading (Palm, 2013), with some programs focusing on subgroups such as incarcerated fathers (Nutbrown et al., 2017) or union members (Wright et al., 2010).

In light of diverse family structures, FL scholars and educators have recognized that other adults and peers are pivotal in cultivating children's literacy (J. Anderson et al., 2010). For instance, extended family, fictive kin, peer groups, and the Black church help nurture Black children's literacy practices (Chaney, 2014). Similarly, Farver et al. (2013) found that shared book reading with older siblings, a culturally relevant yet overlooked practice in extended family households, was related to immigrant children's emergent literacy in English, but not Spanish. Grandparents also influence literacy practices within multigenerational households, which are common in Asia (Ren & Hu, 2013) and other regions. Another line of research explores children as literacy brokers for immigrant and/or refugee parents, thus shaping adults' language and literacy learning and cultural adaptation (Perry, 2009). Studies such as these have broadened our understandings of the multiple people and generations that shape FL practices. However, the paucity of literature on FL pertaining to families with LGBTQ parents or children reflects an underlying assumption of heteronormativity. More research and guidance for FL programs are needed on serving families with same-sex parents, particularly how to create a welcoming atmosphere (e.g., Ryan, 2011).

Family Service-Learning
Service-learning, a structured, reflective, experiential learning activity that serves a local community need, has been widely used in secondary and higher education. Volunteering and service-learning can promote increased school engagement, civic participation, and leadership (Wilson & Musick, 1999), and language development (Riley & Douglas, 2017). To help FL participants strengthen family and community ties, the National Center for Families Learning developed a family service-learning model (Cramer & Toso, 2015). This six-step process is embedded in multigenerational educational programming and is implemented through NCFL's Toyota Family Learning Program, in collaboration with 17 schools and community organizations in 14 states. Parents identify a local need, develop an action plan, and implement it, supported by a facilitator. Projects have included feeding the homeless, school beautification, antibullying, clothing drives, and breast cancer awareness days.

The Goodling Institute's independent evaluation suggests that family service-learning can bolster families' skills in organization, research, planning, reading and writing, technology, teamwork and sharing, civic responsibility, and leadership. Caregivers (primarily Latina immigrants) reported increased confidence, sense of voice, and self-worth and felt more engaged with the community. These findings suggest that incorporating service-learning into FL can benefit the community and participants alike. This model appears to strengthen and extend the benefits of traditional FL programs by building parents' content knowledge, along with civic engagement, employability skills, advocacy, leadership, and social capital (via wider social networks). Additionally, it can counteract the deficit narrative of poor and immigrant families as dependent, unengaged, or unproductive. Providing parents with opportunities to identify, lead, and direct community service projects can enable them to be recognized as experts and invested members of the community.

Conclusion

In many ways, recent FL scholarship and programming have expanded. Researchers and practitioners have a broader view of family that includes fathers, extended family, and differing family configurations. Similarly, conceptions of literacy have extended beyond a focus on print (particularly shared book reading) to include digital literacy and multiple communicative modes. New curricular approaches such as family service-learning position parents as not only recipients of services but also leaders within and beyond their programs. FL programming has also transcended national boundaries and is becoming more attuned to cultural diversity.

In other ways, however, the field has narrowed. Overall, there is less FL funding in the United States, Canada, and the United Kingdom (and perhaps other countries). Some states are still funding FL and practitioners are creatively combining funding, but the diminished funding base is concerning—as is policymakers' and funders' primary focus on children's outcomes. Mirroring national trends in adult basic education and literacy, accountability requirements now emphasize employment for FL participants, goals that may eclipse other worthy aims such as helping parents support children's education or pursue their own personal and educational aspirations. As adult educators, we urge policymakers, researchers, and practitioners to recognize that adults bring many purposes to FL programs and that the benefits of FL extend to not only children but also their caregivers.

References

Al-Maadadi, F., Ihmeideh, F., Al-Falasi, M., Coughlin, C., & Al-Thani, T. (2017). Family literacy programs in Qatar: Teachers' and parents' perceptions and practices. *Journal of Educational and Developmental Psychology, 7*(1), 283–296.

Anderson, A., Anderson, J., & Gear, A. (2015). Family literacy programs as intersubjective spaces: Insights from three decades of working in culturally, linguistically and socially diverse communities. *Language and Literacy, 17*(2), 41–58.

Anderson, J., Anderson, A., Friedrich, N., & Kim, J. E. (2010). Taking stock of family literacy: Some contemporary perspectives. *Journal of Early Childhood Literacy, 10*(1), 33–53. https://doi.org/10.1177/1468798409357387

Auerbach, E. R. (1995). Deconstructing the discourse of strengths in family literacy. *Journal of Reading Behavior, 27*(4), 643–661.

Baker, C. E. (2013). Fathers' and mothers' home literacy involvement and children's cognitive and social emotional development: Implications for family literacy programs. *Applied Develpomental Science, 17*(4), 184–197.

Beckett, L., Glass, R. D., & Moreno, A. P. (2013). A pedagogy of community building: Re-imagining parent involvement and community organizing in popular education efforts. *Association of Mexican American Educators Journal, 6*(1), 5–14.

Belzer, A. (2017). Focusing or narrowing: Trade-offs in the development of adult basic education, 1991–2015. *New Directions for Adult and Continuing Education, 2017*(155), 11–18.

Brooks, G., Hannon, P., & Bird, V. (2012). Family literacy in England. In B. H. Wasik (Ed.), *Handbook of Family Literacy* (2nd ed., pp. 325–338). Routledge.

Brooks, G., Pahl, K., Pollard, A., & Rees, F. (2008). *Effective and inclusive practices in family literacy, language and numeracy: A review of programmes and practice in the UK and internationally*. CfBT Education Trust.

Carpentieri, J. (2013). Evidence, evaluation and the "tyranny of effect size": A proposal to more accurately measure programme impacts in adult and family literacy. *European Journal of Education, 48*(4), 543–556.

Chaney, C. (2014). Bridging the gap: Promoting intergenerational family literacy among low-income, African American families. *Journal of Negro Education, 83*(1), 29–48.

Clymer, C., Toso, B. W., Grinder, E., & Sauder, R. P. (2017). *Changing the course of family literacy*. Goodling Institute for Research in Family Literacy. https://ed.psu.edu/goodling-institute/policy/changing-the-course-of-family-literacy

Compton-Lilly, C., Rogers, R., & Lewis, T. Y. (2012). Analyzing epistemological considerations related to diversity: An integrative critical literature review of family literacy scholarship. *Reading Research Quarterly, 47*(1), 33–60.

Cramer, J., & Toso, B. W. (2015). *Family service-learning brief*. Goodling Institute for Research in Family Literacy. https://ed.psu.edu/goodling-institute/research/family-literacy-service-learning-brief

Desmond, S. (2012). Family literacy programmes in South Africa. In B. H. Wasik (Ed.), *Handbook of family literacy* (2nd ed., pp. 370–384). Routledge.

Desmond, S., & Elfert, M. (2008). *Family literacy: Experiences from Africa and around the world*. UNESCO Institute for Lifelong Learning.

Devlin, K. M. (1991). Kentucky's Parent and Child Education (PACE) Program. *Innovations*. (ED357876). https://eric.ed.gov/?id=ED357876

Di Santo, A., Timmons, K., & Pelletier, J. (2016). "Mommy that's the exit": Empowering homeless mothers to support their children's daily literacy experiences. *Journal of Early Childhood Literacy, 16*(2), 145–170.

Duursma, A. E. (2014). The effects of fathers' and mothers' reading to their children on language outcomes of children participating in Early Head Start in the United States. *Fathering: A Journal of Theory and Research About Men as Parents, 12*(3), 283–302.

Farver, J. A. M., Xu, Y., Lonigan, C. J., & Eppe, S. (2013). The home literacy environment and Latino Head Start children's emergent literacy skills. *Developmental Psychology, 49*(4), 775–791.

Furness, J. (2013). Principles and practices in four New Zealand family focused adult literacy programs: Towards wellbeing in diverse communities. *Literacy and Numeracy Studies, 21*(1), 33–58.

Gadsden, V. L. (2012). Father involvement and family literacy. In B. H. Wasik (Ed.), *Handbook of family literacy* (2nd ed., pp. 151–165). Routledge.

Gadsden, V. L. (2017). Family literacy. In B. V. Street & S. May (Eds.), *Literacies and language education* (3rd ed., pp. 181–195). Springer International.

Gardner, M., Brooks-Gunn, J., & Chase-Lansdale, P. L. (2017). The two-generation approach to building human capital: Past, present, and future. In E. Votruba-Drzal & E. Dearing (Eds.), *The Wiley handbook of early childhood development programs, practices, and policies* (pp. 330–362). Wiley.

Goodling Institute for Research in Family Literacy. (2012). *Research agenda*. https://ed.psu.edu/goodling-institute/publications/gi-research-agenda-update-logo-accessibility

Griffith, A., & Smith, D. (2005). *Mothering for schooling*. RoutledgeFalmer.

Hanemann, U., McCaffery, J., Newell-Jones, K., & Scarpino, C. (2017). *Learning together across generations: Guidelines for family literacy and learning programmes*. UNESCO.

Hannon, P., Nutbrown, C., & Morgan, A. (2019). Effects of extending disadvantaged families' teaching of emergent literacy. *Research Papers in Education* (pp. 1–27). https://doi.org/10.1080/02671522.2019.1568531

Hart, B., & Risley, T. R. (1995). *Meaningful differences in the everyday experience of young American children*. Paul H Brookes.

Hays, S. (1996). *The cultural contradictions of motherhood*. Yale University Press.

Hegarty, A. (2016). Stars are yellow, hearts are red, and the tree would be green . . . Photovoice: Liberating counter-hegemonic narratives of masculinity. *The Journal of Men's Studies*, 24(3), 294–311. https://doi.org/10.1177/1060826516661320

Hill, S., & Diamond, A. (2013). Family literacy in response to local contexts. *Australian Journal of Language and Literacy*, 36(1), 48–55.

Janks, H. (2010). *Literacy and power*. Routledge.

Kress, G. (2003). *Literacy in the new media age*. Psychology Press.

Kucirkova, N. (2017). New literacies and new media: The changing face of early literacy. In N. Kucirkova, C. E. Snow, V. Grøver, & C. McBride (Eds.), *The Routledge international handbook of early literacy education* (pp. 40–54). Routledge.

Lareau, A. (2003). *Unequal childhoods: Class, race, and family life*. University of California Press.

Lee, V. J., Hoekje, B., & Levine, B. (2018). Introducing technology to immigrant families to support early literacy development and two-generation learning. *Language Arts*, 95(3), 133–148.

Leung, C. B., & Li, Y. (2012). Family literacy in China. In C. B. Leung & J. Ruan (Eds.), *Perspectives on teaching and learning Chinese literacy in China* (pp. 199–210). Springer Netherlands.

Marsh, J., Hannon, P., Lewis, M., & Ritchie, L. (2017). Young children's initiation into family literacy practices in the digital age. *Journal of Early Childhood Research*, 15(1), 47–60.

Mendive, S., Lissi, M. R., Bakeman, R., & Reyes, A. (2017). Beyond mother education: Maternal practices as predictors of early literacy development in Chilean children from low-SES households. *Early Education and Development*, 28(2), 167–181.

Moje, E. B., Lewis, C., & Enciso, P. (2006). *Identity, agency, and power: Reframing sociocultural research on literacy*. Lawrence Erlbaum.

Morgan, A., Nutbrown, C., & Hannon, P. (2009). Fathers' involvement in young children's literacy development: Implications for family literacy programmes. *British Educational Research Journal*, 35(2), 167–185. https://doi.org/10.1080/01411920802041996

Nutbrown, C., Clough, P., Stammers, L., Emblin, N., & Alston-Smith, S. (2017). Family literacy in prisons: Fathers' engagement with their young children. *Research Papers in Education*, 1–23. https://doi.org/10.1080/02671522.2017.1402085

Pahl, K. (2011). My family, my story: Representing identities in time and space through digital storytelling. *National Society for the Study of Education*, 110(1), 17–39.

Palm, G. (2013). Fathers and early literacy: A global analysis. In J. Pattnaik (Ed.), *Father involvement in young children's lives* (pp. 13–29). Springer.

Park, M., McHugh, M., & Katsiaficas, C. (2016). *Serving immigrant families through two-generation programs: Identifying family needs and responsive program approaches*. Migration Policy Institute.

Perry, K. H. (2009). Genres, contexts, and literacy practices: Literacy brokering among Sudanese refugee families. *Reading Research Quarterly*, 44(3), 256–276.

Perry, K. H. (2012). What is literacy? A critical overview of sociocultural perspectives. *Journal of Language and Literacy Education*, 8(1), 50–71.

Prins, E. (2017). Digital storytelling in adult basic education and literacy programming. *New Directions for Adult and Continuing Education*, 2017(154), 29–38. https://doi.org/10.1002/ace.20228

Prins, E., & Schafft, K. (2009). Individual and structural attributions for poverty and persistence in family literacy programs: The resurgence of the culture of poverty. *Teachers College Record*, 111(9), 2280–2310.

Prins, E., & Toso, B. W. (2008). Defining and measuring parenting for educational success: A critical discourse analysis of the parent education profile. *American Educational Research Journal*, 45(3), 555–596.

Prins, E., Toso, B. W., & Schafft, K. (2009). "It feels like a little family to me": Social interaction and support among women in adult education and family literacy. *Adult Education Quarterly*, 59(4), 335–352.

Ren, L., & Hu, G. (2013). Prolepsis, syncretism, and synergy in early language and literacy practices: A case study of family language policy in Singapore. *Language Policy, 12*(1), 63–82.

Riley, T., & Douglas, S. R. (2017). The multicultural café: Enhancing authentic interaction for adult English language learners through service-learning. *TESL Canada Journal, 34*(1), 25–50.

Rose, A. (2013). Building on existing informal learning in Traveller communities through family literacy programmes: An Irish case study. *International Journal of Inclusive Education, 17*(2), 174–91. https://doi.org/10.1080/13603116.2011.629688

Rose, A., & Atkin, C. (2011). Family literacy programmes: A comparative study of gender roles in England, Ireland, and Malta. *Early Child Development and Care, 181*(6), 775–790. https://doi.org/10.1080/03004430.2010.490297

Ryan, C. L. (2011). Talking, reading, and writing about gay and lesbian families in classrooms: The consequences of different pedagogical approaches. In C. Compton-Lilly & S. Green (Eds.), *Bedtime stories and book reports: Connecting parent involvement and family literacy* (pp. 96–108). Teachers College Press.

Sabol, T. J., Sommer, T. E., Chase-Lansdale, P. L., Brooks-Gunn, J., Yoshikawa, H., King, C. T., Kathawalla, U., Alamuddin, R., Gomez, C.J., & Ross, E. C. (2015). Parents' persistence and certification in a two-generation education and training program. *Children and Youth Services Review, 58*, 1–10. https://doi.org/10.1016/j.childyouth.2015.08.012

Santos, R. A., & Alfred, M. V. (2016). Literacy, parental roles, and support systems among single Latino father families. *Journal of Research and Practice for Adult Literacy, Secondary, and Basic Education, 5*(3), 5–17.

Schaub, M. (2010). Parenting for cognitive development from 1950 to 2000. *Sociology of Education, 83*(1), 46–66.

Shohet, L. (2012). Family literacy in Canada. In B. H. Wasik (Ed.), *Handbook of family literacy* (2nd ed., pp. 307–324). Routledge.

Simon, K. (2017). Daughters learning from fathers: Migrant family literacies that mediate borders. *Literacy in Composition Studies, 5*(1), 1–20.

Sims, M., & Bogle, M. (2016). *Making tomorrow better together*. Aspen Institute.

Singh, S., Sylvia, M. R., & Ridzi, F. (2015). Exploring the literacy practices of refugee families enrolled in a book distribution program and an intergenerational family literacy program. *Early Childhood Education Journal, 43*(1), 37–45. https://doi.org/10.1007/s10643-013-0627-0

Smythe, S., & Isserlis, J. (2004). The good mother: Exploring mothering discourses in family literacy texts. *Literacy & Numeracy Studies, 13*(2), 23–38.

Sommer, T. E., Gomez, C. J., Yoshikawa, H., Sabol, T., Chor, E., Sanchez, A., Chase Lansdale, C., & Brooks-Gunn, J. (2018). Head Start, two-generation ESL services, and parent engagement. *Early Childhood Research Quarterly, 52*, 63–73. https://doi.org/10.1016/j.ecresq.2018.03.008

Sommer, T. E., Sabol, T. J., Chor, E., Schneider, W., Chase-Lansdale, P. L., Brooks-Gunn, J., Small, M., King, C., & Yoshikawa, H. (2018). A two-generation human capital approach to anti-poverty policy. *RSF: The Russell Sage Foundation Journal of the Social Sciences, 4*(3), 118–143.

Sperry, D. E., Sperry, L. L., & Miller, P. J. (2018). Reexamining the verbal environments of children from different socioeconomic backgrounds. *Child Development*. https://doi.org/10.1111/cdev.13072

Swain, J., Brooks, G., & Bosley, S. (2014). The benefits of family literacy provision for parents in England. *Journal of Early Childhood Research, 12*(1), 77–91.

Tett, L. (2000). Excluded voices: Class, culture, and family literacy in Scotland. *Journal of Adolescent & Adult Literacy, 44*(2), 122–128.

Toso, B. W., & Clymer, C. (2017, October). *Meeting the challenge: Incorporating employability* [Paper presentation]. Families Learning Conference, Tucson, AZ, United States.

Toso, B. W., & Krupar, A. (2016). *Building employability skills in family literacy programs: Lessons from the Toyota Family Learning Program*. Goodling Institute for Research in Family Literacy. https://ed.psu.edu/goodling-institute/professional-development/practitioners-guide-7-1

van Steensel, R., Herppich, S., McElvany, N., & Kurvers, J. (2012). How effective are family literacy programs for children's literacy skills? In B. H. Wasik (Ed.), *Handbook of family literacy* (2nd ed., pp. 135–148). Routledge.

Wasik, B. H., & Hermann, S. (2004). Family literacy: History, concepts, services. In B. H. Wasik (Ed.), *Handbook of family literacy* (pp. 3–22). Lawrence Erlbaum.

Wilson, J., & Musick, M. (1999). The effects of volunteering on the volunteer. *Law and Contemporary Problems, 62*(4), 141–168.

Workforce Innovation and Opportunity Act. (2014). H.R.803, 113th Cong., 1st Sess.

Wright, A. E., Bouchard, M., Bosdotter, K., & Granberg, R. (2010). "LÄS för mej, Pappa": A Swedish model for addressing family literacy. *Childhood Education, 86*(6), 399–403.

CHAPTER 22

Prison Education

Dominique T. Chlup

Correctional education for adults is a responsibility that has long been shared by the fields of corrections and adult education. Some adult education scholars provide critical perspectives on prison education arguing that adult education is a form of control (Davidson, 1995, 2000). Others argue that it is possible for educators to create meaningful and equitable learning experiences for incarcerated people while they are incarcerated (Alfred & Chlup, 2009; Chlup, 2005, 2009, 2017; Chlup & Baird, 2010). This movement from prisons as places for punishment to sites for adult learning can help us reimagine prisons. Prison education in this way can be seen as forward-looking and innovative, a part of the next-generation of criminal justice reform.

Hopeful prison education can be found in the words of incarcerated adults themselves. To borrow the words of prison poet Michael Knoll (1984):

Something in the darkness

has given birth to a sky

spinning with a fierce impossible light. (p. 179)

Learning to write poetry in a correctional training facility, Knoll's words, reprinted here with permission of the publisher, demonstrated how inside a prison classroom he moved from a passive inmate to a knower, teacher, and learner. To be engaged in education allows a prisoner to proclaim that when they are writing they do not feel as if they are inside a prison (Klein, 1988). Or, as Malcolm X (1964) declared in his *Autobiography,* "Prison enabled me to study far more intensively than I would have if my life had gone differently and I had attended some college" (p. 196).

As sites of learning, prisons can provide the field of adult education opportunities to both learn from and contribute to the correctional education programming of incarcerated adults. Prison education can be evolutionary and revolutionary. As adult educators, we can find much to inspire us and guide us as we work directly with incarcerated people and their communities. Because a prison education chapter has not appeared in the *Handbook* in the last 20 years, this chapter aims to provide descriptive information that summarizes the current view of corrections and provide a review of the landscape of prison education in the United States. Emerging issues and trends for adult educators working in correctional education environments will be discussed in an effort to consider how to create equitable and meaningful learning opportunities for incarcerated adults.

This chapter challenges the field to embrace correctional education as a viable form of adult education while also questioning and engaging in critical educational issues. Providing correctional education is an investment that has the potential to create opportunities and change lives. From the perspective of the field of adult education, the prevailing notion has been that correctional education can improve the lives of not just incarcerated individuals but also their families, their communities, and society at large.

Key Definitions and Terms

Prison education is any educational activity that occurs inside a prison. Educational programming can include courses in basic literacy programs, high-school equivalency programs, vocational education, adult and continuing education, and college degree programs (Correctional Officer, 2018). The terms *prison education* and *corrections education* or *correctional education* are used interchangeably. The term *corrections* refers to the federal and state criminal justice systems' network of agencies that supervise individuals that are in a state of incarceration, rehabilitation, on parole, or on probation. However, prisons do not incorporate jail settings or community supervision settings, such as parole or probation. In those instances, it would be more accurate to use the term *corrections education* rather than prison education. An additional term worth noting is *prisoner education*—terminology sometimes used to describe the situation when prisoners educate themselves or others with no formal education program in place. For instance, "jailhouse lawyers" or inmates who engage in informal learning to educate themselves and familiarize themselves with the legal system are said to be engaging in prisoner education.

Overview of the Current Correctional Education Landscape in the United States

At the end of 2016, the most current year for which statistics were available at the time of the writing of this chapter, there were an estimated 1.5 million prisoners under state and federal correctional authority jurisdiction (Carson, 2018). In addition, an estimated 6.6 million persons were in jail, on probation, parole, or under community supervision (Kaeble & Cowhig, 2018). While the population of the United States accounts for less than 5% of the world's population, it accounts for 25% of the world's inmates (Walmsley, 2015).

In order to understand the correctional education landscape, there are other facts worth noting. It is estimated to cost $70 billion a year to operate the U.S. prison system (Walker, 2015). Over 800,000 incarcerated adults are parents of children under age 18, resulting in 2.7 million children with a parent in prison (Pew Charitable Trusts, 2010). The most current statistics available for inmates, broken down by gender, indicate that males represent 93% of inmates, females represent 7% (Federal Bureau of Prisons Statistics, 2018b), and over 3,000 incarcerated individuals identify as transgender (Beck, 2014).

When considering the incarceration rates across races, 30% of the sentenced prison population is White, compared to a national population that is 64% White (U.S. Census Bureau, 2015). In contrast, 36% of the prison population is Black compared to a national population that is 13% Black (Carson, 2018). Historically, the numbers have been higher. Yet recent research indicates that the gap between the number of Blacks and Whites in prison is shrinking (Gramlich, 2018). Hispanics are 22% of the prison population and 17% of the national population (Carson, 2018). Additionally, it is important to note how immigration is represented in these numbers. For instance, while 80.7% of inmates have U.S. citizenship, 12.1% of Hispanic inmates are originally from Mexico, 0.8% from the Dominican Republic, 0.6% from Cuba, 0.9% from Colombia, and 4.9% fall under the category of other/unknown (Federal Bureau of Prisons Statistics, 2018a).

Effectiveness of Correctional Education Programs

In 2010, the Office of Justice Programs' Bureau of Justice Assistance awarded the nonprofit RAND Corporation a cooperative agreement to undertake a study investigating the state of correctional education for incarcerated adults and juveniles. The first report, published in 2013, titled *Evaluating the Effectiveness of Correctional Education: A Meta-Analysis of Programs That Provide Education to Incarcerated Adults,* provided a systematic review of the scientific literature and shared the findings from a meta-analysis on the effectiveness of correctional education programs in helping to improve post-release employment outcomes and reduce recidivism (Davis et al., 2013). A later report, titled *How Effective Is Correctional Education, and Where Do We Go from Here? The Results of a Comprehensive Evaluation*, included the results of a national survey of state correctional directors (Davis et al., 2014). Both reports provide the most comprehensive information we have on the effectiveness of correctional education.

The RAND research dispels the myth that correctional education "does nothing," and instead shows that correctional education is more cost-effective than the direct costs of reincarceration—every dollar spent on education saves $4 to $5 on 3-year reincarceration costs (Davis et al., 2014). RAND's analysis of 71 effect sizes from 50 empirical studies indicated that correctional education programs have a positive impact on incarcerated adults. The 2013 RAND report included a meta-analysis of more than 30 years of previous research, which concluded that individuals participating in correctional education programs were, on average, 43% less likely to recidivate—commit future crimes that return them to prison (Davis et al., 2013). Research also indicates that incarcerated adults who participated in either academic or vocational/career and technical education programs upon release were 13% more likely to obtain employment than those who did not. Overall, the research conducted shows that "the debate should no longer be about *whether* correctional education is effective or *cost-effective* but rather on *where the gaps in our knowledge are and opportunities to move the field forward*" (Davis et al., 2014, p. iv, emphasis in original).

Furthermore, scholars such as Zamani-Gallaher and Fuller (2016) argue for the building of a new pipeline—the prison to school to society pipeline. Specifically, they argue for the increased role of community colleges as postsecondary education behind bars, which increases the employability rates postincarceration; results in lower recidivism rate; and, over time, costs the states less (Davis et al., 2014). A study found that for every $1 million invested in correctional education, nearly 600 crimes are prevented, in contrast to the 350 crimes prevented when funding incarceration only (Bazos & Hausman, 2004). Community colleges are a viable option for educational prison programming since they are often located in the same communities as prisons, which allows for ease of access by adult educators. Additionally, their affordability and open-door policies provide for meaningful and equitable educational experiences for incarcerated people (Zamani-Gallaher & Fuller, 2016).

Educational Attainment Levels of the Incarcerated Population

In spite of the long-standing debate about whether or not correctional education is effective and/or cost-effective, what is much harder to debate—given the alarming statistics—is the fact that the incarcerated adult population, on average, is less educated than the general population. For instance, 37% of individuals in state prisons have less than a high school education, compared with 19% of the U.S. general population. Only 16.5% of state prisoners possess a high school diploma (Davis et al., 2014) compared with 88% of the general population (Ryan & Bauman, 2016). The numbers indicate the inequitable educational attainment levels of the incarcerated population, and thereby point to the need for educational programming in the U.S. prison system.

Incarcerated individuals without a high school diploma have varied racial demographics: 27% of Whites, 44% of Blacks, and 53% of incarcerated Hispanics respectively do not possess a high school diploma or its equivalent (Davis et al., 2014). Research indicates young, Black men aged 20 years to 24 years old who do not possess a high school diploma (or an equivalent credential) have a greater chance of being incarcerated than of being employed (Neal & Rick, 2014). Also, the majority of incarcerated individuals without a high school diploma reported a disability: 59% reported a speech disability, and 66% reported a learning disability (Davis et al., 2014). Additionally, only 14.4% of state inmates have obtained a postsecondary education (Davis et al., 2014) compared with 58.9% of the U.S. adult population (Ryan & Bauman, 2016). The educational attainment levels of men and women in prisons are fairly equal up to obtaining a high school diploma or GED. However, women inmates are 27% more likely to have obtained some college or other postsecondary education compared to incarcerated men. Women inmates are also 35% more likely to be college graduates (Cogswell, 1994; Harlow, 2003).

Skills, Work Experience, Education, and Training of Incarcerated Adults

In 2016, the National Center for Education Statistics (NCES) of the U.S. Department of Education released a report titled the *Highlights from the U.S. PIAAC Survey of Incarcerated Adults: Their Skills, Work Experience, Education, and Training* (Rampey et al., 2016). The Program for the International Assessment of Adult Compentencies (PIACC) survey of incarcerated adults assessed competencies in the areas of literacy, numeracy, and technology use. It also explored these competencies across various demographics of the prison population, such as age, gender, race/ethnicity, health status, educational attainment level, learning disabilities, and parents' educational attainment level. The data were then compared to the general

U.S. household population. The survey found 29% of incarcerated adults have low literacy skills and 52% have low numeracy skills, compared to 19% and 29% respectively of the U.S. general population. However, less than 25% of incarcerated adults participate in secondary education programs, and far less participate in postsecondary programs (Rampey et al., 2016). Yet 70% of incarcerated adults, when surveyed, indicated a desire to advance their education (Crayton & Neusteter, 2008).

Variation in Correctional Education Programming Across the States

Most states offer adult basic education, GED courses, and vocational education/career technical education (CTE) programs, and most report having special education courses available. A small number of states, approximately 15, report offering correspondence courses. An emerging trend is the emphasis on vocational education that will lead to a nationally recognized industry certification. In fact, smaller states are more likely to emphasize vocational/CTE courses of study that lead directly to certification (Davis et al., 2014).

Adult secondary education and postsecondary education are offered in 32 states. In 23 states, postsecondary education is primarily paid for by the individual inmate or through family finances. State funding is used in 16 states, and 12 states report using college or university funds. In 24 states, participation in correctional education is mandatory for individuals who do not possess a high school diploma or GED. Smaller states are less likely to require mandatory participation (Davis et al., 2014).

Inmate Participation in Prison Education Programs

Participation in college-level courses, high-school equivalency, or postsecondary vocational classes is less common for those in correctional populations than for persons in the general population. While this might not be the case in all prisons, the RAND report indicated that almost 58% (three in five incarcerated adults) completed no further formal education beyond the level they had upon their entry into prison. In one study, when inmates were asked directly why they did not enroll in academic programs, 20% of inmates felt the programs offered at their facilities were either not useful or were of poor quality (Rampey et al., 2016).

Furthermore, approximately 21% (one in five) obtained a high school credential (a GED) during their current period of incarceration. Zero percent were listed as completing a bachelor's degree and 2% completed an associate degree, while 4% were listed as completing pre-associate education. A certificate from a college or trade school was completed by 7%, and 8% completed grades 7 to 9 (Rampey et al., 2016).

The research of Davis et al. (2014) provides comprehensive figures on the number of states offering educational programs to adult state prisoners. Table 22.1 summarizes the types of educational programs available to adult state prisoners.

TABLE 22.1. Number of States Offering Educational Programs to Adult State Prisoners, by Program Type

Type of Program	Number of States
Adult basic education	44
Adult secondary education	32
GED test preparation	44
Adult postsecondary education/college courses	32
Vocational skills training/CTE	44
English as a second language (ESL) courses	33
Special education	40
Other	17
Total states responding	46

Source: Davis et al. (2014).

Policy and Prison Education

Several legislative, social, and economic factors—alone and in combination—have created a challenging context for prison education going into the third decade of the 21st century. The impacts of the 2007 Second Chance Act, the 2008 economic recession, and the elimination of so-called Specter funds to finance prison education will be described. The impact of the Second Chance Pell Pilot program, which provided grants to prisoners for postsecondary education, has also been significant. Finally, the shift to computer-based testing has impacted prison education programs' budgets.

Impact of the Second Chance Act of 2007

The Second Chance Act of 2007, which became public law in 2008, and the Second Chance Reauthorization Act of 2018 amended the Omnibus Crime Control and Safe Streets Act of 1968. The purpose of the Second Chance Act was to reduce recidivism and provide grant assistance to states and communities to address the growing population of inmates returning to communities. Approximately 650,000 people are released each year from state and federal prisons, and approximately 9 million are released from jails; 95% of incarcerated adults are released back into their communities (Beck, 2006; Carson, 2018).

A series of historic programs stemmed from the one-time discretionary grant opportunities provided by the Bureau of Justice Assistance's Second Chance Act. One example was Promoting Reentry Success through Continuity of Educational Opportunities (PRSCEO). PRSCEO aimed to create an educational continuum by bridging the divide between community-based education/training programs and prison education programs. PRSCEO sought to address the chronic issue of ex-offenders' underemployment and to give those under community supervision educational based ways to spend their time. At the core of PRSCEO was the reentry education model.

In 2012, the Office of Career, Technical, and Adult Education (OCTAE) revealed its reentry education model, an evidence-based model designed to promote reentry success through the continuity of educational opportunities. "The model focuses on establishing a strong program infrastructure, strengthening and aligning correctional and reentry education services, and integrating education into the correctional system" (Erisman, 2015, p. xi). Grants were awarded to adult education providers at three sites, in Kansas, Pennsylvania, and Wisconsin.

Impact of the 2008 Recession on Prison Education

Often, prison programs are some of the most adversely affected during economic downturns. The RAND report documents that the 2008 recession and its long aftermath led to a reduction in spending on correctional education and a decrease in the number of incarcerated adults participating in educational programs. According to the RAND report, between the fiscal years 2009–2012, states reduced the number of course offerings for academic programs by an average of 6%. States with large prison populations cut program offerings by 10% on average. States with medium-sized populations cut funding by an average of 20% (Davis et al., 2014).

Impact of the Elimination of the Specter Funds

Beginning in 2011, Congress failed to renew federal funding for the Specter funds. The Specter funds, named for the late U.S. senator Arlen Specter, provided funding to finance higher education courses for prisoners. The funds had been provided through the Grants to States for Workplace and Community Transition Training for Incarcerated Individuals. The Supporting Knowledge and Investing in Lifelong Skills (SKILLS) Act—part of the legislation introduced in the U.S. House of Representatives in 2013—was designed to reform the nation's job training system. Known as H.R. 803, the Workforce Innovation and Opportunity Act (WIOA) amended the Workforce Investment Act (WIA) of 1998 and became law in 2014. It repealed the statue that authorized the Specter funds and replaced it with a different federal funding initiative for prison education.

Impacts of the 2014 GED Exam, the Use of Information Technology, and Computer-Based Testing

Beginning in 2014, the GED test was realigned to match Common Core State Standards, which eliminated the earlier pencil-and-paper exam version in favor of a computer-based test. Most prisons and jails that offer GED classes felt the effects of this particular change, given the technology and internet limitations within the confines of correctional facilities. Most incarcerated individuals are not allowed to use the internet in prisons, and most prisoners do not have access to computers. In fact, only 10% of incarcerated adults reported using a computer in their prison job assignments (Rampey et al., 2016). Additionally, the change required educators to prepare students to have a certain level of computer literacy, which had implications for agency budgets and presented a number of logistical concerns regarding preparing inmates to take a computer-based test.

Impact of the Second Chance Pell Pilot Program

Despite a period of contraction, there have been some watershed moments in the implementation of funding for prison education programs. In 2016, the launch of the Second Chance Pell Pilot initiative allowed eligible incarcerated individuals to receive Pell Grants—federal financial aid funding that had been denied to inmates since the passage of the 1994 Violent Crime Control and Law Enforcement Act or the "Crime Bill." Pell Grant eligibility for incarcerated individuals came to an end despite evidence that the program reduced recidivism rates (Ali, 2017). Around 1% of current Pell money ($30 million) was put aside for the first year of the 2-year pilot program. The pilot program had 67 prison schools participating with 12,000 inmates enrolled in over 100 prisons.

Current Issues and Challenges in Correctional Education

Significant challenges are present regarding the delivery of education programs in correctional institutions. These include a variety of barriers to prisoners' participation, including the limited resources available to prisons, the national trend to privatize prisons, and the many learning challenges that individual prisoners may present.

Barriers to Participation

One of the main challenges to prison education is the fact that every state has its own budget and criteria for deciding how to allocate funds when it comes to corrections, which means that when state corrections budgets get cut, there has been a trend of drastically reducing prison education programs.

The era of the 1980s and 1990s, which defined itself as "tough on crime," saw an emphasis of punishment over rehabilitation. This unfortunately set the precedent of cutting prison education classes. The 2008 recession resulted in considerable cuts to state budgets and these cuts were felt in prison classrooms for years. For instance, when California's state budget in 2009 was reduced by $1.2 billion, the state opted to cut corrections education programming by 30%, which resulted in the loss of 712 prison education teachers. Texas in 2011 opted to cut its corrections education budget by an average of 27%, which resulted in the loss of 271 prison teachers (Davis et al., 2013). Fortunately, recent efforts such as the Second Chance Pell Program have expanded prison education efforts. Yet, in uncertain times, states opt to reduce correctional education in response to the cuts they face.

Limited Resources, Learning Challenges, and Privatization

Budget cuts, reduction in teaching personnel, and changes to the computer-based GED test are all examples of resource limitations that impact the number of prison education programs offered. Learning challenges include lower levels of educational attainment among prisoners, lower literacy and numeracy skills of inmates, higher rates of learning difficulties, prevalence of mental health illnesses, and a high rate of addiction among prisoners.

As reported earlier, 68% of state prison inmates have not completed high school (Harlow, 2003). As indicated in the PIACC report, 29% of U.S. prisoners perform below Level 2 in literacy, while 52% of U.S. prisoners perform below Level 2 in numeracy (Rampey et al., 2016). According to the U.S. Department of Justice's Bureau of Justice Statistics, 56% of state prisoners and 45% of federal prisoners have symptoms of a serious mental health illness (James & Glaze, 2006). Research found that 65% of all U.S. inmates meet the medical criteria for substance abuse addiction, while only 11% receive any treatment (CASAColumbia, 2010).

The privatization of prisons is another variable to consider. While the number of U.S. inmates housed in private facilities is less than 10%, the U.S. Department of Justice Statistics indicated that the Bureau of Prisons had 21,366 inmates held in 12 privately run facilities (Zapotosky, 2017). Research indicates that the privatization of prisons results in an even greater lack of transparency and accountability (Headley & Garcia-Zamor, 2014).

In early 2017, the Justice Department rescinded the directive that had been put in place a year earlier directing the Bureau of Prisons to end the use of private prisons by phasing them out over time. A report by the Department's Office of Inspector General found that private prisons do not save significantly on costs, nor do they provide the same level of correctional services, resources, or programs as public prisons. Additionally, private prisons do not maintain the same level of safety and security, incurring more assaults—both by inmates on other inmates and by inmates on staff (Zapotosky, 2017).

Discussion, Conclusion, and Implications

Given the current and historic situation of prison education in the United States, where do we go from here? How do adult educators create equitable and meaningful learning opportunities in a resource-constrained prison environment? What role if any can informal learning play in corrections education? What are the emerging trends and opportunities?

To recap, the results of the meta-analysis conducted by Davis et al. (2013) and Davis et al. (2014) shows that correctional education programs are both highly cost-effective and effective at reducing recidivism rates. For every dollar spent on correctional education, $4 to $5 are saved on 3-year reincarceration costs. The study's key finding is that correctional education is dramatically effective in reducing rates of recidivism and indicate that there is some evidence that educational programs, especially vocational education/CTE programs improve individuals' likelihood of postrelease employment. There is less certainty on the effectiveness of correctional education for juveniles given the knowledge base is so thin, but there are still some practices that are clearly promising.

Davis et al. (2014) also concur with MacKenzie's (2008) assessment that the research findings still have not sufficiently gotten inside the so-called black box of what works in correctional education to answer questions about what dosage is associated with effective programs and how does it vary across the different types of students and academic programs, what models of instruction and curriculum delivery (e.g., one-on-one, classroom lectures, computer-based learning) are the most effective, who benefits most from different types of correctional education programs, and what principles of adult learning and adult education may be applicable to correctional education (Davis et al., 2014).

Overall recommendations from the literature include:

- Focus research and evaluation efforts on illustrating different instructional models with the goal of getting inside the "black box"
- Evaluate programs that are trying innovatively to implement technology and distance learning in prison classrooms
- Conduct new research on instructional quality
- Allow for federal monitoring and assessment of the impact of the new GED test on correctional education outcomes
- Provide technical assistance to help educators teach more rigorous content
- Provide an analysis of what lessons from the larger literature on adult education may be applied to correctional education

Additionally, it is important to continue to grapple with the question of how adult educators can work within and against the prison-industrial complex while concurrently creating equitable and meaningful learning opportunities for incarcerated adults (Chevigny, 1999; Chlup, 2017; Hartnett et al., 2013; Jackson & Meiners, 2010). Hartnett (2011) argues the way to challenge the prison-industrial complex is through activism, arts, and educational alternatives. Alexander (2011) and Sohnen (2011) claim that classrooms in prisons foster educational goals and creative pursuits throughout prisons, thereby changing the environment and prison culture. Berman & Adler (2018) offer a road map for how to reduce the number of people sent to jail and prison in the first place. Their innovative work highlights successful programs across the country that involve the public in preventing crime, treat defendants with dignity and respect, and link individuals to effective community-based interventions rather than incarcerating them.

Adult educators are often looking for tested paths toward action. Unfortunately, in the punishment-driven society that spurs the U.S. prison system, it is often hard to see the ideological and practical framework for empowering and educating prisoners as opposed to incarcerating them. Like the hammer and anvil pounding out the long days of a prison sentence, it is easy to get stuck and encumbered in old ways of thinking. Yet there is much to encourage us to think again about prison education and to offer clear-eyed alternatives that emphasize working directly with incarcerated people and their communities. The last decade has seen emerging trends and opportunities, such as the historic legislation of the Second Chance Act and the publication of the RAND reports on the effectiveness of correctional education. It is necessary to continue in this vein to work with and for the humanity of incarcerated people when we recognize that there are roughly 8 million men and women under the supervision of the U.S. correctional system. We owe it to each other to continue considering this major social issue of our democracy. In this way, corrections education can live up to the perspective that the field of adult education can improve not just the lives of incarcerated individuals, but their families, their communities, and society at large.

References

Alexander, B. (2011). "A piece of the reply": The prison creative arts project and practicing resistance. In S. J. Hartnett (Ed.), *Challenging the prison-industrial complex: Activism, arts, & educational alternatives* (pp. 149–178). University of Illinois Press.

Alfred, M. V., & Chlup, D. T. (2009). Neoliberalism, illiteracy, and poverty: Framing the rise in Black women's incarceration. *The Western Journal of Black Studies, 33*(4), 240–249.

Ali, D. (2017, September 22). *Pell Grants for prisoners: Considerations in the new administration*. NASPA Student Affairs Administrators in Higher Education. https://www.naspa.org/rpi/posts/pell-grants-for-prisoners-considerations-in-the-new-administration

Bazos, A. & Hausman, J. (2004, March). *Correctional education as a crime control program*. UCLA School of Public Policy and Social Research.

Beck, A. J. (2006, June 27). *The importance of successful reentry to jail population growth* [Paper presentation]. Urban Institute's Jail Reentry Roundtable, Washington DC, United States.

Beck, A. J. (2014). *Sexual victimization in prisons and jails reported by inmates 2011–12: Supplemental tables*. U.S. Department of Justice, Office of Justice Programs, Bureau of Justice Statistics.

Berman, G., & Adler, J. (2018). *Start here: A road map to reducing mass incarceration*. New Press.

Carson, A. E. (2018). *Prisoners in 2016*. U.S. Department of Justice, Bureau of Justice Statistics. https://www.bjs.gov/content/pub/pdf/p16.pdf

CASAColumbia. (2010). *Behind bars II: Substance abuse and America's prison population*. The National Center on Addiction and Substance Abuse at Columbia University.

Chevigny, B. G. (1999). *Doing time: 25 years of prison writing*. Arcade.

Chlup, D. T. (2005). The pendulum swings: 65 years of corrections education. *Focus on Basics, 7D*, 21–24.

Chlup, D. T. (2009). The right to write: Teaching creative writing to women inmates. In M. Miller & K. P. King (Eds.), *Empowering women through literacy: Views from experience* (pp. 27–35). Information Age.

Chlup, D. T. (2017). Critical points of resistance: Preparing adult educators to educate inside the U.S. prison system. *Dialogues in Social Justices: An Adult Educational Journal, 2*(2), 4–15.

Chlup, D. T. & Baird, I. (2010). Literacies from the inside: Learning from and within a culture of corrections. In M. V. Alfred (Ed.), *Learning for economic self-sufficiency: Constructing pedagogies of hope among low-income, low literate adults* (pp. 191–209). Information Age.

Cogswell, S. (1994). *Education behind bars: Opportunities and obstacles* (ED392942). Ohio Legislative Office of Educational Oversight. ERIC. https://eric.ed.gov/?id=ED392942

Correctional Officer. (2018). *The U.S. correctional system defined*. http://www.correctionalofficer.org/us-correctional-system

Crayton, A., & Neusteter, S. R. (2008). *The current state of correctional education*. John Jay College of Criminal Justice, Prisoner Reentry Institute.

Davidson, H. S. (1995). *Schooling in a "total institution": Critical perspectives on prison education*. Bergin & Garvey.

Davidson, H. S. (2000). Control and democracy in adult correctional education. In A. L. Wilson & E. R. Hayes (Eds.), *Handbook of adult and continuing education* (pp. 392–407). Jossey-Bass.

Davis, L. M., Bozick, R. Steele, J. L., Saunders, J., & Miles, J. N. V. (2013). *Evaluating the effectiveness of correctional education: A meta-analysis of programs that provide education to incarcerated adults*. RAND Corporation.

Davis, L. M., Steele, J. L., Bozick, R., Williams, M., Turner, S., Miles, J. N. V., Saunders, J., & Steinberg, P. S. (2014). *How effective is correctional education, and where do we go from here? The results of a comprehensive evaluation*. RAND Corporation.

Erisman, W. (2015). *Reentry education model implementation study: Promoting reentry success through continuity of educational opportunities*. U.S. Department of Education Office of Career, Technical, and Adult Education. https://www2.ed.gov/about/offices/list/ovae/pi/AdultEd/reentry-education-model-implementation-study.pdf

Federal Bureau of Prisons Statistics (2018a). *Inmate citizenship*. Federal Bureau of Prisons. https://www.bop.gov/about/statistics/statistics_inmate_citizenship.jsp

Federal Bureau of Prisons Statistics (2018b). *Inmate gender*. Federal Bureau of Prisons. https://www.bop.gov/about/statistics/statistics_inmate_gender.jsp

Gramlich, J. (2018). *The gap between the number of Blacks and Whites in prison is shrinking*. Pew Research Center. http://pewrsr.ch/2mwYQOI

Harlow, C. W. (2003, January, revised April 15). *Education and correctional populations*. Bureau of Justice Statistics Special Report. U.S. Department of Justice Office of Justice Programs. https://www.bjs.gov/content/pub/pdf/ecp.pdf

Hartnett, S. J. (Ed.). (2011). *Challenging the prison-industrial complex: Activism, arts, & educational alternatives*. University of Illinois Press.

Hartnett, S. J., Novek, E., & Wood, J. K. (Eds.). (2013). *Working for justice: A handbook of prison education and activism*. University of Illinois Press.

Headley, A., & Garcia-Zamor, J. (2014). The privatization of prisons and its impact on transparency and accountability in relation to maladministration. *International Journal of Humanities Social Sciences and Education, 1*(8), 23–34.

Jackson, J. L., & Meiners, E. R. (2010). Feeling like a failure: Teaching/learning abolition through the good the bad and the innocent. *Radical Teacher, 88*, 20–30.

James, D. J., & Glaze, L. E. (2006, September, revised December 14). *Mental health problems of prison and jail inmates*. Bureau of Justice Statistics Special Report. U.S. Department of Justice Office of Justice Programs. https://www.bjs.gov/content/pub/pdf/mhppji.pdf

Kaeble, D., & Cowhig, M. (2018). *Correctional populations in the United States, 2016*. Bureau of Justice Statistics. U.S. Department of Justice Office of Justice Programs. https://www.bjs.gov/index.cfm?ty=pbdetail&iid=6226

Klein, R. (1988, January). Molding a cry & a song: American prisoners as poet. *Commonweal, 115*, 14–18.

Knoll, M. (1984). An overture. In J. Bruchac (Ed.), *The light from another country: Poetry from American prisons*. The Greenfield Review Press.

MacKenzie, D. L. (2008). *Structure and components of successful education programs* [Paper presentation]. Reentry Roundtable on Education. http://www.educationjustice.net/home/wp-content/uploads/2012/09/Mackenzie-2008.pdf

Neal, D., & Rick, A. (2014). *The prison boom and the lack of Black progress after Smith and Welch* (Working Paper 20283). National Bureau of Economic Research. http://www.nber.org/papers/w20283

Pew Charitable Trusts (2010). *Collateral costs: Incarceration's effect on economic mobility*. The Pew Charitable Trusts.

Rampey, B. D., Keiper, S., Mohadjer, L., Krenzke, T., Li, J., Thornton, N., and Hogan, J. (2016). *Highlights from the U.S. PIAAC Survey of incarcerated adults: Their skills, work experience, education, and training: Program for the international assessment of adult competencies: 2014* (NCES 2016-040). U.S. Department of Education. National Center for Education Statistics. http://nces.ed.gov/pubsearch.

Ryan, C. L., & Bauman, K. (2016). Educational attainment in the United States: 2015. *Current population reports*. U.S. Census Bureau.

Sohnen, R. (2011). Each one reach one: Playwriting and community activism as redemption and prevention. In S. J. Hartnett (Ed.), *Challenging the prison-industrial complex: Activism, arts, & educational alternatives* (pp. 181–200). University of Illinois Press.

U.S. Census Bureau (2015, September). *U.S. Census Bureau: State and county quick facts*. U.S. Census Bureau.

Walker, J. (2015). *Unlocking minds in lockup: Prison education opens doors*. Plicata Press.

Walmsley, R. (2015). *World prison population list*. Institute for Criminal Policy Research.

X., M. (1964). *The autobiography of Malcolm X*. Ballantine Books.

Zamani-Gallaher, E. M., & Fuller, K. (2016). *Altering the pipeline to prison and pathways to postsecondary education* (ED574524). Office of Community College Research and Leadership. https://files.eric.ed.gov/fulltext/ED574524.pdf

Zapotosky, M. (2017, February 23). Justice department will again use private prisons. *The Washington Post*. https://www.washingtonpost.com/world/national-security/justice-department-will-again-use-private-prisons/2017/02/23/da395d02-fa0e-11e6-be05-1a3817ac21a5_story.html?utm_term=.d550a35f8a73

CHAPTER 23

Workforce Development

Past, Present, and Future

Ellen Scully-Russ and Ximena Vidal De Col

The relationship between education and skill on the one hand, and labor market outcomes on the other, is a topic of debate in the labor market literature. Research shows that, although work has become more knowledge-intensive (Carnevale et al., 2010), lower-skilled jobs are among the fastest growing in the United States (Kalleberg, 2011). Regardless of their education and skill level, however, all workers are vulnerable to new economic forces that can wipe out or relocate their jobs, virtually overnight. Amid this intense labor market instability, many communities are investing in the knowledge and skill of the workforce to build new capacity to withstand rapid economic change. Workforce development, once considered a second-chance employment and training system for adults poorly served by primary and secondary education (Giloth, 2004), has emerged as a strategic imperative in the 21st-century economy. Communities now seek ways to encourage and support lifelong learning for all adults.

Certainly, as the demand for workforce development programs expands beyond the populations traditionally served, stakeholders, including educators, community leaders, and—most importantly—industry leaders must reexamine their responsibilities and commitments to advancing the skills and competence of the entire workforce. The field of adult education, inherently related to workforce development programs, may also need to revisit its technical and political role and possible influence. At a broad level, the field of adult education may need to refresh its mission, theories, and practices to contribute to the development of effective workforce programs for workers at all wage and skill levels.

Indeed, many adult educators are contributing to the reformulation of policies and institutions to support lifelong learning in a rapidly changing society and economy. However, their efforts are not without controversy in the field as some scholars and practitioners are highly critical of efforts to align adult education to workforce needs on the grounds that it commodifies education and narrows its scope to the skills required for work. Under these conditions, it is argued, education is limited to those with the resources to access it. Rather than equalizing society, the unequal distribution of educational opportunity contributes to rising inequality in society (Grubb & Lazerson, 2005).

While we acknowledge these historical critiques, we also recognize the rich stream of adult education research and practice focused on understanding and responding to adult career and workplace learning interests and needs. The central premise of this chapter is that these practices, as well the resistance to them, need to be reexamined and leveraged in new ways to ensure a robust workforce development system that can deliver quality programs as well as develop new opportunity structures in the labor market. A more aligned workforce development system would also ensure all adults with access to lifelong learning that can also provide a measure of labor market stability in a turbulent economy.

The chapter begins with a summary of the current and emerging workforce development framework for the 21st-century economy primarily in the United States, pointing out issues of equity and certain challenges in addressing the learning needs of adults in and excluded from the workforce. Next is a discussion of how educators can leverage public investments in the workforce to support lifelong learning and foster greater social equity. Last are the implications for adult education theory, research, practice, and policy.

Workforce Development Framework: Purpose, Institutions, and Systems

Workforce development in the United States is a fragmented system consisting of multiple institutions responsible to enact public and private sector policies and programs that provide workers with skills and connect them to jobs (Jacobs & Hawley, 2009). Although hampered by the fragmented policy and program landscape, the historical mission of the system is to advance both economic and social goals of a community by preparing adults for meaningful employment, career advancement, and social mobility (Torraco, 2007). In the past, the focus of the system was to respond to the needs of groups facing barriers to employment, such as low-skilled workers, ex-offenders, youth-at-risk, and others, to prepare them and connect them to jobs. In this system, employed workers turned to employers for training, which was provided through structured internal training programs and, in many cases, supported by other incentives for trained workers to remain with the employer and gain the skills necessary to perform in higher level jobs (Lerman, 2015).

Today, as more employers adopt flexible and contingent work arrangements (Cappelli, 2012), their investments in workers' training and development has declined (Waddoups, 2016). At the same time, the focus of employer-provided training has narrowed to the skill needs of workers in key talent pools (Boudreau & Ramstad, 2005; Cappelli, 2008), leaving others with limited access to valuable training. These shifts in employers' training investments have had the effect of socializing the cost of broad workforce development for many workers once served by employer-sponsored trainings. Public systems now must stretch to help an increased number of people in need, while innovating workforce planning processes to anticipate and respond to the skill demands in rapidly changing occupations.

Systems in and Across Workforce Development

Historically, the U.S. workforce development system comprises a loosely coupled network of labor market institutions and systems of scholarship and practice (Schrock, 2014) that determine the nature of jobs and the quality and availability of the education and training in the community. The system, which is largely fragmented (Holland, 2016; Schrock, 2014) has been critiqued for its disjointed, irrelevant, and ineffective programs (Giloth, 2004) and incoherent institutional structures and processes. Recent economic and policy trends have prompted a tighter coupling among labor market institutions (Pittman & Scully-Russ, 2016) and more alignment of the policies and programs sponsored by the once-separate domains.

The broad sets of institutions and systems that constitute the workforce development system include the public employment and training (ET) system, the systems of career and technical education (CTE), and the human resource development (HRD) systems that operate within and across firms in a local economy (Schrock, 2014). Practitioners and researchers in each system approach workforce development differently, according to their distinct institutional priorities (Schrock, 2014). The ET system largely consists of publicly funded programs that address the needs of disadvantaged and dislocated workers in finding and maintaining employment. CTE systems, on the other hand, focus on providing job skills, while HRD systems approach workforce development from organizational and sociological perspectives (Schrock, 2014). However, as will be explained, each system comprises more than programs and activities.

In the past, these institutions and systems of practice operated independently, even though they have a common concern for the workforce skill and in some cases were focused on the needs of similar groups. This disjointed service framework created ineffacies and redundancies, leaving many worker and industry needs unmet. A common thread in recent research, policy, and practice is to create a systemic view of these once-separate workforce development systems to more tightly align and coordinate efforts to produce more efficient and impactful outcomes for workers, employers, and communities. This systemic approach captures the complex interrelationship of internal and external variables that include public and private sector programs and services, social and economic policies at different government levels, as well as institutions, processes, frameworks, and strategies that work better when aligned with each other in and across the domains. A systemic understanding of workforce development also considers the skills, education, and social economic disadvantages and opportunities of workers (see Gray & Paryono, 2004, p. 23, for a conceptual model of workforce education and development; Schrock, 2014).

Employment and Training System
In the United States, the Workforce Innovation and Opportunity Act (WIOA) of 2014 forms the core of the public workforce development system. This legislation extended many of the system's functions as established by the original workforce development act, the Economic Opportunity Act (EOA) of 1964, and of its subsequent versions. Although the WIOA preserves the dual-customer—the employers and job seekers—approach of past workforce development systems, it departs from past policies in several ways, most notably by its greater emphasis on employer engagement and new investments in strategies to track and respond to emerging skill gaps in the labor market (Holland, 2016). To this end, the act enables new public investments in customized, on-the-job training and wage subsidies (Barnow & Spaulding, 2015) and the development of industry-led skill standards to drive new curriculum and certifications across the CTE enterprise (Spaulding, 2015). These and other efforts to align the system with the needs of industry are reshaping the public system to reinforce its focus on employment by shoring up its relationship to the demand side of the labor market. Still, this shift has consequences on the individual level that need to be closely examined, as will be discussed further.

While the Workforce Investment Act (WIOA) of 1998 carries forward the goal of its predecessors—the EOA and WIA—of improving employment preparation and opportunities, its funding has steadily decreased (Jacobson, 2017). According to the National Skills Coalition, the federal government has decreased its financial support for adult education by 20% over the past 2 decades (National Skills Coalition, 2018). Additionally, although the 2016 federal budget for adult education is 31 times as large as the 1965 budget and serves 42 times the number of students, it spent 90% less per student in 2016 than it did in 1965 (Jacobson, 2017).

The WIOA, although funded through national legislation, is administered through a network of state and local workforce development boards, consisting of representatives from industry, education, and the community who are appointed by the governor and local officials. These boards are responsible for conducting labor market research, setting priorities for the system, and overseeing state and local programs. While this decentralization grants flexibility for boards to meet local and state workforce development needs, its noted lack of guidance leaves WIOA stipulations up to interpretation by each board (Jacobson, 2017). This ambiguity, therefore, can result in different curricula that may or may not meet the needs of the most vulnerable and can impact workers' mobility across states. The risk of neglecting the needs of those who face the most barriers to employment is heightened by the new law's requirement that local businesses comprise two thirds of the board. The law also calls for the removal of the previous legislation's requirement that representatives from the labor organizations and adult education sector be members of the board (Holland, 2016; Jacobson, 2017). The exclusion of the latter from boards exacerbates the already historically low prioritization of adult education in workforce development planning (Jacobson, 2017).

In addition to sponsoring ongoing job training, retraining, and support services, local boards and other institutional actors in the broader workforce system are making new investments to improve the effectiveness and efficiency of the local skill formation and job matching functions. For example, new workforce intermediary structures (Conway & Giloth, 2014) have emerged to align training to skill gaps in growing industries and connect workers to training and jobs. Workforce intermediaries can take the form of a variety of organizational structures, such as formal partnerships, local organizations, or public agencies, to name a few. Overall, workforce intermediaries coordinate the efforts of a variety of public and private sector organizations and attempt to deeply engage employers to foster innovation in the planning and development of workforce development programs. A largely shared critique of this approach is that it targets high growth and value-added industries and occupations, leaving other sectors without a broad, holistic strategy to address skills mismatches and other labor market dysfunctions (Conway & Giloth, 2014).

Another key element of the U.S. workforce institutional framework are American Job Centers, once known as local One-Stop employment centers (Nightingale & Eyster, 2018). These centers integrate the resources of a variety of state-level employment security agencies and local service providers to offer job seekers access to publicly available employment data, case-management and job-matching services, and basic and job-related education and training. However, only a small portion of the centers' clients get referred to degree- or certificate-granting training programs. Reflecting the broader systemic work-first philosophy, a significant portion of the funding for these programs is tied to performance on job placement targets, or the number of learners placed in jobs. Although the WIOA expanded previous legislations' support for people with disabilities, veterans and their spouses, and other people who face barriers to employment (e.g., ex-offenders, low-income individuals, single parents, among others) (Eyster & Nightingale, 2017), the new performance metrics lead programs to enroll those with the fundamental skills to succeed, while marginalizing those that need the most support in entering and staying in the workforce (Pickard, 2016).

Another major area of investment and reform is in new, robust labor market information systems to provide timely and accurate data on both the supply (knowledge, skills, and credentials of the workforce) and demand (employer skill requirements) (Giloth, 2004). Occupation information systems such as O*NET, sponsored by the U.S. Department of Labor/Employment and Training Administration, support the work of the American Job Centers, and provide information that informs policy and the contents of CTE programs. Technical advancements in the areas of big data and artificial intelligence will likely influence the future direction and power of these systems.

CTE

The primary focus of workforce institutions and domains is on the development of the basic and career and technical skills of the workforce. Historically, the CTE system focused on preparing non-college-bound youth to enter a trade or industry job. Now, as employment and income security require continuous education, this system has expanded to include a focus on the lifelong learning and retraining of adults. In recent decades, the institutional locus of this domain has shifted from high school to community colleges with the capacity to offer a dynamic combination of postsecondary degree and certificate programs, noncredit continuing education, and contract-based customized training for employers.

The Federal Perkins Career and Technical Education Act, reauthorized in 2018, plays a measured role in funding the broader CTE system but has had an oversized influence in shaping the structure and direction of this system. This is because the federal government, through Perkins, has invested in myriad of initiatives, including the new career pathways model that is realigning the CTE curriculum to link education and training in high school to postsecondary and degree credentials in community colleges and 4-year colleges and universities. The idea is to make it easier for learners to move from one level of education to the next and from school to work to earn degrees and advance in their careers.

Adult basic education (ABE), which receives its funding from local workforce development boards, is also being integrated into the career pathways framework. As ABE aligns more closely with public ET and CTE programs, adult education is increasingly framed as work preparation (Belzer & Kim, 2018). ABE programs are now also held to job placement metrics and performance outcomes and give preference to students who are more likely to achieve the new target outcomes (Eyster & Nightingale, 2017), rather than providing incoming low-scoring students with the necessary scaffolding to achieve literacy competency and educational growth (Pickard, 2016).

CTE curriculum tends to be highly technical, preparing learners for middle-skilled jobs—those jobs requiring education and training beyond high school but less than a college degree (Holzer & Lerman, 2007). The community college is a key pivot point in this emerging continuum of education, for its credentials connect the foundational education provided in high school to the technical education and training required for many high-growth occupations and fields of practice. In addition to building new connections across the continuum of education, many community colleges are building new strategic relationships with the workforce boards, American Job Centers, as well as public economic development agencies and local businesses, positioning them as a central actor in the preparation and career advancement of the workforce (Hughes & Karp, 2006).

The recent reauthorization of Perkins V in 2018 continues the trend toward aligning the ET and CTE systems at the state and local level. For example, the new provisions permit the integration of education and employment data within the state labor market information systems to improve workforce planning and labor market research, facilitate the alignment of performance measures related to labor market outcomes of programs across the two systems, and expand investments in industry partnerships and new career pathways.

Adult educators and others caution against trends that tightly integrate all publicly sponsored ET, including ABE, into the emerging CTE system because of concerns that the emphasis on workforce preparation will divert attention and resources once devoted to supporting the developmental needs of disadvantaged learners and underserved communities. Adults previously underserved by education, specifically those with limited foundational skills that enable continuous learning, are not receiving the basic education support they require to obtain and maintain a good job in a workforce development system dominated by the needs of the economy and labor market.

Firm-Based HRD
The HRD practices of firms is another, often overlooked, domain of workforce development, particularly in the United States, which has long lacked an industrial policy to influence the human resources practices in private firms. Instead, individual firms have been left to construct an internal labor market, including the nature and structure of work, wage classifications, qualifications and skill requirements for jobs, and policies and practices governing the internal training and mobility of workers. In the past, the internal labor market and associated HRD strategies aligned the size and capacities of the workforce with the performance needs of the firm, while assuring some workers with job stability and career advancement opportunities in the workplace.

Today, economic and technological shifts provide opportunities for firms to innovate the way work is organized and conducted. Work locations, structures, and processes can change seemingly overnight and in unexpected ways. One impact of these trends is the segmentation of the labor market (Scully-Russ, 2005). Today many firms maintain a lean primary labor market that offers high wages and continuous learning opportunities and a secondary one where wages are low and jobs are both routine and contingent. Firms will often make significant investments in the career experiences and the training and development of workers in the primary labor market (Cappelli, 2012), and these workers enjoy career opportunities across an industry as either permanent workers or expert contracted labor.

In addition, employer investment in the skills of the primary workforce is largely focused on the development of employees already in higher-level positions. A 2018 report on learning and training initiatives in organizations found that businesses prioritize managerial and supervisory skills (13% of the employer training initiatives) and dedicate less than 1% of their learning budget to basic skills (Association for Talent Development, 2018). Of the employer training delivery methods available, on average 53% of employer training hours were delivered live in an instructor-led face-to-face classroom setting. When considering other instructor-led delivery methods, such as virtual classrooms (9%) and non-online remote classrooms (5%), the percentage of instructor-led training rises to 67%. Education and training in organizations also takes place through self-paced methods (29%), as well as non-computer-based learning (less than 1%), the latter experiencing a quick rate of obsolescence.

While workers with education credentials in the primary labor market are more likely to have access to employer-provided training, workers in the secondary labor markets are not well served by employer training. Because many of these workers conduct routine work that is typically low-waged and contingent, the return on investment in training cannot be justified by many employers. The impact is that these workers are increasingly disadvantaged and marginalized because they cannot leverage their experiences and develop new skills required to find good jobs or advance in a career (Cappelli, 2012).

Another fallout of these trends is the diminishing returns to investments in conventional approaches to workforce planning and development both within and across firms. Internally, codified and static classifications, skill standards, and structured training programs cannot hold up to this rapid change, as the number of jobs and nature of work are moving targets. In addition, employers are reluctant to invest in training for workers in jobs they may change or eliminate or who may choose to leave for opportunities outside the firm. Externally, workers cannot easily leverage firm-specific skills for new jobs or career advancement in growing occupations or firms. Workers who lack access to systematic and continuous education in broad knowledge domains and skill sets are at increased risk of long-term unemployment or underemployment (Schrock, 2014).

The public policy imperative is to enact what Schmitt (2011) calls *active labor market policies* to influence firms' internal HRD policies and practices. These policies would encourage or require the provision of incentives and/or tariffs to secure employer investments in a new workforce development system. The system could provide all workers with the continuous education and transition support, such as income security, they need to navigate more frequent labor market disruptions. On the demand or job side, these policies would lead employers to craft new value-added, skilled jobs that provide meaningful work and support a high degree of learning and skill formation on the job (Appelbaum, 2012).

The new workforce intermediaries, career pathways model, and efforts to align publicly sponsored education and training to the needs of jobs can be seen as attempts to fill widening gaps in opportunity structures in the emerging labor market. The long-term success of these initiatives rests, however, upon deep employer engagement and investment. There are several systemic barriers to employers rising to this challenge. First, the practices to plan and develop workforce development programs need to be updated and modernized to make public programs more nimble and responsive to quickly changing labor market needs (Pittman & Scully-Russ, 2016). Second, employers need to see value in partnering with workforce programs—research shows that employers find that engagement in public programs take too much time (Clymer, 2003). In addition, engagement in the public system often requires employers to adopt new behaviors that they may be reluctant to do so, such as collaborating with competitors in the development of curriculum and programs (Barnow & Spaulding, 2015) or hiring from the population groups targeted by public programs that they have not recruited from in the past.

Implications of Workforce Development for Adult Education and Educators

Schrock (2014) observed a new workforce development system emerging as the three workforce development systems or domains cross traditional boundaries to coordinate and align policies and programs. The career pathways model, for example, is expanding the focus of the ET system's basic skills development and job placement for disadvantaged populations to the upward mobility potential of jobs in the community. In other words, the ET domain is branching out to also consider issues of job quality—once the purview of the HRD domain. In turn, the HRD domain, pressured by skills and labor market gaps, is looking to the ET domain to build new sector partnerships that, in turn, make the public ET more responsive to the needs of industry and the workforce. Finally, the CTE domain is branching out beyond its historic focus on vocational skills to develop new relationships with employers and community groups to promote and support continuous education and lifelong learning among adults.

There are challenges to expanding and modernizing the workforce development system and making it more accessible and equitable, as well as broadening its offerings to ensure adults have access to broad educational opportunities that support their personal and career development. As we discuss in this section, adult educators can help to address these challenges through more active engagement in shaping workforce policy and developing programs.

The alignment of the public workforce development system to the needs of industry, and in particular efforts to eliminate developmental support and narrow training to the requirement of jobs is a controversial move for some adult education scholars and practitioners. However, it is very risky for the field to resist full engagement in a more tightly aligned workforce development system. Labor market data show that, although 63% of U.S. adults with lower skills are employed, 40% of these workers have incomes at the bottom fifth of the wage spectrum and many report higher levels of unemployment, which further diminishes their lifetime earnings. Further studies

(Bernhardt, 1999; Grusky & MacLean, 2016) have shown that workers with lower skills and diminished earnings can easily get caught up in a vicious cycle of marginalization; disadvantage builds or accumulates due to a continued lack of access to the education and experiences needed to develop and maintain skills, advance in a career, and experience a large measure of social mobility. The data also show that this is a structural problem for disadvantaged groups. Older persons, women, and Blacks and Hispanics are more likely to fall into the underprepared labor pools (St. Clair, 2015) primarily because they lack access to valuable knowledge and skills.

Adult educators' extensive expertise in responding to the learning needs of adults is essential but insufficient in addressing these and other structural gaps. Also required is a new activist agenda to influence the public workforce development system and employer organizational and human resources policies and practices. Adult educators may possess untapped power in a new knowledge economy that has grown more reliant on the competencies of the workforce. The field needs effective strategies to leverage its position to create innovative training programs, while also building new opportunity structures in a changing economy to ensure education equity for all adults.

A key leverage point for adult education to garner influence in the emerging system, according to Hake (2003), is located in the workforce intermediaries that are intentionally designed to link ET and CTE and to align workforce development programs with the needs of employers. As discussed, these partnerships work with employers to determine skills standards and then coordinate ET and CTE to deliver programs to the industrial sector in the region. These partnerships are also likely to provide HRD consulting to firms on issues of internal training, work organization, and job design to ensure the organization is positioned to make use of workers' new skills and capabilities and to develop internal programs to support continuous learning and reskilling. Hake (2003) observed that these partnerships also include educators, unions, community groups, and philanthropy organizations who share responsibility for the content and quality of the education and training available through the workforce development system. So, ironically, as these partnerships align education and workforce development with business interests, they also open the system to the influence of a range of community stakeholders. There is opportunity for adult educators to leverage their work in these partnerships to broaden programs and make education more responsive to learners (Hake, 2003) and to also influence employer labor market policies and practices.

Sector partnerships follow the career pathways model to program development; it is the central mechanism for articulating education content and credentials across all levels of education—and purportedly for also aligning education to the occupational requirements in the sector. By intent, career pathways are a series of credentials to connect education to work in ways that allow people to work and learn as they move across firms to advance in a career (Scully-Russ, 2013). However, in many communities the dominant focus in the development of these pathways is on the education side of the labor market while the nature of work is largely ignored. Employers are still left to design jobs and to choose whether and how to align their internal hiring and promotional requirements to the credentials. Therefore, often, the model is not fully implemented. The model could be greatly improved if employers were encouraged, either through incentives or other means, to structurally realign jobs to enable the use of skills developed in pathways education and connect all jobs to a system of career ladders within and across firms to promote career advancement for workers.

Adult educators can leverage their efforts to develop career pathways to counter policies and practices that narrow education by using career pathways to structurally intervene into the workplace to upgrade jobs and create new opportunity structures. For example, educators should use their work in the partnership to develop deep insights into how the industry is changing and the impacts on the nature and structure of jobs. In particular, educators should focus on whether and how jobs are being upgraded or deskilled and the factors that employers consider, or should consider, in making consequential decisions about the structure and nature of work. Sector partnerships potentially expose educators to a number of firms and provide them the opportunity to compare HRD practices across the sector. This knowledge can then be leveraged to influence employers to align with the best practices in the region to gain or maintain a competitive advantage in both the labor and general market.

Once inside firms, educators should also work closely with those who are closest to the work—

workers, frontline supervisors, and unions—to develop an understanding of whether and how work design either mobilizes or thwarts the use of skills. Insights into the actual knowledge and skill demands of a job provide educators with credibility, as well as the information they can use to influence the structure of work on the job. Insight into the changing skill demands of work can also be leveraged to expand education programs to respond to a range of adult learning and development needs and interests.

Finally, a new spirit of labor market activism in adult education may be required to address gaps in the opportunity structures. To support these efforts, new research on the links between education, work, and opportunity in a changing economy is required to understand the structural conditions that cut some people off from valuable education and experiences, as well as from other people. In addition, educators must become more knowledgeable of the ET and CTE policies and structures in their state and local areas and develop new relationships within programs and industry to develop and pursue a reform agenda to broaden education.

Conclusion

As discussed throughout this chapter, there are strong trends and powerful interests serving to narrow education to meet the performance needs of industry, yet this outcome is not inevitable. Adult educators can work to expand the debate and the agenda if we also broaden our thinking and practices to take on an expanded role in the work and labor market experiences of adults. First, adult educators must understand the deep shifts in the economy and jobs and identify the structural gaps inside and between workplaces that make it so difficult for some groups to access the knowledge and skills required for labor market success. More important, adult educators need new strategies to leverage the education that is desired by employers to foster new human resource practices and investments to improve the quality of jobs and expand opportunity in firms and the economy. At stake in an effective workforce development system may be the nature of opportunity in a society that has grown more reliant on labor market participation for individual development, income security, and social cohesion. Therefore, we argue here that workforce development may be the significant social justice issue of our time.

References

Appelbaum, E. (2012). Reducing inequality and insecurity: Rethinking labor and employment policy for the 21st century. *Work and Occupations, 39*(4), 311–320.

Association for Talent Development (2018). *State of the industry*. ASTD DBA Association for Talent Development.

Barnow, B. S., & Spaulding, S. (2015). Employer involvement in workforce programs: What do we know? In C. Van Horn, T. Edwards, & T. Greene (Eds.), *Transforming U.S. workforce development policies for the 21st century* (pp. 231–264). W. E. Upjohn Institute for Employment Research Kalamazoo. https://www.kansascityfed.org/~/media/files/publicat/community/workforce/transformingworkforcedevelopment/book/transformingworkforcedevelopmentpolicies.pdf

Belzer, A., & Kim, J. (2018). We are what we do: Adult basic education should be about more than employability. *Journal of Adolescent and Adult Literacy, 61*(6), 603–608.

Bernhardt, A. (1999). *The future of low wage service jobs and the workers that hold them* (IEE Brief No. 25). Institute on Education and the Economy, Teachers College, Columbia University.

Boudreau, J. B., & Ramstad, P. M. (2005). Talentship, talent segmentation, and sustainability: A new HR decision science paradigm for a new strategy definition. *Human Resource Management, 44*(2), 129–136.

Cappelli, P. (2008, March). Talent management for the 21st century. *Harvard Business Review, 86*(3), 74–81.

Cappelli, P. (2012). *Why good people can't find jobs: The skills gap and what companies can do about it*. Wharton Digital Press.

Carnevale, A. P., Smith, N., & Strohl, J. (2010). *Help wanted: Projections of jobs and education requirements through 2018*. Georgetown University Center on Education and the Workforce.

Clymer, C. (2003). *By design: Engaging employers in workforce development organizations*. Public/Private Ventures.

Conway, M., & Giloth, R. P. (Eds.) (2014). *Connecting people to work: Workforce intermediaries and sector strategies*. The Aspen Institute. https://assets.aspeninstitute.org/content/uploads/2014/06/Final-Version-Connecting-People-to-Work.pdf

Eyster, L., & Nightingale, D. S. (2017). *Workforce development and low-income adults and youth: The future under the Workforce Innovation and Opportunity Act of 2014*. Urban Institute. https://www.urban.org/sites/default/files/publication/93536/workforce-development-and-low-income-adults_and-youth.pdf

Giloth, R. P. (2004). Introduction: A case for workforce intermediaries. In R. P. Giloth (Ed.), *Workforce intermediaries for the twenty-first century (pp. 1–30). Temple University Press.

Gray, K., & Paryono, P. (2004). A conceptual model of workforce education and development systems. In. J. W. Rojewski (Ed.), *International perspectives on workforce education and development* (pp. 17–42). Information Age.

Grubb, W. N., & Lazerson, M. (2005). The educational gospel and the role of vocationalism in American education. *American Journal of Education, 111*(3), 297–319. https://doi.org/10.1086/429112

Grusky, D. B., & MacLean, A. (2016). The social fallout of a high-inequality regime. *Annals of the American Academy of Political and Social Science, 663*(1), 33–52.

Hake, B. (2003, June). Fragility of the "employability agenda": Flexible life courses and the reconfiguration of lifelong learning. [Commissioned report]. *Making lifelong learning a reality: Emerging patterns in Europe and Asia* (pp. 3–51). International Institute for Education Planning, UNESCO.

Holland, B. (2016). Both sides now: Toward the dual customer approach under the Workforce Innovation and Opportunity Act in the United States. *Local Economy, 31*(3), 424–441. https://doi.org/10.1177/0269094216640476

Holzer, H. J., & Lerman, R. I. (2007, November). *America's forgotten middle-skill jobs: Education and training requirements in the next decade and beyond*. The Workforce Alliance. https://www.urban.org/sites/default/files/publication/31566/411633-America-s-Forgotten-Middle-Skill-Jobs.PDF

Hughes, K. L., & Karp, M. M. (2006). *Strengthening transitions by encouraging career pathways: A look at state policies and practices* (Community College Research Center Brief No. 30). Community College Research Center, Columbia University.

Jacobs, R. L., & Hawley, J. D. (2009). The emergence of "workforce development": Definition, conceptual boundaries and implications. In R. Maclean & D. Wilson (Eds.), *International handbook of education for the changing world of work* (pp. 2537–2552). Springer.

Jacobson, E. (2017). The workforce investment and opportunity act: New policy developments and persistent issues. *New Directions for Adult and Continuing Education, 2017*(155), 19–35.

Kalleberg, A. L. (2011). *Good jobs, bad jobs: The rise of polarized and precarious employment systems in the United States, 1970s to 2000s*. Russell Sage Foundation.

Lerman, R. I. (2015, June). Are employers providing enough training? Theory, evidence, and policy implications. In *Supply chain for middle-skill jobs: Education, training, and certification pathways* [Symposium]. National Academy of Sciences, Engineering, and Medicine. https://www.nationalacademies.org/event/06-24-2015/the-supply-chain-for-middle-skill-jobs-education-training-and-certification-pathways

National Skills Coalition (2018, August). *America's workforce: We can't compete if we cut*. https://www.nationalskillscoalition.org/resources/publications/file/Americas-workforce-We-cant-compete-if-we-cut-1.pdf

Nightingale, D. S., & Eyster, L. (2018). Results and returns from public investments in employment and training. In S. Andreason, T. Greene, H. Prince, & C. E. Van Horn (Eds.), *Investing in America's workforce: Improving outcomes for workers and employers: Vol. 3. Investing in systems for employment opportunity* (pp. 99–111). W. E. Upjohn Institute for Employment Research.

Pickard, A. (2016). WIOA: Implications for low-scoring adult learners. *Journal of Research and Practice for Adult Literacy, Secondary, and Basic Education, 5*(2), 50–55.

Pittman, P., & Scully-Russ, E. (2016). Workforce planning and development in times of delivery system transformation. *Human Resources for Health, 14*(56), 1–15. https://doi.org/10.1186/s12960-016-0154-3

Schmitt, J. (2011, May). *Labor market policy in the great recession: Some lessons from Denmark and Germany*. Center for Economic and Policy Research.

Schrock, G. (2014). Connecting people and place prosperity: Workforce development and urban planning in scholarship and practice. *Journal of Planning Literature, 29*(3), 257–271. https://doi.org/10.1177/0885412214538834

Scully-Russ, E. (2005). Agency versus structure: Path dependency and choice in low-wage labor markets. *Human Resources Development Review, 4*(3), 254–278. https://doi.org/10.1177/1534484305278349

Scully-Russ, E. (2013). Are green jobs career pathways a path to a 21st-century workforce development system? *Adult Learning, 24*(1), 6–13. https://doi.org/10.1177/1045159512467323

Spaulding, S. (2015). *The Workforce Innovation and Opportunity Act and child care for low-income parents: Opportunities and challenges under the new law*. Urban Institute. https://www.urban.org/sites/default/files/publication/64706/2000309-the-workforce-innovation_1.pdf

St. Clair, R. (2015). House of cards: Analyzing "making skills everybody's business." *Journal of Research and Practice for Adult Literacy, Secondary, and Basic Education, 4*(2), 37–42.

Torraco, R. (2007). Low-skilled adults in the United States: A case of human resource underdevelopment. *Human Resource Development Review, 6*(4), 343–352. https://doi.org/10.1177/1534484307308045

Waddoups, C. F. (2016). Did employers in the United States back away from skills training during the early 2000s? *ILR Review, 69*(2), 405–434.

CHAPTER 24

Military Education

Evolution and Future Directions

Sarah Cote Hampson and Nancy Taber

Military organizations must use education to improve personnel performance. However, military education is in fact far deeper and more complex than teaching people how to follow orders or perform in the drill square. In this chapter, we present a historical overview of military education in the United States, applying a critical feminist analysis to its current educational practices.

First, we discuss the various forms of education in which the U.S. military is engaged and distinguish *training* from *education*, parsing the evolution of U.S. approaches to professional military education (PME). Second, we apply Habermas's educational paradigms to the context of the military, discussing how the U.S. military has engaged in each of these changes in ways that are beginning to address diversity, decrease othering, and strengthen the cause of social justice as the U.S. Armed Forces move into an increasingly complex and dynamic future.

Defining (Adult) Education in the U.S. Military

Drawing on Nesbit's (2013) definition, *adult education* refers to "all the approaches, processes and activities having to do with the education of, and learning by, adults" (p. xiv). In applying this definition to military education, one can see how all forms of education taking place within the military—everything from very specific job training to officer training in large-scale strategy, to traditional academic training within military academies—are part of the military engaging in adult education. Yet there is a second part to Nesbit's definition that is also useful in focusing this chapter on one aspect of military education: professionalization. Adult education, Nesbit says, is also "the professional, practitioner, and scholarly commitment to . . . long-term educational and society development" (p. xx). Socialization and the process of defining what kind of a society we live in, therefore, is an important aspect of the adult education process.

In the military context, adult education plays a very particular role of socialization—or *professionalization*. In their 1957 book *Soldiers and Scholars: Military Education and National Policy*, Masland and Radway make a distinction between military training and military education in the following way:

> Training identifies instruction that is oriented to a particular military specialty and that is designed to develop a technical skill. . . . Education . . . implies instruction or individual study for the purpose of intellectual development and the cultivation of wisdom and judgment. It prepares a man [*sic*] to deal with novel situations. (as quoted in Simons, 2000, p. vii)

Military adult education, therefore, is about more than simply training members of the armed forces to do their daily jobs. Education in the military is an ongoing process of professionalization—of learning what it means to be a service member as well as how to serve. Throughout its history, the U.S. military's education of its service members has often had a mutually constitutive relationship with U.S. society—simultaneously reflecting society's approach to education and shaping education within the larger U.S. society.

Evolution of PME in the United States

The U.S. Department of Defense (DoD) employs more than 1.3 million active duty service personnel, and 826,000 National Guard and Reserve forces (U.S. DoD, n.d.). As the nation's largest employer, the DoD is also the largest provider of adult education, with an annual training budget of almost $9 billion (Office of the Under Secretary of Defense Comptroller/Chief Financial Officer, 2017). Military education includes everything from basic training for new recruits to graduate-level higher education for its more advanced officers, as well as technical skills training and foreign language training for more specialized personnel. Since World War II, the U.S. military has seen itself as necessarily responsible for the basic education of all of its members beyond training. Moreover, the need to improve and manage morale in times of major conflict has driven the development and reform of educational efforts throughout modern U.S. military history—through the 20th century to the present day.

Specialist training in the technical skills to operate weapons and basic training to instill order and a sense of common purpose have always been necessary components of large-scale militaries, and the newly founded U.S. military looked to Europe as an early model for its educational practices. West Point, the first of the military academies, founded in 1802 and the first institution to engage in PME, was modeled on the British and French military academies in existence at the time (Van Riper, 2016). West Point and, later, military schools such as Norwich University (founded in 1819) provided training and education, with a focus on practical skills such as engineering, for officers in both the professional military and state militia in the United States for much of the 19th century (Coulter, 2017). The purpose of these academies, however, largely reflected a commitment to educating military *leadership*, with the assumption that education was something reserved for the elites.

The systematic and formal education of enlisted service members emerged later in U.S. military history. According to Houle et al. (1947), the U.S. Army engaged in a formal literacy campaign during World War II in order to improve the ability of its members to receive and follow orders. These programs were designed specifically to prepare service*men* for the needs of modern warfare. Moreover, the War Department saw educational services as an important contributor to morale. Houle et al., for instance, cite a 1945 War Department memorandum, which states, "All armies now recognize the need for training the soldier's mind in order to protect his [*sic*] morale" (p. 28). During World War II, the authors report that between 1943 and 1945, approximately 10% of the U.S. Army was illiterate.[1] The Army (and the Navy, which had a similar program) placed these servicemen into special units, designed to make them ready for "regular training" that would allow them to be "warfare ready" (p. 189). It is estimated that approximately 84% of the over 300,000 men enrolled in the Army program graduated successfully to participate fully in the services.

After World War II, the Servicemen's Readjustment Act of 1944, otherwise known as the GI Bill, was enacted, allowing veterans of the war to enroll in 4-year colleges, certificate programs, and vocational training with the assistance of substantial government subsidies. A decade later, by 1954, more than 7.8 million former GIs (or half of all World War II veterans) had taken advantage of the benefits ("GI Bill—10 Years After," 1954). The popularity of this bill with returning service members did not wane; even after the Korean War–era bill offered more meager benefits, as much as 80% of Korean- and Vietnam-era veterans made use of their GI Bill benefits (Altschuler & Blumin, 2009). While the GI Bill is typically viewed as a benefit affording veterans a means of attaining a 4-year degree, these ongoing benefits are also applicable to multiple forms of adult and ongoing education. For instance, by 1952, six million veterans had used their GI Bill benefits to pursue vocational training (Giordano, 2009).

Also aimed at improving the effectiveness of American recruits, the U.S. Armed Forces Institute (USAFI) made literacy, college, and vocational courses available through correspondence (distance learning) until the program's termination in 1974 by Congress (Persyn & Polson, 2012). As part of its educational initiatives, USAFI developed a series of tests designed to measure the completion of 4 years of high school education, which became known as the General Educational Development (GED) tests and was adopted into U.S. civilian use to measure high school equivalency. Just as had been the intention for literacy training in World War II, these adult educational courses, initiated by the U.S. military, were seen as essential to maintaining the morale of the service members fighting in the long-running war in Vietnam.

As a result of the failures in Vietnam—significantly, the low morale of U.S. service members during and after the conflict—the DoD underwent a series of reorganization efforts, which included the 1986 Goldwater–Nichols Act, a law designed to encourage the branches to work more closely with one another. Interbranch cooperation was widely seen as one of the sore points of morale and inefficiency during the Vietnam conflict. Post-Vietnam, each of the branches of the U.S. military consolidated its efforts in forming centralized training commands, the oldest of which is the Army's Training and Doctrine Command (TRADOC), formed in 1973. From its inception, U.S. Army TRADOC (2003) was "built around training the individual soldier" (p. 3), and its early tasks included significant changes in the delivery of training from a more centralized method to a decentralized "systems approach" (p. 41) that would place the responsibility of training more with the individual units. These changes took into account developing adult educational andragogical pedagogies, which emphasized greater self-directed and problem-based learning activities (Persyn & Polson, 2012). Other branches followed suit over the intervening decades, with interoperability being a key feature of these commands' approaches to education.

Perhaps the best example of the most recent evolution in U.S. military adult education is the *Army Learning Concept for Training and Education 2020–2040* (ALC-TE). Released in 2017, and presaged by the 2015 Army Learning Concept, this document represents yet another attempt by the U.S. military to reshape its approach to the education of its members. The Army Learning Concept is a statement by TRADOC of the Army's systematic and ongoing approach to learning. In its foreword, the TRADOC commanding general, David G. Perkins, states: "The Army is a learning organization. Therefore, the Army's vision is to immerse soldiers and Army civilians in a progressive, continuous, learner-centric, competency-based learning environment from their first day of service" (U.S. Army TRADOC, 2017, p. iii). These changes came on the heels of drawn-out conflicts in Afghanistan and Iraq. They represent the Army (and the services as a whole) rethinking its approach to education as necessary to the morale and effectiveness of service members. It lays out its goal that "learners commit to continuous career-long learning to become adaptable, agile, innovative soldiers" (U.S. Army TRADOC, 2017, p. 7). However, the new approach also recognizes the value of "critical analysis" for fostering "innovative thinking":

> Education is largely defined through *cognitive* learning (defined as content knowledge and development of intellectual skills) and *affective* learning (defined as the manner in which people deal with things emotionally: values, motivations, attitudes, enthusiasms, feelings, appreciation), and fosters breadth of view, diverse perspectives, jointness, *critical analysis*, abstract reasoning, comfort with ambiguity and uncertainty, innovative thinking, and ethical reasoning, particularly with respect to complex, nonlinear problems. . . . Training and education are not mutually exclusive. (U.S. Army TRADOC, 2017, p. 10, emphasis added)

While there has long been a focus on skills training, morale building, and leadership development, the specific reference to critical analysis as a required capability for all service members is relatively new. Next, we use a Habermasian adult education lens to explore and problematize this multifaceted approach to education.

A Habermasian Adult Education Lens

Jürgen Habermas (1971), an educational theorist of the Frankfurt School, distinguished between three areas of knowledge or "types of knowing": analytic, hermeneutic, and critical. Analytic knowledge, such as that derived from the physical sciences, allows one to "know that," while hermeneutic knowledge, such as that derived from the humanities, allows one to "know how." Critical knowledge is "emancipatory" in nature. It allows one to "know why" and requires the practice of self-reflection. Plumb and Welton (2001), in their application of his work to adult education, distill these paradigms into three educational approaches: technical, humanistic, and critical. Each paradigm comes with its own sets of understandings and priorities that underlie decision-making and action. All three of these paradigms are required for members to competently, safely, and efficiently perform their jobs; understand how diversity, interpersonal relations, and leadership intersect with organizational culture; and learn to engage in critical thinking with a societal focus. We further describe these paradigms and apply them to military education.

Those educators who subscribe to the technical paradigm aim for "efficient control of an objectified reality" via the "transfer of knowledge and skills to students" (Plumb & Welton, 2001, p. 70). This matches Freire's (2000) description of banking education in which the educator deposits information into students' brains, who can withdraw and utilize it as needed. This paradigm is often found in the physical sciences, where there is a focus on measurement and objectivity. It is applied in ways that aim for efficient and effective results. In the military, the technical paradigm is found in competency-based skill education, such as learning how to fire a weapon, fly an aircraft, or repair a ship engine. In the U.S. military, education has been conducted under this paradigm in relation to military practical skills (Coulter, 2017), weapons and basic training (Van Riper, 2016), GED equivalencies (Persyn & Polson, 2012), and literacy improvement (Houle et al., 1947).

The humanistic paradigm aims to "establis[h] harmonious relations through understanding others" (Plumb & Welton, 2001, p. 71). This paradigm is often found in the humanities, with educators assisting learners to become "more ethical, more just and more humane" (Plumb & Welton, p. 72). Knowles's andragogical approach to self-directed learning and meaning-making for self-actualization fits here (Cranton, 2013). This paradigm is concerned with helping people to understand themselves and each other in order to work better together. It is found in military education that focuses on ethics, leadership, and antiharassment training. Examples of U.S. military education that is humanistic includes morale boosting (Houle et al., 1947), self-directed learning (Persyn & Polson, 2012), PME/leadership training (Van Riper, 2016), and sexual assault prevention education (U.S. DoD, 2014).

The critical paradigm is "undergirded by an interest in minimizing the distorting influences of power" (Plumb & Welton, 2001, p. 72). The goal of educators within this paradigm, often located in the critical social sciences, is for radical change in order to "overcome oppressive social relationships" (Plumb & Welton, p. 73). Freire's (2000) description of problem-posing education, with the self-reflection and social action of learners, fits here. There are a variety of theories that operate under this paradigm, such as transformative learning, critical race theory, queer theory, feminist theories, and postmodernism (Nesbit et al., 2013). This paradigm intersects with the military in a much more complex way than the technical and humanistic due to its culture and, therefore, warrants a more detailed discussion.

Militaries are based on hierarchy, obedience, discipline, and commonality (Soeters et al., 2006; Taber, 2020). These values and attributes are in contradiction to a paradigm that problematizes power, culture, and society. As Freire (2000) says, "No oppressive order could permit the oppressed to begin to question: Why?" (p. 86). Military education within the critical (and, often, humanistic; see Taber, 2005, 2007) paradigm is highly contested as it may be perceived as obstructing the core mission of the military: to defend the country (Taber, 2018, 2020). As Feinman (2000) argues, "the military is too important" (p. 40) in society and therefore must be critiqued and challenged. The U.S. military serves a democratic government and thus can only benefit from an educational approach that encourages critical organizational reflection to the betterment of the institution and the country. If a military is tasked with defending democracy, it must do so in ways that reflect the nation's democratic values, even if the military itself is not a democracy. The Civil Rights Act (1964) outlaws discrimination in American society. Polls demonstrate that Americans "dislike" these forms of oppression (Rohall et al., 2017a). Discrimination and oppression of women and other marginalized groups should therefore be concomitantly unacceptable in the military. For instance, as gender discrimination, sexual harassment, and sexual assault are linked, if women were treated equitably in the military, violence against them should decrease. Making such changes requires a critical social justice approach aimed at culture change.

Although the TRADOC definition of *education* cited previously includes the term *critical analysis*, it is—unsurprisingly, given the oppressiveness of military culture—more specifically based on analytic thinking than on an organizational or societal critique. However, aspects of a critical paradigm are creeping into the U.S. military in limited but important ways. Johnson-Freese (2012), in her thorough and critical examination of PME, notes several ways in which America's military academies must change in order to achieve a more adaptive work force. Notably, she calls out the general lack of academic freedom within the PME system. Johnson-Freese accepts that the limitations on academic freedom will necessarily look different in a war college than in a civilian institution (although we contend that limits on academic freedom inhibit higher learning and the search for knowledge), but argues that a greater degree of academic freedom for faculty is required in order to encourage the critique and reexamination of policy without fear of reprisal. Moreover, she notes that a more faculty-driven, rather than top-down, common curriculum, which dominates most of the PME system, is necessary to encourage the development of critical thinking skills. "If education and intellectual agility are the goals, then educators at PME institutions must create a curriculum that forces students to get over their predilection for certainty and comfort, and for black-and-white issues with clear answers" (Johnson-Freese, 2012, p. 124).

This transition toward a more critical approach may already be underway in some war colleges, according to Carter (2010), a professor of history at the U.S. Army Command and General Staff College (CGSC). Carter, a civilian, argues that, in his experience, "the military seeks to be an adaptive, self-correcting culture" (p. 181) where the development of critical pedagogies is possible. While Carter's experiences may indeed reflect a changing culture that embraces more criticality, it is still a far cry from the U.S. military's central educational paradigm, which remains largely technically based (Bruscino, 2010). Increased academic freedom at war colleges, however, may be one of the more straightforward ways to initiate questions of power into military education.

In a connected but somewhat different manner, Dietz and Schroeder (2012) discuss the need for "full-spectrum (holistic) critical thinking" (p. 29). They argue for "problem-based learning" (p. 38) that looks "outside of doctrine" (p. 37) to assist military members in thinking "critically and creatively about military interventions" (p. 39). Likewise, Cornell-d'Echert (2012) argues for the need for "adaptive thinking, individual initiative, [and] collective agility" (p. 25; see also Zacharakis & Van Der Werff, 2012, with respect to PME). While it is important to engage in this type of out-of-the-box and adaptive thinking, it is not designed to result in organizational cultural change in the way that a truly critical paradigm would be.

Other scholars note the importance of introducing an intentionally more diverse and intersectional lens to military education. Oler (2011), for instance, makes a strong case for the development of a comprehensive education program for U.S. forces on the history of Islam. In addition to being informative for those service members who are deployed to predominantly Muslim regions such as Iraq and Afghanistan, Oler also makes the case that this historical perspective will allow for service members to combat anti-Muslim narratives at home and abroad. The author notes, for instance, "teaching future policy makers about the Golden Age of Islam in particular will help prospective strategists recognize and counter assumptions that are rooted in anti-Muslim rhetoric, instead of historical fact" (p. 78).

Beyond curricular strategies aimed at improving critical thinking in the U.S. military, some scholars have pointed to the significance of an increasingly diverse population serving in the military for expanding the capacity of the forces to think innovatively. Rohall et al.'s (2017b) collection of essays on inclusion in the U.S. military, for instance, opens with an acknowledgment of the value of organizational diversity for limiting "groupthink" (p. 3) and allowing for "outside of the box" (p. 3) thinking. We would push this analysis even further, suggesting that ground-level leadership training, for instance at the noncommissioned officer level, include self-reflective education on intersectional and/or marginalized identities, as well as critical examinations of power relationships within units. Such critical self-reflection could lead to increased trust, self-knowledge, and communication among unit members. Scholarship on diversity demonstrates that group cohesion is not necessary for group performance, that group performance may be a better indication of group cohesion than vice versa (Mullen & Copper, 1994). For instance, in Canada, research demonstrates that the inclusion of women and LGBTQ+ members in the Canadian Armed Forces (CAF) has not negatively affected group cohesion (Belkin & McNichol, 2000/2001; Okros & Scott, 2015; Winslow & Dunn, 2002). Moreover, researchers have demonstrated that diversity leads to greater group performance in many circumstances (Herring, 2009). Given the ability for an increasingly diverse group to achieve greater performance, the possible effects of an increased criticality and inclusion on unit performance should not be underestimated.

Finally, we suggest that an increased commitment to critical pedagogical methods could transform U.S. military culture in positive ways, from a national security emphasis to a greater emphasis on *human* security (Enloe, 2016). The U.S. military prides itself on its ostensible commitment to protecting democratic values throughout the world. Yet, its human rights record even in more recent interventions, such as in Iraq and Afghanistan, points to cracks in its dedication to these values. The massacre of civilians in Kandahar, Afghanistan, by a U.S. Army staff sergeant and the abuse of prisoners at Abu Ghraib prison in Iraq (among others) scandalized the United States and the world, and may have even led to greater threats to U.S. national security (Bartone, 2008; Enloe, 2016). A greater emphasis on cultural competency and critical assessments of race, class, gender and other power structures (such as that proposed by Davis, 2009, in relation to the Canadian military), may lead the U.S. military to develop a stronger organizational culture, one less prone to the othering mind-sets that played a factor in these atrocities. In this way, a greater emphasis on human security may in fact lead to a greater ability to achieve national security as well.

With this scholarship in mind, we recommend the increased inclusion of critical approaches in U.S. military education at all levels, beginning with the already more academia-like PME institutions and then reaching into the more humanistic educational strategies at work in programs such as harassment and diversity training. Encouraging U.S. service personnel to ask questions, to critique policy and practice, and to offer innovative solutions developed from self-reflection, can only serve to further the military's interests in self-improvement as well as in national and international human security.

Critical PME?: A Canadian Case Study

While we are recommending the increased inclusion of critical approaches to military education in the United States, we appreciate that a comparative case study may be helpful in illustrating what this might look like. The CAF, originally focused on occupational skills and leadership training, moved to add in humanistic training such as the Standardization for Harassment and Racism Prevention (SHARP) and is now engaged in Gender-Based Analysis Plus (GBA+) education (i.e., Taber, 2005, 2018, 2020), which aims to explore issues through the lens of gender as well as other forms of marginalization based on characteristics such as race, class, religion, and culture. The training was implemented after much attention on sexual harassment and assault in the CAF, including an investigative report in a national news magazine (Mercier & Castonguay, 2014), the report of an External Review Authority (Deschamps, 2015) appointed at the behest of the CAF, and the results of a Statistics Canada survey (Statistics Canada, 2016). The training aims to eliminate gender discrimination, sexual harassment, and sexual assault by familiarizing members with applicable policies, introducing supports, and providing strategies to respond to inappropriate behavior. However, despite its GBA+ lens, the training fits more in the humanistic paradigm at the moment, with insufficient focus on cultural change that would address the CAF's hypermasculine military culture. Nonetheless, it provides an important first step in moving toward critical education (Taber, 2020). This training (and related supportive policies) in Canada are taking place in a political context where progressive changes in public policy around gender are fairly consistent.

In contrast, U.S. military training is being developed and implemented in a relatively shifting political context. For example, the "Don't Ask Don't Tell" policy, requiring lesbian and gay members to stay closeted, was rescinded in 2011 (Rohall et al., 2017a) and transgender members were allowed to serve openly in 2016 (Rosenstein, 2017), both under the Obama administration. In contrast, under the Trump administration, the military service of transgender people has been limited (Tatum, 2018). Nonetheless, there has been progress within the U.S. military, such as the training involved in the Sexual Assault Prevention Strategy (SAPS) (U.S. DoD, 2014). Again, however, this training does not appear to stem from a critical transformative lens, but its focus on the differential power relationships that intersectional identities can create is a beginning.

Conclusion

The turn toward a critical paradigm in adult education in the U.S. military is an important shift in light of recent social and historical developments, with which military personnel must contend. As the United States continues to rely on a volunteer force, it must deal more directly with the diversity of its members, who are increasingly more diverse along lines of race, ethnicity, religion, gender, and sexuality (Rohall et al., 2017b). Additionally, U.S. service members are facing a new era of warfare, where the ability to think creatively and innovatively will be key to the continuing effectiveness of the armed forces (Zacharakis & Van Der Werff, 2012). Furthermore, the ways in which the military (often negatively) affects society, both domestically and internationally, and the ways in which society affects the military must be acknowledged and problematized (Enloe, 2016; Hampson et al., 2018; Taber, 2009, 2015). Critical education could transform the policies, practices, and even the purpose of militaries in order to create a world in which human security, not national security (see Enloe, 2016), is the aim.

Note

1. Non-English speakers are included in this number, so while a majority was composed of English speakers who were illiterate, some of the soldiers in these special units were simply unable to read English as it was not their mother tongue.

References

Altschuler, G., & Blumin, S. (2009). *The GI bill: The new deal for veterans*. Oxford University Press.

Bartone, P. T. (2008, November). Lessons of Abu Ghraib: Understanding and preventing prisoner abuse in military operations. *Defense Horizons, 64*, 1–8.

Belkin, A., & McNichol, J. (2000/2001). Homosexual personnel policy in the Canadian Forces: Did lifting the gay ban undermine military performance? *International Journal, 56*, 73–88.

Bruscino, T. (2010). Naval gazing Google deep: The expertise gap in the academic-military relationship. In D. Higbee (Ed.), *Military culture and education: Current intersections of academic and military cultures* (pp. 139–148). Routledge.

Carter, B. (2010). No holidays from history: Adult learning, Professional military education, and teaching history. In D. Higbee (Ed.), *Military culture and education: Current intersections of academic and military cultures* (pp. 168–182). Routledge.

Civil Rights Act of 1964, Pub.L. 88-352, 78 Stat. 241 (1964).

Cornell-d'Echert, B. Jr. (2012). Beyond training: New ideas for military forces operating beyond war. *New Directions for Adult and Continuing Education, 2012*(136), 17–27.

Coulter, J. A. (2017). *Cadets on campus: History of military schools in the United States*. Texas A&M Press.

Cranton, P. (2013). Adult learning theory. In T. Nesbit, S. Brigham, N. Taber, & T. Gibb (Eds.), *Building on critical traditions: Adult education and learning in Canada* (pp. 95–106). Thompson.

Davis, K. D. (2009). Sex, gender, and cultural intelligence in the Canadian Forces. *Commonwealth & Comparative Politics, 47*(4), 430–455.

Deschamps, M. (2015). *External review into sexual misconduct and sexual harassment in the Canadian Armed Forces*. External Review Authority.

Dietz, A. S., & Schroeder, E. A. (2012). Integrating critical thinking in the U.S. Army: Decision support red teams. *New Directions for Adult and Continuing Education, 2012*(136), 29–40.

Enloe, C. (2016). *Globalization and militarism: Feminists make the link* (2nd ed.). Rowman & Littlefield.

Feinman, I. R. (2000). *Citizenship rites: Feminist soldiers & feminist antimilitarists*. New York University Press.

Freire, P. (2000). *Pedagogy of the oppressed: 30th anniversary edition*. Continuum.

"GI Bill—10 years after." (1954, June 22). *The Washington Post and Times Herald*, p. 14.

Giordano, G. (2009). GI bill of rights (Servicemen's Readjustment Act). In E. F. Provenzo Jr. & A. B. Provenzo (Eds.), *Encyclopedia of the social and cultural foundations of education* (pp. 365–367). SAGE.

Goldwater–Nichols Department of Defense Reorganization Act of October 4, 1986. Pub.L. 99–433.

Habermas, J. (1971). *Knowledge and human interests*. Beacon Press.

Hampson, S. C., Lebel, U., & Taber, N. (2018). Introduction: Mothers, military and society in conversation. In S. C. Hampson, U. Lebel, & N. Taber (Eds.), *Mothers, military and society* (pp. 9–20). Demeter Press.

Herring, C. (2009). Does diversity pay? Race, gender and the business case for diversity. *American Sociological Review, 74*(2), 208–224.

Houle, C. O., Burr, E. W., Hamilton, T. H., & Yale, J. R. (1947). *Armed services and adult education*. American Council on Education.

Johnson-Freese, J. (2012). *Educating America's military*. Routledge.

Masland, J. W., & Radway, L. I. (1957). *Soldiers and scholars: Military education and national policy*. Princeton University Press.

Mercier, N., & Castonguay, A. (2014, May 5). Our military's disgrace: A special investigation. *Maclean's*, 18–26. https://www.macleans.ca/news/canada/our-militarys-disgrace/

Mullen, B., & Copper, C. (1994). The relation between group cohesiveness and performance. *Psychological Bulletin*, 115, 210–227.

Nesbit, T. (2013). Canadian adult education: A critical tradition. In T. Nesbit, S. M. Brigham, N. Taber, & T. Gibb (Eds.), *Building on critical traditions: Adult education and learning in Canada* (pp. 1–13). Thompson.

Nesbit, T., Brigham, S. M., Taber, N., & Gibb, T. (2013). The continuing imperative of Canadian adult education and learning. In T. Nesbit, S. M. Brigham, N. Taber, & T. Gibb (Eds.) (2013), *Building on critical traditions: Adult education and learning in Canada* (pp. 355–360). Thompson.

Office of the Under Secretary of Defense Comptroller/Chief Financial Officer. (2017). *Operations and maintenance overview: Fiscal year 2018 budget estimates*. https://comptroller.defense.gov/Portals/45/Documents/defbudget/fy2018/fy2018_OM_Overview.pdf

Okros, A., & Scott, D. (2015). Gender identity in the Canadian Forces: A review of possible impacts on operational effectiveness. *Armed Forces & Society*, 41(2), 243–256.

Oler, A. (2011, Spring). A critical but missing piece: Educating our professional military on the history of Islam. *Parameters*, 4(1), 71–85.

Persyn, J., & Polson, C. (2012). Evolution and influence of military adult education. *New Directions for Adult and Continuing Education*, 2012(136) 5–16.

Plumb, D., & Welton, M. (2001). Theory building in adult education: Questioning our grasp of the obvious. In D. Poonwassie & A. Poonwassie (Eds.), *Fundamentals of adult education* (pp. 3–75). Thompson.

Rohall, D. E., Ender, M. G., & Matthews, M. M. (2017a). Diversity in the military. In D. E. Rohall, M. G. Ender, & M. M. Matthews (Eds.), *Inclusion in the military: A force for diversity* (pp. 1–15). Rowman & Littlefield.

Rohall, D. E., Ender, M. G., & Matthews, M. M. (Eds.). (2017b). *Inclusion in the military: A force for diversity*. Rowman & Littlefield.

Rosenstein, J. E. (2017). The integration of trans people into the military. In D. E. Rohall, M. G. Ender, & M. M. Matthews (Eds.), *Inclusion in the military: A force for diversity* (pp. 149–167). Rowman & Littlefield.

Simons, W. E. (2000). *Professional military education in the United States*. Greenwood Press.

Soeters, J., Winslow, D., & Weibull, A. (2006). Military culture. In G. Caforio (Ed.), *Handbook of the sociology of the military* (pp. 237–254). Springer.

Statistics Canada. (2016). *Sexual misconduct in the Canadian Armed Forces, 2016*. Author.

Taber, N. (2005). Learning how to be a woman in the Canadian Forces/unlearning it through feminism: An autoethnography of my learning journey. *Studies in Continuing Education*, 27(3), 289–301.

Taber, N. (2007). *Ruling relations, warring, and mothering: Writing the social from the everyday life of a military mother* [Unpublished doctoral dissertation]. University of South Australia.

Taber, N. (2009). Exploring the interconnections between adult education, militarism, and gender: Implications for our field. *Studies in Continuing Education*, 31(2), 189–196.

Taber, N. (Ed.). (2015). *Gendered militarism in Canada: Learning conformity and resistance*. University of Alberta Press.

Taber, N. (2018). After Deschamps: Men, masculinities, and the Canadian armed forces. *Journal of Military and Veteran Health Research* 4(1), 100–107.

Taber, N. (2020). The Canadian armed forces: Battling between Operation Honour and Operation Hop on Her. *Critical Military Studies*, 6(1): 19–40.

Tatum, S. (2018, Mar. 24). White House announces policy to ban most transgender people from serving in the military. *CNN*. https://www.cnn.com/2018/03/23/politics/transgender-white-house/index.html

U.S. Army Training and Doctrine Command. (2003). *Transforming the army: TRADOC's first thirty years: 1973–2003* (TRADOC 30th Anniversary Commemoration ed.). Military History Office, U.S. Army Training and Doctrine Command.

U.S. Army Training and Doctrine Command. (2017). *The U.S. Army Learning Concept for Training and Education 2020–2040*. TRADOC Pamphlet 525-8-2. https://adminpubs.tradoc.army.mil/pamphlets/TP525-8-2.pdf

U.S. Department of Defense. (n.d.) *Our story*. https://www.defense.gov/our-story/

U.S. Department of Defense. (2014). *2014–2016 sexual assault prevention strategy*. Author.

Van Riper, J. K. (2016). *American professional military education, 1776–1945: A foundation for failure*. https://search.proquest.com/docview/1825271521?accountid=14784

Winslow, D., & Dunn, J. (2002). Women in the Canadian forces: Between legal and social integration. *Current Sociology*, 50(5), 641–667.

Zacharakis, J., & Van Der Werff, J. A. (2012). The future of adult education in the military. *New Directions for Adult and Continuing Education*, 2012(136), 89–98.

CHAPTER 25

International Development Education

Jill Zarestky, Maren Elfert, and Daniel Schugurensky

The concept of international development is a contested one, but usually refers to efforts undertaken to improve people's well-being worldwide, generally by alleviating poverty and reducing inequalities (Haslam et al., 2016; Sen, 1999). Scholars have pointed to the colonial and imperial legacy of development education that perpetuates Western hegemonic power in developing countries and does not account for the vast diversity of learners, learning needs, and historical, cultural and linguistic contexts (Abdi, 2009; Carnoy, 1974). The commonly used classifications of *developed* (e.g., United States, Canada, and most of Western Europe), *developing*, and *least developed countries* (e.g., most of sub-Saharan Africa) reflect a Western view of what development means and are constantly shifting. The term *third world* emerged in the context of the Cold War but is still in use. New terms have emerged like *Global South*, which, rather than designating a geographic location, "is a metaphor that indicates regions of the world at the receiving end of globalization and suffering the consequences" (Mignolo, 2011, p. 165); *emerging economies* (denoting the rapid economic development of formerly underdeveloped countries such as Brazil, China, and South Africa); and *fourth world*, which refers to Indigenous populations (Haslam et al., 2016).

During the second half of the 20th century, two main explanations were advanced to explain why some regions were more economically developed than others. Modernization theory, which became popular in the 1960s, argued that all societies go through the same stages of development, and the key to accelerate progress is the adoption of "modern" attitudes, practices, knowledge, and investments in human capital through educational expansion (Rostow, 1960). Dependency theory contended that modernization theory was rooted in a colonialist worldview and a reductionist conceptualization of development that ignored issues of power and claimed that the development of the Global North and the underdevelopment of the Global South (Africa, Asia, and Latin America) were two sides of the same coin: a world economic system that perpetuated unequal dynamics of production and trade (Wallerstein, 2004).

To resolve some of these tensions, more contemporary perspectives call for South–South dialogue rather than North–South intervention as a tool of development (Abdi & Kapoor, 2009; Willinsky, 1998) and emphasize respect for cultural and social diversity, holistic well-being, quality of life, and sustainable development based on alternative and indigenous worldviews (UNESCO, 2015a). Sen's (1999) capability approach, which influenced debates about international development, understands poverty not as the absence of resources, but as "deprivation of basic capabilities" (p. 20). In Sen's view, development goes beyond material or physical well-being. Rather, development is the removal of unfreedom that keeps human beings from realizing their full potential (see also Nussbaum, 2011).

Achieving such potential requires the support of educational opportunities. International development education (IDE) is embedded in notions of international development; any effort to improve people's lives arguably involves the acquisition of knowledge and skills. Literacy has traditionally occupied a central role in education for development, but IDE for adults has taken many other forms, including vocational education and training, adult basic education, health education, agricultural extension, community development, a variety of capacity building, intergenerational programs, and education for women and girls.

This chapter begins with a short historical account of adult and continuing education (ACE) in the context of international development. Next, it presents key stakeholders in IDE, followed by examples of programs. The last section presents a summary and conclusions.

Historical Perspectives on Adult Education and Development

Although the idea of "developing" poor countries is rooted in colonialism, international development as a field of practice began during the post–World War II period (Haslam et al., 2016) and included the creation of the United Nations (UN) (Sogge, 2016) and its specialized agencies like UNESCO (Singh, 2011). These organizations played a key role in institutionalizing adult education in development frameworks. The First International Conference on Adult Education (CONFINTEA) organized by UNESCO in 1949 in Elsinore, Denmark, advanced the concept of fundamental education, which would become UNESCO's first flagship program of international development. This agenda, prominent during the 1950s, understood adult education as a strategy for community development and the promotion of human rights (Watras, 2010). The subsequent discontinuation of the fundamental education program resulted in a shift in focus from a community-based approach to schooling (Watras, 2010) and marked the first occurrence of the adult education versus schools pattern that runs through the history of IDE (Elfert, 2019).

Adult education as an important tool of community development and social progress is rooted in late 19th-century and early 20th-century initiatives like the Scandinavian Folk Schools and the Canadian Antigonish movement. Scandinavian development aid facilitated the spread of the Folk School idea to African countries, and the Antigonish cooperative movement model was influential in Latin America (LeGrand, 2016; Nordvall, 2018; Rogers, 2000). These movements promoted a more humanistic approach to development, prioritizing the development of people rather than the economy (Draper, 1988). They also represent the strong emancipatory dimension of adult education that emerged in the 1950s and 1960s in different contexts like the Highlander Folk School in the United States (Horton, 1990), the literacy circles in Brazil (Freire, 1970), and the self-reliant model in Tanzania (Nyerere, 1968).

The 1960s also witnessed the ascendance of human capital theory (Schultz, 1961), which promoted education as an investment and economic growth factor and focused on the acquisition of knowledge skills and abilities connected to labor markets. During that period, education became a major pillar of social and economic development in both industrialized and developing countries under the influence of new actors in the system of global governance like the World Bank, the United Nations Development Programme (UNDP), and aid agencies such as the United States Agency for International Development (USAID). Manpower planning, focused on training skilled personnel (e.g., engineers and other technical professionals), increased because, in the logic of donors, industrial infrastructure investments make sense only if there are workers with the skills to make use of that infrastructure. The civil unrest of the late 1960s and the economic crisis of the 1970s turned attention away from this technocratic approach toward the idea of comprehensive education systems allowing for lifelong education opportunities (Elfert, 2018; Govinda, 2011).

By the 1980s, the *Washington consensus* advanced market-oriented economic principles, like trade liberalization, privatization, labor market flexibility, deregulation, and fiscal austerity to developing countries, to promote economic growth. For several decades, these neoliberal principles were applied in developing countries through economic stabilization measures and structural adjustment programs (Jones & Coleman, 2005; Stiglitz, 2002).

The neoliberal influence on adult education worldwide manifests as an increasing focus on skills required for employment (Allais, 2012). This influence has resulted in skills development strategies (e.g., Department of Higher Education and Training, Republic of South Africa, 2015) and skills measurement programs such as the World Bank's Skills Toward Employment and Productivity (STEP), which follows the model of the Organization for Economic Cooperation and Development's (OECD) Program for the International Assessment of Adult Competencies (PIAAC). Additionally, several developing countries have introduced national qualification frameworks as a way of recognizing and standardizing skills and competencies (Aitchison & Alidou, 2009; Allais, 2011).

Literacy as an IDE Focus

Literacy has traditionally played a central role in IDE. In the context of decolonization in the 1950s and 1960s, many developing countries called for literacy campaigns. Several international organizations like UNESCO pursued literacy campaigns as a development strategy. Based on its human rights approach to education, UNESCO's strategy involved raising the entire population's literacy levels. In contrast, other donors such as the UNDP and the World Bank did not support mass literacy campaigns as these organizations focused on raising the literacy levels only of population sectors considered instrumental for economic development (Elfert, 2019).

In the tense Cold War climate, when the United States and the Soviet Union competed over the developing world as a sphere of influence, adult literacy programs gained a reputation as being political and equated with communism (Dorn & Ghodsee, 2012). Literacy campaigns were regarded with suspicion by the United States and other Western countries due to their association with revolutionary governments and progressive educators like Julius Nyerere and Paulo Freire. Freire's work in Brazil in the 1960s connected adult literacy to the experiences of the learners, to their understanding of systems of oppression, and to their potential to become agents of change (Freire, 1970). Nyerere, the first prime minister of Tanzania after it gained independence from Britain, carried out an adult literacy campaign in 1971. Both Freire's liberation pedagogy and Nyerere's ideas of self-reliant development continue to inspire contemporary development efforts and adult education theory and practice (Ireland, 2018; Mulenga, 2001). Freire's literacy approach, which consists of simultaneously "reading the word" and "reading the world," is still used in many adult education programs (e.g., ActionAid, 1996; Finger & Asún, 2001; Freire & Macedo, 1987). Despite the decline of mass literacy campaigns there are examples of 21st-century literacy campaigns driven and funded by national governments, such as Kha Ri Gude in South Africa and Brazil Alfabetizado in Brazil (Hanemann, 2015). Launching "comprehensive and effective literacy campaigns" (African Union, 2016, p. 24) constitutes one of the strategic objectives of African education. However, with limited resources, developing countries typically prioritize investments in children's education. The lack of commitment to adult literacy is reflected in the fact that the number of illiterate adults has dropped by just 1% since 2000 (Hanemann, 2015; Ireland, 2016). Massive drop-out rates and stagnating literacy rates seem to support development educators who cite the strong correlation between adult literacy and school success (ActionAid & Global Campaign for Education, 2005).

International Frameworks, the Right to Adult Education, and Lifelong Learning

A number of international protocols have guided adult education for development since World War II. Two of the earlier ones were UNESCO's CONFINTEA conferences (held every 12 years since 1949) and the UN Development Decades (1960–1990). At the turn of the century, three important initiatives emerged: Education for All (EFA; 1990–2015), the Millennium Development Goals (MDGs; 2000–2015), and the Sustainable Development Goals (SDGs; 2015–2030). Education initiatives are now aligned around Goal 4 of the Sustainable Development Goals, which states: "Ensure inclusive and equitable quality education and promote lifelong learning opportunities for all" (United Nations, 2015, p. 19). These international protocols set directions for education and adult education. However, there is always a gap between the normative international discourse and the reality on the ground in each nation-state due to education's comparatively low priority and diverging views among international donors, national governments, and civil society.

Conflicting dogmas have shaped IDE. On one hand, the focus on primary education was driven by the argument that universal schooling will generate future literate generations. For instance, the EFA initiative, in which the UN and all major international organizations were involved, entailed a narrowing of education by emphasizing primary education (Torres, 2001). For this reason, Khan (2000), then vice president of the International Council of Adult Education (ICAE), argued that EFA in practice meant "Except for Adults." However, through the CONFINTEA conferences and other policy recommendations, UNESCO was instrumental in expanding the adult learners' right to education. According to Ireland (2016), the last two CONFINTEA conferences (1997 and 2009) "present two core messages: a vision of lifelong learning for all as the basic tenet for the organization of educational policy and the concept of development as a human right firmly anchored in human beings" (p. 8). However, the view that education or adult education is a human right is contested, and other international organizations such as the World Bank and the OECD emphasize a human capital approach. This means that these organizations consider education and adult education a social and economic investment rather than a right. The United States does not support the view that education is a human right and, to date, is not one of the 169 nations that have ratified the International Covenant on Economic, Social and Cultural Rights (United Nations Treaty Collection, 2019).

Since the 1970s, lifelong learning has risen to prominence as a leading paradigm of educational policies and as the overarching framework for adult learning and education (UIL, 2017a). Because lifelong learning as a policy concept emerged in the West, some consider it "a luxury of the Developed World" (Rubenson, 2006, p. 71). As a consequence, in many developing countries lifelong learning remains more a vision than a reality (UIL, 2009). In recent years, lifelong learning has been accepted in the development discourse, but scholars from developing countries debate the concept's value (Avoseh, 2001; Regmi, 2015). Although lifelong learning has been largely absent in the MDGs, its prominence in the SDGs is likely to reinvigorate interest in the concept.

Funding and Implementation of IDE

Some countries have legislation and policies pertaining to ACE (UIL, 2009), but generally responsibility for adult education is divided among different ministries, government agencies, and nongovernmental stakeholders. Funding and delivery of adult education is diffuse and complex, involving a wide array of international organizations, aid agencies, philanthropic and religious organizations, nongovernmental organizations (NGOs), and civil society organizations and cross-ministry collaborations. This complexity entails many challenges, including sporadic funding and limited coordination and accountability.

In terms of official development assistance, the three UN International Conferences on Financing for Development provide reference points: Monterrey, in 2002; Doha, in 2008; and Addis Ababa, in 2015. In these conferences, heads of state and international organizations agreed developed countries would allocate 0.7% of gross domestic income to development. Several countries still remain below that target (UNESCO, 2017a; UIL, 2017b). Additionally, the financial crisis of 2008 greatly impacted donors' investments in IDE. At the national level, very few countries allocate at least 6% of gross national product to education as recommended by the UN. Adult education is a low budgetary priority within an already underfunded system (UNESCO, 2016). Aid for adult education is at the bottom of the list of educational priorities. Although several countries reported some progress in political commitment to adult education and improved stakeholder coordination, the negligible funding is an indicator of its marginalization. Currently, most countries spend less than 2% of the national education budget on adult education, and 42% of countries spend less than 1% (OECD, 2018; UNESCO, 2018; UIL, 2017c).

At the CONFINTEA conferences, UNESCO member states deliver national reports about the status of adult education and provide a mechanism for monitoring adult education in developing countries. UNESCO's monitoring capacity has increased with the regular publication of the *Global Report on Adult Learning and Education* (GRALE), since 2009, and the Global Education Monitoring Reports (e.g., UNESCO, 2006; 2015b), both of which present contemporary developments and trends in adult education regarding international development. Data on adult education, including literacy rates, are provided by agencies like the OECD and the UNESCO Institute for Statistics (UIS). Several initiatives have been undertaken to measure literacy and skills in developing countries, such as UNESCO's LAMP initiative (now followed by the World Bank's STEP program) and UNESCO's Action Research on Measuring Literacy Program Participants' Learning Outcomes project, known by its French acronym RAMAA (UIL, 2017c).

The International Council for Adult Education (ICAE) is the major civil society organization for adult education. Founded in 1972, its mission is to promote youth and adult education within the framework of social justice, democracy, human rights, and sustainable development. ICAE represents over 800 organizations in 75 countries and includes regional civil society organizations like the Asia South Pacific Association for Basic and Adult Education (ASPBAE), the Association for the Development of Education in Africa (ADEA) and Consejo de Educación de Adultos de América Latina (CEAAL). In these regions, ICAE works to strengthen links between adult education and other social movements (e.g., peace, indigenous, women's, environmental) and nurture connections among activists, organizations, and networks. Among other activities, ICAE regularly organizes regional and international conferences and produces monitoring reports for CONFINTEA, representing civil society and NGOs in governmental forums.

Adult Education in Least Developed Countries

While the historical origins of ACE for development focused largely on literacy, the application of the SDGs and broader views of development's purpose (Sen, 1999; Nussbaum, 2011) have expanded more recent conceptions of IDE. Indeed, a vast spectrum of IDE programs exists for adults in terms of actors, content, and purpose. In addition to literacy, many programs and organizations strive to address agricultural practices, health outcomes, entrepreneurship and economic development, environmental conservation, food security, sustainability, civic and political participation, job training, and gender equity, among other purposes. Many of these efforts derive their mandates from the SDGs and/or regional and national frameworks such as the African Union Commission's *Agenda 2063: The Africa We Want* (African Union Commission, 2015) and the already mentioned *CESA 2016–2015* (African Union, 2016). Other efforts emerge from specific needs in local contexts.

As one example of IDE efforts, Tostan (2018), an international nonprofit organization based in Senegal, works to improve the health and empowerment of women in six sub-Saharan African countries. By applying a human rights–based approach grounded in the values of the communities it serves, Tostan's educational programs have decreased occurrences of female genital cutting, increased the age at which young women marry, and facilitated women's selection into local leadership positions (Gillespie & Melching, 2010). Similarly, Participatory Research in Asia (PRIA, 2018) seeks to improve health outcomes and local capacity through participatory education programs. PRIA focuses specifically on basic services such as clean water and sanitation, as well as women's safety and inclusion. In Latin America, Centro de Cooperación Regional para la Educación de Adultos en América Latina y el Caribe (CREFAL, 2018) was established in 1950 in Pátzcuaro, Mexico, to promote regional cooperation in youth and adult education programs. Since then, it has undertaken activities devoted to research, program evaluation, and the training of adult education and community development practitioners and policymakers in Latin America and the Caribbean.

While Tostan, PRIA, and CREFAL are well established, there are many examples of less prominent programs that bridge ACE theory, research, and practice. For instance, Mayombe (2017) highlights nonformal adult education as a means to encourage and support entrepreneurs in South Africa to start their own businesses. Similar programs are implemented in Kerala, India, with a focus on economic cooperation among poor women (Panackal et al., 2017). The success of the programs translated to economic growth within the local communities and participants' ability to become economically self-reliant. In Latin America, a vibrant movement of adult education and community organizing for social change known as *popular education* has been active since the 1970s. Inspired by liberation theology and Freire's (1970) ideas on education and society, the principles of popular education have influenced adult education practices in Latin America and beyond (Ireland, 2018).

Generally speaking, the following are the key categories of adult education programs: (a) literacy and basic skills, (b) continuing work-related training and vocational skills, and (c) popular and community education (UIL, 2019). The *Fourth Global Report on*

Adult Learning and Education (GRALE; UIL, 2019) recognized that greater numbers of adults participate in the first two categories. This finding is consistent with studies (e.g., Hoff & Hickling-Hudson, 2011; McGrath, 2012) pointing to the neoliberal influences that restrict adult education's focus to economic productivity and employment, to the detriment of transformative, emancipatory adult education programs.

Conclusion

Many observers have noted with interest the reemergence of the concept of lifelong learning in goal 4 of the SDGs. Given the established historical connection of lifelong learning and adult education, open questions remain regarding the role of adult education in the SDGs and the Education 2030 process (Elfert, 2019). While some commentators emphasize the broader vision of the SDGs that represents an opportunity for adult education and lifelong learning (UIL, 2016), others believe this vision calls for "the need for a stable system to promote adult learning and education" (UIL, 2017a, p. 23). Will adult education receive more attention under the SDGs after a long period of neglect at the expense of primary education? Answers to this question vary and are speculative. The monitoring of SDG 4 will be a complex process (UNESCO, 2017a); it will take time to realistically assess achievement of the targets. The road map to realizing the 10 targets of the SDG 4 is the Education 2030 Framework for Action, also known as the Incheon Declaration (World Education Forum, 2015). A key mechanism for monitoring progress of SDG 4 is the High Level Political Forum (United Nations, n.d.). Annual events will review the progress of specific SDGs. A report published by UNESCO ahead of the first review meeting of the High Level Political Forum notes that in order to meet the SDG targets, "aid to education would need to increase sixfold from its 2010 levels" (UIS-GMR, 2019, p. 11). The *Global Education Monitoring Report*, which documents monitoring of SDG 4, notes: "There is consensus that current levels of funding are inadequate to meet the ambitious SDG 4 goals" (UNESCO, 2017b, p. 264). Given the scarce resources available for IDE, expansion of adult education in developing countries is unlikely (Elfert, 2019). Moreover, although SDG 4 calls for learning opportunities for all, there is a persistent gap between inclusive discourses (e.g., EFA) and practical implementation, in which formal education is prioritized and adult education is an afterthought (Burnett, 2017; Fredriksen, 2017; Ireland, 2016). Arguably, in some regions like sub-Saharan Africa, not enough attention is given to job training in the informal sector of the economy (where most people work), creating a disconnect between the emphasis on universal education and the high level of youth unemployment (Fredriksen, 2017; Oyomo, 2017).

Youth unemployment is a major problem in many developing countries and in industrialized ones. If we apply Sen's (1999) "capability approach" (p. 87) to youth unemployment, unemployment not only results in a lack of income and resources but also has other serious effects—unemployment can cause a loss of self-confidence and motivation and disrupt communities by forcing the unemployed into unlawful work, disruptive social behaviors, or mass migration. McGrath (2018) applies the capability approach to vocational education and training, which in his view should go beyond training workers for the economy, but is important to "maximize the capabilities . . . of . . . young people" and should "be concerned about developing the person more than the worker" (p. 139).

The notorious underfunding of education for development and the emphasis on schooling points to a marginalization of adult education, as seen in the MDGs, the previous development framework (Elfert, 2019). Indeed, there is widespread agreement that the EFA goal related to adult literacy has not been achieved (UNESCO, 2015a). As Benavot and Stepanek Lockhart (2016) point out, "despite the integrated nature of the agenda, certain SDG targets are being prioritized, often to the exclusion of those related to ALE [adult learning and education]" (p. 4). The authors argue that the "skills" agenda might make it difficult to monitor progress in adult education as the lack of a common definition of "relevant skills" in some of the targets in SDG 4 might undermine their monitoring (p. 5; see also King, 2017). Another challenge is the lack of available data for participation in nonformal education in developing countries (Benavot & Stepanek Lockhart, 2016), creating a need for more formal scholarship.

There is no doubt that ACE is foundational for development. The delegates of the last CONFINTEA Conference, held in 2009 in Brazil, stated their "conviction that adult learning and education equip people with the necessary knowledge, capabilities, skills, competences and values to exercise and advance their rights and take control of their destinies" (UIL, 2010, p. 6). The 4th GRALE refers to several studies that show "important social and community benefits of learning" (UIL, 2019, p. 89) regarding intergenerational health improvement, impacts on the quality of life of elderly people, and a lower risk of crime. It also emphasizes the benefits of adult education for the increasing number of migrants and refugees worldwide. These benefits of adult learning and education present vast possibilities for supporting the achievement of the SDGs and advancing development education worldwide.

References

Abdi, A. A. (2009). Presidential address—Education and social development: Global perspectives. *Canadian and International Education / Education canadienne et international, 38*(2), Article 2.

Abdi, A. A., & Kapoor, D. (Eds.). (2009). *Global perspectives on adult education*. Palgrave Macmillan.

ActionAid. (1996). *The Reflect mother manual: A new approach to literacy. Regenerated Freirean literacy through empowering community techniques*. Author.

ActionAid & Global Campaign for Education. (2005). *Writing the wrongs: International benchmarks on adult literacy*. Author.

African Union. (2016). *Continental education strategy for Africa 2016–2025*. African Union Headquarters. https://au.int/sites/default/files/documents/29958-doc-cesa_-_english-v9.pdf

African Union Commission (2015). *Agenda 2063: The Africa we want*. https://au.int/Agenda2063/popular_version

Aitchison, J., & Alidou, H. (2009). *The state and development of adult learning and education in sub-Saharan Africa: Regional synthesis report*. UNESCO Institute for Lifelong Learning. http://uil.unesco.org/adult-education/confintea/state-and-development-adult-learning-and-education-subsaharan-africa

Allais, S. M. (2011). The impact and implementation of national qualifications frameworks: A comparison of 16 countries. *Journal of Education and Work, 24*(3–4), 233–258.

Allais, S. (2012). Will skills save us? Rethinking the relationships between vocational education, skills development policies, and social policy in South Africa. *International Journal of Educational Development, 32*(5), 632–642.

Avoseh, M. B. M. (2001). Learning to be active citizens: Lessons of traditional Africa for lifelong learning. *International Journal of Lifelong Education, 20*(6), 479–486.

Benavot, B., & Stepanek Lockhart, A. (2016). Monitoring the education of youth and adults: From EFA to SDG4. *International Perspectives in Adult Education*. DVV International. http://www.academia.edu/35507385/Monitoring_the_Education_of_Youth_and_Adults_From_EFA_to_SDG_4

Burnett, N. (2017, March 13). Unfinished business in global education. *Norrag Blog*. http://www.norrag.org/unfinished-business-in-global-education/

Carnoy, M. (1974). *Education as cultural imperialism*. David McKay.

Centro de Cooperación Regional para la Educación de Adultos en América Latina y el Caribe. (2018). *Historical background*. https://www.crefal.org/index.php?option=com_content&view=article&id=27&Itemid=182

Department of Higher Education and Training, Republic of South Africa. (2015). *National skills development strategy (NSDS III)*. Department of Higher Education and Training. https://www.nationalskillsauthority.org.za/wp-content/uploads/2015/11/NSDSIII.pdf

Dorn, C., & Ghodsee, K. (2012). The Cold War politicization of literacy: Communism, UNESCO and the World Bank. *Diplomatic History, 36*(2), 373–398.

Draper, J. A. (1988). Canadian studies in international adult education. *Canadian Journal of Development Studies, 9*(2), 283–299.

Elfert, M. (2018). *UNESCO's utopia of lifelong learning: An intellectual history*. Routledge.

Elfert, M. (2019). Lifelong learning in SDG 4: What does it mean for UNESCO's rights-based approach to adult learning and education? *International Review of Education, 65*, 537–556. https://doi.org/10.1007/s11159-019-09788-z

Finger, M., & Asún, J. M. (2001). *Adult education at the crossroads: Learning our way out*. Zed Books.

Fredriksen, B. (2017, June 8). Creating productive jobs for Africa's youth. A huge challenge with global implications. *Norrag NewsBite*. http://www.norrag.org/creating-productive-jobs-africas-youth-huge-challenge-global-implications/

Freire, P. (1970). *Pedagogy of the oppressed*. Continuum.

Freire, P., & Macedo, D. (1987). *Literacy: Reading the word & the world*. Bergin & Garvey.

Gillespie, D., & Melching, M. (2010). The transformative power of democracy and human rights in nonformal education: The case of Tostan. *Adult Education Quarterly, 60*(5), 477–498.

Govinda, R. (2011). Nonformal education and poverty alleviation. In M. Bray, & M. V. Varghese (Eds.), *Directions in educational planning. International experiences and perspectives* (pp. 165–178). IIEP.

Hanemann, U. (2015). *The evolution and impact of literacy campaigns and programmes 2000–2014.* UNESCO Institute for Lifelong Learning. http://unesdoc.unesco.org/images/0023/002341/234154e.pdf

Haslam, P. A., Schafer, J., & Beaudet, P. (Eds.). (2016). *Introduction to international development: Approaches, actors, issues, and practice.* Oxford University Press.

Hoff, L., & Hickling-Hudson, A. (2011). The role of international non-governmental organisations in promoting adult education for social change: A research agenda. *International Journal of Educational Development, 31*(2), 187–195.

Horton, M. (1990). *The long haul: An autobiography.* Doubleday.

Ireland, T. (2016). Reflections on CONFINTEA and the global agendas for education and development post-2015. *Voices Rising, 497.* http://www.ceaal.org/v2/archivos/publicaciones/carta/reflectionson_CONFINTEA_ti.pdf

Ireland, T. (2018). The relevance of Freire for the post-2015 international debate on development and education and the role of popular education. In A. Melling & R. Pilkington (Eds.), *Paulo Freire and transformative education.: Changing lives and transforming communities* (pp. 15–27). Palgrave Macmillan.

Jones, P. W., & Coleman, D. (2005). *The United Nations and education. Multilateralism, development, and globalisation.* Routledge Falmer.

Khan, M. (2000). Does EFA stand for "Except for Adults"? *Adult Education and Development, 55,* 171–174.

King, K. (2017). Lost in translation? The challenge of translating the global education goal and targets into global indicators. *Compare: A Journal of Comparative and International Education, 47*(6), 801–817.

LeGrand, C. C. (2016). The Antigonish Movement of Canada and Latin America: Catholic cooperatives, Christian communities, and transnational development in the Great Depression and the Cold War. In S. J. C. Andes & J. G. Young (Eds.), *Local church, global church. Catholic activism in Latin America from Rerum Novarum to Vatican II* (pp. 207–244). Catholic University of America Press.

Mayombe, C. (2017). Success stories on nonformal adult education and training for self-employment in microenterprises in South Africa. *Education + Training, 59*(7/8), 87–887.

McGrath, S. (2012). Vocational education and training for development: A policy in need of a theory? *International Journal of Educational Development, 32,* 623–631.

McGrath, S. (2018). *Education and development.* Routledge.

Mignolo, W. (2011). The Global South and world dis/order. *Journal of Anthropological Research, 67,* 165–188.

Mulenga, D. C. (2001). Mwalimu Julius Nyerere: A critical review of his contributions to adult education and postcolonialism. *International Journal of Lifelong Education, 20*(6), 446–470.

Nordvall, H. (2018). The global spread of the Nordic Folk High School idea. In M. Milana, S. Webb, J. Holford, R. Waller, & P. Jarvis (Eds.), *The Palgrave international handbook on adult and lifelong education and learning* (pp. 721–735). Palgrave Macmillan.

Nussbaum, M. C. (2011). *Creating capabilities: The human development approach.* Belknap Press of Harvard University.

Nyerere, J. (1968). *Essays on socialism.* Oxford University Press.

Organization for Economic Cooperation and Development. (2018). *Education-related aid data at a glance.* http://www.oecd.org/dac/financing-sustainable-development/development-finance-data/education-related-aid-data.htm

Oyomo, E. (2017, February 8). Obsession with ending poverty is where development is going wrong. *The Guardian.* https://www.theguardian.com/global-development-professionals-network/2017/feb/08/obsession-with-ending-poverty-is-where-development-is-going-wrong

Panackal, N., Singh, A., & Hamsa, S. (2017). Kudimbashree and women empowerment in Kerala. An overview and theoretical framework. *Indian Journal of Commerce and Management Studies, 8*(1), 16–21.

Participatory Research in Asia. (2018). *About us.* https://www.pria.org/about-pria-3-2-0

Regmi, K. D. (2015). Can lifelong learning be the post-2015 agenda for the Least Developed Countries? *International Journal of Lifelong Education, (34)*5, 551–568.

Rogers, A. (2000). Cultural transfer in adult education: The case of the Folk Development Colleges in Tanzania. *International Review of Education, 46*(1–2), 67–92.

Rostow, W. W. (1960). *The stages of economic growth: A comparative manifesto.* Cambridge University Press.

Rubenson, K. (2006). Constructing the lifelong learning paradigm: Competing visions from the OECD and UNESCO. In S. Ellers (Ed.), *Milestones in adult education* (pp. 63–78). Danish University Press.

Schultz, T. W. (1961). Investment in human capital. *The American Economic Review, 51*(1), 1–17.

Sen, A. (1999). *Development as freedom.* Random House.

Singh, J. P. (2011). *United Nations Educational, Scientific and Cultural Organization (UNESCO): Creating norms for a complex world.* Routledge.

Sogge, D. (2016). The United Nations and multilateral actors in development. In P. A. Haslam, J. Schafer, &

P. Beaudet (Eds.), *Introduction to international development: Approaches, actors, issues, and practice* (pp. 180–199). Oxford University Press.

Stiglitz, J. E. (2002). *Globalization and its discontents.* W. W. Norton.

Torres, R. M. (2001). What happened at the World Education Forum? *Adult Education and Development, 56,* 45–68.

Tostan. (2018). *Home | Tostan International.* https://www.tostan.org/

UNESCO. (2006). *Global Monitoring Report. Literacy for life.* Author. http://unesdoc.unesco.org/images/0014/001416/141639e.pdf

UNESCO. (2015a). *Rethinking education: Towards a global common good?* Author. http://unesdoc.unesco.org/images/0023/002325/232555e.pdf

UNESCO. (2015b). *Global Monitoring Report. Education for All 2000–2015: Achievements and challenges.* http://unesdoc.unesco.org/images/0023/002322/232205e.pdf.

UNESCO. (2016). *Global Monitoring Education Report 2016: Education for people and planet: Creating sustainable futures for all.* Author. http://unesdoc.unesco.org/images/0024/002457/245752e.pdf

UNESCO. (2017a, June 6). *Aid to education falls for the sixth consecutive year.* Author. http://en.unesco.org/news/aid-education-falls-sixth-consecutive-year

UNESCO. (2017b). *Global Education Monitoring Report. Accountability in education: Meeting our commitments.* https://en.unesco.org/gem-report/report/2017/accountability-education

UNESCO. (2018). *The power of adult learning and education: A vision towards 2030.* UNESCO Institute for Lifelong Learning.

UNESCO Institute for Lifelong Learning. (2009). *Global report on adult learning and education* (GRALE). Author.

UNESCO Institute for Lifelong Learning. (2010). *CONFINTEA VI. Belém Framework for Action.* Author. https://uil.unesco.org/adult-education/confintea/belem-framework-action

UNESCO Institute for Lifelong Learning. (2016). Key messages and executive summary. *3rd Global report on adult learning and education* (GRALE III) (pp. 81–84). Author. http://unesdoc.unesco.org/images/0024/002459/245917e.pdf

UNESCO Institute for Lifelong Learning (prepared by Rangachar Govinda). (2017a). CONFINTEA IV, midterm review 2017, regional report. *The status of adult learning and education in Asia and the Pacific.* Author.

UNESCO Institute for Lifelong Learning. (2017b). *Progress, challenges and opportunities: The status of adult learning and education.* CONFINTEA VI. Midterm review 2017. Summary of the Regional Reports. Author. http://unesdoc.unesco.org/images/0025/002597/259707E.pdf

UNESCO Institute for Lifelong Learning. (2017c). CONFINTEA VI, midterm review 2017, regional report. *The status of adult learning and education in sub-Saharan Africa.* Author. http://unesdoc.unesco.org/images/0025/002597/259720E.pdf

UNESCO Institute for Lifelong Learning. (2019). *4th Global report on adult learning and education* (GRALE IV). Author.

UNESCO Institute for Statistics and Global Education Monitoring Report. (2019). *Meeting commitments. Are countries on track to achieve SDG4?* UIS and Author. https://en.unesco.org/gem-report/sites/gem-report/files/UNESCO-2019-HLPF_UIS_Meeting-EN-v7-web_aer.pdf

United Nations. (n.d.). *High-level political forum on sustainable development.* Department of Economic and Social Affairs. https://sustainabledevelopment.un.org/hlpf

United Nations. (2015). *Transforming our world: The 2030 Agenda for Sustainable Development.* https://sustainabledevelopment.un.org/post2015/transformingourworld

United Nations Treaty Collection. (2019). *Status as at: 12-07-2019.* https://treaties.un.org/pages/ViewDetails.aspx?src=TREATY&mtdsg_no=IV-3&chapter=4&clang=_en

Wallerstein, I. (2004). *World-systems analysis: An introduction.* Duke University Press.

Watras, J. (2010). UNESCO's program of fundamental education, 1946–1959. *History of Education, 39*(2), 219–237.

Willinsky, J. (1998). *Learning to divide the world: Education at empire's end.* University of Minnesota Press.

World Education Forum. (2015). *Incheon Declaration. Education 2030: Towards inclusive and equitable quality education and lifelong learning for all.* UNESCO, World Education Forum 2015 and Ministry of Education, Republic of Korea. http://uis.unesco.org/en/document/education-2030-incheon-declaration-towards-inclusive-equitable-quality-education-and

CHAPTER 26

Health Professions Education and Adult and Continuing Education

Working Collaboratively to Foster Educator Development

Barbara J. Daley and Ronald M. Cervero

According to the Institute of Medicine (IOM; 2003), the preparation of health professionals needs major revision as clinical education has not kept pace with changes in patient demographics, modifications in the health-care delivery system, new technologies, and the increased focus on quality outcomes and evidence-based practice. These changes within the health-care delivery system have led to a demand for different types of education for all health professionals, resulting in a recognition that educators who teach in health professions programs need to be prepared differently. In today's health-care environment, there is a growing recognition that dual preparation as an expert in clinical practice and an educator is needed for those who teach health professionals.

This chapter explores the developing area of *health professions education* (HPE), which is a broad term with two different meanings. First, the term refers to prelicensure, postgraduate residency, and continuing professional development programs that prepare individuals to function as professionals in one of the health professions, such as medicine or nursing. This field is differentiated from *health education*, which is focused on individual patients and patient populations (Cottrell et al., 2009). Second, HPE refers to master's degrees, doctoral degrees, or certificate programs that prepare professionals who are already licensed (e.g., physicians and nurses) to be educators. In this chapter, we refer to HPE as the preparation of health professionals to be educators and educational leaders. Because of the current emphasis on dual preparation, there has been an increase in the number of HPE programs worldwide. In 1996 there were only 7 master's level programs worldwide in HPE; by 2013 there were 121 programs that prepared health professionals for teaching roles across the education continuum (Tekian & Artino, 2013). HPE program content, which focuses on curriculum development, teaching and assessment, and leadership, is often drawn from educational psychology, curriculum and instruction, and K–12 teaching. However, learners in these programs work in health-care contexts where they teach adults in prelicensure, postlicensure, graduate, and faculty development programs.

This chapter explores ways in which adult and continuing education can serve as the foundation for HPE programs, enhancing and expanding approaches to educational practice. The chapter covers the changing context driving the need to change how health

249

professionals are educated across the life span. It then provides an overview of worldwide trends of HPE graduate programs. The chapter concludes with the need to incorporate the theory, research, and practice of adult and continuing education into these graduate programs.

The Changing Context for Educating Health Professionals Across the Life Span

It is axiomatic that the changing social and organizational contexts for improving the health of individuals and populations has created an urgency for reforming HPE. Although this urgency had been evident for some time, the 2001 IOM report, *Crossing the Quality Chasm: A New Health System for the 21st Century*, defined the characteristics of an effective health-care system. As the title of IOM's 2003 follow-up report (*Health Professions Education: A Bridge to Quality*) indicates, the preparation of health professionals is a key strategy for enabling the success of this new health-care system. IOM (2003) articulated the vision and desired outcomes for clinical education in the health professions as: "All health professionals should be educated to deliver patient-centered care as members of an interdisciplinary team, emphasizing evidence-based practice, quality improvement approaches, and informatics" (p. 3). IOM extended this vision through the entire continuum of health professionals' careers with its 2010 report, *Redesigning Continuing Education in the Health Professions*. These educational changes provided a curriculum framework to achieve the Triple Aim goals of improving the patient experience of care, reducing the per capita cost of care, and improving the health of the population (Paterson et al., 2015). There was widespread understanding that the challenges to implementing this new approach to professional preparation would require culture changes and closer ties between the classroom and practice settings (Thibault, 2013b).

The need and urgency for reform continued unabated with the 2010 Lancet Commission report published on the centennial of the Flexner report (Frenk et al., 2010). The commission argued that professional preparation has not kept pace with the new health challenges, primarily due to the "fragmented, outdated, and static curricula that produce ill-equipped graduates. . . . What is clearly needed is a thorough and authoritative reexamination of health professional education, matching the ambitious work of a century ago" (p. 1923). The Global Forum on Innovation in Health Professional Education took stock of progress 5 years after the Lancet Commission report and found that the "chasm" was increasing between what future health-care professionals are being taught and how they will need to practice in the existing health-care delivery system. Students are being prepared for a system that no longer exists, and the report emphasized that education should be structured to produce lifelong learners across the continuum of health professionals' practice (National Academies of Sciences and Medicine, 2016). Nevertheless, there exists a tremendous amount of experimentation and examples of reform related to interprofessional education (Lutifyya et al., 2016), social determinants of health (Lypson et al., 2016), evidence-based practice (Thomas et al., 2016), continuing professional development (Balmer, 2012), and lifelong learning (Mylopoulos et al., 2016).

Preparing Clinician Educators and Educational Leaders

HPE graduate programs are now seen as a key strategy to positively impact health professionals' transformation from clinicians to educators and educational leaders for prelicensure, residency, and continuing professional development programs. Even though some professions (e.g., nursing and physical therapy) have PhD level preparation as clinicians, this does not ensure educational preparation. This professionalization of the HPE workforce has been driven by several major institutional dynamics (Cervero et al., 2017; Tekian & Artino, 2013; Tekian et al., 2014). The first is that many clinicians have made education the focus of their professional roles, and institutions have responded by creating career tracks, such as clinician educator/scholar. As part of this move, many institutions worldwide now require an HPE master's degree for those serving in these roles. Second, accreditation bodies increasingly require a demonstration of expertise in curriculum design, instruction, assessment, and program evaluation. For example, these requirements are set for educators and leaders in medical education in the United States by the Liaison Committee on Medical Education and the Accreditation Council for Graduate Medical

Education. Similar standards are set in Canada by the Royal College of Physicians and Surgeons and in the United Kingdom by the UK General Medical Council. Finally, this professionalization recognizes that a common set of knowledge, skills, and dispositions exists across the health professions and that there is value in being immersed in the medical education environment where effective approaches to education, leadership, and scholarship can be fostered.

The master of health professions education (MHPE) degree is the most common credential for preparing educators and educational leaders, and by 2013 there were 121 programs that prepared health professionals (e.g., physicians, nurses, pharmacists, physical therapists) for educational roles and responsibilities. New MHPE programs continue to be developed each year due to increased demand for individuals with specialized knowledge concerning how to best educate future health professionals. Approximately 43% of these programs exist in Europe and 20% in North America, with the vast majority housed in medical schools and a handful of programs housed in schools of education. The core content of HPE programs varies widely; however, most master's degree programs provide foundational knowledge and skills focused on the theory, research, and practice of education as applied to the health professions. In many HPE programs, the core content can be categorized into five domains of knowledge and skills: teaching and learning, curriculum development, evaluation and assessment, research methods, and leadership and management (Tekian & Artino, 2013). Typically, these programs are composed of 32 to 36 credits, with very prescriptive course work and few electives.

Doctoral programs in HPE have also increased with 24 structured EdD or PhD programs identified in 2014 (Tekian, 2014; Tekian & Artino, 2014). This traditional North American model requires coursework, research, publications, and a dissertation. These programs are located in Europe (10), the United States (8), Canada (2), Australia (2), and Africa (2). In a number of other programs students could earn a PhD by choosing to specialize in HPE or medical education under the umbrella of a broader programmatic area, such as higher and adult education, psychology, sociology, or kinesiology. There were also some programs that did not follow a structured curriculum, with candidates completing a number of publishable research projects meeting the requirements for a doctoral degree through guidance, supervision and apprenticeships (Tekian, 2014). These doctoral graduates are employed by a range of institutions, including schools of medicine and health sciences, professional associations and boards (e.g., Association of American Medical Colleges), and health-care delivery systems.

Integrating Adult Education Within HPE

Changes within the health-care delivery system have led to a demand for different types of education in all health professions, resulting in a recognition that educators who teach in health professions programs need to be prepared to meet this challenge. With the increase in the number of HPE programs it is imperative that the fields of adult and continuing education and HPE work together so that the knowledge base in each area is expanded and enhanced (Daley & Cervero, 2018). Yet, the question exists, how can these two areas be integrated for the benefit of both and for the students they serve?

Thibault (2013a) provides one framework to support this integration. Thibault, at a keynote address to the American Association of Colleges of Osteopathic Medicine, advanced the following six areas of innovation for HPE:

1. Interprofessional and interdisciplinary education
2. New models of clinical education
3. New content to complement the biological sciences
4. Competency-based education
5. Increased efficiency and individualization of education
6. Incorporation of new educational and information technologies

Even though Thibault's (2013a) six areas of innovation were drawn primarily from medical education, it is evident that meeting the call for these 6 innovations in HPE will rely on the incorporation of adult and continuing education concepts, theories, and principles.

For example, within interprofessional and interdisciplinary education (Brandt, 2018), adult education and learning can assist HPE educators to understand and incorporate team-based learning, problem-based learning, and learning in context within their practice. Each of these areas has the potential to move interprofessional education and practice from a developing concept to an actual practice reality. The importance of interprofessional education cannot be underestimated. According to the IOM (2015), poor preparation of health professionals for working together is reflected in a range of adverse health-care outcomes including lower provider and patient satisfaction, greater numbers of medical errors and other patient safety issues, low workforce retention, system inefficiencies resulting in higher costs, and suboptimal community engagement. IPE experts have identified that effective interprofessional teaching methods need to incorporate strategies focused on how adults learn, interactive learning in interprofessional groups, collaborative learning, reflective learning and ideally are problem focused and related to interprofessional collaborative practice (Barr et al., 2005). However, as Brandt (2018) identified health professions educators tend to bring their own approaches to teaching and learning within their disciplines to IPE work. Most often the underlying theoretical premise of these beliefs is not identified even though HPE educators may use behavioral, competency-based, or humanistic approaches to learning. Brandt (2018) identifies that there are areas of adult learning and education that are untapped and could strengthen HPE approaches to interdisciplinary education. These include workplace learning (Marsick & Watkins, 2001) and informal learning. Incorporating these approaches into HPE has the potential to strengthen both the learning design of IPE along with the systems approach to IPE implementation, ultimately advancing interdisciplinary education within HPE programs.

Thibault (2013a) also calls for new models of clinical education. Bierema (2018) expands this view by identifying that: "[HPE] that focuses on updating individual professionals and teaching them new skills without regard for their work contexts serves neither the profession nor the public well" (p. 29). Adult learning can again assist in fostering the development of new models of clinical education by incorporating principles of situated cognition, authentic learning and assessment, along with specific concepts on apprenticeship advocated by Pratt et al. (2016), who indicate, "The apprenticeship perspective focuses on context-physical, temporal, social and cultural contexts-where people are learning how to engage and work in relation to others" (p. 117). In addition, Bierema's (2018) model of the T-shaped professional has implications for new models of clinical education. According to Bierema, who builds on the work of Harris (2009), the T-shaped professional is one who possesses deep expert knowledge in their own discipline and yet has the ability to cross boundaries, solving problems and collaborating within and across the health-care system. In this model, the vertical line of the T represents the deep expert knowledge and the horizontal line represents the broader-based system knowledge. Bierema and Callahan (2014) propose that HPE programs should focus on developing T-shaped professionals in four areas: learning, relating, changing, and leading. This is a much more in-depth approach to clinical education and, as Bierema (2018), indicates:

> Professional education that strives to be T-shaped and balances both depth and breadth of learning helps ensure HPE makes a positive impact on the professions in the face of ambiguous, uncertain, and shifting landscape of healthcare and paves the way for it to become more transformative and interdependent. (p. 38)

Thibault (2013a) goes on to advocate for new content to complement the biological sciences. It appears there are two components driving this need. First, the fact that within all health-care education there is a huge level of content saturation. The amount of knowledge incorporated into health professions curricula has exploded, and biological sciences is no exception. Second, there needs to be a much tighter link between biological sciences, such as physiology and pathophysiology and the clinical practice of a health-care discipline. Nursing education has dealt with these issues by developing a concept-based curriculum (Giddens & Brady, 2007). Within a concept-based curriculum, faculty identify major concepts that students need and define these concepts across patient populations, life span, and specialty areas. Then specific concept-based teaching and learning strategies are incorporated to assist the students in applying and integrating the concepts within their practice.

Adult educators are well versed in the program planning and curriculum approaches to developed concept-based curricula. Schmidt and Lawson (2018) identify that program planning and curriculum development from an adult education perspective deals with the complexity of the process. They state:

> Both Sork's (2000) framework and Caffarella and Daffron's (2013) model emphasize the often non-linear process of program planning by focusing more on key issues to consider and questions to ask throughout the process and focusing less on specific steps to take and the order in which those steps are taken. (p. 42)

Developing curriculum to link biological sciences and clinical practice is a multifaceted and challenging process that could be assisted by incorporating some of the planning models identified by Schmidt and Lawson (2018).

Additionally, the integration of theoretical components with clinical practice will need to be supported with conceptual teaching and learning approaches, such as concept maps (Daley, 2010; Torre et al., 2013), case studies, and clinical exemplars. These conceptual approaches to teaching and learning provide strategies by which the learner can find meaningful ways to assimilate their overall knowledge within their delivery of patient centered care.

Thibault's (2013a) fourth innovation is competency-based education. Competency-based education requires the identification of specific outcomes or knowledge, skills, and attitudes that students demonstrate upon completion of a course, unit, or program. Within a competency-based framework, assessment of student learning is essential. As Moore (2018) demonstrates, adult educators are well positioned to offer assistance in this area to HPE programs and faculty. Moore explains that the overall purpose of assessment is to determine if students developed the expected levels of competence, and yet assessment can also focus on helping a learner develop the expected competencies within a course. Moore sees assessment as a continuum with three components, including needs assessment, formative assessment, and summative assessment. For a competency-based education program to be effective it is first important to understand what the learner currently knows and what the learners are expected to know by the end of the course. Then formative assessment in the form of feedback and guidance is provided continually throughout the course. Finally, summative assessment determines if the learner has achieved the expected level of competency.

Competency-based education programs also require a change in the role of the teacher and the learner. The learner needs to adapt by developing skills to search out knowledge and information to support and enhance their own learning. The teacher needs to adapt by focusing on the assessment of learning versus the presentation of content. These are major shifts in the teaching–learning interaction and will most likely require practice and advanced study on both the part of the learner and teacher. Torre and Durning (2018) highlight this point in their explanation of the transition from clinician to educator. When describing their pursuit of an advanced degree in HPE they state:

> I am a better physician and a teacher as a result of my health professional education degree. Through having an in-depth understanding of learning, feedback, motivation, emotion, and assessment I am better able to instruct my patients (as well as my learners) and this was an unexpected consequence of getting an advanced degree. (p. 91)

Increased efficiency and individualization of education is the fifth innovation in the Thibault (2013a) framework. Adult educators have a long history of implementing efficient and individualized education through the use of learning contracts, development of self-learning projects (Merriam et al., 2006), and the creation of mentored and precepted learning experiences. As mentioned previously, careful curriculum and program planning, developing competency-based education, and using conceptual approaches in teaching can all lead to more efficient and individualized education.

In addition, for education to be truly individualized, the educator needs to understand how adults develop so that educational interventions can be linked to adult developmental stages. Tisdell and Palmer (2018) identify that there are many adult development theories, but most often they are grouped in the following areas: (a) the stage and phase theories, (b) narrative perspectives on development, and (c) life events and transitions perspectives (Anderson et al., 2011; Merriam et al., 2006). Understanding the developmental stage of adult learners can assist the health professions educator to not only plan the education but also tailor it to the specific individual needs of the learner. As Tisdell and Palmer (2018) identify, understanding adult development allows the educator to interpret "how each person makes meaning of their lives in light of sociocultural factors, the historical context, and their professional status as health care providers/educators" (p. 19).

Finally, Thibault (2013a) calls for the incorporation of new educational and information technologies. Online learning, blended learning, along with the initiation of clinical simulation training are areas in which adult educators practice. A significant amount of the research in distance education has been conducted by adult educators and disseminated in various formats worldwide (Zawacki-Richter et al., 2009). Additionally, adult educators have created and implemented both high-fidelity and low-fidelity simulations with faculty in various health professions programs.

So, as we see here, Thibault's (2013a) call for multiple innovations in HPE can be supported and enhanced by collaboration and cooperation with adult education programs and faculty. One such example of this collaboration is the master of education in health professions education (MEHPE) described by Hansman (2018). The MEHPE program is a collaborative graduate program between Cleveland State University and the Cleveland Clinic.

As HPE program development moves forward, interdisciplinary education, new models of clinical education, new content linking biological sciences with clinical practice, competency-based education, efficiency and individualization of education, and information technologies will all require individuals with both expertise in clinical disciplines along with expertise in facilitating learning and delivering education. As Bierema (2018) suggests this will necessitate the development of a cadre of T-shaped HPE professionals, with the T crossing both axes of adult education and clinical practice.

Conclusion

This chapter has explored the developing area of HPE, along with the ways in which adult and continuing education can serve as the foundation for HPE programs. The health-care context is changing in dramatic and unprecedented ways. This change will require a new type of educator to foster the development of practitioners who can deliver quality health care in this evolving and intensifying environment. To assist in providing this type of educator, HPE and adult and continuing education programs will need to work side-by-side to draw on the strengths of each discipline in new and innovative ways.

As IOM (2003) has indicated, most HPE programs are preparing practitioners for a health-care system that no longer exists. In order for this to change, HPE educators need to work across boundaries and systems in order to create new ways to foster learning, education, leadership, and change. As Godin (2012) indicates, "Our job is obvious: we need to get out of the way, shine a light, and empower a new generation to teach itself and to go further and faster than any generation ever has" (p. 187).

References

Anderson, M., Goodman, J., & Schlossberg, N. (2011). *Counseling adults in transition* (4th ed.). Springer.

Balmer, J. T. (2012). Transforming continuing education across the health professions. *Journal of Continuing Education in Nursing, 43*(8), 340–341. https://doi.org/10.3928/00220124-20120725-02

Barr, H., Koppel, I., Reeves, S., Hammick, M., & Freeth, D. S. (2005). *Effective interprofessional education: Argument, assumption and evidence*. Blackwell.

Bierema, L. (2018). Adult learning in health professions education. *New Directions for Adult and Continuing Education, 2018*(157), 27–40.

Bierema, L. L., & Callahan, J. L. (2014). Transforming HRD: A framework for critical HRD practice. *Advances in Developing Human Resources, 16*(4), 429–444.

Brandt, B. (2018). Rethinking health professions education through the lens of interprofessional practice and education. *New Directions for Adult and Continuing Education, 2018*(157), 65–76.

Caffarella, R., & Daffron, S. (2013). *Planning programs for adult learners: A practical guide* (3rd ed.). Jossey-Bass.

Cervero, R. M., Artino, A., Daley, B. J., & Durning, S. J. (2017). Health professions education graduate programs are a pathway to strengthening continuing professional development. *Journal of Continuing Education in the Health Professions, 37*(2), 147–151. https://doi.org/10.1097/CEH.0000000000000155

Cottrell, R. R., Girvan, J. T., & McKenzie, J. F. (2009). *Principles and foundations of health promotion and education*. Benjamin Cummings.

Daley, B. (2010). Concept maps: Practice applications in adult education and human resource development. *New Horizons in Adult Education and Human Resource Development, 24*(2), 31–37. https://doi.org/10.1002/nha3.10383

Daley, B. J., & Cervero, R.M. (Eds.). (2018). Adult and continuing education: Foundations for health professions education programs [Themed issue]. *New Directions for Adult and Continuing Education, 2018*(157).

Frenk J., Chen L., Bhutta Z. A., Cohen J., Crisp N., Evans T., Fineberg H., Garcia P., Ke Y., Kelley P., Kistnasamy B., Meleis A., Naylor D., Pablos-Mendez A., Reddy S., Scrimshaw S., Sepulveda J., Serwadda D., & Zurayk H. (2010). Health professionals for a new century: Transforming education to strengthen health systems in an interdependent world. *The Lancet, 376*, 1923–1958.

Giddens, J. F., & Brady, D. P. (2007). Rescuing nursing education from content saturation: The case for a concept-based curriculum. *Journal of Nursing Education, 46*(2), 65–69.

Godin, S. (2012). *Stop stealing dreams*. http://www.sethgodin.com/sg/docs/stopstealingdreamsscreen.pdf

Hansman, C. A. (2018). Starting a health professions education graduate program. *New Directions for Adult and Continuing Education, 2018*(157), 77–86.

Harris, P. (2009). Help wanted: "T-shaped" skills to meet 21st century needs. *T+D, 63*(9), 42–47.

Institute of Medicine. (2001). *Crossing the quality chasm: A new health system for the 21st century.* The National Academies Press.

Institute of Medicine. (2003). *Health professions education: A bridge to quality* (A. C. Greiner & E. Knebel, Eds.). The National Academies Press.

Institute of Medicine. (2010). *Redesigning continuing education in the health professions.* The National Academies Press.

Institute of Medicine. (2015). *Measuring the impact of interprofessional education on collaborative practice and patient outcomes. Board on Global Health: Institute of Medicine.* National Academies Press.

Lutifyya, M. N., Brandt, B. F., & Cerra, F. (2016). Reflections from the intersection of health professions education and clinical practice: The state of the science of interprofessional education and collaborative practice. *Academic Medicine, 91*(6), 766–771.

Lypson, M. L., Woolliscroft, J. O., Roll, L. C., & Spahlinger, D. A. (2016). Health professions education must change: What educators need to know about the changing clinical context. *Academic Medicine, 91*(4), 602. https://doi.org/10.1097/acm.0000000000000984

Marsick, V., & Watkins, K. (2001). Informal and incidental learning: What informal and incidental learning look like. *New Directions for Adult and Continuing Education, 2001*(89), 25–34.

Merriam, S. B., Caffarella, R. S., & Baumgartner, L. M. (2006). *Learning in adulthood: A comprehensive guide* (3rd ed.). Jossey-Bass.

Moore, D. (2018). Assessment of learning and program evaluation in health professions education programs. *New Directions for Adult and Continuing Education, 2018*(157), 51–64.

Mylopoulos, M., Brydges, R., Woods, N. N., Manzome, J., & Schwartz, D. L. (2016). Preparation for future learning: A missing competency in health professions education? *Medical Education, 50*(1), 115–123. https://doi.org/10.1111/medu.12893

National Academies of Sciences and Medicine. (2016). *Envisioning the future of health professional education: Workshop summary.* The National Academies Press.

Paterson, M. A., Fair, M., Cashman, S. B., Evans, C., & Garr, D. (2015). Achieving the triple aim: A curriculum framework for health professions education. *American Journal of Preventive Medicine, 49*(2), 294–296. https://doi.org/10.1016/j.amepre.2015.03.027

Pratt, D., Smulders, D., & Associates. (2016). *Five perspectives on teaching: Mapping a plurality of the good* (2nd ed.). Krieger.

Schmidt, S., & Lawson, L. (2018). Program planning in health professions education. *New Directions for Adult and Continuing Education, 2018*(157), 41–50.

Sork, T. J. (2000). Planning educational programs. In A. L. Wilson & E. R. Hayes (Eds.), *Handbook of adult and continuing education,* (pp. 171–190). Jossey-Bass.

Tekian, A. (2014). Doctoral programs in health professions education. *Medical Teacher, 36*(1), 73–81. https://doi.org/10.3109/0142159x.2013.847913

Tekian, A., & Artino, A. R., Jr. (2013). Master's degree in health professions education programs. *Academic Medicine, 88*(9), 1399. https://doi.org/10.1097/ACM.0b013e31829decf6

Tekian, A., & Artino, A. R., Jr. (2014). Overview of doctoral programs in health professions education. *Academic Medicine, 89*(9), 1309. https://doi.org/10.1097/acm.0000000000000421

Tekian, A., Roberts, T., Batty, H. P., Cook, D. A., & Norcini, J. (2014). Preparing leaders in health professions education. *Medical Teacher, 36*(3), 269–271. https://doi.org/10.3109/0142159x.2013.849332

Thibault, G. E. (2013a, April). *Innovations in health professions education and the future of health care* [Keynote address]. American Association of Colleges of Osteopathic Medicine Conference.

Thibault, G. E. (2013b). Reforming health professions education will require culture change and closer ties between classroom and practice. *Health Affairs, 32*(11), 1928–1932. https://doi.org/10.1377/hlthaff.2013.0827

Thomas, D. C., Berry, A., Djuricich, A. M., Kitto, S., Kreutzer, K. O., Van Hoof, T. J., Carney, P. A., Kalishman, S., & Davis, D. (2016). What is implementation science and what forces are driving a change in medical education? *American Journal of Medical Quality, 32*(4), 438–444. https://doi.org/10.1177/1062860616662523

Tisdell, L., & Palmer, C. (2018). Adult development in health professions education: The need for self-care. *New Directions for Adult and Continuing Education, 2018*(157), 17–26.

Torre, D. M., & Durning, S. J. (2018). Making the transition: Clinical practitioner to health professions educator. *New Directions for Adult and Continuing Education, 2018*(157), 87–96.

Torre, D. M., Durning, S. J., Daley, B. J. (2013). Twelve tips for teaching with concept maps in medical education. *Medical Teacher, 35,* 201–208. https://doi.org/10.3109/0142159X.2013.759644

Zawacki-Richter, O., Bäcker, E.M., & Vogt, S. (2009). Review of distance education research (2000–2008): Analysis of research areas, methods and authorship patterns. *The International Review of Research in Open and Distributed Learning, 10*(6), 21–50. http://www.irrodl.org/index.php/irrodl/article/view/741/1433

CHAPTER 27

Continuing Professional Education

Maureen Coady

The need for lifelong learning is stressed throughout the formal education that professionals receive before they enter into service. Yet learning as a preservice student within a controlled framework and focusing on assessable outcomes is significantly different than learning in professional practice. Indeed, as individuals become professionals and participate in professional practice, they acquire knowledge, gain skills, and increase occupational sensibilities through practical experiences or through informal or formal study (Cervero & Daley, 2016). This area of emphasis in adult and continuing education that concerns professional groups and their learning and development beyond initial preparation is typically referred to as continuing professional education (CPE). *CPE* is used as an umbrella term in this chapter to describe a continuum of learning opportunities (formal, nonformal, informal) that enable practicing professionals to continue to learn and to maintain professional competence across their careers (Coady, 2016).

The overall aim of this chapter is to provide a historical account of critical issues and debates that have shaped the field and CPE practice over time, beginning with the remarkable growth of professionalization of occupations in the 1970s and 1980s. As the chapter will reveal, although CPE as an area of study and educational practice has existed since the 1960s, the landscape of CPE remains highly contested terrain. One key tension is that, despite recognition that professionals learn and construct knowledge by connecting concepts from their practice experiences and CPE activities, systems and practices of CPE continue to focus primarily on the delivery of content rather than on enhancing learning (Cervero & Daley, 2016; Fenwick & Nerland, 2014; Webster-Wright, 2009, 2010). Not surprisingly, education scholars have long contested such conceptualizations of CPE that assume "knowledge is a commodity that is transferable to practice; that outcomes can be standardized and controlled, leading to a greater certainty in professional practice; and that professionals are deficient in areas of their practice and in need of development" (Cervero & Daley, 2016, p. 11). This pull between the more mechanistic and "input-led" approaches to CPE, and those that are learning focused, accentuating the vital importance of experiential learning, is an ongoing tension in the CPE literature (Coady, 2016; Cole, 2006).

Recent debates reconceptualize professional development, less as a checklist of required professional competencies or accumulated points or hours of CPE, but as a process of development acquired through continuous learning in and from practice. In this context, professionals are assumed to have the inherent ability to draw on previous experience and navigate through new learning opportunities by their own merits, and through the assistance rather than the enforcement of others (Witnebel, 2012). This reflective capacity is regarded as an essential characteristic in the process of maintaining professional competency across a professional career (Kinsella & Pitman, 2012; Schön, 1983, 1987).

History and Background of CPE

Some notion of *continuing education* has been with us since at least the Middle Ages, although prior to the 1960s, little systematic thought was given to the need for *continuing professional education* beyond the 3 to 6 years of a professional's initial education. Many leaders in the professions believed that the years of preservice professional education, along with some refreshers, were sufficient for a lifetime of work (Queeney, 2000). By the 1970s, however, rapid social change, the explosion of research-based knowledge, and societal demands for greater professional accountability and consumer protection gave rise to the professionalization of occupations, and the need to prepare people continually through CPE became evident (Cervero, 2000, 2001; Cervero & Wilson, 2001, 2006; Houle, 1980).

Fueled by the remarkable growth of professionalization in the 1970s and 1980s, standardized bodies of accredited knowledge were developed, and organized programs of continuing education began to be developed and delivered (Cervero & Daley, 2011, 2016). Steadily rising acceptable levels of performance has led CPE to become increasingly mandated and tied to credential renewal (licensure), certification, ensuring the professional's accountability and ability to keep up to date with the profession's knowledge base (Cervero & Daley, 2016). Today, remaining in good standing in many professions requires that individuals provide evidence of having engaged with the profession's required training and the appropriate number of continuing education units (Jeris, 2010).

Notwithstanding these developments, most professions today embrace the importance of lifelong professional education, and their members regularly participate in a diverse array of CPE offerings to increase their knowledge and competence in professional practice. These CPE offerings are made available by a pluralistic group of providers (e.g., workplaces, private organizations, professional associations/regulatory agencies, universities, etc.) who use a variety of terms to describe the concept of CPE, including *continuing professional development*, *professional learning*, and *staff development*, and who deliver CPE in different settings using a variety of modalities (see Cervero & Daley, 2011, 2016).

Houle, Lifelong Learning, and CPE (1960–1980)

CPE as a distinct area of interest within adult and continuing education emerged in the 1960s largely as a result of the work of Houle, who explored the learning and development needs of 17 different occupational groups, ranging from traditional to emergent professions, over 20 years. Houle's work explored the experience of postqualification professionals as they worked to keep up with new developments, gain mastery, understand the connection of their field to related disciplines, and grow as people as well as professionals. Having noted similarities in the CPE efforts across professions, Houle wondered whether understanding these similarities might yield a fresh exchange of ideas, practices, and solutions to commonly shared problems. This work, culminated in the seminal text *Continuing Learning in the Professions* (Houle, 1980) and was groundbreaking, establishing a strong link between continuing education and lifelong learning (Jeris, 2010). For example, one of Houle's key findings was the recognition that across these professional groups, experiential knowledge (informal learning) acquired from practice was often more useful than what was acquired through more formal forms of continuing education (Queeney, 2000). Considering this, Houle emphasized *continuous* and *self-directed learning*—a desire and obligation to continue to learn over the course of one's professional career—as a primary concern and focus of CPE. He espoused that professionals were agentic individuals, capable of determining their own learning needs, and he saw the educational systems and processes serving those needs as secondary (Jeris, 2010).

The work of Donald Schön (1983, 1987), published in the same decade, reinforced Houle's thinking. Schön argued that those who are competent may have developed their capability through more self-directed methods rather than formal educational opportunities. His work emphasized the value and potential for reflective practices (experiential learning rather than classroom learning) to support the development of professional competency.

CPE Developments Post-Houle (1980–2000)

New developments and insights that built on the work of Houle and Schön have broadened and deepened thinking about professional learning, professional competency, and CPE practices. Yet, in some areas, little has changed. For example, 20 years later, scholars Mott and Daley (2000) lamented that while CPE had undergone significant changes, little progress had been made toward establishing it as a field of educational practice. In fact, they noted that in many ways CPE was even more fragmented than in Houle's earlier conceptualization and vision for how professionals might proceed in the 20th and 21st centuries:

> The task for this generation is to move ahead as creatively as possible, amid all the distractions and complexities of practice to aid professions . . . constantly to refine their sensitiveness, enlarge their concepts, add to their knowledge, and perfect their skills so that they can discharge their responsibilities within the context of their own personalities and the needs of society of which they are collectively a part. (Houle, 1980, p. 316)

Indeed, in stark contrast to Houle's holistic vision, Cervero (2000) claimed that what remained prevalent was a rather universally narrow conceptualization and belief that the aim of CPE was to keep professionals up to date on the profession's knowledge base. Like Houle, Cervero observed the race toward professionalization and the growing use of CPE to regulate practice as having shaped a deeply embedded view that professional practice consisted of instrumental problem-solving made rigorous by the application of scientific theory and technique (Schön, 1987). Like Schön, Cervero questioned the underlying assumptions, arguing that this conceptualization of professional practice was insufficient, given that in the "swampy lowlands" (Schön, 1983, p. 43) of professional practice, messy and confusing problems often defy technical solutions.

Like Houle and Schön, Cervero (2000) believed in the expert knowledge held by practitioners and in their capacity to determine their own need for updating, upskilling, or development. He contended that to be truly effective in CPE, a model of learning must be at the heart of educational practice, and he expanded understanding of the multiple forms of knowledge needed in professional practice. He proposed a more expansive conceptualization, encompassing not only technical knowledge but also practical knowledge—the accumulation of tacit knowledge from experience, which is recognized to contribute to a professional's wisdom and ability to exercise discretionary judgment in practice (Cole, 2006; Goodfellow, 2003; Kinsella & Pitman, 2012). This prompted Daley (2000) to imagine that a valuable model of learning might extend to consider—beyond knowledge requirements—how professionals learn and make meaning of new knowledge from CPE in their distinctive practice contexts—those places where they provided care or delivered services.

What Daley (2000) and Mott (2000) discovered was that professionals made knowledge meaningful through constructivist learning—by establishing connections among the knowledge learned through CPE, previous experiences, and the context in which they found themselves, as well as how they perceived that context. Daley extended this notion of constructivist thinking, emphasizing transformative learning as a way of explaining how professionals acquire new information and then potentially change their understanding of that information (i.e., construct new meaning frames) based on experience. Daley proposed that professionals develop from novice to expert, along a continuum, as they learn to "rely on past concrete experiences rather than on abstract principles, as they understand situations as integrated wholes rather than as discrete parts, and as they begin to act as involved performers rather than detached observers" (p. 39). As they developed into exemplary practitioners along this continuum, it seemed that the development of reflective skills—self-awareness, description, critical analysis, synthesis and evaluation—was an important learning dimension to be incorporated into both preservice and CPE efforts (Daley & Cervero, 2016). Reflection and critical reflection encourage practitioners to critically examine the "common-sense" premises underlying their day-to-day actions, potentially leading to altered perceptions (Mezirow, 1990), changes in behavior, and, ultimately, improvements in service quality (i.e., transformative learning).

Daley (2000) acknowledged that basing one's CPE practice on a model of learning or a learning system involves a significant change in mind-set for most CPE providers who work from the assumption that professionals merely transfer information to their practice. She had discovered that transfer of learning and adoptions of innovation are part of the knowledge construction process and an integral part of a professional's learning (Daley, 2001). As such, she advocated that shifting the role of CPE provider from developer of specific program content to facilitator of learning, and including methods that encourage the participants to link the content of the CPE program to their actual practice and work environment, significantly enhances the meaning they can derive from CPE.

Wilson (2000, 2001) observed that the large-scale organization and systemized delivery of professional services in the 1990s was creating an emphasis on *system competency*, such that systems, not individual practitioners, provided services. The result, he feared, was that professionals were "constantly producing and reproducing the institutional and social mechanism by which they were required to operate, leading to the increasing loss of professional autonomy, and corresponding organizational rather than client allegiance" (p. 78). The growing dominance of these expert systems, he argued, was superseding and undermining the traditional power and autonomy of the individual professional expert, such that they were experiencing a "failure of professional knowing" (Schön, 1987, p. 78) and were uncertain about how to use their expertise to serve client needs. To counteract this, Wilson (2001) encouraged continuing professional educators (while continuing to provide knowledge and technique updates) to more deeply consider the fundamental nature of professional practice, and ways to support professionals in reclaiming their professional (i.e., discretionary) power and capacity for client advocacy.

New Conceptual Horizons (2000–2010)
A year later, Cervero (2001) turned his gaze to persistent issues that impeded progress in building an effective system of CPE across professions. His analysis revealed political and ethical struggles and the need for clarification and consensus on at least three issues, which he framed using the following questions: *Continuing education for what?* (the struggle between updating professionals' knowledge versus improving practice); *Who benefits from continuing education?* (the struggle between the learning agenda and the political and economic agendas of continuing educators); and *Who will provide continuing education?* (the struggle for turf versus collaborative relationships). Subsequently, Jeris and Conway (2003) added the following question: *What impact does the workplace as the site for CPE have on its planning, design, delivery, content, and participation and outcomes?* (the struggle between continuing education learning agenda and the goal of performance improvement through increased productivity).

Scholars have field-tested these critical questions in diverse practice contexts. For example, Umber et al. (2001) investigated power relationships within the context of a continuing education program in public health and discovered that the practice of CPE was shaped by power relationships rooted in complex historical organizational processes, such that courses often did not meet the interests of some stakeholders. They found interests, power relations, and programs were not static and needed to be continually negotiated. Similarly, Daley (2002) found that in addition to the organizational culture, the level of professional autonomy and the sociocultural background (including class, race, gender, and sexual orientation) and positionality of the individual shaped professional learning, and so needed to be considered in planning CPE.

Cervero's (2001) critical questions also served as a useful critical lens for examining the broader discourses guiding the practice of CPE. For example, with these questions in mind, Tobias (2003) examined the underlying ideology and essentialist nature of existing models and discourses on professional development, including discourses on professionalization. He found tensions and contradictory tendencies were inherent in all forms of initial and continuing professional development and corresponding CPE. For example, while the processes of professionalization had played a key role in raising the standards of technical competence of members, thus enabling them to achieve higher levels of excellence in their fields, the same processes and standardized performance guidelines often limited creativity. Moreover, while the drive to regulate practice ensured observable measurable professional skills, these skills were sometimes valued over more ephemeral professional qualities such as empathy. Tobias's work highlighted the limitations of a "one size fits all" approach and the need to consider important political and ethical questions—such as those posed by Cervero—in any debate about the boundaries or the aims, structure, and purposes of continuing professional development and CPE.

The integrated nature of the multiple providers in CPE, and the multiple goals of these providers, was further probed by Dirkx and Austin (2002, 2005) as they searched to locate a common framework for professionals to understand their work, irrespective of context. Their subsequent conceptual model depicted the aims of CPE to include technical, practical, and emancipatory goals, and it provided for consideration of contexts and aims from the point of view of the focus on the organization or individual. The intended advantages for CPE planners was that it helped them to identify and think about aims, purposes, and practice boundaries.

Slightly earlier research had examined practice boundaries. For example, Jeris and Daley (2004) examined the boundaries between CPE and human resource development (HRD). They were interested in ways that both fields could share and learn from each other to enhance the performance and value of CPE to organizations and individuals. What scholars in their collection discovered was that CPE has traditionally conceptualized learning and change largely from an individualistic or psychological perspective, while HRD stressed organizational culture and broader institutional factors that needed to be considered in any change initiative (Bierema & Eraut, 2004).

In continuing their comparative analysis, Dirkx et al. (2004) took a deeper look at change theory within CPE and HRD and their underlying assumptions, concluding that both fields needed to be grounded in a more holistic understanding of work-related learning and change and how it could be facilitated. Like others, they challenged assumptions of lifelong learning that viewed professional development knowledge as objective, distinct from the practitioners who act on it, and not related to the particular sociocultural context (Daley, 2001, 2002; Houle, 1980). Inspired by scholars who were exploring the spiritual nature of work and learning (e.g., English et al., 2003; Palmer 2004; West, 2001), they offered a more expansive conceptualization of lifelong learning, proposing that the professional's identity was deeply intertwined with the processes of developing and sustaining knowledge in practice.

In Dirkx et al.'s (2004) view, professional development knowledge is influenced by the many subjective and richly felt, embodied dimensions of practice, including the concrete relationships, feelings, emotions, and instincts that shape professionals. Like Daley (2001, 2002) and Fenwick (2000) before them, they argued that how people come to understand new information and techniques varies and acquires meaning and purpose, "when filtered through the experience and existing understandings that the practitioner brings to the tasks, as well as sociocultural context in which these tasks are performed" (p. 40). In this conceptualization, *the self* is viewed as active in the coconstruction of knowledge, and lifelong learning in professional practice is characterized by "an evolving awareness of the self in relationship with itself, with others and with the social and cultural context" (Dirkx et al., 2004, p. 40). As such, a major aim in preservice and continuing professional development, they argued, should be to foster self-understanding.

Dirkx (2008) further pursued the notions of self-understanding and self-formation—the iterative cycles of self-forming, re-forming, and transforming throughout one's life (Palmer, 1998, 2004)—as central dynamics of professional learning. Rational processes alone, he argued, do not fully explain how professionals come to know how to navigate the messy and ill-structured nature that makes up much of what constitutes professional practice (Schön, 1983)—that place where there are no pat strategies, methods, or specific models to guide the way. In his view, the constructive, intuitive, and subjective dimensions provide a more expansive way of understanding the process of knowing in action (Schön, 1983, 1987). As such, Dirkx (2008) argued for the "augmentation of highly technical and rational conceptualizations of professional training and continuing education, with an emphasis on the ongoing importance of self-formative processes within the lives of [preservice] students and practicing professionals" (p. 66).

Expanding Conceptualizations of CPE (2010–2018)

Delving more deeply into the spiritual dimensions of practice, Dirkx (2013) explored the potential for meaning and purpose in work—those elements that contribute to "leading lives that matter" (p. 358). He and others (see Palmer, 1998, 2004; Tennant, 2012) postulated that meaningful work arises from deep integration of these inner and outer aspects of professional work—the *inner work* involves learning that allows us to connect with our souls and ourselves (embodied learning), and the *outer work* as learning (often beyond our control) associated with navigating: "the physical or structural organization of one's work, the individuals with whom one works, the culture of the organization in which one works, and the perception of the power and authority relations that characterize one's work environment" (p. 361). These inner and outer dimensions, Dirkx contends, provide a fundamental focus for lifelong learning and CPE, such that professionals are able to develop a more authentic presence and relationships in their work. In this sense, the knowledge developed and deployed for use in practice is always unique to the individual, and, in that sense authentic; this authentic activity provides a basis for thinking about conceptualizations of professional development, and how to support professional learning through CPE.

This notion of *authenticity*—used in education with respect to authentic tasks as genuine and embedded in real life—has been taken up more recently by scholars to more vividly convey this more holistic way of thinking about professional learning. For example, Webster-Wright (2009, 2010) advances a concept of *authentic professional learning* to emphasize professional learning as a personal, complex, and *lived* phenomenon, unique to individuals as they navigate multiple transitions. Like Houle's study (1980), her large-scale studies investigated professional learning from the perspective of professionals themselves, in order to gain insights on their learning, and how it can be supported. Webster-Wright (2010) discovered that professionals learn in situations that are important to them and that these situations "usually are areas they care about enough to engage with effortlessly and with intentionality, yet as the same time, experience uncertainty and doubt" (p. v). She isolated *personal experience* and *intentionality* as the key premises for a professional's ongoing learning, placing pedagogical emphasis on professional learning as a self-directed activity, encompassing not only activity directed by others but also what the individual wishes to achieve.

Webster-Wright (2010) acknowledged that constructive strategies need to be developed to enable change from the practice of delivering CPE to that of supporting authentic professional learning. She identified two interdependent challenges to be changing organizational culture and supporting individual professionals and groups of professionals. What is needed to bridge the gap, she suggested, is a reframing of PD discourses in a way that respects and values professionals' abilities to direct their own learning, while remaining cognizant of the requirements of the contemporary context of standards, accountability, efficiency, and evidence-based outcomes. Any serious effort to support "authentic professional learning" at the organizational level, Webster-Wright contended, must take account of these existing contextual constraints. For example, there is the reality that efforts to regulate practice and maintain standards through CPE are likely to increase, and the learning activities amenable to measurable outcomes are more likely to be those that are officially supported. As a way of broadening this focus, she has advocated for an expansive framework of supports and guiding principles to ensure that professionals are supported to continue to learn in their own authentic manner, while at the same time responding to the realities of their workplace and their professional responsibilities.

Having entered the 21st century, CPE scholars are examining the changing nature and context of professional practice in the knowledge economy. Technological developments are advancing at a rapid pace, challenging the very nature of work and professional practice. For example, Bierema (2016), writing on CPE in organizations and workplaces, draws attention to the fluidity of life for highly interdependent and interconnected professionals who struggle to keep pace with relentless change and unpredictable outcomes. She contends that improvement, understanding complex systems, and promoting innovation are all part of the landscape of learning and coping in the 21st-century workplace. Individuals are expected to be ready to change and adapt in order to stay current with technology, respond to regulations, and stay relevant within a globally competitive context.

Beyond disciplinary knowledge, knowledge and skill requirements are also shifting. Creativity, critical thinking, digital literacy, leadership, and interpersonal communication in a multidisciplinary world are recognized as 21st-century skills (Livingstone & Guile, 2012). At the same time, technologies are being used in a rich range of ways to teach and to support continuous professional learning. Technology-enabled spaces and adaptive technologies that offer new and exciting opportunities in terms of contextual, ambient, augmented, distributed, and social networked learning are emerging (Console, 2013).

Within newer contextual debates, other researchers are working to expand the boundaries and delivery mechanisms of CPE, with a view to greater professional impact on complex societal issues. For example, Rocco et al. (2018) highlight that a critical theory of HRD is emerging that is helping to move the field (HRD) beyond its usual focus on performance, to increased awareness of social issues and causes (i.e., workers' needs and workplace power issues). They argue that this potentially provides new avenues for collaboration of HRD with the field of adult education.

More recent work by Cervero and Daley (2017) highlights the growing prevalence and potential of evidence-based practice and expectations that professionals incorporate the latest research evidence along with their individual expertise and CPE efforts. As professionals study the latest research relevant to their practice, decide how to implement their practice, make changes to their performance and document the results, the potential exists to incorporate formal CPE with more self-directed processes into evidenced based practice.

Highlighting the growing concern with teamwork and inter/multidisciplinary collaboration, collective dialogues and the construct of *communities of practice* (CoPs) (Wenger, 1998) are being examined as a highly relevant space, both within and across professions, for generative learning and innovation. In this context, where professionals collectively reflect on practice and share and create knowledge, Wenger-Trayner et al. (2015) see the real "body of knowledge" (p. 13) of a profession as the community of people who contribute to the continued vitality, application, and evolution of practice, and in this sense, "a profession is best understood as a 'landscape of practice' consisting of a complex system of communities of practice and the boundaries between them" (p. 13). DeGroot et al. (2013) extend this thinking, exploring the potential for transformative learning when the focus in such professional learning communities extends "beyond 'best practices' (collaborative planning, curriculum study, learning assessment) to critical reflection (with others) on their actions, and the social and policy contexts within which these actions are framed" (p. 66). To achieve this, Cranton (2016) suggests strategies for CPE that enable professionals to develop communicative and emancipatory knowledge that helps them be more socially aware, self-determining, and self-reflective. Hansman (2016) agrees that such constructive dialogues, whether constituted as dyadic or group reflection, can also transform the organizational status quo and encourage a bottom-up culture of learning in organizations that can be driven by the real and urgent needs of professionals in the execution of their day-to-day practice and aspirations for social change.

Taking Stock—Moving Forward

In 1980, Houle challenged scholars and practitioners to listen to the *experience* of professionals as a basis for supporting their professional learning. A process of taking stock has revealed that much progress has been made on this agenda. In the subsequent 38 years, scholars including Schön, Cervero, Daley and Mott, Dirkx, Webster-Wright, and others have engaged professionals, significantly deepening understanding about the nature of professional knowledge and how it is constructed and reconstructed through different types of learning transitions. Their collective works reinforce that professional knowing is embodied, contextual, and embedded in practice. Their collective wisdom highlights that changes in learning occur through practice, experience, and critically reflective action within contexts that may pose dilemmas. In this sense, professional learning is situated, social, constructed, and influenced by identity.

These scholars have articulated a reformulated vision of CPE practice and an expanded understanding of the role of CPE providers in supporting learning. They have advanced a vision that the business of CPE is the identification of problems in professional practice and the determination of how education can foster professional development programs that ultimately promote the ability to work in an uncertain, confusing, and dynamic world of professional practice for the betterment of clients.

Apparent, however, is a noticeable disparity between this vision and CPE practice in most professions. Although the theory of and evidence for professional learning is well established, a coordinated system of continuing education—or arriving at any unifying picture of effective CPE across professions—remains elusive decades after Houle and Schön's work.

Looking back, one might ask why this body of knowledge about how professionals learn has not served to support more significant change in the direction envisioned by Houle? Why do CPE providers not embrace the view that developing a professional community and fostering involvement in professional work affects learning? What more needs to be known for providers to shift their focus from creating and transmitting generalizable knowledge to enhancing the knowledge-creating capacities of individuals and professional communities? A closer look, as undertaken more recently by

Cervero and Daley (2016, 2017), reveals that the task of building a coordinated system of continuing education or arriving at any unifying picture of effective CPE across professions is fundamentally a longer-term and more complex process involving multiple stakeholders with distinctive, diverse, and competing professional, social, institutional, and educational agendas. As these agendas are negotiated toward a more integrated approach to CPE in the future, the opportunity exists for this body of knowledge to inform efforts to negotiate agendas. To the extent that these scholars continue to pose critical questions and probe for deeper understandings of professional practice and how professionals learn and come to know, it is likely that their work will continue to shape and reshape understandings and practices of CPE.

References

Bierema, L. (2016). Navigating professional white water: Rethinking continuing professional education at work. *New Directions for Adult and Continuing Education*, 2016(150), 43–53.

Bierema, L., & Eraut, M. (2004). Workplace-focused learning: Perspectives on continuing professional education and human resource development. *Advances in Developing Human Resources*, 6(1), 52–68. https://doi.org/10.1177/1523422303260859

Cervero, R. M. (2000). Trends and issues in continuing professional education. *New Directions for Adult and Continuing Education*, 2000(86), 3–12.

Cervero, R. M. (2001). Continuing professional education in transition. *International Journal of Lifelong Learning*, 20(1–2), 16–30. https://doi.org/10.1080/09638280010008282

Cervero R. M., & Daley, B. J. (2011). Continuing professional education: Multiple stakeholders and agendas. In K. Rubenson (Ed.), *Adult learning and education* (pp. 140–145). Elsevier.

Cervero, R. M., & Daley, B. (2016). Continuing professional education: A contested space. *New Directions for Adult and Continuing Education*, 2016(150), 9–19.

Cervero, R. M., & Daley, B. J. (2017). Continuing professional education: History and influences. In L. Martin, S. Conceição, & A. Knox (Eds.), *International compendium of adult and continuing education*, (Vol. 3, pp. 441–444). Stylus; American Association for Adult and Continuing Education.

Cervero, R. M., & Wilson, A. L. (2001). *Power in practice: Adult education and the struggle for knowledge and power in society*. Jossey-Bass.

Cervero, R. M., & Wilson, A. L. (2006). *Working the planning table: Negotiating democratically for adult, continuing and workplace education*. Jossey-Bass.

Coady, M. (Ed.). (2016). Contexts, practices, and challenges: Critical insights from continuing professional education (CPE) [Themed issue]. *New Directions for Adult and Continuing Education*, 2016(150).

Cole, M. (2006). Learning through reflective practice: A professional approach to effective continuing professional development among healthcare professionals. *Research in Post-Compulsory Education*, 5(1), 23–38. https://doi.org/10.1080/13596740000200067

Console, G. (2013). Tools and resources to guide practice. In H. Beetham & R. Sharpe (Eds.), *Rethinking pedagogy for a digital age: Designing for 21st century learning* (pp. 78–102). Routledge.

Cranton, P. (2016). Continuing professional education for teachers and university and college faculty. *New Directions for Adult and Continuing Education*, 2016(150), 43–53.

Daley, B. J. (2000). Learning in professional practice. *New Directions for Adult and Continuing Education*, 2000(86), 33–43.

Daley, B. J. (2001). Learning and professional practice: A study of four professions. *Adult Education Quarterly*, 52(1), 39–54. https://doi.org/10.1177/074171360105200104

Daley, B. J. (2002). Continuing professional education: Creating the future. *Adult Learning*, 13, 15–17. https://doi.org/10.1177/104515950201300406

Daley, B. J., & Cervero, R. M. (2016). Learning as a basis for continuing professional education. *New Directions for Adult and Continuing Education*, 2016(150), 19–31.

deGroot, E., Maaike, D., Endedijk, A., Jaarsma, A. D., Jan-Simmons, R., & van Beukelen, P. (2013). Critically reflective dialogues in learning communities of professionals. *Studies in Continuing Education*, 35(1), 1–23. https://doi.org/10.1080/0158037X.2013.779240

Dirkx, J. (2008). Care of the self: Mythopoetic dimensions of professional preparation and development. In T. Leonard & P. Willis (Eds.), *Pedagogies of the imagination: Mythopoetic curriculum in educational practice* (pp. 65–83). Springer.

Dirkx, J. (2013). Leaning in and leaning back at the same time: Toward spirituality of work-related learning. *Advances in Developing Human Resources*, 15(4), 356–369. https://doi.org/10.1177/1523422313498562

Dirkx, J., & Austin, A. (2002). *A model of theoretical orientations in professional development*. Unpublished figure included in graduate coursework. Michigan State University.

Dirkx, J. M., & Austin, A. E. (2005, February). *Making sense of continuing professional development: Towards an integrated vision of lifelong learning in the professions* [Paper presentation]. AHRD Preconference on Continuing Professional Education: Exploring a Model of Theoretical Orientations in Professional Development.

Dirkx, J., Gilley, J. W., & Maycunich-Gilley, A. (2004). Change theory in CPE and HRD: Toward a holistic view of learning and change in work. *Advances in Developing Human Resources, 6*(1), 35–51. https://doi.org/10.1177/1523422303260825

English, L. M., Fenwick, T. J., & Parsons, J. (2003). *Spirituality of adult education and training.* Krieger.

Fenwick, T. J. (2000). Expanding conceptualizations of experiential learning. A review of five primary perspectives on cognition. *Adult Education Quarterly, 50*(4), 243–272.

Fenwick, T. J., & Nerland, M. (Eds.). (2014). *Reconceptualizing professional learning: Sociomaterial knowledges, practices and responsibilities.* Routledge.

Goodfellow, J. (2003). Practical wisdom in professional practice: The person in the process. *Contemporary Issues in Early Childhood, 4*(1), 48–63.

Hansman, C. (2016). Mentoring and informal learning as continuing professional education. *New Directions for Adult and Continuing Education, 2016*(150), 53–69.

Houle, C. O. (1980). *Continuing learning in the professions.* Jossey-Bass.

Jeris, L. H. (2010). Continuing professional education. In C. E. Kasworm, A. D. Rose, & J. M. Ross-Gordon (Eds.), *Handbook of adult and continuing education* (pp. 275–282). SAGE.

Jeris, L. H., & Conway, A. E. (2003). Time to regrade the terrain of continuing professional education: Views from practitioners. *Adult Learning, 14*(1), 34–36. https://doi.org/10.1177/104515950301400110

Jeris, L. H., & Daley, B. (2004). Orienteering for boundary spanning: Reflections on the journey to date and suggestions for moving forward. *Advances in Developing Human Resources, 6*(1), 101–115. https://doi.org/10.1177/1523422303260420

Kinsella, E. A., & Pitman, A. (Eds.). (2012). *Phroneiss as professional knowledge: Practical wisdom in the professions.* Sense.

Livingstone, D. L., & Guile, D. (Eds.). (2012). *The knowledge economy and lifelong learning: A critical reader.* Sense.

Mezirow, J. (1990). How critical reflection triggers transformative learning. In J. Mezirow & Associates (Eds.), *Fostering critical reflection in adulthood: A guide to transformative and emancipatory learning* (pp. 1–20). Jossey-Bass.

Mott, V. W. (2000). The development of professional expertise in the workplace. *New Directions for Adult and Continuing Education, 2000*(86), 23–33.

Mott, V. W., & Daley, B. J. (Eds.). (2000). Charting a course for continuing professional education [Themed issue]. *New Directions for Adult and Continuing Education, 2000*(86).

Palmer, P. J. (1998). *The courage to teach: Exploring the inner landscape of a teacher's life.* Jossey-Bass.

Palmer, P. J. (2004). *A hidden wholeness: The journey towards an undivided life.* Jossey-Bass.

Queeney, D. S. (2000). Continuing professional education. In A. Wilson & E. Hayes (Eds.), *Handbook of adult and continuing education* (pp. 375–392). Jossey-Bass.

Rocco, T. S., Munn, S. L., & Collins, J. C. (2018). The critical turn in human resource development. In M. Milano, S. Webb, J. Holford, R. Waller, & P. Jarvis. (Eds.). *The Palgrave international handbook on adult and lifelong learning* (pp. 227–245). Palgrave.

Schön, D. A. (1983). *The reflective practitioner: How professionals think in action.* Arena.

Schön, D. A. (1987). *Educating the reflective practitioner: Toward a new design for teaching and learning in the professions.* Jossey-Bass.

Tennant, M. (2012). *The learning self: Understanding the potential for transformation.* Jossey-Bass.

Tobias, R. (2003). Continuing professional education and professionalization: Travelling without a map or compass? *International Journal of Lifelong Education, 22*(5), 445–456.

Umber, K. E., Cervero, R. M., & Langone, C. A. (2001). Negotiating about power, frames, and continuing education: A case study in public health. *Adult Education Quarterly, 15*(2), 128–145. https://doi.org/10.1177/07417130122087188

Webster-Wright, A. (2009). Reframing professional development through understanding authentic professional learning. *Review of Educational Research, 79*(2), 702–739. https://doi.org/10.3102/0034654308330970

Webster-Wright, A. (2010). *Authentic professional learning: Making a difference through learning at work. Professional and Practice Based Learning Series.* Springer.

Wenger, E. (1998). *Communities of practice: Learning, meaning, and identity.* Cambridge University Press.

Wenger-Trayner, E., Fenton-O'Creevy, M., Hutchinson, S., Krubiak, C., & Wenger-Trayner, B. (Eds.). (2015). *Learning in landscapes of practice: Boundaries of identity, and knowledgeability in practice-based learning.* Routledge.

West, L. (2001). *Doctors on the edge: General practitioners, health and learning in the inner city.* Free Association Books.

Wilson, A. L. (2000). Professional practice in the modern world. *New Directions for Adult and Continuing Education, 2000*(86), 80–86.

Wilson, A. L. (2001). Professionalization: A politics of identity. *New Directions for Adult and Continuing Education, 2001*(91), 73–84.

Witnebel, L. (2012). Business as usual? A review of continuing professional education and adult learning. *Journal of Adult & Continuing Education, 18*(2), 80–88. https://doi.org/10.7227/JACE. 18. 2, 6.

CHAPTER 28

Adult Learners in Higher Education

Matt Bergman

Adult learners, generally defined as students over the age of 24, have been enrolling in U.S. higher education since the mid-1800s when legislation was created and passed by school reformers such as Horace Mann and James Gordon Carter (Remenick, 2019). This legislation provided funding to improve public primary education which increased the need for qualified teachers. State Normal Schools were created to train the teachers, thus opening the door to adult and nontraditional students in higher education (Ogren, 2005). However, it was not until the end of World War II that veterans' GI Bill education benefits "democratized" the collegiate population by making college a viable option for men from a range of sociodemographic backgrounds, including minorities, first-generation Americans, and those from lower income households (Bound & Turner, 2002). Over time, nontraditional and adult student enrollment has grown due to national policies that spurred the advent of Normal Schools, the veteran influx after World War II, the availability of federal financial aid to students, the rise of the community college, and the 1990s online learning boom (Remenick, 2019). Not since the end of World War II have these adult learners played such a key role in the health and viability of higher education (Bowers & Bergman, 2016; MacDonald, 2018). For the purposes of this chapter, I will use the terms *adult learner*, *adult student*, *nontraditional student*, and *mature students* interchangeably, although small distinctions exist among these subpopulations in higher education.

While most depictions of college today feature traditional-age students (18–23 years old) engaging in the campus community as residential students, the fact is that these depictions represent only 26% of U.S. college students today (Bash, 2003; NCES, 2015). The remaining 74% of the entire college-going population in this country exhibits some form of nontraditional characteristics, including students who are enrolled part time, living off campus, working full time, are financially independent, and/or have dependents (NCES, 2015). While students who have nontraditional characteristics are often also adults over the age of 24, they are not always.

Currently, nearly 37% of college students are age 25 years or older, 38% attend part time, 26% are parents, and roughly 41% attend 2-year or nonbachelor's-granting institutions (NCES, 2018b). These percentages are likely to only increase in the coming decade as demographic shifts are signaling a potential 15% reduction in traditional-age college enrollment in the next 6 years due to low birth rates during the 2008–2010 Great Recession (Grawe, 2018). Despite their increased numbers in higher education, of all student subpopulations, adult students continue to be the least understood (Kasworm, 2005), the most difficult to recruit (Hadfield, 2003), and the least likely to persist (Langrehr et al., 2015; Markle, 2015; Osam et al., 2017).

The competing professional and personal responsibilities for adult learners prompts them to identify as workers, parents, or community members first and students second, leading to tenuous enrollment and higher levels of attrition than traditional-age students. Often, these pressures are even greater for female adult students because many of these students are also expected to bear a greater share of domestic and care-giving responsibilities (Deutsch & Schmertz, 2011). This means that colleges and universities in the United States are under more pressure than ever to evolve their operating and delivery models to provide an exceptional student experience with limited operating budgets (Bergman et al., 2018). As changes in the global marketplace drive adult students back into the classroom, it is necessary that institutions of higher learning provide appropriate services and resources to ensure these adults have what they need to attain a baccalaureate degree (Brown, 2002; Hoffman et al., 2011).

Past generations were able to secure any number of jobs in the public sector with a high school diploma; in today's marketplace, however, possession of a high school diploma alone is no longer an adequate qualification for even entry-level positions (Klein-Collins et al., 2010). In the nation's changing economy, a baccalaureate-level degree is a necessity for jobs that never before required one (Bragg et al., 2009). According to Cabrera et al. (2005), "A bachelor's degree is no longer considered a potential stepping-stone to a better life; it is fully acknowledged as the gatekeeper to a myriad of social and individual benefits" (p. 2). Today, there are more than 31 million adults with some college credit but no degree, posing an opportunity for colleges and universities to reengage and graduate those that stopped out last year or long ago (Shapiro et al., 2014). Accordingly, adult learners are garnering added consideration in recruitment, retention, and graduation strategies across the country.

This chapter will discuss the current literature around adult learner–friendly practices that increase the likelihood of persistence to graduation. This chapter is designed to reflect on and add to the body of literature aimed at improving interventions both at a programmatic and policy level for adult and continuing higher education. First, I provide some defining characteristics of nontraditional students. Second, I describe some of the current initiatives and interventions currently used to support these students. Third, I conclude the chapter with some recommendations for future research and practice.

Adult Learners and Their Challenges

Adult learners now comprise close to 40% of higher education enrollment (NCES, 2018b). Yet, defining the word *adult* can be somewhat challenging (Wlodkowski, 1999). Dinmore (1997) argued that adult learners might be better defined by their level of experience instead of chronological age. However, the most widely accepted criteria for identifying this subpopulation of students is age. Consequently, the most consistently recognized criteria for establishing one's classification as an adult learner is the age of 24 and older (Bergman et al., 2014; Horn & Berger, 2004).

Furthermore, Horn and Carroll (1996) defined *nontraditional students* as individuals that meet one of seven characteristics: delaying enrollment after high school, being a part-time student, working more than 35 hours a week, being financially independent, having dependents, being a single parent, or lacking a high school diploma. Horn and Carroll (1996) further differentiated these traits by categorizing nontraditional students as minimally nontraditional (having one of the characteristics), moderately nontraditional (two to three characteristics), or highly nontraditional (four or more characteristics). Researchers have concluded that more than 75% of the undergraduate student population can be classified as nontraditional (having one of the nontraditional characteristics) and most adult learners have at least one or more characteristic of nontraditional status (Choy, 2002; Colvin, 2013; NCES, 2015).

The life experiences and responsibilities of adult and nontraditional students differentiate them from their traditional counterparts. Many adult students have various responsibilities including marriage, children, employment, and civic and social responsibilities (Bergman et al., 2014; Wlodkowski et al., 2001) that limit their ability to engage in academic degree programs. Many of them maintain full-time or part-time employment and have years of work experience. Often nontraditional students are raising children, caring for aging parents, and trying to maintain good health for themselves and their families. They often return to higher education to improve the prospect of career advancement or increase their earning potential in the workforce. Many nontraditional students also report returning to school to fulfill a lifelong goal or to set an example for their families (Bergman et al., 2014). These demands on and motivations of adult students result in educational needs that may differ from what higher education institutions have historically provided. For example, adult students benefit from course scheduling outside of regular business hours, coursework designed to be immediately applicable, and faculty and staff who understand the competing demands placed on these students.

There are many factors that dissuade adults from engaging in higher education; however, no one variable can be identified as the primary reason. By looking at the variables as a cluster, or typology, there are certain groups of variables that rise to the top as the major reason adults do not persist to graduation. Some of the primary reasons include lack of time or energy, cost of tuition, and childcare concerns (Malhotra et al., 2007). Woosley (2004) also reported that stop-out and drop-out students identified financial concerns, family responsibilities, and job conflicts as the leading reasons for not returning to school. These temporary withdrawal habits increase the difficulty in identifying specific variables that contribute to the interruption or might be used to develop a recruitment or retention strategy. Most of these studies found significant indicators related to work and family responsibilities as leading predictors for the withdrawal decisions of students. While some students are able to cope with the multiple demands on their time and persist to completion, others resign themselves to not completing an academic program. Numerous researchers have recently advocated further research on the impact of work and family on nontraditional students to create effective retention strategies (Kasworm, 2018; Kirby et al., 2004; Langrehr et al., 2015). If there is a secret to successful retention, it lies in the willingness of institutions to involve themselves in the social and intellectual development of their students (Tinto, 1998). That institutional commitment often reflects and influences students' commitment to the institution and their involvement in their own learning.

Supporting Adult Students

Over the past several decades, U.S. colleges and universities have increased their support of students on their campuses. These kinds of supports include professional advising, physical and mental health-care providers, bridge programs, peer tutoring and mentoring, career fairs, alternative spring breaks, and other student affairs programming. All of these interventions are designed to foster student engagement (Bergman et al., 2014; Tinto, 2006) and ultimately increase a student's chances of degree attainment. For many nontraditional students, these kinds of supports are either unnecessary or inaccessible. In response, colleges and universities are reimagining institutional support for adult students.

One example of this reimagination is academic advising and student-faculty interactions. Advising services are often the single point of contact on campus outside of instructors for adult learners. Traditionally, academic advising has been provided on campus and during regular business hours. This delivery model disenfranchises nontraditional students who may work during regular business hours or who may not live in geographic proximity to campus. Langrehr et al. (2015) posited that inadequate academic and faculty advising was one of the largest impediments to student retention. Adults view advising as customer service that needs to be prompt and efficient in the dissemination of quality information that assists students to efficiently move toward a baccalaureate degree (Bergman et al., 2014).

Kuh (2008) found academic advising and faculty interaction to be an integral part of any retention, persistence, and student-success initiative. Academic advising that accommodates a flexible schedule or that is provided virtually is a pathway to greater levels of engagement and persistence. Furthermore, academic advisers who are adequately trained and knowledgeable in serving nontraditional students and understanding their unique circumstances is crucial.

Additionally, student-instructor interactions are key to adult student success. Instructors must be both able and willing to support adult students through their instruction, course delivery, and mentoring. For example, instructors should consider instruction and evaluation that incorporates tenets of andragogy such as honoring past experiences and considering the immediate applicability of learning (Knowles et al., 2011). Instructors might also reconsider the notion of office hours by either having flexible office hours or by meeting with students online or off campus.

Online Course Options
Distance education is becoming a more vital part of the higher education system. Today, nearly every major U.S. university offers distance education

courses, which reach a broader student audience and use the principles of modern learning pedagogy (Fitzpatrick, 2001). The latest reports on the characteristics of higher education students show that while overall postsecondary enrollment dropped by almost 90,000 students—nearly half a percentage point—from fall 2016 to fall 2017, the number of all students who took at least some of their courses online grew by more than 350,000 (NCES, 2018a). In 2017, the total number students fully online or enrolled in some online courses eclipsed 6.6 million students. In an analysis of the National 2002 Postsecondary Student Aid Study (NPSAS), Ashby (2002), reported the average age for distance learning students was 30, and students were more likely to be married, working full time and studying part time, with women comprising 65% of the online undergraduate population.

Public as well as political interest in distance education is especially high in geographic regions where the student population is widely distributed. Adult learners are engaging in distance education at an unparalleled rate. Sikora (2002) postulated that the flexibility of distance education attracted nontraditional students because it allowed them the ability to balance their studies with their other life commitments. She further implied that the flexibility and mobility of the online environment will become increasingly more appealing to adult learners who are trying to balance work, family, and education. As previously discussed, this has important implications for female students in particular, who often take on the majority of caretaking and domestic responsibilities. Consequently, distance education courses can provide similar learning outcomes with relevant, rigorous, and research based pedagogy.

Active Learning and Social Integration
Adult students, in particular, exhibit a more problem-centered or skills development focus in the learning environment (Knowles et al., 2011). One way to address this desire of adult students is to utilize components of active learning (Bonwell & Eison, 1991), including real-world problem-solving, peer review and feedback, discussing contemporary issues, and other engaging learning strategies. This population seeks out more active learning because they are self-directed, experiential, problem-centered, and internally motivated (Knowles et al., 2011). Moreover, research findings from other studies confirm that positive involvement with peers and faculty encourages adult students to persist (Tinto, 1998). The study of persistence among traditional age students has stressed the importance of social integration (Tinto, 1998), as students who become involved on campus and make friends, join clubs, and participate in activities are far more likely to persist. It is important to rework this concept to address the persistence of adult students. For adults, social integration and active learning may be better defined as how one integrates pursuit of education into one's overall life (Kerka, 1997; Tinto, 2006). Tinto (2006) posited that students tend to succeed in universities that are committed to student success, hold high expectations for student success, and provide needed academic, social, and financial support structures and policies on campus. Providing frequent and timely feedback and active involvement and engagement with the university faculty and staff have been linked with greater levels of institutional commitment and improved active learning (Kasworm, 2010; Kerka, 1997; Tinto, 2006). Faculty can have a positive or negative influence on a student's sense of fitting in, loyalty, perception of institutional quality, satisfaction with content, self-development, self-confidence and self-efficacy, connection between course content and workforce practice, and stress (Tinto, 2006). Thus, both student and institutional experiences shape subsequent learning outcomes and overall engagement.

Maintaining Consistent Enrollment
Part-time enrollment in higher education has grown dramatically since 1970 in absolute terms and relative to full-time enrollment. Between 1970 and 1990, the share of part-time students grew from 28% of the total to 42%, and there were 5 million part-time students in 1990, which meant that two of every three students aged 30 and older were part time (McCormick et al., 1995). Part-time attendance meets the needs of a wide range of students for whom full-time attendance may not be practical or feasible, thereby permitting postsecondary institutions to be accessible to the widest possible array of students. For example, the part-time student population includes students who are casual course takers, taking only one or two courses for personal enrichment, but not seeking a degree; returning students who want to complete a degree or upgrade their skills, but who cannot afford to give up their jobs to do so; teachers who take courses for professional development, concurrent with full-time employment;

high-school graduates seeking a degree but who are restricted by employment or family circumstances; previously full-time students whose remaining degree requirements constitute less than a full load; and, finally, students who are unsure about their educational plans and want to try out postsecondary education at a lower cost and with less disruption than full-time attendance would require. By allowing students to attend part time, institutions meet a variety of needs and extend educational opportunity to students who otherwise might be dissuaded from participation or shut out of the system entirely (McCormick et al., 1995). The movement back and forth between full-time and part-time status occurs frequently as students who near graduation accelerate a job search or as part-time teacher education students move into a full-time status as they engage in student teaching.

Although part-time status has become much more common, its effect on persistence is generally negative (Markle, 2015; Witkowsky et al., 2016). Adult students who are able to enroll on a full-time basis persist at much higher levels than do part-time students due to increased pace to graduation. The more hours the student takes per term, the more likely they are to persist and graduate in fewer years because of faster overall credit accumulation (Bean & Metzner, 1985; Markle, 2015; McCormick et al., 1995; Witkowsky et al., 2016). Taniguchi and Kaufman (2005) reported similar findings about persistence for both part-time enrollment and number of women enrolling in postsecondary education. They investigated nontraditional student graduation rates from 4-year institutions. The outcome variable was whether or not the adult student completed a 4-year degree program. The primary independent variable was part-time enrollment. The study found that part-time students are significantly less likely to complete a degree than those enrolled full time.

Adult-Focused Degree Programs

Adult degree completion programs are increasingly relevant within the higher education community, and they are growing at a rapid pace across the nation (Johnson & Bell, 2014). An adult-degree completion program is one designed especially to meet the needs of the working adult who, having acquired 60 or more college credit hours during previous enrollments, is returning to school after an extended period of absence to obtain a baccalaureate degree. The institution's promise that the student will be able to complete the program in fewer than 2 years of continuous study is realized through provisions such as establishing alternative class schedules, truncating the traditional semester/quarter time frame, organizing student cohorts, and awarding credit for prior learning experiences equivalent to approximately 25% of the bachelor's degree credit total (Task Force on Adult Degree Completion Programs, 2000). Adult degree programs share common characteristics including but not limited to distance (online) options, evening course options, weekend course options, test-out (CLEP and DSST) options, and college credit for prior learning in the workplace.

One particular characteristic of an adult-focused program that is worth highlighting is prior learning assessment (PLA). PLA is a process that colleges use to evaluate college-level knowledge, skills, and abilities gained outside the confines of the classroom for academic credit (Klein-Collins, 2010). There are two primary forms of PLA: course-specific PLA and the broader portfolio form. In course-specific PLA, adult learners can test out of courses via challenge exams or take College-Level Examination Program (CLEP) or DANTES Subject Standardization (DSST) tests that are universally accepted as the equivalent of various core courses. If students are able to demonstrate mastery of any of a number of content areas, they are exempted from those courses and awarded college credit for that requisite knowledge. The second form of prior learning assessment is the portfolio compilation. Students eligible for elective portfolio credit assemble documents to demonstrate competency in a specific area of knowledge that is deemed college-level equivalency.

Knowledge acquired in noncollege instructional programs, military training, travel, civic engagement, volunteer service, and employment is evaluated through a structured PLA class that documents college-learning outcomes achieved outside the confines of university walls. This PLA credit might include a computer programmer who demonstrates competence in programming by writing a reflective essay outlining their knowledge in conjunction with validating documents including certificates for various programming certifications in their specialty. Another example would be the police officer who serves as the departmental spokesperson and is thus able to test out of a course in oral communication by completing a challenge exam and assembling examples of television appearances that demonstrate mastery of this core content area. The course-specific PLA portfolio and test-out options help experienced adult students avoid taking a course that would be redundant. This process allows students to convert mastery of a subject into academic credits and provides an opportunity to increase the pace and likelihood of graduating. PLA recognizes and legitimizes significant learning in which adults have engaged in many parts of their lives (CAEL, 2000).

Programs that offer PLA are designed to encourage persistence to graduation for adult learners in higher education (Bergman & Herd, 2017). The Council on Adult and Experiential Learning (Klein-Collins, 2010) collected data from 62,475 students at 48 postsecondary institutions and found PLA students had better academic outcomes, particularly in terms of graduation rates and persistence, than other non-PLA students. More than 56% of PLA students earned a postsecondary degree, while only 21% of non-PLA students did so (Klein-Collins, 2010). The CAEL study also revealed that many PLA students graduate sooner than other non-PLA students. Travers (2011) reports that students who earn PLA credit also have increased "self-awareness and self-regulation; problem-solving, study, and reflection skills; use of tacit knowledge; and a better understanding of the role of faculty and mentors" (p. 45). Another study by the College Board Advocacy (2009) of 1,500 adults rated credit for prior learning policy as more important than small class size or availability of financial aid. When compared to students who earned credit through introductory college course work, students who earn CLEP credit had higher overall GPAs at the end of their undergraduate education (Scammacca & Dodd, 2005).

Students who complete the portfolio report feelings of satisfaction, pride, and accomplishment, as well as the appreciation for saving time and money (Rust & Ikard, 2016). Rust and Ikard (2016) also found that adult students who complete the portfolio process find it strengthens core values, like independence, freedom, learning, tenacity, hard work, nonconformity, pride, aspiration, and goal commitment. A well-structured PLA process changes students' thinking about not only their pasts but also the present and their futures (McGinley, 1995). Adult students suggest that the PLA portfolio preparation is "full of revelations" (Burris, 1997, p. 116). The PLA portfolio process certifies readiness for further learning and gives students a forum to investigate the structure of college-level learning through its requirement that they equate their learning from experience to the structure of the curriculum.

Conclusion

There is an ever-present need for more students to graduate from U.S. colleges and universities. By 2025, the U.S. workforce will require one million more college graduates than produced (Carnevale et al., 2010). Due to declining birth rates, adults will likely make up more of the overall percentage of college enrollment. Current research indicates that adult students experience college differently and act on the college experience in ways that differ from those of the traditional college student (Kasworm, 2005). It is important and necessary to understand the nuances of how institutional, personal, and environmental factors impact adult learners' ability to persist to graduation.

One key issue in addressing the puzzle to increase persistence is the need to address affordability and accessibility. Although progress has been made on finding additional scholarships, grants, and loans specifically for adults, the amount of funding in comparison to that of traditional high school seniors is miniscule. Since adult learners are coming back in droves, it is necessary for institutions and legislatures to designate more aid for this growing population. The federal government has made strides in its reform of the GI Bill, but adults outside of the military and those in lower socioeconomic groups find it difficult to secure scholarships or financial aid.

Additionally, it is essential that programs empower academic advisers and instructors with the skills to serve this student population. Adults are focused on real-world relevance and expect a level of service that they receive in the business environment. Unfortunately, the innovative adult degree completion programs and the strategies to develop them described in this chapter are rarely found in traditional university departments (Ross-Gordon, 2011). Therefore, it is essential that more adult-friendly practices (e.g., prior learning assessment, convenient course options, and evening and online student support) become integrated into the fabric of traditional 4-year colleges and universities. If programs are able to manage the demands of students that identify as worker, spouse or partner, parent, caregiver, and community member with timely and informed feedback and guidance, higher levels of student engagement and persistence is sure to follow.

Adult learners continue to represent a growing and widely studied subpopulation in U.S. higher education. It is also important for faculty and administrators to learn how to effectively work with these students as they deal with different challenges than their traditional counterparts. While much of the retention literature has focused on traditional-aged students, researchers should also concentrate on the experiences of adult learners, and together find ways to positively impact recruitment, retention, and graduation. Understanding how entry/background, internal campus/academic environment, and external environment variables interact can assist colleges and universities in identifying at-risk adult students and then implementing interventions that support them. Additional research can also help local and state officials identify new policies that promote adult student persistence to improve bachelor degree attainment rates in this country.

References

Ashby, C. (2002). *Report on adult learners and distance education.* Government Accountability Office. http://www.gao.gov/new.items/d03905.pdf

Bash, L. (2003). *Adult learners in the academy.* Anker.

Bean, J. P., & Metzner, B. S. (1985). A conceptual model of nontraditional student attrition. *Review of Educational Research, 55*(4), 485–540.

Bergman, M., Gross, J. P. K., Berry, M., & Shuck, B. (2014). If life happened but a degree didn't: Examining factors that impact adult student persistence. *The Journal of Continuing Higher Education, 62*(2), 90–101. https://doi.org/10.1080/07377363.2014.915445

Bergman, M., & Herd, A. (2017). Proven leadership = college credit: Enhancing employability of transitioning military members through prior learning assessment. *Advances in Developing Human Resources, 19*(1), 78–87. https://doi.org/10.1177/1523422316682949

Bergman, M., Strickler, B., Osam, K., & Ash, D. (2018). Engineering the benefits of learning in the new learning economy. *The Journal of Continuing Higher Education. 66*(2), 67–76. https://doi.org/10.1080/07377363.2018.1469083

Bonwell, C. C., & Eison, J. A. (1991). *Active learning: Creating excitement in the classroom.* ASHE-ERIC Higher Education Report. School of Education and Human Development, George Washington University.

Bound, J., & Turner, S. (2002). Going to war and going to college: Did World War II and the G.I. bill increase educational attainment for returning veterans? *Journal of Labor Economics, 20*(4), 784–815. https://doi.org/10.1086/342012

Bowers, A., & Bergman, M. (2016). Affordability and the return on investment of college completion: Unique challenges and opportunities for adult learners, *The Journal of Continuing Higher Education, 64*(3), 144–151. https://doi.org/10.1080/07377363.2016.1229102

Bragg, D. D., Townsend, B. K., & Ruud, C. M. (2009, January). *The adult learner and the applied baccalaureate: Emerging lessons for state and local implementation.* Office of Community College Research and Leadership.

Brown, S. M. (2002). Strategies that contribute to nontraditional/adult student development and persistence. *PAACE Journal of Lifelong Learning, 11*, 67–76.

Burris, J. (1997). The adult undergraduate's experience of portfolio development: A multiple case study. *Dissertation Abstracts International, 58,* 2742.

Cabrera, A. F., Burkum, K. R., & LaNasa, S. M. (2005). Pathways to a four-year degree: Determinants of transfer and degree completion. In A. Seidman (Ed.), *Student retention: Formula for student success* (pp. 155–214). Rowman & Littlefield. https://doi.org/10.1002/nha.20014

Carnevale, A. P., Smith, N., & Strohl, J. (2010). *Help wanted: Projections of jobs and education requirements through 2018.* Georgetown University Center on Education and the Workforce.

Choy, S. (2002). *Nontraditional students. The condition of education 2002 (NCES 2002–012).* National Center for Education Statistics, U.S. Department of Education.

College Board Advocacy. (2009). *How colleges organize themselves to increase student persistence: Four-year institutions.* http://pas.indiana.edu/cb.index.cfm

Colvin, B. B. (2013). Where is Merlin when I need him? The barriers to higher education are still in place: Recent re-entry experience. *New Horizons in Adult Education and Human Resource Development, 25*(2), 19–32.

Council for Adult and Experiential Learning. (2000). *Prior learning assessment.* http://www.cael.org/index2.html

Deutsch, N. L., & Schmertz, B. (2011). "Starting from ground zero": Constraints and experiences of adult women returning to college. *Review of Higher Education, 34,* 477–504. https://doi.org/10.1353/rhe.2011.0002

Dinmore, I. (1997). Interdisciplinarity and integrative learning: An imperative for adult education. *Education, 117*(3), 452–467.

Fitzpatrick, R. (2001). Is distance education better than the traditional classroom? *Clear Point Inc.com.* http://www.clearpnt.com/accelepoint/articles/r_fitzpatrick_060101.shtml

Grawe, N. (2018). *Demographics and the demand for higher education*. Johns Hopkins University Press.

Hadfield, J. (2003). Recruiting and retaining adult students. *New Directions for Student Services, 102*, 17–25.

Hoffman, L., Reindl, T., & Bearer-Friend, J. (2011) *Compete to complete - Improving postsecondary attainment among adults*. National Governor's Association (NGA) Center for Best Practices.

Horn, L., & Berger, R. (2004). *College persistence on the rise?: Changes in 5-year degree completion and postsecondary persistence rates between 1994 and 2000*. U.S. Department of Education.

Horn, L., & Carroll, C. D. (1996). *Nontraditional students: Trends in enrollment from 1986 to 1992 and persistence and attainment among 1989–90 beginning postsecondary students (NCES 97-578)*. U.S. Department of Education.

Johnson, N., & Bell, A. (2014). *Scaling completion college services as a model for increasing adult degree completion*. Indianapolis, IN: Lumia Foundation. ERIC Document No. ED555863.

Kasworm, C. (2005). Adult student identity in an intergenerational community college classroom. *Adult Education Quarterly, 56*, 3–20. https://doi.org/10.1177/0741713605280148

Kasworm, C. E. (2010). Adult learners in a research university: Negotiating undergraduate student identity. *Adult Education Quarterly, 60*(2), 143–160. https://doi.org/10.1177/0741713609336110

Kasworm, C. E. (2018). Adult students: A confusing world in undergraduate higher education, *The Journal of Continuing Higher Education, 66*(2), 77–87. https://doi.org/10.1080/07377363.2018.1469077

Kerka, S. (1997). *Adult career counseling in a new age: Social integration for adults* (ED167). ERIC. https://www.ericdigests.org/1996-3/age.htm

Kirby, P. G., Biever, J. L., Martinez, I. G., & Gomez, J. P. (2004). Adults returning to school: The impact on family and work. *The Journal of Psychology, 138*(1), 65–76.

Klein-Collins, R. (2010). *Fueling the race to postsecondary success: A 48-institution study of Prior Learning Assessment and adult student outcomes*. Council for Adult and Experiential Learning.

Klein-Collins, R., Sherman, A., & Soares, L. (2010). *Degree completion beyond institutional boarders: Responding to the new reality of mobile and nontraditional learners*. Center for American Progress; Council for Adult and Experiential Learning. http://www.cael.org/Forum_and_News/IndexNov2010_files/CAPandCAELExecSummary.pdf

Knowles, M. S., Swanson, R. A., & Holton, E. F. (2011). *The adult learner: The definitive classic in adult education and human resource development*. Butterworth-Heinemann.

Kuh, G. (2008). Diagnosing why some students don't succeed. *Chronicle of Higher Education, 55*(16), A72.

Langrehr, K. J., Phillips, J. C., Melville, A., & Eum, K. (2015). Determinants of nontraditional student status: A methodological review of the research. *Journal of College Student Development, 56*(8), 876–881.

MacDonald, K. (2018). A review of the literature: The needs of nontraditional students in postsecondary education. *Strategic Enrollment Management Quarterly, 5*(4), 159–164. https://doi.org/10.1002/sem3.20115

Malhotra, N. K., Shapero, M., Sizoo, S., & Munro, T. (2007). Factor structure of deterrents to adult participation in higher education. *Journal of College Teaching and Learning, 4*(12), 81–90. https://doi.org/10.19030/tlc.v4i12.1515

Markle, G. (2015). Factors influencing persistence among nontraditional university students. *Adult Education Quarterly, 65*(3), 267–285.

McCormick, A., Geis, S., Vergun, R., & Carroll, D. (1995). *Profile of part-time undergraduates in postsecondary education: 1989-90* (NCES 95-173). U.S. Department of Education, Office of Educational Research and Improvement; National Center for Education Statistics.

McGinley, L. (1995). *Transformative learning and prior learning assessment*. Paper presented at the National Conference on Alternative and External Degree Programs for Adults, Columbus, OH. ERIC Document No. ED 402 510.

National Center for Education Statistics. (2015). *Demographics and enrollment characteristics of nontraditional undergraduates: 2011–12*. U.S. Department of Education. https://nces.ed.gov/pubs2015/2015025.pdf

National Center for Education Statistics. (2018a). *The condition of education: Characteristics of postsecondary students*. U.S. Department of Education. https://nces.ed.gov/programs/coe/indicator_csb.asp

National Center for Education Statistics. (2018b). *IPEDS 2018–19 data collection system: Survey materials glossary*. U.S. Department of Education. https://surveys.nces.ed.gov/ipeds/Downloads/Forms/IPEDSGlossary.pdf

Ogren, C. A. (2005). The American state normal school: "An instrument of great good." *History of Education Quarterly, 46*(4), 653–655. https://doi.org/10.1111/j.1748-5959.2006.00052.x

Osam, E. K., Bergman, M., & Cumberland, D. M. (2017). An integrative literature review on the barriers impacting adult learners' return to college. *Adult Learning, 28*(2), 54–60. https://doi.org/10.1177/1045159516658013

Remenick, L. (2019). Services and support for nontraditional students in higher education: A historical literature review. *The Journal of Adult and Continuing Education, 25*(1), 113–130. https://doi.org/10.1177/1477971419842880

Ross-Gordon, J. M. (2011). Research on adult learners: Supporting the needs of a student population that is no longer nontraditional. *Peer Review, 13*, 26–29.

Rust, D. Z. & Ikard, W. L. (2016). Learning assessment portfolio completion: Improved outcomes at a public institution. *The Journal of Continuing Higher Education, 64(2)*, 94–100. https://doi.org/10.1080/07377363.2016.1177871

Scammacca, N. K., & Dodd, B. G. (2005). *An investigation of educational outcomes for students who earn college credit through the college-level examination program.* College Board Research Report No 2005-5.

Shapiro, D., Dundar, A., Yuan, X., Harrell, A., Wild, J., & Ziskin, M. (2014). *Some college, no degree: A national view of students with some college enrollment, but no completion* (Signature Report No. 7). National Student Clearinghouse Research Center.

Sikora, A. C. (2002). *A profile of participation in distance education: 1999–2000 (NCES 2003-154).* National Center for Education Statistics. U.S. Department of Education.

Taniguchi, H., & Kaufman, G. (2005). Degree completion among nontraditional college students. *Social Science Quarterly, 86(4)*, 912–927. https://doi.org/10.1111/j.0038-4941.2005.00363.x

Task Force on Adult Degree Completion Programs. (2000, June). *Adult degree completion programs.* http://www.ncacihe.org/resources/adctf/ADCPRept.pdf

Taylor, J. A. (2000). *Adult degree completion programs: A report to the board of trustees from the Task Force on Adult Degree Completion Programs and the award of credit for prior learning at the baccalaureate level.* Commission on Institutions of Higher Education.

Tinto, V. (1998). Colleges as communities: Taking research on student persistence seriously. *The Review of Higher Education, 21*, 167–177.

Tinto, V. (2006). Research and practice of student retention: What next? *Journal of College Student Retention, 8(1)*, 1–19.

Travers, N. L. (2011). United States of America: Prior learning assessment (PLA) research in colleges and universities. In J. Harris, M. Breier, & C. Wihak (Eds.), *Researching the recognition of prior learning: International perspectives.* (pp. 248–283). NIACE.

Witkowsky, P., Mendez, S., Ogunbowo, O., Clayton, G., & Hernandez, N. (2016). Nontraditional student perceptions of collegiate inclusion. *The Journal of Continuing Higher Education, 64(1)*, 30–41.

Wlodkowski, R. J. (1999). *Enhancing adult motivation to learn: A comprehensive guide for teaching all adults.* Jossey-Bass.

Wlodkowski, R. J., Mauldin, J. E., & Gahn, S. W. (2001). *Learning in the fast lane: Adult learners' persistence and success in accelerated college programs.* Lumina Foundation for Education.

Woosley, S. (2004). Stop-out or drop-out? An examination of college withdrawals and re-enrollments. *Journal of College Student Retention, 5*, 293–303.

CHAPTER 29

Human Resource Development and Workplace Learning

Henriette Lundgren and Rob F. Poell

The workplace has long been recognized as an impactful site for learning. Whether an employee participates in a workshop, shadows a colleague in a new role or "accidentally" stumbles across new insights by performing a task—these instances can lead to enhanced understanding of and improved performance in the workplace. According to an industry report, large corporations in the United States spend on average $1,299 per employee on direct learning (ATD, 2019), most of which goes toward in-house and outsourced training provisions. As technology-based learning continues to displace instructor-led classroom training (which declined from 59.43% of total learning hours used by organizations in 2011 to 51.16% in 2016 [ATD, 2017]), traditional formats and expected outcomes of learning in the workplace are being challenged.

Human resource development (HRD) describes a comprehensive set of facilitated interventions, while workplace learning (WPL) includes a number of less formal and more learner-driven developmental activities. HRD and WPL can be of interest to adult and continuing education (ACE) scholars and practitioners as both groups have the capacity to reach adult learners who do not currently participate in other forms of lifelong learning or have limited access to formal education. Against this backdrop, HRD and WPL offer a dynamic and conceptually rich environment that strives to serve (employed) adult learners in their workplace. The purpose of this chapter is to provide an overview of the key definitions, perspectives, dynamics, and outcomes that are currently characterizing HRD and WPL (Figure 29.1).

This overview of HRD and WPL will lead us through the chapter, starting with a definition of *HRD* and four conceptual frames that help us view the field from different perspectives. We will continue our discussion with formats and outcomes of HRD and WPL, before comparing them to ACE highlighting their interactions, frictions, and differences.

Defining HRD

According to Watkins (1989), "HRD is the field of study and practice responsible for the fostering of a long-term, work-related learning capacity at the individual, group, and organizational level of organizations" (p. 427). The phrase *long-term learning capacity* stands out as Watkins emphasizes the capacity building aspect of HRD that can be sustained over an extended period and, from the employee's perspective, across various jobs. This type of long-term capacity building can take place at different levels, starting from the individual, expanding across teams, and finally reaching whole departments and organizations (Yorks, 2004).

In comparison, McLean and McLean (2001) define *HRD* as "any process or activity that, either initially or over the long term, has the potential to develop

Figure 29.1. Overview of HRD and WPL terms.

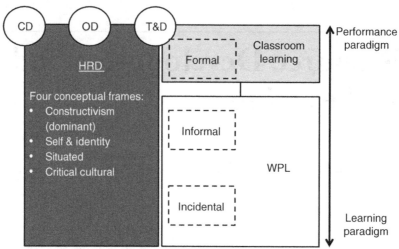

Note. CD: Career development, OD: Organizational development, T&D: Training & development

adult work-based knowledge, expertise, productivity, and satisfaction, whether for personal or group/team gain, or for the benefit of an organization, community, nation" (p. 322). McLean and McLean explicitly formulate a definition that can be applied to HRD practice across the globe, with the possibility that HRD benefits an entity beyond the individual.

Last, we turn to Wang et al. (2017), who suggest that HRD is "a mechanism in shaping individual and group values and beliefs and skilling through learning-related activities to support the desired performance of the host system" (p. 1175). While we find a parallel between those three definitions in the various levels at which HRD takes place, Wang et al. emphasize "productivity" as one of the desired outcomes that will benefit the organization. This tension between learning on the one hand and productivity or performance on the other hand has fueled an ongoing debate among HRD scholars (Bierema, 1996, 2000; Swanson, 1995; Swanson & Arnold, 1996; Watkins & Marsick, 1995). Wang et al. (2017) further describe *learning-related activities* as the means to achieve performance goals of the *host system*—an all-encompassing term that applies to various sociopolitical, cultural, and organizational contexts. Wang et al. offer a definition that was derived through content analysis and that, like McLean and McLean's, can be applied to non-Western contexts, too.

Lee (2001) voices her concerns in her "refusal to define HRD" (p. 327). Lee shares her main definitional dilemma: HRD is a relatively young field that feeds from different disciplines and schools of thought, and defining HRD would impose one's (limiting) view which could deny others opportunities to shape the field. As Lee (2014) states, "seen from an ontology of *becoming*, HRD is contextual, situated, dynamic, and continually negotiated through the interpretations made by organizational actors as cocreators" (p. 108).

Other authors have chimed in on the debate and have suggested that, in order to overcome these definitional dilemmas, a convergence of various HRD-related disciplines into a "people and organization development" domain would be required (Hamlin & Stewart, 2011), along with the need for strong HRD principles and practices (Werner, 2014) and a look at the field's identity boundaries and how they have shifted over time (Ghosh et al., 2014). While we agree on these notions in general, the limited room available in this overview chapter prevents us from providing a more in-depth discussion.

Three Main Areas of HRD

When looking at the field of practice, McLagan (1989) divides HRD into three areas, all of which use development as their primary process:

1. *Career Development* (CD) describes the work area within HRD that ensures alignment between individual career planning and organizational career management processes, with the goal to achieve a match between individual and organizational needs.

2. *Organization Development* (OD) depicts those HRD interventions that look after inter- and intraunit relationships within an organization; often HRD professionals engage with groups to initiate and manage change as part of their OD role.
3. *Training and Development* (T&D) describes those activities within HRD that help identify, assess, and develop key competencies that support individuals and teams to perform current or future jobs.

According to McLagan (1989), HRD distinguishes itself from other business functions through "its use of development as a core process, not by who does it. It is a process, not a department" (p. 4). However, the process to develop employees to enhance performance and increase productivity can also be seen as a power struggle dilemma (Fenwick, 2005) as it portrays a hierarchical arrangement between educator and individual (or group of employees). It implies that these individuals carry a skills deficit that needs to be worked on (Rocco et al., 2018). From this point of view, development plans are constructed and given to employees to close the performance gap. Here, the educator may be seen as the main actor in initiating T&D in formal WPL settings—a scene more typically depicted in traditional HRD.

Defining WPL

From the mid-1980s, adult education (AE) and organization scholars started to put an emphasis back on learning in the workplace (rather than in a training room). Fueled by emerging evidence that the effectiveness of classroom training in terms of transfer to the workplace was often limited (Poell, 2017), these scholars started to pay more attention to the characteristics of the workplace itself as a learning environment as well as to those of the learner (Marsick, 1987; Marsick & Watkins, 1990). Around the same time, the expression "learning company" trended in the United Kingdom, describing an organization that facilitates the learning of all its members and that strives for continuous self-transformation (Pedler et al., 1991). In the United States, Peter Senge (1990) coined the term *learning organization* where, based on a systems thinking approach, he described interventions that would help organizations transform themselves using group problem-solving methods.

These seminal publications helped put learning back on the agenda of HRD practitioners, at a time when T&D was the dominant theme, with WPL strengthening the role of the employee and highlighting the impact that the organizational environment had on learning outcomes. Nowadays, many WPL scholars have adopted a more situated perspective that describes learning as being rooted in the situation in which the employee participates (Fenwick, 2000b). Viewed from the situated perspective, learning emerges in the interaction between individuals within their (professional) environment, including the use of tools and systems (Bell & Mladenovic, 2015; Jordan, 2010; Lundin & Nuldén, 2007; Ovens & Tinning, 2009).

In WPL the learner is the main actor in the learning plot. Described as a natural and largely autonomous process derived from the characteristics of the work process and its inherent social interactions (Poell & Van Woerkom, 2011), WPL is often implicit to performing a task; differentiating WPL from doing the daily work can be hard. The learning that goes on in the workplace embraces everyday work activity, including on-the-job and off-the-job learning (Fuller et al., 2009).

The workplace in itself is "a learning environment focusing on the interaction between the affordances and constraints of the social setting, on the one hand, and the agency and biography of the individual participant, on the other" (p. 312), according to Billett (2004). Hence, WPL facilitates the interface and exchange between individuals and their environment—a concept that has also been described by Lave and Wenger (1991) in their situated learning approach and in learning-network theory (Poell & Van Der Krogt, 2015, 2017a, 2017b). According to Poell and Van Der Krogt, WPL has its own dynamics, shaped by its cultural-historical context and influenced by constant actions undertaken by organizational actors.

Performance Versus Learning

One of the big deliberations within the circles of HRD and WPL is the "learning versus performance" debate. On the one hand, some scholars accentuate the change that can be achieved through learning, where they place the development of individuals as their main goal (Bierema, 1996, 2000; Watkins & Marsick, 1995). Proponents of the *learning paradigm* see training and development activities aligned with Watkins's (1989) definition of HRD that aims at fostering "long-term, work-related learning capacity" (p. 427). On the other hand, some scholars state that HRD's main goal is to contribute to strategic goals of the organization by bettering employee performance (Swanson, 1995; Swanson & Arnold, 1996). Supporters of the *performance paradigm* strive "to advance the mission of the performance system that sponsors the HRD efforts by improving the capabilities of the individuals working in the system" (Swanson & Holton, 2001, p. 137). In this paradigm, learning is merely one of the tools that "the system" can use to improve performance.

This debate has tended to overlook that both learning and performance are necessary in contemporary organizations. Kuchinke (1998) tried to move the field ahead by suggesting a synthesis of the two paradigms that could become a comprehensive foundation on which HRD theory and practice can be built—without much success. More recently, Yoon et al. (2014) suggested revisiting this tension from a performance improvement perspective. They argue, still very much within the performance paradigm, that "the field must move beyond this dualism because, whether it is training or culture change, HRD's ultimate value is the degree to which it contributes to the organization's overarching goal" (Yoon et al., 2014, p. 102). In our view, learning and performance are two sides of the same coin, although the added value of a learning focus over a narrow performance outlook seems crucial especially when reasoning from an employee's perspective. After all, employees' learning and development stays with them throughout their careers and lives, whereas, in the modern economy, their current organization's performance might not be any more important than that of the competitors when all are under constant threat of down-sizing and layoffs.

What role does the educator play in all of this? Practitioners working in HRD and WPL perform their roles under different names and titles, including workplace educator, trainer, content specialist, knowledge manager, development lead, HRD professional, facilitator, or learning coach. An ATD study conducted in the 1980s identified how changes in the environment were affecting the various roles that HRD practitioners performed and what competencies were required to be effective in those roles (McLagan, 1989). In a follow-up study conducted in the Netherlands, Nijhof (2004) asserted that the role of the HRD professional had hardly changed since the 1980s; it was still mainly the "classical type of trainer" (p. 68).

Role descriptions may give an indication where practitioners stand on the performance versus learning debate. Although no specific research has been conducted in this area, HRD professionals who identify as "trainers" or "managers of training strategies" may carry a role understanding that leans more toward the performance paradigm where business strategy alignment and measurable training outcomes prevail. On the other hand, those who see themselves as "learning coaches," "facilitators," or "knowledge managers" may feel closer alignment with the learning paradigm.

Conceptual Frames

Traditionally, HRD and, especially, T&D have been depicted as cognitive activities where the learning that results from (training) interventions takes place inside the learner's head. According to the school of thought known as constructivism (Piaget, 1950; von Glasersfeld, 1984), individuals bring their prior life and work knowledge, skills, beliefs, interests, and motivation into the training room and when exposed to new experiences and through the interaction with others "construct" meaning (Marsick et al., 2011). Learning from this perspective is essentially understood as an individual process.

Although constructivism has been a dominant paradigm in describing and researching HRD, alternative lenses, perspectives, frames and conceptualizations on learning (Davis & Sumara, 1997; Greeno, 1997; Mezirow, 1996) and reflection (Justice et al., 2020; Lundgren et al., 2017) in the workplace have been brought forward and discussed. According to Fenwick (2000a), "Experience embraces reflective as well as kinesthetic activity, conscious and unconscious dynamics, and all manner of interaction among subjects, texts, and contexts" (pp. 244–245). In other words, an experience impacts both a learner's mind as well as a learner's body. The learner might not always be aware of the experience and hence does not automatically account for that experience as "learning" in their head. However, these experiences do impact the learner, even beyond cognition. Fenwick (2000a, 2000b, 2001) offers alternative conceptual frames that help us understand and describe actors, focus points, dynamics and the role of the educator in HRD:

- Self and identity
- Situated learning and development
- Critical cultural analysis

These alternative viewpoints are important as they depict "accepted examples of actual scientific practice" (Kuhn, 1996, p. 10). The frames help us see learning from different angles on the continuum of perspectives between the technical-rational and the social justice views (Rocco et al., 2018). It is one of the core ideas of *critical* HRD (CHRD) to accept multiple truths that are gained through different forms of knowledge construction (Sambrook, 2008, 2014). Furthermore, CHRD is concerned with recognizing power and power dynamics in HRD and the management of learning (Schied et al., 2001), questioning traditions and challenging today's practices (Bierema, 2015; MacKenzie et al., 2012), and facilitating emancipation (Raelin, 2008; Sambrook, 2014).

Self and Identity
Drawing from the fields of developmental psychology and psychoanalysis, the main focus of the self and identity conceptual frame of learning lies in the discovery of self (Fenwick, 2000b). Employees are confronted with varied situations in the workplace, and this perspective pays attention to the affective and self-reflective aspects that are provoked in the individual on their journey to discover self. Feedback from a study on women in WPL shows that participants found most value in naming, appreciating, and recovering the power of their "authentic self" (Fenwick, 1998).

From a self and identity perspective, the role of the educator is to consider unconscious dynamics—although the unknown cannot be known directly—and to offer different viewpoints for WPL and reflection, including the use of symbols and metaphors, dialogue with the self, transformation, interference, and self-discovery in the context of relationships (Lundgren et al., 2017). Educators further support discovery by valuing learners' self-dilemmas; encouraging the sharing of experiences that reconnect the past, present, and future; and helping to "make meaning from the fragments of perplexing experience" (Fenwick, 2000b, p. 300).

Situated Learning and Development
The situated learning and development frame begins with foundational beliefs of the *constructivist* view. In constructivism, learners are seen as separate from each other, from the tools and activities with which they engage, and context is depicted as a container into which learners are dropped (Lave & Wenger, 1991). While affected by the context, the learner is seen as a separate entity with his or her own cognition and meaning-making system that is separate and distinct from its environment.

In the situated learning and development perspective, however, learning is rooted in the situation in which the employee participates (Fenwick, 2000b). The focus is on the interaction between learners and on their participation with the environment, where knowledge can develop from the interplay between individuals and their work-based tools (e.g., work instruments, artifacts, resources). Work-based tools and systems trigger collaboration between learners, which in turn requires a minimum of organizing or formal intervention (Lundgren et al., 2017).

The educator plays a minimal role in this context because learning happens in informal spaces with the tools and systems available. Educators can support the interaction by assisting to name what is emerging by tracing and recording interactions and by helping to make sense of "the patterns emerging among these complex systems" (Fenwick, 2000b, p. 302). Educators can also enhance reflection within situated learning by incorporating mindfulness techniques in their instructional strategies (Stoner & Cennamo, 2018).

Critical Cultural Analysis
The main focus of *critical cultural analysis*, a conceptual frame that is informed by critical-cultural pedagogy (Giroux, 2005), centers on dominance structures and power dynamics in the workplace. Power dynamics are socially constructed and historically developed, and they influence what is valued and shape how people conceptualize agency in the workplace (Lundgren et al., 2017). Through this conceptual frame, questions around gender, culture, postcolonialism, ideology, race, identity, and critical-cultural pedagogy come to the foreground. Employees engage in critical cultural

analysis by interrogating their surroundings as part of their learning journey to challenge "how these beliefs and values are constructed" (Fenwick, 2000b, p. 307).

The role of the educator in critical cultural analysis is to make power dynamics evident by encouraging participants to ask questions on how work culture is practiced and by depicting the politics and constraints of HRD and WPL. By examining the dominant rhetoric, educators can help employees imagining and enacting alternatives that oppose existing contradictions and power dynamics. Educators can make a positive impact around social justice, greater equity and democracy in the workplace as well as improvements in learning, transfer, and productivity can be achieved (Rocco et al., 2018).

Formats Evolving Into Learning Paths

HRD and learning in the workplace come in different, mutually related formats leading to certain combinations of learning activities and outcomes.

Formal learning, the traditional T&D format, describes interventions within structured, formal settings where a trainer has created a program or curriculum that the learner pursues. In formal settings, it is assumed that the trainee follows directions in the form of listening to the trainer, discussing with others in small group interventions, generating ideas from guided coaching or mentoring, or working on a capstone project and presenting findings back to the trainer.

Self-initiated learning, often referred to as *informal learning* (the term has its caveats, see Billett, 2002), is an intentional, conscious pursuit on the part of the learner. Here, the employee is the main actor in the endeavor to learn as part of performing the regular job, taking on new tasks, interacting with colleagues, looking for available knowledge and information, or transferring "lessons learned" from outside working life into the workplace. All of these activities happen intentionally, where the employee is making a conscious effort to learn and expand. To what extent the learner acts strategically in his or her pursuit is an area of research that has more recently been studied (Poell et al., 2018). For more readings on informal learning at work see Messmann et al. (2018).

Incidental learning (Justice & Yorks, 2018; Marsick & Watkins, 1990; Watkins et al., 2018) describes unintentional learning that occurs as a byproduct of the working process. Incidental learning may happen when visiting a museum (Carliner, 2013), when attending a science festival (Brookfield et al., 2016), or when helping out in the community (Jones & Gasiorski, 2008). There is no conscious effort to (encourage someone to) learn; however, learning follows from the work that is being conducted. For example, an employee forced to replace a sick colleague one morning may find afterward that they have learned a good number of new things while doing so. Unlike formal learning, both incidental and informal learning have traditionally been associated with WPL, since the employee is the main learning actor in both.

Employees combine informal, incidental, and formal work-related learning activities into their own individual *learning path*, in the context of the organization's *learning network* (Poell & Van Der Krogt, 2010) (Figure 29.2).

A learning path describes "a set of learning activities that are both coherent as a whole and meaningful to the employee" (Poell & Van Der Krogt, 2010, p. 217); these learning activities can be either actualizations of already available learning opportunities in the organization (e.g., a team brainstorming meeting) or they can be newly added to the organization's learning network (e.g., a new quality improvement project).

The learning network of an organization encompasses employees, HRD professionals, and managers, among other actors; "they interact with each other to develop learning programs, policies, and activities. These interaction processes gradually become institutionalized in certain structural arrangements, regarding the content and the organization of learning programs, and the learning climate" (Poell et al., 1998, p. 36). Many of the learning activities occur as part of the daily work; with the intentional learning programs offered by HRD professionals they form the context from which employees can create their individual learning paths (Poell et al., 2003).

In the learning-network theory, the learner is the main actor and active participant in curating and creating various types of learning opportunities within the context of their organization's learning network (Poell et al., 2000; Poell & Van Der Krogt, 2015, 2017a, 2017b). From this perspective, a formal training program can therefore be seen as a "temporary interruption" (Poell, 2017, p. 11) of the learning path, with the HRD practitioner ultimately having relatively little influence over the employees' choices and decisions regarding learning. Not all scholars and practitioners in the field of HRD acknowledge the powerful role that learners play in creating their own learning paths. As Poell (2017) concludes, "The HRD field as a whole would be stronger and more relevant to practice if scholars would expend as much attention on employees creating learning paths as they do on training transfer matters" (p. 14).

Outcomes: Transfer of Training

When it comes to the outcomes of HRD and WPL, a key question is: How can HRD practitioners tell that their T&D interventions have been successful? What is the way to know that someone has "learned" something in the workplace, and how can learning and performance outcomes be evaluated? The term *transfer of training* describes "the degree to which knowledge, skills, and abilities learned in training are applied to the job" (Bates et al., 2014, p. 386). Therefore, transfer of training can be used as a proxy to evaluate certain outcomes in T&D.

Referring to Web of Science (WoS) statistics, 37 publications were found between 1980 and 1989 that had *transfer of training* (or *training transfer*) in their title or topic fields (Poell, 2017). In 2020, the same WoS search yields 506 publications in the 2010 to mid-2019 time period, showing that there has been an increased interest in showing how T&D may lead to performance outcomes. While transfer of training has thus been a highly researched topic in the effort to evaluate HRD outcomes since the 1980s (Baldwin & Ford, 1988), Poell (2017) notes a transfer of training paradox where first learning is formalized and detached from work in the form of formal training and then researchers and practitioners are surprised that it is hard to prove the relevance and effectiveness of these interventions.

Transfer of training research confirms that both the characteristics of the learners (Bates et al., 2014; e.g., through their motivation to transfer [Gegenfurtner et al., 2009; Massenberg et al., 2017]) as well as the characteristics of the workplace (Govaerts et al., 2017; Nijman et al., 2006; e.g., through supervisory support [Van Der Klink et al., 2001]) contribute to effective learning in the workplace. The latest thinking on transfer of training aligns with the more situated approach of learning-paths research (Poell & Van Der Krogt, 2010), in which the learner is the dominant actor in formulating a learning-path strategy and choosing learning activities available in the workplace that may serve the learner strategically (Poell et al., 2018). While transfer of training remains important,

Figure 29.2. Learning path creation in the context of classroom and WPL.

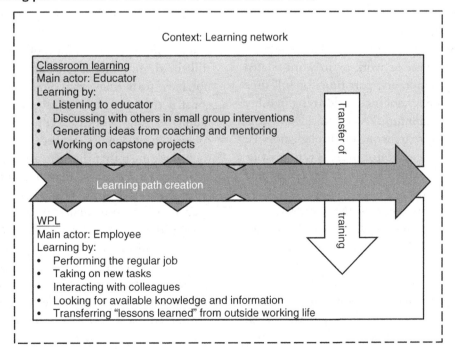

the concept is often measured using perception data and hence does not always lend itself to drawing conclusions on actual changes in performance.

Interactions With ACE

The workplace is a meaningful context for adult learning where WPL and HRD represent the opportunity to reach adults who do not participate in or have limited access to formal education (Bierema, 2000; Unwin, 2004). WPL and HRD have a lot in common with the mission of ACE, that is, create engagement and provide a platform for social inclusion and justice (Rubenson, 2018). According to Watkins (1989), employee training is the largest single "delivery system" (p. 427) for AE. However, there are also a number of frictions and differences between HRD/WPL and ACE (Watkins & Marsick, 2014).

Frictions and Differences
From a definitional point of view, ACE focuses on education and hence is most parallel with the T&D part of HRD. However, there is little overlap between the self-directed parts of WPL and continuing education (CE), which is all formal, classroom-based learning. In AE, informal learning has been of particular interest as the locus of control resides within the learner (Bierema, 2000), in contrast to HRD, where the locus of control rests with the organization.

In terms of audiences, ACE is broader in scope as it concerns all adults whether they are employed or not. In comparison, HRD and WPL focus only on learning that takes place at work or in work-related settings, assuming temporary, part-time, or full-time employment, and it does not include learning in other spaces, such as in community volunteering, in folk high schools, during retirement, or through popular culture. The role of the educator in ACE is to provide formative education, which is driven by policy and standardized curricula.

In terms of functions, ACE in the workplace covers areas such as retraining (Watkins, 1989), literacy development (King, 2010; Peterson, 2010), diversity and inclusion (Peterson, 2010), and lifelong learning opportunities (King, 2010)—themes that are rather distant from the performance paradigm promoted by parts of the HRD community. From an ACE point of view, HRD and WPL should benefit more than the organization; they also carry social responsibility to "promote human development in the workplace" (Bierema, 2000, p. 281).

Peterson (2010) has been critical toward the diversity and inclusion agenda that is proclaimed by HRD, as she doubts whether a standard leadership development program sufficiently accommodates people with disabilities. Also, there is a lack of role models for aspiring women, immigrants, and other minorities in leadership positions (Peterson, 2010), which makes it harder for employees from minority groups to land these positions, due to the uneven split of power and authority at work (Spencer, 2010). Finally, HRD can be portrayed as the "new HRM control strategy" (Spencer, 2010, p. 254) that has moved away from personnel procedures and rules and toward a "management of culture" (Storey, 2007, as quoted in Spencer, 2010, p. 254). Consequently, HRD has been used to incorporate employees into management culture, which means that democratic values have been sacrificed for a more unitarist and "pretend-democratic culture" (Spencer, 2010, p. 254).

Overcoming Challenges
All of these aspects exemplify the frictions and differences that exist between ACE and HRD/WPL approaches to learning. How to overcome these challenges?

First, practitioners in HRD and WPL need to acknowledge power and authority at work. If you set up formal classroom training and have a facilitator stand in front of the room and everyone else is seated, that setting represents a form of power. This setting is still the default when we think of HRD, but it does not have to be that way. Similar to challenging the constructivist perspective as the default perspective on (adult) learning, workplace educators need to stand up (or maybe sit down?) and reconfigure the spaces that they work in so that the structure liberates ideas, participation, and personal development outcomes.

Second, HRD and WPL practitioners are encouraged to create informal learning opportunities. As King (2010) puts it: "Creating a hunger for independent, informal learning . . . is an essential element of providing the skills to accomplish it" (p. 425). Too often workplace educators are measured on the hours trained or the number of workshops conducted—a trend that aligns with the performance paradigm where training effectiveness and return on investment considerations trump anecdotal evidence of progress and personal stories of development. To counteract this tendency, practitioners should organize spaces where informal learning experience can be shared—an ambition that aligns well with the situated learning and development approach.

Third, and for positive individual development outcomes, workplace educators need to practice respect and equity while providing programs that address the whole person (Peterson, 2010). By supporting discovery of self-dilemmas, by encouraging the sharing of experiences and by valuing the self and identity perspective on learning, educators acknowledge the broader potential of employees (beyond their job function) that will impact their family, communities, and society.

Fourth, HRD practitioners should be more critical and self-reflective when wandering through the "corporate jungle" (Bierema, 2000, p. 290). Along the lines of the critical cultural analysis perspective, they need to surface assumptions and assess the systemic impact of what they say, do, and represent.

Fifth, as technology-based learning grows and hence pushes instructor-led classroom training to the margins of HRD formats, the question going forward needs to be: What role will HRD practitioners play in the era of virtual, technology-based, and robot-enhanced learning? From a situated perspective, new technologies are tools that the learner uses in order to create learning paths. However, self-directed learning is not as easy as it seems, and no assurance is given that—without the guidance of HRD/WPL practitioners—relevant content is being accessed and put to effective use by employees. It is therefore possible that HRD/WPL practitioners—in their role as content curators, WPL facilitators and development coaches—will be even more important in virtual contexts.

Finally, here is an appeal to researchers in the HRD community: If we can demonstrate that personal growth *and* organizational improvement are possible together in a symbiotic relationship, then we will make a huge stride toward overcoming the performance versus learning debate. This in turn would facilitate the five actions to overcome common challenges as described previously. The "wicked question" (Kimball, 2011, p. 11) to ask is: How can we promote organizational advancement and success and at the same time also help individuals to experience personal growth and development through HRD and WPL?

References

ATD. (2019). *State of the industry report.* https://www.atd.org/research-reports/state-of-the-industry

Baldwin, T. T., & Ford, J. K. (1988). Transfer of training: A review and directions for future research. *Personnel Psychology, 41*(1), 63–105. https://doi.org/10.1111/j.1744-6570.1988.tb00632.x

Bates, R., Cannonier, N., & Hatala, J.-P. (2014). Linking motivation to workplace learning transfer. In N. F. Chalofsky, T. S. Rocco, & M. L. Morris (Eds.), *Handbook of human resource development* (pp. 386–401). Wiley.

Bell, A., & Mladenovic, R. (2015). Situated learning, reflective practice and conceptual expansion: effective peer observation for tutor development. *Teaching in Higher Education, 20*(1), 24–36. https://doi.org/10.1080/13562517.2014.945163

Bierema, L. L. (1996). Development of the individual leads to more productive workplaces. *New Directions for Adult and Continuing Education, 1996*(72), 21–28.

Bierema, L. L. (2000). Moving beyond performance paradigms in human resource development. In A. L. Wilson & E. R. Hayes (Eds.), *Handbook of adult and continuing education* (pp. 278–293). Wiley.

Bierema, L. L. (2015). Critical human development to enhance reflexivity, change discourse, and adopt a call-to-action. *Human Resource Development Review, 14*(2), 119–124. https://doi.org/10.1177/1534484315585206

Billett, S. (2002). Critiquing workplace learning discourses: Participation and continuity at work. *Studies in the Education of Adults, 34*(1), 56–67. https://doi.org/10.1080/02660830.2002.11661461

Billett, S. (2004). Workplace participatory practices: Conceptualising workplaces as learning environments. *Journal of Workplace Learning, 16*(6), 312–324. https://doi.org/10.1108/13665620410550295

Brookfield, K., Tilley, S., & Cox, M. (2016). Informal science learning for older adults. *Science Communication, 38*(5), 655–665. https://doi.org/10.1177/1075547016655358

Carliner, S. (2013). How have concepts of informal learning developed over time? *Performance Improvement, 52*(3), 5–11. https://doi.org/10.1002/pfi.21330

Davis, B., & Sumara, D. (1997). Cognition, complexity, and teacher education. *Harvard Educational Review, 67*(1), 105–126. https://doi.org/10.17763/haer.67.1.160w00j113t78042

Fenwick, T. J. (1998). Women composing selves, seeking authenticity: A study of women's development in the workplace. *International Journal of Lifelong Education*, *17*(3), 199–217. https://doi.org/10.1080/0260137980170306

Fenwick, T. J. (2000a). Expanding conceptions of experiential learning: A review of the five contemporary perspectives on cognition. *Adult Education Quarterly*, *50*(4), 243–272. https://doi.org/10.1177/07417130022087035

Fenwick, T. J. (2000b). Putting meaning into workplace learning. In A. L. Wilson & E. R. Hayes (Eds.), *Handbook of adult and continuing education* (pp. 294–311). Wiley.

Fenwick, T. J. (2001). *Experiential learning: A theoretical critique from five perspectives*. ERIC Document No. 454418. https://eric.ed.gov/?id=ED454418

Fenwick, T. J. (2005). Conceptions of critical HRD: Dilemmas for theory and practice. *Human Resource Development International*, *8*(2), 225–238.

Fuller, A., Felstead, A., Unwin, L., & Jewson, N. (2009). *Improving working as learning*. Routledge.

Gegenfurtner, A., Veermans, K., Festner, D., & Gruber, H. (2009). Motivation to transfer training: An integrative literature review. *Human Resource Development Review*, *8*(3), 403–423. https://doi.org/10.1177/1534484309335970

Ghosh, R., Kim, M., Kim, S., & Callahan, J. (2014). Examining the dominant, emerging, and waning themes featured in select HRD publications: Is it time to redefine HRD? *European Journal of Training and Development*, *38*(4), 302–322. https://doi.org/10.1108/EJTD-02-2013-0012

Giroux, H. A. (2005). *Border crossings: Cultural workers and the politics of education*. Taylor & Francis.

Govaerts, N., Kyndt, E., Vreye, S., & Dochy, F. (2017). A supervisors' perspective on their role in transfer of training. *Human Resource Development Quarterly*, *28*(4), 515–552. https://doi.org/10.1002/hrdq.21286

Greeno, J. G. (1997). Theories and practices of thinking and learning to think. *American Journal of Education*, *106*, 85–126. https://doi.org/10.1086/444177

Hamlin, B., & Stewart, J. (2011). What is HRD? A definitional review and synthesis of the HRD domain. *Journal of European Industrial Training*, *35*(3), 199–220. https://doi.org/10.1108/03090591111120377

Jones, S. R., & Gasiorski, A. (2008). Service-learning, civic and community participation: Contributions to adult development. In M. C. Smith & N. DeFrates-Densch (Eds.), *Handbook of research on adult learning and development* (pp. 658–691). Routledge.

Jordan, S. (2010). Learning to be surprised: How to foster reflective practice in a high-reliability context. *Management Learning*, *41*(4), 391–413. https://doi.org/10.1177/1350507609357388

Justice, S. B., Bang, A., Lundgren, H., Marsick, V. J., Poell, R. F., & Yorks, L. (2020). Operationalizing reflection in experience-based workplace learning: A hybrid approach. *Human Resource Development International*, *23*(1), 66–87. https://doi.org/10.1080/13678868.2019.1621250

Justice, S. B., & Yorks, L. (2018). Incidental learning as an enacted encounter with materiality. *New Directions for Adult and Continuing Education*, *2018*(159), 91–102. https://doi.org/10.1002/ace.20289

Kimball, L. (2011). Liberating structures: A new pattern language for engagement. *OD Practitioner*, *43*(3), 8–11.

King, K. (2010). Informal learning in a virtual era. In C. E. Kasworm, A. D. Rose, & J. M. Ross-Gordon (Eds.), *Handbook of adult and continuing education* (pp. 421–430). SAGE.

Kuchinke, K. P. (1998). Moving beyond the dualism of performance versus learning: A response to Barrie and Pace. *Human Resource Development Quarterly*, *9*(4), 377–384. https://doi.org/10.1002/hrdq.3920090408

Kuhn, T. S. (1996). *The structure of scientific revolutions* (3rd ed.). University of Chicago Press.

Lave, J., & Wenger, E. (1991). *Situated learning: Legitimate peripheral participation*. https://doi.org/10.1017/CBO9780511815355

Lee, M. (2001). A refusal to define HRD. *Human Resource Development International*, *4*(3), 327–341. https://doi.org/10.1080/13678860110059348

Lee, M. M. (2014). Dilemmas in defining HRD. In N. F. Chalofsky (Ed.), *Handbook of human resource development* (pp. 97–111). Wiley.

Lundgren, H., Bang, A., Justice, S. B., Marsick, V. J., Poell, R. F., Yorks, L., Clark, M., & Sung, S. (2017). Conceptualizing reflection in experience-based workplace learning. *Human Resource Development International*, *20*(4), 305–326. https://doi.org/10.1080/13678868.2017.1308717

Lundin, J., & Nuldén, U. (2007). Talking about tools: Investigating learning at work in police practice. *Journal of Workplace Learning*, *19*(4), 222–239. https://doi.org/10.1108/13665620710747915

MacKenzie, C. A., Garavan, T. N., & Carbery, R. (2012). Through the looking glass: Challenges for human resource development (HRD) post the global financial crisis—business as usual? *Human Resource Development International*, *15*(3), 353–364. https://doi.org/10.1080/13678868.2012.669236

Marsick, V. J. (Ed.). (1987). *Learning in the workplace*. Croom Helm.

Marsick, V. J., & Watkins, K. E. (1990). *Informal and incidental learning in the workplace*. Routledge.

Marsick, V. J., Watkins, K. E., & O'Connor, B. (2011). Researching workplace learning in the United States. In M. Malloch, L. Cairns, K. Evans, & B. O'Connor (Eds.), *The SAGE handbook of workplace learning* (pp. 198–209). SAGE.

Massenberg, A.-C., Schulte, E.-M., & Kauffeld, S. (2017). Never too early: Learning transfer system factors affecting motivation to transfer before and after training programs. *Human Resource Development Quarterly, 28*(1), 55–85. https://doi.org/10.1002/hrdq.21256

McLagan, P. A. (1989). Models for HRD practice. *Training & Development Journal, 43*(9), 49–60.

McLean, G. N., & McLean, L. (2001). If we can't define HRD in one country, how can we define it in an international context? *Human Resource Development International, 4*(3), 313–326. https://doi.org/10.1080/13678860110059339

Messmann, G., Segers, M. S., & Dochy, F. (Eds.). (2018). *Informal learning at work: Triggers, antecedents, and consequences.* Routledge.

Mezirow, J. (1996). Contemporary paradigms of learning. *Adult Education Quarterly, 46*(3), 158–172. https://doi.org/10.1177/074171369604600303

Nijhof, W. J. (2004). Is the HRD profession in the Netherlands changing? *Human Resource Development International, 7*(1), 57–72. https://doi.org/10.1080/1367886022000032363

Nijman, D.-J. J., Nijhof, W. J., Wognum, A., & Veldkamp, B. P. (2006). Exploring differential effects of supervisor support on transfer of training. *Journal of European Industrial Training, 30*(7), 529–549. https://doi.org/10.1108/03090590610704394

Ovens, A., & Tinning, R. (2009). Reflection as situated practice: A memory-work study of lived experience in teacher education. *Teaching and Teacher Education, 25*(8), 1125–1131.

Pedler, M., Burgoyne, J., & Boydell, T. (1991). *The Learning Company: A strategy for sustainable growth.* McGraw-Hill.

Peterson, S. L. (2010). Employer sponsored learning in the workplace. In C. E. Kasworm, A. D. Rose, & J. M. Ross-Gordon (Eds.), *Handbook of adult and continuing education* (pp. 243–252). SAGE.

Piaget, J. (1950). *The psychology of intelligence* (M. Piercy and D. Berlyne, trans.). Routledge.

Poell, R. F. (2017). Time to 'flip' the training transfer tradition: Employees create learning paths strategically. *Human Resource Development Quarterly, 28*(1), 9–15. https://doi.org/10.1002/hrdq.21279

Poell, R. F., Chivers, G. E., Van der Krogt, F. J., & Wildemeersch, D. A. (2000). Learning-network theory: Organizing the dynamic relationships between learning and work. *Management Learning, 31*(1), 25–49. https://doi.org/10.1177/1350507600311004

Poell, R. F., Lundgren, H., Bang, A., Justice, S. B., Marsick, V. J., Sung, S., & Yorks, L. (2018). How do employees' individual learning paths differ across occupations? A review of 10 years of empirical research. *Journal of Workplace Learning, 30*(5), 315–334. https://doi.org/10.1108/JWL-01-2018-0019

Poell, R. F., Pluijmen, R., & Van Der Krogt, F. (2003). Strategies of HRD professionals in organising learning programmes: A qualitative study among 20 Dutch HRD professionals. *Journal of European Industrial Training, 27*(2/3/4), 125–136. https://doi.org/10.1108/03090590310468949

Poell, R. F., & Van Der Krogt, F. (2003). Learning-program creation in work organizations. *Human Resource Development Review, 2*(3), 252–272. https://doi.org/10.1177/1534484303256996

Poell, R. F., & Van Der Krogt, F. (2010). Individual learning paths of employees in the context of social networks. In S. Billett (Ed.), *Learning through practice* (pp. 197–221). Springer.

Poell, R. F., & Van Der Krogt, F. (2015). The Learning-Network Theory: Actors organize dynamic HRD networks. In R. F. Poell, T. S. Rocco, & G. L. Roth (Eds.), *The Routledge companion to human resource development* (pp. 134–146). Routledge.

Poell, R. F., & Van Der Krogt, F. (2017a). Why is organizing human resource development so problematic? Perspectives from the learning-network theory (Part I). *The Learning Organization, 24*(3), 180–193. https://doi.org/10.1108/TLO-12-2016-0093

Poell, R. F., & Van Der Krogt, F. (2017b). Why is organizing human resource development so problematic? Perspectives from the learning-network theory (Part II). *The Learning Organization, 24*(4), 215–225. https://doi.org/10.1108/TLO-12-2016-0094

Poell, R. F., Van Der Krogt, F., & Warmerdam, J. H. (1998). Project-based learning in professional organizations. *Adult Education Quarterly, 49*(1), 28–42. https://doi.org/10.1177/074171369804900104

Poell, R. F., & Van Woerkom, M. (2011). Introduction: Supporting workplace learning. In R. F. Poell & M. Van Woerkom (Eds.), *Supporting workplace learning* (pp. 1–7). Springer.

Raelin, J. A. (2008). Emancipatory discourse and liberation. *Management Learning, 39*(5), 519–540. https://doi.org/10.1177/1350507608096039

Rocco, T. S., Munn, S. L., & Collins, J. C. (2018). The critical turn in human resources development. In M. Milana, S. Webb, J. Holford, R. Waller, & P. Jarvis (Eds.), *Palgrave international handbook on adult and lifelong education and learning* (pp. 227–244). Palgrave. https://doi.org/10.1057/978-1-137-55783-4_13

Rubenson, K. (2018). Conceptualizing participation in adult learning and education: Equity issues. In M. Milana, S. Webb, J. Holford, R. Waller, & P. Jarvis (Eds.), *The Palgrave international handbook on adult and lifelong education and learning* (pp. 337–357). Palgrave Macmillan.

Sambrook, S. A. (2008). Critical HRD: A concept analysis. *Personnel Review, 38*(1), 61–73.

Sambrook, S. A. (2014). Critical HRD. In N. F. Chalofsky, T. S. Rocco, & M. L. Morris (Eds.), *Handbook of human resource development* (pp. 145–163). Wiley.

Schied, F. M., Carter, V. K., & Howell, S. L. (2001). Silent power: HRD and the management of learning in the workplace. In R. M. Cervero & A. L. Wilson (Eds.), *Power in practice: Adult education and the struggle for knowledge and power in society* (pp. 42–59). Jossey-Bass.

Senge, P. (1990). *The fifth discipline: The art and science of the learning organization.* Currency Doubleday.

Spencer, B. (2010). Workers' education for the 21st century. In C. E. Kasworm, A. D. Rose, & J. M. Ross-Gordon (Eds.), *Handbook of adult and continuing education* (pp. 253–262). SAGE.

Stoner, A. M., & Cennamo, K. S. (2018). *Enhancing reflection within situated learning: Incorporating mindfulness as an instructional strategy.* Springer.

Swanson, R. A. (1995). Human resource development: Performance is the key. *Human Resource Development Quarterly, 6*(2), 207–213. https://doi.org/10.1002/hrdq.3920060208

Swanson, R. A., & Arnold, D. E. (1996). Part one: What is the purpose of human resource development? The purpose of human resource development is to improve organizational performance. *New Directions for Adult and Continuing Education, 1996*(72), 13–19. https://doi.org/10.1002/ace.36719967204

Swanson, R. A., & Holton, E. F. (2001). *Foundations of human resource development.* Berrett-Koehler.

Unwin, L. (2004). *Taking an expansive approach to workplace learning: Implications for guidance* (pp. 2–10). Centre for Guidance Studies. http://www.derby.ac.uk/cegs/publications/LornaUnwinOccPape-Annual%20Lecture-2003.pdf

Van Der Klink, M., Gielen, E., & Nauta, C. (2001). Supervisory support as a major condition to enhance transfer. *International Journal of Training and Development, 5*(1), 52–63. https://doi.org/10.1111/1468-2419.00121

von Glasersfeld, E. (1984). An introduction to radical constructivism. In P. Watzlawick (Ed.), *The invented reality* (pp. 17–40). W. W. Norton.

Wang, G. G., Werner, J. M., Sun, J. Y., Gilley, A., & Gilley, J. W. (2017). Means vs ends: Theorizing a definition of human resource development. *Personnel Review, 46*(6), 1165–1181.

Watkins, K. E. (1989). Business and industry. In S. B. Merriam & P. M. Cunningham (Eds.), *Handbook of adult and continuing education* (pp. 422–435). Jossey-Bass.

Watkins, K. E., & Marsick, V. J. (1995). *The case for learning* [Paper presentation]. Academy of Human Resource Development Annual Conference, St. Louis, MO, United States.

Watkins, K. E., & Marsick, V. J. (2014). Adult education & human resource development: Overlapping and disparate fields. *New Horizons in Adult Education and Human Resource Development, 26*(1), 42–54.

Watkins, K. E., Marsick, V. J., Wofford, M. G., & Ellinger, A. D. (2018). The evolving Marsick and Watkins (1990) theory of informal and incidental learning. *New Directions for Adult and Continuing Education, 2018*(159), 21–36.

Werner, J. M. (2014). Human resource development (does not equal) human resource management: So what is it? *Human Resource Development Quarterly, 25*(2), 127–139. https://doi.org/10.1002/hrdq.21188

Yoon, S. W., Lim, D. H., & Willging, P. A. (2014). Goals and means for HRD. In R. F. Poell, T. S. Rocco, & G. L. Roth (Eds.), *The Routledge companion to human resource development* (pp. 99–109). Routledge.

Yorks, L. (2004). Toward a political economy model for comparative analysis of the role of strategic human resource development leadership. *Human Resource Development Review, 3*(3), 189–208. https://doi.org/10.1177/1534484304266260

CHAPTER 30

Labor Education Programs

Radical Beginnings, McCarthyist Backlash, and the Rise of Neoliberal Education

Corey Dolgon and Reuben Roth

> You're going to make goddamned revolutionaries out of people. We're not interested in turning people into revolutionaries. We want goddamned workers who'll be productive.—*George Morris, General Motors Vice President for Industrial Relations, 1979 (White, 1987, p. 151).*

The history of labor education has long been characterized by a tension between radical and conservative approaches to teaching adult workers. Conservative and neoliberal educators peddled a pedagogy that served corporate interests and those of the polity, while labor educators aspired to train workers in the use of the limited legislative tools at their disposal—all the while teaching against those very political limitations. From a radical perspective, labor education programs aim to emancipate the working-class from wage slavery while conservative efforts support modest improvements in pay and working conditions linked strictly to increasing economic growth and market-based individualism (Byrd & Nissen, 2003). More radical efforts not only addressed the drudgery of scientifically managed labor processes and starvation wages but also challenged more fundamental, macro issues of capitalist economic and political legitimacy (Dolgon & Roth, 2016). By contrast, more conservative projects reaffirmed the status quo by presuming corporate property rights and managerial imperatives—capital's control over economic, political, and social processes—were a given. In short, radical workers' education programs in the United States focused on empowering people to negotiate existing working conditions at the same time that they gained the political education and organizing skills to struggle for control over the means of production. Yet conservative projects, always with greater resources and mainstream political support (often influenced by anticommunist, procorporate interests) successfully competed with radical efforts, and usually remained the only educational vehicles available for adult laborers (Barrow, 1990). Workers' rank-and-file attempts to own their own, class-conscious curricula through popular education movements were always filled with hope and possibility but fraught with peril (e.g., Barrow, 1990; Cummins, 1936; Green, 1982).

Worker education began in the United States rooted in institutions that focused on political and cultural knowledge to liberate the working class. The courses simultaneously prepared individuals for leadership positions to serve the formal labor movement and its goals (Keane, 1989; Schied, 1989). Such efforts were often called *tools* courses, as they emphasized the nuts and bolts of organizing within the context of learning about labor history, economics, and politics. According to Richard Altenbaugh (1990a), these programs "served liberating rather than adjustive outcomes, and upheld working-class culture, providing adult worker-students with the knowledge and skills necessary to serve the labor movement" (p. 36). These projects faced powerful opposition from conservative unions and corporate interests, as well as fascist political elements, Cold War politics, and mass consumption culture (Kincheloe, 2018). Commenting on the rise and fall of worker education around the globe, Dieter Buse (1995) noted, "Many studies have shown a similar pattern for Europe where, during the 1920s, the cultural endeavors by unions and leftist parties reached their height and then were destroyed by fascism, the Cold War, and the commercialization of culture" (p. 269). Even labor leaders, like the American Federation of Labor's (AFL's) Samuel Gompers, tried to limit radical educators by arguing that workers' education "should concentrate mainly on developing simple English literacy . . . [and] insisted [it] should not have any relation to 'politics' or the 'isms'" (Barrow, 1990, p. 398; Robinson, 1968). Radical educators flourished in the first half of the 20th century, but such approaches would be countered by red-baiting, corporate power, and conservative business unionism. Today, radical worker education in the United States has almost completely disappeared.

This chapter will offer a brief look at the history and politics of 20th-century labor education in the United States. After examining the more radical programs and how they challenged, and were challenged by, monopoly capitalism and bourgeois democracy, we present how such dynamics set the stage for late 20th- and early 21st-century labor politics where workers' education is dominated by neoliberal economics, politics, and culture. In fact, we argue that a major problem plaguing radical politics and worker education is the disappearing working class (and its attendant class-consciousness), particularly in higher education (Bousquet, 2008; Noble, 1998). While research continues to show a decades-old decline in the number and stability of university-based labor studies programs (Byrd & Nissen, 2003; United Association for Labor Education, 2017; Worthen, 2015), studies of student activism expose almost no interests or links to labor unions or labor issues with minimal exceptions for international solidarity with workers through Students Against Sweatshops in the 2000s and the Fair Labor Association (Featherstone & United Students Against Sweatshops, 2002; Jason, 2018). Unlike the first half of the 20th century, when union membership grew and student activism on campus was often linked to labor struggles and class politics, student consciousness of labor history and issues hardly registers these days (Altbach, 2007; Braungart & Braungart, 1990; Broadhurst, 2014). The neoliberal university produces triumphant stories of corporate hegemony while still promoting *some* rhetorical and severely circumscribed semblance of democratic and public mission. These narratives always serve economic growth frameworks and celebrate increasing individual marketability as tools to succeed in the age of austerity. We conclude with some suggestions for rebuilding radical programs for re-envisioning class-consciousness and class struggle for the future.

In the Beginning: Mass Public Education and Labor

In the United States, mass public education began in the early to mid 19th century. The main focus of mass schooling was creating racial and ethnic assimilation, an efficient and obedient workforce, and a patriotic and civic-minded citizenry (Bowles & Gintis, 1976; Boyles, 2018). Thus, early notions of education and civics often bolstered the exploitation of labor and class inequality while suggesting that education developed individual opportunity and civic capacity (Adams, 1995; Faler, 1974). This irony, that capitalist institutions of education promise individual growth and improvement while primarily supporting the increased power and profit of neoliberal capitalism, has not been lost on some critics of neoliberalism and capitalism's impact on the civic engagement movement in higher education today (Dolgon, 2017; Giroux, 2002; Raddon & Harrison, 2015). Some early, agricultural extension programs—often linked to land-grant colleges and universities—allowed for farmer-driven knowledge production and used the grange model of local organizing and cooperative approaches to production and distribution (Peters, 2017). The dominant model, however, remained "a one-way process of transferring knowledge and technology from the university (as the source of expertise) to its key constituents" (Kellogg Commission on the Future of State and Land-Grant Institutions, 1999, pp. 18–19). Such programs primarily emphasized the rationalization of production and the profitability of agricultural and related industries (Anderson & Feder, 2004; Bennett, 1996; Rivera, 2000). To find a more independent, anticorporate, and anticapitalist worker education in the United States, one would have to point toward the rise of the labor college movement in the first part of the 20th century.

While prototypes of workers' colleges began in New York (e.g., United Hebrew Trades union) and Duluth, Minnesota (the Work People's College), the most notable and substantive establishments were the Work People's College (Chicago, Ilinois) (Altenbaugh, 1990b), Commonwealth College (Mena, Arizona), and Brookwood Labor College (Katonah, New York), as well as the Rand School of Social Science (New York City, New York), and eventually the Highlander School (New Market, Tennessee). A focus on political education and voter registration distinguished these schools from other labor training and union programs. Altenbaugh (1990a) argues that such institutions stood "in sharp contrast to the cultural and economic reproductive functions of the formal education system" (pp. 36–37), as they upheld and reinforced ethnic and regional working-class cultures while also providing adult worker-students with the knowledge and skills necessary to serve the labor movement (Altenbaugh & Paulston, 1978; Dwyer, 1977; Edwards & McCarthy, 1992; Howlett & Charles, 1993).

In Oregon, Portland Labor College founders explained the mission as preparing

> the individual as well as the organization for a share in the responsibilities of democratic control of industry, such preparation requiring the knowledge of the history of the practices, problems, and policies of the labor movement and of the fundamental principles of the production and distribution of wealth. (Lembcke, 1984, pp. 118–119)

Even more conservative approaches to worker education, such as those promoted by Horace Kallen (1924) of the New School for Social Research, suggested that an educated workforce could exert autonomy and creativity in the solution of workplace problems for the improvement of workers and industry. According to Shawn Taylor (1998), "in a few short years (early 1920s), there were upward of 75 workers' colleges, labor temples, and study programs in 21 states across the country" (p. 86). By 1926, workers' education had reached its peak with an enrollment of 40,000 worker-students spread over 300 industrial centers in 30 states throughout the nation.

A second wave of workers' colleges, often with greater focus on a broader and more political class analysis, occurred throughout the 1930s. Socialist and Communist Party efforts arose in Boston, Washington DC, Chicago, Philadelphia, Denver, Seattle, and San Francisco. The very successful Rand School was run primarily by the Socialist Party in New York City, and the Communist Party USA developed the Jefferson School of Social Science to coordinate their national labor education movement (Epstein, 1921; Gettleman, 2002). These projects, while often hosting college and university faculty, evolved primarily as off-campus and independent institutions with goals similar to those as espoused by the Seattle Labor College in their newsletter, *The Vanguard*:

- For the organization of the unorganized along industrial lines and the amalgamating of the present craft unions into departmentalized industrial forum
- For an independent political party of farmers and workers rather than nonpartisan political action
- Support every move on the part of organized workers to better their condition through the 5-day week, higher wages, old age pension, workmen's compensation, unemployment insurance, etc.
- For the recognition of the Soviet Russia by the United States
- For a spirit of international solidarity on the part of American labor and against imperialism and militarism
- For militant unionism as opposed to business unionism
- For support of public ownership of public utilities, municipal or state
- For workers' education based on broad progressive lines (Eigner, 2009)

Over time, the workers' education movement would be mainstreamed by projects that grew under the auspices of the New Deal's Federal Emergency Relief Act (FERA) and the moderately progressive leadership of Hilda Smith, a former social worker and suffragist. Smith founded Bryn Mawr College's Summer School for Women Workers in Industry in 1921, stressing women's role in bringing about social harmony and middle class values (Heller, 1984; McGuire, 2009). In Joyce Kornbluh's (1987) definitive chronicle of the

Workers' Education Project, she suggests that, despite its brief existence and the demise of so many of the era's labor colleges and education programs, "they left an enduring legacy of the democratic educational ideals and practices of the progressive adult educators of the 1920s to the union activists of today" (p. 125).

By the second half of the 20th century many of these institutions, programs, and projects had disappeared. Some suffered from inadequate funding and poor administration. Others were torn apart by internal conflicts over ideological dogma or radical party and sectarian fights. More often than not, however, attacking those with left-wing sympathies—red-baiting—and local political pressure—sometimes including conservative vigilantism and violence—terminated worker education programs in both major urban areas as well as small rural hamlets. The only surviving institution of any significance has been the Highlander Center, whose combination of local cultural integration with an uncanny ability to embrace a changing social justice landscape has made it a mainstay for radical, class-based, political organizing up to the present day (Glen, 1996; Glowacki-Dudka & Griswold, 2016; Kohl, 1991).

Still, some university-sponsored labor programs have endured. Originating during the same period as the independent workers college movement were John Commons's efforts at the University of Wisconsin and Richard Ely's project at Johns Hopkins University in the 1920s and 1930s. Labor studies in higher education grew dramatically after World War II and then again in the 1970s and early 1980s under the guise of linking higher education and public service. These programs often served dual purposes of offering academically substantive courses about labor history, economics, politics, and culture while also offering pragmatic, nuts-and-bolts lessons on labor organizing, contract negotiations, labor law, and so on. Ironically, according to Francis Ryan (2006), "The stronger alliance between organized labor and higher education in the post-1945 period reflected a corresponding decline in class consciousness among American workers" (p. 395). For Ryan, the disappearance of independent labor schools suggests the parallel decline of a separate working-class culture that had characterized the initial rise of labor education in the United States. Gone were the days when radical faculty went into their communities to work as part of the labor movement. Instead, workers as individuals were invited onto college campuses with increasingly neoliberal agendas. In fact, we contend that the infusion of labor studies with higher education may have had a *depoliticizing* impact on practices and resulted in some of the taming of radical knowledge production and anticorporate/anticapitalist movement building.

In the Present: The Current State of Labor Education Programs . . .

During the 1960s and 1970s, when radical social movements changed racial, ethnic, and gender politics and resulted in changing curriculum and staffing on campus, labor studies programs also addressed the challenges of the burgeoning hegemonic role colleges and universities played in elite knowledge production (Byrd & Nissen, 2003). But like many of the ethnic, women's, and peace studies programs that began as anticolonial, antihierarchical, and antimilitary, labor studies, too, seemed hardly counterhegemonic by the 1980s (Lichtenstein, 2013; Moody, 1988). Eventually,

> by the early 1980s corporate capitalists and the state elite were working closely together on a common agenda to restructure the industrial regime. . . . The gains that unionized and nonunionized workers had made in the thirty years after World War II were now at risk. (Heron, 1996, p. 108)

Reagan's war on labor and the rapid right-wing turn in American political life took its toll on progressive programs in higher education in general, and in particular on formal college and university links to labor studies. Still, in the late 1990s and early 2000s, labor programs seemed to make a slight comeback, according to Byrd and Nissen (2003). But by 2005, students at the University of Massachusetts were fighting to save their graduate labor studies program and campus-based labor centers across the country came under attack. *The Daily Kos* reported,

> As conservative state governments and university administrators gain power, programs about unions and workers' organizing have been among their first targets. The Labor Studies program at the University of Indiana suffered huge cuts, and California Governor Arnold Schwarzenegger reached into the University of California's budget to take $3.8 million out of its labor research and education programs. (Weinbaum & Juravich, 2005, para. 5)

Recently, Michigan legislators threatened to *fine* Michigan State University $500,000 for any course found to be promoting unionization (Weinbaum & Juravich, 2005).

As a whole, college- and university-based labor education programs in the United States have lost tremendous ground in tandem with union's own decline since the 1980s. These losses are, in part, a result of expanding and conservative business union models that focus solely on better wages and benefits linked to market-based dynamics and economic growth (Heron, 1996). These organizations bow to the power of courts and electoral politics to provide "representation" to their members but never discuss the need to challenge for power and control over production and governance. They never threaten the status quo premise of corporate capital and property ownership over the means of production. It is clear that the continued success of conservative politics and procapitalist hegemony has not only diminished the ranks of radical and progressive labor studies programs but also influenced the practice and strategies of worker education itself.

Thus, once again, the great irony exists that the *ethos* of civic engagement and democratically driven experiential education have triumphed on college campuses at the same time that university-supported labor studies programs—the very embodiment of democratically driven experiential education—are now on life support. To some degree, civic engagement has been more successful at partnering with the neoliberal project, suggesting that volunteer service, educational access, and economic development are the tools for reducing inequality and fostering democracy. While experiential pedagogy and other community partner programs emanate from worker education programs, labor's historical and integral struggle against corporate triumphalism resulted in a different kind of welcome at most colleges and universities. Unfortunately, the dynamic seems to have inspired all too many labor education programs to emulate civic engagement and look for alliances with the more liberal wing of corporate hegemony through public–private partnerships.

In his book *Retooling the Mind Factory: Education in a Lean State*, Alan Sears (2003) described the lean state as "an emerging regime of social policy designed to further the process of capitalist restructuring" that formed in reaction to declining profitability in the 1970s (p. 2). He continues:

The most important feature of this restructuring process has been the developments of lean production methods in the workplace. Lean production is a set of management strategies to eliminate the waste in work processes by increasing flexibility, reducing the core workforce to an absolute minimum. . . . The social policy of the lean state aims to secure the conditions for the spread of lean production methods. Lean production requires a more polarized workforce, with large sections of the population working in lower pay sectors offering little to no security. . . . Social programs are being slashed at the same time as policing and immigration controls are being dramatically increased. (pp. 2–3)

The lean state also requires its citizenry to adapt to the dictates of the "free market" and thus requires that we reorient ourselves to individual rather than collective endeavors, view the private market as sacrosanct and the collective state as "dead," and see competition as "natural" (Sears, 2003, p. 3). According to Sears (2003), lean state orientation includes educational reforms designed to "shift the focus of schools, colleges and universities" (p. 3) to prepare people for new market relations instead of preparing them with the tools of citizenship. The collective orientation of the labor movement is cast aside in this newly rationalized, neoliberal landscape.

Still, public institutions and higher education cannot simply produce knowledge and pedagogy to legitimize labor precarity and corporate hegemony. While colleges and universities largely ignore issues of class and class-based analyses, new, publicly and politically engaged movements within higher education (e.g., the growth of civic engagement programs and pedagogy) echo neoliberal triumphalism but promise that acts of charity and community service can humanize the lean state. Capitalism has defeated not only socialism but also the idea of a social democracy (although we note that attitudes are quickly shifting, especially among youth). Students are consumers; administrators are managers, and teachers and staff are independent contractors all in service of capital (Dolgon, 2017; Shor, 1987). As we will argue later, university staff and resources once supplied radical workers' educations programs but now they engage in the practices of, and produce the ideological justification for, labor's own immiseration.

In the End . . . A Hopeful Future for Labor Education Programs

The contemporary corporatization of the academy in general and adult workers' education programs in particular seem not just ascendant, but complete. In response, we call for a retrenchment of traditional labor education and class-conscious principles and a decisive turn *away* from the neoliberal values that university extension and trade union programs now adopt. To some this prescription may sound like a hackneyed, "back to the past if we ever expect a future" approach, but we believe it is fortified by the fact that a new generation of workers apparently has little fear of left-wing, socialist/communist-tainted values. New Left activists watch in envy as youth—both students and workers—embrace old and new left positions of radically higher taxation on corporations and the wealthy, free or heavily subsidized education, and socialized health care and Pharmacare. An analysis of the youth support for Bernie Sanders in the 2016 and both Sanders and Warren in the 2020 election campaigns is a clear demonstration of this progressive political thrust (Kight, 2019). In short, we see a rise in support for collectivist principles embodied by New Deal liberalism (at a minimum) and various kinds of socialism and beyond.

We conclude that only an independent and genuinely democratic workers' education movement focused on working class, grassroots organizing that brings workers and intellectuals together as educators, researchers, and brothers and sisters in struggle can truly revitalize workers' education in particular and social justice movements in general. Today, in response to the rise of alt-right, conservative, and White nationalist political movements we have seen a resurgence in activism on the left. This has led to the rise of a social-democratic/socialist movement that has spurred a largely female and non-White movement independent of the "old" labor and socialist left. African American, Latinx, and LGBTQ working-class, grassroots organizing is uniting women, men, and transgender workers, and intellectuals from all sectors. These concurrent struggles not only revitalize social justice movements in general but also could have significantly positive impacts on adult workers' education.

As we have seen, union-based adult education's earliest roots were deeply enmeshed in the socialist and communist movements of the early 20th century, and today's activists are rediscovering these origins and applying the lessons of the past century in an attempt to instill a class-conscious education in a new generation based on the principles of the old, with a reemphasis on democratic principles and practices. Taking a page from previous popular movements and intellectuals, these efforts are broad based and steeped in streetcentric populism and notions of freedom and democracy itself.

Gindin and Robertson (1992) make the point that "democracy" not only emphasizes "popular control over the economy, but also equal access to participation (democracy must be universal) and the development of individual capacities (democracy must aspire to meeting and developing each individual's potential)" (pp. 33–34). This is also in keeping with the classical pronouncement by Marx and Engels (1848/1985) that "we shall have an association, in which the free development of each is the condition for the free development of all" (p. 105). According to Michael Lebowitz (2004) such a perspective encompasses

> the idea of human capacity that Marx advanced [stressing] the actual development of human ability—the idea of "the totally developed individual, for whom the different social functions are different modes of activity he takes up in turn." Variation of labor, mobility of the producer in all directions, points to capacities which, once developed, can be applied to new challenges, to the overcoming of new obstacles which is "in itself a liberating activity" and, thus, a process of self-realisation. (p. 15)

Lebowitz (2004) further explains that Marx conceived of a society free of barriers to "the full development of human beings" (p. 3). It would be a society where every person would maximize their potential capabilities as a human, including the "absolute working-out of his creative potentialities," and the "development of all human powers as such the end in itself" (Marx, 1973, in Lebowitz, 2004, p. 3). What better place for this process of self-realization than the adult education classroom?

But we shouldn't halt our efforts at self-realization at the door of the classroom. A more expansive analysis of education that views knowledge production as taking place in a variety of nonclassroom arenas—including workplaces and union halls—holds the greatest potential for social change and consciousness-raising. Brazilian educator Paulo Freire's educational practice of *cultural action* embraces the self-realization that Marx and Engels espoused. "Freire's term utilizes an anthropological concept of culture that includes all products, ideas and practices of human beings" (Allman, 1999, p. 85). In this vision, the roles of learner and teacher are reversed, while teachers "relinquish authoritarianism, but not authority" in a complex dance that requires that

> learners accept the challenge that the actual, collective struggle to transform the relations begins. . . . In other words, *being or relating differently is inextricably bound up with knowing differently* . . . a task that is all the more difficult in bourgeois societies because our relations to knowledge and our concepts of knowledge, our epistemologies, are constituted within and penetrated by bourgeois ideology. (Allman, 1999, p. 97, italics in original)

This combination of Freirian-Gramscian educational methodology aims at liberating working-class consciousness from the shackles of neoliberalism and the drudgery of wage slavery.

Perhaps the most important element of a new workers' studies movement (as part of a new labor movement) will entail a more complex reconceptualization of class consciousness and collective identity as well. The sophistication of new organizing methods and theories of radical practice hold the potential for reinvigorating class struggle and political movements. Recently, Movement for Black Lives (M4BL) leaders combined Freirian pedagogy and civil rights educational experiences to create their policy provisions and platform. Marbre Stahly-Butts, a M4BL policy coordinator described the process: "We formed working groups, facilitated multiple convenings, drew on a range of expertise, and sought guidance from grassroots organizations, organizers, and elders. As of today, well over 60 organizations and hundreds of people have contributed to the platform" (Kelley, 2016, para. 3)

Radical historian Robin D.G. Kelley (2016) explains M4BL goals are not simply Band-Aids for the wounds of existing racist and exploitive social and economic structures—the point is "to change those structures" (para. 5) Thus, M4BL's "A Vision for Black Lives" proclaims the goals of "community control, self-determination, and collective ownership" (para. 6) of certain economic institutions including control over police and school departments, municipal budgeting, and economic development. Kelley (2016) continues:

> Democratizing the institutions that have governed black communities for decades without accountability will go a long way toward securing a more permanent peace since it will finally end a relationship based on subjugation, subordination, and surveillance. And by insisting that such institutions be more attentive to the needs of the most marginalized and vulnerable—working people and the poor, the homeless, the formerly incarcerated, the disabled, women, and the LGBTQ community— "A Vision for Black Lives" enriches our practice of democracy. (para. 6)

The convergence of antiracist, antipatriarchal, and anticapitalist politics and organizing can be seen in the recent "Fight for 15" campaign and the open coalition-building between organized labor and M4BL. According to United Steelworkers' Maria Somma, the union's first Asian American female director of organizing,

> Young workers get it that you can't organize without a social justice approach. . . . I've been in the movement for a good number of years and I believe it's a big change. It's not coming from union, it's coming directly from our members and I love it. (Elk, 2018, p. 1)

A new generation of workers has been provided with strong analysis and vision by groups such as the Coalition of Black Trade Unions International and is reflected in their report *A Future for Workers: A Contribution from Black Labor* (Melvin et al., 2015). This treatise outlines the "contours of an agenda that focuses on power rather than on grievances . . . an agenda that would emerge later through discussions among workers, their unions and their communities about the needs of working people" (pp. 4–6). The document provides a blended approach to radically transformative and integrative goals addressing economic development and jobs; the environment; criminal justice; the distribution of wealth; education, tolerance and equity; and the labor movement. The authors declare the need for a transformed, energized labor movement—authentically inclusive and clearly perceived by workers as an instrument for justice and equity. They conclude:

Our trade union movement must align itself with a broader labor movement that is welcoming janitors as well as adjunct professors (Fight for 15). Above all, it is totally not acceptable for our movement to debate and adopt an agenda and then adjourn. The final version of a workers' agenda must be a blueprint that guides and is guided by the ongoing efforts of workers to create a humane, sustainable future worthy of their sacrifices and the hopes of the next generation. (Melvin et al., 2015, p. 6)

But these hopes are already finding realization in the actions and education of workers together on the front lines (Dolgon & Roth, 2016).

In response to privatization efforts and the challenges of union organizing in the Right to Work South, workers at various campuses throughout the state of Tennessee have created a union along the lines of the old industrial union model. Anyone who works on a college campus can join United Campus Workers (UCW) and, despite the inability for most workers to bargain collectively, workers have successfully created the solidarity necessary to win better wages and working conditions. In their biggest victory yet, UCW fought back and won against their billionaire governor's attempt to privatize all public land and public services. Their growth and power have now inspired similar movements in Georgia and Mississippi.

UCW efforts are on the cutting edge of not only the labor movement but also adult workers' education. The union understands its efforts to build a base and a place and multitudes of spaces where workers can empower themselves on multiple levels. UCW Lead Organizer Cassie Watters explains that public workers in right-to-work states don't have access to many traditional labor organizing tools (Brooks, 2017). They have responded with creativity and coalition building by

> partnering with students and community organizations in order to be visible and reach workers through different means—doing joint events with student organizations like fall cookouts, tabling, holding happy hours for adjuncts, registering voters at work with the League of Women Voters and student groups, petitioning for early voting locations to be open on campuses, marching in the MLK Day Parade, or holding a Juneteenth event (Brooks, 2017, para. 46).

Watters suggests the future of the union movement will be its ability to recognize that class-consciousness and identity emanate from both the structural position of workers to capital as well as myriad daily experiences with social and political institutions, communities, coworkers and neighbors.

UCW also explains that political power and economic power can no longer be separated. Workers must engage with electoral politics by preparing and running candidates of their own who will stand up for workers' rights and change corporate-friendly legislation. And they echo what is becoming a more common framework for labor organizing in the 21st century: a focus on "social justice unionism" (Brooks, 2017, para. 41) that addresses the intersectionality of class, race, gender, LGBTQ rights, anti-immigrant movements, and so on. UCW leaders suggest such unionism can

> look like many things—for example, supporting workers facing court dates with tactics like community defense, in which members train themselves to participate as advocates with those facing unjust charges. . . . We write letters in defense of their character, providing the judge with the details of their personal story. And it will take creativity and a political will to take risks. This includes finding ways to talk with members about what's happening in the world—for example, Charlottesville and the issue of Confederate monuments on public grounds [, which] opens the door for us as a local to engage on racism and white supremacy with our members. (Brooks, 2017, para. 41–42)

The future of labor education, the revolutionary movement itself, will not be theorized only in classrooms or taught academically in union halls or libraries—it will be lived and learned in the practice of organizing and struggle. Collective actions, knowledge production and mass mobilization will not occur in any particular place but must occur in *every* space available and woven into the fabric of everyday life.

References

Adams, D. W. (1995). *Education for extinction: Native Americans and the boarding school experience, 1875–1928*. University of Kansas Press.

Allman, P. (1999). *Revolutionary social transformation: Democratic hopes, political possibilities and critical education*. Bergin & Garvey.

Altenbaugh, R. J. (1990a). *Education for struggle: The American labor colleges of the 1920s and 1930s*. Temple University Press.

Altenbaugh, R. J. (1990b). Workers' education as counter hegemony: The educational process at Work Peoples' College, 1907–1941. In R. Wahl Rohfeld (Ed.), *Breaking new ground: The development of adult and workers' education in North America*. Syracuse University. http://roghiemstra.com/altenbaugh.html

Altenbaugh, R. J., & Paulston, R. G. (1978). Work People's College: A Finnish folk high school in the American labor college movement. *Paedagogica Historica, 18*(2), 237–256.

Altbach, P. G. (2007). Student politics: Activism and culture. In J. F. Forest & P. G. Altbach (Eds.), *International handbook of higher education* (pp. 329–345). Springer.

Anderson, J. R., & Feder, G. (2004). Agricultural extension: Good intentions and hard realities. *The World Bank Research Observer, 19*(1), 41–60.

Barrow, C. (1990). Counter-movement within the labor movement: Workers' education and the American Federation of Labor, 1900–1937. *The Social Science Journal, 27*(4), 395–417.

Bennett, C. F. (1996). Rationale for public funding of agricultural extension programs. *Journal of Agricultural & Food Information, 3*(4), 3–25.

Bousquet, M. (2008). *How the university works: Higher education and the low-wage nation* (Vol. 3). NYU Press.

Bowles, S. & Gintis, H. (1976). *Schooling in capitalist America: Educational reform and the construction of economic life*. Haymarket Books.

Boyles, D. (2018). *American education and corporations: The free market goes to school*. Routledge.

Braungart, R. G., & Braungart, M. M. (1990). Political generational themes in the American student movements of the 1930s and 1960s. *JPMS: Journal of Political and Military Sociology, 18*(2), 177–192.

Broadhurst, C. J. (2014). Campus activism in the 21st century: A historical framing. *New Directions for Higher Education, 2014*(167), 3–15.

Brooks, C. (2017, September 1). After Nissan: Can we organize the South? *Labor Notes*. https://www.labornotes.org/2017/09/after-nissan-can-we-organize-south

Buse, D. (1995). Weir Reid and Mine Mill: An alternative union's cultural endeavours. In M. Steedman, P. Suschnigg, & D. Buse (Eds.), *Hard lessons: The Mine Mill Union in the Canadian labour movement* (pp. 269–286). Dundurn Press.

Byrd, B., and Nissen, B. (2003). *Report on the state of the labor education in the United States*. Center for Labor Research and Education. https://uale.org/document-table/news/330-summary-byrd-and-nissen

Cummins, E. E. (1936). Workers' education in the United States. *Social Forces, 14*(4), 597–605. https://doi.org/10.2307/2571128

Dolgon, C. (2017). *Kill it to save it: An autopsy of capitalism's triumph over democracy*. Polity.

Dolgon, C., & Roth, R. (2016). Twenty-first-century workers' education in North America: The defeat of the left or a revitalized class pedagogy? *Labor Studies Journal, 41*(1), 89–113. https://doi.org/10.1177/0160449XI16634575

Dwyer, R. (1977). Workers' education, labor education, labor studies: An historical delineation. *Review of Educational Research, 47*(1), 179–207.

Edwards, B., & McCarthy, J. D. (1992). Social movement schools. *Sociological Forum, 7*(3), 541–550.

Eigner, E. (2009). Vanguard and unemployed citizen, a report. *The Labor Press Project: Pacific Northwest labor and radical newspapers*. http://depts.washington.edu/labhist/laborpress/Vanguard.htm

Elk, M. (2018, February 10). Justice in the factory: How Black Lives Matter breathed new life into unions. *The Guardian*. https://www.theguardian.com/us-news/2018/feb/10/black-lives-matter-labor-unions-factory-workers-unite

Epstein, A. (1921). Education of adult working classes. *Monthly Labor Review, 12*(6), 185–194.

Faler, P. (1974). Cultural aspects of the Industrial Revolution: Lynn, Massachusetts, shoemakers, and industrial morality 1828–1860. *Labor History, 15*(3), 367–394.

Featherstone, L., & United Students Against Sweatshops. (2002). *Students against sweatshops*. Verso.

Gettleman, M. (2002). "No varsity teams": New York's Jefferson School of Social Science, 1943–1956. *Science & Society, 66*(3), 336–359.

Gindin, S., & Robertson, D. (1992). Alternatives to competitiveness. In D. Drache (Ed.), *Getting on track: Social democratic strategies for Ontario* (pp. 32–45). McGill-Queen's University Press.

Giroux, H. (2002). Neoliberalism, corporate culture, and the promise of higher education: The university as a democratic public sphere. *Harvard Educational Review, 72*(4), 425–464.

Glen, J. M. (1996). *Highlander: No ordinary school*. University of Tennessee Press.

Glowacki-Dudka, M., & Griswold, W. (2016). Embodying authentic leadership through popular education at Highlander Research and Education Center: A qualitative case study. *Adult Learning, 27*(3), 105–112.

Green, J. (1982). Worker education and labor history in America. *History Workshop, 14*, 168–170.

Heller, R. (1984). Blue collars and bluestockings: The Bryn Mawr Summer School for women workers, 1921–1938. In J. L. Kornbluh & M. Frederickson (Eds.), *Sisterhood and solidarity: Workers' education for women, 1914–1984* (pp. 107–145). Temple University Press.

Heron, C. (1996). *The Canadian labor movement: A short history*. Lorimer.

Howlett, R., & Charles, F. (1993). *Brookwood Labor College and the struggle for peace and justice in America*. Edwin Mellen.

Jason, Z. (2018, Fall). Student activism 2.0: A look back at the history of student activism and whether today's protesters are making a difference. *Harvard Education Magazine*. https://www.gse.harvard.edu/news/ed/18/08/student-activism-20

Kallen, H. M. (1924). *Culture and democracy in the United States*. Transaction Publishers.

Keane, P. (1989). *Early interpretations of workers' education* [Paper presentation]. Breaking New Ground: The Development of Adult and Workers' Education in North America. http://roghiemstra.com/altenbaugh.html

Kelley, R. D. G. (2016, August). What does Black Lives Matter want? *Boston Review*. https://www.filmsforaction.org/articles/what-does-black-lives-matter-want/

Kellogg Commission on the Future of State and Land-Grant Institutions. (1999). *Returning to our roots: The engaged institution*. https://www.aplu.org/library/returning-to-our-roots-the-engaged-institution/file

Kight, S. (2019). Exclusive poll: Young Americans are embracing socialism. *Axios Newsletter*. www.axios.com/exclusive-poll-young-americans-embracing-socialism-b051907a-87a8-4f61-9e6e-0db75f7edc4a.html

Kincheloe, J. (2018). *How do we tell the workers? The socioeconomic foundations of work and vocational education*. Routledge.

Kohl, H. (1991). A tradition of radical education: Highlander in context. *Social Policy*, 21(3), 36–43.

Kornbluh, J. (1987). *A new deal for workers' education: The workers' service program 1933–1944*. University of Illinois Press.

Lebowitz, M. A. (2004, May). *"The rich human being": Marx and the concept of real human development* [Paper presentation]. The Marx Conference, Havana, Cuba.

Lembcke, J. (1984). Labor and education: Portland Labor College, 1921–1929. *Oregon Historical Quarterly*, 85(2), 117–134.

Lichtenstein, N. (2013). *State of the union: A century of American labor* (rev. ed.). Princeton University Press.

Marx, K., & Engels, F. (1985). *Manifesto of the communist party*. Penguin Classics. Originally published 1848.

McGuire, J. (2009). Maintaining the vitality of a social movement: Social justice feminism, class conflict, and the Bryn Mawr summer school for women workers, 1921–1924. *Pennsylvania History: A Journal of Mid-Atlantic Studies*, 76(4), 393–421.

Melvin, T. L., Redmond, F., Fletcher, B., Pitts, S., Hudson, G., Johnson, L., Gresham, G., Lucy, W., Talley, P., Spriggs, W., Williams, R., Harmon, A., & Berkley, C. (2015). *A future for workers: A contribution from Black labor*. www.cbtu.org/pdf/a_future_for_workers.pdf

Moody, K. (1988). *An injury to all: The decline of American unionism*. Verso.

Noble, D. F. (1998). Digital diploma mills: The automation of higher education. *Science as Culture*, 7(3), 355–368.

Peters, S. (2017). Recovering a forgotten lineage of democratic engagement: Agricultural and extension programs in the United States. In C. Dolgon, T. Mitchell, & T. Eatman (Eds.), *The Cambridge University handbook for service learning and community engagement* (pp. 71–80). Cambridge University Press.

Raddon, M., & Harrison, B. (2015). Is service-learning the kind face of the neoliberal university? *Canadian Journal of Higher Education*, 45(2), 134–153.

Rivera, W. M. (2000). The changing nature of agricultural information and the conflictive global developments shaping extension. *The Journal of Agricultural Education and Extension*, 7(1), 31–42.

Robinson, J. W. (1968). The expulsion of Brookwood Labor College from the Workers' Education Bureau. *Labor History: A Journal of Labor and Social History*, 15, 64–69. https://doi.org/10.2307/27507910

Ryan, F. (2006). Trade unions and workers' education. In E. Arnesen (Ed.), *Encyclopedia of U.S. labor and working-class history* (pp. 395–396). Routledge.

Sears, A. (2003). *Retooling the mind factory: Education in a lean state*. Garamond Press.

Schied, F. (1989). Education and working class culture: German workers' clubs in nineteenth century Chicago. In R. W. Rohfield (Ed.), *Breaking new ground: The development of adult and workers' education in North America*. Syracuse University. https://roghiemstra.com/schied.html

Shor, I. (1987). *Critical teaching and everyday life*. University of Chicago Press.

Taylor, S. (1998). Horace Kallen's workers' education for industrial democracy. *Labor Studies Journal*, 23(3), 84–102.

United Association for Labor Education. (2017). *What is the current status of labor education?* https://uale.org/news/306-what-is-the-current-status-of-labor-education

Weinbaum, E., & Juravich, T. (2005, November 8). Labor studies under attack: Faculty and students file charges. *Daily Kos*. https://www.dailykos.com/stories/2005/11/8/163218/-

White, B. (1987). *Hard bargains: My life on the line*. McLelland and Stewart.

Worthen, H. (2015). *The status of labor education in higher education in the United States: A report commissioned and released by the Executive Board of the United Association for Labor Education*. United Association for Labor Education. https://www.academia.edu/28919703/The_Status_of_Labor_Education_in_Higher_Education_in_the_United_States

CHAPTER 31

Adult Education for Human Flourishing

A Religious and Spiritual Framework

Davin Carr-Chellman, Michael Kroth, and Carol Rogers-Shaw

Religious adult education and spiritual adult education deal with profound concerns. As reflected in adult education theory and practice, the purposes of religious and spiritual adult education are many and varied. Contemporary discussion of adult education programs, processes, and purposes in religious settings and spiritual contexts reflects this pluralistic sensibility. Scholars study religious and spiritual adult education. Practitioners apply it for human resource development in the for-profit realm and for spiritual fulfillment in the nonprofit realm. This chapter will highlight the development and current status of inquiry into religious and spiritual adult education, offering historical resources but primarily concentrating on new research over the last decade. Potential avenues for future research are also suggested.

Review of the Literature, 2010 to 2018

Our review is limited to literature found in the adult and continuing education field since the 2010 *Handbook of Adult and Continuing Education* was published. We have summarized religious and spiritual adult education as it has been published in seven primary publications of our field. In a review of the literature from *Adult Education Quarterly, Adult Learning, Canadian Journal for the Study of Adult Education, Studies in the Education of Adults, New Horizons in Adult Education and Human Resource Development, Journal of Adult and Continuing Education,* and *New Directions for Adult and Continuing Education,* including the years 2010–2018, we located 42 articles in which religion, spirituality, religious adult education, or spiritual adult education figured prominently. Our search terms included multiple forms of the words *religion, spirituality, faith, belief, monotheism,* and *divinity*; descriptors of formal religions and their followers, such as *Christianity* and *Buddhist*; formal and informal names for a deity, such as *Allah* or *supreme being*; and words related to nonbelief, such as *atheism* and *agnostic*. In reviewing those 42 articles, we found 11 articles drawing on data-based research, which suggests minimal progress toward a strong empirical foundation. There also appears little progress toward building a theoretical framework, with some progress toward a phenomenological elaboration of spiritual experience in adult education contexts.

Historical Context

The themes derived from our literature review may be interpreted through the lens of the late 1990s and early 2000s scholarship. In that era, distinctions between spiritual adult education and religious adult education were reinforced and advanced through the emphasis on spiritual adult education in certain essential texts (English, 2001, 2005, 2013; English et al., 2005; English & Gillen, 2000; English & Mayo, 2012; English

& Tisdell, 2010; Fenwick & English, 2004; Tisdell, 2000; Tisdell & Tolliver, 2003; Welton, 2000, 2005). These texts provide a sense of the historical development and context for the current state of inquiry into religious and spiritual adult education. More specifically, they provide an understanding of the historical role played by religious adult education in framing the current dialogue, including the relationship between religion and spirituality. For example, the invigoration of spiritual adult education in the late 1990s and early 2000s relied on early religious adult educators and social activists, such as Basil Yeaxlee and Moses Coady, for inspiration and direction (English, 2000).

The terms defining the parameters of this chapter are *religion, spirituality, religious adult education*, and *spiritual adult education*. Distinctions exist in the ways different fields of study approach these topics. For example, Elias (2012) concluded that "adult religious education is a main focus of all religions of the world" (p. 11). Elaborating on adult religious education as it occurs in institutionalized religions, Elias (2012) summarized definitions of *religion* as follows:

> The existentialist theologian Paul Tillich (1964) gave religion a functional definition when he described it as what concerns humans ultimately. The sociologist of religion Robert Bellah (1969) analyzed religion as a set of symbolic forms and actions that relate persons to the ultimate conditions of their existence. A widely referenced description comes from the cultural anthropologist Clifford Geertz (1977): Religion is (1) a system of symbols which acts to (2) establish powerful, pervasive, and long-lasting moods and motivations, in persons by (3) formulating conceptions of a general order of existence and (4) clothing these conceptions with such an aura of factuality that (5) the moods and motivations seem uniquely realistic. (p. 90)

In contrast to Elias's emphasis on institutional religion, we limit our discussion to the professional field of adult and continuing education. Religion and religious adult education are now mostly addressed by scholars working outside of the field of adult and continuing education within their own religious institutions and journals.

This divergence of religious adult education and spiritual adult education was characterized in the 2010 handbook. English and Tisdell (2010) explained the difference between religious and spiritual adult education thus:

> Religion in contemporary literature refers to an organized community of faith, with an official creed and codes of regulatory behavior (determined by those with the most power in these institutions), as well as formalized ritual and sacred story or text. Spirituality, on the other hand, refers to an individual's personal experience of making meaning of the sacred, often in relationship to what is perceived as God or an interconnecting life force. Given that one's personal experience of the sacred can happen anywhere, spirituality is not necessarily related to religion. (p. 287)

Since the last handbook was published, the field of adult and continuing education, as it is manifested in the field's journals, conferences, and associations, has moved decisively in the direction of spirituality and spiritual adult education and away from a discussion of formal religious adult education and the relationship between the two.

Findings

The emphasis on spiritual adult education has carried into current research trends and interests. The state of the research into religious and spiritual adult education was reviewed by English (2013) and English and Tisdell (2010), and many of the themes they identified have continued with recent scholarship including explorations of spirituality in the workplace (Crossman, 2010, 2011; Dirkx, 2013), community development (Pigza & Welch, 2010), higher education (Anye et al., 2013; Chickering et al., 2015), Indigenous workplaces (Muller, 2014; Munroe et al., 2013), and church-related institutions (Rowland & Isaac-Savage, 2014).

This literature review shows that contemporary scholarly work in our field has been predominantly conducted and applied outside of religious contexts. For example, the spiritual dimensions of secular learning (Le Cornu, 2009; Mahmoud, 2015; Moyer & Sinclair, 2016; Tan, 2017) are currently broadly recognized, representing a shift from characterizations of learning prior to the 1990s, which did not generally include spiritual dimensions. Academic credibility, however, does not necessarily translate to practical application, although a few scholars have connected religion and spirituality with educational practice (Ramezanzadeh, 2017; Ryu & Cervero, 2011). For example, there has been an effort to bring spiritual adult education and social work education to bear on each other (Groen et al., 2013). The elaboration of spirituality's role in professions and contexts not traditionally interpreted as spiritual has broadened the contextual palette of our field.

This elaboration has been facilitated by developments in psychology; 20th- and 21st-century psychology's science of the self (Carrette & King, 2005; Mischel & Morf, 2003; Rose, 1990, 1998) has enabled the application of spiritual development to human resource development, recreation, and self-help (Altaf & Awan, 2011; Crossman, 2010, 2011; Gupta et al., 2014; Jirásek et al., 2017; Miller & Ewest, 2013; Neal, 2012). Interest in spirituality in the workplace and in its relationship to leadership (Hodges et al., 2016; Isaac, 2012; McKendry, 2017) is evident. There has been some adult education scholarship connecting spirituality to social justice and the environment (Groen, 2016, 2017; Hitzhusen, 2012; Larrotta, 2017; Mareschal, 2012; Moyer & Sinclair, 2016; Uzama & Walter, 2018; Walter, 2013). On the other hand, this review reveals that adult and continuing education journals are not harvesting potential areas of inquiry like spirituality research into health and lifestyle-related concerns such as mindfulness, meditation, and stress reduction (Daniel, 2015; Gillum & Griffith, 2010; Homan & Boyatzis, 2010; Rowland & Chappel-Aiken, 2012). For example, health-care professionals such as nurses have investigated the role of spirituality in their work with patients (Cobb et al., 2012; Hodge & Horvath, 2011; Lewinson et al., 2015). While adult and continuing education scholarship into spirituality is active, we are missing some of these important opportunities.

A characteristic of current scholarship is the limited but increasing acceptance and use of spiritual adult education research in fields both inside and outside of adult and continuing education. The most cited researchers and writers in this area (English, 2005; Tisdell, 2000, 2006) are referenced more frequently in other areas of education research as well as outside education entirely as evidenced by database searches. This recognition of the quality and usefulness of this research represents only a small portion of the scholarship happening in this area and signals a dissemination opportunity for adult education as a field.

Research into adult education in religious contexts such as congregations, synagogues, churches, and mosques is present in the literature (Carr-Chellman, 2019; Elias, 2012; Findsen, 2006; Frye, 2014; Hodges et al., 2016; Mareschal, 2012; Rowland & Isaac-Savage, 2014), but not as prominently as in the past. As English and Tisdell (2010) argued, "while such adult education programs are growing in number, there is scant systematic research to substantiate their effectiveness or contribution to adult education" (p. 290). Overlooking research opportunities within traditional religious contexts helps explain the minimal influence of adult and continuing education research in these areas of practice.

Discussion

Considering religious adult education apart from spiritual adult education has provided clarity of purpose for researchers investigating spiritual development independent of religious institutions. Part of this shift places priority on the individual, effectively moving the conversation away from what happens in religious communities. English and Tisdell (2010) recognized

> the division between spirituality and religion in the West is somewhat artificial. . . . Nevertheless, the experience of engaging in such practices [as meditation and yoga] is indeed an individual experience. So, like other contemporary scholars, we do separate religion and spirituality but note that the division is somewhat problematic. (p. 288)

The separation is troublesome and its effects within research have become clearer. We will discuss some of these effects and offer ways to reunify religious and spiritual adult education.

Effects of Separating Religious and Spiritual Adult Education

Separating the study of the individual and the community provides a framework for selfhood that is "private, autonomous, and free . . . [and] has been interiorized, individualized, and psychologized away from the institutionalized, social, and collective forms of relations and expressions" (Rhee & Subedi, 2014, p. 344). Within this framework, the individual learner in spiritual adult education research can too easily become a self that is oriented toward and understood primarily as a free-market economic agent. The emergence of psychology as the science of the self facilitates a situation in which "spirituality now takes part in the individual pursuit of wealth and happiness without any concerns and actions for community building and collective well-being" (Rhee & Subedi, 2014, p. 345). One risk of our field's move toward spiritual adult education is a growing emphasis on transactional individualized spirituality—an expression of the psychology of the self—shifting the object of analysis from social, economic, and legal structures to individualized adaptive processes that can help one's personal prosperity and happiness. A strong critique of workplace spirituality research is grounded in this perspective (Fenwick & Lange, 1998; Milacci & Howell, 2002).

This separation has also opened the door for new ways of interpreting human learning. Spiritual learning has been applied to newer areas of inquiry such as somatic and embodied learning (Freiler, 2008) and holistic learning (Merriam & Kim, 2008). However, separating the individual/spiritual and communal/religious aspects of human experience without also considering the symbiotic relationship between the two mitigates the potential power of its application; considering spirituality and religion as an either/or proposition does not take into consideration the interrelationship between the two theoretically or practically.

This separation is a false dichotomy, as Elias (2012) has observed. Religious organizations and groups, he said, "with all their limitations and faults, remain the principal source for nurturing the spiritual or religious impulse or spirit in individuals and societies. Spiritual persons most often draw from religious writings, rituals, practices, and leaders of world religions" (p. 6). While separating religion and spirituality can be helpful for analysis, as Elias suggested, in reality they are interwoven and inseparable threads of one cloth. As an example, walking the Camino di Santiago (Tisdell, 2013) is both an individual spiritual experience and one that is steeped in the traditions and history of the Catholic church. The individual experience might be extracted from the historical and institutional context for purposes of discussion or study, but like all situated learning, religious and spiritual experiences are inextricably tied together.

Reconnecting Religious and Spiritual Adult Education

Moving forward, it will be useful to generate new knowledge through interpreting religious and spiritual experience as mutually dependent and mutually influential. The following represents approaches for pursuing this additional perspective.

The first approach is for adult religious and spiritual educators to ask what learning processes and practices are most likely to move learners more deeply toward community and a relationship with the divine. What is truly relevant to human well-being? How can people accommodate the burdens of being—the inherent and inevitable suffering of life? What is a good life, how do we assess one, what are the elements of actually living it and, perhaps more importantly for adult educators, what learning strategies move learners to develop those fundamental capacities and qualities? To answer these questions, it will be useful for our field to maintain its interest in spiritual adult education. It will also be useful to answer these questions through communities in general, and religious communities in particular. As Elias (2012) highlighted, these communities are central to the learning that happens in religious and spiritual experiences. The concepts of intersubjectivity and communities of truth illustrate Elias's point.

Interpreting religious and spiritual experience through intersubjectivity and communities of truth offers a second approach. Erdreich (2015) wrote about female Palestinian instructors at an Islamic university in Israel. Her research, drawing on some spiritual adult education scholarship (English, 2000; English et al., 2005; Tisdell, 2006; Tisdell & Tolliver, 2003), highlighted the centrality of these educators' concrete and specific religious identities to their success in the academy. Over the course of several articles, Erdreich (2004, 2006a, 2006b, 2010, 2015) built a strong case supporting the emergence of an emancipatory epistemology through the socially embodied argument of a living religious tradition, a situation providing sophisticated access to a meaningful, shared, symbolic system. Rhee and Subedi (2014) emphasized the inextricable connection between spirituality and people, place, and history; such grounding provides transformative possibilities for spirituality as an epistemology and an ontology. Spirituality, then, "offers ways to recover, reconnect, and rebuild the decolonized ways of being and knowing through an ongoing process of healing, forgiving, loving, envisioning, and hoping" (Rhee & Subedi, 2014, p. 353).

The third approach uses the disciplines of spiritual formation that have developed and been practiced by religious communities for generations and centuries; they are integral for the depth of commitment required to make true and lasting social change. A challenge for adult educators is to remember that the roots of spiritual formation are also the foundation for social action (Tisdell, 2000). While doctrine, dogma, ideology, and institutions might constrain and reinforce power structures, specific practices within religious institutions such as prayer or service might inculcate values such as humility and compassion that contribute to human flourishing in a civil and inclusive society.

Applications of Reconnected Religious and Spiritual Adult Education

The concrete lived reality of religious communities and individual spiritual seekers is expressed in and developed through their practices and disciplines such as prayer, meditation, fasting, and reconciliation (Carr-Chellman & Kroth, 2017; Foster, 1998; Willard, 1990). An emancipatory epistemology will value and embrace a broader, postmodern paradigm that lessens the constraints of reified creeds and accepted "truth" by giving equivalent status to experience, practice, and the construction of knowledge gained from that experience and discipline over time. These practices and disciplines are important sites of non-commoditized resistance to unhealthy social forces. They lay the groundwork for a different kind of human encounter which values mutual recognition, reconciliation, healing, belonging, dialogue, and critical reflection. This encountering-within-community is as much a divergent as a convergent process, providing insight and access into a less transactional, precarious, volatile, and fearful existence. These practices, thus, are less compliance-focused and more liberatory and transcendent. They are less concerned with institutional control and are more concerned with the metaphysical. They are more interested in orthopraxy than in orthodoxy. They are as or more desirous of metaphysically received knowledge than knowledge mediated by religious authority. These practices are, in fact, at least as concerned with *being* as they are with *knowing*. Practices, disciplines, and virtues provide a necessary balance and synergy to established doctrine and dogma, giving them life, resonance, and relevance.

The lived reality of intersubjectivity and communities of truth frames these practices and emphasizes social arrangements that treat each person as an end while also safeguarding pluralism in values. It can ground a religious and spiritual selfhood that is more than transactional. Religious and spiritual adult education built on a more generous version of selfhood will be grounded in intersubjectivity and communities of truth. These are two characteristics that should provide a foundation for practices that embellish human well-being and flourishing.

These practices take seriously that human experience is necessarily grounded in people and communities, places, and histories. These intersubjective, concrete, and lived realities reveal aspects of human relations, social structures, and mutual recognition that facilitate emancipatory knowledge. Religious and spiritual adult education can benefit from pursuing intersubjectivity and communities of truth as areas of inquiry and practice. This move will effectively reconnect religious adult education and spiritual adult education in useful, powerful, and generative ways.

Conclusion

Many scholars and practitioners are drawn to adult education by a desire to improve lives. Religious and spiritual adult education guides its practitioners to ask some profound questions about existence, values, and choices. One's answers to these questions inform and shape one's intentions, goals, and decisions. In confronting these life decisions, there are ancient and well-worn traditions, practices, and disciplines that help integrate our visions of the people we want to become.

Another purpose of religious and spiritual education is vocational. This area of research, which is related to life and organizational mission, careers, leadership, ethics, and educating adults in the practical pursuits of day-to-day living and work has received attention over the last decade. This area seems particularly pertinent in a global, diverse, world with many challenging issues in play. In general, the research being conducted in spiritual and religious adult education seems vital and relevant. It also is an area ripe for investigation by scholars and application by practitioners.

References

Altaf, A., & Awan, M. A. (2011). Moderating effect of workplace spirituality on the relationship of job overload and job satisfaction. *Journal of Business Ethics*, 104(1), 93–99.

Anye, E. T., Gallien, T. L., Bian, H., & Moulton, M. (2013). The relationship between spiritual well-being and health-related quality of life in college students. *Journal of American College Health*, 61(7), 414–421. https://doi.org/10.1080/07448481.2013.824454

Carr-Chellman, D. J. (2019). Adult ethical development in Christian congregations: A phenomenological study of pastor's perceptions. *New Horizons in Adult Education and Human Resource Development*, 31(2), 5–26. https://doi.org/10.1002/nha3.20246

Carr-Chellman, D. J., & Kroth, M. (2017). The spiritual disciplines as practices of transformation. *International Journal of Adult Vocational Education and Technology*, 8(1), 23–35. https://doi.org/10.4018/ijavet.2017010103

Carrette, J., & King, R. (2005). *Selling spirituality: The silent takeover of religion*. Routledge.

Chickering, A. W., Dalton, J. C., & Stamm, L. (2015). *Encouraging authenticity and spirituality in higher education*. Wiley.

Cobb, M., Puchalski, C. M., & Rumbold, B. (Eds.). (2012). *Oxford textbook of spirituality in healthcare*. Oxford University Press.

Crossman, J. (2010). Conceptualising spiritual leadership in secular organizational contexts and its relation to transformational, servant and environmental leadership. *Leadership & Organization Development Journal*, 31(7), 596–608.

Crossman, J. (2011). Environmental and spiritual leadership: Tracing the synergies from an organizational perspective. *Journal of Business Ethics*, 103(4), 553–565.

Daniel, J. L. (2015). Workplace spirituality and stress: Evidence from Mexico and U.S. *Management Research Review*, 38(1), 29–43. https://doi.org/10.1108/MRR-07-2013-0169

Dirkx, J. M. (2013). Leaning in and leaning back at the same time: Toward a related learning. *Advances in Developing Human Resources*, 15(4), 356–369. https://doi.org/10.1177/1523422313498562

Elias, J. L. (2012). Adult religious education. *New Directions for Adult and Continuing Education*, 2012(155), 5–12.

English, L. M. (2000). Spiritual dimensions of informal learning. *New Directions for Adult and Continuing Education*, 2000(85), 29–38.

English, L. M. (2001). Reclaiming our roots: Spirituality as an integral part of adult learning. *Adult Learning*, 12(3), 2–3. https://doi.org/10.1177/104515950101200301

English, L. M. (2005). Historical and contemporary explorations of the social change and spiritual directions of adult education. *Teachers College Record*, 107(6), 1169–1192.

English, L. M. (2013). For whose purposes? Examining the spirituality agenda in adult education. In J. Groen, D. Coholic, & J. R. Graham (Eds.), *Spirituality in social work and education: Theory, practice, and pedagogies* (pp. 17–33). Wilfrid Laurier University Press.

English, L. M., Fenwick, T. J., & Parsons, J. (2005). Interrogating our practices of integrating spirituality into workplace education. *Australian Journal of Adult Learning*, 45(1), 7–28.

English, L. M., & Gillen, M. A. (2000). *Addressing the spiritual dimensions of adult learning: What educators can do*. Jossey-Bass.

English, L. M., & Mayo, P. (2012). Spirituality and adult education. In L. M. English & P. Mayo (Eds.), *Learning with adults: A critical pedagogical introduction* (pp. 179–187). Sense.

English, L. M., & Tisdell, E. (2010). Spirituality and adult education. In C. E. Kasworm, A. D. Rose, & J. M. Ross-Gordon (Eds.). *Handbook of adult and continuing education* (pp. 285–293). SAGE.

Erdreich, L. (2004). *Opening identities for change: Multiple literacies of Palestinian Israeli women at the university* [Unpublished doctoral dissertation]. Hebrew University.

Erdreich, L. (2006a). Degendering the honor/care conflation: Palestinian Israeli university women's appropriations of independence. *Ethos*, 34(1), 132–164.

Erdreich, L. (2006b). Strategies against patriarchy: Sexualized political activism of Palestinian Israeli women on campus. *Israel Studies*, 35–58.

Erdreich, L. (2010). To the university and back: Palestinian Israeli women's paths of repositioning. In S. Abu-Rabia-Queder & N. Wiener-Levy (Eds.), *Native Palestinian women in Israel: Struggle and confrontation from the margins* (pp. 123–147). Van Leer Institute and Hakibbutz Hameuchad.

Erdreich, L. (2015). Sacralized citizenship: Women making known selves in an Islamic teachers' college in Israel. *International Journal of Qualitative Studies in Education*, 28(4), 415–436. https://doi.org/10.1080/09518398.2014.916001

Fenwick, T., & English, L. (2004). Dimensions of spirituality: A framework for adult educators. *Journal of Adult Theological Education*, 1(1), 49–64. https://doi.org/10.1558/jate.1.1.49.36052

Fenwick, T., & Lange, E. (1998). Spirituality in the workplace: The new frontier of HRD. *Canadian Journal for the Study of Adult Education*, 12(1), 63–87.

Findsen, B. (2006). Social institutions as sites of learning for older adults: Differential opportunities. *Journal of Transformative Education, 4*(1), 65–81. https://doi.org/10.1177/1541344605282429

Foster, R. J. (1998). *Celebration of discipline: The path to spiritual growth* (20th anniversary ed.). Harper.

Freiler, T. J. (2008). Learning through the body. *New Directions for Adult and Continuing Education, 2008*(119), 37–47.

Frye, S. B. (2014). Becoming an adult in a community of faith. *New Directions for Adult and Continuing Education, 2014*(143), 51–61.

Gillum, F., & Griffith, D. M. (2010). Prayer and spiritual practices for health reasons among American adults: The role of race and ethnicity. *Journal of Religion and Health, 49*(3), 283–295. https://doi.org/10.1007/s10943-009-9249-7

Groen, J. (2016). Rediscover, awaken, renew: The potential role of spiritual retreat centres in environmental adult education. *Canadian Journal for the Study of Adult Education, 28*(1), 83–96.

Groen, J. (2017). The St. Ignatius Jesuit retreat and training centre: Cultivating ecological awareness and connection with the earth. *New Directions for Adult and Continuing Education, 2017*(153), 31–39.

Groen, J., Coholic, D., & Graham, J. R. (Eds.). (2013). *Spirituality in social work and education: Theory, practice, and pedagogies*. Wilfrid Laurier University Press.

Gupta, M., Kumar, V., & Singh, M. (2014). Creating satisfied employees through workplace spirituality: A study of the private insurance sector in Punjab (India). *Journal of Business Ethics, 122*(1), 79–88. https://doi.org/10.1007/s10551-013-1756-5

Hitzhusen, G. E. (2012). Going green and renewing life: Environmental education in faith communities. *New Directions for Adult and Continuing Education, 2012*(133), 35–44.

Hodge, D. R., & Horvath, V. E. (2011). Spiritual needs in health care settings: A qualitative meta-synthesis of clients' perspectives. *Social Work, 56*(4), 306–316. https://doi.org/10.1093/sw/56.4.306

Hodges, T. L., Rowland, M. L., & Isaac-Savage, E. P. (2016). Black males in Black churches. *New Directions for Adult and Continuing Education, 2016*(150), 47–57.

Homan, K. J., & Boyatzis, C. J. (2010). Religiosity, sense of meaning, and health behavior in older adults. *The International Journal for the Psychology of Religion, 20*(3), 173–186. https://doi.org/10.1080/10508619.2010.481225

Isaac, E. P. (2012). Expanding the boundaries of adult religious education. *New Directions for Adult and Continuing Education, 2012*(133), 83–87.

Jirásek, I., Veselský, P., & Poslt, J. (2017). Winter outdoor trekking: Spiritual aspects of environmental education. *Environmental Education Research, 23*(1), 1–22.

Larrotta, C. (2017). Immigrants to the United States and adult education services. *New Directions for Adult and Continuing Education, 2017*(155), 61–69.

Le Cornu, A. (2009). Meaning, internalization, and externalization: Toward a fuller understanding of the process of reflection and its role in the construction of the self. *Adult Education Quarterly, 59*(4), 279–297. https://doi.org/10.1177/0741713609331478

Lewinson, L. P., McSherry, W., & Kevern, P. (2015). Spirituality in pre-registration nurse education and practice: A review of the literature. *Nurse Education Today, 35*(6), 806–814. https://doi.org/10.1016/j.nedt.2015.01.011

Mahmoud, M. M. A. (2015). Culture and English language teaching in the Arab world. *Adult Learning, 26*(2), 66–72. https://doi.org/10.1177/1045159515573020

Mareschal, T. L. (2012). Adult Jewish education and participation among reform Jewish women. *New Directions for Adult and Continuing Education, 2012*(133), 59–70.

McKendry, V. (2017). The "Tse tsa watle" speaker series: An example of ensemble leadership and generative adult learning. *New Directions for Adult and Continuing Education, 2017*(156), 9–19.

Merriam, S. B., & Kim, Y. S. (2008). Non-Western perspectives on learning and knowing. *New Directions for Adult and Continuing Education, 2008*(119), 71–81.

Milacci, F., & Howell, S. L. (2002). Marketing God: A critical inquiry into spirituality in the workplace. *Proceedings of the Adult Education Research Conference.* https://newprairiepress.org/aerc/2002/

Miller, D. W., & Ewest, T. (2013). The present state of workplace spirituality: A literature review considering context, theory, and measurement/assessment. *Journal of Religious & Theological Information, 12*(1–2), 29–54. https://doi.org/10.1080/10477845.2013.800776

Mischel, W., & Morf, C. C. (2003). The self as a psycho-social dynamic processing system: A meta-perspective on a century of the self in psychology. In M. R. Leary & J. P. Tangney (Eds.), *Handbook of self and identity* (pp. 15–43). Guilford Press.

Moyer, J. M., & Sinclair, A. J. (2016). Stoking the dialogue on the domains of transformative learning theory: Insights from research with faith-based organizations in Kenya. *Adult Education Quarterly, 66*(1), 39–56. https://doi.org/10.1177/0741713615610625

Muller, L. (2014). *A theory for Indigenous Australian health and human service work*. Allen & Unwin.

Munroe, E., Borden, L., Murray Orr, A., Toney, D., & Meader, J. (2013). Decolonizing aboriginal education in the 21st century. *McGill Journal of Education/Revue des sciences de l'éducation de McGill, 48*(2), 317–337.

Neal, J. (Ed.). (2012). *Handbook of faith and spirituality in the workplace: Emerging research and practice.* Springer Science & Business Media.

Pigza, J. M., & Welch, M. J. (2010). Spiritually engaged pedagogy: The possibilities of spiritual development through social justice education. *Spirituality in Higher Education Newsletter, 5*(4), 185–207.

Ramezanzadeh, A. (2017). Language educators' understanding of authenticity in teaching and its impacts on their practices. *Adult Education Quarterly, 67*(4), 286–301. https://doi.org/10.1177/0741713617721971

Rhee, J. E., & Subedi, B. (2014). Colonizing and decolonizing projects of re/covering spirituality. *Educational Studies, 50*(4), 339–356. https://doi.org/10.1080/00131946.2014.924941

Rose, N. (1990). *Governing the soul: The shaping of the private self.* Routledge.

Rose, N. (1998). *Inventing our selves: Psychology, power, and personhood.* Cambridge University Press.

Rowland, M. L., & Chappel-Aiken, L. (2012). Faith-based partnerships promoting health. *New Directions for Adult and Continuing Education, 2012*(133), 23–33.

Rowland, M. L., & Isaac-Savage, E. P. (2014). As I see it: A study of African American pastors' views on health and health education in the Black church. *Journal of Religion and Health, 53*(4), 1091–1101. https:doi.org/10.1007/s10943-013-9705-2

Ryu, K., & Cervero, R. M. (2011). The role of Confucian cultural values and politics in planning educational programs for adults in Korea. *Adult Education Quarterly, 61*(2), 139–160. https://doi.org/10.1177/0741713610380440

Tan, C. (2017). A Confucian perspective of self-cultivation in learning: Its implications for self-directed learning. *Journal of Adult and Continuing Education, 23*(2), 250–262. https://doi.org/10.1177/1477971417721719

Tisdell, E. (2000). Spirituality and emancipatory adult education in women adult educators for social change. *Adult Education Quarterly, 50*, 308–335. https://journals.sagepub.com/doi/10.1177/074171360005000404

Tisdell, E. J. (2006). Spirituality, cultural identity, and epistemology in culturally responsive teaching in higher education. *Multicultural Perspectives, 8*(3), 19–25. https://doi.org/10.1207/s15327892mcp0803_4

Tisdell, E. J. (2013). We make the way by walking: Spiritual pilgrimage and transformative learning while walking the Camino De Santiago. *Proceedings of the Adult Education Research Conference.* https://newprairiepress.org/aerc/2013/papers/

Tisdell, E. J., & Tolliver, D. E. (2003). Claiming a sacred face: The role of spirituality and cultural identity in transformative adult higher education. *Journal of Transformative Education, 1*(4), 368–392. https://doi.org/10.1177/1541344603257678

Uzama, A., & Walter, P. (2018). Incorporating ecotourism into social education (shakai kyouiku 社会教育) and lifelong learning (shougai gakushuu 生涯学習) in Japan. *Journal of Adult and Continuing Education, 24*(1), 18–36. https://doi.org/10.1177/1477971417753975

Walter, P. (2013). Greening the net generation: Outdoor adult learning in the digital age. *Adult Learning, 24*(4), 151–158. https://doi.org/10.1177/1045159513499551

Welton, M. R. (2000). *Little Mosie from the Margaree: A biography of Moses Michael Coady.* Thompson Educational Publishers.

Welton, M. R. (2005). "Fraught with wonderful possibilities": Father Jimmy Tompkins and the struggle for a Catholic progressivism, 1912–1922. *Studies in Continuing Education, 27*(2), 117–134. https://doi.org/10.1080/01580370500169886

Willard, D. (1990). *The spirit of the disciplines: Understanding how God changes lives.* Harper.

CHAPTER 32

Cultural Institutions

Robin S. Grenier

Whether they are cultural institutions with well-established reputations and large paid and volunteer staff (e.g., the Louvre in Paris, the Gettysburg battlefield in Pennsylvania, or the Beijing Zoo) or much smaller organizations that operate largely on donations and grants with a mostly volunteer staff (e.g., the McFaddin-Ward House in Beaumont, Texas, or the New Iceland Heritage Museum in Gimli, Manitoba, Canada), such sites are visited annually by hundreds of millions of people worldwide (Miller et al., 2011). Cultural institutions include not just museums and historic sites, but galleries, zoos, aquariums, nature and science centers and field stations, gardens, state and national parks, and libraries, as well as pop-up and virtual sites. According to a 2013 report from Mandala Research, 76% of all U.S. leisure travelers participated in cultural or heritage activities on their last trip. This included various forms of nonformal learning—from museum tours and artist lectures to library-run book clubs, city walking tours, Audubon-led bird watching, and hearth cooking classes. This chapter looks more closely at cultural institutions to better understand their role as sites of adult learning. To do this, the following questions guide the structure of the chapter: (a) How are these sites defined, and whom do they serve? (b) How do cultural institutions create opportunities for and facilitate adult learning? (c) What are the trends for adult learning in cultural institutions and what challenges might exist?

How Are Cultural Institutions and Visitors Defined?

Theorization of *cultural institutions* as a concept is largely absent. The lack of a clear definition is due to the general and inclusive definition of *culture* as used by scholars. Eagleton (2000) notes that "the phrase 'cultural institution' is a tautology, since there are no noncultural ones" (p. 35). The definition of culture can include everything from "the organization of production, the structure of the family, the structure of institutions . . . [to] the characteristic form through which members of society communicate," and thus it is "excessively generous, leaving almost nothing out" (p. 35). To contend with this vagueness, scholars often focus on specific kinds of institutions that house or promote culture, such as museums or libraries. This is the case with David Carr's (2003) definition: "places to hold and preserve objects and texts, to expand the boundaries of public knowledge associated with these artefacts and words, and to open the possibilities of learning in the context of everyday life" (p. xiii). This works for more traditional institutions that preserve and promote tangible cultural items such as artifacts or monuments, but falls short in addressing organizations that engage in the preservation and promotion of *intangible heritage*, which UNESCO (n.d.) defines as "traditions or living expressions inherited from our ancestors and passed on to our descendants" (para. 1), such as handcraft or music. To attend to both these purposes, I suggest *cultural institutions* might be generally defined as organizations that have (or had) cultural significance to a particular community (geographical, social, virtual, etc.) and protect, promote, and honor culture, education, and/or sciences.

Broad definitions of cultural institutions address cultural sustainability (Loach et al., 2017), which includes preserving a community's heritage and constructing and interpreting the past. But, for many, such cultural sustainability is problematic because it can reinforce aristocratic hegemony. When "culture" is dominated by affluent, White, European perspectives, many people don't "see themselves" in the objects and art, narratives, or content, resulting in limited visitor participation (Garibay, 2011; Hood, 2004; Kinsley 2016).

Cultural institutions are addressing this limitation with a more populist view of inclusion that is based in public pedagogy (Sabeti, 2015). Cultural institutions are offering new participatory and relevant experiences and learning opportunities that suit the needs of their communities (Davies, 1994) by envisioning innovative ways of *using* objects and exhibits. This new defining role emphasizes dialogue (with visitors) over monologue (for visitors) (Sandell & Nightingale, 2013), with heavy importance on visitor outreach, engagement, and learning. This shift from merely collecting and displaying objects or presenting facts "impartially" is influenced by organizations like the Museums Association of the United Kingdom, who now acknowledge that impartiality is an illusion and cultural institutions are not neutral (Museums Association, 2020). In other words, cultural institutions present a culturally specific way of seeing the world. That means that everything—organizational mission, collections, installations, programming, and events—is determined and framed by someone or something—curators, staff and volunteers, donors, historians, government, or communities. And while these choices can reflect the experiences and worldviews of some visitors, more often institutions present content and views that conflict with the cultures that visitors bring to the experience (Adams, 2007), which can lead visitors to try out "alternative ways of being" (Rounds, 2006, p. 146).

Embracing this new role, many cultural institutions today are addressing social, political, and cultural conditions and are defined by their desire to bring attention to global changes and conditions by promoting diverse, humanitarian, and democratic values. Such a mission is an inherent strength of cultural institutions as empathy engines—aiding people in understanding the "other" and strengthening social bonds (AAM, 2017). Take, for example, the Harriet Beecher Stowe Center. The center, in a once-wealthy area of Hartford, Connecticut, is surrounded by massive oaks and manicured lawns and neighbors Mark Twain's home—it could easily remain just an object representing the past. Instead, the center situates its outreach in the present. Aware of Hartford's racial diversity and its high rates of violent crime and poverty, the center seeks to preserve and interpret the home and inspire a commitment to social justice and positive change (Harriet Beecher Stowe Center, n.d.). Consistent with their mission based on the work, advocacy, and writings of Harriet Beecher Stowe, the center hosts Salons at Stowe; these parlor conversations founded in 19th-century issues of race, class, and gender are framed in modern day society, often within the context of Hartford current events.

The Exploratorium in San Francisco also embraces this new role of cultural institutions that bring attention to global changes and conditions. One of its projects is the Wired Pier (Exploratorium, 2019). Instruments stationed around the Exploratorium and outside along the pier in San Francisco Bay are used to measure and record environmental conditions, including weather and water pollution in the bay. The live data and webcam feed are on the Exploratorium website and displayed in the Fisher Bay Observatory Gallery. The data are collected for both public and scientific use to better understand and inform the public about patterns and trends in the atmosphere, oceans, and urban landscape. In doing so, the Exploratorium offers a way for visitors to frame discussions and take action against climate change that is based in data from the local environment.

To situate cultural institutions as sites of adult learning and education, it is important to understand visitors to these sites. The American Alliance of Museums found that about 2.5 million people visit a museum or other cultural institutions each day and an additional 5 million visit a library (Miller et al., 2011). These visitors can include a vast range of adults, but certain characteristics are consistent. Older adults visit cultural institutions more frequently than younger ones (CASE, 2010), which is further supported by a long-term trend among adults aged 18 years to 34 years that shows a declining interest and participation in cultural institutions (NEA, 2012). Visitor characteristics also include prior childhood experiences with cultural institutions, higher levels of education and socioeconomic status, a significant underrepresentation of Latinx and African Americans, more females than males, and greater likelihood of adults visiting as part of a family (Farrell & Medvedeva, 2010). The most typical adult patron is a first-time, one-off visitor to a specific site, such as a couple visiting the Polynesian Cultural Center during their honeymoon. To a lesser extent, adult visitors have memberships for an institution, returning on a regular basis, or visit for a particular purpose, like attending a film festival, invited talk, or special programming, such as a guided tour for low-vision and blind patrons at an aquarium.

Most adults' visits to cultural institutions are voluntary, and it is likely that the visitors are expected "to author their own experiences and to engage in agenda setting" (Scott, 2016, p. xii). Visits and engagement are most often curiosity-driven, with visitors having no specialized prior knowledge of the site content. They are more likely visiting with a social agenda and are seeking engaging experiences during time-limited leisure (Serrel, 2006). With the exception of library patrons, who most often visit with a specific intent, like seeking out a particular book or researching genealogy (Smith, 2014), for most people, education is not the primary reason for visiting a cultural institution. Yet Serrel (2006) notes that these visitors are ready to learn if it can happen easily and quickly. Adult visitors to cultural institutions most often come in groups (with other adults or with children), but commonly engage in what Smith (2014) calls "visit together-look alone" (p. 22). Groups of visitors enter a space together, but scatter to be alone to interact with an installation, object, or activity. And increasingly, visitors show an interest in "authentic" experiences that are local or unusual (Garibaldi et al., 2017). This is particularly important to Millennials visiting cultural institutions. They seek experience over education (Bello & Matchette, 2018) and as such are more likely drawn to programs like the Foods of the Lower East Side tour offered by the Tenement Museum in New York or a homestay arranged by the National Park of American Samoa.

How Do Cultural Institutions Create Opportunities for and Facilitate Adult Learning?

Today, most cultural institutions abide by the notion of learning opportunities conceived through a social constructivist lens, due in large part to the social dimension inherent in the visits. Knowledge is constructed not through formal instruction, but through the visitors' direct experience with the site and with others in their group, other visitors, or staff. Constructivism is appealing to those designing learning in cultural institutions because, according to Hein (2001), "it encourages interactive exhibit development, it legitimizes play as a form of learning, and it is compatible with the progressive tradition of object learning exemplified in museums for decades" (p. 3).

Constructivism is supported in Sitzia's (2018) framework addressing how museums might undertake the fundamental pedagogical shift where the role of the educator in a cultural institution is to become a master mediator and create a joint community with relevance for visitors. This relevance leads visitors to new thinking or understanding by adding information, meaning, or bringing new value to existing knowledge (Simon, 2016). The need for relevance is also at the core of the interactive experience model, which serves as a guide for practitioners that emphasizes the personal, social, and physical contexts of the cultural institution (Falk & Dierking, 2000). Falk and Dierking (2000) describe the lessons of the *personal* context as (a) motivation and emotional cues initiate learning, (b) personal interest facilitates learning, (c) knowledge is constructed from prior knowledge and experience, and (d) learning is expressed in an appropriate context. The *sociocultural* context points out that learning is an individual as well as a group endeavor. The *physical* context is the last part of the interactive experience model, and the authors emphasize the notion that learning is dependent on a person's ability to place prior experiences within the context of their physical setting. These three contexts combine in an attempt to explain what, how, why, where, with whom people learn in cultural institutions. This model offers educators a way to frame their services and highlights the role of educational theory in the process of exhibit development, interpretation, and programming.

Framed by these constructivist, sociocultural, and interactive experience approaches, cultural institutions apply both explicit and implicit educational purposes and practices to their nonformal and informal learning environments. *Nonformal learning* is organized and falls outside of educational institutions (Merriam et al., 2012)—such as in cultural institutions, where there is the opportunity for education but, unlike a university, it is not the main purpose of the organization. Nonformal learning involves intentional planning and is structured as a time- and/or location-specific program, activity, or event. The most common form of nonformal learning in cultural institutions is the guided tour or lecture. Regardless of form, this type of learning calls on an educator or someone in a similar role to determine the likely audience, learning objectives, activities, and outcomes, and in most cases these programs are imagined, designed, and facilitated by the cultural institution. For example, at Mystic Seaport in Connecticut, classroom teachers from across New England meet for a week-long institute that allowed them to develop curriculum inspired by the collections of and activities in the seaport. During this professional development, teachers sail on a replica of the *Amistad*, row a whaling boat, and sing sea shanties—all activites organized and planned by the Seaport (Grenier, 2010). Other institutions have developed nonformal learning events such as reminiscence programs for senior citizens (Smiraglia, 2016) and hosted community-led archeological digs (Coen et al., 2017) and even adult-only sleepovers, like the one hosted by the American Museum of Natural History. The audiences for these learning events overwhelmingly attend voluntarily, signing up based on interest, need, or curiosity. However, some may be required to attend, as is the case for law enforcement training at the Museum of Tolerance in Los Angeles. The programming is provided by the museum and is compulsory for many police departments in California and beyond.

Informal learning, or what Falk and Dierking (2000) term *free-choice* when referring to museums, emphasizes learner/visitor choice and control over the whole of the learning event. Individuals may come voluntarily (they see an advertisement on a tourist website) or involuntarily (a spouse chooses a place for date night), but once there, an informal learning experience may occur if the visitor is intrinsically motivated by their desire to discover more about the world, gain information, or in some way enhance their current understanding (Falk & Dierking, 2000). That is to say, the individual decides what to look at, listen to, participate in, and engage with at the site (Heimlich & Horr, 2010). Unlike nonformal learning, it is a nonlinear process in which the visitor brings their own awareness and interests to the experience to create a variety of learning outcomes. The learning tends to be nonhierarchical, with the visitor (learner) and the facilitator on equal ground (Jarvis, 1987).

Examples of informal learning include a self-guided tour through the Alamo or walking among the monuments on the National Mall in Washington DC. Learning at these sites can occur through a number of ways, including: choosing to speak with a stationed interpreter, like a National Parks ranger; stopping to read panels of text; chatting with another visitor while sitting on the steps of the Lincoln Memorial; deciding to punch in a number on a headset to hear more from a recorded message; or looking at a diorama model of a Spanish mission. The cultural institution can make learning opportunities available to visitors, but in informal learning, it is the learners themselves who are in control to determine if, how, and to what extent they engage. For cultural institutions, this means they must offer opportunities for voluntary engagement during the visit, and in some cases before and after the visit through the use of social media.

What Are the Trends and Challenges for Adult Learning in Cultural Institutions?

There are myriad trends affecting cultural institutions. Groups like the American Alliance of Museums' (AAM) Future of the Museum produce a yearly trend watch to help those working in museums and other cultural institutions to identify and plan for the future. For example, the 2019 trend watch (AAM, 2019) explores the concepts of truth and fake news, blockchain, decolonization, homelessness and housing insecurity, and self-care. In this final section of the chapter, three trends and challenges that may influence how cultural institutions will continue to serve as resources for adults engaged in lifelong learning are addressed: a demand for more environmentally conscious experiences, the increase in technology to facilitate learning, and institutions' role in supporting and facilitating social justice.

The UN World Tourism Organization (UNWTO) (2019) predicts a continuation of growth in international tourism with a large move toward responsible tourism, including issues of ecology, ethics, geography, poverty, and sustainability. This means that tour companies and cultural sites and centers of all sizes, as well as aquariums and zoos, are facing new challenges related to providing meaningful, short-term learning experiences to culturally and geographically diverse audiences that limit harm and do not burden the environment and nearby residents. In particular, sites are balancing access to environmentally sensitive areas to educate visitors while protecting the same areas from overexposure and environmentally dangerous practices by ill-informed visitors. For example, whale watching is an important economic resource both in the United States and abroad and may aid in promoting and enacting conservation efforts through public education and support (Luck, 2003). But, with an estimated 13 million tourists taking trips to see whales, dolphins, and porpoises (cetaceans) in their natural habitat (O'Connor et al., 2009), the cultural experience comes at a cost to the whales' habitat when it is poorly regulated and aggressively marketed (Parsons, 2012).

Janes (2008) urged cultural institutions to take the lead in environmental action because they are in a position to shape conversation and learning around "the meaning and implications of our excessive consumption and deteriorating environment" (p. 23). Furthermore, adult educators such as Clover et al. (2013) have championed the need for learning about ecological systems at all levels and our place within them. This is meaningful because previous research demonstrates that when individuals gain more environmental knowledge, there is an increase in their environmental concern (Hines et al., 1987) and sense of responsibility for protecting the environment (Huang & Shih, 2009). To achieve this, cultural institutions need to be aware of their role in supporting environmental awareness and designing programs that are both responsive to visitors' desires to be environmentally responsible and limit effects on nature. Thus, these sites will need to incorporate conservation and environmental education that provide learners with awareness, knowledge, attitudes, skills, and participation (UNESCO, 1978).

A second trend is growth in the use of technology: virtual, immersive environments, mobile apps, and social media creating both opportunities and challenges for cultural institutions. Notably, there is the emergence of a new form of cultural institution that uses technology as the primary or sole means for engaging "visitors." TED Conferences and their popular TED Talks are cultural institution that reaches audiences primarily through their website and YouTube. The short (18–20 minutes), recorded lectures offer on-demand talks on a wide range of topics, often by university-based researchers who speak about their scholarly expertise (Ludewig, 2017). Though the videos are popular for their flashy style and easy access, some have criticized the talks, calling them middlebrow and "pretty packaged messages for those who don't want to think too hard" (Kandur, 2007, para. 22). Despite this critique, the medium is its own discursive genre that is consistent with the needs and interests of adult learners (Ludewig, 2017).

The more common application of technology by cultural institutions is supplemental (Subramanian et al., 2017), For instance, the Art Institute of Chicago is supplementing their visitor experiences with mobile apps allowing visitors to look up artwork in the collection and hear guided audio tours while in or out of the building that, according to the organization, incorporate "an unscripted style, a diversity of voices, and sound design that accentuates the narrative" (Art Institute of Chicago, n.d.) and the Museo dell'Opera del Duomo in Pisa, Italy, used virtual reality to allow visitors to experience sculptures through tactile stimuli that simulated the hand's contact with a digital copy of a real statue (Carrozzino & Bergamasco, 2010). But with the arrival of coronavirus 2019 (COVID-19) cultural institutions had to rethink the supplemental role of technology.

With policies in place to "flatten the curve," people around the world were largely confined to their homes. Social gatherings were banned and places for learning and entertainment, including theaters, museums, zoos, libraries, and historic sites were closed. Capitalizing on (or reacting to) the unprecedented situation, cultural institutions utilized technology, providing virtual classes, tours, and programming on their websites and through social media platforms. In doing so they were able to engage people with their mission, while simultaneously entertaining many who sought distraction. The result is what Packer and Ballantyne (2004) call the "synergy of education and entertainment" (p. 63).

Offerings ranged from the traditional to the downright unexpected. When the Tate Museum in London was forced to close just 5 days after opening a new Andy Warhol exhibit, they released a collection of resources on their website that included a podcast, videos, and exhibit guide (Machemer, 2020). In New York, the Museum of Modern Art offered free, self-paced classes via the online platform Coursera using their modern art collection (Fox, 2020). Other cultural institutions found a whole new audience during the pandemic through their imaginative use of Twitter. The Shedd Aquarium in Chicago took advantage of the closure by letting followers "tag along" with penguins as they moved freely through the exhibits and met the other animals (Lee, 2020), while the head of security at the National Cowboy and Western Heritage Museum in Oklahoma took over the museum's Twitter account because he was the only one left in the building. Using his own captions and pictures, each day "Tim" guided followers through the museum's artifacts and exhibits. What started out as a way to keep the public engaged with the museum during the closure turned into a viral sensation—going from 9,789 followers to over 285,900 in less than a month (Cohn, 2020).

Although all these examples demonstrate tremendous growth and application of technology for learning and demonstrate the outreach potentially for these cultural institutions, it should be remembered that technology is still limited to those with means and access. Even with the tremendous growth in internet access, the fact remains that it is not equally distributed (Amir Hatem Ali, 2011). Those designing learning experiences for cultural institutions should be aware of the digital divide and work to provide learning access through a variety of means (technologies and otherwise) to expand participation and inclusion.

Finally, as a reaction to the ever apparent economic, cultural, and political inequities in the justice system, growth of cultural institutions' community involvement and public pedagogy, there is increased demand for cultural institutions' advocacy for social justice (Clover & Bell, 2013). Cultural institutions can foster innovation and incorporate diverse viewpoints that can aid in addressing issues including racism, sexism, class bias, and homophobia (Vázquez & Wright, 2018). To achieve this, sites are hosting dialogues and bringing attention to current events and dominant systems of power. For example, AAM (2017) notes that museums are giving increased attention to criminal justice reform, migration, and refugees. This is vital, and according to Bailey (2017) there is a need for spaces where individuals, including new immigrants, can "engage in informed and open dialogue across difference on the enduring and sensitive issue of immigration" (p. 3).

One such space is the Jane Addams Hull-House Museum (JAHHM) in Chicago, Illinois. Located at the original Hull House site, the museum represents the house and mission of Jane Addams, the first American female to win the Nobel Peace Prize for her work to provide services to the immigrant and poor population in Chicago. Although this cultural institution began primarily as a building/museum that preserved its historical significance in Chicago, today the house is the site of exhibitions such as the 2016 Aram Han Sifuentes collaborative exhibit, *Official Unofficial Voting Station: Voting for All Who Legally Can't*. As a legal alien in the United States, Sifuentes is barred from voting. She, along with other artists, came together to object to their exclusion from this central democratic process by asking visitors to Hull House (and additionally at locations in Baltimore/Washington DC, Philadelphia, Ithaca, Detroit, and Oaxaca/Chiapas, Mexico) to cast ballots at their own "voting stations," which were then collected, counted, and used as part of an art installation at JAHHM. The result was a way for the community to engage in important dialogues around the larger issues of immigration, citizenship, and the country's electoral process while situating those conversations within the local community. The work at JAHHM is consistent with the increased role of cultural institutions as sites of social movement learning (Grenier & Hafsteinsson, 2016). Such engagement results in new ways of defining and framing the role of these institutions in society, as well as emerging forms of learning for adults. It also challenges these sites to reconsider how current exhibitions, content, and programming are framing community narratives and privileging certain voices while marginalizing others (Mayo, 2013) and how they might reimagine physical environments in order to better refine services, deliver content in multiple ways, and meet the needs of the community (Pritchard, 2008).

Conclusion

Cultural institutions are, according to Clover (2015), "contested, problematic, [and] challenging," as some sites cling to outdated ideas and perpetuate elitism, yet sites are "equally progressive, critical and creative pedagogical spaces" (p. 301). So many cultural institutions around the world are endeavoring to provide learning experiences, both through nonformal and informal means that are engaging and promote extended discovery, return visits, and changes in attitudes. Through participatory learning and access to museums and other cultural institutions we have the opportunity to engage and contribute to the cultural development of society, which is vital for maintaining a true democracy (Anderson, 2000). And although some organizations are content to simply display and tell, those highlighted in this chapter are embracing the opportunity to act as facilitators of cultural sustainability (Loach et al., 2017), identity work (Rounds, 2006), and public pedagogy (Sabeti, 2015).

References

Adams, J. D. (2007). The historical context of science and education at the American Museum of Natural History. *Cultural Studies of Science Education, 2*(2), 393–440.

American Alliance of Museums. (2017). *Trend watch 2017.* http://labs.aam-us.org/trendswatch2017/

American Alliance of Museums. (2019). *Trend watch 2019.* https://www.aam-us.org/programs/center-for-the-future-of-museums/trendswatch-2019/

Amir Hatem Ali, A. (2011). The power of social media in developing nations. *Human Rights Journal, 24*(1), 185–219.

Anderson, D. (2000). A conceptual framework. In A. Chadwick & A. Stannett (Eds.), *Museums and adult learning: Perspectives from Europe* (pp. 4–11). NIACE.

Art Institute of Chicago. (n.d.). The new mobile experience. http://extras.artic.edu/new-mobile/

Bailey, D. A. (2017). *Interpreting immigration at museums and historic sites.* Rowman & Littlefield.

Bello, J., & Matchette, S. (2018). Shifting perspectives: The millennial influence on museum engagement. *Theory and Practice,* Vol. 1. http://articles.themuseumscholar.org/tp_vol1bellomatchette

Carr, D. (2003). *The promise of cultural institutions.* Altamira Press.

Carrozzino, M., & Bergamasco, M. (2010). Beyond virtual museums: Experiencing immersive virtual reality in real museums. *Journal of Cultural Heritage, 11*(4), 452–458. https://doi.org/10.1016/j.culher.2010.04.001

Clover, D. E. (2015). Adult education for social and environmental change in contemporary public art galleries and museums in Canada, Scotland and England. *International Journal of Lifelong Education, 34*(3), 300–315. https://doi.org/10.1080/02601370.2014.993731

Clover, D. E., & Bell, L. (2013). Contemporary adult education philosophies and practices in art galleries and museums in Canada and the UK. *Adult Learner: The Irish Journal of Adult and Community Education, 1*(1), 29–43.

Clover, D. E., Hall, B. L., & Follen, S. (2013). *The nature of transformation: Environmental adult education* (2nd ed.). Ontario Institute for Studies in Education.

Coen, S., Meredith, J., & Condie, J. (2017). I dig therefore we are: Community archaeology, place-based social identity, and intergroup relations within local communities. *Journal of Community & Applied Social Psychology, 27*(3), 212–225. https://doi.org/10.1002/casp.2299

Cohn, A. (2020, April 8). National cowboy museum goes viral during coronavirus closure thanks to security guard. *The Hill.* https://thehill.com/blogs/blog-briefing-room/news/491730-national-cowboy-museum-goes-viral-during-coronavirus-closure

Culture and Sport Evidence. (2010, July). *Understanding the drivers, impact and value of engagement in culture and sport—An over-arching summary of the research.* https://www.gov.uk/government/uploads/system/uploads/attachment_data/file/71231/CASE-supersummaryFINAL-19-July2010.pdf.

Davies, S. (1994). Attendance records. *Leisure Management, 15*(2), 41–44.

Eagleton, T. (2000). *The idea of culture.* Wiley.

Exploratorium. (2019). *Wired Pier environmental field station.* https://www.exploratorium.edu/environmental-field-station

Falk, J. H., & Dierking, L. D. (2000). *Learning from museums: Visitor experiences and the making of meaning.* Altamira Press.

Farrell, B., & Medvedeva, M. (2010). *Demographic transformation and the future of museums.* AAM Press.

Fox, A. (2020, April 14). The Museum of Modern Art now offers free online classes. *Smithsonian Magazine.* https://www.smithsonianmag.com/smart-news/get-sophisticated-moma-now-offers-free-art-courses-online-180974671/

Garibaldi, R., Stone, M. J., Wolf, E., & Pozzi, A. (2017). Wine travel in the United States: A profile of wine travellers and wine tours. *Tourism Management Perspectives, 23,* 53–57. https://doi.org/10.1016/j.tmp.2017.04.004

Garibay, C. (2011, February 11). *Responsive and accessible: How museums are using research to better engage diverse cultural communities.* Association of Science and Technology Centers. http://www.astc.org/astc-dimensions/responsive-and-accessiblehow-museums-areusing-research-to-better-engage-diversecultural-communities/

Grenier, R. S. (2010). "Now this is what I call learning!" A case study of museum-initiated professional development for teachers. *Adult Education Quarterly, 60*(5), 499–516. https://doi.org/10.1177/0741713610363018

Grenier, R. S., & Hafsteinsson, S. B. (2016). A case of public pedagogy in Icelandic museums. *Studies in the Education of Adults, 4*(2), 142–154. https://doi.org/10.1080/02660830.2016.1219487

Harriet Beecher Stowe Center. (n.d.). *Mission*. https://www.harrietbeecherstowecenter.org/about/why-visit-the-stowe-center/

Heimlich, J., & Horr, E. E. (2010). Adult learning in free-choice environmental settings: What makes it different? *New Directions for Adult and Continuing Education, 2010*(127), 57–66.

Hein, G. E. (2001, November 15). *The challenge and significance of constructivism* [Paper presentation]. Hands On! Europe Conference, London, England.

Hines, J. M., Hungerford, H. R., & Tomera, A. N. (1987). Analysis and synthesis of research on responsible environmental behavior: A meta-analysis. *Journal of Environmental Education, 18*(2), 1–8.

Hood, M. G. (2004). Staying away: Why people choose not to visit museums. In G. Anderson (Ed.), *Reinventing the museum: Historical and contemporary perspectives on the paradigm shift* (pp. 150–157). Altamira Press.

Huang, P. S., & Shih, L. H. (2009). Effective environmental management through environmental knowledge management. *International Journal of Environmental Science & Technology, 6*(1), 35–50.

Janes, R. (2008). Museums in a troubled world: Making the case for socially responsible museums. *MUSE, 26*(5), 20–25.

Jarvis, P. (1987). Meaningful and meaningless experience: Towards an analysis of learning from life. *Adult Education Quarterly, 37*(3), 164–172.

Kandur, J. L. (2017). Influence of TedTalks. *Daily Sabah*. https://www.dailysabah.com/feature/2017/07/22/influence-of-ted-talks

Kinsley, R. P. (2016). Inclusion in museums: a matter of social justice. *Museum Management and Curatorship, 31*(5), 474–490. https://doi.org/10.1080/09647775.2016.1211960

Lee, A. (2020, March 16). With the aquarium closed to humans, penguins take opportunity to explore and visit other animals. *CNN Travel*. https://www.cnn.com/2020/03/15/us/coronavirus-penguins-shedd-aquarium-trnd/index.html

Loach, K., Rowley, J., & Griffiths, J. (2017). Cultural sustainability as a strategy for the survival of museums and libraries. *International Journal of Cultural Policy, 23*(2), 186–198. https://doi.org/10.1080/10286632.2016.1184657

Luck, M. (2003). Education on marine mammal tours as agent for conservation—but do tourists want to be educated? *Ocean and Coastal Management, 46*(9–10), 943–956.

Ludewig, J. (2017). TED talks as an emergent genre. *CLCWEB-Comparative Literature and Culture, 19*(1), 1–9.

Machemer, T. (2020, April 9). Take a virtual tour of Tate Modern's Andy Warhol Exhibition. *Smithsonian Magazine*. https://www.smithsonianmag.com/smart-news/explore-tate-moderns-andy-warhol-exhibit-online-180974630/

Mandala Research. (2013). *The American traveler report*. Mandala Research.

Mayo, P. (2013). Museums as sites of critical pedagogical practice. *Review of Education, Pedagogy, and Cultural Studies, 35*(2), 144–153. https://doi.org/10.1080/10714413.2013.778661

Merriam, S. B., Caffarella, R. S., & Baumgartner, L. M. (2012). *Learning in adulthood: A comprehensive guide*. Wiley.

Miller, K. A., Swan, D. W., Craig, T., Dorinski, S., Freeman, M., Isaac, N., O'Shea, P., Schilling, P., & Scotto, J. (2011). *Public libraries survey: Fiscal year 2009 (IMLS-2011–PLS-02)*. Institute of Museum and Library Services.

Museums Association. (2020). *Museums change lives: The MA's vision for the impact of museums*. Author.

National Endowment for the Arts (NEA). (2012). *National Endowment for the Arts' 2012 survey of public participation in the arts*. https://www.arts.gov/sites/default/files/2012-sppa-feb2015.pdf

O'Connor, S. O, Campbell, R., Cortez, H., & Knowles, T. (2009). *Whale watching worldwide: Tourism numbers, expenditures and expanding economic benefits*. International Fund for Animal Welfare, IFAW and Economists.

Packer, J., & Ballantyne, R. (2004). Is educational leisure a contradiction in terms? Exploring the synergy of education and entertainment. *Annals of Leisure Research, 7*(1), 54–71.

Parsons, E. C. M. (2012). The negative impacts of whale watching. *Journal of Marine Biology*, 1–9.

Pritchard, S. M. (2008). Deconstructing the library: Reconceptualizing collections, spaces and services. *Journal of Library Administration, 48*(2), 219–233. https://doi.org/10.1080/01930820802231492

Rounds, J. (2006). Doing identity work in museums. *Curator, 49*, 133–150.

Sabeti, S. (2015). "Inspired to be creative?": Persons, objects, and the public pedagogy of museums. *Anthropology & Education Quarterly, 46*(2), 113–128. https://doi.org/10.1111/aeq.12094

Sandell, R., & Nightingale, E. (Eds.). (2013). *Museums, equality and social justice*. Routledge.

Scott, C. A. (Ed.). (2016). *Museums and public value: Creating sustainable futures*. Routledge.

Serrel, B. (2006). *Judging exhibitions: A framework for excellence.* Left Coast Press.

Simon, N. (2016). *The participatory museum.* Museum 2.0.

Sitzia, E. (2018). The ignorant art museum: Beyond meaning-making. *International Journal of Lifelong Education, 37*(1), 73–87. https://doi.org/10.1080/02601370.2017.1373710

Smiraglia, C. (2016). Targeted museum programs for older adults: A research and program review. *Curator: The Museum Journal, 59*(1), 39–54. https://doi.org/10.1111/cura.12144

Smith, J. K. (2014). *The museum effect: How museums, libraries, and cultural institutions educate and civilize society.* Rowman & Littlefield.

Subramanian, A., Barnes, J., Vemulapalli, N., & Chhawri, S. (2017). Virtual reality museum of consumer technologies. In J. Kantola, T. Barath, S. Nazir, & T. Andre (Eds.), *Proceedings of the AHFE 2016 International Conference on Human Ractors, Business Management and Society* (pp. 549–560). Springer.

UNESCO. (n.d.). *What is intangible heritage?* Intangible Cultural Heritage. https://ich.unesco.org/en/what-is-intangible-heritage-00003

UNESCO. (1978, April). *Intergovernmental conference on environmental education: Final Report.*

United Nations World Tourism Organization. (2019, May). World tourism barometer and statistical annex. https://www.e-unwto.org/doi/pdf/10.18111/wtobarometereng.2019.17.1.2

Vázquez, K. E., & Wright, M. (2018). Making visible the invisible: Social justice and inclusion through the collaboration of museums and Spanish community-based learning projects. *Dimension, 2018*, 113–129.

CHAPTER 33

Adult Environmental Education

Pierre Walter

Since the advent of the U.S. environmental movement in the 1960s, adult environmental education (AEE) has aimed to advance public understanding of environmental problems, and to promote environmental, political, economic, and social solutions (Clover, 2003; Dentith & Thompson, 2017; Gottlieb, 2005). Approaches to AEE have evolved over time in concert with changes in larger U.S. society. As critical understandings of social and environmental justice have become more present in U.S. public and educational discourses, AEE has moved from a focus on single-issue environmental education and activism (e.g., toxic waste, clean water, nuclear power) toward an intersectional analysis of environmental problems (Clover et al., 2013; Dentith & Griswold, 2017; Kluttz & Walter, 2018). In tandem with this change, the educational practice of AEE has shifted from a predominantly White "malestream" focus on the solving of discrete environmental problems, reliance on environmental science, and the promotion of behavioral change, to a more diverse and critical range of educational practices.

This chapter provides an updated typology of contemporary approaches to AEE theory and educational practice using Walter's (2009) five philosophical approaches to AEE—liberal, progressive, behaviorist, humanist, and radical. The typology is based on the philosophies of adult education described by Elias and Merriam (2005) in their book *Philosophical Foundations of Adult Education*. In the following sections of this chapter, each philosophy of AEE is discussed.

This is followed by a review of new directions in AEE, which have emerged from radical AEE philosophies, echoing trends in the wider adult and continuing education (ACE) scholarship. These new AEE directions include ecojustice adult education, critical place-based education, and land-based education. The chapter concludes with some brief remarks on the importance of AEE to U.S. society.

Typology of AEE Philosophies and Pedagogies

Adult educators and programs engage in AEE in a variety of ways, depending on their philosophies of education, including educational aims, beliefs about learners and educators, and preferred instructional strategies. Five major philosophies of AEE are liberal, progressive, behaviorist, humanist, and radical (Walter, 2009). In practice, adult environmental educators will adopt more than one philosophy in their teaching practices, and there are overlapping boundaries between philosophies. However, to better understand each philosophical tradition, they are considered separately here. Notably, this typology of five AEE philosophies is illustrative rather than comprehensive, is limited in scope and depth, and emphasizes AEE in natural areas. However, as noted by Walter (2009),

> The hope is that this typology, however imperfect, will stimulate others to think reflectively, in both philosophical and practical terms, about their own

educational practice in adult environmental education, and allow for a wider consideration of these issues to flourish in the field of adult education as a whole. (p. 8)

The AEE philosophies involve informal learning and nonformal education, outside of formal schooling in degree-granting educational institutions. *Informal learning* refers to adult learning which occurs naturally and socially in the context of family, community, the workplace, and social movements (Foley, 1999). *Nonformal education* is organized and purposeful and occurs in dedicated educational settings: in ACE short courses, workshops, and training programs and structured educational activities like interpretive nature walks, museum and ecotourism tours, and outdoor education programs (Merriam et al., 2009; Walter, 2009). Nonformal education can take place in a variety of nonschool settings—in parks, zoos, community centers, community gardens, environmental protests and elsewhere. Nonformal education is voluntary and short term and has a curriculum and educators directing learning activities. It is flexible and adaptable to the needs and interests of adult learners, does not involve the granting of degrees, but may offer learning credits or certification. The key features of each AEE philosophy are now explained, including aims, beliefs about learners, the role of educators, instructional strategies, and common topics of AEE.

Liberal philosophies of AEE are rooted in (Eurocentric) liberal arts traditions. They aim to expand the intellect, inculcate morality and cultural sensibility in adult learners, and teach academic knowledge of environmental science and environmental issues (Walter, 2009). Liberal educators see adults as rationale, capable learners, who, through rigorous training of the mind, can master the knowledge needed to become informed, enlightened citizens in democratic societies (Elias & Merriam, 2005). Liberal AEE in particular hopes to equip learners with the knowledge they need to understand and solve environmental problems (Walter, 2009). Liberal AEE may include critical analysis of the underlying structural roots of environmental problems and the complexity of interlocking environmental and social issues, but usually does not advocate action for change. The liberal focus is primarily on knowledge and understanding. As such, liberal educators generally see themselves as knowledge experts. They share a strong faith in the importance of scientific knowledge, logical thinking, and rational debate, and use lecture, readings, and Socratic dialogue as teaching tools.

Outside of formal courses or lectures, liberal AEE can be seen in the adult learning opportunities offered by documentary films, libraries, zoos, aquariums, museums, botanical gardens and nature centers (Falk, 2005; Packer & Ballantyne, 2010). Liberal AEE is used to teach about environmental issues such as climate change, threats to wildlife, toxic waste, and water, land, and air pollution. It is also used to educate learners more generally about the natural environment: plant and animal species, weather, watersheds, geology, ecosystems, and so on.

In contrast to liberal approaches, progressive philosophies of AEE are less knowledge-centered, more experience-based, and more learner-centered. Their aim is to not only educate democratic citizens but also promote social reform, the betterment of humanity, and the conservation of the natural environment (Walter, 2009). Progressive educators believe that adults have unlimited potential for growth and development. These educators value the centrality of experience rather than academic knowledge in learning and believe that the body can learn as well as the mind. Muscle memory can be developed, the five senses honed, and the spirit enlightened through experiences in nature. Progressive educators act as guides, mentors, and facilitators of learning experiences rather than didactic teachers of knowledge in the liberal tradition. Progressive AEE involves hands-on problem-solving, embodied learning, and apprenticeship in learning new skills related to environmental issues.

Progressive AEE programs include initiatives like Citizen Science, Outward Bound, International Wilderness Leadership School, the Audubon Expedition model, and the Master Gardener program (Jeffs & Ord, 2017; Merenlender et al., 2016; Waliczek et al., 2002; Wittmer & Johnson, 2000). In these programs, learners may study plants, mammals, birds, fish, and insects in their natural habitats; participate in practical lab work; learn about, plant, and tend gardens; work in outdoor environmental conservation projects; and learn more informally through activities like backpacking, kayaking, camping, and climbing. In general, progressive AEE teaches adults to be comfortable, confident, capable and skilled learners in the outdoors, to appreciate natural environments, and to work toward environmental conservation of wilderness, biodiversity and ecosystems.

Behaviorist AEE, as opposed to liberal and progressive philosophies, aims to carefully design the learning environment and shape learners' behavior to decrease the human tendency toward self-gratification, aggression, and destruction and thus allow the survival and prosperity of our species (Elias & Merriam, 2005; Walter, 2009). In this approach, human behavior is seen to result from prior conditioning. Moreover, humans are believed to be preprogrammed to act in certain predictable ways in response to stimuli. As such, behaviorist educators purposely create learning environments that provide positive and negative reinforcement for desired environmental learning or behavioral change. That is, learners are motivated to learn not internally, but externally, through structured behavioral objectives, benchmarked curricula and tests, rewards (high grades, prizes, social acclaim), and punishments (low grades, fines, and disapprobation). Changing the behavior of discrete individuals, taken together, may then add up to collective change in society.

Outside of formal education, the behaviorist philosophy is evident in the informal adult learning found in AEE campaigns and personal challenges like recycling, ending plastic use, zero waste initiatives, decreasing carbon footprints, no smoking initiatives, picking up dog excrement, reducing food waste, and bike to work programs (Ariza & Leatherman, 2011; Jason et al., 1980; Wyles et al., 2017). Local, citizen-run, or governmental organizations may, for instance, promote community AEE programs on how to properly separate household, workplace, and community trash alongside public education on recycling and the urban solid waste system. These behavioral initiatives usually come with behavioral incentives and disincentives, like fines for misuse of trash and for littering, bottle and can deposits, charges for using plastic bags, and prizes for ocean, river, or community clean-ups. The topics taken up by behaviorist approaches are mainly issues of environmental conservation and preservation: for instance, reducing electricity or gas consumption, removing invasive species, recycling waste, and following nature-friendly rules in public parks, campsites, and wilderness areas.

Humanist AEE does not aim at this sort of behavioral change, nor progressive experiential learning, nor liberal experts teaching scientific knowledge. It is about encouraging human happiness, self-actualization, autonomy, and transcendence (Elias & Merriam, 2005; Walter, 2009). Humans here are taken as inherently good, internally motivated, and self-directed. Thus, they have no compelling need for their behaviors to be conditioned toward goodness and away from badness, as is the case with behaviorist approaches. Learners are also seen as emotional and spiritual beings with minds and bodies, unlimited potential for growth, within a supportive community of other learners, and with impassioned, creative facilitators. Humanist AEE is often employed to catalyze public awareness and social change in the environmental and climate change movements. It is also used in AEE courses, workshops, therapy, and nonformal seminars for groups of adult learners interested in personal and spiritual development, often in outdoor settings (Groen, 2017).

In humanist AEE, learners connect emotionally, bodily, mentally, and spiritually to nature and to environmental issues and learn through song, music, art, and drama, at times with personally transformative results (Clover et al., 2013; Groen, 2017). Humanist AEE may include a wide range of learning activities such as "comedy sketches, street theater and narrative sketches, culture jamming, creative costumery, poetry, puppetry, satirical song, photos, videos, internet memes" (Walter & Earl, 2017, p. 155). In the public realm, humanist AEE may involve eco-artists and adult educators like Marina DeBris ("marine debris"), who creates clothing from beach trash ("trash fashion") to raise awareness of ocean pollution, or Mr. Floatie, a costumed educator dressed as giant piece of excrement who teaches about sewage pollution and solid waste management as he strolls by waterfront restaurant tables in Victoria, Canada (Walter, 2012; Walter & Earl, 2017). As a creative, arts-based philosophy, humanist AEE can be employed to teach environmental knowledge, raise awareness, and catalyze individual and public action in creative engagement with almost any environmental issue, from sea level rise, oil spills, air pollution, and the extinction of animals, to deforestation, solid waste management, and global climate change.

Finally, unlike the other four philosophies, radical AEE is rooted in traditions of critical theory that explicitly question the status quo. Radical AEE works against inequality and inequity and aims to liberate humans (and at times the nonhuman world) from all forms of oppression (Elias & Merriam, 2005; Walter, 2009). Radical AEE promotes adult learning and education for social and environmental change, within the environmental, climate, and Earth justice, ecofeminism, and Indigenous rights movements. Adult learners are seen as active agents in creating their world, culture, and history, both individually and collectively. Radical AEE educators act as facilitators, organizers, and activists, and often follow Freirean lines of problem-posing (rather than problem-solving) AEE (Walter, 2009). This approach stresses the analysis of the structures and intersections of oppression, and the development of collective consciousness and collective action (rather than individual behavioral change) around issues of social and environmental justice (Clover, 2002; Hall, 2009). Radical AEE may involve informal learning in protest camps, marches, workshops, storytelling, music, direct actions, creative public artwork, and social media (Walter & Earl, 2017; Walter, 2007).

In crafting the theory, principles, and practices of radical AEE, the prolific work of Darlene E. Clover has been crucial (Clover, 2002, 2003, 2004; Clover et al., 2013). As Clover (2003) explains, "the most toxic environmental problems result from the practice of capitalist globalization" (p. 10), including the economic commodification of human and natural resources and relations, unchecked consumerism, and corporatization of our society and economy. Clover (2003, 2004) further argues that these are the primary forces responsible for environmental degradation, war, poverty and social inequalities, both locally and globally. Moreover, these inequalities are exacerbated by interlocking oppressions of class, race, and gender whereby Indigenous peoples, poor people, women, people of color, and the working class disproportionately bear the environmental costs of globalization. Thus, radical AEE aims to not only educate about environmental problems caused by global capitalism but also work "toward the democratization of power by challenging underlying racial, class and gender biases and other inequities" (Clover, 2003, p. 11).

The issues, theory, sites, and educational practices of radical AEE are also considered by several scholar-activists working in AEE. Among these are (a) Robert Hill's critical scholarship on the intersectionality of oppressions and environmental justice (2003), radical AEE and green jobs (2013), AEE in the right-wing "popular" environmental movement (2002), and community knowledge in relation to struggles around toxic waste (2004); (b) Walter's (2012) study of cultural codes as catalysts for collective conscientization in radical AEE; (c) Barndt's (2014) work on AEE, arts-based education, food security, labor activism, and justice for migrant workers; (d) Bowles's (2007) study of Black activist women's learning in the environmental justice movement in the southeastern United States; and (e) Tan's (2004) research on antiracist AEE by immigrant groups in Toronto. New directions in radical AEE have been taken up in ecojustice adult education, critical place-based education, and land education.

New Directions in AEE Scholarship

Since the mid-1980s, scholars, educators, and activists in AEE have grappled with the difficult issues of racism, sexism, poverty, homophobia, patriarchy, Indigeneity, and other intersecting axes of privilege and oppression, mainly in radical approaches to AEE. In the late 2010s, work done on the margins of AEE has helped to generate new directions in the field within the radical AEE philosophy. This section summarizes recent AEE literature found at the margins of the field, including scholarship on ecojustice adult education, critical place-based education and land education.

In a recent issue of *New Directions for Adult and Continuing Education*, Dentith and Griswold (2017) provide an overview of theory and educational practice in the emerging field of ecojustice adult education. Drawing on the work of Chet Bowers on ecojustice and revitalizing the commons, ecojustice adult education calls for AEE to promote a cultural shift in society toward two "commons," namely, the environmental commons—"air, water, land, vegetation, . . . [and] the 'cultural commons,'. . . comprised of [sic] the long-term sustaining activities, tangible and abstract, that have been known for centuries" (Dentith & Thompson, 2017, p. 68). Ecojustice AEE recognizes connections among environmental, social, and economic issues, responds to "the educational needs of people, not corporations," and strives to "(re)educate adults about productive but sustainable work, stronger local community living, within an understanding of the relational being and the interdependency of all living and nonliving things" (Dentith & Griswold, 2017, p. 5). The overall aim is to "develop a citizenry capable of re-creating the world to ensure a healthy and equitable existence for all" (Griswold, 2017, p. 11). As such, ecojustice AEE "opposes the dominance of one group over another, of humans over nonhumans, or humans over nature" (Dentith & Thompson, 2017, p. 68). As illustrated in an ecojustice seminar held at Appalachian State University in North Carolina, ecojustice adult education is taught both by example—incorporating case studies of active engagement around environmental issues into AEE curriculum—and through action plans developed by adult learners for "a sustainable future and the recognition of a moral effort to develop ecological intelligence and sustainable cultural life" (Dentith & Thompson, 2017, p. 73).

Like ecojustice adult education, place-based education engenders in learners not only a sense of responsibility for nature, community, and environmental problems but also a realization that positive change is possible and that learners and communities have the capacity to enact it. In place-based education, as a form of intergenerational AEE, youth, elders, and adults learn and work together on local learning projects addressing community problems like food security, waste management, pesticide pollution, plant restoration, hunger, and homelessness (Sobel, 2004).

Building on place-based education and the adult education theories of Paulo Freire, Gruenewald (2003a, 2003b) advances the idea of a *critical* place-based environmental education (EE). In this, Gruenewald (2003a) proposes that all EE, including AEE, should include two fundamental concepts: (a) *decolonization* to investigate and address the exploitation and oppression of marginalized peoples and land for the benefit of the privileged and powerful and (b) *reinhabitation* as the means to mend exploitative human and earth relations, restore damaged ecosystems and revitalize social systems. As Gruenewald (2003a) puts it,

> If reinhabitation involves learning to live well socially and ecologically in places that have been disrupted and injured, decolonization involves learning to recognize disruption and injury and to address their causes. From an educational perspective, it means unlearning much of what dominant culture and schooling teaches, and learning more socially just and ecologically sustainable ways of being in the world. (p. 319)

Greenwood (formerly known as Gruenewald) (2014) understands critical place-based AEE as embracing critical pedagogies (e.g., Freire, Giroux) and a "radical multiculturalism" to acknowledge the "dynamics of race, power, and place" shaping education (p. 312). Most important, his aim is to add a recognition of place—of the human-injured Earth and our responsibility for it—as a key aspect of critical place-based education.

Taking Greenwood's (2014) ideas a step further, Tuck et al. (2014) and a host of others (Bang et al., 2014; Calderon, 2014; Corntassel & Hardbarger, 2019; Datta, 2018; Engel-Di Mauro & Carroll, 2014; Meyer, 2014; Paperson, 2014; Simpson, 2014) have explored the idea of a land-based EE premised on research, pedagogy, and cooperation with local communities, broadly intersecting with AEE. Land-based education is built on the recognition that all lands of colonial states such as the United States, Canada, and the nations of Latin America are in fact part of the vast traditional territories of Indigenous Peoples (i.e., Native Americans) currently living in the Americas. It further acknowledges that this system of White European settler-colonialism dispossessed Native Americans of these lands historically and continues to do so to the present day. As Tuck et al. (2014) explain,

> One of the notable characteristics of settler colonial states is the refusal to recognize themselves as such, requiring a continual disavowal of history, Indigenous peoples' resistance to settlement, Indigenous peoples' claims to stolen land, and how settler colonialism is indeed ongoing, not an event contained in the past. Settler colonialism is made invisible within settler societies. . . . most non-Indigenous people living in settler societies, if they think of colonizers and/or settlers at all, think of Captain James Cook, Christopher Columbus, colonies, and forts. . . .They think of colonization as something that happened in the distant past, as perhaps the unfortunate birthpangs of a new nation. They do not consider the fact that they live on land that has been stolen, or ceded through broken treaties, or to which Indigenous peoples claim a pre-existing ontological and cosmological relationship. They do not consider themselves to be implicated in the continued settlement and occupation of unceded Indigenous land. Indeed, settler colonial societies "cover" the "tracks" of settler colonialism by narrating colonization as temporally located elsewhere, not here and now. (p. 7)

Land education further recognizes that our system of settler-colonialism takes White settlers as the normalized, dominant citizen of the United States,

Canada, and Latin America and positions them as superior to all others, both historically and in the present day. This White supremacist perspective presumes Eurocentric cultures as more "civilized" than others and embraces the White settler-colonial idea of Manifest Destiny in the occupation of Indigenous land (Calderon, 2014). Historically, this allowed not only mass killings of Native Americans and forced removal from their lands but also the violent removal and enslavement of African people from distant African homelands forced to perform slave labor for White settlers in the United States. Moreover, this colonial system allows the continued exploitation of Native Americans, African Americans, and other racialized minorities and immigrant workers today (Calderon, 2014; Tuck & Yang, 2012). As Tuck et al. (2014) note, White colonial hierarchies "are established through force, policy, law, and ideology, and are so embedded that they become naturalized" (p. 7) and largely invisible in U.S. society and other settler-colonial societies.

In land education, decolonization starts with the premise that all lands in the United States are the traditional territories of Native Americans. That is to say, all of our natural environment, all of our wilderness, parks, farms, and cities, all the places we live and work, and all of the sites where we practice AEE in the United States, are located on lands that belonged to Native Americans for at least 15,000 years before any other people arrived from elsewhere (LaDuke, 2017; Spence, 1999). These Native Americans, dispossessed of their lands and homes, continue to face severe environmental racism and injustices today, alongside other racialized minority groups and poor people in the United States—impoverished Latinx, African Americans, and rural poor White people in particular (Gottlieb, 2005; Zimring, 2017). White, Indigenous, African American, Asian American, and Latinx scholars of land-based education acknowledge the importance of learning the history of U.S. settler colonialism, reconnecting to and healing the land, and challenging the power-laden intersections of humans, land, and place (Bang et al., 2014; Calderon, 2014; Engel-Di Mauro & Carroll, 2014; Meyer, 2014; Paperson, 2014; Simpson, 2014). Land education not only promotes a greater awareness of the environmental and human destruction wreaked by settler-colonialists against Native Americans and their lands but also addresses the continuing legacy of settler colonialism and White supremacy. This legacy is found in the toxic, industrial, and hazardous waste poisoning of land, air, and water, for example, in impoverished, disenfranchised African American and Latinx communities in Flint, Michigan; New Orleans, Louisiana; San Antonio, Texas; the Central Valley of California; and Warren County, North Carolina, to name just a few (Gottlieb, 2005; Zimring, 2017).

Several examples of land-based education in the United States illustrate how the approach works in AEE practice. In Hawai'i, for example, the ancestral notion of "land as teacher" is used as a form of AEE to help "awaken Hawaiian communities to develop and host youth projects dedicated to gardens, healthy eating and conscious relationship with lands, moon and each other" (Meyer, 2014, p. 100). Native Hawaiian foods such as taro are being sustainably grown in traditional ways on ancestral lands, thereby providing both food security and land education for Hawaiian and other communities. In urban Chicago, local Ojibwe, Lakota, Choctaw, Chippewa-Cree, Miami, and Navajo educators working with Native American youth, families, and communities have worked to "articulate a pedagogical vision for ourselves in which land was our teacher and our job as teachers was to support our youth in developing right relations with land" (Bang et al., 2014, p. 48). In developing an Indigenous land-based pedagogy for Chicago, first, these educators have "re-storied" the city by unearthing both the history of thousands of years of Native American settlement on pre-Chicago lands and the more recent filling in of Chicago wetlands by colonial settlers. Second, they have revitalized Indigenous epistemologies and ontologies to construct a land-based curriculum and pedagogy for AEE in Chicago. Other scholar-educators on the east coast of the United States have proposed an African-centered approach drawing not on Native American AEE pedagogies, but on Indigenous African approaches to land-based education (Engel-Di Mauro & Carroll, 2014). In this approach, "Ancient Africa" serves as both "historical marker and exemplary" (Engel-Di Mauro & Carroll, 2014, p. 75) to facilitate "people's reconnection to places and the environments/lands they inhabit in ways that do not reduce them, as in settler colonial perspectives, to separable objects of conquest or things to be exploited for profit" (Engel-Di Mauro & Carroll, 2014, p. 78). This requires a recognition of the continuity of African diasporic history, and of U.S. genocidal settler-colonialism history toward both Africans and Native Americans, in this way bringing to "prominence diasporic connections to places erased by settler colonial approaches" (Engel-Di Mauro & Carroll, 2014, p. 79). Still other educators working in San Francisco show land education can be an important "connecting node between Indigenous struggle and Black resistance" (Paperson, 2014, p. 126). These critical AEE connections are made through participatory community mapping; a "decolonizing cartography" (Paperson, 2014, p. 115) that promotes an analysis of settler colonialism as land education.

Conclusion

The United States is facing difficult times as we grapple with the ongoing and future effects of climate change; local, regional, and national environmental crises; an increasingly polarized society; openly racist, sexist, nativist, homophobic, and "anti-environment" government leaders; and a lack of political capacity to face the realities of change. As such, there is now a growing environmental, climate, and social justice imperative for AEE. Since the 1960s, AEE programs, educators, and learners have employed a diverse range of educational philosophies and approaches to address the environmental problems that have plagued, and continue to plague, our society. In the 2010s, ecojustice adult education, critical place-based education, and land-based education have emerged as new areas of AEE thought and practice to meet the social and environmental challenges of the present day. These approaches address not only environmental problems but also the complex and difficult issues of U.S. settler colonialism, human-earth relations, White supremacy, race, gender, poverty, and the intersections of power and privilege in relation to the environment. In doing so, these AEE approaches, like those developed and enacted before them, bring hope to the earth, to its people and to its nonhuman inhabitants.

References

Ariza, E., & Leatherman, S. P. (2011). No-smoking policies and their outcomes on US beaches. *Journal of Coastal Research*, 28(1A), 143–147.

Bang, M., Curley, L., Kessel, A., Marin, A., Suzukovich, E. S., III, & Strack, G. (2014). Muskrat theories, tobacco in the streets, and living Chicago as Indigenous land. *Environmental Education Research*, 20(1), 37–55. https://doi.org/10.1080/13504622.2013.865113

Barndt, D. (2014). Blessings on the food, blessings on the workers: Arts-based education for migrant worker justice. *Canadian Journal of Environmental Education*, 18, 59–79.

Bowles, T. A. (2007). The dimensions of Black women's learning in the environmental justice movement in the Southeastern US. In D. Plumb (Ed.), *Proceedings of the Joint International Adult Education Research Conference and the Canadian Association for the Study of Adult Education* (pp. 55–60). Canadian Association for the Study of Adult Education.

Calderon, D. (2014). Speaking back to manifest destinies: A land education-based approach to critical curriculum inquiry. *Environmental Education Research*, 20(1), 24–36.

Clover, D. E. (2002). Traversing the gap: Concientización, educative-activism in environmental adult education. *Environmental Education Research*, 8(3), 315–323.

Clover, D. E. (2003). Environmental adult education: Critique and creativity in a globalizing world. *New Directions for Adult and Continuing Education*, 2003(99), 5–15.

Clover, D. E. (Ed.) (2004). *Global perspectives in environmental adult education*. Peter Lang.

Clover, D. E., Jayme, B. D., Hall, B. L., & Follen, S. (2013). *The nature of transformation: Environmental adult education*. Sense.

Corntassel, J., & Hardbarger, T. (2019). Educate to perpetuate: Land-based pedagogies and community resurgence. *International Review of Education*, 65(1), 87–116.

Datta, R. K. (2018). Rethinking environmental science education from Indigenous knowledge perspectives: An experience with a Dene First Nation community. *Environmental Education Research*, 24(1), 50–66.

Dentith, A. M., & Griswold, W. (2017). Editors' notes. *New Directions for Adult and Continuing Education*, 2017(153), 5–6.

Dentith, A. M., & Thompson, O. P. (2017). Teaching adult ecojustice education. *New Directions for Adult and Continuing Education*, 2017(153), 65–75.

Elias, J. L., & Merriam, S. B. (2005). *Philosophical foundations of adult education* (3rd ed.). Kreiger.

Engel-Di Mauro, S., & Carroll, K. K. (2014). An African-centred approach to land education. *Environmental Education Research*, 20(1), 70–81.

Falk, J. H. (2005). Free-choice environmental learning: Framing the discussion. *Environmental Education Research*, 11(3), 265–280.

Foley, G. (1999). *Learning in social action: A contribution to understanding informal education*. Zed Books.

Gottlieb, R. (2005). *Forcing the spring: The transformation of the American environmental movement*. Island Press.

Greenwood, D. A. (2014). Culture, environment, and education in the anthropocene. In M. P. Mueller, D. J. Tippins, & A. J. Stewart (Eds.), *Assessing schools for Generation R (responsibility)* (pp. 279–292). Springer.

Griswold, W. (2017). Sustainability, ecojustice, and adult education. *New Directions for Adult and Continuing Education, 2017*(153), 7–15.

Groen, J. (2017). The St. Ignatius Jesuit Retreat and Training Centre: Cultivating ecological awareness and connection with the Earth. *New Directions for Adult and Continuing Education, 2017*(153), 31–39.

Gruenewald, D. A. (2003a). The best of both worlds: A critical pedagogy of place. *Environmental Education Research, 14*(3), 308–324.

Gruenewald, D. A. (2003b). Foundations of place: A multidisciplinary framework for place-conscious education. *American Educational Research Journal, 40*(3), 619–654.

Hall, B. L. (2009). A river of life: Learning and environmental social movements. *Interface: A Journal for and About Social Movements, 1*(1), 46–78.

Hill, R. J. (2002). Pulling up grassroots: A study of the right-wing "popular" adult environmental education movement in the United States. *Studies in Continuing Education, 24*(2), 181–203.

Hill, R. J. (2003). Environmental justice: Environmental adult education at the confluence of oppressions. *New Directions for Adult and Continuing Education, 2017*(153), 27–38.

Hill, R. J. (2004). Fugitive and codified knowledge: Implications for communities struggling to control the meaning of local environmental hazards. *International Journal of Lifelong Education, 23*(3), 221–242.

Hill, R. J. (2013). A deeper shade of green: The future of green jobs and environmental adult education. *Adult Learning, 24*(1), 43–46.

Jason, L. A., McCoy, K., Blanco, D., & Zolik, E. S. (1980). Decreasing dog litter: Behavioral consultation to help a community group. *Evaluation Review, 4*(3), 355–369.

Jeffs, T., & Ord, J. (Eds.). (2017). *Rethinking outdoor, experiential and informal education: Beyond the confines.* Routledge.

Kluttz, J., & Walter, P. (2018). Conceptualizing learning in the climate justice movement. *Adult Education Quarterly, 68*(2), 91–107.

LaDuke, W. (2017). *All our relations: Native struggles for land and life.* Haymarket Books.

Merenlender, A. M., Crall, A. W., Drill, S., Prysby, M., & Ballard, H. (2016). Evaluating environmental education, citizen science, and stewardship through naturalist programs. *Conservation Biology, 30*(6), 1255–1265. https://doi.org/10.1111/cobi.12737

Merriam, S. B., Caffarella, R. S., & Baumgartner, L. M. (2009). *Learning in adulthood: A comprehensive guide* (3rd ed.). Jossey-Bass.

Meyer, M. A. (2014). Hoea Ea: land education and food sovereignty in Hawai'i. *Environmental Education Research, 20*(1), 98–101.

Packer, J., & Ballantyne, R. (2010). The role of zoos and aquariums in education for a sustainable future. *New Directions for Adult and Continuing Education, 2010*(157), 25–34.

Paperson, L. (2014). A ghetto land pedagogy: An antidote for settler environmentalism. *Environmental Education Research, 20*(1), 115–130.

Simpson, L. B. (2014). Land as pedagogy: Nishnaabeg intelligence and rebellious transformation. *Decolonization: Indigeneity, Education & Society, 3*(3), 1–25.

Sobel, D. (2004). Place-based education: Connecting classroom and community. *Nature and Listening, 4*(1), 1–7.

Spence, M. (1999). *Dispossessing the wilderness: Indian removal and the making of national parks.* Oxford University Press.

Tan, S. (2004). Anti-racist environmental adult education in a trans-global community: Case studies from Toronto. In D. Clover (Ed.), *Global perspectives in adult environmental education* (pp. 3–22). Peter Lang.

Tuck, E., McKenzie, M., & McCoy, K. (2014). Land education: Indigenous, post-colonial, and decolonizing perspectives on place and environmental education research. *Environmental Education Research, 20*(1), 1–24.

Tuck, E., & Yang, K. W. (2012). Decolonization is not a metaphor. *Decolonization: Indigeneity, Education & Society, 1*(1), 1–40.

Waliczek, T. M., Boyer, R., & Zajicek, J. M. (2002). The Master Gardener program: Do benefits of the program go beyond improving the horticultural knowledge of the participants? *Horticulture Technology, 12*(3), 432–436.

Walter, P. (2007). Adult learning in new social movements: Environmental protest and the struggle for the Clayoquot Sound rainforest. *Adult Education Quarterly, 57*, 248–263.

Walter, P. (2009). Philosophies of adult environmental education. *Adult Education Quarterly, 60*(1), 3–25.

Walter, P. (2012). Cultural codes as catalysts for collective conscientisation in environmental adult education: Mr. Floatie, tree squatting and Save-Our-Surfers. *Australian Journal of Adult Learning, 52*(1), 114–133.

Walter, P., & Earl, A. (2017). Public pedagogies of arts-based environmental learning and education for adults. *European Journal for Research on the Education and Learning of Adults, 8*(1), 145–163.

Wittmer, C., & Johnson, B. (2000). Experience as a foundation of environmental adult education: The Audubon Expedition Institute model. *Convergence, 33*(4), 111.

Wyles, K. J., Pahl, S., Holland, M., & Thompson, R. C. (2017). Can beach cleans do more than clean-up litter? Comparing beach cleans to other coastal activities. *Environment and Behavior, 49*(5), 509–535.

Zimring, C. A. (2017). *Clean and white: A history of environmental racism in the United States.* NYU Press.

CHAPTER 34

Education to Change the World

Learning Within/Through Social Movements

Jude Walker and Shauna Butterwick

As we write this chapter, many liberal democracies, including the United States, are in crisis. Populist strongmen lead on platforms of xenophobia; "facts" are up for debate. We exist within a corporately colonized lifeworld; traditional social structures of the welfare state, such as unions or jobs for life, have been continuously dismantled over decades. We are, also, arguably living within a social movement moment, with #MeToo, #BlackLivesMatter, or #TakeAKnee—likely familiar to many reading this chapter. The possibilities for learning from and within social movements are arguably unparalleled.

Adult learning and education have always been central to social movements (Cunningham, 1998), from teaching financial literacy to fishermen in Antigonish, Nova Scotia, in the 1920s, to supporting African Americans to read and write at the Highlander Folk School as part of a massive enfranchisement effort of the civil rights movement (Lovett et al., 1993). As Foley (1999) pointed out more than 2 decades ago, learning occurs through social action—most of it incidental and informal. Social movements are also both generators and disseminators of knowledge (Flowers & Swan, 2011).

This chapter focuses on the growing adult education subfield of social movement learning (SML) (Hall & Clover, 2005). While SML is a relatively new adult education research field, the study of learning in and from social movements is not (e.g., Coady, 1939).

Indeed, before the deployment of the term *SML*, many studies of resistance movements, consciousness-raising groups, and activism have occurred with varied foci on adult learning (e.g., Bartky, 1975; Foner, 1970). As the significance of SML has grown, so too has the scholarship and development of the SML subfield, starting around the 1990s (e.g., Dykstra & Law, 1994; Foley, 1999; Kilgore, 1999; Walters & Manicom, 1996; Welton, 1993).

Diani (1992) defines *social movements* as "networks of informal interactions between a plurality of individuals, groups and/or organizations, engaged in political or cultural conflicts, on the basis of shared collective identities" (p. 1). We consider all social movements as both cultural and political, taking an expansive definition to include broad-based movements, submovements, and protests. We include movements concerned with more than one social issue or concern (e.g., Indigenous rights movements are often necessarily also eco/climate justice movements; or the Occupy movement, which was more broadly concerned with an overhaul of global capitalism and transforming society), and movements that might be questioned as examples of social movements (e.g., the Tea Party movement; breast cancer survivors in lobbying for health-care support).

In what follows, we draw primarily on SML literature published in the 21st century to explore the following themes: (a) the various ways scholars have described and interpreted SML, (b) the various learning outcomes of SML, (c) the pedagogies and methods employed in SML, and (d) the role of social media. Given the text limits for this chapter, we can offer only a glimpse into the growing SML scholarship.

Approaches to the Study of SML

SML scholars have sought to understand SML in a variety of ways. We note that research methodologies such as participatory action research (Langdon & Larweh, 2015) and other qualitative approaches that pay close attention to ethical considerations and questions of positionality (Curnow, 2013) have been used to explore SML. For example, narrative inquiry and life history methodologies can capture the stories of social movement activists (Butterwick & Elfert, 2014). In what follows we report on the categories, typologies, and theoretical frameworks deployed in the study of SML.

Categories

Social movements have often been categorized as either old social movements (OSMs) or new social movements (NSM). OSMs comprise labor/union/class-based (i.e., Marxist proletariat) movements emerging over the 19th and first part of the 20th century. NSMs began in the 1960s focusing on identity markers (e.g., women's, civil rights, LGBT, and Indigenous movements) (Holst, 2002). SML scholars have been roughly divided between these categories. OSMs privilege class-based, explicitly anticapitalist, and often Marxist analyses, including feminist approaches (e.g., Carpenter & Mojab, 2016; Choudry, 2015; Holst, 2002), emphasizing anticapitalist struggle and how social movements will always necessarily be subsumed into capitalism's workings. NSM scholars, while also critical of capitalism, focus on the transformative potential of social movements and center issues other than class, such as environmental degradation and LGBT rights (see Hall, 2006; Hill, 2002; Scandrett et al., 2010; Schugurensky, 2016).

Much SML scholarship since the 1990s focuses on NSMs with some (neo)Marxist scholars lamenting the lack of attention on capitalist structures that maintain income inequality (e.g., Choudry, 2015). Some scholars (e.g., Boltanski & Chiapello, 2005) have even argued that the 1968 student, civil rights, and peace movements actually heralded in an era of hypercapitalism, individualism, and the "me generation." Some question the old/new divide (Holst, 2011). For example, the women's movement arguably predates the labor movement and there are direct connections between them. Holst (2011) notes how International Women's Day was created by the Socialist party (thanks to the urging of suffragist labor activist Theresa Malkiel). The politics of Indigenous struggle also does not easily fit within this divide. Further, the OSM/NSM division fails to adequately capture significant changes in employment, including the growing numbers of independent contractors and millions of "subaltern" workers existing outside of social structures (see Kapoor, 2007).

Progressive versus conservative (and, more recently, the alt-right) is another categorization evident in the SML literature. "Progressive" social movements promote the rights and positions of marginalized and oppressed groups. Right-wing, conservative, and even outwardly racist and xenophobic movements are "movements that act on behalf of relatively advantaged groups with the goal of preserving, restoring and expanding the rights and privileges of its members and constituents" (McVeigh, 2009, p. 32). As Kincaid (2017) has shown, mainstream social movement theory fails to include the activities of the radical right (or alt-right), which tends to "create rhetorical frames that effectively blend symbolic and material grievances" (p. 5). Rightwing movements are an underexplored area, with the exception of Hill's (2002) research into the "alternative" adult environmental education movement. He found that individuals and groups within this movement were using logging companies' teaching materials and the arguments of antienvironmentalist and conservative think tanks, including academics. Their discourse provides legitimacy for "reasonable" countereducational measures positioning progressive movement claims as extremist and the alt-right as a besieged minority, existing in opposition to the liberal "mainstream." These alt-right movements have learned progressive campaign tools, which they now employ against them (Hill, 2002; Main, 2018). Not all social movements, however, are easily located on this continuum. For example, Smith's (2015) study of the (primarily online) North American Urban Homestead movement found it attracted a diverse group of women (hippies, Christians, Jews, and Republicans) who seek to "reclaim the lost skills and healing arts of the traditional farm wife" (p. 142).

Typologies of SML

SML has also been explored using various typologies: formal, nonformal, or informal and individual or collective. For example, formal, nonformal, and informal contexts are all sites of adult learning, including SML. Formal contexts include university-based programs such as women's studies, labor education, and environmental programs (emerging from social movements). Nonformal contexts include workshops, seminars, talks, or short courses offered outside of higher education by many organizations, including unions and feminist groups. Popular education activities are also nonformal (Manicom & Walters, 2012) sites of learning where communities identify problems and explore solutions, often using story and theater.

Much adult learning is informal, especially SML (Foley, 1999). Schugurensky (2000) classifies informal SML as self-directed (intentional), incidental (unintentional but with an awareness that something was learned), and tacit or through socialization (unintentional and generally without awareness that something was learned). Similarly, Hall (2006) noted three main types of SML: experiential learning through participating, intentional learning through engagement with structured initiatives, and learning through observation.

The individual-collective relationship of SML is another dimension of SML taken up by scholars. Studies of SML have drawn on sociologists Eyerman and Jamison's (1991) notion of "cognitive praxis" (e.g., Hall & Clover, 2005; Holford, 1995) to capture the knowledge that "constitutes, sustains, and evolves social movements" (VanWynsberghe & Herman, 2015, p. 273). Scandrett et al. (2010) considered the levels of individual and collective learning at the micro, meso, and macro levels (see also Kluttz & Walter, 2018). *Micro* learning occurs when individuals gain new knowledge about issues; *meso* learning refers to learning new frames and understanding that are internalized and acted upon (related here, perhaps, to the concept of perspective transformation, see Cranton, 2016); and *macro* learning involves individuals and groups challenging existing social structures and power differentials.

Theorizing SML

A variety of theoretical resources have been used in the study of SML. Mezirow's transformative learning (TL) and Freire's consciousness raising (CR) are commonly found in SML research pointing to how SML involves shifts in meaning perspectives (TL) through processes of conscientization (CR) (Sandlin, 2010). Foley (1999) examined the inextricable, dialectical, and iterative connections among learning and action with the ultimate goal of some sort of transformation. While not labelled as such, a sociocultural approach to TL is found in feminist research, which has noted where and how women learn that the personal is political—that their individual struggles are shared and grow out of powerful and deep race, class, and gender structures and norms (e.g., Bartky, 1975; Greaves, 2018). The role of emotions in TL has been the focus of more recent SML studies (e.g., Cranton, 2016) that explore how anger, sadness, guilt, or shame can accompany disorienting dilemmas and how a "pedagogy of discomfort" (Boler, 1999, p. 175) can be a productive trigger for radical shifts in one's habits of mind and behavior.

Scholars have also explored SML through the lens of public pedagogy. Biesta (2014) differentiated between pedagogy *for, by,* and *with* the public. This latter orientation is what Sandlin et al. (2011) argue is the public pedagogy dimensions of SML that involve "public intellectualism and social activism" (p. 338); or learning through participation in everyday life. Some examples of public pedagogy include: learning through watching and making documentary films (Roy, 2016); creating and viewing public works of arts and by visiting museums (Clover, 2015); creating performances, such as fashion shows, to tell stories of struggle and resilience (Butterwick et al., 2015); becoming involved with new pedagogies of flash mobs (Sandlin, 2010); and engaging in social media (Terranova & Donovan, 2013).

Scholars have also turned to other theoretical models of learning. For example, Stetsenko (2008) brought a social justice lens to Vygotsky's sociocultural theory of learning, arguing that "collaborative purposeful transformation of the world is the core of human nature" (p. 471). Cunningham (1998) turned to Gramsci's theory and his notion of organic intellectuals whose knowledge arises from day-to-day struggle, in contrast to traditional intellectuals who maintain "official knowledge" (p. 15). She called for a sociocultural view of TL rather than a psychological one, which, she argued, stripped away attention to power and politics. Others have employed Lave and Wenger's (1991) "communities of practice" (p. 42) and the process of legitimate peripheral participation (e.g., Curnow, 2013) to understand SML. Sandlin and Walther (2009) brought identity theory, including learning organizational identity, tactical identity, and activist identity, to study SML at both individual and collective levels.

SML can be studied through a decolonial lens, challenging the hierarchy of scientific and academic knowledge versus Indigenous knowledge (Maldonado-Torres, 2011). Feminist theory contributes an important lens to the study of SML (Anzaldúa & Keating, 2002). Köpsén's (2011) study of trade unions built on theories of workplace learning. Lavendar (2005) used UNESCO's four pillars of lifelong learning to study SML: learning to know, learning to do, learning to be, and learning to live together.

Learning Outcomes

The learning outcomes of SML are numerous and diverse. SML leads significantly to the development of new knowledge and theory (Choudry, 2015; hooks, 1984) and to critical understandings of the taken-for-granted practices and structures and how the world works to maintain hierarchies of privilege and penalty (Lavendar, 2005). SML leads to critical consciousness of gender, class, and race relations and globalization (Curnow, 2013). SML is also about developing relational/personal and technical skills. SML involves learning democratic processes and how to work collaboratively (Larrabure et al., 2011). Skills in self-management, collective organizing, planning, efficiency, and accountability are developed (Bleakney & Choudry, 2013) as are skills in assertiveness, critical analysis, and convincing argumentation (Butterwick & Elfert, 2014; Crowther et al., 2012).

Personal skills developed through SML also include how to adapt, persevere, co-opt, and infiltrate (at the level of the individual and the collective) (Crowther et al., 2012). SML also involves becoming savvy with technology and media (Terranova & Donovan, 2013) (we expand on this later in this chapter). Not all learning outcomes are positive, as Flowers and Swan (2011) note. For example, English and Irving (2015) questioned some of the problematic organizational practices women learn within equality-seeking organizations, which they show are linked to the tension between maintaining a relationship with the state to secure funding and following feminist principles.

Pedagogies of SML

SML research has explored the pedagogies and processes used to enable individual and group learning, which are obviously myriad. Some are not necessarily specific to social movements but are particularly predominant and powerful. Dykstra and Law (1994) pointed to the following SML pedagogies: (a) putting forth a vision of a different society; (b) reflecting critically on issues and making change in that direction; and (c) mobilizing, sustaining, and maintaining the movement (e.g., Jubas, 2018; Sandlin & Walther, 2009). Within these different foci, attention has been given to how creative expression (visual imagery, poetry, dance, theater, and so on) can create spaces for speaking truth to power, articulating lived experiences of those on the margins, and imagining a different future (Greene, 1995). These processes can build empathy and solidarity as found in Miller's (2018) study of how theater of witness built bridges across political polarizations in Northern Ireland. Artistic and creative expression involve both a process and product. The process of making something can be a pathway to activism (e.g., Butterwick et al., 2015). Creative processes can enable critical reflection and a deepening understanding at both a personal and collective level; sharing the products of creative expression can support conditions for marginalized voices to be heard (Butterwick & Roy, 2016).

Appreciation for the affective and emotional elements of adult learning, particularly SML, is growing (Clover, 2015; Walker & Palacios, 2015). The emotional labor of activism and public pedagogy is important to recognize, including activist burnout, where feelings of powerlessness and overcommitment can arise (Gorski, 2015), as can difficult interpersonal relationships. In educating nonmarginalized people to care about social justice issues (Curry-Stevens, 2007), guilt and discomfort often occur.

Vertical learning, or how recent movements learn from past movements, is also receiving attention, as is evident in Grayson's (2011) study of the alliances between middle-class professionals and the working class in South Yorkshire in the United Kingdom, with its strong labor movement in manufacturing and mining. He found an "interplay between old and new grammars of political action" (p. 126) evident in the early 2000s, as activists who fought the deportation of recent migrants joined with Workers Educational

Associations (WEA) (formed earlier in the 20th century). Vertical learning occurs as current social movements learn from 1960s and 1970s movements. Indeed, 1968 remains an inspiration for university-based movements today such as the Chilean student movement (Cabalin, 2012) and the Quebec student movement (Giroux, 2013). The technology-driven Egyptian Arab Spring received inspiration from the silk-screened poster-art of the Paris protests of 1968 (Edgar, 2018), and Black Lives Matter turns to Black Power and the Black Panthers both directly and indirectly for inspiration (Edgar, 2018). Hamilton (2013) found the content and process of the Poor People's Campaign (PPC) of 1968 evident in the global unfurling of Occupy movements in 2011. PPC, led by Martin Luther King Jr., established Resurrection City of 6,000 people in Washington DC which, like Occupy, had a people's university freedom school offering workshops on "problems of human communications, . . . man's first literature, and the politics of race" (p. 12). Similarly, Occupy's University, which grew out of the Education and Empowerment working group, offered similar courses on social action, the humanities, and other courses. Larrabure et al. (2011) noted how Latin American cooperative movements learned from previous cooperative movements.

The Role of Media in SML

Many recent social movements have become synonymous with social media, preceded by Twitter hashtags, spreading across local and global communities. That said, many social movements have arguably always involved a global dimension (e.g., student protests of 1968)—and not all current social movements exist at a global level (e.g., protesting pollution of a local river). As English and Irving (2015) argue, "it is difficult to speak of social movements without considering the impact of [Information and Communication Technologies]" (p. 57). The intensification of globalization and development of social media technologies and capabilities enable more recent social movements to connect the local with a global information network (Castells, 2012).

Social movements have long relied on media to educate the broader local and global community about the social/political/cultural issues they care about. Donovan and Boyd (2018), writing in the *Guardian*, noted that in the 1920s, media coverage was a key recruitment tactic for the Ku Klux Klan. Media mediates the message of social movements and acts as translator of ideas—some of which might actually work against the social movement or social issue, or otherwise provide partial truths. For example, the *New York Times* was shown to ridicule the women's movement of the 1970s (Ashley & Olsen, 1998).

Recent social movements, such as Standing Rock (Walker & Walter, 2018), have relied heavily on media, both social and traditional, for archiving, disseminating, planning, and communicating within and outside the movement. Terranova and Donovan's (2013) engagement with the Occupy movement found them learning how to engage with media outlets, conduct interviews with *New York Times* or Al Jazeera journalists, and use online tools to engage social media to publicize arrests, disseminate information, and help enact deliberative democracy. Social media, particularly Twitter, was a key communication tool for the Idle No More movement in Canada, a self-determination movement of Indigenous activists (Atleo, 2016). Through Twitter, participants learned about actions taking place as well as what worked and did not work.

Using social media can be a double-edged sword, as noted by White (2010), who described how action has been reduced to clicking on an online petition or forwarding an email from a social movement organization. Furthermore, social movement technologies have also been used to support nonprogressive initiatives. For example, Donovan (2017) showed how Occupy's ubiquitous documentation and direct uploading of mobile phone videos to an archival website was used by police departments developing new social surveillance techniques.

Finally, new media and technologies are being brought together with older adult education traditions of the Folk School and the Freedom School. In drawing on his learning from Occupy and the people's university (as well as elsewhere), Micah White recently created an online noncredit activist graduate school, which teaches courses on such topics as How to Change the World and Why Do Protests Fail? (Activist Graduate School, 2019). Faculty include professors from different institutions as well as involved activists. The first cohort began in September 2018.

Conclusion

In this chapter, we have highlighted some of the ways SML has been categorized, studied, and theorized. We have noted some of learning outcomes of social movement participation and the various pedagogies and methods of learning. We have also brought attention to the significant role of media in social movements. While the ways people learn through social movements are not necessarily unique, it is important to take note of how SML contributes to educating for a better and more just world. We urge students and scholars of adult education to consider this vital arena of adult learning and education and to expand their range of vision to include SML. Attention to SML is needed, not just so we have a more comprehensive understanding of our field, but because it is a significant source of new knowledge and theory. At the heart of SML is the interrogation of where knowledge comes from, whose knowledge is being put forth, and how it is being disseminated: three key questions guiding emancipatory visions of adult education.

References

Activist Graduate School. (2019). *Home page.* https://www.activistgraduateschool.com

Anzaldúa, G., & Keating, A. (2002). *This bridge we call home.* Routledge.

Ashley, L., & Olsen, B. (1998). Constructing reality: Print media's framing of the women's movement, 1966 to 1986. *Journalism & Mass Communication Quarterly, 75*(2), 263–277.

Atleo, M. (2016). All my relations: Networks of First Nations/Métis/Inuit women sharing the learnings. In D. Clover, S. Butterwick, & L. Collins (Eds.), *Women, adult education, leadership in Canada* (pp. 33–44). Thompson Educational.

Bartky, S. L. (1975). Towards a phenomenology of feminist consciousness. *Social Theory and Practice, 3*(4), 425–439.

Biesta, G. (2014). Making pedagogy public: For the public, of the public, or in the interest of publicness? In J. Burdick, J. Sandlin, & M. O'Malley (Eds.), *Problematizing public pedagogy* (pp. 15–25). Routledge.

Bleakney, D., & Choudry, A. (2013). Education and knowledge production in workers' struggles: Learning to resist, learning from resistance. *McGill Journal of Education, 48*(3), 569–586.

Boler, M. (1999). *Feeling power: Emotions and education.* Routledge.

Boltanski, L., & Chiapello, E. (2005). *The new spirit of capitalism.* Verso.

Butterwick, S., Carrillo, M., & Villagante, K. (with the Philippine Women's Centre of BC). (2015). Women's fashion shows as feminist transformation. *Canadian Journal for the Study of Adult Education, 27*(2), 79–99.

Butterwick, S., & Elfert, M. (2014). Women social activists of Atlantic Canada: Stories of re-enchantment, authenticity, and hope. *Canadian Journal for the Study of Adult Education, 27*(1), 15–32.

Butterwick, S., & Roy, C. (2016). *Working the margins of community-based adult learning: The power of arts-making in finding voice and creating conditions for seeing/listening.* Sense.

Cabalin, C. (2012). Neoliberal education and student movements in Chile: Inequalities and malaise. *Policy Futures in Education, 10*(2), 219–228.

Carpenter, S., & Mojab, S. (2016). *Revolutionary learning: Marxism, feminism and knowledge.* Pluto Press.

Castells, M. (2012). *Networks of outrage and hope: Social movements in the internet age.* Polity Press.

Choudry, A. (2015). *Learning activism: The intellectual life of contemporary social movements.* University of Toronto Press.

Clover, D. (2015). Adult education for social and environmental change in contemporary public art galleries and museums in Canada, Scotland, and England. *International Journal of Lifelong Education, 34*(3), 300–315.

Coady, M. (1939). *Masters of their own destiny: The story of the Antigonish movement of adult education through economic cooperation.* Harper.

Cranton, P. (2016). *Understanding and promoting transformative learning: A guide to theory and practice* (3rd edition). Stylus.

Crowther, J., Hemmi, A., & Scandrett, E. (2012). Learning environmental justice and adult education in a Scottish community campaign against fish farming. *Local Environment, 17*(1), 115–130.

Cunningham, P. (1998). The social dimensions of transformative learning. *PAACE Journal of Lifelong Learning, 7,* 15–28.

Curnow, J. (2013). Fight the power: Situated learning and conscientisation in a gendered community of practice. *Gender and Education, 25*(7), 834–850.

Curry-Stevens, A. (2007). New forms of transformative education: Pedagogy for the privileged. *Journal of Transformative Education, 5*(1), 33–58.

Diani, M. (1992). The concept of social movement. *The Sociological Review, 40*(1), 1–25.

Donovan, J. (2017, April). From social movements to social surveillance. *XRDS*. https://xrds.acm.org/article.cfm?aid=3055151

Donovan, J., & Boyd, D. (2018, June 1). The case for quarantining extremist ideas. *The Guardian*. https://www.theguardian.com/commentisfree/2018/jun/01/extremist-ideas-media-coverage-kkk

Dykstra, C., & Law, M. (1994). Popular social movements as educative forces: Towards a theoretical framework. In *Proceedings of the 35th Adult Education Research Conference* (pp. 121–126). University of Tennessee.

Edgar, D. (2018, May 10). The radical legacy of 1968 is under attack. We must defend it. *The Guardian*. https://www.theguardian.com/commentisfree/2018/may/10/radical-legacy-1968-neoliberalism-progressive

English, L., & Irving, C. (2015). *Feminism and community: Adult education for transformation*. Sense.

Eyerman, R., & Jamison, A. (1991). *Social movements: A cognitive approach*. Pennsylvania State University Press.

Flowers, R., & Swan, E. (2011). "Eating at us": Representations of knowledge in the activist documentary film *Food Inc*. *Studies in the Education of Adults, 43*(2), 234–250. https://doi.org/10.1080/02660830.2011.11661615

Foley, G. (1999). *Learning in social action: A contribution to understanding informal education*. Zed Books.

Foner, P. S. (1970). *The Black Panthers speak*. Da Capo Press.

Giroux, H. (2013). The Quebec student protest movement in the era of neoliberal terror. *Journal for the Study of Race, Nation, and Culture, 19*(5), 515–535. https://doi.org/10.1080/13504630.2013.835510

Gorski, P. C. (2015). Relieving burnout and the "martyr syndrome" among social justice education activists: The implications and effects of mindfulness. *Urban Review, 47*, 696–716.

Grayson, J. (2011). Organising, educating, and training: varieties of activist learning in left social movements in Sheffield (UK). *Studies in the Education of Adults, 43*(2), 197–215. https://doi.org/10.1080/02660830.2011.11661613

Greaves, L. (Ed.) (2018). *Personal and political: Stories from the women's health movement 1960–2000*. Second Story Press.

Greene, M. (1995). *Releasing the imagination: Essays on education, the arts, and social change*. Jossey-Bass.

Hall, B. (2006). Social movement learning: Theorizing a Canadian tradition. In T. Fenwick, T. Nesbit, & B. Spencer (Eds.), *Contexts of adult education: Canadian perspectives* (pp. 230–238). Thompson Educational.

Hall, B., & Clover, D. (2005). Social movement learning. In L. English (Ed.), *International encyclopedia of adult education* (pp. 584–589). Palgrave Macmillan.

Hamilton, R. (2013). Did the dream end there? Adult education and resurrection city 1968. *Studies in the Education of Adults, 45*(1), 4–26.

Hill, R. J. (2002). Pulling up grassroots: A study of right-wing "popular" adult environmental education movements in the United States. *Studies in Continuing Education, 24*(2), 181–203.

Holford, J. (1995). Why social movements matter: Adult education theory, cognitive praxis, and the creation of knowledge. *Adult Education Quarterly, 45*, 95–111.

Holst, J. (2002). *Social movements, civil society, and radical adult education*. Praeger.

Holst, J. (2011). Frameworks for understanding the politics of social movements. *Studies in the Education of Adults, 43*(2), 117–127.

hooks, b. (1984). *Feminist theory: From margin to center* (1st ed.). South End Press.

Jubas, K. (2018). Courting change on the field: Lessons from the "Take a Knee" movement about pop culture's potential for critical public pedagogy. In R. McGray & V. Woloshyn (Eds.), *Proceedings of the 37th CASAE/ACEEA Annual Conference* (pp. 127–130). Canadian Association for the Study of Adult Education.

Kapoor, D. (2007). Subaltern social movement learning and the decolonization of space in India. *International Education, 37*(1), 10–41.

Kilgore, D. (1999). Understanding learning in social movements: A theory of collective learning. *International Journal of Lifelong Education, 18*(3), 191–202.

Kincaid, R. (2017). Theorizing the radical right: Directions for social movement's research on the right-wing social movements. *Sociology Compass, 11*(5). https://doi.org/10.1111/soc4.12469

Kluttz, J., & Walter, P. (2018). Conceptualizing learning in the climate justice movement. *Adult Education Quarterly, 68*(2), 91–107.

Köpsén, S. (2011). Learning for renewal: Learning in a trade union practice. *Journal of Workplace Learning, 23*(1), 20–34.

Langdon, J., & Larweh, K. (2015). Moving with the movement: Collaboratively building a participatory action research study of SML in Ada, Ghana. *Action Research, 13*(3), 281–297.

Larrabure, M., Vieta, M., & Schugurensky, D. (2011). The "new cooperativism" in Latin America: Worker-recuperated enterprises and social production units. *Studies in the Education of Adults, 43*(2), 181–196.

Lave, J., & Wenger, E. (1991). *Situated learning: Legitimate peripheral participation*. Cambridge University Press.

Lavendar, P. (2005). Connecting with new social movements. *Adults Learning, 16*(7), 18–19.

Lovett, T., Clarke, C., & Kilmurray, A. (1993). *Adult education and community action: Adult education and popular social movements*. Routledge.

Main, T. (2018). *The rise of the alt-right*. Brookings Institution Press.

Maldonado-Torres, N. (2011). Thinking through the decolonial turn: Post-continental interventions in theory, philosophy, and critique—An introduction. *Journal of Peripheral Cultural Production of the Luso-Hispanic World, 1*(2), 1–14.

Manicom, L., & Walters, S. (2012). *Feminist popular education in transnational debates: Building pedagogies of possibility*. Palgrave Macmillan.

McVeigh, R. (2009). *The rise of the Ku Klux Klan: Right-wing movements and national politics*. University of Minnesota Press.

Miller, J. (2018). The transformative and healing power of theatre of witness. *Canadian Journal for the Study of Adult Education, 30*(2), 47–56.

Roy, C. (2016). *Documentary film festivals: Transformative learning, community building, and solidarity*. Sense.

Sandlin, J. (2010). Learning to survive the "Shopocalypse": Reverend Billy's anti-consumption "pedagogy of the unknown." *Critical Studies in Education, 51*(3), 295–311.

Sandlin, J., O'Malley, M. P., & Burdick, J. (2011). Mapping the complexity of public pedagogy scholarship: 1894–2010. *Review of Educational Research, 81*(3), 338–375.

Sandlin, J., & Walther, C. (2009). Complicated simplicity: moral identity formation and social movement learning in the voluntary simplicity movement. *Adult Education Quarterly, 59*(4), 298–317.

Scandrett, E., Crowther, J., Hemmi, A., Mukherjee, S., Shah, D., & Sen, T. (2010). Theorising education and learning in social movements: Environmental justice campaigns in Scotland and India. *Studies in the Education of Adults, 42*(2), 124–140.

Schugurensky, D. (2000). *The forms of informal learning: Towards a conceptualisation of the field* [NALL working paper, 19]. Centre for the Study of Work & Education, OISE/UT.

Schugurensky, D. (2016). Social pedagogy in North America. Historical background and current developments. *Pedagogía Social: Revista Interuniversitaria, 27*, 225–251.

Smith, A. (2015). The Farm Wife Mystery School: Women's use of social media in the contemporary North American urban homestead movement. *Studies in the Education of Adults, 47*(2), 142–159.

Stetsenko, A. (2008). From relational ontology to transformative activist stance on development and learning: expanding Vygotsky's (CHAT) project. *Cultural Studies of Science Education, 3*, 471–491.

Terranova, T., & Donovan, J. (2013). Occupy social networks: The paradoxes of using corporate social media in networked movements. In G. Lovink & M. Rash (Eds.), *Unlike us reader: Social media monopolies and their alternatives*. Institute of Network Cultures. http://hdl.handle.net/11574/37273

VanWynsberghe, R., & Herman, A. (2015). Education for social change and pragmatist theory: Five features of educative environments designed for social change. *International Journal of Lifelong Education, 34*(3), 268–283.

Walker, J., & Palacios, C. (2015). A pedagogy of emotion in teaching about SML. *Teaching in Higher Education, 21*(2), 175–190.

Walker, J., & Walter, P. (2018). Learning about social movements through news media: Deconstructing *New York Times* and Fox News representations of Standing Rock. *International Journal of Lifelong Education, 37*(4), 401–418. https://doi.org/10.1080/02601370.2018.1485184

Walters, S., & Manicom, L. (1996). *Gender in popular education: Methods for empowerment*. Zed Books.

Welton, M. (1993). Social revolutionary learning: The new social movements as learning sites. *Adult Education Quarterly, 43*(3), 152–164.

White, M. (2010, August 12). Clicktivism is ruining leftist activism. *The Guardian*. https://www.theguardian.com/commentisfree/2010/aug/12/clicktivism-ruining-leftist-activism

CHAPTER 35

Peace-Building and Conflict Resolution Education

Robin Neustaeter and Jessica Senehi

The ability to draw on wisdom achieved through life experience is especially relevant to conflict resolution and peace-building skills. Often people are working to address interpersonal and intergroup conflicts, bridge differences, address social inequalities, and build community in ways that they may not name peace-building—for example, establishing and running foodbanks and women's and men's shelters, or advocating for affordable housing (Neustaeter, 2015). These experiences are significant spaces for learning peace-building and conflict resolution. UNESCO (2009) states, "Adult learning and education are a valuable investment which brings social benefits by creating more democratic, peaceful, inclusive, productive, healthy and sustainable societies" (p. 3). The purpose of this chapter is to examine peace education and conflict resolution education in relation to adult and continuing education, with specific attention on nonformal and informal learning.

Toward these ends, this chapter first clarifies the following terms: *peace, conflict, conflict resolution,* and *peace education*. Second, the linkages among adult, peace, and conflict resolution education are explored, with a focus on nonformal and informal learning. Third, community mediation and conflict resolution are discussed as less formal and informal sites of learning communication, problem-solving, and peacemaking skills. Fourth, the role of informal learning in social justice action and positive social change is examined. Fifth, dialogue processes as informal learning is explored. Finally, suggestions for the future of informal adult education and peace education are shared.

Clarifying Terminology

This chapter is grounded in four foundational concepts: peace, conflict, conflict resolution, and peace education, which are defined in the following sections.

Peace

Understandings of peace are context-dependent and informed by individual and collective current and historical experiences, popular and accepted narratives, religion, values, tradition, and cultures (Bar-Tal, 2002; Mizzi, 2010). How peace is defined informs perceptions of its presence and absence in our everyday lives, societies, and the world. In peace theory a distinction is made between *negative peace* and *positive peace*. Negative peace is the absence of war and violent conflict and the presence of sociocultural, economic, and political systems and beliefs that discriminate and oppress (Galtung, 1969, 1990). For example, while refugees from war and conflict zones flee direct violence, often they find themselves in negative peace where policies, behaviors, and beliefs discriminate against refugees and migrants, limit their rights and access to services including medical and judicial, or confine them to camps or detention centers.

Positive peace is the presence of social justice, including gender and racial equity and equality, and the equal distribution of justice, power, and wealth among individuals, families, communities, societies, and states (Brock-Utne, 1989; Galtung, 1969, 1990; Reardon, 1993; Smoker & Groff, 1996; Turay, 2005). The annual *Positive Peace Report* (Institute for Economics and Peace, 2018) conceptualizes and analyzes a scale of eight measurements (pillars) of positive peace, rather than a single static point. These pillars include a well-functioning government, equitable distribution of resources, the free flow of information, good relations with neighbors, high levels of human capital, acceptance of the rights of others, low levels of corruption, and a sound business environment. According to the Institute for Economics and Peace (2008), positive peace is associated with "better economic outcomes, measures of wellbeing, levels of gender equality and environmental performance" (p. 2). Vellacott (2000) and Lederach (1996, 1998), among others, discuss peace as an active, organic, intentional, individual, and collective peace seeking to engage and transform individuals, societies, and systems to foster and reflect positive peace. Peace is action.

Conflict

Conflict, like peace, is better known by our perceptions and experiences than by a universally accepted definition. Folger et al. (2013) define *conflict* as "the interaction of interdependent people who perceive incompatibility and the possibility of interference from others as a result of this incompatibility" (p. 4). Interdependent relationships, perception, and behavior are core interrelated elements of conflicts (Folger et al., 2013; Hocker & Wilmot, 2018). Conflict in itself is not problematic; it is the destructive, disrespectful, and violent behaviors and ideologies in response to conflict that are problematic. Conflict can clarify goals, beliefs, and relationships; strengthen relationships; and be a catalyst for change (Hocker & Wilmot, 2018).

Conflict Resolution

Broadly speaking, *conflict resolution* is the nonviolent "informal or formal process that two or more parties use to find a peaceful solution to their dispute" (Shonk, 2019, para. 2) and the theory/knowledge and analysis that inform these processes. Examples of conflict resolution include, but are not limited to, negotiation, mediation, arbitration, dialogue, and sharing circles. Awareness, analysis, and reflection of self, others, and society; values; needs; power; relationships; and behaviors that inform and ignite conflict, as well as building reflective constructive resolution skills are some elements considered in conflict resolution (Folger et al., 2013; Hocker & Wilmot, 2018).

Peace Education

Peace education is a philosophy and a process that engages learners "to empower themselves with knowledge, skills, attitudes, values and beliefs which build cultures of peace, non-violence and sustainability" (Turay, 2005, p. 465). Peace education seeks to identify, confront, and address the roots and causes of violence; to teach people alternative and constructive conflict behaviors; to transform the systems and structures within societies that maintain injustice and discrimination, and identify existing and imagine new peaceable ways of doing and being (Askerov, 2010; Bajaj, 2014; Boulding, 2000; Harris & Morrison, 2003; Reardon, 1988, 2001). Much learning for peace and conflict resolution is tacit and negotiated through experience. Peace education happens in formal, nonformal, and informal spaces for all learners (Harris, 2008; Turay, 2005). Throughout history and across cultures, peace has been the dedication to resolve conflicts without deadly force (Harris, 2008, p. 15).

Historically, most conflict resolution and peace education happens through storytelling, including historical stories, proverbs, and religious-based stories. Peace education includes human rights education, social justice education, democracy education, development education, and environmental education, to name a few. Conflict resolution education is a branch of peace education. For example, since 2009, the U.S.-based National Peace Academy (NPA) facilitates accessible and affordable learning and dialogue opportunities for community leaders and changemakers to foster healthy, sustainable, peaceable communities and address local and national sociocultural tensions (NPA, n.d.).

Adult Education, Peace-Building, and Conflict Resolution Education

In 1981, Finnish peace and adult educator Helena Kekkonen stated "peace education should be integral to adult education. Adult educators are in a decisive position for putting into practice educational work for peace" (p. 56). Adult education's goals of individual and social transformation for social justice are shared by peace education (Turay & English, 2008). Phyllis Cunningham (1991) called on adult educators to create and support spaces for critical thinking and action on injustice and social justice; she also asked whether adult educators are already doing this under a different name and to see and name their peace education as such. Around the globe, adult education, past and present, examines and addresses injustice and violence, including relational, religious, cultural, social, economic, and political. Adult education imagines and supports learning for individual, community, and societal transformation (Turay, 2005). Examples include the Highlander Research and Education Center in the United States, the Antigonish Movement and Coady International Institute in Canada, and the Swedish Folk School Movement.

Larry Fisk (2000) identified three strands of peace education applicable to adult education. First, *education about peace* emphasizes peace as the subject matter. Learning about human rights, social issues, violence, and nonviolence can increase knowledge and awareness about peace topics. Attending a workshop or presentation on human rights or a social issue, such as gender-based violence or the UN Convention 1325 of Women, Peace, and Security, informs participants about peace. Second, *education for peace* has peace as the learning goal. Continuing professional education in conflict resolution and management, negotiation, and mediation are examples of education for peace, as its goals are to build knowledge and skills in constructive and sustainable means to address conflict in relationships at home, work, and in the community. Popular education focused on social justice action aims to address injustice and bring about positive peace. Social movement learning (Choudry, 2015; Hall et al., 2012; Hall & Turay, 2006) reflects principles of education for peace, although it is rarely explicitly named as such. Education for peace includes international and cultural education though which people learn about cultures and the realities of the world and others around the globe to build tolerance and empathy. Third, *peace through education* focuses on facilitation with an andragogy informed by dialogue, participation, respect, criticality, democracy, relationship, empathy, and reflecting values of social justice; that is, the learning experience is peace (Fisk, 2000; Turay & English, 2008). Examples of peace through education are formal, nonformal, and informal collaborative learning negotiated by learners-facilitators to reflect the aforementioned values.

The goals, needs, and concerns of peace education are informed by the societal conditions in which it is happening (Bar-Tal, 2002; Harris, 2004; Turay, 2005). In war, postwar, postgenocide, interethnic and interracial conflict, and postcolonial societies the needs, goals, and concerns of educators and learners differ. Adult education can address immediate needs such as low literacy due to interrupted schooling as a result of violence and war (Boughton, 2018) and economic empowerment through cooperatives in conflict and postconflict zones (Sentama, 2009). Addressing these needs engages simultaneously in individual and community empowerment, conflict resolution learning, relationship-building, and reconciliation.

Conflict resolution education brings peace education to a more personal level to address interpersonal and community conflicts. Through socialization, everybody has learned skills and knowledge for resolving conflicts, for better or for worse (Folger et al., 2013; Hocker & Wilmot, 2018). Beliefs we hold about conflict—for example, "Conflict is bad," "I have to act first or I'll be taken advantage of," or "This is an opportunity to learn more and fix the matter"—develop over time and through our experiences with conflict. Critically reflecting on beliefs and assumptions of what conflict is, whether or not it is destructive and should be avoided, and what are appropriate and acceptable behaviors for addressing it (e.g., fighting, avoiding, or talking) can lead to new ways of thinking of and being in conflict (Braman, 1999). The desire to develop more positive and effective ways to deal with conflict at the interpersonal level, in the workplace, and in community is an impetus for many adults to pursue conflict resolution learning opportunities. For example, Cornell University, in Ithaca, New York, offers a certificate in organizational conflict management. Mediation Services, in Winnipeg, Canada, offers certificates in conflict management, mediation, and leadership.

Community Mediation and Conflict Resolution

Since the 1970s, community mediation has emerged as a major dimension of alternative dispute resolution in the United States, from a handful of early centers to more than 500 today. This development has been characterized as a social movement (Hedeen & Coy, 2005), with its own ideology (e.g., Engle Merry & Milner, 2010). Community mediation draws on a body of community volunteer mediators, who are prepared for this role through training provided by the center the volunteer is serving. All are welcome to participate in these trainings, which are often offered for free to the public. Community mediation encompasses diverse types of mediation and handles a variety of disputes, including, for example, conflicts between neighbors, as well as family mediation, divorce and custody mediation, and victim-offender mediation (e.g., Umbreit, 1995).

Community mediation is considered to have developed along two lines (Hedeen & Coy, 2005). The first branch are neighborhood justice centers, which grew out of the social movement mobilization in the 1960s, with a focus on community empowerment, of which the San Francisco Community Boards is an iconic example (e.g., Engle Merry & Milner, 2010). The second branch developed in the United States largely in response to critiques of the justice system. Throughout the world, mediation is seen as a way to alleviate the burden on the courts, especially in regions where the ratio of lawyers to citizens is very steep (e.g., Ali, 2018).

Mediation training designed and delivered by mediation centers forms a large body of inclusive adult education on conflict resolution. While some of this curriculum is set by standards for mediation certification, community mediation becomes a site for less formal and informal adult education. The core ideas in these trainings coalesce around key skills and themes, for example, communication and the role of empathy for defusing intense emotions, sensitivity to cultural contexts and power relations, and the ethics of mediation (e.g., Hedeen et al., 2010). While community mediation aims to empower individuals in the community who use its services, Edward Schwerin (1995) argues that the people who are most empowered are the mediators themselves, whose self-report of empowerment is especially high immediately after training, likely boosted by the inspirational quality of the training.

While it is more formalized in the West, mediation practice has roots in the traditional conflict resolution practices of Indigenous communities and traditional societies throughout the world. Indigenous and traditional conflict resolution rely on the leadership of elders who share a body of cultural values and practices to both teach peace and resolve conflicts (e.g., Stobbe, 2015). Although there may be a range of practices involving diverse rituals and social structures, there may be some common principles across these forms (e.g., Moore, 2014). These leaders may be informed by their own early childhood training and cultural learning—that is, a transgenerational transmission of knowledge about conflict resolution and peace through informal learning. Such informal learning has been a means for the survival of cultural practices that might have been erased and replaced by the institutions of colonizers. Now in the West, these may be taken up to address social injustice. For example, peace circles drawing on First Nations' practices in North America are used by a variety of civil society organizations in cooperation with court systems (e.g., Pranis et al., 2003). In Asia, traditional, cultural, and local forms of mediation practice simultaneously inform, coordinate, and resist state-based legal processes (Stobbe, 2018).

Social Justice Awareness and Learning
Adult education has a long tradition and practice of teaching and learning for critical thinking and reflection and effectively addressing conflict and sociocultural, political, and economic issues for individual, collective, and societal change (Brookfield & Holst, 2010; English, 2005; Freire 1970; MacKerarcher, 2004; Preskill & Brookfield, 2009). In the United States and throughout the world, movements addressing positive, nonviolent, social change in order to bring about a peace characterized by racial and economic justice and gender equality have relied on developing educational processes outside formal institutions. Social movements whether community organizing or collective action—are important sites of informal adult education, often running counter to formal education, which may emphasize different education goals or competencies. Peacebuilding and social justice work seeks to define a vision of peace and social justice, develop strategies for social change, and use teaching approaches that put into practice the principles of peace they espouse—that is, as Fisk (2000) would put it, education about peace, for peace, and through peace.

A historic example of this peace educational process can be located in 1932 Tennessee, where the Highlander Folk School was established to build civic and political leadership for democratic social change (Horton, 1990; Schneider, 2014) and train people like Martin Luther King Jr. and Rosa Parks. Working toward social change often runs counter to existing power structures and norms and requires an alternative space for colearners who want to be a part of such a project. MacLean (1966) reported that the Highlander Folk School faced "systematic abuse and misrepresentation" (p. 489) from critics because it challenged the norms of segregation. The school's charter was revoked by the legislature on February 16, 1960, due to three arguably spurious, or at least minor charges. In 1961, the founders of the Folk School were granted a charter from the state of Tennessee to open the Highlander Research and Education Center (MacLean, 1966).

After years of activist work, Rosa Parks was renewed and inspired by workshops at Highlander with Septima Clark and others (Theoharis, 2013). Parks drew on what she learned in these workshops in her historically significant act of resisting racism and racialization by not relinquishing her seat on the bus to a male youth, demonstrating the impact of this type of alternative educational space. Rosa Parks is one of four citizens to ever lie in honor in the U.S. Capitol Rotunda. Social action that had its roots in resistance to the status quo and alternative adult education prevailed and became a symbol and standard for the highest values of the nation.

Some education and training centers explicitly envision a peaceful and just society. For example, in Philadelphia, Training for Change (2018) provides training for "social justice and radical change" (para. 1) to activists and organizers. They focus on strengthening facilitation and training skills for people from numerous civil society organizations working on environmental issues, racial justice, gender and LGBTQ rights, and food justice, among others. Training for Change uses the *direct education* approach, developed by Quaker activist and sociologist George Lakey, that builds on participants' experience and direction in the learning process and their accessing their own wisdom (Training for Change, 2018). The Southern Poverty Law Center (2019), established in 1971 by Morris Dees, publishes resources that educators and others can access at no cost on the topic of teaching tolerance. In their training, social justice organizations raise awareness with evidence-based information about social issues. They draw on educational methods that are considered peaceful because, following Freire, they reject the notion of a teacher depositing knowledge into a passive student and are characterized by inclusion, shared power, and a sense of who should benefit from education (Horton & Freire, 1990).

Intergroup Dialogue and Building Peace

Throughout the world, civil society organizations provide training for facilitating dialogue around social concerns and issues (e.g., Saunders, 1999; van Tongeren et al., 2005). Sustained Dialogue (SD) is an intergroup peace-building process, developed by the late U.S. diplomat Harold Saunders (1999), envisioned as a "political process to change conflictual relationships" (p. 88) with five stages: deciding to engage, mapping and naming problems and relationships, probing problems and relationships to choose a direction, scenario-building to experience a changing relationship, and acting together to make change happen. The Sustained Dialogue Institute (2018), established by Saunders in collaboration with the Kettering Foundation, is considered a hub for sustained dialogue training in the United States and globally.

In another example, the Kettering Foundation (2019) holds a Deliberate Democracy Institute every summer in Dayton, Ohio, for participants from around the world, with a focus on "exploring the idea of a deliberative public and considering new ways for organizing political work in communities" (para. 7). The Institutes are "learning exchanges" (Kettering Foundation, 2019, para. 1) on critical issues, where the presenters share information that the foundation has developed over many years and participants share their experiences and insights. Other approaches taught and practiced through less formal community-based organizations include Deep Democracy, which values the minority voice, and World Café, which provides a process for intimate conversations among larger groups, among numerous other approaches (Pioneers of Change, 2006).

Where there are people building peace who are working in innovative ways to develop knowledge and skills, there is less formal and informal education to identify and share these skills. The Forgiveness Project, based in London, the United Kingdom, provides programming, training, and educational resources bringing people together, in the aftermath of trauma, to tell their stories and seek mutual understanding (Cantacuzino, 2016). The Green String Network (2018), working mostly in South Sudan and Somalia, developed a trauma-informed resilience framework. Community members are trained, and then train others in the community to understand and address the impact of trauma and political violence. Such community-based training makes it possible to provide mental health care and other necessary support in a social crisis. Such a context is considered to be a *complex emergency*, that is, "a social catastrophe marked by the destruction of the affected population's political, economic, sociocultural, [formal educational], and healthcare infrastructures" (Mollica et al., 2004, p. 2058).

The arts have also been a means of informal education about social issues. These have taken the form of theater, storytelling, and photography to create a kind of virtual dialogue. Approaches such as theater of the oppressed (Boal, 1992), and its offshoots—theater for living (Diamond, 2007); theater for community, conflict, and dialogue (Rohd, 1998); and dramatic problem-solving (Hawkins, 2012)—blend theater and popular education. In theater of witness, participants work with and develop stories based on their own lives that become the basis of a play that is then shared with others (Sepinuck, 2013). Another example is the Winnipeg International Storytelling Festival in Canada, which reaches thousands of students in grades kindergarten through 12 each year and seeks to promote crosscultural storytelling and students' peacemaking skills through StoryShops and StoryShows (Senehi, 2013). The festival's school program provides informal learning for teachers who bring their students to the festival, a few of whom enrolled in graduate programs in related areas. The festival's public program offers workshops on storytelling for peacebuilding for adults.

Throughout the world, there are people who have developed grassroots organizations and/or innovative projects for peacebuilding. Most of these involve an aspect of training and public education. Because conflict involves differences in understanding, and because peace requires changing insights, peace can be seen as interconnected with knowledge and colearning. That is, experiences of sustained dialogue are education. As has been said, power often precedes knowledge (e.g., Foucault, 1972/1993). Less formal and informal education can provide a liberating environment for those marginalized from mainstream knowledge systems—such as academia (e.g., Foucault, 1972/1993; Franklin, 1978), the high arts (Bakhtin, 1986; Said, 1993), and Western journalism (e.g., Gugelberger & Kearney, 1991; Randall, 1991)—to shape social thought and action.

Concluding Thoughts

As the goal of peace and conflict resolution education is to foster responsible and respectful relations, address injustices, and create and nurture social justice and collaboration, it is imperative that such learning critically engage, bring in and bring up diverse actors, thinking, and voices. This requires critically examining how peacebuilding and conflict resolution are racialized, genderized, heteronormative, classed, and ableist (Byrne et al., 2017; Dueck-Read, 2016, 2018; Mizzi & Byrne, 2015); and the positionality of curriculum, educators, and learners. Identifying how conflict resolution and peace education are racialized, gendered, and stratified by class is crucial to moving toward the diversity that accounts for the plethora of lived knowledges, practices, and experiences that exist.

Civil society organizations and peace institutes are taking peace and conflict resolution learning online via webinars, podcasts, games, workshops, and courses. Examples include offerings by the U.S. Institute of Peace Academy, the Rotary Positive Peace Academy (in partnership with the Institute for Peace Economics), and the Global Human Rights Education and Training Centre. Online learning presents new education opportunities for peace and conflict resolution practitioners and educators. Comparable critical analysis of learning theories and practice of face-to-face learning need to be applied to online learning. While online learning can address some concerns such as accessibility, including more flexible scheduling and reduced costs for travel, other challenges remain, such as access to the required hardware (computer, tablet, or smartphone), software, reliable electricity and internet, and state censorship.

Peace-building and conflict resolution education are significant to individual and collective learning for individual, community, and societal transformation. This learning informs and is informed by adult education concepts and practice. Within adult and continuing education this learning explicitly exists in small pockets, past and present, also found in social movement learning (Hall et al., 2012; Hall & Turay, 2006) and community development learning (English & Irving, 2015; Kane, 2010). In a world where the ongoing call for peace and transformation of conflict resounds, recognizing how adult education can advance peace and conflict resolution is paramount for social transformation.

References

Ali, S. (2018). *Court mediation reform: Efficiency, confidence and perceptions of justice.* Edward Elgar.

Askerov, A. (2010). Peace education and conflict resolution: A critical review. *Innovative Issues and Approaches in Social Sciences, 3*(1), 5–35. https://libres.uncg.edu/ir/uncg/f/A_Askerov_Peace_2010.pdf

Bajaj, M. (2014). "Pedagogies of resistance" and critical peace education praxis. *Journal of Peace Education, 12*(2), 154–166. https://doi.org/10.1080/17400201.2014.991914

Bakhtin, M. (1986). *Speech genres and other late essays.* University of Texas Press.

Bar-Tal, D. (2002). The elusive nature of peace education. In G. Salomon & B. Nevo (Eds.), *Peace education: The concept, principles and practice in the world* (pp. 27–36). Lawrence Erlbaum.

Boal, A. (1992). *Games for actors and non-actors* (2nd ed.) (A. Jackson, Trans.). Routledge.

Boughton, B. (2018). Timor-Leste: Adult literacy, population education and post-conflict peacebuilding. In M. Milana, S. Webb, J. Holford, R. Waller, & P. Jarvis (Eds.), *The Palgrave international handbook on adult and lifelong education and learning* (pp. 629–647). Palgrave Macmillan.

Boulding, E. (2000). *Cultures of peace: The hidden side of history.* Syracuse University Press.

Braman, O. R. (1999). Teaching peace to adults: Using critical thinking to improve conflict resolution. *Adult Learning, 10*(2), 30–32.

Brock-Utne, B. (1989). *Feminist perspectives on peace and peace education.* Pergamon Press.

Brookfield, S. D., & Holst, J. D. (2010). *Radicalizing learning: Adult education for a just world.* Wiley.

Byrne, S., Mizzi, R.C., & Hansen, N. (2017). Living in a liminal peace: Where is social justice for LGBTQ and disability communities living in post peace accord Northern Ireland? *Journal for Peace and Justice Studies, 27*(1), 24–51.

Cantacuzino, M. (2016). *Forgiveness project: Stories for a vengeful age.* Jessica Kingsley.

Choudry, A. (2015). *Learning activism: The intellectual life of contemporary social movements.* University of Toronto Press.

Cunningham, P. (1991). What's the role of adult educators? *Adult Learning, 3*(1), 15–16, 27.

Diamond, D. (2007). *Theatre for living: The art and science of community-based dialogue.* Trafford Publishing.

Dueck-Read, J. (2016). *Transnational activism: Intersectional identities and peacebuilding in the border justice movement* [Unpublished doctoral dissertation]. University of Manitoba.

Dueck-Read, J. (2018). Racialized and gendered peacebuilding in the U.S.–Mexico border justice movement. In L. E. Reimer, K. Standish, & C. Thiessen (Eds.), *Conflict transformation, peacebuilding, and storytelling: Research from the Mauro Centre* (pp. 127–142). Lexington Books.

Engle Merry, S., & Milner, N. (Eds.). (2010). *The possibility of popular justice: A case study of community mediation in the United States.* University of Michigan Press.

English, L. M. (2005). Third-space practitioners: Women educating for justice in the global south. *Adult Education Quarterly, 55*(2), 85–100.

English, L. M., & Irving, C. J. (2015). *Feminism in community: Adult education for transformation.* Sense.

Fisk, L. J. (2000). Shaping visionaries. In J. Schellenberg & L. Fisk (Ed.), *Patterns of conflict, paths to peace* (pp. 159–193). Broadview Press.

Folger, J., Poole, M. S., & Stutman, R. K. (2013). *Working through conflict: Strategies for relationships, groups, and organizations.* Routledge.

Foucault, M. (1993). *The archaeology of knowledge and the discourse on language* (A. M. Sheridan Smith, Trans.). Barnes and Noble. (Original work published 1972)

Franklin, B. H. (1978). *The victim as criminal and artist: Literature from the American prison.* Oxford University Press.

Freire, P. (1970). *Pedagogy of the oppressed.* Continuum.

Galtung, J. (1969). Violence, peace, and peace research. *Journal of Peace Research, 6*(3), 167–191.

Galtung, J. (1990). Cultural violence. *Journal of Peace Research, 27*(3), 291–305.

Green String Network. (2018). *Our approach.* https://www.green-string.org/approach

Gugelberger, G., & Kearney, M. (1991). Voices for the voiceless: Testimonial literature in Latin America. *Latin American Perspectives, 18*(3), 3–14.

Hall, B. L., Clover, D. E., Crowther, J. I. M., & Scandrett E. (Eds.). (2012). *Learning and education for a better world: The role of social movements.* Sense.

Hall, B. L., & Turay, T. (2006). *A review of the state of the field of adult learning: Social movement learning.* Canadian Council on Learning. http://en.copian.ca/library/research/sotfr/socialmv/socialmv.pdf

Harris, I. (2004). Peace education theory. *Journal of Peace Education, 1*(1), 5–20. https://doi.org/10.1080/1740020032000178276

Harris, I. (2008). History of peace education. In M. Bajaj, (Ed.), *Encyclopedia of peace education* (pp. 15–23). Information Age.

Harris, I., & Morrison, M. (2003). *Peace education.* McFarland.

Hawkins, S. T. (2012). *Dramatic problem solving: Drama-based group exercises for conflict transformation.* Jessica Kingsley.

Hedeen, T., & Coy, P. (2005). A stage model of social movement co-optation: Community mediation in the United States. *The Sociological Quarterly, 46*(3), 405–435. https://doi.org/10.1111/j.1533-8525.2005.00020.x

Hedeen, T., Raines, S., & Barton, A. (2010). Foundations of mediation training: A literature review of adult education and training design. *Conflict Resolution Quarterly, 26*(2), 157–182. https://doi/libproxy.stfx.ca/10.1002/crq.20018

Hocker, J., & Wilmot, W. (2018). *Interpersonal conflict* (10th ed.). McGraw-Hill.

Horton, M. (1990). *The long haul: An autobiography.* Doubleday.

Horton, M., & Freire, P. (1990). *We make the road by walking: Conversations on education and change.* Temple University Press.

Institute for Economics and Peace. (2018). *Positive peace report 2018.* http://visionofhumanity.org/app/uploads/2018/11/Positive-Peace-Report-2018.pdf

Kane, L. (2010). Community development: Learning from popular education in Latin America. *Community Development Journal, 45*(3), 276–286. https://doi.org/10.1093/cdj/bsq021

Kekkonen, H. (1981). Peace education is integral to adult education. *Convergence, 14*(4), 53–58.

Kettering Foundation. (2019). *Deliberative Democracy Institute.* https://www.kettering.org/shared-learning/ddi

Lederach, J. P. (1996). *Preparing for peace.* Syracuse University Press.

Lederach, J. P. (1998). *Building peace: Sustainable reconciliation in divided societies.* United States Institute of Peace Press.

MacKerarcher, D. (2004). *Making sense of adult learners.* University of Toronto Press.

MacLean, K. T. (1966). Myles Horton and the Highlander Folk School. *The Phi Delta Kappan, (47)*9, 487–489.

Mizzi, R. C. (2010). Let's get this straightened out: Finding a place and presence for sexual/gender identity-difference in peace education. *Journal of Peace Education 7*(2), 139–156.

Mizzi, R. C., & Byrne, S. (2015). Queer theory and peace and conflict studies: Some critical reflections. In M. Flaherty, S. Byrne, H. Tuso, & T. Matyok (Eds.), *Gender and peacebuilding: All hands required* (pp. 359–374). Lexington Books.

Mollica, R. F., Cardoza, B. L., Osofsky, H. J., Raphael, B., Ager, A., & Salama P. (2004). Mental health in complex emergencies. *Lancet, 364*(9450), 2058–67. https://doi.org/10.1016/S0140-6736(04)17519-3

Moore, C. W. (2014). *The mediation process* (4th ed.). Jossey-Bass.

National Peace Academy (NPA). (n.d). *About us.* https://nationalpeaceacademy.us/about-us

Neustaeter, R. (2015). "It's not the icing, it's the glue": Rural women's volunteering in Manitoba, Canada. In M. Flaherty, S. Byrne, H. Tuso, & T. Matyok (Eds.), *Gender and peacebuilding: All hands required* (pp. 195–212). Lexington.

Pioneers of Change. (2006). *Mapping dialogue.* Nelson Mandela Foundation.

Pranis, K., Stuart, B., & Wedge, M. (2003). *Peacemaking circles: From crime to community.* Living Justice Press.

Preskill, S., & Brookfield, S. D. (2009). *Learning as a way of leading: Lessons from the struggle for social justice.* Jossey-Bass.

Randall, M. (1991). Reclaiming voices: Notes on new females practices in journalism. *Latin American Perspectives, 18*(3), 103–113.

Reardon, B. (1988). *Comprehensive peace education: Educating for global responsibility.* Teachers College Press.

Reardon, B. (1993). *Women and peace: Feminist visions of global security.* SUNY Press.

Reardon, B. A. (2001). *Education for a culture of peace in a gender perspective.* UNESCO.

Rohd, M. (1998). *Theatre for community, conflict & dialogue: The hope is vital training manual.* Heinemann.

Said, E. W. (1993). *Culture and imperialism.* Alfred A. Knopf.

Saunders, H. H. (1999). *A public peace process: Sustained dialogue to transform social and ethnic conflicts.* St. Martin's Press.

Schneider, S. A. (2014). *You can't padlock an idea: Rhetorical education at the Highlander Folk School, 1932–1961.* University of North Carolina Press.

Schwerin, E. (1995). *Mediation, citizen empowerment, and transformation.* Praeger.

Senehi, J. (2013). Storytelling on the path to peace. *English Quarterly, 44*(1–22), 117–126.

Sentama, E. (2009). *Peacebuilding in post-genocide Rwanda: The role of cooperatives in the restoration of interpersonal relationships.* University of Gothenburg.

Sepinuck, T. (2013). *Theatre of witness: Finding the medicine in stories of suffering, transformation, and peace.* Jessica Kingsley.

Shonk, K. (2019). *What is conflict resolution, and how does it work? How to manage conflict at work through conflict resolution.* Program on Negotiation: Daily Blog. https://www.pon.harvard.edu/daily/conflict-resolution/what-is-conflict-resolution-and-how-does-it-work/

Smoker, P., & Groff, L. (1996). Creating global-local cultures of peace. *Peace and Conflict Studies, 3*(1), 3–40. https://nsuworks.nova.edu/cgi/viewcontent.cgi?article=1170&context=pcs/

Southern Poverty Law Center. (2019). *Teaching tolerance.* https://www.tolerance.org

Stobbe, S. P. (2015). *Conflict resolution and peacebuilding in Laos: Perspective for today's world.* Routledge.

Stobbe, S. P. (Ed.). (2018). *Conflict resolution in Asia: Mediation and other cultural models.* Lexington Books.

Sustained Dialogue Institute. (2018). *Our work.* https://sustaineddialogue.org/our-work

Theoharis, J. (2013). *The rebellious life of Mrs. Rosa Parks.* Beacon.

Training for Change. (2018). *Direct education.* https://www.trainingforchange.org/about/#direct-education

Turay, T. (2005). Peace education. In L. M. English (Ed.), *International encyclopedia of adult education* (pp. 465–467). Palgrave Macmillan.

Turay, T., & English, L. (2008). Toward a global culture of peace: A transformative model of peace education. *Journal of Transformative Education, 6*(4), 286–301. https://doi.org/10.1177/1541344608330602

Umbreit, M. (1995). *Mediating interpersonal conflicts: A pathway to peace.* CPI Publishing.

UNESCO. (2009). *Harnessing the power and potential of adult learning and education for a viable future: Belém framework for action.* https://unesdoc.unesco.org/ark:/48223/pf0000181414

van Tongeren, P., Brenk, M., Hellema, M., & Verhoeven, J. (Eds.). (2005). *People building peace II: Successful stories of civil society.* European Centre for Conflict Prevention.

Vellacott, J. (2000). Dynamic peace and the practicalities of pacifism. In L. J. Fisk, & J. L. Schellenberg (Eds.), *Patterns of conflict, paths to peace* (pp. 202–205). Broadview Press.

PART FIVE

CONTEMPORARY ISSUES

CHAPTER 36

Decolonizing Adult Education

Cindy Hanson and JoAnn Jaffe

Colonization is a complex, historical process in which political and economic systems wield power over other nations or groups and appropriate their land and resources. Colonization thus involves the subjugation of one people over another where both the colonizer and the colonized are agents in a contradictory relationship. According to Memmi (1956/1991), colonization transforms the subjectivities of both colonizer and colonized by enlisting them in oppositional relations of domination and subordination in which each is convinced and complicit in their role. This oppositional relationship is maintained through a cultural, educational, and psychological hegemony in which the colonized come to believe in their own inferiority and that they must become Whiter (Fanon, 1967); they gain self-worth and prestige to the degree they come to adopt the culture of the colonizers (Fanon, 1967; Memmi, 1956/1991; Rodney, 1973). According to Du Bois (1903/1996), the oppressed come to internalize the subjectivities of both sides of the antagonistic relationship, resulting in *double consciousness* or *two-ness*, in which the dominator's hatred and disdain is felt in the very center of the oppressed's awareness.

Socially, colonization conveys the "mark of the plural" (Memmi, 1956/1991, p. 129) onto dominated populations through its handmaidens: racism, classism, and sexism, via binary and hierarchical discourses that characterize individuals using stereotypical, generic qualities of the collective. Collins (1990) noted that archetypes form around clusters of these qualities—creating, for example, the Mammy and the Jezebel in the case of White characterizations of Black women—which are then put to work in political goals.

Colonization usually involves the resettlement of populations new to the colonized place, but typically many are people who have been disadvantaged, but whose movement serves the interests of the colonizing power. (Dis)advantage and (dis)privilege still attach to historical categories created by colonialization, including former enslaved Africans, Indigenous peoples, housewives (Mies, 1986), low-wage workers, family farmers, and newcomer populations. However, although some people may be dominated—for example, farmers, workers, or women, or due to their ethnicity—they are often also enlisted in the colonization project via their identification with the colonizer. Education plays a key role in this (Willinsky, 1998).

Western colonization is maintained through a hegemony that positions the dominant Western spiritual, ontological, and epistemological positions on knowledge as superior. While the details are shaped by location and history, since the 1500s, Western colonization and its impact cannot be separated from the development of capitalism and nation-states, the Enlightenment, science, patriarchy, evangelism, and White supremacy. Colonial structures, such as institutions, languages, and doctrines, work to undermine and destroy beliefs, symbols, values, and epistemologies of the colonized to establish universal models that are prejudged as modern and rational (Quijano, 2007). All non–colonial-derived methodologies or beliefs are thus stigmatized as irrational and in need of change, but their existence helps to legitimize the superiority of the colonizers' authority. Thiong'o (1986) characterized this process as a *cultural bomb* that "annihilate[s] a people's belief in their names, in their languages, in their environment, in their heritage of struggle, in their unity, in their capacities and ultimately in themselves. It makes them see their past as one wasteland of nonachievement" (p. 3). Colonial institutions and models of education added to and supplanted earlier systems of learning—both formal and informal. The racist, capitalist, and patriarchal biases and orientations implicit in the colonial paradigm have been instilled into the (hidden) curriculum and an education that advanced the values, virtues, culture, and practices of the West, as Rodney (1973) argued: "Colonial schooling [is] education for subordination, exploitation, the creation of mental confusion and the development of underdevelopment" (p. 61).

In *Education for Self-Reliance*, former teacher and founding president of Tanzania, Julius Nyerere (1968), similarly argued that Tanzania's colonial educational system

> was motivated by a desire to inculcate the values of the colonial society and to train individuals for service of the colonial state. . . . It was a deliberate attempt to change values and to replace traditional knowledge with the knowledge from a different society. (pp. 416–417)

For Nyerere and other scholars from the Global South, colonial education, including adult education, played a central role in upholding systems of hierarchy and inequality and supported the domination of the weak by the strong—socially, politically, and, especially, economically. But Nyerere (1976) argued that adult education that inspires and creates social change plays a critical role in decolonizing society.

While there are legitimate accomplishments of Western ways of knowing, it is imperative to challenge the epistemic injustice resulting from colonization. Maori scholar L. Tuhiwai Smith (2012) explains that Indigenous populations continue to be subordinated and *othered* because universalisms used in colonial structures, including educational institutions, construct colonized peoples and their knowledge as intrinsically different, threatening, superstitious, and incorrect. Because decolonizing education means examining who speaks for whom (Spivak, 1994); how knowledge about *others* is expressed, understood, and valued (Said, 1978); and how knowledge is embedded in colonial systems of meaning and power, the decolonizing journey is never straightforward. In the absence of a decolonizing shift, all forms of education—including adult and continuing education (ACE)—contribute to the oppression of colonized populations (Battiste, 2013) and to devaluing diverse knowledge systems.

Decolonizing methodologies involve confronting positionality. In this regard, the contributors to this chapter, who hold different immigrant-ally positions, acknowledge that origins and identities are complex, nuanced, and dynamic. We both work in solidarity with a range of groups whose goals are linked to decolonization. For the sake of representation and, as Regan (2010) states, of unsettling the settler project, we acknowledge our positions in the process of decolonizing ACE.

Decolonizing Approaches to ACE

Decolonizing ACE involves deconstructing colonial systems of knowledge by rewriting, rethinking, and reassessing how we teach, learn, and conduct research. Decolonizing can strengthen the field of ACE because it builds on principles of equity, epistemic pluralism, and social justice. It remains challenging to do this, however, because colonial practices are built into structures such as the state and church from which adult education emerged. In this section, four distinct approaches to decolonization are discussed: liberal, emancipatory, sentimental, and emerging. These approaches are not straightforward but meander like tributaries of a river—each constituting different ideas, at times coming together in confluence and shared view, and other times diverging.

Liberal approaches tend to see the problem of colonization as one of exclusion and misrepresentation of marginalized groups and knowledge. Solutions are to be found, therefore, in diversity, inclusion, and representation, both of people and texts. Ironically, liberal approaches see the endpoint of decolonizing ACE as bringing marginalized individuals into the mainstream, positing this will create inclusion for the whole underrepresented group. Many extension programs are liberal in approach.

Emancipatory approaches view decolonization as an ongoing disruption of colonization and essential to creating education as the "practice of freedom" (Freire, 1970, p. 60). In this case, decolonizing education takes the form of a collective process aimed at transforming political and socioeconomic structures and healing relations ruptured by domination and subordination. Women-only labor schools aimed at transforming male-dominated union leadership are an example of an emancipatory approach (Hanson et al., 2019).

Sentimental approaches contain nostalgia for a lost past and may see the answer to the ills of colonization as being a return to the knowledge and relationships of precolonization or, conversely, may understand colonization as an unabashed good. Many museum education programs that glorify pioneer experiences are examples of this.

As discussed in the following sections, new or *emerging approaches* are arising from Indigenous, African American, feminist, and other decolonizing spaces (Grace, 2013; Gregorčič, 2009; Hall & Tandon, 2017; hooks, 1994). These four approaches—emancipatory, liberal, sentimental, and emerging—are not mutually exclusive in their theorization or practice; rather, the sociohistorical embeddedness of ACE means that any actuality of decolonization will emerge as a mixture of approaches.

As Indigenization emerged as a challenge to dominant Western systems of knowledge, Afrocentrism developed "as an attempt to reclaim a sense of identity, community, and power in the face of Eurocentric cultural hegemony" (Guy, 1996, p. 21). Indigenization and Afrocentricity share many of the same premises and prescribe similar remedies to address hegemonic and colonizing practices in ACE. They also demonstrate how tensions between liberal and emancipatory approaches to ACE may emerge in attempts to deal with the social legacy of colonization. In the African American movement, this is reflected in the contrast between the educational philosophies of Booker T. Washington and W. E. B. Du Bois.

Washington (1903) supported racial solidarity but argued that self-help and accommodation to the racial status quo would be necessary until Black people could gain respect from Whites through patience, hard work, thrift, and training in crafts, farming, and industrial skills. In contrast, Du Bois (1903) contended Washington's approach would serve to condemn Black people to permanent second-class status; he argued instead that education must support social change, political action, and civil rights. His solution was to utilize the abilities of the "talented tenth," that fraction who could use their advantages, access to higher education, and office to uplift their less fortunate brethren. These debates are echoed today in arguments between Black conservatives who continue to endorse individual self-help approaches, and Black activist educators, such as hooks (1994) and Collins (1990), who promote emancipatory approaches to education.

Indigenous resistance to colonial education continues to emerge organically, as seen in revolutionary movements of the Zapatistas in Mexico and campesinos in Honduras (Gregorčič, 2009). Western knowledges are fragmented, homogenous forms of knowing very different from the Indigenous or emerging pedagogies discussed by Gregorčič (2009), who notes that revolutionary movements in Mexico "have begun to develop non-Cartesian and anti-capitalist approaches to pedagogy that invigorate collective work, imagination, human creativity, and human capital" (p. 357). These autonomous forms of community-based education, called *potencias,* demonstrate how diverse knowledges can be developed and shared, even in adverse situations.

Historical Examples From ACE

In the past, ACE participated in colonizing adult learners largely because it operated within domains financed and led by state- and church-related institutions. State-sponsored programs operate mainly as formal and nonformal education systems, but informal adult learning, such as individual learning on the internet, may also have colonizing impacts. As will be explained, examples of ACE programs that have colonizing elements include extension programs, citizenship education, literacy programs, community development, lifelong learning, labor education, cooperative education, religious education, and women's clubs. These ACE programs were supported by legislation and postsecondary institutions, which, among other things, denied Indigenous spirituality (Atleo, 2013), non-Western curricula, and community-centered leadership.

Extension Programs and Development

Today, the largest ACE organization in the United States is the Cooperative Extension System (CES) (Franz

& Townson, 2008). Started in 1914, CES works on behalf of land-grant universities and colleges. Initially, the programs focused on agriculture, home economics, and, later, 4-H and had a racialized character due to the segregated admissions and geographic concentration of land-grant universities in 1862, historically Black colleges and universities in 1890, and the 1994 expansion into tribal colleges and universities. Within the CES, educational approaches vary from traditional content transmission to more transformational models, although Franz (2007) asserts more participatory learning in extension is required.

In Canada, extension programs generally replicated examples from Oxford and Cambridge universities, which offered courses to a wider constituency of learners using less traditional methods (Welton, 2013). Still, Welton's characterization of the men who carried out these efforts as "pioneers and pedagogues" (p. 95) and his descriptions of their predominantly Christian values and passion for science-based, Western models of farming clearly paint a sentimental picture of settler-colonialism. Despite their differences, both U.S. and Canadian models of extension continued to promote colonized knowledge systems by being embedded in conventional epistemologies and ontologies of scientific disciplines and oriented toward a gendered and racialized public and private divide, and by following the archetype of capitalist modernity as its goal.

Internationally, health and agricultural extension activities continue to be the primary means of ACE in rural and remote locations, but many remain colonial replications from the North despite being critical to development projects (Boughton, 2016). Recently, the combination of fiscal restraint, cultural concerns, and widespread need have allowed the emergence of participatory and hybrid extension practices that combine local and Western knowledge, although the degree to which they are emancipatory is undetermined. In general, however, both health and agricultural extension are dominated by corporate entities and promote private sector practices (IAASTD, 2009).

Lifelong Learning: From Communities to Commodities

Cunningham (2000) describes lifelong learning as divisive and concerned with "commodity production not quality of living" (p. 579). This reflects a shift in emphasis, from ACE with an essential philosophy of empowerment and programs that focused on working in communities to a market-based, cost-recovery model of lifelong learning, with individuals from the community coming to the university. Thus, ACE, as originally linked to social welfare and community development, shifted to lifelong learning, which is often linked to neoliberalism.

Although some adult educators advocate taking more critical approaches to lifelong learning (Grace, 2013; Guo & Maitra, 2019), UNESCO's emphasis on lifelong learning demonstrates how the move was institutionalized at international levels. Widely criticized for replicating Western ideological assumptions and having a weak epistemological and pedagogical foundation (Finger & Asun, 2001), lifelong learning is increasingly situated as a credentializing practice with considerable emphasis on individualized, cost-recovery programs, not on community engagement. An example of this is the building of colonial identities among transnational migrants who are uncritically assimilated into Western, lifelong molds of citizenship education (Guo & Maitra, 2019).

Social Justice and Worker's Education

Some of the earliest forms of nonformal education aimed at decolonizing communities and workplaces built on hierarchical, capitalist management-worker relations and their associated discriminations came out of the labor movement. By the early 1900s, education for democracy and improved socioeconomic conditions resonated clearly. Among labor educators, however, ideological conflicts—particularly between social democrats and socialists/communists—led to undermining labor education overall. Brookwood Labor College, New York (established 1921) had a curriculum centered on labor, social justice, and peace, but floundered due to the declining militancy of its supporting union. These clashes were not restricted to the United States.

The Workers' Education Association (WEA) in the United Kingdom (established in 1903) was plagued by ideological clashes. The WEA made inroads into Canada and, by the mid-1940s, sponsored labor education including courses, radio broadcasts, study circles, summer schools, and university-level courses (Spencer & Taylor, 2006). Its support also waned when it was denounced as communist-oriented. A more radical Canadian example is Frontier College, started in 1899 by Alfred Fitzpatrick, who believed educated workers could change power relations in their workplaces.

Canadian socialist parties and the Industrial Workers of the World taught them that "capitalist exploitation was the source of workers' ills" (Taylor, 2001, p. 13).

The divide between adult education with its civic goals and the class goals of labor education were identified by A. J. Muste, faculty chair of Brookwood Labor College (Rose & Jeris, 2011). Other early examples of labor education included the Wisconsin School for Workers (started 1925); the Highlander Institute (started 1932); and the University and College Labor Education Association (started 1960s). The latter merged in 2000 with the Workers Education Local #189 (a union for labor educators started in the 1920s) to develop the United Association for Labor Education.

Proactive politicized labor education is still needed to examine critically the way unions are adapting to liberal ideas of diversity and hegemonic neoliberal discourse (Briskin, 2013). Movement-building education in unions is largely a form of emancipatory education with Freirean and popular education roots. Popular education is thus designed to deepen consciousness-raising and build critical awareness among workers about collective oppression. Individualism, increasingly pervasive in ACE contexts, is challenged when educators work collectively and toward movement building.

Women's Clubs and Institutes

In North America, the Progressive Era (1890–1930) saw reform movements with strong ACE components focused on and often initiated by marginalized groups. Many of these efforts continue to this day. In Canada, Women's Institutes developed in the early 20th century primarily to support rural women. Most of the learning was in hygiene and homemaking. By the 1980s, the Federated Women's Institutes of Canada "was speaking out on pornography, violence against women, reproductive technology, and abortion" (Carbert, 1996, p. 21), while the local chapters were singing hymns and reading scriptures. Their role in women's history, particularly for rural women, was central and the values were entrenched in the colonialism of the day, as this quote illustrates:

> At one time membership in the Women's Institute (WI) marked a rite of passage for women in rural Canada. New brides typically received a year's free membership in the local branch of the WI and thus were introduced into a women's world of home-making, teas, and community service. (Carbert, 1996, p. 21)

In the United States, the Black women's club movement began in the 1890s in response to intensified racism and as an alternative to segregated White women's clubs (Parker, 2010). The first clubs followed the philosophy of Du Bois and understood the problems of Black people were caused by unjust social structures; club women were thus involved in projects of sociopolitical transformation, such as advocating for suffrage and antilynching laws, fighting against antimiscegenation, and creating social welfare institutions for children, women, and the elderly. They supported their own education through a variety of nonformal educational clubs, including civic and literary clubs, wherein women read, discussed, debated, and wrote articles and literary works. Mothers' clubs promoted economic self-sufficiency for poorer and rural Black women, along with refinement in child-rearing, home-making, and character development (Powell, 2014). Black women's clubs played an important role in the formation of other Black civil rights organizations, such as the NAACP. The Black women's clubs ideology of "racial uplift" (Powell, 2014, para. 3) expressed the deep ambiguities and contradictions in which Black and other colonized women may still find themselves as they strive to improve their conditions.

Intergenerational Impacts

Similar to the segregation of Black students in the United States and Canada, governments and churches engaged in a process of assimilation of Indigenous peoples through compulsory schooling—the most notorious being Indian Residential Schools, which lasted into the 1990s. Segregation in schools officially ended in both Canada and the United States in 1954, but as late as 1994 the Black Learners Advisory Committee in Canada noted poor achievement, high dropout rates, high unemployment, and institutional racism in communities previously segregated (Brigham, 2013).

For Indigenous students, colonial education took the form of religious or secular education that aimed to assimilate the student and deny them citizenship rights (Tuhiwai Smith, 2012). Intergenerational impacts of residential schools began when children were removed from their families, causing trauma, grief, and long-term irreconcilable senses of loss to families and communities. Where, traditionally, Indigenous communities shared responsibility for children's well-being, the schools taught Christian and patriarchal values (Monture-Angus, 2014). The school's survivors sometimes internalized experiences and reentered communities with negatively learned behaviors (Harrison, 2009), perpetuating colonial violence.

The scope of the intergenerational residential schools' legacy continues to be broad and devastating, as documented in the Truth and Reconciliation Commission of Canada Report (2015) and its 94 calls to action. The calls challenge workplaces, postsecondary institutions, and settler populations to move beyond denial and guilt and to take political and social action (Regan, 2010), including Indigenizing and decolonizing postsecondary institutions. In this, they follow Tuhiwai Smith's (2012) recommendation that attention be paid to "what counts as knowledge, as language, as curriculum and as the role of intellectuals" (p. 68).

Transforming Adult Education

Although ACE in North America widely embraces community activism and social movements, it also struggles with contradictions that reinforce colonial values and worldviews. For colonial legacies to end, educators are called upon to trouble histories of unequal relations (e.g., Indigenous–settler relations) and engage in postcolonial commitments, such as disrupting colonial patterns through attention to reciprocity, reconciliation, reflexivity, and equity (Hanson, 2018).

Emerging pedagogies offer sites for learning decolonization and the development of more reflexive practices. We suggest that examining practices at the interplay of knowledge and power from other locations can build efforts toward decolonization. Potential sites for decolonizing theories and pedagogies are heeding attention to contextualized, local knowledge sources, and via knowledge solidarities, epistemic justice (Jaffe, 2017), and participatory methodologies, including those emerging from social movements.

Knowledge Solidarities and Epistemic Pluralism
Decolonizing approaches that unsettle settler-colonial relationships, honor non-Western worldviews, and query the contemporary politics of reconciliation can foreground Indigenous, African American, or other worldviews, including cultural practices and knowledge. Such approaches include understanding knowledge is not objective or value-free because people are accountable for knowledge and its outcomes (Collins, 1990). Because experience and position determine the outcomes of knowledge production, the outcomes can be unjust and cause (differential) harm. Reflexive attention to our own experience and position, and recognition of the value and experience of others (locally and grounded in context), are pedagogical imperatives for emancipatory learning. Alternatives may be envisioned through Freirean (1970), multiepistemic, or feminist postcolonial (Anzaldúa, 1987) imaginings and through conceptualizing knowledge as collective and belonging to human heritage and linked realities (Harding, 1998).

Epistemic pluralism asks for varied accounts and multiple perspectives from diverse players and knowledges. A recent study on learning and conducting research across Western, intersectional feminist, and Indigenous knowledge systems, for example, suggests that neglecting to honor and learn from diverse knowledge systems eliminates opportunities for creativity, hope, guidance, and learning, which limits the creation of knowledge that can build collective solutions (Levac et al., 2018). The same study lists 19 different frameworks for integrating knowledge systems, thus suggesting multiple emerging approaches to decolonization.

Decolonizing Practice and Pedagogies
Epistemic pluralism requires using pedagogies that develop critical consciousness about the ways in which knowledge is acquired and practiced. As we are reminded by Freire (1970) and Vygotsky (1978), learners are not empty vessels waiting to be filled with knowledge from experts who may have little relevant experience. Issues such as whose voices are heard, and whose histories are told, require continuous reflexivity and engagement with uneasy moments between, and emerging from, colonial relations.

Emancipatory, decolonizing learning requires attention to how multiple epistemologies or knowledges can be brought into juxtaposition in order to challenge hierarchical practices. The Western vision of building a more democratic society, for example, is made more robust through knowledge solidarity, by honoring views from and with the *other* that position human societies in congruence and conversation with the natural world, as in Indigenous worldviews. According to Cunningham (2000), "These alternative visions do not reject time and space (science and rationality) for time and space (interrelationship in face-to-face groups) or vice versa, but [act] as two paradigms that can be brought together in a critical practice" (p. 582).

Emancipatory education practices, particularly in developing nations, also draw attention to questions of representation and the need for decolonizing solidarities. Working with women in popular education to dismantle apartheid in South Africa, Walters and Butterwick (2017) explained that participants stressed similar goals but held very different representational positions. They learned about the need to learn "radical vulnerability," make mistakes, and be open to getting feedback through a process they call "stepping forward, standing with and staying connected" (p. 27). This example suggests an emancipatory approach to decolonizing ACE.

According to Indigenous scholars, relationship building, story-work, art, dance, music, intergenerational learning, and community-based practices are ways to move beyond historically entrenched patriarchal, Western values. A location for learning in communities is public spaces, such as museums. As English and Mayo (2012) state, "There is room for adult education initiatives that deconstruct the 'orientalist' representations, often found in these museums, to convert these institutions into de-colonizing spaces" (p. 72). Decolonizing museums and civic spaces (e.g., decolonizing tours or the hacking of monuments) are tangible ways adult educators are challenged to question colonial relationships. Although this may create discomfort, such tensions are necessary for transformation.

Interrupting Hegemony: Social Movements and Participatory Methodologies

Necessary parts of epistemic pluralism and knowledge solidarities are actions and pedagogies that interrupt or challenge hegemonic sites of knowledge. Challenging hegemony is possible only when marginalized groups are conscious of dominant ideologies that support structures of power. Gramsci (1971) suggested that this is more likely when intellectuals are part of the subordinated group. As Mayo (2007) stated, "adult educators engaging in counter-hegemonic cultural activity are . . . as intellectuals who are organic to the 'subaltern' groups aspiring to power. This implies that they should be politically committed to those they teach" (p. 426). Community-engaged ACE has the potential to be a catalyst for new ideas grounded in nontraditional sites of intellectualism. These could include Indigenous elders, Black leaders, and disability activists with knowledge from experience and practical engagement with the world. The ideas emerging from these positions can create new structures, spaces, democracies, and resistances to capitalism and neocolonialism.

The movement to decolonize ACE is possible only through conversations on multiple levels. For example, the work of Deshler and Grudens-Schuck (2000) in democratizing knowledges; Franz (2007) in cooperative extension; Hall and Tandon (2017) in higher education and community-based approaches; and Chilisa (2012) in Indigenous methodologies all suggest using more participatory approaches to achieve emancipatory goals. The practices of social movements such as the women's movement, Black Lives Matter, Idle No More (Indigenous rights), *Animation Rurale* (rural development), the World Social Forum, Training for Transformation, popular literacy campaigns, and many others, demonstrate diverse and varied examples of how social movements use participatory methodologies, and secondly, how they engage with processes of decolonizing ACE.

Conclusion

Structures and locations of class, racialization, ethnicity, gender, place, age, sexuality, and (dis)ability continually play on how we see the world and our position within it. As Collins (1990) suggests, however, recognition of our contradictory positions requires constant reflexivity and further development of decolonizing pedagogies appropriate for ACE. The politics of identity, when they are contextualized and understood within structures, help to situate experience and social positionality. The politics of identity cannot, however, abrogate our collective responsibility to communities and to each other—knowledge solidarities and democracy depend on this.

No approach to decolonization is without contradictions or ambiguities similar to the multiple and meandering tributaries of the river analogy discussed earlier. They provide powerful, creative, and dynamic confluences—each with potential for transformation. We propose that decolonizing spaces can be found in the hinterlands of epistemic pluralism, solidarity, and reflexivity, where complex, emerging, and varied approaches are possible.

References

Anzaldúa, G. (1987). *Borderlands/la frontera: The new Mestiza*. Aunt Lute Books.

Atleo, M. (2013). The zone of Canadian Aboriginal adult education: A social movement approach. In T. Nesbit, S. M. Brigham, N. Taber, & T. Gibb (Eds.). *Building on critical traditions: Adult education and learning in Canada.* (pp. 39–50). Thompson Educational Publishing.

Battiste, M. (2013). *Decolonizing education: Nourishing the learning spirit*. Purich.

Boughton, B. (2016). Radical international adult education: A pedagogy of solidarity. In R. C. Mizzi, T. S. Rocco, & S. Shore (Eds.), *Disrupting adult and community education: Teaching, learning, and working in the periphery* (pp. 257–273). SUNY Press.

Brigham, S. (2013). Theorizing race in adult education: Critical race theory. In T. Nesbit, S. M. Brigham, N. Taber, & T. Gibb (Eds.), *Building on critical traditions: Adult education and learning in Canada.* (pp. 119–128). Thompson Educational Publishing.

Briskin, L. (2013). Merit, individualism and solidarity: Revisiting the democratic deficit in union women's leadership. In S. Ledwith & L. Hansen (Eds.). *Gendering and diversifying trade union leadership* (pp. 138–161). Routledge.

Carbert, L. (1996). For home and country: Women's institutes in Ontario. *Women and Environments, 15*(2), 21.

Chilisa, B. (2012). *Indigenous research methodologies*. SAGE.

Collins, P. H. (1990). *Black feminist thought: Knowledge, consciousness, and the politics of empowerment*. Routledge.

Cunningham. P. (2000). A sociology of adult education. In A. Wilson & E. R. Hayes (Eds.), *Handbook of adult and continuing education* (pp. 573–591). Jossey-Bass.

Deshler, D., & Grudens-Schuck, N. (2000). The politics of knowledge construction. In A. Wilson & E. R. Hayes (Eds.), *Handbook of adult and continuing education* (pp. 592–611). Jossey-Bass.

Du Bois, W. E. B. (1903). The talented tenth. In B. T. Washington (Ed.), *The Negro problem: A series of articles by representative American Negroes of Today* (pp. 31–75). James Pott.

Du Bois, W. E. B. (1996). *The souls of Black folk*. Penguin. (Original work published 1903).

English, L. M., & Mayo, P. (2012). *Learning with adults: A critical pedagogical introduction*. Sense.

Fanon, F. (1967). *Black skin, white masks*. Grove.

Finger M., & Asun, J. M. (2001). *Learning our way out: Education at a crossroads*. Zed Books.

Franz, N. (2007). Adult education theories: Informing Cooperative Extension's Transformation. *Journal of Extension, 45*(1). https://www.joe.org/joe/2007february/a1.php?pagewanted=all

Franz, N. K., & Townson, L. (2008). The nature of complex organizations: The case of Cooperative Extension. *New Directions for Evaluation, 2008*(120), 5–14. https://doi.org/10.1002/ev.272

Freire, P. (1970). *Pedagogy of the oppressed*. Continuum.

Grace, A. (2013). *Lifelong learning as critical action: International perspectives on people, politics, policy, and practice*. Canadian Scholar's Press.

Gramsci, A. (1971). *Selections from the prison notebooks*. International Publishers.

Gregorčič, M. (2009). Cultural capital and innovative pedagogy: A case study among Indigenous communities in Mexico and Honduras, *Innovations in Education and Teaching International, 46*(4), 357–366.

Guo, S., & Maitra, S. (2019). Decolonising lifelong learning in the age of transnational migration. *International Journal of Lifelong Education, 38*(1), 1–4. https://doi.org/10.1080/02601370.2018.1561534

Guy, T. C. (1996). *Africentricism and adult education: Outlines of an intellectual tradition with implications for adult education* (ED409457). ERIC. https://eric.ed.gov/?id=ED409457

Hall, B., & Tandon, R. (2017). Decolonization of knowledge, epistemicide, participatory research and higher education. *Research for All, 1*(1) 6–19.

Hanson, C. (2018). Stitching together an arts-based inquiry with Indigenous communities in Canada and Chile. *Canadian Journal for the Study of Adult Education, 30*(2), 11–22.

Hanson, C., Paavo, A., & Sisters in Labour Education. (2019). *Cracking labour's glass ceiling: Transforming lives through women-only union education*. Fernwood.

Harding, S. (1998). *Is science multicultural?: Postcolonialisms, feminisms, and epistemologies*. Indiana University Press.

Harrison, P. (2009). Dispelling ignorance of residential schools. In G. Younging, J. Dewar, & M. DeGagné (Eds.), *Response, responsibility, and renewal: Canada's truth and reconciliation journey* (pp. 149–160). Aboriginal Healing Foundation.

hooks, b. (1994). *Teaching to transgress: Education as the practice of freedom*. Routledge.

International Assessment of Agricultural Knowledge, Science, and Technology for Development. (2009). *Agriculture at a crossroads: Global report*. International Assessment of Agricultural Knowledge, Science, and Technology for Development Earthscan/United Nations. www.agassessment-watch.org/report/Global%20Report%20(English).pdf

Jaffe, J. (2017). Knowledge equity as social justice. *Rural Sociology*, *82*(3), 391–410. https://doi.org/10.1111/ruso.12143

Levac, L., Mcmurtry, L., Stienstra, D. Baikie, G., Hanson, C., & Mucina, D. (2018, May). *Learning across Indigenous and Western knowledge systems and intersectionality: Reconciling social science research approaches* [Unpublished research report]. University of Guelph. www.criaw-icref.ca/images/userfiles/files/Learning%20Across%20Indigenous%20and%20Western%20Knowledges FINAL.pdf

Mayo, P. (2007). Antonio Gramsci and his relevance for the education of adults. *Educational Philosophy and Theory*, *40*(3), 418–435.

Memmi, A. (1991). *The colonized and the colonizer*. Beacon Press. (Original published 1956)

Mies, M. (1986). *Patriarchy and capital accumulation on a world scale: Women in the international division of labor*. Zed Books.

Monture-Angus, P. (2014). Standing against Canadian law: Naming oppressions of race, culture, and gender. In E. Comack (Ed.), *Locating law: Race, class, gender, sexuality connections* (pp. 68–79). Fernwood.

Nyerere, J. (1968). Education for self-reliance. *CrossCurrents*, *18*(4), 415–434.

Nyerere, J. (1976). *Adult education and development*. DVV International. https://www.dvv-international.de/adult-education-and-development/editions/aed-672006/ica-e7th-world-assembly/adult-education-and-development/

Parker, A. M. (2010). *Clubwomen, reformers, workers, and feminists of the Gilded Age and Progressive Era*. History Faculty Publications. https://digitalcommons.brockport.edu/hst_facpub/10

Powell, C. (2014). African American women's clubs' activism in Chicago: The remaining strength of extended kinship solidarity. *Nuevo Mundo Mundos Nuevos*. http://journals.openedition.org/nuevomundo/67421

Quijano, A. (2007). Coloniality and modernity/rationality. *Cultural Studies*, *21*(2–3), 168–178.

Regan, P. (2010). *Unsettling the settler within: Indian residential schools, truth telling and reconciliation in Canada*. UBC Press.

Rodney, W. (1973). *How Europe underdeveloped Africa*. Howard University Press.

Rose, A. D., & Jeris, L. H. (2011). Finding the worker: Adult education and workers' education. *Adult Learning*, *22*(1), 28–31. https://doi.org/10.1177/104515951102200106

Said, E. W. (1978). *Orientalism*. Pantheon.

Spencer, B., & Taylor, J. (2006). Labor education. In T. Fenwick, T. Nesbit, & B. Spencer (Eds.), *Contexts of adult education: Canadian perspectives* (pp. 208–217). Thompson Educational Publishing.

Spivak, G. C. (1994). Can the subaltern speak? In P. Williams & L. Chrisman (Eds.). *Colonial discourse and postcolonial theory* (pp. 66–111). Columbia University Press.

Taylor, J. (2001). *Union learning: Canadian labor education in the twentieth century*. Thompson Educational Publishing.

Thiong'o, N. wa. (1986). *Decolonising the mind: The politics of language in African literature*. Heinemann.

Truth and Reconciliation Commission. (2015). *Truth and Reconciliation Commission of Canada: Calls to action*. TRC Commission.

Tuhiwai Smith, L. (2012). *Decolonizing methodologies: Research and Indigenous peoples*. Zed Books.

Vygotsky, L. S. (1978). *Mind in society: The development of higher psychological processes*. M. Cole, V. John-Steiner, S. Scribner, & E. Souberman (Eds. & Trans., pp. 7–29). Harvard University Press.

Walters, S., & Butterwick, S. (2017). Moves to decolonize solidarity through feminist popular education. In A. von Kotze & S. Walters (Eds.), *Forging solidarity: Popular education at work* (pp. 27–38). Sense.

Washington, B. T. (1903). *The negro problem*. James Pott.

Welton, M. (2013). *Unearthing Canada's hidden past: A short history of adult education*. Thompson Educational Publishing.

Willinsky, J. (1998). *Learning to divide the world: Education at the empire's end*. University of Minnesota Press.

CHAPTER 37

Adult Education, Welfare, and New Evidence on Helping Low-Income Adults Improve Their Skills

Julie Strawn

What role can and should adult education play to reduce poverty in the United States? In the past, adult education as a poverty-reduction strategy was most often viewed through the lens of welfare reform and bound up with a more general debate about the relative effectiveness of skill-building versus rapid job placement in welfare-to-work programs. This question of what role adult education should play in public assistance programs, however, has become less and less relevant over time for several reasons.

First, sweeping changes in the U.S. safety net in the last 20 years have resulted in far fewer low-income families receiving cash assistance. For those who remain on welfare, funding for and policymaker interest in skill development have fallen dramatically during this period. Many who might have participated in adult education through that route had to find other sources of support to upgrade their skills. Second, changes in the labor market sharply increased the payoff to postsecondary credentials and further disadvantaged those having only a high school education or less. Having a high school credential alone no longer allows many people to earn a living wage, regardless of whether it is a traditional diploma, GED, or other high school equivalent. Third, emerging research on welfare-to-work programs, and on education and training for low-income adults more generally, shed new light on what works—and what has not—with important implications for the content and delivery of adult education.

Adult education programs have had to adapt to this evolving landscape and think differently about how to reach and serve low-income adults if they seek to help reduce poverty. This has contributed to a stronger focus by these programs on transitions to postsecondary education and to employment, and more integration of academic and occupational content. These shifts likely mean adult education is positioned to support the goals of public assistance programs, such as increasing employment and earnings, reducing the need for government aid, and ultimately improving individual and family well-being. Unfortunately, though, without changes in federal and state funding and policy governing cash assistance programs, adult education can expect little renewed interest and investment from these programs for basic skills services for recipients.

Instead, we need to expand our vision and broaden the focus beyond what role adult education plays in welfare programs to larger questions, such as who should be responsible—which programs and systems—for helping low-income adults improve their basic skills and gain credentials that can help them advance in the labor market? And what are the most effective ways to do that? Researchers can make important contributions to answering those questions and informing needed changes in policy and practice.

Role of Adult Education in Welfare Reform

Historically, the primary rationales for public assistance programs to partner with adult education have been that helping recipients increase their basic skills and earn education credentials will

- increase their employment and earnings;
- reduce their reliance on public assistance;
- ameliorate poverty; and
- for parents, improve their children's educational outcomes.

Proponents have posited other benefits as well, including improved health outcomes and, among noncustodial parents, increased employment and earnings (and therefore better ability to pay child support) and reduced prison recidivism.

The Early Years of Welfare Reform

Financial and political support to help public assistance recipients improve their skills has ebbed and flowed over the years, and with it, the extent of adult education provided to recipients. Until the mid-1980s, welfare-to-work policies at the federal and state levels for recipients of Aid to Families with Dependent Children (AFDC) tended to emphasize rapid employment through job search and, after 1981, unpaid community work experience or *workfare*. California's creation, in 1985 of the Greater Avenues to Independence (GAIN) program helped move the focus of welfare reform toward skill development. GAIN was the largest welfare-to-work program in the country. GAIN sought to deliver a comprehensive set of mandatory education, training, and employment services, with a strong focus on improving basic skills (Riccio et al., 1994). Though rigorous evidence on GAIN's results would not emerge until the early 1990s, Congress took many aspects of the GAIN approach nationwide in 1988 through creation of the Job Opportunities and Basic Skills Training (JOBS) program as part of passage of the Family Support Act.

JOBS imposed work participation requirements on welfare recipients while also requiring states to provide a comprehensive set of assessment, education, training and employment services, as well as guaranteed childcare for AFDC recipients engaged in work activities. Importantly, JOBS included funding dedicated to these comprehensive services, though states had to provide matching funds and typically did not draw down all available JOBS funding. At the same time, states continued to experiment through waivers with customizing their welfare-to-work strategies in various other ways, and the federal government began requiring rigorous evaluations of those waiver demonstration programs (Falk, 2019b; Gueron, 2016).

The JOBS program led to a substantial increase in the number of welfare recipients without a high school diploma being referred to adult education programs. In some cases, programs received additional funding to expand hours of instruction to meet the 20-hour-a-week JOBS work activity requirement or otherwise customize their classes. More often, programs did not receive direct JOBS funding but, importantly, students in JOBS gained access to publicly funded supports, such as childcare and transportation, which was not generally available to other adult education students. Adult education programs had to grapple with the fact that their historically voluntary services were now mandatory for welfare recipients sent to them under JOBS.

JOBS mandates and supports had a big effect on adult education. A study of adult education in three welfare-to-work programs during the JOBS era found that the programs substantially increased participation in adult education, similar to what an earlier study of GAIN adult education found. Without the programs, about one in five welfare recipients without a high school diploma or GED enrolled in adult education. Under the JOBS programs, more than half did. Furthermore, the JOBS students received, on average, three times as many hours of instruction as control group members not in the programs. Those who participated in adult education (excluding those referred but who did not participate) were enrolled for 488 hours, far higher than control group members. The study found that the content of adult education services for JOBS students, however, generally did not change, but continued to focus on traditional adult basic education and GED preparation instruction (Bos et al., 2002).

By the mid-1990s the pendulum concerning quick employment versus skill development in welfare reform had begun to swing back again, in large part because of early findings from a random assignment evaluation of California's GAIN program. Short-term impacts from the study suggested "work first" job search–focused strategies were more effective than was education. As described later, subsequent research revealed that neither work first–focused nor basic skills–focused programs had lasting effects over the long term, but those findings came too late to inform late 1990s welfare reform policy. The debate over work-first versus skill-building approaches culminated in 1996 in passage of the Personal Responsibility and Work Opportunity Reconciliation Act (PRWORA), which replaced the AFDC entitlement program, first established in 1935, with the Temporary Assistance to Needy Families (TANF) block grant.

Adult Education in the TANF Era

TANF had both immediate and long-term effects on the provision of adult education and other skill development activities to welfare recipients. TANF curtailed skill-building activities in direct ways, by strictly limiting the extent to which education and training counted toward meeting work requirements. Except for teens, basic skills education can never be counted toward work rates by itself; it must always be combined with 20 hours a week of a TANF "core" activity, such as employment or community service, or integrated into vocational education training, which is itself limited. There were also indirect impacts. TANF had the effect of reducing investment in welfare-to-work activities generally, including adult education, by freezing overall funding to states (replacing open-ended entitlement funding with a capped block grant), eliminating any dedicated funding for welfare-to-work activities, and allowing states to meet work participation rates by reducing caseloads rather than placing recipients in jobs or welfare-to-work activities.

Two decades later the effects have been dramatic:

- Between FY 1997 and FY 2017 the total real value of the TANF block grant, adjusted for inflation, fell by more than a third (36%), with deeper effective cuts in some states whose share of families in poverty grew in that time (Falk, 2019a; Floyd et al., 2018).
- States have used TANF's flexibility to shift block grant spending away from cash assistance and welfare-to-work activities to other purposes, especially child welfare, refundable tax credits, prekindergarten, and childcare. By federal FY 2017, states were spending just 23% of the TANF block grant and state match on cash assistance and 11% on any work, education, and training activities. Only about half of that—5%—was spent on education and training (Office of Family Assistance, 2018a).
- Much of the population that adult education served under AFDC and the JOBS program simply no longer receives cash assistance, though poverty has not decreased commensurately. Both federal and state policy changes under TANF have driven steep caseload declines since 1996. The current strong economy has also contributed to a more recent, smaller drop in caseloads since 2012. TANF now assists only one in five poor children nationally (20%) with basic needs, down from the 59% helped by AFDC in 1996 just prior to adoption of the block grant (Falk, 2019a).

These changes all contribute to fewer than 10,000 TANF recipients who participated in adult education or high school completion, on average, each month in federal fiscal year 2017. This represented just 1.6% of all of those participating in TANF work activities (Office of Family Assistance, 2018b). By contrast, GAO estimated that in mid-1994 in the JOBS program 75,000 AFDC recipients participated in adult basic education or English as a second language classes, with an additional 85,000 completing high school or enrolled in high school equivalency classes, for a total of 160,000 (27% of those participating in JOBS activities) (General Accountability Office, 1995). While there are some limitations in comparing TANF and JOBS participation data, and there was an uptick in adult education participation during the recession, it is nonetheless clear that the main trend has been a huge drop in welfare recipient participation in adult education in the years since the TANF block grant went into effect. Factors other than TANF, such as reduced adult education spending in real terms, may explain some of this decline. Overall enrollment in adult education also declined over this same period, though much less precipitously than among welfare recipients (Office of Vocational and Adult Education, 2013; Office of Career, Technical, and Adult Education, 2018).

In theory, low-income adults formerly receiving education and training through the welfare system could now be receiving support for the same services through other programs. While this is likely happening to some extent, the decline in TANF resources for education activities has coincided with a more general decline in public funding for adult education and job training. Over the last 20 years, federal adult education funding has fallen in inflation-adjusted dollars by 17%. Funds for federal postsecondary programs that adult education students might also hope to benefit from have declined more rapidly. Job training funding through the Workforce Innovation and Opportunity Act (WIOA) and its predecessor is down by 40% while career and technical education funding is down by 28% (Spiker, 2019). The largest source of federal funding for postsecondary training, Pell Grants, has failed to keep up with college tuition and related living expenses. The current maximum Pell Grant covers less than one third (28%) of the cost of attending a 4-year public college (Institute for College Access & Success, 2018); it also leaves many (71%) community and technical college students with substantial unmet financial need, averaging $4,920 (Center for Law and Social Policy, 2018).

Rising Importance of Education for Earnings and Evidence on Skill-Building Strategies

Ironically, the disinvestment by the federal government in skill-building activities for welfare recipients and for low-income adults more generally has coincided with a growing body of evidence about the importance of skills and credentials for helping low-income adults improve their economic well-being. This evidence is two-pronged. First, labor market changes that increasingly place a premium on postsecondary education have widened the gap between the educational attainment of public assistance recipients, and low-income adults generally, and the credentials needed to obtain middle-class jobs. Second, new workforce development strategies have emerged that show promise for bridging that gap more effectively than past approaches did, such as sectoral training and integrated basic education and training.

The Changing Labor Market

Figure 37.1 illustrates how the economy has increasingly rewarded postsecondary education, not only 4-year degrees but also other credentials such as 2-year degrees and certificates. In 1970 about three out of

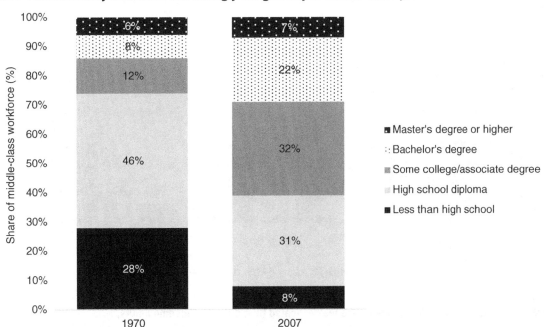

FIGURE 37.1 Postsecondary education increasingly the gateway to middle-class jobs.

Source: Adapted from Carnevale et al., 2010. Middle-class jobs in this study were defined as ones paying between $35,000 and $70,000 in 2010 dollars.

four workers (74%) in middle class jobs had only a high school diploma or less education; by 2007, only 39% of those in middle class jobs did (Carnevale et al., 2010). The trend toward employers requiring higher skills for jobs paying family-sustaining wages is projected to continue for the foreseeable future. About half of all job openings over the next decade are expected to be for middle-skill jobs that require some education or training beyond high school, but less than a 4-year degree (National Skills Coalition, 2017).

Given these economic realities, the fact that the majority of low-income adults do not have any postsecondary education poses a major hurdle to improving their economic lot. While TANF recipients are markedly less educated, and especially likely not to have even finished high school, other public assistance recipients, such as those in the Supplemental Nutrition Assistance Program (SNAP, formerly known as food stamps) and low-income adults generally also possess substantially less education than the general U.S. population (Figure 37.2). Clearly, education is not the only factor at play here in holding down earnings, because more than a third of low-income adults do have some postsecondary education. Other individual and labor market characteristics, such as mental and physical health issues, justice system involvement, lack of jobs in a region, and discrimination, are important drivers of earnings, too, which is critical to keep in mind when devising strategies to help low-income adults improve their economic well-being. Still, the skills gap is striking.

Emerging Evidence on Skill Development Strategies
As noted earlier, the earliest rigorous evidence on helping welfare recipients find jobs quickly, as opposed to helping them improve their skills first, suggested that the work-first approach was more effective. That conclusion was based on a relatively short-term follow-up data, and as researchers followed participants for a longer period (5 years, and eventually 15 years), those early results turned out to be misleading. Over the long run, both the work-first and education-first models from the 1980s and 1990s generated relatively small and short-lived increases in employment and earnings. Work-first programs were less expensive to run and got participants into jobs more quickly; basic education-focused models eventually produced similar outcomes

FIGURE 37.2 Educational attainment of TANF and SNAP recipients versus low-income and all U.S. adults (25 years and older).

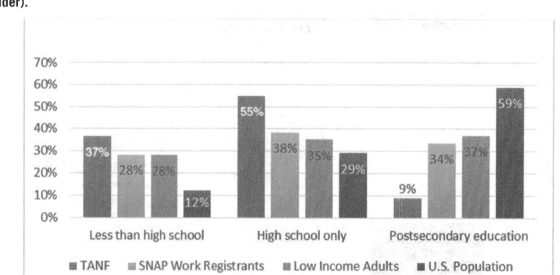

Note. Figure demonstrates that TANF recipients are less educated than other low-income adults.

Source. Adapted from Center for Poverty Research, University of California, Davis, 2015; Office of Family Assistance, Administration for Children and Families, U.S. Department of Health and Human Services, 2018c; Rowe et al., 2017

but took longer to produce them. (It should be noted that education in these programs typically consisted of stand-alone, academically focused adult education, not job training or other postsecondary education.) Both approaches ultimately left participants working in low-wage jobs, without steady employment, and no better off than similar parents who did not receive program services (the control group in these studies).

The best welfare-to-work results from that early era came from a program that offered a mix of employment and training services, helping some participants to find jobs quickly and enrolling others in employment-focused education or training, which was typically of short duration. While this boosted employment and earnings more than work first or education first, even this program's effects faded over the long run (though it should be noted that the program shifted away from skill-building partway through the study). Across these various approaches, long-term analyses of welfare-to-work participants found that many remained in low-wage jobs with unstable employment 10 or even 15 years later. None of the three approaches described here lifted participants out of poverty. Evaluations of job training programs during this same period suggested that occupational training could provide a higher boost in earnings for some than job search or basic education alone, but the results varied considerably by program and earnings increases were not sustained over the long term (Hamilton, 2012; Hendra & Hamilton, 2015; Martinson & Strawn, 2002).

These sobering findings have helped sparked a reassessment and a wave of innovation in the workforce development field in the years since. These include efforts to link basic skills education much more closely to employment and training and partnerships between business and an array of service providers to train workers in industry sectors and to help them advance along career pathways over time. Rigorous evidence is now emerging that suggests these new strategies may be more effective than past approaches, though longer-term follow-up data are needed. While public assistance programs have not played the central role in these programs that they did in the 1980s and 1990s, many of the participants in them received at least SNAP benefits; TANF aid seems to have been much less common. Many of the interventions focus on those who have completed high school and possess eighth-grade or higher academic skills, but some are tailored to those with lower skills and/or without a high school credential.

Contextualized Basic Skills and Integrated Basic Education and Training Instruction

Recent experimental and quasiexperimental research on approaches that contextualize basic skills instruction to occupational training and/or integrate it with training shows these strategies can produce higher high school equivalency completion, higher postsecondary transition rates, greater accumulation of college credits, and increased attainment of occupational certificates when compared with traditional basic skills approaches.

Washington State's I-BEST model provides integrated basic education and occupational training instruction in defined pathways in a number of in-demand industries. A core feature of I-BEST is team teaching, in which a basic skills instructor and an occupational instructor are teaching together for at least 50% of occupational training class time. New findings from the Pathways for Advancing Careers and Education (PACE) evaluation provide the first rigorous evidence about the effects of I-BEST on educational outcomes, from follow-up data at about 2 years after study enrollment. The study found that I-BEST more than tripled completion of occupational certificates and other credentials, as compared to a control group, and students earned twice as many college credits (see Figure 37.3). Other key findings include that I-BEST students were significantly more likely to attend college courses, particularly occupational training courses, and to complete "gatekeeper" college math and English classes essential for entering higher-level college courses. These positive education impacts are notable given that students testing as low as fourth- and fifth-grade reading and math could enter the I-BEST programs in the study. Future PACE reports will examine I-BEST employment and earnings impacts (Glosser et al., 2018).

The accelerating opportunity (AO) initiative was based on the I-BEST model, though with more concurrent education and training and substantially less team teaching and integrated instruction. The four states studied varied in which populations they targeted for AO but, in general, AO programs allowed students with sixth-grade skills or higher to enroll. The quasiexperimental evaluation found that, in the first 3 years of participation, AO had a positive impact on the number of college-awarded credentials earned overall, with wide variation between states. AO

FIGURE 37.3 I-BEST impacts on enrollment and credential receipt.

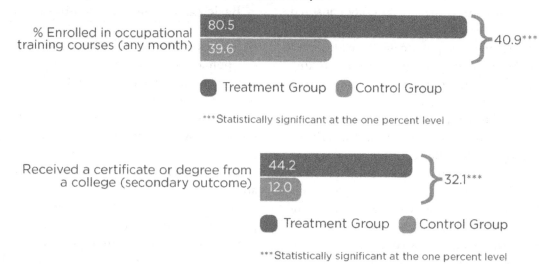

Source: Adapted from Glosser et al., 2018.

students tended to earn more credentials while taking fewer credits, which may have reflected accelerated learning. Earnings impacts were more mixed, but AO did produce strong and sustained increases in earnings for two subgroups: AO students recruited from adult education in Kentucky and AO students recruited from career technical education in Kansas (Anderson et al., 2017).

The Carreras en Salud (Careers in Health) program, operated by Instituto del Progreso Latino in Chicago, Illinois, focuses on training low-income Latinxs for employment in health-care occupations, primarily certified nursing assistant (CNA) and licensed practical nurse (LPN). Like I-BEST, it is one of the nine career pathways programs being evaluated in the PACE study. The Carreras en Salud program consists of the following elements: (a) a structured health-care training pathway, starting at about the fourth grade; (b) contextualized and accelerated basic skills and English as a second language instruction; (c) academic advising and nonacademic supports; (d) financial assistance; and (e) employment services. The PACE study found that Carreras en Salud increased hours of occupational training and basic skills instruction received, as compared to the control group, and participants were more likely to earn education credentials within an 18-month follow-up period. The program also increased employment in the health-care field and resulted in a reduction of participants reporting financial hardship. Future reports will examine whether these effects translate into gains in earnings (Martinson et al., 2018).

The Bridge to Health and Business program at LaGuardia Community College in New York helped adults and out-of-school youth earn a GED while also learning about careers in health and business. In addition to contextualizing the curriculum, the program offered group and individualized counseling to help students transition to college. The Bridge Program served somewhat lower-skilled students than regular GED preparation classes at the college, with about half of the students testing at the seventh- and eighth-grade levels. Students in the program were twice as likely to earn a high school diploma and three times as likely to enroll in college as students in traditional GED Prep classes (Martin & Broadus, 2013).

Career Pathways

The goal of career pathways is to help people advance over time to higher skills, recognized credentials, and better jobs with higher pay. The key elements of the model are: (a) articulated education and training steps along a pathway in an industry sector; (b) support services, including proactive career and academic advising and financial aid; (c) various levels at which to enter and exit a pathway, depending on prior skills and experience; and (d) partnerships with employers and service providers. Career pathways combine elements of other approaches, including integrated basic education and training, sector training, and guided pathways. Recent examples of large career pathways initiatives include the PACE evaluation noted earlier, the Health Profession Opportunity Grant program (HPOG, especially the second round), and the Trade Adjustment Assistance Community College and Career Training grants (TAACCCT)—especially the later rounds.

Because the career pathways model is relatively young and has been evolving over time, in the research there is wide variation in what the programs were actually implementing. For example, some offered more fully developed pathways with multiple steps of training offered while others provided only one-step of training, which was often for entry-level jobs. For low-skilled adults, some career pathways programs offer bridge courses and integrated basic education and training courses that provide on-ramps for them into higher-level pathways training. In many other programs, those without a high school diploma or equivalent or with lower than eighth-grade skills are shut out of training opportunities. Because career pathways approaches are relatively new, rigorous research on results have only recently begun to be available and they generally rely on fairly short-term follow-up data.

A 2019 scan of career pathways research to date found 96 studies that examined the impact of programs through experimental or quasiexperimental research designs. In the short-to mid-term, those evaluations found

- consistently positive effects across studies on education outcomes such as training completion, credentials earned, and others (83% of studies);
- more mixed short-term impacts on employment and earnings, though majority of projects had positive effects (62% and 63% of studies, respectively); and
- wide variation in magnitude of study impacts even within same research project, which points to the importance of how the model is implemented and local context.

Figure 37.4 also shows that a substantial minority of evaluations (30%–40%) found no impacts on economic outcomes in the short- to mid-term. Future reports from projects such as PACE and HPOG will shed light on whether early positive education impacts translate into increased earnings later on or not.

Sector-Focused Training

Sectoral training strategies typically involve partnerships that bring employers within one industry together along with employment, education, and training providers to focus on the workforce needs of that industry within a regional labor market. A 2010 study of three well-established sectoral training programs found large increases in earnings and suggested that a sector focus may result in deeper knowledge

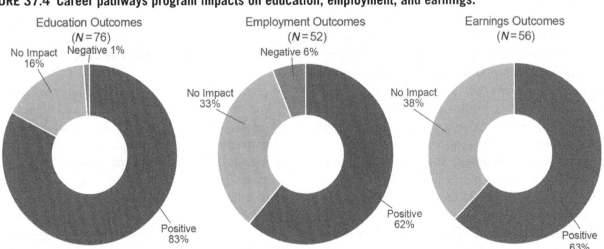

FIGURE 37.4 Career pathways program impacts on education, employment, and earnings.

Source: Schwartz et al., 2020. *N* = the number of impact evaluations. Percentages do not sum to 100% due to rounding.

of the labor market and stronger relationships with employers which, in turn, creates a better match between training and in-demand skills than past job training efforts (Maguire et al., 2010). Since then several other sectoral training studies—of four programs in the WorkAdvance evaluation, of Project Quest, and of the Year Up program—have also found substantial earnings gains, though these impacts varied greatly across the programs studied, pointing to the importance of the details of program design, implementation, and maturity (Fein & Hamadyk, 2018; Roder & Elliott, 2019; Schaberg, 2017).

Despite impressive results, one critique of sector training programs generally is that they tend to be highly selective, in terms of basic skills, educational attainment, and motivation. One notable exception is Project Quest, which supported access and completion in occupational certificate and degree programs in health care. The program targeted low-income individuals and while a high school diploma or GED was required, nearly two thirds of participants required help increasing their basic skills before they could enroll in postsecondary education and training.

Project QUEST brought an adult basic education instructor from the San Antonio Independent School District on site to help students improve their math and reading skills so that they could pass the colleges' placement tests and avoid taking regular college remedial classes. These QUEST Prep classes were held 25 hours per week and customized to the needs of students. The combination of this basic skill instruction, prerequisite courses, and the length of the targeted training programs themselves (ranging from 7 months to 2 years) meant a long road to completion—participants took 23 months on average to finish (Roder & Elliott, 2018, 2019). The end result, however, was some of the most impressive earnings gains ever seen in a workforce development program, with earnings increases that continued to grow even 9 years later, and average earning increases large enough to move participants into the middle class. Project Quest's earnings impacts took more than 2 years to materialize, which illustrates why it is so important not to draw conclusions prematurely from short-term impacts when assessing effectiveness of skill development programs.

There are examples of other well-established sector training programs that serve lower-skilled individuals than Project Quest does. For example, the Jane Addams Resource Corporation (JARC), which began in Chicago in 1985 and has now expanded to Baltimore, offers a Manufacturing Bridge that serves those with fifth- to eighth-grade skills and feeds into their sector training programs in manufacturing. JARC has a strong reputation; however, there is not a rigorous evaluation of its results.

Transitional Jobs

Transitional jobs are an employment strategy for those facing significant obstacles to finding steady work, sometimes called the "hard to employ." The model offers publically subsidized temporary jobs that seek to help participants improve work readiness skills and gain work experience. In general, transitional jobs have shown they can greatly increase employment and earnings while the subsidized jobs are in place but impacts tend to fade when the jobs end. Recent research from the Enhanced Transitional Jobs Demonstration (ETJD) provides some intriguing results for those without a high school diploma, with somewhat larger impacts on earnings over 30 months of follow-up and significantly larger impacts on employment in the final year of the follow-up period. These programs provided little skill development, which raises the question of whether the ETJD results suggest that transitional jobs could have larger and more sustained impacts for low-skilled adults if combined with basic skills and job training (Barden et al., 2018). Two large demonstration projects targeting the hard to employ, funded by the U.S. Department of Health and Human Services, were just getting started in 2019 and may ultimately shed light on strategies for those with low skills, among other barriers to employment.

The Path Forward

So where does this leave low-skilled adults who need help to compete in the labor market and improve their economic well-being? What role can adult education play in reducing income inequality and poverty, and can welfare programs still be a viable partner? In some states and localities, public assistance programs are assisting these adults gain skills and credentials by expanding access within TANF to adult education. In the most recent data on TANF work activity participation, Arizona, Nebraska, Oklahoma, Rhode Island, and South Dakota were the states with the highest percentages in "education related to employment" (the category under which adult education generally falls; it is possible some other states are also supporting significant adult education activity and recording it under "vocational educational training," "job skills training," or other categories if adult education is being combined with job training) (Office of Family Assistance, 2018b). In the states identified here, the share of work activity participants who were in adult education ranged from 7.6% to 11.8% (Office of Family Assistance, 2018b). Supportive state TANF policies are making this possible. For example, Nebraska allows parents on cash assistance to combine education and employment activities in their self-sufficiency plans and counts most education and training as core work activities, in contrast to federal policy. The state also allows vocational education participation to count for up to 36 months, in contrast to the 12-month limit in federal policy (Hall, 2016).

In the SNAP program in recent years, the federal government has encouraged states to expand employment and training activities and to invest in skill development for in-demand jobs, among other strategies. In some cases, this includes adult education services. While those efforts are still relatively small at the moment, the SNAP Employment and Training program has the potential to grow, especially since states can qualify for additional federal matching funds if they enlist third-party partners, such as community colleges and nonprofit organizations, to contribute resources toward these services (USDA Food and Nutrition Services, 2016). In some cases, states are incorporating into these public assistance efforts the relatively new evidence-based strategies described earlier. In Oregon, for example, a community college consortium led by Portland Community College is partnering with the state's SNAP E&T program to expand career pathway services for SNAP recipients. In Kansas, TANF recipients can receive a scholarship to support their participation in the state's version of I-BEST, called AO-K (Bergson-Shilcock, 2016; Strawn, 2017).

Nevertheless, absent major changes in federal and state funding and policy governing cash assistance programs, it appears that adult education can expect little renewed interest and investment in basic skills services from that quarter for low-income adults with low skills. Instead, such individuals will have to look toward more universal approaches for help in upgrading their skills. There have been some encouraging national policy developments in this respect. Changes adopted in 2014 to federal adult education and job training policy, as part of the Workforce Innovation and Opportunity Act, encourage adoption of innovation strategies noted here, such as sector training, career pathways, and integrated basic education and training. In 2015 Congress changed federal student aid policy toward those without a high school diploma—the Ability to Benefit provision—to make it fairer and more consistent with WIOA policy, so that these students can now receive larger Pell Grants and colleges can implement the policy more easily Subsequent guidance from the U.S. Department of Education clarified for states and for colleges how federal student aid under the Ability to Benefit policy can be combined with adult education funding to support integrated basic education and job training models (Walizer, 2016; Walizer & Mortrude, 2017). Pending legislation in Congress would expand Pell Grants to cover noncredit training as short as 8 weeks in length; this could increase access to federal aid for those with lower skills who are more likely to enroll in short-term certificate programs. Outside of student aid, though, the funding picture remains bleak for adult education and job training services.

Despite resource constraints, these federal policy developments, combined with long-standing state and local innovation (including ones in adult education outside the scope of this chapter, such as managed enrollment, more active learning techniques, and digital literacy efforts), have contributed to a stronger focus in adult education on transitions to postsecondary education and to employment; more integration of academic and occupational content; and closer ties to community college, workforce agency, community organization partners, and businesses. These shifts likely mean adult education is better positioned than ever before to support adult learners, together with other partners, to increase their employment and earnings and ultimately improve their individual and family well-being. The challenge is summoning the political will to devote resources to these learners and continuing to build the evidence base to guide policymakers and practitioners toward more effective interventions.

Researchers can make important contributions to informing policy and practice. In the policy realm, for example, they could seek to learn from the various natural experiments underway in the states on expanding student aid—such as Washington State's landmark

Workforce Education Investment Act—to understand the extent to which lower-skilled adults can participate in and benefit from these more universal approaches to adult learning, which garner more political support for funding than basic skills education alone. Does the presence of integrated basic education and training options in Washington through I-BEST, for example, mean that lower-skilled adults will see expanded access to student aid, too, as a result of the new law? Are there lessons for the current debate nationally about expanding Pell aid to noncredit, short-term programs? To what extent is it possible or desirable to have a unified funding source for all forms of adult learning? Other issues deserving of more research include the extent to which structural issues in the labor market, such as neighborhoods or regions with high unemployment, poor infrastructure and few public transportation options, constrain how effective employment, education, and training strategies can be for low-skilled adults and the implications for policy.

Beyond these broad questions, there are many gaps concerning lower-skilled adults in the program evaluation literature that researchers could help fill. For example, what can sectoral training and career pathways programs do to serve lower-skilled adults than they do now while still successfully meeting the needs of their business and industry partners? How can programs help those with multiple challenges to employment, beyond low skills, address those issues and gain marketable basic and job skills at the same time? What kinds of researcher-program partnerships could help local programs learn from their data and improve their services for low-skilled adults in real time? Lower-skilled adults are frequently left out of policy and program evaluation research in this field; meaningful advances toward solutions to reduce poverty will be difficult unless that changes.

References

Anderson, T., Kuehn, D., Eyster, L., Barnow, B., & Lerman, R. (2017). *Final impact report for accelerating opportunity*. Urban Institute.

Barden, B., Juras, R., Redcross, C., Farrell, M., & Bloom, D. (2018). *The enhanced transitional jobs demonstration: new perspectives on creating jobs: Final impacts of the next generation of subsidized employment programs*. MDRC.

Bergson-Shilcock, A. (2016). *Integrated education and training policy toolkit*. National Skills Coalition.

Bos, J. M., Scrivener, S., Snipes, J., & Hamilton, G. (with Schwartz, C., & Walter, J.) (2002). *National evaluation of welfare-to-work strategies. improving basic skills: The effects of adult education in welfare-to-work programs*. MDRC.

Carnevale, A. P., Smith, N., & Strohl, J. (2010). *Help wanted: Projecting jobs and education requirements through 2018*. Georgetown Center on Education and the Workforce.

Center for Law and Social Policy. (2018). *When financial aid falls short: New data reveals students face thousands in unmet need*. https://www.clasp.org/publications/report/brief/when-financial-aid-falls-short-new-data-reveal-students-face-thousands

Center for Poverty Research, University of California, Davis. (2015). *How does level of education relate to poverty?* https://poverty.ucdavis.edu/faq/how-does-level-education-relate-poverty

Falk, G. (2019a). *The temporary assistance for needy families (TANF) block grant: A legislative history*. Congressional Research Service.

Falk, G. (2019b). *The temporary assistance for needy families (TANF) block grant: Responses to frequently asked questions*. Congressional Research Service.

Fein, D., & Hamadyk, J. (2018). *Bridging the opportunity divide for low-income youth: Implementation and early impacts of the year up program* [Pathways for Advancing Careers and Education (PACE) evaluation, OPRE Report #2018-65]. Office of Planning, Research, and Evaluation, Administration for Children and Families, U.S. Department of Health and Human Services.

Floyd, I., Burnside, A., & Schott, L. (2018). *Policy brief: TANF reaching few poor families*. Center on Budget and Policy Priorities.

General Accountability Office. (1995). *Welfare to work: Most AFDC training programs not emphasizing job placement* [GAO/HEHS-95-113]. General Accountability Office.

Glosser, A., Martinson, K., Cho, S. W., & Gardiner, K. (2018). *Washington state's integrated basic education and skills training (I-BEST) program in three colleges: Implementation and early impact report* [OPRE Report No. 2018-87]. Office of Planning, Research, and Evaluation, Administration for Children and Families, U.S. Department of Health and Human Services.

Gueron, J. (2016). *The politics and practice of social experiments: Seeds of a revolution*. MDRC.

Hall, R. (2016). *Expanding education and training opportunities under TANF: A path to stable employment in today's economy*. Center for Law and Social Policy.

Hamilton, G. (2012). *Improving employment and earnings for TANF recipients*. Urban Institute.

Hendra, R., & Hamilton, G. (2015). Improving the effectiveness of education and training programs for low-income individuals: Building knowledge from three decades of rigorous experiments. In C. Van Horn, T. Edwards, & T. Greene (Eds.), *Transforming U.S. workforce development policies for the 21st century* (pp. 411–440). W. E. Upjohn Institute for Employment Research.

Institute for College Access & Success (2018). *Pell Grants help keep college affordable for millions of Americans* [Fact sheet]. Institute for College Access & Success. https://ticas.org/sites/default/files/pub_files/overall_pell_one-pager.pdf.

Maguire, S., Freely, J., Clymer, C., Conway, M., & Schwartz, D. (2010). *Tuning in to local labor markets: Findings from the sectoral employment impact study.* Public Private Ventures.

Martin, V., & Broadus, J. (2013). *Enhancing GED instruction to prepare students for college and careers: Early success in LaGuardia Community College's Bridge to Health and Business Program.* MDRC.

Martinson, K., Copson, E., Gardiner, K., & Kitrosser, D. (2018). *Instituto del Progreso Latino, Carreras en Salud Program: Implementation and early impact report* [OPRE Report # 2018-06]. Office of Planning, Research, and Evaluation, Administration for Children and Families, U.S. Department of Health and Human Services.

Martinson, K., & Strawn, J. (2002). *Built to last: Why skills matter for long-run success in welfare reform.* Center for Law and Social Policy.

National Skills Coalition. (2017). *United States forgotten middle* [Fact sheet]. National Skills Coalition. https://www.nationalskillscoalition.org/resources/publications/2017-middle-skills-fact-sheets/file/United-States-MiddleSkills.pdf.

Office of Career, Technical, and Adult Education, U.S. Department of Education (2018). *Program year 2016–17 national summary of the statewide performance report for the adult education program, WIOA Title II.* Author. https://www2.ed.gov/about/offices/list/ovae/pi/AdultEd/spr/py2016/nationalsummary.pdf.

Office of Family Assistance, Administration for Children and Families, U.S. Department of Health and Human Services. (2018a). *TANF and MOE Spending and transfers by activity, FY 2017: United States.* Author. https://www.acf.hhs.gov/sites/default/files/ofa/fy2017_tanf_moe_national_data_pie_charts.pdf.

Office of Family Assistance, Administration for Children and Families, U.S. Department of Health and Human Services. (2018b). *Temporary Assistance for Needy Families (TANF) and Separate State Programs—Maintenance of Effort (SSP-MOE) work participation rates and engagement in work activities, fiscal year (FY) 2017, Tables 6a and 6b.* Author. https://www.acf.hhs.gov/ofa/resource/work-participation-rates-fiscal-year-2017

Office of Family Assistance, Administration for Children and Families, U.S. Department of Health and Human Services. (2018c). *Characteristics and financial circumstances of TANF recipients, fiscal year 2017. Table 20.* https://www.acf.hhs.gov/sites/default/files/ofa/fy17_characteristics.pdf

Office of Vocational and Adult Education, U.S. Department of Education (2013). *An American heritage—federal adult education: A legislative history 1964–2013.* Author.

Riccio, J. A., Friedlander, D., & Freedman, S. (1994). *GAIN: Benefits, costs, and three-year impacts of a welfare-to-work program.* MDRC.

Roder, A., & Elliott, M. (2018). *Escalating gains: The elements of Project QUEST's success.* Economic Mobility Corporation.

Roder, A., & Elliott, M. (2019). *Nine year gains: Project QUEST's continuing impact.* Economic Mobility Corporation

Rowe, G., Brown, E. & Estes, B. (2017). *SNAP employment and training (E&T) characteristics study: Final report.* U.S. Department of Agriculture, Food and Nutrition Service. https://www.mathematica.org/our-publications-and-findings/publications/snap-employment-and-training-e-t-characteristics-study-final-report

Schaberg, K. (2017). *Can sector strategies promote longer-term effects? Three-year impacts from the WorkAdvance demonstration.* MDRC.

Schwartz, D., Sarna, M., & Adam, T. (2020). *Evidence on career pathways strategies: Highlights from a scan of the research.* U.S. Department of Labor, Chief Evaluation Office. https://www.dol.gov/sites/dolgov/files/OASP/legacy/files/2-Career-Pathways-Research-and-Evaluation-Synthesis.pdf

Spiker, K. (2019, March 12). *Despite focus from the administration, budget falls short on much needed investment in workforce and education programs.* National Skills Coalition. https://www.nationalskillscoalition.org/news/blog/despite-focus-from-the-administration-budget-falls-short-on-much-needed-investment-in-workforce-and-education-programs

Strawn, J. (2017). *Integrating SNAP E&T into career pathway systems to boost outcomes* [SNAP to Skills Initiative, Policy brief 6]. Food and Nutrition Service, U.S. Department of Agriculture.

USDA Food and Nutrition Services. (2016). *About SNAP to Skills.* SNAP to Skills. https://snaptoskills.fns.usda.gov/about-snap-skills

Walizer, L. (2016). *Federal guidance explains how the ability to benefit provision aligns with a career pathway.* CLASP. https://www.clasp.org/blog/federal-guidance-explains-how-ability-benefit-provision-aligns-career-pathway.

Walizer, L., & Mortrude, J. (2017). *Ability to benefit: Understanding it & implementing it at your institution.* Center for Law and Social Policy. https://www.clasp.org/sites/default/files/ATB-Implementation-Guide.pdf

CHAPTER 38

Activism in/and Struggle

Teaching for a Different World

Dianne Ramdeholl and Rusa Jeremic

Tomorrow belongs to those of us who conceive of it as belonging to everyone; who lend the best of ourselves to it, and with joy.
—Audre Lorde (1988, p. 96)

Karl Marx (Marx & Engels, 1846/1976) said the point of the world is to change it, and one way to do this is through social activism. Lorde (1988) explicitly speaks of activism as a collective struggle for more joyful tomorrows for and with everyone, pointing out that a revolution is not a onetime event. One purpose of teaching activism is to make visible and transform what has been made habit and normalized through dominant systems in the interests of unearthing a more equitable world. Given the lightning-paced erosion of human rights—including the state-sponsored violent deportation of immigrants, women's and trans peoples' rights coming under attack publicly, and the climate crisis threatening human extinction—it is both urgent and critical for educators to think of, and act in, ways that go against the grain of instrumentalization that undermines adult education's potential for critical and collective action (Boggs, 1998; Brookfield & Holst, 2010; Davis, 2016). Social activism is thinking about collectively implementing equitable systems that care for ourselves/each other and creating shared resources instead of using labor from certain groups to create wealth for others (Dixon, 2014).

Adult education has long had roots in social activism aimed at a more just world (Brookfield & Holst, 2010; Heaney, 2000). Adult education must therefore include action, whether in the form of student advocacy, participating in classroom or program decision-making, or taking to the streets to protest social injustices; otherwise, it can become a sterile exercise that replicates systems of domination and dispossession. In the United States (and globally), this is especially urgent given the history of violence perpetuated through state-sponsored policies. Adult education for social change is explicitly situated in a long human rights struggle for democratic social change, standing in solidarity with marginalized groups that can only be produced in and through social activism. This chapter contextualizes current educational trends within a capitalist, neoliberal context, demonstrating how adult education must be necessarily intertwined with teaching social activism, and offers examples of best practices to challenging power and teaching social justice. In this chapter, we define *teaching for social justice* as curricula and pedagogy that reflect and unpack structural inequities impacting marginalized populations living in precarity. These frameworks are informed by Paulo Freire, Myles Horton, Augusto Boal, and other critical adult educators. We define *social activism* as lineages of struggle that have created visions of social transformation and revolutionary strategies to achieve those visions (Dixon, 2014).

Teaching Social Activism in a Neoliberal World

Neoliberalism plays a pivotal role in understanding the injustices and inequities prevalent today and how we can, as educators, offer alternative visions through teaching social activism. While social activism existed long before neoliberal policies emerged in the late 1970s, neoliberalism has, over the last 3 decades, impacted our lives, societies, cultures, ideologies, and our political systems both globally and locally. Now, decades in, we can see that the results of neoliberalism have been nothing short of an extreme concentration of wealth, which has eroded notions of a middle class and dramatically increased the gap between rich and poor both nationally and globally. This has not only "fueled unparalleled inequalities in income wealth" (Brodie, 2007, p. 93) but also impacted the life chances of future generations. Deeply embedded neoliberal thought has become the unquestioned lens through which we see and interact with the world, that is, "the common-sense way many of us interpret, live in and understand the world" (Harvey, 2007, p. 3). Muhammad (2014) defines this way of seeing and interacting with the world as an "age of individualism" (pp. 11–12), where everything revolves around the self-absorbed individual, which is now compounded in what Giroux (2015) calls a narcissistic selfie culture.

As such, neoliberalism has negatively impacted adult education. Hadley (as cited in Holborow, 2015) notes a "McDonaldization" (p. 4) of higher education, where the fast food model of food production and its lessons of quick, mass production of goods (in this case graduates) are applied to universities and community colleges. Through neoliberal policies and ideology, all levels of formal schooling and the education students receive are being negatively impacted (Tatelman & MacMillan, 2013). College-level job training programs, which emphasize technical aspects of education, are trumping the thinking aspects of education. While adult educators have tried to combat this through media literacy strategies and critical literacy education (Dehli, 2009; Rogers et al., 2009), it appears that students are graduating with fewer critical thinking skills—that is, if they can even afford to attend a postsecondary institution. Ledwith (2001) calls this "an anti-intellectual, antipraxis backlash—in which adult education is distracted by skills and competencies at the expense of ideas—all of which is located in a political context of anticollective individualism" (p. 174).

Adult education increasingly has become an entrepreneurial instrument, stressing methodology (*how to*) over purpose (*what for*) (Merriam & Caffarella, 1999). Degree programs offering adult education are currently not as connected to a social purpose as they once were even as recently as 20 years ago (Brookfield & Holst, 2010). This is reflected in a marked reduction of the number of U.S. higher adult education programs offering degrees focusing on social change. Decisions about programs are made solely based on profits. Because adult education degree programs have generally tended to be smaller and, ultimately, less profitable, they have been more vulnerable to cuts (T. Heaney, personal communication, August 17, 2012). With few exceptions, there is little in the curricula of many programs that aligns their mission with social justice and activism in explicit, unapologetic ways (T. Heaney, personal communication, May 22, 2015). National Louis University's doctoral program in adult education, which no longer exists (Brookfield, 2013), was one of a handful of examples that explicitly held social justice principles at its core. Though by no means conclusive, it provides some evidence of the lack of importance placed on social justice-driven education and activism by dominant higher education.

The general devaluing of education coupled with the emergence of increasing authoritarianism in political leadership is dangerous for any society. Such authoritarianism in leadership promotes what Giroux (2018) identifies as a purposeful civic illiteracy, the spreading of half-truths, fake news, and wild opinions with no factual basis. In this terrain, another vision based on truth and social justice becomes even more crucial, and teaching social activism becomes more imperative, provoking educators to think creatively about how we move students to action through transformative pedagogical approaches that rely on nontraditional methods of delivery.

Teaching Social Activism

Social activism is about change, and in order for there to be social change, there need to be shifts in power. Power circulates and is everywhere, in all social relations (Foucault, 1984). Activism teaches us ways to shift power by interrogating the status quo, supporting us in understanding how to critique dominant neoliberal capitalist systems, and disrupting traditions that wrap around disciplinary silo thinking in adult education. Activist thinking uproots dominant social and political structures that view certain groups as disposable as well as understands how capitalism serves to perpetuate violence, racism, and colonialism (Davis, 2016).

The concept of hegemony as presented by Gramsci (1971) identifies that dominant power and its replication occur through society's institutions, including official educational spaces, cultural initiatives, and societal priorities. In this way, one group or class builds hegemony through a moral or ethical leadership, an ideology where meanings, values, and ideas of a society are determined by the ruling classes, as Karl Marx famously observed (Marx & Engels, 1846/1976). At the same time, Gramsci insisted that hegemony needs the will of the people—their consent—to function, allowing for hegemony to be seen as a fluid, dynamic process that opens the door to counter-hegemonic struggle and resistance. The Gramscian framework of hegemony identifies how power is replicated. More importantly, this framework posits that replication of status quo is not static or monolithic, rather it allows space for challenging dominant ideas. Thus, for Gramsci, both formal and informal sites of education play crucial roles in what we would now identify as activist struggles or social activism.

Social activism (or activist pedagogy) involves understanding and acknowledging privilege such as racial and economic and how they serve to preserve the hegemony of dominant groups (e.g., White supremacy) in which less effort is required to thrive in a world assembled around one's own dominant ideologies. However, if you happen to be minoritized in some way, the wrong shape/color, you must make more effort to fit into dominant spaces in the world (Ahmed, 2017). Being racialized in higher education or female in a male-dominated profession demonstrates this. Activist pedagogies focused on social change must adopt an intersectional approach to social justice that recognizes multiple layers of oppression and includes elements such as human rights discourses both incorporating an understanding of universal rights and addressing inequities through antioppressive practice (Baines, 2006; Kumashiro, 2015), critical race theory (Brigham, 2013) that encapsulates understandings of White supremacy and privilege, and decolonization practices (Tuck & Yang, 2012) that go beyond lip service to examine hard truths. In doing so, they help frame a deeper analysis and understanding of what is happening and how people can resist oppressive power. Any revolutionary adult education project, including teaching social activism, needs to understand the ways in which oppressions/struggles are connected to each other with social relations of race, gender, and class (Davis, 2016). Carpenter et al. (2013) remind us of the importance of connecting the micro (individual) to the macro (societal) discourses and warns of the danger of only "conceptualizing experience as an individualized phenomenon" (p. 6), rather than as systemic.

Social Activist and Justice Centered Pedagogy Examples

> Every social action group should be at the same time an adult education group, and I go even so far as to believe that all successful adult education groups will sooner or later become social action groups. (Lindeman, 1945, p. 12)

Lindeman, in these words, intertwines social action with adult education. Adult education, historically, has had a strong relationship with social action and activism. There are many historical examples connecting adult education to activism. One is the important work that occurred at Highlander Folk School in Tennessee, an adult education social justice and activist school whose philosophy was that education had the possibility of affecting profound social change. A hallmark of the school was working on justice and equity for and with marginalized, invisibilized populations. Highlander played an essential role during the civil rights movement and beyond, training social activists, and community and labor leaders. They held adult literacy classes for African Americans who were nonproficient readers to register to vote. Septima Clark worked at Highlander and with her cousin, Bernice Robinson, and Esau Jenkins (a bus driver from Johns Island, South Carolina) developed citizenship schools on Johns Island. Rosa Parks also attended Highlander before refusing to give up her bus seat, an act which ignited the Montgomery bus boycott.

Another example of social activism and adult education was in the 1990s in New York City, when students and instructors organized together in response to impacts on adult literacy programs by welfare reform enacted by former president Bill Clinton. Welfare reform, under the Clinton administration, stipulated that adult literacy students could no longer attend programs of their choice and mandated that students work at a series of dead-end jobs in exchange for public benefits. Adult literacy students (primarily poor people of color) were outraged. The Welfare Literacy Coalition (a group of teachers, students, and program directors) began organizing around the welfare battle and adult literacy students' right to attend adult education programs of their choice. Students and instructors spoke out against what many saw as the criminalization of adult literacy students on welfare or an effort to frame Black and Brown poor people as lazy and undeserving (Ramdeholl, 2011). Ultimately, through these and other social activist actions, adult literacy students involved in this struggle began to feel their sense of collective power. Through activism, there was a sense of reconceptualizing oneself and one's roles in the world.

In response to the 2008 financial crisis, Occupy Wall Street emerged and specifically focused on political education and organizing (Dixon, 2014), which was grounded in activism training, grassroots organizing, and nonviolent direct action. Occupy encampments across the country and globally contained libraries and classes were held focusing on radical economics, labor, and radical pedagogy such as Theater of the Oppressed, developed by Augusto Boal (1974) who demonstrated political theater could provide ordinary people active opportunities to understand and change their social/political situations. In New York City, the Occupy movement was successful in bringing to the mainstream questions of inequality and injustice. In mini communities they set up in the financial district, they held classes on social, racial, and economic inequalities; invited guest speakers; and engaged in modeling alternative ways of living with and being with one another. Supporters of the movement (e.g., myself, Dianne Ramdeholl) who were unable to join full time, donated our time, clothing, cooked meals, and provided other resources.

Since 2011–2012 there has been a surge of grassroots movements seeking to counter the multiplicity of oppressions and inequities that they face. For instance, Movement for Black Lives, which seeks to highlight the need for equitable rights in Black communities and police oppression; Fight for 15, which seeks to raise the minimum wage to a living wage of $15.00 per hour; and #MeToo, which seeks to highlight systemic sexual harassment, have all relied on adult education techniques to advance their goals and challenge power—a key component of teaching social activism.

Components and Strategies of Activist Pedagogy and Taking Action

Some key components of social activism as teaching include raising critical consciousness, experiential learning, thinking critically, and connecting to values and worldviews. Heaney (2000) states that if adult educators adopt a neutral position and avoid challenges to the status quo, we inevitably serve the status quo. To leave structural inequities unattended is to not fight for a world that supports the dignity of the most invisible and marginalized among us (Brookfield & Holst, 2010; Choudry, 2015).

While social justice education and activist discourses have played a crucial role in encouraging students to become active participants in the world around them (Johnson-Bailey et al., 2010), the purpose has not always aligned with the methodology. Focusing on charitable acts is more widespread in educational institutions than enacting notions of solidarity. As Marullo and Edwards (2000) point out, promoting acts of charity in higher education, while well intentioned, often serves to reproduce the status quo rather than "transforming institutions of higher education into agents of social transformation" (p. 911). Acts of charity are prevalent within neoliberalism where "helping" people rather than working with people becomes an individual choice, instead of a collective necessity. What has become a common occurrence is to stop with charity (meeting immediate or temporary needs), thereby making murky the differences between charity and social justice. The emphasis on voluntarism, raising funds, donating to food banks, or marathon running for a cause are excellent examples of charity that students first experience in school at a young age. They are rewarded and valued for participating in these acts that stop short of engaging the structures that are creating the social problems (poverty, lack of living wages, privatized health care, affordable housing). In order to move beyond charity to a social justice rooted in solidarity, raising critical consciousness becomes key. Paulo Freire (as cited in Fischman & Haas, 2014) understood critical consciousness to be a process and stated that "conscientization is more of a process of commitment. I do not have to be already critically self-conscious in order to struggle. By struggling I become conscious/aware" (p. 46).

An activist pedagogy, then, is situated in deep understandings of social justice and our collective responsibility to transform the roots of injustice so that everyone can live a life with dignity as is their human right. Expanded notions of citizenship help us go beyond narrow definitions of who is/isn't a citizen and beyond traditional rights (civil, political) to understanding engagement and social justice as part of enacting our citizenship rights (Sparks, 1997). Social activism is seen as part of our civic duty and educational institutions play a role in how those rights are framed and teacher-activists help define that framing. Social justice education demands engagement with the world, questioning the status quo, owning (students' and activists') power, and a self-perception as potential change-makers (Kirylo et al., 2010). By linking experiential learning to lived practice and theory, teaching social activism (Freire, 1970; hooks, 2010; Mayo, 2014) is firmly rooted to a dialogical educational perspective that incorporates peoples' lived experiences and encourages learning that goes beyond understanding structures to feeling injustice. Learners are empowered through valuing lived experience as knowledge (Choudry, 2015), which connects to our core beliefs and value system (Nussbaum, 2013). Horton and Freire (1990) state that people cannot just read about visions for new worlds; they have to be able to experience them for themselves. They added that, if you want to change people's ideas, you should not convince them intellectually; instead you need to get them into a situation where they will act on those ideas. Experiential learning can assist learning in thinking critically and connecting values and worldviews. An assignment to attend a protest or community meeting that occurs simultaneously to learning about power, resistance, and organizing can raise critical consciousness, empower students as activists, and encourage social activism. Attending a political march or community meeting is a new experience that can be a transformative exercise for many adult learners who attend school, take care of their families, and work. By tying their participation to a self-reflective exercise that connects to theories of protest, students have the opportunity to engage in social activism in a collective manner and to reflect on their participation. The exercise can dispel common myths around protestors, protesting, and power. It can often serve to empower the students themselves as they can feel part of something bigger and gain a sense of their own power within the collective movement context. This straightforward exercise helps students engage with a variety of social movements and social issues as they are happening in the moment, such as attending Black Lives Matter sit-ins, protests in support of migrant rights, and community vigils against Islamophobia. Exercises of this sort promote solidarity. Davis (2016) framed *solidarity* as a (a) political action and practice, (b) way of living that supports communities in living with dignity and self-determination, (c) way of helping people restore confidence in their own collective people power, and (d) way to resist cultural domination of capitalism. Solidarity can be conceived as a political act of living and loving in the communities we reside, a way of being in the world that considers how each of our actions impact others and the planet. Navigating our lives in ways that are caring/respectful to both is necessary and urgent. In teaching activism, cocreated spaces in courses where power is shared with students are a way of practicing what is being learned and engaging solidarity. Practicing consensus decision-making structures around aspects of course content, group teach-ins, or Theater of the Oppressed techniques embodying political situations relevant to course themes are ways to teach activism. The course methodology needs to be liberatory in ways that reflect the content being studied. Strategies for achieving this include student-developed curricula in which themes relevant to students' lives are coconstructed with the instructor. Students could also join relevant collectives where they can gain experience and struggle around particular issues. Students have also made posters with adult literacy students, as well as attended rallies against repealing Deferred Action for Childhood Arrivals (DACA) and upholding the Muslim travel ban.

It is important to experience collective processes and nonhierarchical power structures directly. Recognizing this, one of the courses we teach requires students to volunteer for a minimum of 20 hours throughout the semester in various community-based adult literacy programs such as Make the Road New York or Arab American Association of New York, which offers students an immersion into a larger conversation about privilege, race, and power. Students come to better appreciate the struggles experienced by learners in the adult literacy programs (primarily, poor people of color), understand more deeply how adult literacy in the United States is inextricably linked to structural inequities, and recognize that dismantling these inequities is an ongoing struggle requiring collective efforts. During their field site experience, they hear first-hand from students of the desolation wreaked by the Muslim travel ban (a decision upheld by the Supreme Court in June 2018) and come to better understand that who is deemed a U.S. security threat has little to do with justice and more to do with upholding imperialist agendas (Davis, 2016). Students are better able to connect how state-sponsored policies such as the Muslim ban trigger violence such as the mosque terror attacks in Quebec City (Canada) in January 2017 or in Christchurch, New Zealand, in March 2019. While the context in New Zealand is different than North America's, there is a long, deeply racist history there regarding Indigenous populations and immigrants. These are no longer abstract issues for the students but struggles involving real people organizing to challenge dominant power and solve their problems.

In grappling with issues of social change, larger questions of positionality emerge: What does it mean to be an ally in struggles when one's own positionality is so vastly different from those with whom you are working? How, in recognizing one's privilege, can one be an effective ally knowing that your positionality displaces certain other groups in the world? Through Freire's (1970) problem posing, deeper understandings of ways in which using one's privilege to call out injustice is possible (and necessary) in struggles and being an ally, regardless of positionality, is possible when one acts with care and integrity. To reinforce this, in another classroom activity, students coauthor short skits (or codes) embodying situations affecting literacy programs (composites of conversations they heard at their sites) and together we analyze what is happening and why, and what is needed to change/shift the underlying root causes that produced this situation. In doing so, we come to better understand how it is possible to stand in solidarity with oppressed groups in ways that are respectful to those groups while considering one's racial/economic privilege.

Learning Through Discomfort: The Blanket Exercise
The Blanket Exercise is another strategy for teaching social activism. It capitalizes on what is known as the pedagogy of discomfort (Boler, 1999). As a mandatory classroom exercise, it helps to challenge structural injustice by connecting to our morals, values, and worldviews (Zembylas, 2015) and our beliefs. Feminist pedagogies have brought to the forefront how "transformation of consciousness requires attention to this intersection of emotional experiences, theories, and analysis of social institutions" (Boler, 1999, p. 117). Students learn the hidden history and impact of colonization on Indigenous (Native American) peoples through Indigenous voices by participating in the KAIROS Blanket Exercise, an exercise originally created for a Canadian context but now adapted to other contexts including American (United States) and Central American (Guatemala). It provides an opportunity to engage students on an emotional level before moving to theoretical considerations. In order to uncover the hidden history of colonial oppression, the Blanket Exercise situates students in the true history of colonization.

Strong emotional reactions are evoked as the history (often not really understood or known)—a history in which governments have been complicit and open in engaging in widespread oppression and genocide—comes alive. Emotional reactions can be connected to White settler guilt, the shattering of newcomers' belief that they were in a new land different and better from where they have come, being Indigenous, and histories of oppression from their own life experience, among others. Students are warned that they might feel uncomfortable with what they hear and feel and are encouraged to take the opportunity to "sit" in the discomfort (Boler, 1999) as a way of seeing, knowing, and understanding at a deeper level. This helps them to recognize how "emotional investments shape . . . attachments to particular worldviews" (Boler, 2014, pp. 27–30). The pedagogy of discomfort is for not only those who share a progressive worldview but also those who don't hold the same values.

Creating space for sitting in the discomfort that confronts the "common sense" of neoliberal authoritarianism at its core can "challenge the hegemonic narratives of everyday life that manipulate people to think and behave according to a dominant set of cultural beliefs" (Ledwith, 2011, p. 72). By understanding "how emotions function as a key site of ideological control" (Boler, 1999, p. 127), we are better positioned to engage in the transformative process of critical consciousness-raising in the public education milieu. The role play exercise is an experiential activity facilitated by an Indigenous person and a settler—understood to be anyone who is not original or indigenous to the land—and ends with a talking circle that provides participants an opportunity to reflect on their experience with others. Through this experiential emotional activity based in pedagogy of discomfort, the potential for learning and understanding oppression are varied but deep. This exercise always makes a big impact on students and there are more than a few (good) tears shed. Learning can happen through uncomfortable or unsettling moments and emotions. Later, this experience is connected to government policies and also resistance to those policies. It compels students to more fully understand and also provokes many to be in solidarity with Indigenous peoples' who continue to experience widespread oppression. Connecting to emotions to provoke contextualized learning is a powerful tool.

Conclusion: Moving Forward Toward Tomorrow

Freire (1970) points out that education can never be neutral, while Heaney (2000) sees the essence of the field as a quest to disrupt the status quo and subvert existing social order. As adult educators, it is important to ask: For whom? In whose interests? Teaching social activism requires students to read critically, asking the texts: What is truth? How do we know this to be true? Whose truth is this particular text privileging? Who does it benefit to believe this is true? Who does it harm? Whether acknowledged or not, traditional adult learning theories such as andragogy and other self-directed frameworks reframe adult education in terms in which successes and failures fall upon individuals as opposed to structural forces such as race, class, and gender, which affect us all.

Teaching activism must be grounded in understanding that this work is a profoundly anticapitalist project in which justice cannot be retributive but must be restorative in nature. It requires learning how to be compassionate with each other and understanding that living in such a highly capitalist society dehumanizes everyone—the oppressed and oppressor. It demands unlearning aspects of ourselves that have internalized the qualities rewarded in capitalism (competition, individual success, one person succeeding at the expense of another's failure, wealth being defined as solely monetary). To teach activism and its relationship to adult education is to learn about examples such as the Highlander Folk School in which groups who have suffered the most have stood up and to understand that when this happens, it enables everyone to stand up. It enables us to teach about connections between state violence and individual violence and the refusal to do the dirty work of capitalism.

To commit to a social activist pedagogy says we were here and we did not get used to it. This involves the cocreation and nurturing of collective intellectual and psychic spaces that are supportive/healing (Dixon, 2014). It forces us to ask how we can practice being more *human* human beings when capitalism not only surrounds us but also resides inside us, defining what we consider valuable, how we live, and what we believe possible (Boggs, 1998). It gives us the courage to resist and eject this internalization that everything can be commodified/is transactional, even core emotions such as love and encourages us to live in ways that don't perpetuate this toxicity. We need to be able to practice visionary organizing (Boggs, 1998), develop well-defined critiques and analyses of capitalism, and be able to eject the harm this system has inflicted on our souls and consciousness. Dominant neoliberal ideology has internalized unconscious emotions of individualism and alienation and a sense of Us versus Them that is manifesting itself today through the support of populist leaders and policies that mostly work in direct contradiction to the majority of peoples' best interests. As critical theory practitioners our emotions must be connected to our values in this age of half-truths, grandstanding, and media distortion, and these must be situated within a context of understanding social injustices in order to truly work for change.

We are at a critical crossroad in social activism teaching, with the rise of more strident thinking and a shrinking space for critical analysis. Teaching social activism is one way to counter the prevalent neoliberal ideology and rising authoritarianism. Teaching social activism can happen in a multitude of contexts and classes both formal and informal. Teaching social activism connects to students' hearts, minds and feet and helps adult learners become fully engaged citizens participating, responding, and working for social change in the world around them. To teach activism is to create collective visions that are worth fighting for, to do better for and with each other, to become more human. It is about seeking magical elsewheres to create what could be and being and staying attuned to more hopeful tomorrows, summoning those into today.

References

Ahmed, S. (2017). *Living a feminist life*. Duke University Press.

Baines, D. (Ed.). (2006). *Doing anti oppressive practice: Building transformative, politicized social work*. Fernwood.

Boal, A. (1974). *Theatre of the oppressed*. Theatre Communications Group.

Boggs, G. L. (1998). *Living for change*. University of Minnesota Press.

Boler, M. (1999). *Feeling power: Emotions and education*. Routledge.

Boler, M. (2014). Teaching for hope: The ethics of shattering worldviews. In V. Bozalek, B. Leibowitz, R. Carolissen, & M. Boler (Eds.), *Discerning critical hope in educational practices* (pp. 26–39). Routledge.

Brigham, S. (2013). Theorizing race in adult education: Critical race theory. In T. Nesbit, S. Brigham, N. Tabor, & T. Gibb (Eds.), *Building on critical traditions: Adult education and learning in Canada* (pp. 119–128). Thompson Educational Publishing.

Brodie, J. M. (2007). Reforming social justice in neoliberal times. *Studies in Social Justice, 1*(2), 93–107.

Brookfield, S. D. (2013). *Powerful techniques for teaching adults: Tools and techniques for democratic classrooms*. Jossey-Bass.

Brookfield, S. D., & Holst, J. D. (2010). *Radicalizing learning: Adult education for a just world*. Jossey-Bass.

Carpenter, S., Ritchie, G., & Mojab, S. (2013). The dialectics of praxis. *Socialist Studies/Études Socialistes, 9*(1), 1–17.

Choudry, A. (2015). *Learning activism: The intellectual life of contemporary social movements*. University of Toronto Press.

Davis, A. (2016). *Freedom is a constant struggle: Ferguson, Palestine, and the foundations of a movement*. Haymarket Books.

Dixon, C. (2014). *Another politics*. University of California Press.

Dehli, K. (2009). Media literacy and neoliberal government: Pedagogies of freedom and constraint. *Pedagogy, Culture & Society, 17*(1), 57–73. https://doi.org/10.1080/14681360902742860

Fischman, G., & Haas, E. (2014). "That's scary. But it's not hopeless": Critical pedagogy and redemptive narratives of hope worldviews. In V. Bozalek, B. Leibowitz, R. Carolissen, & M. Boler (Eds.), *Discerning critical hope in educational practices* (pp. 57–68). Routledge.

Foucault, M. (1984). Truth and power. In P. Rabinow (Ed.), *The Foucault Reader* (pp. 51–75). Pantheon.

Freire, P. (1970). *Pedagogy of the oppressed*. Seabury Press.

Giroux, H. A. (2015). Selfie culture in the age of corporate and state surveillance. *Third Text, 29*(3), 155–164.

Giroux, H. A. (2018). *The public in peril: Trump and the menace of American authoritarianism*. Routledge.

Gramsci, A. (1971). *Selections from the Prison Notebooks* (Q. Hoare & G. Smith, Eds.). Lawrence and Wishart.

Harvey, D. (2007). *A brief history of neoliberalism*. Oxford University Press.

Heaney, T. (2000). Adult education and society. In A. I. Wilson & E. R. Hayes (Eds.), *Handbook of adult and continuing education* (pp. 559–57). Jossey-Bass.

Holborow, M. (2015). Neoliberalism. In C. A. Chappelle (Ed.), *The encyclopedia of applied linguistics* (pp. 1–6). Wiley. https://doi.org/10.1002/9781405198431.wbeal1475

hooks, b. (2010). *Teaching critical thinking: Practical wisdom*. Routledge.

Horton, M., & Freire, P. (1990). *We make the road by walking*. Temple University Press.

Johnson-Bailey, J., Baumgartner, L. M., & Bowles, T. A. (2010). Social justice in adult and continuing education: Laboring in the fields of reality and hope. In C. Kasworm, A. Rose, & J. Ross-Gordon (Eds.), *Handbook of adult and continuing education* (pp. 339–349). SAGE.

Kirylo, J. D., Thirumurthy, V., Smith, M., & McLaren, P. (2010). Issues in education: Critical pedagogy: An overview. *Childhood Education, 86*(5), 332–334. https://doi.org/10.1080/00094056.2010.10521420

Kumashiro, K. (2015). *Against common sense: Teaching and learning toward social justice* (3rd ed.). Routledge.

Lorde, A. (1988). *A burst of light: Essays*. Firebrand Books.

Ledwith, M. (2001). Community work as critical pedagogy: Reenvisioning Freire and Gramsci. *Community Development Journal, 36*(3), 171–182.

Ledwith, M. (2011). *Community development: A critical approach* (2nd ed.). Policy Press.

Lindeman, E. (1945). The sociology of adult education. *The Journal of Educational Sociology, 19*(1), 4–13. https://doi.org/10.2307/2263073

Marullo, S., & Edwards, B. (2000). From charity to justice: The potential of university-community collaboration for social change. *American Behavioral Scientist, 43*(5), 895–912.

Marx, K., & Engels, F. (1976). *The German ideology*. International. (Original work published 1846)

Mayo, P. (2014). Gramsci and the politics of education. *Capital & Class, 38*(2), 385–398. https://doi.org/10.1177/0309816814533170

Merriam, S. B., & Caffarella, R. S. (1999). *Learning in adulthood: A comprehensive guide* (2nd ed.). Jossey-Bass.

Muhammad, U. (2014). *Confronting injustice: Social activism in the age of individualism*. Creative Commons Press.

Nussbaum, M. C. (2013). *Political emotions*. Harvard University Press.

Ramdeholl, D. (2011). *Adult literacy in a new era*. Paradigm Press.

Rogers, R., Mosley, M., & Folkes, A. (2009). Focus on policy: Standing up to neoliberalism through critical literacy education. *Language Arts*, *87*(2), 127–138.

Sparks, H. (1997). Dissident citizenship: Democratic theory, political courage, & activist women. *Hypatia*, *12*(4), 74–110.

Tatelman, S., & MacMillan, S. (2013). Are budget cuts being made in your child's school? *Canadian Family*. http://www.canadianfamily.ca/kids/are-budget-cuts-being-made-in-your-childs-school/

Tuck, E., & Yang, K. W. (2012). Decolonization is not a metaphor. *Decolonization: Indigeneity, Education & Society*, *1*(1), 1–40.

Zembylas, M. (2015). "Pedagogy of discomfort" and its ethical implications: The tensions of ethical violence in social justice education. *Ethics and Education*, *10*(2), 163–174. https://doi.org/10.1080/17449642.2015.1039274

CHAPTER 39

Sexual Diversity and Allyship in Adult and Continuing Education

Mitsunori Misawa and Craig M. McGill

Sexuality is one of the most complicated, yet understudied aspects of human behavior. A person's sexual identity, or *sexual orientation*, is inclusive of their sexual, romantic, emotional, or intellectual attraction to another person or to multiple people (American Psychological Association, 2018). Importantly, sexual orientation is about a person's attraction or feelings and not necessarily sexual *behavior* (e.g., a gay man having sex with women in the past or present does not mean he identifies as straight or bisexual). Despite sexuality being "the source of our most profound private emotional and physical experiences" (Edwards & Brooks, 1999, p. 49), the subject remains off limits in society at large, including adult and higher education, and conversations about sexuality rarely move beyond our most basic understandings of sexual orientation. Adult and continuing education (ACE) places value on diverse perspectives and multicultural understandings; however, this is the first chapter dedicated to sexual diversity issues to appear in an ACE handbook. The previous handbook (Kasworm et al., 2010) covered gender and sexuality broadly (Bracken & Nash, 2010), but issues experienced by sexual minorities—lesbian, gay, bisexual, trans, and queer (LGBTQ) people—was a small section of that chapter. Along with facing potential developmental and cultural obstacles due to their orientation, sexual minorities are often "denied civil rights, the right to work, and other human rights because of their sexuality and sexual orientation" (Rocco et al., 2009, p. 8).

Although the terms *gay* (often used to refer to homosexual men) and *lesbian* (often used to refer to homosexual women) have become commonplace, some people choose an alternate term, *queer*, or not to self-identify with any labels for their sexual orientation. Initially a pejorative term, queer has now come into the academic lexicon to represent ideologies/identities falling outside of the status quo. Queer also serves as a larger theoretical framework in which to problematize identity structures, such as being labelled "straight" or "gay." Introduced into academic discourse by theorist Teresa de Lauretis in 1990, queer "focuses on mismatches between sex, gender, and desire" (Jagose, 1996, p. 3). Thus, queer serves

> as an umbrella term for a coalition of culturally marginal sexual self-identifications . . . [and as] a category in the process of formation. It is not simply that queer has yet to solidify and take on a more consistent profile, but rather that its definitional indeterminacy, its elasticity, is one of its constituent characteristics. (p. 1)

Because dominant discourse in ACE remains heterocentric (Grace, 2013), conversations about sexual minorities rarely move beyond advocating acceptance. We aim to deepen this discussion. In this chapter, we contextualize historical and political contexts of sexual diversity, discuss sexual diversity within ACE, and offer implications for ACE practitioners. We use the acronym LGBTQ or the terms *sexual diversity* or *sexual minorities* as an umbrella for the queer community. However, we will vary deployment of the acronym based on the context and explore other terminologies and acronyms as appropriate.

Historical and Political Contexts of Sexual Diversity

Although an entire history of sexual diversity is out of the scope of this chapter, significant events within the 19th, 20th, and 21st centuries are worth highlighting. In the 19th century, the words *homosexual* and *heterosexual* were created to categorize human sexual behavior (Foucault, 1990). Previously, there were no distinctions, in a Western sense, related to sexual orientation because people assumed everyone was (a) heterosexual, (b) a sexual pervert, or (c) experiencing a Freudian stage leading to heterosexuality. In the late 19th century and the early 20th century, nonheterosexual behaviors were characterized as deviant (Foucault, 1990). This action was possible because early models of sexual orientation were based on heteronormative, conservative essentialist presumptions. In response, queer people were often subjected to conversion treatments to "fix" them to align to heterosexual norms. An exception to this prevailing Western notion was found within Indigenous communities. For instance, Two-Spirited people of North America were honored for their queerness and had special status in their tribes (Tafoya, 2003).

During the early 20th century, some queer people living in large cities had small opportunities to experience their sexual identity publicly. For instance, in New York City during the 1920s, the Harlem Renaissance "provided an informal and communal public pedagogical queer space for a coterie of musicians, artists, writers, and intellectuals" (Grace & Hill, 2004, p. 169). Alain Locke, a gay, African American man who was the first African American Rhodes Scholar (in 1910) and became the president of the American Association for Adult Education (AAAE, the precursor to AAACE), made significant contributions to the intellectual and artistic revolution of the Harlem Renaissance (Guy, 1996).

During and after World War II in the 1940s and 1950s, Americans were impacted by various social changes. For example, middle- and upper-class women entered the paid work force for the first time and gained economic independence. After the war, soldiers returned home, and women lost some of the economic gains they had made. As part of his witch hunts during the 1950s to eliminate communism in the United States, Senator McCarthy alleged links between gay people and communism, suggesting the USSR was infiltrating U.S. life by using gay people as spies (Faderman, 2015). This forced most LGBTQ people to hide their sexual orientation.

The period between 1960s and 1970s was pivotal for LGBTQ advancement. More LGBTQ people began publicly congregating for social and entertainment needs. The 1969 Stonewall Riots in New York City was a watershed moment, which marked the public shift of the LGBTQ experience from accepting violence, isolation, and homophobia to seeking safety and equality. Amid the sexual revolution, LGBTQ people gained visibility and worked to counter the prevailing notion that homosexuality was a mental illness. As a result, in 1973, the American Psychological Association eliminated homosexuality from mental illness diagnostic categories. Since this decision, homosexuality has not been considered a mental illness by credible psychological institutions, researchers, and practitioners, and many scholars now recognize homosexuality as healthy human development.

The LGBTQ movement grew globally and expanded to include greater social and individual human rights goals as society acknowledges LGBTQ people and becomes more inclusive of people's sociocultural identities (Hill & Grace, 2009b). Worldwide, the Pride Movement gradually took many forms including: annual marches and celebration of LGBTQ rights and freedom from oppression (Pride Month and Pride Parades); political and legislative efforts to attain legal rights, and protections for LGBTQ people equivalent to those of heterosexuals; increased and balanced portrayals of LGBTQ persons in news media, arts, and entertainment; and the right to marry same-sex partners (Bronski, 2011).

The last 35 years have been characterized by major issues, which have been taken up by researchers of sexual orientation, particularly activists and ACE scholars, including the AIDS epidemic (Baumgartner, 2002), the military policy of "Don't Ask, Don't Tell"

(Belkin & Bateman, 2003), the same-sex marriage debates (King, 2010), and eventually marriage equality (*Obergefell v. Hodges*, 2015).

In spite of these advances, there is still much LGBTQ oppression across the globe. This is complicated by international differences around the types of legal jurisdictions regarding homosexuality (Mendos, 2019). While the UN and other international reports document LGBTQ rights and protections and progress in some countries in the past few decades, they identify persistent areas of concern (ACHPR-IACHR-UN, 2016). There are countries with progressive laws and social changes (e.g., Netherlands, Canada, Sweden, New Zealand), countries with progressive laws and little social change (e.g., South Africa, Ecuador), countries with social change and little legal change (e.g., Eastern European countries), countries with mixed internal legal and social systems and municipalities or states with a mixture of progressive and conservative laws (e.g., United States, Australia), and countries with little legal change and little social progress (e.g., Uganda, Saudi Arabia, Pakistan, Russia).

Sexual Diversity in ACE Contexts

Although queer and sexuality studies have appeared as issues in some social science fields since the 1970s, it was not until the 1990s that LGBTQ issues first appeared in adult education (Hill, 1995) and human resource development (Gedro et al., 2004). Prior to the 1990s, ACE scholars often neglected sexual diversity as part of their curriculum/programs because, in being characterized as a sickness, sin, and/or perversion, homosexuality had been culturally ignored and legally excluded (Hill, 2004). In 1993, a Lesbian, Gay, Bisexual, Transgender, and Queer & Allies Caucus (LGBTQ&AC) was held for the first time at the Adult Education Research Conference (AERC), and the first AERC LGBTQ&A Preconference was hosted to celebrate that event's 10th anniversary at San Francisco State University in 2003 (Hill & Grace, 2009a).

The integration of LGBTQ issues into ACE curriculum was not without controversy. In 2009, Robert Hill faced persecution from the Georgia State Legislation, who called for his firing due to his teaching of queer issues (Mizzi et al., 2016). When Hill's vita revealed his "heinous educational agenda" (p. 105) to the legislature, his home university opened an investigation of his teaching, research, and service activities. When investigators determined this work was within scope of a legitimate academic field, Hill was exculpated and publicly declared a "nationally and internationally recognized scholar" (p. 105). That this occurred within the last decade indicates the immense struggle to legitimize queer issues within academe and a religiously zealous society and speaks to how the topic has been silenced in our educational systems, reifying exclusion in the broader society (King, 2009; Misawa, 2010). To follow we present the predominant issues of sexual diversity in ACE contexts: health care, workplace, transnationalism and globalization, and queer knowledge and praxis.

Health Care

ACE scholars and researchers have explored a variety of issues related to sexual minorities relative to health care. Their research has clear implications for health and wellness educators and providers. LGBTQ healthcare issues identified in the ACE literature include marginalization (Collins & Rocco, 2014a) and disparities in access and knowledge (Collins & Rocco, 2014b; Collins et al., 2014; Hill, 2011). Good health care is predicated in part on having open and trusting relationships with providers. Due to stigma, sexual minorities are marginalized and may have difficulty coming out to their physician, precluding a full consideration of the health issues they might be experiencing. Even if a sexual minority has established a trusting relationship with their caregiver, homophobia is pervasive in the medical profession. Collins and Rocco (2014a) point out, "Communication may be hindered by differences in levels of education between medical professionals and patients, community understandings about certain health conditions, prejudice, and cultural differences and in/sensitivities" (p. 9). This contributes to disparities in access and knowledge, creating barriers for sexual minorities to receive proper health care. Barriers might include "insurance status, knowledge of health and wellness, community attitudes toward authority or the medical community, discrimination, and trust, among others" (p. 9). For example, HIV-negative gay men with autoimmune diseases experience exclusion and dismissal based on incorrect assumptions about their HIV status (Collins & Rocco, 2014b). Thus, these men are an underserved, underexamined population who are not afforded full access to health-care services and knowledge. Collins and Rocco (2014a) note that "educat[ing] those sexual minorities who have been disowned/shunned from communities of 'birth' (e.g., family), health and wellness campaigns may be more effective in resource centers and other social venues in which sexual minorities gather for fellowship" (p. 10). Finally, lesbians are at higher risk (as a double minority) for alcohol abuse due to facing marginalization and stigmatization. Like other sexual minorities, lesbians "have 'special treatment concerns' in addition to recovery, such as grappling with and recovering from internalized homophobia" (Gedro, 2014, p. 59).

Sexual Diversity in the Workplace

Issues of sexual diversity in the workplace/organizational culture have also been discussed (Schmidt et al., 2012), especially in relation to the dis/comfort sexual minorities experience in the workplace (Mizzi, 2013). For instance, masculinized industries are "historically dominated by men embodying masculine, heterosexual work styles" (Collins & Callahan, 2012, p. 455). Due to their sexual orientation, gay men may not experience the male privilege afforded by straight men working in masculinized industries. The result is often an organization steeped in heteroprofessionalism, "a professional value that screens out homosexuality" (Mizzi, 2013, p. 1602). Organizations reify heteroprofessionalism by expecting gay men to "to think and behave in a heteroprofessional way" (p. 1617), which involves the following:

- Reassert[ing] heteromasculinist dominance as a normative functioning of an organization
- Operat[ing] through discourses of professionalism to devalue homosexual histories, identities, and understandings
- Silenc[ing], undervalu[ing], or marginaliz[ing] workers who try to address heteronormativity in the workplace
- Create[ing] policies and programs that do not take into account homosexuality. (pp. 1617–1618)

Heteroprofessionalism certainly impacts the tone of workplace culture and the experiences of queer workers. Rocco et al. (2009) articulated five workplace perspectives—hostility, compliance, inquiry, inclusion, and advocacy—and what a variety of organizational activities would look like within each of these perspectives. The organizational activities included new employee orientation, diversity/sexual harassment training, career development/progression, organizational development, strategic planning, and work/life balance. These perspectives and the ways the organization operates have implications for sexual minorities in terms of individual, career, and organizational development. The degree of openness an organization has to issues that impact sexual minorities can affect people working in these organizations. Organizational backlash to diversity efforts "includes diversity resisters' refusal to transition into new, more inclusive structures" (Hill, 2009, p. 42). Some of the backlash efforts include threats to major group entitlement, resentment for what is labeled "LGBTQ special rights," fear of LGBTQ people *taking* majority rights, religious intolerance, negative stereotypes about LGBTQ people, and government/politician-sponsored antigay speech. Hill examined the *AHRD Standards on Ethics and Integrity*, which are that

- difference is a fundamental human right that must be recognized in all organizational venues;
- justice, equity, and fairness are about "inclusion for all," not preferential treatment; and
- *diversity* must be redefined to not just embrace "minorities" . . . but also to welcome "nonminorities"—those who are from *dominant*, and historically *dominating* groups. (Hill, 2009, pp. 48–49)

By implementing these principles, human resource development (HRD) practitioners and scholars can diminish backlash. From these principles, LGBTQ workers and the dilemmas they face in workplaces should be discussed in ongoing programmatic efforts to diversify the workplace and make it a safe place for all employees. Commenting on the difficulty of designing universal HR policies, Gedro (2010) notes:

> Because there is no global consensus that LGBT people deserve legal protections against discrimination in employment, it is necessary for an HRD professional to understand the legal status of LGBT people within the appropriate geopolitical context for the training curriculum being developed. This lack of consistency in protections mirrors the persistent marginalization of LGBT people all over the world. (p. 357)

Transnationalism and Globalization

Related to Gedro's point, LGBTQ issues in ACE contexts have been examined from international and transnational perspectives. For example, studies have examined sexual minority "clandestine" work in a global context (Mizzi et al., 2016), the challenges of LBGT expatriates crossing international borders (Gedro et al., 2013), the adult teaching experiences of North American gay males overseas (Mizzi, 2015), intercultural dynamics of teaching sexualities in challenging contexts (Mizzi, 2016), and the effect of heteroprofessional norms on the workplace experiences of foreign gay men (Mizzi, 2013). Grace (2016) examined the role of media in countering homophobia in Uganda. These studies illustrate issues LGBQ people face worldwide and how LGBQ developments in one country can have effects on people in another. For instance, Hill (2007) participated in the International Conference on Adult Education (CONFINTEA V) in Hamburg, Germany, and, with others, discussed the negligence of LGBQ issues in the education of adults. The group worked toward three objectives: "advocate for justice in gender relations, promote education for 'another possible world', and advance learning for nondiscrimination and inclusion in difference spaces throughout life" (Hill, 2007, p. 172). To enact these objectives to benefit LGBQ people, Hill advised advocating for the "rights and dignity" (p. 172) of LGBTQ people who, in most places, live as second-class citizens, to include queer issues across all educational curricula, and nondiscrimination education for those who hold heterosexual privilege.

Queer Knowledge and Praxis

Finally, ACE scholars have written about epistemology and what constitutes queer knowledge/praxis. Because of societal heteronormativity, much of the learning adults must do to challenge the patriarchy involves "unlearning" societal messages they have internalized over their lifetimes. ACE has a history of encouraging behaviors such as counter-learning (Kucukaydin, 2010) or resisting commonly accepted norms and knowledge bases, within communities of oppressed or stigmatized people (Hill, 2004). Queering knowledge means:

> building adult education as a lived and knowable community that involves deliberate engagements with queer—a term representing our spectral community that incorporates a diversity of sex, sexual, and gender differences—and queerness—our ways of being, believing, desiring, becoming, belonging, and acting in life-and-learning spaces. (Grace & Hill, 2004, p. 168)

Thus, queer knowledge is a site of learning for queer praxis, "a practical, expressive, and reflective encounter with sex, sexual, and gender differences historically considered taboo terrain and relegated to fugitive spaces" (p. 168). Queer praxis destabilizes taken-for-granted (and often, hierarchical) binaries (e.g., male/female or straight/gay) and challenges assumptions like the conflation of sex and gender, and the privileging of "private acts over public ones" (p. 182). It recognizes the complexities of society and challenges adults to think about issues as more than either/or propositions. In this way, queer praxis "opens up the possibility of 'straight queers'" and accepts that some heterosexuals are "on the margins of heteronormativity" (p. 182). An example of "straight queers" are heterosexuals in the kink community whose sexual practices, however "heterosexual" they might be (one man/one woman), are not sanctioned as "healthy" sexual behavior by a heteronormative society. By problematizing heteronormative assumptions, queer praxis offers a "site of learning in adulthood, offering potential for personal development" and the possibility "for self-reinforcement and for queer persons to write themselves into an alien (heteronormative) world" (p. 182).

Implications for ACE

Providing awareness of sexual diversity is foundational to learning environments because it creates a more inclusive learning environment and improves understanding in ACE (Hill & Grace, 2009a). We believe adult educators can initiate, integrate, and perform queer praxis through queering spaces and pedagogical practice, infusing queer theory and LGBTQ topics into traditionally heteronormative curricula, and developing allyship and consciousness.

Queering Spaces/Pedagogy/Curriculum

We use the term *queering space* to mean that spaces should feel safe for those outside of the status quo (Misawa, 2009). Everyone is affected by homophobia, not just LGBTQ people. Although practices have been adopted by many higher education staff to promote welcoming, inclusive, and safe environments (e.g., SafeZone training, gender-neutral bathrooms), LGBTQ students continue to be marginalized in college environments (Misawa, 2009). Several authors have suggested there needs to be a more inclusive and welcoming environment for LGBTQ and other minority students in higher education (Cuyjet et al., 2012; Misawa, 2010; Stewart et al., 2015). Once faculty and staff begin to understand how an environment can impact a student's experience of sexual orientation, they can begin to appreciate the need to construct environments that embrace LGBTQ students and their sexual identity (Rhodes, 2019).

By building a culture of sexual diversity, workplaces can also benefit by having workers who feel included and supported. For instance, queering these spaces "can reduce discriminatory structures and processes; it can improve a company's image, and it can facilitate learning within the organization in order to enhance performance" (Gedro, 2010, p. 355). ACE practitioners and educators can listen to better understand the multiple dimensions (intersectionality) of their students' identities, their concerns, and learning needs to actively teach inclusively so that students can feel physically and psychologically safer (Misawa, 2015). They can advocate on the inside of organizations for policy changes (Hornsby & Munn, 2009). Another way is by creating a gay–straight alliance in their organizations as a means of establishing a professional and support network (Githens, 2009).

Teaching, pedagogy, and curriculum can be queered in several ways. The adult education classroom is an important site for learning about sexual diversity (Misawa, 2009). Students enter the classroom "with preconceptions about how the world works" (Hill, 2004, p. 91), and thus, the classroom provides an opportunity for adult educators to challenge and dismantle heterocentric ideas through queering teaching. As a site for the confluence of theory and activism, adult educators can use the classroom "to offer students new ways of seeing and being in the world" (p. 91). Infusing queer theory into pedagogy "offers an alternative paradigm, a richer possibility of insights into ways to facilitate individual and organizational learning because it questions relations of power, privilege, and identity" (Gedro, 2010, p. 355). For a queer-identified instructor, this may involve disclosing their sexual identity, which can be difficult in a heteronormative society. This creates vulnerability and requires building rapport with students. However, if they know how to disclose their sexual identities or how to address sexual diversity, they can create richer learning opportunities for their students.

Queering pedagogy should go beyond an instructor revealing their sexual identity. Queering pedagogy can be done by utilizing established teaching models such as the culturally responsive teaching model (CRTM). This model focuses on envisioning and designing adult learning experiences that will help adult learners to be intrinsically motivated. CRTM's four foundational conditions are to establish inclusion, develop a positive attitude, enhance meaning, and engender competence (Ginsberg & Wlodkowski, 2009). Instead of LGBTQ learners constantly seeking to find their space in heteronormative classrooms, this approach provides them with learning experiences that support their sexual orientation and welcomes sexual diversity.

Queering a curriculum involves deconstruction of heterocentric representation and associations of sexuality in the curriculum (Misawa, 2009), which challenges the status quo and questions power dynamics among diverse groups. Heterosexual instructors can, for instance, queer the curriculum by including LGBTQ issues "within lecture, reading, and assignments" which "decenters the heterosexist assumption of the classroom" (p. 101). Decentering heteronormativity and intentionally bringing in queer issues can broaden the perspectives of all classroom participants by helping them appreciate the struggles of queer people (Allen, 1995). In so doing, adult educators perform the difficult, but ethically responsible, task of creating "pedagogical play spaces" (Plumb, 2009, p. 17) in which people who may not normally think about different sexualities are exposed to a "mosaic of difference" (Edwards & Brooks, 1999, p. 56). Potential sites might be secondary school sex education classrooms, as well as LGBTQ resource centers in communities and on college campuses. Educational outreach should focus on healthy benign sexual variance. That is, healthy differences spanning a range of sexualities and gender expressions as opposed to death and illness of LGBTQ people (McGill & Collins, 2015). In so doing, education may reveal to students their "attachments to heteronormality, homophobia, and heterosexual privilege" (Hill, 2004, p. 91). So, considering those privileges in teaching, pedagogy, and curriculum would be important for ACE practitioners to create a queer space for LGBTQ populations.

Developing Allyship for Social Justice

To achieve the fundamental social justice purposes of adult education, adult educators must work to become allies. Becoming an ally is challenging; unlike advocating for other underrepresented people, there is a threat of being perceived as LGBTQ, and possibilities for verbal abuse or ostracism echoing the experience of being LGBTQ. Intrinsic benefits of allyship include greater ability to relate to and work with all members of society, building broader interpersonal relationships, development of a stronger sense of self-efficacy, increased self-esteem, and congruence between one's values and one's actions (McIntosh, 1998). However, most people are unable to become an ally instantly; allyship involves a long adjustment, described as a *cycle of socialization/liberation* (Harro, 2000), through which people of the dominant culture discern their role in an unjust society. As allies become aware of contradictions inherent in the system—a disjunction between current observations and what they believed true—creates dissonance. They must unlearn assumptions and stereotypes they have been taught to believe. As part of this process, people begin redefining their identity as belonging to the dominant group. Although defining oneself as part of the dominant group does not inherently make one a "bad" or "good" person, discerning one's identity in such a way can cause feelings of anger and guilt. But it can also produce feelings of pride and empowerment in pursuit of challenging systemic oppression. In so doing, people realize there may be negative social consequences for undertaking such actions, which leads to further consciousness raising about their surroundings causing reflection and a need to find others who experience dissonance, too.

Although models of multicultural and diversity competency have abounded, in recent years there is a shift to reframe the discourse to one of *consciousness* (Cuyjet et al., 2012). Social justice and equity issues should not be satisfied with *competence*, but rather, a more comprehensive reframing and understanding of social issues. Conscientization provides a strong foundation for cultivating critical consciousness and sociopolitical and sociocultural responsibility (Freire, 1973). Regardless of one's sexual orientation, consciousness requires one to take responsibility for guarding, securing, and fighting for LGBTQ rights, equality, protection, and practices. Such LGBTQ consciousness spans ACE contexts and organizations for opportunities to be more welcoming, inclusive, and supportive of people of all sexual orientations. It is a tremendous challenge to transform social and organizational cultures and practices while also transforming our personal and professional understanding and practices. Such practices constitute *resistance education*, leading "to powerful identity transformations in individuals" (Hill, 1995, p. 148). Practicing consciousness may pose discomfort but getting out of our comfort zone allows us to expand our learning. When people unlearn things they have taken to be truths, they can confront stigmatization, homophobia, and heteronormativity. Adult education programs, pedagogy, and statements of purpose, whether through educational institutions or classrooms, influence learners' perceptions of environments.

Conclusion

The fight for justice is not over simply because marriage equality has been enacted in many countries. There are policy reversals and homophobic attitudes expressed at state and federal levels. ACE educators need to be deeply committed to the cause during these difficult times and use any momentum as an opportunity for teaching a better understanding of inclusion and diversity (Edwards & Brooks, 1999). We believe this is the case for all people, queer-identified or not. We also believe this requires commitment to unlearning social scripts deeply undergirding societal heteronormativity. Without unlearning these scripts, adults reify homophobia and "cultural practices that are expressions of a politics of complicity that perpetuates heterosexism and homophobia. Such unlearning requires that educators conceive of their educational project as an active engagement in a politics of hope and possibility" (Grace & Hill, 2004, p. 186). So, ACE practitioners must commit to this unlearning process so that they can create a queer space where sexual diversities are valued and there is no judgment for LGBTQ populations.

References

African Commission on Human and Peoples' Rights, Inter-American Commission on Human Rights, and United Nations (ACHPR-IACHR-UN). (2016). *Ending* violence and other human rights violations based on sexual orientation and gender identity. Pretoria University Law Press.

Allen, K. R. (1995). Opening the classroom closet: Sexual orientation and self-disclosure. *Family Relations, 44*, 136–141.

American Psychological Association (2018). *Lesbian, gay, bisexual, transgender.* http://www.apa.org/topics/lgbt/index.aspx

Baumgartner, L. M. (2002). Living and learning with HIV/AIDS: Transformational tales continued. *Adult Education Quarterly, 53*(1), 44–59. https://doi.org/10.1177/074171302237203

Belkin, A., & Bateman, G. (Eds.). (2003). *Don't ask, don't tell: Debating the gay ban in the military.* Lynne Rienner.

Bracken, S. J., & Nash, H. (2010). Struggles for utopia(s)? Gender and sexuality in adult and continuing education. In C. E. Kasworm, A. D. Rose, & J. M. Ross-Gordon (Eds.), *Handbook of adult and continuing education* (pp. 351–358). SAGE.

Bronski, M. (2011). *A queer history of the United States.* Beacon Press.

Collins, J. C., & Callahan, J. L. (2012). Risky business: Gay identity disclosure in a masculinized industry. *Human Resource Development International, 15*(4), 455–470. https://doi.org/10.1080/13678868.2012.706427

Collins, J. C., & Rocco, T. S. (2014a). Disparities in healthcare for racial, ethnic, and sexual minorities. *New Directions for Adult and Continuing Education, 2014*(142), 5–14.

Collins, J. C., & Rocco, T. S. (2014b). HIV-negative gay men and autoimmune diseases. In J. C. Collins, T. S. Rocco, & L. O. Bryant (Eds.), *Health and wellness concerns for racial, ethnic, and sexual minorities* (pp. 73–80). John Wiley.

Collins, J. C., Rocco, T. S., & Bryant, L. O. (Eds.). (2014). Health and wellness concerns for racial, ethnic, and sexual minorities [Themed Issue]. *New Directions for Adult and Continuing Education, 2014*(142).

Cuyjet, M. J., Howard-Hamilton, M. F., & Cooper, D. L. (Eds.). (2012). *Multiculturalism on campus.* Stylus.

Edwards, K., & Brooks, A. K. (1999). The development of sexual identity. *New Directions for Adult and Continuing Education, 1999*(84), 49–57. https://doi.org/10.1002/ace.8406

Faderman, L. (2015). *The gay revolution: The story of the struggle.* Simon & Schuster.

Foucault, M. (1990). *The history of sexuality: An introduction* (Vol. 1). Random House.

Freire, P. (1973). *Education for critical consciousness.* Continuum. https://doi.org/10.1177/1523422310375029

Gedro, J. (2010). Understanding, designing, and teaching LGBT issues. *Advances in Developing Human Resources, 12*(3), 352–366. https://doi.org/10.1080/1367886042000243790

Gedro, J. (2014). Alcoholism and lesbians. *New Directions for Adult and Continuing Education, 2014*(142), 73–80.

Gedro, J. A., Cervero, R. M., & Johnson-Bailey, J. (2004). How lesbians learn to negotiate the heterosexism of corporate America. *Human Resource Development International, 7*(2), 181–195. https://doi.org/10.1080/1367886042000243790

Gedro, J., Mizzi, R. C., Rocco, T. S., & van Loo, J. (2013). Going global: Professional mobility and concerns for LGBT workers. *Human Resource Development International, 16*(3), 282–297. https:doi.org/10.1080/13678868.2013.771869

Ginsberg, M. B., & Wlodkowski, R. J. (2009). *Diversity and motivation: Culturally responsive teaching in college.* John Wiley.

Githens, R. P. (2009). Capitalism, identity politics, and queerness converge: LGBT employee resource groups. *New Horizons in Adult Education & Human Resource Development, 23*(3), 18–31. https://doi.org/10.1002/nha3.10347

Grace, A. (2013). Gay rights as human and civil rights: Matters of degree in culture, society, and adult education. In T. Fenwick, T. Nesbit, & B. Spencer (Eds.), *Contexts of adult education: Canadian perspectives* (pp. 72–81). Thompson Educational Publishing.

Grace, A. P. (2016). Counteracting fabricated anti-gay public pedagogy in Uganda with strategic lifelong learning as critical action. *International Journal of Lifelong Education, 35*(1), 51–73.

Grace, A. P., & Hill, R. J. (2004). Positioning queer in adult education: Intervening in politics and praxis in North America. *Studies in the Education of Adults, 36*(2), 167–189.

Guy, T. C. (1996). Alain Locke and the AAAE movement: Cultural pluralism and negro adult education. *Adult Education Quarterly, 46*(4), 209–223.

Harro, B. (2000). The cycle of liberation. *Readings for diversity and social justice, 2*, 52–58.

Hill, L. H. (Ed.). (2011). Adult education for health and wellness. [Themed Issue]. *New Directions for Adult and Continuing Education, 2011*(130).

Hill, R. J. (1995). Gay discourse in adult education: A critical review. *Adult Education Quarterly, 45*(3), 142–158.

Hill, R. J. (2004). Activism as practice: Some queer considerations. *New Directions for Adult and Continuing Education, 2004*(102), 85–94.

Hill, R. J. (2007). Finding a voice for sexual minority rights: Some comprehensive policy considerations. *Convergence, 40*(3/4), 169–179.

Hill, R. J. (2009). Incorporating queers: Blowback, backlash, and other forms of resistance to workplace diversity initiatives that support sexual minorities. *Advances in Developing Human Resources, 11*(1), 37–53.

Hill, R. J., & Grace, A. P. (Eds.) (2009a). *Adult and higher education in queer contexts: Power, politics, and pedagogy*. Discovery Association.

Hill, R. J., & Grace, A. P. (2009b). Introduction: Queer silence no more—Let's make some noise. In R. J. Hill & A. P. Grace (Eds.), *Adult and higher education in queer contexts* (pp. 1–10). Discovery Association.

Hornsby, E. E., & Munn, S. L. (2009). University work—life benefits and same-sex couples. *Advances in Developing Human Resources*, *11*(1), 67–81. https://doi.org/10.1177/1523422308329199

Jagose, A. (1996). *Queer theory: An introduction*. New York University Press.

Kasworm, C. E., Rose, A. D., & Ross-Gordon, J. M. (Eds.). (2010). *Handbook of adult and continuing education*. SAGE.

King, K. P. (2009). Crossroads for creating my space in the workforce: Transformative learning helps understand LGBTQ sexual identity development among adults. In R. J. Hill & A. P. Grace (Eds.), *Adult and higher education in queer contexts* (pp. 139–155). Discovery Association.

King, K. P. (2010). A personal journey into gay marriage in a heteronormative society: Or . . . how many times do we have to get "married" in order to have our rights in the USA? *New Horizons in Adult Education & Human Resource Development*, *24*(1), 71–77.

Kucukaydin, I. (2010). Counter-learning under oppression. *Adult Education Quarterly*, *60*(3), 215–232. https://doi.org/10.1177/0741713609358448

McGill, C. M., & Collins, J. (2015). Creating fugitive knowledge through disorienting dilemmas: The issue of bottom identity development. *New Horizons in Adult Education and Human Resource Development*, *27*(1), 32–43. https://doi.org/10.1002/nha3.20091

McIntosh, P. (1998). White privilege: Unpacking the invisible knapsack. In E. Lee, D. Menkart, & M. Okazawa-Rey (Eds.), *Beyond heroes and holidays: A practical guide to K–12 anti-racist, multicultural education and staff development* (pp. 79–82). Teaching for Change.

Mendos, L. R. (2019). Author's preface. In L. R. Mendos (Ed.), *State-sponsored homophobia* (13th ed). (pp. 13–16). International Lesbian, Gay, Bisexual, Trans and Intersex Association.

Misawa, M. (2009). Where is our citizenship in academia? Experiences of gay men of color in higher education. In R. J. Hill & A. P. Grace (Eds.), *Adult and higher education in queer contexts* (pp. 111–126). Discovery Association.

Misawa, M. (2010). Queer race pedagogy for educators in higher education. *International Journal of Critical Pedagogy*, *3*(1), 26–25.

Misawa, M. (2015). Cuts and cruises caused by arrows, sticks, and stones in academia: Theorizing three types of racist and homophobic bullying in adult and higher education. *Adult Learning*, *26*(1), 6–13. https://doi.org/10.1177/1045159514558413

Mizzi, R. C. (2013). "There aren't any gays here": Encountering heteroprofessionalism in an international development workplace. *Journal of Homosexuality*, *60*(11), 1602–1624. https://doi.org/10.1080/00918369.2013.824341

Mizzi, R. (2015). Sexualities on the move: A comparison of the work experiences of gay male educators teaching overseas. *Canadian Journal of Educational Administration and Policy*, *173*, 73–92.

Mizzi, R. C. (2016). Tackling cultural blinders: Towards an understanding of a sexuality, adult education, and intercultural dynamic. In G. Strohschen (Ed.), *The metagogy project: A theorem for a contemporary adult education praxis* (pp. 257–273). American Scholars Press.

Mizzi, R. C., Hill, R., & Vance, K. (2016). Beyond death threats, hard times, and clandestine work: Illuminating sexual and gender-minority resources in a global context. In R. Mizzi, T. Rocco, & S. Shore (Eds.), *Disrupting adult and community education: Teaching, learning, and working in the periphery* (pp. 101–115). SUNY Press.

Obergefell v. Hodges, 576 U.S. 644 (2015).

Plumb, D. (2009). Intimacy and ethical action in adult education. *New Horizons in Adult Education and Human Resource Development*, *23*, 6–21.

Rhodes, C. M. (2019). A practical guide to queering the adult English language classroom. *Adult Learning*, *30*(4), 160–166. https://doi.org/10.1177/1045159519840334

Rocco, T. S., Landorf, H., & Delgado, A. (2009). Framing the issue/framing the question: A proposed framework for organizational perspectives on sexual minorities. *Advances in Developing Human Resources*, *11*(1), 7–23.

Rubin, G. (1984). Thinking sex: Notes for a radical theory of the politics of sexuality. In C. Vance (Ed.), *Pleasure and danger: Exploring female sexuality* (pp. 143–178). Routledge.

Schmidt, S. W., Githens, R. P., Rocco, T. S., & Kormanik, M. B. (2012). Lesbians, gays, bisexuals, and transgendered people and human resource development: An examination of the literature in adult education and human resource development. *Human Resource Development Review*, *11*(3), 326–348. https://doi.org/10.1177/1534484312447193

Stewart, D. L., Brazelton, G. B., & Renn, K. A. (Eds.). (2015). LGBTQ college student success [Themed issue]. *New Directions for Student Services*, *2015*(152).

Tafoya, T. (2003). Native gay and lesbian issues: The two-spirited. In L. D. Garnets & D. C. Kimmel (Eds.). *Psychological perspectives on lesbian, gay, and bisexual experiences* (pp. 401–409). Columbia University Press.

CHAPTER 40

Gender and Its Multiple Forms

Laura L. Bierema and André P. Grace

Laura: I am a White, U.S. cisgender heterosexual woman (she/her), first-generation college graduate. I began researching women in organizations during the 1990s, viewing gender from a feminist perspective that emerged during my early career in automotive manufacturing. During that time, I held a binary view of gender (female-male), overlooked heterosexual privilege, and lacked intersectional understanding. I have become increasingly critical in my work over the past 20 years, with the realization that interlocking systems of power and oppression in organizations and society need to be interrogated and restructured. Writing this chapter scared me a bit. Indeed, the way we think and talk about gender has changed radically, and making sense of the shifts and how they impact research and practice is intimidating. I believe we all need to engage in work to value gender diversity. I continue my learning on a daily basis as an educator, researcher, and ally.

André: I am a White, Canadian cisgender gay man (he/him). My history of struggle as I came out and came to terms with my sexual orientation involved dealing with both internalized and cultural homophobia and consequential comprehensive health issues. Focusing on the trans "T" in LGBT+, understanding gender identity and sexual orientation as separate personal characteristics, and interrogating transphobia came later. Over the past decade, I have engaged in continuous learning about gender diversity. I have also grappled with my own gender identity as a male who grew up seeing the world through female lenses provided by strong women in my life. I know my core is feminine in disposition. My worldview is a construction solidified by the influences of my mother Joan, my aunts Mary and Anne, and my grandmothers Mary Ellen and Margaret. I am pieces of each woman in terms of my attitudes, values, and beliefs. These days, I am fortunate to learn and work with gender diverse individuals in academe and in my inner-city community through a comprehensive health education and outreach project I initiated a few years ago. Today, I see gender as something big, intriguing, and beyond historical binary limits. It is an unbounded focal point for being, learning, and acting in the world.

We decided to begin with these narrative vignettes locating ourselves as gender subjects because we believe educators need to know and name their gender subjectivities as part of their work to develop broader, relational understandings of gender and its multiple forms. The spectral nature of gender as a sociocultural construction is embodied in conceptions of the body, identity, and expression. How we understand and position gender deeply affects how we navigate life, learning, and work. In contemporary times, constructing gender is an intricate socioecological process shaped by self, others, culture, history, social expectations, geography, and politics, as well as by our interpretations of their effects on personal agency and how we act in the world (Grace, 2015). These days, with the move to position gender as spectral, those who construct and self-affirm their gender against the grain of the male-female binary contest conventional sociocultural norms delimiting gender to either male or female. For adult and continuing education, this contestation challenges educators and learners to build knowledge and understanding of the spectrum of gender identities that includes such designations as cisgender, transgender, and nonbinary. *Cisgender* describes a person whose lived gender identity as male or female is coterminous with natal or birth sex. *Transgender* describes a person whose self-affirmed gender identity does not align with natal sex/gender assigned at birth. While it is a nebulous term defined differently by different people, *nonbinary* generally describes a person who does not fit into the male-female binary as discretely male or female. There is also Indigenous or other culturally distinguished gender diversity, signifying that culture plays an important role in locating and giving meaning to gender identities.

In this chapter, we investigate gender and its multiple forms. We discuss what it means to integrate a focus on gender diversity to meet learner needs, address organizational issues, and develop inclusive adult and continuing education. In doing so, we interrogate the historical conception of gender as a binary construction and introduce scaffolding for more broadly conceptualizing and incorporating gender as a complex formation in teaching and learning contexts. We begin with an examination of gender and gender identity as they are understood in contemporary times. We then review how gender and its multiple forms have been studied in particular U.S. adult education and human resource settings. As examples, we explore prior versions of the U.S. *Handbook of Adult and Continuing Education*, beginning with the controversial 1989 handbook. This edition was much critiqued for its failure to address diversity of women in intersections with other relational differences, notably race. We also examine 25 years of Adult Education Research Conference (AERC) proceedings, starting with the 1993 conference where Robert J. Hill initiated the Lesbian, Gay, Bisexual, Transgender, Queer & Allies Caucus (Hill & Grace, 2009). We then consider the meager attention paid to gender in recent handbooks of human resource development (HRD) as well as journals sponsored by the Academy of Human Resource Development. We cover 2010 to 2018 for the HRD focus, which coincides with a time frame when sexual and gender minority inclusion was increasingly taken up in U.S. law, legislation, and institutional policy making. In sum, we note how these various mainstream ventures in adult and continuing education have predominantly focused on limited binary interpretations of gender. We then continue to develop perspectives on gender diversity, speaking to negative consequences of genderism. Finally, we discuss ways to affirm gender diversity and promote inclusion in classrooms and organizations.

Understanding Gender and Gender Identity in Contemporary Times

As new knowledge and understanding of gender and its spectrum of gender identities emerge, it is increasingly accepted that the parameters of gender exceed birth sex/gender assigned at birth. For some time now, the American Psychiatric Association (APA) has deliberated the nature of gender diversity and what it means for someone to be gender healthy. APA positions have profound ramifications in individual and institutional contexts. In 2013, the organization decided to remove the pathological diagnosis of gender identity disorder (GID) from its Diagnostic and Statistical Manual of Mental Disorders in its DSM-5 edition (Byne et al., 2012). Indeed, the APA (2013) now holds that "gender nonconformity is not in itself a mental disorder" (p. 1). Thus, GID, which located gender variation outside the male-female binary as psychopathology from 1980 in DSM-3, was replaced with what is perhaps the less-stigmatizing diagnosis of *gender dysphoria* (GD). The change in diagnosis to GD was the result of persistent community advocacy and intensive academic deliberations within the APA (Scharrón-del Río et al., 2014). Pragmatically, the diagnostic term *GD* was included in the DSM-5 in order to "facilitate clinical care and access to insurance coverage that supports mental health" (APA, 2013, p. 1). Notably, GD moves beyond historical pathologizing of the individual, denoting "the presence of clinically significant distress" (APA, 2013, p. 1) is due to systemic stressors like genderism and transphobia. While the delisting of GID was indeed groundbreaking, it was nevertheless controversial, with deliberations demonstrating that U.S. psychiatry remains challenged in setting standards and determining approaches to address variations in gender identity (Drescher & Byne, 2012). Considering this, and noting the history of psychologization in U.S. academic adult education (Grace, 2012, 2013), adult educators ought to problematize gender discourses in psychiatry and psychology as part of considering how sources of disciplinary knowledge on topics like gender identity and expression impact field dynamics.

Progressive psychiatrists who advocated for the removal of GID from the DSM-5 locate gender identity as a personal characteristic that can transcend natal sex (Byne et al., 2012; Ehrensaft, 2011). In their professional discourse, they use *transgender* as a "collective term to incorporate all and any variance from imagined gender norms" (Valentine, 2007, p. 14). As Valentine (2007) relates, disciplinary deliberations (notably in psychiatry) along with public policy work, media coverage, and grassroots activism have increased the visibility of transgender as a social and analytic category. Acknowledging that transgender itself does not encompass all gender variation, this visibility challenges us to consider how we rearticulate the social, cultural, and institutional constructions of gender and gender identity and expression beyond binary cisgender limits (Grace, 2015).

There is much work to do here, because it is still a sociocultural norm to contain gender within the fixity of the male-female binary. Those who do so in culture, society, and its educational and other institutions are subscribing to genderism as a hegemonic and systemic stressor that works against recognizing and accommodating gender diversity (Grace, 2015). Genderism has historically fueled hetero-patriarchy marked by cisgender male dominance and cisgender female subjugation. It resists transgender and begets transphobia, which is a fear of gender differences sparked by ignorance and expressed in forms of symbolic and physical violence toward those whose gender identities are deemed nonnormative (Grace, 2015). When individuals experience dissonance between their natal sex/gender assigned at birth and the gender they desire to affirm, their health, happiness, and functionality in life, learning, and work contexts are jeopardized. Fortunately, however, the gender landscape is changing. There are increasing demands for alterations in law, legislation, and institutional policy making focused on recognizing and accommodating differences in gender identity (APA, 2013; Grace, 2015). In this regard, progressives recognize that genderist systems and structures are the problem, not individuals exhibiting variation in gender identity and expression. If individuals experience gender dysphoria, then it is because they are victimized by systemic genderism. In the end, gender identity is a human characteristic constructed in alignment with what the mind knows and the heart feels (Ehrensaft, 2011). With new ways of knowing and understanding gender and its multiple forms, there is a need to reflect on absences and new moves as we focus on gender and gender identity in research, theory, policy, and practice in adult and continuing education.

Studying Gender and Gender Identity in Education for Adults

Competing discourses on gender and gender identity juxtaposed with resistance to sociality that recognizes and accommodates perceived nonconforming gender identities are quite evident in U.S. culture and society. They provide reasons for educators in adult and continuing education to interrogate and make sense of the ways gender and gender identity are constructed from social and cultural perspectives. With this in mind, we review sample literature in adult education and HRD to better understand scholarship related to gender and gender identity.

Review of Handbooks of Adult and Continuing Education *(1989–2010)*

A review of the past three *Handbooks of Adult and Continuing Education* (Kasworm et al., 2010; Merriam & Cunningham, 1989; Wilson & Hayes, 2000) was revealing. Notably, gender discussions were primarily cisgender in focus. Problematically, the 1989 handbook (Merriam & Cunningham, 1989) dealt with women as a relatively homogenous group, with no significant discussion of positionality and intersectionality. With so many women across relational differences ignored in this handbook, it spurred deliberations about the presence and place of gender and the need to bring the field of study and practice into times concerned with diversity and inclusion. Still, there were chapters raising key gender issues. Deshler and Hagan (1989) noted that the women's movement had led to wide recognition that gender issues are crucial in all cultures around the globe. They concluded that research in this area was promising, noting how little was known about gender differences across cultures and the extent to which these differences were socially or biologically based. Boucouvalas and Krupp (1989) recognized Carol Gilligan (1982) as a vanguard of adult development with her thesis that women tend to strive for attachment and connection and men for separation. Wolford (1989) discussed gender discrimination in the U.S. corrections system. Rice and Meyer (1989) noted the discontinuous versus continuous education experience women have due to socialized expectations of women to provide caregiving, and Ohliger (1989) imagined a future for alternative adult education that would be characterized by feminism rather than brute masculine power.

The 2000 handbook (Wilson & Hayes, 2000) featured more discussions about gender that elevated women's ways of knowing (Belenky et al., 1986) as a valued mode of connected knowing (Brookfield, 2000). The handbook also addressed positionality in learning (Tennant, 2000; Tisdell et al., 2000), intersectionality (Johnson-Bailey & Cervero, 2000), and feminist poststructural culture and its effects on positionality (Brooks, 2000). Sork (2000) lamented a gulf between dominant program planning methods and feminism, questioning whether program planning would be rethought from a feminist perspective. The workplace was assessed with Bierema's (2000) critique of HRD from a feminist perspective and Fenwick's (2000) appraisal of women's development in organizations. Distance education was discussed as having predominantly women learners (Gibson, 2000). The 2000 edition brought discussions of complicated heterogenous women's identities and women's locations in learning and work to the fore. Many authors who engaged these topics in the 2000 edition tended to understand feminist theory as a philosophical branch of poststructuralism.

The 2010 *Handbook of Adult and Continuing Education* (Kasworm et al., 2010) advanced field discourse on gender, with chapters advocating race, gender, and class as interlocking systems of oppression, particularly for people of color (Boucouvalas & Lawrence, 2010); using feminist theory as a key unit of analysis (Brookfield, 2010; Monaghan, 2010); exploring ecofeminism (Lange, 2010); investigating gender as affecting the distribution of social power and privilege (Johnson-Bailey et al., 2010); and delineating an intersectional feminist agenda (Bracken & Nash, 2010).

Review of Adult Education Research Conference (AERC) Proceedings (1993–2017)
A review of proceedings of the U.S. AERC (1993–2017), which are archived at Kansas State University, indicates that studies of gender were generally from cisgender perspectives, with varying attention given to intersections with race, sexual orientation, and ethnocultural differences. In taking up gender, critical analyses contested hetero-patriarchal limits placed on gender, bringing the political ideals of modernity—democracy, freedom, and social justice—to bear on possibilities for being and acting in the world. Positional analyses explored how knowledge, language, culture, and power influence how we understand gender and its performance. Intersectional analyses observed how these understandings change when gender interacts with race, ethnicity, sexual orientation, class, and other differences. These particular and competing social analyses examined relational, contextual, and dispositional elements of researching gender.

Eclectic social analyses found in AERC papers and symposia during the 1990s constituted a multiperspective critique of the deliberate and systematic ways a cisgender male lens has framed how we make sense of society and adult and continuing education. This critique points out an inherent male bias in educational and other institutional contexts, as well as an oppressive masculinity that positions men as subjugators of women. Of importance, the critique emanated from expanding spaces for feminisms and politics and pedagogies of resistance at AERC. These inroads have been incremental, particularly in terms of concomitantly addressing oppression in relation to sexual orientation and gender identity. In 1996, Diane Resides presented the first lesbian-themed paper, which examined the implications of lesbian development and life experiences for adult education. While papers on lesbian and gay sexual orientations have become more prevalent at AERC since then, there has been little focus on perceived nonnormative gender identity and expression. If transgender is mentioned, it is commonly as part of the LGBT+ acronym used in papers predominantly or exclusively exploring sexual orientation. This erroneously conflates sexual orientation and gender identity, because these two characteristics of individuals are distinct and separate (Grace, 2015). Robert J. Hill (2000) spoke to this distinction in the first paper on transgender issues presented at AERC. He referred to transfeminism as an emergent "menacing feminism" (p. 1) that challenges the institutionalized gender binary, providing a basis for actively transgressing how gender is understood in the social context of adult learning. Also of historical significance, Hill presented the first paper on sexual orientation, speaking about heterosexist discourse in adult education at the 35th annual AERC in 1994 (Hill & Grace, 2009). While many progressive adult educators supported an emerging LGBT+ presence at AERC, there was palpable resistance during the early years to what some perceived as the incursion of sexual and gender differences into hetero-patriarchal conference space (Hill & Grace, 2009).

Since the 1990s, discourses on gender at AERC have been mainly cisgender focused, considering such concepts as privilege, difference, authority, voice, empowerment, agency, emancipation, inclusion, advocacy, socioeconomic status, literacy, justice, spirituality, and transnationalism, and such dynamics as new knowledge production, transgressive identity politics, feminist praxis, and culture–power interactions. Importantly, an increasing number of papers in this period engaged gender in intersections with race, ethnicity, Indigeneity, immigrant status, class/poverty, sexual orientation, age, and ability. The turns in theorizing to understand these concepts, dynamics, and intersections brought feminisms including critical feminism, poststructural feminism, and lesbian feminism to bear on adult education as an enterprise needing to build gender consciousness in transgressive and transformative ways. Synergistically, these feminisms focused on the personal, the political, and matters of connection, collaboration and relationship, albeit from different and sometimes competing perspectives. Sadly, while there were postfoundational turns involving critical race theory, queer theory, and cultural studies, transfeminism was largely invisible.

Moving into the 2000s, the increasing prominence of feminist analyses in AERC papers and symposia reflected the growing presence of feminist pedagogies, notably in positional and intersectional forms, in academic adult education (Grace & Gouthro, 2000). In a review of these pedagogies, Grace and Gouthro (2000) provided this synopsis. As formations focused on how women learn, feminist pedagogies variously placed emphases on gender consciousness and emancipation, the multiple subjectivities of learners and educators, knowledge production by and for whom, authority, voice, and social transformation. As these pedagogies focused on gender as a category of analysis, postfoundational versions contested the idea of gender as a universal construct. Instead, they advanced the perspective that gender is a multifaceted and unsettled category altered by culture and experience, and further altered in intersections with race, ethnicity, class, sexual orientation, and other relational differences. Feminist pedagogies opened up possibilities for adult learning and research as they explored the synergy between theory and practice; exposed social, cultural, and institutional limits placed on gender in terms of being and acting in the world; and interrogated ways the dominant knowledge–language–culture–power nexus impacts how gender is taken up in political and sociological terms in adult and continuing education and learning.

Feminist adult educators have a well-established history of critiquing principles and assumptions guiding adult education as a field of study and practice (Carpenter, 2009). At AERC, this work has cemented a place for employing feminist theorizing and pedagogy in these analyses. Concomitantly, it has helped in identifying timely research topics for adult educators to study. Research is still needed to continue building feminist social theories and pedagogies. For example, in their ongoing work probing patriarchal biases and practices in adult education, critical feminist adult educators have to keep gender consciousness and the impact of experience at the heart of interrogations leading to the further development of feminist epistemologies and pedagogies (Carpenter, 2009). The work of Mojab (2009) is instructive here. Utilizing Marxist-feminist theorizing to focus on learning for Iraqi women who had experienced war, militarization, and violence, she complicates adult learning by challenging adult educators to conceptualize critical consciousness and praxis in the intersection of adult education, gender, and imperialism. Mojab speaks to the danger of adult learning that favors dominant ideology, saying it constitutes learning by dispossession. As she relates, such learning reflects the duality of learning new knowledge and skills while also subjecting the self/mind/consciousness to alienation, fragmentation of self/community, and confusion of differences between forces like capitalism and imperialism. Mojab's research reminds us of the need to conduct investigations that continue to grapple with intention, purpose, and context in researching learning for women. With the subjugation of women a persistent and troubling norm in many nations, such research remains crucial in adult education as a field of study.

In recent years, there is also recognition of the need for field research that studies contemporary social and cultural phenomena contributing to alienation and fragmentation of self/community in the United States. For example, the Black Lives Matter movement raised public consciousness about the negative impacts of systemic racism on Blacks, particularly cisgender males, in such forms as racial profiling, targeting by police, and overrepresentation in the criminal justice system. This movement accentuates the need for research intersecting race and gender that focuses on factors affecting recognition, accommodation, and success for men of color engaging in adult education and navigating life in culture and society. Schwartz's (2012) research provides an example of such useful research. In her phenomenological study of trauma that young men of color experienced, she found participants perceived a lived experience of trauma as normal. Moreover, she concluded this experience impeded their ability to have an optimum GED or college learning experience. Drawing on critical race theory to speak to complexities of studying race in the intersection with masculinity, Schwartz speaks to the importance of considering larger social and cultural contexts in dealing with educational opportunities and counseling supports for those traumatized and still dealing with disenfranchisement, social and educational inequities, and injustices perpetrated against them. In another example demonstrating the need for field research that intersects gender with race, Alfred and Chlup (2010) spoke to the importance of considering intersectionality, relationality, and societal structures in investigating the impacts of poverty and low literacy on the overrepresentation of cisgender Black women in prisons. Employing critical race theory in their sociostructural analysis that included policy critique, they located neoliberal policies of welfare reform and the racism inherent in crime control laws as key causes of a rapid increase in Black women's incarceration. Alfred and Chlup called for gender-responsive strategies that attend to the intersectionality of poverty, culture, race, ethnicity, class, and gender in planning and implementing educational programming for women in and out of the criminal justice system. In a different example speaking to the need for field research that intersects gender identity with race, Jackson (2010) studied outreach programming supporting urban African American transgender sex workers. Her research speaks to the importance of researching culturally responsive education and developing outreach models that promote client self-efficacy so they might engage in safer sex work and stay healthier.

Further expanding research terrain, the Me Too movement is another prominent U.S. social and cultural phenomenon that ought to trigger adult education research on gender and the violent outcomes of subjugating cisgender women in workplace and other sociocultural contexts. This movement has raised public consciousness of the impacts of sexual harassment and sexual assault on women in relation to their abilities to function in life, learning, and work contexts. The kind of research needed is exemplified by Nikischer's (2014) study of the influence of sexual assault on the educational outcomes and life choices of women. She called on adult educators who engage in comprehensive health education to build knowledge and understanding of sexual assault, the characteristics of victims, the negative outcomes that can affect their successful participation as adult learners and workers, and the kinds of pedagogy and resources needed to deal with topics including sexual assault, sexuality, and healthy sexual behaviors. In light of the social crisis the Me Too movement exposes, there is much field research to be done on these topics in order to inform policy making, programming, and service provision.

Adult education as social education always has to examine the ways social policy affects people as they navigate life, learning, and work. The Deferred Action for Childhood Arrivals (DACA) provides a poignant example. As a U.S. immigration policy, DACA raised issues about identity and belonging for Latinxs who were brought to the United States illegally as children and have no guarantees when it comes to daily existence in the only country they have known as "home." There is a need for field research on adults in this predicament. Research that Toso and Prins (2010) conducted with Mexican immigrant women enrolled in a family literacy program is relevant here. They studied the calculated agency of these cisgender women as they took up dominant discourses of mothering and parent involvement in their pursuit of personal and academic goals. What is important in this research is the focus on agency that involved debunking demeaning stereotypes and developing identities as advocates. Adult educators conducting research with DACA recipients need to study agency and advocacy in relation to paradoxes shaping how they live, learn, and work. Toso and Prins stress this point, calling on adult educators to study what constitutes strategic adult learning for those disenfranchised.

Review of HRD Publications

While there are intersections with gender in some chapters (Byrd, 2014; Gedro & Tyler, 2014, Sambrook, 2014), the 2014 *Handbook of Human Resource Development* (Chalofsky et al., 2014) has only one chapter specifically focused on feminism (Bierema & Cseh, 2014). Moreover, the 2017 *Handbook of International Human Resource Development* makes no mention of gender throughout an otherwise comprehensive examination of the field on a global scale (Garavan et al., 2017). This trend is replicated in journals sponsored by the Academy of Human Resource Development including *Advances in Developing Human Resources (ADHR)*, *Human Resource Development International (HRDI)*, *Human Resource Development Quarterly (HRDQ)*, and *Human Resource Development Review (HRDR)*. A review of these journals from 2008 to 2018 echoes findings from prior analyses and critiques of the HRD literature that draw two key conclusions: The literature has been grounded in dominant masculinist rationality (Bierema, 2009), and it has taken a compliance, financial, and instrumental focus regarding diversity (Bierema, 2010). Earlier, Bierema and Cseh (2003) analyzed over 600 AHRD Conference Proceedings according to a feminist framework, finding that less than 1% of the studies included research focused on women, challenges to power, topics of racism or sexism, or advocacy for social justice. Indeed, Swanson (2004) has advocated for "unisex research" in HRD that minimizes gender based on his argument that research should be bias free and detached from researcher passions.

Topics considered less safe than feminism are even more rare in the HRD literature and create trepidation in professional communities. For example, Schmidt and Githens (2010) recounted their difficulties in proposing and running a preconference focused on LGBT+ issues in HRD for the 2008 Academy of Human Resource Development Conference. Although the preconference was the highest attended that year, the reviews of their proposal were uneven, with an overall recommendation to refocus it more broadly on "workplace diversity." Schmidt and Githens chose to keep the LGBT+ focus, although the session name was changed to "Workforce Diversity" in the program schedule and signage. Despite such erasure, they concluded that there is strong interest in developing cultural competence to address LGBT+ concerns in organizations, despite an unexpected reaction from AHRD. This is disconcerting, because AHRD is apparently "an organization that prides itself on being at the forefront of HRD research and practice" (p. 60). In sum, this scan indicates there has been resistance to work that threatens hetero-patriarchal intellectual and conference spaces in HRD.

Genderism and Its Consequences

As our review of particular U.S. adult education and human resource settings indicates, genderism has affected research, policy, and practice in education for adults. Of course, programming using the gender binary to delimit gender identity starts long before adulthood. Parents-to-be and others engage in gendering behaviors prebirth, with the most glaring contemporary example being "gender reveal parties" that ceremoniously uncover whether the unborn child is a "boy" or a "girl." Here gender stereotyping begins early and frivolously, reflecting the strong social tendency to foist hegemonic gender expectations on children. As a counterpoint, Morris (2018) details the rise of the "theyby" whereby parents attempt to raise a child in a gender affirming way without imposing gender binary designations or revealing the biological sex of their child. These parents face formidable resistance and anger, with pressures coming from family members, friends, teachers, and health-care providers to disclose their child's gender. The behaviors of these nonconforming parents are deemed highly threatening in an age where gender is still dominantly conceived in binary cisgender terms that embody gender stereotypes whereby men eschew and avoid traditional "female" roles at home and at work (Haines et al., 2016). From childhood to adulthood, society has not progressed much beyond what Acker (1990) described as the ideal worker archetype: a socialized preference for a White, heterosexual male who is wholly devoted to his work and prioritizes it over family, health, and personal life. This ideal worker bias serves to marginalize anyone who does not fit the image, particularly women, people of color, and members of the LBGT+ community. Two key ways genderism impacts workplaces and classrooms are through provoking an inhospitable culture and perpetuating discrimination.

Provoking an Inhospitable Culture
Culture reinforces genderism, which is about maintaining the dominant status quo embodied in the cisgender male-female binary. Thus, workers identifying as female are marginalized by patriarchal culture, even though women attain higher levels of education than men at every level, and organizational leaders often claim their policies and practices are gender-blind (Bierema, 2017). Yet, dedicated efforts to eradicate gender bias are lacking. Priola et al.'s (2014) research indicated genderism in discourse. They also found that heteronormative discourse in five organizations created a culture of silence preventing LGBT+ employees from constructing a work identity encompassing their sexual identity. This kept the organizations from being fully inclusive workplaces. In education for adults, classroom culture can also perpetuate silence and microaggressions, especially when learning is about transmitting rather than transgressing and transforming the hetero-patriarchal status quo. Educators have the dual responsibility to be informed on issues of diversity, equity, and inclusion that affect learners and classrooms and to be equipped to handle them with professionalism and care (Robinson et al., 2017).

Gender-affirming practices in educational settings and workplaces matter; still, they are lacking. Moreover, LGBT+ workplace experiences are hardly uniformly positive, and there is minimal integration of gender identity (Grace, 2013; Ozturk & Tatli, 2016). Workplace attitudes toward sexual and gender diversity can be vitriolic and misogynistic, with virtual and in-person harassment being common (Banet-Weiser & Miltner, 2016). Consequently, Hill (2009) observed that sexual minorities experience the debilitating dynamics of "invisibility, erasure, and silence, both self- and other- imposed" (p. 38). Furthermore, transgender employees experience the highest discrimination rates (ILO, 2013), and may suffer misgendering and gender microaggressions such as the lack of all-gender restrooms, continuous exposure to sexist language, sexual harassment, stereotyping, wage gaps, implicit bias, gaslighting, or inappropriate questions such as "Are you a man or a woman?" or "Have you had your surgery yet?"

In most organizations, the male–female binary is a staple of dominant culture that imperiously generates unspoken rules governing gender presentation, behavior, and employment practices (Elias et al., 2018). For example, women are expected to exhibit feminine behaviors such as gentleness, empathy, compassion, and deference. When women exhibit masculine behaviors such as aggressiveness, forcefulness, or courage, they do not conform to expected gender behaviors and may suffer consequences such as being viewed as too tough, uncooperative, or not promotable. While gender expectations prevail for both women and men, as Connell (1987) argued, "There is no femininity that is hegemonic in the sense that the dominant form of masculinity is hegemonic. . . . All forms of femininity in this society are constructed in the context of the overall subordination of women to men" (pp. 186–187).

Perpetuating Discrimination
Discrimination on the basis of gender is nothing new. Women have been historically marginalized in educational and work-life experiences by segregation into gender-appropriate degree programs and work roles. Yet, cisgender people have privilege, regardless of gender. As Robinson et al. (2017) maintain,

> Cisnormativity is the root of unawareness about transgender experiences, because it suggests that transgender people do not exist or, that if they do, their numbers are so miniscule that the average person does not need to know about their existence. (p. 303)

Indeed, gender-diverse employees are expected to conform to traditional gender binary roles and receive little help from leaders when transitioning. Some organizations attempt to respond by adopting transgender policies and procedures, although if steps are not taken to educate the organization and enforce policies, they can do more harm than good (Elias et al., 2018). Those who fail to meet expected gender norms are likely to encounter harassment (Dietert & Dentice, 2009) and stigmatization (Collins et al., 2015).

From this sorry perspective, we need to ask: How do we bring visibility, safety, and comfort to issues related to gender identity so we can contest cisgender hegemony and stop perpetuating discrimination? After all, the workplace is often unsafe for gender minority individuals. Ozturk and Tatli (2016) interviewed 14 transgender individuals about their experiences at work and concluded that the failure to address gender diversity is a key shortcoming in human resources and diversity management research and practice. Transgender employees are also at higher risk of being isolated and bullied. They often lack support from their managers and are disadvantaged by a general lack of awareness about the challenges they face in navigating a hetero-patricarchal, genderist organizational culture and sociality. These workers face discrimination and harassment ranging from being denied a job, getting fired, being passed over for promotion, or receiving less compensation and desirable assignments (Chung et al., 2015). The discrimination they face may be more ecological and informal, such as exposure to an inhospitable climate, isolation by coworkers, and experiencing jokes, vandalism, or even physical assault (Chung, 2001). Grant et al. (2011) reported that 90% of transgender and gender-nonconforming respondents in a U.S. study ($N = 6,450$) experienced workplace harassment or mistreatment, or took actions to avoid it. They also found that 71% of transgender employees sought to hide their gender transitions and 57% postponed their transitions to avoid discrimination.

According to Elias et al. (2018), policies and practices are needed to support transgender workers. Thus, it is important to understand how to shape policy and practice based on new understandings of sex and gender for transgender individuals. This is challenging, particularly because personal and professional dimensions are intertwined (Elias et al., 2018). Nevertheless, genderism is countered when awareness of privilege and oppression is heightened and actions are taken to bolster inclusion. This is not easy work. Contributing to the trepidation of accepting gender diversity and becoming more gender affirming are the challenges of learning new labels and potentially making mistakes while unsettling our binary views of gender. Indeed, a new lexicon is evolving in relation to naming gender identity and expression. The array of terms in a growing list includes *trans, transgender, transmasculine, transfeminine, cisgender, gender nonconforming, gender variant, gender fluid, genderqueer, transsexual, female-to-male* (FTM), *male-to-female* (MTF), and *Two Spirit Indigenous* (Grace, 2015; Singh, 2018). Gender-affirming language practices also include using preferred pronouns including such variations as *she/her/hers, he/him/his, ze/hir,* and *they/them/theirs* (Lowrey, 2017). For some people, pronoun use is also part of affirming gender identity. But again, the difficulty is having mainstream society accept, remember, and use descriptors and pronouns that people across gender differences prefer (Teich, 2012; Valentine, 2007). Ultimately, creating safe, welcoming, and accommodating environments for gender-diverse people is the ultimate test of inclusivity aimed at equity. As Brooks and Edwards (2009) conclude, gender minority workers, like sexual minority workers, want inclusion, safety, and freedom from ostracization. Indeed, strides can be made to build safe and caring educational, workplace, and community spaces by creating an open, inclusive, gender-affirming culture; using affirmative language; implementing policy focused on gender diversity; fostering authentic gender identity expression; supporting people during transition; and developing gender identity awareness.

To enable these positive interventions, employees and managers need ongoing education about transpeople in order to recognize and effectively manage their own responses and implicit biases (Robinson et al., 2017). This involves creating a community of learners, with educators facilitating deliberations that help learners build gender consciousness and knowledge of systems and structures that impede recognition, respect, and accommodation of gender minorities (Bierema, 2002; Grace, 2015). Here educators need to introduce the concept of "doing gender" as a performative, everyday recurring routine embedded in social interactions (Butler, 1990; West & Zimmerman, 1987). This can enable cisgender students to reflect on their gender privilege, and it can help transgender and nonbinary students feel included and safe enough to speak up and educate others. Connell (2010) asserted that transpeople undo and redo gender. Exposed to this notion, all learners can understand gender as a more fluid social and cultural construction. They can interrogate how gender operates in the classroom, workplace, or community, and they can become more aware of the ways transgender individuals experience these sociocultural spaces. To help here, resources can be accessed using local university or community LGBT+ centers. In addition, inviting transgender speakers can help students humanize the unfamiliar; challenge their hegemonic conceptualization of gender; and develop awareness, understanding, and the capacity to be more inclusive. Importantly, bringing transgender issues into the classroom can also serve specific needs of learners with gender differences (Robinson et al., 2017). In the end, "the test of true inclusiveness is the degree to which most marginalized groups are taken into consideration, valued, and safeguarded in the [classroom and] organization" (Ozturk & Tatli, 2016, p. 796).

References

Acker, J. (1990). Hierarchies, jobs, bodies: A theory of gendered organizations. *Gender & Society, 42*(2), 139–158.

Alfred, M. V., & Chlup, D. T. (2010, June 3). Beyond illiteracy and poverty: Theorizing the rise in Black women's incarceration. *Proceedings of the Adult Education Research Conference.* http://newprairiepress.org/aerc/2010/papers/1

American Psychiatric Association. (2013). *Gender dysphoria.* http://www.dsm5.org/Documents/GenderDysphoria Fact Sheet.pdf

Banet-Weiser, S., & Miltner, K. M. (2016). #MasculinitySoFragile: Culture, structure, and networked misogyny. *Feminist Media Studies, 16*(1), 171–174.

Belenky, M. F., Clinchy, B. M., Goldberger, N. R., & Tarule, J. M. (1986). *Women's ways of knowing: The development of self, voice, and mind.* Basic Books.

Bierema, L. L. (2000). Moving beyond performance paradigms in workplace development. In A. Wilson & E. Hayes (Eds.), *Handbook of adult and continuing education* (pp. 278–293). Jossey-Bass.

Bierema, L. L. (2002, May 24–26). The role of gender consciousness in challenging patriarchy. *Proceedings of the Adult Education Research Conference.* http://newprairiepress.org/aerc/2002/papers/4

Bierema, L. L. (2009). Critiquing HRD's dominant masculine rationality and evaluating its impact. *Human Resource Development Review, 8*(1), 68–96.

Bierema, L. L. (2010). Resisting HRD's resistance to diversity. *Journal of European Industrial Training, 34*(6), 565–576.

Bierema, L. L. (2017). No woman left behind: Critical leadership development to build gender consciousness and transform organizations. In S. R. Madsen (Ed.), *Handbook of research on gender and leadership* (pp. 145–164). Edward Elgar.

Bierema, L. L., & Cseh, M. (2003). Evaluating HRD research using a feminist research framework. *Human Resource Development Quarterly, 14*(1), 5–26.

Bierema, L. L., & Cseh, M. (2014). A critical, feminist turn in HRD: A humanistic ethos. In N. E. Chalofsky, T. S. Rocco, & M. L. Morris (Eds.), *The handbook of human resource development* (pp. 125–144). Wiley.

Boucouvalas, M., & Krupp, J. A. (1989). Adult development and learning. In S. B. Merriam & P. M. Cunningham (Eds.), *Handbook of adult and continuing education* (pp. 183–200). Jossey-Bass.

Boucouvalas, M., & Lawrence, R. L. (2010). Adult learning. In C. E. Kasworm, A. D. Rose, & J. M. Ross-Gordon (Eds.), *Handbook of adult and continuing education* (pp. 35–48). SAGE.

Bracken, S. J., & Nash, H. (2010). Struggles for utopia(s)?: Gender and sexuality in adult and continuing education. In C. E. Kasworm, A. D. Rose, & J. M. Ross-Gordon (Eds.), *Handbook of adult and continuing education* (pp. 351–358). SAGE.

Brookfield, S. D. (2000). The concept of critically reflective practice. In A. L. Wilson & E. R. Hayes (Eds.), *Handbook of adult and continuing education* (pp. 33–49). Jossey-Bass.

Brookfield, S. D. (2010). Theoretical frameworks for understanding the field. In C. E. Kasworm, A. D. Rose, & J. M. Ross-Gordon (Eds.), *Handbook of adult and continuing education* (pp. 71–82). SAGE.

Brooks, A. K. (2000). Cultures of transformation. In A. L. Wilson & E. R. Hayes (Eds.), *Handbook of adult and continuing education* (pp. 161–170). Jossey-Bass.

Brooks, A. K., & Edwards, K. (2009). Allies in the workplace: Including LGBT in HRD. *Advances in Developing Human Resources, 11*(1), 136–149.

Butler, J. (1990). *Gender trouble: Feminism and the subersion of identity.* Routledge.

Byne, W., Bradley, S. J., Coleman, E., Eyler, A. E., Green, R., Menvielle, E. J., Meyer-Bahlburg, H. F. L., Pleak, R. R., & Tompkins, D. A. (2012). Report of the American Psychiatric Association task force on treatment of gender identity disorder. *Archives of Sexual Behavior, 41*(4), 759–796.

Byrd, M. (2014). A social justice paradigm for HRD: Philosopical and theoretical foundations. In N. E. Chalofsky, T. S. Rocco, & M. L. Morris (Eds.), *The handbook of human resource development* (pp. 281–298). Wiley.

Carpenter, S. (2009, May 28). Experience, learning, & consciousness: Advancing a feminist-materialist theory of adult learning. *Proceedings of the Adult Education Research Conference.* http://newprairiepress.org/aerc/2009/papers/14

Chalofsky, N. E., Rocco, T. S., & Morris, M. L. (2014). *The handbook of human resource development.* Wiley.

Chung, Y. B. (2001). Work discrimination and coping strategies. *The Career Development Quarterly, 50,* 33–44.

Chung, Y. B., Chang, T., K., & Rose, C. S. (2015). Managing and coping with sexual identity at work. *Psychologist, 28*(3), 212–215.

Collins, J. C., McFadden, C., Rocco, T. S., & Mathis, M. K. (2015). The problem of transgender marginalization and exclusion: Critical actions for human resource development. *Human Resource Development Review, 14*(2), 205–226.

Connell, C. (2010). Doing, undoing, or redoing gender? Learning from the workplace experiences of transpeople. *Gender & Society, 24*(1), 31–55.

Connell, R. W. (1987). *Gender and power.* Polity Press.

Deshler, D., & Hagan, N. (1989). Adult education research: Issues and directions. In S. B. Merriam & P. M. Cunningham (Eds.), *Handbook of adult and continuing education* (pp. 147–167). Jossey-Bass.

Dietert, M., & Dentice, D. (2009). Gender identity issues and workplace discrimination: The transgender experience. *Journal of Workplace Rights, 14*(1), 121–140.

Drescher, J., & Byne, W. (2012). Gender dysphoric/gender variant (GD/GV) children and adolescents: Summarizing what we know and what we have yet to learn. *Journal of Homosexuality, 59*(3), 501–510.

Ehrensaft, D. (2011). *Gender born, gender made: Raising healthy gender-nonconforming children.* The Experiment.

Elias, N. M., Johnson, R. N., Ovando, D., & Ramirez, J. (2018). Improving transgender policy for a more equitable workplace. *Journal of Public Management & Social Policy, 24*(2), 53–81.

Fenwick, T. J. (2000). Putting meaning into workplace learning. In A. L. Wilson & E. R. Hayes (Eds.), *Handbook of adult and continuing education* (pp. 294–311). Jossey-Bass.

Garavan, T., McCarthy, Carbery, R. (Eds.). (2017). *The handbook of international human resource development: Context, process, and people.* Edward Elgar.

Gedro, J., & Tyler, J. (2014). Sexual orientation and HRD. In N. E. Chalofsky, T. S. Rocco, & M. L. Morris (Eds.), *The handbook of human resource development* (pp. 314–325). Wiley.

Gibson, C. C. (2000). Distance education for lifelong learning. In A. L. Wilson & E. R. Hayes (Eds.), *Handbook of adult and continuing education* (pp. 423–437). Jossey-Bass.

Gilligan, C. (1982). *In a different voice: Psychological theory and women's development.* Harvard University Press.

Grace, A. P. (2012). The decline of social education and the rise of instrumentalism in North American adult education (1947–1970). *Studies in the Education of Adults, 44*(2), 225–244.

Grace, A. P. (2013). *Lifelong learning as critical action: International perspectives on people, politics, policy, and practice.* Canadian Scholars' Press.

Grace, A. P. (2015). Part II with K. Wells. *Growing into resilience: Sexual and gender minority youth in Canada.* University of Toronto Press.

Grace, A. P., & Gouthro, P. A. (2000). Using models of feminist pedagogies to think about issues and directions in graduate education for women students. *Studies in Continuing Education, 22*(1), 5–28.

Grant, J. M., Mottet, L. A., Tanis, J., Herman, J. L., Harrison, J., & Keisling, M. (2010). *National transgender discrimination survey report on health and health care.* National Center for Transgender Equality and the National Gay and Lesbian Task Force.

Haines, E. L., Deaux, K., & Lofaro, N. (2016). The times they are a-changing . . . or are they not? A comparison of gender stereotypes, 1983–2014. *Psychology of Women Quarterly, 40*(3), 353–363.

Hill, R. J. (2000, June 2–4). Menacing feminism, educating sisters. *Proceedings of the Adult Education Research Conference.* http://newprairiepress.org/aerc/2000/papers/.

Hill, R. J. (2009). Incorporating queers: Blowback, backlash, and other forms of resistance to workplace diversity initiatives that support sexual minorities. *Advances in Developing Human Resources, 11*(1), 37–53.

Hill, R. J., & Grace, A. P. (Eds.). (2009). *Adult and higher education in queer contexts: Power, politics, and pedagogy.* Discovery Association.

International Labor Organization. (2013). *Discrimination at work on the basis of sexual orientation and gender identity. Results of pilot research.* http://www.ilo.org/wcmsp5/groups/public/---ed_norm/---relconf/documents/meetingdocument/wcms_221728.pdf

Jackson, N. E. (2010, June 3). Expanding the application of the African centered paradigm model, use of its social components as tools in the provision of mobile HIV AIDS outreach with transgender dropout youth and adults, expanding the empirical study. *Proceedings of the Adult Education Research Conference.* http://newprairiepress.org/aerc/2010/papers/33

Johnson-Bailey, J., Baumgartner, L. M., & Bowles, T. A. (2010). Social justice in adult and continuing education: Laboring in the fields of reality and hope. In C. E. Kasworm, A. D. Rose, & J. M. Ross-Gordon (Eds.), *Handbook of adult and continuing education* (pp. 339–349). SAGE.

Johnson-Bailey, J., & Cervero, R. M. (2000). The invisible politics of race in adult education. In A. L. Wilson & E. R. Hayes (Eds.), *Handbook of adult and continuing education* (pp. 147–160). Jossey-Bass.

Kasworm, C. E., Rose, A. D., & Ross-Gordon, J. M. (Eds.). (2010). *Handbook of adult and continuing education.* SAGE.

Lange, E. A. (2010). Environmental adult education: A many-voiced landscape. In C. E. Kasworm, A. D. Rose, & J. M. Ross-Gordon (Eds.), *Handbook of adult and continuing education* (pp. 305–316). SAGE.

Lowrey, S. (2017, November 8). A guide to nonbinary pronouns and why they matter. *Huffpost.* https://www.huffingtonpost.com/entry/non-binary-pronouns-why-they-matter_us_5a03107be4b0230facb8419a

Merriam, S. B., & Cunningham, P. M. (1989). *Handbook of adult and continuing education.* Jossey-Bass.

Mojab, S. (2009, May 28). Learning by dispossession: Gender, imperialism and adult education. *Proceedings of the Adult Education Research Conference.* http://newprairiepress.org/aerc/2009/papers/42

Monaghan, C. H. (2010). Management and leadership. In C. E. Kasworm, A. D. Rose, & J. M. Ross-Gordon (Eds.), *Handbook of adult and continuing education* (pp. 177–188). SAGE.

Morris, A. (2018, 13 April). It's a theyby! Is it possible to raise your child entirely without gender from birth? Some parents are trying. *New York Magazine: The Cut.* https://www.thecut.com/2018/04/theybies-gender-creative-parenting.html

Nikischer, A. B. (2014, June 4–7). Dreams deferred: The impact of sexual assault during adolescence on the educational outcomes and life choices of women. *Proceedings of the Adult Education Research Conference.* http://newprairiepress.org/aerc/2014/papers/58

Ohliger, J. (1989). Alternative images of the future in adult education. In S. B. Merriam & P. M. Cunningham (Eds.), *Handbook of adult and continuing education* (pp. 628–639). Jossey-Bass.

Ozturk, M. B., & Tatli, A. (2016). Gender identity inclusion in the workplace: Broadening diversity management research and practice through the case of transgender employees in the UK. *The International Journal of Human Resources Management, 27*(8), 781–802.

Priola, V., Lasio, D., De Simone, S., & Serri, F. (2014). The sound of silence. Lesbian, gay, bisexual and transgender discrimination in "inclusive organizations." *British Journal of Management, 25*(3), 488–502. https://doi.org/10.1111/1467-8551.12043

Resides, D. (1996, Oct 24–26). Learning and new voices: Lesbian development and the implications for adult education. *Proceedings of the Adult Education Research Conference.* https://newprairiepress.org/aerc/1996/papers/43/

Rice, J. K., & Meyer, S. (1989). Continuing education for women. In S. B. Merriam & P. M. Cunningham (Eds.), *Handbook of adult and continuing education* (pp. 550–568). Jossey-Bass.

Robinson, M. J., Van Esch, C., & Bilimoria, D. (2017). Bringing transgender issues into management education: A call to action. *Academy of Management Learning & Education, 16*(2), 300–313.

Sambrook, S. (2014). Critical HRD. In N. E. Chalofsky, T. S. Rocco, & M. L. Morris (Eds.), *The handbook of human resource development* (pp. 145–163). Wiley.

Scharrón-del Río, M. R., Dragowski, E. A., & Phillips, J. J. (2014). Therapeutic work with gender-variant children: What school psychologists need to know. *School Psychology Forum: Research in Practice, 8*(1), 38–55.

Schmidt, S. W., & Githens, R. P. (2010). A place at the table? The organization of a preconference symposium on LGBT issues in HRD. *New Horizons in Adult Education & Human Resource Development, 24*(1), 59–62.

Schwartz, J. M. (2012, June 1–3). A new normal: Young men of color, trauma and engagement in learning. *Proceedings of the Adult Education Research Conference.* http://newprairiepress.org/aerc/2012/papers/41

Singh, A. (2018). *The queer and transgender resilience handbook: Skills for navigating sexual orientation and gender expression.* New Harbinger.

Sork, T. J. (2000). Planning educational programs. In A. L. Wilson & E. R. Hayes (Eds.), *Handbook of adult and continuing education* (pp. 171–190). Jossey-Bass.

Swanson, R. A. (2004). Unisex research. *Human Resource Development Quarterly, 15*(1), 117–119.

Teich, N. M. (2012). *Transgender 101: A simple guide to a complex issue.* Columbia University Press.

Tennant, M. (2000). Adult learning for self-development and change. In A. L. Wilson & E. R. Hayes (Eds.), *Handbook of adult and continuing education* (pp. 87–100). Jossey-Bass.

Tisdell, E. J., Hanley, M. S., & Taylor, E. W. (2000). Different perspectives on teaching for critical consciousness. In A. L. Wilson & E. R. Hayes (Eds.), *Handbook of adult and continuing education* (pp. 132–146). Jossey-Bass.

Toso, B.W., & Prins, E. (2010, June 3). Educational and mothering discourses and learner goals: Mexican immigrant women enacting agency in a family literacy program. *Proceedings of the Adult Education Research Conference.* http://newprairiepress.org/aerc/2010/papers/79

Valentine, D. (2007). *Imagining transgender: An ethnography of a category.* Duke University Press.

West, C., & Zimmerman, D. H. (1987). Doing gender. *Gender & Society, 1*(2), 125–151.

Wilson, A. L., & Hayes, E. (Eds.). (2000). *Handbook of adult and continuing education.* Jossey-Bass.

Wolford, B. I. (1989). Correctional facilities. In S. B. Merriam & P. M. Cunningham (Eds.), *Handbook of adult and continuing education* (pp. 356–368). Jossey-Bass.

CHAPTER 41

Adult Education and Disability

Jovita M. Ross-Gordon and Greg Procknow

Disability is a relatively recent and contentious term. The nomenclature used to refer to those *debilitated* or *diseased* has evolved from *handicapped* or *disabled people* to *people with disabilities* (Rocco & Delgado, 2011). Yet, some question the use of "people first language" when we don't say "person with a gender or race" (Rocco & Delgado, 2011, p. 8). Meanwhile, bearers of bodily, cognitive, and mental difference are reclaiming *mad*, *cripple*, and *disabled*, and an array of other signifiers and embracing them as not only descriptors but also badges of pride.

Traditional Perspectives on Disability

While disability has been largely overlooked in the literature of the field, where they appear, conceptions of disability within the field have been influenced over time by the educational setting, legislative mandates, and perspectives on disability prominent in related fields. Over the last several decades different models have been used to understand disability and its relationship to educational policy, best practices, and global concerns, each with different assumptions and emphases.

Medical Model of Disability
The foremost model of understanding disability remains the medical model of disability that posits how bodily, cognitive, and mental variations are grounded in one's genetics and individualized within its bearer (Oliver & Barnes, 2012). These variations are presumed to follow from bad biology or biochemistry, disease, or trauma and inhibit the full physiological, mental, or cognitive functioning of those deemed disabled. This model regulates bodily/mental "otherness" and treats the sick, ill, and debilitated as "deficient" and "less than" (Beresford & Menzies, 2015). It stresses the need for intrusive treatment and cure regimes to remedy illness and disability through biomedical fixes. Through the 1960s and into the early 1970s, medical perspectives were dominant as the framework for understanding disability in related fields, including special education, rehabilitation, and vocational education (Rocco & Fornes, 2010). Discussions of disability focused on clinical and psychoeducational assessments to diagnose physical, cognitive, or mental conditions, viewed as impairments to be addressed by medical procedures, medications, or psychoeducational interventions.

Functional Model of Disability
In some ways, the functional model mirrors the medical model by conceiving of disability as arising from "deficits" in one's physiological, psychic, or cognitive makeup. This model relates that the limitations these disorders impose on those differently abled prevent them from engaging in life-fulfilling activities such as employment or education (Rocco & Fornes, 2010). Adult educators will likely be familiar with Section 504 of the Rehabilitation Act and the Americans with Disabilities Act of 1990 (ADA), both of which can be viewed as reflecting a functional model of disability.

The Rehabilitation Act of 1973 defines *individuals with a disability* as those having a physical or mental impairment that substantially limits one or more major life activities or those who have a record of such impairment (Section 504 of the Rehabilitation Act). Almost 20 years later, Congress enacted the ADA as an extension of the Rehabilitation Act. The ADA is a broad civil rights law prohibiting discrimination in all areas of public life, including jobs, schools, transportation, and all public and private places utilizing the same definition for individuals with disabilities as the Rehabilitation Act. Title I of the ADA, focuses on equal opportunity in employment and so has implications for adult education in the workplace. Title II prohibits discrimination against qualified individuals with disabilities in all programs, activities, and services of public entities. Title III, in contrast, also extends to accommodations within private organizations (ADA National Network, 2017) and therefore has implications for private organizations offering educational opportunities for adults. Essentially, then, all public and private organizations providing adult education are expected to be accessible to students with disabilities. The ADA Amendments Act of 2008 (Public Law 110-325, ADAAA) was intended to make it easier for an individual seeking protection under the ADA to establish that they have a disability. In adult and continuing education (ACE) literature, disability tends to be discussed through the prism of functional and medical models (Rocco & Fornes, 2010). Adult educators and systems of higher education then consult these models to engage with or accommodate students with diverging bodies and minds (Fernando, 2016). Adult educators are beginning to rethink categories of disablement using critical theory (Rocco & Delgado, 2011; Rocco & Fornes, 2010).

Contemporary Perspectives on Disability

Disability studies grew out of disability rights activism in the United States and Europe. This activism shifted the focus from medicalizing disability as a personal pathology to be treated and cured, to understanding body and mind variance as a political and social cause for concern (Ross-Gordon, 2017). Disability studies maintains that (a) persons with disabilities (PWD) are marginalized, (b) PWD constitute a minority group, and (c) disability should be rethought as a social problem (Roulstone et al., 2013). Disability studies does not appeal or speak to all PWD; for instance, this discipline hardly ever refers to *madness* (Rose, 2017).

Mad studies was, in part, created to address this lacuna. Mad studies entered into the academy via departments of critical disability studies (LeFrançois et al., 2016); yet the infiltration of mad studies into disability studies continues piecemeal (Jones & Brown, 2013). Mad studies is an "exercise in critical pedagogy—in the radical coproduction, circulation, and consumption of knowledge" (Menzies et al., 2013, p. 14). The purpose of mad studies is bifold: (a) to counter the hegemony of biopsychiatry and to dispute that distress and madness has its origins in genetics and (b) to restore power and epistemic voice to people who have been diagnosed or labeled as mentally ill (Menzies et al., 2013). Mad studies bears "mutual affinities" (Menzies et al., 2013, p. 14) with disability studies insofar as both counter pathological models of disablement and discuss disablement from a critical stance rather than a clinical one.

Social Model

Created as an alternative to the reductionist medical and functional paradigms, the social model of disablement redirects the blame from one's bodily, cognitive and mental composition to their socioeconomic surroundings (Goodley, 2011). The social model severs "impairment" from "disability" and supposes that disabilities are the oppressions layered on top of or attached to impairments (Procknow & Rocco, 2016). Social model theorists accept "impairments" as functional limitations. No social meaning is imputed to impairments (Withers, 2012). The radical model of disability is dissimilar from the social model insomuch as both "impairments" and "disabilities" are viewed as socially constituted (Withers, 2012). This model argues that there is no biological cause for impairments. That having been said, the social model was created with only people with physical and cognitive disabilities in mind (Withers, 2012). While the social model does not entirely attend to mad matters, a revised social model—the social model of mental distress and illness—considers issues that are specific to self-identifying mad people (Beresford et al., 2010). The social model of mental distress is not a replacement but an extension of the social model of disability (Beresford et al., 2010).

Discussions of adults with disabilities embedded within a social model of disability place greater emphasis on factors inherent to discrimination against those whose physical, cognitive, and mental characteristics or capacities are different from what is viewed as normal—calling out attitudes of ableism and sanism on the part of others (McRuer, 2013; Poole et al., 2012). *Ableism* involves "discriminatory, oppressive or abusive behavior arising from the belief that disabled people are inferior to others" (Miller et al., 2004, p. 9). Further to this, *sanism* is regarded as the discrimination and the mental "othering" of those maligned as "mad" or "crazy" and those branded with psychiatric diagnoses (Diamond, 2013). Ableism and sanism are invisible, pervasive, and forms of disability oppression (Perlin, 2008). Like ableism, sanism can be the cause of, or reflected in other "prevailing social attitudes of racism, sexism, homophobia, and ethnic bigotry" (Perlin, 2008, p. 590).

Selected discussions in disability studies and mad studies move beyond the social model to include the wider imbricated social categories of identity that are imprinted on disabled bodies and minds (Ross-Gordon, 2017). Interestingly, both studies consider that two or more marginal identity markers can be collocated in one body as with: *gender*—using feminist disability studies to reimagine the possibilities when nesting feminism within disability studies rather than merely blending the former into the latter (Garland-Thomson, 1997); *race*—whereby, racial, diasporic and disabled citizens of the Global South have found little resonance with a "White" disability studies (Bell, 2011) or mad studies (Gorman, 2013); and *sexual orientation*—queering disability studies by using analogies critically to twine queer identity and disabled identity through their comparable experiences of coming out (McRuer, 2013).

Biopsychosocial Model of Disability

Shakespeare (2012) points to the need for a multifactorial or integrated approach to disability. Although he critiques interpretations of the social model that minimize impairments, he acknowledges that environments are disabling to people with impairments. Thus, he contends that "adequate accounts of disability should make space for medical, psychological, social, and political factors in the lives of people with disabilities" (p. 129).

Building on this biopsychosocial model of disability, the World Health Organization has developed the International Classification of Functioning, Disability, and Health (ICF), a tool intended as a way of classifying the functioning, disability, and health of individuals worldwide. Disability is viewed as

> a complex phenomena [*sic*] that is both a problem at the level of a person's body, and a complex and primarily social phenomena. Disability is always an interaction between features of the person and features of the overall context in which the person lives, but some aspects of disability are almost entirely internal to the person, while another aspect is almost entirely external. (World Health Organization 2002, p. 10)

This tool is intended to assess both personal and environmental factors so that appropriate interventions can be individually designed. Adult educators who similarly argue for holistic, interactional, or integrative understandings of disability incorporating biological, psychological, cultural, and sociopolitical dimensions of the experience of disability include Rule and Modipa (2012) and Ross-Gordon (2017).

Only a few academics have cross-fertilized adult education with disability studies (Clark, 2006; Rocco, 2005). Thus far this examination has indicated that (a) rarely does disability ever enter centrally into discussions of workplace learning (Procknow & Rocco, 2016), (b) teaching about disability studies in education is an ethic of responsibility where educators are called on to dismantle structural ableism (McLean, 2011), (c) some impairments are "deemed more amenable to education than others" (Goodley, 2007, p. 320), and (d) certain bodies and minds are bestowed more access to disability supports (Liasidou, 2014).

Traditional Approaches to Psychoeducational and Training Needs of Adults With Disabilities

As defined by Donker et al. (2009), "*psychoeducational interventions* are interventions in which education is offered to individuals with psychological disorders or physical illnesses" (p. 2, emphasis added). While their meta-analysis focused on psychoeducation for depression, anxiety, and psychological distress, psychoeducational interventions have empowered women with chronic physical disabilities (Vail & Xenakis, 2007), developed life skills in incarcerated individuals with learning disabilities (Hearne et al., 2007), and assisted formerly homeless individuals with co-occurring mental illness and substance abuse through various transition programs (Sun, 2012).

Adult Basic Education and Literacy Programs
Adults with disabilities have long been a focus within the context of adult basic education literacy practice; however, with few exceptions (Moni et al., 2011; Silver-Pacuilla, 2006), this discussion has focused on adults in literacy programs *known or suspected* to have specific learning disabilities (Belzer & Ross-Gordon, 2011). Much of this literature has focused on identifying effective instructional strategies for improving basic skills performance (Hock, 2012; Mellard & Scanlon, 2006; Pannucci & Walmsley, 2007), while another prominent strand focused on assessment issues (defining learning disabilities, determining the prevalence of learning disabilities, and screening for learning disabilities in adult basic education programs) (Reynolds et al., 2012; Taymans, 2012). Yet, Covington (2004) cautioned adult basic education teachers and administrators that "danger arises when this label—or any other label—serves the needs of those who apply it at the expense of those who receive it" (p. 101) and suggested instead that "by incorporating a variety of strategies in an emotionally safe and accepting environment, teachers will help not only those with learning disabilities, but all students" (p. 100). Similarly, in an analysis of the limited research examining instructional and testing accommodations made for learning with learning disabilities within adult basic education, Gregg (2012) first pointed to the limited use of accommodations in this setting and evidence of their effectiveness when used, then called for greater use of universal instructional design likely to benefit both those with diagnosed learning disabilities and the many adults in basic education who cannot afford the cost of evaluation procedures needed to acquire the documentation required for accommodations.

Accommodations Within Higher Education
Within higher education, the predominant provision for learners who qualify as disabled under ADA and Section 504 of the Rehabilitation Act has been through instructional accommodations coordinated through an office for disability services (Oslund, 2015). Students are sometimes reluctant to seek accommodations, given their desire to avoid stigmatization they have experienced in the past (Couzens et al., 2015). Others struggle with securing the requisite documentation needed to access disability supports, given these costs are not covered by the institution. Furthermore, nonvisibly disabled students are least likely to be believed by their instructors due to the disablist "assumptions at play in accommodation policies" (Landry & Church, 2016, p. 180). Recalcitrant professors may deny students requests for support or riddle the request process with so many hurdles that students may not receive accommodations before the class ends (Poole et al., 2012). In some instances, disability disclosures are made too late in the semester or surface only when students are at risk of flunking (Summers, 2008).

Job-Related Accommodations and Training
Shortages in job training to remedy disabled employees' skills deficits continue to hamstring their job growth (Augustin, 2011). Even when training occurs, disabled learners are disadvantaged by exclusionary curricular aspects, such as handout materials printed using small fonts (Procknow & Rocco, 2016). For ADA protection to apply, the employee should communicate their need for accommodation before the training begins (Clardy, 2003). Where group training fails to include disabled learners, then personalized training and development should be offered. Personalized workplace learning for workers with intellectual disabilities can enhance job performance and empowerment (Fornes et al., 2008). Supplying cognitively impaired workers ongoing training and maintenance of job skills can lessen their chances of turnover (Fornes et al., 2008).

Moving Beyond Traditional Approaches: Promoting Greater Disability Inclusion and Equity Across Sectors of ACE

An alternative or supplementary model to providing educational and workplace accommodations to those who qualify under ADA and Rehabilitation Act 504 is the creation of courses, programs, and worksites that are designed for greater inclusion. The next section discusses ways in which ACE can nurture diversity, inclusion, and equity for PWD within and beyond the academy.

Inclusive Education
ACE educators can model openness and inclusion by accepting students who bear mental, cognitive, and bodily variance and altering the environment to better meet their needs. Citing Nirje's *normalization principle* (1969) as the origin of the concept of inclusion, Renzaglia et al. (2003) suggest that

> individuals both with disabilities and without disabilities must acquire skills needed for living and learning in inclusive settings. These skills include those needed to interact with each other, support each other, cooperate with each other, and compliment [*sic*] each other's strengths. (p. 141)

For instance, openness involves educating able-minded students to be tolerant of students in unsane states of mind and their ways of being and knowing in the world (Burstow, 2003).

Inclusive educators confer credence to students' claims to alternate realities, such as students who hear voices (Burstow, 2003). Students who are divergent from what Garland-Thompson (1996) termed the *normate*—those with unmarked privileges of White, male, cisgender, heterosexual, able-bodied, and middle-class bodies—will feel included when they sense they are adequately represented. Increased representation communicates to learners with mental, physical, and cognitive disabilities that community exists within the university and that they no longer need to go it alone (Poole & Grant, 2018). ACE endorses the equity of students in mad or distressed states of mind by rethinking what constitutes healthy states of behaving and being. This includes destabilizing categories of sanity as the ideal state of neurodiversity. Adult educators need to start to rethink how able-bodiedness, neurotypicality, and saneness are reified in their pedagogical praxis as normative and, specifically, how hegemonies of saneness exclude students that experience its obverse, insanity.

Adaptive Leadership
Disabled students need to know that their teachers are receptive to their need to be included. *Adaptive leadership* is a style of leadership that demands leaders adapt to disabled persons' debilitated minds and bodies (Anderson et al., 2015; Maxey et al., 2016). Instructors assuming this leadership style adjust to the divergence of their students' experience in cognition, mental, or physical functioning (Maxey et al., 2016). Adaptive leadership is similar to the social model of disablement, insomuch as environments are expected to adapt to and accommodate student disabilities. Instructors exhibiting adaptive leadership work collaboratively with students in identifying and solving complex problems (Anderson et al., 2015). For example, teachers that exercise adaptive leadership in class reorient their praxis to become *mad positive*; to practice mad positivity is to not identify as "mad" but "support [the] goals of those who do" (Reville, 2013, p. 170). Mad positive teachers enact "mad-enabling pedagogies" (Castrodale, 2017). These pedagogies guide teachers on how best to bring about mad positivity in the classroom by dialoguing about recovery, nonpsychiatric alternatives, peer support, and allowing for mad subjectivities to be shared. In mad-positive classroom cultures, madness is rethought of as only one tile in a mosaic of marginality (Castrodale, 2017).

Universal Design
Universal design (UD) approaches constitute one means of minimizing barriers for individuals with varying types of minds and bodies. Originating in the field of architecture, UD is a way of designing a building or facility so it is attractive and functional for all people, disabled or not (Hamraie, 2013). Universal design for instruction (UDI) is a modification of UD. Scott et al. (2003) developed the nine principles of UDI—including equitable use (concerned with accessibility to a broad range of individuals), flexible use (to accommodate individual abilities), and a welcoming instructional climate.

More recently, the focus has turned to universal design for learning (UDL) (Rogers-Shaw et al., 2018). Like UDI, it shifts the focus from the student with disabilities to the "disabled curriculum" (Rappolt-Schlichtmann et al., 2012, as cited in Rogers-Shaw et al., 2018, p. 23). The Center for Applied Special Technology (CAST) interprets UDL in terms of providing multiple means of engagement, representation, and action and expression for learners, and has developed guidelines for UDL, presented in the form of an evolving graphic organizer (CAST, 2018). UDL enables students to access flexible learning environments. First, flexibility is structured into the design of the curriculum, permitting the loose attendance of students (Burstow, 2003) or scheduling classes for the afternoon to accommodate mad learners that deal with the residual effects of neuroleptics such as lethargy in the morning (Poole & Grant, 2018). Second, instructors grant flexibility when it comes to completing assignments, for example, allowing coursework alternatives if requested (Castrodale, 2018; Jones & Brown, 2013) or extensions on due dates (Poole & Grant, 2018). UDL has been touted as offering pedagogical practices to adult educators that benefit all adult students "with a lack of language fluency, or with weak basic skills" who struggle in formalized educational settings (Rogers-Shaw et al., 2018, p. 22). Yet, UD concepts are not without their problems. There are concerns that UD does not avail all mad learners equally. For instance, White, mad-identified students are more "likely to be registered with disability services than students of color" with comparable behavioral or emotional disturbances (Gorman, 2013, p. 279). For these reasons and others, Gorman (2013) maintains that mad identity is articulated as a position of privilege and that this privilege redounds to White mad students the greatest benefits and access.

ACE has also taken steps toward developing communities supportive of differently abled bodies and minds outside the academy (Fernando, 2016). For instance, mental health service providers have enlisted the help of outpatients as "coproducers" to deliver destigmatization campaigns and community mental health awareness workshops alongside clinicians (Ledger & Slade, 2015). To involve service users in the coproduction of educational programs is in line with ACE, disability studies, and mad studies insofar as coproduction privileges the frenetic voices and realities of said users. In a different vein, "madvocates" are nested within user/survivor activist circles and the academy, where their pedagogy informs their community praxis (Landry & Church, 2016; Reville, 2013). They teach *with* community rather than about community (Castrodale, 2018)—this "requires a special pedagogy that brings students to the community and brings mad people into the academy" (Faulkner, 2017, p. 515). Similarly, adult educators can create pathways back to academia for those with diagnosed mental disorders through supported education (SE). SE eases mentally ill learners' (re)entry into college or university following hospitalization to redress skills and capacity shortages (Fernando et al., 2014).

Supporting Self-Determination and Self-Advocacy

Early activists paved the way for an ongoing social movement that has contributed to key policy changes such as ADA, and which continues today through the work of organizations such as the American Association for People with Disabilities (AAPD, 2018), Self Advocates Becoming Empowered (SABE, 2020), and the Hearing Voices Network (HVN, 2020). For example, Faigin and Stein (2015) studied individuals with psychiatric disabilities who served as actors in theater troupes that performed works about mental illness and recovery designed to educate as well as entertain audiences. Study findings revealed actor-participants experienced personal growth as well.

Ryan and Griffiths (2015) examined the literature on self-advocacy from a transformational learning perspective. They uncovered personal impacts of self-advocacy, including growth in leadership abilities and changes in self-concept. They also discovered impacts on advocacy advisers, who improved their capacities to play a supportive rather than a directive role in working alongside adults with intellectual disabilities. Finally, they identified positive impacts on boards and communities that took seriously the input of self-advocates with disabilities.

Similarly, in studying transitions of secondary students to postsecondary education and work, Wehmeyer et al. (2018) present evidence of enhanced well-being and functioning resulting from the use of a strengths-based approach to disability, grounded in positive psychology and an ecological model of disability. They argue for a paradigm shift from the disability services systems nearly ubiquitous in postsecondary education, to a personalized supports paradigm. This model places more emphasis on self-determination, "as enabling people to act as causal agents in their own lives becomes an important means to enable people to live, learn, work, and play in their communities. People with disabilities become, in essence, their own supports" (Wehmeyer et al., 2018, p. 57).

Implications for ACE Research and Practice

We would be remiss to end this chapter without including recommendations for ACE research and practice. The literature reviewed for this chapter has drawn from related fields such as disability studies and mad studies. This points to the urgent need for research focused on adult education and PWD. While historically much of the writing on disability from within the field has been based in medical and functional models of disability, it is important that those doing research today also incorporate social, radical, ecological, and integrative models of disability. It is equally important that adult education and training move beyond simply accommodating PWD as required by legal mandates, to incorporating principles of UD (for environments), UDI (for instruction), and UDL (for fostering self-determination and self-advocacy among learners who are PWD). In order to reduce disability-based discrimination it is important that educational interventions extend beyond PWD alone, to educate members of the public, employers and potential employers, and last but not least, ourselves as adult educators. The consequences of ableism and sanism lead to significant loss of human potential. Thus, it is crucial that through formal and informal professional development we become more aware of these "-isms" as well as others compounding the negative impacts for individuals with intersectional identities, starting with the examination of our personal biases and their potential impact on our educational practice.

References

ADA Amendments Act of 2008, Pub. L. 110–325 Stat. 3406.

ADA National Network. (2017). *Postsecondary institutions and students with disabilities.* https://adata.org/factsheet/postsecondary.

American Association for People with Disabilities. (2018). https://www.aapd.com/

Americans with Disabilities Act of 1990, Pub. L. 101-336, 104 Stat. 328.

Anderson, R. A., Bailey, D. J., Wu, B., Corazzini, K., McConnell, E. S., Docherty, S. L., & Thygeson, N. M. (2015). Adaptive leadership framework for chronic illness framing a research agenda for transforming care delivery. *Advances in Nursing Science, 38*(2), 83–95.

Augustin, M. L. (2011). *Breaking the silence: Exploring the workplace experiences of six women with learning disabilities* [Unpublished master's thesis]. Brock University St. Catherines. https://dr.library.brocku.ca/handle/10464/4021

Bell, C. (2011). Introduction: Doing representational detective work. In C. Bell (Ed.), *Blackness and disability: Critical examinations and cultural interventions.* (pp. 1–8). Michigan State University Press.

Belzer, A., & Ross-Gordon, J. (2011). Revisiting debates on learning disabilities in adult education. *New Directions for Adult and Continuing Education, 2011*(132), 75–84.

Beresford, P., & Menzies, R. (2015). Developing partnerships to resist psychiatry within academia. In B. Burstow, B. A. LeFrançois, & S. Diamond (Eds.), *Psychiatry disrupted: Theorizing resistance and crafting the (r)evolution* (pp. 77–95). McGill-Queen's University Press.

Beresford, P., Nettle, M., & Perring, R. (2010). *Towards a social model of madness and distress? Exploring what service users say.* Joseph Rowntree Foundation. https://www.jrf.org.uk/sites/default/files/jrf/migrated/files/mental-health-service-models-full.pdf

Burstow, B. (2003). From pills to praxis: Psychiatric survivors and adult education. *The Canadian Journal for the Study of Adult Education, 17*(1), 1–18.

CAST. (2018). *Universal design for learning guidelines version 2.2 [Graphic organizer].* Author.

Castrodale, M. (2017). Critical disability studies and mad studies: Enabling new pedagogies in practice. *The Canadian Journal for the Study of Adult Education, 29*(1), 49–66.

Castrodale, M. (2018). Teaching (with) dis/ability and madness. In M. S. Jeffress (Ed.), *International perspectives on teaching with disability: Overcoming obstacles and enriching lives* (pp. 188–204). Routledge.

Clardy, A. (2003). The legal framework of human resources development, Part II: Fair employment, negligence, and implications for scholars and practitioners. *Human Resource Development Review, 2*(2), 130–154.

Clark, M. (2006). Adult education and disability studies, an interdisciplinary relationship: Research implications for adult education. *Adult Education Quarterly, 56*(4), 308–322.

Couzens, D., Poed, S., Kataoka, M., Brandon, A., Hartley, J., & Keen, D. (2015). Support for students with hidden disabilities in universities: A case study. *International Journal of Disability, Development and Education, 62*(1), 24–41.

Covington, L. E. (2004). Moving beyond the limits of learning: Implications of learning disabilities for adult education. *Journal for Adult Literacy Educational Planning, 14*(2), 90–103.

Diamond, S. (2013). What makes us a community? Reflection on building solidarity in anti-sanist praxis. In B. A., LeFrançois, R. Menzies, & G. Reaume (Eds.), *Mad matters: A critical reader in Canadian mad studies* (pp. 64–78). Canadian Scholar's Press.

Donker, T., Griffiths, K. M., Cuijpers, P., & Christensen, H. (2009). Psychoeducation for depression, anxiety and psychological distress: A meta-analysis. *BMC Medicine, 7,* 79. https://doi.org./libproxy.txstate.edu/10.1186/1741-7015-7-79

Faigin, D. A., & Stein, C. H. (2015). Community-based theater and adults with psychiatric disabilities: Social activism, performance and community engagement. *American Journal of Community Psychology*, (1–2), 148. https://doi.org/10.1007/s10464-014-9695-6

Faulkner, A. (2017). Survivor research and mad studies: The role and value of experiential knowledge in mental health research. *Disability & Society, 32*(4), 500–520.

Fernando, S. (2016). Adult educators as community developers: Combatting the structural violence of job insecurity. *Proceedings of the 35th CASAE Conference* (pp. 70–75). University of Calgary.

Fernando, S., King, A., & Loney, D. (2014). Helping them help themselves: Supported adult education for persons living with mental illness. *The Canadian Journal for the Study of Adult Education, 27*(1), 15–28.

Fornes, S. L., Rocco, T., & Rosenberg, H. (2008). Improving outcomes for workers with mental retardation. *Human Resource Development Quarterly, 19*(4), 373–395. https://doi.org/10.1002/hrdq.1246.

Garland-Thomson, R. (1997). *Extraordinary bodies: Figuring disability in American culture and literature.* Columbia University Press.

Goodley, D. (2007). Towards socially just pedagogies: Deleuzoguattarian critical disability studies. *International Journal of Inclusive Education, 11*(3), 317–334.

Goodley, D. (2011). *Disability studies: An interdisciplinary introduction.* SAGE.

Gorman, R. (2013). Thinking through race, class, and mad identity politics. In B. A. LeFrançois, R. Menzies, & G. Reaume (Eds.), *Mad matters: A critical reader in Canadian mad studies* (pp. 269–280). Canadian Scholars' Press.

Gregg, N. (2012). Increasing access to learning for the adult basic education learner with learning disabilities. Evidence-based accommodation research: Adults with learning disabilities in adult education. *Journal of Learning Disabilities, 45*(1), 47–63.

Hamraie, A. (2013). Designing collective access: A feminist disability theory of Universal Design. *Disability Studies Quarterly, 33*(4).

Hearing Voices Network. (2020). http://www.hearingvoicesusa.org/

Hearne, S., Garner, K., O'Mahony, B., Thomas, C., & Alexander, R. (2007). The Life Skills group—An introductory multimodular group programme in forensic learning disability. *The British Journal of Forensic Practice, 9*(2), 3–13.

Hock, M. F. (2012). Effective literacy instruction for adults with specific learning disabilities: Implications for adult educators: Adults with learning disabilities in adult education. *Journal of Learning Disabilities, 45*(1), 64–78.

Jones, N., & Brown, R. (2013). The absence of psychiatric C/S/X perspectives in academic discourse: Consequences and implications. *Disability Studies Quarterly, 33*(1).

Landry, D., & Church, K. (2016). Teaching (like) crazy in a mad positive school: Exploring the charms of recursion. In J. Russo & A. Sweeney (Eds.), *Searching for a rose garden: Challenging psychiatry, fostering mad studies* (pp. 172–182). PCCS Books.

Ledger, A., & Slade, B. (2015). Coproduction without experts: A study of people involved in community health and well-being service delivery. *Studies in Continuing Education, 37*(2), 157–169. https://doi.org/10.1080/0158037X.2015.1022718

LeFrançois, B. A., Beresford, P., & Russo, J. (2016). Editorial: Destination mad studies. *Intersectionalities, 5*(3), 1–10.

Liasidou, A. (2014). Critical disability studies and socially just change in higher education. *British Journal of Special Education, 41*(2), 120–134. https://doi.org/10.1111/1467-8578.12063

Maxey, E. C., Moore, J., & Hanson, W. (2016). Catalysts for change: Disabled workforce actualizes adaptive leadership and organizational learning. In A. T. Amayah (Ed.), *Academy of Human Resource Development International Conference Proceedings.* Academy of Human Resource Development.

McLean, M. A. (2011). Challenging ableism through adult learning. *New Directions for Adult and Continuing Education, 2011*(132), 13–22.

McRuer, R. (2013). Compulsory able-bodiedness and queer/disabled existence. In L. Davis (Ed.), *The disability studies reader* (pp. 369–378). Routledge.

Mellard, D., & Scanlon, D. (2006). Feasibility of explicit instruction in adult basic education: Instructor-learner interaction patterns. *Adult Basic Education, 16*, 21–37.

Menzies, R., LeFrançois, B.A., & Reaume, G. (2013). Introducing mad studies. In B. A. LeFrançois, R. Menzies, & G. Reaume's (Eds.), *Mad matters: A critical reader in Canadian mad studies* (pp. 1–21). Canadian Scholar's Press.

Miller, P., Park, S., & Gillinson, S. (2004). *Disablism: How to tackle the last prejudice.* Demos.

Moni, K. B., Jobling, A., Morgan, M., & Lloyd, J. (2011). Promoting literacy for adults with intellectual disabilities in a community-based service organisation. *Australian Journal of Adult Learning, 51*(3), 456–478.

Nirje, B. (1969). The normalization principle and its human management implications. In R. Kugel & W. Wolfensberger (Eds.), *Changing patterns in residential services for the mentally retarded* (pp. 179–195). President's Commission on Mental Retardation.

Oliver, M., & Barnes, C. (2012). *The new politics of disablement* (2nd ed.). Palgrave Macmillan.

Oslund, C. M. (2015). *Disability services and disability studies in higher education: History, contexts, and social impacts.* Palgrave Macmillan.

Pannucci, L., & Walmsley, S. A. (2007). Supporting learning-disabled adults in literacy. *Journal of Adolescent & Adult Literacy, 50*(7), 540–546.

Perlin, M. (2008). "Simplify you, classify you": Stigma, stereotypes and civil rights in disability classification systems. *Georgia State University Law Review, 25*(3), 607–639.

Poole, J. M., & Grant, Z. (2018). When youth get mad through a critical course on mental health. In S. Pashang, N. Khanlou, & J. Clarke (Eds.), *Today's youth and mental health* (pp. 305–320). Springer.

Poole, J. M., Jivraj, T., Arslanian, A., Bellows, K., Chiasson, S., Hakimy, H., Pasini, J., & Reid, J. (2012). Sanism, "mental health," and social work/education: A review and call to action. *Intersectionalities, (1),* 20–36.

Procknow, G., & Rocco, T. S. (2016). The unheard, unseen, and often forgotten: An examination of disability in the human resource development literature. *Human Resource Development Review, 15*(4), 379–403. https://doi.org/10.1177/1534484316671194

Rehabilitation Act of 1973. Pub. L. No. 93-112, 87 Stat. 355.

Renzaglia, A., Karvonen, M., Drasgow, E., & Stoxen, C. C. (2003). Promoting a lifetime of inclusion. *Focus on Autism & Other Developmental Disabilities, 18*(3), 140–149.

Reville, D. (2013). Is mad studies emerging as a new field of inquiry? In B. A. LeFrançois, R. Menzies, & G. Reaume (Eds.), *Mad matters: A critical reader in Canadian mad studies* (pp. 170–180). Canadian Scholars' Press.

Reynolds, S. L., Johnson, J. D., & Salzman, J. A. (2012). Screening for learning disabilities in adult basic education students. *Journal of Postsecondary Education and Disability, 25*(2), 179–195.

Rocco, T. S. (2005). From disability studies to critical race theory: Working towards critical disability theory. In R. J. Hill & R. Kiely (Eds.), *Proceedings of the 46th Annual Adult Education Conference* (pp. 369–374). University of Georgia Press.

Rocco, T. S., & Delgado, A. (2011). Shifting lenses: A critical examination of disability in adult education. *New Directions for Adult and Continuing Education, 2011*(132), 1–12.

Rocco, T. S., & Fornes, S. (2010). Perspectives on disability in adult and continuing education. In A. Rose, C. Kasworm, & J. Ross-Gordon (Eds.), *The handbook of adult and continuing education* (pp. 379–388). SAGE.

Rogers-Shaw, C., Carr-Chellman, D., & Choi, J. (2018). Universal design: Guidelines for accessible online instruction. *Adult Learning, 29*(1), 20–31.

Rose, D. (2017). Service user/survivor-led research in mental health: Epistemological possibilities. *Disability & Society, 32*(6), 773–789.

Ross-Gordon, J. M. (2017). Disabilities and adult and lifelong education. In M. Milano, S. Webb, J. Holford, R. Walker, & P. Jarvis (Eds.), *International handbook of on adult and lifelong education and learning* (pp. 879–898). Palgrave Macmillan.

Roulstone, A., Thomas, C., & Watson, N. (2013). The changing terrain of disability studies. In N. Watson, A. Roulstone, & C. Thomas (Eds.), *Routledge handbook of disability studies* (pp. 3–11). Routledge.

Rule, P., & Modipa, T. R. (2012). "We must believe in ourselves": Attitudes and experiences of adult learners with disabilities in KwaZulu-Natal, South Africa. *Adult Education Quarterly, 62*(2), 138–158.

Ryan, T. G., & Griffiths, S. (2015). Self-advocacy and its impacts for adults with developmental disabilities. *Australian Journal of Adult Learning, 55*(1), 31–53.

Scott, S. S., McGuire, J. M., & Shaw, S. F. (2003). Universal design for instruction: A new paradigm for adult instruction in postsecondary education. *Remedial & Special Education, 24*(6), 369–379.

Self Advocates Becoming Empowered. (2020). *Home.* https://www.sabeusa.org/

Shakespeare, T. (2012). Still a health issue. *Disability and Health Journal, 5*(3), 129–131.

Silver-Pacuilla, H. (2006). Access and benefits: Assistive technology in adult literacy. *Journal of Adolescent & Adult Literacy, 50*(2), 114–125.

Section 504 of the Rehabilitation Act of 1973, as amended 29 U.S.C. §794.

Summers, T. (2008). Teaching adults with disabilities in the postsecondary setting: Examining the experiences of faculty members [Paper presentation]. Adult Education Research Conference, St. Louis, MO, United States. http://newprairiepress.org/aerc/2008/papers/63/

Sun, A. P. (2012). Helping homeless individuals with co-occurring disorders: The four components. *Social Work, 57*(1), 23–37. https://doi.org/10.1093/sw/swr008

Taymans, J. M. (2012). Legal and definitional issues affecting the identification and education of adults with specific learning disabilities in adult education programs. *Journal of Learning Disabilities, 45*(1), 5–16. https://doi.org/10.1177/0022219411426857

Vail, S., & Xenakis N. (2007). Empowering women with chronic, physical disabilities: A pedagogical/experiential group model. *Social Work in Health Care, 46*(1), 67–87.

Wehmeyer, M. L., Shogren, K. A., & Thompson, J. R. (2018). Self-determination and adult transitions and supports. *New Directions for Adult and Continuing Education, 2018*(160), 53–62.

Withers, A. (2012). *Disability politics and theory.* Fernwood.

World Health Organization. (2002). *Towards a common language for functioning, disability, and health.* ICF. http://www.who.int/classifications/icf/en/

CHAPTER 42

Older Adults

Learning and Identity

Kathy D. Lohr, Brian Findsen, and Vivian W. Mott

This chapter focuses on older adults' learning and the influences of identity, motivation, and access. Discussion includes relevant theoretical constructs, governmental (and other mandated or legislated) impact, sociocultural factors, and best practices in the development and implementation of learning in later life. The chapter concludes with a brief discussion of trends affecting education and learning for older adults.

Who Are Older Adults?

Chronological age has been a popular measure of aging, providing consistency across large data sets and simplification in adult development textbooks. The U.S. Census Bureau applies the term *older adult* to those 65 years and older. Although grouping by age provides a convenient statistic, such numbers fail to reflect variances in physiological health and abilities, sociocultural differences, historical cohorts, and individual life events. Even characteristics tied to chronological age, such as life expectancy, are not static. For instance, a male born in the United States in 1930 had an estimated life expectancy of 58 while males born in 2015 have an estimated life expectancy of 76. New measures accounting for changes in life expectancy and disability have been developed (Sanderson & Scherbov, 2010), but these also fail to portray the vast diversity of the U.S. population.

To address the heterogeneity of older adults, Neugarten (1974) differentiated *young-old* (age 55 to 75) from *old-old* (75 and older). A revised breakdown beginning at 65 instead of 55 considers four categories: young-old (65–74), old-old (75–84), oldest-old (85–99), and centenarians (100 years and older) (Moody, 2018). To illuminate recent demographics of older adults in the United States, we provide further statistics.

Based on life expectancy, birth and death rates, and immigration and migration estimates, we know that the U.S. population is aging. The U.S. Census Bureau projects that the number of individuals 65 and older will increase from 49 million (16%) in 2016 to 73 million (21%) by 2030. Beyond 2030, this growth is expected to slow as the last of the Baby Boomers (those born between 1946 and 1964) cross the 65-year mark. However, the projection of the 85-and-over population is expected to double by 2035 and nearly triple by 2060 (Vespa et al., 2018).

Overlaying age statistics with race and ethnicity figures, the trend of an increasingly diverse U.S. population continues. By 2060, it is projected that 1 in 3 or 32%, of the U.S. population will be a race other than White (Vespa et al., 2018). In 2016, 23% of individuals 65 and older were members of a racial or ethnic minority (using the U.S. Census Bureau's four categories of non-Hispanic White, Black or African American, Asian and Pacific Islander, and Hispanic). The fastest growing racial or ethnic group—people who identify as two or more races—is projected to grow 200% by 2060 (Vespa et al., 2018).

Regarding gender, 2010 census figures continue to show a gender difference, with older females outnumbering older males, but that gap is narrowing (Werner, 2011). Another gender difference is in median income. Older males in 2016 received a median income of $31,618, while females collected a median income of $18,380. In 2015, Social Security constituted 90% of income received by 34% of its beneficiaries. Other income sources included pensions, income from assets, and earnings (Administration on Aging, 2017).

Greater financial insecurity among women is evident in higher rates of poverty. Lower salaries and interrupted income from caregiving reduce women's Social Security earnings and retirement savings. White women fare better than women from other racial and ethnic groups, not because of a higher status, but because of their present or previous positions as wives of relatively privileged White men (Calasanti, 2010). Pay inequity and other social constructs lead to a cumulative disadvantage over the life course not linked to individual choice or action (Ferraro & Shippee, 2009).

Finally, education level of older adults (65 years and older) is increasing in the United States. Between 1970 and 2017, the percentage of older persons completing high school rose from 28% to 86%. This varies considerably by race and ethnicity. For instance, in 2017, 91% of non-Hispanic Whites graduated high school, while only 58% of Hispanics graduated (Braddock et al., 2017). The figures for higher education reflect even more disparity by race and ethnicity. The truism of "those who have, get more" is valid for older adult learning. Hence, older adult education, as in other stages of educational provision, is enveloped in a social justice framework supporting the notion that the quality of life of significant numbers of seniors is diminished through insufficient educational participation (Findsen, 2005).

Identifying as a Student/Learner

There is a subtle difference between being an older student (usually associated with engagement with a provider or institution) and being an older adult learner. Given that so much of learning for seniors is not linked to being a student (depicted in higher education literature as "nontraditional"), the idea of older people seeing themselves as learners can seem quite remote. Typically, older people construct multiple identities (e.g., historian; grandparent; mentor) as they transition through different stages of the life course (Ecclestone et al., 2010). Seldom is the identity of "learner" one of them. Hence, the concept of older people as learners is closely connected to an engagement in activities having the potential for learning/ education (Boulton-Lewis, 2010; Hammond, 2004; Withnall, 2010).

> People's sense of self (identity), their capacity for autonomous, empowered action (agency) and the effects of structural factors (class, gender, race and economic and material conditions) have long been a concern of researchers hoping to understand questions of inequality, access to educational and life opportunities, and learners' responses to particular forms of teaching. (Ecclestone, 2007, p. 121)

When focusing specifically on older adults' identities, agency, and structural supports or barriers, it is helpful to review a timeline of theories of aging and how this explains older adult learning.

Theories of Aging, Learning, and Education

Initial theories of aging came out of medical research and practice and attempted to explain physical and cognitive decline. These theories continue to inform geriatric medicine and provide preventative measures such as immunizations and healthy lifestyle coaching but do not reflect sociocultural shifts and emerging educational needs of older adults.

Social theories of aging that emerged in the 1950s and 1960s included Cumming and Henry's (1961) disengagement theory and Havighurst and Albrecht's (1953) activity theory. The assumption of declining health, a developmental need to disengage, and society's dogmatic belief in individual productivity left many older adults in the first half of the 1900s with little motivation to engage in educational endeavors. While the perceived and real limitations of older adults' physical abilities are sensible, the tendency to describe all seniors in terms of decrepitude (Findsen, 2005) has been and is inaccurate.

Activity theory seemed a better match for the American ideals of independence, autonomy, and freedom (Settersten, 2017), ideals that did not disappear on one's 65th birthday. By the 1960s, longer life expectancy and a steady decline in average retirement age resulted in courses on transitioning to retirement and discovering new roles. This trend extended into the 1970s, with some states allowing adults 65 and older to enroll in public colleges and universities tuition free (Manheimer, 2005). This was a time of multipurpose senior centers and national funding of arts and humanities programming for seniors.

Elderhostel, a travel/learning program for seniors 55 and older, was organized in 1975. Around this same time, Shepard Centers, Older Adult Service Information Centers (OASIS), and Institutes of Learning in Retirement (ILRs) opened (Manheimer, 2005). Interestingly, in an effort to attract Baby Boomers, who tend to be age-sensitive, Elderhostel has become Road Scholar and Institutes for Learning in Retirement refer to themselves as Lifelong Learning Institutes. Even the American Association for Retired Persons, founded in 1958, has formally adopted its acronym AARP.

Activity theory spawned additional theories, including productive aging (Butler & Gleason, 1985) and successful aging (Rowe & Kahn, 1997). While successful aging moved research from disease and disability to health and growth, it was criticized for its lack of inclusion, particularly those with disabilities and functional impairments. In response, Freedman et al. (2017) suggested successful accommodation for older adults such as those desiring to age in place and resilient aging, which aims to capture an individual's resilient responses to adversity over the life course, becoming trajectories of adaptation and growth (Pruchno et al., 2015). Once thought to be an innate trait, resilience is both a process and outcome, and as a process, it is likely teachable (APA, 2011; Lohr, 2018; Southwick et al., 2014).

One aspect of resilient aging is spirituality or a belief in a higher power. Tornstam's theory of gerotranscendence (2005), the conscious aging conferences by the New York State-based Omega Institute (1977), and Rabbi Schachter-Shalomi's book *From Age-ing to Sage-ing* (1995), correspond to this more cosmic perspective. Educational programming reflecting a cosmic perspective includes courses in mind-body awareness, self-development, wisdom, and comparative religion (Manheimer, 2005).

Over recent decades the emancipatory component of learning by and for older adults has come to the forefront. The emergence of *critical educational gerontology* is significant as theorists incorporate critical theory into the discourse. The primary goals of this critical dialogue are to avoid homogenizing older adults, lessen the dominance of psychological and cognitive theories of deficit, and pose the sociological consideration of whose interests are being served (Battersby, 1987; Battersby & Glendenning, 1992). In the 2000s more emphasis has been placed on the concept of learning in later life, reflecting the life-wide side of older people's learning (Findsen & Formosa, 2011; Jarvis, 2001; Withnall, 2010), coupled with how some groups in society remain marginalized in terms of access (Formosa & Higgs, 2013).

Older Adult Education and Learning

One scheme for developing learning and educational opportunities for older adults is the conventional needs assessment that distinguishes between "lower level" needs (*coping, expressive*) and moving toward more aspirational needs of *contribution, influence* and *transcendence* (McClusky, 1974). In the 1980s, Peterson (1980) developed a model based on *educational gerontology* as "the field of study and practice at the interface of adult education and social gerontology" (p. 62). Peterson identified three subfields: education for older adults, public education about aging, and education of professionals and paraprofessionals in the field of aging.

In the case of education for older adults, it is useful to broaden the notion of education not only *for* but also *with* older adults. The idea of older adults framing their own opportunities for learning/education is the cornerstone of many current educational/social movements. The insertion of *with* lessens the prospect that older people are patronized by education provided *for* them (Moody, 2002).

Public education *for* older adults provided by state and federal agencies is usually quite limited, though there are some exceptions. The rhetoric of educational institutions regarding older adult education may change as more higher education institutions offer age-friendly educational options (Talmage et al., 2016). Given that many older people may feel somewhat estranged from active engagement with younger learners, educators might well employ extra sensitivity to seniors' diverse needs. Some marginalized groups of older adults may require different ways of participating to ensure their concerns are considered. Older people's voices need to be heard as key stakeholders in establishing relevant curriculum and learning strategies (Talmage et al., 2016).

With more seniors working beyond typical retirement age, one of the significant challenges facing older adults is equal access to learning opportunities in the workplace (Beatty & Visser, 2005). A cursory glance at statistics of older workers and their educational participation levels reveals significant disparities between older and younger workers (Boston & Davey, 2006). Carefully crafted intergenerational programs offer ample opportunity for engagement across the age span. Such programs benefit both older workers who have considerable expertise and life experience to contribute and younger employees who are so-called digital natives ready to offer skills advice (Newman & Hatton-Yeo, 2008; Thalhammer, 2014). The challenge is to use—and continue to develop—the wisdom and accumulated expertise of these workers to the benefit of not only the individual but also the workplace and wider society.

Learning can occur anywhere, any time, and include an informal, incidental activity or a formal setting involving instruction. In the case of older adults, learning is more commonly informal or nonformal, such as volunteer work or newly acquired skills from daily engagement. However, even in nonformal and informal learning venues, differential opportunity is prevalent in voluntary activities located in many social institutions such as places of worship, the workplace, or service agencies (Findsen, 2005, 2006). A focus on *learning in later life* (Findsen & Formosa, 2011) offers an expansive notion of learning and highlights greater self-determination among seniors, broader motives and outcomes, and lessened constraints of institutional provision. It often incorporates a political economy perspective where the role of government is examined, and how social stratification (i.e., gender, race/ethnicity, social class, sexual orientation, religious affiliation—and their intersections) affects who gets access to particular forms of knowledge (Estes et al., 2003; Jamieson et al., 1997).

Public education *about* aging has become more important in postmodern society because information and knowledge about aging are often clouded in ageist stereotypes. It is still commonplace to connect older adulthood to perceptions of declining mental and physical capabilities (Fisher, 1998). Butler (1969), who coined the term *ageism*, called for more research on the widespread, negative attitudes toward older adults. Later, in 2005, Nelson found comparatively little research focused on age prejudice compared to research on the other two preeminent social perceptions of race and gender. In his 2016 follow-up article, Nelson found a slight increase in ageism research, likely attributable to the aging Baby Boomers; but ageism continues to fly under the radar in the media and with the general public. Levy and Macdonald (2016) identified three areas associated with ageism: prejudicial beliefs, discriminatory behaviors, and institutionalized bias in programs and policies. While older adults actually vary greatly in health, financial situation, and functional status, the stereotype of older adults as sick, frail, senile, or at least unhappy prevails (Lindland et al., 2015).

In 2015, a report on the first phase of a collaboration between the AARP, the American Federation for Aging Research, the American Geriatrics Society, the American Society on Aging, the Gerontological Society of America, the National Council on Aging, and the National Hispanic Council on Aging was released. *Gauging Aging: Mapping the Gaps Between Expert and Public Understandings of Aging in America* (Lindland et al., 2015) found numerous challenges facing the United States as an aging society. These included deep negative perceptions of aging, the ideal of self-sufficiency, and lack of productive thinking about policies required to improve well-being and contribution in later life.

Public education on aging is particularly relevant as more paraprofessionals and policymakers need training and professional development to work on behalf of greater numbers of older people. In the private sector, many agencies are poised to take advantage of the *silver economy* (older people with strong economic capital). Examples abound of private agencies offering training and staff development for professionals working with seniors. Some private industry is taking advantage of the relative wealth of the older middle class by gearing programs to leisure, travel, and recreation (Findsen & Formosa, 2011).

Adjustments are needed in numerous social structures, including employment, health care, transportation, urban planning, housing, and community development. Specifically, workplaces may be restructured to allow older individuals to work longer and with more flexibility. Opportunities can be increased for civic, social, and economic contribution—from mentoring and volunteerism to second (and even third) careers. Institutional ageism must be acknowledged and addressed as a major barrier to older adults' participation in society. Geriatric training and care should be made more available and long-term-care insurance options made more affordable. Improved institutional and social supports must be made readily available for caregivers. Finally, greater investment in research on aging will provide valuable data about aging and the educational needs for and about the elderly (Lindland et al., 2015).

Future Trends and Research Implications

The field of older adult learning is gaining in both importance and prominence based on the proliferation of new books, journals, and social media sites addressing the well-being and educational prospects of older people. Findsen and Formosa's (2016) *International Perspectives on Older Adult Education: Research, Policies and Practice* provides a useful framework for issues impacting learning/education among older citizens in both developed and developing country contexts. Trends identified in this and other relevant resources suggest opportunity for advocacy and intervention for learning in later life.

Older People in the Workforce
Without doubt, more people beyond traditional retirement age are continuing to engage in the labor market, whether out of economic necessity or for other reasons such as personal fulfilment. This is especially well demonstrated in most advanced economies (Rothwell et al., 2008). While ageism is still prevalent in the workplace (Nelson, 2016), many older workers need to assert their rights for ongoing employment and point to the numerous advantages of employing older workers, including accumulated experience and expertise (DeLong, 2004; Hedge et al., 2006; Shea & Haasen, 2005). At the federal level, policy and legal conditions need to be conducive to the employment of older people.

When provided favorable working conditions, older workers contribute both hard and soft skills. Brooke and Taylor's (2005) research on mixed-age teams found older workers showing younger workers how to work "smarter" and avoid mistakes. These older employees also imparted stability and maintained quality standards. At the same time, younger workers excelled at new technology, adding this dimension to the team dynamic. Brooke and Taylor (2005) determined that age management practices, like mixed-age group work, must come from formalizing "an intergenerational workforce development approach" (p. 426). Incorporating age-inclusive practices; age-neutral recruiting, promotion, and training; and promoting initiatives that create age-diverse workplaces and corporate cultures will be key in the future success of companies (Boehm et al., 2013).

Technological Access and Competency
Older adults are gaining in technological skills and ownership of various technological devices, including smartphones, ereaders and tablets, and laptop computers. Seniors are among the fastest growing group of new Facebook users; for instance, general internet use by those 65 and older is virtually the same as those aged 65 and younger (Anderson & Perrin, 2017). Although the Pew Research Center found that internet and broadband use drops off around age 75, this is expected to change as the young-old become the old-old. Internet access and use is shown to support skill enhancement, social access, and intellectual stimulation; however, there are dramatic differences in access and competency impacted by affluence and educational attainment (Smith, 2014). Seniors with an annual income of $75,000 or more are three times as likely to have internet or broadband at home than seniors earning less than $30,000. Seniors with a college degree are twice as likely to go online than seniors who have not attended college. Physical condition and health issues also create barriers to technology use. Skepticism toward connectivity was widely documented in early studies of older adults and computer usage, but newer studies suggest that once seniors learn to use the internet, they find it useful and integrate it into their daily lives (Huber & Watson, 2014).

Adult Literacy
One area of innovation via technology is (older) adult literacy education that can be individualized, self-paced,

and made available in remote locations (Roman, 2004). In much of the world, older cohorts are often among the least literate members of society and are thus potentially more marginalized, isolated, and at risk. Data collected from the National Adult Literacy Survey (NALS) in 1992 found that 44% of adults over age 65 were functionally illiterate (Kirsh et al., 2002). The National Assessment of Adult Literacy (NAAL) survey in 2003 found the age group of 65 years and above still had the largest percentage of illiterate adults but the percentage was dropping compared to the 1992 numbers in the NALS (White, 2007). This is likely more a cohort effect than age related. More telling is the fact that illiteracy is a result of economic, social, and educational inequities.

Health literacy is one aspect of functional literacy—an aspect that is attracting research and funding. "Education is arguably the most critical social determinant of health and proximate health determinants such as health behaviors, economic resources, and stress" (Yamashita et al., 2017, p. 242). Given more opportunity for both formal and nonformal education, seniors can gain increased literacy skills, along with the associated advantages of social engagement, life enrichment, and better health. Recognition of this trend posits opportunities for both private and public agencies and institutions to provide such relevant learning opportunities.

Limited Resource Allocation

Financial allocation to adult education in the United States is minimal, with resources available for *older* adult education even more limited. A related issue is that research, advocacy, development, and implementation of learning for older adults have largely been unrecognized by funding agencies, state or federal institutions, or private providers. While lifelong learning may receive indirect support through other channels of social provision/support, learning aimed at older learners' needs is undersupported. Improved resource allocation may benefit from explicit strategic connections with other related fields where funding is less competitive.

The Fourth Age

Laslett (1991) coined the term *the third age,* representing seniors still in good health with relatively high level of functioning and well-being; and *the fourth age,* referring to the period of life immediately before death, usually of short duration when individuals return, as in early childhood, to a state of dependency (Formosa, 2015). A reality is that the fourth age is usually described as one of considerable decrepitude and dependence where many older people need considerable care. Given the virtual lack of useful institutional policy and intervention where poor health and dependence exist, elder care often falls to family and typically to women. With the growing numbers of seniors, issues of care for our elderly within the family unit is of significant interest. If models demonstrating seniors' centrality to the family structure such as those found in more collective societies where older people are revered for their wisdom and *mana* (a Māori term similar to prestige) are adopted in the United States, a return to multigenerational households may result.

Because many adults in Western cultures hold a self-image of independence and a perception of seeking help as forced reliance (Tam, 2014), the way forward is two-pronged. First, a better understanding of help-seeking attitudes and abilities is needed so that older adults and caregivers are better informed, able, and willing to take advantage of the services available (Wacker & Roberto, 2016). Second, educating service providers in the many layers of physical, social, and cultural nuances that impact an extremely heterogeneous older adult population is essential.

Conclusion

Older adults, defined differently in varying contexts, have assumed increasing importance in most societies globally out of sheer numbers. However, their significance and influence belie any simple mathematical estimation. While people have multiple identities beyond what their chronological age might suggest, the notion of an older learner is not well understood. While the idea of older students is better comprehended, in many institutional settings they are still treated as "other" or "nontraditional" in formal education circles.

Yet the majority of learning by older people goes well beyond what educational providers capture. Most learning occurs in more incidental ways and through membership within community organizations (e.g., through volunteering). Increasingly, learning is self-directed and largely separate from education structures and policy. While a myriad of adult education agencies supports learning opportunities for seniors, an ageist attitude, while challenged more often, still persists in wider society.

References

Administration on Aging. (2017). *A profile of older Americans: 2017*. Administration on Aging. https://acl.gov/aging-and-disability-in-america/data-and-research/profile-older-americans.

American Psychological Association. (2011). *The road to resilience*. Author.

Anderson, M., & Perrin, A. (2017). *Tech adoption climbs among older adults*. Pew Research Center. http://www.pewinternet.org/2017/05/17/technology-use-among-seniors/

Battersby, D. (1987). From andragogy to geragogy. *Journal of Educational Gerontology, 2*(1), 4–10.

Battersby, D., & Glendenning, F. (1992). Reconstructing education for older adults: An elaboration of first principles. *Australian Journal of Adult and Community Education, 32*(2), 115–121.

Beatty, P. T., & Visser, R. M. S. (Eds.). (2005). *Thriving on an aging workforce: Strategies for organizational and systematic change*. Krieger.

Boehm, S. A., Kunze, F., & Bruch, H. (2013). Spotlight on age diversity climate: The impact of age-inclusive HR practices on firm-level outcomes. *Personnel Psychology, 67*(3), 667–704.

Boston, J., & Davey, J. A. (2006). *Implications of population ageing: Opportunities and risks*. Institute of Policy Studies, Victoria University of Wellington.

Boulton-Lewis, G. (2010). Education and learning for the elderly: Why, how, what. *Educational Gerontology, 36*(3), 213–228. https://doi.org/10.1080/03601270903182877

Braddock, D., Hemp, R., Tanis, E. S., Wu, J., & Haffer, L. (2017). *The state of the states in intellectual and developmental disabilities: 2017*. American Association on Intellectual and Developmental Disabilities

Brooke, L., & Taylor, P. (2005). Older workers and employment: Managing age relations. *Ageing and Society, 25*, 415–429.

Butler, R. (1969). Age-ism: Another form of bigotry. *The Gerontologist, 9*(4), 243–246.

Butler, R., & Gleason, H. (1985). *Productive aging: Enhancing vitality in later life*. Springer.

Calasanti, T. (2010). Gender relations and applied research on aging. *The Gerontologist, 50*(6), 720–734.

Cumming, E., & Henry, W. (1961). *Growing old: The process of disengagement*. Basic Books.

DeLong, D. W. (2004). *Lost knowledge: Confronting the threat of an aging workforce*. Oxford University Press.

Ecclestone, K. (2007). An identity crisis? Using concepts of "identity," "agency," and "structure" in the education of adults. *Studies in the Education of Adults, 39*, 121–131.

Ecclestone, K., Biesta, G. & Hughes, M. (2010). Transitions in the lifecourse: The role of identity, agency and structure. In K. Ecclestone, G. Biestra, & M. Hughes (Eds.), *Transitions and learning through the lifecourse* (pp. 1–15). Routledge.

Estes, C. L., Biggs, S., & Phillipson, C. (2003). *Social theory, social policy and ageing: A critical introduction*. Open University.

Ferraro, K., & Shippee, T. (2009). Aging and cumulative inequality: How does inequality get under the skin? *The Gerontologist, 49*(3). 333–343.

Findsen, B. (2005). *Learning later*. Krieger.

Findsen, B. (2006). Social institutions as sites of learning for older adults: Differential opportunities. *Journal of Transformative Education, 4*(1), 65–81.

Findsen, B., & Formosa, M. (2011). *Lifelong learning in later life: A handbook on older adult learning*. Sense.

Findsen, B., & Formosa, M. (Eds.). (2016). *International perspectives on older adult education: research, policies and practice*. Springer.

Fisher, J. C. (1998). Major streams of research probing older adult education. *New Directions for Adult and Continuing Education, 1998*(77), 41–53.

Formosa, M. (2015). *Ageing and later life in Malta: Issues, policies and future trends*. Book Distributors.

Formosa, M., & Higgs, P. (Eds.) (2013). *Social class in later life: Power, identity and lifestyle*. The Policy Press.

Freedman, V. A., Kasper, J. D., & Spillman, B. C. (2017). Successful aging through successful accommodation with assistive devices. *The Journals of Gerontology. Series B, Psychological Sciences and Social Sciences, 72*(2), 300–309.

Hammond, C. (2004). Impacts of lifelong learning upon emotional resilience, psychological and mental health: Fieldwork evidence. *Oxford Review of Education, 30*(4), 551–568.

Havighurst, R., & Albrecht, R. (1953). *Growing old*. Longmans.

Hedge, J., Borman, W., & Lammlein, S. (2006). *The aging workforce: Realities, myths, and implications for organizations*. American Psychological Association.

Huber, L., & Watson, C. (2014). Technology: Education and training needs of older adults. *Educational Gerontology, 40*, 16–25. https://doi.org/10.1080/03601277.2013.768064

Jamieson, A., Harper, S., & Victor, C. (Eds.). (1997). *Critical approaches to ageing and later life*. Open University Press.

Jarvis, P. (2001). *Learning in later life: An introduction for educators and carers*. Kogan Page.

Kirsh, I., Jungeblut, A., Jenkins, L., & Kolstad, A. (2002). *Adult literacy in America: A first look at the findings of the National Adult Literacy Survey*. National Center for Education Statistics.

Laslett, P. (1991). *A fresh map of life: The emergence of the third age* (rev. ed.). Harvard University Press.

Levy, S., & Macdonald, J. (2016). Progress on understanding ageism. *Journal of Social Issues, 72*(1), 5–25.

Lindland, E., Fond, M., Haydon, A., & Kendall-Taylor, N. (2015). *Gauging aging: Mapping the gaps between expert and public understandings of aging in America*. FrameWorks Institute.

Lohr, K. (2018). Tapping autobiographical narratives to illuminate resilience: A transformative learning tool for adult educators. *Educational Gerontology, 44*(2–3), 163–170.

Manheimer, R. (2005). The older learner's journal to an ageless society: Lifelong learning on the brink of a crisis. *Journal of Transformative Education, 3*(3), 198–220.

McClusky, H. Y. (1974). Education for ageing: The scope of the field and perspectives for the future. In A. Borowski, & W. D. Mason (Eds.), *Learning for ageing* (pp. 324–355). Adult Education Association of the USA.

Moody, H. (2002). The changing meaning of aging. In R. S. Weiss & S. A. Bass (Eds.), *Challenges of the third age* (pp. 41–54). Oxford University Press.

Moody, H. (2018). *Aging: Concepts and controversies* (9th ed.). SAGE.

Nelson, T. (2005). Ageism: Prejudice against our feared future self. *Journal of Social Issues, 61*(2), 207–221.

Nelson, T. (2016). The age of ageism. *Journal of Social Issues, 72*(1), 191–198.

Neugarten, B. (1974). Age groups in American society and the rise of the young-old. The *Annals of the American Academy of Political and Social Science, 415*(1), 187–198.

Newman, S., & Hatton-Yeo, A. (2008). Intergenerational learning and the contributions of older people. *Ageing Horizons, 8*, 31–39.

Omega Institute. (1977). *Mission, history, and values*. https://www.eomega.org/mission-history-values

Peterson, D. A. (1980). Who are the educational gerontologists? *Educational Gerontology, 5*, 65–77.

Pruchno, R., Heid, A., & Genderson, M. (2015). Resilience and successful aging: Aligning complementary constructs using a life course approach. *Psychological Inquiry, 26*, 200–207.

Roman, S. (2004). Illiteracy and older adults: Individual and societal implications. *Educational Gerontology, 30*, 79–93.

Rothwell, W. J., Sterns, H. L., Spokus, D., & Reaser, J. M. (2008). *Working longer: New strategies for managing, training, and retaining older employees*. American Management Association.

Rowe, J., & Kahn, R. (1997). Successful aging. *The Gerontologist, 37*(4), 433–440.

Sanderson, W., & Scherbov, S. (2010). Remeasuring aging. *Science, 329*(10), 1287–1288.

Schachter-Shalomi, Z. (1995). *From age-ing to sage-ing: A profound new vision of growing older*. Time Warner Book Group.

Settersten, R. (2017). Some things I have learned about aging by studying the life course. *Innovation in Aging, 1*(2), 1–7. https://doi.org/10.1093/geroni/igx014

Shea, G., & Haasen, A. (2005). *Older worker advantage: Making the most of our aging workforce*. Praeger.

Smith, A. (2014). *Older adults and technology use: Adoption is increasing, but many seniors remain isolated from digital life*. Pew Research Center. http://www.pewinternet.org/2014/04/03/older-adults-and-technology-use/

Southwick, S., Bonanno, G., Masten, A., Panter-Brick, C., & Yehuda, R. (2014). Resilience definitions, theory, and challenges: Interdisciplinary perspectives. *European Journal of Psychotraumatology, 5*.

Talmage, C. A., Mark, R., Slowey, M., & Knopf, R. C. (2016). Age friendly universities and engagement with older adults: Moving from principles to practice. *International Journal of Lifelong Education, 35*(5), 537–554. https://doi.org/10.1080/02601370.2016.1224040

Tam, M. (2014). Understanding and theorizing the role of culture in the conceptualizations of successful aging and lifelong learning. *Educational Gerontology, 40*, 881–893. https://doi.org/10.1080/03601277.2014.907072

Thalhammer, V. (2014). Elearning: An opportunity for older persons. In B. Schmidt-Hertha, S. J. Jelenc Kravosec, & M. Formosa (Eds.). *Learning across generations in Europe: Contemporary issues in older adult education* (pp. 47–58). Sense.

Tornstam, L. (2005). *Gerotranscendence: A developmental theory of positive aging*. Springer.

Vespa, J., Armstrong, D., & Medina, L. (2018). *Demographic turning points for the United States: Population projections for 2020 to 2060*. U.S. Census Bureau.

Wacker, R., & Roberto, K. (2016). Theories of help-seeking behavior: Understanding community service use by older adults. In V. L. Bengtson & R. A. Setterson, Jr. (Eds.), *Handbook of theories of aging* (pp. 505–530). Springer.

Werner, C. (2011). *The older population: 2010*. United States Census Bureau.

White, S. (2007). *Literacy in everyday life: Results from the 2003 National Assessment of Adult Literacy*. National Center for Education Statistics.

Withnall, A. (2010). *Improving learning in later life*. Routledge.

Yamashita, T., Lopez, E., Stevens, J., & Keene, J. (2017). Types of learning activities and life satisfaction among older adults in urban community-based lifelong learning programs. *Activities, Adaptation & Aging, 41*(3), 239–257. https://doi.org/10.1080/01924788.2017.1310583

CHAPTER 43

Adult Education and Race

A Critical Race Theory Analysis

Lorenzo Bowman and Jeremy Bohonos

Adult education has long claimed to embrace social justice as one of its foundational pillars. However, the past actions of the field have often been inconsistent with this claim. For example, observations of the early actions of the field suggest complicity in oppression. It is our observation that the field's involvement in the education of slaves was not to advance liberation and social awareness regarding the inherent inhumanity of slavery, but rather to increase the productivity of slaves. Writing in Neufeldt and McGee's important work on the education of the African American adult slave, Whiteaker (1990) points out that "adult education for slaves took shape on two levels: the training of skilled workers and the teaching of reading, writing, and other elementary subjects" (p. 3).

In this chapter, we will review the treatment of race within the field of adult education from its initial years of professionalization through today. The review will be situated within a critical race theory (CRT) critique in an attempt to unveil motives for action or inaction in the field across time. The use of CRT for such an analysis will offer insight and reveal possible changes that the field can make in the future to advance its social justice agenda. We begin by providing a short introduction to CRT.

CRT began as a movement comprising activists and scholars who were interested in studying and transforming "the relationship among race, racism, and power" (Delgado & Stefancic, 2001, p. 2). Unlike the civil rights movement, which embraced incrementalism, CRT interrogates the foundations of liberalism, including the various legal structures that maintain the American system of racial hegemony (Delgado & Stefancic, 2001).

Colonial exploitation of Native Americans as well as the marriage of chattel slavery to skin color form the foundation of the racism experienced by people of color in America today. Even in the face of clear evidence that there is no scientific proof to support the notion of race, as advanced in the failed "science" of eugenics, its significance has not diminished (Nyborg, 2019). In fact, the birth defect in the founding of America, as noted by former Secretary of State Condoleezza Rice, is racism (Bumiller, 2007). Critical race theorists posit that the long period of slavery's existence resulted in widespread social and psychological acceptance of the inferiority of African Americans. Thus, racism is permanently ingrained into the social reality of our nation (Bell, 1992).

CRT embraces several major ideas relevant to this chapter: (a) counterstorytelling, (b) the permanence of racism, (c) Whiteness as property, (d) interest convergence, (e) the critique of liberalism, and (f) differential racialization (Bell, 1992; Delgado & Stefancic, 2001; Harris, 1993). The tenet of counterstorytelling gives voice to the experiences of the oppressed by confronting racist characterizations of social life and exposing race neutral discourses that work to disadvantage the racially oppressed. Through the use of counterstories in adult education, faculty, students, and practitioners of color are provided a voice to tell their narratives involving marginalization in the field (Merriweather et al., 2006). Merriweather et al. (2006) noted in their work that experiences in the adult education classroom may be interpreted differently depending on race. Counterstorytelling provides a means to challenge majority stories that reinforce racial hegemony. Counterstorytelling gives voice to the silent. The use of counternarratives could reveal opportunities for further research on becoming inclusive and not remaining superficially diverse.

The permanence of racism embraces the reality that racism in our society is not the exception: It is the norm (Bell, 1992). The Black Lives Matter movement can be argued to be a reaction to the reality of the permanent continuing prominence of racism in our society (Miller & Schwartz, 2016). Racism is an endemic factor of the American social landscape that privileges White people over people of color in most areas of life including—but not limited to—education (DeCuir & Dixon, 2004; Delgado, 1995; Ladson-Billings, 1998; Ladson-Billings & Tate, 1995).

As a result of the ingrained racism in American society, Whiteness can be viewed as a property interest. The notion of property interest in Whiteness is "the idea that White skin and identity are economically valuable" (Delgado & Stefancic, 2001, p. 153). White people have the right to use and enjoyment, the right of disposition, and the right of exclusion from the ascribed benefits of White skin (DeCuir & Dixon, 2004; Harris, 1993; Ladson-Billings & Tate, 1995). This right of disposition and exclusion results in power and control over people of color and maintains the White power structure. This tenet plays out in the adult education classroom, where White educators have free rein to deliver courses as they see fit without the fear of challenge by students. Students dare not challenge their authority, legitimacy, or subject matter expertise. In stark contrast, educators of color report that they are frequently challenged by White students in the classroom (Johnson-Bailey & Cervero, 2000). Institutional power in organizations of higher learning reinforces the belief that being White is more valuable and carries much more social capital than being a person of color (DiAngelo, 2018).

Interest convergence is the notion that the White majority "tolerates advances for racial justice only when it suits its interest to do so" (Delgado & Stefancic, 2001, p. 149). Interest convergence acknowledges the reality that White people are the primary beneficiaries of civil rights legislation (DeCuir & Dixon, 2004; Ladson-Billings, 1998). A review of the primary policies and laws resulting from civil rights legislation reveals the reality of interest convergence. For example, affirmative action has long been viewed as a policy and law that unfairly discriminates against White people in favor of people of color who are frequently not qualified or less qualified. Yet White women have been the major beneficiaries of affirmative action (Rocco & Gallagher, 2004). White women are members of families where White men and children live; thus, it can be argued that White women, men, and children are beneficiaries of affirmative action, and as such it was in the interest of White people to support affirmative action.

The critique of liberalism provides insight into how liberalism acts to maintain racial barriers or create them for the benefit of the majority. Liberalism advances the perspective that the law is colorblind and neutral and is enough in and of itself to address and correct the vestiges of racism in our society. The notion of colorblindness allows society to ignore the reality of racist policies that perpetuate social inequity (DeCuir & Dixon, 2004). When unmasked, liberalism becomes fuel feeding the permanence of racism in modern American society because it ignores the origins of the racialization of America. Addressing symptoms of an illness without curing the underlying disease allows the underlying disease to thrive until it devours its host.

CRT's differential racialization thesis argues that dominant groups have racialized minoritized groups differently across history in response to factors such as shifting labor market needs and geopolitical conflicts (Delgado & Stefancic, 2001). This leads to changes in what stereotypical images are attached to different groups and even what privileges and rights of citizenship groups have access to at different times. In this chapter, we use CRT to interrogate the actions of the field as we review the field's actions over the years with regards to race.

Dominant Trends in the Early Years

Analysis of the previous editions of the *Handbook of Adult Education in the United States* (Ely, 1948;

Rowden, 1934, Rowden, 1936) as well as historical bibliography of adult education (Rachal, 1992) revealed that between 1910 and 1950 there were two dominant trends regarding race and adult and continuing education: the Americanization of European immigrants and Black adult education under Jim Crow.

The Americanization Movement and Adult Education

At the founding of the United States, there was a decided preference for immigrants whose race was White and of a certain Western European ancestry. White skin carried cultural value. European ethnic groups with darker skin colors were less desirable (Olneck, 1989). For example, Italian immigrants were less desirable. *Race* refers to physical differences that groups and cultures consider socially significant, such as skin color (Brace, 2005). As such, race is a social construct. *Ethnicity* refers to shared cultural values such as language, ancestry, or practices and beliefs. European immigrants to America had to quickly adapt to the cultural norms of America to be fully accepted. This process of becoming "American" is referred to as *Americanization*. The Americanization process resulted in the delegitimization of the collective ethnic identity that many European immigrants possessed upon arriving to America. These European groups needed to part with their ethnic identities to become American (Olneck, 1989).

In the early 20th century, the terms *Americanization* and *adult education* were regarded as synonymous by many Americans—owing to the field's heavy involvement in this area (Ross-Gordon et al., 2017). The first *Handbook of Adult Education in the United States* (Lewis, 1934) asserted that educating the foreign born for citizenship is the oldest form of adult education in the United States, but prior to World War I there was little coordinated effort to provide citizenship classes. In the Americanization movement, adult education facilitated the rapid acculturation of immigrants, especially from Europe. The war spurred interest in "Americanizing," driven by fears of labor unrest or disloyalty among unassimilated immigrant groups, as well as by industry and military needs for workers with improved English language skills. Teaching English was seen as a first step in the process of achieving "complete amalgamation with American ideas and ideals" (Mahoney & Herligy, 1918, p. 4). Learning English was considered a valuable skill that could prevent immigrants from experiencing the types of exploitation that could push them toward disloyalty or communistic labor agitation. Authors of Americanization texts saw various European "races" as having the potential to become "good Americans" (Talbot, 1917, p. 89) and provided detailed discussions of the content, pedagogical approaches, and philosophies that guided this form of education.

The process of Americanization was exposed by Du Bois (1996) as providing economic opportunities to European Americans who assimilated, while barring African Americans from both acceptance in and the economic opportunities that came with Americanization. Building on Du Bois's insights, contemporary scholarship has connected this assimilation process to the development of the White racial category as it exists today, while arguing that Europeans did not learn how to be American so much as they learned to be White Americans (Roediger, 2005). This Whitening process established the foundation for present embodiments of social ills such as race prejudice and the socioeconomic privileges associated with Whiteness (Bohonos, 2019; Ignatiev, 1995; Roediger, 2005). Given adult education's deep involvement in the Americanization movement, contemporary adult educators must grapple with our discipline's complicity in the construction and popularization of the White racial category as well as White supremacy and White privilege.

The Americanization movement is a classic example of CRTs differential racialization thesis, as specific efforts were devoted to the assimilation of European groups in response to military and labor market needs. This led to a shift in which previously minoritized European "races" became White—thus transforming the Anglo-Saxon hegemony the nation was founded on to allow all Christian European-descended people access to the privileges of Whiteness, while continuing to exclude people of African, Asian, and American Indian descent. Differential racialization drove the development of privilege for those racialized as White. Given that much of the early work in the field of adult education focused on the "Americanization" of immigrants and "race assimilation," and the fact that the field has yet to come to terms with the responsibility we may bear for complicity in forming and sustaining the current racial hierarchy, we argue that the field needs to acknowledge and work toward restorative justice that includes efforts to deconstruct Whiteness.

Jim Crow and Adult Education

Johnson-Bailey and Cervero (2000) argued that early handbooks (Ely, 1948; Rowden, 1934), by limiting the discussion of race to chapters describing programs for "Negroes" and "Indians," failed to address the centrality of race and racism in American society and ignored Jim Crow practices that affected adult education—and all other aspects of American life. Additionally, they criticize early adult educators' interest in race for an overestimation of the capacity for education alone to remedy racial issues, as well as for failing to consider the substantive social and political changes that would be required for people of color in America to enjoy life chances on par with those enjoyed by Whites. However, leading Black adult educators of this era, including Alain Locke and W. E. B. Du Bois, did attempt to address such issues but encountered repressive tolerance (Marcuse, 1965) from White adult educators and funding agencies, who quashed attempts to link adult education to critique of and advocacy against systemic racism and Jim Crow segregation (Guy & Brookfield, 2009). Repressive tolerance can be seen at work in the ways Locke was pressured to cut Du Bois from the Bronze Book series on Black Adult Education. Du Bois's contribution attempted to link adult education to calls for socialistic, economic, and political reorganization (Guy & Brookfield, 2009). Repressive tolerance was seen in Du Bois having his Encyclopedia of the Negro project canceled by financial backers who deemed him too biased to complete the project after putting years of work into the compilation process (Lewis, 2009) and, also, the disconnect between the systematic discussion of antiracist and anticolonial sentiments expressed by Locke elsewhere (Stewart, 2018). It was also evident in the relatively restrained writing Locke contributed to the early handbooks (Johnson-Bailey & Cervero, 2000). The role of so-called bad money (James-Gallaway, 2019)—donations from White philanthropists seeking to control Black education—can be seen in each of these instances. The Carnegie Foundation was either the sole or primary underwriter for the three examples mentioned and used the considerable influence their donations bought them to shape the publications they sponsored. These examples suggest that the repressive tolerance of White liberal adult educators and the bad money of their financial backers restrained the efforts of progressive Black intellectuals to publish visions that connected adult education to broader critiques or critical arguments of systemic racism.

Johnson-Bailey and Cervero's (2000) criticism of adult education's historical overreliance on education as a remedy to racial issues—without addressing the important social and political structural changes that need to occur—provides a vivid example of why CRT critiques liberalism. One of the assumptions of liberalism is that the reduction of prejudice and movement toward a "colorblind" society would result in the elimination of racism. Racism cannot be eliminated because it is a core part of the social infrastructure of the nation. It was in the interest of adult educators to advance education as a panacea for racism. When we acknowledge that education is not enough to end racism, we risk losing our status as experts who can fix it. Advancing the argument that education is the key to change is in the best interest of a liberally conceived view of our field because it privileges our pedagogical skill sets—but it does so in a way that does not seriously challenge the existing racial order. This argument is the embodiment of the interest convergence tenet in CRT.

Johnson-Bailey and Cervero's (2000) observation that early adult education did not address the central role of racism in American society, and evidence that early adult educators' calls for systemic change were excluded from prominent adult education publications (Guy & Brookfield, 2009) speaks to the need for counternarratives. White people controlled the narrative in early adult education work. We now need a corrective counternarrative that embraces both historical and contemporary voices that have been deemed "too radical" for the field. The movement toward the explicit acknowledgment of race and racism in the current era is positive; however, much more is needed in the way of counterstorytelling that links to political organizing around racial justice. We challenge the notion that the field is rooted in social justice. Our CRT analysis suggests that the field claims its social justice roots when it is beneficial to do so; viewing the field's commitment through the lens of interest convergence, we conclude that it is fair to question the field's sincere commitment to social justice.

The Civil Rights and Black Power Era

A review of the 1960, 1970, and 1980 editions of the *Handbook of Adult Education in the United States* show that during the civil rights and Black Power era, discussions of race were excluded and reveal White perspectives to be highly privileged (Johnson-Bailey & Cervero,

2000). Similarly, analysis of articles published in *Adult Education* (later renamed *Adult Education Quarterly*—hereafter *AEQ*) between 1950 and 1990 shows that discussions about race received only marginal attention.

Between 1950 and 1970 only two articles in *AEQ* devoted more than a few paragraphs to race. Of these two, one was a reprint from *Phylon, the Atlanta University Review of Race and Culture* (Prothro & Smith, 1954), leaving only one original research article published on the topic during this time period (Rubin, 1967). Additionally, the conservatism in adult education research can be seen in many articles where race is mentioned but not substantively addressed or where it is addressed in ways that expose reactionary views. For example, some studies identified "Negros" among the subjects of a study or as participants in an educational program, but their experiences are not explored (Johnson et al., 1968; Knox & Videbeck, 1963).

Other articles demonstrated reactionary views on issues of race by the way they discussed racial minorities. For example, Hewes (1956) warned adult educators of the "considerable hazard" (p. 216) of bringing adult students' prior experiences into the classroom and giving the example of a class of adult women who began demanding that the organization sponsoring the classes racially desegregate and start paying women equally. The general conservatism toward race in the field is further suggested by the number of studies addressing race that are mentioned in *AEQ*, relative to the number of full articles published on the topic. For example, over several years the editors published lists of research, including new books and dissertations which contained at least 13 studies focused on Black adult education, none of which were ever published in *AEQ* in article form.

The ways that White adult educators were able to exclude Black radical thought from prominent publications in the field (Guy & Brookfield, 2009) is an example of Whiteness as property. In this example, White people had the power to determine what Black thought was acceptable to their political visions and determine whether or not it should be published. Similarly, the lack of studies examining issues related to racialized minorities and the noninclusion of studies regarding racialized minorities in the early decades of *AEQ* show a lack of interest in the experiences of people of color. The tenet of Whiteness as property explains why the experiences of Blacks were not deemed important enough for substantive inclusion in *AEQ*. Whiteness as property advances and prefers the experiences of those with White skin color—their lives matter!

Acknowledging Systemic Racism in Adult Education

Johnson-Bailey and Cervero (2000) found, from the analysis of past handbooks, that the 1970s presented a major turning point in the treatment of race in adult education. They noted the emergence of perspectives that located the problems associated with minority groups with "the insidious character of White racism that infects our society" (London, 1970b, p. 13) and calls for systemic change. As in the handbooks during this time period, *AEQ* begins to break with established patterns by pushing the field to consider both the degree to which social class effects the life chances of Americans and the ways racial discrimination compounds the barriers faced by lower-class Blacks (London, 1970a). We also see discussions of how the middle-class assumptions that most adult educators bring to their work act as an impendent to participation of the working class, and that both more responsive programing and better institutional support are needed for adult educators to more effectively engage with diverse learners. The decade also saw an increase in publications about race, with eight articles focusing on the topic.

The 1980s saw a decline in research articles focused on race relative to the 1970s, with only two such articles published in the decade (Heisel, 1985; Heisel & Larson, 1984). These papers both focused on the literacy experiences of older Black Americans and broke important ground in adult education by recognizing that standards of measurement used to assess White populations may be inappropriate for application in Black communities. These studies noted that previous measures of literacy—developed using the experiences of White learners as the norm—perpetuated misconceptions of Black illiteracy by overrepresenting the degree of illiteracy in older Black Americans. Previous assessments relied too heavily on years of formal education completed to serve as proxies for literacy. This assumption failed to consider that older Black adults often left formal schooling early because of limited opportunities under segregation, but that they often continued their learning in informal spaces. These articles also note that older Blacks expressed great interest in further improving their literacy, but generally expressed very little interest in doing so in formal adult education settings. This led the authors to conclude that adult educators need a conceptual shift in the way that literacy education in Black communities is approached and which will include the use of more relevant teaching approaches and materials when working in Black communities. We assert that such a shift requires a much more open and explicit acknowledgment of the relevance of race in teaching. CRT offers a viable explanation for this failure to acknowledge the relevance of race in teaching at this juncture in the field's history. The voices of disenfranchised students and scholars were largely missing. The counterstories of older Black adults would have unveiled the error in using the experiences of White learners as the norm.

Ross-Gordon (2017) noted a turn in the field toward a more explicit analysis of race and racism in the 1990s. Prior to this turn, adult education commonly addressed the issue of race and racism from within a multicultural framework (Cassara, 1990; Ross-Gordon, 1991). The problem with a purely multicultural framework is that multiculturalism is defined broadly, which allowed multicultural researchers to address any marker of diversity under that umbrella. While diversity is an important topic that should be addressed by the field, there is a critical need for the field to address race and racism given its relevance in our society. Merriam (1993) acknowledged that multiculturalism was similar to adult education because of its broad definition. It could be "interpreted to mean different things by different people" (p. 57). It is interesting to note that even though multiculturalism could have been used to address race and racism in the field, on the whole, scholars did not. Ross-Gordon (1991) challenged adult educators to embrace a multicultural perspective in adult education research after pointing out the lack of research in the field addressing multiculturalism relative to other education fields.

There were works during this era that addressed the topic of race within the field; most of these works were produced by the growing number of scholars of color in the field. For example, Peterson (1996) edited her important work, *Freedom Road: Adult Education of African Americans*, during this era. This work comprised six chapters by different authors that addressed the history of African American contributions and participation in adult education. Another example was the study conducted by Johnson-Bailey and Cervero (1998) that sought to determine the ways in which power relations that exist in the greater society play out in the teaching and learning exchange in the adult learning environment. They found that the positionality of instructors and learners, particularly with respect to race, was key in mediating classroom dynamics.

During this same time period (1990–2000), it appears that the field was changing at the program level, especially relative to the makeup of the graduate student population. Several universities housing large programs in the field of adult education made concerted efforts to recruit a more diverse student population. As a result, the scholarship started to directly address race and racism. Additionally, new faculty of color founded a preconference around 1992 (now the African Diaspora Preconference) for students of color with the goal of creating a safe environment for students to present research focused on issues important to members of the African Diaspora. This preconference became fertile ground for fostering future research presented at the annual Adult Education Research Conference (AERC) that addresses race.

Examples of scholarship from the 1990–2000 era that directly addressed race and racism in the field can be found in Guy's (1999) *New Directions for Adult and Continuing Education* monograph, *Providing Culturally Relevant Adult Education: A Challenge for the 21st Century*, and in Johnson-Bailey and Cervero's (2000) chapter published in the *Handbook of Adult and Continuing Education*. Chapters in Guy's monograph introduced adult education to polyrhythmic realities (Sheared, 1999) and CRT (Peterson, 1999). Johnson-Bailey and Cervero (2000) noted that there are no generic teachers. All teachers develop a teaching philosophy based on their unique positionality. This means that the role of race in teaching cannot and should not be ignored.

With the publication of the important book *Making Space: Merging Theory and Practice in Adult Education* (Sheared & Sissel, 2001), the field of adult education challenged adult educators to reflect on their "complicity in marginalizing others" (p. 12). The events leading to the publication of this book can be viewed as an inflection point that moved the field forward toward a far greater degree of inclusion. The book was in response to the second "black book" (Peters & Jarvis, 1991) published in adult education. The goal of the "black book "was to characterize the field . . . and consider its future possibilities" (p. 12). The Commission on Professors of Adult Education and its new "black book" were "rejected as being Eurocentric, racist, gender insensitive, elitist and exclusionary" (p. 12). Following a vote at the general business meeting of the 1992 Adult Education Research Conference, it was decided that American Association For Adult and Continuing Education (AAACE) would sponsor the publication of an alternative book that would project the field as inclusive. However, the inclusive proposal submitted by Sheared and Sissel was rejected by AAACE. The organization had substantial influence over the publisher Jossey-Bass, so the selected editors secured another publisher (Sheared & Sissel, 2001). The actions of AAACE provides another example of repressive tolerance. The 1992 research conference and the events which followed emboldened scholars of color and their allies to make space for alternative perspectives and move the field forward. The scholarship which followed reflected this embrace of alternative voices and counterstories.

Johnson-Bailey and Alfred's (2006) work is an example of alternative voices being incorporated into the literature as a result of the changes the field had undergone in the prior decade. They used the classroom experiences of two Black women professors as a lens to examine how transformational theory affects learning and teaching. Transformational learning speaks to how adults use learning to make meaning of major life events (Mezirow, 1975). Johnson-Bailey (in Johnson-Bailey & Alfred, 2006) wrote that she was challenged by a colleague to write the piece. She noted that she was asked why there were no Black women scholars in adult education writing about transformational learning. Johnson-Bailey and Alfred's work indicated that Black scholars felt empowered enough to bring their experiences as Black women front and center in connection with the analysis of major theories in the field.

Additional examples of the emergence of other voices in adult education include feminist pedagogy. Johnson-Bailey and Lee (2005) argued that the combination of feminist pedagogy and Women of Color feminism (WOC) can be a powerful force in the classroom where the pedagogy is intentional and incorporates the pedagogical practices of mastery, voice, positionality, and authority. Sheared (1996) noted the importance of including the Africentric feminist perspective in the literature. The Africentric feminist perspective expressly embraces the polyrhythmic reality of individuals. According to Sheared, the intersection of race, class, gender, and other realities are polyrhythmic realities. Polyrhythms are the multiple rhythms or realities that flow through a person's being—the multiple intersecting bits of identity that make each person unique. In acknowledging polyrhythmic realities, we acknowledge the effect of race, class, gender, and other realities on the educational process whereas, a feminist perspective only acknowledges the effects of gender and class.

Rosser-Mims (2010) used Black feminism to conduct a historical review of the forces that impact the development of Black women's leadership development. She found that in using a Black feminist lens for analysis, she was able to identify leadership development needs that might otherwise have remained invisible. While Black feminism had been used in works in the field prior to this time (Johnson-Bailey & Cervero, 1996), scholars in this era appear to have become more comfortable producing works using the Black feminist lens.

The inclusion of other voices allowed for the inclusion of sexual identity as well as race. Misawa (2010a) addressed the intersection of race and sexual identity in the adult education classroom. In his work, he advanced the need for a queer race pedagogy for educators in higher education. Such a pedagogy would need to address the reality of dynamics and positionality in lesbian, gay, bisexual, transgender, and queer students of color. *Intersectionality* (like polyrhythmic realities) is a reference to the simultaneous experience of social classifications including but not limited to race, class, gender, and sexuality (Weldon, 2008). For example, gender does not occur apart from race. There is no such thing as a raceless woman. Ignoring the intersectional nature of identity means that we "overlook the experiences of many different groups and by default focus on the most privileged" (Weldon, 2008, p. 195) in society. Misawa (2010) also analyzed narratives of gay men of color in higher education to unveil the manifestation of racist and homophobic bullying in higher education. His important work gave voice to the experiences of Black gay men in education that had largely been neglected by the field.

Including other voices in the literature emboldened scholars of color to add their perspectives to the adult education literature. For example, Bowman et al. (2013) felt that adult education literature failed to address pedagogical issues specific to the reality of Black faculty. They used their firsthand personal teaching experiences as Black faculty to demonstrate a need for a race pedagogy for Black faculty in adult education. They argued the need for a pedagogical approach that embraces the identity and racial experiences of Black faculty. Their work captured the reality of how Black faculty often avoid racial topics in order not to be viewed as the "angry" Black man or woman. Even when teaching about race, they noted, Black faculty often distance themselves from the topic in order to be taken seriously and to avoid personalizing the topic. They further argued that Black faculty must be conscious of the following dimensions that are important in pedagogical decision-making and which impact praxis: (a) authenticity of experiences, (b) authority of Whiteness, and (c) presentation of self and style.

Authenticity of experiences allows Black faculty to confirm objective historical content and to offer counternarratives to illuminate materials. The authority of Whiteness contradicts Blackness and Black experience as legitimate. Blackness is often delegitimized, resulting in the dismissal of anything associated with Blackness such as history, experience, and realities. Whiteness is regarded as the basis for authority. Presentation of self and style considers the affective demeanor of the educator and the manner in which the material is presented. Black faculty often find themselves shifting back and forth between demeanors. This constant shifting can lead to racial battle fatigue (Bowman et al., 2013). Race pedagogy challenges Black faculty to teach with their authentic selves and to use their racial identity as an asset in their teaching endeavors. They argued that Black professors should be intentional in their pedagogy when teaching about race.

More recently, evidence of repressive tolerance (Marcuse, 1965) can be seen in relation to the slow adoption of CRT in adult education. Derrick Bell and other germinal contributors in CRT began their work in the 1970s, and substantive work using CRT was done in education in the 1990s. Peterson (1999) was the first to introduce CRT to the field of adult education. Yet the field did not publish its first research articles embracing CRT as a valid approach to interrogating the role of race in society until the early 2000s. Some in adult education were skeptical about incorporating the CRT lens into the field because they found it to be overly pessimistic and without solutions (Closson, 2010).

Many other adult educators are not comfortable with the use of CRT, finding it to be too radical (Closson, 2010). The reality is that racism itself is radical and, as such, a response of equal measure is required. If most people in our society understood racism as a radical social and structural plague, no one would have been surprised at the election of Donald Trump as president of the United States in 2016 and the "safety net" that his presidency has provided for those who would like to publicly display their racism. There is power in being at the helm of the dominant racial group in our society (White males). We assert that White males are well aware of their social status. Any threat to this status should expectedly be met with resistance and rebellion. As the demographics of America continue to change and non-Whites become the majority, more resistance should be expected. Adult education should place itself in a position to respond to this resistance in an effective manner.

Reflecting on past errors, the field must embrace the reality of racism as described in CRT and respond with solutions that address the permanence of racism in America. For example, rather than teaching adults how to eradicate racism, teach adults how to navigate through a society in which racism should be expected because it is a norm. Embracing this perspective can be invaluable in helping adult educators to recognize the danger in relying on the fickle and temporary support of self-interested liberal White allies (interest convergence), and avoiding the pitfall of pursuing tactics informed by illusionary visions of progress that ultimately lead to racial retrenchment (permanence of racism) and will likely include the development of racisms that are subtler, more insidious, and more difficult to directly confront (differential racialization).

Adult educators' responses to racism should proceed from mindfulness of Derrick Bell's (1992) admonition that antiracism is about finding meaning and human dignity in the struggle against injustice while working toward solutions that challenge established liberal dogmas and consider much more foundational changes than are typically entertained by liberals. These could include deeper integrations of adult education's racial justice vision with reform efforts for economic justice. This would have the potential to move the field toward an embrace of Du Bois's (1935/1998) vision of a reformed American political system in which "the deliberate distribution of property and income by the state on an equitable and logical basis will be looked upon as the state's prime function" (p. 591).

Conclusion

Adult education's treatment of the topic of race has been inconsistent over the decades. We assert that most of the scholarship in the field addressing the issue of race has embraced the Black/White binary as the embodiment of the racial issue in America. Without argument, the centrality of slavery and White racism against African Americans is at the core of American history. However, to ignore the experience of race for other marginalized groups empowers liberals to advance arguments of racial progress by looking at the experiences of each racialized group as if they are separate and without connection or overlap. It is critical to understand the effect of racism on all people of color so that adult educators can facilitate interracial group understanding in an effort to forge effective liaisons that can combat racism. The field should engage in much more scholarship addressing the connectedness of the experiences of racialized groups in order to accomplish this objective. Nevertheless, the treatment of race must be expanded beyond the Black/White binary.

The field of adult education identifies itself as rooted in social justice. Indeed, the success of the Highlander Institute is an example of the field's involvement in social justice. The Highlander Institute played an important role in training major civil rights leaders, including Martin Luther King Jr. and Rosa Parks. The institute believes that "innovative educational practices are a catalyst for social change" (Highlander Institute, 2019, para. 1). Nevertheless, it appears that the Highlander Institute, as notable as its accomplishments may be, is not the norm for the field. The field must make racial justice and inclusiveness a pillar that permeates the identity of the field at every level. This means that the field must pay close attention to the decisions and identity of the "gatekeepers." Including the voices of scholars of color in adult education in significant numbers changed the nature of the scholarship and ushered in the present era of explicit scholarship on race and inclusivity. However, more must be done. The multiple spaces where gatekeepers' actions can impact inclusiveness must always be scrutinized. These spaces include admissions into adult education programs of study, faculty hiring and promotion, conference attendance, and publications. It can no longer be acceptable to hide behind notions like blind publication review or faculty hiring decisions based solely on teaching expertise. Publication reviewers often draw conclusions about the author based on the topic. Topics addressing race and inclusivity must be given equal standing with all other topics. Faculty hiring decisions should take race and gender into consideration as well as teaching expertise. Diversity and inclusivity do not result from unintentional actions; rather, they are the direct result of decisions made with an eye toward diversity and inclusivity. The field cannot live up to its call of social justice if it is not listening to the voices of marginalized groups. The final assessment as to whether or not the field lives up to its social justice calling will begin and end with the "gatekeepers."

References

Bell, D. (1992). *Faces at the bottom of the well: The permanence of racism*. Basic Books.

Bohonos, J. W. (2019). Including critical Whiteness studies in the critical human resource development family: A proposed theoretical framework. *Adult Education Quarterly, 69*(4), 315–337. https://doi.org/10.1177/0741713619858131

Bohonos, J. W., Otchere, K. D., & Pak, Y. (2019). Artistic expression as a teaching strategy for social movements: Deepening understandings of the civil rights and #BlackLivesMatter movements. *Advances in Developing Human Resources, 21*(2), 250–266. https://doi.org/10.1177/1523422319827942

Bowman, L., Merriweather, L. R., & Closson, R. B. (2013). Teaching race, being other: Development of a race pedagogy. *Proceedings of the Adult Education Research Conference*. https://pdfs.semanticscholar.org/17d1/193b5467a973d49beb11ad46ac3738ff9d8a.pdf

Brace, C. L. (2005). *Race is a four-letter word*. Oxford Press.

Bumiller, E. (2007). *Condoleezza Rice: An American life*. Random House.

Cassara, B. (1990). *Adult education in a multicultural society*. Routledge.

Closson, R. B. (2010). Critical race theory and adult education. *Adult Education Quarterly, 60*(3), 261–283. https://doi.org/10.1177/0741713609358445

DeCuir, J. T., & Dixon, A. D. (2004). So when it comes out, they aren't surprised that it is there: Using critical race theory as a tool of analysis of race and racism in education. *Educational Researcher, 33*(5), 26–31.

Delgado, R. (Ed.). (1995). *Critical race theory: The cutting edge*. Temple University Press.

Delgado, R., & Stefancic, J. (2001). *Critical race theory: An introduction*. New York University Press.

DiAngelo, R. (2018). *White fragility: Why it's so hard for White people to talk about racism.* Beacon Press.

Du Bois, W. E. B. (1996). *The Philidelphia negro: A social study.* University of Pennsylvania Press. (Originally published 1899)

Du Bois, W. E. B. (1998). *Black reconstruction in America, 1860–1880.* Free Press. (Originally published 1935)

Ely, M. L. (Ed.). (1948). *Handbook of adult education in the United States.* Columbia University Bureau of Publications.

Guy, T. C. (Ed.). (1999). *Providing culturally relevant adult education: A challenge for the 21st century.* Jossey-Bass.

Guy, T. C., & Brookfield, S. (2009). W. E. B. Du Bois's basic American Negro creed and the associates in Negro folk education: A case of repressive tolerance in the censorship of radical Black discourse on adult education. *Adult Education Quarterly, 60*(1), 65–76. https://doi.org/10.1177/0741713609336108

Harris, C. L. (1993). Whiteness as property. *Harvard Law Review, 106*(8), 1709–1791. https://doi.org/10.2307/1341787

Heisel, M. A. (1985). Assessment of learning activity level in a group of Black aged. *Adult Education Quarterly, 36*(1), 1–14. https://doi.org/10.1177/0001848185036001001

Heisel, M. A., & Larson, G. (1984). Literacy and social milieu: Reading behavior of the Black elderly. *Adult Education Quarterly, 34*(2), 63–70. https://doi.org/10.1177/0001848184034002001

Hewes, A. (1956). Early experiments in workers' education. *Adult Education, 6*(4), 211–220. https://doi.org/10.1177/074171365600600403

Highlander Institute. (2019). *Our history.* https://highlanderinstitute.org/

Ignatiev, N. (1995). *How the Irish became White.* Routledge.

James-Gallaway, A. D. (2019). All money ain't good money: The interest convergence principle, white philanthropy, and Black education of the past and present. *Mid-Western Educational Researcher, 31*(3), 348–374.

Johnson, R. L., Cortright, R. W., & Cooper, J. V. (1968). Attitude changes among literacy teachers coincident with training and experience. *Adult Education, 18*(2), 71–80. https://doi.org/10.1177/074171365600600403

Johnson-Bailey, J., & Alfred, M. V. (2006). Transformational learning and the practices of Black women adult educators. *New Directions for Adult and Continuing Education, 2006*(109), 49–58.

Johnson-Bailey, J., & Cervero, R. M. (1996). An analysis of the educational narratives of reentry Black women. *Adult Education Quarterly, 46*(3), 142–157. https://doi.org/10.1177/074171369604600302

Johnson-Bailey, J., & Cervero, R. M. (1998). Power dynamics in teaching and learning practices: An examination of two adult education classrooms. *International Journal of Lifelong Education, 17*(6), 389–399. https://doi.org/10.1080/0260137980170605

Johnson-Bailey, J., & Cervero, R. M. (2000). The invisible politics of race in adult education. In A. L. Wilson & E. R. Hayes (Eds.), *Handbook of adult and continuing education* (pp. 147–160). Jossey-Bass.

Johnson-Bailey, J., & Lee, M-Y. (2005). Women of color in the academy: Where's our authority in the classroom? *Feminist Teacher, 15*(2), 111–122.

Knox, A. B., & Videbeck, R. (1963). Adult education and adult life cycle. *Adult Education, 13*(2), 102–121. https://doi.org/10.1177/074171366301300207

Ladson-Billings, G. (1998). Just what is critical race theory and what's it doing in a nice field like education? *International Journal of Qualitative Studies in Education, 11*(1), 7–24.

Ladson-Billings, G., & Tate, W. F., IV (1995). Toward a critical race theory of education. *Teachers College Record, 97*(1), 47–68. https://doi.org/10.1080/095183998236863

Lewis, D. L. (2009). *W. E. B. Du Bois: A biography 1868-1963.* Henry Holt and Company.

Lewis, R. (1934). Adult education and the foreign born. In D. Rowden (Ed.), *Handbook of adult education in the United States* (pp. 58–62). American Association for Adult Education.

London, J. (1970a). The influence of social class behavior upon adult education participation. *Adult Education, 20*(3), 140–153.

London, J. (1970b). The social setting for adult education. In R. M. Smith, G. F. Aker, & J. R. Kidd (Eds.), *Handbook of adult education* (pp. 2–23). Macmillan.

Mahoney, J. J., & Herligy, C. M. (1918). *First steps in Americanization: A handbook for teachers.* Houghton Mifflin.

Marcuse, H. (1965). Repressive tolerance. In R. P. Wolff, B. Moore, & H. Marcuse (Eds.), *A critique of pure tolerance.* Beacon Press.

Merriam, S. B. (1993). Multiculturalism and adult education: Questions to guide our research. *PAACE Journal of Lifelong Learning, 3,* 57–60.

Merriweather, L. R., Guy, T. C., & Manglitz, E. (2006). Who can speak for whom: Using counterstorytelling to challenge racial hegemony. *Proceedings of the Adult Education Research Conference.* https://newprairiepress.org/aerc/2006/papers/32/

Mezirow, J. (1975). *Education for perspective transformation.* Teachers College, Columbia University, Center for Adult Education.

Miller, B., & Schwartz, J. (2016). The intersection of Black Lives Matter and adult education: One community college initiative. *New Directions for Adult and Continuing Education, 2016*(150), 13–23.

Misawa, M. (2010a). Queer race pedagogy for education in higher education: Dealing with power dynamics and positionality of LGBTQ students of color. *International Journal of Critical Pedagogy, 3*(1), 26–35.

Misawa, M. (2010b). Racist and homophobic bullying in adulthood: Narratives from gay men of color in higher education. *New Horizons in Adult Education and Human Resource Development, 24*(1), 7–23.

Nyborg, H. (2019). Race as social construct. *Psych, 1*(1), 139–165. https://doi.org/10.3390/psych1010011

Olneck, M. R. (1989). Americanization and the education of immigrants, 1900–1925: An analysis of symbolic action. *American Journal of Education, 97*(4), 398–423.

Peters, J. M., & Jarvis, P. (1991). *Adult education: Evolution and achievement in a developing field of study*. Jossey-Bass.

Peterson, E. A. (Ed.). (1996). *Freedom road: Adult education of African Americans*. Krieger.

Peterson, E. A. (1999). Creating a culturally relevant dialogue for African American adult educators. *New Directions for Adult and Continuing Education, 1999*(82), 79–91.

Prothro, J. W., & Smith, C. U. (1954). The psychic cost of segregation. *Adult Education, 5*(3), 179–181.

Rachal, J. R. (1992). *Adult education: A bibliography of English-language books and selected non-periodical Literature*. https://files.eric.ed.gov/fulltext/ED356382.pdf

Rocco, T., & Gallagher, S. (2004). Discriminative justice: Can discrimination be just? *New Directions for Adult and Continuing Education, 2004*(101), 29–41.

Roediger, D. R. (2005). *Working toward Whiteness: How American immigrants became White: The strange journey from Ellis Island to the suburbs*. Basic Books.

Ross-Gordon, J. M. (1991). Needed: A multicultural perspective for adult education research. *Adult Education Quarterly, 42*(1), 1–16. https://doi.org/10.1177/074171369104200101

Ross-Gordon, J. M. (2017). Racing the field of adult education—Making the invisible visible. *PAACE Journal of Lifelong Learning, 26*, 55–77.

Ross-Gordon, J. M., Rose, A. D., & Kasworm, C. (2017). *Foundations of adult and continuing education*. Jossey-Bass.

Rosser-Mims, D. (2010). Black feminism: An epistemological framework for exploring how race and gender impact Black women's leadership development. *Advancing Women in Leadership Journal, 30*(15), 1–10. https://doi.org/10.18738/awl.v3010.10/

Rowden, D. (1934). Adult education for Negroes. In D. Rowden (Ed.), *Handbook of adult education in the United States* (pp. 124–130). American Association for Adult Education.

Rowden, D. (Ed.). (1936). *Handbook of adult education in the United States*. American Association for Adult Education.

Rubin, I. M. (1967). The reduction of prejudice through mass media. *Adult Education, 18*(1), 43–52. https://doi.org/10.1177/074171366701800105

Sheared, V. (1996, May). *An Africentric feminist perspective on the role of adult education for diverse communities* [Paper presentation]. International Adult & Continuing Education Conference.

Sheared, V. (1999). Giving voice: Inclusion of African American students' polyrhythmic realities in adult basic education. *New Directions for Adult and Continuing Education, 1999*(82), 33–48.

Sheared, V., & Sissel, P. A. (Eds.) (2001). *Making space: Merging theory and practice in adult education*. Greenwood Publishing Group.

Stewart, J. C. (2018). *The new Negro: The life of Alain Locke*. Oxford University Press.

Talbot, W. (1917). *Americanization*. H. W. Wilson.

Weldon, S. L. (2008). Intersectionality. In G. Goertz, & A. G. Mazur, A.G. (Eds.), *Politics, gender, and concepts: Theory and methodology* (pp. 193–218). Cambridge University Press.

Whiteaker, L. H. (1990). Adult education within the slave community. In H. G. Neufeldt & L. McGee (Eds.), *Education of the African American adult: An historical overview* (pp. 3–10). Greenwood Press.

CHAPTER 44

Working Class, Social Class, and Literacy Classism

Jeff Zacharakis, Margaret Becker Patterson, and Allan Quigley

An invisible caste system exists in North American society, one that is burdened by wage inequalities, educational discrepancies, and government policies and is forgotten in most university and college adult education degree programs. Another term for this "caste system" is *social class*, whereby lower "castes" are typically the undereducated, underemployed or unemployed low-wage earners. This caste system has major implications for adult education since, as Boshier (2018) describes, "sociocultural impediments to learning and education are deep-rooted and related to socioeconomic status" (p. 7). Nesbit (2006) argues that we need to be aware of social class, its implications to adult and continuing education, and how it shapes not only our curricula but also our policies. He posits that education can be a liberating and empowering experience, or it can be designed to maintain the status quo and keep students within existing class boundaries. In a society that values individualism, hard work, and personal motivation, the issues and problems of social class are often not discussed or analyzed as structures that underlie our career and educational pathways, behaviors, or social networks.

As adult educators, we regularly see class differences among our students—how they dress, speak, present themselves, and act can affect their academic performance (Nesbit, 2006). Beyond our classrooms, we see how those without a formal education, including the millions of adults living with low literacy skills, are often ignored in our discourse (Patterson, 2016; Quigley, 2017). Depending upon our personal biases and political values, some believe we should not use social class to analyze and address social problems, arguing that one's class is not a barrier to achieving one's goals. By contrast, in this chapter we explore the relationship between class, classism, and adult education using adult literacy education (ALE) to illustrate how related government policies can shape our practice. Our thesis is that class does matter, and classism does affect adult education policies, practices, and outcomes.

What Is Class and Classism?

What is class and how does classism manifest itself? Bourdieu's (1987) notion of *class* is consistent with Marx and Durkheim's views: social structures that differentiate people and communities by their economic, cultural, and social status. Bourdieu defines these relations as *capital*, that which is fungible (i.e., has exchange value), and explains class structures as invisible and obscure, meaning that most people are unconscious of their own class other than having a "sense of one's place" and "a sense of the place of others" (p. 5). Using his sociological framework, a social class is a group of people who share the same three-dimensional space defined by economic, cultural, and social capital. Each class is shaped in part by its educational structures.

Social class shapes goals and beliefs, defines power, and determines access to resources required to make basic decisions and frame choices. Class divisions at their most basic level are divided into lower (unemployed and low-wage earners), lower middle, middle, upper middle, and upper classes (Reeves, 2015). The American Psychological Association Task Force on Socioeconomic Status (Saegert et al., 2006) defines social class by income, occupation, and education, concluding: "Socioeconomic factors and social class are fundamental determinants of human functioning across the life span, including development, well-being, and physical and mental health. These are all primary concerns for psychological research, practice, education, policy, and advocacy" (p. 1). A recent Brookings Institute report (Reeves, 2015) showed the top 20% of society has seen consistent income and wealth grow from 1973 to 2013, especially the top 1%, while the lower 80% have seen stagnation and declining income and wealth. This report also shows a strong correlation between income and education, especially related to professional and graduate degrees. Income disparities have especially widened between the top 20% and lower 80% between 1983 and 2013. Moreover, the income disparity between working and middle class is not large, nor has it changed in the last 30 years. Education results in only a small percentage of students rising from a lower class and, in fact, serves more effectively in reproducing class structures (Chetty, Friedman et al., 2017). These trends have been exacerbated since World War II, as each group of adults is less and less likely to earn more than their parents (Chetty, Grusky et al., 2017). The essence of these reports is that educational level not only correlates with income but also strengthens class boundaries for lower socioeconomic groups.

Associated with social class is *classism*, denoting a negative relation between classes where one class treats another class differently based on the first group's perception of a second group's cultural values and social status. According to Lott (2012), members of each class see value and power in their own class, which gives significance to their membership and reifies the social-cultural boundaries between classes. Classism is amplified by conscious and unconscious biases that reinforce one class as better than another. Lott points out that higher-class membership allows access to and benefits from "society's economic and political resources" (p. 650) while enhancing the member's sense of power and self-worth. As these boundaries become more distinct, they become more impenetrable. Movement from lower class to higher classes seldom occurs spontaneously.

As noted, education is an important form of capital and, when accumulated, sometimes enables one to move from one class to another (Chetty, Friedman et al., 2017). Yet the proportion is small, with 90% of early school leavers not pursuing education (Patterson, 2018). Of those who do pursue adult education, low-income students are especially disadvantaged in the ALE system due to textbook shortages, overcrowded classrooms, low academic expectations, and chronic under-funding (Quigley, 2017). If they enroll in 4-year institutions, low-income students are often less likely to graduate than peers from families with the highest incomes (Snyder et al., 2018). When 4-year colleges are not academically or financially attainable, students will often apply to community colleges and trade schools, take low-skilled, low-pay jobs or, if they qualify, enlist in the military. Compounding this educational disparity, approximately 45% of low-income students in the United States leave 2-year institutions without completing degrees (Snyder et al., 2018).

Classism also manifests itself in state and national policies and programs, often reflecting the biases of elected officials and policy makers who predominantly represent upper classes. Jensen (2012) describes classism as a form of prejudice permeating all aspects of civil society and reproducing structures that strengthen class divisions and class identities. In short, classism not only shapes one's identity, values, and beliefs but also sets up power relations that benefit certain classes, as seen in many state, provincial, and national literacy policies and resource disparities.

Historical Context of Adult Education and Literacy

To illustrate how social class has shaped the development of adult education as a field of study we examine the historical roots of ALE. The genesis and purpose of ALE in the early 20th-century United States was aligned with serving the impoverished and working class. Roots can be traced to Walter Rauschenbusch (1908) and the social gospel, which strongly influenced progressive educators such as John Dewey, Jane Addams, and, later, Reinhold Niebuhr and

Myles Horton (Fisher, 1997; Zacharakis & Holloway, 2016). Similarly, in Canada, the social gospel was the driving force for ALE landmarks such as the YMCA, Frontier College, and the Antigonish Movement (Quigley, 2006). Providing necessary literacy education for new immigrants and the underclass was an important strategy to enfranchise the disenfranchised into civil society. However, the struggle to achieve this in the face of literacy classism has deep historical roots.

During the Roman Empire, considered the first literate empire: "An illiterate was not a person who could not read, but someone who could not read Latin, the vehicle of Christendom and all learning. Only someone who could read Latin was a *litteratus*" (Fischer, 2003, p. 149). As Fischer observed, privileging a dominant language "demonstrates how literacy in any society is not simply a question of who can read and write, but rather the accommodation of prevailing values" (p. 149). In the United States today, "literacy" means instruction in English, no other written language. In Canada, English and French alone formally qualify as "literacy." No native or Indigenous languages, no other European languages, not even regional majority languages such as Spanish or Chinese officially qualify as "literacy" in North America. This centuries-old social construct is still defined and quantified by the dominant classes—today's *litteratus* (Quigley, 1997).

Significantly, the starting point for ALE through history has been to first "justify" its social benefits. As early as 1816, Thomas Pole argued the case for adult literacy for the "illiterate poor" by discussing the success of the Bristol School Movement (Verner, 1967). Here was the archetypal justification for ALE. According to Pole, teaching the "illiterate poor" to read using the Bible would increase the morality of the illiterate lower classes: "Industry, frugality, and economy will be their possession. They will have also learned better to practise [sic] meekness, Christian fortitude, and resignation" (Pole cited in Verner, 1967, p. 19). In addition, England would see economic benefits: "Our poor rates will thus be lightened, our hospitals, alms-houses, dispensaries, and other public charities less encumbered" (Pole cited in Verner, 1967, p. 19). The justification of literacy education for the economy and morality were the first imperatives for sponsoring ALE. Led by various religious groups, especially the Methodists, the Bristol School model swept England, Sierra Leone, China, New York, and Philadelphia, becoming the 19th-century model for countless adult education programs across North America (Quigley, 2006).

In March 1862, Rev. William Richardson and 40 members of the Gideonite religion sailed from New York to Port Royal to establish adult schools for the more than 10,000 freed slaves. The goal of this "Port Royal Experiment" was to help Freedmen learn to read and write (with the Bible central to the curriculum) and encourage a postwar takeover of plantations and farms by freed slaves (Rachal, 1986). Importantly, the controversy around this "experiment" was whether freed slaves were even capable of learning to read and write (Quigley, 2006). Richardson and colleagues found themselves working tirelessly to try to convince Northerners that African Americans were their intellectual equals.

Likewise, in 1889, Jane Addams and her female colleagues established Hull House, a landmark settlement house in Chicago's worst slums. They sought to help immigrants learn English and gain citizenship but faced fierce social class opposition. They began by inviting Chicago's elite to witness the poverty surrounding Hull House, and focused their efforts on teaching English, adult literacy, and trades training. But they ultimately realized that the struggles of thousands of immigrants were not due to lack of motivation or intelligence, but to an exploitive class structure. The very concept of an 8-hour workday was "connected in the minds of many employers not only with laziness but with anarchy" (Linn, 1935, p. 101). Addams and her colleagues ultimately led the fight for rights of immigrants and the working class (Linn, 1935) and are today credited with leading the way into the 20th century for rights for the disenfranchised.

A final example, in 1911 Cora Wilson, superintendent of schools and editor of the local newspaper, created a night school movement in Rowan County, Kentucky, that swept America. If the moon was shining, adults were invited to rural schoolhouses to learn to read and write. The Moonlight Schools of Kentucky saw 1,200 engage across Rowan County in its first year. The movement swept the entire United States within a decade (Cook, 1977; Quigley, 2006). Nevertheless, despite her successes both nationally and internationally, including being named adviser to President Calvin Coolidge for the first national literacy crusade in 1926 and Army adviser on literacy through World War I, when Stewart requested further funding to continue her work, her Kentucky superintendent colleagues refused her request, calling the Moonlight Schools a quixotic "fad and a failure" (Estes, 1988, p. 251). They argued adults would not learn to read and write, insisting all funding should go to the school system, a policy argument still heard today.

The goal of these North American adult education pioneers was to not only address individual issues of poverty, exploitation, and access to education and civil rights but also enfranchise every citizen into civil society. These ideals helped shape President Roosevelt's New Deal and gave life to land-grant university extension programs, post–World War II veteran education programs, the community college movement, and the higher levels of state/federal assistance for education. These ideals spawned an adult education movement in the 1950s, as exemplified by the Center for the Study of Liberal Education for Adults (Liveright, 1961) and the first graduate programs in adult education in both the United States and Canada. The unifying theme across both nations has been high-quality educational opportunities at an affordable cost that should extend to everyone, regardless of class or social status. Education was to be a primary pillar of an equitable, fair, democratic society.

Historically, literacy classism has been ever-present. However, while today's mainstream adult, postsecondary, and higher education is realizing such goals for some, for the voiceless millions living with low literacy and undereducation, their best hope is today's marginalized system of ALE—a system that has become dependent on competing ideologies and the political will of government sponsors on both sides of the U.S.-Canada border.

Political Context in Adult Education and Literacy

During the 1960s and 1970s, "it seemed the years of struggle were over" (Thomas, 2001, p. xiii). President Johnson's 1964 Economic Opportunity Act initiated a surge of literacy campaigns promising to "eradicate illiteracy" (Quigley, 1997, p. 17). U.S. Commissioner of Education James Allen called the federal Right to Read campaign the "moonshot for the seventies" (Harman, 1987, p. 1). In Canada, the 1967 federal Adult Occupational Act saw, "Media attention . . . at an all-time high with new partners, new alliances, new coalitions, everything from, travelling musicals . . . to T-shirts and mugs making adult literacy initiatives extremely popular" (Thomas, 2001, p. xxiii). North America's war on illiteracy would be won with an army of volunteers and supported with an infusion of federal funding to build ALE programs across North America. By the late 1980s, this surge was over.

Despite the heroic efforts of individuals and innovative programs through time, literacy education has come to be shaped by neoliberal government policies that often reproduce the dominant patterns of literacy's history. In the United States, ALE programs are primarily funded by federal government through the Workforce Innovation and Opportunity Act (WIOA, 2014) with varying levels of matching funds from individual states, much of which is dedicated to increasing the number of adults who can gain skills and credentials for high-demand jobs. The purpose of federal funding is articulated on the U.S. Department of Education's webpage: "*WIOA* is designed to strengthen and improve the nation's public workforce development system by helping Americans with barriers to employment, including individuals with disabilities, achieve high quality careers and helping employers hire and retain skilled workers" (OCTAE, 2019, Overview section, para. 1). At the same time, minimal funding through Title II of WIOA, approximately $509 million in 2017–2018, or $364 per adult learner, is awarded for ALE. As a result, fewer and fewer adults who qualify for these programs and need skills actually receive services. By our calculations of National Reporting System data, enrollment in Title II programs has declined nationally from 2.5 million adult learners in 2005–2006 to 1.4 million adult learners in 2017–2018.

Canadian federal and provincial/territorial policies have followed a similar path over the past 2 decades. ALE programs in Canada are today supported by the national Office of Literacy and Essential Skills (OLES), the mandate of which is "to help adult Canadians improve their literacy and essential skills to better prepare for, get and keep a job, and adapt and succeed at work" (OLES, 2017, From employment and social development Canada section, para. 1). Federal funding exists to support "the integration of essential skills into employment and training programs" (OLES, para. 1). While Canada's provinces and territories have the constitutional mandate for adult literacy education, their policy priorities today basically mirror the human capital formation goals of the federal government.

Implications to Adult Education and Literacy

As we move further into the 21st century, the skills gap continues to widen between income levels of the educational "haves" and "have-nots" (Patterson & Paulson, 2016). In the United States, one in seven young adults leaves high school early, and only half of this group receives a high school equivalency (HSE) credential. Of those with an HSE credential, 45% enroll in postsecondary education by age 26, and only 18% of those earn a postsecondary certificate or associate degree (National Center for Education Statistics, 2016). It is not surprising then, that by age 26, four in five of these graduates were earning no more than $35,000 annually. Moreover, the more a family relies on the income of an adult learner, the less likely the adult learner is to enroll in and complete college (Smith & Gluck, 2016). Without credentialed skills, adults remain firmly "have-nots" with minimal economic opportunities (Patterson & Paulson, 2016).

Despite historical examples of heroism and pedagogical exceptions, the fact is that the voices of adult literacy learners and the disenfranchised have been rarely heard at the practice level, and are absent at the level of policy making (Patterson, 2016, 2018; Quigley, 2006). This is not something new. In the first nationwide U.S. evaluation of adult basic education, Mezirow et al. (1975) wrote that "involving students in any kind of evaluation of methods, materials, teacher performance, scheduling, classroom facilities or anything else for that matter, is almost unheard of" (p. 28). While the field of adult education has long prided itself in seeking to meet the needs of adult learners, policymakers and sponsors influence and determine funding levels, curricula, delivery methods, and the very purposes of ALE programs.

As practitioners of adult education and ALE, we understand the importance of being able to support a family; earn an income; and have the reading, numeracy, and career skills needed for employment. We understand that millions of adults have been helped to achieve those objectives through ALE programs. However, we also understand that a fundamental social value and first principle of contemporary adult education is that adult learning is a personal choice.

Zacharakis and Holloway (2016) deconstructed how neoliberalism has become the dominant paradigm in adult education practice today at all levels, including preparing future educators in ALE, higher education, and human resource development. Using Rhoades and Slaughter's (1997) concept of academic capitalism and Bagnall's (1999) critique of open marketeering, they argue that faculty in higher education, including adult education faculty, often are reduced to recruiting students who have financial means to pay for education. A situation exists where only "entrepreneurial faculty and universities will survive" (Zacharakis & Holloway, 2016, p. 228). This reality is reflected in how choices that enhance an adult student's opportunity to increase status, income, and marketability are often made at the expense of other courses that would prepare them to work in low-status positions, such as teaching in ALE programs. Adult education programs in higher education increasingly reflect societal priorities and the norms of literacy classism. Students that faculty are most likely to recruit are rarely interested in literacy education because ALE typically serves the unemployed and low-wage earners. As such, ALE is not a high social priority in higher education unless attached to research grants and contracts. It is hardly surprising that very few departments of education in universities across North America today offer degrees, majors, or even standalone courses on adult literacy.

The question that we raise for further discussion is, "Do these trends in educational policies and programs create a more equitable society or do they reify existing class structures?" If the future of ALE is to be built on learner needs as well as societal and economic priorities, a literacy pedagogy that builds critical thinking and increases adults' life chances will be essential. Narrowing ALE programs to be "the handmaiden of job training" (Mezirow et al., 1975, p. 141) does not fulfill this promise. We argue for a pedagogy that introduces how social structures can become personal barriers. We advocate for more politically based curricula to help adult learners understand and access the political system, to help them identify their rights as adult citizens, and build their capacities to see and challenge literacy classism into the 21st century.

One promising approach for doing so is through development of adult learner empowerment where the impoverished and working class can establish control over their own learning and success. If *adult learner leadership* was a central objective—defined as involvement in all components of an ALE program (Patterson, 2016)—the experiences and prior knowledge of adult learners could lead them to become advocates for ALE and mentors to others. We need pedagogy in

ALE that provides adequate opportunities and practice in building leadership (Greene, 2007). Leadership skills such as problem-solving, critical thinking, communication, and interpersonal skills are critical for the future of ALE. An example is an ALE program that is showing real promise as learners develop transferrable skills for the workplace, family, and community (Black et al., 2006; Jurmo, 2010; Toso et al., 2009). Engaging adult learners in supported and structured leadership activities encourages them into more formal positions of leadership and community activism (Bolívar & Chrispeels, 2011; Toso & Gungor, 2012).

Findings from a recent experimental evaluation could expand the limited ALE knowledge base of adult learner leadership in the United States (Patterson, 2016). Envisioned and developed by VALUEUSA, a nonprofit organization comprising adult learner alumni, this evaluation allowed 13 ALE programs in 7 states to be randomly selected for an intervention including leadership training and developing a learner-led project. By the final year of the evaluation, adult learner leaders had heightened scale scores in both reasoning and information processing measures. After controlling for first-year scores in information processing, growth on information and processing scale scores was also higher.

Over time, adult learner leaders from such programs have found their voice in leading interactions within learning settings where teachers have traditionally led, and learners have passively listened (Hunt et al., 2019). Adult learner leaders experienced significant growth from baseline to final year in proportion of time in leading interactions, compared with control learners who tended to lead fewer interactions as time went on (Patterson, 2016). Adult learners who participated as leaders also saw themselves as more inclined to volunteer to help in the program or lead an activity than staff thought they would (Patterson, 2016). Based on these findings, VALUEUSA is expanding leader-training efforts with a goal of involving even more adult learners in ALE program administration and capacity building in the 2020s.

In closing, over the past half-century, we have seen marginalized groups with disabilities, African Americans and African Canadians, Canadian First Nations, Métis, Native Americans, and the LGBTQ community gain greater voice and more rights by challenging classism. This type of counterhegemonic challenge is needed in adult literacy. As Cervero (2017) stated, "Learning needs should not be treated as deficiencies. . . . Rather, learning needs should be treated as the adult's right to know" (p. 39). In a 2018 study on reasons why adults do not participate in adult education, a low-income adult addressed national policymakers saying:

> Everybody needs an education. Provide the education for people who want one. Make sure you go all out for them. Because they [at the national level] are the ones saying it is very important to have education, so provide the way so people are able to get it. (Patterson & Song, 2018, p. 67)

In this chapter we explored working class, social class, literacy classism, and their combined influences on teaching and learning in ALE. We introduced *invisible caste* as a metaphor for class and classism using adult literacy in both Canada and the United States to illustrate the complexities of this issue. We argue that we have a choice to either support a status quo that often sustains income disparity and maintains class structures, or seek programs that emphasize that all citizens have a *right to know* and a right to act on the political and social structures that shape their life chances.

References

Bagnall, R. G. (1999). *Discovering a postmodern agenda in adult education: Building a postmodern agenda in adult education*. Peter Lang.

Black, S., Balatti, J., & Falk, I. (2006). Social capital outcomes: The new focus for adult literacy and numeracy courses. *Australian Journal of Adult Learning, 46*(3), 317–336.

Bolívar, J., & Chrispeels, J. (2011). Enhancing parent leadership through building social and intellectual capital. *American Educational Research Journal, 48*(1), 4–38. https://doi.org.10.3102/0002831210366466

Boshier, R. W. (2018). Learning cities: Fake news or the real deal. *International Journal of Lifelong Education, 37*(4), 419–434. https://doi.org/10.1080/02601370.2018.1491900

Bourdieu, P. (1987). What makes a social class? On the theoretical and practical existence of groups. *Berkeley Journal of Sociology, 32*, 1–17.

Cervero, R. M. (2017). Professionalization for what? Fulfilling the promise of adult and continuing education. PAACE *Journal of Lifelong Learning, 26*, 1–20.

Chetty, R., Friedman, J. N., Saez, E., Turner, N., & Yagan, D. (2017). *Mobility report cards: The role of colleges in intergenerational mobility*. National Bureau of Economics Research.

Chetty, R., Grusky, D., Hell, M., Hendren, N., Manduca, R., & Narang, J. (2017). The fading American Dream: Tends in absolute income mobility since 1940. *Science, 356*(6336), 398–406.

Cook, W. D. (1977). *Adult literacy education in the United States*. International Reading Association.

Estes, F. (1988). *Cora Wilson Stewart and the Moonlight Schools of Kentucky* [Unpublished doctoral dissertation]. University of Kentucky, Lexington.

Fischer, S. (2003). *A history of reading*. Reaktion Books.

Fisher, J. C. (1997). The social gospel: Lindeman's overlooked inspiration. In S. J. Levine (Ed.), *Proceedings of the 16th Annual Midwest Research to Practice Conference in Adult, Continuing, and Community Education* (pp. 42–48). Michigan State University.

Greene, D. (2007). Gatekeepers: The role of adult education practitioners and programs in social control. *Journal for Critical Education Policy Studies, 5*(2), 411–437.

Harman, D. (1987). *Illiteracy: A national dilemma*. Cambridge Book Company.

Hunt, T., Rasor, A, & Patterson, M. B. (2019). "We are the voice to speak up": Cultivating learner voice through leadership. *COABE Journal, 8*(2), 22–32.

Jensen, B. (2012). *Reading classes: On culture and classism in America*. Cornell University Press.

Jurmo, P. (2010). Productive and participatory: Basic education for high performing and actively engaged workers. *New Directions for Adult and Continuing Education, 2010*(128), 45–57.

Linn, J. (1935). *Jane Addams: A biography*. Appleton-Century.

Liveright, A. (1961, September 19–21). *The role of the university in an undirected society* [Paper presentation]. Annual Conference on Instruction of the University College.

Lott, B. (2012). The social psychology of class and classism. *American Psychologist, 67*(8), 650–658.

Mezirow, J., Darkenwald, G, & Knox, A. (1975). *Last gamble on education*. Adult Education Association of the USA.

National Center for Education Statistics. (2016). *Education Longitudinal Study of 2002 (ELS:2002)*. https://nces.ed.gov/surveys/els2002.

Nesbit, T. (2006). What's the matter with social class? *Adult Education Quarterly, 56*(3), 171–181.

OCTAE. (2019, June). *RSA: Workforce Innovation and Opportunity Act (WIOA)*. Office of Career, Technical, and Adult Education, U.S. Department of Education. https://www2.ed.gov/about/offices/list/osers/rsa/wioa-reauthorization.html

Office of Literacy and Essential Skills. (2017, May). *The Office of Literacy and Essential Skills*. Employment and Social Development Canada. https://www.canada.ca/en/employment-social-development/programs/literacy-essential-skills.html

Patterson, M. (2016). *Adult learner leadership in education services (ALLIES) final year leadership report. Part 1: Key quantitative findings*. VALUEUSA. http://valueusa.org/projects/

Patterson, M. (2018). The forgotten 90%: Adult nonparticipation in education. *Adult Education Quarterly, 68*(1), 41–62.

Patterson, M., & Paulson, U. (2016). Adult transitions to learning in the USA: What do PIAAC survey results tell us? *Journal of Research and Practice for Adult Literacy, Secondary, and Basic Education, 5*(1), 5–27. https://static1.squarespace.com/static/55a158b4e4b0796a90f7c371/t/57995d789f7456dc5697a96a/1469668780681/COABE+Journal+Spring+2016.pdf#page=7

Patterson, M. B., & Song, W. (2018). Adult nonparticipation in education: Deterrents and solutions. *The Nontraditional Journal (ANTSHE), 19*, 59–68. https://drive.google.com/file/d/1gYqW_Ua9Ci0FYpdbqMEPZqpFz7v1dWY5/view

Quigley, B. A. (1997). *Rethinking literacy education: The critical need for practice-based change*. Jossey-Bass.

Quigley, B. A. (2006). *Building professional pride in literacy*. Krieger.

Quigley, B. A. (2017). Will anything be different in the 21st century? How 107 million adults and the field for adult literacy became so marginalized. *PAACE Journal of Lifelong Learning, 26*, 39–54.

Rachal, J. (1986). Freedom's crucible: William T. Richardson and the schooling of freed men. *Adult Education Quarterly, 1*(37), 14–22.

Rauschenbusch, W. (1908). *Christianity and the social gospel*. MacMillan.

Reeves, R. (2015). *The dangerous separation of the American upper middle class*. Brookings Institute.

Rhoades, G., & Slaughter, S. (1997). Academic capitalism, managed professionals, and supply-side higher education. *Social Text, 51*(15), 9–38.

Saegert, S., Adler, N., Bullock, H., Cauce, A., Liu, W., & Wyche, K. (2006). *Report of the APA task force on socioeconomic status*. American Psychological Association.

Smith, C., & Gluck, L. (2016). *Adult transitions longitudinal study: Final report to the Nellie Mae Foundation*. University of Massachusetts Press.

Snyder, T., de Brey, C., & Dillow, S. (2018). *Digest of Education Statistics 2016 (NCES 2017-094)*. National Center for Education Statistics, Institute of Education Sciences, U.S. Department of Education.

Thomas, A. (2001). How adult literacy became of age in Canada. In M. C. Taylor (Ed.), *Adult literacy now!* (pp. xvii–xxv). Culture Concepts.

Toso, B., & Gungor, R. (2012). Parent engagement and parent leadership. In B. Wasik (Ed.), *Handbook of family literacy* (2nd ed., pp. 223–236). Routledge.

Toso, B., Prins, E., Drayton, B., Gnanadass, E., & Gungor, R. (2009). Finding voice: Shared decision-making and student leadership in a family literacy program. *Adult Basic Education and Literacy Journal, 3*(3), 151–160.

Verner, C. (1967). *Pole's history of adult schools*. Adult Education Associates of the USA. (Original work published 1812)

Workforce Innovation and Opportunity Act. (2014, July). Public Law No. 113-128. US Congress. https://www.congress.gov/bill/113th-congress/house-bill/803

Zacharakis, J., & Holloway, J. (2016). The murky waters of neoliberal marketizations and commodification on the education of adults in the United States. *European Journal for the Research on the Education and Learning of Adults, 7*(2), 223–236. https://doi.org/10.3384/rela.2000-7426.rela9083

CHAPTER 45

Whiteness and Privilege

Elaine Manglitz and Stephen D. Brookfield

This chapter is the first time that White racial identity and its associated power and privilege has been the focus of a particular entry in the *Handbook of Adult and Continuing Education* series. Reviewing the 1934, 1938, 1948, 1960, 1970, and 1980 handbooks, one can see that race is absent. Additionally, the 1981 handbook titled *Examining Controversies in Adult Education* (Kreitlow, 1981) does not probe whether or not Eurocentric models of adult education are being inappropriately applied across multiple racial and cultural groups of learners, nor does it mention racism or racial inequity. It is not until the 1990 volume that a chapter appears examining racial and ethnic minorities (Briscoe & Ross, 1989). The 2000 volume began with a meta review of the previous handbooks (Wilson & Hayes, 2000) and initiated a philosophical break by organizing the book's chapters around the concept of critically reflective practice. One of the profession's concerns explored was the invisible politics of race (Johnson-Bailey & Cervero, 2000). In the 2010 handbook the centrality of social justice concerns was identified for the first time as an important subsection, with one of that section's chapters focusing specifically on race (Isaac et al., 2010). This chapter will discuss the racialization of adult education, specifically examining White privilege and White supremacy as often-unspoken norms that undergird much theory and practice within the field. It will also offer strategies for how adult educators can create learning environments to bring Whites into an awareness and then analysis of their own privilege, thus moving toward the goal of furthering social justice on both individual and institutional levels.

The Racialization of Adult Education

In his analysis of race and philosophy Lucius Outlaw (1996) argues that every field of study is racialized. By that he means that a field's dominant conceptualizations, and the mechanisms it has in place for the production and dissemination of knowledge, are grounded in one particular racial group's experiences and the forms of thought that flow from these. In the case of American adult education, the field is racialized in favor of White Euro-Americans. The most valorized and frequently cited concepts that purport to define what is distinctive about the field and that comprise its dominant discursive boundaries—andragogy, self-direction, critical reflection, transformative learning—are identified mostly with scholarship conducted by White European Americans, Europeans, and Commonwealth males. The Eurocentric valorization of rational, autonomous, critical thought endemic to these four discourses is supremely powerful in its unremarkableness. Such thought is taken for granted as the natural, cognitive modality to which all adults should clearly aspire.

Central to this racialization of adult education is the fact that it is deemed so obvious as to need no justification. Consequently, the racialization of adult education theorizing—the way it is viewed through the lens of Eurocentric Whiteness, with Whiteness regarded as the positively valued, unspoken norm—is rarely commented on. The gatekeepers of the field who function as editors of the handbooks issued by, in turn, the American Association for Adult Education (AAAE), the Adult Education Association of the USA, and most recently the American Association for Adult and Continuing Education, have been overwhelmingly White. Only in the 2010 handbook and the current volume have we had scholars of color as members of the editorial team.

Reracializing the field of adult education so that it decenters Whiteness and addresses privilege fits squarely in the adult education's traditional concern with progressive social issues. As the AAAE was established and grew between the 1930s and the 1950s, two of its most emphasized projects were to clarify and extend adult education's role in community development (Kempfer, 1955) and to understand its contribution to preserving and revitalizing democracy, particularly after World War II (Brookfield, 1987; Smith & Lindeman, 1951). In the 1970s, 1980s, and 1990s the Freirean turn (Freire, 1970, 1994) foregrounded critical and emancipatory pedagogies that aimed to help adults learn how to examine their privilege (Shor & Freire, 1987). At the same time, Myles Horton's (1990) legacy began to be celebrated, largely as a result of his work organizing and educating against racial and economic disparities (Horton, 2003; Horton & Freire, 1990). Moving into the 21st century, the current dominant theoretical paradigm in the field—transformative learning—also connects directly to the project of examining Whiteness and privilege.

Adult transformative learning theory, as articulated initially by Mezirow (1991) and then developed by Cranton (2016), Taylor and Cranton (2012), and others, focuses on the study of how adults reflect critically on their assumptions and open themselves to new perspectives. Mezirow builds on Habermas's (1990) contention that the signifier that one has entered adulthood is realizing that you should stop universalizing your own experience and understand that different people experience the world in fundamentally different ways. Transformative learning theory holds that as adults do this, their meaning perspectives become more discriminating and comprehensive; in other words, they are able to understand that contexts constantly change, situations continuously alter and that complexity is the fundamental reality of adult human experience. This causes fundamental changes in how they view the world at large and their own place within it. Learning that one's experience as a White person is an unreliable guide to understanding how large swathes of the population spend their days negotiating racist structures and environments is the disorienting dilemma that awakens the need to learn what it means to be White. Recognizing and deconstructing one's White identity and its associated privilege is a complex project of transformative learning.

Whiteness

The year 2010 signaled a readiness by U.S. adult education scholars to move race and White privilege to the center stage of the field's discourse. In the first published U.S. volume dealing specifically with White privilege, the coeditors noted how the field of American adult education had not sufficiently addressed "the linkages between White racist ideology, White privilege, and White racist behaviors and attitudes that are reflected in sociocultural and intellectual racism" (Colin & Lund, 2010, p. 1). That same year *The Handbook of Race and Adult Education* (Sheared et al., 2010) featured a whole section on Whiteness, supremacy, and privilege that included chapters on White racial identity development (Baumgartner, 2010), White ontology and epistemology (Paxton, 2010), the experience of Whiteness (Manglitz & Cervero, 2010), and White humility (European-American Collaborative Challenging Whiteness, 2010).

At the same time that race has moved into the discourse of the field, critics have noted how its discussion is too often framed in terms of enhancing diversity or including minority perspectives, rather than confronting the reality of White supremacy (Johnson-Bailey, 2002). Non-White perspectives can become represented as the exotic other, the alien tradition of different racial experience that is added on to the White center. Shore (2001) commented on how the desire to make the Other visible "often involves legitimizing from the center a space in which the Other can speak, where the Other gets to operate or be visible, only because of the largesse of the center" (p. 51). This meant that supposedly emancipatory initiatives to widen the field's discourse were experienced by scholars, practitioners, and learners of color as condescending; patronizing attempts by the White center to empower the margins—when empowerment cannot be given, only claimed. Johnson-Bailey (2002) called this the "add-difference-and-stir approach" (p. 43) and noted its presence in most adult education textbooks. In her words,

> authors trivialize the significance of race in their authored or edited texts by adding a final chapter that pertains to minority concerns. These chapters are usually offered to placate the concerns of politically conscious publishers or readers to whom they would not want to appear exclusionary. (p. 43)

In this sense, an afterthought chapter or two on race comprises a perfect example of what Herbert Marcuse (1965) termed *repressive tolerance*. Adult education as a field claims to embrace, even celebrate, the presence of multiple positionalities while simultaneously positioning racially based Africentric or indigenous traditions of adult learning as interesting diversions existing chiefly to broaden the horizons of Whites.

Whiteness is a category of identity more than an empirical reality. However, the unexamined identity of Whiteness—what it means to be White—is at the core of the dominant ideology of White supremacy (Brookfield, 2018). Critical theory contends (Brookfield, 2004) this ideology legitimizes—makes normal—the fact that a clear and deep-rooted imbalance of wealth and poverty, access and exclusion, advantage and disadvantage, exists between Whites and people of color. The ideology holds that these imbalances are the result of nature and hereditary reality. As critical theorists point out (Delgado & Stefancic, 2017; Zamudio et al., 2010), White supremacy's claim that Whites' more highly developed cognitive capacity and ethic of hard work means they deserve to occupy their positions of power ensures that racism remains endemic to the culture of the United States. Whites are deemed to have an innately higher level of intelligence and a more developed ability to think objectively, logically, and rationally compared to people of color, who are portrayed as too emotional, unpredictable, and passionate. This presumed inability to control one's emotions is then used to justify the belief that people of color do not have the cognitive capacity to make decisions for the good of the whole (Kendall, 2013; Sue, 2015).

A defining character of Whiteness is not being aware of one's White racial identity, or of believing it represents a "natural" order. As Dyson (2018) comments, Whiteness "is a category of identity that is most useful when its existence is denied. That's its twisted genius" (p. ix). Being White is assuming oneself not to have a race and viewing oneself as the universal norm for humanity. Hence, Whiteness means viewing race as "a marker for 'other' and not for Whites" (Manglitz, 2003, p. 127). Whiteness holds that racial identity is something only enacted by people of color. Accepting this view means that Whites can choose not to think about race as they move through their daily lives, a choice denied to people of color. When asked about race, many Whites present themselves as good, compassionate people (Sullivan, 2014) who claim to be color blind. They say they do not see race and that they take people as they are, judging them purely on their character and actions, not skin pigmentation. This ignores the reality that for many people of color race is the primary lens through which everything is viewed. So Whiteness as an identity category effectively destructuralizes and decontextualizes race, reducing it to a matter of individual action and choice. This White view permeated *Crash* (Haggis, 2004), the Oscar-winning film on race, in which the White characters were presented at different times opting to be good, nonracist Whites or to act in clearly racist ways. Whiteness as a worldview bypasses systemic and structural factors and argues that being racist is up to the individual involved. "Good" Whites can then resolve to gird up their moral loins and choose to be fair and compassionate in their individual dealings with people of color.

Paxton (2010) argues that behind the Whiteness paradigm lies a particular ontology and epistemology that derives from a Eurocentric and Enlightenment worldview. European aesthetic standards determine what constitutes real culture and what counts as legitimate forms of artistic expression such as music, art, and poetry. Epistemologically, Whiteness values rationality, logic, and proof, and argues that legitimate truth arises from the application of the scientific method. It tends to see the world as dualistic, dividing conduct into moral or immoral categories such as racist and nonracist behavior. This epistemology undergirds adult educational attempts to identify best practices that can then be applied in a standardized way across multiple contexts. It ignores complexity, contextuality, and mess.

However, Whites can identify and problematize their White identity and work to become less racist. As individuals, White people are at different stages of racial identity development (Baumgartner, 2010) and obviously exhibit major differences and divisions in terms of class, ethnicity, ideology, and culture. Work on White identity development (Frankenberg, 1993; Helms, 1990) presents models of how adults become increasingly aware of their Whiteness and move to a more structural understanding of how racism is a systemic reality rather than an individual experience. One of the barriers to adult White racial identity development is that of White fragility (DiAngelo, 2018) in which "the mere suggestion that being White has meaning often triggers a range of defensive responses" (p. 2). Here methodologies drawing on transformative learning theory are useful in guiding adult educators on how to create disorienting dilemmas (moments of cognitive and experiential dissonance) around race and then use support groups to move people through sustained critical reflection on racial identity (Cranton, 2016; Mezirow & Taylor, 2009).

White Privilege

Whiteness as a category of identity is inextricably linked to the White privilege that accompanies it and the system of White supremacy and racism that it supports (Colin & Lund, 2010; Kendall, 2013). Whiteness is not just a racial classification. It is a social and institutional identity "imbued with legal, political, economic, and social rights and privileges that are denied to others" (DiAngelo, 2018, p. 24). In 1988, when Peggy McIntosh identified and published a list of unearned advantages and benefits that accrued to her just for being White, it opened other educators' eyes to consider and do the same analysis within their own lives. In 2018, now 30 years later, many of the same advantages and unearned privileges still hold true, with additional advantages accruing based on the current context and political milieu and aligned with other dimensions of positionality. No matter where one believes we are in the challenge of addressing racism in our society, it is still the case that our social, political, and educational institutions support the ideology of White supremacy when one considers who is in leadership positions, what the curriculum entails, who accumulates the most wealth, or has access to the best health care among many other dimensions of institutional and daily life. In addition, Whites, no matter their class or gender, still have a choice as to whether to address White privilege and racism in themselves and in society, without expecting any negative repercussions or consequences to ensue if they choose not to do so.

In the field of adult education and other disciplines, there has been encouragement for Whites, including White adult educators, to start with themselves and their own lives to acknowledge, address, and challenge White privilege and racism (Colin & Lund, 2010; Kendall, 2013; Sue, 2015). However, the barriers that keep Whites from acknowledging their race and their privilege are many and have been carefully constructed and supported over hundreds of years. Whites have been socialized into a system that centers them and is contingent on assumptions of individualism, meritocracy, and objectivity. Because that system is invisible and the norm, Whites have very little awareness of belonging to a racial group and bringing it up in any setting often causes defensive reactions in addition to guilt, anger, and blaming. Kendall (2013) believes that not seeing social structures is a part of Whites' anesthetizing themselves; if patterns and structures are not acknowledged, then one does not have to deal with them. Racism is instead viewed as intentional acts of discrimination or hatred by individuals; those Whites who do not see themselves as taking part in hateful acts do not see themselves as part of the problem and subsequently feel they have nothing to learn or contribute to a conversation about race. There is also a fear among Whites that seeing race or talking about race may mean they will be perceived as being racist, especially if they say the wrong thing. The impetus to remain silent is powerful.

Since many Whites believe we are in a postracial period, there is a tendency for them to use a belief in colorblindness to neutralize any attempt to talk about the experiences of different racial groups. When Whites view racial relations through the prism of colorblindness, it presents a definite barrier to talking about White privilege and racism and effectively shuts down the conversation. Comments such as "I don't see color" or "we are all human beings" or "we are all one race," and so on, serve to deny the experiences of people of color and, as Sue (2015) notes, are examples of microaggressions that can occur in any setting, whether race is an expressed topic or not. Further, if

Whites see their own racial membership, they may then have to acknowledge the benefits they have based on their White privilege, which further challenges the myth of meritocracy and colorblindness (DiAngelo, 2018) and leads to a reluctance to even begin a dialogue on race.

Adult education classrooms, university settings, community settings, and workplaces are all microcosms of our society and enact the same structural systems of privilege and oppression that occur everywhere. The barriers that make it difficult for Whites to address their own privilege and complicity in racism also make it difficult to have and facilitate effective cross-racial discussions and to address Whiteness and privilege within the classroom. Many adult educators have experienced the result of these barriers within their own learning environments, and some of them have written about ways to address them.

Adult Education and Strategies for Examining Whiteness and Privilege

Since 2010, adult education has recognized the importance of addressing inequities related to the system of White supremacy. Several publications have advanced the practice of conducting effective cross-racial dialogues, including how to create learning environments to bring Whites into an awareness and then an analysis of their own Whiteness. In 2014, a special issue of *Adult Learning* (Bowman et al., 2014) and in 2018, the book *Teaching Race: How to Help Students Unmask and Challenge Racism* (Brookfield, 2019) offered practical strategies for the teaching and discussion of racial issues and for bringing often reluctant White students in to the ongoing process to examine their own White identity.

A way that White adult educators can address the resistance most Whites have to discussing race is to talk openly about their own racialized assumptions and their lifelong journey to move toward a more antiracist identity. Building on the work that the European-American Collaborative Challenging Whiteness (2010) has done for years, Brookfield (2014) notes how he came to understand that education about racism was done more effectively through narrative disclosure rather than a discussion of techniques or an analysis of institutional policies and practices. Sharing with others how one learned and how one enacts racism and White privilege also models the vulnerability that educators are asking students to have. Pawlowski (2019) completes the same writing assignments as students, including one that locates herself within the stages of racial identity development, demonstrating for students that race is learned, can be relearned, and how one can move toward a more antiracist state of being and acting. The willingness of White adult educators to explicate their own racist assumptions and behaviors can provide an opening for other students to be vulnerable despite the strong impetus not do to so. The practice also honors the admonition of many antiracists and people of color who have repeatedly suggested to Whites that they begin addressing racism by examining themselves.

Smith (2019) highlights her own vulnerability in a discussion of a classroom experience where she asked the participants to examine the workshop on race and privilege she had just completed with them for assumptions, inconsistencies, omissions, and the reasons behind those. A pedagogy where one is willing to examine mistakes is counter to the (White) narrative that keeps us afraid of failure and unwilling to immerse ourselves in the complexity and messiness that is a reality of working to challenge White supremacy and racism.

The barriers that make it difficult for Whites to address their own privilege and complicity in racism also make it difficult to facilitate effective cross-racial discussions. Pawlowski (2019) discussed ways to create conditions where authentic learning that entails risk and controversy, along with opportunities for growth can occur. In delineating between safe space and brave space for her writing classroom, Pawlowski (2019) identifies the characteristics also noted by Arao and Clemens (2013) in their reframing of uncritical spaces to brave spaces more conducive to growth and exploration. Pawlowski (2019) engages her students from the beginning to develop classroom norms that contrasts the differences between safe and brave spaces and the assumptions behind each one. Openly countering the assumptions behind such guidelines as "agreeing to disagree," "not taking things personally," and "respect" set the tone for a class where comments do not go unaddressed and learners are held accountable.

Critical race theory is used by adult educators and others to assist learners in uncovering and addressing the racism endemic to our society (Bell, 2010;

Closson, 2010). The use of counterstorytelling, along with a comparison of stock (dominant) stories and counterstories can help uncover how everyday knowledge is influenced by and tied to racialized structures. Just as in classrooms where brave spaces rather than safe spaces are enacted, educators emphasize the need to carefully attend to the dynamics based on the different social positions of the learners when discussing racialized stories. Bell (2010) describes the building of a community of learners who agree to hold stories up to analysis and hold each other accountable for taking risks to scrutinize the stories and their relationship to power and privilege. Chapman (2004) also notes that narratives and the analysis that follows can quickly become discourses about individualism that further inscribes the status quo; thus, the importance of monitoring who gets to speak and how to set up the conditions necessary for dialogue to occur is paramount, as not all stories are equally acknowledged, valued, or even heard (Bell, 2010).

Bell (2010), a social justice educator, uses narratives, visual arts, spoken word and poetry, theater, and other media as one way to engage body, mind, and heart and open up learning to provide opportunities for a broader understanding of societal patterns and practices. In Bell's storytelling project model, educators and learners create a community that moves progressively through an examination of stock (dominant) stories, concealed stories, resistance stories, and emerging/transforming stories to analyze and critique then to re-create more inclusive, just stories. Along the way aesthetic engagement with various art and media allow learners to use their imagination and formulate connections between the personal and the structural that they may not have been able to access through abstract analysis alone (Bell, 2010). Ramdeholl and Jones (2019) find this to be the case as they use films in their classrooms to analyze structural inequities, understand the political economy of racism, and re-imagine the ending of a film that reflects the current climate of U.S. race relations, among other objectives.

For many Whites, becoming aware of their racial identity and the ways they are unconsciously complicit in the perpetuation of racist structures and systems is one of the hardest learning projects they can imagine. The work done in the classroom indeed creates "disorienting dilemmas" and elicits opportunities for learners and educators to reframe their assumptions. It requires a high degree of vulnerability, critical reflection on previously unexamined assumptions, and a movement to reformulate a new way of being, all characteristics of transformative learning experiences (Cranton, 2016; Mezirow & Taylor, 2009). Adult educators *can* create learning environments to help bring Whites into an awareness and then an analysis of their own Whiteness and privilege. These approaches involve complexities, multilayered realities, strong emotions, and messiness and may also counter the epistemology of Whiteness that primarily values rationality, logic, proof, and dualistic thinking (Paxton, 2010), leading toward a way of thinking that is both/and instead of either/or. Learners may begin to see the possibility that they can be White and antiracist or at least moving toward that direction. The impetus for Whites to maintain the system of White supremacy and the status quo is indeed powerful. It is up to us as adult educators to do the intentional and sustained work that shows them another way.

References

Arao, B., & Clemens, K. (2013). From safe spaces to brave spaces. In L. Landreman (Ed.), *The art of effective facilitation: Reflections from social justice educators* (pp. 94–102). Stylus.

Baumgartner, L. M. (2010). White whispers: Talking about race in adult education. In V. S. Sheared, J. Johnson-Bailey, S. A. Colin III, E. Peterson, & S. D. Brookfield (Eds.), *The handbook of race and adult education: A resource for dialogue on racism* (pp. 105–118). Jossey-Bass.

Bell, L. A. (2010). *Storytelling for social justice: Connecting narrative and the arts in antiracist teaching*. Routledge.

Bowman, L., Merriweather, L. R., & Closson, R. B. (Eds.). (2014). The pedagogy of teaching race. *Adult Learning, 25*(3).

Brookfield, S. D. (Ed.). (1987). *Learning democracy: Eduard Lindeman on adult education and social change*. Croom Helm.

Brookfield, S. D. (2004). *The power of critical theory: Liberating adult learning and teaching*. Jossey-Bass.

Brookfield, S. D. (2014). Teaching our own racism: Incorporating personal narratives of Whiteness into antiracist practice. *Adult Learning, 25*(3), 89–95. https://doi.org/10.1177/1045159514534189

Brookfield, S. D. (2018). Transformative learning and the awareness of White supremacy. *Phronesis, 7*(3), 62–68.

Brookfield, S. D. (2019). *Teaching race: How to help students unmask and challenge racism*. Jossey-Bass.

Briscoe, D. B., & Ross, J. M. (1989). Racial and ethnic minorities and adult education. In S. B. Merriam & P. M. Cunningham (Eds.), *Handbook of adult and continuing education* (pp. 583–598). Jossey-Bass.

Chapman, V. L. (2004). Using critical personal narratives: A poststructural perspective on practice. *New Directions for Adult and Continuing Education, 2004*(102), 95–103.

Closson, R. B. (2010). An exploration of critical race theory. In V. S. Sheared, J. Johnson-Bailey, S. A. Colin III, E. Peterson, & S. D. Brookfield (Eds.), *The handbook of race and adult education: A resource for dialogue on racism* (pp. 173–185). Jossey-Bass.

Colin, S. A. J., III, & Lund, C.A. (Eds.). (2010). White privilege and racism: Perceptions and actions [Themed issue]. *New Directions for Adult and Continuing Education, 2010*(125).

Cranton, P. (2016). *Understanding and promoting transformative learning: A guide to theory and practice* (3rd ed.). Stylus.

Delgado, R. & Stefancic, J. (2017). *Critical race theory: An introduction* (3rd ed.). NYU Press.

DiAngelo, R. (2018). *White fragility: Why it's so hard for White people to talk about racism.* Beacon Press.

Dyson, M. E. (2018). Foreword. In R. DiAngelo, *White fragility: Why it's so hard for White people to talk about racism* (pp. ix–xii). Beacon Press.

European-American Collaborative Challenging Whiteness. (2010). White on White: Developing the capacity to communicate about race with critical humility. In V. S. Sheared, J. Johnson-Bailey, S. A. Colin III, E. Peterson, & S. D. Brookfield (Eds.), *The handbook of race and adult education: A resource for dialogue on racism* (pp. 145–157). Jossey-Bass.

Frankenberg, R. (1993). *White women, race matters: The social construction of race.* University of Minnesota Press.

Freire, P. (1970). *Pedagogy of the oppressed.* Continuum.

Freire, P. (1994). *Pedagogy of hope.* Continuum.

Habermas, J. (1990). *Moral consciousness and communicative action.* MIT Press.

Haggis, P. (Director). (2004). *Crash* [Film]. Lionsgate.

Helms, J. E. (1990). *Black and White racial identity: Theory, research and practice.* Greenwood Press.

Horton, M. (1990). *The long haul: An autobiography.* Doubleday.

Horton, M. (2003). *The Myles Horton reader: Education for social change.* University of Tennessee Press.

Horton, M., & Freire, P. (1990). *We make the road by walking: Conversations on education and social change.* Temple University Press.

Isaac, E. P., Merriweather, L. R., & Rogers, E. E. (2010). Chasing the American dream: Race and adult and continuing education. In C. E. Kasworm & A. D. Rose (Eds.), *Handbook of adult and continuing education* (pp. 359–368). SAGE.

Johnson-Bailey, J. (2002). Race matters: The unspoken variable in the teaching-learning transaction. In J. M. Ross-Gordon (Ed.), *Contemporary viewpoints on teaching adults effectively* (pp. 39–50). Jossey-Bass.

Johnson-Bailey, J., & Cervero, R. M. (2000). The invisible politics of race in adult education. In A. L. Wilson & E. R. Hayes (Eds.), *Handbook of adult and continuing education* (pp. 147–160). Jossey-Bass.

Kempfer, H. (1955). *Adult education.* McGraw-Hill.

Kendall, F. E. (2013). *Understanding White privilege: Creating pathways to authentic relationships across race* (2nd ed.). Routledge.

Kreitlow, B. W. (1981). *Examining controversies in adult education.* Jossey-Bass.

Manglitz, E. (2003). Challenging White privilege in adult education: A critical review of the literature. *Adult Education Quarterly, 53*(2), 119–134.

Manglitz, E., & Cervero, R. M. (2010). Adult education and the problem of the color (power) line: Views from the Whiter side. In V. S. Sheared, J. Johnson-Bailey, S. A. Colin III, E. Peterson, & S. D. Brookfield (Eds.), *The handbook of race and adult education: A resource for dialogue on racism* (pp. 133–144). Jossey-Bass.

Marcuse, H. (1965). Repressive tolerance. In R. P. Wolff, B. Moore, & H. Marcuse (Eds.), *A critique of pure tolerance* (pp. 81–123). Beacon Press.

McIntosh, P. (1988). *White privilege and male privilege: A personal account of coming to see correspondences through work in Women's Studies* [Working paper 189]. Wellesley College Center for Research on Women.

Mezirow, J. (1991). *Transformative dimensions of adult learning.* Jossey-Bass.

Mezirow, J., & Taylor, E. W. (2009). *Transformative learning in practice: Insights from community, workplace, and higher education.* Jossey-Bass.

Outlaw, L. T., Jr. (1996). *On race and philosophy.* Routledge.

Pawlowski, L. (2019). Creating a brave space classroom through writing. In S. Brookfield (Ed.), *Teaching race: How to help students unmask and challenge racism* (pp. 68–97). Jossey-Bass.

Paxton, D. (2010). Transforming White consciousness. In V. S. Sheared, J. Johnson-Bailey, S. A. Colin III, E. Peterson, & S. D. Brookfield (Eds.), *The handbook of race and adult education: A resource for dialogue on racism* (pp. 119–132). Jossey-Bass.

Ramdeholl, D., & Jones, J. (2019). Helping students uncover positionality. In S. Brookfield (Ed.), *Teaching race: How to help students unmask and challenge racism* (pp. 258–280). Jossey-Bass.

Sheared, V., Johnson-Bailey, J., Colin, S. A. J., III, Peterson, E., & Brookfield, S. D. (Eds.). (2010). *The handbook of race and adult education: A resource for dialogue on racism*. Jossey-Bass.

Shor, I., & Freire, P. (1987). *A pedagogy for liberation: Dialogues on transforming education*. Bergin & Garvey.

Shore, S. (2001). Talking about Whiteness: Adult learning principles and the invisible norm. In V. Sheared & P. Sissel (Eds.), *Making space: Merging theory and practice in adult education* (pp. 42–56). Bergin & Garvey.

Smith, B. (2019). Examining mistakes to advance antiracist teaching. In S. Brookfield (Ed.), *Teaching race: How to help students unmask and challenge racism* (pp. 303–320). Jossey-Bass.

Smith, T. V., & Lindeman, E. C. (1951). *The democratic way of life*. New American Library.

Sue, D. W. (2015). *Race talk and the conspiracy of silence: Understanding and facilitating difficult dialogues on race*. Wiley.

Sullivan, S. (2014). *Good White people: The problem with middle-class White antiracism*. SUNY Press.

Taylor, E. W., & Cranton, P. (Eds.). (2012). *The handbook of transformative learning: Theory, research, and practice*. Jossey-Bass.

Wilson, A. L., & Hayes, E. R. (2000). A selective history of the adult education handbooks. In A. L. Wilson & E. R. Hayes (Eds.), *Handbook of adult and continuing education* (pp. 3–14). Jossey-Bass.

Zamudio, M. M., Russell, C., Rios, F. A., & Bridgeman, J. L. (2010). *Critical race theory matters: Education and ideology*. Routledge.

CHAPTER 46

Migration and Migrant Education

Hongxia Shan and Shibao Guo

Permanent migration to Organisation for Economic Co-operation and Development (OECD) countries, such as the United States or Canada, continues to grow. In 2018, more than 5.3 million people settled permanently in OECD countries. Temporary migration, which is undertaken for a limited period of time for purposes such as term employment, business, and study, is also increasing, but at a slower pace than permanent migration, sitting at about 4.9 million in 2017 (OECD, 2019). The United States remains a primary destination country for not only permanent and temporary migrants but also other migrants, including undocumented migrants. The total foreign-born population residing in the United States was 44.5 million in 2016, or 13% of the population. Among them, 10.5 million were unauthorized immigrants, which is a number that has been largely unchanged since 2009. In the last few years, however, the number of migrants in most categories has declined in the United States (OECD, 2019).

With the rise of right-wing populism in the United States, antimigrant policies targeting both legal and undocumented migrants have been introduced—including the notorious 2017 travel ban directed against citizens from a number of Muslim-majority countries. In the face of the recent Syrian refugee crisis, countries such as Canada, Germany, and Sweden have stepped up their humanitarian efforts to resettle refugees, but the United States has taken legislative measures to restrict the admission of refugees and asylum seekers. As a result, the number of refugees and asylum seekers admitted into the United States has reached a historic low. In contrast, the number of temporary workers admitted into the country increased by 11.5% in 2016 and 5.7% in 2017 (OECD, 2018).

Upon arrival in the new country, some migrants, especially those with racialized backgrounds, find it a challenge to access quality employment, rights to health and safety at work, and citizenship. In addition to the need to develop crucial language skills, employment skills, and cultural knowledge in the host societies, many migrants also have to cope with issues of credential recognition, racism, xenophobia, institutional marginalization, and labor market segregation. In countries such as the United States, with the rise of exclusive nationalism and recent enforcement of populist radical right policies, the political climate for migrants' reception and integration has become even more precarious (Pierce et al., 2018). In this context, it is important to turn to the field of adult learning and education, which has an important role to play for enhancing migrants' capacities to participate in the social and economic lives in the host societies. This chapter continues with a global survey of migrant education. It introduces the major players in migrant education, followed by a number of migrant education models emerging in different contexts that demonstrate deliberate efforts to engage migrant newcomers across social, cultural, and other relations of differences. This chapter concludes with a discussion of the strengths and limitations of migrant education as a field of practice.

Migrant Education: Major Players in the Field

Typically, each country has its immigration policies and national approaches to migrants' integration, ranging from the assimilationist model in France, to the melting pot of the United States, and to the multiculturalist model in Canada (Moreno et al., 2018). However, there is rarely an overarching design for migrant education at the national level. Migrant education is shaped by a multitude of forces, including the policies and politics of migration and integration; national and subnational policies and practices related to work, health, and training; and the emergence of supranational agreements and conventions. It also involves a host of actors, including multiple national and subnational (i.e., state and municipal) governmental stakeholders; supranational organizations; and nongovernmental actors, such as community organizations, educational and other social institutions, unions, and activist organizations.

National and Subnational Governments

National and subnational governments today are typically involved, albeit to varying degrees, in the funding and coordination of migrant training and services. In the United States, the federal government plays a role in the areas of refugee resettlement, citizenship training, and English as a second language (ESL) funding (Siemiatycki & Triadafilopoulos, 2010). In 1980, the U.S. Congress enacted the Refugee Act, which enabled the building of a web of support for refugees and a comprehensive framework for resettlement (de Graauw & Bloemraad, 2017). The federal government provides limited funding for permanent migrants. The assumption is that migrants should access available public services and facilities, such as schools, to integrate into society. Starting from 2009, the U.S. Citizenship and Immigration Services (USCIS) has funded community-based organizations to provide citizenship-related language training and support services. However, only $80 million so far has been distributed to relevant community organizations (USCIS, n.d.). Due to the underprovision of language training, a large number of migrants end up not applying for citizenship out of fear of not passing the citizenship test (Siemiatycki & Triadafilopoulos, 2010).

State and municipal governments in the United States are not subsumed within the same politics as the federal government. Driven by the needs of a growing migrant population in local communities, many of these governments have joined efforts with nongovernmental actors to foster more constructive discourses about migration and migrants and to promote policies and practices that provide migrants, including undocumented migrants, opportunities for inclusion in society (de Graauw & Bloemraad, 2017). One of these initiatives is Cities for Action, which is a coalition of over 175 mayors and county executives advocating for proimmigrant policies and promoting inclusive programs and policies in local communities (Cities for Action, n.d.).

Unlike the United States, the Canadian federal government has long been involved in not only refugee resettlement but also language training and employment support for permanent migrants. Migrant integration in Canada is visualized as a two-way street involving the mutual adaptation of both newcomers and the Canadian society. The administrative model of integration programs has shifted over time (Shan, 2015). Today, migrant integration has increasingly become a shared responsibility between the federal and provincial governments. In the wake of the Syrian refugee crisis, a whole-of-society approach has been proposed and it involves a shared governance where "the federal, provincial/territorial and municipal governments play a central role to facilitate immigrant integration, in partnership with many societal actors in diverse communities across Canada" (Prince-St-Amand, 2016, p. 6). While this model may reflect the will of the large civil society in Canada to provide better reception for migrants, it is uncertain as to how much control the civil society can exercise over these partnerships.

In newer migrant destination countries such as Germany and Sweden, governments have also worked in collaboration with nongovernmental stakeholders to integrate migrants. In Germany, for instance, with the provision of the Residence Act in 2005, the new Federal Office for Migration and Refugees has worked with the civil society to deliver integration courses, which include language training and an introduction to German culture, history, and the legal system (Siemiatycki & Triadafilopoulos, 2010). In Sweden, subsequent to the Syrian refugee crisis, the government invited organizations, such as folk high schools and study associations, to apply for funding that could provide asylum seekers with courses on Swedish language and society (Mešić et al., 2019). Both cases show that when national governments become invested in migrant settlement, there is potential to mobilize the civil society in the training and education of migrants.

Supranational Organizations

Supranational organizations, such as the United Nations (UN), International Organization for Migration, and the European Union (EU), have influenced people's experiences of migration and settlement. The advocacy of universal human rights by supranational organizations supplements and, at times, challenges national citizenship rights, based on which migrant programs are administered. To give an example, the UN is a core body in the global governance of migration and migrant settlement. The 1951 UN Refugee Convention, for instance, defines the term *refugee* and outlines the rights of the displaced and the obligations of nation states to protect them. This convention has provided the principle framework for countries and other stakeholders to work with refugees.

The human rights discourses promoted at the supranational level have also influenced migrants' access to training and services, which is particularly true in the case of temporary migrant workers. Temprorary workers, especially those working in low-end sectors such as farming and construction, are one of the most vulnerable groups as they are susceptible to exploitation, abuse, health hazards, and social isolation (Sawchuk & Kempf, 2008). Yet they do not normally have access to state-funded migrant programs because they are not typically destined to become citizens in the host societies. International agreements, however, such as the UN International Convention on the Protection of the Rights of Migrant Workers and Members of their Families, have extended the concept of citizenship from "a state-based to a more 'individual-based' and 'universal' conception of rights" (Basok, 2004, p. 48). In other words, by advocating individual human rights beyond national borders, these conventions challenge policies and practices that restrict rights to individuals based on citizenship. This reconceptualization of citizenship and rights at the global level has provided an alternative framework for the public to debate the rights of temporary migrant workers, with implications for who is entitled to education and services. In 2017, reflecting this changing discourse around citizenship and entitlement, Canada announced a grant of CA$93,000 to the Migrant Workers' Dignity Association to develop workshops, information tools, and materials to inform temporary workers on topics such as housing, health care, and access to rights and benefits (Employment and Social Development Canada, 2017).

Nongovernmental Actors

Multiple nongovernmental actors are involved in the design and delivery of training and services for migrants. Settlement houses, ethnic communities, and religious organizations were among the first organizations to provide settlement assistance in countries such as Canada and the United States. Often, however, such assistance has been delivered with a missionary and paternalistic orientation (de Graauw & Bloemraad, 2017; Shields et al., 2016). Community-based organizations remain the main service providers for migrant newcomers. The role that they play in migrants' integration process has, however, been mixed and contested. On the one hand, when community organizations receive funding from government agencies, they need to follow governmental priorities and demonstrate immediate economic efficiency, effectiveness, and accountability in order to keep their funds for operational support. These organizations can easily become part of the state apparatus, or a shadow state, perpetuating existing stratification of the labor market along social differences such as gender and race (Evans & Shields, 2010; Ng, 1988). On the other hand, community organizations can potentially afford a space through which migrants negotiate identities and forge new communities (see Gibb et al., 2008). In the case of Sweden, for example, the radical tradition of the workers' movement in popular education has enabled some state-funded agencies to respond to the needs of refugees beyond state-defined mandates (Mešić et al., 2019). Additionally, in the United States and Canada, activist community organizations have also worked to organize learning and training opportunities and helped migrant workers deal with issues related to health, labor, and civil rights—issues that often fall out of the scope of integration programs (e.g., Butterwick et al., 2015; Luque et al., 2007; Perry, 2018).

Educational institutions can potentially enhance the social, cultural, and economic opportunities for migrants across countries (Alfred, 2015; Morrice, 2009; Salerno & Kibler, 2015; Webb, 2015). In Germany, for instance, the dual system of vocational training, which combines on-the-job training with learning based in vocational schools, has to some extent equalized employment opportunities for migrant youths (Burkert & Seibert, 2007). Higher education and research institutions have also worked with migrant communities and community-based organizations to address specific issues facing migrant communities, such as health and safety at work (Abdelrahman Amin & Brigham, 2009; Arcury et al., 2010; Green & Kearney, 2011). Some of these programs tap into national regulations and funding designed to promote health, occupational safety, and community development rather than state funding for migrant integration and settlement.

Models of Migrant Education

Migrant education is a heterogeneous field of practice. It takes the form of formal education (i.e., school-based certificate, diploma, and degree programs), nonformal training (i.e., short-term workshops, seminars, and study groups), as well as informal learning that is fostered in people's everyday work and life encounters. Some programs are generic mainstream programs extended to migrant newcomers. Some programs are initiatives created by educators, researchers, and workplace professionals to address selected issues facing specific migrant communities (e.g., Arcury et al., 2010; Gallo, 2001; Green & Kearney, 2011; Perry, 2018). The majority are migrant (re)settlement and integration programs. In the process of designing and implementing educational programs for migrants, notably, adult educators have consciously navigated two common pitfalls: the "difference as deficit" mentality and the "sameness" approach, which assumes all learners have similar backgrounds and learning needs (Guo, 2015). When considering how the programs are set up to deal with social, cultural, and linguistic differences, four main programmatic approaches are salient: culturally relevant education, bridging programs, participatory programming and active learning, and learning through everyday practices.

Culturally Relevant Education
Culturally relevant or responsive education is education that endeavors to create learning environments that respond to diverse needs (Au, 2007; Guo & Jamal, 2007). In migrant education, culturally relevant education encompasses pedagogical orientations that range from transmitting knowledge in a culturally appropriate manner to foster transformative social change. In the United States, there has long been a call to develop culturally relevant education and educational materials for migrants. The purpose here is to connect migrant communities with meaningful information so that they change their behaviors and inform themselves about issues such as health (e.g., Ikeda et al., 2002), parenting practices (e.g., Powell et al., 1990), and safety in labor intensive sectors, such as agriculture (Arcury et al., 2010; Austin et al., 2001) and construction (Brunette, 2005). Research on migrant education and learning experiences in Canada also stresses the importance of validating migrants' prior knowledge, which is believed to be instrumental in enhancing their confidence, self-esteem, and sense of control over their lives (Fursova, 2013).

In some unique cases, programs go beyond cultural relevance and take on a transformative role. These programs typically challenge historical and systematic exploitation of migrant workers by critically and creatively engaging migrant workers (e.g., Butterwick et al., 2015; Gallo, 2001; Perry, 2018). For example, Gallo (2001) introduced an English learning program for migrant and refugee workers in a U.S. manufacturing plant. The program is based on learner-generated photography to help workers gain English reading and writing skills. Participants not only became more confident, having strengthened their English language skills, but also began to question the meaning of some English words that are used by supervisors and coworkers to marginalize and exploit them in the workplace. Programs such as this demonstrate the power of critical pedagogies, which can deepen the impacts of culturally relevant education.

Bridging Programs
Bridging programs are designed to connect skilled migrants to their fields of practice. Bridging programs arose in Canada in the past few years as a response to the notorious phenomenon called *deprofessionalization*, or the underemployment of immigrant professionals, which costs the country's economy billions of dollars annually (Reitz et al., 2014). One exemplary bridging program is the Internationally Educated Engineers Qualification Program (IEEQ) conducted out of the University of Manitoba (Canada), which aims to pave the pathway of qualification recognition for migrant engineers (Friesen, 2013). IEEQ is composed of academic requirements, paid co-op

experiences, development of sociolinguistic and communication skills, and socialization to the culture and values of the profession. Rather than dismissing migrants' prior training as irrelevant, the program recognizes migrants' prior knowledge and encourages the participants to draw comparisons and contrasts to Canadian engineering practices. The program also fosters language and communication development in the specific context of the engineering profession, and it immerses participants within practicing engineering environments.

The IEEQ program tries to live up to the principle of substantive equality. It recognizes that the starting point for different individuals may be unequal or unfair, and thus it is necessary and just to address the cultural, social, economic, and historical disadvantages that have led to inequality of opportunities in the first place (Government of Canada, 2018). The program addresses migrants' lack of access to professional employment by enabling them to accumulate the social and cultural capital needed within their profession (Friesen, 2011). Bridging programs are not, however, without their challenges. Due to employers' negative to grudgingly tolerant responses toward cultural differences (Friesen & Ingram, 2013), it is difficult for some programs to assist migrant professionals to gain employment beyond entry-level positions (e.g., McCoy & Masuch, 2007). Also, when there is a lack of program articulation with or endorsement by regulatory bodies, these programs may fail to significantly impact migrants' lives (e.g., Kleef & Werquin, 2013).

Participatory Programs and Active Learning

Migrants, particularly those with temporary status and low language literacy, are among the populations most vulnerable to poor health, safety hazards, workplace exploitation, discrimination, and social isolation. Health agencies, migrant community organizations and advocacy groups, and research institutes have worked to extend training and education to specific migrant communities (Arcury et al., 2010; Austin et al., 2001; Luque et al., 2007). Many of these programs target groups of migrants to promote certain types of learning. Some programs also engage community-based participatory approaches or partnerships with migrant communities (e.g., Abdel-rahman Amin & Brigham, 2009; Green & Kearney, 2011). These participatory programs merit special attention because they not only offer the opportunity for migrants to participate in the coconstruction of knowledge and program but also help migrants develop their capacity for both individual and community development.

An example of this participatory approach is a unique initiative in Australia, where researchers from Griffith University conducted a community-based participatory action research project with a Pacific Island community (Green & Kearney, 2011; Kearney & Zuber-Skerritt, 2012). The project produced a leadership program which was based on the needs identified by elders in the community. The program adopted an active learning system developed by the Global University for Lifelong Learning (2020). The system comprised a self-nominated personal coach/mentor and a "learning set" for a support group of colearners to ask questions, explore assumptions, and collaboratively identify and overcome learning barriers, and establish guidelines for completing specific tasks. Researchers found that this partnership project not only enhanced the personal and professional development of individuals within the community (e.g., problem-solving) but also contributed to sustainable community development (Green & Kearney, 2011; Kearney & Zuber-Skerritt, 2012).

Learning Through Everyday Practices

Recently, researchers in Australia, Canada, and the EU have looked into methods that can foster and mobilize everyday informal adult learning for migrants as well as the broader society. Some of these initiatives include the development and introduction of portable technologies, such as smartphones and specialized apps, to support migrants' language learning and social integration (Bradley et al., 2017; Jones et al., 2017; Kluzer et al., 2011). For example, a European project, Mobile Assistance for Social Inclusion & Empowerment of Immigrants with Persuasive Learning Technologies & Social Network Services (MASELTOV), involves the development of a prototype context-aware smartphone app for migrants. It comprises an integrated suite of navigation, information, social interaction, language learning, and game playing services. Examining a trial of the project in the United Kingdom, Jones et al. (2017) found that the app helped migrants practice language skills, expanded their socioemotional support system, and enhanced their confidence in language use.

Another form of informal learning is mediated through everyday multiculturalism, or the "everyday practice and lived experience of diversity in specific situations and spaces of encounter" (Wise & Velayutham, 2009, p. 3) through which people negotiate cultural difference and social identities. Learning associated with everyday multiculturalism is often spontaneous, organic, and incidental in nature (Flowers & Swan, 2017; Shan & Walter, 2015). Facilitated everyday multiculturalism, however, can extend cross-cultural learning to both migrants and the host communities. The Welcome Dinner Project (WDP) in Australia is an example of facilitated everyday multiculturalism (Flowers & Swan, 2017). This program aims to bring together new migrants and "established Australians" (p. 270) to meet and share stories over a potluck meal in the comfort of their homes. The purpose is to create meaningful connections, friendships, and social solidarities across cultural differences. Trained facilitators lead activities associated with the meals and manage contacts among people of different backgrounds. There is no report on the impact of this program to date. The program's existence nonetheless demonstrates an interest from the host society to include newcomers.

Discussion and Conclusion

Adult education and learning has an important role to play in migrants' integration into their host countries. This chapter offers an overview of migrant education, with a focus on the major players in the field and the key approaches used to engage migrants. Several country contexts were described where migration and integration have been identified as national priorities. Although governmental involvement in migrant integration has been historically uneven across the globe, there is a converging pattern for governments and civil society to form partnerships in the coordination and provision of migrant integration services. Some research (e.g., Evans & Shields, 2010; Ng, 1988) has been skeptical of the roles that states play in the orientation of integration services given the contractual relationship between the state and community-based organizations. The field of migrant education may benefit from a comparative study of the mode of governance across several countries in the future.

In summary, there are four major ways in which educational programs have engaged migrants. These are culturally relevant education, bridging programs, participatory programs and active learning, and learning through everyday practices. Many of the programs are geared toward teaching the necessary language and skills for success in the labor market or extending migrants' social and cultural capitals. Some promising practices include: (a) grounding teaching and learning within the cultural realities of migrants; (b) validating migrants' prior knowledge as a ground to build further learning; and (c) engaging migrants in the design, development, and delivery of programs and working toward enhancing migrants' capacity for self and community development.

Migrant education programs are becoming more diversified and creative with the integration of new technologies, new forms of gathering, and new research methodologies such as arts-informed research (e.g., Butterwick et al., 2015; Perry, 2018). Despite these promising developments, there is some caution that when migrant education solely focuses on the normative needs of the host labor markets, it perpetuates the existing cultural and social hierarchy dominant in the host society (e.g., Maitra, 2015; Ng, 1988; Slade, 2012). Migrant programs do not typically address issues of power and differences that affect how skills are differentially constructed, valorized, and recognized in host societies. Nor are they typically positioned—with the exception of critical, activist-led programs—to deal with the systematic issues that affect migrants' control over their sociocultural and economic opportunities and general wellbeing (Austin et al., 2001). To increase the impact of migrant education as a social force of change, a global forum might be helpful, where adult educators, researchers, and practitioners can exchange and learn from related policies, practices, and politics across countries and foster new ways to explore migrant education as a social enterprise.

References

Abdelrahman Amin, M., & Brigham, S. M. (2009). Exploring the boundaries of lifelong learning for lifelong health: Immigrant women's knowledge, beliefs, attitudes, and perceptions about cancer. In S. Carpenter, M. Laiken, & S. Mojab (Eds.), *Proceedings of the 28th Canadian*

Association for the Study of Adult Education Conference (pp. 7–14). Canadian Association for the Study of Adult Education.

Alfred, M. V. (2015). Diaspora, migration, and globalization: Expanding the discourse of adult education. *New Directions for Adult and Continuing Education, 2015*(146), 87–97. https://doi.org/10.1002/ace.20134

Arcury, T. A., Estrada, J. M., & Quandt, S. A. (2010). Overcoming language and literacy barriers in safety and health training of agricultural workers. *Journal of Agromedicine, 15*(3), 236–248. https://doi.org/10.1080/1059924X.2010.486958

Au, K. H. (2007). Culturally responsive instruction: Application to multiethnic classrooms. *Pedagogies: An International Journal, 2*(1), 1–17. https://doi.org/10.1080/15544800701343562

Austin, C., Arcury, T. A., Quandt, S. A., Preisser, J. S., Saavedra, R. M., & Cabrera, L. F. (2001). Training farmworkers about pesticide safety: Issues of control. *Journal of Health Care for the Poor and Underserved, 12*(2), 236–249. https://doi.org/10.1353/hpu.2010.0744

Basok, T. (2004). Post-national citizenship, social exclusion and migrants rights: Mexican seasonal workers in Canada. *Citizenship Studies, 8*(1), 47–64. https://doi.org/10.1080/1362102042000178409

Bradley, L., Lindström, N. B., & Hashemi, S. S. (2017). Integration and language learning of newly arrived migrants using mobile technology. *Journal of Interactive Media in Education, 2017*(1), 1–9. https://doi.org/10.5334/jime.43

Brunette, M. J. (2005). Development of educational and training materials on safety and health: Targeting Hispanic workers in the construction industry. *Family & Community Health, 28*(3), 253–266. https://doi.org/10.1097/00003727-200507000-00006

Burkert, C., & Seibert, H. (2007). *Labour market outcomes after vocational training in Germany: Equal opportunities for migrants and natives?* Institut für Arbeitsmarkt- und Berufsforschung der Bundesagentur für Arbeit. http://doku.iab.de/discussionpapers/2007/dp3107.pdf.

Butterwick, S., Carrillo, M., & Villagante, K. (2015). Women's fashion shows as feminist trans-formation. *The Canadian Journal for the Study of Adult Education/La Revue canadienne pour l'etude de l'education des adultes, 27*(2), 79–99.

Cities for Action. (n.d.). *About Cities for Action.* http://www.citiesforaction.us/mission

de Graauw, E., & Bloemraad, I. (2017). Working together: Building successful policy and program partnerships for immigrant integration. *Journal on Migration and Human Security, 5*(1), 105–123. https://doi.org/10.1177/233150241700500106

Employment and Social Development Canada. (2017). *Government of Canada offers support to vulnerable migrant workers in Canada.* https://www.canada.ca/en/employment-social-development/news/2017/12/government_of_canadaofferssupporttovulnerablemigrantworkersincan.html

Evans, B., & Shields, J. (2010). The third sector and the provision of public good: Partnerships, contracting and the neo-liberal state. In C. Dunn (Ed.), *The handbook of Canadian public administration* (2nd ed., pp. 305–318). Oxford University Press.

Flowers, R., & Swan, E. (2017). Bring a plate: Facilitating experimentation in the Welcome Dinner project. *Studies in the Education of Adults, 49*(2), 269–287. https://doi.org/10.1080/02660830.2018.1453117

Friesen, M. (2011). Immigrants' integration and career development in the professional engineering workplace in the context of social and cultural capital. *Engineering Studies, 2,* 79–100. https://doi.org/10.1080/19378629.2011.571260

Friesen, M. (2013). Critical perspectives in a qualifications recognition programme for immigrant engineers in Canada. *Global Journal of Engineering Education, 15*(1), 6–12.

Friesen, M., & Ingram, S. (2013). Advancing intercultural competency: Canadian engineering employers' experiences with immigrant engineers. *European Journal of Engineering Education, 38*(2), 219–227. https://doi.org/10.1080/03043797.2013.766677

Fursova, J. (2013). *A journey of her own: A critical analysis of learning experiences among immigrant women* [RCIS working paper no. 2013/3]. Ryerson Centre for Immigration and Settlement.

Gallo, M. L. (2001). Immigrant workers' journeys through a new culture: Exploring the transformative learning possibilities of photography. *Studies in the Education of Adults, 33*(2), 109–117. https://doi.org/10.1080/02660830.2001.11661446

Gibb, T., Hamdon, E., & Jamal, Z. (2008). Re/claiming agency: Learning, liminality and immigrant service organizations. *Journal of Contemporary Issues in Education, 3*(1), 4–16.

Global University for Lifelong Learning. (2020). www.gullonline.org

Government of Canada. (2018). *Jordan's principle: Substantive equality principles.* https://www.canada.ca/en/indigenous-services-canada/services/jordans-principle/jordans-principle-substantive-equality-principles.html

Green, A., & Kearney, J. (2011). Participatory action learning and action research for self-sustaining community development: Engaging Pacific Islanders in Southeast Queensland. *The Australasian Journal of University-Community Engagement, 6*(2), 46–68.

Guo, S. (2015). The changing nature of adult education in the age of transnational migration: Toward a model of recognitive adult education. *New Directions for Adult and Continuing Education, 2015*(146), 7–17. https://doi.org/10.1002/ace.20127

Guo, S., & Jamal, Z. (2007). Nurturing cultural diversity in higher education: A critical review of selected models. *Canadian Journal of Higher Education, 37*(3), 27–49.

Ikeda, J. P., Pham, L., Nguyen, K., & Mitchell, R. A. (2002). Culturally relevant nutrition education improves dietary quality among WIC-eligible Vietnamese immigrants. *Journal of Nutrition Education and Behavior, 34*(2), 151–158. https://doi.org/10.1016/s1499-4046(06)60084-5

Jones, A., Kukulska-Hulme, A., Norris, L., Gaved, M., Scanlon, E., Jones, J., & Brasher, A. (2017). Supporting immigrant language learning on smartphones: A field trial. *Studies in the Education of Adults, 49*(2), 228–252. https://doi.org/10.1080/02660830.2018.1463655

Kearney, J., & Zuber-Skerritt, O. (2012). From learning organization to learning community: Sustainability through lifelong learning. *The Learning Organization, 19*(5), 400–413.

Kleef, J. V., & Werquin, P. (2013). PLAR in nursing: Implications of situated learning, communities of practice and consequential transition theories for recognition. *Journal of International Migration and Integration, 14*(4), 651–669.

Kluzer, S., Ferrari, A., & Centeno, C. (2011). *Language learning by adult migrants: Policy challenges and ICT responses*. Joint Research Centre Institute for Prospective Technological Studies. http://ftp.jrc.es/EURdoc/JRC63889_TN.pdf1

Luque, J. S., Monaghan, P., Contreras, R. B., August, E., Baldwin, J. A., Bryant, C. A., & McDermott, R. J. (2007). Implementation evaluation of a culturally competent eye injury prevention program for citrus workers in a Florida migrant community. *Programs in Community Health Partnerships, 1*(4), 359–369. https://doi.org/10.1353/cpr.2007.0040

Maitra, S. (2015). Between conformity and contestation: South Asian immigrant women negotiating soft skill training in Canada. *Canadian Journal for the Study of Adult Education, 27*(2), 64–75.

McCoy, L., & Masuch, C. (2007). Beyond "entry-level" jobs: Immigrant women and nonregulated professional occupations. *Journal of International Migration and Integration, 8*(2), 185–206.

Mešić, N., Dahlstedt, M., Fejes, A., & Nyström, S. (2019). Use-values for inclusion: Mobilizing resources in popular education for newly arrived refugees in Sweden. *Social Inclusion, 7*(2), 85–95.

Moreno, K. A. V., Shields, J., & Drolet, J. (2018). Settling immigrants in neoliberal times: NGOs and immigrant well-being in comparative context. *Alternate Routes: A Journal of Critical Social Research, 29*, 65–89.

Morrice, L. (2009). Journeys into higher education: The case of refugees in the UK. *Teaching in Higher Education, 14*(6), 661–672. https://doi.org/10.1080/13562510903315282

Ng, R. (1988). *The politics of community services: Immigrant women, class and state*. Garamond Press.

OECD. (2019). *International migration outlook*. Author.

Perry, A. (2018). Play-making with migrant farm workers in Ontario, Canada: A kinesthetic and embodied approach to qualitative research. *Qualitative Research, 18*(6), 689–705.

Pierce, S., Bolter, J., & Selee, A. (2018). *U.S. immigration policy under Trump: Deep changes and lasting impacts*. Migration Policy Institute. https://observatoriocolef.org/wp-content/uploads/2018/07/TCMTrumpSpring2018-FINAL.pdf

Powell, D. R., Zambrana, R., & Silva-Palacios, V. (1990). Designing culturally responsive parent programs: A comparison of low-income Mexican and Mexican-American mothers' preferences. *Family Relations, 39*(3), 298–304. https://doi.org/10.2307/584875

Prince-St-Amand, C. (2016, December 1–2). *Immigrant integration in Canada: A whole-of-society approach to help newcomers succeed* [Paper presentation]. Pathways to Prosperity Conference, Ottowa, ON, Canada.

Reitz, J., Curtis, J., & Elrick, J. (2014). Immigrant skill utilization: Trends and policy issues. *International Migration and Integration, 15*, 1–26.

Salerno, A. S., & Kibler, A.K. (2015). Vocational training for adolescent English language learners in newcomer programs: Opportunities or isolations? *TESOL Journal, 6*(2), 201–224. https://doi.org/10.1002/tesj.140

Sawchuk, P., & Kempf, A. (2008). Guest worker programs and Canada: Towards a foundation for understanding the complex pedagogies of transnational labour. *Journal of Workplace Learning, 20*(7/8), 492–502. https://doi.org/10.1108/13665620810900319

Shan, H. (2015). Towards a participatory model of governance: Settlement services in the training and education of immigrants. *New Directions for Adult and Continuing Education, 2015*(146), 19–28.

Shan, H., & Walter, P. (2015). Growing everyday multiculturalism: Practice-based learning of Chinese immigrants through community gardens in Canada. *Adult Education Quarterly, 65*(1), 19–34. https://doi.org/10.1177/0741713614549231

Shields, J., Drolet, J., & Valenzuela, K. (2016). *Immigrant settlement and integration services and the role of nonprofit service providers: A cross-national perspective on trends, issues and evidence* [RCIS working paper no. 2016]. Ryerson Centre for Immigration and Settlement.

Siemiatycki, M., & Triadafilopoulos, T. (2010). *International perspectives on immigrant service provision.* Mowat Centre for Policy Innovation. School of Public Policy and Governance.

Slade, B. (2012). From high skill to high school: Illustrating the process of deskilling immigrants through reader's theatre and institutional ethnography. *Qualitative Inquiry, 18*(5), 401–413. https://doi.org/10.1177/1077800412439526

U.S. Citizenship and Immigration Services. (n.d.). *About the citizenship and assimilation grants.* https://www.uscis.gov/citizenship/organizations/grant-program

Webb, S. (2015). "It's who you know not what': Migrants" encounters with regimes of skills as a misrecognition. *Studies in Continuing Education, 37*(3), 67–285.

Wise, A., & Velayutham, S. (Eds.). (2009). *Everyday multiculturalism.* Palgrave. https://doi.org/10.1080/0158037X.2015.1007938

Conclusion

Reflecting on Struggles, Achievements, and Cautions in Complex Times

M Cecil Smith, Robert C. Mizzi, Joshua D. Hawley, Tonette S. Rocco, and Lisa R. Merriweather

"Prediction is very difficult, especially if it's about the future."

—*Nils Bohr, Nobel Laureate in Physics*

Editing the 2020 *Handbook of Adult and Continuing Education* has been a humbling experience for each member of the editorial team. Over the years leading up to the publication, we have engaged in deeply important conversations with an array of researchers, considered a plethora of perspectives across a vast field of topics, and witnessed a rich passion for subject matter that people have spent their lives studying. The handbook has a long tradition in the field of adult and continuing education and it is an immense honor for us to provide editorial service to the profession and to shed light on important topics, novel approaches, and new developments in the field over the past decade. To this end, our goals for this handbook were to offer

- an orientation to the broad field of adult education for practitioners who have come into the field lacking an understanding of adult and continuing education;
- a synthesis of foundational principles, practices, and related theory and research on adult learning and its facilitation;
- an overview of key contemporary organizational structures and programs reflecting the profession of adult and continuing education;
- diverse examinations of the touchstone perspectives framing current debates, advocacy, and commitments to social justice;
- analyses of current issues reflecting the nexus of global forces and the contemporary practices and beliefs within adult and continuing education; and
- a closer look at understanding what the current perspectives, knowledge, and practices might offer for the future of the field going forward into the next decade—and beyond.

While prediction of the future is difficult, as Nils Bohr says in the opening epigraph, we have obtained a clue into the current struggles and achievements in our field, and have begun to conceptualize what is on the horizon.

Adult and Continuing Education in Complex Times

We believe that we have assembled an excellent collection of chapters written by many of the leading theorists, researchers, practitioners, activists, and administrators working in adult and continuing education today. The contributors (and the editors as well) represent diverse social identities and backgrounds, philosophical and methodological perspectives, theoretical locations, contexts of practice, and interdisciplinary and epistemological orientations to adult and continuing education. The contributors have identified and expanded on extant understandings of adult learner populations as well as described adult learner populations that have been previously invisible, unexamined, or marginalized by policymakers and educators. Traversing across time through a handbook shows some unique trends, but it also delivers cautions of what may unfold over the next 10 years if we are not vigilant in our defense of the field.

In conceptualizing the 2020 handbook, we wanted to not only consider the current state of adult and continuing education, in all of its diversity and complexity, but also invite our contributors and our readers to ponder how our current understandings and practices will give rise to new ideas, collaborations, and practices to emerge and advance the field over the coming decade. We hope that our conclusions serve as conversation starters in your work and learning situations as they have in our work as editors for the 2020 handbook. Concluding our editorial work, we—along with readers of the handbook—can draw some important insights about where the field stands at the end of 2019 with regard to questions of critical importance to society—and to the profession. These insights lead us to ask: Where does the field go from here? What critical actions are necessary to advance the field so that it achieves (finally) prominence and stature equivalent to that of pre-K–12 and higher education? What new questions and debates will emerge over the next decade?

When the 2010 handbook was published, it is likely that few professionals in the field could have imagined the difficult times and uncertainty in which the global community finds itself a decade on. Adding to this difficulty is a tangle of complexities that can be difficult to unravel. Western nations have seen the rise of nationalism and populism, fueled in seemingly equal parts by economic uncertainties and outright distress among some layers of the socioeconomic strata, and by waves of unchecked immigration driven by wars and poverty and the personal despair that accompanies these tragic circumstances. Alongside these trends are: the rise of White nationalist groups in the United States and Europe, the so-called alt-right; an embrace of "alternative facts" by political leaders; the forced separation of immigrant families and internment of immigrant children in conditions that threaten their emotional health and physical well-being; the demonization of institutions that have long been considered the vanguards of democracy (journalism, in particular); and the takeover and radical transformation of a major political party in United States by a real estate mogul and television personality with a distinctly authoritarian bent. The results of this transformation have included, but not been limited to: threats to reproductive rights and the health of women of childbearing years; denial or roll-back of protections for transgender individuals in workplaces and in schools; the undermining of science and open skepticism of global climate change; opening up of public lands for extraction and environmental degradation; and ongoing wars in Afghanistan, with other conflicts involving U.S. troops and/or material support in Yemen, Nigeria, and Syria. We now have a generation of U.S. service personnel physically and psychologically maimed in war seeking our support. We have seen leftist governments or leaders come under fire or publicly shamed for their "liberal" ways, as well as the apparent embrace of authoritarian and dictatorial leaders with ruthless aims, which can only lead to further political and social division—in the United States and around the world. Further, there are mass shootings in schools, places of worship, entertainment centers, and festivals—seemingly any place with large crowds and low levels of security—inviting disturbed individuals to inflict carnage on innocent people. There is apparently little political will to confront and take the concrete and bold actions needed to solve this societal problem—a problem that is unique to the United States. Adult education's role in facilitating social awareness of this complexity and how these developments connect to one another is paramount, more than ever.

In response to these and other developments, there is a rise of important social and political movements—Black Lives Matter, #MeToo, #TimesUp, the Occupy movement, and so forth. Labor unions—particularly public school teachers' unions in states such as West Virginia, Oklahoma, and Arizona, and cities such as Chicago—have reasserted themselves, demanding and, in some cases, striking for fair compensation and appropriate resources for their students. The enormous influence local union leaders are playing in education, such as Karen Lewis in Chicago, harkens back to earlier eras in the 1920s and the 1960s, when education unions strongly opposed business elites. There is greater emphasis on the significant (and often not positive) influence of social media in politics, news media, and entertainment. Without question, as a society we have revisited important issues in equity and diversity over the past decade, such as with legalization of same-sex marriage in the United States. These movements ask important questions of adult educators and adult education as a field. Can adult and continuing education, as a mechanism for individual growth and change, offer any viable solutions to these social, political, and economic challenges? What can a field that has been historically marginalized offer to not only improve people's lives but also alter the social and political landscape to reflect positive change? How can we, in a Freirean (1985) sense, help individuals to read the world and the word, in a context that is rife with technological advancements, massive wealth imbalance, and political uncertainty? Participation in learning throughout the lifespan—both within and outside of formal educational institutions—is not only a concept but also a practice, and perhaps a way of life for many adults as they look to learn and grow their personal, community, and occupational capacities.

In facilitating adult learner growth, educators must recommit to teaching with moral courage in these fraught and uncertain times. Some adult educators will say that social justice is not a part of their curriculum, so they cannot connect important foundational values (e.g., human rights, social inclusion) in the classroom. However, as Dianne Ramdeholl and Rusa Jeremic illustrate in chapter 38, if we are educators, then we must take responsibility to make that kind of critical learning space in our pedagogy—regardless of obvious curricular connections. Taking time and making the effort to discuss these and other pressing social matters means being proactive, committed, and dedicated to creating safe spaces both in classrooms and in the broader society. One such pressing matter is the rise of neoliberalism that came through so strongly in several of the chapters.

Neoliberalism in Adult and Continuing Education

Education is no stranger to cutbacks and cutthroats, and education stakeholders cannot assume that they have some protection from neoliberal forces that are affecting other aspects of society. Belzer and Kim (chapter 19) and Rhodes and Schmidt (chapter 20) describe influencing legislative debates about public funding for education and social services. As such funding diminishes, organizational systems are increasingly led into competition with one another, resulting in camps of "winners" and "losers." Neoliberalism sometimes operates under the guise of equity so that it is shielded from critique and robust evaluation of its impacts. From an equity standpoint, most adult educators would agree that programs should be accessible to everyone who desires to learn. It is hard to imagine how access will be possible to everyone where neoliberal policies predominate and where "best practices" are only those that yield the largest return on investment (e.g., improved test scores; cost-efficient training that leads to ever-higher worker productivity; see Deggs & Boeren, chapter 10). Yet, for many adult educators, there are no "best practices," but only a rich array of *different* practices designed to meet the needs of adult learners who have diverse characteristics, circumstances, and abilities, and have important personal, educational, and occupational goals.

In recent years, questions about the purposes and skepticism about the value of higher education have arisen among certain segments of the population. Further contributing to such views are neoliberal influences regarding public obligations to fund education and social welfare programs (see Prins et al., chapter 21; Shan & Guo, chapter 46; Strawn, chapter 37). Education, as a result, becomes increasingly viewed as a private rather than a public good, or a "choice" rather than a "right." As the chapters illustrate, devaluing or shifting the role of higher education or devaluing adult education programs within higher education is a dangerous move. Research, innovation, and critical thinking must continue so that we do not repeat the harms of the past, become unable to challenge new waves of oppression, or respond to existential threats such as climate change, social isolation, or nuclear proliferation.

At the national policy level, the current U.S. Secretary of Education has shown little knowledge of, or interest in, adult education policy, programs, and practices. Thus, there has been little policy leadership regarding how to best promote adult and continuing education as a vital conduit to greater employment opportunities, improved workplace training, and increased worker productivity. Given this federal retreat from adult and continuing education policy development, it has been left to U.S. states to take the lead in advocating for adult education as a remedy. Several states, including Ohio, Kentucky, and Alabama, have established a single administrative agency for adult and community college, including vocational education.

All of these contemporary political, economic, and societal issues provide a context and a backdrop for the consideration of adult and continuing education and how the field might respond and offer leadership and potential solutions. Without question, adult and continuing education must be prepared to lead the way in educating adults to become informed, globally connected, capable citizens who are knowledgeable, skilled, and open and adaptive to change and uncertainty. Collaboration across borders and across cultures needs to be foundational in the field, so that we can learn new approaches, orientations, and perspectives.

Adult and Continuing Education as Collaborative Practice

Adult and continuing education can only grow, prosper, and have meaningful social and economic impacts if its many and varied professional organizations join forces, work to create a unified and overarching identity (inclusive of all subfields, such as military education, religious education, or literacy education), develop cohesive and sustained public relations campaigns, and become a strong voice in public policy at the local, regional, and national levels (see Roumell & Martin, chapter 4). The challenge, as some would see it, is that the adult educators that deliver or facilitate educational content work within many distinct fields (e.g., see Belzer & Kim, chapter 19; Carr-Chellman et al., chapter 31; Coady, chapter 27), and the general public does not know what "adult and continuing education" actually does for different populations of adults (e.g., see Bowman & Bohonos, chapter 43 or Misawa & McGill, chapter 39). This lack of a public understanding of adult education makes it easy for legislatures to deny funding and for higher education administrators to close academic programs, leaving program administrators and practitioners to struggle simply to maintain the status quo. As Roumell and Martin observe in chapter 4, the field of adult and continuing education lacks any "formal architecture" (p. 44, this volume) that incorporates the various adult education stakeholders into a comprehensive domain for policy advocacy. The next decade must see adult and continuing education evolving to become a unified profession that can advocate on behalf of its varied fields, myriad stakeholders, and adult learners.

The American Medical Association (AMA) offers a compelling—if imperfect—example for the field. The AMA is a national professional organization consisting of member physicians that work in distinct areas of medicine (e.g., obstetrics, orthopedics, oncology) and participate in distinct roles—as researchers, as practitioners, and as administrators. As a field, medicine did not always enjoy the positive reputation that it holds today among the public (Starr, 1984). Medicine has endured periodic national scandals (from the Tuskegee Medical Study to Henrietta Lacks); occasionally, members of the AMA have been found to have violated ethical standards or engaged in fraud and some have been appropriately sanctioned (i.e., loss of medical license or, less often, prison). Yet, despite these and other ethical concerns, the AMA, as a professional association, has been a strong voice in the public arena for many decades and has contributed to the generally high regard for the medical profession that is observed today. While adult and education may not be life-saving, it is certainly a *life-changing* endeavor for those who participate in its various forms—and this is clearly a cause for rallying.

To increase its visibility and reputation, adult and continuing education needs to form new professional, organizational, and institutional partnerships that cross-fertilize disciplines, orientations, and perspectives. Prioritizing adult education as a shared and important contributor (and, sometimes, leader) in social change establishes a seat at the interdisciplinary table for adult education theorists and practitioners. How do subfields such as health professions education (see Daley & Cervero, chapter 26), prison education (see Chlup, chapter 22), or military education (see Hampson & Taber, chapter 24) interact with and influence one another? How should they do so—and to what ends? What are their linkages to other professions and their contributions to social and economic growth? How might initiatives in international development (see Zarestky et al., chapter 25) and peace education (see Neustaeter & Senehi, chapter 35) be joined to improve the living conditions and educational and economic opportunities for individuals? If adult education needs to be decolonized (as suggested by Hanson & Jaffe, chapter 36), then how can more Indigenous peoples and perspectives be involved and included to minimize the corrosive effects of colonialism? When viewing adult and continuing education foremost as a collaborative practice, we begin to realize more fully the *life-changing* potential of the field.

A number of the handbook's chapters reveal how past theory and practices continue to influence current approaches in adult and continuing education (e.g., see Bowling & Henschke, chapter 16). Although it is important to be mindful of the past, we cannot glue ourselves to history. Nor can we rest upon the many accomplishments of the field as a form of self-celebration. Critical reflection creates room for critique, generates dialogue, and inspires innovation. However, where we can become trapped as a field is when we try to maintain a historical tradition in a different and rapidly evolving era or conceptualize a positive utopia through lofty ideas. For example, Elizabeth Ellsworth (1992) describes critical pedagogy as a "repressive myth that perpetuates relations of domination" (p. 91). She delivers us a useful caution: We should not assume that our theoretical or practical advancements will be entirely inclusive or meaningful to everyone. Though we want to honor our past achievements, tradition might find itself running at odds with new approaches, identities, theorizing, and equities that were not yet conceived or part of the discussion in even the recent past. We need to view the past as having some useful—and not so useful—legacies if we are going to move forward. The next decade may bring to light some of the tensions noted here, as well as some direction.

As Amy D. Rose noted in her discussion of the history of adult and continuing education (chapter 2), studies examining the field's history are rare. Moreover, adult education scholars in the 19th and beginning of the 20th centuries did not agree about the boundaries of the field as it was emerging—a problem that persists today. For example, many scholars of adult basic education (ABE) share more in common with scholars in the field of reading (from the K–12 arena) or in measurement (i.e., within educational psychology) than with the adult education scholars who focus on adult learning theory or critical theory. One result is that important work may be marginalized or ignored and significant opportunities for improving both scholarship and practice may be lost or slowed.

While these ongoing discussions and debates are important, what we noticed is that the scholarship in the field is devoid of topics that are increasingly being studied in American colleges and universities such as, for example, data analytics and artificial intelligence, health-care innovation, and knowledge management. We can imagine that scholarly collaborations with theoreticians, researchers, and scientists within these and other emerging disciplines can establish a foundation for increased scholarly growth within the adult education profession. Certainly, an understanding of adult learning, and of the systems and the institutions that support learning is terrain that adult educators know well and would be vital knowledge to investigators who are not only studying but also teaching the adult students who now pursue degrees and training in these new scientific, technical, and health-related fields. We urge greater collaboration and cross-fertilization of the research "silos" in both adult education and the applied social sciences that is likely to benefit investigators in both arenas. Our readings of the assembled chapters assure us that there are tremendous opportunities for new directions in adult education theory and practice. But we must be ready and willing to embrace these opportunities.

Moving Forward in the Field of Adult and Continuing Education

In light of our review of the chapters submitted for this handbook, and on our reading of the extant literature of the chapters, we provide a few suggestions for future scholars and students working within adult and continuing education. We offer these ideas for new scholarly directions as merely examples—and which are hardly exhaustive of the many potentially new lines of theorizing and investigation—of the work that the field might undertake. We also point to areas where new scholarship could yield greater attention to adult and continuing education, lead to more extensive interdisciplinary work and cross-fertilization of theoretical innovations, increase the field's visibility and impact, and contribute to improved instructional practices and adult learner outcomes. Our goal with these suggestions is to consider a broader "re-view" of the field and to consider where stronger interventions and participation of researchers, educators, and others can take place.

Strengthening Adult and Continuing Education Scholarship

The different sections of the handbook provide evidence that, independently, scholars have continued to advance core theories in the field (e.g., Bowling & Henschke, chapter 16), as well as to expand the use of critical theory through case studies (e.g., Neustaeter & Senehi, chapter 35; Walker & Butterwick, chapter 34). Adult education scholars' work is often empirical in orientation, leading to testable methods for teaching, for example, subjects such as reading or numeracy for adults. Other empirical questions also loom for ABE, including the issue of the return on investment for basic literacy instruction for adult learners, as illustrated by Belzer and Kim (chapter 19).

Adult and continuing education scholars may wish to expand on their applications of various research methods. One possible direction is through arts-based and participatory research methods so that adult learners and adult learning can be researched in ways that appeal to a wider audience of "storytellers" and can appeal to audiences who may wish to achieve a more creative understanding of human experiences.

In contrast to arts-based and participatory research methods, there can also be stronger utilization of quantitative (i.e., statistical) methods for a variety of reasons. First, scholarship in many education subdisciplines is focused on the application of quantitative methods. Often, the knowledge developed and applied in these subfields feeds into adult education theory and practice. Thus, this kind of quantitatively oriented scholarship needs to be understood and valued in adult and continuing education graduate programs, journals, and associations. Second, the federal government focuses much of its research funding toward projects that employ quantitative methods, thereby having a profound effect on the methods used in education research. Scholars in adult education risk losing opportunities to engage with government and the private sector and may be ceding important questions to other fields that emphasize statistical methods, such as economics and psychology. That said, it is completely plausible that adult education can function as a form of activism against government funding schemes and explore quantitative approaches within and by community organizations. The point being is that, without methodological adaptation and plurality, adult and continuing education risks having specializations in one methodology (qualitative), but less developed insights into others.

Nontraditional Students in Higher Education

Colleges and universities are increasingly becoming significant sites for adult education scholarship—in large part due to demographic shifts. With fewer U.S. high school graduates on the horizon, higher education institutions will need to attract nontraditional (i.e., older) adult learners to remain viable, both financially and politically (see Bergman, chapter 28 for further discussion). In all of postsecondary education, nontraditional students make up nearly three quarters (71%) of all enrolled students (U.S. Department of Education, 2019). These percentages are expected to significantly increase over the next decade. There is a need to develop a better corpus of scholarship on topics as diverse as the following: learning theories are useful for understanding adult learning? How are higher education institutions changing in response to the surge of adult students? What academic programs are providing better learning and employment outcomes for adults in college? Adult education scholars can offer much to the policy debates taking place in higher education.

Alternative Education Programs

Before college, more than 400,000 people enter high school every year but do not earn a diploma. Also, many incarcerated persons in U.S. prisons are high school dropouts (see Chlup, chapter 22). Those adults lacking a high school diploma face a lifetime of diminished employment opportunities, unsteady employment, and low wages. High school equivalency programs enable these adults to earn a diploma through successful completion of the GED test, which is now keyed to the Common Core State Standards (adopted by nearly every U.S. state) and the College and Career Readiness Standards for Adult Education (Pimentel, 2013). School dropouts who have been out of school for many years often struggle to attain the GED certificate. Many have learning and other disabilities that make test-taking difficult without appropriate supports and compensations. In response to these and related concerns, some U.S. states are promoting school-based alternatives, including night schools or online schools that provide more formal instruction to help learners achieve an actual high school diploma and, in some cases, may prepare them for career training or college (see Belzer & Kim, chapter 19, for further information). Increasingly, employers expect to hire people that have some college experience, even for jobs that do not require strong literacy or numeracy skills. Thus, it seems paramount to study these issues from an adult-education perspective. How effective are these alternative programs for increasing the numbers of adults that complete a high school education? And, how can career and technical education be integrated with high school equivalency programs? Hopefully these questions provoke a more nuanced discussion on alternative education as we move forward.

Educational Technology

There is a phenomenal amount of scholarship on educational technology, including the benefits of online or distance education, and challenges that learning outside of a traditional classroom present for adult learners (see Bennett & McWhorter, chapter 18). The field of educational technology tends to be value-neutral, and critical perspectives could strengthen this area. Exploring how marginalized people experience educational technology differently may be a worthwhile endeavor to ensure relevance to content and inclusion of various ages, abilities, and backgrounds. It will be equally important, as the workforce ages and diversifies, to ensure that employers understand how to teach the existing workforce new technology skills. Adult education scholarship is necessary to study how organizations are responding to this challenge and consider planning for resistances to resolving these challenges.

In conclusion, contributors throughout this handbook have offered their perspectives on the critical questions and the associated work needed to address them—work that is essential as the field goes into the next decade and beyond. We do not doubt that incredible opportunities are present for the adult and continuing education field. With an aging population and the increasing importance of education and training to economic development and personal fulfillment, adult and continuing education—as a critical contributor to a skilled, knowledgeable, and compassionate citizenry—can and must be essential to conversations occurring within and across academic, political, business, and community spaces. This handbook, like its predecessors, has provided a basis for both action and scholarship.

References

Ellsworth, E. (1992). Why doesn't this feel empowering?: Working through the repressive myths of critical pedagogy. In C. Luke & J. Gore (Eds.), *Feminisms and critical pedagogy* (pp. 90–119). Routledge.

Freire, P. (1985). Reading the world and reading the word: An interview with Paulo Freire. *Language Arts, 62*(1), 15–21.

Pimentel, S. (2013). *College and career readiness standards for adult education*. Office of Vocational and Adult Education. U.S. Department of Education.

Starr, P. (1984). *The social transformation of American medicine: The rise of a sovereign profession and the making of a vast industry*. Basic Books.

U.S. Department of Education, National Center for Education Statistics (2019, May). *Characteristics of postsecondary students*. IES NCES. https://nces.ed.gov/programs/coe/indicator_csb.asp

Epilogue

Considerations of the COVID-19 Pandemic and Black Lives Matter

Joshua D. Hawley, Lisa R. Merriweather, M Cecil Smith, Robert C. Mizzi, and Tonette S. Rocco

The 2020 *Handbook of Adult and Continuing Education* is being published during a time that the world faces both immense social and economic transformation and heightened awareness of how one's positionality results in differential impact of the same experience. Since December 2019, the severe acute respiratory syndrome coronavirus 2 (SARS-CoV-2; hereafter COVID-19) pandemic has killed over 500,000 and sickened over 10 million people worldwide (as of July 3, 2020) (Johns Hopkins Coronavirus Resource Center, 2020). The United States alone has had more than 130,000 deaths—a number likely to dramatically increase as the world waits for a vaccine. Black Americans, as well as Native Americans and Latinx, are disproportionately affected by the pandemic (Centers for Disease Control and Prevention, 2020), as well as by the economic decline (Lopez et al., 2020). At the same time that the pandemic gripped the nation, the United States and other nations watched in horror as yet another unarmed Black man was murdered at the hands of those sworn to protect and serve. This recurring phenomenon has uniquely impacted the Black American community. The *Washington Post* (Berman et al., 2020) reports that Blacks are killed by the police using deadly force at higher rates than are Whites. Both George Floyd in Minneapolis on May 25, 2020 and Eric Garner in New York City in 2014 were murdered by police by asphyxiation—cutting off the airway by exerting pressure on the neck. In response, massive protests to systemic racism, specifically the impact of police violence, have erupted across the United States and the world. Recent protests have united people in social activism and have spread across large urban areas, small cities, and towns in the United States to international protests.

The pandemic and the continued devaluation of Black lives are the backdrop for two of the major challenges resulting during this unprecedented time: economic and social disruption. Adult and continuing education has an important role to play in helping the United States and all nations grapple with these challenges. The most direct roles are in expanding the delivery of education and training—people need adult vocational training, community colleges, and literacy and numeracy instruction to build skills that will help them earn a living in the coming years. With 40 million currently unemployed in the United States as a direct consequence of the pandemic, adults need access to state supported training, degrees, and certificates.

Those already employed need access to continuing professional education, especially in areas of bias and culturally responsive training. Military and law enforcement education, for instance, is focused on vocationalism—learning the skills needed to complete their tasks (see Hampson & Taber, chapter 24). Although adult and continuing education has a long and somewhat neglected history in labor, military, and law enforcement education, adult education's social justice sensibilities and practices could help change the direction of police unions. Principles of adult education should be introduced into the training and continuing professional education of law enforcement personnel. Professional training must include a focus on persistent racism and injustice and increased understanding that law enforcement skills and practices are not neutral. For instance, being trained to use a choke hold to restrain a suspect is not an excuse for indiscriminate use of this "tool," nor does the sanctioning of any enforcement tool by police departments mitigate the responsibility of individuals to consider whether or not such a tool is ever necessary or morally correct to use. Racial profiling is another byproduct of the current training. It is used to stop and detain Black men disproportionately compared to any other group (Stanford Open Policing Project, 2020). Adult education can help facilitate an awareness of how organizations such as police forces can better reflect and practice equity, justice, and fairness.

The greater challenge, however, lies in America's unwillingness and inability to appreciate that it has continually failed to honor its social contract with Blacks living in America. At both the individual and societal level, White people—in particular—need to recognize that the social contract with Black Americans has long been broken and understand their culpability resulting from White privilege and engrained White supremacist ideology. Vocational training and education are needed to prepare individuals for 21st-century employment, but these do little to impact hiring practices undergirded by white dominance and anti-Black racism. Black Americans occupy vocational positions with low earning potential and continue to earn less even with advanced degrees and training (Patten, 2016). They continue to be at the bottom in terms of receiving adequate medical care (Taylor, 2019) and continue to lead in arrests and incarcerations (Hinton et al., 2018).

An example of how the health care system mistreats Black and Brown Americans is in a *Newsweek* (Rahman, 2020) story of a Black family who became infected with the coronavirus. The story details how after visiting the grandfather, who would later be diagnosed with the coronavirus, the father and mother developed COVID-19 symptoms. The grandfather's condition worsened, and he was admitted to the hospital. During this same time, the mother and father attempted to get treatment and testing but were refused by several Detroit, Michigan, area hospitals. The grandfather died in the hospital, and the father died within hours of the grandfather at home, in the absence of any medical care. The mother's condition finally received treatment but only after being turned away again from several Detroit area hospitals in spite of health-care providers being aware of documented exposure, presenting with a high fever of 103 degrees, and dry cough. This is all in contrast to a White woman who presented with symptoms of food poisoning and was treated immediately in the very same emergency room that refused the Black mother. Other family members were eventually tested but only after being repeatedly denied in the face of having symptoms consistent with COVID-19, and three family members with confirmed cases, two of whom died. This is not a unique or new story for Black and Brown people. This is a centuries-long, commonplace experience. In the face of such harsh realities, even the best-intentioned efforts fail to afford Black Americans the same level of humanity experienced by White Americans when navigating complex social systems like health care, criminal justice, and education.

These moments are difficult, and we must not ignore that adult education has played a role in the oppression of racialized minorities. For example, the exclusion of DuBois' *Negro Creed* from the Bronze Booklets in the 1930s is largely considered the result of the American Association of Adult Education's conservativism and exercise of White privilege (Cain, 2004). The Atlanta and Harlem "experiments" are another early example in which the education of Black Americans was subjugated to the interests of White America (Guy, 1996). And Sheared and Sissel (2001) exposed how key authoritative texts, known as the Black Book (Jensen, 1964) and Blue Book (Peters & Jarvis, 1991), demonstrated the raced and oppressive nature of adult education. The books, and by extension adult education, were condemned by Sheared and Sissel (2001) as "Eurocentric, racist, gender insensitive, elitist and exclusionary" (p. xi). More contemporarily, we continue to see evidence of the raced and biased nature of adult education through its practices and theory: access to and quality of mentoring for Black Americans in academic and workplace spaces, pervasiveness of Whiteness as the normative experience for learners, formal, informal and nonformal, and anti-Black racism in planning, facilitation, and evaluation of various

EPILOGUE

adult learning experiences such as in museum spaces, in graduate education, and in human resource and organizational development, among others.

These examples of the broken social contract in adult education and society at large present an opportunity for adult and continuing education to play a meaningful role in addressing the deeper, seemingly recalcitrant problems facing society. Addressing systemic racism requires collective action, action that includes support to facilitate community development as well as organizational change. But these actions cannot begin without adult educators reflecting on their complicity in instigating, supporting, and maintaining anti-Black racism. We need to assess how our theories, practices, and policies have historically been and continue to be used in service of inequity and social injustice (Ross-Gordon, 2017). We should ask ourselves: How has adult and continuing education mitigated or perpetuated social inequality?

While we acknowledge the racism and oppression, we also recognize that adult and continuing education has played a role in significant American and, indeed, global transformations. For instance, the national literacy campaigns in the 1950s and 1960s brought millions of adults around the world out of the darkness of illiteracy (Arnove & Graff, 1987). Looking back even further, adult education and training had a significant role in both World War I and II, as the U.S. government provided many soldiers literacy and vocational training (Dorn, 2007; Rose, 1991). Finally, the civil rights movement was assisted by significant adult education institutions such as Highlander in Tennessee, which pioneered education to register Black Americans to vote (Highland Center, 2020). Adult education's history has been punctuated with moments of socially just actions built in particular from interracial cooperative efforts such as antislavery abolition, Highlander, and the civil rights movement. The interracial protests of Floyd's murder are reminiscent of such efforts.

We appreciate and are grateful that our awareness of historic injustice in 2020 is different than 100 years ago or even 1 year ago thanks to the watershed moment catalyzed by COVID-19 and the murder of George Floyd by the police. There is greater awareness that despite 50 years of job training through the U.S. federal government that such funding and effort are never going to change the future of the nation unless we also simultaneously grapple with economic inequality and systemic racism. It will be impossible for cities and states to transform police departments, impact disparities in access to and delivery of health care, and create equitable systems of education among others unless as a society we use tools pioneered by adult educators to ensure that people confront their individual biases and change perspectives (see Barlas et al., 2000; Bozalek & Biersteker, 2010; Rocco & West, 1998). Increasing protections for workers, reducing inequality among adults, dramatically increasing the quality of education, and addressing the historic legacy of slavery and contemporary manifestations of anti-Black racism are all necessary to ensure that we are united as a nation.

We assert that no efforts to deploy adult education for economic justice will be successful without larger changes in society for racial justice. This is our challenge to the adult education community. COVID-19 and the unmasked racialized injustice have laid bare our vulnerabilities as a nation, exposing our weaknesses and spotlighting awareness of the need to do and be better. Ten years from now when the 2030 *Handbook of Adult and Continuing Education* is published will we be able to look back and see the change we, as a field, claimed to be, what difference will adult education have made? This can be our moment as a professional field to impact and influence the direction of our nation but only if it propels us to approach our work differently, with greater intentionality, with dogged determination to make adult education count for the common good which means good for all, not just for the privileged few. The 2020 *Handbook of Adult and Continuing Education* is the benchmark against which we should check our progress over the ensuing decade. This epilogue should be the foreword for 2030. It represents where we are now but not where we will be if we commit our practice, theory and policy to the project of racial justice. The question is will we?

Peace and Justice.

References

Arnove, R. F., & Graff, H. J. (1987). *National literacy campaigns: Historical and comparative perspectives.* Plenum Press.

Barlas, C., Kasl, E., Kyle, R., MacLeod, A., Paxton, D., Rosenwasser, P., & Sartor, L. (2000). Learning to unlearn white supremacist consciousness. In *Proceedings of the 41st annual Adult Education Research conference* (pp. 26–30). Adult Education Research Conference.

Berman, M., Sullivan, J., Tate, J., & Jenkins, J. (2020, June 8). Protests spread over police shootings. Police promised reforms. Every year, they still shoot and kill nearly 1,000 people. *Washington Post.* https://www.washingtonpost.com/investigations/protests-spread-over-police-shootings-police-promised-reforms-every-year-they-still-shoot-nearly-1000-people/2020/06/08/5c204f0c-a67c-11ea-b473-04905b1af82b_story.html

Bozalek, V., & Biersteker, L. (2010). Exploring power and privilege using participatory learning and action techniques. *Social Work Education, 29*(5), 551–572. https://doi.org/10.1080/02615470903193785

Cain, R. (2004). *Alain Leroy Locke: Race, culture, and the education of African American adults.* Rodopi.

Centers for Disease Control and Prevention. (2020). *COVID-19 in racial and ethnic minority groups.* https://www.cdc.gov/coronavirus/2019-ncov/need-extra-precautions/racial-ethnic-minorities.html

Dorn, R. D. (2007). *Investing in human capital the origins of federal job training programs, 1900 to 1945.* [Unpublished doctoral dissertation]. Ohio State University.

Guy, T. (1996). Alain Locke and the AAAE Movement: Cultural pluralism and Negro adult education. *Adult Education Quarterly, 46*(4), 209–223. http://doi.org/10.1177/074171369604600403

Highland Center (2020, June 30). *Our history.* https://www.highlandercenter.org/our-history-timeline/

Hinton, E., Henderson, L., & Reed, C. (2018). *An unjust burden: The disparate treatment of Black Americans in the criminal justice system.* Vera Institute of Justice. https://www.vera.org/downloads/publications/for-the-record-unjust-burden-racial-disparities.pdf

Jensen, G. (1964). *Adult education: Outlines of an emerging field of university study.* Adult Education Association.

John Hopkins Coronavirus Resource Center (2020). *COVID-19 case tracker.* Retrieved July 3, 2020, from https://coronavirus.jhu.edu/

Lopez, M. H., Rainie, L., & Budiman, A. (2020). *Financial and health impacts of COVID-19 vary widely by race and ethnicity.* Pew Research Center. https://www.pewresearch.org/fact-tank/2020/05/05/financial-and-health-impacts-of-covid-19-vary-widely-by-race-and-ethnicity/

Patten, E. (2016). *Racial, gender wage gaps persist in U.S. despite some progress.* Pew Research Center. https://www.pewresearch.org/fact-tank/2016/07/01/racial-gender-wage-gaps-persist-in-u-s-despite-some-progress/

Peters, J., & Jarvis, P. (1991). *Adult education: Evolution and achievements in a developing field of study.* Jossey-Bass.

Rahman, K. (2020, April 24). Michigan man died after being repeatedly denied test just hours after his father died of coronavirus, family say. *Newsweek.* https://www.newsweek.com/michigan-man-dies-coronavirus-repeatedly-turned-away-1499818

Rocco, T. S., & West, G. W. (1998). Deconstructing privilege: An examination of privilege in adult education. *Adult Education Quarterly, 48*(3), 171–184. https://doi.org/10.1177/074171369804800304

Rose, A. D. (1991). Preparing for veterans: Higher education and the efforts to accredit the learning of World War II servicemen and women. *Adult Education Quarterly, 42*(1), 30–45. https://doi.org/10.1177/074171369104200103

Ross-Gordon, J. (2017). Racing the field of adult education—Making the invisible visible. *PAACE Journal of Lifelong Learning, 26,* 55–22

Sheared, V., & Sissel, P. (Eds.) (2001). *Making space: Merging theory and practice in adult education.* Bergin & Garvey.

Stanford Open Policing Project (2020, June 30). *The open policing project.* https://openpolicing.stanford.edu/

Taylor, J. (2019). *Racism, inequality, and health care for African Americans.* The Century Foundation. https://tcf.org/content/report/racism-inequality-health-care-african-americans/?agreed=1

Editors

Joshua D. Hawley is a professor in the John Glenn College of Public Affairs at The Ohio State University. He is also associate director for the Center of Human Resource Research and director of the Ohio Education Research Center. He received his EdD and EdM from the Harvard Graduate School of Education and MA and BA in history and Asian studies from the University of Wisconsin–Madison.

Lisa R. Merriweather is an associate professor of adult education at the University of North Carolina, Charlotte, and cofounder and senior editor of *Dialogues in Social Justice: An Adult Education Journal*. She received her PhD in adult education with a graduate certificate in qualitative inquiry from the University of Georgia in 2004. Her research interests include anti-Black racism and race pedagogy; equity and social justice in adult education; and mentoring in doctoral education. Merriweather is dedicated to the project of communalism and is guided by the spirits of Sankofa and Ubuntu that provide the ideological culturally informed grounding for the work in which she engages.

Robert C. Mizzi is an associate professor and Canada Research Chair in queer, community, and diversity education in the Faculty of Education at the University of Manitoba, Canada. He is also former president of the Canadian Association for the Study of Adult Education and the current editor-in-chief of the *Canadian Journal for the Study of Adult Education*. He has worked in over 15 countries as a researcher or educator, has authored over 50 articles on his research, and has published five books. His research in adult education includes topics relating to sexual and gender diversity, transnational identities and work, and social justice.

Tonette S. Rocco serves as a professor in adult education and human resource development at Florida International University in Miami, Florida. She is a Houle Scholar; member of the 2016 class of the International Adult and Continuing Education Hall of Fame; 2016 Outstanding HRD Scholar; and recipient of more than 25 awards for scholarship, mentoring, and service. Her other books include *Challenging the Parameters of Adult Education: John Ohliger and the Quest for Social Democracy* (with Grace; Jossey-Bass, 2009); *Handbook of Scholarly Writing and Publishing* (with Hatcher, Jossey-Bass, 2011); *Handbook of Human Resource Development* (with Chalofsky and Morris, Wiley, 2014); *The Routledge Companion to Human Resource Development* (with Poell and Roth, Routledge, 2014); and *Disrupting Adult and Community Education: Teaching, Working, and Learning in the Periphery* (with Mizzi & Shore, SUNY, 2016). She is editor-in-chief of *New Horizons in Adult Education and Human Resource Development*.

M Cecil Smith is dean of the new School of Education at Southern Illinois University Carbondale. He has held previous academic and administrative appointments at West Virginia University and Northern Illinois University. In addition to publications in several leading journals in education, he has edited books on reading, adult literacy, adult learning and development, and teaching methods for educational psychology. He earned a PhD in educational psychology from the University of Wisconsin–Madison.

Contributors

Mary V. Alfred is professor of adult education at Texas A&M University. Her research interests include international adult education; sociocultural contexts of migration and adult learning; and issues of equity, inclusion, and social justice in education and the workplace. In 2016 she was inducted into the International Adult and Continuing Education Hall of Fame.

Geleana D. Alston, associate professor in the Department of Leadership Studies and Adult Education at North Carolina A&T State University, is a former editor for *Adult Learning*, former editorial assistant and the inaugural social media coordinator for *Adult Education Quarterly*, and a recipient of the CPAE Early Career Award.

Alisa Belzer is a professor at Rutgers University Graduate School of Education and program coordinator for Rutgers University's online master of education in adult and continuing education program. Prior to that, she was an adult literacy practitioner and professional development facilitator. Currently she coedits *Adult Literacy Education: The International Journal of Literacy, Language, and Numeracy*.

Elisabeth E. Bennett, PhD, is associate teaching professor of organizational leadership studies at Northeastern University. Her research includes virtual human resource development, technology, knowledge forms, organizational culture, and informal learning. Bennett is a University of Georgia Circle of 50 honouree and serves on editorial boards for *Adult Education Quarterly*, *Advances in Developing Human Resources*, *Human Resource Development Quarterly*, and *New Horizons in Adult Education and Human Resource Development*.

Matt Bergman is an assistant professor at the University of Louisville. His research is focused on adult learner persistence, prior learning assessment, and degree completion programs. His work is highlighted in international media outlets including the *Wall Street Journal*, the *Washington Post*, *The Chronicle of Higher Education*, and *TIME*.

Laura L. Bierema is a professor in the University of Georgia, College of Education's Adult Learning, Leadership, and Organization Development program. Bierema holds both bachelor's and master's degrees from Michigan State University and a doctorate in adult education from the University of Georgia. She has published over 60 articles and 7 books.

Ellen Boeren, professor at the University of Glasgow, United Kingdom, has published on participation in postcompulsory education and won the 2017 Cyril O. Houle Award for Outstanding Contribution to Adult Education for her book *Lifelong Learning Participation in a Changing Policy Context: An Interdisciplinary Theory* (Palgrave MacMillan, 2016). She was one of the coeditors of UNESCO's fourth *Global Report on Adult Learning and Education* (GRALE 4) and is a coeditor of *Adult Education Quarterly*.

Jeremy Bohonos is an assistant professor of adult education at Texas State University and an assistant editor for *New Horizons in Adult Education and Human Resource Development*. His research focuses on organizational (in)justice with a special emphasis on race and racism in the workforce.

Marcie Boucouvalas, professor emerita of human development at Virginia Tech, serves as vice president for North America to the International Council for Adult Education, immediate-past director of the Commission for International Adult Education, and editor of *Journal of Transpersonal Psychology*. A Fulbright scholar, she was inducted into the Adult and Continuing Education Hall of Fame in 2003.

Jerry Bowling is a professor of Christian education and formation at Harding University. He received a PhD and MDiv from Southern Baptist Theological Seminary in curriculum, teaching, and adult education and an MA in religion from Harding School of Theology.

Lorenzo Bowman, JD, PhD, is currently a professor of business and management at the Keller Graduate School of Management/DeVry University in Atlanta, Georgia. He has taught in the adult education program at the University of Georgia and the educational psychology program at Georgia State University. He is the author of numerous journal articles, conference papers, and book chapters on race, critical race theory, and LGBTQ issues in adult education.

Stephen D. Brookfield is the John Ireland Endowed Chair and Distinguished University Professor at the University of St. Thomas, Minneapolis–St. Paul. He has published 19 books on adult learning, teaching, critical thinking, discussion methods, critical theory, and teaching race, six of which have won the Cyril O. Houle World Award for Literature in Adult Education.

Jake Burdick is an assistant professor in curriculum studies at Purdue University. His research interests include public and popular sites of education, activist studies, and community knowledge and perceptions of education. Burdick coedited *The New Henry Giroux Reader: The Role of the Public Intellectual in a Time of Tyranny* (with Giroux & Sandlin, Myers Education, 2019), *Problematizing Public Pedagogy* (with Sandlin & O'Malley, Routledge, 2013), and the *Handbook of Public Pedagogy: Education and Learning Beyond Schooling* (with Sandlin & Schultz, Taylor & Francis, 2010), and he has published in *Qualitative Inquiry, Curriculum Inquiry, Review of Research in Education*, and *Review of Educational Research*.

Shauna Butterwick is a professor emeritus at the University of British Columbia where she taught in the Adult Learning and Education program for over 2 decades. Her teaching and research is informed by feminist approaches. Her inquiries have focused on women's learning in state training programs, community engagement, and activism.

Davin Carr-Chellman is an associate professor of education in the Department of Educational Administration in the School of Education and Health Sciences at the University of Dayton. His research agenda focuses on individual, organizational, and community capacity building, especially within the framework of adult learning and agency.

Ronald M. Cervero is a professor in the School of Medicine's Graduate Programs in Health Professions Education at the Uniformed Services University of the Health Sciences. He has provided intellectual and organizational leadership for health professions education over the span of his career, with special emphasis on continuing professional development.

Dominique T. Chlup is a Harvard University educated tenured faculty member turned certified life coach. Her career has been spent researching lives on the periphery with a focus on prison education. A lifelong scholar, Chlup now uses her signature methodologies to help her coaching clients achieve their most expansive dreams (dominiquechlup.com).

Carol Clymer is codirector of the ISAL/Goodling Institute at Penn State University. She has more than 40 years of experience implementing and evaluating programs related to workforce development, college access, adult education, and family literacy. She has made numerous presentations and published extensively.

Maureen Coady is an associate professor of adult education and chair of the Faculty of Education at St. Francis Xavier University in Antigonish, Nova Scotia, Canada. Her research focuses on health and learning and all aspects of professional learning including lifelong continuing professional education.

Royce Ann Collins is an associate professor and graduate program director for adult learning and leadership in the Department of Educational Leadership at Kansas State University. Her research interests focus on the adult learner across the themes of assessment, elearning, and accelerated/intensive program format.

Barbara J. Daley retired from the University of Wisconsin–Milwaukee after 23 years as a professor of adult and continuing education. Her research and teaching focused on how adults develop their thinking and learning, specifically in the context of professional practice.

CONTRIBUTORS

David Deggs is executive director of college access programs and research associate professor of education policy and leadership in the Simmons School of Education at Southern Methodist University. He is responsible for leadership, oversight, and evaluation of programs that support student success and transition at the secondary and postsecondary levels. His research focuses on how social capital is manifested in communities to support or negate educational attainment. He earned his PhD in adult and human resource education at Louisiana State University.

Corey Dolgon is professor of sociology at Stonehill College, past president of the Association for Humanist Sociology, and president-elect of the Society for the Study of Social Problems. Dolgon has published five books, including the award-winning *Kill It to Save It: An Autopsy of Capitalism's Triumph Over Democracy* (Policy Press, 2016) and *The End of the Hamptons: Scenes From the Class Struggle in American Paradise* (NYU Press, 2005). He is also a folksinger who has released three CDs and performed singing lectures on folksongs and social movements (as well as played numerous bar gigs) all around the world. He has recently returned from a Fulbright Award teaching and performing in Austria.

Maren Elfert is lecturer in education and society at King's College London and a 2018 National Academy of Education/Spencer Postdoctoral Fellow. Her research focuses on global governance of education and the influence of international organizations on educational ideas and policies. She is author of *UNESCO's Utopia of Lifelong Learning: An Intellectual History* (Routledge, 2018).

Brian Findsen has worked in adult and continuing education for over 35 years, in his home country of New Zealand and Glasgow, Scotland, from 2004 to 2008. His main research interests include learning in later life, the sociology of adult education, social equity issues, and international adult education. Findsen has (co)written and edited several books, been guest editor for journals of special issues, and published extensively in later-life learning.

Margery B. Ginsberg is a consultant who specializes in instructional improvement through a motivational lens. Recipient of the American Educational Research Association's Relating Research to Practice Award, her books include *Enhancing Adult Motivation to Learn: A Comprehensive Guide for Teaching All Adults* (4th ed., with Wlodkowski, Jossey-Bass, 2017) and *Excited to Learn: Motivation & Culturally Responsive Teaching* (Corwin, 2015).

André P. Grace, PhD, is Canada Research Chair in sexual and gender minority studies (Tier 1) in the Faculty of Education, University of Alberta, Edmonton, Canada. Visit his academic website at www.andrepgrace.com and his community website at chewprojectyeg.org for more information regarding his research, policy work, and advocacy.

Robin S. Grenier is an associate professor of adult learning in the Department of Educational Leadership at the University of Connecticut. She conducts research, writes, and presents on informal and experiential learning and learning in cultural institutions and works with graduate students, faculty, and organizations as a qualitative methodologist.

Janet Groen is the associate dean of graduate programs and professor of adult learning in the Werklund School of Education at the University of Calgary, Canada. Her research and writing focuses on spirituality and transformative learning in multiple contexts, including higher education settings, workplaces, and environmental education programs and contexts.

Shibao Guo is professor in the Werklund School of Education at the University of Calgary. He specializes in adult and lifelong education, comparative and international education, and citizenship and immigration. He has numerous publications including books, journal articles, and book chapters. His latest book is *Immigration, Racial and Ethnic Studies in 150 Years of Canada: Retrospects and Prospects* (Brill/Sense, 2018).

Sarah Cote Hampson is an assistant professor in the School of Interdisciplinary Arts and Sciences at the University of Washington Tacoma. Her work includes *The Balance Gap: Working Mothers and the Limits of the Law* (Stanford University Press, 2017) and *Mothers, Military, and Society* (with Udi Lebel and Nancy Taber, Demeter Press, 2018).

Catherine A. Hansman, professor and director of the MEd in health professions education at Cleveland State University, is a recipient of the Cyril O. Houle Emerging Scholar in Adult and Continuing Education Scholarship, a recipient of the CSU Distinguished Faculty Research Award, and a member of the International Adult and Continuing Education Hall of Fame.

Cindy Hanson is a professor of sociology at the University of Regina, Canada, and past director of the Adult Education, Community Engagement, and Human Resource Development Unit. Her scholarship and activism is community-based, and she specializes in nonformal, feminist, and Indigenous learning. She is the president elect of the Canadian Association for the Study of Adult Education (CASAE) and past president of the Canadian Research Institute for the Advancement of Women.

John A. Henschke, EdD, is emeritus professor of andragogy at Lindenwood University; was 2014 and 2015 Board Chair International Adult, Continuing Education Hall of Fame; has researched/tested/facilitated andragogy in the United States and 19 countries since 1970; and has developed and Cronbach Alpha validated three times his andragogical Modified Instructional Perspectives Inventory, which was used in 30 completed dissertations.

Lilian H. Hill is professor of adult education at the University of Southern Mississippi. Her research interests are in adult health learning, professional education, and assessment and evaluation. Hill served on the assessment committees of two universities, and her past administrative roles have involved assessment, evaluation, and accreditation responsibilities.

JoAnn Jaffe is professor of sociology and social studies at the University of Regina, Saskatchewan, Canada. As an educator, researcher, and activist who uses adult education approaches in all domains, Jaffe works on questions of rural development, environment, agri-food systems and practices, and local/Indigenous knowledge. She is past-president of the North American Rural Sociological Society.

Rusa Jeremic is a professor and researcher at a local city college in Toronto, Canada. She teaches community organizing, human rights, and social movement building. She is a long-time activist who is currently completing her PhD in social justice education at the University of Toronto/OISE.

Kaela Jubas is an associate professor in adult learning at the University of Calgary, focused on consumption, social movement, and work-related learning, and feminist/critical gender studies. Jubas's current projects explore popular culture in professional education and female students' learning from #MeToo about professional identity and opportunities. Recent publications include *Equity and Internationalization on Campus: Intersecting or Colliding Discourses for LGBTQ People?* (Brill, 2018) and *Popular Culture as Pedagogy* (with Taber & Brown, Sense, 2015).

Anna Kaiper-Marquez is the associate director and assistant teaching professor of the Institute for the Study of Adult Literacy and the Goodling Institute for Research in Family Literacy at Penn State University. Her research interests include adult and family literacy, English language learning, and qualitative methodologies in national and international contexts.

Colleen Kawalilak is the associate dean international, professor, and chair of adult learning in the Werklund School of Education, University of Calgary, Canada. Her research spans adult learning, comparative education, cross/intercultural awareness and responsiveness, and professional learning communities. Qualitative methodologies that include narrative and autoethnography inform her research.

Jeounghee Kim is an associate professor at the Rutgers School of Social Work with research interests in policy analyses and low-wage labor market issues. She is currently writing about socioeconomic returns on investment in adult basic education with Alisa Belzer and the economic consequences of nonstandard and informal employment for low-skilled direct care workers.

Michael Kroth is professor of education at the University of Idaho. He has written or coauthored six books, including *Transforming Work: The Five Keys to Achieving Trust, Commitment, and Passion in the Workplace* (with Boverie, Basic Books, 2001); *Managing the Mobile Workforce: Leading, Building, and Sustaining Virtual Teams* (with Clemons, McGraw-Hill, 2010); and *Stories of Transformative Learning* (with Cranton, Sense Publishers, 2014).

Kathy D. Lohr, EdD, is a teaching assistant professor at East Carolina University with more than a decade of instructing graduate coursework in adult education.

Her research is on identity development and resilience through autobiographical narratives. She has facilitated a monthly life-story writing group through a lifelong learning institute for the past 12 years. Lohr is a consulting editor for *Adult Learning* and presents on formal and informal writing as learning.

Henriette Lundgren is an international scholar-practitioner in the human resource development (HRD) field with an interest in adult education, organizational psychology, and talent management. Educated in the Netherlands, Italy, and Germany, Lundgren holds a PhD in human resource studies from Tilburg University. Lundgren publishes regularly in workplace learning and HRD journals.

Elaine Manglitz worked in the field of public education for 30 years in K–12 and higher education settings before retiring in August 2018 as vice president for student affairs at Clayton State University. Manglitz's scholarly interests include research and writing on facilitating effective cross-racial dialogues in educational settings, White privilege, and other similar topics.

Larry G. Martin is professor emeritus of adult and continuing education leadership at the University of Wisconsin-Milwaukee. An editor of eight books and the author of numerous articles and book chapters, he was a 2015 inductee into the International Adult and Continuing Education Hall of Fame.

Craig M. McGill is an assistant professor at Kansas State University. He holds a doctorate in adult education and human resource development from Florida International University. His research agenda is focused on social justice, queer studies, and the professionalization of academic advising.

Rochell R. McWhorter is an associate professor of human resource development (HRD) in the Soules College of Business at The University of Texas at Tyler. Her passion for emerging technologies includes virtual HRD, visual social media, augmented and virtual reality, cybersecurity, and artificial intelligence. Additionally, she is a champion of eservice-learning.

Mitsunori Misawa is an associate professor and associate department head of the Department of Educational Psychology and Counseling at the University of Tennessee, Knoxville. His areas of scholarship include social justice, adult bullying in academia and at work, context-oriented learning, qualitative research, professionalism, and transformative education.

Vivian W. Mott, PhD, is professor emerita and former associate dean in the College of Education at East Carolina University in Greenville, North Carolina. Mott holds a PhD from The University of Georgia and is a Cyril O. Houle Research Scholar (UGA) and Fellow of the Institute of American Studies in Salzburg, Austria.

Robin Neustaeter is an assistant professor in adult education at St. Francis Xavier University and program teaching staff at the Coady International Institute in Antigonish, Canada. Her teaching and research focus on adult education, conflict, peace, and community development learning, particularly in regard to women.

Margaret Becker Patterson is a senior researcher with Research Allies for Lifelong Learning near Washington DC (www.researchallies.org). She partners with nonprofit organizations, postsecondary institutions, and state agencies to apply research that supports adult educators and learners. She administered and taught in adult education in Nebraska, Nevada, and Kansas and presents extensively throughout the United States.

Rob F. Poell is a professor of human resource development (HRD) at Tilburg University, the Netherlands. His key area of expertise within HRD is workplace learning, focusing especially on how employees organize their own learning at work, and how organizations attempt to influence this. His work appears in all four AHRD journals as well as other human resource and adult education–related international journals.

Esther Prins is a professor in the lifelong learning and adult education program at Penn State. She serves as codirector of the Goodling Institute for Research in Family Literacy and the Institute for the Study of Adult Literacy. Her research focuses on critical and sociocultural approaches to adult and family literacy.

Greg Procknow is an independent scholar who has published two books and articles in top journals in human resource development, adult education, and qualitative methods. His work focuses on mad studies, cultural pedagogy, and recruitment and training. Procknow is a peer support worker with Mood Disorders Association of Ontario.

Allan Quigley, now semiretired, was professor of adult education at St. Francis Xavier University, Nova Scotia, Canada, for 14 years. He was on faculty at Penn State before that and a public servant with the Saskatchewan government and colleges in Saskatchewan and Alberta earlier. His primary area of research is adult literacy.

Dianne Ramdeholl is an associate professor of adult education at SUNY Empire State College in NYC. Before that, she was a grassroots community-based adult literacy practitioner. Committed to adult education for democratic social change and justice centered practice/research, her work has focused on developing educational projects with marginalized populations.

Thomas G. Reio Jr. is professor of adult education and human resource development at Florida International University. Reio earned his PhD in adult and continuing education from Virginia Tech University. He has served as editor or coeditor of *New Horizons in Adult Education and Human Resource Development* and *Human Resource Development Review*. He is currently editor of *Human Resource Development Quarterly*.

Christy Rhodes is an assistant professor of adult education at East Carolina University. She previously taught adult English language learners in Florida and the United Arab Emirates. Her scholarship centers on the role of cultural identity in learning and culturally inclusive teaching. She is an active member of AAACE.

Carol Rogers-Shaw, PhD, graduated from Pennsylvania State University with a degree in lifelong learning and adult education. Her research interests include expanding access and inclusion in higher education and lifelong learning for learners with disabilities (stigma, disclosure, identity development), distance education, universal design for learning, profound learning, and graduate study.

Amy D. Rose is professor emerita of adult education at Northern Illinois University. She writes on history and policy issues in adult education. She coedited the *Handbook of Adult Continuing Education* (with Kasworm & Ross-Gordon, 2010, SAGE); coauthored *Professional Foundations of Adult and Continuing Education* (with Kasworm & Ross-Gordon, Wiley, 2017); coedited *Adult Education Quarterly*; and currently coedits *Adult Literacy Education: The International Journal of Literacy, Language, and Numeracy*.

Reuben Roth is an associate professor in the workplace and labour studies program in the School of Northern and Community Studies at Laurentian University, Canada. A former assembly worker at General Motors of Canada in Oshawa, Ontario, he has written about work-related topics including labor education, occupational health and safety, and working-class consciousness.

Jovita M. Ross-Gordon is professor emeritus of adult, professional, and community education at Texas State University and has focused on adult/higher education and on diversity and equity as related to race, gender, and (dis)ability. She was inducted into the International Adult and Continuing Education Hall of Fame and received the AAACE Cyril A. Houle Award with Amy D. Rose and Carol Kasworm for their publication, *Foundations of Adult and Continuing Education* (Wiley, 2017). She serves as coeditor-in-chief of *New Directions for Adult and Continuing Education* (Wiley).

Elizabeth A. Roumell is an associate professor and program leader of adult education at Texas A&M University. Roumell teaches graduate courses in adult learning, teaching methods for adults, globalization and social justice, qualitative research, feminist pedagogy, and evaluation research. Her research interests include identity development, distance learning, and policy analysis.

Jennifer A. Sandlin is a professor in the School of Social Transformation, Arizona State University (ASU). Focused on intersections of education, learning, and consumption, she is exploring The Walt Disney Corporation's globalized pedagogical function. She coedits the *Journal of Curriculum and Pedagogy* and recently published *Paranoid Pedagogies: Education, Culture, and Paranoia* (with Wallin, Palgrave/MacMillan, 2018) and *The New Henry Giroux Reader: The Role of the Public Intellectual in a Time of Tyranny* (with Burdick & Giroux, Myers Education, 2019). She received ASU's College of Liberal Arts Zebulon Pearce Teaching Award in 2018.

CONTRIBUTORS

Clea A. Schmidt is a professor of teaching English as an additional language at the University of Manitoba. She has taught English language learners in Canada, Korea, and Nepal and has provided teacher development in the United States, Canada, Europe, and South America. Her scholarship includes a focus on teacher development and intersections of diversity.

Steven W. Schmidt is professor of adult education and the coordinator of the Adult Education Program in the College of Education at East Carolina University, in Greenville, North Carolina. He served as president of AAACE in 2014 and is currently a member of the AAACE Board of Directors.

Daniel Schugurensky is a full professor at Arizona State University with a joint appointment in the School of Public Affairs and the School of Social Transformation. He is also the director of the Program in Social and Cultural Pedagogy. His areas of interest include adult education, community development and participatory democracy.

Leodis Scott, EdD, is assistant professor of educational leadership at DePaul University, Chicago; adjunct professor of quantitative research methods at Teachers College, Columbia University, New York; and researcher of learning cities and lifelong learning policy at LearnLong Institute. Scott received his doctorate of education in adult learning and leadership from Teachers College, Columbia University.

Ellen Scully-Russ, EdD, is an associate professor and department chair of human and organizational learning at The George Washington University. Her research interest is in the changing nature of work and the implications for adult learning and the structure and distribution of opportunity in the labor market.

Jessica Senehi is associate professor of peace and conflict studies at the University of Manitoba, Winnipeg, Canada. She is coeditor, with Joseph Sobol, of *Storytelling, Self, Society: An Interdisciplinary Journal of Storytelling Studies*. In 2006, she established the Winnipeg International Storytelling Festival: Storytelling on the Path to Peace / *Festival international du conte de Winnipeg: Se raconter une nouvelle histoire paix*.

Hongxia Shan is associate professor in the Department of Educational Studies at the University of British Columbia. Her work focuses on im/migrant education and learning, professional learning and knowledge transfer, lifelong learning, politics of skills and competency, and the changing organization of work in the context of globalization and transnationalism.

Thomas J. Sork is a professor in the adult learning and education group at the University of British Columbia. His research and writing focus on program planning, professional ethics, and international collaboration. He received a BSc and MEd from Colorado State University and a PhD from Florida State University.

Julie Strawn is a principal associate at Abt Associates with 30 years of experience in research, policy analysis, and technical assistance on education and training for low-income adults. Strawn has also worked at the Center for Law and Social Policy, the National Governors' Association, the U.S. Department of Health and Human Services, and the U.S. House of Representatives.

Nancy Taber is a professor in the Department of Educational Studies in the Faculty of Education at Brock University. She teaches in the areas of critical adult education and sociocultural learning, with a focus on gender and militarism. Her research explores the ways in which learning, gender, and militarism interact in daily life, popular culture, museums, academic institutions, and military organizations.

Blaire Willson Toso is an independent consultant. Her work focuses on adult and intergenerational literacy and engagement. She supports organizations to effectively realize their goals and initiatives through evaluation, research, professional development, project management, and product development.

Ximena Vidal De Col is a doctoral candidate in human and organizational learning at The George Washington University. Her two main research interests are the integration of our public and shadow selves and the relation between workforce development and adult learning.

Jude Walker is assistant professor in adult learning and education at the University of British Columbia. Coming to adult education initially through the ideas of Paulo Freire, she is interested in understanding both the ways in which adult education can transform individuals and societies, as well as the broader political and policy landscape within which adult learning and education takes place.

Pierre Walter works in the adult learning and education graduate program at the University of British Columbia in Vancouver, Canada. He teaches courses on theories of adult learning, environmental education, and education for sustainability. His research focuses on environmental adult education, community-based ecotourism and decolonizing living history museums.

Raymond J. Wlodkowski is professor emeritus in the College for Professional Studies at Regis University in Denver, Colorado. He is a member of the International Adult and Continuing Education Hall of Fame. His work encompasses adult motivation and learning. Among his recent publications is *Living a Motivated Life: A Memoir and Activities* (Brill/Sense, 2019).

Robin Redmon Wright is an associate professor in lifelong learning and adult education at Pennsylvania State University Harrisburg. Employing a critical/feminist perspective on popular culture, socioeconomic class, opportunity, and identity development, she has published in the *International Journal of Lifelong Education*, *International Journal of Qualitative Studies in Education*, and *American Journal of Health Behavior*. With colleagues, Wright received the 2017 Imogene Okes Award for Outstanding Research in Adult Education.

Jeff Zacharakis is professor of adult learning and leadership at Kansas State University (KSU). His research includes history and philosophy of education, adult learning, and organizational and leader development. Prior to joining KSU, he was an area community development specialist for Iowa State University Extension and program coordinator for Northern Illinois University's Lindeman Center.

Susan M. Yelich Biniecki serves as associate professor of Adult Learning and Leadership at Kansas State University. She serves on major editorial boards such as *Adult Education Quarterly*, *Adult Learning*, and the *Journal of Military Learning*. She is coauthor of the book *Organization and Administration of Adult Education Programs* (with Schmidt, Information Age, 2016).

Jill Zarestky is an assistant professor in the School of Education at Colorado State University. Her research interests include informal, nonformal, and community-based education, particularly in international nongovernmental and nonprofit organizations and STEM education. Zarestky is the former secretary of the American Association of Adult and Continuing Education.

Name Index

Abdelrahman Amin, M., 439–40
Abdi, A. A., 66, 240
Acker, J., 386
Adam, 357
Adams, D. W., 288
Adams, J. D., 306
Adams, J. T., 22–23
Addams, Jane, 27, 310, 421–22
Adhiya, D., 177
Adler, J., 220
Adler, Mortimer, 12–13
Adorno, T., 169
Ahissar, E., 92
Ahmadian, M., 198
Ahmed, S., 364
Ainsworth, M. D. S., 85
Aitchison, J., 242
Akintunde, A. L., 82
Alamprese, J. A., 190
Albrecht, R., 402
Alexander, B., 220
Alexander, R., 159–60
Alfred, Mary V., 5, 61, 66–67, 200–201, 209, 214, 385, 415, 438
Alhadeff-Jones, M., 14
Ali, D., 219
Ali, S., 333
Alidou, H., 242
Alkire, S., 94
Allais, S. M., 241–42
Allen, E. I., 95–96
Allen, James, 423
Allen, K. R., 376
Allman, P., 153, 293
Al-Maadadi, F., 209
Alston, Geleana D., 5, 55, 107, 109–11
Altaf, A., 299
Altbach, P. G., 61, 288
Altenbaugh, Richard, 288–89
Altschuler, G., 233
Alvermann, D. E., 172–73

Ambrose, S. A., 141–43
Amir Hatem Ali, A., 310
Anderson, A., 207–8
Anderson, Chris, 194–95
Anderson, D., 311
Anderson, J., 205, 207, 210
Anderson, J. R., 288–89
Anderson, M., 84, 125, 253, 405
Anderson, R. A., 396
Anderson, T., 356
Andrade, M. S., 184
Andreotti, V. D. O., 66
Anthias, F., 197
Anthony, E., 160
Anye, E. T., 298
Anzaldúa, G., 325, 346
Appelbaum, E., 228
Apple, M. W., 147
Apps, J. W., 153
Arao, B., 153, 432
Archer, A., 161
Archer, W., 178
Arcury, T. A., 439–40
Aristotle, 12
Ariza, E., 316
Arnett, J. J., 86, 93
Arnold, D. E., 276, 278
Arnold, M. E., 131
Artino, A. R., Jr., 249–51
Ashby, C., 269
Ashley, L., 326
Askerov, A., 331
Asún, J. M., 242, 344
Atkin, C., 209
Atkinson, R. C., 84
Atleo, M., 326, 343
Au, K. H., 439
Audesirk, T., 93
Auerbach, E. R., 207
Augustin, M. L., 395
Augustine, 12

Austin, A. E., 260–61
Austin, C., 439–41
Avolio, B., 123
Avoseh, M. B. M., 243
Awan, M. A., 299

Bagnall, R. G., 17, 424
Bailey, D. A., 310
Bailyn, B., 25
Bain, A., 142, 159
Baines, D., 364
Baird, I., 214
Bajaj, M., 331
Baker, C. E., 209
Bakhtin, M., 335
Baldwin, T. T., 281
Ball, S. J., 64
Ballantyne, R., 309, 315
Balmer, J. T., 250
Baltes, P., 81–87
Baltes, P. B., 81
Banet-Weiser, S., 387
Bang, M., 318–19
Banta, 142
Banta, T. W., 140, 142
Baptiste, I., 155
Barbezat, D. P., 160
Barden, B., 358
Barndt, D., 317
Barnes, C., 392
Barnes, P., 95
Barnow, B. S., 193, 225, 228
Barr, H., 252
Barrett, L. F., 92–93
Barron, K. F., 92
Barrow, C., 287–88
Barry, C. M., 88
Bar-Tal, D., 330, 332
Barthelemy, J. J., 2
Bartky, S. L., 322, 324
Bartolomé, J., 132
Barton, G. E., 18
Bartone, P. T., 237
Bash, L., 266
Basok, T., 438
Batalova, J., 66, 198
Bateman, G., 372
Bates, R., 281
Battersby, D., 403

Battiste, M., 342
Bauman, K., 216
Baumgartner, L. M., 74, 372, 429, 431
Bazos, A., 216
Bean, J. P., 270
Beard, C., 77
Beatty, P. T., 404
Becher, T., 31–32
Beck, A. J., 215, 218
Beckett, L., 209
Bedau, H., 17
Bekinschtein, P., 83
Belenky, M. F., 78, 383
Belkin, A., 237, 372
Bell, A., 270, 277
Bell, B. S., 132
Bell, C., 394
Bell, Derrick, 409–10, 416
Bell, L., 310, 432–33
Bellah, Robert, 298
Bello, J., 307
Belzer, Alisa, 3, 6, 42, 143–44, 189, 192, 208, 226, 395, 447–48, 450–51
Benavot, B., 245
Benne, K., 11
Bennett, C. F., 288–89
Bennett, Elisabeth E., 5, 177, 180–84, 451
Benowitz, June Melby, 26
Beresford, P., 392–93
Berg, R., 142
Bergamasco, M., 309
Berger, R., 267
Bergevin, Paul, 13
Bergman, Matt, 6, 266–68, 271, 450
Bergson-Shilcock, A., 359
Berman, G., 220
Bernhardt, A., 228–29
Berry, J., 64–65
Bersch, G., 23, 25–26
Bertram, G., 158
Bhattacharyya, D. K., 120
Bierema, Laura L., 2–3, 6, 13, 73–74, 102–3, 105, 109–10, 125, 154, 159–60, 173–74, 178, 180, 252, 254, 261–62, 276–79, 282–83, 380, 383, 386–88
Biesta, G., 324
Billett, S., 104, 161, 277, 280
Bin, B., 133
Black, J., 183

NAME INDEX

Black, S., 425
Blackburn, S., 17–18
Blake, R., 122, 124
Blanchard, K. H., 122
Bleakney, D., 325
Blee, K. M., 26
Bloemraad, I., 437–38
Blumin, S., 233
Boal, A., 335, 362, 365
Boehm, S. A., 405
Boeke, M., 96
Boeren, Ellen, 5, 44, 100–101, 103, 105, 447
Boggs, G. L., 362, 368
Bogle, M., 206
Bohonos, Jeremy, 6, 409, 411, 448
Bohr, Nils, 445
Boler, M., 324, 367
Bolívar, J., 425
Boltanski, L., 323
Bolton, S., 83
Bonner, F., 142
Bonwell, C. C., 269
Bordas, J., 123
Bos, J. M., 351
Boshier, R., 23, 48, 129, 420
Boston, J., 404
Botta, A., 180
Bouchard, P., 3
Boucouvalas, Marcie, 3, 5, 47, 49, 61–62, 73, 75–76, 78, 81, 383
Boud, D., 142–43, 147
Boudreau, J. B., 224
Boughton, B., 332, 344
Boulding, E., 331
Boulton-Lewis, G., 402
Bound, J., 266
Bourdieu, P., 420
Bousquet, M., 288
Boverie, P., 102
Bowers, A., 266
Bowers, Chet, 317
Bowlby, J., 85
Bowles, S., 288
Bowles, T. A., 317
Bowling, Jerry, 5, 158, 160, 449–50
Bowman, Lorenzo, 6, 409, 415–16, 432, 448
Boyatzis, C. J., 299
Boyce, F. A., 146–47
Boyd, D., 326

Boyles, D., 288
Brace, C. L., 411
Bracken, S. J., 132–33, 371, 383
Braddock, D., 402
Bradley, L., 440
Brady, D. P., 252
Bragg, D. D., 267
Braman, O. R., 332
Branch, L. M., 122
Brandt, B., 251–52
Braungart, M. M., 288
Braungart, R. G., 288
Breuing, M., 160
Brigham, S., 345, 364, 439–40
Briscoe, D. B., 428
Briskin, L., 345
Broadhurst, C. J., 288
Broadus, J., 356
Brockett, R. G., 18, 154
Brock-Utne, B., 331
Brodie, J. M., 363
Bromwich, J. E., 129
Bronfenbrenner, U., 88
Bronski, M., 372
Brooke, L., 405
Brookfield, K., 280
Brookfield, Stephen D., 2–3, 5–6, 13–14, 18–19, 25, 27, 33, 75, 132, 150, 152–56, 170, 172, 333, 362–63, 365, 383, 412–13, 428–30, 432
Brooks, A. K., 55, 147, 371, 376–77, 383, 388
Brooks, Chris, 294
Brooks, G., 208
Brophy, J., 91
Brown, E., 34, 354
Brown, M. E., 2
Brown, R., 393, 397
Brown, S. M., 267
Brown, T., 170
Bruner, J., 161
Brunette, M. J., 439
Bruscino, T., 236
Bryant, I., 13
Bryant, L., 32
Bumiller, E., 409
Burbules, N. C., 62–63
Burdick, Jake, 168–70
Burgess, K. R., 110
Burkert, C., 438–39
Burnett, N., 245

Burnette, D. M., 133
Burris, J., 271
Burstow, B., 396–97
Buse, Dieter, 288
Bush, George H. W., 191
Bush, M., 160
Bushway, D. J., 135
Butler, J., 388
Butler, R., 403–4
Butterwick, Shauna, 6, 33, 77, 322–25, 347, 438–39, 441, 450
Byne, W., 381–82
Byrd, B., 287–88, 290
Byrd, M., 386
Byrne, S., 335

Cabalin, C., 326
Cabrera, A., 123, 267
Caffarella, R., 107, 128–29, 134, 145–46, 253, 363
Cahalan, M., 96
Calasanti, T., 402
Calderon, D., 318–19
Callahan, J., 125, 252, 374
Campbell, M., 15
Canfield Fisher, Dorothy, 25
Cantacuzino, M., 334
Cappelli, P., 224, 227
Capps, R., 198
Carbert, L., 345
Carliner, S., 280
Carnevale, A. P., 223, 271, 353–54
Carnoy, M., 240
Carpenter, S., 153, 323, 364, 384
Carpentieri, J., 207
Carr, David, 305
Carr-Chellman, Davin, 6, 297, 299, 301, 448
Carrette, J., 299
Carroll, C. D., 267
Carroll, K. K., 318–20
Carrozzino, M., 309
Carson, A. E., 215, 218
Cartensen, L. L., 82
Carter, B., 236
Carter, James Gordon, 266
Cashman, K. D., 81–82
Cassara, B., 414
Castells, M., 326
Castonguay, A., 237
Castro, C., 111

Castrodale, M., 396–97
Celce-Murcia, M., 200
Cennamo, K. S., 279
Cercone, K., 163
Cervero, Ronald M., 6, 110, 129, 131–36, 155, 249–51, 257–60, 263–64, 298–99, 383, 412–15, 425, 428–29, 448
Chalofsky, N. E., 386
Chan, J. F., 132
Chandler, D. E., 113
Chaney, C., 210
Chapman, V. L., 433
Chappel-Aiken, L., 299
Charlemagne, 12
Charles, F., 289
Charters, Alex, 51, 62
Charters, Jessie Allen, 25
Cherrstrom, C. A., 112
Chetty, R., 421
Chevigny, B. G., 220
Chiapello, E., 323
Chickering, A. W., 298
Chilisa, B., 347
Chlup, Dominique T., 3, 6, 214, 220, 385, 448, 450
Choudry, A., 323, 325, 332, 365–66
Choy, S., 267
Chrispeels, J., 425
Christensen, C., 183
Christenson, S. L., 92
Christian, N., 183
Christie, M., 15
Chung, Y. B., 388
Church, K., 395, 397
Cicero, 12
Cincinnato, S., 103
Clardy, A., 395
Clark, M., 394
Clark, Septima, 334, 364
Clemens, K., 153, 432
Clinton, Bill, 364–65
Closson, R. B., 33, 416, 432–33
Clover, D. E., 33, 77, 155, 309–10, 314, 316–17, 322, 324–25
Clymer, Carol, 194, 205–8, 228, 447
Coady, Maureen, 3, 6, 257, 448
Coady, Moses, 298, 322
Cobb, M., 299
Cochran-Smith, M., 111
Coen, S., 308

NAME INDEX

Cogswell, S., 216
Cohen, H., 33
Cohen, N. H., 107–8
Cohn, A., 143, 310
Cole, M., 257, 259
Coleman, D., 241
Colin, S. A. J., III, 429, 431
Collard, S., 201
Colley, H., 100
Collins, J. B., 153
Collins, J. C., 373–74, 376, 387
Collins, P. H., 341, 343, 346–47
Collins, Royce Ann, 5, 31, 42, 144
COLLO. *See* Coalition of Lifelong Learning Organizations
Columbaro, N. L., 110
Columbus, Christopher, 318
Colvin, B. B., 267
Comenius, Johann Amos, 49, 58, 162
Commons, John, 290
Commons, M. L., 83
Compton-Lilly, C., 207
Connell, C., 388
Connell, E. O., 110
Connell, R. W., 387
Consedine, N. S., 87
Console, G., 262
Conway, A. E., 260
Conway, M., 225–26
Cook, James, 318
Cook, W. D., 422
Coolidge, Calvin, 422–23
Coombs, P. H., 73
Cooney, M., 181
Cope, B., 177, 180, 183
Copper, C., 236–37
Cordie, L. A., 43
Cornell-d'Echert, B. Jr., 236
Corntassel, J., 318
Coryell, J., 34, 61–62, 65–67
Coryn, C. L. S., 146
Cottrell, R. R., 249
Coulter, J. A., 233, 235
Counts, D., 190
Couzens, D., 395
Covington, L. E., 395
Cowhig, M., 215
Coy, P., 332–33
Cozolino, L., 76

Cramer, J., 207, 210
Cranton, P., 76, 96, 153, 155, 172, 235, 263, 324, 431, 433
Crayton, A., 217
Cremin, L. A., 25
Crookes, G., 198
Crooks, V. C., 82
Cropley, A. J., 56
Cross, K. P., 102
Cross-Durrant, A., 50
Crossman, J., 298–99
Crow, G. M., 112
Crowther, J., 325
Cseh, M., 386
Csikszentmihalyi, M., 94
CTE. *See* Career and Technical Education
Cumming, E., 402
Cummins, E. E., 287
Cummins, J., 200
Cunningham, P., 3–4, 31, 322, 324, 332, 344, 347, 382
Curnow, J., 323–25
Curran, V., 177
Curry-Stevens, A., 325
Cuyjet, M. J., 376–77

Daffron, S. R., 134, 145–46, 253
Daley, Barbara J., 6, 44, 249, 251, 253, 257–61, 263–64, 448
Daloz, L. A., 107, 109, 153
Damsa, C., 161
Daniel, J. L., 299
Darkenwald, G. G., 11, 14
Datta, R. K., 318
Dave, R. H., 55
Davey, J. A., 404
Davidson, H. S., 214
Davidson, K., 3
Davies, K., 48
Davies, S., 306
Davis, A., 362, 364, 366–67
Davis, B., 278
Davis, K. D., 237
Davis, L. M., 215–20
DE. *See* Department of Education
DeBris, Marina, 316
Deci, Edward, 93–94, 96
De Col, Ximena Vidal, 3, 6, 223
DeCuir, J. T., 410

Dees, Morris, 334
Deggs, David, 5, 100, 102, 447
De Graauw, E., 437–38
deGroot, E., 263
Dehli, K., 363
Delgado, A., 392–93
Delgado, R., 409–10, 430
de Linares, Y., 125
DeLong, D. W., 405
DeLors, J., 52, 55
DeMarco, R., 111
Dentice, D., 387
Dentith, A. M., 314, 317–18
De Rick, K., 104
Desai, A. R., 130
Deschamps, M., 237
Deshler, D., 347, 382–83
Desjardins, R., 100
Desmond, S., 209
Dess, G., 122, 125
Deutsch, N. L., 267
Devlin, K. M., 206
Dewey, J., 12–13, 16, 33, 78, 421–22
de Wit, H., 65
Diamond, A., 208
Diamond, D., 335
Diamond, S., 394
DiAngelo, R., 410, 431–32
Diani, M., 322
Dierking, L. D., 307–8
Dietert, M., 387
Dietz, A. S., 236
Dinevski, D., 183
Dinmore, I., 267
DiPietro, L., 82
Dirkx, J. M., 77, 174, 260–63, 298
Di Santo, A., 206
Dixon, A. D., 410
Dixon, C., 362, 365, 368
Dodd, B. G., 271
DOL. *See* Department of Labor
Dolgon, Corey, 3, 6, 287, 288, 291, 294
Donker, T., 394
Donovan, J., 324–26
Dorn, C., 242
Douglas, S. R., 210
Doxsee, C., 197, 199, 202
Draper, J. A., 241
Drescher, J., 381–82

Dreyfus, H. L., 136
Dreyfus, S. E., 136
Du Bois, W. E. B., 27, 341, 343, 345, 411–12, 416
Dueck-Read, J., 335
Dunn, J., 237
Dunton, L. E., 190
Durkheim, Émile, 420
Durks, D., 134
Durning, S. J., 253
Duursma, A. E., 209
Dweck, C., 95
Dwyer, R., 289
Dykstra, C., 322, 325
Dyson, M. E., 430
Dzakiria, H., 161

Eagleton, T., 305
Earl, A., 316–17
Ecclestone, K., 402
Edgar, D., 326
Edwards, B., 289, 365
Edwards, K., 371, 376–77, 388
Edwards-Groves, C., 162
Egan, J., 33
Egetenmeyer, R., 61–62, 66–67
Ehrensaft, D., 382
Eigner, E., 289
Eison, J. A., 269
Eldredge, L. K. B., 131, 134
Elfert, Maren, 209, 240–42, 245, 323, 325, 449
Elias, J. L., 11–13, 16–19, 298–300, 314–16, 387–88
Elk, M., 293
Elliott, D., 65
Elliott, M., 358
Ellis, J. M., 172
Ellis, R., 200
Ellsworth, Elizabeth, 449
Ely, Mary, 25, 150, 410–12
Ely, Richard, 290
Engel-Di Mauro, S., 318–20
Engelhardt, M., 82
Engels, Friedrich, 292–93, 362, 364
Engle Merry, S., 332–33
English, L. M., 77, 147, 152, 261, 297–300, 325–26, 332–33, 335, 347
Enloe, C., 237–38
EOA. *See* Economic Opportunity Act
Eraut, M., 261

NAME INDEX

Erdreich, L., 300
Erichsen, E. A., 35
Erikson, E. H., 86
Erikson, Joan, 86
Eriksson, P. S., 83
Erisman, W., 218
Essert, P. L., 150
Estes, B., 354
Estes, C. L., 404
Estes, F., 422–23
Etzioni, A., 184
Etzioni, O., 184
Eubanks, V., 177
Evans, B., 438, 441
Evans, C., 159
Ewell, 142
Ewest, T., 299
Eyerman, R., 324
Eynon, B., 144
Eyre, G. A., 101
Eyster, L., 226

Faderman, L., 372
Faerm, S., 160
Faigin, D. A., 397
Faler, P., 288
Falk, G., 351–52
Falk, J. H., 307–8, 315
Fanon, F., 341
Farrell, B., 307
Farver, J. A. M., 210
Faulkner, A., 397
Faure, E., 48–49, 52, 56
Featherstone, L., 288
Feder, G., 288–89
Fein, D., 358
Feinman, I. R., 235
Fenwick, T., 2, 75, 143, 147, 257, 261, 277–80, 297–98, 300, 383
Fernandes, M. A., 144
Fernando, S., 393, 397
Ferraro, K., 402
Fetterman, D., 146
Fiedler, F. E., 122–23
Field, John, 61–62
Findsen, Brian, 299, 401–5
Finger, M., 242, 344
Fingeret, H. A., 191
Finnegan, F., 41, 43

Fischer, M., 27
Fischer, S., 422
Fischman, G., 365–66
Fish, S., 3
Fisher, J. C., 404, 421–22
Fisher, R., 171
Fisk, L. J., 332–33
Fitzpatrick, Alfred, 344
Fitzpatrick, J., 144–46
Fitzpatrick, R., 268–69
Fleige, M., 133
Fletcher, S., 109
Flowers, R., 322, 325, 441
Floyd, I., 352
Foley, G., 315, 322, 324
Folger, J., 331–32
Folkman, D. V., 62
Foner, P. S., 322
Fong, C. J., 97
Ford, J. K., 281
Fordjor, P., 15–16
Formosa, M., 403–6
Fornes, S., 392–93, 395
Foster, M., 190
Foster, R. J., 301
Foucault, Michel, 155, 335, 363, 372
Fowler, J. W., 88
Fox, A., 310
Frankenberg, R., 431
Franklin, Benjamin, 28, 50
Franklin, B. H., 335
Franz, N., 129, 343–44, 347
Fredriksen, B., 245
Freedman, V. A., 403
Freeman, M., 32
Freiler, T. J., 76–77, 300
Freire, Paulo, 12–13, 49, 74, 151–53, 156, 159–60, 235, 241–42, 244, 293, 318, 324, 333–34, 343, 346, 362, 365–68, 377, 429, 447
Frenk, J., 250
Freud, Sigmund, 372
Friedenberg, J. E., 199
Friedman, J. N., 421
Friesen, M., 439–40
Frye, S. B., 299
Fuller, A., 277
Fuller, K., 216
Furness, J., 208
Fursova, J., 439

Gaard, G. C., 159–60
Gaby, R., 77
Gadsden, V. L., 206, 209
Galbraith, M. W., 107–8, 140
Gale, Cathy, 171
Gallagher, S., 410
Gallo, M. L., 439
Galtung, J., 330–31
Gambino, L. M., 144
Ganglbauer, S., 133
Ganzglass, E., 192–93
Garavan, T., 386
Garcia-Zamor, J., 219
Gardner, M., 206
Gardner, W., 123
Garibaldi, R., 307
Garibay, C., 306
Garland-Thomson, R., 394, 396
Garrison, D. R., 160–61, 178
Gasiorski, A., 280
Gedro, J., 373–76, 386
Geertz, Clifford, 92, 298
Gegenfurtner, A., 281
Gettleman, M., 289
Ghodsee, K., 242
Ghosh, R., 276
Giangregorio, L. M., 82
Gibb, T., 438
Gibson, C. C., 383
Giddens, J. F., 252
Gieseke, W., 133
Gillen, M. A., 297–98
Gillespie, D., 244
Gillig, T. K., 171–72
Gilligan, Carol, 86–87, 383
Gillum, F., 299
Giloth, R. P., 223–26
Gindin, S., 292
Ginsberg, Margery B., 5, 91, 95–97, 154, 200–202, 376
Gintis, H., 288
Giordano, G., 233
Giroux, H. A., 62–64, 169, 279, 288, 318, 326, 363
Githens, R. P., 376, 386
Glass, D. S., 123
Glassman, M., 24
Glaze, L. E., 219
Glazer, N., 26
Gleason, H., 403

Glen, J. M., 290
Glendenning, F., 403
Glosser, A., 355–56
Glowacki-Dudka, M., 123, 290
Gluck, L., 424
Godin, S., 254
Godinez, E., 123
Goldenstein, C., 35
Gomez, C. J., 207
Goodfellow, J., 259
Goodley, D., 393–94
Goolsby, M. J., 110
Gorman, M., 177
Gorman, R., 393–94, 397
Gorski, P. C., 325
Gottlieb, R., 314, 319
Gouthro, P. A., 172–73, 384
Govaerts, N., 281
Govers, E., 135
Govinda, R., 241
Grace, André P., 2–3, 6, 26, 55, 75, 147, 163, 343–44, 371–73, 375, 377, 380–84, 387–88
Graham, C., 161
Gramlich, J., 215
Grams, S. L., 77
Gramsci, A., 154, 168–72, 293, 324, 347, 364
Grant, J. M., 388
Grant, Z., 396–97
Grattan, C. H., 22–23
Grawe, N., 266
Gray, K., 225
Grayson, J., 325–26
Greaves, L., 324
Green, A., 439–40
Green, J., 287
Green, L. W., 131, 134
Green, W., 31
Greenberg, D., 143–45
Greene, D., 424–25
Greene, M., 325
Greeno, J. G., 278
Greenwood, D. A., 318
Greer, J., 27
Gregg, N., 105, 183, 395
Gregorčič, M., 343
Grenier, Robin S., 3, 6, 305, 308, 310
Griffin, V. R., 77
Griffith, A., 205, 207
Griffith, D. M., 299

NAME INDEX

Griffiths, S., 397
Griswold, W., 290, 314, 317
Groen, Janet, 5, 73–74, 77–78, 299, 316
Groff, L., 331
Grosik, S. A., 199
Grover, K. S., 125
Grubb, W. N., 223
Grudens-Schuck, N., 347
Gruenewald, D. A., 318
Grusky, D., 421
Grusky, D. B., 228–29
Gueron, J., 351
Gugelbeger, G., 335
Guile, D., 262
Gungor, R., 425
Guo, Shibao, 2–3, 5–6, 61–62, 65–67, 344, 436, 439, 447
Guo, Y., 65–66
Gupta, M., 299
Gutek, G. L., 12
Guy, C. A., 109–10
Guy, T. C., 25, 27, 170, 173, 343, 372, 412–14

Haas, E., 365–66
Haasen, A., 405
Habermas, J., 232, 234–37, 429
Hadfield, J., 266
Hadley, 363
Hafsteinsson, S. B., 310
Hagan, N., 382–83
Haggis, Paul, 430
Haines, E. L., 386
Hake, B., 229
Hall, B., 322–24, 343, 347
Hall, B. L., 317, 332, 335
Hall, G. Stanley, 86
Hall, R., 359
Hall, S., 170
Hallam, S., 159
Hallenbeck, Wilbur, 50, 183
Hamadyk, J., 358
Hamilton, G., 355
Hamilton, R., 326
Hamlin, B., 276
Hammond, C., 402
Hampson, Sarah Cote, 6, 232, 238, 448
Hamraie, A., 396
Han, 147
Hanemann, U., 209, 242

Hanley, M. S., 150
Hannon, P., 207
Hansman, Catherine A., 5, 24, 26, 107–12, 254, 263
Hanson, Cindy, 2–3, 6, 341, 343, 346, 449
Haras, C. A., 97
Hardbarger, T., 318
Harding, L., 77
Harding, S., 346
Harlow, C. W., 216, 219
Harman, D., 423
Harnecker, M., 132
Harris, C. L., 409–10
Harris, I., 331–32
Harris, P., 252
Harrison, B., 288
Harrison, P., 346
Harro, B., 377
Hart, B., 207
Hartle, T., 96
Hartnett, S. J., 220
Hartree, A., 75
Harvey, D., 3, 363
Haslam, P. A., 240–41
Haslinda, A., 133
Hathaway, M., 77
Hattie, J., 83
Hatton-Yeo, A., 404
Hausman, J., 216
Havighurst, R. J., 81, 402
Hawkins, M. R., 198
Hawkins, S. T., 335
Hawley, Joshua D., 1, 224, 445
Hayes, E. R., 1, 31, 33, 40, 150, 382–83, 428
Hays, S., 107, 205
Hazan, C., 85
Headley, A., 219
Heaney, T., 362–63, 365, 368
Hearne, S., 394–95
Hedeen, T., 332–33
Hedge, J., 405
Hegarty, A., 209
Heimlich, J., 308
Hein, G. E., 307
Heinrich, C. J., 193
Heisel, M. A., 413
Heller, R., 289
Helms, J. E., 431
Hendra, R., 355
Henehan, S., 171

Henry, W., 402
Henschke, John, 5, 34, 158–59, 162–64, 449–50
Herbart, John F., 159, 162
Herd, A., 271
Herligy, C. M., 411
Herman, A., 324
Hermann, S., 206
Hermes, M., 78
Heron, C., 290–91
Herring, C., 237
Hersey, P., 122
Hewes, A., 413
Hickling-Hudson, A., 245
Higgs, P., 403
Hill, D., 125
Hill, K., 63
Hill, Lilian H., 2, 5, 23, 140–42, 373
Hill, R. J., 2, 317, 323, 372–77, 381, 383–84, 387
Hill, S., 208
Hines, J. M., 309
Hiok, O. M., 133
Hitzhusen, G. E., 299
Hobson, A. J., 108
Hock, M. F., 395
Hocker, J., 331–32
Hodge, D. R., 299
Hodge, S., 17
Hodges, T. L., 299
Hoff, L., 245
Hoffman, 267
Hoggan, C., 76
Holborow, M., 363
Holford, J., 324
Holland, B., 224–25
Holloway, J., 421–22, 424
Holst, J. D., 19, 26, 132, 152, 323, 333, 362–63, 365
Holton, E. F., 278
Holzer, H. J., 226
Homan, K. J., 299
Hood, M. G., 306
hooks, b., 325, 343, 366
Horkheimer, M., 169
Horn, L., 267
Horn, M. B., 43
Hornsby, E. E., 376
Horr, E. E., 308
Horrocks, N., 154

Horton, Myles, 152, 241, 333–34, 362, 366, 421–22, 429
Horvath, V. E., 299
Houle, C. O., 1, 12–14, 31, 40, 100, 233, 235, 258–59, 261–63
Hovsepian, F., 177
Howell, S. L., 300
Howlett, R., 289
Hu, G., 210
Huang, P. S., 309
Huang, Y., 23
Huber, L., 405
Hughes, K. L., 226–27
Hulleman, C. S., 92
Husén, T., 48
Hutchings, 142
Hutchins, H. M., 173–74
Hutchins, Robert M., 48

Ibrahim, S., 94
ICAE. *See* International Council for Adult Education
Ignatiev, N., 411
Ikard, W. L., 271
Ikeda, J. P., 439
Illeris, K., 17
Imel, S., 23, 25–26
Ingram, S., 440
Institute of Medicine, 32–33
Inverso, D. C., 177–78
Ireland, T. D., 62, 66, 242–45
Ireson, J., 159, 162
Irving, C., 325–26, 335
Isaac, E. P., 14, 299, 428
Isaac-Savage, E. P., 298–99
Isabella, L. A., 111
Isen, A. M., 87–88
Isserlis, J., 207

Jackson, J. L., 220
Jackson, N. E., 385
Jacobs, R. L., 224
Jacobson, E., 225
Jaeger, W., 49
Jaffe, JoAnn, 2–3, 6, 341, 346, 449
Jagose, A., 371
Jamal, Z., 439
James, D. J., 219

NAME INDEX

James-Gallaway, A. D., 412
Jamieson, A., 404
Jamison, A., 324
Janes, R., 309
Janks, H., 206
Jarvis, C., 172–74
Jarvis, P., 18, 31–32, 62–63, 66, 308, 403, 414
Jason, L. A., 316
Jason, Z., 288
Jeffs, T., 315
Jelfs, A., 178
Jenkins, Esau, 364
Jensen, B., 421
Jeremic, Rusa, 2, 6, 362, 447
Jeris, L. H., 258, 260–61, 345
Jiannine, L. M., 81–82
Jirásek, I., 299
Johnson, B., 315
Johnson, Lyndon B., 423
Johnson, N., 270
Johnson, R. L., 413
Johnson, S., 121
Johnson-Bailey, J., 35, 110–11, 365, 383, 412–15, 428–30
Johnson-Freese, J., 236
Johnston, D., 63–64
Johnston, R., 13
Johnstone, D. B., 64
Johnstone, K., 170–71
Jones, A., 440
Jones, J., 433
Jones, M. S., 140
Jones, N., 393, 397
Jones, P. W., 241
Jones, S. R., 280
Jordan, S., 277
Jordi, R., 33
Jubas, Kaela, 5, 168, 172–73, 325
Juravich, T., 290–91
Jurmo, P., 425
Jurowetski, R., 77
Justice, B., 25
Justice, S. B., 278, 280

Kaeble, D., 215
Kahn, R., 403
Kail, R., 84
Kaiper, Anna, 205

Kalantzis, M., 177, 180, 183
Kalleberg, A. L., 223
Kallen, Horace, 12–13, 289
Kandiko, C. B., 63–64
Kandur, J. L., 309
Kane, L., 335
Kapoor, D., 240, 323
Kapp, Alexander, 35, 162
Käpplinger, B., 129, 133
Karp, M. M., 226–27
Kasworm, C. E., 1–2, 11, 23, 32, 35, 141–42, 150, 266, 268–69, 271, 371, 382–83
Kaufman, G., 270
Kaufman, R., 125
Kawalilak, Colleen, 5, 73–74, 77–78
Keane, P., 22–23, 26, 31–32, 287
Kearney, J., 439–40
Kearney, M., 335
Keating, A., 325
Kekkonon, Helena, 331–32
Keller, K., 82
Kelley, Robin D. G., 293
Kempf, A., 438
Kempfer, H., 429
Kendall, F. E., 430–31
Kerka, S., 269
Kett, J. F., 23, 28
Kettner, P. M., 131
Khan, M., 243
Khatiwada, I., 189
Khoo, S. M., 65
Kibler, A. K., 438
Kidd, J. R., 51, 53
Kight, S., 292
Kilgore, D., 322
Kim, Jeounghee, 3, 6, 189, 226, 447–48, 450–51
Kim, Y., 11, 14–15, 300
Kimball, L., 283
Kincaid, R., 323
Kincheloe, J., 288
King, K., 163, 245, 282
King, K. P., 15, 104–5, 110, 155, 178, 372–73
King, Martin Luther Jr., 326, 333–34, 417
King, P. M., 32–33
King, R., 299
Kinsella, E. A., 257, 259
Kinsley, R. P., 306
Kirby, P. G., 268

Kirkpatrick, D. L., 146
Kirsh, I., 406
Kirylo, J. D., 366
Kitchener, K. S., 32–33
Kleef, J. V., 440
Klein, J. T., 31, 77
Klein, R., 214
Klein-Collins, R., 144, 267, 270–71
Kleingeld, P., 34
Kloubert, T., 28
Kluttz, J., 314, 324
Kluzer, S., 440
Knight, J., 61, 65
Knipprath, H., 104
Knoll, J. H., 61–62
Knoll, Michael, 214
Knowles, Malcolm, 13–14, 23, 31, 33, 35, 50, 75, 81, 150–52, 158–60, 162–65, 183, 200, 235, 268–69
Knox, A. B., 154, 413
Knutson, P., 172–73
Kockelmans, J. J., 31
Kohl, H., 290
Kohlberg, Lawrence, 86–87
Kok, G., 134
Kolb, D., 32, 75
Koning, P., 193
Kop, R., 3
Köpsén, S., 325
Kornbluh, Joyce, 290
Kozlowski, S. W. J., 132
Kram, K. E., 107, 111–12
Kreber, C., 33
Kreitlow, B., 32–33, 428
Kress, G., 206, 209
Kreuter, M. W., 134
Kroth, Michael, 96, 102, 297, 301, 448
Krupar, A., 207
Krupp, J. A., 383
Kuchinke, K. P., 278
Kucukaydin, I., 375
Kuh, G. D., 92, 145, 268
Kuhn, T. S., 279
Kumar, R., 125
Kumaravadivelu, B., 198
Kumashiro, K., 364
Kunzman, U., 81, 87

Labouvie-Vief, G., 83, 87
Lacks, Henrietta, 448

Ladson-Billings, G., 201–2, 410
LaDuke, W., 319
Lakey, George, 334
Lambert, N. M., 91
Landry, D., 395, 397
Langdon, J., 323
Lange, E., 2, 300, 383
Langrehr, K. J., 266, 268
Lareau, A., 205
Larrabure, M., 325–26
Larrotta, C., 299
Larson, G., 413
Larson, L. L., 109
Larweh, K., 323
Laslett, P., 406
Lather, P., 160, 170
Lauretis, Teresa de, 371
Lave, J., 161, 277, 279, 324–25
Lavendar, P., 325
Law, M., 322, 325
Lawler, P. A., 104–5
Lawrence, R. L., 77, 122–23, 172, 383
Lawson, K. H., 13, 17–18
Lawson, L., 135, 252–53
Lazerson, M., 223
Lazowski. R. A., 92
Leaker, C., 146–47
Leask, B., 65
Leatherman, S. P., 316
Lebel, U., 238
Lebowitz, Michael, 292
Le Cornu, A., 298
Lederach, J. P., 331
Ledger, A., 397
Ledwith, M., 363, 367
Lee, A., 198, 310
Lee, Edwin, 57
Lee, J. M., 97
Lee, M., 147, 276
Lee, M-Y., 415
Lee, R., 133
Lee, V. J., 209
Lee, W., 91
LeFrançois, B. A., 393
LeGrand, C. C., 241
Lehner, A., 198
Lembcke, J., 289
LeNoue, M., 163
Lerman, R. I., 224, 226

NAME INDEX

Leslie, B. B., 123
Leslie, L. L., 64
Leung, C. B., 209
Levac, L., 346
Levidow, L., 64
Levinson, D. J., 107–8
Levy, S., 404
Lewin, K., 122
Lewinson, L. P., 299
Lewis, D. L., 412
Lewis, Karen, 447
Lewis, R., 411
Lewis, T. Y., 209
Li, Y., 209
Liasidou, A., 394
Lichtenstein, N., 290
Lifelong Learning Act of 1976, 53–54
Lin, M., 182
Lindeman, Eduard, 12–13, 17, 28, 32, 43, 50, 73, 150, 364, 429
Lindland, E., 404–5
Linkon, S., 172
Linn, J., 422
Lipson Lawrence, R., 73, 75–76, 78
Liu, S., 111
Liveright, A., 423
Livingstone, D. L., 262
Livingstone, S. R., 87
Loach, K., 306, 311
Locke, Alain, 25, 27, 372, 412
Lohr, Kathy, 6, 401, 403
London, J., 128, 413
Longfellow, Henry Wadsworth, 47
Longworth, N., 56
Lorde, Audre, 362
Lott, B., 421
Lovett, T., 322
Lovey, I., 125
Lowe, J., 51
Lowrey, S., 388
Luck, M., 309
Ludewig, J., 309
Luke, A., 65, 169
Luke, Carmen, 173
Lund, C. A., 429, 431
Lundgren, Henriette, 3, 6, 275, 278–79
Lundin, J., 277
Luque, J. S., 438, 440
Luria, A. L., 84

Lutifyya, M. N., 250
Lynch, A., 58
Lypson, M. L., 250

Macdonald, J., 404
MacDonald, K., 266
MacGregor Burns, J, 151
Machemer, T., 309–10
MacKenzie, C. A., 279
MacKenzie, D. L., 220
MacKerarcher, D., 333
MacLean, A., 228–29
MacLean, K. T., 334
MacMillan, S., 363
Magai, C., 87
Mager, R. F., 132
Maguire, S., 357–58
Mahmoud, M. M. A., 298
Mahoney, J. J., 411
Main, T., 323
Maitra, S., 344, 441
Malcolm X, 214
Maldonado-Torres, N., 325
Malhotra, N. K., 268
Malkiel, Theresa, 323
Manglitz, Elaine, 2–3, 6, 428–30
Manheimer, R., 403
Manicom, L., 322, 324
Mann, Horace, 266
Marbley, A. F., 142, 146
Marcus, L. J., 123
Marcuse, H., 412, 416, 430
Mareschal, T. L., 299
Marienau, C., 76, 141–42, 154
Markle, G., 266, 270
Markus, H. R., 109
Marsh, J., 209
Marsick, V. J., 31, 96, 168, 174, 252, 276–78, 280, 282
Martens, K., 39
Martin, Larry G., 5, 38, 145–46, 448
Martin, V., 356
Martinson, K., 355–56
Marullo, S., 365
Marx, Karl, 151–52, 292–93, 362, 364, 420
Masland, J. W., 232
Maslow, A. H., 74, 78
Massenberg, A.-C., 281
Mastro, D., 171

Masuch, C., 440
Matchette, S., 307
Mathes, V. S., 28
Mathews-Aydinli, J., 199, 202–3
Mathison, S., 32
Maudlin, J. G., 169
Maxey, E. C., 396
Mayer, 96–97
Mayes, A., 159
Mayo, P., 147, 152, 297–98, 310, 347, 366
Mayoh-Bauche, J., 135
Mayombe, C., 244
McCarthy, J. D., 289
McCarthy, Joseph, 372
McClusky, H. Y., 32, 403
McCombs, B. L., 91
McCormick, A., 269–70
McCoy, L., 440
McGee, L., 409
McGhee, P., 48
McGill, Craig M., 2–3, 6, 371, 376, 448
McGill, I., 75
McGinley, L., 271
McGrath, S., 245
McGreal, R., 182
McGuire, J., 289
McHugh, M., 197, 199, 202
McIntosh, P., 377, 431
McKendry, V., 299
McKenzie, Leon, 13–14, 17
McLagan, P. A., 276–78
McLean, G. N., 275–76
McLean, L., 275–76
McLean, M. A., 394
McLean, S., 33
McLendon, L., 143–44, 190
McNichol, J., 237
McRuer, R., 394
McVeigh, R., 323
McWhorter, Rochell R., 5, 177, 180, 182–84, 451
Medvedeva, M., 307
Meiners, E. R., 220
Mejiuni, O., 111
Melching, M., 244
Mellard, D., 395
Melvin, T. L., 293–94
Memmi, A., 341
Mendive, S., 209
Mendos, L. R., 373

Menzies, R., 392–93
Mercier, N., 237
Merenlender, A. M., 315
Merriam, S. B., 3–4, 11–19, 32, 73–74, 102–3, 105, 107, 109–10, 154, 159–60, 178, 253, 300, 308, 314–16, 363, 382, 414
Merrifield, J., 192–93
Merriweather, Lisa R., 1, 11, 111, 410, 445
Mešić, N., 437–38
Messmann, G., 280
Mettler, S., 50
Metzner, B. S., 270
Meyer, K. A., 95–96
Meyer, M. A., 318–19
Meyer, S., 383
Mezirow, J., 76, 155, 259, 278, 324, 415, 424, 429, 431, 433
Mies, M., 341
Mignolo, W., 240
Milacci, F., 300
Milana, M., 38
Miller, B., 2, 410
Miller, D. W., 299
Miller, J., 325
Miller, K. A., 305–6
Miller, M. T., 125
Miller, P., 394
Mills, L. A., 172
Milner, H., 161
Milner, N., 332–33
Miltner, K. M., 387
Misawa, Mitsunori, 2–3, 6, 371, 373, 375–76, 415, 448
Mischel, W., 299
Mitchell, D. E., 42, 63–65
Mixue, L., 133
Mizzi, Robert C., 1, 11, 330, 335, 373–75, 445
Mladenovic, R., 277
Modipa, T. R., 394
Mohammed, A. J., 52, 55
Mojab, S., 153, 323, 384–85
Moje, E. B., 206
Moles, J., 107
Mollica, R. F., 335
Monaghan, C. H., 383
Mondale, Walter, 53
Moni, K. B., 395
Monture-Angus, P., 346
Moody, H., 401, 403

NAME INDEX

Moody, K., 290
Moon, B., 159
Moore, A., 159
Moore, C., 132, 145–46, 333
Moore, D., 253
Moore, D. E., 142, 145–46
Morcom, L. A., 16
More, W. S., 18
Moreno, K. A. V., 437
Morf, C. C., 299
Morgan, A., 207, 209
Morgan, A. J., 111
Morrice, L., 438
Morris, A., 386
Morris, George, 287
Morrison, M., 331
Mortimore, P., 159
Mortrude, J., 359
Mott, Vivian W., 110, 259, 263, 401
Mouton, J., 122, 124
Moyer, J. M., 298–99
Muhammad, U., 363
Mukhlaeva, T., 133
Mulenga, D. C., 242
Mullen, B., 236–37
Mullen, C. A., 108–9, 112
Muller, L., 74, 298
Mumford, Lewis, 52, 56
Munn, S. L., 376
Munroe, E., 298
Murphy, M. M., 12
Murray, I., 161
Murray, T. S., 189
Murray-Johnson, K., 33
Musick, M., 210
Muste, A. J., 345
Musu-Gillette, L., 95
Mutamba, C., 15
Myers, K., 100
Mylopoulos, M., 250
Myrsiades, K., 62

Nadler, L., 31
Nakamura, J., 94
Nanton, C. R., 136
Nash, H., 371, 383
Neal, D., 216
Neal, J., 299
NeCamp, S., 27

Nellum, C., 96
Nelson, T., 404–5
Nembhard, J. G., 28
Nerland, M., 257
Nesbit, T., 38, 74, 150, 155, 232, 235, 420
Netting, F. E., 135
Neufeldt, H. G., 409
Neugarten, B., 401
Neustaeter, Robin, 6, 330, 449–50
Neusteter, S. R., 217
Newell, W., 31
Newfield, D., 161
Newman, S., 404
Ng, R., 438, 441
Nguyen, T. T. H., 142
Niebuhr, Reinhold, 421–22
Nielsen, S. Y., 63–65
Nieto, S., 200
Nightingale, D. S., 226
Nightingale, E., 306
Nijhof, W. J., 278
Nijman, D.-J. J., 281
Nikischer, A. B., 385
Nind, M., 160–61
Nirje, B., 396
Nissen, B., 287–88, 290
Noble, D. F., 288
Nocera, A., 27
Noddings, N., 17
Nordvall, H., 241
Northouse, P., 122
Notthoff, N., 82
Nuldén, U., 277
Nurius, P., 109
Nussbaum, M. C., 240, 244, 366
Nutbrown, C., 206–7, 209–10
Nyborg, H., 409
Nyerere, Julius, 241–42, 342

Obama, Barack, 237
O'Brien, D., 92
O'Connell, K. M., 15, 17–19
O'Connor, M. K., 135
O'Connor, S. O., 309
Ogden C. L., 82
Ogren, C. A., 266
Ohliger, John, 48, 55, 383
Okros, A., 237
Oler, A., 236

Oliver, M., 392
Olneck, M. R., 411
Olsen, B., 326
Olssen, M., 63
Ord, J., 315
Osam, E. K., 266
Osborne, M., 56
Oslund, C. M., 395
O'Sullivan, E., 155
Outlaw, Lucius, 428
Ovens, A., 277
Owen, J. A., 135
Oyomo, E., 245
Ozturk, M. B., 387–89

Packer, J., 309, 315
Pahl, K., 209
Palacios, C., 325
Palm, G., 209–10
Palmer, C., 253–54
Palmer, P. J., 261
Palomba, C. A., 140, 142
Panackal, N., 244
Panksepp, J., 87
Pannucci, L., 395
Paperson, L., 318–20
Paris, C., 111
Park, M., 206, 208
Park, Y., 84
Parker, A. M., 345
Parks, Rosa, 333–34, 364, 417
Parsons, E. C. M., 309
Paryono, P., 225
Paterson, M. A., 250
Paterson, R. W. K., 13, 18
Patrick, F., 42–43
Patterson, Margaret, 44, 103, 420–21, 424–25
Paul, J. L., 17
Paulson, K., 96
Paulson, U., 424
Paulston, R. G., 289
Paus, T., 83
Pawloski, R., 101, 432
Paxton, D., 429–30, 433
Pedler, M., 277
Pericles, 49, 58
Perkins, Carl D., 41
Perkins, David G., 234
Perlin, M., 394

Perna, L., 96
Perna, L. W., 104
Perrin, A., 405
Perry, A., 438–39, 441
Perry, K. H., 205, 210
Perry, W. G., 32–33, 83, 86
Persyn, J., 233–35
Pestalozzi, 159
Peters, J. M., 414
Peters, M. A., 63
Peters, S., 288
Peterson, D. A., 403
Peterson, E. A., 414, 416
Peterson, S. L., 282–83
Philo, 158
Piaget, J., 74, 83–86, 278
Pickard, A., 194, 226
Pierce, S., 436
Piercy, G., 77
Pigza, J. M., 298
Pimentel, S., 450
Pipe, P., 132
Pitman, A., 257, 259
Pittman, P., 224, 228
Plato, 12, 158
Platt, R. E., 23
Plumb, D., 235, 376
Poell, Rob F., 3, 6, 275, 277, 280–81
Pogson, J., 31, 33
Pole, Thomas, 422
Polson, C., 233–35
Polyani, M., 77
Poole, J. M., 394–97
Porter, C. M., 134
Powell, C., 345
Powell, D. R., 439
Powell, J. W., 11
Pranis, K., 333
Pratt, D., 252
Pratt, D. D., 74, 150, 152–53
Preskill, S., 333
Prince-St-Amand, C., 437
Prins, Esther, 6, 143, 192, 194, 205–7, 209, 385–86, 447
Priola, V., 387
Pritchard, S. M., 310
Procknow, Greg, 6, 392–95
Prothro, J. W., 413
Pruchno, R., 403

NAME INDEX

Pushpanathan, T., 15

Quail, C. M., 171
Queeney, D. S., 258
Quigley, Allan, 40, 42, 420–24
Quijano, A., 341
Quintilian, 12

Rachal, J. R., 24, 33, 36, 410–11, 422
Rad, S. E., 198
Raddon, M., 288
Radovan, M., 183
Radway, L. I., 232
Raelin, J. A., 279
Ramdeholl, Dianne, 2, 6, 362, 365, 433, 447
Ramezanzadeh, A., 298–99
Rampey, B. D., 216–19
Ramstad, P. M., 224
Randall, M., 335
Ransom, T., 97
Rappolt-Schlichtmann, 396
Ratey, J. J., 91
Rauschenbusch, Walter, 421–22
Reagan, Ronald, 290
Reardon, B., 331
Reder, S., 189
Rees, F., 111
Reeve, J., 91
Reeves, R., 421
Regan, P., 342, 346
Regmi, K. D., 243
Reindl, 267
Reio, Thomas G., Jr., 5, 81–82, 85, 111
Reischmann, J., 35
Reitz, J., 439
Remenick, L., 266
Ren, L., 210
Renzaglia, A., 396
Repko, A., 32–33
Resides, Diane, 383
Reville, D., 396–97
Reynolds, S. L., 395
Rhee, J. E., 299–301
Rhoades, G., 424
Rhodes, 64
Rhodes, Christy, 6, 197, 447
Rhodes, C. M., 95, 202, 376
Rhoten, D., 31–32
Riccio, J. A., 351

Rice, Condoleezza, 409
Rice, J. K., 383
Richardson, J. T. E., 178
Richardson, William, 422
Rick, A., 216
Riegel, K. F., 83
Riley, T., 210
Risku, M., 77
Risley, T. R., 207
Rittel, H., 129–30
Ritzer, G., 63
Rivera, W. M., 288–89
Roberto, K., 406
Robertson, D., 292
Robertson, R., 63
Robinson, Bernice, 364
Robinson, J. W., 288
Robinson, M. J., 387–89
Rocco, Tonette S., 1, 55, 122–23, 262–63, 277,
    279–80, 371, 373–74, 392–95, 410, 445
Roder, A., 358
Rodney, W., 341–42
Roediger, D. R., 411
Roessger, K., 33, 44, 145–46
Rogers, A., 154, 241
Rogers, C. R., 74
Rogers, R., 363
Rogers, T., 92
Rogers-Shaw, Carol, 297, 396–97, 448
Roh, K-R., 133
Rohall, D. E., 235–38
Rohd, M., 335
Roman, S., 405–6
Roosevelt, Franklin D., 39, 423
Rose, Amy D., 5, 11, 22–26, 28, 34–35, 39, 150,
    191–92, 208–9, 345, 449
Rose, D., 393
Rose, N., 299
Rosenstein, J. E., 237
Ross, J. M., 428
Rosser-Mims, D., 415
Ross-Gordon, Jovita, 6, 11, 14, 18, 23, 27–28, 92,
    144, 202, 271, 392–95, 411, 414
Rossiter, M., 109
Rostow, W. W., 240
Roth, H. D., 160
Roth, Reuben, 3, 6, 287, 294
Rothwell, W. J., 405
Roulstone, A., 393

Roumell, Elizabeth A., 5, 38–42, 448
Rounds, J., 306, 311
Rowden, D., 410–12
Rowe, J., 354, 403
Rowland, M. L., 298–99
Roy, C., 324–25
Rubenson, K., 144, 243
Rubin, I. M., 413
Rule, P., 394
Runes, D. D., 18
Rust, D. Z., 271
Ruther, N, L., 68
Ruvolo, A. P., 109
Ryan, C. L., 210, 216
Ryan, Francis, 290
Ryan, Richard, 93–94, 96
Ryan, T. G., 397
Ryu, K., 133, 298–99

Saad-Filho, A., 63–64
Saar, E., 102
Sabatini, J., 144
Sabeti, S., 306, 311
Sabol, T. J., 206–7
Saegert, S., 421
Said, E. W., 335, 342
Salerno, A. S., 438
Sally, David, 194–95
Salmon, R., 125
Sambrook, S. A., 279, 386
Sandell, R., 306
Sanders, Bernie, 292
Sanderson, W., 401
Sanders-Reio, J., 111
Sandlin, Jennifer A., 33, 75, 168–70, 174, 324–25
Sandoe, K. J., 171–72
Santos, R. A., 209
Sappho, 12
Sarna, 357
Saunders, Harold, 334
Savicevic, D., 158–59, 162
Sawchuk, P., 438
Scammacca, N. K., 271
Scandrett, E., 323–24
Scanlon, D., 395
Schaberg, K., 358
Schachter-Shalomi, Z., 403
Schafft, K., 206–7
Schaie, K. W., 85

Scharrón-del Río, M. R., 381
Schaub, M., 205
Scheil, K. W., 28
Scherbov, S., 401
Schied, F. M., 62, 279, 287
Schleicher, A., 189
Schmertz, B., 267
Schmidt, Clea, 6, 197, 447
Schmidt, Steven, 2, 5, 119–25, 134, 252–53
Schmidt, S. W., 135, 374, 386
Schmidt, W. H., 122, 150
Schmitt, J., 228
Schmitt, M. H., 135
Schneider, S. A., 333–34
Schön, Donald, 257–61, 263
Schreiner, P., 162
Schrock, G., 224–25, 228
Schroeder, E. A., 236
Schugurensky, Daniel, 66, 240, 323–24, 449
Schultz, L., 66
Schultz, T. W., 241
Schunk, D. H., 112
Schwab, K., 177
Schwartz, J. M., 2, 33, 385, 410
Schwarzenegger, Arnold, 290
Schwerin, Edward, 333
Scott, C. A., 307
Scott, D., 237
Scott, J. C., 28
Scott, Leodis, 5, 11, 57
Scott, S. S., 396
Scully-Russ, Ellen, 3, 6, 223–24, 227–29
Seaman, J., 95–96
Sears, Alan, 291
Seibert, H., 438–39
Selleck, R., 159
Semali, L., 16
Sen, A., 240, 244–45
Senehi, Jessica, 6, 330, 335, 449–50
Senge, P., 122, 277
Sentama, E., 332
Sepinuck, T., 335
Serrel, B., 307
Settersten, R., 403
Sexton, C. A., 25
Shakespeare, T., 394
Shan, Hongxia, 2–3, 6, 436–37, 441, 447
Shapiro, D., 267
Sharma, V., 88

NAME INDEX

Shaver, P., 85
Shea, G., 405
Sheared, V., 1, 18, 414–15, 429
Shernoff, D. J., 92
Shields, J., 438, 441
Shiffrin, R. M., 84
Shih, L. H., 309
Shippee, T., 402
Shohet, L., 208
Shonk, K., 331
Shor, I., 152, 156, 429
Shore, S., 429
Shuck, B., 123
Siegel, R., 128
Siemiatycki, M., 437
Sifuentes, Aram Han, 310
Sikora, A. C., 269
Silva, E., 92
Silver-Pacuilla, H., 395
Simmie, G. M., 107
Simmons, A. J., 122
Simon, B., 159
Simon, K., 209
Simon, N., 307
Simons, W. E., 232
Simpson, L. B., 318–19
Sims, M., 206
Sinclair, A. J., 298–99
Singh, A., 388
Singh, J. P., 241
Singh, S., 206
Single, P., 109
Sink, A., 171
Sinnott, J. D., 83
Sissel, P. A., 1, 414–15
Sitzia, E., 307
Skilton, M., 177
Skinner, B. F., 12–13, 74, 159
Slade, B., 397, 441
Slaughter, S., 64, 424
Smiraglia, C., 308
Smith, A., 323, 405
Smith, A. P., 353
Smith, B., 432
Smith, C., 424
Smith, C. U., 413
Smith, D., 205, 207
Smith, Hilda, 289
Smith, J. K., 307

Smith, M Cecil, 1, 150, 445
Smith, R. O., 150
Smith, T. V., 429
Smoker, P., 331
Smythe, S., 207
Snyder, T. D., 95, 198, 421
Sobel, D., 318
Socrates, 12
Sodhi, M., 33
Soeters, J., 235
Sogge, D., 241
Sohnen, R., 220
Sokolova, I., 133
Soler, R., 142–43, 147
Somma, Maria, 293
Sommer, T. E., 206–7
Song, W., 425
Sork, Thomas J., 5, 128–30, 132, 136, 253, 383
Southwick, S., 403
Spalding, D., 154
Sparks, H., 366
Spaulding, S., 225, 228
Specht, I., 133
Specter, Arlen, 218
Spence, M., 319
Spencer, B., 282, 344
Sperry, D. E., 207
Spezia, C. J., 62, 66
Spiker, K., 353
Spivak, G. C., 342
Sprokay, S., 76
Sprow, K., 74
Squires, G., 35
Stahly-Butts, Marbre, 293
Stalker, J., 110–11, 201
Standing, M., 111
Starr, P., 448
Stavredes, T., 95
St. Clair, R., 134, 229
Stefancic, J., 409–10, 430
Stein, C. H., 397
Stein, P., 161
Stepanek Lockhart, A, 245
Stetsenko, A., 324
Stewart, Cora Wilson, 27, 422–23
Stewart, D. L., 376
Stewart, J. C., 25, 27–28, 276, 412
Stewart, S., 110
Sticht, T. G., 40, 189–91

Stifter, C. H., 133
Stiglitz, J. E., 241
Stobbe, S. P., 333
Stogdill, R., 122
Stoner, A. M., 279
Storey, 282
Stowe, Harriet Beecher, 306
Strachan, R., 142
Strawn, Julie, 6, 350, 355, 359, 447
Strohl, J., 353
Stubblefield, H. W., 22–24, 26, 31–32
Stufflebeam, D. L., 146
Su, Y., 141–42
Subedi, B., 299–301
Subramanian, A., 309
Sue, D. W., 430–31
Sullivan, S., 430
Sumara, D., 278
Summers, T., 395
Sun, A. P., 394–95
Sungsri, S., 15, 17
Svenson, E. V., 150
Swain, J., 207–8
Swan, E., 322, 325, 441
Swanson, R. A., 276, 278, 386
Swartz, A. L., 33, 74

Taber, Nancy, 6, 171, 173, 232, 235, 237–38, 448
Tafoya, T., 372
Tagore, Rabindranath, 15, 17
Talbot, W., 411
Talmage, C. A., 403–4
Tam, M., 406
Tan, C., 298, 317
Tandon, R., 343, 347
Taniguchi, H., 270
Tannehill, D. B., 164
Tannenbaum, A. S., 122
Tate, P., 144
Tate, W. F., IV, 410
Tatelman, S., 363
Tatli, A., 387–89
Tatum, S., 237
Taylor, E. E., 155–56
Taylor, E. W., 13, 76, 150, 155, 431, 433
Taylor, J., 344–45
Taylor, K., 76, 109, 154
Taylor, M. M., 155
Taylor, P., 405

Taylor, Shawn, 289
Taymans, J. M., 395
Teich, N. M., 388
Tekian, A., 249–51
Tennant, M., 31–33, 261, 383
Terranova, T., 324–26
Tett, L., 208
Thalhammer, V., 404
Thayer-Bacon, B. J., 78
Theoharis, J., 334
Thibault, G. E., 250–54
Thiong'o, N. wa., 342
Thomas, A., 48, 423
Thomas, D. C., 250
Thomas Aquinas, 12
Thompson, O. P., 314, 317–18
Thompson, P. M., 172
Thorndike, Edward L., 12–13, 50, 73, 150
Ticknor, Anna, 28
Tighe, E. L., 144
Tillich, Paul, 298
Tinning, R., 277
Tinto, V., 268–69
Tisdell, E. J., 13, 18, 33, 35, 57, 74, 77, 150, 170, 172–73, 297–301, 383
Tisdell, L., 253–54
Tobias, R., 260
Tobin, J., 33
Tolliver, D. E., 61–62, 66–67, 297–98, 300
Tornstam, L., 403
Torraco, R., 224
Torre, D. M., 253
Torres, C. A., 62–63
Torres, R. M., 242–43
Toso, Blaire, 205–8, 210, 385–86, 425, 447
Tough, Allen, 13–14, 75
Townson, L., 343–44
Traianou, A., 160
Travers, N. L., 271
Treff, M. E., 123
Triadafilopoulos, T., 437
Triscari, J., 33
Trowler, P., 31–32
Trump, Donald, 237, 416
Trutko, J. W., 193
Tuck, E., 318–19, 364
Tuhiwai Smith, L., 77, 342, 345–46
Tukachinsky, R., 171
Turay, T., 331–32, 335

NAME INDEX

Turner, S., 266
Tusting, K., 147
Twain, Mark, 306
Tyler, J., 386
Tyler, R. W., 12–13

Umber, K. E., 260
Umbreit, M., 333
Unruh, G., 123
Unwin, L., 282
Usher, R., 13, 19, 75
Uzama, A., 299

Vail, S., 394–95
Vaira, M., 63
Valentine, D., 382, 388
Valentine, T., 31, 33
Van Der Klink, M., 281
Van Der Krogt, F., 277, 280–81
Van Der Werff, J. A., 236, 238
van Emmerik, I. J. H., 112
Van Riper, J. K., 233, 235
van Steensel, R., 205, 207
Van Tongeren, P., 334
Van Woerkom, M., 277
VanWynsberghe, R., 324
Vaughn, N. D., 160
Vázquez, K. E., 310
Velayutham, S., 441
Vella, J., 154
Vellacott, J., 331
Verner, C., 422
Vespa, J., 401–2
Vickers, J., 32
Videbeck, R., 413
Visser, R. M. S., 404
Vodde, R. F., 163–64
Voelkel, M., 171
Von Glasersfeld, E., 278
von Hippel, A., 133
Vygotsky, L. S., 74, 83–84, 86, 112, 161, 324, 346

Wacker, R., 406
Waddoups, C. F., 224
Waliczek, T. M., 315
Walizer, L., 359
Walker, Judith, 6, 215, 322, 325–26, 450
Walker, M., 142
Wallerstein, I., 240

Wallis, J. D., 93
Wallo, A., 122
Walmsley, R., 215
Walmsley, S. A., 395
Walshaw, M., 160
Walter, Pierre, 6, 299, 314–17, 324, 326, 441
Walters, S., 130, 322, 324, 347
Walther, C., 325
Walumbwa, F., 123
Wang, G. G., 276
Wang, V., 15
Wanstreet, C. E., 25
Warhol, Andy, 309–10
Waring, M., 159
Warren, Elizabeth, 292
Warriner, D. S., 197–98
Washington, Booker T., 343
Wasik, B. H., 206
Watkins, C., 159
Watkins, K. E., 96, 168, 174, 252, 275–78, 280, 282
Watras, J., 241
Watson, C., 405
Watters, Cassie, 294
Webb, S., 438
Webber, M. M., 129–30
Weber, M., 122
Webster-Wright, A., 257, 262–63
Wehmeyer, M. L., 397
Weil, S. W., 75
Weinbaum, E., 290–91
Weiner, B., 91
Welch, A. R., 63
Welch, M. J., 298
Weldon, S. L., 415
Wells, J. M., 146
Welton, M. R., 23, 235, 297–98, 322, 344
Wenger, E., 112, 161, 263, 277, 279, 324–25
Wenger-Trayner, E., 263
Werner, C., 402
Werner, J. M., 276
Werquin, P., 440
West, C., 388
West, L., 261
Wheeler, A., 134
White, B., 287
White, K. E., 63
White, Micah, 326
White, S., 406
White, T., 92

Whiteaker, L. H., 409
Whitehead, Alfred North, 50
Wiggs, G., 31
Willard, D., 301
Williams, R., 168–70
Willinsky, J., 240, 341
Willis, S. L., 85
Wilmot, W., 331–32
Wilson, A. L., 1, 33, 107, 129, 131–36, 150, 155, 258, 260, 382–83, 428
Wilson, J., 210
Wilson, J. P., 77
Winslow, D., 237
Wise, A., 441
Withers, A., 393
Withnall, A., 402
Witkowsky, P., 270
Witnebel, L., 257
Wittmer, C., 315
Wittnebel, L., 147
Wlodkowski, Raymond J., 5, 91, 95–97, 154, 200–202, 267, 376
Wolford, B. I., 383
Woo, A., 128
Woosley, S., 268
Worthen, H., 64–65, 288
Wright, A. E., 209–10
Wright, G. L., 171
Wright, M., 310
Wright, Robin Redmon, 168, 170–72, 174
Wyles, K. J., 316

Xenakis N., 394–95
Xiao, J., 61–62, 66

Yamashita, T., 46, 406
Yang, K. W., 319, 364
Yarborough, D. B., 145–46
Yeaxlee, Basil, 50, 58, 298
Yelich Biniecki, Susan, 2, 5, 119–25, 134
Yoon, S. W., 278
Yorks, L., 275, 280
Youde, A., 160
Young, S., 2

Zacharakis, Jeff, 3, 6, 55, 123, 236, 238, 420–22, 424
Zachary, L. J., 109, 153, 156
Zajonic, A., 160
Zamani-Gallaher, E. M., 216
Zamudio, M. M., 430
Zapotosky, M., 219
Zarestky, Jill, 6, 240, 449
Zawacki-Richter, O., 254
Zembylas, M., 367
Zigarelli, J., 95
Zimmerman, D. H., 388
Zimring, C. A., 319
Zinn, L. M., 11–12, 14
Zinth, J., 143–44
Zong, J., 66
Zorrilla, A., 33
Zuber-Skerritt, O., 440
Zull, J. E., 93

Subject Index

AAACE. *See* American Association for Adult and Continuing Education
AAAE. *See* American Association for Adult Education
AAM. *See* American Alliance of Museums
ABE. *See* adult basic education
Ability to Benefit policy, 359
ableism, 394, 398
Abu Ghraib prison, 237
academic advising services, for adult students, 268
academic capitalism, 63–65
Academy of Human Resource Development, 381
accelerating opportunity (AO), 355–56
access, 55–56, 101–6, 125, 311, 405
accountability, 145, 147, 192–93
accreditation, of prior learning, 151
Accreditation Council for Graduate Medical Education, 250–51
ACE. *See* adult and continuing education
ACS. *See* American Community Survey
ActionAid, 242
action mapping, 132
Action Research on Measuring Literacy Program Participants' Learning Outcomes (RAMAA), 243–44
active labor market policies, 228
active learning, 269, 440
activism, social, teaching, 363–69
Activist Graduate School, 326
activist pedagogy, 364–68
activity theory, of aging, 402–3
ADA. *See* Americans with Disabilities Act of 1990
ADA Amendments Act of 2008, 393
adaptive leadership, 396
ADDIE model, 132
ADEA. *See* Association for the Development of Education in Africa
administration, of ACE programs, 2, 122–26
administrative leadership, 122–24
adolescents, 86, 151
adult and continuing education (ACE), 4. *See also specific topics*

administrative leadership in, 122–24
AI and, 180–82
assessment, 141, 146–47
bias in assessment and evaluation, 146–47
business models in, 125
colonizing adult learners, historical examples, 343–46
decolonizing, 342–47
democratic ideals in, 182
digital technologies for, 177–84
disability inclusion and equity in, 395–98
discipline and, 31, 35–36
effective administration in, 122–24
epistemology and, 17–19
ESL and, 197
essential philosophical questions and terms, 16–19
ethics and, 18–19
evaluation, 145–47
extension programs, 343–44
funding and delivery of, 243
historical perspectives on, 241–42
history of, 22–29
HRD, WPL and, 275, 282–83
interdisciplinarity and, 31–35
IoT and, 180–81
legislation, federal, 39–41
life-changing potential of, 448–49
logic and, 17–18
metaphysics and, 17
neoliberalism and, 125, 447–48
non-Western philosophical foundations, 15–16, 19–20
philosophical foundations of, 11–20
policy arena, 38–39, 44
policy development, 39–45
policy domain, 39
program administration, management, and organization, 119–26
public education policy, 38–45
research, interdisciplinarity in, 34
scholarship, strengthening, 450

489

sexual diversity in, 371–77
Western philosophical foundations, 11–14, 19–20
adult basic education (ABE), 43, 424
adults with disabilities and, 395
curriculum, narrowing, 193–94
FL programs and, 208
funding, 189–92, 226
performance accountability and, 192–93
policy, evolution of, 191–94
programs, 190–94, 208
in state prisons, 217
workforce development and, 192, 226
adult development, 81–88, 109
adult education. *See specific topics*
Adult Education Act of 1966, 24, 39, 101, 202
Adult Education and Family Literacy Act of 1998 (AEFLA), 40, 191, 194, 207–8
Adult Education and Family Literacy Act of 2016, 24
Adult Education Association of the USA, 429
adult education associations, policy interests and, 43–45
Adult Education Committee of the British Ministry of Reconstruction, 49
adult education journals, 44
adult education programs, 1
ABE, 190–94, 208
administration of, 2, 122–26
alternative, 450–51
correctional, 215–17
evaluation of, 145–46
FL, 194, 205–11, 385
HPE, 135, 249–54
IDE, 244
labor, 287–88, 290–94
leadership in administration of, 122–24
lifelong learning, 47–48
literacy, 40, 199, 242, 364–67, 395, 423–25
management of, 119–20
organization of, 120–21, 124–26
participatory, for migrants, 440
policies and, 40–42
poverty reduction and, 350
support for, 104–5
technology and, 43
for vulnerable populations, 3
WIA and, 40
WIOA and, 41–42
workforce development, 208, 223, 225–26

Adult Education Quarterly (*AEQ*), 23–24, 34, 44, 412–13
Adult Education Research Conference (AERC), 67, 381, 383–86, 414–15
adult educators, 3, 78
administrative leaders and, 124
adult developmental principles and, 81
adult learners and, 101–2, 105, 141, 150–51, 153–54, 158, 168
andragogy and, 151
authentic, 123
Black, 412
critical theory and, 74
CRT and, 416
DACA and, 385–86
disability and, 394
ESL and, 197, 203
feminist, 384
gender discourses and, 382
on history, 26
HPE, 251–52
HRD and, 279
inclusion of PWD, 396
labor education and, 287
leadership and, 122–23
on lifelong learning, 223, 344
mentorship and, 109
peace education and, 331–32
philosophical foundations for, 11
physical development and, 81–82
popular culture and, 172, 174
on sexual assault, 385
social class and, 420
social justice and, 332
teaching perspectives and, 153
White, 412–13, 432
workforce development and, 227–30
adult environmental education (AEE), 314–20
adulthood, 82, 86
The Adult Learner (Knowles), 150
adult learner leadership, 424–25
adult learners, 92, 424–25
access, participation, and support of, 100–106
adult educators and, 101–2, 105, 141, 150–51, 153–54, 158, 168
andragogy for, 163–64
assessment and, 140
barriers to participation, 102–3
behaviorism on, 315–16

challenges of, 267–68
characteristics of, 93
colonization of, historical examples in ACE, 343–46
ESL for, 200–202
in higher education, 266–67
HRD and, 278–79
humanism on, 316
media literacy of, 172
mentoring models and frameworks for, 111–13
motivational framework for teaching, 95
older, 402
TED Talks and, 309
underserved and low-income, 96–97

Adult Learners' Week, 51

adult learning. *See also* lifelong learning
andragogy, 75
clinical education models and, 252
contemporary theories of, 73, 76–77
cultural institutions and, 307–10
curiosity and, 82–83, 87
digital technologies and, 178, 180, 183–84
e-mentoring and, 110
emotions and spirituality in, 77
experiential, 75
Facilitating Interdisciplinary Research on, 32–33
foundational theories of, 73–76
helping-adults-learn paradigm, 154–56
holistic and blended pedagogy, 161
HPE and, 252
integrated ways of, 76–77
intrinsic motivation and, 93–94
IoT and, 180–81
life mission and, 102
mentoring relationships and, 109
power relations in, 414
relationality in, 77–78
self-directed, 74–75
SML and, 322, 324–25
social context of, 73–74
traditional learning theories and, 74, 78
transformative, 76–77
ZPD in, 84

Adult Learning (periodical), 55, 432
Adult Learning (Thorndike), 150
adult learning theory, 151, 200
adult literacy education (ALE), 405–6
assessment in, 143–44
ESL and, 198–99, 202–3

historical context of, 421–23
political context in, 423
programs, 40, 199, 242, 364–67, 395, 423–25
social class and, 420–21, 423–25
adult literacy skills, 6, 189–95
adult motivation to learn, 91–97, 102
Adult Occupational Act of 1967, 423
adult students. *See also* adult learners
active learning and social integration, 269
in colleges, 266–72
consistent enrollment of, 269–70
degree programs for, 270–71
literacy, 365
older, 402
PLA for, 270–71
adult worker-students, 288–89
AEA. *See* American Evaluation Association
AEE. *See* adult environmental education
AEFLA. *See* Adult Education and Family Literacy Act of 1998
AEQ. *See* Adult Education Quarterly
AEQ. See Adult Education Quarterly
AERA. *See* American Educational Research Association
AERC. *See* Adult Education Research Conference
aesthetics, 18
AFDC. *See* Aid to Families with Dependent Children
affirmative action, 410
African Americans, 23–25, 27–28, 319, 322, 343, 364. *See also* Black people
Americanization movement and, Du Bois on, 411
older, 413
White racism against, 410, 412–13, 416–17
African art, 27
African Diaspora Preconference, 414
African philosophy, 15–16
African Union, 242, 244
Africentric feminist perspective, 415
Afrocentricity, 343
Age-ing to Sage-ing (Schachter-Shalomi), 403
ageism, 404–5
Agenda 2030, 48, 52, 55–58, 242–46
Agenda 2063 (African Union Commission), 244
aging, 402–4
brain, 83–85
AHRD Conference Proceedings, 386
AHRD Standards on Ethics and Integrity, 374
AI. *See* artificial intelligence

Aid to Families with Dependent Children (AFDC), 351–52
ALC-TE. *See Army Learning Concept for Training and Education 2020-2040*
ALE. *See* adult literacy education
allyship, for LGBTQ people, 377
alternative education programs, 450–51
alt-right movement, 323, 446
Alzheimer's disease, 82
AMA. *See* American Medical Association
Amazon Echo, 181
American Alliance of Museums (AAM), 306, 308, 310
American Association for Adult and Continuing Education's (AAACE), 34, 52, 55, 68, 415, 429
American Association for Adult Education (AAAE), 24–25, 27, 50, 372, 429
American Association of Colleges of Osteopathic Medicine, 251
American Association of Community Colleges, 97
American Community Survey (ACS), 198
American Educational Research Association (AERA), 145
American education system, 3–4, 33
American Evaluation Association (AEA), 145
Americanization movement, 411
Americanization programs, 27
American Job Centers, 226–27
American Library Association, 207–8
American Medical Association (AMA), 448
American Museum of Natural History, 308
American Psychiatric Association (APA), 381–82
American Psychological Association (APA), 4, 145, 371
Americans with Disabilities Act of 1990 (ADA), 392–93, 395, 397
analytical philosophical foundation, of ACE, 13, 18
ancient China, lifelong learning in, 49
ancient Greek philosophy, 12, 14, 49
ancient India, lifelong learning in, 49
andragogy, 35, 74–75, 81, 150–52
    applications and characteristics of, 163–64
    historical development of, 162
    MIPI and, 163
    pedagogy and, 75, 151, 158–59, 162, 165
Antigonish movement, 241
anti-racism, 432
AO. *See* accelerating opportunity
AO-K program, 359

APA. *See* American Psychiatric Association; American Psychological Association
Apartheid, in South Africa, 347
apprenticeship teaching perspective, 153
Arab American Association of New York, 366
Army, U.S., 233–34, 236
Army Learning Concept for Training and Education 2020-2040 (ALC-TE), 234
artificial intelligence (AI), 177, 180–82, 184
Art Institute of Chicago, 309
arts, in informal education about social issues, 335
arts-based learning, 77
Asia South Pacific Association for Basic and Adult Education (ASPBAE), 244
assessment, 140–48
Association for the Development of Education in Africa (ADEA), 244
Association of American Medical Colleges, 251
ATD, 227, 275, 278
attachment theory, of adult development, 85–86
audit culture, 147
Australian Indigenous tradition, 15
authentic assessments, 142–43
authenticity, 262, 307
authentic leadership, 123
authentic professional learning, 262
authoritarian *versus* authoritative teaching, 152, 156
The Autobiography of Malcolm X (Malcolm X), 214
The Avengers (TV show), 171

banking education, 152
Barbara Bush Foundation, 207–8
basic education, 24, 28, 101, 141
Basic English Skills Test (BEST), 143
basic skills, contextualized, 355–58
behaviorism, 12, 18–19, 74, 159, 315–16
BEST. *See* Basic English Skills Test
bias, in assessment and evaluation, 146–47
bilingualism, 200
bioecological theory, 88
biopsychosocial model, of disability, 394
Birmingham School, 170
Black activism, environmental justice and, 317
Black adult educators, 412
Black African personhood, 16
"black books" of adult education, 414–15
Black children's literacy practices, 210
Black education, 412
Black faculty, race pedagogy for, 415–16

SUBJECT INDEX

Black feminism, 14, 415
Black gay men, 415
Black Learners Advisory Committee, 345
Black Lives Matter movement, 2, 130, 293, 322, 326, 347, 365, 385, 410
Blackness, 416
Black people
    Du Bois and Washington on movement of, 343, 345
    literacy of older, 413–14
    in prison population, 215–16
Black Power era, 412–13
Black students, at community colleges, 97
Black/White binary, in adult education scholarship, 417
Black women, 341, 385, 415–16
Black women's club movement, 345
The Blanket Exercise, 367–68
blended pedagogy, 160–62
body, 33, 76–77
Bolshevik revolution, 84
both-ways education, 15
brains
    aging, 83–85
    cultural socialization and, 92
    development, 83–86
    motivation and, 93
    neuroscience and, 32–33, 74, 76, 91, 93
    SEEKING system of, 87
Bridge to Health and Business program, 356
bridging programs, 439–41
Bristol School Movement, 422
Brookings Institute, 421
Bryn Mawr College, Summer School for Women Workers, 289
Buddhism, 15
Bureau of Justice Statistics, 219
business models, in ACE, 125
business unionism, 288–89, 291

CAEO. *See* Coalition of Adult Education Organizations
CAF. *See* Canadian Armed Forces
Canada
    Adult Occupational Act, 423
    ALE programs in, 423
    Antigonish movement, 241
    bridging programs in, 439–40
    critical PME in, 237–38
    extension programs in, 344
    FL programs in, 207
    Frontier College in, 344–45
    Indigenous activists in, 326
    international students in, 67
    migrants to, 436–38
    Royal College of Physicians and Surgeons, 251
    social gospel in, 421–22
    Truth and Reconciliation Commission of Canada Report, 346
    WEA in, 344
    WI of, 345
    women in military, 237
Canadian Armed Forces (CAF), 237
Canadian Association for the Study of Adult Education (CASAE), 67–68
Canadian Starbucks stores, racial bias training, 128, 131
capability approach, 245
capital, 420–21
    human, 104
capitalism, 154–55, 290, 368
    academic, 63–65
    colonization and, 341
    global, 63, 172
    labor education and, 287–88
    neoliberal, 170, 363–64
care, relationships and, 107
Career and Technical Education (CTE), 41–42, 217, 220, 224, 226–30
career development (CD), 107–8, 276
career pathways, 41–42, 45, 191, 194, 202, 229, 356–57
Careers in Health (Carreras en Salud), 356
Carl D. Perkins Career and Technical Education Act of 2006, 41, 226–27
Carnegie Corporation, 28
Carnegie Foundation, 50, 164, 412
Carreras en Salud (Careers in Health), 356
CASAE. *See* Canadian Association for the Study of Adult Education
CASAS. *See* Comprehensive Adult Student Assessment Systems
CASE. *See* Culture and Sport Evidence
CAST. *See* Center for Applied Special Technology
caste system, social class and, 420
CBE. *See* competency-based assessments; competency-based education
CCR. *See* College and Career Readiness

CD. *See* career development
CEAAL. *See* Consejo de Educación de Adultos de América Latina
Census Bureau, U.S., 198, 401–2
Center for Applied Linguistics, 198–99
Center for Applied Special Technology (CAST), 396
Center for Community College Student Engagement, 97
Center for Law and Social Policy, 353
Center for the Study of Liberal Education for Adults, 423
Centro de Cooperación Regional para la Educació de Adultos en América Latina y el Caribe (CREFAL), 244
Century Foundation, 97
CES. *See* Cooperative Extension System
CESA. *See* Continental Education Strategy for Africa
CGSC. *See* Command and General Staff College
change, assessment principles and, 142
change, managing, 125
charity, neoliberalism and, 365
Chautauqua Institution, 28
Chicago, Indigenous land-based pedagogy in, 319
children, pedagogy for, 158–59
children and adolescents, 151
CHRD. *See* critical HRD
cisgender, 380–81, 384–88
citizenship education, 343–44, 423
civic engagement, 288, 291
Civil Affairs Training School, 25
Civil Rights Act of 1964, 235
civil rights movement, 2, 25, 40, 322, 409, 412–13, 417
class, social, 420–21, 423–25
classism, 420–21, 425
CLEP. *See* College Level Examination Program
clinician educators, 250–52
COABE. *See* Coalition on Adult Basic Education
coaching, 108
Coalition of Adult Education Organizations (CAEO), 53
Coalition of Black Trade Unions International, 293
Coalition of Lifelong Learning Organization (COLLO), 52–53, 56, 58
Coalition on Adult Basic Education (COABE), 43
cognitive aging, 83–85
cognitive development, 83–86
Cold War, 242
collaboration, 33, 130, 448–49

College and Career Readiness (CCR), 101
College Level Examination Program (CLEP), 144, 270
college students, adult, 266–71
COLLO. *See* Coalition of Lifelong Learning Organization
colonial education, 342, 345
colonial institutions, 341–42
colonialism, 16, 25, 240–41
    decolonization and, 318–19, 342–48, 364
    of White settlers, 318–20, 367
colonization, 341–43
    of adult learners, in ACE, 343–46
    Indigenous populations and, 342–43, 345–46, 367, 409
colorblindness, White privilege and, 431–32
Comenius Medal, UNESCO, 49
Command and General Staff College (CGSC), 236
Commission of Professors of Adult Education (CPAE), 32, 68, 415
Common Core, 143–44
Common Core State Standards, 218
the commons, revitalizing, 317
common sense, 169
communalism, 15
communication, multimodal, 161
Communist Party, 289
communities of practice (CoP), 112, 161, 263, 324–25
community, 15, 26
    development, 241, 244
    education, 244
    mediation, conflict resolution and, 332–33
    of peer mentors, 112
community-based education, 241, 343, 347
community-based training, for trauma aftermath, 334–35
community colleges, 97, 216, 226–27, 356–57
compensatory education, 206
competence, culturally responsive teaching and, 202
competency-based assessments (CBE), 144
competency-based education (CBE), 135, 235, 253
complex emergency, 335
complexity theory, 74
Comprehensive Adult Student Assessment Systems (CASAS), 143
computer literacy, 218
concept-based curriculum, 252
CONFINTEA. *See* International Conferences on Adult Education

conflict, 330–31
conflict resolution, 330–33, 335
Conrad N. Hilton Foundation, 57
conscientização (*conscientization*), 74
consciousness raising (CR), 324
Consejo de Educación de Adultos de América Latina (CEAAL), 244
conservation, 315
conservative social movements, 323
constructionism, 74
constructivism, 278–79, 307–8
constructivist epistemology, 17
constructivist learning, 259
contemplative pedagogy, 160
Continental Education Strategy for Africa (CESA), 242, 244
continuing education. *See specific topics*
Continuing Learning in the Professions (Houle), 258
continuing professional development, 258
continuing professional education (CPE), 257–64
continuous and self-directed learning, 258
continuum of learning, 75
contract workers, 3
conventional/rational planning models, 135–36
Cooperative Extension System (CES), 343–44
CoP. *See* communities of practice
Coronavirus 2019 (COVID 19), 309
corporate hegemony, 288, 291
correctional education, 214–17, 219–20
cosmic perspective, on aging, 403
cosmopolitanism, 34
Council of Chief State School Officers, 143–44
counterstorytelling, 409–10, 432–33
COVID 19. *See* Coronavirus 2019
COVID-19 pandemic, 53–55
CPAE. *See* Commission of Professors in Adult Education
CPE. *See* continuing professional education
CR. *See* consciousness raising
Crash, 173, 430
creaming, 193
credentialing, training and, 55
CREFAL. *See* Centro de Cooperación Regional para la Educació de Adultos en América Latina y el Caribe
Crime Bill of 1994, 218–19
critical analysis, in military education, 234, 236
critical consciousness, 346, 365–66
critical cultural analysis, 279–80

critical educational gerontology, 403
critical HRD (CHRD), 279
critical knowledge, 235
critical learning, 173
critical media literacy, 173
critical paradigm, of adult military education, 235, 237–38
critical pedagogy, 151–52, 160, 237, 318
critical place-based EE, 314, 318, 320
critical PME, 237–38
critical race theory (CRT), 409–12, 414, 416, 432–33
critical reflection, 1, 263, 325, 332
critical theory, 74, 132, 154, 262–63
cross-cultural mentoring relationships, 110
Crossing the Quality Chasm (IOM), 250
CRT. *See* critical race theory
CRTM. *See* culturally responsive teaching model
CTE. *See* Career and Technical Education
cultural action, 293
cultural bomb, 342
cultural consumption, 168–70, 174
cultural institutions, 305–11
culturally relevant or responsive education, 439
culturally responsive teaching, motivational framework for, 201–2
culturally responsive teaching model (CRTM), 376
cultural pluralism, 12
cultural sustainability, 306
culture, 305–6, 387
Culture and Sport Evidence (CASE), 306–7
culture market, 13
culture of poverty perspective, 207
Cultures of Program Planning in Adult Education (Käpplinger), 133
curiosity, 82–83, 87
curriculum, 155, 193–94
  colonialism and, 342
  concept-based, 252
  CTE, 226
  of HPE programs, 249, 252–53
  LGBTQ issues in, 373
  queering, 376
  UDL and, 396–97
cycle of socialization/liberation, 377

DACA. *See* Deferred Action for Childhood Arrivals
The Daily Kos, 290
DANTES Subject Standardization (DSST), 270

daytime talk shows, 171
DE. *See* Department of Education, U.S.
decision-making processes, 132
decolonization, 318–19, 342–48, 364
deconstruction, 13
Deep Democracy, 334
deep learning, 182
Deferred Action for Childhood Arrivals (DACA), 366, 385–86
degree programs, adult-focused, 270–71
Deliberate Democracy Institute, 334
dementia, 82
democracy, 23, 27–28, 63–64, 182, 292
democratic socialism, 132
Department of Defense, U.S. (DOD), 40, 233–34
Department of Education, U.S. (DE), 40–41, 143, 190, 192–93, 359, 447–48
    NCES of, 4, 199, 216–17, 267, 269, 424
    on WIOA, 423
Department of Health and Human Services, U.S., 206, 358
Department of Justice, U.S., 219
Department of Labor, U.S. (DOL), 40–42, 45, 226
deprofessionalization, 439
development, 81–88, 109, 151, 279, 325. *See also* human resource development
developmental networks, mentoring and, 113
developmental teaching perspective, 153
Development Decades, UN, 242
Diagnostic and Statistical Manual of Mental Disorders (DSM), 381–82
differential racialization thesis, in CRT, 411
digital literacies, 209
digitally mediated learning (DML), 163
digital technologies, 177–84
direct education, 334
direct learning, 275
disability, 392–98
disability studies, 393–94, 397
discipline, ACE and, 31, 35–36
discrimination
    ableism and sanism, 394, 398
    genderism perpetuating, 387–88
    racism and, 155, 385, 431
discussion groups, 150
disorienting dilemmas, 155
dispositional barriers, to participation, 102
diversity
    adult and continuing education and, 2–4, 42

    consciousness, 377
    of educational programs, 121
    in ESL classes, 197–99
    of family structures, FL and, 210
    gender, 380, 387–88
    inclusivity and, 417
    language, 200
    in methodical research approaches, 44
    sexual, 371–77
    in U.S. military, 232, 236–38
    of viewpoints, at cultural institutions, 310
DML. *See* digitally mediated learning
doctoral education, e-mentoring in, 110
Doctor Who, 171
DOD. *See* Department of Defense
DOL. *See* Department of Labor
"Don't Ask Don't Tell" policy, of U.S. military, 237, 372
double consciousness, 341
DSM. *See* Diagnostic and Statistical Manual of Mental Disorders
DSST. *See* DANTES Subject Standardization
dynamic assessment, 143

EAP. *See* English for Academic Purposes
Eastern philosophy, 15
e-books, 181
ecojustice, 317–18
ecojustice adult education, 314
Economic and Philosophical Manuscripts (Marx), 151–52
Economic Bill of Rights, 1944, 39
Economic Opportunity Act of 1964 (EOA), 40, 225, 423
Educating Rita, 171
Education 2030, 245
education about peace, education for peace and, 332
educational attainment levels, of incarcerated population, 216
educational configurations, 25
educational gerontology, 403
educational leaders, 250–51
Education as a Science (Bain), 159
Education Commission of the States, 143–44
Education for All (EFA), 242–43, 245
Education for Self-Reliance (Nyerere), 342
education philosophies, 11–20
education policy, of ACE, 38–44
EE. *See* environmental education
EFA. *See* Education for All

SUBJECT INDEX

effective administration, 122–24
effective assessment principles, 141–42
effective feedback, in assessment, 142
effective program evaluation, 145
Elderhostel, 403
elite democratic liberalism, 27
emancipatory approaches, to decolonizing ACE, 343, 346–47
emancipatory epistemology, 17, 301
e-mentoring, 109–10
emergent approaches, to program planning, 135
emerging adulthood theory, 86
emerging approaches, to decolonizing ACE, 343
emerging economies, 240
emotional development, 87–88, 325
emotions, 77, 87–88, 92, 367
empathy, cultural institutions and, 306
Employment and Training program, SNAP, 359
Employment and Training (ET) system, 224–30
empowerment evaluation, 146
English as a Second Language (ESL), 190–91, 437
    adultcentric approaches to, 200–202
    adult learning theory and, 200
    ALE and, 198–99, 202–3
    Career Pathways and, 202
    diversity in classes, 197–99
    EPI Model and, 202
    IEP, 199
    TESOL, 199–200
English for Academic Purposes (EAP), 199
English for Specific Purposes (ESP), 199
English language
    immigrants to U.S. and, 411
    literacy and, 422
    in migrant education, 439
English-Plus Integration (EPI) Model, 202
Enhanced Transitional Jobs Demonstration (ETJD), 358
Enlightenment, 12
entrepreneurship, 64
environmental education (EE), 309, 318–20. *See also* adult environmental education
environmentalism, 309, 316–18
environmental racism, 319
EOA. *See* Economic Opportunity Act of 1964
EPI. *See* English-Plus Integration Model
epistemic pluralism, 346
epistemology, 17–19
ESL. *See* English as a Second Language

ESP. *See* English for Specific Purposes
ET. *See* Employment and Training system
ethics, 18–19
ethnicity, 411
ETJD. *See* Enhanced Transitional Jobs Demonstration
eugenics, 409
European-American Collaborative Challenging Whiteness, 429, 432
European immigrants, Americanization of, 411
European Parliament, 65
Evaluating the Effectiveness of Correctional Education (RAND Corporation), 215
evaluation, 140–41, 144–48
Even Start program, 206–8
everyday experience, learning in, 168
everyday practices, learning through, 440–41
evidence-based evaluation policy, 145
Examining Controversies in Adult Education (Kreitlow), 428
experience, 33, 168, 262–63, 307–8, 334
experiential learning, 75, 316, 324
expert systems, 260
The Exploratorium, San Francisco, 306
extension programs, ACE, 343–44
External Review Authority, CAF and, 237

Facebook, 405
Facilitating Interdisciplinary Research (IoM), 32
facilitation, 150, 152
faculty, higher education, 64, 67, 268, 415–16
Fair Labor Association, 288
faith and hope, 88
false consciousness, 152
family literacy (FL) programs, 194, 205–11, 385
family service learning, 210
family skills, 206
Family Support Act of 1988, 351
Far Right, 26
Federal Bureau of Prisons Statistics, 215
Federal Emergency Relief Act (FERA), 289
federal funding, adult education and, 189–91, 207–8, 225
feminism, 383–86, 394
    Black, 14, 415
feminist critiques, of mentoring, 111
feminist program planning, 132–33, 135
FERA. *See* Federal Emergency Relief Act
films, education and, 170–72

firm-based HRD, 227–30
First Nations, peace circles of, 333
five-stage theory of skill acquisition, 136
FL. *See* family literacy programs
"flatten the curve" policies, 309
Flexner report, 250
flow experiences, 94
Food and Nutrition Services, USDA, 359
Forgiveness Project, 334
formal education, 257, 316
formal learning, 73, 172, 183, 280
formal mentoring programs, 108
formative assessment, 141–42
four-level model of evaluation, 146
four stages of cognitive development, Piaget's theory of, 83, 85
the fourth age, 406
Fourth World, 240
Frankfurt School, 169–72, 234
free-choice, 308
Freedom Road (Peterson), 414
Freedom School, 326
From Pedagogy to Andragogy (Knowles), 151
Frontier College, 344–45
functionalism, 15
functional model, of disability, 392–93
funding
    for ABE, 189–92, 226
    federal, 189–91, 207–8, 225
    for FL programs, 207–8
    for IDE, 243–44
    research activities and, 64
A Future for Workers (Melvin), 293–94

GAIN. *See* Greater Avenues to Independence
GAO. *See* General Accountability Office
"gatekeepers," 417
Gauging Aging (Lindland), 404
GBA+. *See* Gender-Based Analysis Plus education
GD. *See* gender dysphoria
GED. *See* General Educational Development; General Equivalency Diploma; high school equivalency degree
gender-affirming language, 388
Gender-Based Analysis Plus (GBA+) education, 237
gender differences, of older adults, 402
gender diversity, 380, 387–88
gender dysphoria (GD), 381–82
gender identities, 380–88, 394

gender identity disorder (GID), 381–82
genderism, 381–82, 386–88
General Accountability Office (GAO), 352
General Educational Development (GED), 101, 217–20, 234
General Equivalency Diploma (GED), 143–44, 351, 356, 450
General Medical Council, UK, 251
Germany, migrants to, 437
gerontology, 403
Ghanaian philosophy, 15–16
G.I. Bill, 40, 50, 233, 266
GID. *See* gender identity disorder
Global Campaign for Education, 242
global capitalism, 63, 172
Global Conference on Learning Cities, 57
global education, 65
Global Education Monitoring Reports, 55, 243, 245
Global Forum on Innovation in Health Professional Education, 250
globalism, 78
globalization, 4, 61–62
    in adult education access, 125
    adult education participation and, 105
    knowledge society and, 103
    neoliberalism, academic capitalism and, 63–65
    transnationalism and, 375
global leadership, 123
global learning, 66
Global Monitoring Report (GMR), UNESCO, 55
Global Network of Learning Cities (GNLC), UNESCO, 57
Global North, 240
Global Report on Adult Learning and Education (GRALE), 243–46
Global South, 240, 342, 394
Global University for Lifelong Learning, 440
GMR. *See* Global Monitoring Report
GNLC. *See* Global Network of Learning Cities
Goldwater-Nichols Act of 1986, 234
Goodling Institute, 210
GRALE. *See* Global Report on Adult Learning and Education
Great Britain Ministry of Reconstruction, 49
The Great Didactic (Comenius), 162
Greater Avenues to Independence (GAIN), 351–52
Green String Network, 334
Grey's Anatomy, 172
Guardian, 326

SUBJECT INDEX

Handbook of Adult and Continuing Education (Ely), 150
Handbook of Adult and Continuing Education (Kasworm), 1–2, 7
Handbook of Adult and Continuing Education (Wilson & Hayes), 1, 73, 107, 414, 429, 446
Handbook of Adult Education (Adult Learning) (Thorndike), 73
Handbook of Adult Education in the United States (English & Tisdell), 297
Handbook of Adult Education in the United States (Knowles), 128, 150
Handbook of Adult Education in the United States (Lewis), 411
Handbooks of Adult and Continuing Education (1934-1948), 410–12
Handbooks of Adult and Continuing Education (1934-1980), 428
Handbooks of Adult and Continuing Education (1989-2010), 382–83
Harlem Experiments, 27
Harriet Beecher Stowe Center, 306
Hawai'i, land-based EE in, 319
HBCUs. *See* historically Black colleges and universities
healthcare, LGBTQ issues and, 373–74
health care delivery system, 251
health care professionals, spirituality in workplace of, 299
health education, 249
health literacy, 406
Health Profession Opportunity Grant program (HPOG), 357
health professions education (HPE), 135, 249–54
Health Professions Education (IOM), 250
health promotion programs, 134–35
hearables, 182
hegemony, 169, 172, 341
    corporate, 288, 291
    decolonizing ACE and, 347
    Eurocentric cultural, 343
    Gramsci on, 364
Helping Adults Learn (Knox), 154
helping-adults-learn paradigm, 154–56
HEQ. *See History of Education Quarterly*
heterocentric discourse, in ACE, 371
heteroprofessionalism, 374
heterosexuals and heterosexuality, 372, 374–77, 380, 386–87

higher education
    academic disciplines in, 31
    adult learners in, 266–67
    disability accommodations within, 395
    e-mentoring in, 110
    faculty, 64, 67, 268, 415–16
    in films, 170–71
    globalization and, 63–65
    internationalization of, 65–67
    labor studies in, 290
    LGBTQ students and, 375–76
    market orientation of, 64
    nontraditional students in, 450
    Normal Schools and, 266
    PLA and, 144
higher education institutions, corporate model in, 3
Higher Education Reconciliation Act of 2005, 144
Highlander Center, 290
Highlander Folk School, 152, 241, 322, 326, 334, 364, 368
Highlander Institute, 417
Highlander Research and Education Center, 123, 334
Highlights from the U.S. PIAAC Survey of Incarcerated Adults (Rampey), 216–17
high school equivalency (HSE), 101, 424
high school equivalency degree (GED), 3–4
High School Equivalency Test (HiTest), 143–44
Hilton Foundation, 57
Hispanics, in prison population, 215
historically Black colleges and universities (HBCUs), 133
historiography, of ACE, 22–23
history, of ACE, 22–29
history, of education, 25
History of Education Quarterly (HEQ), 23–24
history writing, 22
HiTest. *See* High School Equivalency Test
HIV, 373
holism, 16, 259
holistic pedagogy, 159–62
homophobia, 372–77, 415
homosexuality, 372–73
host system, 276
How Effective Is Correctional Education, and Where Do We Go from Here? (RAND Corporation), 215
HPE. *See* health professions education
HPOG. *See* Health Profession Opportunity Grant program

HRD. *See* human resource development
HSE. *See* High School Equivalency
Hull House, 310, 422
human capacity, 292
human capital, 104, 241
humanism, 74, 235, 316
humanistic paradigm, of adult education, 235
humanistic philosophical foundation, of ACE, 14, 19
human resource development (HRD), 224
    CD and, 276
    conceptual frames for, 278–79
    CPE, 261–63
    critical, 279
    critical cultural analysis and, 279–80
    critical theory of, 262–63
    defining, 275–76
    firm-based, 227–30
    gender identities and, 386
    learners and, 278–79
    learning paths and learning networks in, 280–81
    LGBTQ workers and, 374, 386
    long-term learning capacity in, 275
    OD and, 276–77
    performance *versus* learning in, 277–78
    productivity in, 276–77
    publications, 386
    self and identity in, 279
    situated learning and development in, 279
    T&D in, 276–78, 280–82
    terms, 276
    transfer of training and, 281–82
    WPL and, 275–78, 280–83
human rights, 237, 243, 364, 438
The Hunger Games, 171

I-BEST, 355–56, 359
ICAE. *See* International Council for Adult Education
ICF. *See* International Classification of Functioning, Disability, and Health
IDE. *See* international development education
identities
    gender, 380–88, 394
    in HRD, 279
    mentoring relationships and, 109–11, 113
    narrating notion of, 77
    politics of, 347
    sexual, 415
    White, 430–31, 433
    of women, 383
identity-culture relationship, 169
identity markers, 323
ideological transmission, pedagogy and, 169
Idle No More movement, 326, 347
IEEQ. *See* Internationally Educated Engineers Qualification Program
IEP. *See* Institute for Economics and Peace; Intensive English Programs
IET. *See* Integrated Education and Training
ILAs. *See* interactive parent-child literacy activities
IM. *See* intervention mapping
immigrants, to U.S., 198–99, 206, 210, 310, 385, 411, 436
impartiality, cultural institutions and, 306
incarcerated population, 215–21
Incheon Declaration, 245
incidental learning, 73, 280
inclusion, 3–4, 201, 395–98, 417
Inclusion and Education report, GMR, 55
inclusive education, 396
Indian Residential Schools, 345–46
Indigenization, 343
Indigenous activists, in Canada, 326
Indigenous African land-based EE, 319–20
Indigenous conflict resolution practices, 333
Indigenous knowledge, 77–78, 325
Indigenous philosophy, 15–16
Indigenous populations, colonization and, 342–43, 345–46, 367, 409
Indigenous students, 345–46
Indigenous worldviews, 346–47
Industrial Workers of the World, 344–45
inequality, 103–4, 223, 316
informal learning, 73, 100, 172, 178, 183, 280, 282
    in AEE, 315–16
    arts in, 335
    cultural institutions and, 307–8, 310–11
    multiculturalism and, 441
    peace education and, 332
    in social justice action, 330
    social movements and, 324, 333
informal mentoring, 108
information, in assessment and evaluation, 141, 144–45
information processing (IP) theory, of cognitive development, 84
information technology, prison education and, 218
inner work, outer work and, 261–62
Institute for College Access & Success, 353

SUBJECT INDEX

Institute for Economics and Peace (IEP), 199, 331
Institute for Lifelong Learning, UNESCO, 57
Institute of Medicine (IOM), 249–50, 252, 254
institutional barriers, to participation, 102
institutional education, as banking education, 152
institutionalized religions, adult religious education in, 298
Instituto del Progreso Latino, 356
instrumental (situational) epistemology, 17
intangible heritage, 305–6
Integrated Education and Training (IET), 191
integrated ways of learning, 76–77
intelligence, genotypic and phenotypic expressions of, 85
Intensive English Programs (IEP), 199
intentionality, 262
intentionality, internationalization and, 65
interactive experience model, 307–8
interactive parent-child literacy activities (ILAs), 206
interactive planning model, 134
interdisciplinarity, ACE and, 31–35
intergenerational learning and literacy, 205–6, 209
intergroup dialogue, peace-building and, 334–35
international adult education frameworks, 242–43
International Adult Learning Survey, 144
International Classification of Functioning, Disability, and Health (ICF), 394
International Conferences on Adult Education (CONFINTEA), 62, 241–46, 375
International Conferences on Financing for Development, UN, 243
International Convention on the Protection of the Rights of Migrant Workers and Members, UN, 438
International Council for Adult Education (ICAE), 51–53, 62, 66, 68, 243–44
International Covenant on Economic, Social and Cultural Rights, UN, 243
international development, 240, 243–44
international development education (IDE), 240–46
international FL programming, 208–9
internationalization, 61–62, 65–68
Internationally Educated Engineers Qualification Program (IEEQ), 439–40
International Perspectives on Older Adult Education (Findsen and Formosa), 405
international students, 65–67
international tourism, 308–9
internet access, 55–56, 405

Internet of Things (IoT), 180–81, 183–84
interprofessional education (IPE), 251–52
interrelationality, 78
intersectionality, 294, 317, 364, 376, 415
intertextuality, 169
intervention mapping (IM), 134
interventions, in social work, 135
intrinsic motivation, 93–94
invisible caste, 425
IOM. *See* Institute of Medicine
IoT. *See* Internet of Things
IP. *See* information processing theory
IPE. *See* interprofessional education
Italian immigrants, 411

Jane Addams Hull House (JAHHM), 310
Jane Addams Resource Corporation (JARC), 358
Al Jazeera, 326
Jefferson School of Social Science, 289
Jim Crow, 411–12
Job Opportunities and Basic Skills Training (JOBS), 351–52
job-related accommodations and training, for adults with disabilities, 395
JOBS. *See* Job Opportunities and Basic Skills Training
Joint Committee on Standards for Educational Evaluation, 145
Juntos, of Benjamin Franklin, 28, 50

Kenya, 66–67
Kettering Foundation, 334
kinesthetic learning, 76–77
knowledge, 17–19, 63, 132, 301
    body and, 33
    construction of, 307
    in CPE, 257–63
    critical, 235
    democratizing, 347
    disciplinary, 262
    epistemic pluralism, 346
    Habermas on types of, 234–35
    Indigenous, 77–78, 325
    narrative and, 77–78
    power and, 335
    queer, 375
    radical, 290
    SML and, 327
    solidarities, 346–47

knowledge economy, 262
knowledge society, 102–3
Korea, program planning in, 133
Korean War, 233
Ku Klux Klan, 26, 326

labor, mass public education and, 288–90
labor activism and movement, 289, 325
Labor College, New York, 344
labor education, 287–94, 344–45
    programs, 287–88, 290–94
labor market, 223–30, 241, 267, 350, 353–54, 357–58
labor studies programs, 290–91
labor unions, 64–65, 152, 294
LAMP initiative, UNESCO, 243–44
Lancet Commission, 2010, 250
land-based EE, 314, 318–20
Land Grant universities, 423
language learning, cultural context of, 200
Latinos, low-income, 356
Latino students, at community colleges, 97
Latinx communities, 319
leadership, 122–24, 151–52, 233, 396, 424–25
lean state, 291
learning. *See also* adult learning; lifelong learning; workplace learning
    assessment principles and, 142–43
    in cognitive development, 83
    contexts, popular culture and, 170–74
    critical, 173
    deep, 182
    digital technologies and, 177–78
    through discomfort, 367–68
    in everyday experiences, 168
    formal, 73, 172, 183, 280
    informal, 73, 100, 172, 178, 183
    motivation and, 91–92
    online, 95–96, 163, 266, 335
    participatory, 311, 344
    performance *versus*, WPL and, 277–78
    service, 210
    sociocultural context for, 307–8
    transformative, 76–77, 96, 155, 324, 429
Learning (DeLors), 52
learning cities, 56–57
learning disabilities, 395
learning in later life, 404

learning management systems (LMS), 178, 183
learning networks, 280–81
learning opportunities, typologies of, 100–101
learning organization, 277
learning paradigm, 278
learning paths, 280–81
learning-related activities, 276
learning skills, of children, 206
learning society, 48–49, 56–57
The Learning Society (Hutchins), 48
Learning to Be (Faure), 52
Learning to Be (UNESCO), 48–49
least-developed countries, adult education in, 244–45
left-wing activism, 292
Lesbian, Gay, Bisexual, Transgender, and Queer & Allies Caucus (LGBTQ&AC), 373, 381
LGBTQ movement, 372
LGBTQ parents and children, FL and, 210
LGBTQ people, 371–77, 384, 386
LGBTQ+ soldiers, 237
"LGBTQ special rights," 374
LGBTQ students, 375–76
Liaison Committee on Medical Education, 250–51
liberal approaches
    to AEE, 315
    to decolonizing ACE, 342
liberal democracies, in crisis, 322
liberal education, 160
liberalism, CRT on, 409–10, 412
liberal philosophical foundation, 12, 18–19, 315
liberation pedagogy, 242
liberation theology, 151–52
lifelong education, 48, 53, 56
Lifelong Education (Yeaxlee), 50
lifelong learning, 15, 43, 47
    adult development and, 88
    adult education, societal transformation and, 56–58
    adult educators on, 223, 344
    in ancient and earlier times, 49
    commodity production and, 344
    controversies and tensions, 55–56
    CPE and, 258
    developing countries and, 243
    dimensions of, 53
    formal education and, 257
    intrinsic motivation and, 94
    legislation, 53–54

lifelong education and, 48, 53, 56
meaning and usefulness of concept, 52–54
movement, 48–52
multiple levels of meaning in, 56
programs, 47–48
social justice and, 55
UNESCO and, 48–53, 55, 57, 344
workforce development and, 223–24
in workplace, 111
Lifelong Learning Act of 1976, 53–54
life mission, adult learning and, 102
linguistics, in TESOL, 200
literacy. *See also* family literacy
of adult students, 365
computer, 218
digital, 209
English language, 422
family, 194, 205–11, 385
fathers in development of, 209–10
Freire's approach to, 242
health, 406
IDE and, 241–42
intergenerational learning and, 205–6, 209
media, 172–73
of older Black people, 413–14
as social practice, 205–6
literacy classism, 423
literacy skills, 6, 44, 189–95
litteratus, 422
LMS. *See* learning management systems
logic, 17–18
logic model, 131
long-term learning capacity, 275
low-income adults, 96–97, 350, 353–54, 356, 358–59
low skills, adults with, 189–90, 193, 360
Lyceum movement, 28

M4BL. *See* Movement for Black Lives
mad-enabling pedagogies, 396
mad studies, 393–94, 396–97
Make the Road New York, 366
Making Space (Sheared & Sissel), 414–15
managing change, 125
Mandala Research, 305
marketing, 124–25
marketization, 64–65, 241, 424
marriage equality, 372

Marxism, 132, 152
Marxist-feminism, 384
MASELTOV. *See* Mobile Assistance for Social Inclusion & Empowerment of Immigrants with Persuasive Learning Technologies & Social Network Services
mass public education, labor and, 288–90
Master's in Health Professions Education (MHPE), 251
Matthew principle, 103
maximimalist and minimalist approaches, to lifelong learning, 56
MDG. *See* Millennium Development Goals
meaning, culturally responsive teaching and, 201–2
meaning making, assessment principles and, 142
The Meaning of Adult Education (Lindeman), 73, 150
Mechanics Institutes, 28
media, in SML, 326–27
media literacy, 172–73
mediation, 332–33
medical education, 250–51
medical model, of disability, 392
medicine wheel, 16
medieval educational philosophers, 12
mentoring constellations and mosaics, 112
mentoring relationships, 107–13
mentorship, 108–13
metaleadership, 123
#MeToo movement, 2, 111, 322, 365, 385
Mexico, Zapatistas in, 343
MHPE. *See* Master's in Health Professions Education
middle-class jobs, postsecondary education and, 353–54
migrant education, 437–41
migrant integration and settlement, 437–39
migrants, 103, 436–40
Migrant Workers' Dignity Association, 438
migration, 201, 436
military education, 232–38
military leadership, 233
Millennium Development Goals (MDG), 242–43, 245
MIPI. *See* Modified Instructional Perspectives Inventory
Mobile Assistance for Social Inclusion & Empowerment of Immigrants with Persuasive Learning Technologies & Social Network Services (MASELTOV), 440

Modern Era philosophies of education, 12
modernization theory, 240
The Modern Practice of Adult Education (Knowles), 150–51
Modified Instructional Perspectives Inventory (MIPI), 163
Moonlight Schools, 27, 422–23
moral development, 86–87
motivation, 91–96, 201–2
motivation to learn, 91–97, 102
Movement for Black Lives (M4BL), 293, 365. *See also* Black Lives Matter movement
multiculturalism, 14, 318, 371, 414, 441
multicultural leadership, 123
multidisciplinary perspective, 32, 91–92
multimodality, 161
multinational corporations, 63–64
Museo dell'Opera del Duomo, 309
Museum of Modern Art, 310
museums, decolonizing, 347
Museums Association of the United Kingdom, 306
Muslim ban, 366–67, 436
mutuality, 161
Mystic Seaport, Connecticut, 308

NAAL. *See* National Assessment of Adult Literacy
NALS. *See* National Adult Literacy Survey
narrating notion of identity, 77
narrative, disrupting, 27–28
narratives, in adult learning, 77–78
National Academies of Sciences and Medicine, 250
National Adult Education Professional Development Consortium, 43–44
National Adult Literacy Survey (NALS), 144, 406
national and subnational governments, in migrant education, 437–38
National Assessment of Adult Literacy (NAAL), 406
National Center for Disease Prevention and Health Promotion, 82
National Center for Education Statistics (NCES), 4, 199, 216–17, 267, 269, 424
National Center for Families Learning, 207–8
National Center for Family Literacy (NCFL), 206, 210
National Conference of Adult Education, 1961, 48
National Cowboy and Western Heritage Museum, 310
National Educational Association (NEA), 145, 306–7

national educational systems, 64
National Governors Association, 143–44
National Guard and Reserve, 233
nationalism, 78, 436, 446
National Literacy Act of 1991 (NLA), 190–93
National Peace Academy (NPA), 331
National Postsecondary Student Aid Study, 2002 (NPSAS), 269
National Reporting System (NRS), 101, 143, 192–94, 423
National Skills Coalition, 225, 354
Native American land-based pedagogy, 319–20
Native Americans, 23, 28–29, 318–19, 409
NCES. *See* National Center for Education Statistics
NCFL. *See* National Center for Family Literacy
NEA. *See* National Educational Association
negative emotions, 87–88
negative peace, 330–31
Neo-Confucianism, 15, 133
neo-Gramscian approaches, to pedagogy, 169–70, 172
neoliberalism, 41–43, 62, 197, 241–42, 292, 344
  in ACE, 125, 447–48
  acts of charity in, 365
  capitalism and, 170, 363–64
  globalization and, 63–65
  managerialism and, 64
  social activism teaching and, 363, 368
neo-Piagetians, 83
neuroscience, 32–33, 74, 76, 91, 93
New Deal, 289, 292, 423
New Directions for Adult and Continuing Education, 317
New Federalism, 40
new social movements (NSM), 323
New York Times, 326
NGOs. *See* nongovernment organizations
Night School, 143
NLA. *See* National Literacy Act of 1991
nonbinary, 381
nonformal learning, 73, 307–8, 310–11, 315
nongovernmental actors, in migrant education, 438–39
nongovernment organizations (NGOs), 51–52, 56, 243
nontraditional learners, 92
nontraditional students, 266–67, 450
non-Western philosophies, of ACE, 15–16, 19–20
normalization principle, 396

SUBJECT INDEX

Normal Schools, 266
Northern European countries, adult education in, 103
novice and expert program planners, 136
NPA. *See* National Peace Academy
NPSA. *See* National Postsecondary Student Aid Study, 2002
NRS. *See* National Reporting System
NSM. *See* new social movements
nursing education, 252
nurturing teaching perspective, 153

Obergefell v. Hodges, 2015, 372
Occupy movement, 326
Occupy Wall Street, 365
OCTAE, 24, 218
OD. *See* Organization Development
OECD. *See* Organisation for Economic Cooperation and Development
Office of Education, U.S., 101
Office of Family Assistance, 352, 359
Office of Literacy and Essential Skills (OLES), 423
Office of Management and Budget, 190–91
Office of the Under Secretary of Defense, 233
Official Unofficial Voting Station exhibition (Sifuentes), 310
OISE. *See* Ontario Institute for Studies in Education
older adult education and learning, 403–7
older adults, 401–5, 413–14
older students/learners, 402
older workers, 404–5
old social movements (OSMs), 323
OLES. *See* Office of Literacy and Essential Skills
Omnibus Crime Control and Safe Streets Act of 1968, 218
Once Upon a Time, 171
One-Stop employment centers, 226
O*NET, 226
online courses, for adult students, 268–69
online education, 64, 134, 177
online learning, 95–96, 163, 266, 335
Ontario Institute for Studies in Education (OISE), 51
On the Meaning of Adult Education (Lindeman), 50
openness, inclusion and, 396
oppression, 33, 160, 235, 242, 316–17
    colonization and, 341
    counterstorytelling and, 409–10
    disability and, 394
    of LGBTQ people, 372–73, 377
Organisation for Economic Cooperation and Development (OECD), 100, 144, 191, 241–43, 436
organization, of adult education programs, 120–21, 124–26
organizational-administrative perspective, on planning, 134
Organization Development (OD), 277
OSMs. *See* old social movements
othering, 342, 429
outer work, inner work and, 261–62

PACE. *See* Pathways for Advancing Careers and Education
paideia, 49
Pampaedia (Comenius), 49
Parent Promise programs, 102
participation
    in adult education, 100–106
    digital technologies and, 183
    in prison education, 217, 219
participative leadership theory, 122
participatory/collaborative evaluation, 146
participatory learning, 311, 344
participatory programs, in migrant education, 440
Participatory Research in Asia (PRIA), 244
part-time status, for adult students, 270
Pathways for Advancing Careers and Education (PACE), 355–57
peace, 330–31
peace-building, 330, 334–35
peace circles, 333
peace education, 330–35
peace through education, 332
pedagogies, 396
    activist, 364–68
    in AEE, 314–17
    in ALE, 424–25
    in ancient times, 158–59
    andragogy and, 75, 151, 158–59, 162, 165
    blended, 160–62
    for children and adults, 158
    conceptualizations of, 159–62
    contemplative, 160
    critical, 151–52, 160, 237, 318
    decolonizing practice, 346–47
    of discomfort, 367
    in education history, 158–59

Freire on, 152
holistic, 159–62
Indigenous land-based, 319
liberation, 242
mad-enabling, 396
neo-Gramscian approaches to, 169–70, 172
public, 33, 169–70, 306, 325
queering, 376
race, 415–16
SML, 324–26
traditional, 159
White supremacy, racism and, 432
WOC feminism, 415
workplace, 104
Pedagogy of the Oppressed (Freire), 151–52, 160
peer mentoring, 111–13
Pell Grants, 353, 359–60
Pell Institute for the Study of Opportunity in Higher Education, 96
performance, learning *versus*, 277–78
performance paradigm, 278
personal context, for learning, 307
personal development, motivation and, 95
personal experience, 262
Personal Responsibility and Work Opportunity Reconciliation Act of 1996 (PRWORA), 40, 352
persons with disabilities (PWD), 393–98
Pew Charitable Trusts, 215
Pew Research Center, 405
Philadelphia Starbucks, racial bias incident, 2018, 128
philosophical foundations, of ACE, 11–20
Philosophical Foundations of Adult Education (Elias and Merriam), 314
physical context, for learning, 307
physical development, 81–82
PIAAC. *See* Program for the International Assessment of Adult Education Competencies
Pioneers of Change, 334
PLA. *See* prior learning assessment
place-based education, critical, 314, 318, 320
PME. *See* professional military education
policy
    ABE, 191–94
    ACE, 38–45
    advocates, adult education programs and, 105
    lifelong learning, 223
    prison education and, 217–19

political education, 289
political liberation, education and, 152
political program planning, 132
Polynesian Cultural Center, 307
polyrhythmic realities, 415
Poor People's Campaign (PPC), 326
popular culture, 168–74
popular education, 244, 345, 347
Portland Labor College, 289
positive peace, 330–31
Positive Peace Report (IEP), 331
possible selves, mentoring relationships and, 109
postmodern paradigm, 301
postmodern philosophical foundation, of ACE, 13, 18–19
postsecondary education, middle-class jobs and, 353–54
postsecondary international students, 66
post–World War II period, 39, 50
potencias, 343
poverty, 40, 207
    illiteracy and, 422
    low-income adults and, 96–97, 350, 353–54, 356, 358–59
    reduction, 350, 355
power
    activism and, 363–65
    analysis, of teaching, 155–56
    critical cultural analysis of, 279–80
    dynamics and cultural characteristics, in mentoring relationships, 110–11
    knowledge and, 335
    relations, in adult learning environment, 414
    relations, program planning and, 132–34
PPC. *See* Poor People's Campaign
PRECEDE-PROCEED health promotion model, 134
PRIA. *See* Participatory Research in Asia
Pride Movement, 372
primary education, 242–43
prior learning, accreditation of, 151
prior learning assessment (PLA), 144, 270–71
prison education, 214–15, 217–21
    GED exam of 2014 and, 218
    policy and, 217–19
    programs, inmate participation in, 217
    reentry model, 218
    Specter funds and, 218
    2008 recession and, 218

prisoner rehabilitation, 3
prison-industrial complex, 3
prison population, 215–21
privatization, 219, 294
processes and products, of learning, 75
productivity, in HRD, 276–77
professional development, 110, 261
professionalization, 233, 258, 260, 409
professional learning, 258–62
professional military education (PME), 232–38
program evaluation standards, 145–46
Program for the International Assessment of Adult Education Competencies (PIAAC), 44, 100, 103, 144, 189–90, 194, 216–17, 219, 241–42
program management, 119–20
program organization, 120–21
program planners, 129–32, 135–36
program planning
    contexts, 129–36
    curriculum development and, 252–53
    feminist, 132–33, 135
    five-stage theory of skill acquisition and, 136
    political, 132
    power relations and, 132–34
    Starbucks racial bias incident and, 128–31
    wicked problems and, 129–30, 134
programs. *See* adult education programs
Progressive Era, 345
progressive philosophical foundation, 13, 19, 315
progressive social movements, 323
Project QUEST, 358
ProLiteracy, 52
Promise Programs, 101–2
Promoting Reentry Success through Continuity of Educational Opportunities (PRSCEO), 218
propaganda, education and, 28
property, Whiteness and, 410, 413
PROQUEST database, 34
protégés, in mentoring relationships, 108–9, 112–13
Providing Culturally Relevant Adult Education (Guy), 414
PRSCEO. *See* Promoting Reentry Success through Continuity of Educational Opportunities
PRWORA. *See* Personal Responsibility and Work Opportunity Reconciliation Act of 1996
psychoeducational and training needs of PWD, traditional approaches to, 394–95
psychology, 32–33, 74
psychosocial mentors, 107–8

psychosocial theory, of adult development, 86
public education, for older adults, 403–4
public education policy, of ACE, 38–44
public health workforce, 110
public pedagogy, 33, 169–70, 306, 325
PWD. *See* persons with disabilities

quadrivium, 12
queering disability, 394
queering space, 375–76
queer knowledge and praxis, 375
queer studies, 373

Rabbinic Judaism, 158–59
race, 110–11, 409–11, 414–15, 417
race-based philosophical foundation, of ACE, 13–14
race pedagogy, for Black faculty, 415–16
racial bias incident at Philadelphia Starbucks, 2018, 128–31
racialization, of adult education, 428–29
racism, 409
    anti-racism and, 432
    discrimination and, 155, 385, 431
    environmental, 319
    liberalism and, 410, 412
    systemic, in adult education, 413–16
    Trump and, 416
    Whiteness and, 429–31
    White people and, 410, 412–13, 416–17
    White privilege and, 431–32
radical AEE, 316–17
radical/critical philosophical foundation, of ACE, 13, 18–19
radical labor education programs, 288
radical multiculturalism, 318
RAMAA. *See* Action Research on Measuring Literacy Program Participants' Learning Outcomes
RAND Corporation, 215–18, 220
Rand School, 289
rational planning models, 135
Redesigning Continuing Education in the Health Professions (IOM), 250
reentry education model, 218
Reformation, 12
Refugee Act of 1980, 437
Refugee Convention, UN, 438
Rehabilitation Act of 1973, 392–93, 395
reinhabitation, 318
relationality, 77–78

relational learning, 78
relationships, 85–86, 107–13
religious and spiritual adult education, 297–301
Renaissance, 12
repressive tolerance, 412, 430
Residence Act of 2005 (Germany), 437
resistance education, 377
resource allocation, for older adult education, 406
responsibility, in adult motivation, 93
Resurrection City, 326
Rethinking Education (Mohammed), 52, 55
Retooling the Mind Factory (Sears), 291
Right to Read campaign, 423
right-to-work states, 294
right-wing populism, 322–23, 436, 446
Royal College of Physicians and Surgeons, 251
Royal Pains, 171–72

San Francisco Community Boards, 333
sanism, 394, 398
SAPS. *See* Sexual Assault Prevention Strategy
Scandinavian Folk Schools, 241
School of New Learning (SNL), 66
SD. *See* Sustained Dialogue
SDGs. *See* Sustainable Development Goals, UN
SDL. *See* self-directed learning
SE. *See* supported education
Seattle Labor College, 289
Seattle Longitudinal Study (SLS), 85
2nd Chance Act of 2007, 217–18, 220
2nd Chance Pell Pilot program, 217–19
secondary education, 24
Second Chance Reauthorization Act of 2018, 218
second language teaching theory, 200
sector-focused training, 357–58
SEEKING system, of brains, 87
self, 279, 300. *See also* identities
self-actualization, 74
self-advocacy, 397
Self-Authored Integrated Learning app, 183
self-determination, 397
self-directed learning (SDL), 74–75, 151, 258
self-direction, 102
self-help, 26
self-initiated learning, 280
self-understanding, self-formation and, 261
sentimental approaches, to decolonizing ACE, 343
servant education, 151
service learning, family, 210

Servicemen's Readjustment Act of 1944, 40, 50, 233
sex education, 376
sexual assault, adult educators and, 385
Sexual Assault Prevention Strategy (SAPS), 237
sexual diversity, 371–77
sexual identity, race and, 415
sexuality, 371, 375
sexuality studies, 373
sexual minorities, 371–74
sexual orientation, 371–72, 377, 383, 394
SHARP. *See* Standardization for Harassment and Racism Prevention
Shedd Aquarium, Chicago, 310
situated learning and development, 279
situational barriers, to participation, 102
skill-building/development
    contextualized basic skills, 355–58
    labor market and, 353–54
    strategies, emerging evidence on, 354–55
    welfare reform and, 350–52
skill level, education and, 223
skills
    adult literacy, 6, 189–95
    adults with low, 189–90, 193, 360
    family, 206
    five-stage theory of acquisition, 136
    literacy, 6, 44, 189–95
    military, 235
    SDGs and, 245
    SML and, 325
    workforce development and, 223–29
SKILLS Act, 218
Skills Toward Employment and Productivity (STEP), 241–44
slavery, 409, 417
SLS. *See* Seattle Longitudinal Study
SML. *See* social movement learning
SNAP. *See* Supplemental Nutrition Assistance Program
SNL. *See* School of New Learning
social activism, 362–69
social background, in adult education access, 103
social capital, 104
social change, adult education and, 26, 75, 263, 292–93, 333–34
social change movements, 26, 316
social class, 420–21, 423–25
social constructionism, 74
social-democratic welfare states, 103

SUBJECT INDEX

social development, 85–87
social gospel, 421–22
social integration, active learning and, 269
socialism, 132, 292
Socialist Party, 289
social justice, 409, 412, 428
   adult educators and, 332
   allyship for, 377
   awareness, learning and, 333–34
   cultural institutions and, 310
   environmental, 316–17
   erosion of, multinational corporations and, 63–64
   informal learning through action, 330
   lifelong leaning and, 55
   programs, social change and, 26
   social activist pedagogy and, 364–66
   social justice education and, 31
   sociocultural theory and, 324
   training for, 334
   in U.S. military, 232
   workers and, 293
   worker's education and, 344–45
social justice unionism, 294
social media, 326
social model, of disability, 393–94
social movement learning (SML), 310, 322–27, 333
social movements, 446–47
   ACE, colonialism and, 346
   Black Lives Matter, 2, 130, 293, 322, 326, 347, 365, 385, 410
   civil rights movement, 2, 25, 40, 322, 409, 412–13, 417
   defining, 322
   informal learning and, 324, 333
   LGBTQ, 372
   media and, 326
   old and new, 323
   progressive *versus* conservative, 323
social problems, interdisciplinarity in addressing, 33
social reform teaching perspective, 153
social theories, of aging, 402
social work, interventions in, 135
societal transformations, lifelong learning and, 56–58
society, education and, 48–49, 52
Society to Encourage Study at Home, 28
sociocultural context, for learning, 307–8
sociocultural theory, 83–84, 86, 201, 324
sociology, 32–33
Soldiers and Scholars (Masland and Radway), 232

solidarity, 346–47, 366
somatic learning, 76–77
South Africa, 66–67
South African Family Literacy Project, 209
Southern Poverty Law Center, 334
Soviet Union, 242
Spanish language speakers, ESL and, 198
Specter funds, 218
spirals model of emergent planning, 135
spiritual adult education, 297–301
spiritual formation, 301
spirituality, 77, 88, 160, 261, 299–300
stackable credentials, 41
staff development, 258
Standardization for Harassment and Racism Prevention (SHARP), 237
Standing Rock, 326
Starbucks, racial bias incident, 2018, 128–31
State Normal Schools, 266
STEP. *See* Skills Toward Employment and Productivity
strategic planning, 125
student activism, 288
student aid, 359–60
student college choice, 104
student-instructor interactions, for adult students, 268
Students Against Sweatshops, 288
student standards, 143–44
summative assessment, 141–42
Summer School for Women Workers, Bryn Mawr College, 289
superstructure, 169
Supplemental Nutrition Assistance Program (SNAP), 354–55, 359
support, mentoring relationships and, 107
support, of adult learners, 100, 104–6
supported education (SE), 397
Supporting Knowledge and Investing in Lifelong Skills (SKILLS) Act of 2013, 218
supranational organizations, in migrant education, 438
sustainable assessment, 143
Sustainable Development Goals, UN (SDGs), 48, 52, 55–58, 242–46
Sustained Dialogue (SD), 334
Sweden, migrants to, 437
Syrian refugee crisis, 436
system competency, 260
systemic racism, in adult education, 413–16

TAACCCT. *See* Trade Adjustment Assistance Community College and Career Training
TABE. *See* Tests of Adult Basic Education
tacit learning, 73
TANF. *See* Temporary Assistance for Needy Families
Tantum Quantum, 153
Tanzania, colonial education system of, 342
TASC. *See* Test Assessing Secondary Completion
task/issue, 86
Tate Museum, 309–10
T&D. *See* Training and Development
teachable moment, 81
teaching, 150
    contemporary perspectives, in adult education, 152–54
    culturally responsive, 201–2
    with digital technology, 184
    helping-adults-learn paradigm, 154–56
    power analysis of, 155–56
    queering, 376
    social activism, 363–69
Teaching English to Speakers of Other Languages (TESOL), 199–200
teaching perspectives inventory (TPI), 153
Teaching Race (Brookfield), 432
technical paradigm, of adult education, 235
technology, 43, 103, 262
    at cultural institutions, 309–10
    digital, 177–84
    educational, 451
    e-mentoring, 109–10, 113
    information, prison education and, 218
    older adults' access and competency, 405
TED Conferences and TED Talks, 309
television, 171–72
Temporary Assistance for Needy Families (TANF), 40, 190, 352, 354–55, 358–59
terminal education, 48
TESOL. *See* Teaching English to Speakers of Other Languages
Test Assessing Secondary Completion (TASC), 143–44
Test of English as a Foreign Language (TOEFL), 199
Test of English for International Communication (TOEIC), 199
Tests of Adult Basic Education (TABE), 143
texts, popular culture, 169
Theater of the Oppressed, 335, 365–66
theory of change, 131

theyby, 386
the third age, 406
Third World, 240
Title II, of the WIOA, 24, 207–8, 423
Title II, of WIA, 40–41, 101, 191
Title IV, of Higher Education Reconciliation Act, 144
TL. *See* transformative learning
TOEFL. *See* Test of English as a Foreign Language
TOEIC. *See* Test of English for International Communication
Tostan, 244
Toyota Family Learning Program, of NCFL, 210
TPI. *See* teaching perspectives inventory
Trade Adjustment Assistance Community College and Career Training (TAACCCT), 357
traditional pedagogy, 159
TRADOC. *See* Training and Doctrine Command
training, 224
    adult education and, 100
    for adults with disabilities, 395
    credentialing and, 55
    education and, 38–39, 44
    HRD and, 227, 281–82
    mediation, 333
    military, 232–34
    racial bias, 128, 131
    sector-focused, 357–58
    social justice, 334
    VET, 100–101
    workplace, 132
Training and Development (T&D), 276–78, 280–82
Training and Doctrine Command (TRADOC), 234, 236
Training for Change, 334
trait theory, 122
transfeminism, 383–84
transfer of training, 281–82
transformative learning (TL), 76–77, 96, 155, 324, 429
transgender, 380–85, 388–89
transitional jobs, 358
transmission teaching perspective, 153
transnationalism, globalization and, 375
transnational migration, 201
transphobia, 380–82
trivium, 12
Truth and Reconciliation Commission of Canada Report, 346

SUBJECT INDEX

Turing test, 182
Twitter, 310, 326
two-generation (2Gen), 206
two-ness, 341
2008 recession, 218

Ubuntu, 15
UCW, 294
UD. *See* universal design
UDI. *See* universal design for instruction
UDL. *See* universal design for learning
UFS. *See* University of Free State
UIL. *See* UNESCO Institute for Lifelong Learning
UIS. *See* UNESCO Institute for Statistics
UN. *See* United Nations
underserved and low-income adult learners, 96–97
UNDP. *See* United Nations Development Program
UNESCO
    CONFINTEA of, 62, 241–46, 375
    on EE at cultural institutions, 309
    on FL, 209
    GMR of, 55
    GNLC, 57
    ICAE and, 62, 66, 68
    on intangible heritage, 305–6
    international conferences of, 62
    LAMP initiative, 243–44
    on learning societies, 57
    on lifelong learning, 48–53, 55, 57, 344
    literacy campaigns, 242
    on peace-building, 330
    SDGs and, 245
    SML and, 325
    United States' withdrawal from, 3, 51
UNESCO Institute for Lifelong Learning (UIL), 57
UNESCO Institute for Statistics (UIS), 243, 245
United Association for Labor Education, 288, 345
United Kingdom, 67, 251, 306
United Nations (UN), 123
    Convention 1325 of Women, Peace, and Security, 332
    creation of, 241
    Development Decades, 242
    ICAE and, 52
    International Conferences on Financing for Development, 243
    International Convention on the Protection of the Rights of Migrant Workers and Members, 438
    International Covenant on Economic, Social and Cultural Rights, 243
    Refugee Convention, 438
    SDGs, 48, 52, 55–58, 242–46
United Nations Development Program (UNDP), 241–42
United States (U.S.)
    adult education articles in publications, 34
    adult education participation in, 103
    AEE in society, 314
    antimigrant policies, right-wing populism and, 436
    Black women's club movement in, 345
    correctional educational programs in, 217
    diversity of foreign-born population in, 198–99
    economy, postwar, 39
    education history, 25
    HBCUs, program planning and, 133
    higher education, internationalization and, 66–67
    immigrants to, 198–99, 206, 210, 310, 385, 411, 436
    low skills, economy and, 189
    military, "Don't Ask, Don't Tell" policy, 237, 372
    military education in, 232–38
    pedagogy in, 159
    poverty in, 40
    prison system, 215–16, 220
    Promise Programs in, 101–2
    racism in society, 410
    safety net, changes in, 350, 416
    SDGs and, 57–58
    slavery, 409, 417
    social gospel in, 421–22
    Soviet Union and, 242
    UNESCO withdrawal, 3, 51
    violence in, 55
    whale watching tourism in, 309
    White settler colonialism, 318–19
United States Agency for International Development (USAID), 241
United Steelworkers, 293
United Students Against Sweatshops, 288
universal design (UD), 396–97
universal design for instruction (UDI), 396, 398
universal design for learning (UDL), 396–98
University of Free State (UFS), 66
UN World Tourism Organization (UNWTO), 308–9
Urban Homestead movement, 323

USAFI. *See* U.S. Armed Forces Institute
USAID. *See* United States Agency for International Development
U.S. Armed Forces Institute (USAFI), 233–34

value neutrality, 154–55
VALUEUSA, 425
The Vanguard, Seattle Labor College newsletter, 289
VET. *See* vocational education and training
veterans, 40, 50, 266
Vietnam War, 233–34
Violent Crime Control and Law Enforcement Act of 1994, 218–19
virtual reality, at cultural institutions, 309
"A Vision for Black Lives" (M4BL), 293
visitors, at cultural institutions, 305–9
vocational education, 217
vocational education and training (VET), 100–101
voluntary learning, 23

WAAE. *See* World Association of Adult Education
War Department, U.S., 233
Washington consensus, 241
WDP. *See* The Welcome Dinner program
WEA. *See* Workers Educational Associations
weak-link problem, 194–95
Web of Science (WoS), 281
The Welcome Dinner (WDP) program, 441
Welfare Literacy Coalition, 365
welfare reform, 350–53, 365, 385
welfare-to-work policies, 351–52, 355
Welfare-to-Work Program, of DOL, 40
Western colonization, 341
Western philosophies, of ACE, 11–14, 19–20
West Point, 233
White adult educators, 412–13, 432
White Americans, European immigrants and, 411
White fragility, 431
White identity, 430–31, 433
White men, 402, 416
White nationalism, 446
Whiteness, 410–11, 413, 416, 429–33
White people, racism and, 410, 412–13, 416–17
White privilege, 411, 428, 431–33
White settlers, colonialism of, 318–20, 367
White supremacy, 153, 155, 318–19, 341, 364, 411, 428–32
White women, affirmative action and, 410
White women's clubs, 345

whole learner, 16
WI. *See* Women's Institutes
WIA. *See* Workforce Investment Act of 1998
wicked problems, in program planning, 129–30, 134
Winnipeg International Storytelling Festival, 335
WIOA. *See* Workforce Innovation and Opportunity Act of 2014
WOC. *See* Women of Color feminism
WOI. *See* Workforce Innovation Act
women
 Black, 341, 385, 415–16
 feminism and, 383–85
 in FL programs, 207
 identities of, 383
 in male-female binary, 387
 in militaries, 235–37
 older, financial insecurity of, 402
 sexual assaults of, 385
 White, affirmative action and, 410
Women of Color (WOC) feminism, 415
women's clubs and groups, 26, 345
Women's Clubs and Institutes, 345
Women's Institutes (WI) of Canada, 345
Women's National Indian Association, 28
worker education, 287–90, 292, 344–45
workers
 colleges, 289–90
 contract, 3
 labor education and, 287–94
 LGBTQ, 374, 386
 migrant, 438
 older, 404–5
 social justice and, 293
Workers Educational Associations (WEA), 325–26, 344
Workers' Education Project, 290
workfare, 351
workforce, older people in, 405
workforce development
 ABE and, 192, 226
 adult education and, 191–92, 202
 adult educators and, 227–30
 community colleges and, 226–27
 CTE, 224, 226–30
 ET system, 224–30
 FL programs and, 208
 HRD practices of firms and, 224, 227–30
 labor market and, 223–30

local, 40–42
programs, 208, 223, 225–26
skills and, 223–29
systems, 224–29
Workforce Development Boards, 191–92
Workforce Education Investment Act, 359–60
Workforce Innovation Act (WOI), 143
Workforce Innovation and Opportunity Act of 2014 (WIOA), 39, 44, 143, 190–94, 353, 359
adult education programs and, 41–42
ALE programs and, 423
employment outcomes and, 208
ESL and, 197, 199, 202
Title II of, 24, 207–8, 423
WIA and, 218
in workforce development system, 225–26
workforce intermediaries, 225, 228
Workforce Investment Act (WIA) of 1998, 40–41, 101, 191–94, 218
working class, 288, 290, 292, 422
work participation, welfare reform and, 351
workplace
genderism and, 386–87
pedagogy, 104
sexual diversity in, 374, 376
spirituality in, 299
training, 132

workplace learning (WPL), 104, 110–11, 252, 325
defining, 277
for disabled learners, 395
HRD and, 275–78, 280–83
learning paths and, 281
performance *versus* learning in, 277–78
terms, 276
World Assemblies on Adult Education, UNESCO, 51
World Association of Adult Education (WAAE), 61–62, 66, 68
World Bank, 64, 241–44
World Café, 334
World Education Forum, 245
World Health Organization, 394
worldview, 17
World War I, 40, 49
World War II, 25, 61–62, 143, 233, 290
social changes and, 372
veterans, 40, 50, 266
WoS. *See* Web of Science
WPL. *See* workplace learning

youth unemployment, 245

Zapatistas, 343
zone of proximal development (ZPD), 84

The American Association for Adult and Continuing Education (AAACE) is a professional association providing leadership for the field of adult, community, and continuing education through publications, conferences, advocacy, and dissemination of research and best practices. AAACE was founded in 1982.

The mission of AAACE is to provide leadership for the field of adult and continuing education by expanding opportunities for adult growth and development; unifying adult educators; fostering the development and dissemination of theory, research, information, and best practices; promoting identity and standards for the profession; and advocating relevant public policy and social change initiatives. AAACE is dedicated to the belief that lifelong learning contributes to human fulfillment and positive social change. AAACE members envision a more humane world made possible by the diverse practice of the members in helping adults acquire the knowledge, skills, and values needed to lead productive and satisfying lives. AAACE publishes the leading adult education journals in the field: *Adult Education Quarterly (AEQ)*, *Adult Learning (AL)*, and the *Journal of Transformative Education (JTED)*. In addition, the organization publishes the *Handbook of Adult and Continuing Education* every 10 years. The AAACE annual conference is held in different regions of the country on a rotating basis, often in partnership with state, regional, or other national and international associations. Several AAACE commissions offer preconferences and coconferences during the annual conference, including the Commission on International Adult Education, the Commission of Professors of Adult Education, and the Commission for Distance Learning and Technology.

Made in the USA
Monee, IL
12 May 2025